TRIAL MANUAL 8
FOR THE DEFENSE OF CRIMINAL CASES 2023 EDITION

Anthony G. Amsterdam and Randy Hertz

© 2023 by The American Law Institute. All rights reserved
First Edition 1967. Eighth Edition 2023

TRIAL MANUAL 8 FOR THE DEFENSE OF CRIMINAL CASES
by Anthony G. Amsterdam and Randy Hertz

The *Trial Manual 8 for the Defense of Criminal Cases* is a guidebook for criminal defense lawyers at the trial level. It covers the information a defense attorney has to know, and the strategic factors s/he should consider, at each of the stages of the criminal trial process. It is organized for easy access by practitioners who need ideas and information quickly in order to jump-start their work at any given stage.

The allocation of material among the four volumes of the book is intended to facilitate defense attorneys' use of the book:

- *Volume One* (Chapters 1-16) provides an overview of criminal procedure and then focuses on the issues a defense attorney is likely to confront, and the steps s/he will need to take, at the early stages of a criminal case, including: the first steps to be taken to locate, contact and protect a client who has been arrested or summoned or who fears s/he is wanted for arrest; arguing for bail or other forms of pretrial release; conducting the initial client interview; developing a theory of the case; dealing with police and prosecutors; planning and overseeing the defense investigation; conducting the preliminary hearing; grand jury practice; handing arraignments; and plea bargaining. This volume also addresses the additional considerations that may arise when representing a client who is mentally ill or intellectually disabled.

- *Volume Two* (Chapters 17-27) begins with a checklist of matters for counsel to consider between arraignment and trial, and then focuses extensively on pretrial motions practice. In addition to discussing strategic and practical aspects of drafting motions and handling motions hearings and non-evidentiary motions arguments, this volume covers the substantive law and procedural aspects of each of the types of motions that defense attorneys commonly litigate in criminal cases: motions for discovery (along with a discussion of all other aspects of the discovery process); motions to dismiss the charging paper; motions for diversion or for transfer to juvenile court; motions for a change of venue or for disqualification of the judge; motions for severance or for consolidation of counts or defendants; and motions to suppress tangible evidence, to suppress statements of the defendant, and to suppress identification testimony. These chapters provide detailed information about federal constitutional doctrines and a large number of state constitutional rulings that confer heightened protections.

- *Volume Three* (Chapters 28-40) starts with the immediate run-up to trial: issues relating to the timing of pretrial and trial proceedings; interlocutory review of pretrial rulings; and the concrete steps that counsel will need to take to prepare for trial, including working with expert witnesses where appropriate. It then begins the book's coverage of the trial stage, discussing the decision to elect or waive jury trial; jury selection procedures and challenges before and at trial; general characteristics of trials; opening statements; evidentiary issues and objections; techniques and tactics for handling prosecution and defense witnesses; and trial motions. Issues, procedures, and strategies unique to bench trials are discussed in tandem with the parallel aspects of jury-trial practice.

- ***Volume Four*** (Chapters 41-49) concludes the coverage of the trial by discussing the renewed motion for acquittal; closing arguments; requests for jury instructions; objections to the court's instructions; and jury deliberations. This volume then discusses posttrial motions and sentencing and concludes with a short summary of appellate and postconviction procedures and a précis of the first steps to be taken in connection with them.

The structure and presentation of material are designed to facilitate the conversion of text into defense motions and other types of briefing. Three of the documents in the text are available for direct downloading from the ALI website: section 2.5's flow-chart of procedures in summary, misdemeanor, and felony cases; section 4.5's questionnaire for obtaining information pertinent to bail from the client; and section 6.15's checklist for interviewing the client. The bail questionnaire and the interview list are in Word format that can be edited and thus customized to an individual user's practice and/or turned into a form for use in taking notes in real time during client interviews. **The downloadable versions of these documents are available at www.ali.org/trial-manual.**

The conventions the book uses for gender pronouns are designed to be fully inclusive. As societal conventions for gender pronouns change, the book's terminology is updated.

ABOUT THE AUTHORS

Anthony G. Amsterdam is a University Professor and Professor of Law *Emeritus* at the N.Y.U. School of Law. He previously taught at the University of Pennsylvania and at Stanford. Throughout and following his fifty years of law teaching (which were preceded by a stint as an Assistant United States Attorney in the District of Columbia), he has engaged in extensive *pro bono* litigation in criminal, civil-rights, and civil-liberties cases. He has also served as counsel, as a consultant, or as a member of the board of directors or advisors for numerous public-defender and civil-rights organizations.

Randy Hertz is the vice dean of N.Y.U. School of Law. He has been at the law school since 1985, and regularly teaches the Juvenile Defender Clinic, 1L Criminal Law, Criminal Procedure, and a simulation course titled Criminal Litigation. Before joining the N.Y.U. faculty, he worked at the Public Defender Service for the District of Columbia, in the juvenile, criminal, appellate and special litigation divisions.

TABLE OF CONTENTS

VOLUME TWO

PART THREE: PROCEEDINGS BETWEEN ARRAIGNMENT AND TRIAL

Chapter 17
Defense Procedures and Considerations Between Arraignment and Trial

A. Checklist of Matters for Counsel to Consider Between Arraignment and Trial

B. Selecting and Drafting Pretrial Motions:
Strategic and Practical Considerations

Chapter 18
Pretrial Discovery; The Pretrial Conference

A. *Introduction*

B. *Informal Discovery*

C. *Formal Discovery: Mechanisms and Legal Bases*

Chapter 19
Motions Practice in General

A. *Motions Hearings*

B. *Non-Evidentiary Motions Arguments*

Chapter 20
Motions to Quash or Dismiss the Charging Paper

Chapter 21
Removing the Case from the Criminal Court's Docket:
Motions for Diversion, ACD, or Stetting; Transfer to Juvenile Court

A. *Motions for Diversion, ACD, Stetting*

B. *Transfer to Juvenile Court*

Chapter 22
Motions for a Change of Venue or for Disqualification of the Judge

A. *Motions for a Change of Venue*

B. *Motions for Recusal or Disqualification of the Judge*

Chapter 23
Motions for Severance or for Consolidation of Counts or Defendants

A. *Motions Challenging the Joinder of Counts or Seeking Consolidation of Counts*

B. *Motions Challenging the Misjoinder of Defendants or Seeking Severance of Defendants*

Chapter 24
Suppression Hearings

Chapter 25
Motions To Suppress Tangible Evidence

A. Introduction: Tools and Techniques for Litigating Search and Seizure Claims

Chapter 26
Motions To Suppress Confessions, Admissions, and Other Statements of the Defendant

A. *Introduction*

B. *Involuntary Statements*

Chapter 27
Motions To Suppress Identification Testimony

PART THREE: PROCEEDINGS BETWEEN ARRAIGNMENT AND TRIAL

Chapter 17

Defense Procedures and Considerations Between Arraignment and Trial

A. *Checklist of Matters for Counsel to Consider Between Arraignment and Trial*

17.1. *Matters Looking Backward to Arraignment and Prearraignment Proceedings: Considering Whether to Change the Plea Entered at Arraignment*

17.1.1. *Changing a Previously Entered "Not Guilty" Plea*

If the defendant entered a plea of not guilty at arraignment and thereafter the defendant decides to enter a guilty plea, it is ordinarily easy to obtain leave of the court to do so. See §§ 14.7, 15.7.2 *supra*. For discussion of the factors that counsel and the client should consider in assessing a plea offer, see §§ 15.3-15.7 *supra*. For discussion of the matters counsel should take into account when counseling a client about a guilty plea, see §§ 15.2, 15.14-15.17 *supra*.

In some cases, counsel may want to strike a defendant's not guilty plea in order to enter special pleas (see §§ 14.5-14.6 *supra*) or to make pre-plea motions (see § 13.1 *supra*) that are ordinarily waived by the general plea of not guilty. The usual mechanism for the purpose is a motion to withdraw the plea entered at arraignment. Some judges will grant the motion as a matter of course. Others will require a showing of good cause (*e.g.*, changed circumstances; inadequate information or time to make a fully advised decision before pleading at arraignment). The Sixth Amendment doubtless requires that leave be granted (a) if the defendant was unrepresented by counsel at the arraignment (*see Hamilton v. Alabama*, 368 U.S. 52 (1961); *cf. Stevens v. Marks*, 383 U.S. 234, 243-44 (1966)), or (b) if the plea at arraignment was entered after valid defense objections that counsel was being forced to plead despite inadequate opportunity to consult with the client or to research and investigate the case (see §§ 3.23.3, 14.3 *supra*).

17.1.2. *Vacating or Withdrawing a Guilty Plea*

If the defendant entered a plea of guilty at arraignment and counsel thereafter wishes to withdraw or vacate it in order to plead specially, raise prearraignment matters, or plead not guilty (see §§ 13.1, 14.5-14.6, 15.3 *supra*), s/he will have to file a motion for relief from the plea.

If the plea was arguably invalid for any of the reasons identified in § 14.8 *supra*, counsel should file a motion to vacate it. The motion should be made before sentencing unless the claim of invalidity of the plea is based on disappointment with the sentence (see § 14.8 subdivision (c)). In most jurisdictions, appellate review of defects in a guilty plea cannot be obtained without prior exhaustion of trial-level remedies, such as a motion to vacate (or "strike") the plea. *See, e.g.*, *State v. Dortch*, 317 So.3d 1074 (Fla. 2021); *State v. Lavy*, 121 Idaho 842, 828 P.2d 871

(1992).

In federal practice, withdrawal is governed by FED. RULE CRIM. PRO. 11(d), which provides:

> " A defendant may withdraw a plea of guilty or nolo contendere:
> (1) before the court accepts the plea, for any reason or no reason; or
> (2) after the court accepts the plea, but before it imposes sentence if:
> (A) the court rejects a plea agreement under Rule 11(c)(5); or
> (B) the defendant can show a fair and just reason for requesting the withdrawal."

See United States v. Freeman, 17 F.4th 255, 262 (2d Cir. 2021) (clarifying that ("the government bears the burden of proving that the error was harmless . . . when . . . [a] defendant [has] moved to withdraw . . . [an accepted] guilty plea based on an alleged . . . violation" of the protective provisions of Rule 11(b) and (c) that prescribe the procedures to be followed in taking a plea).

If the plea colloquy satisfied constitutional and state-law standards and the guilty plea was valid, it may subsequently be withdrawn only by leave of court, in the court's discretion, usually for good cause shown. *See, e.g., United States v. Rivera*, 62 F.4th 778 (3d Cir. 2023); *United States v. Pacheco-Romero*, 2023 WL 3736877, at *2 (11th Cir. 2023); *Commonwealth v. Carrasquillo*, 631 Pa. 692, 115 A.3d 1284 (2015); *Greene v. Commonwealth*, 475 S.W.3d 626 (Ky. 2015); *McCard v. State*, 78 P.3d 1040, 1042-43 (Wyo. 2003) (Wyoming Criminal Rule 32(d) "provides that if a motion for withdrawal of a guilty plea is made before sentence is imposed, the court may permit withdrawal upon a showing by the defendant of any fair and just reason. A defendant has no absolute right to withdraw a plea of guilty before sentence is imposed, and where the strictures of . . . [Rule 11, governing the procedure for entering a plea of guilty] have been met, and the defendant intelligently, knowingly, and voluntarily entered into his plea of guilty, the district court's decision to deny such a motion is within its sound discretion. . . . Seven factors have been suggested as pertinent to the exercise of the court's discretion: (1) Whether the defendant has asserted his innocence; (2) whether the government would suffer prejudice; (3) whether the defendant has delayed in filing his motion; (4) whether withdrawal would substantially inconvenience the court; (5) whether close assistance of counsel was present; (6) whether the original plea was knowing and voluntary; and (7) whether the withdrawal would waste judicial resources."); *accord, United States v. Williams*, 852 Fed. Appx. 992 (6th Cir. 2021); *cf. State v. Anthony D., Sr.*, 320 Conn. 842, 134 A.3d 219 (2016); *United States v. De Leon*, 915 F.3d 386 (5th Cir. 2019). Illustrative cases finding an abuse of discretion in refusing to allow withdrawal of a guilty plea before sentencing include *State v. Barnes*, 2022-Ohio-4486, 2022 WL 17684072, at *1 (Ohio 2022) ("This discretionary appeal asks us to determine whether a defendant in a criminal case has a reasonable and legitimate basis to withdraw his guilty plea when, before sentencing, he discovers evidence that (1) his attorney withheld from him and (2) would have negated his decision to plead guilty had he known about it. We hold that he does. Accordingly, we reverse the judgment of the Eighth District Court of Appeals affirming the trial court's judgment denying appellant Terry Barnes Sr.'s motion to withdraw his guilty plea."); *Hernandez v. Commonwealth*, 67 Va. App. 67, 70, 793 S.E.2d 7, 9 (2019) ("We find that the trial court erred by denying the [defendant's] motion [to withdraw his guilty plea before sentence] because . . . [his] counsel misadvised her client concerning a valid insanity defense" (*id.* at 70, 793 S.E.2d at 9) and no prejudice to the prosecution was shown); *State v. Bowley*, 282 Mont. 298, 938 P.2d 592 (1997) ("[T]hree factors . . . show that good cause existed to permit Bowley to withdraw his guilty plea – the District Court's pre-plea interrogation [of the defendant, in which judge failed to inquire whether defense had advised the defendant competently and well] was inadequate, Bowley's motions to withdraw his guilty plea were prompt, and the State breached . . .[its] Pre-Trial Agreement [to recommend a suspended sentence, by implicitly endorsing the probation officer's recommendation of a custodial sentence]. Accordingly, we hold that the District Court abused its discretion by denying Bowley's motions to withdraw his guilty plea, and in so doing, erred." *Id.* at 312, 938 P.2d at 600); *Commonwealth v. McLaughlin*, 469 Pa. 407, 366 A.2d 238 (1976) (finding an abuse of discretion when a trial court denied a motion to withdraw a guilty plea before sentence in a case in which it appeared that "a total lack of co-operation, communication and trust existed between . . . [the defendant] and his former defense counsel [who had represented him at the time of the plea]" (*id.* at 413, 366 A.2d at 241) and where no prejudice to the prosecution was shown).

Judges differ considerably in their willingness to permit guilty pleas to be withdrawn. In multi-judge courts in which the judges rotate assignments from time to time, defense counsel should inquire of experienced criminal lawyers concerning the respective judges' attitudes, obtain the assignment schedule, and time the motion accordingly. Of course, the motion should not, for this purpose, be delayed beyond any deadline set by local rules for a motion to withdraw. Some jurisdictions, for example, disallow withdrawal after the end of the term of court in which the defendant was sentenced on the plea. *E.g., Brooks v. State*, 301 Ga. 748, 751-52, 804 S.E.2d 1, 3-4 (2017). Nor should a withdrawal motion be delayed until after sentence has been pronounced (unless, of course, the basis for the motion arises from the sentence, as in a case in which the sentence violates the terms of a plea bargain, see §§ 14.8 subdivision (c), 15.13 *supra*), because courts ordinarily grant leave to withdraw a plea more freely prior to sentencing than after sentencing, whether or not the applicable rules explicitly so provide. *See State v. Pedro*, 149 Hawai'i 256, 270, 488 P.3d 1235, 1249 (2021) ("[HAWAI'I RULE PENAL PRO.] 32(d) governs plea withdrawals. It specifies that sentenced defendants who move for plea withdrawal within ten days after the imposition of sentence are entitled to withdraw guilty or no contest pleas to 'correct manifest injustice.' It also provides that at any later time, a defendant seeking to withdraw a plea may do so only by petition pursuant to HRPP Rule 40. But HRPP Rule 32(d) omits a standard controlling plea withdrawal *before* sentencing. We introduced such a standard in [*State v.*] *Jim*, [58 Hawai'i 574, 574 P.2d 521 (1978)], explaining that courts evaluating pre-sentence requests for plea withdrawals should take a 'liberal approach' and grant them 'if the defendant has presented *a fair and just reason* for [the] request and the State has not relied upon the guilty plea to its substantial prejudice'. . . (emphasis added)."); *State v. Slater*, 198 N.J. 145, 156, 966 A.2d 461, 467 (2009) ("[T]he court rules set forth two standards that are dependent on the time a plea withdrawal motion is made. Motions filed at or before the time of sentencing will be granted in the 'interests of justice,' R. 3:9–3I; post-sentencing motions must meet a higher standard of 'manifest injustice' to succeed, R. 3:21–1; *Dodge v. State*, 2020 ND 100, 942 N.W.2d 478, 483 (N.D. 2020) (discussing N.D. RULE CRIM. PRO. 11 (d)(1)(b)(ii) and 11(d)(2); "'After a court has accepted a guilty plea and imposed a sentence, a defendant cannot withdraw a plea unless withdrawal is necessary to correct a manifest injustice.'"); *State v. Romero*, 2019-Ohio-1839, 156 Ohio St. 3d 468, 129 N.E.3d 404 (2019) (Ohio Criminal Rule 32.1 "provides that a trial court may grant a defendant's postsentence motion to withdraw a guilty plea only to correct a manifest injustice. . . . A defendant bears the burden of establishing the existence of manifest injustice." *Id.* at 471, 129 N.E.2d at 410. "We conclude that the trial court abused its discretion by denying Romero's motion to withdraw his guilty pleas without considering the two-prong test for ineffective assistance of counsel established in *Strickland* [*v. Washington*, 466 U.S. 668 (1984)]." *Id.* at 476, 129 N.E.2d at 414.). And if the probation department has invested time in preparing a PSI in a guilty-plea case, that alone may make the judge testy and unsympathetic to allowing the defendant to change his or her plea. All told, absent strong reasons for delaying a motion to withdraw, counsel is ordinarily well advised to make it as soon as possible after the defendant indicates that s/he wants to take the case to trial.

The argument that an accused should be routinely permitted to withdraw a guilty plea before sentence, at least when neither the prosecutor nor the court has relied upon it to their disadvantage, has so far failed to command a majority of the Supreme Court of the United States (*see Neely v. Pennsylvania,* 411 U.S. 954 (1973) (opinion of Justice Douglas, dissenting from denial of *certiorari*); *Dukes v. Warden,* 406 U.S. 250 (1972)), and has been rejected by a substantial number of state high courts. *See, e.g., Osborn v. State*, 672 P.2d 777, 788 (Wyo. 1983) ("There is a general consensus that the withdrawal of a plea of guilty is not an absolute right and the right to do so is within the sound discretion of the trial court. . . . A presentencing withdrawal motion is measured by whether it would be fair and just to allow it. . . . The burden is on the defendant to establish good grounds for withdrawing his plea. . . . Most of the foregoing cited authority also set out the policy to be that withdrawal of a plea of guilty before sentencing should be freely allowed but, as also indicated, that policy is frequently qualified. It has been considered an abuse of discretion to not hold a hearing whereby a defendant may develop support of his reasons for wanting to change his guilty plea."); *but see Mendoza v. State*, 590 S.W.3d 57 (Tex. App. 2019), and cases cited. Nevertheless, the argument is worth making as a matter of state and federal constitutional due process. "Identification of the specific dictates of due process generally requires consideration of three distinct factors: First, the private interest that will be affected by the official action; second, the risk of an erroneous deprivation of such interest through the procedures used, and the probable value, if any, of additional or substitute procedural safeguards; and finally, the Government's interest, including the function involved and the fiscal and administrative burdens that the additional or substitute procedural requirement would entail." *Mathews v. Eldridge*, 424 U.S. 319, 335 (1976). "Several federal constitutional rights are involved in a waiver that takes place when a plea of guilty is entered in a state criminal trial. First, is the privilege against compulsory self-incrimination guaranteed by the Fifth Amendment and applicable to the States by reason of the Fourteenth. . . . Second, is the right to trial by jury. . . . Third, is the right to confront one's accusers." *Boykin v. Alabama*, 395 U.S. 238, 243 (1969). *And see Mendoza v. State, supra,* 590 S.W.3d at 60: "[W]hen a defendant seeks to withdraw a guilty plea before the jury retires, his right to do so is unqualified and the trial court has no discretion to deny the request. . . . This right is derivative of the defendant's constitutional right to be tried by a jury." Unless *some* state interest is served by holding a defendant to a waiver of these basic rights, due process and the Fifth and Sixth Amendments should forbid a state to insist on doing so.

In any event, a trial court's refusal to permit a defendant to withdraw a guilty plea on timely motion before sentencing is assailable on appeal for abuse of discretion. *See, e.g., Commonwealth v. McCall*, 320 Pa. Super. 473, 467 A.2d 631 (1983); *United States v. Gardner*, 5

F.4th 110 (1st Cir. 2021) (a plea agreement provided that if it was not accepted by the court it would be null and void and the defendant could withdraw it; the court initially accepted it but later granted the government's motion to withdraw from the agreement on the ground that the defendant had violated one of its provisions by committing an assault while in custody awaiting sentence; the defendant then moved to withdraw his guilty plea; his motion was denied; the court of appeals holds this denial an abuse of discretion because the terms of the agreement specifically assured the defendant an opportunity to withdraw his plea if the agreement was not accepted – terminology which the appellate court reads as meaning if the plea agreement was not implemented by imposing the agreed-upon sentence.). And if a defendant can demonstrate that trial judges have been exercising their discretion in an inexplicable pattern, denying leave to withdraw in some cases while granting it in others that present indistinguishable circumstances, the argument for finding an abuse of discretion will be a strong one. *See Williams v. Georgia*, 349 U.S. 375, 388-90 (1955), and cognate cases collected in § 14.5 *supra*.

A factor often considered by courts in determining whether to exercise their discretion in favor of permitting withdrawal of the plea is whether the defendant puts forth a credible assertion of innocence. Such an assertion of innocence will be treated as particularly compelling in cases in which the plea was an *Alford* plea (see § 15.16.1 *supra*), and the defendant therefore has never admitted guilt.

In the event that a guilty plea is vacated or withdrawn by leave of the court, it may not be used against the defendant as evidence of guilt at a subsequent trial on the charge to which the defendant initially pleaded guilty. This proposition was settled in federal practice by *Kercheval v. United States,* 274 U.S. 220 (1927); *see also* FED. RULE CRIM. PRO. 11(f); FED. RULE EVID. 410; *but cf. United States v. Mezzanatto,* 513 U.S. 196 (1995); and the *Kercheval* rule appears to have been constitutionalized by a dictum in *Hutto v. Ross,* 429 U.S. 28, 30 n.3 (1976) (per curiam).

17.2. *Matters Looking Forward to Trial*

During the period between arraignment and trial, counsel will need to attend to a number of important matters, including:

(1) *Required notices.* Depending upon the rules of the jurisdiction and the circumstances of the case, the defendant may be required to file, within a designated period prior to trial, specified notices relating to matters s/he intends to raise at trial. The most commonly required are notices of intention to present evidence of alibi or of insanity. See § 14.6 subdivisions (G) and (H)) *supra*. Failure to file the notice precludes the presentation of the defense except in the discretion of the court. But see § 14.6 subdivision (H) *supra*, regarding potential challenge to the arbitrary exercise of this discretion. Local practice should be consulted regarding the time and form of required notices.

(2) *Filing of pretrial motions.* See § 17.4 *infra*. See also §§ 17.3, 17.5-17.11 *infra*.

(3) *A pretrial conference or conferences.* See §§ 18.14-18.15 *infra*.

(4)   *Election or waiver of jury trial.* See § 32.2 *infra.*

(5)   *Challenges to the venire of petit jurors.* See § 32.4 *infra.*

(6)   *Investigation of prospective jurors.* See § 32.5 *infra.*

(7)   *The timetable for proceedings.* See § Chapter 28 *infra.*

B. *Selecting and Drafting Pretrial Motions: Strategic and Practical Considerations*

17.3. *The Importance of Motions Practice; The Objectives to Be Sought*

Pretrial motions practice is crucial to effective defense work. Successful litigation of motions can win the case – either by producing outright dismissal of the charging paper (for example, when the defense prevails on a motion challenging the legal sufficiency of the charging paper) or by excluding evidence that the prosecution needs in order to win the case at trial (for example, when the defense prevails on a motion to suppress tangible evidence, incriminatory statements, or identification testimony).

Even when the defense loses a motion, there are often net benefits to litigating it. Motions practice serves as a highly effective discovery technique. The prosecutor's written and oral responses to a defense motion may provide defense counsel with information about the prosecution's case that it would not otherwise be able to obtain before trial. Evidentiary hearings on motions provide invaluable opportunities to ferret out such information in detail and also to pin down prosecution witnesses on the record, developing transcripts that can be used at trial to impeach the witnesses with prior inconsistent statements.

The defense also gains other fringe benefits from motions practice. The judge's ruling on the motion may provide a fertile source of reversible error on appeal. In cases in which a guilty plea is under consideration but counsel is not sure about the strength of the government's case, an evidentiary hearing on a motion to suppress can provide a preview of the prosecution's evidence that will enable counsel to realistically evaluate the wisdom of taking the offered plea. Or if counsel has concluded that a plea is wise but the client is unconvinced, the client's observation of the prosecution's witnesses at an evidentiary suppression hearing may change the client's mind and enable him or her to reach the right decision. In instances in which police conduct is particularly reprehensible, the unpleasant prospect of its exposure at a motions hearing may occasionally persuade the prosecutor to drop the charges or may give the defense considerable leverage in plea bargaining. Hearings on motions, whether they are evidentiary hearings or oral arguments, may also strengthen the attorney-client relationship and lead the client to place greater trust in the attorney's advice generally, since the client sees the attorney fighting for him or her in court.

17.4. *The Motions That Counsel Should Consider*

Counsel will need to make a decision early in the case about what motions to file. In most jurisdictions a statute or court rule establishes a deadline (usually a specified number of days after arraignment or a specified number of days before trial) for filing motions. See § 17.7 *infra*.

Counsel should begin by examining the charging paper to determine whether it suffers from deficiencies that render it subject to a motion to dismiss. See §§ 20.4-20.7 *infra*. Counsel also should consider whether the charging paper can be challenged on double jeopardy grounds. See § 20.8 *infra*. If the charges are based on more than one incident, counsel should consider a motion to sever counts (see §§ 23.1-23.4 *infra*), and if the client is charged jointly with one or more codefendants, counsel should consider a motion for severance of defendants (see §§ 23.6-23.9 *infra*). In rare cases motions for consolidation of charges or defendants may be advisable. See §§ 23.5, 23.10 *infra*.

On the basis of counsel's interviews with the client (see §§ 3.21.2, 6.9-6.10, 6.15 *supra*), informal discovery obtained from the prosecutor (see §§ 8.1.4, 8.4, 15.9-15.10 *supra*) or at the preliminary hearing (see §§ 11.7-11.8), and independent defense investigation (see §§ 9.15, 9.20 *supra*), counsel should determine whether the prosecution's case is likely to include any tangible evidence obtained by searches or seizures, any confessions or incriminating admissions by the defendant, or any identification testimony. If so, counsel should evaluate the potential of a motion to suppress evidence under the doctrines summarized in Chapters 25 (tangible evidence), 26 (confessions and admissions), and 27 (identifications).

If the informal discovery process has proven inadequate and the prosecutor has refused to turn over information that the defense requires, counsel should file motions for discovery. See § 18.7 *infra*. Counsel should also consider motions for sanctions if counsel learns that evidence has been destroyed (see §§ 18.9.26, 18.9.27 *infra*) or that the prosecutor has told witnesses not to talk with counsel or defense investigators (see § 9.14 *supra*).

If the client has a limited prior record and the charged offense is not extremely serious, counsel might consider any remedies available in the jurisdiction for diverting the case out of the criminal justice system. See Chapter 21 *infra*. In some jurisdictions, diversion can be sought by means of a pretrial motion. See §§ 21.1, 21.3-21.4 *infra*.

Counsel should give thought to the trial forum. If there are reasons to believe that the defendant would not receive a fair trial in the jurisdiction in which the case is presently pending, counsel can file a motion for a change of venue. See §§ 22.1-22.3 *infra*. If there are reasons to believe that the judge presiding over the case may not be impartial, counsel can file a motion for recusal. See §§ 22.4-22.7 *infra*.

Depending upon the jurisdiction and the circumstances of the case, there may be grounds for a motion to challenge aspects of juror selection. See § 32.4 *infra*.

Depending upon the defense theory of the case (see § 7.2 *supra*), counsel may need to retain an investigator (see § 9.4 *supra*) and expert consultants or expert witnesses (see § 16.2 *supra*; §§ 30.1-30.2 *infra*). If so, and if the client is indigent, counsel will have to file a motion for state funds. See §§ 5.1.2-5.4, 16.3, 16.5 *supra*; § 30.3 *infra*.

Developments during the pretrial stage may necessitate motions addressed to the timing of pretrial proceedings and trial. It may become strategically desirable to advance the dates of pretrial hearings, the trial, or both. See § 28.2 *infra*. Or counsel may want to file a motion for a continuance in order to gain more time for investigation and preparation. See § 28.3 *infra*. If the prosecution seeks a continuance, counsel may respond with a motion to dismiss for want of prosecution (see § 28.4 *infra*) or on grounds of denial of a speedy trial (see § 28.5 *infra*) or both.

17.5. *Deciding Whether to Raise an Issue in a Pretrial Motion or at Trial*

Local practice may give the defense the option of raising certain defenses and contentions either by pretrial motion or at trial. Counsel should consider the following reasons for and against litigating a motion prior to trial.

17.5.1. *Reasons for Litigating an Issue by Pretrial Motion*

Election of the pretrial motion forum ordinarily results in an earlier adjudication of the issues raised. This may be important not only when success on the issues will require dismissal of the entire prosecution, so that termination of the case in the defendant's favor is expedited, but also when success on the issues will weaken the prosecution's litigating posture or morale and thereby increase the defense's leverage in plea bargaining. Conversely, when there is a substantial likelihood that the defense will lose the issues no matter when they are presented, they may be more effective bargaining counters if mentioned to the prosecutor during plea negotiations as contentions that the defense intends to raise at trial rather than being raised and definitively lost prior to the negotiation.

A major reason to opt for the pretrial motion forum exists whenever defense motions may produce discovery of the prosecution's case that can be used to guide defense investigation and improve defense trial preparation (see, *e.g.*, § 9.14 *supra*; §§ 17.9, 24.2, 24.4.2 *infra*) or provide an opportunity to cross-examine prosecution witnesses and get them committed on record to statements which will curb their trial testimony or be usable to impeach it (see §§ 17.9, 24.2, 24.4.3 *infra*).

If interlocutory appellate review of adverse rulings on pretrial motions is available (see § 31.1 *infra*), the motion procedure will give counsel a chance to obtain appellate remedies for errors that, as a practical matter, are uncorrectable after verdict.

The pretrial motion procedure also minimizes the risk of lengthy sidebar proceedings or proceedings in the jury's absence that will bore or irritate the jurors. It reduces the risk that prejudicial material exposed in these proceedings will be leaked to the jury. See § 40.4 *infra*.

If counsel is seeking dismissal on a legal issue that is both technical and close, litigating it in a pretrial motion forum rather than at trial may also improve the defense's chances of prevailing. Judges are understandably reluctant to dismiss a case on a narrow legal point after the parties have prepared and all of the witnesses have appeared for trial.

Depending upon the idiosyncrasies of local practice, there may be various other benefits to litigating certain issues by pretrial motion. In jurisdictions in which motions scheduled in advance of the trial date are heard by a motions judge rather than the trial judge, counsel can use the choice of forum to select the more favorable judge. In such jurisdictions, litigating issues before a judge other than the trial judge also avoids the risk that the trial judge will hear evidence during the motions hearing that is inadmissible at trial but may unconsciously prejudice the judge's verdict in a bench trial or rulings in a jury trial. And if the motions judge happens to be an especially favorable sentencer, counsel may be able to take advantage of an appearance before that judge as an occasion for withdrawing the defendant's not guilty plea and pleading guilty. See §§ 15.7.2, 17.1.1 *supra*.

17.5.2. *Reasons for Litigating an Issue at Trial Rather Than in a Pretrial Motions Forum*

On the other hand, there may be considerable advantages to postponing the presentation of certain defenses and contentions until after trial has begun. Some defense contentions will be more compelling in the context of the case as it develops at trial than in isolation as they appear on pretrial motion. Also, there may be circumstances under which a defect in the prosecution can be cured if the defendant brings it to the attention of the court and prosecutor before trial but cannot be cured after the trial has begun. *See, e.g., United States v. Muresanu*, 951 F.3d 833 (7th Cir. 2020) (the indictment charged the defendant with attempting to commit aggravated identity theft; substantive federal law does not make criminal an attempt to commit this particular crime; the defendant did not challenge the indictment before trial but moved for an acquittal after the government rested its case; the trial judge then deleted the attempt language from the jury instructions and charged the jury on the elements of the completed crime; on appeal, the resulting conviction was reversed because of *Stirone* error (see § 12.2.1 *supra*)).

A consideration militating strongly in favor of delaying various issues until trial is that this plan of action can prevent the prosecutor from ever obtaining appellate review of a ruling favorable to the defense. Local practice may permit prosecutorial appeals (or petitions for prerogative writs) following pretrial rulings but not following rulings made in the course of trial. *See, e.g.*, 18 U.S.C. § 3731; *United States v. Park*, 938 F.3d 354 (D.C. Cir. 2019); *Commonwealth v. Surina*, 438 Pa. Super. 333, 652 A.2d 400 (1995). Moreover, the beginning of trial marks the point at which jeopardy attaches for purposes of the federal constitutional guarantee against double jeopardy. See § 20.8.2.1 *infra*. Rulings in favor of the defendant prior to that point may be appealed by the prosecution to the extent permitted by local practice (*see, e.g., Serfass v. United States*, 420 U.S. 377 (1975); *United States v. Miller*, 61 F.4th 426 (4th Cir. 2023); *United States v. Rundo*, 990 F.3d 709 (9th Cir. 2021); *United States v. Gissantaner*, 990 F.3d 457 (6th Cir. 2021)), whereas rulings in favor of the defendant after that point may not be appealed if either: (a) they are tantamount to an acquittal, or (b) they result in an acquittal. Probably also they cannot be appealed if they result in the termination of the trial without a general verdict or finding of guilty, other than upon the defendant's own motion – such as, for example, when the charges are dismissed by the court *sua sponte* or at the instance of the prosecution following a trial ruling in favor of the defendant upon a motion or objection that does not affirmatively request dismissal or a mistrial – at least in the absence of "a manifest necessity" for terminating the trial. See §§ 20.8.3, 20.8.5 *infra*. Although the law in this area is tortuous and confused, the bottom line is that serious, often insurmountable practical, statutory, and constitutional difficulties impede prosecutorial appeals from midtrial rulings in the defendant's favor, whereas pretrial (or post-trial) rulings of identical purport can be readily appealed by the prosecutor.

17.5.3. *Casting the Issue in the Form of a Pretrial Motion When the Pretrial Forum Is Preferable*

If, after weighing the competing considerations, counsel concludes that they favor motions litigation, counsel should employ any applicable pretrial motion procedure provided by statute or court rule. If neither statutes nor rules authorize any such procedures, counsel will have to be resourceful in inventing them. In a number of jurisdictions, for example, courts will entertain common-law motions *in limine* seeking pretrial rulings on (a) issues of law whose disposition importantly affects defense trial strategy (such as the admissibility of evidence that the prosecution is expected to offer to impeach the defendant if the defendant elects to testify), *e.g., People v. Patrick,* 233 Ill. 2d 62, 73, 908 N.E.2d 1, 7, 330 Ill. Dec. 149, 155 (2009) ("We conclude that a trial court's failure to rule on a motion in limine on the admissibility of prior convictions when it has sufficient information to make a ruling constitutes an abuse of discretion."); *State v. Lamb*, 321 N.C. 633, 365 S.E.2d 600 (1988); *State v. Lariviere*, 527 A.2d 648 (R.I. 1987); *compare New Jersey v. Portash,* 440 U.S. 450 (1979), *with Luce v. United States*, 469 U.S. 38 (1984); (b) the admissibility of prosecution evidence when its preclusion "'renders the state's proof with respect to the pending charge so weak in its entirety that any reasonable possibility of effective prosecution has been destroyed'" (*City of Defiance v. Kretz*, 60 Ohio St. 3d 1, 4, 573 N.E.2d 32, 35 (1991)); *cf. People v. Smith*, 248 Ill. App. 3d 351, 617 N.E.2d 837, 187 Ill. Dec. 380 (1993); (c) the admissibility of prosecution evidence which, if mentioned in the prosecutor's opening statement or proffered at trial, may prejudice the defendant despite an eventual ruling by the trial judge sustaining a defense objection to the evidence (*e.g., United States v. Jones*, 930 F.3d 366 (5th Cir. 2019), summarized in § 36.3.3 *infra*; *United States v. Wells*, 879 F.3d 900, 914-18 (9th Cir. 2017); *United States v. Shelley*, 405 F.3d 1195, 1201 (11th Cir. 2005); *United States v. Mejia-Alarcon*, 995 F.2d 982 (10th Cir. 1993); *People v. Johnson*, 215 Ill. App. 3d 713, 575 N.E.2d 1247, 159 Ill. Dec. 187 (1991); *Gasaway v. State,* 249 Ind. 241, 231 N.E.2d 513 (1967); *State v. Nakamitsu*, 138 Hawai'i 51, 375 P.3d 1289 (Table) (Hawai'i App. 2016), *ruling on other issues aff'd,* 140 Hawai'i 157, 398 P.3d 746 (2017); *State v. Rushton*, 260 Or. App. 765, 320 P.3d 672 (2014); *Commonwealth v. Padilla*, 2007 PA Super 130, 923 A.2d 1189 (Pa. Super. 2007); *State v. Latham,* 30 Wash. App. 776, 638 P.2d 592, 594-95 (1982), *aff'd,* 100 Wash. 2d 59, 667 P.2d 56 (1983); *State v. Gaston*, 192 Wash. App. 1032, 2016 WL 398317 (2016)); *cf. State v. Hoffman*, 321 Or. App. 330, 515 P.3d 912 (2022); (d) the permissibility of particular prosecution arguments in opening or closing (*e.g., State v. Martinez*, 319 Conn. 712, 728-31, 127 A.3d 164, 173-75 (2015); *Carruthers v. State*, 272 Ga. 306, 528 S.E.2d 217 (2000); Michael D. Cicchini, *Combatting Prosecutor Misconduct in Closing Arguments*, 70 OKLA. L. REV. 887 (2018)); (e) the admissibility of defense evidence (*United States v. Dingwall*, 6 F.4th 744 (7th Cir. 2021) (evidence of battered woman syndrome and PTSD in support of a defense of duress)); or (f) issues of law whose disposition renders the presentation of certain defense evidence unnecessary or irrelevant (*e.g., Lewis v. United States,* 445 U.S. 55 (1980)). *See* Stephen H. Peskin, *Innovative Pre-Trial Motions in Criminal Defense,* 1 AM. J. TRIAL ADVOCACY 35, 64-73 (1977), and authorities collected; *Luce v. United States, supra,* 469 U.S. at 41 n.4 (1984) (dictum)). The latter two kinds of motions *in limine* are particularly useful when defense counsel expects to lose the motion at the trial level but wishes to preserve the legal issue for appeal and when the defense evidence in question is difficult or costly to gather or present or is inconsistent with alternative defense trial strategies or may be less persuasive factually than is the legal claim for its admissibility.

17.6. *Choosing Between Oral and Written Motions*

When local practice gives the defense the option to make pretrial motions orally or in writing, it is ordinarily better to make them in writing. Written motions assure that both the relief sought by the defense and the grounds upon which it is sought are preserved in the record, whereas oral motions entail the risk that counsel may omit to make (or the court reporter may fail to hear) significant points. Many state appellate courts will not entertain claims of error unless the record shows that the specific legal contention sought to be raised on appeal was presented to the trial court; and federal constitutional contentions must ordinarily be made in state trial courts with explicit reference to the provision of the Constitution on which counsel relies in order to support subsequent Supreme Court review (see § 49.2.2 *infra*) and to avoid the danger that the federal claim will be held to have been waived for purposes of postconviction federal habeas corpus (see § 49.2.3.2 *infra*). If, for any reason, a motion *is* made orally, counsel should be sure that a stenographer or reporter is present. Similarly, a stenographer or reporter should be present when the judge rules orally on any matter.

17.7. *Timely Filing of the Motion: Methods for Extending the Filing Deadline and for Obtaining Relief from Forfeitures Entailed as a Consequence of Untimely Filing*

In most jurisdictions the applicable state statute or court rule specifies a certain time period within which all motions must be filed. Counsel must pay careful attention to the deadline; failure to meet it will almost always result in the court refusing to entertain the motion.

If counsel finds that s/he will be unable to file a motion on time (because, for example, counsel cannot obtain discovery from the prosecutor within the specified time period or because counsel's heavy trial schedule precludes the preparation and timely filing of the motion), counsel will need to take one of the following measures to protect the client's rights: (i) at arraignment, request that the court extend the normal period for filing motions; (ii) on or before the deadline, file a motion for an extension of time (commonly called an "EOT") for filing a particular motion or all defense motions, as the situation warrants; (iii) if the impediment is a lack of necessary factual information resulting from insufficient discovery or investigation, file the motion on time but in an incomplete or even skeletal form, and explain in the body of the motion that the supporting facts will be supplemented at a later time after discovery or investigation has been completed; (iv) secure a firm commitment from a trustworthy prosecutor that s/he will consent to (or will not oppose) defense counsel's filing of the motion *nunc pro tunc* after the expiration of the normal filing period.

It cannot be emphasized too strongly that defense attorneys must not rely on longstanding local customs of permitting late filing of motions without prior leave of court. All too many defense attorneys have found, to their dismay, that theirs was the first case in which the customary informality and relaxed filing procedure was suddenly abrogated.

In the event that counsel does encounter the unfortunate situation in which s/he missed a filing deadline without prior leave or prosecutorial assent, all is not necessarily lost. Depending upon the facts of the case, counsel may be able to argue that the usual procedural requirement of timely filing is unenforceable or should be waived for one or more of the following reasons:

1. The state procedural rule establishing the deadline was not "'firmly established and regularly followed' by the time as of which it is to be applied" (*Ford v. Georgia*, 498 U.S. 411, 424 (1991)). *See also James v. Kentucky*, 466 U.S. 341 (1984), and cognate cases collected in § 14.5 *supra*.

2. Prior to the expiration of the filing period, the defense did not know, and could not reasonably have known, the facts that provide the basis for filing a motion. *Gouled v. United States,* 255 U.S. 298, 305 (1921); *United States v. Johnson,* 713 F.2d 633, 649 (11th Cir. 1983) (defense lacked knowledge of facts because the prosecutor failed to provide adequate discovery); *DiPaola v. Riddle,* 581 F.2d 1111, 1113-14 (4th Cir. 1978) (circumstances of the incident prevented the defendant from knowing of the illegal aspects of the police officers' actions, and therefore defendant could not have told counsel); *and see Murray v. Carrier,* 477 U.S. 478, 488 (1986) (dictum). This doctrine would also justify the waiver of the timeliness requirement if the client's inability to communicate effectively with counsel (because of, for example, the client's intellectual limitations or educational deficits) prevented counsel from learning the relevant facts from the client in time to meet the filing deadline.

3. Prior to the expiration of the filing period, the defense did not know, and could not reasonably have known, of the legal basis for the motion because the caselaw giving rise to such a motion had not yet been decided. *Reed v. Ross,* 468 U.S. 1, 16 (1984); *see Murray v. Carrier, supra,* 477 U.S. at 488 (dictum).

4. Prosecutorial interference or some other external factor beyond counsel's control prevented counsel from filing the motion in a timely fashion. *Amadeo v. Zant,* 486 U.S. 214 (1988); *see also Banks v. Dretke,* 540 U.S. 668, 691-98 (2004); *Strickler v. Greene,* 527 U.S. 263, 283-90 (1999); *Murray v. Carrier, supra,* 477 U.S. at 488 (dictum).

5. Counsel reasonably relied on a longstanding local practice under which late-filing was always permitted. *See Spencer v. Kemp,* 781 F.2d 1458, 1470-71 (11th Cir. 1986).

6. Regardless of whether there was or was not good cause for counsel's procedural default, filing of the motion *nunc pro tunc* should be permitted because, at this stage, there will be no prejudice to the prosecution or to the administration of justice if the defense is permitted to file the motion, whereas preclusion of the motion may well result in a later finding of ineffectiveness of counsel (*see Kimmelman v. Morrison,* 477 U.S. 365 (1986); *see, e.g., Grumbley v. Burt,* 591

Fed. Appx. 488, 499-501 (6th Cir. 2015); *Tice v. Johnson*, 647 F.3d 87, 106-08 (4th Cir. 2011); *Thomas v. Varner*, 428 F.3d 491, 499-504 (3d Cir. 2005); *People v. Ferguson*, 114 A.D.2d 226, 228-31, 498 N.Y.S.2d 800, 801-03 (N.Y. App. Div., 1st Dep't 1986)) and a retrial that will be costly both to the parties and to the administration of justice.

The foregoing arguments may result in the court's agreeing to entertain the motion on the merits despite its lateness. If the court does not do so, counsel will have to put on the record any facts that bring the case within one of the six enumerated principles or could otherwise be viewed as excusing counsel's procedural default, so as to lay the groundwork for an appeal contending that the trial judge abused his or her discretion in holding the motion procedurally barred. Counsel should not expect to prevail on many such appeals. The watchword here is to be *very* careful not to miss motions deadlines.

17.8. *The Form of the Motion; The Need for Affidavits*

Requirements regarding the form of the motion vary considerably among jurisdictions, and counsel will need to check the applicable statutes and court rules as well as local practice and custom in his or her particular court. In some jurisdictions law and facts are combined in a single pleading; in other jurisdictions the motion is limited to factual averments and may or must be accompanied by a separate memorandum of points and authorities setting forth the law.

Some jurisdictions require the attachment of affidavits or affirmations. Often, this requirement can be satisfied by an affirmation of counsel, setting forth all the facts that s/he has a good-faith basis for believing to be true. Depending upon local rules, counsel may or may not have to specifically identify the sources of each of the facts which s/he is affirming and may or may not have to state that any facts of which she has no personal knowledge are asserted "on information and belief." In those jurisdictions in which counsel is required to attach affidavits by the witnesses themselves, counsel should keep these affidavits as cursory as possible to avoid giving the prosecutor material with which to impeach the witness at an evidentiary hearing on the motion or at trial.

17.9. *Deciding Whether to Seek an Evidentiary Hearing for Claims That Can Be Proven with Affidavits Alone*

When counsel's position on a motion depends upon the establishment of facts that are not already in the record, counsel should decide whether to request an evidentiary hearing of the motion or to file supporting factual affidavits with the motion. Of course, local practice may compel one of these procedures or the other for certain motions. In the case of motions to suppress evidence, for example, the defense is ordinarily required to prove the facts by oral testimony and authenticated documents at an evidentiary hearing and may also be required to make a factual proffer or to file affidavits as a threshold matter in order to establish his or her entitlement to a hearing. See § 17.8 *supra;* § 17.10 *infra.*

On the other hand, in many jurisdictions, counsel will have the option of proceeding by affidavit or seeking an evidentiary hearing on motions such as a motion for a continuance to procure the attendance of a defense witness, or a motion to dismiss the charging paper because prosecutorial delay has violated the defendant's right to a speedy trial, or a motion for change of venue on the ground of prejudicial publicity, or a motion for sanctions against the prosecution for concealing or destroying potential defense evidence or harassing defense witnesses or instructing prosecution witnesses to refuse to talk to the defense. When local practice leaves the option to the movant, counsel should consider the following factors in making the choice: (a) the relative persuasiveness of the factual showings that can be made, respectively, by affidavit and by live testimony; (b) the opportunities that an evidentiary hearing may give the defense for pretrial discovery of the prosecution's case and for locking potential prosecution witnesses into impeachable positions by cross-examination; (c) the opportunities that an evidentiary hearing may give the prosecution for pretrial discovery of the defendant's case and for locking defense witnesses into impeachable positions by cross-examination; (d) the delay of the trial that may be necessitated by a pretrial evidentiary hearing; and (e) in courts in which "long" or evidentiary pretrial motions are heard by a different judge from "short" or on-the-papers motions, the judge who will be most favorable to the defense.

17.10. *Drafting the Motion So as to Gain Relief Without Unduly Disclosing the Defense Case*

In drafting written motions that will have to come on for an evidentiary hearing – which will usually include all motions to suppress evidence – counsel should be careful to avoid unnecessary disclosure of either the facts or law that s/he intends to rely upon at the hearing. If a motion gives the prosecutor unnecessary advance notice of the points on which counsel intends to cross-examine prosecution witnesses, the prosecutor can coach those witnesses to avoid traps and undermine defense strategies. For example, if a suppression motion sets out in detail the police conduct that counsel is challenging, the police officers (who are, by nature, deeply interested in sustaining their arrests, searches, and confessions) are likely to conform their testimony to fit whatever theories validate their conduct. In addition, undue disclosure of counsel's factual and legal theories will give the prosecutor the time and opportunity to gather rebuttal witnesses and adjust the prosecution's proof.

Thus the best practice in drafting evidentiary motions is (a) to state the relief wanted with great clarity, (b) to state the source of law relied on (statute, rule of criminal procedure, state constitutional provision, federal constitutional provision, leading precedent (*e.g.*, "*Miranda v. Arizona*"), or whatever) specifically, but (c) to disclose as little as possible of the legal theory and the factual matter that will be presented in support of the motion. If counsel thinks it desirable to clarify the defense's factual and legal contentions for the court, this can best be done by a brief filed and served at the close of the evidentiary hearing.

This approach may need to be modified, however, in jurisdictions in which local statutes or court rules require a threshold showing of law and fact in order to get an evidentiary hearing. The key in such jurisdictions is (a) to draft the motion so as to meet the applicable standard just marginally, without revealing any additional facts or law, and (b) to the extent possible, to stick to the facts already known to the prosecution and the legal theories that will be obvious to the prosecutor or that cannot be cured by prosecutorial coaching of witnesses. Thus, for example, if counsel moves to suppress an identification from a photo spread, counsel should cite the federal and state due process clauses, document the general proposition that unreliable and unnecessarily suggestive police-staged identification procedures violate due process (see §§ 27.2, 27.3.3 *infra*), and then relate one or more obvious defects in the photo spread without mentioning other less obvious defects and particularly without adverting to defects that can be patched up testimonially by the prosecutor (such as the suggestive writing on the backs of the photographs, which the identifying witness can be coached to say s/he never saw) and without revealing any materials that counsel will use in cross-examining prosecution witnesses (such as a statement the identifying witness gave to a defense investigator, admitting that s/he saw the suggestive writing and also mentioning suggestive comments by the police).

A sufficient reason for sometimes diverging from the general strategy of keeping the legal expositions in defense motions as sparse as possible is that there are some judges who will be impressed by an elaborately reasoned, thoroughly documented legal analysis and will take the motion more seriously, according the defense more latitude at the evidentiary hearing, than they would on a bare-bones motion. They believe that short, boilerplate motions are likely to be nonmeritorious; consequently, they will insist that hearings on such motions be kept to a bare minimum of fact development and will truncate counsel's examinations of witnesses. Experienced criminal practitioners in the locality will know which judges are of this bent. Even when drafting a motion which will be heard by one of them, though, counsel should refrain from spelling out its *factual basis* in any greater detail than is necessary to provide a point of entry for counsel's learned legal arguments.

17.11. *Invoking State Constitutional Provisions in the Motion*

In the years since the Warren Court era, the Supreme Court of the United States has increasingly cut back on the protections that the federal Constitution's Bill of Rights gives criminal defendants, particularly in regard to searches and seizures, interrogations and confessions. Quite a few state supreme courts have reacted by construing the parallel provisions of their state constitutions so as to preserve some of the safeguards eliminated by the United States Supreme Court. *State v. Short*, 851 N.W.2d 474, 486 (Iowa 2014) ("As a result of the United States Supreme Court's retreat in the search and seizure area, there has been a sizeable growth in independent state constitutional law. A survey of jurisdictions in 2007 found that a majority of the state supreme courts have departed from United States Supreme Court precedents in the search and seizure area to some degree."); LaKeith Faulkner & Christopher R. Green, *State-Constitutional Departures from the Supreme Court: The Fourth Amendment*, 89 MISS. L. J. 197 (2020). *See generally* Shirley S. Abrahamson, *Criminal Law and State Constitutions: The Emergence of State Constitutional Law*, 63 TEX. L. REV. 1141 (1985); William J. Brennan, Jr., *The Bill of Rights and the States: The Revival of State Constitutions as Guardians of Individual Rights*, 61 N.Y.U. L. REV. 535 (1986); William J. Brennan, Jr., *State Constitutions and the Protection of Individual Rights*, 90 HARV. L. REV. 489 (1977); Judith S. Kaye, *State Courts at the Dawn of a New Century: Common Law Courts Reading Statutes and Constitutions*, 70 N.Y.U. L. REV. 1 (1995); Judith S. Kaye, *Dual Constitutionalism In Practice And Principle*, 42 RECORD BAR ASS'N CITY OF NEW YORK 285 (1987); Hans E. Linde, *First Things First: Rediscovering the States' Bills of Rights*, 9 U. BALT. L. REV. 379 (1980); Robert F. Utter, *The Practice of Principled Decision-Making in State Constitutionalism: Washington's Experience*, 65 TEMP. L. REV. 1153 (1992).

State courts are, of course, free to construe state constitutional provisions as providing greater protection for individual rights than the Constitution of the United States (*PruneYard Shopping Center v. Robbins*, 447 U.S.74, 81 (1980); *Arkansas v. Sullivan*, 532 U.S. 769, 772 (2001) (per curiam); *New Jersey v. T.L.O.,* 469 U.S. 325, 343 n.10 (1985); *Oregon v. Hass,* 420 U.S. 714, 719 (1975)), although they may not drop below the protections afforded by federal constitutional guarantees (*Burgett v. Texas,* 389 U.S. 109, 114 (1967)).

In urging state courts to rely on the state constitution to reach a result contrary to a holding of the Supreme Court of the United States, counsel should provide the court with a rationale for interpreting the state constitutional provision more expansively than its federal analogue. Although the state courts need not cite a rationale for resorting to the state constitution, counsel's identification of a rationale may prove decisive in persuading a trial judge – and later the state appellate courts – to adopt state grounds of decision. So:

(a) When dealing with a state constitutional provision whose wording differs from its federal counterpart, or whose history suggests the framers' intent to establish a standard different from the federal constitutional standard, counsel can argue that "well established rules governing judicial construction of constitutional provisions . . . [forbid courts to] . . . presume . . . that the framers of the . . . [state] Constitution chose the . . . [distinctive state] form 'haphazardly,' nor may we assume that they intended that it be accorded any but its ordinary meaning" (*People v. Anderson*, 6 Cal. 3d 628, 637, 493 P.2d 880, 886, 100 Cal. Rptr. 152, 158 (1972); *see, e.g., State v. Mefford*, 2022 MT 185, 410 Mont. 146, 153, 517 P.3d 210, 216 (2022) ("Apart from Article II, Section 11 [prohibiting unreasonable searches and seizures], and its federal counterpart, the Montana Constitution provides an express right to individual privacy against government intrusion. Mont. Const. art. II, § 10 . . . [which] states that '[t]he right of individual privacy . . . shall not be infringed without the showing of a compelling state interest.' . . . 'Together, Article II, Sections 10-11, provide a heightened state right to privacy, broader where applicable than the privacy protection provided under the Fourth and Fourteenth Amendments to the United States Constitution.'"); *People v. Parks,* 510 Mich. 225, 987 N.W.2d 161 (2022) (considerations that warrant holding the Michigan Constitution's cruel-or-unusual punishments clause more protective than its federal counterpart include (1) "textual differences between the state and federal Constitutions . . . [:] a bar on punishments that are either cruel *or* unusual is necessarily broader than a bar on punishments that are both cruel *and* unusual" (*id.* at 242, 987 N.W.2d at 170), and (2) "by 1963, the words 'cruel' and 'unusual' had been understood 'for more than half a century to include a prohibition on grossly disproportionate sentences,' indicating that the framers and adopters of the 1963 Constitution had intended a broader view of the state constitutional protection" (*id.*)); *General Contractors, Inc. v. State through Division of Administration, Office of State Purchasing*, 95-2105 (La. 3/8/96), 669 So.2d 1185 (La. 1996); *State v. Glass,* 583 P.2d 872 (Alaska 1978); *State v. Simpson,* 95 Wash. 2d 170, 622 P.2d 1199 (1980)). *See* William W. Berry III, *Cruel State Punishments*, 98 N.C. L. REV. 1201 (2019-20).

(b) When dealing with a state constitutional provision whose wording mirrors the federal constitutional guarantee and whose constitutional history proves of no avail, counsel can:

(i) argue that the U.S. Supreme Court's precedents are unworkably vague (*see, e.g.*, *Commonwealth v. Upton*, 394 Mass. 363, 373, 476 N.E.2d 548, 556 (1985) ("We reject the 'totality of the circumstances' test now espoused by a majority of the United States Supreme Court. That standard is flexible, but is also 'unacceptably shapeless and permissive.' . . . The Federal test lacks the precision that we believe can and should be articulated in stating a test for determining probable cause."); *People v. Griminger*, 71 N.Y.2d 635, 640, 524 N.E.2d 409, 412, 529 N.Y.S.2d 55, 58 (1988) ("[W]e have recognized that the more structured 'bright line' *Aguilar–Spinelli* test better served the highly desirable 'aims of predictability and precision in judicial review of search and seizure cases', and that 'the protection of the individual rights of our citizens are best promoted by applying State constitutional standards.'")), or otherwise dysfunctional (*see, e.g.*, *State v. Pierce*, 136 N.J. 184, 211, 642 A.2d 947, 961 (1994) ("We also perceive that the *Belton* rule, as applied to arrests for traffic offenses, creates an unwarranted incentive for police officers to 'make custodial arrests which they otherwise would not make as a cover for a search which the Fourth Amendment otherwise prohibits'"); *State v. Jacumin*, 778 S.W.2d 430, 436 (Tenn. 1999) ("We agree with the Courts cited above that the principles developed under *Aguilar v. Texas* . . . and *Spinelli v. United States* . . . if not applied hypertechnically, provide a more appropriate structure for probable cause inquiries incident to the issuance of a search warrant than does *Gates*."));

(ii) identify specific aspects of "policy, justice and fundamental fairness" that compel a more protective state constitutional standard (*People v. P.J. Video, Inc.*, 68 N.Y.2d 296, 303, 501 N.E.2d 556, 560, 508 N.Y.S.2d 907, 911 (1986)). *See, e.g., State v. Novembrino*, 105 N.J. 95, 146, 519 A.2d 820, 850 (1987) ("the privacy rights of our citizens and the enforcement of our criminal laws . . . [are] matters of 'particular state interest' that afford an appropriate basis for resolving . . . [the] issue on independent state grounds"); *State v. Stoddard*, 206 Conn. 157, 537 A.2d 446 (1988) (declining to follow *Moran v. Burbine*, 475 U.S. 412 (1986), and construing the state constitution as establishing more exacting due process protections for the right to counsel because of Connecticut's history of rigorous enforcement of the right to counsel); *Commonwealth v. Hernandez*, 456 Mass. 528, 532, 924 N.E.2d 709, 712 (2010) (declining to follow *Virginia v. Moore*, 553 U.S. 164 (2008) because "the exclusion of evidence is an appropriate remedy when a defendant is prejudiced by an arrest made without statutory or common-law authority. . . . [Earlier Massachusetts cases] explained that the application of the exclusionary rule is appropriate where it is 'inherent in the purpose of a statute which the government has violated,' and that such a purpose is inherent in 'statutes closely associated with constitutional rights.'"); *State v. Bauder*, 2007 VT 16, 181 Vt. 392, 396, 924 A.2d 38, 42 (2007) ("we have . . . long held that our traditional Vermont values of privacy and individual freedom – embodied in Article 11 [of the state constitution] – may require greater protection than that afforded by the federal Constitution"); *State v. Jones*, 706 P.2d 317, 324 (Alaska 1985) ("In previous cases, we have stated that the state constitutional guarantee against unreasonable searches and seizures is broader in scope than Fourth Amendment guarantees under the United States Constitution. In part, this broader protection results from the more extensive right of privacy guaranteed by Article I, Section 22 of our state constitution."); *State v. Brown*, 356 Ark. 460, 467-72, 156 S.W.3d 722, 727-31 (2004) ("our right-to-privacy tradition in Arkansas is "'rich and compelling'" (*id.* at 472, 156 S.W.3d at 731); and/or

(iii) cite state constitutional decisions from other States rejecting that ruling of the Supreme Court, commentators' criticisms of the Supreme Court ruling, and analyses in the opinions of the dissenting Supreme Court Justices. *See, e.g., Commonwealth v. Johnson*, 231 A.3d 807, 824-26 (Pa. 2020); *State v. Glenn*, 148 Hawai'i 112, 120, 468 P.3d 126, 134 (2020); *State v. Pierce, supra*, 136 N.J. at 200-03, 642 A.2d at 955-57; *State v. Novembrino, supra*, 105 N.J. at 152-56 & nn.35-38, 519 A.2d at 853-56 & nn.35-38; *State v. Cordova*, 1989-NMSC-083, 109 N.M. 211, 217, 784 P.2d 30, 36 (1989); *State v. Brown, supra*, 356 Ark. at 470-72, 156 S.W.3d at 729-31.

In any event, counsel should always invoke parallel state constitutional guarantees when making any federal constitutional claim, even in States whose highest court has adopted the posture that it will construe its Bill of Rights provisions as coextensive with those of the federal Constitution as construed by the United States Supreme Court, and whether the federal precedents are unfavorable, favorable, or nonexistent. If counsel wins a friendly state-court decision based exclusively on federal constitutional grounds, it will be subject to review and reversal by an unfriendly U.S. Supreme Court. *See, e.g., Kansas v. Marsh*, 548 U.S. 163 (2006). Were the same ruling based on the state constitution, or on alternative federal and state constitutional grounds, it would be immune against U.S. Supreme Court tampering. *See, e.g., Colorado v. Nunez*, 465 U.S. 324 (1984). "If the state court decision indicates clearly and expressly that it is alternatively based on bona fide separate, adequate, and independent grounds, we, of course, will not undertake to review the decision." *Michigan v. Long,* 463 U.S. 1032, 1041 (1983).

C. *Resisting Prosecution Attempts to Freeze a Defendant's Assets*

17.12. *Statutory and Sixth Amendment Bases for Opposing Government Applications for Asset Freezing*

In federal criminal prosecutions and in some state jurisdictions, statutes authorize courts to freeze a defendant's assets before trial, in order to assure the preservation of funds that may later be tapped, in the event of conviction, to pay fines, forfeitures and restitutionary orders. The statutory texts specify the criminal charges to which the authorization applies, the categories of assets subject to freezing, the procedures that the prosecution must follow, and the showing that it must make, in order to obtain a pre-conviction order enjoining the defendant from transferring or expending property or funds (and, in some cases, the appointment of a receiver to administer the sequestered assets). These texts tend to be dense and require close scrutiny for implicit as well as explicit limitations on the sequestration power. *See, e.g., United States v. Chamberlain*, 868 F.3d 290 (4th Cir. 2017) (en banc). The Sixth Amendment to the federal Constitution also provides a narrow sphere of protection: Assets which are not "tainted" (as contraband or the proceeds or instruments of crime) and which a defendant requires in order to "pay a reasonable fee" to retain the services of counsel of choice in defending against the criminal charges s/he is facing may not be ordered frozen (*Luis v. United States*, 578 U.S. 5, 23 (2016) (plurality opinion)). *See United States v. Kahn*, 890 F.3d 937, 938 (10th Cir. 2018) (a defendant is entitled to a pretrial "hearing to challenge the seizure of assets that he contends are necessary for him to retain an attorney to represent him in his upcoming criminal trial. The district court denied a hearing because he has *some* unseized assets with which to pay an attorney. We reverse and remand because the proper test is whether he has sufficient unseized assets to pay for the reasonable cost of obtaining counsel of his choice.").

Chapter 18

Pretrial Discovery; The Pretrial Conference

A. *Introduction*

18.1. *Scope and Organization of the Chapter*

As a matter of practice, criminal discovery involves two processes or phases: *informal* and *formal* discovery. Most prosecutors are willing to hand over to the defense upon request certain categories of materials which it is clear that a court would order the prosecutor to divulge if the defense made a motion to discover them. Informal discovery devices (such as the *discovery letter* (see § 18.5 *infra*) and the *discovery conference* (see § 18.6 *infra*)) provide a quick route to obtaining this material. When the informal devices fail because the prosecutor refuses voluntarily to divulge information requested by the defense, counsel must turn to formal discovery devices, such as motions to compel the prosecutor to disclose the information.

Part B of this chapter examines informal methods for obtaining discovery. Part C canvasses formal discovery procedures, describing the devices that can be employed and exploring constitutional doctrines that can be invoked in support of motions for court-ordered discovery going beyond that provided by statutes and local common law. Part D discusses the prosecutor's right to discovery from the defense.

While employing informal and formal discovery devices, defense counsel should not lose sight of opportunities to use other pretrial proceedings to acquire information about the prosecution's case. The recognized mechanisms for overt discovery in criminal cases – both informal and formal – remain far more limited than those in civil practice and are usually inadequate to advise the defense of everything it needs to know to prepare fully for trial. In this current state of the practice, defense counsel's ingenuity in devising self-help techniques is distinctly at a premium.

A pretrial conference, customary in many jurisdictions and usually available upon defense request even when it is not a standard practice, often provides a valuable opportunity for such unofficial discovery, as well as serving a number of other functions that are important to the defense. Part E discusses the pretrial conference.

Other chapters discuss other mechanisms that counsel can employ to obtain discovery. Discussions with the police and/or prosecutor will often yield useful information. See §§ 8.1.3, 8.1.4, 8.3.1, 8.4, 9.15, 13.5 *supra*. Applications for bail or for the reduction of bail sometimes can operate as a discovery device. See § 4.3.3 *supra*. A grand jury hearing may offer opportunities for learning the identity of prosecution witnesses. See § 12.10 *supra*. Several motions that counsel can file may lead to the prosecutor's disclosing facts not previously known to the defense. See § 17.3 *supra*. Evidentiary hearings, such as the preliminary hearing (see § 11.8.2 *supra*) and suppression hearings (see §§ 24.2, 24.4 *infra*) present invaluable opportunities to uncover information. Police and court records and transcripts of prior judicial proceedings are also important sources to delve into. See §§ 9.17-9.18, 9.20 *supra*. Section 34.7

infra discusses additional discovery processes that are available at trial.

18.2. *The General Position of the Defense on Discovery*

It is frequently said that no discovery was allowed by the common law in criminal cases. This is not strictly accurate; and at least since Chief Justice Marshall presided at the trial of Aaron Burr, American trial courts have exercised a discretionary power to compel the production of materials requested by a defendant and found by the court to be necessary for adequate preparation of the defense. *United States v. Burr*, 25 Fed. Cas. 30 (No. 14,692d) (C.C.D. Va. 1807). Nonetheless, most States largely follow the "closed-book" policy of the common law by precluding some of the most effective tools of civil discovery (like interrogatories and depositions) and, even for those discovery devices that are allowed, employing procedures that are far more restrictive than in civil matters.

When arguing in support of specific discovery requests, counsel will often find it useful to take the position that the same general policy that supports "wide-open" discovery in civil cases should be applied as well in criminal cases. "We have elected to employ an adversary system of criminal justice in which the parties contest all issues before a court of law. The need to develop all relevant facts in the adversary system is both fundamental and comprehensive." *United States v. Nixon*, 418 U.S. 683, 709 (1974). The quest for truth at trial is better served, under an adversary system, if the evidence of one party does not come as a surprise to the other but, having been disclosed in advance while there is still time to check it out through adequate investigation, appears in court subject to meaningful cross-examination and rebuttal. This assures "the reliability of the adversarial testing process" (*Kimmelman v. Morrison*, 477 U.S. 365, 385 (1986)). "Discovery is one of the most important tools of a criminal defendant. . . . ¶ . . . We believe that it is necessary in most criminal cases for the State to share its information with the defendant if a fair trial is to result. Furthermore, we find that complete and reasonable discovery is normally in the best interest of the public. One consequence of full and frank discovery is that it may very well encourage plea negotiations. . . . ¶ '. . . It may be impossible for counsel to make any intelligent evaluation of the alternatives if he knows only what his client has told him and what he has discovered on his own.'" *State ex rel. Rusen v. Hill*, 193 W. Va. 133, 139, 454 S.E.2d 427, 433 (1994). *See also* AMERICAN BAR ASSOCIATION, STANDARDS FOR CRIMINAL JUSTICE, Commentary to Standard 11-1.1(a) (3d ed. 1996) ("[P]reparation is essential to the proper conduct of a trial. Experienced trial counsel know that effectiveness at trial depends upon meticulous evaluation and preparation of the evidence to be presented. Where counsel's evaluation and preparation are hampered by a lack of information, the trial becomes a pursuit of truth and justice more by chance than by design. This can only lead to a diminished respect for the criminal justice system, the judiciary, and the attorneys who participate." (footnotes omitted)). *See, e.g.*, N.C. GEN. STAT. ANN. § 15A-903(a) ("Upon motion of the defendant, the court must order: (1) The State to make available to the defendant the complete files of all law enforcement agencies, investigatory agencies, and prosecutors' offices involved in the investigation of the crimes committed or the prosecution of the defendant."); N.Y. CRIM. PRO. LAW § 245.20 (effective January 1, 2020, requiring the prosecution to disclose to the defense, with no need for a defense motion, "all items and information that relate to the subject matter of the case and are in the possession, custody or control of the prosecution or persons under the prosecution's direction or control"); *People v. Copicotto*, 50 N.Y.2d 222, 226, 406 N.E.2d 465,

468, 428 N.Y.S.2d 649, 652 (1980) (commenting that an earlier, less extensive New York discovery statute, based on the then extant FED. RULE CRIM. PRO 16, "evinces a legislative determination that the trial of a criminal charge should not be a sporting event where each side remains ignorant of facts in the hands of the adversary until events unfold at trial. Broader pretrial discovery enables the defendant to make a more informed plea decision, minimizes the tactical and often unfair advantage to one side, and increases to some degree the opportunity for an accurate determination of guilt or innocence (see Notes of the Advisory Committee on the Proposed 1974 Amendment to Rule 16 of the Federal Rules of Criminal Procedure). In short, pretrial discovery by the defense and prosecution contributes substantially to the fair and effective administration of justice."

The arguments against this eminently civilized approach to criminal cases are essentially two:

First, it is said that criminal defendants, more than civil litigants, once forewarned are likely to flee the jurisdiction, bribe or intimidate witnesses, or engage in other misbehavior. Counsel may concede that these dangers, if they are real, justify curbing criminal discovery. But quite apart from the fact that there has never been any adequate showing made to support the proposition that the dangers *are* greater in criminal cases generically than in civil cases (*compare NLRB v. Robbins Tire & Rubber Co.*, 437 U.S. 214, 239-41 (1978), finding a special danger of witness intimidation in NLRB proceedings because of the "'peculiar character of labor litigation'" (*id.* at 240)), it is evident that the supposed dangers are differentially present in different sorts of criminal cases and in different sorts of discovery requests. No amount of argument about generalities can make concerns for flight, bribery, or intimidation anything other than preposterous when the defendant is an indigent, is jailed in default of bail, and wants production of the police report. Counsel should, therefore, urge that the liberality of civil discovery practice is appropriate unless the prosecutor can make some particularized showing that in *this* case and with respect to *this* discovery request the speculative dangers have some factual substance to them.

Second, the objection is mounted against criminal discovery that it is a "one-way street": that the privilege against self-incrimination precludes the prosecutor from obtaining discovery against the defendant and that it is inefficient or unfair to give the defendant unilateral discovery against the prosecutor. Defense counsel can disarm this argument if s/he is willing to offer reciprocal disclosure to the prosecution. If s/he is not, s/he may at least be able to point to the caselaw suggesting that the Fifth Amendment is not an absolute bar to criminal discovery in favor of the prosecution but would permit the prosecutor to obtain disclosure of the products of defense investigation in an appropriate case (see §§ 18.11-18.13 *infra*; *cf. Kansas v. Cheever*, 571 U.S. 87 (2014)) – a point that can often be made consistently with arguing vigorously that the present case is not an appropriate one. Yet even if the Fifth Amendment were an absolute bar – or to the extent that it is a bar – the "one-way street" objection is logically unsound. That is so because the "one-way street" in question is no anomalous creation of criminal discovery but is the very hallmark of the American accusatorial system of criminal procedure, preferred and, in large measure, commanded by the Fifth Amendment itself. *See Murphy v. Waterfront Commission*, 378 U.S. 52, 55 (1964). The Fifth Amendment privilege against self-incrimination embodies "'a judgment . . . that the prosecution should [not] be free to build up a criminal case, in whole or in part, with the assistance of enforced disclosures by the accused'" (*Ullmann v. United States*, 350 U.S. 422, 427 (1956)). No one would suppose that because it protects the defendant from being compelled to incriminate himself or herself, the prosecution should be permitted to incriminate the defendant with perjurious or unreliable evidence. See § 18.9.2.5 *infra*. The efficiency and fairness of prescreening the prosecution's evidence for veracity and reliability are not diminished simply because the overriding policy of the Fifth Amendment makes impossible what would be equally, but independently, desirable if constitutionally permissible: the prescreening of defense evidence as well. Any aversion to one-way streets, in this context, is nothing more or less than a rejection of basic Fifth Amendment values. *See State v. Whitaker*, 202 Conn. 259, 267, 520 A.2d 1018, 1023 (1987) ("[U]nderlying the imbalance between prosecutorial and defense discovery are constitutional and general societal concerns. In *Middleton v. United States*, . . . [401 A.2d 109,] 116 n. 11 [(D.C. App. 1979)], the court explained that criminal discovery is strongly influenced by concerns that 'the accused be secure from condemnations resting upon his coerced testimony or the improper annexation of his counsel's labors, and that the safety of the community not be jeopardized by unrestrained access to its prosecutor's files. These concerns, as well as proper deference to the constitutional principles which burden the state alone with proof of criminal charges, and considerations of fairness in light of the normal superiority of the government's investigatory resources, necessarily will frustrate the evolution of a parity of access similar to that embodied in the rules applicable to civil proceedings.'"). Such a rejection is particularly indefensible because the best founded attacks on the policy of the privilege against self-incrimination have always rested upon its tendency to protect the guilty, whereas it is the innocent who are particularly hurt by denial of discovery on "one-way street" logic. Furthermore, the realities of criminal investigation are a one-way street the other way. Police and prosecutors have resources to gather and preserve evidence incomparably greater than those of the accused. *See Wardius v.Oregon*, 412 U.S. 470, 475-76 n.9 (1973). If equal advantage were the measure of fairness in criminal procedure – which the Fifth Amendment denies – discovery in favor of the defense would nevertheless be required in virtually all situations.

18.3. ***The Advisability of Pursuing Informal Discovery Methods Before Resorting to Formal Discovery Devices***

As a general rule, counsel should always pursue informal discovery options, asking the prosecutor for whatever is wanted, before counsel embarks upon discovery motions and other formal discovery devices. Judges understandably dislike being asked for coercive orders when it is not clear that coercion is necessary, and they are likely to tell counsel to pursue informal remedies first. (Indeed, in some jurisdictions, the discovery rules require that defense attorneys employ informal discovery procedures before resorting to discovery motions.) Also, when defense counsel has sought and been denied informal discovery, the balance of goodwill tips in the defense's favor, with the judge blaming the prosecution for the expenditure of court time on a discovery matter.

B. *Informal Discovery*

18.4. *Designing a Strategy for Informal Discovery*

Prior to engaging in informal discovery, counsel will need to thoroughly familiarize himself or herself with local discovery rules and the constitutional doctrines (described in § 18.9 *infra*) that can be invoked in support of defense discovery. Even though counsel will usually not explicitly cite these rules and doctrines, a knowledge of the scope of the defendant's formal discovery rights is important in deciding what information to request and the degree to which counsel can insist that s/he is entitled to the information. And occasionally it may be possible to break through an impasse in informal negotiations by demonstrating to the prosecutor that a particular doctrine or citation supports counsel's discovery request.

Counsel should not restrict informal discovery requests to the information to which the defense is entitled as a matter of law. Instead counsel should seek everything that a liberal and enlightened criminal procedure would allow to the defense. See § 18.2 *supra*. Later in the process, when counsel is seeking judicial relief because of the prosecutor's refusal to disclose information, counsel will need to calculate whether to be venturesome or to limit discovery motions to materials that are plainly discoverable under the recognized statutes, rules, and constitutional doctrines. At that stage, there are considerations to be weighed against over-ambition. See § 18.8 *infra*. But, given the basic notion of informal discovery – that defense counsel is merely asking for whatever information the prosecutor is willing to disclose voluntarily – counsel needs not, and should not, feel restricted to the categories of information that the prosecutor can be compelled to disclose through formal discovery.

18.5. *The Discovery Letter*

Ordinarily, it is preferable to make discovery requests in written form. Discovery letters permit the type of careful phrasing that is difficult to achieve in oral requests. Moreover, if the prosecutor denies the request and counsel moves the court for a discovery order, it will be important to show precisely what counsel requested; a letter serves as the best record that any particular request was made and obviates arguments about how the request was framed. Finally, the written format permits an extended series of requests that would tax a prosecutor's time and patience if made orally in a discovery conference or a phone conversation.

To the extent possible, counsel should make the requests in the discovery letter highly specific. The more precisely a request identifies the item or information sought, the more unreasonable – and potentially unconstitutional – the prosecutor's refusal to produce it will appear. *Cf. United States v. Agurs,* 427 U.S. 97, 106-07 (1976). On the other hand, a discovery request limited to materials that defense counsel has sufficient information to identify with particularity may fail to cover some items that are crucial to the defense. One device for dealing with this problem is to frame discovery requests in the form of a series of concentric circles of increasing breadth and generality. Thus, for example, in an armed robbery prosecution, counsel might request:

    (I)   The following real or physical objects or substances:

(A)   The "thing of value" that it is alleged in Count One of the indictment the defendant took from the complainant, John Smith, on or about May 1, 2021;

(B)   Any other thing that it is claimed was taken from John Smith during the course of the robbery alleged in Count One;

(C)   The "pistol" described by Detective James Hall at page 6, line 4 of the transcript of the preliminary hearing in this case;

(D)   Any other weapon that it is claimed was used by the defendant during the course of the robbery alleged in Count One of the indictment;

(E)   Any other thing that it is claimed was used by the defendant as an instrumentality or means of committing the robbery alleged in Count One;

(F)   Any real or physical object or substance that:

    (1)   the prosecution intends to offer into evidence at any trial or hearing in this case;

    (2)   the prosecution is retaining in its custody or control for potential use as evidence at any trial or hearing in this case;

    (3)   is being retained for potential use as evidence at any trial or hearing in this case by, or within the custody or control of:

        (a)   any personnel of the Oak City Police Department;

        (b)   any personnel of the State Bureau of Investigation;

        (c)   any personnel of the Oakland County Criminalistics Laboratory;

        (d)   [following paragraphs designate other relevant agencies];

    (4)   has been submitted to any professional personnel [as defined in a "Definitions" paragraph of the discovery request, encompassing all forensic science experts and investigators] for examination, testing, or analysis in connection with this case by:

        (a)   the District Attorney's office;

        (b)   any person previously described by paragraph (I)(F)(3)(a), (b), (c) or (d);

(5)   has been gathered or received in connection with the investigation of this case by:

    (a)   the District Attorney's office;

    (b)   any personnel previously described by paragraph (I)(F)(3)(a), (b), (c), or (d);

(6)   is relevant to:

    (a)   the robbery alleged in Count One of the indictment;

    (b)   the identity of the perpetrator of that robbery;

    (c)   the investigation of that robbery;

    (d)   the physical or mental state, condition, or disposition of the defendant at the time of:

        (i)   that robbery;

        (ii)   the confession allegedly made by the defendant, described by Detective James Hall at page 10, lines 12-23 of the transcript of the preliminary hearing in this case;

        (iii)   any other confession, admission, or incriminating statement allegedly made by the defendant;

        (iv)   the present stage of the proceedings or any previous or subsequent stages of the proceedings;

(G)   Every real or physical object or substance within the categories previously described by paragraphs (I)(A) through (I)(F), which hereafter comes into the possession, custody, or control of, or is, or hereafter becomes, known to:

(1)   the District Attorney's office;

(2)   any person previously described by paragraph (I)(F)(3)(a), (b), (c), or (d).

(II)   [The following paragraphs would describe other categories of materials – defendant's statements, witnesses' statements, police and investigative reports and records, lab test results, exculpatory materials, and so forth – in a similar manner.]

Discovery requests in this form have the virtue of covering everything that might be discoverable, whether known or unknown to defense counsel, while insulating counsel's requests for narrower or more specific categories from denial on the ground that the broader or more general categories are impermissible "fishing expeditions" or include undiscoverable material.

Counsel should always include in every discovery letter a paragraph stating that each request for discovery should be construed as seeking not only information presently in the possession of the prosecution or its agents, but also "all like matter that hereafter comes into the possession of, or becomes known to, an attorney for the prosecution, the police, any other law enforcement or investigative agency, or any other agent of the prosecution."

18.6. *The Discovery Conference*

As a general rule, counsel should attempt to meet with the prosecutor for a discovery conference in addition to sending the type of discovery letter described in § 18.5 *supra*. The conference often will yield information not produced in the prosecutor's written response to a discovery letter.

The key to conducting a discovery conference effectively is to set an informal, conversational tone from the beginning. See §§ 8.1.2, 15.12 *supra*. If counsel treats the conference as governed by strict rules, s/he will soon find the prosecutor denying every request on the theory that discovery in criminal cases is very limited. If, on the other hand, counsel suggests that the two attorneys simply "talk over the case," the give-and-take of ordinary conversation usually will result in the prosecutor's disclosing information to which the defense is not technically entitled. Of course, "give-and-take" means precisely that: prosecutors usually will not give information that they are not required to give unless they feel that they are getting information in exchange. Accordingly, counsel should decide in advance what bits of information can be disclosed to the prosecutor as barter without in any way damaging the defense case or giving away too much of the defense strategy.

In addition to seeking information about the case, counsel should use the discovery conference as a vehicle for learning the prosecutor's attitude toward the seriousness of the offense and for discussing the possibility of dismissing or reducing the charges (see § 8.4 *supra*) or diverting the prosecution (see §§ 2.3.6, 3.19, 8.2.2-8.2.4, 8.4 *supra*; Chapter 21 *infra*).

It may also be useful to let the prosecutor know that counsel intends to work hard at the case (either explicitly, by saying so and explaining counsel's concern for the client, or implicitly, by describing the motions that counsel intends to file or other work counsel intends to do on the case). The pros and cons of this approach are canvassed in § 8.1.4 *supra*.

Finally, if the defendant is interested in cutting a deal with the state – furnishing testimony against a codefendant or other persons, or supplying criminal-intelligence wanted by law enforcement, in exchange for dismissal of the prosecution or reduction of charges or acceptance of a plea to a lesser charge (see §§ 6.12, 8.6, 15.10, 15.11 subdivision (9), 15.13 *supra*) – counsel might begin discussing this possibility with the prosecutor at the discovery conference.

C. *Formal Discovery: Mechanisms and Legal Bases*

18.7. *Types of Formal Discovery Procedures*

Local practice varies widely with regard to whether and which discovery procedures are available. Statutes and court rules in an increasing number of jurisdictions require that the prosecution produce specified categories of information to the defense upon request and, in some cases, without a request. *See, e.g., Watkins v. State*, 619 S.W.3d 265 (Tex. Crim. App. 2021); VERNON'S ANN. TEX. CODE CRIM. PRO. art. 39.14 (amendment effective September 1, 2017, requiring that the prosecution routinely disclose detailed information about the record and performance of custodial snitches whom it intends to call as witnesses; this automatic disclosure supplements an extensive list of other prosecutorial material discoverable upon defense request); OKLA. STAT. ANN., title 22, § 2002(A)(4) (effective November 1, 2020) (requiring similar disclosure of material relating to snitches); MINN. STAT. ANN. § 634.045, summarized in § 37.15 *infra*; VA. SUPREME COURT RULE 3A:11 (amended effective July 1, 2019); *and see* National Association of Criminal Defense Lawyers, *Discovery Reform Legislative Victories: Summary of recent discovery reforms adopted by states* (May 21, 2020), *available at* https://www.nacdl.org/Content/DiscoveryReformLegislativeVictories. Also, unwritten customs in some localities may offer discovery procedures that are more liberal than those authorized by statutes and formal rules. Counsel who is not thoroughly familiar with local practice will therefore want not only to consult the State's statutes, court rules, and caselaw, but also to confer with experienced defense attorneys practicing in the jurisdiction, to ascertain what types of discovery devices are conventional, as well as what sanctions for discovery violations the local judges commonly employ. *See, e.g., City of Seattle v. Lange*, 18 Wash. App. 2d 139, 491 P.3d 156 (2021) (approving the trial court's suppression of blood test results as a sanction for the prosecution's failure to disclose a corrective action report showing that the crime lab forensic expert who conducted the test had made a mistake resulting in a false positive in another DWI case; the Court of Appeals holds that although the report was in the possession of the lab and was unknown to the prosecution, Washington's discovery rules "'impose[ ] a continuing obligation on the prosecutor to seek the disclosure of [defense-requested] discoverable information not in his or her control'" (*id.* at 152, 491 P.3d at 164); that those rules "do not require proof of materiality before mandating disclosure, and . . . that the absence of constitutional materiality 'does not relieve prosecutors of the obligation to disclose impeachment evidence'" (*id.* at 149, 491 P.3d at 162); and that the rules give a trial judge discretion to suppress prosecution evidence as a sanction for discovery violations without making the finding of prejudice which would be required to establish a constitutional *Brady* violation (see § 18.9.1 *infra*): "Nothing in the language of the [applicable] rule requires a finding of prejudice before remedying a discovery violation with something less than dismissal." *Id.* at 155, 491 P.3d at 165.); *State ex rel. Rusen v. Hill*, 193 W. Va. 133, 144, 454 S.E.2d 427, 438 (1994) (upholding a trial court order dismissing a prosecution as a sanction for a long-running discovery violation: "[A] circuit court is not required to find actual prejudice to be justified in sanctioning a party for pretrial discovery violations. Prejudice may be presumed from repeated discovery violations necessitating numerous continuances and delays."); *State ex rel. Jackson County Prosecuting Attorney v. Prokes*, 363 S.W.3d 71 (Mo. App. 2011) (upholding a trial court order excluding all prosecution evidence as a sanction for repeated, egregious violations of discovery orders); *State v. Montgomery*, 901 N.E.2d 515, 523 (Ind. App. 2009) ("The State did not comply with [a] request [for discovery of a fire investigator's photographs of a purported arson scene for] . . . over three years and five months . . . . Montgomery's expert witness, . . . believed that some of the photographs were exculpatory, but Montgomery was unable to prepare his defense in time for trial. In light of the State's pattern of failure in complying with Montgomery's discovery requests and the trial court's orders, we do not find clear error in the trial court's grant of Montgomery's motion for discharge."); *and see CNN News: State v. Yallow*, https://www.cnn.com/2023/03/22/us/lori-vallow-death-penalty-idaho-ruling/index.html (as a sanction for belated discovery, an Idaho trial court in a capital case precludes the prosecution from seeking the death penalty; the court explains that this sanction is not punitive but is designed to protect the defendant's right to adequate time to prepare for a penalty trial; the prosecution's argument that a continuance would provide an adequate remedy is rejected because the defendant has unequivocally asserted her right to a speedy trial).

Even if certain devices are not recognized by applicable local legislation, rules, or practice, counsel can argue that they should be made available in the case at bar in the exercise of the trial court's inherent discretionary power to regulate the proceedings before it. *See, e.g., State ex rel. Keller v. Criminal Court of Marion County, Division IV*, 262 Ind. 420, 423, 317 N.E.2d 433, 435 (1974) ("A trial court may, sua sponte, affirmatively order discovery. We have specifically so held: 'Discovery may be provided for by statute, court rule or granted by the inherent power of the trial court.' . . . The object of a trial is the discovery of the truth. A trial judge has the responsibility to direct the trial in a manner which facilitates the ascertainment of that truth. The power to order discovery is 'grounded in the inherent power of the trial court to guide and control the proceedings.'"); *State v. Richardson*, 452 N.J. Super. 124, 132, 171 A.3d 1270, 1274 (2017) ("Notably, our courts' power to order discovery is not limited to the express terms of the automatic discovery provisions of . . . [the State's criminal procedure rules]. The courts have 'the inherent power to order discovery when justice so requires.'"); *accord, State v. Chambers*, 252 N.J. 561, 583, 288 A.3d 12, 25 (2023); *State v. Laux*, 167 N.H. 698, 704 117 A.3d 725, 730 (2015) ("we hold that the circuit court has the inherent authority, within its sound discretion, to order discovery prior to the preliminary hearing when the accused has made a particularized showing that the discovery is needed to show a lack of probable cause and the court concludes that the interests of justice require disclosure"); *United States v. Villa*, 2014 WL 280400 (D. Conn. 2014), quoted in § 18.9.1 *infra*; *cf. State v. Tetu*, 139 Hawai'i 207, 386 P.3d 844 (2016), quoted in §18.7.4 *infra*.

Authorities and arguments supporting the recognition of various devices are found in the following literature, most of which is outspoken in favor of broadened criminal discovery: AMERICAN BAR ASSOCIATION, STANDARDS FOR CRIMINAL JUSTICE MONITORS AND MONITORING, DISCOVERY (4th ed. 2020) [Chapter 11 of the 2017 Standards, updated]; William J. Brennan, Jr., *The Criminal Prosecution: Sporting Event or Quest for Truth?,* 1963 WASH. U. L.Q. 279; Richard M. Calkins, *Criminal Justice for the Indigent,* 42 U. DET. L.J. 305, 334-35, 337-39 (1965); Richard M. Calkins, *Grand Jury Secrecy,* 63 MICH. L. REV. 455 (1965); Daniel J. Capra, *Access to Exculpatory Evidence: Avoiding the* Agurs *Problems of Prosecutorial Discretion and Retrospective Review,* 53 FORDHAM L. REV. 391 (1984); Ronald L. Carlson, *False or Suppressed Evidence: Why a Need for the Prosecutorial Tie?,* 1969 DUKE L.J. 1171; Robert L. Fletcher, *Pre-*

Trial Discovery in State Criminal Cases, 12 STAN. L. REV. 293 (1960); Abraham S. Goldstein, *The State and the Accused: Balance of Advantage in Criminal Procedure,* 69 YALE L.J. 1149, 1172-98 (1960); Sheldon Krantz, *Pretrial Discovery in Criminal Cases: A Necessity for Fair and Impartial Justice,* 42 NEB. L. REV. 127 (1962); David W. Louisell, *Criminal Discovery: Dilemma Real or Apparent?,* 49 CALIF. L. REV. 56 (1961); Robert P. Mosteller, *Discovery Against the Defense: Tilting the Adversarial Balance,* 74 CAL. L. REV. 1567 (1986); Robert P. Mosteller, *Exculpatory Evidence, Ethics, and the Road to the Disbarment of Mike Nifong: The Critical Importance of Full Open-File Discovery,* 15 GEO. MASON L. REV. 257 (2008); Barry Nakell, *Criminal Discovery for the Defense and the Prosecution – The Developing Constitutional Considerations,* 50 N.C. L. REV. 437 (1972); Barry Nakell, *The Effect of Due Process on Criminal Defense Discovery,* 62 KY. L.J. 58 (1973-74); Mary Prosser, *Reforming Criminal Discovery: Why Old Objections Must Yield to New Realities,* 2006 WIS. L. REV. 541; Daniel A. Rezneck, *The New Federal Rules of Criminal Procedure,* 54 GEO. L.J. 1276 (1966); Jenny Roberts, *Too Little, Too Late: Ineffective Assistance of Counsel, the Duty to Investigate, and Pretrial Discovery in Criminal Cases,* 31 FORDHAM URB. L.J. 1097 (2004); Hon. H. Lee Sarokin & William E. Zuckermann, *Presumed Innocent? Restrictions on Criminal Discovery in Federal Court Belie this Presumption,* 43 RUTGERS L. REV. 1089 (1991); Roger J. Traynor, *Ground Lost and Found in Criminal Discovery,* 39 N.Y.U. L. REV. 228, 749 (1964); Peter Westen, *The Compulsory Process Clause,* 73 MICH. L. REV. 71, 121-31 (1974); Bureau Draft, *A State Statute to Liberalize Criminal Discovery,* 4 HARV. J. LEGISLATION 105 (1966); Edward M. Glickman, Note, *Disclosure of Grand Jury Minutes to Challenge Indictments and Impeach Witnesses in Federal Criminal Cases,* 111 U. PA. L. REV. 1154 (1963); Katherine L. Hensley, Note, *Discovery Depositions: A Proposed Right for the Criminal Defendant,* 51 S. CAL. L. REV. 467 (1978).

A general approach to defense counsel's argument for broadened discovery rights is contained in § 18.2 *supra,* and constitutional considerations that may be advanced to support those rights are enumerated in § 18.9 *infra.* The most commonly recognized formal discovery devices are discussed in §§ 18.7.1-18.7.6 *infra.*

18.7.1. *Motion for a Bill of Particulars*

See § 13.7 *supra.*

18.7.2. *Motion for a List of Prosecution Witnesses*

See § 13.7 *supra.* If the prosecutor responds to a motion or order for production of a witness list by serving up an obviously inflated list calculated to hamper defense preparation, counsel can seek the court's intervention to extract a more realistic list. *Cf. Chafin v. State,* 246 Ga. 709, 713-14, 273 S.E.2d 147, 152-53 (1980). If counsel's independent investigation suggests, conversely, that the prosecutor is probably withholding the names of some potential prosecution witnesses, counsel can bring the matter to the court's attention by a motion to compel full disclosure; or alternatively counsel can (1) move at a pretrial conference or other pretrial, post-discovery proceeding to preclude the testimony of an unlisted witness (*see, e.g., State v. Martinez,* 1998-NMCA-022, 124 N.M. 721, 954 P.2d 1198 (N.M. App. 1998)), or (2) await trial and, when the prosecutor calls an unlisted witness, object to his or her testifying (*see, e.g.*, *Rouse v. State*, 243 So.2d 225 (Fla. App. 1971); *People v. White*, 123 Ill. App. 2d 102, 259 N.E.2d 357 (1970)). At trial the judge will have discretion to (a) exclude the testimony of the witness, or (b) allow the witness to testify and allow the defense a continuance to prepare for cross-examining the witness and to gather defense witnesses responsive to the unannounced witness's testimony. *State v. Prieto*, 2016 WI App 15, 366 Wis. 2d 794, 876 N.W.2d 154 (Wis. App. 2015). *See, e.g.*, *Rogers v. State*, 261 Ga. 649, 649-50, 409 S.E.2d 655, 656-57 (1991) ("[I]f a defendant makes a timely written demand for a list of witnesses, a witness whose name does not appear on the list may not testify without defendant's consent. The prosecution's failure to list a witness can be cured in many situations, however, if defendant is granted a continuance or allowed to interview the witness before the testimony is given. ¶ In this case, Rogers made a timely written demand for a list of witnesses . . . . We conclude that the testimony of the witness should not have been allowed without giving Rogers some remedy for the prosecution's noncompliance with the statute. The record is clear that Rogers insisted on his right to a witness list and on his right to a remedy for the failure of the witness to appear on the list."); *People v. Kysar*, 158 A.3d 544, 544, 69 N.Y.S.3d 649, 650 (N.Y. App. Div., 1st Dep't 2018) (reversing a conviction because the trial court failed to grant appropriate relief when the prosecution violated the witness-list rule by presenting the testimony of the complainant, who had been omitted from the witness list because the prosecution was "unable to locate him in the two years between the incident and the trial" and who was located "after the jury was selected, and just before opening arguments"; "[d]efense counsel clearly 'relied to her detriment [in *voir dire*] on her expectation that the People would not call this witness,'" and therefore the trial court, "having denied defense counsel's request to preclude the complainant's testimony, should have granted counsel's alternative request, made prior to opening arguments, to select a new jury").

In a few jurisdictions, the defendant's right to a witness list is not limited to potential prosecution witnesses but extends to witnesses whom the prosecutor knows have exculpatory evidence. *See, e.g.*, FLA. RULE CRIM. PRO. 3.220(b)(1)(A); *Richardson v. State*, 246 So.2d 771 (1971). Local rules should be consulted.

18.7.3. *Discovery Motions*

In addition to the two specific types of discovery motions that have been described thus far – motions for a bill of particulars and motions for a list of witnesses – most jurisdictions provide for a generalized discovery motion in which the defense can seek production of any other information to which it is entitled by statute, court rule, or caselaw.

Depending upon the facts of the case, the defense may wish to move for production or inspection of:

1. *Physical objects.* Counsel should ask that these be released or duplicated for testing by defense experts, if advised (*State v. Grenning*, 169 Wash. 2d 47, 234 P.3d 169 (2010)); or the court can be asked to order that defense experts be allowed to attend testing by prosecution experts.

2. *Police and other investigative reports* (*see, e.g.*, *Minges v. State*, 192 N.E.3d 893 (Ind. 2022) (holding police reports discoverable, subject to work-product

privilege and other applicable privileges)); *records and materials generated by police procedures and activities* (911 telephone calls (*Magallan v. Superior Court*, 192 Cal. App. 4th 1444, 121 Cal. Rptr.3d 841 (2011) (approving a pre-preliminary-hearing discovery order that required the prosecution to disclose the contents of a 911 call and related dispatch communications for the defendant's use in a suppression motion at the PX)); recordings from police body and vehicle vidcams (*People v. Kladis*, 2011 IL 110920, 960 N.E.2d 1104, 355 Ill. Dec. 933 (2011)); police officers' notebooks (*People v. Pierna*, 74 Misc. 3d 1072, 163 N.Y.S.3d 897 (N.Y. Crim. Ct., Bronx Cty. 2022); arrest photographs; booking records (*State v. Grimm*, 165 W. Va. 547, 270 S.E.2d 173 (1980)); eyewitness identification forms; and so forth); *photographs* (*State v. Montgomery*, 901 N.E.2d 515 (Ind. App. 2009); *People v. Coleates*, 86 Misc. 2d 614, 376 N.Y.S.2d 374 (N.Y. County Ct., Ontario Cty. 1975)), *diagrams, and other items generated by law enforcement and prosecutorial evidence gathering*. See § 9.20 *supra* for a roster of the kinds of documents and materials that are commonly accumulated in the course of police processing and prosecutorial working-up of a case. *And see United States v. Soto-Zuniga*, 837 F.3d 992 (9th Cir. 2016) (holding that the defendant's motion for discovery of the number and types of arrests and vehicle searches at an immigration checkpoint should have been granted in connection with a suppression motion claiming that the checkpoint operation violated the Fourth Amendment); *United States v. Washington*, 869 F.3d 193 (3d Cir. 2017) (authorizing limited defense discovery of records and statistics relating to operations of the Bureau of Alcohol, Tobacco, Firearms and Explosives in connection with a prospective motion for dismissal based upon a claim of selective enforcement).

3.   *Medical and scientific reports* (*see, e.g., State v. Desir*, 245 N.J. 179, 206-07, 244 A.3d 737, 753-54 (2021) (in order to permit the defendant an adequate opportunity to litigate a *Franks* challenge to a search warrant (see § 25.17.3 *infra*) in a narcotics case, the New Jersey Supreme Court requires discovery of a lab report that was the basis for the warrant affidavit); *Patrick v. State*, 329 Md. 24, 617 A.2d 215 (1992); *Wester v. State*, 260 Ga. 228, 391 S.E.2d 765 (1990); *State v. Adams*, 481 A.2d 718 (R.I. 1984); *People v. Davis*, 52 A.D.3d 1205, 859 N.Y.S.2d 804 (N.Y. App. Div., 4th Dep't 2008); *State v. Fair*, 164 N.C. App. 770, 596 S.E.2d 871 (2004)) *and materials relating to the expected testimony of prosecution expert witnesses* (*see, e.g., State v. Fair, supra*, 164 N.C. App. at 774, 596 S.E.2d at 873; *State v. Arteaga*, 2023 WL 3859579, at *1, *9, *11, *12 (N.J. Super. Ct., App. Div. 2023) (directing the State to comply with the defendant's motion for "discovery related to the facial recognition technology (FRT) used to develop a picture of him, which was then used to identify and charge him": "The evidence sought here is directly tied to the defense's ability to test the reliability of the FRT. As such, it is vital to impeach the witnesses' identification, challenge the State's investigation, create reasonable doubt, and demonstrate third-party guilt."; "The FRT's reliability has obvious implications for the accuracy of the identification process because an array constructed around a mistaken potential match would leave the witness with no actual perpetrator to choose. The

reliability of the technology bears direct relevance to the quality and thoroughness of the broader criminal investigation, and whether the potential matches the software returned yielded any other viable alternative suspects to establish third-party guilt. Defendant's request for the identity, design, specifications, and operation of the program or programs used for analysis, and the database or databases used for comparison are relevant to FRT's reliability."; "Here, the items sought by the defense have a direct link to testing FRT's reliability and bear on defendant's guilt or innocence. Given FRT's novelty, no one, including us, can reasonably conclude without the discovery whether the evidence is exculpatory or 'merely potentially useful evidence.' . . . For these reasons, it must be produced."; "Defendant must have the tools to impeach the State's case and sow reasonable doubt."); *State v. Pickett*, 466 N.J. Super. 270, 301, 246 A.3d 279, 306-07 (2021) ("We hold that if the State chooses to utilize an expert who relies on novel probabilistic genotyping software to render DNA testimony, then defendant is entitled to access, under an appropriate protective order, to the [proprietary] software's source code and supporting software development and related documentation – including that pertaining to testing, design, bug reporting, change logs, and program requirements – to challenge the reliability of the software and science underlying that expert's testimony at a *Frye* hearing [see § 39.15 *infra*], provided defendant first satisfies the burden of demonstrating a particularized need for such discovery."). *See also People v. Jones*, 2023 IL App (1st) 221311, 2023 WL 3856424, at *1, *7 (Ill. App. 2023) (affirming the trial court's order enforcing the defendant's subpoena to ShotSpotter, Inc., to "produce materials relating to the reliability of its system, both generally and in this incident specifically": "It appears that defendant Jones subpoenaed ShotSpotter primarily in anticipation of filing a motion to suppress the traffic stop [which was initiated by the police receipt of "a ShotSpotter alert of suspected gunfire," that led to police officers driving to the location specified in the alert and then seeing and stopping defendant's vehicle, and] that led to his arrest [for aggravated driving under the influence of alcohol] and the evidence against him."; "Defendant Jones's arrest report indicates that, at the suppression hearing, the ShotSpotter alert will be the officers' primary, and perhaps only, legal justification for seizing defendant Jones. Defendant Jones should be allowed to subpoena evidence regarding the ShotSpotter alert itself, what information ShotSpotter communicated to the arresting officers, and whether the ShotSpotter alert was reliable. The trial court's ruling on ShotSpotter's motion to quash accomplishes those goals. Records reflecting the qualifications, experience, and training of the IRC [Incident Review Center] staff who analyzed the acoustic pulse in this case are relevant to the reliability of the information that the IRC communicated to CPD [Chicago Police Department] officers shortly before defendant Jones's arrest. Policies and procedures that IRC analysts followed in evaluating this acoustic pulse are relevant to understanding why IRC staff took the actions that they did in this incident. Logs reflecting the calibration of the sensors that detected the acoustic pulse in this case are relevant to whether those sensors were working properly on the day of defendant Jones's arrest. Records reflecting reclassifications of acoustic pulses in Chicago in the three months before and after defendant Jones's arrest and studies regarding the performance of the ShotSpotter system in Chicago are relevant to whether ShotSpotter, as a system, is reliably able to identify gunfire and direct police to the firearms that caused it. ¶ . . . Moreover, this discovery will allow defendant Jones to prepare for any testimony or argument that ShotSpotter alerts are reliable and often lead police to illegal firearms. The possibility that the State will present such evidence is not speculative; other courts have accepted such testimony in support of reasonable suspicion. . . . Defendant Jones should be allowed to prepare to cross-examine officers who testify similarly in a motion to suppress hearing by obtaining materials that shed light on ShotSpotter's reliability as a system."). *But see People v. Wakefield*, 38 N.Y.3d 367, 385, 195 N.E.3d 19, 31, 174 N.Y.S.3d 312, 324 (2022) (rejecting "defendant's novel argument that the source code [for TrueAllele software] is . . . [a] declarant [so as to give the defendant a Sixth Amendment right to its discovery]. Even if the TrueAllele system is programmed to have some measure of 'artificial intelligence,' the source code is not an entity that can be cross-examined. '[T]he Confrontation Clause provides two types of protections for a criminal defendant: the right physically to face those who testify against him, and the right to conduct cross-examination'."), *including the standard operating procedures, quality controls and proficiency testing records of prosecution experts who will testify at trial* (*Cole v. State*, 378 Md. 42, 835 A.2d 600 (2003)). Note that in federal practice, an amendment to FED. RULE CRIM. PRO. 16(a), effective December 1, 2022, provides for the following disclosure by the Government:

> (G) Expert Witnesses.
> (i) Duty to Disclose. At the defendant's request, the government must disclose to the defendant, in writing, the information required by (iii) for any [expert] testimony that the government intends to use at trial . . . during its case-in-chief, or during its rebuttal to counter testimony that the defendant has timely disclosed under . . . [parallel provisions of Rule 16 requiring disclosure by the defense]. If the government requests discovery under the . . . [provision relating to defense disclosure of materials relating to expert testimony on the defendant's mental condition] and the defendant complies, the government must, at the defendant's request, disclose to the defendant, in writing, the information required by (iii) for [expert] testimony that the government intends to use at trial . . . on the issue of the defendant's mental condition.
> (ii) Time to Disclose. The court, by order or local rule, must set a time for the government to make its disclosures. The time must be sufficiently before trial to provide a fair opportunity for the defendant to meet the government's evidence.
> (iii) Contents of the Disclosure. The disclosure for each expert witness must contain:
> • a complete statement of all opinions that the government will elicit from the witness in its case-in-chief, or during its rebuttal to counter testimony that the defendant has timely disclosed . . . ;

• the bases and reasons for them;
• the witness's qualifications, including a list of all publications authored in the previous 10 years; and
• a list of all other cases in which, during the previous 4 years, the witness has testified as an expert at trial or by deposition.

. . . .

(v) Signing the Disclosure. The witness must approve and sign the disclosure, unless the government:
• states in the disclosure why it could not obtain the witness's signature through reasonable efforts; or
• has previously provided . . . a report, signed by the witness, that contains all the opinions and the bases and reasons for them required by (iii).

See § 37.14 *infra*.

4. *Written and oral statements of the defendant. See, e.g.,* FED. RULE CRIM. PRO. 16(a)(1)(A), (B), *and United States v. Isa*, 413 F.2d 244 (7th Cir. 1969); *cf. United States v. Vinas*, 910 F.3d 52, 54, 58, 59 (2d Cir. 2018) (vacating a conviction and ordering a new trial because the government's notice of the defendant's statement violated Rule 16(a)(1)(A) by presenting "a misleading description of the circumstances under which the defendant purportedly made . . . [the statement], and so misinformed defense counsel about the possible grounds for suppression" and misled counsel "into not moving to suppress" the statement); KENTUCKY RULE CRIM. PRO. 7.24(1); ME. RULE UNIFIED CRIM. PRO. 16(2)(C); MICH. CT. RULE 6.201(B)(3); *Ex parte Hunter*, 777 So.2d 60 (Ala. 2000); *Jones v. State*, 376 So.2d 437 (Fla. App. 1979); *People v. Boucher*, 62 Ill. App. 3d 436, 379 N.E.2d 339 (1978).

5. *Written and oral statements of any codefendants or other alleged accomplices. See* MICH. CT. RULE 6.201(B)(3); *Walker v. Commonwealth*, 4 Va. App. 286, 356 S.E.2d 853 (1987); and see §§ 29.8, 37.8 *infra*.

6. *Statements of witnesses (see People ex rel. Shinn v. District Court of Fifteenth Judicial District*, 172 Colo. 23, 469 P.2d 732 (1970) (applying the general provision now found in COLO. CRIM. PRO. RULE 18(d)(1): "The court in its discretion may, upon motion, require disclosure to the defense of relevant material and information not covered by . . . [earlier provisions of the rule providing for discovery of specific items] upon a showing by the defense that the request is reasonable."); see also § 37.4 infra), and the names and addresses of all prospective prosecution witnesses (see McKinney v. State*, 482 So.2d 1129 (Miss. 1986)). In some jurisdictions a motion for discovery is the appropriate procedure for obtaining the names of prosecution witnesses (*see, e.g., Foster v. State*, 484 So.2d 1009 (Miss. 1986)); in other jurisdictions there is a specialized procedure for obtaining a witness list (see §§ 13.7, 18.7.2 *supra*).

7. *Official records* (maintained by prisons, jails, hospitals, probation departments, and so forth) relating to the defendant, codefendants, and prosecution and defense witnesses, including materials relevant to credibility in the personnel files of police witnesses (*see People v. Toussaint*, 78 Misc. 3d 504, 506-07, 182 N.Y.S.3d 586, 589 (N.Y. Crim. Ct., Queens Cty. 2023) ("When the People claimed to certify compliance, they also had not disclosed disciplinary records relating to charges against two of their police witnesses. Instead, the People had disclosed only summary letters, which they authored, containing little information about the officers' misconduct. After over 200 days past arraignments, the People finally provided some of the underlying records for one officer. They have never provided any underlying documents for the second. ¶ Under these circumstances, the People failed to properly certify discovery before stating ready for trial."); *People v. Soto*, 72 Misc. 3d 1153, 1157-61, 152 N.Y.S.3d 274, 279-82 (N.Y. Crim. Ct., N.Y. Cty. 2023)); investigative reports relating to previous complaints by the present complainant; and records of all police and prosecutorial transactions with any undercover agents or informants involved.

8. *Criminal records* of the defendant, codefendants, complainant (*see People v. Soto, supra*, 72 Misc. 3d at 1156-57, 152 N.Y.S.3d at 278-79; (*cf. Pitchess v. Superior Court*, 11 Cal. 3d 531, 522 P.2d 305, 113 Cal. Rptr. 897 (1974) (superseded by statute on unrelated issues)), prosecution and defense witnesses, and informants. See §§ 36.4, 37.5, 37.15, 39.13.1 *infra*.

9. *The grand jury transcript.* A special shibboleth of secrecy has traditionally surrounded grand jury proceedings and made courts reluctant to disclose grand jury records. See § 12.5 *supra*. There has, however, been some erosion of this protectionistic attitude, "consonant with the growing realization that disclosure, rather than suppression, of relevant materials ordinarily promotes the proper administration of criminal justice" (*Dennis v. United States*, 384 U.S. 855, 870 (1966)). Some jurisdictions provide for pretrial discovery by the defense of the grand jury transcript or an electronic recording of the grand jury proceedings, either upon defense motion or as a matter of routine (*see, e.g.,* ALASKA RULE CRIM. PRO. 6(m); MASS. RULE CRIM. PRO. 14(a)(1)(A)(ii); N.J. RULE GOVERNING CRIM. PRACTICE 3:6-6(b)), while others provide the more limited pretrial discovery mechanism of allowing the defense to seek disclosure in connection with a motion to dismiss the indictment based upon "a matter that occurred before the grand jury" (FED. RULE CRIM. PRO. 6(e)(3)(E)(ii)) or the insufficiency of the evidence before the grand jury to support the charges in the indictment (N.Y. CRIM. PRO. LAW § 210.30(3)). A number of jurisdictions also provide for discovery *at trial* of the prior statements of prosecution witnesses, for purposes of impeachment (see § 34.7 *infra*), and these provisions ordinarily include witnesses' grand jury testimony.

10. *Photographs and other visual aids* shown to witnesses by investigating officers for purposes of identification. *See Simmons v. United States,* 390 U.S. 377, 388 (1968) (dictum).

11. *Other documents or data* that are "within the government's possession, custody, or control and . . . [that are] material to preparing the defense" (FED. RULE CRIM. PRO. 16(a)(1)(E); *and see, e.g., United States v. Soto-Zuniga*, summarized in subdivision 2 of this section (Federal Criminal Rule 16(a)(1)(E)'s requirement of production of items "'material to preparing the defense'" includes "discovery related to the constitutionality of a search or seizure" (*id.* at 1000)); *State v. Reed-Hansen*, 2019 ME 58, 207 A.3d 191, 192-96 (Me. 2019) (affirming the trial court's order "imposing a significant discovery sanction [of suppressing "'all evidence obtained as a result of the [traffic] stop'"] following the state's failure to provide to the defendant a dash-cam video of the defendant ostensibly committing the [charged] crime" of driving with an expired inspection sticker: although the state asserted that the video was not subject to discovery requirements "because Reed-Hansen's inspection sticker could not be seen on the video," the court concludes that "there can be no question that the video was 'material and relevant to the preparation of the defense'" given that the "video . . . indisputably records . . . Reed-Hansen's operation of the vehicle, an element of the very crime at issue"); *Commonwealth v. Daniels*, 445 Mass. 392, 402, 837 N.E.2d 683, 692-93 (2005) (ordering post-trial discovery of a statement by a friend of the defendant's co-indictee containing information which, if known to the defense, would have provided a basis for discrediting the testimony of the prosecution's sole eyewitness; defense counsel's motion for pretrial discovery of "exculpatory evidence" had been denied but the Massachusetts Supreme Judicial Court holds that: "At the pretrial stage, and where the requested discovery is specific, the requirements of due process mandate that a judge should not refuse to order discovery without either reviewing the specifically requested material or obtaining a representation from the Commonwealth that the specifically requested material contains no favorable evidence. . . . ¶ . . . [W]e do not accept the prosecutor's contention that in the circumstances of this case, the denial of the defendant's pretrial discovery request absolved the Commonwealth of its obligation to disclose the specific materials requested. . . . [O]nce the Commonwealth has notice that the defendant seeks specific favorable information in its possession, it must examine the material and furnish that information to the defense if it is favorable. Where the Commonwealth knows that a judge has not reviewed the specifically requested material, its obligation continues.")) *and documents and data in the possession of parties allied with the prosecution (such as the purported victims of the alleged crimes)* which are material to the prosecution's case or potentially supportive of a defense (*see, e.g., State ex rel. Rusen v. Hill*, 193 W. Va. 133, 454 S.E.2d 427 (1994), quoted in § 18.2 *supra*; *Pitchess v. Superior Court, supra.*)

12. Other materials that are obtainable by law enforcement through special accommodations not available to defense counsel. *See, e.g., Black v. State*, 2017 Wyo. 135, 405 P.3d 1045, 1051 (2017) (conviction reversed, in part because of the prosecution's failure to comply with a discovery order that it obtain and produce to the defense a six-month batch of Verizon cell phone and Facebook

records: "One of the exhibits in support of the motion for sanctions was an email from the prosecutor to defense counsel. The email contained a Facebook policy for addressing record requests from law enforcement. According to the policy, law enforcement 'may expeditiously submit formal preservation requests through the Law Enforcement Online Request System at facebook.com/records, or by email . . . .' Once the request is received, according to the policy, Facebook 'will search for and disclose data that is specified with particularity in an appropriate form of legal process and which we are reasonably able to locate and retrieve.'" 405 P.3d at 1051. Defense counsel's motion for production had alleged that "'[i]t is believed that it is much easier and more convenient for the State to obtain these requested records than the Defendant. It is known, in fact, that such a request for Facebook to provide records is made frequently by law enforcement in Teton County, Wyoming. *See* Records Request at www.facebook.com/records/login (stating that "If you are a law enforcement agent who is authorized to gather evidence in connection with an official investigation, you may request records from Facebook through this system."). Whereas, it is unduly cumbersome and costly, both in time and resources for the Office of the State Public Defender to obtain these records via court subpoena, or subpoena duces tecum, and the required modes of providing notice and service.'" 405 P.3d at 1049.). *Cf. Wardius v. Oregon*, 412 U.S. 470 (1973), discussed in § 18.9.2.7.

13.   Materials relating to any proposed prosecution testimony by snitches (see § 37.15 *infra*) or turncoat accomplices (see §§ 29.8, 37.8 *infra*).

18.7.4. *Other Discovery-Related Motions*

In addition to the foregoing motions, local practice may recognize (or counsel may be able to persuade the judge to recognize) one or more of the following types of motions, which involve the court's ordering the prosecution or prosecution witnesses to participate in certain discovery-related procedures:

1.   Motions for medical or psychiatric examination of the complainant or other prosecution witnesses. *See State v. Ruiz*, 131 N.M. 241, 34 P.3d 630 (N.M. App. 2001); *State v. Chambers*, 252 N.J. 561, 288 A.3d 12 (2023), quoted in §§ 18.9.2.4, 39.1 *infra*.

2.   Motions for independent testing of prosecution forensic evidence. *See State v. Migliore*, 261 La. 722, 260 So.2d 682 (1972).

3.   Motions for an order requiring the complainant and other prosecution witnesses to speak with the defense because of prosecutorial or police interference with the defense right to investigate. See § 9.14 *supra*.

4.   Motions for an order requiring police witnesses to speak with the defense. See § 9.15 *supra*.

5.   Motions for access to the crime scene. *See State v. Tetu*, 139 Hawai'i 207, 214, 386 P.3d 844, 851 (2016) ("The issue of whether a defendant has a right to inspect the crime scene is one of first impression before this court. . . . Because the State was not in possession of . . . [the site of a charged burglary, Hawaii Penal Procedure] Rule 16 does not expressly provide the defense with access to the crime scene. However, the . . . Rule 16 discovery right does not purport to set an outer limit on the court's power to ensure a defendant's constitutional rights. . . . Accordingly, we consider whether there is a constitutional right to access a crime scene when the defendant is alleged to have committed the offense on private property. . . . ¶ A review of several jurisdictions' codes and performance standards for defense attorneys indicates that in order to assure competent representation, defense counsel should investigate the crime scene and consider seeking access as early as possible, unless circumstances suggest it would be unnecessary in a given case." *Id.* at 214-15, 386 P.3d at 851-52. "There is a broad consensus across the United States that competent defense counsel should access the crime scene unless, after a careful investigation of the underlying facts of a case, counsel makes a reasonable determination that access is not necessary to provide effective assistance of counsel. Thus, a defendant's ability to access the crime scene inheres within the right to effective assistance of counsel guaranteed by article I, section 14 of the Hawai'i Constitution." *Id.* at 218, 386 P.3d at 855. "[Also,] under article I, section 5 of the Hawai'i Constitution, a defendant has a due process right to a fair trial. Due process requires that a defendant be given a meaningful opportunity to present a complete defense and that discovery procedures provide the maximum possible amount of information and a level-playing field in the adversarial process. Thus, the due process clause of the Hawai'i Constitution provides a defendant with the right to access the crime scene in order to secure the promises that a fair trial affords." *Id.* at 220, 386 P.3d at 857.); *see also State v. Gonsalves*, 661 S.2d 1281 (Fla. App. 1995).

6.   Motions for a lineup. *See State in the interest of W.C.*, 85 N.J. 218, 426 A.2d 50 (1981); *Evans v. Superior Court*, 11 Cal. 3d 617, 522 P.2d 681, 114 Cal. Rptr. 121 (1974); *Garcia v. Superior Court*, 1 Cal. App. 4th 979, 2 Cal. Rptr. 2d 707 (1991) (voice lineup).

In addition, counsel can, in certain circumstances, move for the detention of persons as material witnesses. See §§ 18.10.1, 29.4.1 *infra*.

18.7.5. *Depositions*

Although depositions are a key feature of discovery in civil cases, most jurisdictions do not authorize depositions in criminal cases, except when it is necessary to preserve the testimony of a witness for trial (*see, e.g.*, FED. RULE CRIM. PRO. 15(a)) or in other exceptional circumstances (see, *e.g.*, § 9.14 *supra*, discussing deposition as a possible remedy for the prosecutor's impermissibly advising a witness to decline to talk with defense counsel or a defense investigator).

In a small number of jurisdictions, depositions are available in criminal cases for their customary function of discovery. *See* Romualdo P. Eclavea, Annot., *Accused's right to depose prospective witnesses before trial in state court*, 2 A.L.R.4th 704 (1980 & Supp.); AMERICAN BAR ASSOCIATION, STANDARDS FOR CRIMINAL JUSTICE 11-5.1, Commentary n.4 (3d ed. 1996) (citing statutes and rules). In these jurisdictions, depositions may be freely available just as in civil cases (FLA. RULE CRIM. PRO. 3.220(h)(1); *Ivester v. State*, 398 So.2d 926 (Fla. App. 1981); VT. RULE CRIM. PRO. 15(a); *and see Archer v. State*, 166 N.E.3d 963 (Ind. App. 2021), *effectively superseded by statute, see Church v. State*, 189 N.E.3d 580, 593 (Ind. 2022) (applying Indiana's three-pronged standard for the allowance of depositions by the defense – "(1) is there a sufficient designation of the items sought to be discovered (particularity), and (2) are the items sought to be discovered material to the defense (relevance); if so, then the request must be granted unless (3) the State makes a sufficient showing of its 'paramount interest' in non-disclosure" (166 N.E.3d at 969) – to reverse a trial court order quashing a defendant's deposition notice: the issue arises in anticipation of the retrial of a child-molestation charge after the defendant's first conviction, seven years earlier, was reversed for ineffective assistance of defense counsel; the court of appeal adverts to "notions of fundamental fairness" in finding that "[i]t would be unfair to the defendant to limit him to a defense strategy, poorly or well-formed, that was adopted to address a victim aged eight or nine, when that victim will be testifying in his new trial from the life experience of a nearly grown adult" (*id.* at 970)) or they may require that counsel seek a court order and make a specified showing of a need for depositions (*see, e.g.*, ARIZ. RULE CRIM. PRO. 15.3(a); N.H. REV. STAT. § 517:13(II)). Some of these jurisdictions bar the defendant from attending the deposition unless there is a stipulation of the parties or unless counsel obtains a court order based upon a showing of good cause. *See, e.g.*, FLA. RULE CRIM. PRO. 3.220(h)(7); VT. RULE CRIM. PRO. 15(b).

In jurisdictions that permit depositions by the prosecution as well as the defense, the applicable statute or rule commonly recognizes that the defendant may not be deposed by the prosecution. *See, e.g.*, ARIZ. RULE CRIM. PRO. 15.3(a); N.H. REV. STAT. § 517:13(II). *See also* FED. RULE CRIM. PRO. 15(e)(1) (procedure for preserving the testimony of a witness in a criminal trial may not be used to depose a defendant "without that defendant's consent"). Even if such a limitation were not set by the relevant statute or rule, the Fifth Amendment's privilege against self-incrimination would preclude the prosecution from deposing the defendant. *See* § 18.12 *infra*.

Where depositions are available to defense counsel, they will ordinarily be an invaluable tool for discovery of the prosecution's case and for locking prosecution witnesses into statements that can be used to impeach the witness at trial if s/he changes his or her account. In these respects, depositions offer the kinds of tactical benefits discussed in other chapters with regard to preliminary hearings (see § 11.8.2 *supra*) and suppression hearings (see §§ 24.2, 24.4 *infra*). But depositions can be even more effective for these purposes because they usually cover a wider range of subjects and because their use as a discovery tool is not merely tolerated but specifically intended.

An issue that may arise at trial in a jurisdiction that affords depositions in criminal cases is whether, in the event that a prosecution witness who was deposed is unavailable at trial, the prosecution can introduce the witness's deposition into evidence. The rule of *Crawford v. Washington*, 541 U.S. 36 (2004), discussed in § 36.3.3 *infra*, should bar such a practice. *See, e.g., Corona v. State*, 64 So.3d 1232, 1241 (Fla. 2011) (discovery depositions, available to the defense in criminal cases under state rules, "do not meet *Crawford*'s cross-examination requirement" of "afford[ing] [the accused] an adequate opportunity to cross-examine the . . . declarant" because, *inter alia*, such depositions are "'not designed as an opportunity to engage in adversarial testing of the evidence against the defendant,'" and they are admissible at trial solely "'for purposes of impeachment'" and not as "'substantive evidence'"). *But see Thomas v. State*, 966 N.E.2d 1267, 1272 (Ind. App. 2012) (concluding that the prosecution's introduction of a deposition of an unavailable witness at trial did not violate *Crawford* because defense counsel had an adequate prior opportunity to cross-examine that witness at the deposition, but ultimately holding that "even assuming that *Crawford*'s requirements were not met, any error in admitting the deposition was harmless"). To make discovery or witness-preservation depositions admissible at trial under *Crawford*, the prosecution must show not only adequate opportunity for cross-examination at the deposition but unavailability of the witness at the time of trial. *State v. Tribble*, 193 Vt. 194, 67 A.3d 210 (2012), summarized in § 1.3 *supra* and § 36.3.3 *infra*. And failure to conduct the deposition in accordance with applicable statutes or court rules may make it inadmissible. *See Avsenew v. State*, 334 So.3d 590 (Fla. 2022) (reversing a conviction because of error in the admission of a preservation deposition conducted remotely using a setup in which the witness could not see the defendant; the applicable Florida rule provides that the defendant is to be kept "in the presence of the witness during the examination" (*id.* at 594)).

18.7.6. *Freedom of Information Laws (FOILs)*

A number of jurisdictions have enacted freedom of information laws (commonly called FOILs), some of them patterned on the federal Freedom of Information Act, 5 U.S.C. § 552. Although the Supreme Court has said of the federal Act that it "was not intended to supplement or displace rules of discovery" (*John Doe Agency v. John Doe Corp.*, 493 U.S. 146, 153 (1989)), and lower courts have said the same of their state FOILs (*e.g., State ex rel. Steckman v. Jackson*, 70 Ohio St. 3d 420, 639 N.E.2d 83 (1994)), these laws may be written sufficiently broadly to reach certain government records that defense counsel would like to examine. *See, e.g., United States Department of Justice v. Julian*, 486 U.S. 1 (1988); *Bartko v. United States Department of Justice*, 898 F.3d 51 (D.C. Cir. 2018); *Evans v. Federal Bureau of Prisons*, 951 F.3d 578 (D.C. Cir. 2020); *Fields v. State*, 432 Md. 650, 69 A.3d 1104 (2013); *Jones v. Medlin*, 302 Ga. 555, 807 S.E.2d 849 (2017); *and see Jimerson v. Payne*, 957 F.3d 916, 922 (8th Cir. 2020); *Phillips v. Valentine*, 826 Fed. Appx. 447, 454 (6th Cir. 2020).

Unless the jurisdiction's statute or other controlling authority explicitly forbids its use by parties to litigation against the government or exempts the types of records counsel is seeking (*compare Arkansas State Police v. Wren*, 2016 Ark. 188, 491 S.W.3d 124 (2016), *with Martin v. Musteen*, 303 Ark. 656, 799 S.W.2d 540 (1990)), counsel may find it profitable to follow the statutory procedures for requesting access to records that arguably fall within its compass. *See, e.g., North v. Walsh*, 881 F.2d 1088, 1096-97 (D.C. Cir. 1989) ("North's need or intended use for the documents is irrelevant to his FOIA action; his identity as the requesting party 'has no bearing on the merits of his . . . FOIA request.' . . . ¶ The fact that a defendant in an ongoing criminal proceeding may obtain documents via FOIA that he could not procure through discovery, or at least *before* he could obtain them through discovery, does not in and of itself constitute interference with a law enforcement proceeding [so as to shield the documents from disclosure under exemption 7(A) of the federal Freedom of Information Act, which provides that "records or information compiled for law enforcement purposes [need not be disclosed], but only to the extent that the production of such law enforcement records or information . . . could reasonably be expected to interfere with enforcement proceedings"]. Rather, the government must show that disclosure of those documents would, in some particular, discernible way, disrupt, impede, or otherwise harm the enforcement proceeding."); *accord, Morgan v. United States Department of Justice*, 923 F.2d 195, 198 (D.C. Cir. 1991); *Chief of Police, Hartford Police Department v. Freedom of Information Commission*, 252 Conn. 377, 386, 746 A.2d 1264, 1269 (2000) ("requests for records under the act are to be determined by reference to the provisions of the act, irrespective of whether they are or otherwise would be disclosable under the rules of state discovery . . . whether civil or criminal"); *In the Matter of Gould v. New York City Police Department*, 89 N.Y.2d 267, 274-75, 675 N.E.2d 808, 811-12, 653 N.Y.S.2d 54, 57-58 (1996) (even though "petitioners seek [to use FOIL] to obtain documents relating to their own criminal proceedings, and . . . disclosure of such documents is governed generally by CPL [Criminal Procedure Law] article 240 [on discovery in criminal cases,] . . . the Criminal Procedure Law does not specifically prelude defendants from seeking these documents under FOIL, [and therefore] we cannot read such a categorical limitation into the statute"; "the Police Department's argument and the dissent's concern that the requests serve not the underlying purposes of FOIL, but the quite different private interests of petitioners in obtaining documents bearing on their [criminal] cases and will produce an enormous administrative burden" are "unavailing as the statutory language imposes a broad duty to make certain records publicly available irrespective of the private interests and the attendant burdens involved"; the rulings below "establishing a blanket exemption from FOIL disclosure for [police] complaint follow-up reports and police activity logs" are reversed and the cases are remitted to the trial courts "to determine, upon an in camera inspection if necessary, whether the Police Department can make a particularized showing that any claimed exemption applies").

FOIL requests are ordinarily submitted in writing directly to the governmental agency whose records are sought. If the agency does not produce them, a civil action is brought against the agency to compel production. The FOIL specifies the court or courts in which the civil action may be brought and the procedure for bringing it. The National Freedom of Information Coalition tracks open records laws in every jurisdiction and provides detailed information about procedures (including sample request letters) and appeals. It is accessible at https://www.nfoic.org/foi-center/.

18.8. *General Strategy When Employing Formal Discovery Procedures*

Section 18.4 *supra* advised that counsel seek as much information as possible through informal discovery procedures. A different tack may be advisable in making formal discovery motions. By limiting these motions to what counsel is likely to get as a matter of settled law and local custom, counsel can display an attitude of undemanding reasonableness that may persuade the court to exercise its discretion in favor of discovery in areas where the prevailing practice allows discovery but does not require it. Since discovery law in most jurisdictions confers broad discretionary power on the trial judge, it often makes sense to get or keep on the judge's good side by requesting nothing that s/he could regard as exorbitant. In deciding whether to employ this strategy, or whether to go for broke and ask for everything that an enlightened criminal procedure would give the defense, or whether to take some intermediate position between these two extremes, counsel will need to assess the temperament of his or her individual judge. When counsel's theory of the case makes one or a few particular items crucial subjects for discovery (see § 7.2.1.4 *supra*), s/he may do best by focusing on those items in his or her requests for court-ordered discovery, and forgoing other items – or at least forgoing any other items which are not routine, unremarkable staples of local discovery practice.

In any event, counsel should make discovery requests as specific as possible, identifying the material that is wanted (*cf. United States v. Agurs,* 427 U.S. 97, 106-07 (1976)) and describing its relevance and importance for the preparation of the defense unless self-evident (*cf. United States v. Valenzuela-Bernal,* 458 U.S. 858, 871-74 (1982)). *See, e.g., People v. Watkins,* 2003 WL 723303 (Cal. App. 2003) ("[We] cannot say that the trial court abused its discretion in denying defendant's motion for discovery without prejudice to filing a more specific motion. First, the broad reach of the discovery request strongly suggests defendant was on a mere 'fishing expedition.' Second, defendant made little effort to demonstrate how the specific information sought would produce or lead to the production of admissible evidence. Third, the critical factual information in the affidavit was not stated on information and belief, but only in the conclusory fashion that 'it is the defense contention.' Fourth, the defense contention did not dispute the essence of what happened, that there was a collision between the truck and the patrol car, but only disputed the characterization of that event, i.e., whether the patrol car was rammed or whether the truck merely rolled into it. ¶ Under these circumstances, the immediate invocation of the in camera procedure would have imposed an undue burden upon the custodian of records to attempt to determine and produce any documents or information potentially relevant to the discovery request. And it would have imposed upon the trial court the burden of examining the record to determine whether some measure of discovery might be appropriate in order to properly narrow the discovery request. Therefore, the court was entitled to insist that defendant present a more narrow and specific discovery request supported by a specific factual showing relevant to the particular information requested."). If counsel is unable to identify with specificity some of the information that s/he wants, counsel should use the concentric-circles approach described in § 18.5 *supra* to guard against the risk that the judge will deny the entire discovery motion as a "fishing expedition."

When requesting a discovery order, counsel should recount his or her attempts to obtain the information through informal discovery, and the prosecutor's refusal to disclose it. See § 18.3 *supra.* If counsel sent a discovery letter to the prosecutor (see § 18.5 *supra*), a copy of the letter as well as any prosecutorial responses should be attached as an appendix to the discovery motion. When seeking materials or information to which the defense is not plainly entitled as a matter of routine under established precedent, counsel should take pains to demonstrate his or her efforts and inability to obtain the information independently: for example, counsel should recite his or her attempts to interview the prosecution witness(es) who know the information and the fact that the witness(es) refused to speak with counsel or the defense investigator. By documenting his or her assiduity, counsel demonstrates that s/he genuinely needs the judge's intervention and is not just being lazy. The absence of any alternative to judicial process as a means for obtaining vital information strengthens counsel's entitlement to the court's assistance.

Compare California v. Trombetta, 467 U.S. 479, 488-90 (1984).

18.9. *Constitutional Doctrines That Can Be Invoked in Support of Defense Discovery*

The *Brady* rule described in § 18.9.1 *infra,* gives the defense a federal constitutional right to discovery of exculpatory information and information that impeaches prosecution evidence. This is a firmly established doctrine, recognized in all jurisdictions. The other doctrines described in this section, which provide constitutional rationales for broader defense discovery rights, have not as yet been authoritatively recognized. Accordingly, when relying on the latter doctrines, counsel will need to fully brief their legal basis and should also present a compelling factual showing of need.

18.9.1. *The* Brady *Doctrine: The Right to Prosecutorial Disclosure of Evidence Helpful to the Defense*

Brady v. Maryland, 373 U.S. 83 (1963), and its progeny require that the prosecution disclose, upon defense request, evidence in the prosecutor's possession that is material and potentially helpful to the defense. The Court ruled in *Brady* that "suppression by the prosecution of evidence favorable to an accused upon request violates due process where the evidence is material either to guilt or punishment, irrespective of the good faith or bad faith of the prosecution" (*id.* at 87). *Accord, Turner v. United States,* 582 U.S. 313 (2017) (dictum); *Wearry v. Cain,* 577 U.S. 385 (2016) (per curiam); *Smith v. Cain,* 565 U.S. 73 (2012); *Cone v. Bell,* 556 U.S. 449, 451, 469-70 (2009); *Banks v. Dretke,* 540 U.S. 668, 691 (2004); *Strickler v. Greene,* 527 U.S. 263, 280-81 (1999); *Kyles v. Whitley,* 514 U.S. 419, 432-38 (1995); *Fontenot v. Crow,* 4 F.4th 982 (10th Cir. 2021); *Dennis v. Secretary, Pennsylvania Department of Corrections,* 834 F.3d 263 (3d Cir. 2016) (en banc); *Gumm v. Mitchell,* 775 F.3d 345, 363-74 (6th Cir. 2014); *United States v. Tavera,* 719 F.3d 705, 711-12 (6th Cir. 2013). "Suppression" in this context simply means a failure to disclose material which is in the possession of the prosecution or of any government actor involved in the case. *See Baugh v. Nagy,* 2022 WL 4589117 (6th Cir. 2022) ("The state willfully, or at least inadvertently, suppressed . . . [a] statement . . . [that could have been used to impeach a key prosecution witness. The defendant] likely did not have access to . . . [this] statement before . . . [its maker] mailed the statement to . . . [the defendant a dozen years after the trial]. Because . . . [the] statement was in the exclusive control of the government and never handed over to . . . [the defendant] or his attorney, . . . [the defendant] has satisfied his burden of proving that the prosecutor at least inadvertently withheld . . . [the] statement." *And see Floyd v. Vannoy,* 894 F.3d 143, 162-63 (5th Cir. 2018) (per curiam) (the prosecution's failure to disclose lab reports indicating that fingerprints lifted at the crime scene did not match the defendant's violated *Brady*: "The State's assertion the fingerprint-comparison results were effectively disclosed through the crime-scene report and list of evidence distorts *Brady*'s requiring prosecutors to offer exculpatory evidence absent a specific request by the defense. . . . Floyd's *Brady* claim does not stem from the fingerprints themselves, but from the results of the State's fingerprint-comparison test. ¶ The State does not demonstrate compliance with *Brady*'s disclosure requirement by asserting a possibility Floyd could deduce that, based on the general evidence provided to him, additional evidence likely existed. . . . Further, the State's assertions the evidence was not withheld because Floyd could have conducted his own analysis are in direct contrast to clearly-established *Brady* law rejecting the defense's ability to conduct their own analysis as justification for prosecutorial non-disclosure."); *United States v. Paulus*, 952 F.3d 717, 725 (6th Cir. 2020) ("The prosecution is not obligated under *Brady* to disclose information to the defense that the defense already 'knew or should have known.' The government argues that Paulus knew the essential facts described in the . . . [undisclosed document] and that he could have gathered the missing [factual] detail with 'minimal investigation.' . . . ¶ . . . But . . . *Brady* 'does not [allow] the State simply to turn over some evidence, on the assumption that defense counsel will find the cookie from a trail of crumbs.' . . . [Here] Paulus would have had to follow a long trail of crumbs to get the missing details"; therefore, the prosecution's nondisclosure violated *Brady*.); *People v. Bueno*, 2018 CO 4, 409 P.3d 320, 328 (Colo. 2018) (alternative ground) ("The People urge us to follow several federal circuit decisions holding that where evidence is otherwise available through reasonable diligence by the defendant, that evidence is not suppressed under *Brady*. . . . The Supreme Court has at least twice rejected arguments similar to the People's assertion that the defense must make reasonable efforts to locate *Brady* materials."); *Bracey v. Superintendent, Rockview SCI*, 986 F.3d 274, 289 (3d Cir. 2021) (recognizing that *Dennis v. Secretary, Pennsylvania Department of Corrections*, *supra*, held that "[t]here is no 'affirmative due diligence duty of defense counsel as part of *Brady*' and 'no support [for] the notion that defendants must scavenge for hints of undisclosed *Brady* material.' . . . Rather, 'the duty to disclose under *Brady* is absolute – it does not depend on defense counsel's actions.' . . . Consequently, the defense 'is entitled to presume that prosecutors have "discharged their official duties"' by sharing all material exculpatory information in their possession, . . . and the defense's diligence in seeking out exculpatory material on its own 'plays no role in the *Brady* analysis,' . . . ."; the *Bracey* court also collects the decisions of other federal circuits that accord with *Dennis*). "When there are multiple *Brady* claims, the Supreme Court instructs that we consider materiality 'collectively.' . . . We must imagine that every piece of suppressed evidence had been disclosed, and then ask whether, assuming those disclosures, there is a reasonable probability that the jury would have reached a different result." *Browning v. Baker*, 875 F.3d 444, 464 (9th Cir. 2017).

"'Information that is favorable to the accused may consist of evidence that "could exonerate the accused, corroborate[ ] the accused's position in asserting his innocence, or possess[ ] favorable information that would have enabled defense counsel to conduct further and possibly fruitful investigation regarding the fact that someone other than the appellant killed the victim."'" . . . Additionally, favorable evidence includes evidence that "'challenges the credibility of a key prosecution witness.'" . . . [E]vidence is favorable under *Brady* if 'it provides grounds for the defense to attack the reliability, thoroughness, and good faith of the police investigation, to impeach the credibility of the state's witnesses, or to bolster the defense case against prosecutorial attacks.'" *Jordan v. State*, 343 S.W.3d 84, 96 (Tenn. Crim. App. 2011). *See Commonwealth v. Caldwell*, 487 Mass. 370, 167 N.E.3d 852 (2021) ("'Evidence is exculpatory if it "provides some significant aid to the defendant's case, whether it furnishes corroboration of the defendant's story, calls into question a material, although not indispensable, element of the prosecution's version of the events, or challenges the credibility of a key prosecution witness."'" *Id.* at 375, 167 N.E.3d 858. . . . ¶ Here, the prosecutor's note indicated that the witness had testified about a jailhouse confession extracted from a then-fellow inmate in a previous case. Further investigation of the case referenced in the note likely would have led defense counsel to discover the witness's significant role in the prosecution of Rancourt. . . . The judge who heard Rancourt's motion to suppress found that the witness had hoped to gain favorable treatment in exchange for the information that he had provided to the trooper. . . . After providing the information, the witness's sentence was revised and he was released two and one-half months before his previously scheduled release date as a protective measure, although there was no evidence that law enforcement officers made any promises to the witness. . . . ¶ If the defendant's trial counsel had known about the witness's previous involvement in the *Rancourt* case, he could have used it to challenge the witness's claim that he had broken the jailhouse 'code of silence' to testify against the defendant with no expectation of any benefit for himself. Defense counsel could have argued that the witness once again was motivated by a desire to secure favorable treatment in his pending cases." *Id.* at 375-76, 167 N.E.3d 858. "[W]e reject the Commonwealth's contention that the information revealed by the prosecutor's note is merely cumulative because the Commonwealth had turned over the police report that noted the witness's previous cooperation with law enforcement, about which defense counsel did not question the witness at trial. The specific facts relating to the witness's cooperation in *Rancourt*, including his hope for favorable treatment and the reduction of his sentence, would have made that evidence far more compelling for a jury than the generic reference to the witness's prior police cooperation contained in the police report." *Id.* at 378, 167 N.E.3d 859-60."). "There are good reasons to think that the threshold for the favorability inquiry should be fairly low." *Phillips v. Valentine*, 826 Fed. Appx. 447, 460 (6th Cir. 2020). *See Long v. Hooks*, 972 F.3d 442, 461 (4th Cir. 2020) (en banc) (finding that a state postconviction court "had an improper view of favorable evidence, conflating favorable evidence with exculpatory evidence": "*Kyles* expressly rejects the notion that evidence must be 'impeachment [ ]or exculpatory evidence' in order to be 'favorable.' 514 U.S. at 450-51. Rather, evidence is favorable under *Brady* if it would have 'some weight' and a 'tendency [to be] favorable' to Petitioner. *Id.* at 451."); *see also, e.g.,* *People v. Ulett*, 33 N.Y.3d 512, 520-21, 129 N.E.3d 909, 914-15, 105 N.Y.S.3d 371, 376-77 (2019) (the prosecution violated *Brady* by "withh[o]ld[ing] a video of the crime scene that captured events surrounding the murder, including the body of the victim as he fell to the ground": "This video evidence could have been used to impeach the eyewitnesses. . . . We reject the People's argument that the impeachment value of the video is cumulative to what was already available to defense counsel. Impeachment with contradictory testimony of other witnesses is hardly the same as being confronted with a videotape of the scene. ¶ The video would also have provided leads for additional admissible evidence . . . and avenues for alternative theories for the defense. The video shows people entering and exiting the building, including other potential eyewitnesses. At a minimum, the presence of unidentified witnesses, at least one of whom was only a few feet away when the shots were fired, could have been used by the defense to argue that the police failed to conduct a thorough investigation (*see Kyles*, 514 U.S. at 446–447 [finding that undisclosed *Brady* material could have been used to attack 'the thoroughness and even the good faith of the investigation']). And the video captures something none of the eyewitnesses reported: an additional person at the scene interacting with the victim as he lay on the ground, which defense counsel could have used at trial in combination with the medical examiner's report to argue that another shooter was potentially responsible for the victim's death after he fell to the ground."); *Bowen v. Maynard*, 799 F.2d 593, 613 (10th Cir. 1986) ("The withheld evidence also raises serious questions about the manner, quality, and thoroughness of the investigation that led to Bowen's arrest and trial. A common trial tactic of defense lawyers is to discredit the caliber of the investigation or the decision to charge the defendant, and we may consider such use in assessing a possible *Brady* violation."); *People v. Rong He*, 34 N.Y.3d 956, 135 N.E.3d 1081, 112 N.Y.S.3d 1 (2019) (*Brady* requires the prosecution to produce contact information for individuals who told investigating officers that they had witnessed the criminal episode or events immediately after it); *People v. Ramunni*, 203 A.D.3d 1076, 1078, 166 N.Y.S.3d 27, 30 (N.Y. App. Div., 2d Dept. 2022) (the prosecution violated *Brady* by disclosing only the content of a 911 call – which contained a description of the perpetrator that "did not match the defendant" – while "fail[ing] to provide the defendant with meaningful access to the caller by redacting the caller's identity and contact information and thereafter denying the defendant's request for this caller's identity"; "While the contents of the 911 call may have provided some clues as to the identity of the caller, the defendant should not be forced to guess as to the identity of this caller.").

In *Brady,* the evidence improperly suppressed by the prosecution was a codefendant's confession that identified the codefendant as the lone triggerman in a robbery-murder. In *United States v. Bagley,* 473 U.S. 667 (1985), the Court made clear that "[i]mpeachment evidence . . . as well as exculpatory evidence, falls within the *Brady* rule," and thus the *Brady* doctrine extends to "evidence that the defense might . . . use[ ] to impeach the Government's witnesses by showing bias or interest" (*id.* at 676). *Accord, Wearry v. Cain, supra,* 577 U.S. at 392 ("the rule stated in *Brady* applies to evidence undermining witness credibility"); *Strickler v. Greene, supra,* 527 U.S. at 280; *Kyles v. Whitley, supra,* 514 U.S. at 433; *United States v. Flores-Rivera,* 787 F.3d 1, 18 (1st Cir. 2015) (finding a *Brady* violation where potential impeachment evidence went undisclosed: "[T]he testimony of the three cooperating [*i.e.*, turncoat] witnesses – especially Delgado – was both essential to the convictions and uncorroborated by any significant independent evidence. Indeed, the absence of such evidence is so marked and surprising in view of the resources devoted to the investigation and the availability of three turned conspirators that it could reasonably cause the factfinder to be dubious about the witnesses' claims. This is therefore a case in which the *Brady* material that was not produced need not be 'highly impeaching' in order to require that the verdict be reversed. . . . ¶ Delgado was the star witness. . . . On cross, . . . Delgado parried any suggestions that his testimony was orchestrated with that of the other witnesses. In fact, he denied even talking about the case with them, telling the jury that to do so was against the rules. So, too, did those other two cooperating witnesses firmly deny a basic premise of the defense: that they coordinated their testimony. ¶ Had defense counsel possessed Delgado's notes, counsel could have either shown Delgado and the others to have perjured themselves, and/or forced them to admit that they had at the very least compared prospective testimony with one another. . . . It was not just the defense who believed the potential for the cooperators to talk about the case in prison jeopardized the government's chances of a conviction. The prosecutor elicited testimony from . . . [another of the three turncoat witnesses] . . . on redirect that suggested male and female prisoners could not talk to each other at the prison."); *Mellen v. Winn,* 900 F.3d 1085 (9th Cir. 2018). *See also Smith v. Cain, supra,* 565 U.S. at 75-76; *United States v. Walter,* 870 F.3d 622, 629-31 (7th Cir. 2017); *Barton v. Warden,* 786 F.3d 450, 465-70 (6th Cir. 2015) (*per curiam*); *Lewis v. Connecticut Comm'r of Correction,* 790 F.3d 109, 113, 123-24 (2d Cir. 2015); *Amado v. Gonzalez,* 758 F.3d 1119, 1133-34, 1138-39 (9th Cir. 2014); *Johnson v. Folino,* 705 F.3d 117, 129-30 (3d Cir. 2013); *United States v. Mahaffy,* 693 F.3d 113, 130-33 (2d Cir. 2012); *State v. Best,* 376 N.C. 340, 852 S.E.2d 191 (2020); *In re Stenson,* 174 Wash. 2d 474, 488-89, 276 P.3d 286, 293-94 (2012). For example, "*Brady* requires prosecutors to disclose any benefits that are given to a government informant, including any lenient treatment for pending cases" (*Maxwell v. Roe,* 628 F.3d 486, 510 (9th Cir. 2010), and cases cited). *Accord, Carter v. State,* 2019 UT 12, 439 P.3d 616, 631

(Utah 2019) ("We agree with the district court that the Tovars' declarations do not allege the prosecutor asked them to alter their testimony in any substantive way. Standing alone, this claim is likely insufficient to create a material dispute of fact regarding materiality. But we do not view this claim in isolation, we view it along with Carter's other claims of misconduct and evidence suppression. *See Kyles*, 514 U.S. at 436 . . . ('The . . . final aspect of . . . materiality to be stressed here is its definition in terms of suppressed evidence considered collectively. . . .'). . . . [T]he Tovars' testimony is inconsistent in meaningful ways. In the same way that it is reasonable to infer that the Tovars' testimony changed over time in response to financial benefits received, it is likewise reasonable to infer that the Tovars' testimony changed over time, at least in part, in response to testimony coaching by the prosecutor. When considered alongside the financial benefits and the threats of deportation and separation, the inferences drawn in favor of Carter from the accusations of testimony coaching become more than mere speculation."); *Simpson v. State*, 344 So.3d 1274, 1283 (Fla. 2022) (a witness's credibility may be attacked by showing bias, including the possible bias arising from the witness's relationship to a party; here "because Little Archie had been an informant in another case, he had a 'relationship to a party' that was a potential source of bias requiring disclosure. And disclosure of a witness' informant status is required even where there is no evidence that the witness was given favorable treatment in exchange for the information."). *Compare Fuentes v. Griffin*, 829 F.3d 233, 247 (2d Cir. 2016) ("if the prosecution has a witness's psychiatric records that are favorable to the accused because they provide material for impeachment, those records fall within *Brady* principles"), *with McCray v. Capra*, 45 F.4th 634 (2d Cir. 2022) (in a case in which federal adjudication is constrained by AEDPA's limitation on federal *habeas corpus* review of state-court decisions (see § 49.2.3.2 *infra*), a divided panel of the Second Circuit rejects a claim that the New York Court of Appeals was unreasonable in holding the prosecution's *Brady* obligation satisfied by the disclosure of a 28-page "representative sample" of a rape victim's 5,000-page medical records after *in camera* screening by the trial judge). *See also Stacy v. State*, 500 P.3d 1023, 1026-27 (Alaska App. 2021), *subsequent history in Stacy v. State*, 2023 WL 380355 (Alaska App. 2023) ("Stacy . . . argues that his due process rights under *Brady v. Maryland* and the Alaska Constitution were violated when the trial court denied his motion to compel the prosecutor to disclose any *Brady* impeachment material that was in the personnel files of the law enforcement officers who testified at his trial. The prosecutor took the position that the State had no duty to learn of any *Brady* material in the personnel files of the law enforcement officers because he personally had no access to their otherwise confidential personnel files. ¶ [W]e conclude that the confidentiality of these files does not, standing alone, absolve a prosecutor of their duty under *Brady v. Maryland* and *Kyles v. Whitley* to take reasonable steps to learn of favorable material evidence in the possession of the prosecution team, including personnel files. Because the prosecutor in this case made no effort to comply with the mandate of *Brady*, we remand this case to the trial court for further proceedings to determine if a *Brady* violation occurred."); *Meyer v. Hawai'i*, 152 Hawai'i 243, 524 P.3d 1267 (Table) (Hawai'i App. 2023) (finding a *Brady* violation in a DUI case where a police officer testified to the results of a field sobriety test and other indicia of intoxication and where the prosecution did not disclose the 17-page report of an internal investigation of that officer for unauthorized use of a computer: the Court of Appeals examines the report and finds that it contains material that could have been used to impeach the officer's credibility under Hawaii Evidence Rule 608(B) as "[s]pecific instances of conduct" that are "probative of untruthfulness."); *In the Matter of a Grand Jury Investigation*, 485 Mass. 641, 152 N.E.3d 65 (2020), quoted in the fifth paragraph of this section.

To satisfy the "materiality" standard of *Brady* and its progeny, the defendant must show that "'there is a reasonable probability' that the result of the trial would have been different if the suppressed documents had been disclosed to the defense." *Strickler v. Greene, supra,* 527 U.S. at 289. The "'reasonable probability' standard . . . is not a particularly demanding one. This is true because the government's burden at the trial level is so demanding. . . . '[A] finding of guilt . . . is permissible only if supported by evidence establishing guilt beyond a reasonable doubt. It necessarily follows that if the omitted evidence creates a reasonable doubt that did not otherwise exist, constitutional error has been committed.' ¶ . . . Since it would have taken only one juror harboring a doubt to change the result, we cannot say that the record survives *Brady* analysis." *United States v. Robinson,* 68 F.4th 1340, 1348 (D.C. Cir. 2023). *See, e.g., Long v. Hooks, supra,* 972 F.3d at 458 (finding that a state postconviction court "unreasonably applied Supreme Court law in imposing an erroneously high burden . . . [when it] required Petitioner to demonstrate the withheld evidence would have changed the result at trial 'by a preponderance of the evidence,' rather than asking him to demonstrate a 'reasonable probability of a different result.'"). "[M]uch of what we focus on in assessing materiality is how the suppressed evidence relates to cross-examination. For example, we have asked whether the suppressed impeachment evidence is the '*only* avenue of impeachment' and whether the suppressed evidence impeaches an already impeached witness. . . . Further, even when our materiality jurisprudence extends beyond the scope of cross-examination, it asks questions that often depend on a full review of the trial evidence. For example, we ask whether the suppressed evidence impeaches a witness at the 'heart of the government's case,' whether the case is close on any element of the crime, and whether the testimony that could be attacked with the suppressed evidence is strongly corroborated. . . . These questions implicate the totality of the evidence presented at trial. Indeed, we have made clear that '[t]he materiality of *Brady* material depends almost entirely on the value of the evidence relative to the other evidence mustered by the state.'"). *United States v. Cessa,* 851 F.3d 121, 129 (5th Cir. 2017). "In determining whether "'there is a reasonable probability" that the result of the trial would have been different[,]' . . . a court must consider 'the aggregate effect that the withheld evidence would have had if it had been disclosed['] . . . . In order to determine 'the aggregate effect' of the withheld evidence, the court must *both* 'add[ ] to the weight of the evidence on the defense side . . . all of the undisclosed exculpatory evidence' *and* 'subtract[ ] from the weight of the evidence on the prosecution's side . . . the force and effect of all the undisclosed impeachment evidence.'" *Juniper v. Zook,* 876 F.3d 551, 568 (4th Cir. 2017). *Cf. Tempest v. State,* 141 A.3d 677, 683 (R.I. 2016) ("With respect to . . . [*Brady* violations], our jurisprudence 'provides even greater protection to criminal defendants than the one articulated [by the United States Supreme Court].' . . . 'When the failure to disclose is deliberate, this [C]ourt will not concern itself with the degree of harm caused to the defendant by the prosecution's misconduct; we shall simply grant the defendant a new trial.'"). Materiality judgments made at the pretrial stage are necessarily predictive and therefore dangerously speculative. For an analysis of this problem and a possible solution, *see* Justin Murray, *Prejudice-Based Rights in Criminal Procedure,* 168 U. PA. L. REV. 277 (2020). Counsel seeking *Brady* disclosure before trial should insist that the applicable standard is *potential* materiality, and that this is a broader measure than the ordinary post-trial "retrospective test, evaluating the strength of the evidence after trial" (*United States v. Olsen,* 704 F.3d 1172, 1183 (9th Cir. 2013)). "[S]ome trial courts . . . have concluded that the retrospective definition of materiality is appropriate only in the context of appellate review, and that trial prosecutors must disclose favorable information without attempting to predict whether its disclosure might affect the outcome of the trial." *Id.* at 1183 n.3; *see United States v. Sudikoff*, 36 F. Supp. 2d 1196, 1198-99 (C.D. Cal. 1999) ("Numerous cases define the *Brady* obligation in the context of appellate review considering the ramifications of a prosecutor's failure to disclose evidence. Using this post-trial perspective, *Brady* held that it would be a due process violation only if the suppressed evidence was 'material.' Courts have concluded that '[e]vidence is considered material "only if there is a reasonable probability that, had the evidence been disclosed to the defense, the result of the proceeding would have been different."' . . . ¶ This standard is only appropriate, and thus applicable, in the context of appellate review. Whether disclosure would have influenced the outcome of a trial can only be determined after the trial is completed and the total effect of all the inculpatory evidence can be weighed against the presumed effect of the undisclosed *Brady* material. . . . ¶ Additionally, the post-trial review determines only whether the improper suppression of evidence violated the defendant's due process rights. However, that the suppression may not have been sufficient to violate due process does not mean that it was proper. . . . ¶ Because the definitions of materiality as applied to appellate review are not appropriate in the pretrial discovery context, the Court relies on the plain meaning of 'evidence favorable to an accused' as discussed in *Brady*. ¶ The meaning of 'favorable' is not difficult to determine. In the *Brady* context, 'favorable' evidence is that which relates to guilt or punishment . . . , and which tends to help the defense by either bolstering the defense's case or impeaching prosecution witnesses . . . . The Court notes again that in the pretrial context it would be inappropriate to suppress evidence because it seems insufficient to alter a jury's verdict. Further, '[t]he government, where doubt exists as to the usefulness of evidence, should resolve such doubts in favor of full disclosure . . . .' Thus, the government is obligated to disclose all evidence relating to guilt or punishment which might reasonably be considered favorable to the defendant's case."); *United States v. Wells*, 2013 WL 4851009, at *3 (D. Alaska 2013) ("[i]n the pretrial context the government should review 'materiality' of exculpatory information as evidence that may be 'favorable to the accused' which, if so, should be disclosed without regard to whether the failure to disclose it likely would affect the outcome of the upcoming trial"); *United States v. Lampkin*, 2016 WL 11680667, at *2 (D. Alaska 2016) ("Compliance with *Brady* in a pretrial context requires a more expansive application of what constitutes evidence favorable to the accused. Evidence that is favorable to the accused should be disclosed and, 'where doubt exists as to the usefulness of evidence, [the government] should resolve such doubts in favor of full disclosure.'"); *United States v. Safavian*, 233 F.R.D. 12, 16 (D. D.C. 2005) ("The prosecutor cannot be permitted to look at the case pretrial through the end of the telescope an appellate court would use post-trial. Thus, the government must always produce any potentially exculpatory or otherwise favorable evidence without regard to how the withholding of such evidence might be viewed – with the benefit of hindsight – as affecting the outcome of the trial. The question before trial is not whether the government thinks that disclosure of the information or evidence it is considering withholding might change the outcome of the trial going forward, but whether the evidence is favorable and therefore must be disclosed. Because the definition of 'materiality' discussed in *Strickler* and other appellate cases is a standard articulated in the post-conviction context for appellate review, it is not the appropriate one for prosecutors to apply during the pretrial discovery phase. The only question before (and even during) trial is whether the evidence at issue may be 'favorable to the accused'; if so, it must be disclosed without regard to whether the failure to disclose it likely would affect the outcome of the upcoming trial."); *and see United States v. Villa*, 2014 WL 280400, at *2 (D. Conn. 2014)

("Some courts have noted that . . . [the] retrospective definition of *Brady* material 'is only appropriate . . . in the context of appellate review.' *United States v. Sudikoff*. . . ; *see also* Ellen Yaroshefsky, *Prosecutorial Disclosure Obligations*, 62 HASTINGS L.J. 1321, 1335 n.70 (2011) (collecting cases). Aside from the inherent difficulty of measuring materiality to a trial that has not yet occurred, the analysis post-trial focuses on a different question – 'whether the improper suppression of evidence violated the defendant's due process rights' rather than whether the material ought to have been disclosed in the first place. . . . While it is not clear if this theory has been accepted in this Circuit, . . . the Second Circuit noted that that it had 'no occasion to consider the scope of a trial judge's discretion to order pretrial disclosures as a matter of sound case management . . . .'"). *Cf.* Riley E. Clafton, Note, *A Material Change to Brady: Rethinking Brady v. Maryland, Materiality, and Criminal Discovery*, 110 J. CRIM. L. & CRIMINOLOGY 307 (2020). And when drafting discovery-request memoranda that cite appellate decisions spelling out *Brady* doctrine, counsel should be sure to quote verbatim the language of *Kyles*, *Cone*, and *Agurs* emphasizing that doubtful questions of materiality should be resolved in favor of disclosure. See the concluding paragraph of this section.

Brady has also been held to apply to prosecutors' failures to disclose factual information which would support a procedural contention (such as the contention that prosecution evidence was unconstitutionally obtained and therefore required to be suppressed), even though the information does not go to the issue of guilt-or-innocence in the strictest sense. *People v. Geaslen*, 54 N.Y.2d 510, 516, 430 N.E.2d 1280, 1282, 446 N.Y.S.2d 227, 229 (1981) ("[W]here, as here, there is in the possession of the prosecution evidence of a material nature which if disclosed could affect the ultimate decision on a suppression motion, and that evidence is not disclosed, such nondisclosure denies the defendant due process of law. The failure of the District Attorney in this instance to disclose to the suppression court the Grand Jury testimony of Officer Wheeler (which on its face can only be classified as 'favorable' to defendant) to allow the suppression court to make an *in camera* inspection to determine whether the testimony should be made available to defendant prior to or at the suppression hearing, constitutes a denial of the due process required by the Federal Constitution under the principles of *Brady v. Maryland* . . . and its progeny."); *Biles v. United States*, 101 A.3d 1012, 1020 (D.C. 2014) ("[T]he suppression of material information can violate due process under *Brady* if it affects the success of a defendant's pretrial suppression motion. We have described as 'eminently sensible' a broad formulation of the government's *Brady* obligation that would reach the kind of evidence 'that would suggest to any prosecutor that the defense would want to know about it,' . . . and a rule prohibiting the government from suppressing favorable information material to a Fourth Amendment suppression hearing would impose little if any additional burden on prosecutors and police beyond the obligations that court rules and professional standards already impose."); *Milke v. Ryan*, 711 F.3d 998, 1019 (9th Cir. 2013) ("Also at issue was . . . [a police detective's] claim – again, unsupported by evidence – that Milke waived her *Miranda* rights and didn't ask for a lawyer. Beyond its effect on . . . [the detective's] credibility, evidence of . . . [his] falsifications and his disregard of *Miranda*, would have been highly relevant to the determination of whether Milke's alleged confession had been lawfully obtained. The suppression of evidence of . . . [the detective's] lies and misconduct thus qualifies as prejudicial for purposes of *Brady* and *Giglio*."); *Jackson v. City of Cleveland*, 925 F.3d 793 (6th Cir. 2019) (a cognizable *Brady* claim was presented by allegations that police officers neglected to inform the prosecuting attorneys that a juvenile who, under the police theory of the case, was an eyewitness and had identified the defendants as the perpetrators of a murder, had in fact not been present at the murder scene and was coerced by the officers into signing a statement falsely asserting that his reason for failing to identify the defendants in a lineup was that he was afraid of them: "The prosecutor did not speak to . . . [the juvenile] prior to bringing charges, and so the false statement constituted the entire basis for his [the prosecutor's] understanding of . . . [the juvenile's] involvement. If . . . [the police officers had not fabricated . . . [the juvenile's] statement, therefore, charges would not have been brought" (*id.* at 816), and the juvenile would not have been called to testify before the grand jury and at trial.); *United States v. Gamez-Orduno*, 235 F.3d 453, 461 (9th Cir. 2000) (dictum) ("The suppression of material evidence helpful to the accused, whether at trial or on a motion to suppress, violates due process if there is a reasonable probability that, had the evidence been disclosed, the result of the proceeding would have been different"); *Smith v. Black*, 904 F.2d 950, 965-66 (5th Cir. 1990), *ruling on another issue vacated*, 503 U.S. 930 (1992); *cf. United States v. McElroy*, 697 F.2d 459, 464 (2d Cir. 1982) (Federal Criminal Rule "16(a)(1)(A) requires the government to disclose the substance not only of the incriminating post-arrest oral statements which it intends to use at trial, but also the substance of the defendant's responses to any *Miranda* warnings which preceded the statements. Disclosure, to be meaningful, must be made of the defendant's responses both to the warnings which immediately preceded his admissions and to any other set(s) of warnings given the defendant from arrest onwards. Requiring the government to make such disclosure will bring to light *Miranda* violations that might otherwise remain hidden because the defendant misunderstands his rights, fails fully to inform defense counsel, or is unable to remember. Disclosure is clearly consistent with the view that pretrial discovery is an important avenue to the protection of defendants' rights. As prudence and long practice require law enforcement officers to record a defendant's responses to the *Miranda* warnings, disclosure imposes no significant additional burden on law enforcement agencies. We believe that our interpretation of Rule 16 will, at little cost to effective law enforcement, help to make meaningful in practice the important rights which motivated the *Miranda* decision.").

The *Brady* "rule encompasses evidence 'known only to police investigators and not to the prosecutor' . . . [and] therefore, 'the individual prosecutor has a duty to learn of any favorable evidence known to the others acting on the government's behalf in this case, including the police'" (*Strickler v. Greene, supra*, 527 U.S. at 280-81 (quoting *Kyles v. Whitley, supra*, 514 U.S. at 437-38)). *See Youngblood v. West Virginia*, 547 U.S. 867 (2006) (per curiam); *Barton v. Warden, supra*, 786 F.3d at 465; *Aguilar v. Woodford*, 725 F.3d 970, 982-83 (9th Cir. 2013); *Roldan v. Stroud*, 52 F.4th 335, 338-39 (7th Cir. 2022) ("Under *Brady v. Maryland,* the government violates a criminal defendant's due process rights when it fails to disclose evidence favorable to the defendant and material to guilt or punishment. . . . *Giglio* extended that rule to impeachment evidence – to information calling into question the credibility of a witness. . . . ¶ The question then becomes who on the law enforcement side – police officers or prosecutors – bears the obligation to disclose. *Brady* and *Giglio* are usually understood to impose a duty on prosecutors to make any required disclosure to the defense. . . . But the disclosure obligation sometimes falls to police officers if they are the only ones who know about the exculpatory or impeachment evidence in question.. . . Officers typically satisfy this obligation when they disclose evidence to the prosecutor."); *State ex rel. Griffin v. Denney*, 347 S.W.3d 73, 78 (Mo. 2011) ("Even if the prosecutor was subjectively unaware that a weapon was confiscated from . . . [a suspect other than the defendant], the State is nonetheless under a duty to disclose the evidence. . . . In this case, the murder occurred in prison, and the prison guards were acting on the government's behalf. Therefore, the State had a duty to discover and disclose any material evidence known to the prison guards."); *McCormick v. Parker*, 821 F.3d 1240 (10th Cir. 2016) (the prosecutor violated *Brady* by failing to disclose to the defense that the alleged Sexual Assault Nurse Examiner (SANE) who testified for the state at trial "wasn't certified as a SANE nurse in Texas when she testified" and that she had "misrepresented herself as a certified SANE nurse 'to patients, court officials and the public'" (*id.* at 1244); there was no indication that "the prosecutor actually knew about [witness] Ridling's lapsed credentials" (*id.* at 1246) but "Ridling was part of the prosecution team for *Brady* purposes . . . [and] [a]ccordingly, we must impute her knowledge of her own lack of certification to the prosecutor" (*id.* at 1247)); *and see Carillo v. County of Los Angeles*, 798 F.3d 1210 (9th Cir. 2015); *People v. Uribe*, 162 Cal. App. 4th 1457, 76 Cal. Rptr. 3d 829 (2008); *In re Brown*, 17 Cal. 4th 873, 952 P.2d 715, 72 Cal. Rptr. 2d 698 (1998); *Martinez v. Wainwright*, 621 F.2d 184 (5th Cir. 1980); *Jackson v. City of Cleveland, supra*; *Stacy v. State, supra,* 500 P.3d at 1033-40; *In the Matter of a Grand Jury Investigation*, 485 Mass. 641, 642, 658, 152 N.E.3d 65, 70, 82 (2020) (rejecting the objections of two police officers to the prosecution's disclosure to defense counsel, in "criminal cases where the petitioners might be witnesses," that the officers "knowingly made false statements in their police reports that concealed the unlawful use of force by a fellow officer against an arrestee and supported a bogus criminal charge of resisting arrest against the arrestee": the court "conclude[s], as did the district attorney, that the prosecutors here have a *Brady* obligation to disclose the exculpatory information at issue to unrelated criminal defendants in cases where a petitioner [police officer] is a potential witness or prepared a report in the criminal investigation. That obligation remains even though that information was obtained in grand jury testimony compelled by an immunity order. And the district attorney may fulfill that obligation without prior judicial approval; a judge's order is needed only for issuance of a protective order limiting the dissemination of grand jury information. ¶ More broadly, we conclude that where a prosecutor determines from information in his or her possession that a police officer lied to conceal the unlawful use of excessive force, whether by him- or herself or another officer, or lied about a defendant's conduct and thereby allowed a false or inflated criminal charge to be prosecuted, the prosecutor's obligation to disclose exculpatory information requires that the information be disclosed to defense counsel in any criminal case where the officer is a potential witness or prepared a report in the criminal investigation."). *A fortiori*, a prosecutor's duty to learn about exculpatory and impeaching evidence "includes evidence held by other prosecutors"; "knowledge of that evidence is imputed to . . . [the trial prosecutor] under *Brady*" (*Aguilar v. Woodford, supra*, 725 F.3d at 982).

"It is well established that the state violates a defendant's right to due process under *Brady* when it withholds evidence that is 'favorable to the defense' (and material to the defendant's guilt or punishment). . . . In describing evidence that falls within the *Brady* rule, the Supreme Court has made clear that impeachment evidence is 'favorable to the defense' even if the jury might not afford it significant weight." *Lambert v. Beard*, 537 Fed. Appx. 78, 86 (3d Cir. 2013). *See also id.* at 85-86 ("We further hold that, to the extent the state court determined that the Police Activity Sheet was not exculpatory or impeaching under *Brady* because it was ambiguous, such determination was an unreasonable application of clearly established Supreme Court precedent."); *Johnson v. Folino*, 705 F.3d 107, 130 (3d Cir. 2013) ("we believe, as do the majority of our sister courts of appeals, that inadmissible evidence may be material if it could have led to the discovery of admissible evidence"); *Jones v. Medlin*, 302 Ga. 555, 560, 807 S.E.2d 849, 854 (2017) ("The admissibility of the undisclosed material itself is not a prerequisite to finding a *Brady* violation; the question is whether, had the material 'been disclosed to the defense, the result of the proceeding would have been different,' in reasonable probability. . . . Thus, 'inadmissible evidence may be material [under *Brady*] if it could have led to the discovery of [material] admissible evidence. . . .'"); *Commonwealth v. Johnson,* 644 Pa. 150, 174 A.3d 1050 (2017) (The prosecution's failure to disclose five police reports relating to criminal investigations of a key prosecution witness (Robles) violated *Brady:* "The reports are textbook impeachment evidence. They suggest that Robles sought to curry favor with the police in the face of ongoing criminal investigations and mounting evidence of his own criminal conduct. And they would have guided defense counsel's efforts to expose to the jury the 'subtle factors' of self-interest upon which Johnson's life or liberty may have depended." *Id.* at 1056-1057. "The withheld evidence also revealed instances where Robles had lied or deceived the police when it was in his interest to do so . . . . In addition, the withheld evidence revealed that Robles had a motive to eliminate rival drug dealers such as Johnson's affiliates." *Id.* at 1057. "The substantive admissibility of impeachment evidence, *vel non*, is not dispositive of a *Brady* claim. . . . Documents like the police reports at issue here – which would not have been admissible as substantive evidence at Johnson's trial – may nevertheless contain information that can be used to impeach a witness." *Id.* at 1056.); *State v. Marshall*, 845 S.W.2d 228, 232-33 (Tenn. Crim. App. 1992) ("The prosecution's duty to disclose is not limited in scope to 'competent evidence' or 'admissible evidence.' The duty extends to 'favorable information' unknown to the accused."). *Compare Turner v. United States, supra*, 582 U.S. at 316, 323-28 (finding that undisclosed evidence, which the Government conceded to have been "'favorable to the accused,'" was not "material" for *Brady* purposes and therefore did not require the reversal of the defendants' convictions, because there was no "'reasonable probability that, had the evidence been disclosed,'" the outcome of the trial "'would have been different'"; prosecution witness Carrie Eleby's undisclosed statement to a prosecutor that "she had been high on PCP during a . . . meeting with investigators" essentially duplicated evidence that "the jury heard multiple times about Eleby's frequent PCP use, including Eleby's own testimony that she and [prosecution witness Linda] Jacobs had smoked PCP shortly before they witnessed Fuller's attack," and "it would not have surprised the jury to learn that Eleby used PCP on yet another occasion"; an undisclosed prosecutorial note reporting that Kaye Porter, "a minor [prosecution] witness," had "changed her mind about having agreed with Eleby's claims," would have added "little . . . [of] significance," given that Porter was "impeached at trial with evidence about changes in her testimony over time"; although the prosecution failed to disclose a detective's note that Linda Jacobs "'vacillated' [during an interview] about what she saw," the "jury was . . . well aware of Jacobs' vacillation, as she was impeached on the stand with her shifting stories about what she witnessed"; the Court explicitly describes its non-materiality holding as "fact-intensive" and as dictated by "the context of this trial, with respect to these witnesses"; and it says that "We of course do not suggest that impeachment evidence is immaterial with respect to a witness who has already been impeached with other evidence," citing *Wearry v. Cain, supra.*). "The dispositive question . . . is whether the guilty verdict . . . is worthy of confidence in the absence of the suppressed evidence." *Thomas v. Westbrooks*, 849 F.3d 659, 663 (6th Cir. 2017) (in a state-court prosecution, "the State violated . . . [the defendant's] due process rights as articulated in *Brady v. Maryland* when the prosecution failed to inform him that . . . [the key prosecution witness] had received $750 from the FBI prior to trial" under the auspices of "the

Safe Streets Task Force – a joint federal-state working group charged with investigating and prosecuting gang-related crime" (*id.* at 661-63)).

The *Brady* obligation trumps any state-law privilege of non-disclosure that the prosecution may assert. *Fontenot v. Crow, supra,* 4 F.4th at 1063 (although "[a]t the time of Mr. Fontenot's trials, Oklahoma law viewed unsworn statements of prosecution witnesses and police investigative reports to fall within the work-product privilege, making them non-discoverable," the Tenth Circuit holds that the prosecutor's failure to turn such materials over to the defense violated *Brady*).

Defense counsel should always make a general *Brady* request in his or her discovery letter to the prosecution (see § 18.5 *supra*) and in discovery motions (see § 18.7.3 *supra*). Such a request might be framed in terms such as the following:

> any and all materials and information within the possession of the prosecution or law enforcement agents which could constitute evidence favorable to the accused, or which could lead to material favorable evidence, including exculpatory or mitigating matters and any matters that could be used to impeach the prosecution's evidence or to undermine the prosecution's case, within the meaning of *Brady v. Maryland,* 373 U.S. 83 (1963).

In addition, counsel should make particularized requests for any specific items or categories of *Brady* information that counsel can identify, on the basis of defense investigation, as likely to be in the hands of prosecuting or law enforcement authorities. While the prosecution does not escape its obligation to turn over *Brady* information when the defense request is "merely a general request" – or even when "there has been no [defense] request at all" – (*United States v. Agurs, supra,* 427 U.S. at 106-07; *Strickler v. Greene, supra,* 527 U.S. at 280; *Kyles v. Whitley, supra,* 514 U.S. at 433-34), the chances of reversal of a conviction may be somewhat improved if the prosecution failed to honor a specific *Brady* request. *See United States v. Bagley, supra,* 473 U.S. at 682-83 (opinion of Blackmun, J.); *Pennsylvania v. Ritchie,* 480 U.S. 39, 58 n.15 (1987). *See also, e.g., People v. Vilardi,* 76 N.Y.2d 67, 71-78, 555 N.E.2d 915, 916-21, 556 N.Y.S.2d 518, 519-24 (1990) (a specific *Brady* request by defense counsel triggers the enhanced protections afforded by the state constitutional version of the *Brady* doctrine).

Because *Brady* and its progeny involved invalidations of convictions in response to post-trial revelations that the prosecutor had failed to disclose information favorable to the accused at any time prior to the conclusion of a trial, they do not speak directly to the requisite timing of *Brady* disclosures. But their rationale implies that disclosure of *Brady* material "must be made at such time as to allow the defense to use the favorable material effectively in the preparation and presentation of its case" (*United States v. Pollack,* 534 F.2d 964, 973 (D.C. Cir. 1976)). *See, e.g., Leka v. Portuondo,* 257 F.3d 89, 100-02 (2d Cir. 2001) ("The district court considered it sufficient that Garcia was identified to the defense "*nine* days before opening arguments and *twenty-three* days before the defense began its case." These are relevant considerations. At the same time, however, the longer the prosecution withholds information, or (more particularly) the closer to trial the disclosure is made, the less opportunity there is for use. One good example is the last-minute identification of Chiusano, whose mis-spelled name was a useless datum without a preliminary investigation aimed at the bus company; another good example is the last-minute identification of Gonzalez, who had moved away. ¶ As to Garcia, the defense evidently had sufficient time to attempt an interview, but we assume that it bungled the contact by a deceptive and aggressive maneuver, and as a result was barred from further contact. It is easy, however, to see this as a blunder precipitated by the prosecution's failure to discharge its duty under *Brady.* In any event, the prosecution is in no position to fault the defense for cutting corners when the prosecution itself created the hasty and disorderly conditions under which the defense was forced to conduct its essential business. All of these circumstances demonstrate how the delayed disclosure of evidence tends to impair the opportunity of the defense to use it . . . ¶ The limited *Brady* material disclosed to Leka could have led to specific exculpatory information only if the defense undertook further investigation. When such a disclosure is first made on the eve of trial, or when trial is under way, the opportunity to use it may be impaired. The defense may be unable to divert resources from other initiatives and obligations that are or may seem more pressing. And the defense may be unable to assimilate the information into its case. *See United States v. Cobb*, 271 F. Supp. 159, 163 (S.D. N.Y. 1967) (Mansfield, J.) ('[T]here may be instances where disclosure of exculpatory evidence for the first time during trial would be too late to enable the defendant to use it effectively in his own defense, particularly if it were to open the door to witnesses or documents requiring time to be marshalled and presented.'). ¶ Moreover, new witnesses or developments tend to throw existing strategies and preparation into disarray. For example, Leka undertook to show on defense that weather conditions might have impaired visibility-a tack he may not have wanted to take if he was going to rely on what Garcia saw from his second-floor window across the street. And in rejecting Leka's arguments on materiality, the district court carefully demonstrated that Garcia's testimony (that the gunfire started as the car pulled over) is in possible tension with the testimony of defense witness Luftim Cira (who testified that he shot Ferati in self-defense), who estimated that his 'car must have been stopped not more than 30 seconds.' . . . By the same token, however, this testimony illustrates how difficult it can be to assimilate new information, however favorable, when a trial already has been prepared on the basis of the best opportunities and choices then available. ¶ For the same reasons, a disclosure made on the eve of trial (or after trial has begun) may be insufficient unless it is fuller and more thorough than may have been required if the disclosure had been made at an earlier stage. Here, it is ridiculous to think that the prosecution did not know what a police officer saw as a witness to a shooting; yet the last-minute disclosure consisted of nothing but Garcia's name and perhaps his address. The only other information available to the defense was the (false) statement during plea negotiations that a police officer could identify Leka and the (true) statement at the *Wade* hearing that he could not. ¶ At that stage of proceedings, we think that such a disclosure afforded insufficient opportunity to use the information. As we stated in *Grant*: ¶ [']We refuse . . . to infer from the failure of defense counsel, when surprised at trial, to seek time to gather other information on [the suppressed witness], that defense counsel would have by-passed the opportunity had the prosecutor apprised him of the [evidence] at a time when the defense was in a reasonable pre-trial position to evaluate carefully all the implications of that information. Given the time for preparation which counsel was denied by the belated disclosure, it seems to us counsel might have pursued a course of inquiry which would have resulted in ferreting out . . . relevant . . . information.['] ¶ *Grant* [*v. Alldredge*], 498 F.2d [376] at 382 [(2d Cir 1974)] . . . ; *see also Blake v. Kemp*, 758 F.2d 523, 352 n.10 (11th Cir. 1985) ('In some instances [disclosure of *Brady* material during trial] may be sufficient. However . . . some [*Brady*] material must be disclosed earlier. This is because of the importance of some information to adequate trial preparation.' . . .); *United States v. Polisi*, 416 F.2d 573, 578 (2d Cir. 1969) ('Under *Brady v. Maryland,* we must look to the prejudice to the accused of the suppression, in its effect upon his preparation for trial.')."); *United States v. Obagi*, 965 F.3d 993 (9th Cir. 2020) (the prosecution's discovery and disclosure of impeachment material for the first time after the government had delivered its closing argument and between the closing arguments of two joined defendants came too late; failure to provide earlier disclosure violated *Brady*, and the violation could not be cured by the trial judge's instructions to the jury to disregard the testimony of the potentially impeached witness and any government arguments based on that witness's testimony); *United States v. Bundy*, 968 F.3d 1019, 1031 (9th Cir. 2020) (affirming an order of the district court which had "concluded that dismissal with prejudice was appropriate because the government withheld key evidence favorable to the defense until after trial was underway – in clear violation of its duties under *Brady* – and dismissing without prejudice would allow the government to cure its mistakes, to the detriment of the defendants."); *Fuentes v. Griffin, supra,* 829 F.3d at 249-50 (the prosecution's failure to turn over a psychiatric report about the complainant was prejudicial for a number of reasons including, "importantly, [that] timely disclosure of the [report] . . . would have provided defense counsel with an opportunity to seek an expert opinion with regard to the [report's] . . . indication of other significant symptoms, in order to establish reasonable doubt in the minds of the jurors because of [complainant] G.C.'s predisposition toward emotional instability and retaliation – an opinion he was able to obtain after he eventually learned of the psychiatric record but not in time to present it to the jury"); *Blakeney v. State*, 236 So.3d 11, 24 (Miss. 2017) ("Because the prosecution's late disclosure of previously undisclosed witnesses left the defense without adequate time to prepare, we find that a continuance should have been granted"). *See also, e.g., Tennison v. City and County of San Francisco*, 570 F.3d 1078, 1093 (9th Cir. 2009); AMERICAN BAR ASSOCIATION, STANDARDS FOR CRIMINAL JUSTICE MONITORS AND MONITORING, DISCOVERY (4th ed. 2020) [Chapter 11 of the 2017 Standards, updated], Standard 11-2.3(b), *Timing of Discovery* ("in all cases, disclosures should be made in sufficient time for each party to use the disclosed information to adequately prepare for hearings, the entry of a plea, trial, or sentencing"). In federal practice, an amendment of FED. RULE CRIM. PRO. 5, effective October 21, 2020, requiring that "[i]n all criminal proceedings, on the first scheduled court date when both prosecutor and defense counsel are present, the judge shall issue an oral and written order to prosecution and defense counsel that confirms the disclosure obligation of the prosecutor under Brady v. Maryland, 373 U.S. 83 (1963) and its progeny, and the possible consequences of violating such order under applicable law" (Rule 5(F)(i)), carries the strong implication that *Brady* disclosure is required early in the pretrial process. *Compare United States v. Ruiz*, 536 U.S. 622, 625, 631, 633 (2002) (the *Brady* doctrine "does not require the Government to disclose material impeachment evidence prior to entering a plea agreement with a criminal defendant," given that pre-plea prosecutorial disclosure of "'information establishing the factual innocence of the defendant'" and other constitutional and systemic protections guard against the risk that "innocent individuals, accused of crimes, will plead guilty"), *with State v. Huebler*, 275 P.3d 91, 96-98 (Nev. 2012) ("the considerations that led to the decision in [*United States v.*] *Ruiz* do not lead to the same conclusion when it comes to material exculpatory information": "While the value of impeachment information may depend on innumerable variables that primarily come into play at trial and therefore arguably make it less than critical information in entering a guilty plea, the same cannot be said of exculpatory information, which is special not just in relation to the fairness of a trial but also in relation to whether a guilty plea is valid and accurate."; "We are persuaded by language in *Ruiz* and due-process considerations that a defendant may challenge the validity of a guilty plea based on the prosecution's failure to disclose material exculpatory information before entry of the plea."), *and Bridgeforth v. Superior Court*, 214 Cal. App. 4th 1074, 1077, 1087, 154 Cal. Rptr. 3d 528, 530, 538 (2013) ("applying the traditional three-factor due process analysis utilized in *Ruiz* . . . [and] the remaining considerations cited in *Ruiz*" to hold that the Due Process clauses of the federal and state constitutions require "the prosecution to disclose, prior to the preliminary hearing, evidence in its possession that is both favorable to the defense and material to the probable cause determination to be made at the preliminary hearing"). And, in any event, both prosecutors and judges should be sensitive to the argument that timely pretrial discovery is a better way to run a system than disclosure at trial, with a constitutionally compelled mistrial and continuance, or postconviction litigation of questions of nondisclosure. "[T]he aim of due process 'is not punishment of society for the misdeeds of the prosecutor but avoidance of an unfair trial to the accused.'" *Smith v. Phillips*, 455 U.S. 209, 219 (1982). This is why, as the Supreme Court noted pointedly in *Agurs*, "the prudent prosecutor will resolve doubtful questions in favor of disclosure" (427 U.S. at 108). *See also Cone v. Bell*, *supra*, 556 U.S. at 470 n.15 ("Although the Due Process Clause of the Fourteenth Amendment, as interpreted by *Brady*, only mandates the disclosure of material evidence, the obligation to disclose evidence favorable to the defense may arise more broadly under a prosecutor's ethical or statutory obligations. . . . As we have often observed, the prudent prosecutor will err on the side of transparency, resolving doubtful questions in favor of disclosure."); *Kyles v. Whitley*, *supra*, 514 U.S. at 439-40 ("Unless . . . the adversary system of prosecution is to descend to a gladiatorial level unmitigated by any prosecutorial obligation for the sake of truth, the government simply cannot avoid responsibility for knowing when the suppression of evidence has come to portend such an effect on a trial's outcome as to destroy confidence in its result. ¶ This means, naturally, that a prosecutor anxious about tacking too close to the wind will disclose a favorable piece of evidence. . . . This is as it should be. Such disclosure will serve to justify trust in the prosecutor as 'the representative . . . of a sovereignty . . . whose interest . . . in a criminal prosecution is not that it shall win a case, but that justice shall be done.' . . . And it will tend to preserve the criminal trial, as distinct from the prosecutor's private deliberations, as the chosen forum for ascertaining the truth about criminal accusations."); *Strickler v. Greene*, *supra*, 527 U.S. at 281 (the *Brady* doctrine reflects "the special role played by the American prosecutor in the search for truth in criminal trials" and the prosecutor's interest in ensuring that "'justice shall be done'" (quoting *Berger v. United States*, 295 U.S. 78, 88 (1935))); *Banks v. Dretke*, *supra*, 540 U.S. at 696 ("[a] rule . . . declaring 'prosecutor may hide, defendant must seek,' is not tenable in a system constitutionally bound to accord defendants due process."); *Turner v. United States*, *supra*, 582 U.S. at 324 ("Consistent with the[ ] principles [that "the *Brady* rule's "'overriding concern [is] with the justice of the finding of guilt'"" and that "the Government's "'interest . . . in a criminal prosecution is not that it shall win a case, but that justice shall be done,"'"], the Government assured the Court at oral argument that subsequent to petitioners' trial, it has adopted a 'generous policy of discovery' in criminal cases under which it discloses any 'information that a defendant might wish to use.' . . . As we have recognized, and as the Government agrees, . . . '[t]his is as it should be.'"); *Fernandez v. Capra*, 916 F.3d 215, 217, 222-23 (2d Cir. 2019) (dictum) (the prosecution violated the obligation to "promptly disclose" *Brady* evidence by delaying disclosure of the lead investigator's involvement in a drug sale until the prosecutor had "reviewed the audiotapes and concomitantly ordered the arrest" of the investigator; "while [prosecutor] Burmeister may have reasonably sought a high degree of certainty in the credibility of the accusation before ordering the arrest of a NYPD officer, it was not reasonable for Burmeister to delay the disclosure to [defendant] Fernandez of credible evidence from an undercover officer that Officer Melino had negotiated a sale of cocaine"; "'if there were questions about the reliability of the exculpatory information, it was the prerogative of the defendant and his counsel – and not of the prosecution – to exercise judgment in determining whether the defendant should make use of it'"); *In re Kline*, 113 A.3d 202, 204, 213 (D.C. 2015) (District of Columbia Rule of Professional Conduct 3.8(e), which "prohibits a prosecutor in a criminal case from intentionally failing to disclose to the defense any evidence or information that the prosecutor knows or reasonably should know tends to negate the guilt of the accused," "requires a prosecutor to disclose all potentially exculpatory information in his or her possession regardless of whether that information would meet the materiality requirements of *Bagley, Kyles*, and their progeny").

For an overview of *Brady*'s enforcement by state and federal courts, *see* Brandon L. Garrett, Adam M. Gershowitz & Jennifer Teitcher, *The Brady Database, available at* https://ssrn.com/abstract=4470780. For an argument that *Brady* doctrine needs an overhaul to take account of evolving prosecutorial technology, *see* Andrew Guthrie Ferguson, *Big Data Prosecution & Brady*, 67 U.C.L.A. L. REV. 180 (2020). For a discussion of the role of *Brady* violations in the conviction of innocent persons, *see* Jon B. Gould, Samantha L. Senn, Belén Lowrey-Kinberg & Linda Phiri, *Mapping the Path of Brady Violations: Typologies, Causes & Consequences in Erroneous Conviction Cases*, 71 SYRACUSE L. REV. 1061 (2021). For an argument that *Brady* should aligned with the ethical standards governing prosecutors, *see* David A. Lord, *Creating Architects of Justice: A Gift from Modern Ethics to* Brady *on Its 60th Anniversary, available at* https://ssrn.com/abstract=4417140.

18.9.2. *Other Bases for Constitutional Contentions of Rights to Discovery*

The following subparagraphs sketch additional constitutional principles that defense counsel can invoke in developing arguments to support discovery requests for particular kinds of materials or information that are not encompassed – or are only dubiously encompassed – by the *Brady* doctrine.

18.9.2.1. *The Sixth Amendment Right to Counsel*

The Sixth Amendment right to counsel, incorporated into the Fourteenth Amendment by *Gideon v. Wainwright,* 372 U.S. 335 (1963); *see also, e.g., Alabama v. Shelton*, 535 U.S. 654, 661-62 (2002) – and recognized as "'a bedrock principle in our justice system'" (*Davila v. Davis*, 582 U.S. 521, 531 (2017), quoting *Martinez v. Ryan*, 566 U.S. 1, 12 (2012)) – guarantees more than that the defendant must have a lawyer. It assures "effective aid in the preparation and trial of the case" (*Powell v. Alabama,* 287 U.S. 45, 71 (1932); *State v. Lindsey*, 271 N.C. App. 118, 132, 843 S.E.2d 322, 332 (2020)), and it is violated whenever defense counsel's performance is inadequate to "ensure that a defendant has the assistance necessary to justify reliance on the outcome of the proceeding" (*Strickland v. Washington*, 466 U.S. 668, 691-92 (1984); *see id.* at 685-86; *Rompilla v. Beard*, 545 U.S. 374, 387-90 (2005); *Wiggins v. Smith*, 539 U.S. 510, 521-22, 524-28, 533, 534-35 (2003); *Williams v. Taylor*, 529 U.S. 362, 390-91, 395-97 (2000)). The Sixth Amendment is not solely – or even primarily – an admonition to defense attorneys to do the best job they can under the circumstances. More basically, it invalidates any state-created procedure that compels counsel to operate under circumstances which preclude an effective defense effort. *Powell v. Alabama, supra,* 287 U.S. at 71-73; *Holloway v. Arkansas,* 435 U.S. 475, 481-86 (1978); *Holt v. Virginia,* 381 U.S. 131 (1965); *Ferguson v. Georgia,* 365 U.S. 570 (1961); *Brooks v. Tennessee,* 406 U.S. 605 (1972); *Geders v. United States,* 425 U.S. 80 (1976); *Cuyler v. Sullivan,* 446 U.S. 335, 344 (1980) (dictum). "[T]he right to the assistance of counsel has been understood to mean that there can be no restrictions upon the function of counsel in defending a criminal prosecution in accord with the traditions of the adversary factfinding process that has been constitutionalized in the Sixth and Fourteenth Amendments." *Herring v. New York,* 422 U.S. 853, 857 (1975). For example, the Sixth Amendment has repeatedly been held to condemn eve-of-trial appointments of counsel that leave the lawyer inadequate time to prepare for trial. *E.g., Jones v. Cunningham,* 313 F.2d 347 (4th Cir. 1963); *Martin v. Virginia,* 365 F.2d 549 (4th Cir. 1966); *Roberts v. United States,* 325 F.2d 290 (5th Cir. 1963); *Townsend v. Bomar,* 331 F.2d 19 (6th Cir. 1964); *People v. Stella,* 188 A.D.2d 318, 318-19, 590 N.Y.S.2d 478, 478-79 (N.Y. App. Div., 1st Dep't 1992). *See also, e.g., Catalan v. Cockrell,* 315 F.3d 491, 492-93 (5th Cir. 2002); *Routhier v. Sheriff, Clark County,* 93 Nev. 149, 151-52, 560 P.2d 1371, 1372 (1977); *Blakeney v. State,* 236 So.3d 11, 24 (Miss. 2017) ("Because the prosecution's late disclosure of previously undisclosed witnesses left the defense without adequate time to prepare, we find that a continuance should have been granted"); and see § 3.23.3 *supra.* Timely appointment of counsel was required by *Powell v. Alabama, supra,* the fountainhead of all right-to-counsel cases, because during the pretrial period "consultation, thoroughgoing investigation and preparation were vitally important" (287 U.S. at 57). If adequate *time* to prepare is a constitutional mandate, adequate *information* to prepare is arguably no less necessary. For, as the Supreme Court has recognized, the pretrial gathering of this information is a vital part of the effective assistance of counsel that the Constitution commands. *See Coleman v. Alabama,* 399 U.S. 1, 9 (1970); *Adams v. Illinois,* 405 U.S. 278, 281-82 (1972); *see also Rompilla v. Beard, supra,* 545 U.S. at 387 ("The notion that defense counsel must obtain information that the State has and will use against the defendant is not simply a matter of common sense."); *Wiggins v. Smith, supra,* 539 U.S. at 522, 524-26, 531-32, 534; *Williams v. Taylor, supra,* 529 U.S. at 396; *Strickland v. Washington, supra,* 466 U.S. at 690-91.

18.9.2.2. *The Right to Fair Notice of Charges*

In *Cole v. Arkansas,* 333 U.S. 196 (1948), the Supreme Court recognized the "principle of procedural due process . . . that notice of the specific charge, and a chance to be heard in a trial of the issues raised by that charge, if desired, are among the constitutional rights of every accused in a criminal proceeding in all courts, state or federal" (*id.* at 201). *See also Dunn v. United States,* 442 U.S. 100, 106-07 (1979). "These standards no more than reflect a broader premise that has never been doubted in our constitutional system: that a person cannot incur the loss of liberty for an offense without notice and a meaningful opportunity to defend." *Jackson v. Virginia,* 443 U.S. 307, 314 (1979). *See Wright v. Beck,* 981 F.3d 719 (9th Cir. 2020), surveying the Supreme Court's caselaw and holding it violated when the police obtained and executed an *ex parte* order for the destruction of a gun collection seized from an individual who had been arrested for possession of an unregistered assault weapon.

"Notice, to comply with due process requirements, must be given sufficiently in advance of scheduled court proceedings so that reasonable opportunity to prepare will be afforded, and it must 'set forth the alleged misconduct with particularity.'" *In re Gault,* 387 U.S. 1, 33 (1967) (juvenile delinquency proceeding). This principle may – though it probably needs not – be derived from the express right given an accused by the Sixth Amendment "'to be informed of the nature and cause of the accusation'" (*see Faretta v. California,* 422 U.S. 806, 818 (1975) (dictum); *Herring v. New York,* 422 U.S. 853, 856-57 (1975)). Even in noncriminal matters the Supreme Court has found a due process right to adequate notice of the issues posed for adjudication in a proceeding affecting individual interests. *E.g., Morgan v. United States,* 304 U.S. 1 (1938); *Gonzales v. United States,* 348 U.S. 407 (1955); *Goldberg v. Kelly,* 397 U.S. 254, 267-68 (1970) (dictum); *cf. Wolff v. McDonnell,* 418 U.S. 539, 563-64 (1974); *Goss v. Lopez,* 419 U.S. 565, 578-82 (1975); *Vitek v. Jones,* 445 U.S. 480, 494-96 (1980); *but see Greenholtz v. Inmates of the Nebraska Penal and Correctional Complex,* 442 U.S. 1, 14 n.6 (1979). A passing *dictum* in *United States v. Agurs,* 427 U.S. 97, 112 n.20 (1976), says that "the notice component of due process refers to the charge rather than the evidentiary support for the charge"; but the line between these two will often be shadowy.

18.9.2.3. *The Sixth Amendment Right to Confrontation*

The extent to which the Sixth Amendment right to confrontation governs pretrial discovery is unclear in the light of *Pennsylvania v. Ritchie,* 480 U.S. 39 (1987). The lead opinion in *Ritchie,* written by Justice Powell, is a majority opinion except on one point: its analysis of the Confrontation Clause. On that point, Justice Powell, with three other Justices concurring, concluded that "the right of confrontation is a *trial* right" and cannot be "transform[ed] . . . into a constitutionally-compelled rule of pretrial discovery" (*id.* at 52). However, three Justices – Justices Brennan and Marshall in dissent, and Justice Blackmun concurring solely in the plurality's result on this point – concluded that the Confrontation Clause does confer upon the defense a constitutional right to discovery of information that would facilitate effective cross-examination. *See id.* at 61-62 (Blackmun, J., concurring) ("In my view, there might well be a confrontation violation if, as here, a defendant is denied pretrial access to information that would make possible effective cross-examination of a crucial prosecution witness"); *id.* at 66 (Brennan, J., dissenting) ("the right of cross-examination . . . may be significantly infringed by . . . the wholesale denial of access to material that would serve as the basis for a significant line of inquiry at trial"; the trial court's "denying access to the prior statements of the victim . . . deprived Ritchie of material crucial to any effort to impeach the victim at trial . . . [and was] a violation of the Confrontation Clause"). The remaining two Justices, Justices Stevens and Scalia, took no position on the Confrontation Clause issue, concluding that the writ of *certiorari* should have been dismissed because the lower court's judgment was not yet final. *See id.* at 78 (Stevens, J., dissenting).

The elements of a Confrontation Clause argument in support of discovery are set forth in Justice Brennan's dissent in *Ritchie. See* 480 U.S. at 66-72. Since the argument has not been rejected by a majority of the Court – and, indeed, was expressly supported by three members of the Court – counsel can continue to press it as a basis for discovery requests. *See, e.g., State v. Anthony*, 440 A.2d 736, 736-37 (R.I. 1982) (per curiam) ("The defendant was charged with the murder of his infant daughter, Melissa. Prior to his trial, defendant caused a subpoena duces tecum to be issued to the Department for Children and Their Families, seeking access to records pertaining to Melissa and her mother (the state's principal witness against defendant). The defendant claims that these records contain certain information supporting his allegation that his wife was responsible for Melissa's injuries. ¶ The Department moved to quash the subpoena on the ground that disclosure of the records is prohibited by . . . [a statute making health-care information confidential]. The trial justice granted the motion to quash and, after a jury trial, defendant was convicted of manslaughter. ¶ The subpoena duces tecum should not have been quashed. Disclosure of the records sought by defendant is not prohibited in cases of known or suspected child abuse. . . . Furthermore, the subpoenaed information may have been defendant's only means of challenging testimony which led to his conviction. ¶ Clearly, the defendant's right to effective cross-examination, guaranteed by the Sixth and Fourteenth Amendments to the United States Constitution and by art. 1, sec 10 of the Rhode Island Constitution, has been denied."); *accord, State v. Parillo*, 480 A.2d 1349, 1353-55 (R.I. 1984); *People v. Thurman*, 787 P.2d 646, 651-52 (Colo. 1990) (relying on the Confrontation Clause, in tandem with the Due Process Clause, to hold that the trial court permissibly dismissed charges against a defendant when the prosecution refused to divulge the identity, address, and current place of employment of a confidential informant: "The government's refusal to reveal the identity of a police informant who is *not* a witness against the defendant has been clearly distinguished from its refusal to do so where the informant is also a witness. The former does not deny the accused's right of confrontation; in the latter situation, the witness's identity generally must be revealed."); *United States v. Arias*, 936 F.3d 793 (8th Cir. 2019); *Burns v. State*, 968 A.2d 1012, 1024 (Del. 2009), *subsequent history in* 979 A.2d 1110 (Table), 2009 WL 2490253 (Del. 2009); *State v. Peseti*, 101 Hawai'i 172, 186, 65 P.3d 119, 133 (2003); *Commonwealth v. Barroso*, 122 S.W.3d 554, 559-60, 561 (Ky. 2003); *State v. Spurlock*, 874 S.W.2d 602 (Tenn. Ct. Crim. App. 1993) (reversing a conviction primarily because the prosecution's failure to disclose recordings of interviews of its key witness by police officers and a prosecutor violated due process; "It is a fundamental principle of law that an accused has the right to cross-examine prosecution witnesses to impeach the credibility or establish the motive or prejudice of the witness. This includes the right to cross-examine a prosecution witness regarding any promises of leniency, promises to help the witness, or any other favorable treatment offered to the witness." *Id.* at 617. "The prosecution knew that [prosecution witness] Apple's testimony was crucial to its case; and, further, the prosecution knew that Apple's prior criminal record, use of illicit narcotics, sparse work record, and other factors made his credibility tenuous at best. It may be reasonably inferred from the evidence and the nature of the . . . recordings that the prosecution made every effort to suppress the recordings. The prosecution knew if the material contained on these tapes was conveyed to defense counsel, an extremely competent, experienced and skilled criminal defense lawyer, Apple's credibility would have been completely destroyed; and the trier of fact would not have believed Apple's testimony." *Id.* at 620.). *But see Church v. State*, 189 N.E.3d 580, 593 (Ind. 2022) ("[t]he right to confrontation is a trial right – not a pretrial right"); *McCray v. Capra*, 45 F.4th 634 (2d Cir. 2022) (in a case in which federal adjudication is constrained by AEDPA's limitation on federal *habeas corpus* review of state-court decisions (see § 49.2.3.2 *infra*), the Second Circuit rejects a claim that the Sixth Amendment Confrontation Clause confers any pretrial discovery rights).

18.9.2.4. *The Right To Present Defensive Evidence*

The Sixth Amendment guarantees a criminal defendant the right "to have compulsory process for obtaining witnesses in his favor." In *Pennsylvania v. Ritchie,* 480 U.S. 39 (1987), a majority of the Court recognized that "[o]ur cases establish, at a minimum, that criminal defendants have the right to the Government's assistance in compelling the attendance of favorable witnesses at trial and the right to put before a jury evidence that might influence the determination of guilt" (*id.* at 56). "[C]onclud[ing] . . . that compulsory process provides no *greater* protections in this area than those afforded by due process," the Court elected to analyze the claim solely as a *Brady* issue (*id.* at 56; see § 18.9.1 *supra*), without "decid[ing] . . . whether and how the guarantees of the Compulsory Process Clause differ from those of the Fourteenth Amendment."

Pending the Court's resolution of the parameters of the compulsory process right, counsel can argue that the Compulsory Process Clause of the Sixth Amendment, when coupled with the Due Process Clause, confers a right to present defensive evidence (*Webb v. Texas*, 409 U.S. 95 (1972) ("'The right to offer the testimony of witnesses, and to compel their attendance, if necessary, is in plain terms the right to present a defense, the right to present the defendant's version of the facts as well as the prosecution's to the jury so it may decide where the truth lies [quoting *Washington v. Texas*, 388 U.S. 14, 19 (1967)]'"); *Holmes v. South Carolina*, 547 U.S. 319, 324 (2006) ("'Whether rooted directly in the Due Process Clause of the Fourteenth Amendment or in the Compulsory Process or Confrontation Clauses of the Sixth Amendment, the Constitution guarantees criminal defendants "a meaningful opportunity to present a complete defense [quoting *Crane v. Kentucky*, 476 U.S. 683, 690 (1986)].'''"); *Chambers v. Mississippi,* 410 U.S. 284, 302 (1973); see § 39.1 *infra*), which, in turn, implies a corollary right to pretrial discovery of information in the sole possession of the prosecution that might lead to defensive evidence. *See State v. Chambers*, 252 N.J. 561, 581-82, 288 A.3d 12, 24-25 (2023) ("Criminal defendants have the constitutional right to a fair trial, which includes the right to effective assistance of counsel, confrontation, compulsory process, and due process. . . . Under both the Federal and the New Jersey Constitutions, criminal defendants also have the right to 'a meaningful opportunity to present a complete defense.' ¶ To be able to present a complete defense, a defendant is entitled to broad, automatic pre-trial discovery in criminal cases in New Jersey, which is governed by our court rules. . . . Our state's robust "'open-file approach to pretrial discovery in criminal matters" is intended "[t]o advance the goal of providing fair and just criminal trials.'" . . . . This Court has emphasized that '[a] criminal trial where the defendant does not have 'access to the raw materials integral to the building of an effective defense is fundamentally unfair.'"); *United States v. Stever*, 603 F.3d 747 (9th Cir. 2010) ("Stever sought to defend on the ground that the marijuana growing operation found on an isolated corner of his mother's 400–acre property was the work of one of the Mexican drug trafficking organizations (DTOs) that had recently infiltrated Oregon. He was prevented from doing so by two district court rulings, the first denying him discovery related to the operations of DTOs and the second declaring that defense off-limits." *Id.* at 750. "Stever claimed that the Government was in possession of law enforcement reports, officer training materials, and other documents bearing on the operations of Mexican DTOs in Eastern Oregon and California. He cited news reports and ongoing prosecutions and noted that Detective Mogle averred in his search warrant affidavit that his training had familiarized him with investigations of drug trafficking organizations. *Id.* at 752. "The requested evidence, if it existed, tended to show that a Mexican DTO planted the marijuana. It also tended to make it more probable that Stever was not involved, as there would then be an alternative explanation for the grow that would not entail the consent, much less the participation, of any of the Stevers. *Id.* at 753. "[T]he Government argues that the evidence would invite the jury to engage in impermissible speculation about Mexican DTOs and their 'correlat[ion] with the Stever property grow.' But the district court is not free to dismiss logically relevant evidence as speculative: '[I]f the evidence [that someone else committed the crime] is in truth calculated to cause the jury to doubt, the court should not attempt to decide for the jury that this doubt is purely speculative and fantastic but should afford the accused every opportunity to create that doubt.'" *Id.* at 754. "From well before the trial, the Government refused to turn over documents – documents it does not deny it possesses and as to which it claims no privilege of any kind – relating to the Mexican drug growing operations in Eastern Oregon. The district court then compounded this error by concluding that the documents were irrelevant to the point of immateriality, without even reviewing the requested documents in camera. Having denied Stever the opportunity to explore this discovery avenue, the district court declared a range of defense theories off-limits, without considering in any detail the available evidence it was excluding. As we have explained, its reason for doing so – that any such evidence was necessarily irrelevant – was deeply flawed. Stever was not only prevented from putting on evidence important to his defense . . . ; he was prevented from making his defense at all. We must conclude that Stever's Sixth Amendment rights were violated." *Id.* at 757.); *and cf. Melnik v. Dzurenda*, 14 F.4th 981, 985-86 (9th Cir. 2021) (in order to prepare for a disciplinary hearing, a prison inmate requested that officials give him envelopes in which they claimed drugs were being sent to him; they refused; the Ninth Circuit holds that this refusal violated his right to due process: "The Supreme Court established in *Wolff v. McDonnell* [418 U.S. 539 (1974),] that there are procedural due process rights that a prisoner must be afforded in the context of a prison disciplinary proceeding prior to being deprived of a protected liberty interest. . . . The Court held that one of the constitutional rights afforded a prisoner in a disciplinary hearing is that the 'inmate facing disciplinary proceedings should be allowed to . . . present documentary evidence in his defense when permitting him to do so w[ould] not be unduly hazardous to institutional safety or correctional goals.' . . . ¶ Many courts have held that for the right articulated in *Wolff* to mean anything, a prisoner must also have the right to access evidence that he might use in preparing or presenting his defense."); *Roviaro v. United States,* 353 U.S. 53 (1957); *United States v. Augenblick,* 393 U.S. 348, 356 (1969) (dictum). *See generally* Jean Montoya, *A Theory of Compulsory Process Clause Discovery Rights*, 70 IND. L.J. 845 (1995). The Supreme Court of Hawai'i has drawn the appropriate conclusion: "'[C]entral to the protections of due process is the right to be accorded a meaningful opportunity to present a complete defense.' . . . Under this 'well-established principle,' 'all defendants must be provided with the basic tool[s] of an adequate defense.' . . . One such basic tool is access to known favorable evidence on which a defense may be based. . . . Therefore, the prosecution has a constitutional obligation to disclose evidence that is material to the guilt or punishment of the defendant. ¶ The duty to disclose evidence that is favorable to the accused includes evidence that may be used to impeach the government's witnesses by showing bias, self-interest, or other factors that might undermine the reliability of the witness's testimony." *Birano v. State*, 143 Hawai'i 163, 181-82, 426 P.3d 387, 405-06 (2018).

18.9.2.5. *The Right Against Prosecutorial Fabrication of False Incriminating Evidence or Concealment of Evidence That Impeaches Prosecution Testimony*

A line of decisions from *Mooney v. Holohan,* 294 U.S. 103 (1935), to *Miller v. Pate,* 386 U.S. 1 (1967), condemns the prosecution's presentation of "evidence that it knew (or should have known) was false." *See e.g., Pyle v. Kansas,* 317 U.S. 213 (1942); *United States v. Butler,* 955 F.3d 1052, 1064 (D.C. Cir. 2020); *Barnes v. City of New York,* 68 F.4th 123, 129-30 (2d Cir. 2023) ("[t]he use of fabricated evidence in initiating a prosecution or at trial may amount to a deprivation of liberty [without due process] even in the absence of a conviction based on the fabricated evidence and even when, as here, a plaintiff simultaneously was charged, detained, tried, and convicted for a separate offense"); *United States v. Ausby,* 916 F.3d 1089, 1092 (D.C. Cir. 2019); *Fogle v. Sokol,* 957 F.3d 148 (3d Cir. 2020); *Burgess v. Goldstein,* 997 F.3d 541, 553 (4th Cir. 2021) ("'We have recognized a due process right not to be deprived of liberty as a result of the fabrication of evidence by a government officer acting in an investigating capacity.'"); *accord, Truman v. Orem City,* 1 F.4th 1227 (10th Cir. 2021); *O'Connell v. Tuggle,* 2021 WL 5973048 (10th Cir. December 16, 2021) (applying the principle to sustain a section 1983 claim of clear due process violation in a case in which a social worker, taking notes during a police interview of the mother of a child whose death was suspicious, deliberately recorded falsely that the mother had confessed to abusing the child); *Frost v. New York City Police Department,* 980 F.3d 231, 244 (2d Cir. 2020) ("The Due Process Clause guarantees a criminal defendant's 'right to a fair trial.' . . . This right is violated '[w]hen a police officer creates false information likely to influence a jury's decision and forwards that information to prosecutors.'"); *Richards v. County of San Bernardino,* 39 F.4th 562, 569 (9th Cir. 2022) ("'[t]here is a clearly established constitutional due process right not to be subjected to criminal charges on the basis of false evidence that was deliberately fabricated by the government'"); *Ricks v. Pauch,* 2021 WL 4775145, at *4 (6th Cir. October 13, 2021) ("[t]he officers do not contest that it was clearly established in 1992 that fabricating evidence to create probable cause to detain a suspect would have violated the suspect's Fourth Amendment right to be free from unreasonable seizures"); *accord, Dennis v. City of Philadelphia,* 19 F.4th 279 (3d Cir. 2021); *Patrick v. City of Chicago,* 974 F.3d 824, 834-35 (7th Cir. 2020) ("We have recently clarified the contours of constitutional claims based on allegations of evidence fabrication. A claim for false arrest or pretrial detention based on fabricated evidence sounds in the Fourth Amendment right to be free from seizure without probable cause. . . . If fabricated evidence is later used at trial to obtain a conviction, the accused may have suffered a violation of his due-process right to a fair trial. . . . And 'misconduct of this type that results in a conviction might also violate the accused's right to due process under the rubric of *Brady* . . . and *Kyles* . . . if government officials suppressed evidence of the fabrication.'"); *Stinson v. City of Milwaukee,* 2013 WL 5447916, at *18 (E.D. Wis. 2013), *rulings on other issues aff'd in part and appeal dism'd in part,* 868 F.3d 516 (7th Cir. 2017) (en banc) ("'a police officer who manufactures false evidence against a criminal defendant violates the due process clause if the evidence is later used to deprive the defendant of her liberty in some way'"); *Morse v. Fusto,* 804 F.3d 538, 541, 547-48 (2d Cir. 2015) (upholding section 1983 relief for a defendant who was "deprived . . . of his constitutional right to a fair trial" as a result of a prosecutor's and state investigator's intentional presentation of "false or misleading evidence" to the grand jury in support of an indictment); *Jackson v. City of Cleveland,* summarized in § 18.9.1 *supra; and see generally Strickler v. Greene,* 527 U.S. 263, 281 & n.19 (1999) (dictum); *United*

States v. Agurs, 427 U.S. 97, 103 (1976) (dictum); *cf. McDonough v. Smith,* 139 S. Ct. 2149, 2155 n.2 (2019); *Coggins v. Buonora,* 776 F.3d 108 (2d Cir. 2015). "'In a classic *Brady* case, involving the state's inadvertent failure to disclose favorable evidence, the evidence will be deemed material only if there would be a reasonable probability of a different result if the evidence had been disclosed. . . .' . . . ¶ When, however, a prosecutor obtains a conviction with evidence that he or she knows or should know to be false, the materiality standard is significantly more favorable to the defendant. '[A] conviction obtained by the knowing use of perjured testimony is fundamentally unfair, and must be set aside if there is any reasonable likelihood that the false testimony could have affected the judgment of the jury.' . . . This standard. . . applies whether the state solicited the false testimony or allowed it to go uncorrected; . . . and is not substantively different from the test that permits the state to avoid having a conviction set aside, notwithstanding a violation of constitutional magnitude, upon a showing that the violation was harmless beyond a reasonable doubt." *Adams v. Commissioner of Correction,* 309 Conn. 359, 370-72, 71 A.3d 512, 519-20 (2013); *accord, Henning v. Commissioner of Corrections,* 334 Conn. 1, 24-25, 219 A.3d 334, 348-49 (2019); *and see Dickey v. Davis,* 69 F.4th 624, 636-37 (9th Cir. 2023) (The United States Supreme Court has "explained that the materiality analysis for a *Napue* violation requires that a conviction 'must be set aside if there is *any reasonable likelihood* that the false testimony *could have* affected the judgment of the jury.' . . . [*United States v. Agurs,* 427 U.S. 97 (1976)] at 103–04 (emphasis added) . . . ¶ *Napue*'s materiality standard is considerably less demanding than the standard for *Brady* claims, which requires that a petitioner show 'there is a reasonable probability that, had the evidence been disclosed to the defense, the result of the proceeding *would have* been different.' . . . The Supreme Court has explained that *Napue*'s materiality threshold is lower 'not just because [*Napue* cases] involve prosecutorial misconduct, but more importantly because they involve a corruption of the truth-seeking function of the trial process.' *Agurs,* 427 U.S. at 104."). "The standard applied under the . . . *Giglio* test [see the following paragraph] has been described as being more "defense-friendly" than the *Brady* standard. . . . The reason for this characterization is that once the defendant establishes that the State knowingly presented false testimony, the burden is on the State to prove beyond a reasonable doubt that the knowing use of the false testimony, or failure to disclose the false testimony once it was discovered, did not affect the verdict." *State v. Dougan,* 202 So.3d 363, 378 (Fla. 2016).

Specifically, the Supreme Court has held that the Due Process Clause invalidates a state conviction obtained after a trial at which the prosecutor has knowingly elicited false testimony from a witness, even on a matter relating to the witness's credibility rather than directly to the defendant's guilt (*Alcorta v. Texas,* 355 U.S. 28 (1957)), or at which the prosecutor has knowingly permitted the witness to testify falsely on such a matter (*Napue v. Illinois,* 360 U.S. 264 (1959)). Under *Napue,* if the prosecution knows of any evidence inconsistent with the testimony of one of its material witnesses and "relevant to his credibility," the defense and "the jury [are] . . . entitled to know of it" (*Giglio v. United States,* 405 U.S. 150, 155 (1972)). *See, e.g., Haskell v. Superintendent Greene SCI,* 866 F.3d 139 (3d Cir. 2017); *Dow v. Virga,* 729 F.3d 1041, 1047-51 (9th Cir. 2013); *Guzman v. Secretary,* 663 F.3d 1336 (11th Cir. 2011); *Sivak v. Hardison,* 658 F.3d 898 (9th Cir. 2011); *Moore v. Illinois,* 408 U.S. 786, 797-98 (1972) (dictum). Like the command of *Brady v. Maryland,* the command of *Napue* and *Giglio* extends to impeachment evidence known to law enforcement officers involved in a case, as well as to the prosecutor. See § 18.9.1 sixth paragraph *supra. And see In re Jackson,* 12 F.4th 604, 611 (6th

Cir. 2021) (holding that a viable *Napue* claim was pleaded by allegations that law enforcement agents had intimidated a prosecution witness into testifying falsely that the defendant had confessed to several murders, and observing that "*Napue* claims . . . have a prejudice-like prong in that 'a new trial is required if the false testimony could in any reasonable likelihood have affected the judgment of the jury.' . . . [and that t]his threshold can be met when the knowingly misleading testimony is offered by a 'key prosecution witness'"); *Phillips v. Ornoski*, 673 F.3d 1168, 1183-85 (9th Cir. 2012) ("*Hayes v. Brown*, 399 F.3d 972 (9th Cir. 2005) (en banc) controls this case. . . . In *Hayes*, as here, the prosecutor had reached a deal with the attorney for a key state witness, James, providing for the dismissal of all felony charges against him . . . if he testified against Hayes at trial. *Id.* at 977. As in this case, the prosecution elicited a promise from James's attorney that James would not be informed of the deal, and at trial James testified that he had received no promise of benefits in exchange for his testimony. *Id.* at 977, 980. As we observed in *Hayes*, and as is equally applicable here, that a witness may have been unaware of the agreement entered into on his behalf may mean that his testimony denying the existence of such an agreement is not knowingly false or perjured, but it does not mean it is not false nevertheless. As we explained in *Hayes*: ¶ '[T]hat the witness was tricked into lying on the witness stand by the State does not, in any fashion, insulate the State from conforming its conduct to the requirements of due process. . . . The fact that the witness is not complicit in the falsehood is what gives the false testimony the ring of truth, and makes it all the more likely to affect the judgment of the jury. That the witness is unaware of the falsehood of his testimony makes it more dangerous, not less so.' ¶ . . . In *Hayes* we made clear in no uncertain terms that the practice of 'insulating' a witness from her own immunity agreement so that she can profess ignorance of the benefits provided in exchange for her testimony is an egregious violation of the prosecution's obligations under *Napue*."); *People v. Smith*, 498 Mich. 466, 870 N.W.2d 299 (2015) ("Four times . . . [prosecution witness] Yancy denied having been paid in connection with the defendant's case – specifically, that he had not been compensated for his testimony at the defendant's trial and also that he had not been otherwise compensated for 'cooperating' 'with regards to this case.' Clearly, the jury could have interpreted this statement to indicate that Yancy had *never* been paid for his involvement with the investigation of the homicide [in issue], not merely that the Genesee County Prosecuting Attorney's office had not compensated him for 'testimony' or cooperation with the defendant's formal prosecution. The latter point might have been true; the former point was plainly misleading and likely untrue, as the prosecutor well knew . . . . This former point, however, was never corrected or clarified at trial, nor was the true nature or extent of Yancy's participation or compensation as an informant put before the jury. Rather, the prosecutor exploited the potential confusion Yancy's testimony created by reminding the jury of Yancy's denials during closing argument, cementing the false notion that Yancy had only been paid for his cooperation in *other cases,* and attempting to advance his credibility as a result of that fact . . . ." *Id.* at 474, 870 N.W.2d at 303. Capitalizing on Yancy's testimony that he had no paid involvement in the defendant's case is inconsistent with a prosecutor's duty to correct false testimony. Indeed, the prosecutor sought to transform testimony that might have been merely confusing on its own into an outright falsity. Irrespective of the veracity of Yancy's claim that he had not been paid to 'testify,' the prosecutor should not have capitalized on Yancy's testimony after Yancy had confusingly denied being paid for cooperating in 'this case.' . . . Her actions served to underscore the jury's false impression that because Yancy had not been paid to 'testify,' he had no questionable incentive for his participation in this case. Simply put, the prosecutor sought to benefit from the problematic testimony and use it to her advantage. This prosecutorial conduct does not comport with due process." *Id.* at 480-81, 870 N.W.2d at 306-07.); *State v. Higgs*, 253 N.J. 333, 357-61, 290 A.3d 1235, 1249-51 (2023) (relying on *Brady*, *Napue, Giglio*, and state law that implements the constitutional requirements of those cases, the Supreme Court holds as follows: "To ensure that defendants in criminal trials are provided with the discovery necessary to adequately prepare for trial, defendants must be allowed, under certain circumstances, to access documents in law enforcement's internal affairs files. This is consistent with the State's obligation to produce exculpatory and impeachment evidence, as the Attorney General has conceded in this matter. That does not, however, mean that defendants should have unbridled access to internal affairs records. To appropriately balance the important interests involved, we adopt the following procedure. ¶ Going forward, a defendant who seeks discovery of information from an internal affairs file must first file a motion with the trial court requesting an in camera review of that file. The motion shall identify the specific category of information the defendant seeks and the relevance of that information to the defendant's case. A general allegation that the defendant is in search of information relevant to a law enforcement officer's credibility for impeachment purposes would be insufficient to obtain review of the file. . . . ¶ . . . [I]n order for a trial court to grant a motion to conduct an in camera review of an internal affairs file, the defendant must point to a specific category or type of evidence and assert that the evidence, if present in the file, has a relevant nexus to an issue in the case. ¶ We anticipate that many defendants will be in a position to meet the relevancy standard and decline to adopt . . . [a] more stringent . . . standard . . . . ¶ If the trial court determines as a threshold matter that the requested information, if present in the internal affairs file, would be relevant to the defendant's case – for impeachment purposes or to support the defense's theory, for example – the trial court shall grant the defendant's motion and conduct an in camera review of the internal affairs records outside the presence of the parties. The in camera review by the trial court would be *solely* for the purpose of determining whether the category of identified information exists in the internal affairs file. If, upon review, the trial court determines that the requested information is present in the file, both parties shall be allowed to review the *relevant* portion of the file, subject to any protective orders entered by the trial court. ¶ Allowing the parties access to the relevant portion of the internal affairs file is not, however, the end of the inquiry. Even if the evidence sought is present in the file and relevant to the case, the court must balance its relevance against potential undue prejudice, as required [by New Jersey Evidence Rule 403], prior to allowing that evidence in at trial."); *People v. Wilcox*, 2023 WL 2144541 (Mich. App. 2023) (affirming a trial court's ruling granting a defendant a new trial because of a *Napue-Giglio* violation: a prosecution witness's trial testimony was more favorable to the defendant than his grand jury testimony and the prosecutor concluded that the trial testimony was perjurious; she did not did not inform the court or the defense of this conclusion but impeached the witness with his grand jury testimony, which was admitted as substantive evidence; "Because . . . the prosecutor failed to fulfill her constitutional obligation to report . . . [the witness's] perjury to defendant and the trial court when she determined that . . . [the witness] lied under oath, . . . she violated defendant's right to due process. With . . . [the witness] on the witness stand, the prosecutor was able to introduce his prior grand jury testimony, which was more consistent with . . . [the complainant's] testimony. If . . . [the witness] had not been allowed to testify untruthfully, there would not have been any testimony to corroborate . . . [the complainant's] version of events. As such, defendant was denied his right to due process." *Id.* at *4); *Commonwealth v. Gray*, 2023 WL 2581859 (Pa. Super. 2023) (at trial the prosecutor informed the jury that the complainant in an assault and sex-abuse case was facing criminal charges; he asked her whether she had been promised or paid anything for her testimony and she answered "no"; in a post-trial motion, the defense presented a plea transcript in the complainant's case showing that the same prosecutor had reduced two felony charges to misdemeanors and had stated that the complainant was cooperative and was providing testimony against the defendant; the prosecutor denied having made any plea deal with the complainant, and defendant's trial judge denied the motion without a hearing; the Superior Court holds that this rejection of a *Napue-Giglio* claim without sufficient record support was an abuse of discretion that requires remand for a hearing). It is but a short step to hold that since the whole of every witness's testimony impliedly asserts its veracity, nondisclosure of any material known to the prosecution that is legally admissible to impeach the witness would also violate due process. *Cf. Giles v. Maryland,* 386 U.S. 66 (1967). The California Supreme Court, for example, has required disclosure of the felony record of a prosecution witness on this theory. *In re Ferguson,* 5 Cal. 3d 525, 487 P.2d 1234, 96 Cal. Rptr. 594 (1971). *See also State v. Ireland,* 11 Or. App. 264, 500 P.2d 1231 (1972).

Some courts hold that a prosecutor who knows a prosecution witness has presented false testimony satisfies *Napue* by informing defense counsel of the perjury. Others hold that the prosecutor has an independent obligation to set the record straight and assure that the jury is made aware of the true facts as the prosecutor knows them. *See Gomez v. Commissioner of Correction,* 336 Conn. 168, 188, 243 A.3d 1163, 1175-76 (2020) (canvassing the federal caselaw on the issue and adopting the latter rule; "[I]t is the prosecutor who is best positioned to repair the damage that is done to 'the efficient and fair administration of justice'. . . ; when a state's witness provides false testimony. In the face of silence – or worse, complicity – on the part of the prosecution and continued dissembling by the state's witness, there is no reason to believe that defense counsel will have any greater success in persuading the jury that the witness has been promised benefits in exchange for his or her testimony than, for instance, that he or she is the true perpetrator. As the United States Court of Appeals for the Ninth Circuit explained in [*United States v.*] *LaPage,* [231 F.3d 488, 492 (9th Cir. 2000)] '[a]ll perjury pollutes a trial, making it hard for jurors to see the truth. No lawyer, whether prosecutor or defense counsel, civil or criminal, may knowingly present lies to a jury and then sit idly by while opposing counsel struggles to contain this pollution of the trial. The jury understands defense counsel's duty of advocacy and frequently listens to defense counsel with skepticism.'").

Perjury by a prosecution witness violates due process even when the prosecutor who examines the witness is unaware of its falsity; "rather, knowledge on the part of any representative or agent of the prosecution is enough" (*People v. Olinger,* 176 Ill. 2d 326, 347, 680 N.E.2d 321, 332, 223 Ill. Dec. 588, 599 (1997)). *See, e.g., Giglio v. United States,* 405 U.S. 150, 154 (1972); *Ex parte Castellano,* 863 S.W.2d 476 (Tex. Crim. App. 1993); *People v. Ellis,* 315 Ill. App. 3d 1108, 735 N.E.2d 736, 249 Ill. Dec. 132 (2000); *People v. Kasim,* 56 Cal. App. 4th 1360, 1380, 66 Cal. Rptr. 2d 494, 506 (1997) ("[t]he scope of the prosecutorial duty to disclose encompasses not just exculpatory evidence in the prosecutor's possession but such evidence possessed by investigative agencies to which the prosecutor has reasonable access"). It follows that, if the witness who testifies perjuriously is a police officer or other state agent, due process is violated whether or not the prosecutor is aware that the testimony is untrue.

Some state court decisions hold that perjurious testimony by any prosecution witness violates due process even when the prosecutor is unaware of its falsity. *E.g.*, *Ex Parte Chabot,* 300 S.W.3d 768 (Tex. Crim. App. 2009).

18.9.2.6. *The Right Against Prosecutorial Suppression of Evidence Favorable to the Defense*

The *Brady* doctrine described in § 18.9.1 *supra* governs prosecutorial disclosure of evidence favorable to the defense. A closely related, but older and conceptually distinct doctrine prohibits the prosecutor from *suppressing* such evidence. This right was recognized as an alternative ground of decision in *Pyle v. Kansas,* 317 U.S. 213 (1942), and *Wylde v. Wyoming,* 362 U.S. 607 (1960). It is best expounded in *United States ex rel. Almeida v. Baldi,* 195 F.2d 815 (3d Cir. 1952). *See also Soo Park v. Thompson*, 851 F.3d 910 (9th Cir. 2017) ("'[I]t is well established that "substantial government interference with a defense witness's free and unhampered choice to testify amounts to a violation of due process."'" *Id.* at 919. "[W]rongful conduct by prosecutors or law enforcement officers can . . . constitute 'substantial government interference' with a defense witness's choice to testify." *Id.* "Detective Thompson contacted Ayala after Park gave notice to the District Attorney of her intention to use Ayala as a defense witness at her criminal trial. During the course of the phone conversation, Thompson told Ayala that 'John [Gilmore] was really upset about the whole thing because he – he feels like they just made you lose faith in him, I guess.' . . . [I]t is plausible to infer that Thompson intended to intimidate Ayala, a domestic violence victim, by informing her that Gilmore, her abuser, was 'really upset' by her potential testimony." *Id.* at 920. "Moreover, Park contends that Thompson's actual motive in asserting Gilmore's innocence, Park's guilt, and the defense team's dishonesty was to dissuade Ayala from testifying. . . . During the phone call in question, Thompson declared, among other things, that Gilmore was certainly innocent and that Park was in fact the killer: 'And first, what I want to tell you is that John [Gilmore] is not the killer . . . . But the two people who showed up at your house two weeks ago . . . they are private investigators who were hired by the defense team that is representing the killer [Park] [in] this case.' *Id.* at 920-21. "Park further alleges that Thompson made false representations of the evidence against Park, incorrectly stating, for example, that Park 'left her blood DNA on the door handle.' Detective Thompson also encouraged Ayala not to 'believe what they're [the defense team] saying,' because they were 'going to tell every lie they can to try and get [Park] off.' Thompson described the defense team as 'private investigators who are hired by [Park's] defense attorneys to try and shoot holes in – in our prosecution of their – of the bad guy' and stated that they 'bent the facts to try to, you know, make you think something else.' Taken together, the allegations regarding Thompson's misrepresentation of the evidence against Park, coupled with her statements about Park's guilt, Gilmore's innocence, and the defense investigators' duplicity (as well as her statement that Gilmore was 'really upset' with Ayala), can reasonably be interpreted as adequately pleading a deliberate intent on the part of Thompson to intimidate and otherwise attempt to persuade Ayala to refuse to testify on behalf of the defense." *Id.* at 921.); *Morse v. Fusto*, 804 F.3d 538, 541, 543, 547-48 (2d Cir. 2015) (the prosecutor's and state investigator's alteration of documents – which were then presented to a grand jury in support of an indictment – to remove exonerating details supported a grant of section 1983 relief for violation of the "'right not to be deprived of liberty as a result of the fabrication of evidence by a government officer acting in an investigative capacity'").

This doctrine is at the heart of the caselaw described in § 9.14 *supra,* establishing a right to judicial relief when the prosecution suppresses evidence by instructing witnesses not to speak with defense counsel or a defense investigator. The doctrine would also seem to imply a right of defense access to any exculpatory or favorable materials that are within the exclusive control of the prosecutor, such as impounded physical objects. The Supreme Court has recognized that if a police officer or prosecutor, acting in "bad faith," destroys evidence "potentially useful" to the defense, its destruction violates the accused's due process rights (*see Arizona v. Youngblood*, 488 U.S. 51, 57-58 (1988) (dictum); *Illinois v. Fisher*, 540 U.S. 544, 547-48 (2004) (per curiam) (dictum). *Accord, Jimerson v. Payne*, 957 F.3d 916, 930-31 (8th Cir. 2020) (finding a *Youngblood* violation where a recording of a turncoat accomplice's confession was lost or destroyed before trial: "After law enforcement and the deputy prosecutor discussed the recording, the prosecutor advised that the recording was inadmissible. The testimony from . . . [law enforcement officers] was not that the prosecutor thought the evidence was inculpatory, but that it could not be used or 'wouldn't have evidentiary value.' Although the substance of the recording is not entirely clear, what the recording contained appears to be significant enough that law enforcement and the prosecution worked together to intentionally conceal its existence from the defense. That intent is demonstrated in several ways. One way is the prosecutor's decision to provide, at a minimum, misleading answers to defense counsel's discovery requests, but more accurately classified as untruthful answers. Another way is the prosecutor's decision not to preserve the recording after he found out about it and opined it was inadmissible. In addition, law enforcement assisted the prosecution's efforts to conceal the existence of the recording by putting together a statement for . . . [an informant] to sign that deliberately left out any mention that a recording took place. The existence of the recording was also omitted from the state police report, which failed to identify . . . [the] informant. Taken together, the uncontroverted evidence establishes bad faith."); *Blakeney v. State*, 236 So.3d 11, 27-28 (Miss. 2017) ("Blakeney argues that the ATF reports [regarding electronic evidence obtained from cell phones and discarded by the prosecution] were forensic evidence that did not support the State's theory that Blakeney had murdered V.V. in order to demonstrate that he was worthy of entry into the Aryan Brotherhood. Moreover, Blakeney contends that in a world that is full of digital photography on cell phones with the ability to share with others, the fact that the cell phone and computer records contained nothing incriminating demonstrates evidence in favor of Blakeney. We find that the prosecutor's failure to disclose the contents of the ATF reports was in error and in bad faith. Clearly, information on Blakeney's and Viner's cell phones and computer potentially could be useful. One of the most monumental defenses that Blakeney presented was an attempt to show that he had pursued membership into the Aryan Brotherhood only after he had been in jail for years and only for protection in prison. Thus, a recent picture of Blakeney without swastika tattoos could have emphasized the defense's point that Blakeney had not been involved with the Aryan Brotherhood before he went to jail. And, as Blakeney argued, the lack of the presence of any incriminatory evidence would be in Blakeney's favor, especially in a case with minimal direct evidence against a capital murder suspect. Surely had any mention of anger or gang initiation been present on the ATF reports, the prosecution would have introduced it into evidence. In addition, the prosecutor's statement that he had engaged in a practice of disposing of exculpatory evidence demonstrates bad faith. Therefore, prosecutorial misconduct also requires reversal in this case."). State constitutional due process protections may be broader in this regard: As Justice Stevens' concurring opinion in *Fisher* notes (540 U.S.at 549 n.*): "Since *Youngblood* was decided, a number of state courts have held as a matter of state constitutional law that the loss or destruction of evidence critical to the defense does violate due process, even in the absence of bad faith." *See State v. Tiedemann*, 2007 UT 49, 162 P.3d 1106, 1115-17 (Utah 2007) (rejecting *Arizona v. Youngblood*'s "bad faith" requirement on state constitutional grounds); *People v. Handy*, 20 N.Y.3d 663, 669, 988 N.E.2d 879, 882, 966 N.Y.S.2d 351, 354 (2013) (declining to reach the question of whether to reject *Youngblood* on state constitutional grounds and instead "resolv[ing] this case, following the approach taken by the Maryland Court of Appeals in *Cost v. State*, 417 Md. 360, 10 A.3d 184 (2010), by holding that, under the New York law of evidence, a permissive adverse-inference instruction should be given when a defendant, using reasonable diligence, has requested evidence reasonably likely to be material, and when that evidence has been destroyed by agents of the State"). As long as the evidence has *not* been destroyed but is still in the state's possession, the language and logic of the Supreme Court's federal Due Process decisions are clear that "the good or bad faith of the prosecution is irrelevant" and that the prosecution "must disclose material exculpatory evidence" (*Illinois v. Fisher, supra*, 540 U.S. at 547). *Accord, Arizona v. Youngblood, supra*, 488 U.S. at 57.

18.9.2.7. *The Right Against an Unfair Balance of Advantage Favoring the Prosecution*

Wardius v. Oregon, 412 U.S. 470, 472 (1973), holds that "the Due Process Clause of the Fourteenth Amendment forbids enforcement of alibi[-disclosure] rules unless reciprocal discovery rights are given to criminal defendants." *See, e.g., United States v. Bahamonde*, 445 F.3d 1225 (9th Cir. 2006) (A regulation of the Department of Homeland Security required the defendant "to state with specificity the testimony he expected from Agent Rodmel but the government was not required at any time to state what evidence it expected to offer in rebuttal, either from Rodmel or anyone else. Nor was there any other requirement in force to compel the government to reveal that information." *Id.* at 1229. "The regulation, as applied in this case, accordingly falls squarely within the rule of *Wardius*." *Id.* at 1230.); *Mauricio v. Duckworth*, 840 F.2d 454, 457-58 (7th Cir. 1988) (In this habeas proceeding "the district court found . . . that . . . [Indiana's facially constitutional] discovery procedures were not applied evenhandedly in Mauricio's case. Thus, although the relevant Indiana alibi statutes do not explicitly impose upon parties an affirmative obligation to disclose alibi and alibi rebuttal witnesses, the district court found that, in the circumstances presented by this case, the trial court's discovery order requiring the defense to list *all* its witnesses should have triggered a corresponding and reciprocal obligation on the part of the State to list *all* its potential witnesses – including likely rebuttal witnesses. In the opinion of Judge Sharp, the trial court's failure to require the State to divulge the identical information it required from the defense altered the balance struck by the statutory discovery provisions and created instead the same type of nonreciprocal discovery scheme held unconstitutional by the Supreme Court in *Wardius*." The Seventh Circuit agrees with this analysis, disagrees with District Judge Sharp's finding that the *Wardius* violation was harmless, and orders habeas relief.); *Camp v. Neven*, 606 Fed. Appx. 322, 326 (9th Cir. 2015) ("We conclude that allowing the State to present unnoticed expert rebuttal testimony when Camp was required to disclose his own expert testimony on the same issues was a violation of the Supreme Court's precedent in *Wardius*, and that the state courts were unreasonable in denying Camp relief on this ground."); *State v. Wooten*, 260 So.3d 1060 (Fla. App. 2018) ("Due process . . . requires that discovery 'be a two-way street.' *Wardius* . . . at 475. . . ."); *United States ex rel. Hairston v. Warden*, 597 F.2d 694 (7th Cir. 1979) (finding a violation of *Wardius* although the defendant did not offer alibi testimony at trial; it was sufficient that defense counsel's reason for this failure was the trial court's ruling that no alibi testimony would be permitted unless the defendant complied with a unilateral pretrial disclosure requirement).

The *Wardius* opinion states more broadly that "the Due Process Clause . . . does speak to the balance of forces between the accused and his accuser" (*id.* at 472). *See also United States v. Ash,* 413 U.S. 300, 309 (1973), noting the Sixth Amendment's concern against "the imbalance in the adversary system that otherwise [that is, without defense counsel] resulted with the creation of a professional prosecuting official." These formulations suggest that Justice Cardozo's famous phrase about keeping "the balance true" (*Snyder v. Massachusetts,* 291 U.S. 97, 122 (1934)) may be more than just a jurisprudential attitude: It may be a constitutionally enforceable right of the defense. Their implication is that if significant procedural tools or benefits are made available to the prosecution by state law or practice, defendants must be given the same or similar tools or benefits. *See State v. Reimonenq,* 2019-0367 (La. 10/22/19), 286 So.3d 412 (La. 2019) (After a trial judge issued a ruling *in limine* excluding the testimony of a proposed prosecution witness, the prosecutor entered a *nol pros* and then reindicted the defendant. The defendant filed a motion to quash, noting that "the state's decision to dismiss and reinstitute criminal charges is a power that defendant does not have. He urged that . . . [the Louisiana Supreme] Court's precedent bars the state from flaunting its power by essentially granting itself a continuance in a way that substantially prejudices defendant's right to a fair trial" (*id.* at 414). The Louisiana Supreme Court holds that the motion to quash must be granted: "Inherent in justice and the concept of fundamental fairness is ensuring a 'balance of forces between the accused and his accuser,' *Wardius v. Oregon,* 412 U.S. 470, 474 . . . . In its brief, the state openly acknowledges it could have sought writs from the appellate court and simply declined to do so. The state also suggests that dismissing and reinstituting these charges was simply 'to put its case together.' We find that in this case, the state's exercise of its statutory right . . . to dismiss and reinstitute charges against defendant upset this 'balance of forces' to such a degree that it violates defendant's right to due process and fundamental fairness." *Id.* at 417.). *See also State v. Williams,* 2021-00205 (La. 6/8/21), 317 So.3d 317, 317-18 (La. 2021) ("After the trial court granted defendant's motion to exclude a cellphone video that the State failed to authenticate, the State dismissed the prosecution during jury selection before the jury was sworn. On the next day, the State reinstituted the prosecution. Defendant then filed a motion to quash, which the trial court granted. . . .¶ . . . Inherent in justice and the concept of fundamental fairness is ensuring a 'balance of forces between the accused and his accuser.' *Wardius v. Oregon,* 412 U.S.470, 474 (1973). As in *Reimonenq,* the State's exercise of its statutory right . . . to dismiss and reinstitute charges against defendant upset this 'balance of forces' to such a degree that it violates defendant's right to due process and fundamental fairness. Thus, under the circumstances presented here, we find the trial court did not abuse its discretion in granting defendant's motion to quash."); *State v. Joekel,* 19-334 (La.App. 5 Cir. 12/20/19), 2019 WL 7044739, at *2-*3 (La. App. 2019) (referring to *Reimonenq*'s citation of *Wardius,* the court of appeal affirms a trial court's pretrial order requiring the prosecution to create and disclose a written report of the proposed testimony of a prosecution expert witness: "We are of the opinion that disclosure of the various examinations and/or test results used by . . . [the expert] to formulate his conclusory opinion is necessary for the defendant's adequate preparation for trial and to cross-examine the expert, and must be given to the defense. Fundamental fairness and due process require that defendant have the opportunity to examine the basis from which . . . [the expert] reached his conclusions.").

Although the balance-of-forces principle is still embryonic, two implications of *Wardius* deserve note.

First, any criminal procedures that provide "nonreciprocal benefits to the State" in regard to the investigation, preservation, and presentation of its evidentiary case should be constitutionally assailable "when the lack of reciprocity interferes with the defendant's ability to secure a fair trial" (*Wardius, supra,* 412 U.S. at 474 n.6). For example, if procedures are available by which the prosecution can detain witnesses or collect and secure other evidence favorable to its case, then either the prosecution should be obliged equally to collect, secure, and make available witnesses and evidence favorable to the defense, or at least the defense should be given equal use of the procedures. If court orders or compulsory process can be issued to assist the prosecution in conducting lineups, fingerprint or handwriting or voice comparisons, or other scientific tests, the results of those investigations must be disclosed to the defense; and judicial process must be made available for the conduct of similar investigations at the instance of the defense, at least to search out "evidence that might be expected to play a significant role in the . . . defense" (*California v. Trombetta,* 467 U.S. 479, 488 (1984)). *See Evans v. Superior Court,* 11 Cal. 3d 617, 522 P.2d 681, 114 Cal. Rptr. 121 (1974) (giving defendants a state constitutional due process right to a pretrial order requiring the prosecution to conduct a lineup); *People v. Mena,* 54 Cal. 4th 146, 277 P.3d 160, 141 Cal. Rptr. 3d 469 (2012) (adhering to *Evans* despite post-*Evans* legislation that might have been read as limiting defense discovery to statutorily enumerated procedures that do not include lineups); *United States v. Ash,* 461 F.2d 92, 104 (D.C. Cir. 1972) (en banc) (dictum), *rev'd on an unrelated point,* 413 U.S. 300 (1973) ("It was the combined interests of fairness and effective police administration that led this court to approve judicial orders, on application of the prosecutor, that reinforced the long-standing police recognition of the need for corporeal lineups for persons taken into custody on photographic identification, by requiring the attendance at a police-conducted lineup of persons released on recognizance or bail. Orders may likewise be issued at the request of defense counsel, as has been done by various district judges in pretrial procedures."); *cf. People ex rel. Gallagher v. District Court,* 656 P.2d 1287 (Colo. 1983) (the defendant was denied due process when police refused to perform forensic testing requested by defense counsel before testing was rendered impossible by the preparation of the homicide victim's body for burial); *Snyder v. State,* 930 P.2d 1274, 1277 (Alaska 1996) ("the Due Process Clause of the Alaska Constitution entitles a DWI arrestee to an independent chemical test even if that person refuses to take the statutorily prescribed breath test"); *and compare* the cases holding that the unnecessary destruction of material evidence in the course of forensic testing by the prosecution, so as to preclude independent testing by defense experts, constitutes a violation of due process (*State v. Vannoy,* 177 Ariz. 206, 209-12, 866 P.2d 874, 878-80 (Ariz. App. 1993); *People v. Gomez,* 198 Colo. 105, 596 P.2d 1192 (1979); *People v. Garries,* 645 P.2d 1306 (Colo. 1982); *State v. Blackwell,* 245 Ga. App. 135, 137-42, 537 S.E.2d 457, 460-63 (2000); *People v. Taylor,* 54 Ill. App. 3d 454, 369 N.E.2d 573, 12 Ill. Dec. 76 (1977); *People v. Dodsworth,* 60 Ill. App. 3d 207, 376 N.E.2d 449, 17 Ill. Dec. 450 (1978); *State v. Morales,* 232 Conn. 707, 726-27, 657 A.2d 585, 594-95 (1995) ("Like our sister states, we conclude that the good or bad faith of the police in failing to preserve potentially useful evidence cannot be dispositive of whether a criminal defendant has been deprived of due process of law. Accordingly, we, too, reject the litmus test of bad faith on the part of the police, which the United States Supreme Court adopted under the federal constitution in *Youngblood* [*infra*]. Rather, in determining whether a defendant has been afforded due process of law under the state constitution, the trial court must employ the *Asherman* balancing test [referring to *State v. Asherman*, 193 Conn. 695, 724-26, 478 A.2d 227, 245-47 (1984)], weighing the reasons for the unavailability of the evidence against the degree of prejudice to the accused. More specifically, the trial court must balance the totality of the circumstances surrounding the missing evidence, including the following factors: 'the materiality of the missing evidence, the likelihood of mistaken interpretation of it by witnesses or the jury, the reason for its nonavailability to the defense and the prejudice to the defendant caused by the unavailability of the evidence.'"); *State v. Matafeo*, 71 Hawai'i 183, 187, 787 P.2d 671, 673 (1990) (dictum) ("This court has held that '"the duty of disclosure is operative as a duty of preservation," [and] that principle must be applied on a case-by-case basis,' . . . ¶ In certain circumstances, regardless of good or bad faith, the State may lose or destroy material evidence which is 'so critical to the defense as to make a criminal trial fundamentally unfair' without it.")) *with California v. Trombetta, supra* (limiting the federal constitutional version of this doctrine to "evidence that both possess[es] an exculpatory value that was apparent before the evidence was destroyed, and [is] of such a nature that the defendant would be unable to obtain comparable evidence by other reasonably available means" (*id.* at 489)), *and Arizona v. Youngblood*, 488 U.S. 51, 57-58 (1988), limiting the doctrine to destruction in "bad faith"). For a summary of the *Trombetta/Youngblood* rules in more defense-friendly terms, *see United States v. Johnson*, 996 F.3d 200, 206 (4th Cir. 2021) (in a case in which the prosecution failed to disclose that it had possession of potentially exculpatory evidence and then permitted that evidence to be lost, the court of appeals holds that the district court is required to make a more complete evidentiary record before adjudicating the defendants' motion to dismiss the prosecution: "A criminal defendant may prove a due process violation based on the prosecution's failure to preserve evidence if the evidence 'possess[es] an exculpatory value that was apparent before the evidence was destroyed' and if it is 'of such a nature that the defendant would be unable to obtain comparable evidence by other reasonably available means.' *See Trombetta* . . . . A showing of bad faith is required, however, when the lost evidence can only be said to be 'potentially useful' to the defendant because the contents of the evidence are unknown. *See Arizona v. Youngblood* . . . . ¶ Even absent a due process violation, a criminal defendant may be entitled to an adverse inference instruction pursuant to the spoliation of evidence rule. Under that evidentiary rule, 'an adverse inference may be drawn against a party who [loses or] destroys relevant evidence.' . . . In order to draw the inference, there must be 'a showing that the party knew the evidence was relevant to some issue at trial and that his willful conduct resulted in its loss or destruction.'"). *See also State v. Richardson*, 452 N.J. Super. 124, 138-39, 171 A.3d 1270, 1279 (2017), collecting "persuasive decisions of other jurisdictions . . . . [that] have found an adverse inference charge was warranted by the State's destruction of potentially useful evidence, even where bad faith was not shown").

Second, *Wardius* raises the question to what extent "the State's inherent information-gathering advantages suggest that if there is to be any imbalance in discovery rights, it should work in the defendant's favor" (*Wardius v. Oregon, supra*, 412 U.S. at 475 n.18). In a case in which counsel can compile a strong record of his or her unsuccessful attempts to obtain important defensive information from the prosecution and his or her equally unsuccessful efforts to acquire the information through independent sources, it may be possible to persuade a court that the traditional plight of the impecunious defendant – going into trial blind in the face of a well-prepared adversary – itself requires the allowance of corrective discovery measures under *Wardius.*

18.9.2.8. *The Obligation of the Equal Protection Clause That a State Not Permit an Indigent Defendant To Be Deprived of "The Basic Tools of an Adequate Defense" by Reason of Poverty*

The equal protection doctrine guaranteeing an indigent defendant "the basic tools of an adequate defense" (*Britt v. North Carolina,* 404 U.S. 226, 227 (1971) (dictum)), is discussed in § 5.2 *supra.* One method of compensating for the investigative disadvantage suffered by impoverished defendants, compared to defendants who have money, is to give the defense full discovery of the products of the prosecution's investigation.

18.10. *Responses to Prosecutorial Assertions That the Information That the Defense Is Seeking Is Privileged*

18.10.1. *The "Informer's Privilege" and the Surveillance Location Privilege*

The courts have recognized an "informer's privilege" that empowers the prosecution to conceal the name of a confidential source of information, upon a claim of the privilege by the prosecutor and a representation that disclosure would endanger the prosecution's interests.

In *Roviaro v. United States,* 353 U.S. 53 (1957), the Supreme Court discussed the applicability of the privilege to block a criminal defendant's request for the name of an informer who appeared, from the trial testimony, to have been a central figure in the narcotics transactions with which the defendant was charged. The Court there required disclosure of the name, concluding "that no fixed rule with respect to disclosure is justifiable. The problem is one that calls for balancing the public interest in protecting the flow of information against the individual's right to prepare his defense. Whether a proper balance renders nondisclosure erroneous must depend on the particular circumstances of each case, taking into consideration the crime charged, the possible defenses, the possible significance of the informer's testimony, and other relevant factors." (*id.* at 62). *See also United States v. Valenzuela-Bernal,* 458 U.S. 858, 870-71 (1982) (dictum); *State v. Jackson*, 239 Conn. 629, 631-37, 687 A.2d 485, 486-89 (1997); *Commonwealth v. Madigan,* 449 Mass. 702, 705-11, 871 N.E.2d 478, 481-86 (2007); *State v. Florez*, 134 N.J. 570, 578-83, 636 A.2d 1040, 1044-46 (1994).

The Court cut back somewhat on the *Roviaro* doctrine in *McCray v. Illinois,* 386 U.S. 300 (1967), upholding a trial court's refusal to order disclosure of the name of an informer at a hearing on a motion to suppress tangible evidence, even though the informer's information was being relied upon to support a warrantless arrest and incidental seizure. However, the diffuseness of the *McCray* decision makes it difficult to ascertain exactly how much of *Roviaro* it retracts. Certainly, "*McCray* does not establish an absolute rule against disclosure," even at a suppression hearing (*State v. Casal,* 103 Wash. 2d 812, 817, 699 P.2d 1234, 1237 (1985)). "*McCray* . . . concluded only that the Due Process Clause of the Fourteenth Amendment did not require the State to expose an informant's identity routinely, upon a defendant's mere demand, when there was ample evidence in the preliminary hearing to show that the informant was reliable and his information credible." *Franks v. Delaware,* 438 U.S. 154, 170 (1978). Moreover, *McCray*'s limitations upon *Roviaro* arguably apply only to informers whose information bears exclusively upon a pretrial search-and-seizure issue and do not affect the *Roviaro* rules governing informers who have information pertinent to the central trial issue of guilt or innocence. So, for the present, defense counsel would be warranted in continuing to press for the disclosure of informers' names, both before and at trial, as defensive needs dictate. *See, e.g., Sheriff of Washoe County v. Vasile*, 96 Nev. 5, 7-8, 604 P.2d 809, 810-11 (1980) ("During cross examination of Officer Douglas at the preliminary examination, defense counsel asked for the name of the person who introduced Officer Douglas to Vasile and who was seated in the car during the purported marijuana sale. The prosecutor's objection, based on the confidential informant privilege, . . . was sustained. ¶ . . . The informant . . . was apparently the only independent witness who could hear and see the transaction in question. He was a material witness whose identity should have been disclosed. The magistrate's refusal to require disclosure or dismiss the charges was error."); *State v. Walston*, 401 Mont. 15, 469 P.3d 716 (2020) (reversing an order of a trial court that denied the defendant's pretrial motion for disclosure of the identity of a confidential informer who was the key witness to a drug transaction with which the defendant was charged or, in the alternative, for dismissal of the charges against the defendant); *State v. Lerma*, 639 S.W.3d 63 (Tex. Crim. App. 2021) ("All of the officers claimed that they failed to make a record of the informant's identity, even though the Task Force's policies and procedures required an informant's information to be thoroughly documented. The Task Force officers admitted, after the trial court posed the defense theory [that the shooting of the homicide victim by his roommate during the defendant's robbery of the two was not in response to the robbery but was motivated by the roommate's independent motive to eliminate the victim as a police informer] to them, that it was possible that the informant could have potentially exculpatory information. Combined with the fact that the State utilized every means available to resist disclosure of the informant's identity, the trial court found that the Task Force officers' claim that they simply did not know the informant's identity lacked credibility. ¶ . . . [The defendant] filed a motion to dismiss pursuant to [Texas Evidence] Rule 508 which provides that, if the trial court finds that there is a reasonable probability that the informant possesses information necessary to a fair determination of guilt or innocence, once the 'public entity elects not to disclose the informer's identity: (i) on the defendant's motion, the court must dismiss the charges to which the testimony would relate[.]'. . . After the defense . . . motion . . . was filed, the State disclosed an e-mail to the defense and the trial court showing that, prior to the *in camera* hearing, the Task Force commander – who testified at the hearing that he did not know the identity of the informant – did in fact know the identity of the informant but would not disclose the identity to the defense. The trial court – considering the e-mail, the fact that the State exhausted every legal remedy possible, and the fact that the testimony of the Task Force officers lacked credibility – granted . . . [the defendant's] motion to dismiss." *Id.*at 65-66. "Rule 508 is not limited to exculpatory information. *Inculpatory* information is equally 'necessary to a fair determination of *guilt* or innocence.' *Id.*at 69. "The Rule 508 burden is not a high one, and Appellee met his burden to make a plausible showing of how the informant's information *may be* important. *Id.* at 70. "From the evidence that the Task Force officers were untruthful to the court about the informant, and the evidence that the Task Force officers had strongly resisted disclosure of information relating to the informant, the trial court's conclusion that the informant had information affecting the capital murder case against Appellee was not unreasonable." *Id.* "The trial court did not abuse its discretion." *Id.* at 71.); *State v. Jones*, 169 N.E.3d 397 (Ind. 2021) (remanding a criminal case on interlocutory appeal to the trial court for a determination whether the defendant is entitled to a court order for a pretrial face-to-face interview with a government informer, the Indiana Supreme Court holds that a defense request for such an order triggers the informer's privilege and requires a *Roviaro*-like case-specific weighing of considerations for and against an exception to the privilege); *Beville v. State*, 71 N.E.3d 13, 17 (Ind. 2017) (the trial court erred in upholding a prosecutor's invocation of the informer's privilege to bar the defendant from joining defense counsel in viewing "a video recording of a controlled drug buy between . . . [the defendant] and a confidential informant"; even if the state had satisfied its threshold burden of "establish[ing] that the informer's privilege applies in the first instance" (which the state failed to do "because it is unclear whether the video would actually reveal the informant's identity"), the state supreme court "find[s] that Beville carried his burden of proving an exception to the privilege because his review of the video was relevant and helpful to his defense"); *State v. Chapman*, 209 Mont. 57, 679 P.2d 1210 (1984). Of course, the attempt should be made to assimilate the case as much to *Roviaro,* and to segregate it as much from *McCray,* as possible. If an informer's identity is needed both to challenge a search and seizure, for example, and to defend on the guilt issue, a pretrial discovery motion should rest on the latter need.

The informer's privilege is a creature of state law, subject to federal constitutional constraint. This means that the States are free to restrict the privilege to a compass narrower than that recognized in federal practice under *Roviaro* (*see, e.g., State v. Delaney*, 58 Hawai'i 19, 24, 563 P.2d 990, 993-94 (1977) ("[W]e have followed the U.S. Supreme Court's decision in *McCray* . . . and held that neither the federal nor state constitutions dictate disclosure of an informer's identity where the sole purpose is to challenge the finding of probable cause. . . . [But a] trial court may, in its discretion, require disclosure if it believes that the officer's testimony is inaccurate or untruthful."); *Little v. Commonwealth*, 553 S.W.3d 220, 224-25 (Ky. 2018) (dictum) (applying a state rule of evidence which exempts from the informer's privilege the names of informers who appear as a prosecution witness at trial, the Kentucky Supreme Court declares it "unacceptable," "unconscionable" and "an abuse of the trial court's discretion" to deal with a defendant's motion for disclosure of such an informer's name 30 days before trial by ordering the disclosure only 48 hours before trial)) although they are not free to expand the privilege so as to shield informers under circumstances which would deny the defendant the fair opportunity to contest the prosecution's case which is a fundamental component of due process (*see, e.g., State v. Bullen*, 63 Hawai'i 27, 32, 620 P.2d 728, 731 (1980) (reversing a conviction because the police arranged to have charges against an informer *nol prossed* so that he could leave the State: the Hawai'i Supreme Court finds that, because the informer was an active participant in the drug transaction for which the defendant was charged, the case was one in which "the government's privilege to withhold from disclosure the identity of persons reporting law violations to the police must give way to the due process requirements of a fair trial. . . . ¶ Merely identifying the informer, however, would not suffice. Knowledge of the informant's name would be useless to the defendant unless he was also made aware of the location of the prospective witness. Where the government chooses to employ an informer in its sponsored enterprise, it must be prepared to supply the defendant with information as to his whereabouts. This would require the government, at the very least, to acquire information which might later be useful in locating the informant, while he is still under police discipline and control.")). Legislation, state or federal, may require more liberal disclosure of materials that reveal an informer's identity than *Roviaro* and *McCray* envision. *See, e.g., United States v. Perez*, 353 F. Supp. 3d 131 (D. Mass. 2018).

Even when the informer's privilege does bar disclosure of an informant's identity, it does not protect "the contents of a communication [when these] will not tend to reveal the identity of an informer"; nor does it protect the informer at all "once . . . [his or her] identity . . . has been [otherwise] disclosed to those who would have cause to resent the communication" (*Roviaro v. United States,* 353 U.S. at 60 (dictum)). *See, e.g., State v. Dexter*, 941 N.W.2d 388 (Minn. 2020). Its purpose is to prevent the improvident unmasking of government undercover agents. *Cf. Weatherford v. Bursey,* 429 U.S. 545, 557-60 (1977). Nothing in the privilege, therefore, precludes inquiry into such matters as a confidential informant's batting average (see § 25.35.2 *infra*), or the terms of the informant's compensation by the government, or the informant's own guilt of criminal offenses, or the promises of immunity made to the informant to induce him or her to inform. Nor, once an informant is known, does the privilege authorize the prosecution to shield that informant from being interviewed by the defense. When counsel ascertains an informant's identity and finds that the informant is evading attempts to be contacted and interviewed or when it otherwise appears that s/he may vanish before trial, counsel should not hesitate to seek his or her arrest as a material witness. See § 29.4.1 *infra.* Police spies, "special agents," and undercover informers often are criminals cooperating with the government in return for nonprosecution; they are exceedingly unstable and likely to disappear without a trace; and the prosecution cannot be relied upon to know of their whereabouts. If defense counsel wants to be assured that they will be around at the time of trial, counsel may have no option but to use material-witness procedures to have them jailed. Less aggressive procedures are available (see § 29.4.7.3 *infra*) but are not sure-fire.

A number of courts recognize a surveillance-location privilege by analogy to, and which has essentially the same rationale and contours as, the informer privilege. *Compare United States v. Harley*, 682 F.2d 1018 (D.C. Cir. 1982), *with United States v. Foster*, 986 F.2d 541 (D.C. Cir. 1993); *and see United States v. Van Horn*, 789 F.2d 1492, 1508 (11th Cir. 1986) ("We hold that the privilege applies equally to the nature and location of electronic surveillance equipment. Disclosing the precise locations where surveillance devices are hidden or their precise specifications will educate criminals regarding how to protect themselves against police surveillance. Electronic surveillance is an important tool of law enforcement, and its effectiveness should not be unnecessarily compromised. Disclosure of such information will also educate persons on how to employ such techniques themselves, in violation of Title III [of the Omnibus Crime Control and Safe Streets Act of 1968 (§§ 25.31, 25.32 *infra*)]."); *accord, United States v. Cintolo*, 818 F.2d 980 (1st Cir. 1987). *Compare People v. Sanders*, 2019 IL App (1st) 160718, 134 N.E.3d 305, 434 Ill. Dec. 4 (2019), *with People v. Palmer*, 2017 IL App (1st) 151253, 92 N.E.3d 483, 419 Ill. Dec. 72 (2017); *compare People v. Haider*, 34 Cal. App. 4th 661, 40 Cal. Rptr. 2d 369 (1995), *with In re Marcos B.*, 214 Cal. App. 4th 299, 153 Cal. Rptr. 3d 778 (2013); *compare State v. Garcia*, 131 N.J. 67, 618 A.2d 326 (1993), *with State v. Zenquis*, 131 N.J. 84, 618 A.2d 335 (1993).

18.10.2. *Work Product*

In federal cases, the "work product" doctrine of *Hickman v. Taylor,* 329 U.S. 495 (1947), and *Upjohn Co. v. United States,* 449 U.S. 383, 397-402 (1981), applies to criminal discovery (*see United States v. Nobles,* 422 U.S. 225, 236 (1975) (dictum)), protecting "the mental processes of the attorney" (422 U.S. at 238), whether that attorney be the prosecutor or defense counsel (*see id.* at 238 & n.12; *cf. United States v. Valenzuela-Bernal,* 458 U.S. 858, 862 n.3 (1982)). *But see Goldberg v. United States,* 425 U.S. 94, 101-08 (1976) ("work product" protection does not bar production at trial of prior statements of government witnesses that are "otherwise producible under the Jencks Act [see § 34.7.1.1 *infra*]" (*id.* at 108)).

Whether such a limitation of defense discovery is recognized in state criminal cases is, of course, in the first instance a matter of local law. Counsel should consult the relevant state statutes, rules and precedents governing the scope of the privilege (*see, e.g., State ex rel. Becker v. Wood,* 611 S.W.3d 510 (Mo. 2020) (en banc)) and its waiver (*see, e.g., People v. Superior Court of San Diego County,* 12 Cal. 5th 348, 499 P.3d 999, 287 Cal. Rptr. 3d 312 (2021), summarized in § 33.3.2 *infra*). But local law cannot extend "work product" protection to any materials that are constitutionally required to be disclosed to the defense. *Fontenot v. Crow,* 4 F.4th 982 (10th Cir. 2021); *see Davis v. Alaska,* 415 U.S. 308 (1974); *cf. Chambers v Mississippi,* 410 U.S. 284 (1973). Thus, for example, a "work product" privilege could not override the prosecutor's due process obligation to disclose exculpatory materials and such impeaching information as the existence of promises made by the prosecutor to prosecution witnesses. See § 18.9.1 *supra.*

18.10.3. *Other Claims of Governmental Privilege*

It is not uncommon for prosecutors to stonewall defense discovery requests by broad claims of some unspecified privilege to protect "governmental secrets" or "government operations" or the "confidential relations" of government employees. If any privilege of this sort is recognized beyond the scope of the informer's privilege (§ 18.10.1 *supra*) and the attorney's work product doctrine (§ 18.10.2 *supra*), it is extremely narrow (*compare Federal Bureau of Investigation v. Fazaga,* 142 S. Ct. 1051 (2022), *with, e.g., United States v. Nixon,* 418 U.S. 683 (1974); *Kerr v. United States District Court,* 426 U.S. 394 (1976); *Schneider v. City of Jackson,* 226 S.W.3d 332, 344 (Tenn. 2007) ("the law enforcement privilege has not previously been adopted as a common law privilege in Tennessee and should not be adopted herein")), and is arguably altogether inapplicable in criminal prosecutions because "it is unconscionable to allow [a government] . . . to undertake prosecution and then invoke its governmental privileges to deprive the accused of anything which might be material to his defense" (*United States v. Reynolds,* 345 U.S. 1, 12 (1953) (dictum)). State statutes creating governmental-operations privileges are narrowly construed in order to maintain consistency with the "'fundamental proposition that [an accused] is entitled to a fair trial and an intelligent defense in light of all relevant and reasonably accessible information'" (*City of Santa Cruz v. Municipal Court,* 49 Cal. 3d 74, 84, 776 P.2d 222, 228, 260 Cal.Rptr. 520, 526 (1989), quoting *Pitchess v. Superior Court,* 11 Cal. 3d 531, 535, 522 P.2d 305, 308, 113 Cal.Rptr. 897, 900 (1974)).

D. *Discovery by the Prosecution Against the Defense*

18.11. *The Prosecution's Right to Discovery*

Most States have enacted statutes requiring that defendants who intend to employ a defense of alibi or insanity must file a pretrial notice of their intention and inform the prosecution of certain particulars relating to the proposed defense, including the names of witnesses who will be called to prove it. See §§ 14.6 subdivisions (G) and (H); 17.2 subdivision (1) *supra*. In addition, in many States, statutes confer upon the prosecution a right to obtain discovery from the defense of certain other categories of information such as the names and sometimes statements of intended defense witnesses, reports of defense experts, and tangible evidence. The latter statutes are generally of one or the other of two types: those that give the prosecution affirmative independent discovery rights; and those that give the prosecution reciprocal discovery rights, allowing the prosecutor to obtain certain types of information from the defense only if and after the defense has first sought similar information from the prosecution.

Even when discovery by the prosecutor is legislatively authorized, it is "limited . . . by . . . constitutional privileges" (*Standefer v. United States,* 447 U.S. 10, 22 (1980) (dictum)). The limitations imposed by the Fifth Amendment privilege against self-incrimination are discussed in § 18.12 *infra,* and those established by the Sixth Amendment right to counsel in § 18.13 *infra.*

If counsel is practicing in a jurisdiction that has no statute authorizing prosecutorial discovery, counsel should oppose all discovery motions by the prosecution on the ground that such a radical change from traditional procedures is a matter for the Legislature and should not be ordered by a court without express legislative authority. *Cf.* § 12.8 concluding paragraph *supra.* It is one thing for the judiciary to institute discovery procedures in favor of the defense, inasmuch as these procedures tend to promote constitutional values that are particularly committed to the care of courts. See § 18.9 *supra; and see Jencks v. United States,* 353 U.S. 657 (1957). It is quite another thing to institute unprecedented procedures in favor of the prosecution – procedures that often raise close constitutional questions and that prosecutors (unlike criminal defendants) surely have the power to obtain from the Legislature if the Legislature deems those procedures advisable. *Cf. People v. Kilgore*, 2020 CO 6, 455 P.3d 746, 751 (Colo. 2020) ("the [trial] court erred in ordering the parties to exchange exhibits thirty days prior to trial": the "court was devoid of authority to require Kilgore to disclose his exhibits to the prosecution before trial because nothing in [Colo.] Rule [Crim. Pro.] 16(II) [which "requires Kilgore to make certain pretrial disclosures to the prosecution . . . [but] does not mention trial exhibits"] permitted the court to do so. . . . ¶ The disclosure order is concerning for an additional reason – it arguably infringes on Kilgore's constitutional rights. The district court, at a minimum, potentially infringed on Kilgore's right to due process because his compliance with the disclosure order may help the prosecution meet its burden of proof."); *United States v. LaSalle National Bank,* 437 U.S. 298, 312-13 (1978) (dictum).

18.12. *Fifth Amendment Limitations Upon Prosecutorial Discovery*

When the Court in *Williams v. Florida,* 399 U.S. 78 (1970), sustained the constitutionality of an alibi-notice statute, the Court's Fifth Amendment analysis started from the premise that the defendant intended to present the alibi information at trial. There could be no viable claim of compelled self-incrimination, the Court said, because the choice to adduce or withhold this information was left entirely to the defendant; all the statutory requirement of an alibi notice did was to advance the *time* of disclosure of material that the defendant had freely elected to spread upon the record at trial in any event (*id.* at 83-86). The corollary of this reasoning is that court-ordered disclosure to the prosecution of any potentially incriminating matter that the defense does *not* intend to produce at trial violates the Fifth Amendment (*see Scott v. State*, 519 P.2d 774 (Alaska 1974) (applying the state constitutional privilege against self-incrimination)) or at least that the prosecution may not make any use of any information thus disclosed unless and until the defendant introduces evidence at trial which the information serves to rebut (*compare Commonwealth v. Sliech-Brodeur,* 457 Mass. 300, 930 N.E.2d 91 (2010), *with Commonwealth v. Hanright*, 465 Mass. 639, 989 N.E.2d 883 (2013); *and compare Prudhomme v. Superior Court,* 2 Cal. 3d 320, 466 P.2d 673, 85 Cal. Rptr. 129 (1970), *with Izazaga v. Superior Court*, 54 Cal. 3d 356, 815 P.2d 304, 285 Cal. Rptr. 231 (1991), *and Maldonado v. Superior Court,* 53 Cal. 4th 1112, 274 P.3d 1110, 140 Cal. Rptr. 3d 113 (2012); *and cf. Lanari v. People*, 827 P.2d 495, 502 (Colo. 1992) (before trial, the defendant listed a named psychiatrist as an expert witness; the prosecution interviewed the psychiatrist; the psychiatrist did not testify at trial but the defendant did, and the prosecution was permitted to impeach him with inconsistent statements that he made to the psychiatrist; the Colorado Supreme Court finds no Fifth Amendment violation because "[t]he defendant's ability to assert . . . [the privilege] remained available to him until he elected to present testimony to the jury that contradicted statements he had voluntarily made to . . . [the psychiatrist]. At that point in the trial proceedings the prosecution . . . was entitled to impeach the defendant by means of his prior inconsistent voluntary statements."); *Richardson v. District Court in and for Eighth Judicial District*, 632 P.2d 595, 599 (Colo. 1981) ("[Colorado Rule of Criminal Procedure 16 (II)(c)'s] exclusion of non-expert witnesses' statements from prosecutorial discovery, far from being an oversight, reflects a purposeful decision to prevent the impairment of constitutional rights that arguably could result from a rule permitting the court to enlarge the categories of prosecutorial discovery on the basis of an ad hoc evaluation of each case."). Indeed, the United States Supreme Court has impliedly so held several times since *Williams. See Brooks v. Tennessee,* 406 U.S. 605 (1972); *New Jersey v. Portash,* 440 U.S. 450 (1979); *United States v. Doe,* 465 U.S. 605 (1984); *compare Estelle v. Smith*, 451 U.S. 454 (1981), *with Buchanan v. Kentucky,* 483 U.S. 402, 422-24 (1987), *and Kansas v. Cheever*, 571 U.S. 87, 93-95 (2014).

Counsel should take the position that no pretrial discovery sought by the prosecution may be ordered – or at least that no such discovery should be ordered without a protective order restricting its use to rebuttal of defense trial evidence – if it would require the defendant, personally or through counsel, to make or reveal any oral or written communication whose contents "would furnish a link in the chain of evidence needed to prosecute the [defendant] . . . for a crime" (*Hoffman v. United States,* 341 U.S. 479, 486 (1951); *see Blau v. United States,* 340 U.S. 159, 161 (1950); *Maness v. Meyers,* 419 U.S. 449, 461 (1975)), or that would provide "'an investigatory lead,' [or produce] . . . evidence . . . by focusing investigation on [the defendant] . . . as a result of his compelled disclosures" (*Kastigar v. United States,* 406 U.S. 441, 460 (1972); *see also United States v. Hubbell,* 530 U.S. 27, 40-46 (2000), discussed in §12.6.4.1 *supra*), unless the information which is ordered to be disclosed is either information that the defendant intends to adduce at trial or information that the prosecutor could properly bring out on cross-examination of the defendant in the light of what the defendant does intend to adduce at trial – that is, material "reasonably related to those [subjects that will be] brought out in direct examination" of the defendant (*United States v. Nobles,* 422 U.S. 225, 240 (1975)), or material constituting proper rebuttal of other defense evidence (*see Buchanan v. Kentucky, supra,* 483 U.S. at 422-24; *Kansas v. Cheever, supra,* 571 U.S. at 93-95, 97). *See also, e.g., United States v. Morton,* 993 F.3d 198, 203 (3d Cir. 2021) ("The Fifth Amendment's protections include more than just 'evidence which may lead to criminal conviction,' extending to 'information which would furnish a link in the chain of evidence that could lead to prosecution, as well as evidence which an individual reasonably believes could be used against him in a criminal prosecution.' . . . As a result, the key inquiry is whether the witness 'reasonably believes' her testimony 'could be used in a criminal prosecution or could lead to other evidence that might be so used.' . . . ¶ Mindful of that focus, where a witness, like Morton here, makes a 'prima facie' invocation of the privilege, . . . it must be '*perfectly clear*, from careful consideration of all the circumstances in the case, that the witness is mistaken, and that the answer[s] *cannot possibly* have such tendency to incriminate . . .'" or she cannot be compelled to make disclosures (emphasis in original).).

Ordering the defendant to disclose tangible evidence, on the other hand, would not violate the Fifth Amendment Privilege because, under currently prevailing doctrine, the Privilege forbids only "testimonial self-incrimination" (*Fisher v. United States,* 425 U.S. 391, 399 (1976)) and accordingly does not extend to the production of physical objects (*see Schmerber v. California,* 384 U.S. 757 (1966) (extracting blood from a drunk-driving suspect for chemical analysis does not violate Fifth Amendment); *United States v. Mara,* 410 U.S. 19 (1973) (requiring a suspect to produce handwriting exemplars does not violate Fifth Amendment); *United States v. Dionisio,* 410 U.S. 1 (1973) (requiring a suspect to speak for voice identification does not violate Fifth Amendment)). The Supreme Court has also applied this doctrine to permit compelled production of preexisting writings (*Fisher v. United States, supra,* 425 U.S. at 414), including an incriminated person's own business records (*United States v. Doe,* 465 U.S. 605 (1984)). *See also State v. Diamond,* 905 N.W.2d 870 (Minn. 2018) (rejecting a Fifth Amendment challenge to a trial court's order requiring a defendant to provide a fingerprint to unlock his cellphone, which had been seized pursuant to a warrant authorizing its seizure and the examination of its contents). The *Mara-Doe* line of cases severely limits but does not completely overrule *Boyd v. United States,* 116 U.S. 616 (1886), insofar as *Boyd* construed the Fourth and Fifth Amendments as forbidding courts to compel the production of a person's papers. *Boyd* is not now good law as to "business records" (*United States v. Doe, supra,* 465 U.S. at 606; *see also Fisher v. United States, supra,* 425 U.S. at 414; *Andresen v. Maryland,* 427 U.S. 463 (1976)), but it may survive as a protection of nonbusiness papers (*see Fisher v. United States, supra,* 425 U.S. at 414 (distinguishing *Boyd*); *United States v. Miller,* 425 U.S. 435, 440 (1976) (same)), or at least of intimate private papers. In cases like *Diamond, supra,* in which clients are ordered to take physical actions that give authorities access to electronically locked cell phones, counsel should document and emphasize that "[c]ell phones . . . place vast quantities of personal information literally in the hands of individuals" (*Riley v. California,* 573 U.S. 373, 386 (2014), summarized with additional helpful quotations in § 25.8.2 *infra*) – a point ignored in the Minnesota Supreme Court's mechanistic opinion. *See People v. Spicer,* 2019 IL App (3d) 170814, 125 N.E.3d 1286, 430 Ill. Dec. 268 (2019), summarized in § 25.8.2 concluding paragraph *infra*. And there is reason to believe that the *Fisher/Miller/Doe* line of cases may be reconsidered in the near future. Given the uncertain state of the law – which is discussed in detail in § 12.8 *supra* – defense counsel is warranted in interposing Fourth and Fifth Amendment objections to any prosecutorial discovery request seeking nonbusiness documents whose contents incriminate a defendant.

The Fifth Amendment unquestionably forbids prosecutorial discovery of any document – business or nonbusiness, and whether written by the defendant or by anyone else – when the *act of producing that document,* as distinguished from the contents of the document, would be incriminating. This is the case whenever (a) the act of production would constitute an admission of the existence or possession of the document, in a context in which such an admission would be probative of the defendant's guilt (*United States v. Hubbell*, 530 U.S. 27, 36 & n.19 (2000); *United States v. Doe, supra*, 465 U.S. at 612-14; *Fisher v. United States, supra*, 425 U.S. at 410-12 (dictum)), or (b) the act of production would constitute an implicit authentication of the document, when such an authentication could be used by the prosecution as part of its case against the defendant (*id.* at 412-13 & n.12 (dictum); *Andresen v. Maryland, supra*, 427 U.S. at 473 & n.7 (dictum)), or (c) the act of production would open the door to the individual's being "compelled to take the witness stand and answer questions designed to determine whether he has produced everything demanded by the subpoena," the "answers [to which] . . . , as well as the act of production itself, may . . . communicate information about the existence, custody, and authenticity of the documents" (*United States v. Hubbell, supra*, 530 U.S. at 38-40, 43-45). In these situations, notably, the prosecution cannot avoid the Fifth Amendment objection by foreswearing evidentiary use of the implications arising from the act of production (*see United States v. Doe, supra*, 465 U.S. at 612-14); if the prosecution *could* use those implications in any way to make its case against the defendant, then the defendant cannot constitutionally be required to produce.

Similarly, the pretrial discovery of other tangible objects possessed by the defendant whose existence or possession is incriminating, or of information obtained by defense counsel from third parties whose identities or connections with the case could lead the prosecution to incriminating evidence should be forbidden because, whatever the original source of that information may have been, it is now being sought from the defendant through compulsory process addressed to the defendant (*compare United States v. Miller, supra*, 425 U.S. at 440-45; *Andresen v. Maryland, supra*, 427 U.S. at 473-77; *Couch v. United States*, 409 U.S. 322 (1973)) for possible use by the prosecutor in prosecuting the defendant. *See People v. Havrish*, 8 N.Y.3d 389, 393-97, 866 N.E.2d 1009, 1012-16, 834 N.Y.S.2d 681, 684-88 (2007) (when the defendant in a domestic violence case was ordered by the court to "surrender any and all firearms owned or possessed," the unlicensed handgun which he surrendered to the police should have been suppressed as a compelled communication in violation of the Fifth Amendment privilege against self-incrimination: "the surrender of evidence can be testimonial if, by doing so, defendant tacitly concedes that the item demanded exists or is in defendant's possession or control when these facts are unknown to the authorities and would not have been discovered through independent means"). Admittedly, *United States v. Nobles,* 422 U.S. 225 (1975), appears to hold that the Fifth Amendment privilege does not cover records of defense interviews with persons other than the accused, at least when those persons are independently available to the prosecution. But *Nobles* was a case involving the prosecution's power to secure discovery of portions of a defense investigator's report after (1) the prosecution had concluded its case-in-chief at trial and (2) the defense had called the investigator to testify concerning interviews with prosecution witnesses. *See Corbitt v. New Jersey*, 439 U.S. 212, 219 n.8 (1978). In this situation the defense has voluntarily presented evidence about a set of facts; its evidence indicates that the underlying facts are not only already known to the prosecution but also have already been the subject of testimony by prosecution witnesses; and its Fifth Amendment claim is therefore necessarily limited to a contention that a particular recorded version of those same facts is privileged merely because it was made by an agent of the defense other than the accused. *Nobles'* rejection of that contention does not imply that a defendant can be compelled by court order to come forward with materials whose existence, possession, or authentication are incriminating *unless and until* s/he has voluntarily elected to adduce those materials at trial. This compulsion would obviously affront the basic policy of the Self-Incrimination Clause that requires the prosecution "'to shoulder the entire load'" (*Miranda v. Arizona*, 384 U.S. 436, 460 (1966); *compare Andresen v. Maryland, supra*, 427 U.S. at 475-76 & n.8).

Counsel should therefore resist, on Fifth Amendment grounds, any and all prosecutorial discovery prior to the time when s/he has had an opportunity to investigate and prepare the defense case; and s/he should insist upon the right to defer decision concerning what s/he will present at trial until s/he has been given ample prior disclosure of the prosecutor's case to enable counsel to make that decision intelligently. If prosecutorial discovery is ever to be ordered, the defendant has a due process right to reciprocal discovery under *Wardius v. Oregon*, 412 U.S. 470 (1973); *see also, e.g., Mauricio v. Duckworth*, 840 F.2d 454 (7th Cir. 1988), summarized in § 18.9.2.7 *supra*; *Camp v. Neven*, 606 Fed. Appx. 322 (9th Cir. 2015); see § 18.9.2.7 *supra;* and the decision in *Brooks v. Tennessee*, 406 U.S. 605 (1972), demonstrates that no disclosure may be required of the defense unless (i) *prior* to the time when the defendant is asked to disclose, (ii) s/he is given a sufficient preview of the prosecutor's case to make an advised and intelligent decision concerning what, if any, defense evidence s/he will present at trial. *Brooks* invalidated a statute requiring that if a defendant was going to testify, s/he must testify before any other defense evidence was presented. That requirement was held to violate the Fifth Amendment on the ground that the constitutional privilege against self-incrimination forbids forcing the defense to decide whether or not to present the defendant's testimony before "its value can be realistically assessed" (*id.* at 610). *See also Portuondo v. Agard*, 529 U.S. 61, 70 (2000) (discussing *Brooks*). But surely, if a criminal defendant cannot be compelled to decide whether to testify and to "subject himself to impeachment and cross-examination at a time when the strength of *his* other evidence is not yet clear" (*id.* at 612 (emphasis added)), a defendant cannot be compelled to furnish the prosecution with information that may be used in any fashion to incriminate him or her – even merely by "focusing investigation on [the defendant] . . . as a result of his compelled disclosures" (*Kastigar v. United States*, 406 U.S. 441, 460 (1972)) – prior to the time when the defendant has been sufficiently informed about the prosecutor's evidence to decide what defense evidence will be "necessary or even helpful to his case" (*Lakeside v. Oregon*, 435 U.S. 333, 339 n.9 (1978) (dictum)). Under *Brooks*, such a requirement violates not merely the Fifth Amendment but also the Sixth Amendment right to counsel, "[b]y requiring the accused and his lawyer to make [an important tactical decision regarding the presentation of defensive evidence] . . . without an opportunity to evaluate the actual worth of their evidence" (*Brooks v. Tennessee, supra*, 406 U.S. at 612). *See also Cuyler v. Sullivan*, 446 U.S. 335, 344 (1980) (dictum).

It is a difficult question whether the Fifth Amendment forbids conditioning defense discovery upon reciprocal disclosures that, if ordered directly, would violate the privilege. Certainly, when the defendant has a constitutional right to discovery under any of the doctrines identified in § 18.9 *supra,* the defendant's enforcement of that right cannot be conditioned upon the waiver of another constitutional right, and in such instances, the reciprocal disclosure requirement would seem to be invalid. *Cf. Simmons v. United States,* 390 U.S. 377, 389-94 (1968), reaffirmed in *United States v. Salvucci,* 448 U.S. 83, 89-90 (1980); *Lefkowitz v. Cunningham,* 431 U.S. 801, 807-08 (1977); *Brooks v. Tennessee, supra,* 406 U.S. at 607-12. In other cases, however, it is likely that a requirement of reciprocation can be imposed and the defense presented with the choice of both giving and getting or neither.

18.13. *"Work Product" Protections Against Prosecutorial Discovery*

When the "work product" doctrine was discussed in § 18.10.2 *supra* in connection with defense discovery of prosecutorial files, it was explained that the prosecution's ability to use the "work product" privilege to insulate its files from defense discovery is initially a matter of state law. However, when the issue is one of whether defense files are "work product," the issue assumes constitutional dimension. The function of the "work product" doctrine is to provide "a privileged area within which [the attorney] . . . can analyze and prepare his client's case" (*United States v. Nobles,* 422 U.S. 225, 238 (1975)), in order to "assure the thorough preparation and presentation of . . . the case" (*id.*); and the Sixth Amendment countenances "no restrictions upon the function of counsel in defending a criminal prosecution in accord with the traditions of the adversary factfinding process" (*Herring v. New York,* 422 U.S. 853, 857 (1975)). The Sixth Amendment right to the effective assistance of counsel (described and documented in § 18.9.2.1 *supra*) therefore arguably requires "work product" protection of defense counsel's trial preparation, in addition to whatever "work product" protection it is given by state law. *See United States v. Alvarez,* 519 F.2d 1036, 1046-47 (3d Cir. 1975), quoted in § 16.6.1 *supra; State v. Mingo,* 77 N.J. 576, 581-82, 392 A.2d 590, 592-93 (1978) (dictum) ("The right to counsel afforded criminal defendants by the Sixth Amendment of the United States Constitution and by Art. I, par. 10 of the New Jersey Constitution comprehends the right to the effective assistance of counsel. To safeguard the defense attorney's ability to provide the effective assistance guaranteed by these constitutional provisions, it is essential that he be permitted full investigative latitude in developing a meritorious defense on his client's behalf. This latitude will be circumscribed if defense counsel must risk a potentially crippling revelation to the State of information discovered in the course of investigation which he chooses not to use at trial. ¶ The particular application of the foregoing principle involved in the present case is a defense attorney's right to seek out expert evidence in aid of the defense without risking its disclosure to the State if for any reason the expert's opinion turns out to be unfavorable to the defense. . . . ¶ We think it makes no difference whether the principle calling for vindication in such a situation is to be denominated the effective representation by counsel or the attorney-client privilege. We regard them as related, and basically subserving the right of a criminal defendant to be effectively represented by counsel. . . . We believe that right to be clearly subverted if an expert report obtained for defense purposes by defendant's counsel is to be made discoverable to the State and utilizable by it, directly or indirectly, at trial, unless a defendant signifies his intention to use the expert evidence at trial or in fact does so." *Id.* at 581-82, 392 A.2d at 592-93. ¶ "We accordingly hold that the report and testimony of a defense-retained expert consultant who will not testify as a defense expert witness and whose report will not be utilized as evidence are not available to the State. This rule will safeguard the internal strategic processes of the defense. The protection such a rule affords will enhance the ability of the defense attorney to provide effective representation by affording him the maximum freedom to seek the guidance of expert advice in assessing the soundness and advisability of offering a particular defense without the fear that any unfavorable material so obtained can be used against his client. A defense attorney should be completely free and unfettered in making a decision as fundamental as that concerning the retention of an expert to assist him. Reliance upon the confidentiality of an expert's advice itself is a crucial aspect of a defense attorney's ability to consult with and advise his client. If the confidentiality of that advice cannot be anticipated, the attorney might well forego seeking such assistance, to the consequent detriment of his client's cause. The protection from unwarranted disclosure we today mandate is an indispensable element of a criminal defendant's constitutional right to the effective assistance of counsel." *Id.* at 587, 392 A.2d at 595.). The *Nobles* case holds nothing to the contrary, although it does permit limited prosecutorial discovery of a defense investigator's report *after* the defense has presented the investigator's testimony at trial and thereby waived both the "work product" and Sixth Amendment protections. *See United States v. Nobles,* 422 U.S. at 240 n.15.

The "work product" doctrine is primarily designed to shield materials that reveal an attorney's analyses and assessments of the case, including evaluations of potential witnesses. For this reason, it is particularly protective of counsel's own summaries of oral statements of witnesses, as distinguished from written or transcribed statements of witnesses or even defense investigators' reports reflecting the oral statements of witnesses. *See Upjohn Co. v. United States,* 449 U.S. 383, 399-402 (1981). In the case of witnesses whose testimony will be favorable to the defense – as distinguished from potential prosecution witnesses (see §§ 9.12-9.13 *supra*) – counsel may wish to increase the likelihood of avoiding prosecutorial discovery by taking oral statements instead of written statements from witnesses and by including appropriate evaluative matter in his or her writeups of those statements. See § 9.11 *supra*. Counsel can obtain maximum protection by (a) refraining from taking written statements from these witnesses; (b) instructing defense investigators to take only oral statements from witnesses and to report their contents orally to counsel; (c) personally interviewing witnesses whose information promises to be favorable; (d) summarizing counsel's interviews of these witnesses in a way that melds the witnesses' own words with counsel's observations of the credibility and potential uses of the witnesses' statements; (e) coding these summaries as suggested in the concluding paragraph of § 6.7 *supra* so as to enable counsel – but not a judge who may later inspect the summary in camera on a prosecution motion for discovery – to distinguish passages that are unmarked direct quotations of the witness from passages that are counsel's commentaries; (f) collecting the summaries of information gotten from two or more witnesses in a single document (or in several documents, each of which contains information from more than a single witness) in which counsel connects the several witnesses' statements and relates them to the defense theory of the case (see § 7.2 *supra*); and (g) captioning the document[s] "strategy memorandum." Anything that discloses counsel's "litigating strategies [is not] . . . the subject of permissible inquiry by his opponent . . ." (*United States v. Valenzuela-Bernal,* 458 U.S. 858, 862 n.3 (1982) (dictum)). Counsel can consult these memoranda while preparing defense witnesses to testify (see § 29.5 *infra*) but should not give them to the witness to read.

State law in the form of statutes, rules of court or common-law doctrines provides work-product protection that may be more extensive than the protection which defense counsel can claim as ancillary to the Sixth Amendment or parallel state constitutional right-to-counsel guarantees. For example, "Florida [and a number of other States] recognize[ ] two forms of work product: opinion work product and fact work product. 'Fact work product traditionally protects that information which relates to the case and is gathered in anticipation of litigation.'... In comparison, opinion work product 'consists primarily of the attorney's mental impressions, conclusions, opinions, and theories.'... ¶ The distinction between the two forms of work product becomes important when disclosure is sought. Fact work product can be discovered upon a determination by an opposing party of need and undue hardship.... Conversely, 'opinion work product generally remains protected from disclosure.'" *Kidder v. State,* 117 So.3d 1166, 1171 (Fla. App. 2013). *See Smith v. State,* 873 So.2d 585 (Fla. App. 2004) (in holding that "a 22-page psycho-social report, prepared by defense counsel with the assistance of other members of the defense team, that is in narrative form and is based on medical records, witness interviews, and mental health evaluations" (*id.* at 587) and that was shown to a defense "expert witness who would be testifying at trial" (*id.* at 591) was opinion work product absolutely protected against discovery by the prosecution, the Court of Appeals finds "the conclusion... inescapable that... [this] report... and its addendum... constitute classic opinion work product. It is a summary of witness statements, italicizing certain portions, which unavoidably combined a selection process achieved through an interpretative filter that emphasized certain information over other, thus disclosing counsel's opinions and strategy.... The act alone of compelling an attorney to disclose a group of documents invariably reveals the counsel's 'assessment of the relative importance of each of those documents, and of their significance as a collection'" (*id.* at 588).); *Thomas v. State,* 191 So.3d 500, 501 (Fla. App. 2016) (applying Florida's work-product rules to reverse a trial court's reciprocal discovery order that allowed the prosecution to interview a fingerprint expert who "was a consultant on the defense team recruited to assist in forming a strategy to challenge the prosecution's fingerprint expert witness, not a testifying witness"). *And see, e.g., In re 2018 Grand Jury of Dallas County,* 939 N.W.2d 50 (Iowa 2020) (applying Iowa's work-product doctrine to hold that "the State cannot subpoena an expert retained by the defense to testify before the grand jury regarding her opinions on the criminal matter being investigated" (*id.* at 52) and that the prosecution could not establish waiver of the privilege by asserting that defense counsel had disclosed the identity of the expert to the prosecutor during plea negotiations (*id.* at 60)); *Commonwealth v. Kennedy,* 583 Pa. 208, 218, 876 A.2d 939, 945 (2005) (relying on the work product doctrine to require the quashing of a prosecution subpoena directed to "an expert, who was originally hired by a criminal defendant's attorney in order to prepare for the defendant's trial,... where the defendant does not plan on calling the expert at trial or using any materials that the expert completed as evidence at trial"); *People v. Spiezer,* 316 Ill. App. 3d 75, 735 N.E.2d 1017, 249 Ill. Dec. 192 (2000) ("we are most persuaded that the work product doctrine protects from disclosure reports and other materials prepared by nontestifying, consulting [defense] experts and also prevents the State from introducing such evidence at trial" (*id.* at 80, 735 N.E.2d at 1020, 249 Ill. Dec. at 195); the court goes on to explain why work product is a more satisfactory basis for this holding than the attorney-client privilege, the constitutional privilege against self-incrimination or the constitutional right to counsel (*id.* at 87-89, 735 N.E.2d at 1025-27, 249 Ill. Dec. at 200-02)); *State v. Pawlyk,* 115 Wash. 2d 457, 479, 800 P.2d 338, 350 (1990) (while upholding a trial court order granting the prosecution discovery of the findings and conclusions of a psychiatrist retained by the defense who examined the defendant but whom defense counsel did not intend to call as a witness in support of a noticed insanity defense, the court observes: "We recognize, nonetheless, that the work product doctrine does apply to some extent in this case. While it does not preclude disclosure of the psychiatrist's factual findings and opinions on the issue of defendant's insanity, it does operate to preclude disclosure of defense counsel's 'opinions, theories or conclusions.' . . . The trial court excluded from disclosure any letters or communications between . . . [the psychiatrist] and defense counsel. It appears that this exclusion was intended to protect this type of information from disclosure, and we agree that this limitation is appropriate. . . . While it seems doubtful that . . . [the psychiatrist's] reports would contain any such information, if defendant believes they do he may request the trial court to examine the materials in camera and to protect any such work product from disclosure."); *Washington v. State*, 856 S.W.2d 184, 188 (Tex. Crim. App. 1993) (en banc) (holding that the trial court erred in overruling the defendant's work-product objection to a mid-trial order granting the prosecutor disclosure of the tape recording of a defense investigator's interview of a prosecution witness who had been cross-examined by defense counsel regarding statements he made in that interview: "[T]he interview at issue here was an attempt both to evaluate the strengths and weaknesses of the State's case and to prepare . . . [the defendant's] case. . . .This Court has held that the work-product privilege applies in similar cases."); *State ex rel. Corbin v. Ybarra*, 161 Ariz. 188, 193, 777 P.2d 686, 691 (1989) (holding that a soil analysis report commissioned upon advice of defense counsel by a corporation under criminal investigation for hazardous waste management violations and containing in the margin handwritten notes which the analyst made in response to questions by defense counsel was protected from discovery by Arizona's work product rule, which protects "reports to the extent they 'contain the opinions, theories or conclusions . . . of defense counsel or his legal or investigative staff'" (*id.* at 193, 777 P.2d at 691): "[The corporation] created the protocol for the investigation report. The creation of the protocol – specifying the type of investigation, the type and location of samples, the method of taking the samples, and the method of their analysis – necessarily constitutes scientific or engineering theories and opinions. The interpretation of gas chromatography tests is more than a mere lay observation; it requires scientific training. The ability to make expert scientific observations necessarily requires professional judgment and, therefore, opinion and conclusion. Thus, the determination that certain compounds or chemicals exist in the soil samples is a conclusion. Additionally, the determination that certain material in the soil samples is a hazardous waste can be made only by applying the Code of Federal Regulations. Thus, determining whether the substances in the soil samples were hazardous wastes requires the application of law to fact and is, in the truest sense, a conclusion."); *cf. Teal v. Superior Court*, 117 Cal. App. 4th 488, 11 Cal. Rptr. 3d 784 (2004) ("Teal . . . served a subpoena duces tecum on the Los Angeles Sheriff's Department (the Sheriff) and the Los Angeles Police Department (LAPD) seeking records on Teal, the victim and two other individuals. . . . ¶ The records were subpoenaed directly to the court, and the trial judge reviewed the documents out of the presence of the prosecution. The court allowed defense counsel to obtain the LAPD records, but required her to provide copies of these records to the prosecution." *Id.* at 490, 11 Cal. Rptr. 3d at 785. "To protect Teal's Fifth Amendment right against self-incrimination and Sixth Amendment right to counsel, the subpoenaed documents were produced in camera to allow defense counsel to present relevancy arguments without having to reveal possible defense strategies and work product to the prosecution. . . . ¶ [I]t is inappropriate to give a defendant 'the Hobson's choice of going forth with his discovery efforts and revealing possible defense strategies and work product to the prosecution, or refraining from pursuing these discovery materials to protect his constitutional rights and prevent undesirable disclosures to his adversary. . . .' The trial court's order to reveal the subpoenaed materials to the prosecution placed Teal in this untenable position. As such, we conclude that the trial court abused its discretion in ordering defense counsel to provide the subpoenaed materials to the prosecution and that the error impinged upon Teal's constitutional rights. . . . Should defense counsel decide to introduce evidence at trial relating to these documents or call any witnesses whose name appears in the documents, she must comply with the requirements of . . . [the applicable reciprocal discovery statute]." *Id.* at 491-92, 11 Cal. Rptr. 3d at 786.); *State v. Martinez*, 461 N.J. Super. 249, 255, 220 A.3d 498, 501-02 (2019), quoted in § 25.31 *infra.*

E. *The Pretrial Conference*

18.14. *Defense Uses of the Pretrial Conference*

In cases in which no statute, rule of court, standing order, or established local practice provides for a regularly calendared pretrial conference, it is customary for the court, the prosecutor, and the defense lawyer to confer briefly at sidebar immediately prior to the commencement of trial, to review the status of pretrial matters (for example, to assure that all the necessary procedural steps required to bring the defendant to trial have been taken; to assure that all pending motions that should be disposed of before trial have been disposed of); to estimate the probable length of trial and to plan convenient recesses; to make special arrangements for the appearance of particular witnesses when appropriate (for example, to schedule an expert witness's appearance to accommodate his or her other commitments); to discuss any problems occasioned by the failure of witnesses to appear; and sometimes to attempt to expedite matters by stipulations.

In many jurisdictions, local law or practice calls for one or more pretrial conferences calendared prior to the trial date. *See, e.g.,* FED. RULE CRIM. PRO. 16.1, 17.1; UNITED STATES DISTRICT COURT FOR THE EASTERN DISTRICT OF OKLAHOMA, LOCAL RULE 17.1.1; KENTUCKY RULE CRIM. PRO. 8.03; N.J. CRIM. RULE 3:9-1; MINN. RULE CRIM. PRO. 11-1 – 11.10, 12.1. The timing, purposes and procedures of these conferences vary widely from jurisdiction to jurisdiction. They may be mandatory in some or all cases, or may be convened by the court *sua sponte* or at the request of a party. The provisions or conventions governing the conferences may or may not prescribe specific matters to be discussed or resolved. Even where they do, there is nothing to prevent defense counsel from raising other matters as well at any meeting with the judge and prosecutor; nor is there anything to prevent defense counsel from requesting an *ad hoc* pretrial conference in courts where no general practice of holding pretrial conferences exists. *See State v. Dickson*, 53 Wis. 2d 532, 543-45, 193 N.W.2d 17, 23 -24 (1972) (considered dictum). Defense counsel should consider using – and, if necessary, filing a motion for an order setting – a pretrial conference whenever it would be to the defendant's advantage to define issues, stipulate to the qualifications of experts, stipulate to the admission of certain items of evidence or to some of the technical predicates for their admissibility in order to dispense with time-wasting foundation testimony, and generally for the same purposes as a pretrial conference in a civil case (not excluding, with some judges, settlement negotiations, see §§ 15.6.2 subdivision (2)(G), 15.7.2 *supra*) – that is, to look for means to make the presentation and disposition of the case more efficient by agreement of the parties upon matters of procedure. Counsel can support a motion by referring, in whole or in part, to Standard 12-4.3(i) of the AMERICAN BAR

ASSOCIATION STANDARDS FOR CRIMINAL JUSTICE (3d ed. 2006) ("There is increasing evidence that, shortly after a case is assigned to a judicial officer for trial or other action, it is desirable for the judicial officer to hold a case scheduling conference at which the prosecutor, defense counsel, and the defendant are present. The early conference provides an opportunity for the judge to review the status of discovery and of negotiations concerning possible non-trial disposition of the case, and to schedule any necessary motion hearings or other events. ¶ The fact that such a conference is scheduled should serve to encourage completion of discovery, preparation of the case by both sides, and pre-conference negotiations between the prosecutor and the defense. If no agreement on non-trial resolution can be reached by the time of the conference, at least the remaining pretrial tasks can be identified, a schedule can be set for completing any further discovery and for conducting motion hearings, and a tentative trial date can be fixed."). A pretrial conference is particularly useful when counsel is dealing with a prosecutor who is overcharging, stonewalling sensible plea offers or otherwise acting highhandedly in ways that the judge is likely to think are unreasonable, or where counsel who is unfamiliar with the judge can invent risk-free issues for discussion that will shed some light on the judge's temperament or attitudes toward the case at hand.

Counsel may be well advised to request such a pretrial conference if one is not routinely held. Its utility should be considered for the following purposes, among others:

(1) *To attempt to enlist some judicial support if counsel feels that the prosecutor is taking an unreasonable position in pressing certain charges which should be dropped* (see §§ 8.2.2-8.2.3, 8.4, 12.13 *supra*); or that the prosecutor is taking an unreasonable position in plea negotiations (see §§ 15.9-15.13 *supra*); *or to "try out" an agreed sentencing recommendation on the judge* (see § 15.6.2 subdivision (2)(G) *supra*). Judges differ considerably on whether they will involve themselves in plea negotiation and what they regard as a reasonable disposition of particular kinds of cases. Counsel must therefore know or inquire about the attitudes of the presiding judge before deciding whether to bring up these subjects.

(2) *To explore the possibility of diverting the prosecution and to discuss the components of an acceptable diversion plan.* See §§ 2.3.6, 8.2.2, 14.12 *supra*; Chapter 21 *infra*.

(3) *To set or change dates for pretrial proceedings and/or for trial (or to arrange a schedule for setting those dates at a later time), and to work out agreements regarding contingencies that may call for reconsideration of whatever timetable is set.* See Chapter 28.

(4) *To anticipate evidentiary problems that will arise at trial and attempt to resolve them.* Particularly important may be the opportunity to alert the judge and prosecutor to defense objections to expected lines or items of prosecution evidence at trial and to arrange (1) that the prosecutor not mention these items in his or her opening statement (see § 35.2 *infra*) and (2) that the prosecutor's examination be conducted in a fashion that will permit both a defense objection and a ruling on it prior to the time when matters have been disclosed to the jury that may cause prejudice and may therefore require a mistrial if the defense objection is sustained (see §§ 11.8.6, 17.5.3 *supra*; §§ 35.2, 35.5, 36.6, 39.10, 40.1, 40.3.2, 40.4, 40.4.2-40.4.4, 40.8 *infra*). Counsel may want to suggest that the prosecutor forgo offering items of evidence that will create problems of admissibility or prejudice at a joint trial, so that, if the prosecutor insists on

presenting these items, counsel can request a severance (see Chapter 23).

(5) *To arrange to stipulate certain matters, in the interest of trial convenience* (for example, see §§ 36.7.1, 39.16.2 *infra*), *and to put certain sorts of exhibits into safe and unexceptionable form.* Before trial, counsel will want to examine all proposed prosecution exhibits carefully because, even when an exhibit is admissible for the most part, it may contain items which are inadmissible and damaging. *See, e.g., State v. Hines*, 131 N.C. App. 457, 508 S.E.2d 310 (1998); and see § 36.4.1 *infra*, discussing the problem of paper documents that are admissible on their face but have damaging notations on the back. Counsel may sometimes want to redact portions of defense exhibits as well, to eliminate distracting or prejudicial material or simply to avoid giving the prosecution some handle for nit-picking objections when the exhibit is offered at trial.

(6) *To obtain agreement that certain witnesses need not be subpoenaed by either party and that neither will request or be entitled to a missing witness charge as a result.* See § 29.4.7 *infra*. Counsel may also want to seek other agreements or advance judicial rulings regarding matters that will determine whether s/he is going to call particular witnesses: for example, rulings on whether certain convictions or arrests may be used by the prosecutor in cross-examining the defendant or character witnesses (see § 17.5.3 *supra*; §§ 39.21-39.24 *infra*).

(7) *To discover what can be discovered of the prosecutor's case through discussion of the foregoing and similar matters.*

(8) *To impress the judge.* A pretrial conference offers an excellent opportunity for defense counsel to become known to the judge, who ordinarily will already be familiar with the prosecutor. If counsel's learning, preparation, and reasoned judgment make a good impression, the judge may be more receptive to counsel's positions on questions that arise at trial than if counsel were entirely unknown.

(9) *To get a sense of the judge's attitude toward the case.* Counsel will want to learn, if s/he can, both how the judge is likely to react to certain kinds of evidentiary issues at trial (for example, whether the judge is disposed to exercise liberally or sparingly the court's discretion to exclude prejudicial matter (see § 36.2.3 *infra*); whether the judge is likely to respond favorably to a highly technical hearsay argument) and how the judge is likely to react to the case and to the defendant at sentencing in the event of conviction. The answer to the latter questions may well cause counsel to decide that a jury waiver or even a guilty plea is advised rather than a trial before this judge. (See § 15.7.2 *supra*.)

18.15. *Memorializing the Pretrial Conference*

If the judge who conducts the pretrial conference drafts an order purporting to record agreements and dispositions reached at the conference, counsel should give it careful study upon its receipt and immediately call to the judge's attention any point on which counsel's recollection differs from the judge's or anything to which counsel objects. If the judge does not draft an order, counsel should make his or her own file memorandum memorializing the conference. If agreements reached there include important matters on which s/he intends to rely, s/he may want to embody them in a proposed pretrial order for the judge's signature; or s/he may want to embody them in a letter of "understanding" to the judge, of which a copy should be sent to the prosecutor and another filed. In this fashion, counsel will be able to document the legitimacy of any complaints s/he may have in the unhappily common event that the court or the prosecution breaches an agreed course of conduct at trial.

Chapter 19

Motions Practice in General

A. *Motions Hearings*

19.1. *Evidentiary and Non-evidentiary Motions Hearings*

Section 17.3 *supra* discusses the various aims that defense motions can serve. Section 17.4 provides a roster of motions counsel should consider. Section 17.5 examines the strategic question whether counsel should raise issues by pretrial motion or at trial when local practice allows both options. It concludes with a discussion of tactics and procedures relating to motions *in limine*. Sections 17.6-17.8 deal with other procedural aspects of motions. Sections 17.10-17.11 discuss the drafting of written motions and the advisability of invoking state constitutional law as well as federal constitutional law in both written and oral motions that raise constitutional claims. Section 17.9 canvasses considerations bearing on the decision whether to present claims in the form of an evidentiary motion or a non-evidentiary motion. That section is the prelude to this one.

Depending upon the type of motion involved and the specific facts at issue on the motion, a motions hearing can be either a non-evidentiary legal argument by the attorneys or a trial-like evidentiary hearing.

Motions that raise purely legal issues, such as motions challenging the sufficiency of the charging paper (see § 20.4 *infra*) and motions for a bill of particulars (see § 13.7 *supra*) are presented at non-evidentiary hearings, since they involve no factual disputes that need to be resolved through the presentation of testimony. The same is true of motions that turn upon facts already known to the court, such as most motions for recusal of the judge (§§ 22.4-22.7 *infra*), or facts fully ascertainable through a review of court records, such as most motions to dismiss the charging paper on double jeopardy grounds (§ 20.8 *infra*) or for a violation of speedy trial guarantees (§ 28.5 *infra*).

The quintessential type of motion that turns upon factual issues and therefore requires an evidentiary hearing is a motion to suppress evidence. Motions to suppress tangible evidence (Chapter 25), incriminating statements (Chapter 26), and identification testimony (Chapter 27) all typically result in an evidentiary hearing followed by legal arguments on the law and facts. In some jurisdictions the defense must demonstrate the right to an evidentiary hearing by arguing, in a non-evidentiary legal argument, the sufficiency of the facts alleged in the suppression motion to state a claim under the applicable law. See §§ 17.8-17.10 *supra*. The prosecutor can, of course, obviate the need for an evidentiary hearing on a motion to suppress by stipulating to the facts alleged by the defense, thereby reducing the hearing to a legal argument on whether the stipulated facts satisfy the legal rules governing suppression.

Local practice may also require that a motion for an evidentiary hearing be supported by affidavits setting out the facts that the defendant intends to establish through testimony at the hearing. See § 17.8 *supra*. This requirement for a *preliminary* demonstration of the factual merits of the defendant's claim to a motions remedy is distinct from the procedure of submitting the motion for final adjudication of the merits on affidavits instead of live testimony. These procedures are discussed in §§ 17.9-7.10 *supra*, together with the relevant tactical considerations in handling them.

Motions for severance (Chapter 23) and motions for discovery (§§ 18.7.3-18.7.5 *supra*) can be either evidentiary or non-evidentiary, depending upon the specific issues and facts that they raise. Thus, for example, a motion to sever codefendants based upon a codefendant's statement implicating the defendant (see § 23.9.1 *infra*) would ordinarily go to a non-evidentiary hearing in which the judge reviews the statement and hears arguments on its legal implications, but a motion to sever based upon the defense's intention to present the testimony of the codefendant in the defense case might necessitate an evidentiary hearing on the contents of the testimony (see § 23.9.2 *infra*). Most motions for discovery turn upon undisputed facts about the general nature of the materials that the prosecution is unwilling to turn over to the defense; but a particular discovery motion could involve an evidentiary hearing on the question, for example, whether witnesses were unconstitutionally instructed by the prosecutor or police officers to refuse to speak with defense counsel and his or her investigator (see § 9.14 *supra*). Motions to dismiss for prosecutorial misconduct might turn upon facts already known to the judge – such as acts of misconduct that occurred in proceedings at which the judge was presiding, or acts reflected in the transcript of a prior proceeding – or they might, in certain cases, require direct and cross-examination of the prosecutor and witnesses to the prosecutor's behavior outside the courtroom.

Motions for a change of venue (§§ 22.1-22.3 *infra*) and motions challenging jury selection procedures (§ 32.4 *infra*) may turn upon case-specific facts (such as the nature and extent of prejudicial pretrial publicity in the case) or upon more general, less disputable facts (such as the county's standard procedure for selecting the venire). Some jurisdictions require that the facts supporting such motions be established through affidavits; other jurisdictions require that the facts be presented at an evidentiary hearing; still others permit the defense to choose between these two options. The factors that counsel should consider in making the choice are summarized in § 17.9 *supra*.

19.2. *Scope of the Chapter*

The following sections deal solely with non-evidentiary motions hearings, describing the procedures followed in such hearings and suggesting approaches to take in arguing motions. Techniques for conducting evidentiary hearings on motions to suppress are covered in Chapter 24; and much of the tactical advice offered in that chapter applies to other evidentiary motions hearings as well. See, *e.g.,* §§ 24.2, 24.4-24.6 *infra*; and see § 18.1 concluding paragraph *supra*.

B. *Non-Evidentiary Motions Arguments*

19.3. *Procedure*

Usually defense counsel, as the proponent of the motion, argues first, and the prosecutor responds thereafter. Depending upon local practice and the preferences of the judge presiding over the motions hearing, defense counsel may or may not be offered the opportunity to reply to the prosecutor's arguments. Counsel should always request leave to reply if s/he has something useful to say, whether or not rebuttal argument is standard operating procedure in this court. When practicing in courts that are less formal, where the question of who argues first is decided by which lawyer starts talking first, defense counsel should usually seize the initiative and speak first. The attorney who argues first has the invaluable opportunity to acquaint the judge with the facts and issues in the light most favorable to the presenter – a matter of particular importance inasmuch as the judge may not have read the motion. To some extent the first speaker can also control the order in which issues are taken up, addressing first the issues on which s/he is strongest.

Most judges conduct motions arguments like appellate arguments, feeling free to interrupt and pepper attorneys with factual and legal questions. Techniques for responding to judges' questions are described in § 19.7 *infra*.

Although counsel has the right to object to statements made by the prosecutor, many judges insist that counsel refrain from interrupting his or her opponent and instead make all objections at the conclusion of the prosecutor's argument. If this is the local custom, counsel should conform to it *unless:* (i) appellate caselaw suggests that "contemporaneous objection" rules require counsel to object at the moment when the prosecutor makes the improper statement; or (ii) the prosecutor is reciting information that is both very likely to be ruled inadmissible and strongly prejudicial to the defendant, in which case defense counsel should object and insist that the judge prohibit the prosecutor from continuing to relate the prejudicial information.

19.4. *Guarding Against Undue Disclosures of Defense Trial Evidence and Trial Strategy*

Whenever s/he is arguing pretrial motions or conducting any type of pretrial hearing, counsel must carefully guard against revealing to the prosecutor aspects of the defense trial evidence or strategy. This is particularly important with respect to matters that involve weaknesses of prosecution witnesses (such as their inconsistent statements to defense counsel's investigator) when the prosecutor does not already know about these matters, because their disclosure could lead to the prosecutor's coaching the witness to avoid defense traps.

Usually, the objective of avoiding revelation of defense secrets will not conflict with the objective of winning a motions argument. Most non-evidentiary motions focus upon aspects of the legal history of the case (such as the length of delays, as pertinent to speedy trial issues; the existence and nature of prior proceedings, as pertinent to double jeopardy issues; and so forth) that do not implicate the facts of the offense and accordingly do not call for any discussion of defense evidence or the defense theory of the case. However, some motions may be problematic. For example, when counsel is litigating a motion for severance of defendants on the ground of conflicting defenses (see § 23.9.3 *infra*), the judge may reject counsel's attempt to describe his or her projected defense in broad, ambiguous terms and may demand of counsel a detailed description of the defense that counsel will offer at trial as a predicate for the judge's assessment of whether that defense so severely conflicts with the codefendant's as to require a severance.

Whenever confronted with the dilemma of whether to reveal defense secrets whose disclosure might win the motion for the defense, counsel must calculate the relative prospects of winning the motion with and without the revelation; whether winning the motion will terminate the case, and, if not, the degree to which winning the motion would improve the defense's chances of winning the trial; and the degree to which revealing the defense evidence or trial strategy would impair the defense's chances of winning the trial. In unusual cases in which the revelation is extremely important to winning the motion, extremely damaging to the defense's chances of winning the trial, and arguably protected by the defendant's Fifth Amendment privilege against self-incrimination (see § 18.12 *supra*), counsel should consider asking leave to present certain facts or arguments to the court *ex parte,* either in a sealed affidavit or in chambers. Judges will be resistant to this suggestion because it is untraditional and deprives the prosecutor, to some extent, of the right of reply. But proceedings conducted partly in the open and partly *ex parte* are becoming customary in a number of contexts (such as defense motions for state-paid expert assistance (see § 5.4 *supra*); prosecution submission of prior statements of prosecution witnesses to the court for screening before their production to the defense at trial (see § 34.7 *infra*); and prosecution submission of electronic surveillance logs to the court for screening and redaction before their production to the defense), and it is therefore possible that the judge will consider a similar procedure in the present context. In theory, the same request could be made in all cases in which the information that counsel seeks to withhold from the prosecutor is defense "work product" (see § 18.13 *supra*). But this is a very dangerous position for the defense to urge in most jurisdictions, because "work product" protection is usually extended to the prosecutor as well as defense counsel, and the defense has much to lose from any general legitimation of *ex parte* proceedings as a means of limiting pretrial disclosure in a system in which the prosecutor has every investigative advantage over the defense. See Chapter 18.

19.5. *The Extent to Which Counsel Should Orally Recite Facts and Law Already Set Forth in the Motion*

In arguing a motion, counsel cannot assume that the judge has read the motions papers or any other pleadings in the case. Many trial judges are so overloaded (or lazy) that they are unable to find the time to read motions papers. Or they are prevented from reading particular motions papers because the administrative processes of the court have caused the motion to sit unread in the clerk's office, awaiting filing in the court file. Nor can counsel assume that the judge will supplement what s/he hears in the oral argument by reading the motion and other pleadings after the argument. Many trial judges rule on motions from the bench at the conclusion of the attorneys' arguments.

Accordingly, unless counsel knows for certain that the judge has read the motion (as, for example, when the judge's opening remarks or questions refer to a particular passage in the motion), counsel will need to recite in oral argument any facts and law that are essential to the defense position. On the other hand, counsel cannot take the risk of offending the judge by stating or even implying counsel's assumption that the judge has not read the motion. For this reason counsel should avoid giving the impression that s/he is reiterating information and legal analysis contained in the motion. Also, as explained in § 19.6 *infra,* counsel typically wants to avoid engaging in detailed legal documentation in the oral argument.

Usually, the best way of reconciling all of these concerns is to touch upon each of the essential facts and legal points, while mentioning the pages of the motion on which important legal points are more extensively developed and supported with citations. As long as counsel couches the references to the body of the motion as if they were shorthand substitutes for lengthier argument rather than directions to the judge to read a motion s/he has never looked at, this approach will be inoffensive. It may also have the salutary effect of inducing the judge to read at least those portions of the motion prior to ruling, if s/he has not done so already.

19.6. *The Inadvisability of String-citing Cases or Analyzing Court Decisions at Length*

Counsel should almost never recite strings of citations to court decisions or engage in complex legal analysis in oral argument. Such matters are extremely tedious, and counsel's dwelling on them may lead the judge either to tune out or to cut counsel's argument short. Moreover, because these are not matters that the judge is going to remember (and few judges take notes during attorneys' arguments), spending time on these matters is unproductive and wastes the opportunity to use the argument to make more memorable and persuasive points.

As a general rule of thumb, counsel should treat the law bearing on the motion merely as a legal framework for organizing the key points to be made about the case at hand. S/he should state the legal framework simply and briefly and then devote most of the argument to fitting facts into that framework. Counsel should focus particularly on things that: (i) are dramatic (speaking to the heart of the case and making the judge *want* to rule in the defendant's favor); (ii) are factually persuasive; and (iii) give the judge some overall feeling about the case, enabling him or her to see the forest rather than the trees.

In those cases in which it is necessary to depend upon detailed analysis of prior caselaw, counsel should ordinarily set forth the analysis in the written motion and then direct the judge's attention to the relevant pages of the motion instead of orally reiterating the analysis. See § 19.5 *supra;* see also § 24.6.4 *infra.* If counsel refrained from setting forth a detailed legal analysis in the written motion for strategic reasons (see § 17.10 *supra*), s/he can sometimes offer to brief the issues in a supplementary memorandum of points and authorities. But this is more commonly done in argument at the close of an evidentiary motions hearing, particularly one in which extensive testimony has been taken. It is often impracticable in a non-evidentiary hearing, either because the judge intends to rule from the bench or because counsel simply has no good reason for failing to brief the issues fully beforehand. When, in these or other situations, counsel's only option is to analyze the caselaw orally, s/he should bring to the argument copies of any court decisions that were not amply covered in the written motion, and, upon reaching the points in the argument that depend on those decisions, offer to hand copies of the decisions to the judge and prosecutor rather than citing and quoting at length. Counsel can then alleviate much of the tedium and confusion of oral legal analysis by directing the judge's attention to relevant passages of the opinion (which should be highlighted, if they are short), essentially using the opinion as a prop in counsel's argument.

19.7. *The Importance of Being Responsive to the Judge's Questions*

The key to arguing motions is to be responsive to the judge's questions and address his or her concerns as thoroughly as possible. Since most judges rule on motions from the bench, they depend upon counsel's answers to their questions to resolve the issues that the judge finds most troublesome. The judge's questions will usually pinpoint the areas in which the judge most sorely needs to be persuaded in order to rule in the defendant's favor.

Counsel cannot afford to give short shrift even to questions that seem irrelevant or uninformed. Anything that is troubling the decision-maker is, by definition, relevant. And questions that betray the judge's unfamiliarity with the issues or caselaw show a need to educate the judge through the answer to the question.

In preparing for oral argument, counsel should attempt to anticipate the questions that the judge is likely to ask and should develop persuasive answers. Since trial judges are generally concerned with staying well within established rules of law, counsel should be prepared to demonstrate that the rule counsel is advocating is wholly consistent with the controlling caselaw, and s/he should bring copies of the cases to the hearing to use as props in the argument if necessary. See § 19.6 *supra*. Since trial judges are usually disinclined to adopt rules of great breadth and scope (either because they are cautious about binding themselves in the future or because they fear that the adoption of sweeping new rules invites appellate reversal), counsel should be prepared to show the limits of the rule s/he is advocating, preferably by distinctions that limit the rule to the unique facts of counsel's own case.

When the judge asks questions of counsel's opponent, counsel should listen to the questions as carefully as if they were directed to counsel himself or herself. As previously noted, the judge's questions usually identify the concerns that are of paramount importance to the judge. Accordingly, counsel cannot afford to allow the prosecutor to be the only party to address these matters. During counsel's reply to the prosecutor, counsel should say that s/he would like to state the defendant's position on the question that the judge addressed to the prosecutor, and then do so. If local practice does not normally afford counsel the opportunity to reply to the prosecutor, but counsel has a very persuasive answer to a question directed at the prosecutor, counsel should – at the close of the prosecutor's argument – ask leave to state the position of the defense in regard to the prosecutor's answer to the judge's question.

Chapter 20

Motions to Quash or Dismiss the Charging Paper

20.1. *Overview of the Grounds for Quashing or Dismissing the Charging Paper*

There are numerous grounds for moving to quash or dismiss a charging paper or one or more of its counts. These include:

1. Denial or inadequacy of a preliminary hearing, and certain other defects in the conduct of the preliminary hearing. See § 20.2 *infra*.

2. Defects in the composition or functioning of the grand jury. See § 20.3 *infra*.

3. Lack of personal or subject-matter jurisdiction. *Compare McGirt v. Oklahoma*, 140 S. Ct. 2452 (2020), *with Oklahoma v. Castro-Huerta*, 142 S. Ct. 2486 (2022); *and see, e.g., In re Hijazi*, 589 F.3d 401 (7th Cir. 2009); *United States v. Davila-Mendoza*, 972 F.3d 1264 (11th Cir. 2020); *United States v. Wahchumwah*, 472 Fed. Appx. 623 (9th Cir. 2012); *Sheridan v. Superior Court in and for Pinal County*, 91 Ariz. 211, 370 P.2d 949 (1962); *A Juvenile v. Commonwealth*, 380 Mass. 552, 556-63, 405 N.E.2d 143, 146-50 (1980); *People v. Cousar*, 191 A.D.3d 694, 137 N.Y.S.3d 736 (N.Y. App. Div., 2d Dep't 2021). Although most other grounds for dismissal of a prosecution must be raised within specified time limits (see § 20.3.4 *infra*), lack of jurisdiction can be called to the court's attention at any time (*see, e.g., State v. Kavajecz*, 139 Idaho 482, 80 P.3d 1083 (2003); *Harrell v. State*, 721 So.2d 1185 (Fla. App. 1998)).

4. Failure to charge an offense. See § 20.4 *infra*.

5. Objections to venue. See § 20.5 *infra*.

6. Technical defects. See § 20.6 *infra*.

7. A statute of limitations. See § 20.7 *infra*.

8. Double jeopardy. See § 20.8 *infra*.

9. Misjoinder. See § 20.10 *infra*.

10. Substantive unconstitutionality of the criminal statute on which the charge is based. *See, e.g., United States v. Stevens*, 559 U.S. 460 (2010); *Ramirez v. Commonwealth*, 479 Mass. 331, 94 N.E.3d 809 (2018); *cf. State v. Spell*, 2021-00876 (La. 5/13/22), 339 So.3d 1125 (La. 2022). Counsel should be alert particularly to the possibility of challenging obscure criminal statutes on grounds of vagueness (*see, e.g., United States v. Davis*, 139 S. Ct. 2319 (2019); *Henry v. Spearman*, 899 F.3d 703 (9th Cir. 2018)), or overbreadth (*see, e.g., Seals v.*

McBee, 898 F.3d 587 (5th Cir. 2018)). *See generally Manning v. Caldwell for City of Roanoke*, 930 F.3d 264 (4th Cir. 2019) (en banc); Anthony G. Amsterdam, *Federal Constitutional Restrictions on the Punishment of Crimes of Status, Crimes of General Obnoxiousness, Crimes of Displeasing Police Officers, and the Like*, 3 (No. 4) CRIM. L. BULLETIN 207 (1967).

11.   Selective prosecution or selective enforcement based on invidious discrimination. Litigation of selective prosecution claims – including issues of discovery necessary to prove such claims – is governed by a body of caselaw rooted in *United States v. Armstrong*, 517 U.S. 456 (1996). *Armstrong* declares in dictum that "the decision whether to prosecute may not be based on 'an unjustifiable standard such as race, religion, or other arbitrary classification'" (*id*. at 464). *See also Whren v. United States*, 517 U.S. 806, 813 (1996) (dictum) ("the Constitution prohibits selective enforcement of the law based on considerations such as race"); *Murguia v. Municipal Court*, 15 Cal. 3d 286, 300, 540 P.2d 44, 53, 124 Cal. Rptr. 204, 213 (1975) ("a criminal defendant may object, in the course of a criminal proceeding to the maintenance of the prosecution on the ground of deliberate invidious discrimination in the enforcement of the law") (discovery standard relaxed by the California Racial Justice Act as construed in *Young v. Superior Court of Solano County*, 79 Cal. App. 5th 138, 294 Cal. Rptr. 3d 513 (2022).). However, a "'presumption of regularity supports' . . . prosecutorial decisions and, 'in the absence of clear evidence to the contrary, courts presume that they have properly discharged their official duties'" (*United States v. Armstrong*, 517 U.S. at 464). "In order to dispel the presumption that a prosecutor has not violated equal protection, a criminal defendant must present 'clear evidence to the contrary.'" *Id*. at 465. This standard makes selective prosecution claims difficult to prove, but "not . . . impossible" (*id*. at 466). *Armstrong* also sets a demanding standard for defense discovery of prosecutorial records in support of a selective prosecution claim: it endorses a rule "'requir[ing] some evidence tending to show the existence of the essential elements of the defense,' discriminatory effect and discriminatory intent"; and it holds that "'some evidence tending to show the existence' of the discriminatory effect element" must include "some evidence that similarly situated defendants of other races could have been prosecuted, but were not" (*id*. at 468-469). *Cf. State v. Ballard*, 190 N.J. 270, 920 A.2d 80 (2005), approved in *State v. Lee*, 190 N.J. 270, 920 A.2d 80 (2007). Some lower courts apply the same exacting requirements to claims of selective enforcement – that is, discrimination on the part of the police and other law-enforcement agencies, as distinguished from prosecutors – while others have adopted more defendant-friendly rules for cases in which *Armstrong*'s concern against exercising too much "judicial power over [prosecutorial judgment –] a 'special province' of the Executive" – is inapplicable. See the discussions of the standards for discovery and proof of selective enforcement claims in, *e.g.*, *United States v. Davis*, 793 F.3d 712 (7th Cir. 2015) (en banc); *United States v. Washington*, 869 F.3d 193 (3d Cir. 2015); *United States v. Sellers*, 906 F.3d 848 (9th Cir. 2018); *United States v. Jackson*, 2018 WL 6602226 (D. N.M. December 17, 2018); *United States v. Lopez*, 415 F. Supp. 3d 422 (S.D. N.Y. 2019).

12.   Prosecution instituted for the purpose of punishing the defendant's exercise of constitutional rights. *See Holt v. Virginia*, 381 U.S. 131 (1965); *cf. Wright v. Georgia*, 373 U.S. 284 (1963); *Sobol v. Perez*, 289 F. Supp. 392 (E.D. La. 1968); *and compare Lozman v. City of Riviera Beach, Florida*, 138 S. Ct. 1945 (2018), *with Nieves v. Bartlett*, 139 S. Ct. 1715 (2019). Targeting political activists or religious groups for surveillance or detention may also raise First Amendment issues. *See, e.g., Fazaga v. Federal Bureau of Investigation*, 916 F.3d 1202, 1244-45 (9th Cir. 2019); *Black Lives Matter v. Town of Clarkstown*, 354 F. Supp. 3d 313 (S.D. N.Y. 2018). The *Nieves* case represents the Supreme Court's current last word on the complex subject of retaliatory arrests. *Cf. Cole v. Encapera*, 758 Fed. Appx. 252 (3d Cir. 2018); *Campbell v. Mack*, 777 Fed. Appx. 122 (6th Cir. 2019).

13.   Violations of due process during the pretrial stages of the case (*compare Hayes v. Faulkner County*, 388 F.3d 669 (8th Cir. 2004), *with United States v. Jones*, 70 F.4th 1109 (8th Cir. 2023); *and see United States v. Wingender*, 790 F.2d 802 (9th Cir. 1986); *United States v. Bogart*, 783 F.2d 1428, 1433 (9th Cir. 1986) (dictum) ("[w]e now reaffirm once again that a defendant may raise a due process-based outrageous government conduct defense to a criminal indictment"); *People v. Newberry*, 265 Ill. App. 3d 688, 638 N.E.2d 1196, 203 Ill. Dec. 70 (1994)), or flagrant governmental misconduct warranting a severe sanction (*compare United States v. Estepa*, 471 F.2d 1132 (2d Cir. 1972), *with United States v. Walters*, 910 F.3d 11 (2d Cir. 2018)).

In most jurisdictions, statutes or court rules require that motions challenging the sufficiency of the charging paper be made in writing, within a specified period of time. See § 17.7 *supra*; § 20.3.4 *infra*.

20.2.   *Motions to Quash or Dismiss an Information or Indictment on Grounds Relating to the Preliminary Hearing*

In nonindictable cases many of the objections to denial or inadequacy of a preliminary hearing that are summarized in § 12.12 *supra* survive the filing of an information. After the information is filed, they may be raisable – depending upon local practice – by the procedures previously available (see the sections referenced by § 12.12) or by a motion to quash or to dismiss the information or by both. *See, e.g., Commonwealth v. Harris*, 2022 PA Super 1, 269 A.3d 534 (Pa. Super. 2022), *app. granted*, 285 A.3d 883 (Table) (Pa. 2022); *State v. Essman*, 98 Ariz. 228, 403 P.2d 540 (1965); *State v. Colvin*, 81 Ariz. 388, 307 P.2d 98 (1957).

Motions to quash or to dismiss informations on the ground that illegally obtained evidence was presented before the magistrate at preliminary hearing are considered in § 20.3.3 *infra*.

A motion to quash or to dismiss an information will also lie to raise the objection that the information charges offenses not shown in the transcript of the preliminary examination or offenses for which the defendant was not bound over (in the jurisdictions where a bind-over on a specific charge is a prerequisite to charging that offense in an information). See §§ 2.3.6, 11.1.1 *supra*.

If the argument made in § 11.4 *supra* – that indictment does not moot the right to a preliminary examination – prevails, certain attacks on the preliminary examination will also survive indictment in an indictable case and may be raised by the procedures enumerated in § 11.6.2 *supra*, including a motion to quash or to dismiss the indictment.

20.3. *Motions to Quash or to Dismiss an Indictment on Grounds Relating to Defects in the Composition or Functioning of the Grand Jury*

20.3.1. *Challenges to the Composition or Procedures of the Grand Jury*

Motions to quash or to dismiss an indictment are available in most jurisdictions on various grounds that challenge the composition or procedures of the grand jury. *E.g.*, UTAH RULE CRIM. PRO. 25(b)(3) ("[t]he court shall dismiss the information or indictment when: ¶ (3) It appears that there was a substantial and prejudicial defect in the impaneling or in the proceedings relating to the grand jury"); N.Y. CRIM. PRO. LAW §§ 210.20(1)(b), (c), 210.35, as construed in *People v. Williams*, 73 N.Y.2d 84, 535 N.E.2d 275, 538 N.Y.S.2d 222 (1989). Particularly important are:

(1)   Challenges to the method of selection of the grand jurors or to their qualifications collectively or individually, including claims of systematic exclusion of a racial, ethnic, religious, economic, gender-based, or other distinctive demographic group; claims that the jury panel was prejudiced by inflammatory publicity; and claims of bias of an individual juror (see §§ 12.1, 12.1.1, 12.3 *supra*);

(2)   Challenges to the manner of proceeding or to the functioning of the grand jury – for example, claims that unauthorized persons were present during the jury's deliberations (*see* Andrea G. Nadel, Annot., *Presence of Unauthorized Persons During State Grand Jury Proceedings as Affecting Indictment*, 23 A.L.R.4th 397 (1983 & Supp.); *cf. United States v. Mechanik*, 475 U.S. 66, 70, 72 & n.2 (1986) (leaving unresolved the status of such objections in federal practice)), or that the prosecutor engaged in prejudicial misconduct before the grand jury (*see, e.g.*, *People v. Huston*, 88 N.Y.2d 400, 668 N.E.2d 1362, 646 N.Y.S.2d 69 (1996); *State v. Martin*, 823 N.W.2d 913 (Minn. App. 2012); *Commonwealth v. Baker*, 11 S.W.3d 585 (Ky. App. 2000); *State v. Joao*, 53 Hawai'i 226, 491 P.2d 1089 (1971) and cognate cases cited in § 12.1.3 *supra*; *cf. Bank of Nova Scotia v. United States*, 487 U.S. 250, 254-56 (1988)), or presented perjured testimony to the grand jury (*People v. Hunter*, 298 Ill. App. 3d 126, 698 N.E.2d 230, 232 Ill. Dec. 392 (1998); *People v. Oliver*, 368 Ill. App. 3d 690, 859 N.E.2d 38, 307 Ill. Dec. 38 (2006)), or that less than a majority of the grand jurors concurred in returning the indictment (see § 12.1.2 concluding paragraph *supra*);

(3)   Claims that the defendant's rights were violated in the course of his or her

appearance before the grand jury, for example, by compulsion of the defendant's testimony in violation of the privilege against self-incrimination (*e.g., State v. Turner*, 300 Kan. 662, 333 P.3d 155 (2014); see §§ 12.6.1-12.6.3, 12.6.4.3 third and fourth paragraphs *supra*); and

(4)   Claims that the indictment was returned in violation of a grant of immunity given the defendant before the grand jury (see §§ 12.6.4.1-12.6.4.2 *supra*).

20.3.2. *Challenges to the Sufficiency of the Evidence Presented to the Grand Jury*

In some jurisdictions a motion to quash or to dismiss an indictment will lie upon the ground that there was insufficient evidence before the grand jury to support a finding of probable cause or to meet whatever other burden of proof is required by local law for the return of an indictment. *See, e.g., Felix F. v. Commonwealth*, 471 Mass. 513, 31 N.E.3d 42 (2015); *People v. Nitzberg*, 289 N.Y. 523, 47 N.E.2d 37 (1943); *People v. Jackson*, 18 N.Y.2d 516, 223 N.E.2d 790, 277 N.Y.S.2d 263 (1966); *State v. Nordquist*, 309 N.W.2d 109, 112-17 (1981) (dictum); *but see Costello v. United States*, 350 U.S. 359 (1956) (federal practice), discussed in § 20.3.3 *infra*. In other jurisdictions there are judicial decisions purporting to authorize these motions on the ground that no evidence was presented to the grand jury which would rationally warrant the submission of the case to a trial jury (*see, e.g., State v. Parks*, 437 P.2d 642, 644 (Alaska 1968) (dictum) ("[W]e would hold an indictment to be insufficient and subject to dismissal if it appeared that no evidence was presented to the grand jury that rationally established the facts. . . . ¶ Under such a rule, the question is one of sufficiency of the evidence – whether it is adequate to persuade reasonable minded persons that if unexplained or uncontradicted it would warrant a conviction of the person charged with an offense by the judge or jury trying the offense.")); but attempts to satisfy the no-evidence standard are obviously rarely successful.

20.3.3. *Challenges to the Admissibility of Evidence Presented to the Grand Jury*

Attacks on the admissibility of evidence received by the grand jury will support a motion to quash or to dismiss an indictment only in jurisdictions that both permit review of the grand jury transcript for probable cause (see § 20.3.2 *supra*) and restrict grand juries to legally competent evidence (see § 12.1.2 *supra*). In these jurisdictions an indictment will be set aside if exclusion of the inadmissible evidence would leave insufficient remaining evidence to support it. *See, e.g., People v. Hardy*, 42 Misc. 3d 211, 976 N.Y.S.2d 774 (Clinton Cty. Ct. 2013), and cases cited.

A more complex question is presented by attacks on an indictment on the ground that illegally or unconstitutionally obtained evidence was presented before the grand jury – for example, coerced confessions, evidence procured by unlawful searches and seizures or electronic surveillance, perjured testimony known by the prosecutor to be perjured. In *United States v. Calandra*, 414 U.S. 338, 344-45, 346 (1974), the Supreme Court of the United States repeated with approval a collection of *dicta* in earlier cases to the effect that, in the federal courts, indictments need not be dismissed by reason of the grand jury's use of unconstitutional evidence (*see Lawn v. United States*, 355 U.S. 339, 349-50 (1958); *United States v. Blue*, 384 U.S. 251, 255 n.3 (1966); *Gelbard v. United States*, 408 U.S. 41, 60 (1972), because "[a]n indictment returned by a legally constituted and unbiased grand jury, . . . if valid on its face, is enough to call for trial of the charge on the merits. The Fifth Amendment requires nothing more" (*Costello v. United States*, 350 U.S. 359, 363 (1956)). But this conclusion manifestly does not follow from its premise. For, *in addition* to the requirements of the Fifth Amendment (or whatever state-law counterpart it may have in any jurisdiction, conferring a right to prosecution by indictment of a grand jury), criminal procedures must satisfy the requirements of other constitutional and statutory safeguards, including those that proscribe impermissible methods of obtaining evidence (see, *e.g.*, Chapters 25, 26, 27 *infra*) and that have been read by implication to exclude the use of evidence obtained by the proscribed methods (*e.g.*, *Mapp v. Ohio*, 367 U.S. 643 (1961)). The purposes of the exclusionary rules discussed in those chapters (see *e.g.*, §§ 25.39-25.42, 26.2, 26.5, 26.16) – as recognized even by Supreme Court opinions that withdraw the exclusionary sanction in certain classes of cases (see, *e.g.*, §§ 25.3 concluding paragraph, 25.17) – should condemn any use of unconstitutionally obtained evidence to aid a prosecution, as Justice Holmes recognized in *Silverthorne Lumber Co. v. United States*, 251 U.S. 385, 392 (1920): "The essence of a provision forbidding the acquisition of evidence in a certain way is that not merely evidence so acquired shall not be used before the Court but that it shall not be used at all." Particularly in light of the doctrine that illegally obtained evidence may not "legally form the basis for an arrest or search warrant" (*Alderman v. United States*, 394 U.S. 165, 177 (1969) (dictum); *cf. United States v. Giordano*, 416 U.S. 505, 529-34 (1974); and see § 25.42 *infra*), it is difficult to comprehend how the same evidence can "legally form the basis for" an indictment. And if the police may not even use the evidence to advance their investigation (*see Wong Sun v. United States*, 371 U.S. 471, 487-88 (1963)), surely the prosecutor should not be permitted to use it to advance the prosecution by obtaining an indictment. So the argument is logically forceful that the federal Constitution does compel the voiding of an indictment based upon evidence obtained in violation of federal statutory or constitutional guarantees. *See* Note, *Disclosure of Grand Jury Minutes to Challenge Indictments and Impeach Witnesses in Federal Criminal Cases*, 111 U. Pa. L. Rev. 1154 (1963); *compare United States v. Tane*, 329 F.2d 848 (2d Cir. 1964). This requirement would apply in both federal and state cases, to the same extent and for the same reasons that the exclusionary rules governing trial evidence do. See §§ 25.39-25.41 *infra*. It would call for the dismissal of indictments whenever the unconstitutional evidence cannot be said to have been harmless in its impact on the grand jury, within the rule of *Chapman v. California*, 386 U.S. 18 (1967); *Harrington v. California*, 395 U.S. 250 (1969); *United States v. Hasting*, 461 U.S. 499, 508-12 (1983); and *Satterwhite v. Texas*, 486 U.S. 249 (1988) – not merely when the other, constitutionally untainted evidence is sufficient to support a finding of probable cause. *Cf. Vasquez v. Hillery*, 474 U.S. 254, 262-64 (1986).

The broad language of the *Calandra* opinion, however, expressly refuses "to extend the exclusionary rule to grand jury proceedings . . . ." (414 U.S. at 390). Technically, this language is *dictum* insofar as it implies that indictments are not to be quashed on the ground of the grand jury's receipt of illegally obtained evidence. *Calandra* did not involve a motion to quash by an indicted defendant but held only that an unindicted grand jury witness was not entitled to a judicial order immunizing the witness from grand jury questioning based upon leads obtained through an unreasonable search and seizure. Counsel may therefore wish to contend:

(a)   That *Calandra* does not foreclose a motion to quash by "a criminal defendant" who has been "indicted by the grand jury" (414 U.S. at 352 n.8), because these motions do not entail the sort of "interruption of the grand jury proceedings" (*id.* at 353 n.8) with which *Calandra* is primarily concerned (*see id.* at 349-50).

Alternatively, it is arguable at least:

(b)   That *Calandra* is limited to cases in which grand jury evidence is challenged on Fourth Amendment grounds, as distinguished from other grounds of illegality – such as the coercion of confessions or incriminating admissions (*see, e.g., Mincey v. Arizona*, 437 U.S. 385, 397-98 (1978)) – which (i) implicate its "trustworthiness" (*cf. Harris v. New York*, 401 U.S. 222, 224 (1971)), or (ii) involve the grand jury more directly in a constitutional violation (*compare United States v. Calandra, supra*, 414 U.S. at 353-54, *with New Jersey v. Portash*, 440 U.S. 450, 458-59 (1979); *cf.* § 25.41 *infra*; *but see United States v. Blue, supra*, 384 U.S. at 255 n.3 (dictum));

or

(c)   That *Calandra* is limited to cases in which no motion to suppress has been filed prior to submission of the case to the grand jury (*see United States v. Calandra, supra*, 414 U.S. at 352-53 n.8, distinguishing *Silverthorne Lumber Co. v. United States*, 251 U.S. 385 (1920); and see § 12.4 *supra*).

These arguments would not bar the defendant's reindictment following new grand jury proceedings in which his or her constitutional rights were observed; they would merely require the dismissal of indictments obtained "'by exploitation of . . . illegality'" (*Wong Sun v. United States*, 371 U.S. 471, 488 (1963); § 25.39 *infra*), so as to provide a "remedy . . . denying the prosecution the fruits of its transgression" (*United States v. Morrison*, 449 U.S. 361, 366 (1981)).

However, the tone of *Calandra* bodes ill for these several distinctions and plainly implies that – at least until the membership of the Supreme Court changes sufficiently – there is no real hope for the argument of a constitutional right to dismissal of indictments based on illegally obtained evidence. *See also United States v. Washington*, 431 U.S. 181, 185 n.3 (1977); *United States v. Ceccolini*, 435 U.S. 268, 275 (1978); *United States v. Blue, supra*, 384 U.S. at 255 n.3; *Bracy v. United States*, 435 U.S. 1301 (Rehnquist, Circuit Justice, 1978).

The hope is stronger that *Calandra* can be distinguished:

(a)   In *information* cases, in which *Calandra*'s solicitude for the "special role" of the grand jury (414 U.S. at 343), is obviously beside the point, upon a motion to quash an information or a magistrate's transcript on the ground of receipt of illegally obtained evidence at the preliminary examination (see § 11.5.4 *supra*; *but see* FED. RULE CRIM. PRO. 5.1(e)); and

(b)   In both information and indictment cases in which the motion to quash is based upon a claim of illegal electronic surveillance in violation of the Omnibus Crime Control and Safe Streets Act of 1968 (see §§ 25.31-25.32 *infra*) and can therefore draw support from 18 U.S.C. § 2515, which "directs that '. . . no part of the contents of [an illegally intercepted] . . . communication and no evidence derived therefrom may be received in evidence in any [trial, hearing or other] . . . proceeding in or before any [court,] . . . grand jury . . . [or other authority of the United States, a State, or a political subdivision thereof] if the disclosure of that information would be in violation of this chapter'" (*Gelbard v. United States*, 408 U.S. 41, 43 (1972)). *Compare id.* at 59-61 *with United States v. Calandra*, *supra*, 414 U.S. at 355-56 n.11.

State law may preclude or limit the presentation of illegally obtained evidence to a grand jury notwithstanding *Calandra. See, e.g., Gathrite v. Eighth Judicial District Court in and for County of Clark*, 135 Nev. 405, 451 P.3d 891 (2019) (applying a statute that provides that "the grand jury can receive none but legal evidence"). This should be the result wherever a state statue, rule or judicial decision provides that informations and indictments may be set aside on the ground that the magistrate's or grand jury transcript contains insufficient legally competent evidence to support them. For this purpose, illegally obtained evidence is not legally competent evidence (*see, e.g., Badillo v. Superior Court*, 46 Cal. 2d 269, 294 P.2d 23 (1956)) – not because of the federal exclusionary rule that *Calandra* declined to apply to grand juries but because the state-law screening function of preliminary examinations and indictments in these jurisdictions forbids magistrates or grand juries to act upon evidence that will not be admissible at trial.

20.3.4. *Deadlines for Filing Motions to Quash an Indictment Due to Defects in the Composition or Functioning of the Grand Jury*

The various motions to quash or to dismiss an indictment on the grounds summarized in the above subsections (§§ 20.1-20.3.3) are ordinarily required to be made within specified time limits (*e.g., x* number of days after the indictment is filed; *x* number of days before arraignment; prior to the defendant's entry of a general plea at arraignment (see § 14.5 *supra*)). Local time limitations should be checked and carefully observed, because untimelinesss can irrevocably forfeit meritorious claims of error in the proceedings leading up to indictment. *See Davis v. United States*, 411 U.S. 233 (1973); *Francis v. Henderson*, 425 U.S. 536 (1976); *cf. Wainwright v. Sykes*, 433 U.S. 72 (1977). For the few grounds on which such forfeitures can be challenged, see § 14.5 *supra*. Concerning the possibility of obtaining an extention of time for filing motions, see § 17.7 *supra*.

20.3.5. *Strategic Considerations*

Success on any of the motions discussed above does not bar reindictment following new grand jury proceedings that avoid the defects of the old. Reindictment is precluded only if the statute of limitations has run; and in many jurisdictions there are provisions that toll the statute during the pendency of a technically deficient indictment or that permit reindictment within a specified time after its dismissal, even though the limitations period has expired. Counsel may sometimes decide that, in light of the probabilities of reindictment, available motions are not advised. But knocking out an indictment is often a victory that demoralizes the prosecution considerably and commensurately improves the bargaining posture of the defense. See § 15.12 *supra*. Fringe benefits of the motions to quash or dismiss should also not be ignored: (1) If denied, they leave a claim of error that may be pressed on appeal from conviction; (2) if granted, they ordinarily delay the trial at least one criminal term (which may, of course, be a blessing or a bane, depending on the circumstances of the defense); and (3) whether granted or denied, they may occasion some inquiry into the proceedings before the grand jury (perhaps even serving as the basis for a defense request to examine all or portions of the grand jury transcript or to interview grand jury witnesses regarding matters relating to their grand jury appearances), knowledge of which may enable counsel to gain some measure of informal discovery of the prosecution's case.

20.4. *Challenges to an Information or Indictment for Failure to Charge an Offense*

A motion to quash or to dismiss an indictment or information, or a demurrer to it, is used to challenge the legal sufficiency of its allegations. They may be legally insufficient for several different reasons, often confusingly grouped under the single rubric, "failure to charge a public offense."

Demurrers and motions to quash or to dismiss that attack the facial sufficiency of a charging paper are ordinarily required to be filed before the defendant's plea, although the contention that what is charged is not a crime (§ 20.4.1 *infra*) will usually be heard at any time. *See, e.g., People v. Tedtaotao*, 2015 WL 6941122 (Guam 2015).

20.4.1. *Failure to Charge Acts That Are Criminal in Nature*

The allegations may state fully and clearly what specific acts the defendant is charged with doing, but these acts may be no crime. *See, e.g., United States v. McKee*, 68 F.4th 1100, 1102 n.2 (8th Cir. 2023) (affirming the dismissal of an indictment charging acts that lay beyond the "'scope, reach, or coverage' of a federal criminal statute"); *United States v. Guertin*, 67 F.4th 445 (D.C. Cir. 2023) (affirming the dismissal of an indictment charging wire fraud because that offense requires devising a scheme to obtain money or property fraudulently, and in the case at bar the fraud charged against the defendant, a federal employee, was aimed solely at getting his security clearance renewed); *Burns v. State*, 2023 WL 3606074, at *3 (Fla. App. 2023) (issuing a writ of prohibition to require the dismissal of an aggravated assault charge against a homeowner who chambered a round in a handgun during an altercation with a tree-cutting crew in his yard; "Florida provides a statutory right to openly carry a weapon or firearm while on one's home property or place of business. Even when one is not at his or her home property or place of business, it is not unlawful in Florida to 'briefly and openly display' a lawfully carried firearm 'to the ordinary sight of another person,' so long as the firearm is not being 'intentionally displayed in an angry or threatening manner' . . . ."); *Payne v. State*, 282 So.3d 432, 437 (Miss. App. 2019) ("Here, the indictment charged Payne with 'knowingly, willfully, unlawfully and feloniously possess[ing] 0.1 grams or more but less than 2.0 grams of ETHYLONE, a SCHEDULE I Controlled Substance . . . .' . . . But 'ethylone' is not listed in Schedule I of the Controlled Substances Act . . . . [I]t is insufficient for an indictment merely to allege an unlisted pseudonym for a controlled substance actually listed on the schedule then leave it to the jury to connect the dots."); *State v. Metzinger*, 456 S.W.3d 84 (Mo. App. 2015); *State v. Cooper*, 396 S.W.3d 603 (Tex. App. 2012); *State v. Isaacs*, 794 N.E.2d 1120, 1123 (Ind. App. 2003); *State v. Miller*, 159 N.C. App. 608, 583 S.E.2d 620 (2003), *aff'd per curiam*, 358 N.C. 133, 591 S.E.2d 520 (2004) (mem.); *State v. Harrison*, 805 S.W.2d 241 (Mo. App. 1991). For example, a defendant might be charged under a statute penalizing one who "resists an officer in the execution of his duty" by an information alleging that the defendant did "run away and refuse to stop when called upon to stop by" the officer. A motion to dismiss or demurrer here tests the prosecution's legal theory. Specifically, it raises the issue of law whether one who runs away from a police officer thereby "resists" the officer within the meaning of the statute.

Ordinarily, the sole focus of this species of motion to dismiss is the text of the charging paper: Do the actions and circumstances which the charging paper sets forth constitute a crime or do they not? However, if there is no dispute between the parties that the factual scenario on which the charge is based includes additional circumstances relevant to the criminality of the actions charged, those circumstances can be considered by the court in ruling on the motion. *See, e.g., United States v. Halseth*, 342 U.S. 277 (1952); *State v. Hankins*, 155 So.3d 1043, 1045-46 (Ala. Crim. App. 2011); *State v. Pagano*, 104 Md. App. 113, 122, 655 A.2d 55, 59-60 (1995), *aff'd*, 341 Md. 129, 669 A.2d 1339 (1996); *State v. Fernow*, 328 S.W.3d 429, 431 (Mo. App. 2010) (the indictment alleged that the defendant "while being held in custody after arrest for burglary, a felony, knowingly escaped from custody" but the facts underlying this allegation, as represented by the parties to the court on the motion to dismiss, were that the defendant "was not in custody after arrest for burglary. At the time . . . [he] absconded, he was being held in custody pursuant to a capias warrant issued for his failure to appear at his probation revocation hearing, where burglary was the underlying offense."). Prosecutors will ordinarily take the position that consideration of any factual information outside the four corners of the charging paper is improper on a motion to dismiss. But where there is no genuine factual debate about what happened when and where, and under what circumstances – so that the only real contest between the prosecution and defense is whether a set of agreed-upon events comes within the terms of a criminal statute – defense counsel can sometimes persuade the prosecutor to stipulate to the specifics of those events as the basis for a ruling on the motion, in order to save the state the cost and trouble of a trial.

Counsel should always check the caselaw to determine whether the courts have previously dealt with the kinds of acts with which the defendant is charged or equivalent acts. Frequently, prosecutors will charge defendants with acts that have previously been deemed insufficient to constitute a crime because the prosecutor is not aware of the prior decision or because the prior decision, while persuasive, is not controlling.

If there is no prior caselaw on the issue, then counsel's motion should be devoted primarily to a construction of the statute. In addition to parsing the statutory language, counsel should examine the statute's overall structure, context, relationship to other criminal provisions, and any relevant legislative history for indications that the legislature (1) considered various factual situations to which the statute was intended to apply and did not mean it to reach facts like those in the defendant's case or (2) enacted the statute to achieve certain goals of policy that do not call for an application of the statute to acts such as those committed by the defendant. *See, e.g., Dubin v. United States*, 143 S. Ct. 1557 (2023); *State v. Lopez*, 907 N.W.2d 112 (Iowa 2018). Potentially relevant canons of statutory construction are referenced in § 48.7 subdivision (3) *infra*.

A motion to dismiss is also appropriate when a charging paper purports to charge a particular offense but the facts which it alleges constitute only a lesser offense. *See, e.g., Corona v. Superior Court for the City and County of San Francisco,* 65 Cal. App. 5th 950, 280 Cal. Rptr. 3d 285 (2021). In this situation, local practice may call for outright dismissal of the charging paper, allowing the prosecution to file a new paper charging the lesser offense, or it may allow the prosecution to amend the charging paper (formally or constructively) so that the case proceeds to trial on the lesser charge only.

20.4.2. *Failure to Allege Facts That Make Out Every Element of Each of the Charged Offenses*

A charging paper may quite simply have something missing. The conduct with which it charges the defendant is perfectly consistent with criminality, but some ingredient of the crime is omitted. Thus, for example: "To constitute an offense under Section 12438, General Code, a breaking and entering or an attempt to break and enter in the night season an uninhabited dwelling or other described building must be 'maliciously and forcibly' done, and an indictment purportedly drawn under such section, which charges merely that the accused in the night season 'did unlawfully attempt to break and enter' a building containing a food store, states no offense, is fatally defective and cannot be remedied by the court." *State v. Cimpritz,* 158 Ohio St. 490, at 490, 110 N.E.2d 416, 417 (1953); *accord, Holcomb v. State,* 573 S.W.2d 814, 815 (Tex. Crim. App. 1978) (reversing a conviction and ordering the indictment dismissed because it "omits the necessary culpable mental state"); *People v. Kidd,* 2022 IL 127904, 2022 WL 17245556 (Ill. 2022) (same); *State v. Singleton,* 285 N.C. App. 630, 634, 878 S.E.2d 653, 656 (2022) (reversing a conviction under a statute providing that a person commits second-degree forceable rape when he "engages in vaginal intercourse with another person" who is "physically helpless" and he "knows or should reasonably know that the other person [is] physically helpless": "The indictment here uses the phrase 'engaged in vaginal intercourse' where the statute requires the phrase 'carnally know and abuse.' While the phrase used in the indictment is a sufficient substitute for 'carnally know,' it is not a sufficient substitute for the word 'abuse'. The verb 'abuse' (or some equivalent) is required as a means of describing the essential element that was omitted from the indictment here, that Defendant 'knew or reasonably should have known' that Jane was physically helpless. The inclusion of 'abuse' is necessary to describe that Defendant knew and took advantage of Jane's physical inability to resist his advances."). *See, e.g., State ex rel. Day v. Silver,* 210 W. Va. 175, 180, 556 S.E.2d 820, 825 (2001) ("We . . . hold that in order for an indictment for larceny to be sufficient in law, it must identify with specificity the particular items of property which are the subject of the charge by specifically describing said property, unless the property is incapable of identification as in cases involving fungible goods, United States currency, or comparable articles. Likewise, in order for an indictment for destruction of property to be sufficient in law, it must identify with specificity the particular items of property which are the subject of the charge by specifically describing said property, unless the property is incapable of identification as in cases involving fungible goods, United States currency, or comparable articles."); *State v. Shaw,* 150 Hawai'i 56, 497 P.3d 71 (2021) ("The State alleged only that Shaw 'did knowingly access a computer . . . with the intent to commit the offense of *theft in the third degree,* [and] thereby committed the offense' of Computer Fraud 3. (Emphasis added.) Because the indictment did not allege Shaw knowingly accessed a computer, computer system, or computer network with the intent to commit the offense of theft in the *fourth degree,* and since none of the individual transactions were greater than $250.00, the State was required to include in the indictment language that Shaw possessed the intent to commit theft in the third degree through a continuing course of conduct over the four-month period. The State failed to do so." *Id.* at 63-64, 497 P.3d at 78-79. "The . . . [Intermediate Court of Appeals] was incorrect when it held that the charge was sufficient merely because the charge 'tracked' the language of the statutory offense and the predicate theft offense, and all the statutory elements were included in the indictment. This court has stated that a charge can be insufficient even when the charge tracks the language of the statute if it fails to sufficiently describe the crime . . . ." *Id.* at 64, 497 P.3d at 79.); *State v. Moavenzadeh*, 135 Wash. 2d 359, 362, 956 P.2d 1097, 1098 (1999) ("this court has held that an information is constitutionally adequate only if it includes all of the essential elements of the crime, both statutory and nonstatutory"); *State v. Rankin*, 257 N.C. App. 354, 809 S.E.2d 358 (2018); *United States v. Qazi*, 975 F.3d 989 (9th Cir. 2020); *Woods v. State*, 361 Ga. App. 844, 850-52, 864 S.E.2d 194, 201-02 (2021).

Local practice varies enormously with regard to the significance that an omission must have in order to be fatal. Most jurisdictions require allegations of: (1) the name of the defendant, (2) a description or characterization of the defendant's conduct that asserts (in factual or conclusory terms) every legal element of the offense charged (including acts done, any circumstances surrounding them that are necessary to make them unlawful, and the requisite mental state or *mens rea*), (3) the place of the crime (disclosing venue in the court, see § 20.5 *infra),* and (4) the approximate date of the crime (within the statute of limitations, see § 20.7 *infra*). Beyond these rudiments, the jurisdictions differ (and often differ from offense to offense) regarding what must be charged. Some jurisdictions require the name of the victim and great particularization of the means or instrumentalities of the offense. Others disregard these matters. Some disregard even the rudiments just described. Conspicuous among the latter are jurisdictions that provide statutory "short forms," declaring that a charging paper shall be sufficient for the crime of *x* if it alleges: "On [date], defendant A committed the crime of *x* against complainant B within the jurisdiction of this Court." Local practice must be consulted.

20.4.3. *Lack of Specificity*

A charging paper may be wholly unspecific and conclusory. It may duplicate the language of the criminal statute (defendant A "did commit a lewd act") without giving the slightest idea what the defendant *did*. Again, the jurisdictions vary considerably in the factual specificity required. Many permit allegations in conclusory statutory language under all but the vaguest statutes. *Cf. Michigan v. Doran*, 439 U.S. 282, 290 (1978) (dictum). However, there are limits. The following formulation of federal pleading rules is also common in state practice: "It is generally sufficient that an indictment set forth the offense in the words of the statute itself, as long as 'those words of themselves fully, directly, and expressly, without any uncertainty or ambiguity, set forth all the elements necessary to constitute the offence intended to be punished.' . . . 'Undoubtedly the language of the statute may be used in the general description of an offence, but it must be accompanied with such a statement of the facts and circumstances as will inform the accused of the specific offence, coming under the general description, with which he is charged.'" (*Hamling v. United States*, 418 U.S. 87, 117-18 (1974)). *See also United States v. Resendiz-Ponce*, 549 U.S. 102, 108-10 (2007); *United States v. Bailey*, 444 U.S. 394, 414 (1980); *Russell v. United States*, 369 U.S. 749, 765-69 (1962); *People v. Burchell*, 2018 IL App

(5th) 170079, 100 N.E.3d 660, 671, 421 Ill. Dec. 643, 654 (2018) (affirming the dismissal of an information that charged the defendant with failing to report his absence for 3 or more days from his address of registration as a sex offender, the court construes the statute as applying only to absences or 3 or more consecutive days and finds that the information failed to specify that the three days were consecutive as distinguished from aggregate: therefore, "we do not believe that the instrument's less-specific allegation that the defendant was temporarily absent for '3 or more days' during . . . [a 3-month] time period contained sufficient particularity to allow the defendant to prepare a defense"); *United States v. Hillie*, 227 F. Supp. 3d 57, 70-71 (D. D.C. 2017) ("It is important to note that, '[i]n order to meet the requirements of the Sixth Amendment, an indictment must contain every element of the offense charged *and* must fairly apprise the accused *of the conduct allegedly constituting the offense* so as to enable him to prepare a defense against those allegations.' . . . Courts have found that it is especially important to include such facts and circumstances in cases where, by solely tracking the statutory language, the indictment's terms create ambiguity regarding the defendant's conduct. . . . ¶ The indictment at issue in this case is, for the most part, a verbatim recitation of the broad and varied statutory elements of the offenses that are charged against Hillie in the various counts. Among other things, Hillie argues that the 'limited facts contained' in the indictment render this charging document constitutionally deficient, because the indictment does not 'sufficiently apprise him of what he must be prepared to meet at trial' or 'enable him to identify the conduct on which the government intends to base its case.' . . . The government responds that 'the charging language is sufficient[ ] because it tracks the language of the statute and provides the defendant with notice of what he has been charged with.' . . . ¶ [T]his Court agrees with Hillie that the federal child-pornography charges . . . do not contain any facts that describe the conduct of Hillie's that the government believes constitutes criminal behavior, and thus, these counts of the indictment fail to provide adequate notice of the factual bases for the myriad, manifestly indistinguishable charges that the government has brought. Nor do the indictment's vague child-pornography allegations provide adequate protection for Hillie's grand jury and double jeopardy rights. As a result, this Court concludes that the federal child pornography counts in the instant indictment . . . are constitutionally deficient and must be dismissed."); *State v. Israel*, 78 Hawai'i 66, 67-68, 890 P.2d 303, 304-05 (1995) (affirming the dismissal of a count of a complaint which "charged Israel with knowingly possessing or intentionally using or threatening to use a firearm while engaged in the commission of a felony . . . [but which failed] to specify which felony Israel was allegedly committed at the time he possessed, used, or threatened to use a firearm": the Hawai'i Supreme Court relies on Article I, § 14 of the state constitution, providing that in all criminal prosecutions "the accused shall enjoy the right . . . to be informed of the nature and cause of the accusation").

Conclusory pleading has several recognized vices. First, it impairs the defendant's right to be "'fairly inform[ed] . . . of the charge against which he must defend'" (*United States v. Resendiz-Ponce, supra*, 549 U.S. at 108, quoting *Hamling v. United States, supra*, 418 U.S. at 117; and see § 18.9.2.2 *supra*). Second, it frustrates the defendant's interest in having "'the record . . . sho[w] with accuracy to what extent he may plead a former acquittal or conviction [that is, double jeopardy (see § 20.8 *infra*)]'" in the event of a subsequent prosecution (*Sanabria v. United States,* 437 U.S. 54, 66 (1978)). Third, it deprives the defendant of any opportunity to test the prosecution's legal theory without contesting its facts (an opportunity traditionally provided by the motion to dismiss and by its progenitor, the common-law demurrer (*see, e.g.,*

Russell v. United States, supra, 369 U.S. at 768-69 ("It has long been recognized that there is an important corollary purpose to be served by the requirement that an indictment set out 'the specific offence, coming under the general description,' with which the defendant is charged. This purpose . . . is 'to inform the court of the facts alleged, so that it may decide whether they are sufficient in law to support a conviction, if one should be had.'"); Robert L. Weinberg, *Iqbal for the Accused?*, 34-JUL THE CHAMPION 28 (2010); and see §§ 20.4.1-20.4.2 *supra*). Fourth, it deprives the defendant, in an indictable case, of any opportunity to obtain judicial review of the concurrence of findings of fact by the grand jury and the trial jury or judge – a concurrence that the right to prosecution by indictment supposes (*see Stirone v. United States*, 361 U.S. 212 (1960); *United States v. Miller*, 471 U.S. 130, 138-40, 142-45 (1985)).

Although some judges seem to think that a vague charging paper can be cured by a bill of particulars (see § 13.7 *supra*), the bill actually remedies only the first two of these four vices. It does not touch the third because of the general rule that a demurrer or motion to dismiss will not lie to a bill of particulars. It does not touch the fourth because the bill is the product of the prosecutor, not the grand jury. Therefore, as long as the defendant's interests are not harmed by delay at the pleading stage, counsel may do well to attack even venerable and accepted forms of conclusory charging papers, particularly indictments, on the ground that these disempower the court to perform its function of testing the sufficiency of the prosecutor's case in law and that they subvert the defendant's constitutional right of indictment by grand jury.

However, when, a court has denied counsel's motion to dismiss and when the factual allegations in the charging paper are not sufficiently specific to enable counsel to investigate and prepare a defense efficiently, counsel should move for a bill of particulars. *See United States v. Montague*, 67 F.4th 520, 531-32 (2d Cir. 2023) ("[If the] allegations [in a charging paper] are . . . subject to the criticism that a defendant might need more notice of the charges . . . [, the] proper way to address such concerns is through a bill of particulars. 'An indictment that fulfills the [pleading] requirements . . . but is nonetheless insufficient to permit the preparation of an adequate defense may be supplemented with a bill of particulars.'").

20.5. *Challenges to an Information or Indictment for Failure to Establish Venue*

A charging paper is generally held fatally defective if it does not allege facts establishing venue in the court where it is filed. Allegations in terms of "*X* street" or "*Y* township" are ordinarily sufficient; the court will judicially notice that *X* street or *Y* township is within the geographical jurisdiction of the court, if it is.

Criminal venue is governed by statute within constitutional limitations. *See, e.g., United States v. Lozoya*, 982 F.3d 648 (9th Cir. 2020) (en banc); *United States v. Petlechkov*, 922 F.3d 762 (6th Cir. 2019). The prevalent state constitutional provision guaranteeing trial by a jury of the vicinage may or may not comport a venue restriction (*see* WAYNE R. LAFAVE, JEROLD H. ISRAEL, NANCY J. KING & ORIN S. KERR, 4 CRIMINAL PROCEDURE §§ 16.1-16.2 (4th ed. & Supp.); Lisa E. Alexander, *Vicinage, Venue, and Community Cross-Section: Obstacles to a State Defendant's Right to Trial by a Representative Jury*, 19 HASTINGS CONST. L. Q. 261 (1991); Drew Kershen, *Vicinage*, 29 OKLA. L. REV. 801 (1976); 30 OKLA. L. REV. 1 (1977)); and even those forms of state jury-trial guarantees that omit explicit reference to "vicinage" may be read as restricting the place of trial or the area from which the trial jury pool can be drawn (*see Alvarado v. State*, 486 P.2d 891 (Alaska 1971)). The Sixth Amendment to the federal Constitution requires trial "by an impartial jury of the State and district wherein the crime shall have been committed, which district shall have been previously ascertained by law." *See United States v. Johnson*, 323 U.S. 273, 275 (1944); *Platt v. Minnesota Mining & Mfg. Co.*, 376 U.S. 240, 245-46 (1964); *cf.* U.S. CONST. art. III § 2, cl. 3. The incorporation of the Sixth Amendment into the Fourteenth by *Duncan v. Louisiana*, 391 U.S. 145 (1968) [§ 4.3.2 *supra*; § 32.1 *infra*], may, therefore, entail some measure of federal constitutional restraint upon state legislative power to manipulate criminal venue. *See Williams v. Florida*, 399 U.S. 78, 92-97 (1970); *Mareska v. State*, 534 N.E.2d 246 (Ind. App. 1989); *but see Price v. Superior Court*, 25 Cal. 4th 104, 625 P.3d 618, 108 Cal. Rptr. 2d 409 (2001); *State v. Bowman*, 588 A.2d 728 (Me. 1991).

The general constitutional and statutory rule is that offenses are triable only in the county (or circuit or other judicial unit) comprising the place where the offense was committed. *See, e.g., United States v. Cores*, 356 U.S. 405, 407 (1958); *United States v. Medina-Ramos*, 834 F.2d 874 (10th Cir. 1987); *United States v. Moran-Garcia*, 966 F.3d 966 (9th Cir. 2020); *Thompson v. Brown,* 288 Ga. 855, 708 S.E.2d 270 (2011); *Tanner v. Commonwealth*, 72 Va. App. 86, 841 S.E.2d 377 (2020). The "crime-committed" formula depends principally on the statutory elements of the offense: If a defendant mails a false application to a state agency in another county, for example, venue may turn on whether the statue punishes "making" a false statement or "filing" one. *See, e.g., United States v. Powers*, 40 F.4th 129, 134-35 (4th Cir. 2022) ("[F]or some offenses, determining where the crime was committed for venue purposes can be complicated. Mail and wire fraud are 'continuing offense[s],' which may be prosecuted anywhere the offense 'was begun, continued, or completed,' including 'any district from, through, or into which' the mail or wire communication moved. . . . Mail and wire fraud are defined by two essential elements: '(1) the existence of a scheme to defraud and (2) the use of the mails or wire communication in furtherance of the scheme.' . . . But only the second element constitutes the 'essential *conduct* element' for purposes of determining venue. . . . In other words, venue will not lie everywhere the fraudster schemed, but venue is proper in any district associated with misuse of the mail or wires in furtherance of the scheme or 'any acts that cause such misuse.'"); *United States v. Seward*, 967 F.3d 57 (1st Cir. 2020); *United States v. Smith*, 22 F.4th 1236, 1242 (11th Cir. 2022), *subsequent history in Smith v. United States*, 143 S. Ct. 1594 (2023) (the determination whether venue is proper involves a "two-step . . . inquiry. . . . First, we identify the essential conduct elements of the . . . [charge]. Then, we 'discern the location of the commission' of the essential conduct elements, which are the only relevant elements for venue, and determine whether the location of their commission is the same as the location of the trial."). Crimes, the operative elements of which occur in more than one county, are generally triable in either. *United States v. Rodriguez-Moreno*, 536 U.S. 275 (1999); *People v. Posey*, 32 Cal. 4th 193, 82 P.3d 755, 8 Cal. Rptr. 3d 551 (2004); *Wakefield v. State*, 2023 WL 2489444 (Miss. App. 2023); *compare Martinez-Guzman v. Second Judicial District Court in and for County of Washoe*, 137 Nev. 599, 603, 496 P.3d 572, 676 (2021) (Nevada Revised Statutes 171.030 "governs venue over criminal offenses committed in more than one county: ¶ [']When a public offense is committed in part in one county and in part in another or the acts or effects thereof constituting or requisite to the consummation of the offense occur in two or more counties, the venue is in either county.['] ¶ . . . The district court's finding of proper venue under this statute depended in part on its finding that intent alone or a preparatory act alone could meet the requirements of that language. We hold that this conclusion was incorrect."), *and United States v. Bowens*, 224 F.3d 302, 308 (4th Cir. 2000) ("Bowens . . . appeals his two convictions for harboring or concealing a fugitive from arrest, arguing that venue for those offenses was not proper in the Eastern District of Virginia. There was no evidence that Bowens engaged in any act in the Eastern District of Virginia to harbor or conceal Beckford or Laidlaw. Nonetheless, the government makes two alternative arguments to support its venue selection: first, that venue was proper in the Eastern District of Virginia because an element of the offense (issuance of the warrant) occurred there; second, that venue was proper because Bowens' offense interfered with the administration of justice in the Eastern District of Virginia. Because both of these arguments fail, we vacate Bowens' harboring convictions."). "[I]n conspiracy cases, 'venue is proper in any district where the agreement was formed or an overt act occurred.'" *United States v. Romans*, 823 F.3d 299, 309-10 (5th Cir. 2016). *Accord, United States v. Geibel*, 369 F.3d 682, 696 (2d Cir. 2004) ("'In a conspiracy prosecution, venue is proper in any district in which an overt act in furtherance of the conspiracy was committed by any of the coconspirators. The defendant need not have been present in the district, as long as an overt act in furtherance of the conspiracy occurred there.'"); *State v. Dent*, 123 Wash. 2d 467, 481, 869 P.2d 392, 400 (1994); *Henry v. Commonwealth*, 2 Va. App. 194, 342 S.E.2d 655 (1986); *compare Jones v. State*, 135 Ga. App. 893, 899-900, 219 S.E.2d 585, 590-91 (1975) ("Venue in a conspiracy prosecution is properly laid either in the jurisdiction where the conspiracy was formed or in any jurisdiction wherein a conspirator committed an overt act in furtherance of the conspiracy. . . . Sub judice, there was no evidence presented as to the place of the formation of the conspiracy. In addition, appellants' alleged participation in the conspiracy consisted of acts committed exclusively in Candler County. Thus, proof of venue rested solely upon the overt acts of co-conspirators Pinkham and Von Bargeron. It was incumbent upon the State to prove, in this respect, that the overt acts were committed in furtherance of the conspiracy and that they took place in Bulloch County. ¶ Did the trial court's failure to instruct the jury on the issue of venue constitute reversible error? We are compelled to answer this question affirmatively. . . . Appellants, by denying participation in the conspiracy and by denying any agreement or concerted action with Pinkham or Von Bargeron, necessarily raised an issue of fact as to venue which properly should have been presented to the jury. . . . Also for the jury's determination was the question of whether the alleged overt acts were proved to have been committed in furtherance of the conspiracy. . . . The trial court's failure to properly charge the applicable law relating to venue removed the above issues from the jury's determination."); *United States v. Williams*, 274 F.3d 1079, 1085 (6th Cir. 2001) ("None of the overt acts in consummation of the conspiracy occurred in Michigan and the conspiracy had no effect in Michigan. Moreover, it was never intended to have any effect there. Carboni, acting [as an informer] for the government, knew when he was making his drug deals with Williams that the drugs would never reach Michigan and that the drugs would be seized and the defendant arrested in Texas. The government's argument notwithstanding, there is no evidence that the *conspirators* fixed the price of the marijuana based upon their determination that the drug could be re-sold for a higher price in Michigan. The conspiracy between Williams and Del Bosque was simply one to sell the marijuana in Texas to a buyer in Texas, who professed that it was *his* purpose (although it was not) to resell the drugs in Michigan. That agreement did not provide the conspirators, Williams and Del Bosque, 'substantial contacts' to Michigan. We do not believe that a government informant may arbitrarily determine venue merely by stating, falsely, where he intends to take the drugs for resale."). (At the trial stage, the rule requiring proof of an overt act in the county or district of prosecution may become quite significant. When forum-shopping, prosecutors – particularly federal prosecutors – frequently pick a jurisdiction having only very attenuated contacts with a conspiracy and allege only one or two overt acts within it. If they fail to prove these specific overt acts at trial, an acquittal is compelled, even though the conspiracy is otherwise abundantly proved. *E.g., Green v. United States*, 309 F.2d 852, 856-57 (5th Cir. 1962).)

In some courts, a defendant who fails to make a pretrial motion to dismiss the charging paper for lack of venue forfeits the right to argue lack of venue as the basis for an acquittal at trial. *E.g., Harper v. United States*, 383 F.2d 795 (5th Cir. 1967); *and see United States v. Carreon-Palacio*, 267 F.3d 381, 392-393 (5th Cir. 2001) ("A defendant indicted by an instrument which lacks sufficient allegations to establish venue waives any future challenge by failing to object before trial. In situations where adequate allegations are made but the impropriety of venue only becomes apparent at the close of the government's case, a defendant may address the error by objecting at that time, and thus preserve the issue for appellate review."). In other courts, such a pretrial motion is not required. *See, e.g., State v. Hampton*, 2012-Ohio-5688, 134 Ohio St. 3d 447, 452, 983 N.E.2d 324, 329 (2012) ("Nothing in the Constitution, statutes, or rules requires a defendant to raise the issue of venue before trial. The state has the obligation to ensure the proper venue within the indictment, for the indictment puts the defendant on notice and the state to its proof."); *United States v. Ghanem*, 993 F.3d 1113 (9th Cir. 2021). Counsel considering a pretrial motion should check the jurisdiction's law on this question. It is important because, where defendants are permitted to delay raising the issue until trial, it is often strategically wise to do so. The relief available on a pretrial motion will be nothing more than a dismissal that leaves the prosecution free to re-charge the defendant in a court of proper venue; also, the prosecution can appeal a ruling in the defendant's favor on a pretrial motion; whereas, if the defendant raises the issue for the first time at trial and obtains an acquittal on that ground, the acquittal will, in most jurisdictions, be unappealable and constitute a bar to re-prosecution. *See, e.g., State v. Hampton, supra*; and see § 17.5.2 *supra*; *but see Derry v. Commonwealth*, 274 S.W.3d 439 (Ky. 2008).

Venue is typically an intricate technical subject, and counsel does well to research the local law and practice thoroughly in any case in which the offense charged has elements based on events or circumstances outside the county or district in which the charging paper is filed.

20.6. *Technical Defects in the Indictment or Information*

Charging papers may be assailed by motion on a host of technical grounds, some relating to the nature of the charging language ("duplicity," "multiplicity," vagueness, noncompliance with prescribed statutory forms), others relating to strictly formal matters (failure of an indictment to carry the signature or endorsement of the grand jury foreperson or the prosecutor as required by law, failure of the indictment to carry an endorsement of the names of the witnesses who testified before the grand jury as required by law, and so forth). Some of these defects are remediable and will be ordered remedied without resubmission of the bill. Others are fatal. *See, e.g., People v. Edmondson*, 191 A.D.3d 1015, 1018, 142 N.Y.S.3d 198, 202 (N.Y. App. Div., 2d Dep't 2021) (an indictment that charged assault in the first degree and robbery in the first degree was multiplicitous, charging two counts that are "essentially identical" and thereby "'creat[ing] the risk that a defendant will be punished for, or stigmatized with a conviction of, more crimes than he actually committed'"; although the defect was "unpreserved for appellate review" and although "dismissal of the multiplicitous count will not affect the duration of the defendant's sentence of imprisonment," the court "review[s] this contention in the exercise of our interest of justice jurisdiction" and "dismiss[es] the count charging assault in the first degree in consideration of the stigma attached to the redundant convictions"); *People v. Alonzo*, 16 N.Y.3d 267, 268, 945 N.E.2d 495, at 495, 920 N.Y.S.2d 302, at 302 (2011) ("where the evidence before a grand jury shows a single, uninterrupted attack in which the attacker gropes several parts of a victim's body, the attacker may be charged with only one count of sexual abuse"); *State v. Brown*, 217 Ariz. 617, 177 P.3d 878 (Ariz. App, 2008) (under a statute prohibiting the sale, transfer or offer to sell or transfer a narcotic drug, separate charges of selling and of transferring the drug, based on a single transaction, were multiplicitous); *compare United States v. Smith*, 54 F.4th 755 (4th Cir. 2022) (two counts of an indictment alleging that the defendant lied twice to an F.B.I. agent during a single interview were multiplicitous, and one count should have been dismissed), *with United States v. Maldonado-Passage*, 56 F.4th 830 (10th Cir. 2022) (alternative ground) (two counts of an indictment charging that the defendant hired two unrelated hitmen to kill the same victim were not multiplicitous), *and United States v. Haas*, 37 F.4th 1256 (7th Cir. 2022) (holding that an indictment containing three counts alleging three threats against an F.B.I. agent made in texts sent over the course of two days is not multiplicitous). Again, local practice must be consulted.

20.7. *Statutes of Limitations*

Statutes of limitations of prosecutions, like statutes of limitations governing civil matters, prescribe the permissible period of time within which a charging paper may be filed after an event, asserting liability based on that event. In many jurisdictions, a charging paper is subject to demurrer or dismissal if it either (a) does not allege the date of the offense charged with reasonable specificity ("on or about" will do) or (b) alleges a date that is beyond the period of limitations. *See, e.g., United States v. Yashar*, 166 F.3d 873 (7th Cir. 1999). The demurrer or motion to dismiss is ordinarily required to be made before plea. In other jurisdictions, questions of limitations are raised by a special plea at arraignment. In still others the defendant must go to trial and raise the issue by a demurrer to the evidence or a motion for acquittal at the close of the prosecution's case. Local practice should be consulted.

20.8. *Challenges to the Indictment or Information on Double Jeopardy Grounds*

At common law, double jeopardy challenges were ordinarily raised by special pleas at arraignment. Today, in many jurisdictions they must be raised by prearraignment motion.

20.8.1. *Introduction: The General Rules Governing Double Jeopardy Challenges*

Guarantees against being "twice put in jeopardy" may be found in the Fifth Amendment to the federal Constitution and in most state constitutions. In *Benton v. Maryland,* 395 U.S. 784 (1969), the Supreme Court incorporated the Fifth Amendment guarantee into the Due Process Clause of the Fourteenth Amendment and thereby made it binding in state criminal prosecutions. See § 4.3.2 *supra*. The Court thereafter declared its *Benton* decision fully retroactive (*Ashe v. Swenson*, 397 U.S. 436, 437 n.1 (1970); *and see Robinson v. Neil*, 409 U.S. 505 (1973)), but it has reserved the question whether "each of the several aspects of the [federal] constitutional guarantee against double jeopardy" developed by its Fifth Amendment cases is applicable in state prosecutions (*Waller v. Florida*, 397 U.S. 387, 390-91 (1970); *cf. Illinois v. Somerville*, 410 U.S. 458, 468 (1973)). Subsequent cases strongly imply an affirmative answer to this question (*see Greene v. Massey*, 437 U.S. 19, 24 (1978); *Crist v. Bretz*, 437 U.S. 28, 32 (1978); *Hudson v. Louisiana*, 450 U.S. 40, 42 n.3 (1981); *and see McDonald v. City of Chicago*, 561 U.S. 742, 764-65 & nn.12-14 (2010) (listing the Fifth Amendment's Double Jeopardy Clause among the rights that have been incorporated and are fully applicable to the States); *Timbs v. Indiana*, 139 S. Ct. 682, 687 (2019) ("Incorporated Bill of Rights guarantees are 'enforced against the States under the Fourteenth Amendment according to the same standards that protect those personal rights against federal encroachment.' . . . Thus, if a Bill of Rights protection is incorporated, there is no daylight between the federal and state conduct it prohibits or requires.")), but these decisions are not categorical on the point (*see Crist v. Bretz, supra*, 437 U.S. at 37-38; *Whalen v. United States*, 445 U.S. 684, 689-90 n.4 (1980)). The argument for full-scale incorporation is supported by numerous decisions involving other incorporated Bill of Rights guarantees, which consistently rely on doctrines and precedents announced in federal prosecutions as establishing the rules to be applied in state cases as well. *See, e.g., Ker v. California*, 374 U.S. 23, 30-34, 46 (1963) (Fourth Amendment guarantee against unreasonable search and seizure); *Malloy v. Hogan*, 378 U.S. 1, 9-11 (1964) (Fifth Amendment privilege against self-incrimination); *Lakeside v. Oregon*, 435 U.S. 333, 336 (1978) (same); *New Jersey v. Portash*, 440 U.S. 450, 456-57 (1979) (same); *Washington v. Texas*, 388 U.S. 14, 22 (1967) (Sixth Amendment right to compulsory process); *Baldwin v. New York*, 399 U.S. 66, 68-69 (1970) (Sixth Amendment right to jury trial); *Apprendi v. New Jersey*, 530 U.S. 466 (2000) (same); *Ring v. Arizona*, 536 U.S. 584 (2002) (same); *Pointer v. Texas*, 380 U.S. 400 (1965) (Sixth Amendment right to confrontation); *Crawford v. Washington*, 536 U.S. 584 (2004) (same); *Argersinger v. Hamlin*, 407 U.S. 25 (1972) (Sixth Amendment right to counsel); *Scott v. Illinois*, 440 U.S. 367 (1979) (same); *Graham v. Florida*, 560 U.S. 48 (2010) (Eighth Amendment prohibition of Cruel and Unusual Punishment); *cf. Ludwig v. Massachusetts*, 427 U.S. 618, 624-30 (1976). "The Court thus has rejected the notion that the Fourteenth Amendment applies to the States only a 'watered-down, subjective version of the individual guarantees of the Bill of Rights.'" *Malloy v. Hogan, supra*, 378 U.S. at 10-11.

Federal and state constitutional double jeopardy guarantees establish the general rule that a defendant may not be reprosecuted for the "same offense" if the first trial ended in acquittal or conviction, or if the first trial passed the stage at which jeopardy "attaches" and then ended in a mistrial declared without some "manifest necessity" or the defendant's assent. Each element of this general rule, however, has been qualified by complex definitions and exceptions. Section 20.8.2 *infra* discusses the concepts of "attachment of jeopardy" and "same offense." Sections 20.8.3, 20.8.4, and 20.8.5 examine, respectively, the double jeopardy doctrines governing reprosecution when there has been an acquittal, conviction, or mistrial.

Sections 20.8.6 and 20.8.7 then discuss other double jeopardy doctrines. Section 20.8.6 describes the collateral estoppel doctrine that applies to retrials. Section 20.8.7 explains the "dual sovereignty" exception to double jeopardy guarantees.

20.8.2. *Definitions*

20.8.2.1. *"Attachment of Jeopardy"*

Double jeopardy protections come into play only after a first trial has passed the stage at which jeopardy "attaches." In a jury trial, jeopardy attaches when the jury is sworn. *Crist v. Bretz*, 437 U.S. 28, 35-38 (1978); *Martinez v. Illinois*, 572 U.S. 833, 839-40 (2014) (per curiam). In a bench trial, jeopardy attaches when the first witness is sworn and the presentation of evidence commences. *Crist v. Bretz, supra*, 437 U.S. at 37 n.15; *Serfass v. United States,* 420 U.S. 377, 388 (1975).

20.8.2.2. *"Same Offense"*

The guarantee against double jeopardy forbids a defendant's "be[ing] subject for the *same offence* to be twice put in jeopardy of life or limb" (U.S. CONST., amend. V (emphasis added)). Thus a threshold issue in double jeopardy analysis is whether the offense for which the defendant is being prosecuted is the "same offense" for which s/he was previously tried. This issue is obviously clear-cut when the second charge leveled against the defendant is a violation of the same criminal code provision that bottomed the first. Another easy call is that all lesser-included-offenses are treated as "the same" as the greater offense which subsumes all of their elements. "Historically, courts have treated greater and lesser-included offenses as the same offense for double jeopardy purposes, so a conviction on one normally precludes a later trial on the other." *Currier v. Virginia*, 138 S. Ct. 2144, 2150 (2018) (dictum). *See, e.g., Price v. Georgia,* 398 U.S. 323 (1970); *De Mino v. New York,* 404 U.S. 1035 (1972) (per curiam); *Harris v. Oklahoma,* 433 U.S. 682 (1977) (per curiam); *United States v. Gries,* 877 F.3d 255 (7th Cir. 2017), quoted in the following paragraph; *State v. Putfark*, 651 S.W.3d 869 (Mo. App. 2022). More difficult issues emerge, however, when the defendant's conduct violates two separate statutory provisions, and s/he is prosecuted first for one statutory violation and then the other.

> "Where the same conduct violates two statutory provisions, the first step in the double jeopardy analysis is to determine whether the legislature . . . intended that each violation be a separate offense. If . . . [the legislature] intended that there be only one offense – that is, a defendant could be convicted under either statutory provision for a single act, but not under both – there would be no statutory authorization for a subsequent prosecution after conviction [or acquittal] of one of the two provisions, and that would end the double jeopardy analysis." (*Garrett v. United States,* 471 U.S. 773, 778 (1985).)

Techniques for divining legislative intent in the common situation in which it is unclear differ considerably among the jurisdictions. In construing federal legislation, the Supreme Court has employed the so-called *Blockburger* test, deriving from *Blockburger v. United States,* 284 U.S. 299 (1932), which "emphasizes the elements of the two crimes . . . [and asks whether] 'each requires proof of a fact that the other does not'" (*Brown v. Ohio,* 432 U.S. 161, 166 (1977)). *See, e.g., Rutledge v. United States*, 517 U.S. 292, 297 (1996); *United States v. Dixon*, 509 U.S. 688, 696 (1993); *Ball v. United States,* 470 U.S. 856, 861 (1985); *United States v. Reyes-Correa*, 971 F.3d 6 (1st Cir. 2020); *United States v. Gries, supra*, 877 F.3d at 259 ("Under the familiar *Blockburger* test, if 'the same act or transaction constitutes a violation of two distinct statutory provisions,' the double-jeopardy inquiry asks 'whether each provision requires proof of a fact which the other does not.'. . . . A lesser-included offense nests within the greater offense and therefore flunks the *Blockburger* test."); *United States v. Morrissey*, 895 F.3d 541 (8th Cir. 2018), quoted in § 48.7 subdivision (3) *infra*. The Court has cautioned that the *"Blockburger* rule[,] . . . [although] a useful canon of statutory construction," is not "a conclusive determinant of legislative intent" and "the *Blockburger* presumption must . . . yield to a plainly expressed contrary view on the part of [the legislature]" (*Garrett v. United States, supra*, 471 U.S. at 779). *See also Missouri v. Hunter,* 459 U.S. 359, 368 (1983); *Wood v. Milyard*, 721 F.3d 1190, 1195 (10th Cir. 2013). But, at least in the context of successive prosecutions – as distinguished from multiple charges joined for simultaneous adjudication in a single trial (see § 48.7 subdivision (3) *infra*) – it is arguable that the *Blockburger* test should prevail and preclude subjecting a defendant to two trials for offenses having identical elements unless the legislature intended specifically to authorize not merely cumulative punishments but multiple trials. And it would be a rare statute that could reasonably be found to manifest the latter intent. *See Ex Parte Chaddock*, 369 S.W.3d 880, 883, 886 (Tex. Crim. App. 2012) (even if "the Legislature manifested its intention that an accused be *punished* for both offenses," the Double Jeopardy Clause nonetheless bars *"successive prosecutions"* for both offenses; "Multiple punishments that result from a single prosecution do not subject a defendant to the evils attendant upon successive prosecutions, namely the 'embarrassment, expense and ordeal' of repetitive trials, 'compelling [the accused] to live in a continuing state of anxiety and insecurity,' and creating 'a risk of conviction through sheer governmental perseverance.'").

In interpreting their state constitutions and statutes, some state courts employ the *Blockburger* test. *See, e.g., State v. Watkins*, 362 S.W.3d 530 (Tenn. 2012); *Gianiny v. State*, 320 Md. 337, 577 A.2d 795 (Md. App. 1990); *May v. State*, 267 So.3d 803, 807-08 (Miss. App. 2018) ("May has two convictions under one statute . . . arising out of the same occurrence: his attack on Jalanivich. The State broke the assault down into two phases, the beating and the strangling, charging each under the same statute. But May's striking and strangling of Jalanivich was during the same assault. 'Whether a transaction results in the commission of one or more offenses is determined by whether separate and distinct acts made punishable by law have been committed.' . . . ¶ . . . May committed one attack to harm Jalanivich. His actions were not each a discrete and separate act but a part of May's single attack on Jalanivich, i.e., one aggravated assault. Even though the statute for aggravated assault has two methods of proof for the one occurrence, May was not charged under a separate statute with differing elements of proof. Therefore, the same-elements test is inapplicable. Because statutes are to be strictly construed against the State, the two methods of proof are to be construed as describing one aggravated assault in this case. ¶ Thus, the right to protection from double jeopardy precludes the second conviction . . . ."). Other courts use the "same transaction" or compulsory-joinder approach articulated by Justice Brennan, concurring, in *Ashe v. Swenson,* 397 U.S. 436, 450-60 (1970). *See, e.g., State v. Boyd*, 271 Or. 558, 533 P.2d 795 (1975), and the authorities collected in *Brooks v. Oklahoma,* 456 U.S. 999, 1000 (1982) (opinion of Justice Brennan, dissenting from the denial of *certiorari*). Still other courts use an idiosyncratic local test. *See, e.g., Wadle v. State*, 151 N.E.3d 227, 235 (Ind. 2020) ("[W]hen a defendant's single act or transaction implicates **multiple** criminal statutes (rather than a single statute) , . . [the court should conduct a two-part inquiry: First, a court must determine, under our included-offense statutes, whether one charged offense encompasses another charged offense. Second, a court must look at the underlying facts

527

– as alleged in the information and as adduced at trial – to determine whether the charged offenses are the 'same.' If the facts show two separate and distinct crimes, there's no violation of substantive double jeopardy, even if one offense is, by definition, 'included' in the other. But if the facts show only a single continuous crime, and one statutory offense is included in the other, then the presumption is that the legislation intends for alternative (rather than cumulative) sanctions. The State can rebut this presumption only by showing that the statute – either in express terms or by unmistakable implication – clearly permits multiple punishment.").

20.8.3. *Reprosecution After An Acquittal*

Double jeopardy guarantees clearly and unequivocally bar reprosecution for the same offense after an individual has been acquitted. *United States v. Martin Linen Supply Co.*, 430 U.S. 564 (1977); *see, e.g., Ball v. United States,* 163 U.S. 662, 671 (1896); *United States v. Scott,* 437 U.S. 82, 91 (1978); *Bullington v. Missouri,* 451 U.S. 430, 437-38, 445 (1981), and cases cited; *Yeager v. United States*, 557 U.S. 110, 117-20, 122-23 (2009); *McDaniels v. Warden Cambridge Springs SCI*, 700 Fed. Appx. 119, 121 (3d Cir. 2017); *and see State v. Allen*, 192 Wash. 2d 526, 431 P.3d 117 (2018) (applying the rule to a sentencing enhancement factor that is viewed as an element of a greater offense). *Cf. Blueford v. Arkansas*, 566 U.S. 599, 605-08 (2012); *Bravo-Fernandez v. United States*, 580 U.S. 5, 9 (2016); *Commonwealth v. Landis*, 2018 PA Super 351, 201 A.3d 768 (Pa. Super. 2018) (the defendant was tried before a jury on charges of first degree murder, third degree murder, voluntary manslaughter, and involuntary manslaughter; the jury found him guilty of first degree murder but acquitted him of the other charges, including third degree murder; after the first degree conviction was vacated on ineffective-assistance grounds in postconviction proceedings, the prosecution petitioned the trial court to reinstate the third degree murder charge, arguing that third degree murder is a lesser included offense of the first degree murder count on which the defendant had been convicted; the Superior Court affirms denial of the petition on the ground that double jeopardy prohibits reprosecution after an acquittal even when the acquittal is logically inconsistent with conviction on a greater charge). "A trial court's actions constitute 'an acquittal on the merits when "the ruling of the judge . . . represents a resolution [in defendant's favor] . . . of some or all of the factual elements of the offenses charged."' . . . In determining whether a trial court's ruling represents a resolution in the defendant's favor of some or all of the factual elements of the offense charged, we consider both the form and the substance of the trial court's ruling. . . . A finding of insufficient evidence to convict amounts to an acquittal on the merits because such a finding involves a factual determination about the defendant's guilt or innocence." *State v. Sahr*, 812 N.W.2d 83, 90 (Minn. 2012) (reviewing relevant decisions of the U.S. Supreme Court and applying them to bar reprosecution after a trial judge has dismissed a charging paper on the basis of the prosecution's "concession that it lacked sufficient evidence to prove an essential element" of the offense initially charged (*id.*) and has denied the prosecution leave to amend that charge by adding a count alleging a lesser-included crime (*id.* at 87)); *Walker v. Commonwealth*, 288 S.W. 3d 729 (Ky. 2009) (at the close of the prosecution case, the defendant moved for a directed verdict on a charge of tampering with evidence; the prosecutor replied that the charge was based on the defendant's having thrown guns away; the judge granted the motion, commenting that he did not recall any evidence to that effect; then, at the close of all evidence, the prosecutor moved for reconsideration of the directed verdict, arguing that the tampering indictment was open-ended and that evidence had been presented that the defendant had disposed of ski masks and clothing bearing on the crime; the judge reinstated the tampering charge and the defendant was convicted on it; the Kentucky Supreme Court holds that the mid-trial directed verdict was an acquittal and that reinstatement of the charge constituted double jeopardy in violation of the Fifth Amendment). *See also, e.g., Deedy v. Suzuki*, 788 Fed. Appx. 549 (9th Cir. 2019) (in the defendant's first jury trial on a charge of second-degree (intentional) murder, both the defense and the prosecution objected to the submission of reckless manslaughter as a lesser included offense and the trial judge agreed, stating in a conference on instructions that "I don't think there's any evidence to support manslaughter"; the jury deadlocked and a mistrial was declared; the Ninth Circuit holds that reprosecution for reckless manslaughter is barred by double jeopardy because the instructional ruling amounted to an acquittal); *Martinez v. Illinois*, 572 U.S. 833, 834, 842 (2014) (per curiam) (the trial judge's grant of defense counsel's motion for "a directed not-guilty verdict" when the state "declined to present any evidence" and instead moved for a continuance after the jury had been empaneled and sworn, "was an acquittal because the court 'acted on its view that the prosecution had failed to prove its case.' . . . And because Martinez was acquitted, the State cannot retry him."). *And see Evans v. Michigan*, 568 U.S. 313, 315-16, 318 (2013) (the trial judge's midtrial entry of a "directed verdict of acquittal" in a jury trial, based upon the judge's "view that the State had not provided sufficient evidence of a particular element of the offense" which "turn[ed] out" not to be "a required element at all," constituted "an acquittal for double jeopardy purposes" and barred a retrial notwithstanding the judge's error: "[A]n acquittal precludes retrial even if it is premised upon an erroneous decision to exclude evidence, . . .; a mistaken understanding of what evidence would suffice to sustain a conviction, . . .; or a 'misconstruction of the statute' defining the requirements to convict, ... In all these circumstances, 'the fact that the acquittal may result from erroneous evidentiary rulings or erroneous interpretations of governing legal principles affects the accuracy of that determination, but it does not alter its essential character.' . . . [O]ur cases have defined an acquittal to encompass any ruling that the prosecution's proof is insufficient to establish criminal liability for an offense."); *State v. Karpov*, 195 Wash. 2d 288, 293, 458 P.3d 1182, 1184-85 (2020) ("A dismissal by a trial judge is a judicial acquittal when it adjudicates the ultimate question of factual guilt or innocence. . . . Thus, when the trial court 'act[s] on its view that the prosecution ha[s] failed to prove its case' and dismisses the case in the defendant's favor, the trial court judicially acquits the defendant. . . . A judicial acquittal triggers the protections of the double jeopardy clauses even when the judge bases the acquittal on an erroneous understanding of the elements of the crime.").

When a jury convicts a defendant only of a lesser-included offense and is silent regarding the offense charged, the verdict constitutes an acquittal of the greater charge and bars reprosecution on it. *Green v. United States*, 355 U.S. 184 (1957); *Price v. Georgia*, 398 U.S. 323 (1970). If the jury returns a verdict stating explicitly that the jurors are unable to agree regarding the offense charged but convicting the defendant of a lesser-included or alternative offense, there is disagreement as to whether reprosecution on the greater charge is permissible. *Compare State v. Martin*, 247 Ariz. 101, 446 P.3d 806 (2019), *and Terry v. Potter*, 111 F.3d 454 (6th Cir. 1997), *with United States v. Bordeaux*, 121 F.3d 1187 (8th Cir. 1997), *and Cleary v. State*, 23 N.E.3d 664 (Ind. 2015). *And see United States v. Candelario-Santana*, 977 F.3d 146, 155, 156 (1st Cir. 2020) (alternative ground) ("We do not disagree with the district court's conclusion that, if the jury truly was 'clear and deliberate in expressing its deadlock' with respect to the death penalty, double jeopardy would not bar the government from seeking the death penalty upon retrial. We are not convinced, however, that the record so clearly supports the government's position that the jury was hopelessly deadlocked on the question of death. [It could be that, "by instructing the jury repeatedly as to the consequences of deadlock (namely, that it would result in an imposition of a life sentence), the district court reduced the jury's choice to a binary one – i.e., to either death or life in prison – and that any decision by the jury other than a unanimous verdict for death acquitted Candelario of the death penalty."] We therefore cannot say that the district court properly concluded that the original penalty-phase jury was deadlocked. . . . Consequently, the government is now barred from seeking the death penalty a second time.").

Unlike jury trials, in which a verdict of "not guilty" obviously is an "acquittal" for purposes of double jeopardy (*Fong Foo v. United States,* 369 U.S. 141 (1962) (per curiam)), there may be questions whether a dismissal in a bench trial constituted an acquittal so as to bar reprosecution (*see, e.g., Smalis v. Pennsylvania,* 476 U.S. 140 (1986)). The rule (which also applies to ambiguous rulings terminating a jury trial) is that "'the trial judge's characterization of his own action cannot control the classification of the action'" (*United States v. Scott, supra,* 437 U.S. at 96 (quoting *United States v. Jorn,* 400 U.S. 470, 478 n.7 (1971) (plurality opinion))). Instead, the test is whether "'the ruling of the judge, whatever its label, actually represents a resolution [in the [defendant's] . . . favor], correct or not, of some or all of the factual elements of the offense charged'" (*United States v. Scott, supra,* 437 U.S. at 97). *See, e.g., Sanabria v. United States,* 437 U.S. 54 (1978); *Martinez v. Illinois, supra,* 572 U.S. at 842.

Although double jeopardy issues ordinarily arise when the government seeks to prosecute an individual after a first trial has concluded (either in a verdict or a mistrial), double jeopardy protections also may come into play if a trial judge grants a mid-trial judgment of acquittal on one or more counts of the charging paper and is inclined to reconsider that ruling after the defense case has already commenced and the defense has begun presenting evidence. If the judge's ruling qualifies as a "judgment of acquittal" for double jeopardy purposes (under the test described in the preceding paragraph) and if state law does not expressly authorize judicial reconsideration of such a ruling (and – arguably – if, in addition, the judge does not reserve the right to reconsider or indicate that the ruling is not final), double jeopardy protections bar the trial judge from reconsidering the ruling. *Smith v. Massachusetts,* 543 U.S. 462, 473-74 (2005). *Compare Price v. Vincent,* 538 U.S. 634 (2003); *Schiro v. Farley,* 510 U.S. 222 (1994).

When a jury convicts a defendant but the trial judge enters a judgment in the defendant's favor N.O.V. (see § 47.2 subdivision (1) *infra*), that judgment does not constitute an acquittal for purposes of the rules summarized in this section even if the judge labels it an "acquittal": the prosecution may appeal it (*see United States v. Wilson,* 420 U.S. 332 (1975), and *e.g., United States v. Filer,* 56 F.4th 421 (7th Cir. 2022); *United States v. Jabar,* 19 F.4th 66 (2d Cir. 2021); *United States v. Rafiekian,* 991 F.3d 529 (4th Cir. 2021)) notwithstanding the rule barring prosecutorial appeal of an acquittal in a bench trial (*see United States v. Martin Linen Supply Co., supra*).

20.8.4. *Reprosecution After Conviction in the First Trial*

Once convicted, a defendant may not be reprosecuted for the same offense. *E.g., Brown v. Ohio,* 432 U.S. 161 (1977); *Harris v. Oklahoma,* 433 U.S. 682 (1977) (per curiam). This rule is said not to preclude a second prosecution in certain "special circumstances" (*Ricketts v. Adamson*, 483 U.S. 1, 8 (1987)). Three such circumstances recognized by the caselaw are: (i) when "the State is unable to proceed on the [second] . . . charge at the outset because the . . . facts necessary to sustain that charge have not occurred or have not been discovered despite the exercise of due diligence" (*Brown v. Ohio, supra*, 432 U.S. at 169 n.7 (dictum); *see Garrett v. United States, supra*, 471 U.S. at 789-92); (ii) when the prosecution makes multiple charges in the alternative at the outset and the defendant elects to obtain a disposition of some of them prior to the others (*Jeffers v. United States,* 432 U.S. 137, 151-54 (1977); *see Ohio v. Johnson*, 467 U.S. 493 (1984)); and (iii) when the conviction on the earlier charges was the result of a plea agreement that the defendant later violates (*Ricketts v. Adamson, supra,* 483 U.S. at 8-12).

Double jeopardy guarantees also do not bar reprosecution of a previously convicted defendant if the defendant succeeded in getting the first conviction set aside by a post-trial motion, an appeal, or postconviction proceedings. *See, e.g., Smith v. United States*, 143 S. Ct. 1594 (2023); *Bravo-Fernandez v. United States*, 580 U.S. 5 (2016); *United States v. Tateo,* 377 U.S. 463, 465-68 (1964); *United States v. Serrano,* 856 F.3d 210 (2d Cir. 2017). However, retrial will be barred even after a conviction has been set aside if the basis for that action was a finding by either the trial court or an appellate court that the evidence was insufficient to support the conviction. *Hudson v. Louisiana,* 450 U.S. 40 (1981); *Burks v. United States,* 437 U.S. 1 (1978); *Monge v. California,* 524 U.S. 721, 729 (1998) (dictum). *But see Tibbs v. Florida,* 457 U.S. 31 (1982) (reprosecution is permissible if the basis for reversal was not insufficiency of the evidence but rather that the appellate court, sitting as a "thirteenth juror," found the conviction to be "against the weight of the evidence" [see § 47.3 subdivision (2) *infra*]).

20.8.5. *Reprosecution After the First Trial Ends in a Mistrial*

Double jeopardy guarantees will not bar reprosecution if the first trial ended in a mistrial, at the request of, or with the acquiescence of, the defendant (*United States v. Dinitz,* 424 U.S. 600 (1976)), except when the defendant's request for the mistrial was occasioned by prosecutorial misconduct "intended to 'goad' the [defendant] into moving for a mistrial" (*Oregon v. Kennedy,* 456 U.S. 667, 676 (1982) (dictum); *compare United States v. Foster*, 945 F.3d 470 (6th Cir. 2019), *with State v. Parker*, 391 S.C. 606, 707 S.E.2d 799 (2011)).

A mistrial declared without the defendant's assent will bar reprosecution (*see, e.g., Downum v. United States,* 372 U.S. 734 (1963); *United States v. Jorn,* 400 U.S. 470 (1971); *State v. Stephenson*, 307 Or. App. 189, 476 P.3d 527 (2020); *State v. Fennell*, 431 Md. 500, 66 A.3d 630 (2013); *Commonwealth v. Balog*, 395 Pa. Super. 158, 576 A.2d 1092 (1990)), except when the mistrial was declared under circumstances of "manifest necessity" (*see, e.g., Illinois v. Somerville,* 410 U.S. 458 (1973); *Arizona v. Washington,* 434 U.S. 497 (1978); *Renico v. Lett,* 559 U.S. 766, 773-75 (2010); *Blueford v. Arkansas, supra,* 566 U.S. at 609-10). Under ordinary circumstances, a hung jury constitutes "manifest necessity" for this purpose. *Richardson v. United States,* 468 U.S. 317 (1984). See §§ 40.8.4.2, 45.4 *infra*. But if the prosecution voluntarily dismisses the charges following a hung-jury mistrial, double jeopardy does bar reprosecution, even though the prosecutor's stated reason for the dismissal is the jury's failure to agree. *State v. Courtney,* 372 N.C. 458, 831 S.E.2d 260 (2019). *Compare Seay v. Cannon,* 927 F.3d 776, 779 (4th Cir. 2019) ("[W]e conclude that the government failed to satisfy its high burden of showing manifest necessity for a mistrial. The record shows that the government allowed the jury to be empaneled knowing that the crucial witness might not appear to testify. Additionally, the state trial court failed to consider possible alternatives to granting the government's mistrial motion."); *Gouveia v. Espinda*, 926 F.3d 1102, 1113 (9th Cir. 2019) (the grant of a mistrial on the prosecutor's motion when members of the jury, after having deliberated and reached a verdict but before announcing it, expressed fear for their safety because of a "scary looking man" on the prosecution's side of the courtroom was not justified by "manifest necessity" and therefore barred retrial: "'A trial court should consider and correctly evaluate the alternatives to a mistrial" and, "once the court considers the alternatives, it should adopt one if less drastic and less harmful to the defendant's rights than a mistrial.'"); *Mansfield v. State*, 422 Md. 269, 290-93, 29 A.3d 569, 581-83 (2011) (the judge's declaration of a mistrial at the close of evidence in a bench trial – based on her knowledge of the defendant's having been twice previously convicted of similar crimes, once in a jury trial over which the judge herself presided – was not justified by a "manifest necessity," and retrial therefore was barred by double jeopardy, because the judge possessed this knowledge before jeopardy attached and, "rather than proceeding to try the petitioner, knowing what she did of his criminal history, the trial judge should have recused herself"); *In the Matter of McNair v. McNamara*, 206 A.D.3d 1689, 1691, 169 N.Y.S.3d 774, 777 (N.Y. App. Div., 4th Dept. 2022) ("there was no manifest necessity for the mistrial, and the court therefore abused its discretion in granting it sua sponte" based on the judge's inability to come to court due to apparent COVID symptoms until testing negative or recovering: "The record establishes that the court did not consider the alternatives to a mistrial, such as a continuance . . . or substitution of another judge"); *In re Morris v. Livote*, 105 A.D.3d 43, 47, 962 N.Y.S.2d 59, 62 (N.Y. App. Div., 1st Dept. 2013) (double jeopardy barred a retrial after the first trial ended with the judge's granting the prosecution's motion for a mistrial based on "defense counsel's improper questioning" of a prosecution witness: "Although defense counsel's disregard of the court's instructions was blameworthy and understandably angered the court, the [defense] cross-examination did not rise to the level of the gross misconduct displayed in cases in which retrial was permitted."); *Commonwealth v. Goods*, 2021 PA Super 206, 265 A.3d 662, 673 (Pa. Super. 2021) (defense counsel's asking two improper questions of a prosecution witness did not constitute "manifest necessity"; therefore, the trial court's granting of the prosecution's motion for a mistrial triggered a double-jeopardy bar to the defendant's retrial).

20.8.6. *Collateral Estoppel*

The Supreme Court has held that the federal Fifth Amendment embodies a "rule of collateral estoppel" (often called "issue preclusion") in criminal cases (*Yeager v. United States*, 557 U.S. 110, 119-20 & n.4 (2009); *Ashe v. Swenson,* 397 U.S. 436, 444 (1970)), so that, following acquittal at a first trial, a criminal defendant may not be retried for any offense – whether or not it is the "same offense" within the definition of § 20.8.2.2 *supra* – if conviction of the offense requires proof of facts that are inconsistent with the facts established in the accused's favor by his or her prior acquittal (*e.g., Yeager v. United States, supra,* 557 U.S. at 119-20; *Simpson v. Florida,* 403 U.S. 384 (1971) (per curiam); *Harris v. Washington,* 404 U.S. 55 (1971) (per curiam); *Turner v. Arkansas,* 407 U.S. 366 (1972) (per curiam); *Wilkinson v. Gingrich*, 806 F.3d 511, 516-20 (9th Cir. 2015). "For . . . [the] doctrine [of collateral estoppel] to apply . . . , an issue of ultimate fact decided in . . . [the defendant's] favor through his acquittal must be fatal to the subsequent prosecution." *United States v. Inman*, 39 F.4th 357, 359 (6th Cir. 2022). *See, e.g.,* *Ferrell v. State*, 318 Md. 235, 567 A.2d 937 (1990) ("[U]nder both the Fifth Amendment [to the federal Constitution] and Maryland common law, it is established that the doctrine of collateral estoppel is embodied in the double jeopardy prohibition. *Id.* at 241, 567 A.2d at 940. "[T]he critical questions in applying collateral estoppel are not whether the victim is the same or whether each offense is the same. The important questions are whether the offense for which the defendant was earlier acquitted, and the offense for which he is being retried, each involved a common issue of ultimate fact, and whether that issue was resolved in the defendant's favor at the earlier trial. *Id.* at 243, 567 A.2d at 941. "[I]n determining whether the State at a subsequent trial is attempting to relitigate an issue which was resolved in the defendant's favor at an earlier trial, a court must realistically look at the record of the earlier trial, including the pleadings, the evidence, the prosecution's theory, the disputed issues, and the jury instructions. A court should not, as did the trial court in the instant case, ignore the evidence and disputed issues at the earlier trial and speculate that the jury's acquittal might have been based on a theory having nothing to do with the evidence and issues presented to the jury. ¶ Moreover, in reviewing the earlier trial to determine the jury's basis for the acquittal, a court 'should not strain to dream up hypertechnical and unrealistic grounds on which the previous verdict might conceivably have rested.'" *Id.* at 245, 567 A.2d at 942.); *People v. Terrance*, 2019 WL 1049701 (Mich. App. 2019) ("Defendant was tried before a jury on charges of first-degree premeditated murder and first-degree felony murder. The predicate felony for the felony-murder charge was torture, though it was not charged as a separate individual crime. The jury was instructed on second-degree murder as a lesser included offense for both charges. After two days of deliberation, the jury acquitted defendant of first-degree murder and the lesser offense of second-degree murder. The jury was unable, however, to reach a verdict on the felony-murder charge. ¶ . . . The prosecutor then charged defendant with torture, and defendant . . . moved to dismiss, arguing that the charge constituted (1) a violation of double jeopardy . . . . *Id.* at *1-*2. "The Double Jeopardy Clause includes the concept of issue preclusion, also known as collateral estoppel." *Id.* at *2. "[T]he jury [in the first trial] was asked to find that defendant murdered Tillman . . . as the final act of an assault in which he also inflicted a severe beating and that the extensive beating and suffocation constituted the crime of torture. The prosecution emphasized that point during closing argument, referring to the beating and killing as a single attack . . . Throughout the trial, the prosecution's evidence and argument were directed toward a finding that defendant was the victim's sole assailant, that the assault was a continuous or near-continuous event, beginning with a beating and culminating in defendant suffocating the victim. The defense asserted that defendant was not the party responsible for either the beating or the murder. The question, therefore, as presented by both sides, was whether defendant was the victim's assailant . . . ; neither side suggested that defendant committed only the murder or only the beating. Accordingly, we conclude that the prosecution's claim that defendant tortured the victim on that day is barred under the doctrine of issue preclusion by the jury's verdict acquitting defendant of murder." *Id.*); *Ex Parte Watkins*, 73 S.W.3d 264, 265 (Tex. Crim. App. 2002) ("[T]he doctrine of collateral estoppel applies in a subsequent prosecution of . . . [a defendant] for attempted capital murder or attempted murder of his wife's lover, when a prior jury found that appellant killed his wife 'in sudden passion' during the same transaction. . . . [T]hough . . . [collateral estoppel] does not preclude the State from prosecuting the charged offenses . . . [, the State is precluded from re-litigating the issue of sudden passion in the second trial."); *Ex parte Taylor*, 101 S.W.3d 434, 443 (Tex. Crim. App. 2002) (en banc) (two passengers were killed when a car driven by the defendant collided with an oncoming vehicle; the prosecution first charged the defendant with intoxication manslaughter based on alcohol inebriation, and a jury acquitted him of that charge; the prosecution then charged him with intoxication manslaughter of the other passenger based on inebriation either by marijuana alone or by marijuana and alcohol; a divided Texas Court of Criminal Appeals examines the evidentiary record of the first trial and finds that "[t]he *source* of . . . [the defendant's] intoxication was not a disputed issue in the first trial. It was only the more general issue of intoxication was he or wasn't he that was disputed, and upon this issue, the . . . [defendant] prevailed"; it accordingly holds that collateral estoppel bars the second prosecution); *Commonwealth v. States*, 595 Pa. 453, 938 A.2d 1016 (2007) (a defendant's bench trial on charges of causing an accident involving death while not properly licensed was conducted simultaneously with a jury trial on charges of homicide by vehicle, homicide by vehicle while driving under the influence of alcohol, and DWI; the trial judge acquitted the defendant of the license-violation charges, expressly finding that the prosecution had failed to prove that the defendant was the driver of the vehicle; the jury hung on all other charges; a divided Pennsylvania Supreme Court holds that collateral estoppel based upon the judge's finding bars the prosecution from retrying the defendant on any of the charges on which the jury deadlocked; *compare Commonwealth v. Jordan*, 256 A.3d 1094, 1096 (Pa. 2021) ("a defendant who elects to proceed with a simultaneous jury and bench trial during aa defendant who elects to proceed with a simultaneous jury and bench trial during a single prosecution is subjected to only one trial and therefore double jeopardy and collateral estoppel do not apply to preclude the guilty verdict rendered by the judge."). *Compare Schiro v. Farley*, 510 U.S. 222, 232-36 (1994), *and Dowling v. United States*, 493 U.S. 342, 350-52 (1990). Conviction of a lesser included offense or degree of the offense almost certainly constitutes an implicit acquittal of the greater offense or degree for this purpose (*Currier v. Virginia*, 138 S. Ct. 2144, 2150 (2018) (dictum)), just as it does for the purpose of the rule barring reprosecution for the "same offense" following an acquittal (*Price v. Georgia,* 398 U.S. 323 (1970); *De Mino v. New York,* 404 U.S. 1035 (1972) (per curiam)). *Compare Yeager v. United States*, *supra*, 557 U.S. at 121-23 (when a jury acquits a defendant on some counts of a multi-count indictment and hangs on others that require a finding of the same "critical issue of ultimate fact" as "an essential element," the prosecution is barred from retrying the defendant on the counts on which the jury hung; "collateral estoppel" or "issue-preclusion analysis" cannot ascribe significance to a jury's inability to reach a verdict on the latter counts "[b]ecause a jury speaks only through its verdict" and thus "there is no way to decipher what a hung count represents"; "To identify what a jury necessarily determined at trial, courts should scrutinize a jury's decisions, not its failures to decide."), *and Roesser v. State*, 294 Ga. 295, 295, 298, 300, 751 S.E.2d 297, 297, 299, 301 (2013) (applying *Yeager v. United States, supra*, to hold that collateral estoppel barred retrial of the defendant for voluntary manslaughter, following a trial in which the jury acquitted the defendant of "malice murder, felony murder, and aggravated assault but was unable to reach a verdict on the lesser included offense of voluntary manslaughter"; "the jury in acquitting Roesser of [the higher counts] . . . necessarily determined that Roesser acted in self-defense and . . . this issue of ultimate fact constitutes a critical element of voluntary manslaughter"), *and In re Moi*, 184 Wash. 2d 575, 577, 580, 360 P.3d 811, 812, 813 (2015) (the doctrine of collateral estoppel barred retrial of the defendant for murder after the jury in the first trial "was unable to reach a verdict on the murder charge" and "[b]ased on the same evidence, Moi was acquitted [in a concurrent bench trial] of unlawful possession of the gun" that was used to commit the murder, and "the State's theory of the case [in the murder retrial] was that he shot the victim with . . . [the] gun he was [previously] acquitted of possessing"), *with*

Bravo-Fernandez v. United States, 580 U.S. 5, 8-9 (2016) (if "a jury returns inconsistent verdicts, convicting on one count and acquitting on another count, where both counts turn on the very same issue of ultimate fact," then the doctrine of "issue preclusion does not apply" because of the rule of *United States v. Powell*, 469 U.S. 57 (1984), which respects both verdicts by allowing the conviction to stand but forbidding reprosecution on the acquittal charge; the *Powell* rule bars issue preclusion even if "the guilty verdicts were vacated on appeal because of error in the judge's instructions unrelated to the verdicts' inconsistency"; the scenario in *Yeager v. United States*, *supra* – where "issue preclusion attend[s] a jury's acquittal verdict if the same jury in the same proceeding fails to reach a verdict on a different count turning on the same critical issue" – differs from the inconsistent-verdict situation because "'there is no way to decipher what a hung count represents'" and "a jury's failure to decide 'has no place in the issue-preclusion analysis'"), *and Bobby v. Bies*, 556 U.S. 825, 835 (2009) (collateral estoppel does not apply to "a subsidiary finding that, standing alone, is not outcome determinative" but does apply to "a determination necessary to the bottom-line judgment").

In *Currier v. Virginia*, 138 S. Ct. 2144 (2018), a fractured Supreme Court revisited *Ashe*. Five Justices subscribed to an opinion which said that the *Ashe* "test is a demanding one. *Ashe* forbids a second trial only if to secure a conviction the prosecution must prevail on an issue the jury necessarily resolved in the defendant's favor in the first trial. . . . A second trial 'is not precluded simply because it is unlikely – or even very unlikely – that the original jury acquitted without finding the fact in question.' . . . To say that the second trial is tantamount to a trial of the same offense as the first and thus forbidden by the Double Jeopardy Clause, we must be able to say that 'it would have been *irrational* for the jury' in the first trial to acquit without finding in the defendant's favor on a fact essential to a conviction in the second." (*Currier*, 138 S. Ct. at 2150). Technically, this is dictum because Currier's double-jeopardy claim was rejected on the ground that by joining the prosecution in a request for severance of two charges, he had waived any double-jeopardy claim he might have had against a second prosecution following acquittal in the first. ("[C]onsenting to two trials when one would have avoided a double jeopardy problem precludes any constitutional violation associated with holding a second trial." *Id.* at 2151.) But it is dictum in command mode. A four-Justice plurality then proceeded to write an extended critique of the principle of issue preclusion in criminal cases, suggesting that *Ashe* would be in trouble if the plurality could gain a fifth vote. Justice Kennedy, the potential fifth vote, abstained from joining this critique; and four dissenting Justices disagreed with both the critique and the majority's holding that Currier had waived his double-jeopardy rights. Counsel will need to be on the *qui vive* for ensuing chapters in the *Ashe* saga.

But whether or not *Ashe* survives as federal constitutional law, a jurisdiction's statutory or common-law doctrines of collateral estoppel will continue in many circumstances to protect defendants from relitigation of issues previously resolved in their favor. *See, e.g., United States v. Arterbury*, 961 F.3d 1095 (10th Cir. 2020); *Crosby-Garbotz v. Fell, Judge Pro Tempore of the Superior Court in and for the County of Pima*, 246 Ariz. 54, 434 P.3d 143 (2019) (holding that "issue preclusion may apply in a criminal proceeding when an issue of fact was previously adjudicated in a dependency proceeding and the other elements of preclusion are met"); *Mason v. State,* 361 Ark. 357, 206 S.W.3d 869 (2005); *Commonwealth v. Williams*, 431 Mass. 71, 725 N.E.2d 217 (2000); *State v. Butler*, 505 N.W.2d 806 (Iowa 1993); *People v. Acevedo,* 69 N.Y.2d 478, 508 N.E.2d 665, 515 N.Y.S.2d 753 (1987); *Harris v. State*, 193 Ga. 109, 17 S.E.2d 573

(1941). Similarly, state-law doctrines of *res judicata* (*see, e.g., Webster v. State*, 376 P.3d 488 (Wyo. 2016); *Highsmith v. Commonwealth*, 25 Va. App. 434, 489 S.E.2d 239 (1997); *State v. Stahley*, 12 Or. App. 579, 507 P.2d 1159 (1973)) and of finality of judgments or law of the case (*see, e.g., State v. Jackson*, 306 So.3d 936 (Fla. 2020); *Okafor v. State*, 306 So.3d 930 (Fla. 2020)) will remain available to bar successive prosecutions in some situations, regardless of the ultimate fate of *Ashe*.

For an argument that principles of collateral estoppel together with other components of double-jeopardy theory outlaw the prosecutorial practice of pursuing convictions of two or more individuals in separate trials on the theory that each alone is the perpetrator of a crime which was committed by a single person, *see* Vedan Anthony-North, Note, *Doubling Down: Inconsistent Prosecutions, Capital Punishment, and Double Jeopardy*, 97 N.Y.U. L. Rev. 235 (2022).

A prosecutor's attempt to invoke collateral estoppel against a criminal defendant is a quite different matter and should always be objected to. *See United States v. Pelullo*, 14 F.3d 881 (3d Cir. 1994); *United States v. Gallardo-Mendez*, 150 F.3d 1240 (10th Cir. 1998); *Allen v. State*, 423 Md. 208, 31 A.3d 476 (2011); *People v. Morrison*, 156 A.D.3d 126, 130, 66 N.Y.S.3d 682, 685-86 (N.Y. App. Div., 3d Dep't 2017) (rejecting the prosecution's argument that it could invoke collateral estoppel to instruct a Grand Jury that an element of the crime had already been determined by a jury in the defendant's prior trial on a related charge for the same crime; "Applying collateral estoppel in the strategic, prosecutorial manner attempted here – in an effort to dispense with proof of the elements of a class A–1 felony that carries a potential life sentence . . . – undermines, if not violates, fundamental principles of due process and the presumption of innocence, among others . . . . These countervailing constitutional protections '"outweigh the otherwise sound reasons for preventing repetitive litigation"' in this manner . . . . ¶ While the People argue that their offensive use of collateral estoppel is fair play, in that had defendant been acquitted of attempted murder, he would defensively rely on collateral estoppel principles to argue against a subsequent murder trial, this analysis overlooks the obvious and critical difference between an accused's defensive use of this doctrine and a prosecutor's strategic use of it against an accused. An accused's defensive invocation of this doctrine implicates and protects constitutional rights – to a jury trial, to present a defense, to due process and to not be placed twice in jeopardy, among others – whereas the People's affirmative use is for matters of expediency and economy and lacks a constitutional imperative . . . ."); *see also id.* at 130 n.*, 66 N.Y.S.3d at 686 n.1 (citing decisions by "other states' high courts" that support the "conclusion that the People's use of collateral estoppel is rarely, if ever, permitted").

20.8.7. *Reprosecution by a Different Sovereign*

The double jeopardy clause does not bar successive prosecutions by different sovereigns. So, for example, a defendant convicted of bank robbery in a state court may subsequently be prosecuted for federal bank robbery of the same bank. *See, e.g., Abbate v. United States,* 359 U.S. 187 (1959); *United States v. Wheeler,* 435 U.S. 313 (1978); *Gamble v. United States*, 139 S. Ct. 1960 (2019); *Puerto Rico v. Sanchez Valle*, 579 U.S. 59, 66-69 (2016) (dictum). Similarly, when two different States are in a position to prosecute a defendant for the same or closely related conduct, the separate prosecutions do not violate the Fifth Amendment. *Heath v. Alabama,* 474 U.S. 82 (1985). (Another route to the same result in the case of successive prosecutions by the federal government and a Native American tribe was plowed in *Denezpi v. United States*, 142 S. Ct. 1838 (2022) ("Because the sovereign source of a law is an inherent and distinctive feature of the law itself, an offense defined by one sovereign is necessarily a different offense from that of another sovereign. . . . That means that the two offenses can be separately prosecuted without offending the Double Jeopardy Clause –even if they have identical elements and could not be separately prosecuted if enacted by a single sovereign.").) The "two sovereignties" principle does not, however, permit successive prosecutions by a state and its political subdivisions (for example, municipalities); these are barred by double jeopardy whenever successive prosecutions by the same prosecuting agency would be (*Waller v. Florida,* 397 U.S. 387 (1970); *United States v. Wheeler, supra,* 435 U.S. at 318-22 (dictum); *Puerto Rico v. Sanchez Valle, supra,* 579 U.S. at 71).

As a matter of executive policy, the federal Government seldom prosecutes persons previously convicted or acquitted of state crimes based on the same conduct. *See Thompson v. United States*, 444 U.S. 248 (1980) (per curiam):

> "The Department of Justice has a firmly established policy, known as the 'Petite' policy, under which United States Attorneys are forbidden to prosecute any person for allegedly criminal behavior if the alleged criminality was an ingredient of a previous state prosecution against that person. An exception is made only if the federal prosecution is specifically authorized in advance by the Department itself, upon a finding that the prosecution will serve 'compelling interests of federal law enforcement.'" (*Id.* at 248.)

20.9. ***Challenges to the Indictment or Information on the Ground of Unconstitutionality of the Statute on which the Charges Are Based***

A pretrial motion to dismiss a charging paper can be based on the claim that the statute grounding the charges is unconstitutional on its face or – in some jurisdictions – that the statute is unconstitutional as applied to the facts alleged. *See, e.g.,* WEST'S ANN. IND. CODE § 35-34-1-6(a)(3); *United States v. L. Cohen Grocery Co*, 255 U.S. 81 (1921) (facial challenge); *United States v. Rahimi*, 59 F.4th 163 (5th Cir. 2023) (facial challenge); *People v. Counterman*, 497 P.3d 1039 (Colo. App. 2021) (deciding the merits of a claim raised by a pretrial motion to dismiss a charge of stalking (serious emotional distress) on the ground that it violates the First Amendment but upholding the statute), *rev'd sub. nom. Counterman v. Colorado*, 2023 WL 4187751 (U.S. 2023) (holding the statute unconstitutional for lack of a *mens rea* element); *State v. Small*, 162 Ohio App. 3d 375, 833 N.E.2d 774 (2005) (as-applied challenge); *People v. Redwood*, 335 Ill. App. 3d 189, 780 N.E.2d 760, 269 Ill. Dec. 288 (2002) (overbreadth-as-applied-challenge: "The offense of disorderly conduct is broadly defined. . . . ¶ Freedom of speech is a fundamental right protected from invasion by the state by the fourteenth amendment. . . . A statute that punishes spoken words alone . . . cannot withstand constitutional attack unless it cannot be applied to speech protected by the first and fourteenth amendments, even if the speech punished is vulgar or offensive. . . . Thus, . . . [the disorderly-conduct statute] may only be applied in this case if the words used are 'fighting words.' . . . ¶ A trial court may dismiss a charge in a criminal case on the grounds that the charge does not state an offense. . . . ." *Id.* at 192, 780 N.E.2d at 762-63, 269 Ill. Dec. at 290-91. "Confining our analysis to the charging instruments, as we must on review of a judgment dismissing for failure to state a crime, we find the comment by defendant did not rise to the level of "fighting words," because the comment did not contain an explicit or implied threat. Because the only conduct alleged to have violated the statute was the use of these words, and because the "fighting words" requirement has not been met, the information charging defendant with disorderly conduct fails to state an offense." *Id.* at 194-95, 195-96, 780 N.E.2d at 765, 269 Ill. Dec. at 293.); *and see State v. Kay Distributing Co., Inc*, 110 Wis. 2d 29, 32, 327 N.W.2d 188, 191 (Wis. App. 1982) (reviewing and reversing on the merits the dismissal of two counts of a complaint on the ground of statutory vagueness: "The state initially argues that the trial court prematurely considered the question of whether . . .[the challenged statute] is unconstitutionally vague because there is no factual record on which to base a determination whether Kay had notice that its conduct was within the statute's prohibitions. We disagree. A statute challenged on vagueness grounds for lack of notice must be examined in light of the conduct with which the defendant is charged."); *State v. Moeller*, 105 Or. App. 434, 806 P.2d 130 (1991) (superseded by statute amending the substantive provision involved) (affirming a trial court order sustaining a demurrer to an indictment which, in addition to charging that the defendants engaged in drug offenses, alleged that the offenses occurred "as a part of a drug cultivation, manufacture or delivery scheme or network" – language copying a guidelines rule (see § *infra*) providing for sentencing enhancement: the Court of Appeals finds the guidelines language void for vagueness and holds that a demurrer is an appropriate procedure for challenging the constitutionality of an enhancement allegation in an indictment); *cf. State v. Metzinger*, 456 S.W.3d 84 (Mo. App. 2015) (upholding dismissal of a prosecution for online terroristic threats on the ground that the defendant's tweets – whose contents were not specified in the information but were specified in the prosecution's answer to the motion to dismiss – were not true threats punishable consistently with the First Amendment); *People v. Sovey*, 77 Misc. 3d 518, 179 N.Y.S.3d 867 (N.Y. Sup. Ct., N.Y. Cty. 2022) (entertaining the defendant's motion to dismiss an indictment on the ground of unconstitutionality of the underlying statute, the court orders a suppression hearing to determine whether there was probable cause for the defendant's arrest; at this hearing, the defendant will have the burden of establishing the factual circumstances that render the statute unconstitutional as applied, thereby laying the foundation for dismissal).

In federal practice, claims of facial unconstitutionality are appropriately addressed on a motion to dismiss but claims of unconstitutionality as applied are not. *United States v. Petrillo*, 332 U.S. 1 (1937); *but cf. United States v. Pearl*, 324 F.3d 310 (10th Cir. 2003) (a motion to dismiss an indictment on grounds of unconstitutional overbreadth of the statutory language sufficed to preserve for appeal the defendant's contention that he could not be convicted under jury instructions that permitted a conviction to be based on the overbroad terminology).

As a matter of strategy, the question whether to challenge the constitutionality of the proscriptive statute before trial turns largely on the question whether and at what later stages the jurisdiction permits the same challenge to be raised. If failure to raise it before trial forfeits the claim, the answer is obvious. If the defendant has no plausible defense at trial other than the claim that the statute is unconstitutional, and if the jurisdiction allows a defendant to move to dismiss the charges for unconstitutionality, plead guilty conditionally (see § 14.8 second paragraph *supra*), and obtain appellate review of the denial of the motion (*compare United States v. Rahimi, supra, and State v. White*, 545 N.W.2d 552, 554 (Iowa 1996), allowing such a procedure where the statute is challenged on its face, *with United States v. Turner*, 842 F.3d 602

(8th Cir. 2016), *and United States v. Pope*, 613 F.3d 1255 (10th Cir. 2010), disallowing the procedure in the case of an as-applied challenge), this procedure will ordinarily offer the quickest and least costly way to get a final ruling resolving the case. If a midtrial motion in a jury trial is available (*see, e.g., State v. Woodard*, 2017 WL 2590216 (Tenn. Crim. App. 2017) (rejecting "the State's claim that the defendant has waived plenary review of her constitutional challenges by failing to challenge the constitutionality of the statute prior to her trial" (*id.* at *6), the court holds that "[b]y its plain language, [Tennessee Criminal] Rule 12 permits claims of a lack of jurisdiction to be raised at any time. . . . A claim that the proscriptive statute is facially unconstitutional amounts to a claim that the trial court lacks jurisdiction to impose a conviction under the statute. . . . Consequently, a *facial constitutional challenge* to the *proscriptive* statute is not subject to the waiver provision of Rule 12." *Id.* at *10.); *Smith v. State*, 194 N.E.3d 118 (Ind. App. 2022) (in reviewing a trial court's order denying a pretrial motion to dismiss an information, the court of appeals declines to reach a potential challenge to the proscriptive statute as applied: although § 35-34-1-6(a)(3) of the Indiana Code, *supra*, permits "a motion to dismiss . . . [to] be made or renewed at any time before or during trial" (*id.* at 125), a pretrial motion "is an inappropriate forum for adjudicating factual questions" (*id.* at 130), and a motion challenging the constitutionality of a statute as applied to the defendant's conduct should be made during trial)), such a motion offers the distinct advantage of disabling the prosecution from appealing a ruling in defendant's favor, both as a matter of state law in most jurisdictions (*see, e.g., State v. Wright*, 91 Mont. 427, 8 P.2d 646 (1932)) and because a prosecution appeal from such a ruling would be barred by double-jeopardy doctrine (*see United States v. Sisson*, 399 U.S. 267 (1970); *cf. Sanabria v. United States*, 437 U.S. 54 (1978)). If the only available alternative to a pretrial motion is a postconviction motion in bar – or in arrest of judgment or for dismissal after verdict – (see § 47.2 subdivision (3) *infra*), the pretrial motion will usually be preferable, because the prosecution can obtain appellate review of a ruling granting the motion at either stage. *See, e.g., United States v. Vuitch*, 402 U.S. 62 (1971) (pretrial motion); *State v. Arrington*, 74 S.3d 482 (Ala. Crim. App. 2011) (motion for judgment of acquittal NOV); and see §§ 17.5.2, 20.8.2.1, 20.8.3 last paragraph *supra*.

20.10. *Misjoinder*

State statutes, rules of court, and common-law doctrines restrict the circumstances under which (a) a single charging paper may charge more than one offense against a single defendant and (b) a single charging paper may charge an offense or offenses against more than one defendant. In some jurisdictions a separate bill of indictment is returned for each offense charged, even though several charges are based on the same event or episode (for example, housebreaking, larceny, receiving, and conspiracy). Other jurisdictions permit the joinder of any number of separate charges in a single charging paper (usually in separate paragraphs, or "counts") if they are based on the same transaction or series of transactions or are part of a "common plan" or "common scheme" by the defendant or if the charges, although based on distinct transactions, are legally the same or similar (for example, housebreaking on May 5 and housebreaking on June 12). More than one defendant may usually be joined if all were involved in the criminal transaction, whether or not conspiracy is alleged.

The usual remedy for misjoinder (or for prejudicial joinder) is severance of the charges for trial. See generally Chapter 23 *infra* and particularly § 23.3. In some jurisdictions, however, charging papers that misjoin offenses or defendants are subject to dismissal on that ground. In researching local law on the question, counsel should keep in mind the possible contention that under a statute permitting joinder in specified circumstances (for example, "common scheme"), a charging paper is defective for misjoinder if it fails to *expressly* allege facts supporting an inference that the specified circumstances ("common scheme") exist. These allegations are frequently omitted, even in traditional forms of charging papers. Another question common under many of the joinder statutes is whether things joinable to joinable things are thereby joinable to each other; that is, whether, under a statute that allows joinder of (a) different offenses arising out of one transaction and (b) the same or similar offenses arising out of different transactions, an indictment may charge: (1) housebreaking and (2) larceny, both on May 5, *plus* (3) housebreaking and (4) arson, both on June 12. The statutes are full of grounds for legal argument, and they should be read with a critical eye.

Chapter 21

Removing the Case from the Criminal Court's Docket:
Motions for Diversion, ACD, or Stetting; Transfer to Juvenile Court

A. *Motions for Diversion, ACD, Stetting*

21.1. *The Nature of the Motion; Defense Counsel's Responsibilities*

As noted in §§ 2.3.6 and 8.2.2 *supra*, many localities have more or less formal procedures for "diverting" criminal cases out of the system. Such diversion procedures go by different names in different jurisdictions (including "adjournment in contemplation of dismissal" ("ACD") and "stetting"). *See, e.g.*, KY. RULE CRIM. PRO. 8.04 *and* http://courts.ky.gov/courtprograms/pretrialservices/Pages/PretrialDiversion.aspx ("pretrial diversion" in misdemeanors and criminal violations); N.J. STAT. ANN. § 2C:43-12 ("pretrial intervention," "ordinarily" limited to first-offenders, but with a presumption against its use in public corruption cases, domestic violence cases in which the defendant was subject to a temporary or permanent restraining order at the time of the crime, and violent crimes involving infliction or a threat to inflict serious or significant bodily injury or involving use of a deadly weapon); N.Y. CRIM. PRO. LAW § 170.55 ("adjournment in contemplation of dismissal" in misdemeanors). *See generally* Anna Roberts, *Dismissals as Justice*, 69:2 ALA. L. REV. 327 (2017); Debra T. Landis, Annot., *Pretrial Diversion: Statute or Court Rule Authorizing Suspension or Dismissal of Criminal Prosecution on Defendant's Consent to Noncriminal Alternative*, 4 A.L.R.4th 147 (1981 & Supp.); Paul J. Larkin, Jr., *Swift, Certain and Fair Punishment: 24/7 Sobriety and Hope: Creative Approaches to Alcohol- and Illicit Drug-Using Offenders*, 105 J. CRIM. L. & CRIM. 39 (2016). More than twenty States now have Mental Health Courts to which some criminal cases can be diverted for formal adjudication as an alternative to prosecution aimed at punitive disposition. *See* National Center for State Courts, Mental Health Courts State Links, *available at* https://www.ncsc.org/topics/alternative-dockets/problem-solving-courts/mental-health-courts/state-links. Specialized Drug/DWI Courts of the sort described in JAMES L. NOLAN, JR., REINVENTING JUSTICE: THE AMERICAN DRUG COURT MOVEMENT (2001), and in NATIONAL DRUG COURT INSTITUTE, BUREAU OF JUSTICE ASSISTANCE, PAINTING THE CURRENT PICTURE: A NATIONAL REPORT CARD ON DRUG COURTS AND OTHER PROBLEM-SOLVING COURT PROGRAMS IN THE UNITED STATES (2011) are also found in many localities. *See* National Center for State Courts, Drug/DWI Courts, *available at* https://www.ncsc.org/topics/alternative-dockets/problem-solving-courts/drug-dwi-courts/resource-guide; Doug Smith, *L.A. criminal court program diverts mentally ill offenders from prosecution*, *Los Angeles Times*, May 26, 2023, *available at* https://www.latimes.com/california/story/2023-05-26/l- a-criminal-court-program-diverts-mentally-ill-offenders-from-prosecution. In 2022, the ABA issued the AMERICAN BAR ASSOCIATION CRIMINAL JUSTICE STANDARDS ON DIVERSION, *available at* https://www.americanbar.org/groups/criminal_justice/standards/diversion-standards/.

The usual features of such diversion programs are that the criminal case is held in abeyance for a designated period of time and one or more conditions are set that the defendant must satisfy in order to obtain its ultimate dismissal. The condition may be solely that the defendant remain arrest-free for a specified period of time. Usually, however, the defendant must successfully complete a community-based program of some sort (*e.g.*, alcohol or drug treatment; counseling of some sort (such as individual or family counseling, or anger management); an educational program (such as a GED program)) and/or that the defendant perform a certain number of hours of community service. Some of the kinds of monitoring, periodic reporting-in, or surveillance mentioned in § 4.10 *supra* may also be ordered. Upon the defendant's satisfaction of the conditions, the charges are dismissed. If the defendant fails to complete the program or violates some other condition of the diversion arrangement, the case is usually restored to the court calendar to resume the customary progression of pretrial stages of a criminal case. *See, e.g., State v. Marino*, 100 Wash. 2d 719, 725-27, 674 P.2d 171, 174-75 (1984) ("The similar rights at stake in probation revocation, plea bargain agreements, and pretrial diversions persuade us that . . . [a defendant] is entitled to have factual disputes resolved by a neutral fact finder [when the prosecutor seeks to terminate a diversion agreement and resume prosecution of criminal charges]. This includes an independent determination that the deferred prosecution agreement was violated, by a preponderance of the evidence with the burden of proof on the State. . . . This requirement best safeguards the . . . [defendant's] right to have the agreement administered equitably, with full protection of the constitutional rights relinquished in the bargain. The State is not unduly burdened as it has no interest in proceeding to prosecution in any case unless a violation has, in fact, occurred. ¶ Once the court has resolved the factual disputes, determining whether a violation of the agreement has occurred, it has a basis for reviewing the reasonableness of the prosecutor's decision to terminate. Clearly, the court is not in a position to require that prosecution be recommenced. Discretion to finally bring the case to trial still rests with the prosecutor. Other options may still be open in a particular case, such as reducing the charges if a plea bargain is reached, offering a new diversion arrangement, or dismissing charges where appropriate. We therefore find that the court's review of a prosecutor's termination decision should consist of assessing its reasonableness in light of the facts the trial court determines at [the] hearing." . . . ¶ . . . The trial court [here] clearly did find the prosecutor's decision to terminate reasonable in light of the facts ascertainable from the evidence. This finding satisfies the standard of review we hold appropriate for pretrial diversion terminations."); *United States v. Hicks*, 693 F.2d 32, 33-34 (5th Cir. 1982) ("The government argues that the district court did not have the power to review the decision to terminate appellant from the [diversion] program. It argues that the court would be participating in the decision to charge. Weaving the argument from the strands of prosecutorial discretion and separation of powers, it seeks to insulate the pretrial diversion program from any and all judicial review. ¶ That would take us too far. The court below, in holding this hearing, was not participating in the decision to charge. The diversion agreement is a contract. The government sought to hold the accused to his side of the bargain, i.e. the waiver of his speedy trial rights. The court was entitled to hear evidence on the violations to make sure that the government had lived up to its side of the bargain. ¶ The court is also charged with the responsibility for safeguarding the constitutional rights of the accused. An apt analogy is the plea bargain. Like pretrial diversion, the plea bargain is an agreement between the prosecutor and the accused. The court has a duty to supervise this process and insure that the defendant's plea is voluntary and that he is informed of his constitutional rights. ¶ . . . [W]e think the analogy sufficiently persuasive to defeat the government's argument that the court lacks jurisdiction to hold a hearing. Our holding is of a limited nature. We do not decide that the court is required to hold a hearing prior to termination of the agreement, with or without request by defendant. We simply hold that in this case the court was entitled to decide whether defendant should be held to his waiver of speedy trial." Because "the trial court found that the defendant had violated the terms of his agreement," the prosecutor's decision to resume prosecution is plenary.).

In many of the jurisdictions that have such a diversion option, the prosecutor has complete discretion whether to employ this option in a particular case. Although judicial approval may be needed if the case has progressed beyond a certain stage – usually arraignment – (*see, e.g.*, KY. RULE CRIM. PRO. 8.04(1)), judges commonly sign off on any diversion arrangement supported by the prosecutor. Dealings with the prosecutor on the subject are discussed in §§ 2.3.6, 3.19, 8.2.2, 8.2.3, and 8.4 *supra*.

In some jurisdictions, however, a statute or rule or local practice authorizes defense counsel to file a motion with the court to seek diversion of the case. *See, e.g.*, CONN. GEN. STAT. ANN. § 54-56e (authorizing a judicial order of pretrial "accelerated rehabilitation" "on motion of the defendant"); N.Y. CRIM. PRO. LAW § 170.55(1) (authorizing a judicial grant of adjournment in contemplation of dismissal "upon motion of . . . the defendant"). Where such a motion is available, a judicial grant of relief may or may not require the prosecutor's consent. *Compare, e.g.*, N.Y. CRIM. PRO. LAW § 170.55(1) (requiring the prosecutor's "consent"), *with* N.J. STAT. ANN. § 2C:43-12(f) ("If the applicant [to the Pretrial Intervention program] desires to challenge the decision . . . of a prosecutor not to consent to . . . enrollment into a supervisory treatment program, a motion shall be filed before the designated judge (or assignment judge) authorized pursuant to the Rules of Court to enter orders"), *and State v. Tucker*, 219 Conn. 752, 755, 761, 762-63, 595 A.2d 832, 834, 837, 838 (1991) (trial judge's grant of defendant's motion for "accelerated rehabilitation" in a drug sale case, which was granted "over the state's objection," is affirmed on appeal, as is the court's early termination of the probationary period and the dismissal of the charge), *and Commonwealth v. Pyles*, 423 Mass. 717, 718-23, 672 N.E.2d 96, 97-100 (1996) (trial court did not improperly "infringe[ ] on the district attorney's authority" by granting the defendant's request, "[o]ver the Commonwealth's objection," to continue the case after a guilty plea without a finding for a period of one year with conditions, the satisfaction of which would result in dismissal of the criminal case – a longstanding state procedure that the Supreme Judicial Court describes as "analogous" to legislatively-established "forms of disposition by means of pretrial diversion"), *and* CAL. PENAL CODE § 1001.95(A) ("[a] judge in the superior court in which a misdemeanor is being prosecuted may, at the judge's discretion, and over the objection of a prosecuting attorney, offer diversion to a defendant pursuant to these provisions").

In jurisdictions that authorize the court to grant diversion over a prosecutor's objection, counsel should consider making a motion supported by a proposed diversion plan in any promising case in which the prosecutor has rejected defense counsel's pre-court request for the favorable exercise of the prosecutor's discretion to divert cases out of the system. Even in jurisdictions in which court-ordered diversion requires prosecutorial consent, such a motion may nonetheless be a valuable tool because a prosecutor who initially rejected a defense attorney's appeal to his or her discretion may thereafter acquiesce in diversion if a judge – who has been persuaded by the motion that diversion is the right outcome – leans on the prosecutor to cooperate. See § 21.4 *infra*.

Counsel's responsibilities to a criminal client include the obligation to explore the possibility of diversion in appropriate cases. *See* AMERICAN BAR ASSOCIATION, STANDARDS FOR CRIMINAL JUSTICE MONITORS AND MONITORING, PLEAS OF GUILTY (4th ed. 2017), Standard 14-3.2(e), *Responsibilities of defense counsel* ("At the outset of a case, and whenever the law, nature and circumstances of the case permit, defense counsel should explore the possibility of a diversion of the case from the criminal process.").

As explained in § 2.3.6 *supra*, counsel should ordinarily consider diversion only in felony and misdemeanor cases, because in summary-offense prosecutions the consequences of diversion tend to be harsher for the client than the relatively mild sentence that is likely to follow a conviction. (In some jurisdictions, the diversion program is structured to guard against such inequitable outcomes. *See, e.g.*, KY RULE CRIM. PRO. 8.04(2) (a pretrial diversion "agreement may not specify a period longer than could be imposed upon probation after conviction of the crime charged").)

21.2. *Invoking the Prosecutor's Discretion in the First Instance*

Generally, in any case in which the circumstances of the crime and/or the defendant's background or other aspects of the case make it realistic to seek diversion, counsel should begin by attempting to persuade the prosecutor to divert the case (or, if judicial approval is required, to join with defense counsel in requesting this relief from the judge). If the prosecutor's agreement can be secured, this is always the easiest way to obtain diversion. For discussion of the types of arguments that may persuade a prosecutor to exercise his or her discretion in the defendant's favor, see §§ 8.2.2-8.2.4 *supra*.

The following two sections discuss what counsel can do if the prosecutor rejects defense counsel's request for diversion. Section 21.3 focuses on jurisdictions in which the applicable statute or rule authorizes a judge to grant diversion upon defense request even though the prosecutor objects. Section 21.4 addresses the types of arguments that counsel can make to a judge when the statute or rule requires prosecutorial consent to diversion.

21.3. *Seeking a Judicial Order of Pretrial Diversion in Jurisdictions In Which Prosecutorial Consent to Diversion Is Not Required*

In some jurisdictions, a statute or court rule or case law identifies specific criteria for a court to consider when assessing whether to grant diversion. *See, e.g., State v. Washington*, 866 S.W.2d 950, 951 (Tenn. 1993) ("Tennessee case law directs that 'the following factors and circumstances should be considered in determining [whether] diversion is warranted: circumstances of the offense; the criminal record, social history and present condition of the defendant, including his mental and physical conditions where appropriate; the deterrent effect of punishment upon other criminal activity; defendant's amenability to correction; the likelihood that pretrial diversion will serve the ends of justice and the best interests of both the public and defendant; and the applicant's attitude, behavior since arrest, prior record, home environment, current drug usage, emotional stability, past employment, general reputation, marital stability, family responsibility and attitude of law enforcement.'"; "while the circumstances of the case and the need for deterrence may be considered as two of many factors, they cannot be given *controlling* weight unless they are 'of such overwhelming significance that they [necessarily] outweigh all other factors'"); *People v. Whitmill*, 86 Cal. App. 5th 1138, 303 Cal. Rptr. 3d 444 (2022) (reversing an order denying a defendant's motion for mental health diversion: "[California Penal Code] § 1001.36 authorizes pretrial mental health diversion for defendants with qualifying mental health disorders. . . . As used in the statute, 'pretrial diversion' means "'postponement of prosecution, either temporarily or permanently, at any point in the judicial process from the point at which the accused is charged until adjudication, to allow the defendant to undergo mental health treatment.'" *Id.* at 1147-48, 303 Cal. Rptr. 3d at 450. The six threshold eligibility requirements are set forth in section 1001.36, subdivision (b)(1)(A)-(F). First, the court must find defendant suffers from a mental disorder as identified in the most recent edition of the Diagnostic and Statistical Manual of Mental Disorders. . . . ¶ Second, the court must find 'the defendant's mental disorder was a significant factor in the commission of the charged offense.' . . . ¶ Third, 'a qualified mental health expert' must opine that 'the defendant's symptoms of the mental disorder motivating the criminal behavior would respond to mental health treatment.' . . . ¶ Fourth, subject to certain exceptions, the defendant must consent to diversion and waive his or her right to a speedy trial. . . . ¶ Fifth, the defendant must agree to comply with treatment as a condition of diversion. . . . ¶ Finally, the court must find defendant will not pose an 'unreasonable risk of danger to public safety . . . if treated in the community.'" *Id.* at 1148-49, 303 Cal. Rptr. 3d at 450-51. "Here, the trial court stated: '[W]hat I have here is a defendant who had three years in the county jail suspended. And that's designed to create a strong disincentive to commit any new crime. That does not give me great confidence.' . . . We find nothing in the diversion statute suggesting the Legislature intended to give courts discretion to deny diversion simply because diversion is or may be less motivating than probation or prison. The trial court appeared to be grafting on a seventh element that defendants show they do not need to be additionally motivated. The trial court's conclusion that diversion is insufficiently motivating is simply a challenge to the underlying premise of diversion itself." *Id.* at 1155, 303 Cal. Rptr. 3d at 456.).

In jurisdictions that lack such an inventory of relevant criteria, counsel may find it useful to cite statutes, rules or caselaw from other jurisdictions as illustrations of the types of factors that legislatures and courts have deemed to be appropriate determinants of the suitability of diversion.

As a general matter, whether the judge is bound by or chooses to consider an itemized list of factors, it is usually safe to assume that the judge will focus particularly on the circumstances of the alleged crime and the circumstances of the defendant's life. Although the arguments that counsel will make about these subjects naturally will turn upon the particulars of the case, the following two subsections offer some general suggestions.

21.3.1. *Addressing the Circumstances of the Crime*

Presumably counsel will want to emphasize any mitigating aspects of the crime. *See, e.g., State v. Tucker*, 219 Conn. 752, 761, 595 A.2d 832, 837 (1991) (affirming the trial judge's grant of "accelerated rehabilitation" in a drug sale case, despite the prosecutor's objection, and also affirming the trial judge's early termination of the probationary period and dismissal of the charge because, *inter alia*, "[t]he defendant was a first time offender, and no evidence before the court suggested that his alleged sale of narcotics had been accompanied by violence or had resulted in harm to another"); *State v. Gutierrez*, 2008 WL 190989, at *1, *4 (N.J. Super. Ct. App. Div. Jan. 24, 2008) (per curiam) (affirming the trial judge's grant of pretrial diversion in a DWI case, "over the objection of the . . . Prosecutor," because, *inter alia*, "no one was injured, defendant did not strike another vehicle or a pedestrian, defendant was not charged with any crimes other than possession of CDS [a controlled dangerous substance], and he did not leave the scene.").

In referring to mitigating aspects of the crime, counsel should scrupulously avoid disclosing to the prosecution the projected trial testimony of defense witnesses, or even revealing the defendant's version of the events. Since counsel cannot count on winning a motion for pretrial diversion, particularly if the prosecutor is opposing it, counsel cannot afford to reveal facts that, although supportive of the motion, would give discovery to the prosecutor and thereby undermine the defendant's chances of winning the trial in the event diversion is denied. Generally, counsel should focus upon mitigating aspects of the prosecution's version of the crime, beginning statements with such phrasing as: "even under the prosecution's version of the events . . . ." For example, counsel might say: "Even under the prosecution's theory of what happened, no one was injured and the complainant recovered her property."

Statements taken by counsel or a defense investigator from potential prosecution witnesses should seldom be submitted on a motion for pretrial diversion. These are too valuable for impeachment at trial, and too vulnerable to prosecutorial undercutting (by coaching the witness to explain away any impeaching material; by procuring additional witnesses to bolster an impeachable witness's weak points; etc.) to jeopardize. Counsel should ordinarily refrain from any use or even mention of such statements that can tip off their existence to the prosecutor. However, in cases where a statement will clearly be of no worth in cross-examining the witness at trial but contains assertions that would be persuasive in a motion for pretrial diversion (such as the assertions that a complainant wishes to drop the charges, or that s/he was not injured, or that s/he and the defendant have resolved their differences since the antagonistic events giving rise to the charges), counsel might consider attaching the statement to the motion.

In rare cases counsel might also consider arranging for the defendant to take a private polygraph test and, if the defendant passes it, attaching the polygraph results to a motion for pretrial diversion. Although most jurisdictions exclude polygraph evidence at trial, the less formal rules of evidence applicable to pretrial motions would likely allow the submission of polygraphic vindication on a diversion motion. Judges who tend to assume that all defendants are guilty may be more inclined to offer diversion over a prosecutor's objection if a polygraph test confirms a defendant's claim of innocence. Recourse to polygraph testing is most useful in cases in which counsel believes a client's exonerating story but can develop little or no evidence to support it other than the defendant's own assertions. Even in this situation, however, the dangers and uncertainties that attend polygraph procedures – including the risk of false positives – call for extreme caution: Counsel who are considering going the polygraph route should (1) *first* commission a confidential polygraph examination by a reputable examiner and (2) submit the results only if (a) the examiner reaches a firm conclusion of the truthfulness of the client's declarations of innocence *and* of all significant aspects of the client's story relating to his or her activities or whereabouts at the time of the crime; and (b) the recorded dialogue between the examiner and the defendant will not give the prosecutor a preview of unobvious aspects of the defense case at trial or provide the prosecutor with material for impeaching the defendant's trial testimony.

In describing the mitigating aspects of the crime on a diversion motion, counsel should not play into rejoinders by the prosecutor or the judge that counsel is inappropriately minimizing the gravity of the offense or the trauma to the victim. It is often an effective tactic to state explicitly that counsel does not wish to minimize the gravity of the offense and then to go on to make the point that nonetheless the offense is less serious than the usual roster of violent crimes prosecuted in criminal court.

21.3.2. *Addressing the Circumstances of the Defendant's Life*

In some jurisdictions, pretrial diversion is limited to defendants who have no prior convictions. Even in jurisdictions where diversion is not so limited, a defendant's lack of prior convictions will usually be an important factor to emphasize. In all jurisdictions, it is always worthwhile to stress the lack of prior *arrests* in any case in which the defendant has never been arrested before. Of course, before making any such assertions about the defendant's prior record, it is essential that counsel not only question the client thoroughly but also check court records, probation records, and, if possible, police records.

The guiding philosophy of diversion in most jurisdictions is that the use of community-based rehabilitative services can obviate the need for expending the resources of the criminal justice system. Thus, it will usually be productive to present a judge with any information counsel can offer to show that the defendant is likely to benefit from rehabilitative services. As §§ 7.2.4 and 12.18 *supra* suggest, counsel will often want to encourage a client with an alcohol or substance abuse problem to voluntarily enroll in a treatment program at the earliest possible opportunity so that s/he has a successful track record of participation in the program that can be cited at sentencing in the event of conviction. If the client is already participating in such a program at the time when pretrial diversion can be requested, evidence of the client's successful performance in the program may be very persuasive to a judge in deciding whether to grant diversion. *See, e.g., State v. Gutierrez*, 2008 WL 190989, at *1 (N.J. Super. Ct. App. Div. Jan. 24, 2008) (per curiam) (affirming the trial judge's grant of pretrial diversion, "over the objection of the . . . Prosecutor," because, *inter alia*, "the probation officer pointed to defendant's enrollment in an outpatient drug and alcohol treatment program, and his 'amenability to treatment, [which] bode well for the likelihood of success with PTI [Pretrial Intervention] services'"). In such cases, counsel should obtain a letter from the program (and, ideally, from the defendant's own counselor), attesting to the client's faithful attendance and the progress s/he has already made. Counsel's advice and assistance to the client in arranging other aspects of his or her daily life so as to support a prediction that s/he will shape up and present no law-enforcement issues in the future will also be very useful. See § 21.5 *infra*. In any case in which the defendant made significant changes in his or her mode of living or sought professional assistance for his or her problems even before the arrest, this is a fact that a judge may view as particularly compelling. *See, e.g., State v. Tucker*, 219 Conn. 752, 761, 595 A.2d 832, 837 (1991) ("As for the defendant's personal potential for rehabilitation, the court could reasonably have inferred from his voluntary act of enlisting in the Navy some two weeks *before* his arrest that he would not resist supervisory authority, and that diversionary measures would be likely to ensure that he would not offend again."). If this was not the case, however, counsel may be able to portray the arrest as having caused the defendant to realize how far s/he had fallen and to finally muster the determination to change.

If the defendant is currently employed, this is always a useful fact to emphasize. The judge will ordinarily appreciate that it is better for society – not only for the defendant and the defendant's family and dependents – to resolve the prosecution without a criminal conviction that may result in the loss of the defendant's current job and make it more difficult to secure other jobs in the future. *See, e.g., Commonwealth v. Pyles*, 423 Mass. 717, 723, 672 N.E.2d 96, 100 (1996) (affirming the trial judge's grant of a "continuance without a finding" because, *inter alia*, the defendant "held a responsible job"); *State v. Washington,* 866 S.W.2d 950, 951-52 (Tenn. 1993) ("As to the merits of the case, we agree fully with the Court of Criminal Appeals's characterization of the defendant's petition for diversion as 'especially compelling.' She is an otherwise respected member of the community who has taught elementary school in Rutherford County for more than 20 years. She holds a bachelor's degree from Middle Tennessee State University and a master's degree from Tennessee State University. She has been active in community affairs and in her church. Her request for diversion was supported by local civic and political leaders, by her pastor, and by school officials. To the extent that her offenses, although apparently aberrant, require chemical dependency treatment, substance abuse counseling, or other correctional response short of incarceration, the trial court is equipped to individualize her diversion program. ¶ Tennessee case law directs that 'the following factors and circumstances should be considered in determining [whether] diversion is warranted: circumstances of the offense; the criminal record, social history and present condition of the defendant, including his mental and physical conditions where appropriate; the deterrent effect of punishment upon other criminal activity; defendant's amenability to correction; the likelihood that pretrial diversion will serve the ends of justice and the best interests of both the public and defendant; and the applicant's attitude, behavior since arrest, prior record, home environment, current drug usage, emotional stability, past employment, general reputation, marital stability, family responsibility and attitude of law enforcement.' *State v. Markham*, 755 S.W.2d 850, 852-53 (Tenn.Crim.App. 1998) . . . . ¶ . . . The proof in this case clearly meets the *Markham* standard. . . . ¶ . . . [T]he case is remanded to the trial court for . . . entry of an appropriate order of diversion."). If the defendant is not currently employed but had a good work history in the past, it is advisable to tell the judge about that, along with information about the defendant's current efforts to find a job. *See, e.g., State v. Gutierrez, supra*, 2008 WL 190989, at *1 ("[t]he probation officer . . . reported that until recently, defendant had maintained 'lawful, gainful' employment"). As the quotation from *State v. Washington* illustrates, the factors favoring diversion mentioned in most of the reported cases are heavily skewed by the influence of middle-class, establishment values, but in trial courts where judges come from sundry backgrounds, counsel should not hesitate to base diversion requests on circumstances more relevant to a broader swath of the population. In locations where there are community resources and programs aimed at strengthening people's ability to overcome problems like unemployment, addiction, poor education, and mental disturbance, counsel should document that the defendant is eligible for their services, willing to use them, and likely to benefit from them and should point out that the very purpose of these programs is to provide a more effective means for dealing with such problems than the criminal process has traditionally provided. In some jurisdictions, indeed, there are special diversion provisions aimed at furthering the rehabilitation of individuals with mental problems or other handicaps. *See, e.g.*, CAL. PENAL CODE §§ 1001.35-1001-36, enacted in 2018 and held retroactive in *People v. Frahs*, 9 Cal. 5th 618, 631, 466 P.3d 844, 850, 264 Cal. Rptr. 3d 292, 300 (2020), because they provide "a potentially ameliorative benefit for a class of individuals – namely, criminal defendants who suffer from a qualifying mental disorder . . [and] the diversion statute states the legislative purpose 'to promote ... [¶] [i]ncreased diversion of individuals with mental disorders to mitigate the individuals' entry and reentry into the criminal justice system while protecting public safety'").

Military service is likely to be viewed by many judges as a strong mitigating factor (*see State v. Bell*, 69 S.W.3d 171 (Tenn. 2002), quoted in § 21.4 *infra*, listing the defendant's "honorable discharge from the United States Army" along with his "stable marriage of thirteen years, high school diploma, and lack of a history of drug or alcohol abuse" as evidence supporting diversion), especially if counsel is able to connect the difficulties the defendant has experienced in civilian life to the lingering effects of combat. *Cf. Porter v. McCollum*, 558 U.S. 30, 30-31, 41, 43 (2009) (per curiam) (finding defense counsel to have been ineffective at the penalty phase of a capital trial because counsel failed to uncover and present evidence of, *inter alia*, Porter's military service: "Petitioner George Porter is a veteran who was both wounded and decorated for his active participation in two major engagements during the Korean War; his combat service unfortunately left him a traumatized, changed man."; because of counsel's failure, the jury and judge never heard about Porter's "struggles to regain normality upon his return from war": "Our Nation has a long tradition of according leniency to veterans in recognition of their service, especially for those who fought on the front lines as Porter did. . . . Moreover, the relevance of Porter's extensive combat experience is not only that he served honorably under extreme hardship and gruesome conditions, but also that the jury might find mitigating the intense stress and mental and emotional toll that combat took on Porter.").

Judges are often also impressed by letters of support from responsible members of the community who know the defendant and can speak to his or her good qualities and prospects for rehabilitation. *See, e.g., State v. Washington*, 866 S.W.2d 950, 951 (Tenn. 1993) (finding that the grounds for diversion were "'especially compelling'" because, *inter alia*, the defendant's "request for diversion was supported by local civic and political leaders, by her pastor, and by school officials").

If counsel is able to obtain a statement from the complainant that s/he supports the handling of the case through a means other than a criminal prosecution (see § 8.5 *supra*), this will often be highly persuasive to a judge. *See, e.g., Commonwealth v. Pyles*, 423 Mass. 717, 718, 724, 672 N.E.2d 96, 97, 100 (1996) (diversion was appropriate, notwithstanding the seriousness of the charge – assault with a dangerous weapon based on allegations that "the defendant, during an argument, cocked and pointed a handgun at his twelve year old nephew, in the presence of the boy's mother (defendant's sister)" – because, *inter alia*, "the victim's mother (defendant's sister) stated that it was unnecessary to incarcerate her brother to deal with the problem that had occurred").

21.4. *Seeking Judicial Relief Despite a Statute or Rule Requiring Prosecutorial Consent to Diversion*

Even in a jurisdiction in which a statute or rule expressly conditions a grant of diversion on prosecutorial consent, it may nonetheless be worthwhile to file a motion for diversion with the court. Notwithstanding the apparently unequivocal language of the applicable statute or rule, it may be possible to persuade a judge that an exception is possible. *See, e.g., State v. Bell*, 69 S.W.3d 171 (Tenn. 2002) ("[W]e hold that when the district attorney general denies pretrial diversion without considering and weighing all the relevant factors, including substantial evidence favorable to the defendant, there is an abuse of prosecutorial discretion. We further hold that in such a case, the proper remedy under the applicable standards of review requires a remand for the district attorney general to consider and weigh all of the relevant factors to the pretrial diversion determination." *Id.* at 173. "The district attorney general denied pretrial diversion because Bell failed to take responsibility for his actions, has a record of traffic offenses, acted recklessly, endangered persons other than the victims, and has an unstable work history. The district attorney general also cited a need to deter irresponsible driving by tractor-trailer drivers. The district attorney general, however, failed to consider evidence favorable to Bell, such as his honorable discharge from the United States Army, stable marriage of thirteen years, high school diploma, and lack of a history of drug or alcohol abuse. Moreover, the district attorney general failed to set forth this favorable evidence in writing, weigh it against the other factors, and reach a conclusion based on the relative weight of all of the factors." *Id.* at 177-78. "[T]his case is remanded for the district attorney general's further consideration of the defendant's pretrial diversion application in a manner consistent with this opinion." *Id.* at 180.); *State v. Leonardis*, 73 N.J. 360, 375 A.2d 607 (1977) (under a pretrial diversion program established by court rule, "our rule-making power must be held to include the power to order the diversion of a defendant into PTI where either the prosecutor or the program director arbitrarily fails to follow the guidelines in refusing to consent to diversion" (*id.* at 375, 375 A.2d at 615). However, "great deference should be given to the prosecutor's determination not to consent to diversion. Except where there is such a showing of patent and gross abuse of discretion by the prosecutor, the designated judge is authorized . . . to postpone proceedings against a defendant only where the defendant has been recommended for the program by the program director and with the consent of the prosecutor." (*id.* at 381, 375 A.2d at 618).); *State v. Dalglish*, 86 N.J. 503, 509-10, 432 A.2d 74, 77 (1981) (under a pretrial diversion program established by statute after the *Leonardis* decision, "a court may not order the enrollment of a defendant in PTI unless he has demonstrated a patent and gross abuse of discretion by the prosecutor, [but] we have recognized that a remand to the prosecutor may be appropriate without such a showing in certain cases. . . . These are cases where a court finds that the prosecutor's decision was arbitrary, irrational, or otherwise an abuse of discretion, but not a patent and gross abuse, and also determines that a remand will serve a useful purpose. A remand might be proper, for example, where 'prosecutorial decision was based upon a consideration of inappropriate factors or not premised upon a consideration of all relevant factors,' . . . where the denial resulted from an incorrect evaluation of relevant factors, . . . where the prosecutor's belief that a particular factor is or is not present was unfounded or based upon unreliable information, . . . or where the prosecutor's statement of reasons is inadequate . . . , either because it lacks the necessary specificity or because it fails to give a rational explanation of the result."); *accord, State v. K.S.*, 220 N.J. 190, 104 A.3d 258 (2015) (remanding to the prosecutor because his decision denying PTI was based upon prior criminal charges that had been dismissed and juvenile charges that had been diverted and dismissed with nothing in the record to support the truth of the factual allegations underlying those charges); *State v. Greenlee*, 228 Kan. 712, 721, 620 P.2d 1132, 1139 (1980) (dictum) ("the prosecutor, although possessing wide discretion, is not immune from judicial review of the exercise of that discretion for arbitrariness"); *People v. Siragusa*, 81 Misc. 2d 368, 371-73, 366 N.Y.S.2d 336, 341-43 (Dist. Ct., Nassau Cty. 1975) (although "[t]he statute makes the District Attorney's consent mandatory before the Court can grant a defendant an A.C.O.D. [adjournment in contemplation of dismissal]," the court nonetheless grants the ACOD over the prosecutor's objection because "[t]he Court finds that the prosecutor had originally given his consent" and subsequently "withdr[e]w that consent solely because the defendant refused to agree to release the County and the police from any civil liability," which "[t]he Court finds . . . to be an unreasonable condition amounting to undue pressure and an act of coercion and duress").

When filing a motion under these circumstances, defense counsel can (and ordinarily will) make the types of arguments described in § 21.3 *supra*. But it is always advisable – and often essential – also to present the judge with a reason to view the prosecutor's objection to diversion as unreasonable. This might be done by "'show[ing] that a prosecutorial veto (a) was not premised upon a consideration of all relevant factors, (b) was based upon a consideration of irrelevant or inappropriate factors, or (c) amounted to a clear error in judgment,'" especially if "'the prosecutorial error complained of will clearly subvert the goals underlying [the pretrial diversion program]'" (*State v. Gutierrez*, 2008 WL 190989, at *1, *3, *5 (N.J. Super. Ct. App. Div. Jan. 24, 2008) (per curiam) (quoting this standard for a judicial override of a prosecutor's objection to diversion, and then applying the standard to hold that the prosecutor's "reject[ion] [of the] defendant from PTI [Pretrial Intervention Program] solely because of his immigration status" was "a patent and gross abuse of discretion that a reviewing court is obliged to overturn")). Cases holding that a prosecutor's discretion to withhold consent to diversion is judicially reviewable and was abused can be cited. *See, e.g., State v. Maguire*, 168 N.J. Super. 109, 116-18, 401 A.2d 1106, 1110-11 (1979) (overriding the prosecutor's objection to diversion of three defendants as "arbitrary and capricious, and a patent and gross abuse of discretion" because the prosecutor's use of "exactly the same wording" in the "three separate letters" of denial, issued "seven months . . . [after] the [timely] applications," show that the prosecutor "failed to deal with defendants on a prompt and individual basis."; "The fact that defendants were involved in a single night of wrongful conduct does not justify grouping them as he did. We are dealing with young persons whose futures hang in the balance, and whose applications for diversion mandate prompt individualized study and consideration. This was not afforded to them here. Rather, it would appear that the prosecutor may have personal reservations about the philosophical underpinnings of PTI and the court's role in connection therewith. Such an attitude, however, should not deter him from acting on the individual merits of each case."); *People v. Siragusa, supra*, 81 Misc. 2d at 372, 366 N.Y.S.2d at 342 ("The practice of a prosecutor demanding releases of defendant's claims against the government and police officers in exchange for his consent to an A.C.O.D. [adjournment in contemplation of dismissal] must be discouraged"); *Commonwealth v. Benn*, 544 Pa. 144, 147, 149, 675 A.2d 261, 262, 264 (1996) (although "[it] is well established that admission to ARD [accelerated rehabilitative disposition program] rests with the discretion of the district attorney," "the district attorney committed an abuse of discretion" by denying the application for ARD based on appellant's previous "probation without verdict and expunged record"; "The abuse was compounded by [the district attorney's] weighing negatively the fact that appellant denied having a prior record. The only way that the district attorney could have known of appellant's record was to have had access to information that, by statute, should have been unavailable. . . . Further, the intent of the probation without verdict and expungement statutes would be obviated if the district attorney could use the ARD questionnaire to force disclosure of matters that the legislature has made private."); *State v. Curry*, 988 S.W.2d 153, 159-60 (Tenn. 1999) ("We agree with the trial court that the prosecutor failed to consider all of the relevant factors and, therefore, abused his discretion in denying the defendant's application for pretrial diversion."; "[T]he prosecutor's denial letter concentrated solely upon the circumstances of the offense and, arguably, a veiled consideration of deterrence. There was no apparent consideration given to the defendant's lack of a criminal record, favorable social history, and obvious amenability to correction. Moreover, the prosecutor did not articulate or state why those factors that were considered, i.e., seriousness of the offense and deterrence, necessarily outweighed the other relevant factors. The evidence presented a close case on the diversion question; however, the failure by the prosecutor to consider and articulate all of the relevant factors constitutes an abuse of discretion."); *State v. Markham*, 755 S.W.2d 850, 852-53 (Tenn. Crim. App. 1988) (the district attorney general's denial of the applications for pretrial diversion was an abuse of discretion because "Appellees do not have criminal records, . . . they are persons of good character and are amenable to correction," "[t]here is no showing that the facts of this case are particularly flagrant in comparison with other criminal conspiracies designed to defraud the State," "[t]here is no evidence in the record which suggests that in this case deterrence is an overriding consideration," and "the district attorney general denied the application for diversion prior to completion of the pretrial investigation authorized by statute, [and thus] his decision was made without the benefit of the report, which found Appellees to be good candidates for diversion").

Even if a judge is unable or unwilling to grant diversion over the prosecutor's objection, bringing the matter to a judge may cause the judge to put some pressure on the prosecutor to acquiesce. It is usually the case that prosecutors are far more willing to accede to a judge's strongly expressed wishes than to a request from a defense attorney.

21.5. *Developing and Implementing a Proposed Diversion Plan*

The key to securing diversion is ordinarily to convince the judge – or the prosecutor and the judge – that the defendant will be "crime-free" (which usually means *no further trouble to the authorities*) and well-behaved (according to the judge's/prosecutor's vision of appropriate social behavior) in the future. Thus, whatever counsel can do to develop and to set in motion a specific, detailed regimen for the future correction of the problematic aspects of the client's life will ordinarily be indispensable. Areas that counsel can profitably mine in working up a diversion plan are outlined in § 12.18 *supra*. Any movement on those fronts that counsel can effectuate before the diversion motion comes on for hearing will be especially valuable. But if none can be made by that time, counsel should try to demonstrate that the specificity and practicality of his or her proposed diversion program make it a sound bet for success in the future.

21.6. *Guilt, Penitence and Future Promise*

Some prosecutors and judges will begin their consideration of a defense diversion motion from the premise that the defendant is almost certainly guilty of the crime charged or a lesser crime (since, in their view, virtually all defendants are). They will want and expect the defendant to admit guilt and to display contrition as an indicator of the likelihood that s/he will behave suitably in the future if the prosecution is resolved without a criminal conviction. This attitude presents some problems for the defense.

Defense counsel will need to ascertain whether the prosecutor and judge on the case are of this mind. If they *may be*, counsel and the client will have to determine whether the defense strategy on the motion should be (1) to concede guilt (a) of the charged offense or (b) of some lesser offense, and to make the defendant's penitence an element of their argument for diversion; or (2) to urge that this is the rare case in which diversion is being sought by an accused person who is genuinely innocent; or (3) to try to keep the prosecutor or the court from getting into the issue of guilt-or-innocence at all, by couching the issue of diversion as wholly future-oriented – not backward-looking – and, if this attempt fails, whether (a) to fall back to position (1); or (b) to fall back to position (2); or (c) to persist in refusing to discuss the defendant's guilt or innocence.

Choosing among these strategies and implementing one's chosen strategy involve considerations and techniques much like those discussed in Chapter 15 *supra*, relating to guilty pleas. If counsel believes that an admission of guilt will be important in obtaining diversion but the client resists it, counsel will need to work to persuade the client – without overbearing the client's will – to make the necessary admission. See §§ 15.2-15.5, 15.7.5, 15.14-15.15 *supra*. If counsel is unsuccessful in this persuasion, counsel will have to work out with the client a game plan for the hearing on the diversion motion which implements strategy (3) with minimal damage. In any event, whether the defense strategy is (1) or (2) or (3), counsel will have to prepare for the motion hearing by explaining to the client exactly what will happen at the hearing and by rehearsing the client to play his or her part in it. See § 15.16 *supra*.

The strategy of admitting guilt poses a complication in the context of diversion motions that it no longer poses, in most jurisdictions, in the context of guilty pleas. Guilty pleas and incriminating statements made in guilty-plea colloquies or during plea negotiations are commonly inadmissible at trial if the plea is vacated or if the negotiations fall through. *See, e.g.,* FED. RULE EVID. 410; §§ 15.3, 17.1.2 concluding paragraph *supra*. The applicable rules and precedents may not be broad enough to encompass incriminating statements made in connection with diversion motions. There is a strong argument that such statements are constitutionally inadmissible: Confessions made to police and prosecutors are held involuntary and inadmissible if "'obtained by any direct or implied promises, however slight, [or] by the exertion of any improper influence'" (*Hutto v. Ross,* 429 U.S. 28, 30 (1976) (per curiam); see the cases collected in § 26.3.3 *infra*); and an admission of guilt which is made in order to obtain the leniency of diversion is no different than an interrogating officer's promise of "leniency – no jail" (*Sharp v. Rohling,* 793 F.3d 1216, 1219 (10th Cir. 2015)). Nevertheless, counsel should check to see whether there is any law in his or her jurisdiction strengthening or weakening the case for inadmissibility if diversion is denied after a defendant has admitted guilt in an effort to obtain it.

B. *Transfer to Juvenile Court*

21.7. *Possible Transfer of a Case to Juvenile Court*

If counsel is representing a client whose age falls within the concurrent jurisdiction of the juvenile court (which usually covers juveniles who were below the age of 18 – or, in some States below the age of 17 – at the time of the crime), and if local law provides for the possibility of transfer of a juvenile's case from adult criminal court to juvenile court (*see, e.g.,* N.Y. CRIM. PRO. LAW §§ 722.20 - 722.23 (as amended in 2017; effective, October 1, 2018); *Hansen v. State*, 904 P.2d 811 (Wyo. 1995)), counsel will need to consider whether to seek transfer of the case to juvenile court.

Usually it is in the client's interest to seek transfer to juvenile court because: (1) the maximum sentence the client would face upon conviction is substantially lower than the likely sentence in adult court (*see* RANDY HERTZ, MARTIN GUGGENHEIM & ANTHONY G. AMSTERDAM, TRIAL MANUAL FOR DEFENSE ATTORNEYS IN JUVENILE DELINQUENCY CASES § 38.03 (2018), *available at* http://njdc.info/trial-manual-for-defense-attorneys-in-juvenile-delinquency-cases-by-randy-hertz-martin-guggenheim-anthony-g-amsterdam/); (2) if the client is detained before trial or sentenced to a term of incarceration by the juvenile court, s/he will probably be held in a facility for juveniles rather than an adult jail or prison (*see id.,* §§ 4.18, 38.03(c)); (3) juvenile court convictions (commonly called "adjudications") may be exempt from some of the collateral consequences that can stem from an adult court conviction of a crime (*see id.,* § 14.07); and (4) local law often provides for sealing and possibly even expungement of a juvenile conviction (*see id.,* §§ 37.03, 39.08).

There may be cases, however, in which a client who is eligible for transfer to juvenile court may fare better by keeping his or her case in adult criminal court. This may be true, for example, if the maximum possible sentence in adult court is roughly comparable to the maximum possible sentence in juvenile court (which may be the case in a misdemeanor or perhaps even a low-level felony prosecution) and if the client is more likely to receive probation if sentenced by an adult court judge who is accustomed to seeing defendants who are older than the client whereas a juvenile court judge would view the client as one of the older youths to appear in juvenile court. Also, if the adult criminal case is eligible for a jury trial (see § 32.1 *infra*), and if local law precludes jury trials in juvenile court (as is true in most jurisdictions, *see* HERTZ, GUGGENHEIM & AMSTERDAM, *supra,* § 21.01), counsel needs to consider whether the case is more likely to be won in adult court in a jury trial (*see generally* Martin Guggenheim & Randy Hertz, *Reflections on Judges, Juries and Justice: Ensuring the Fairness of Juvenile Delinquency Trials,* in *Symposium on Juvenile Justice Reform,* 33 WAKE FOREST L. REV. 553 (1998)).

For further discussion of factors to consider when assessing whether to seek transfer of a criminal case to juvenile court, see HERTZ, GUGGENHEIM & AMSTERDAM, *supra,* § 13.02. For possible arguments to make in support of a transfer motion, see *id.,* §§ 13.08, 13.11, 13.13 - 13.15, setting out the justifications for preferring juvenile-court proceedings in the context of a defense attorney's opposition to transfer of a juvenile delinquency case to adult court.

As with other case-related decisions that depend primarily upon a choice of ultimate objectives, the decision whether to seek transfer of the case to juvenile court is ultimately the client's, but counsel has a responsibility to counsel the client to ensure that s/he makes the decision with as full an understanding as possible of the options and implications, and with the benefit of counsel's professional judgment. *See id.,* § 13.02. *And cf. Clinard v. Lee,* 722 Fed. Appx. 552 (6th Cir. 2018).

In most jurisdictions, a case originally filed in juvenile court can be transferred to adult court at the prosecution's instance under specified circumstances. The propriety of the transfer is initially ruled upon by the juvenile court judge; if the transfer is granted, the defendant can have that ruling reviewed (in some jurisdictions) by appellate courts in an appeal from the transfer order itself (*see, e.g., Ex parte S.B.,* 650 So.2d 953 (Ala. 1994); *In re Stevenson,* 167 Mont. 220, 538 P.2d 5 (1975)), or (in other jurisdictions) by a pretrial motion to the criminal court to dismiss the charging paper and/or to remand the case to the juvenile court – a motion whose disposition is reviewable by appellate courts either immediately through interlocutory-appeal or prerogative-writ proceedings or on post-conviction appeal (*see, e.g., A Juvenile v. Commonwealth,* 380 Mass. 552, 405 N.E.2d 143 (1980)), or (in still other jurisdictions) by the appellate courts in a post-conviction criminal appeal on the record of the juvenile-court transfer hearing (*see, e.g., In re Interest of Tyrone K,* 295 Neb. 193, 887 N.W.2d 489 (2016); *People v. Taylor,* 76 Ill. 2d 289, 391 N.E.2d 366 (1979)). Commonly, the prosecution bears the burden of persuasion that the circumstances warranting transfer exist and are sufficient (*see, e.g., State v. Nicholas,* 2022-Ohio-4276, 2022 WL 17365211, at *6 (Ohio 2022) ("Insofar as the 'burden of persuasion' refers to the risk borne by a party if the trier of fact finds that the evidence is in equilibrium, . . . the state bears that burden when it asks the juvenile court to transfer a juvenile's case to adult court."); *In re William E.,* 29 Neb. App. 44, 49, 950 N.W.2d 392, 396 (2020); *United States v. Leon D.M.,* 132 F.3d 583 (10th Cir. 1997) ("[u]nder 18 U.S.C. §5032, juvenile adjudication is presumed appropriate, and the government bears the burden of establishing that a transfer to adult status is warranted")), but appellate review is restricted to (1) assuring compliance with procedural requisites for transfer, including the necessary factual findings (*see, e.g., A Juvenile v. Commonwealth, supra; Guerrero v. State,* 471 S.W.3d 1 (Tex. Ct. App. 2014); *Commonwealth v. Broome,* 317 Pa. Super. 1, 463 A.2d 1053 (1983); *cf. Kent v. United States,* 383 U.S. 541 (1966) (holding a juvenile court's waiver of jurisdiction invalid "because no hearing was held; because no findings were made by the Juvenile Court; because the Juvenile Court stated no reasons for waiver; and because counsel was denied access to the Social Service file which presumably was considered by the Juvenile Court in determining to waive jurisdiction" (*id.* at 552): the applicable statute, governing the District of Columbia Juvenile Court's waiver of its exclusive jurisdiction so as to permit criminal-court prosecution, "assumes procedural regularity sufficient in the particular circumstances to satisfy the basic requirements of due process and fairness, as well as compliance with the statutory requirement of a 'full investigation'" (*id.* at 553)); *State v. Yard,* 109 Ariz. 198, 507 P.2d 123 (1973) (reversing a transfer order on the ground that the juvenile court's belated appointment of counsel for the juvenile and other irregular proceedings violated due process), (2) sufficiency of the evidence to support any required factual findings (*see, e.g., In re William E., supra; Kevin P. v. Superior Court of Contra Costa County,* 57 Cal. App. 5th 173, 270 Cal. Rptr. 3d 877 (2020) (principal ground)), and (3) abuse of discretion (*see, e.g., State v. Ellis,* 22022-Ohio-147, 183 N.E.3d 65 (Ohio App. 2022)).

Chapter 22

Motions for a Change of Venue or for Disqualification of the Judge

A. *Motions for a Change of Venue*

22.1. *Initial Venue and Change of Venue*

The general principles governing initial venue in criminal cases are sketched in § 20.5 *supra*. As that section indicates, a charging paper filed in the wrong venue is usually subject to a motion to quash or to dismiss. In some jurisdictions, however, the defendant's remedy may be merely a motion for transfer to the court of proper venue.

When the applicable venue doctrine would allow prosecution of a particular offense in more than one court, ordinarily the prosecutor has the initial option. After the commencement of the prosecution, statutes or court rules may permit either party to move for a change of venue to another court in which the prosecution could properly have been begun. In the absence of an explicit authorization by statute or formal court rule, the prosecutor should not be able to obtain a change of venue. *See, e.g., Jacksori v. Superior Court,* 13 Cal. App. 3d 440, 91 Cal. Rptr. 565 (1970). *Cf.* §§ 12.8 concluding paragraph, 18.11 concluding paragraph *supra. But see* Caroline Zane, Annot., *Power of State Trial Court in Criminal Case to Change Venue on its Own Motion,* 74 A.L.R.4th 1023 (1989 & Supp.). In any event, the prosecutor cannot obtain a change of venue, over the defendant's objection, to a place where the prosecution could not initially have been brought, consistent with the state and federal constitutional guarantees mentioned in § 20.5.

The defendant, however, is allowed a venue change to other places under certain circumstances. These are addressed in the next two sections.

22.2. *Motions for a Change of Venue on the Ground That a Fair Trial Cannot Be Had in the Court in Which the Charge Is Pending*

22.2.1. *Grounds for the Motion*

Counsel can seek a change of venue based upon public hostility against the defendant, public belief that the defendant is guilty, public outrage over the offense, and prejudicial news reporting or editorializing that vilifies the defendant or discloses inadmissible evidence against the defendant. In addition to the state-law right to a venue change, the federal constitutional guarantee of a fair trial by an impartial jury is implicated here. *See Sheppard v. Maxwell*, 384 U.S. 333 (1966); *Irvin v. Dowd*, 366 U.S. 717 (1961)), and cases cited together with *Sheppard* and *Irvin* in § 32.1 subdivision 1 *infra.* "This Court has long recognized that adverse publicity can endanger the ability of a defendant to receive a fair trial . . . . To safeguard the due process rights of the accused, a trial judge has an affirmative constitutional duty to minimize the effects of prejudicial pretrial publicity." *Gannett Co. v. DePasquale*, 433 U.S. 368, 378 (1979). "Trial courts must be especially vigilant to guard against any impairment of the defendant's right to a verdict based solely upon the evidence and the relevant law." *Chandler v. Florida*, 449 U.S. 560, 574 (1981) (dictum).

The federal right does not necessarily require change of venue as a remedy. Other procedural devices may sometimes be effective to insulate a jury from the effects of inflammatory publicity and similar prejudicing influences: – a continuance (see § 28.3 *infra*), sequestration of the jurors (see § 34.3.1 *infra*), or scrupulous interrogation on the *voir dire* (see Chapter 33 *infra*), for example. *See Dobbert v. Florida*, 432 U.S. 282, 302-03 (1977); *Nebraska Press Ass'n v. Stuart*, 427 U.S. 539, 563-64 (1976) (dictum); *Richmond Newspapers, Inc. v. Virginia*, 448 U.S. 555, 581 (1980) (plurality opinion) (dictum). But if these devices are not employed or are insufficient, vindication of the federal fair-trial right demands a venue change. *Groppi v. Wisconsin*, 400 U.S. 505 (1971); *Coleman v. Kemp*, 778 F.2d 1487 (11th Cir. 1985), *rehearing en banc denied*, 782 F.2d 896 (11th Cir. 1986); *Ruiz v. State*, 265 Ark. 875, 582 S.W.2d 915 (1979); *People v. Boss*, 261 A.D.2d 1, 701 N.Y.S.2d 342 (N.Y. App. Div., 1st Dep't 1999) (per curiam). *Cf. Skilling v. United States*, 561 U.S. 358, 377-85 (2010). And, of course, the defendant may not be required to waive other significant rights, such as the right to a jury trial (see § 32.1 *infra*) or a speedy trial (see § 28.5.4 *infra*), as the price of a fair trial. *Cf. Jackson v. Denno*, 378 U.S. 368, 387-89 & nn.15, 16 (1964); *Simmons v. United States*, 390 U.S. 377, 389-94 (1968), and cases cited following *Simmons* in § 16.6.1, paragraph 5 *supra*.

Courts commonly hold that a showing of prejudicial publicity or community hostility is not sufficient to require a change of venue on constitutional grounds unless the defendant also demonstrates that as a consequence of these biasing factors it is likely to be impracticable to empanel an impartial jury. *See, e.g., State v. Komisarjevsky*, 338 Conn. 526, 258 A.3d 1166 (2021); *Commonwealth v. Briggs*, 608 Pa. 430, 12 A.3d 291 (2011); *State v. Fowler*, 266 S.C. 203, 222 S.E.2d 497 (1976). The latter demonstration is particularly difficult to make. If the publicity is highly inflammatory or the hostility particularly intense, a doctrine of "presumed prejudice" that finds support in *Sheppard, supra,* may render evidentiary proof of impracticality unnecessary. *See Rideau v. Louisiana*, 373 U.S. 723 (1963); *Estes v. Texas*, 381 U.S. 532 (1965); *compare Skilling v. United States, supra*. But "[f]or prejudice to be presumed under this standard, the defendant must show: 1) that the pretrial publicity was prejudicial and inflammatory and 2) that the prejudicial pretrial publicity saturated the community where the trial was held. *See Coleman v. Kemp*, 778 F.2d 1487 (11th Cir. 1985). Under this standard, a defendant carries an extremely heavy burden of proof. ¶ . . . The presumptive prejudice standard is 'rarely' applicable, and is reserved for only 'extreme situations'." *Brown v. State*, 74 So.3d 984, 1031-32 (Ala. App. 2010), *aff'd,* 74 So.3d 1039 (Ala. 2011). *See also, e.g., Gonzalez v. State*, 222 S.W.3d 446 (Tex. Crim. App. 2007); *Commonwealth v. Casper*, 481 Pa. 143, 151, 392 A.2d 287, 291 (1978) ("[i]t is trite but true to note that a presumption of prejudice pursuant to this exception requires the presence of exceptional circumstances."). Ordinarily, counsel who is seeking a change of venue will want to proceed on alternative theories of actual prejudice and presumed prejudice. *See Daniels v. Woodford*, 428 F.3d 1181 (9th Cir. 2005) ("To support a change of venue motion, Daniels must demonstrate either actual or presumed prejudice. . . . To demonstrate actual prejudice, Daniels must show that 'the jurors demonstrated actual partiality or hostility that could not be laid aside.' . . . Prejudice is presumed only in extreme instances 'when the record demonstrates that the community where the trial was held was saturated with prejudicial and inflammatory media publicity about the crime.' . . . ¶ Three factors should be considered in determining presumed prejudice: (1) whether there was a 'barrage of inflammatory publicity immediately prior to trial, amounting to a huge . . . wave of public passion'; (2)

whether the news accounts were primarily factual because such accounts tend to be less inflammatory than editorials or cartoons; and (3) whether the media accounts contained inflammatory or prejudicial material not admissible at trial. . . . ¶ Applied here, these factors compel a finding 'that the venue [wa]s saturated with prejudicial and inflammatory media publicity about the crime' sufficient for a presumption of prejudice."). But in some cases in which counsel anticipates that s/he will fail to persuade the court of either actual or presumed prejudice, s/he may nevertheless be well advised to file a change-of-venue motion and present the sorts of evidence suggested in § 22.2.3 *infra*. A trial judge who is convinced that the local atmosphere is tainted by a defendant's notoriety or damaging portrayal in widespread media may grant the motion as a matter of discretion without insisting on the showing of impracticality that the constitutional caselaw demands. *See, e.g., United States v. Cortez*, 251 F.R.D. 237 (E.D. Tex. 2007); *and see Meadows v. Mutter*, 243 W. Va. 211, 228, 842 S.E.2d 764, 781 (2020). High-publicity cases are labor-intensive and costly to the court and prosecution; savvy trial judges understand that by denying a change-of-venue motion they will risk appellate reversal of a conviction obtained after a laborious trial; they may choose to avoid that risk or simply to escape the burden of trying a troublesome case.

When a defendant charged in county *A* moves for a change of venue to county *B* on the grounds that s/he cannot get a fair trial in *A*, the court is ordinarily allowed discretion to transfer the case instead to county *C*. The defendant's right is only to get out of *A*, not to get into *B*. For this reason, considerable caution is advised before counsel decides to file a change-of-venue motion. Counsel should ascertain from knowledgeable local attorneys or court personnel *where*, in granting such motions, the court (or this particular judge) has been sending cases; and, after investigating those localities, counsel should thoroughly investigate the risks and costs of being transferred there. In particular, the pattern has developed in a number of metropolitan counties to transfer venue almost invariably to one or more nearby rural counties – possibly because it is thought that the jurors there will have been less exposed to inflammatory publicity but more likely simply because court calendars in the rural counties are not so badly backlogged. These counties may be unmitigated disaster areas for the transferred defendant. Adverse publicity there may be less voluminous and less provable without being less pervasive in fact. Even if it is less pervasive, the local jurors may also be (a) less sophisticated and skeptical in their reactions to the adverse publicity to which they have been exposed; (b) more homogeneous (see §§ 33.4.2.2 concluding paragraph and 33.10 *infra*); (c) more punitive; (d) less likely to include members of a minority defendant's race and social class; and (e) unprovably but unmistakably hostile to "foreigners" – including both defendants and their lawyers. *Compare People v. Boss, supra*, 261 A.D.2d 1, 3, 8, 701 N.Y.S.2d 342, 343, 347 (N.Y. App. Div., 1st Dep't 1999) (upon granting the defense's request for a change of venue in the "case of the four police officers accused of murdering Amadou Diallo" in the Bronx, the court rejects the defendants' request to shift the case to an adjoining county that "carries the advantage of convenience" because "'within reasonable limits, the community to which the trial is transferred should reflect the character of the county where the crime was committed'" and "[a] change of venue should, of course, not afford defendants an unfair demographic advantage"; the court orders that the case "be removed to an urban county rather than a suburban or rural county. Counties where substantial numbers of New York City law enforcement officers reside are particularly undesirable. We have examined data published by the United States Bureau of the Census which reveal that several counties containing urban areas, namely Albany, Erie, Monroe, and Onondaga, have populations featuring a reasonable degree of ethnic diversity. Since the demographics of each of these counties are approximately the same, we have chosen, as the place of trial, Albany County, which is geographically closest to Bronx County.").

Statutes sometimes delimit the geographic bounds within which a venue change may be allowed. If circumstances render fair trial anywhere within the area of allowed change impossible, the statutes may be attacked as unconstitutional. *See Groppi v. Wisconsin, supra; Nebraska Press Ass'n v. Stuart, supra*, 427 U.S. at 563 n.7 (dictum).

22.2.2. *Timing of the Motion*

In some jurisdictions, a motion for venue change from a court in which the defendant asserts that s/he cannot be fairly tried must await the conclusion of *voir dire* examination of prospective jurors (see Chapter 33). Only after an attempt to empanel a fair jury has been made and – in the opinion of the presiding judge – has failed, may venue be shifted. In other jurisdictions, a motion for change of venue may be made before trial. Local practice governing the timeliness of motions should be checked.

22.2.3. *Evidence that Can Be Presented in Support of the Motion*

The motion is customarily supported by affidavits, and the defendant is allowed an evidentiary hearing if the motion and affidavits are facially sufficient. The following sorts of evidence should be considered by counsel who is attempting to prove that a fair trial cannot be had in the locality:

(1) *Newspaper articles, internet and social media postings, video recordings, audio recordings, and TV or radio scripts. See, e.g., Sheppard v. Maxwell, supra*, 384 U.S. at 345-49; *Coleman v. Kemp, supra*, 778 F.2d at 1491-1533; *Ruiz v. State, supra*, 265 Ark. at 885-86, 582 S.W.2d at 919-20. These may be attached as riders to affidavits and presented as exhibits at a hearing. The prosecutor will ordinarily stipulate their authenticity. If s/he does not, the news reporters or editorial personnel who published them will have to be called to authenticate them. If the news media are uncooperative, subpoenas *duces tecum* are in order. *See Coleman v. Zant*, 708 F.2d 541, 546-48 (11th Cir. 1983). Counsel should be sure particularly to put into the record texts and recordings of publicity containing inadmissible inculpatory or inflammatory material. *Cf. Gannett Co. v. DePasquale*, 443 U.S. 368, 378 (1979).

(2) *Testimony of persons knowledgeable about public opinion.* Individuals whose occupations bring them in touch with prevalent public opinions may be called as witnesses or their affidavits attached to a motion. *See, e.g., Coleman v. Kemp, supra*, 778 F.2d at 1533-37; *Ruiz v. State, supra*, 265 Ark. at 885-86, 582 S.W.2d at 919-20. News reporters, political ward leaders, and members of the service trades (cab drivers, bartenders, barbers, delivery people, shopkeepers, and so forth) are frequently used. After a foundation is laid by showing that the witness (a) has occasion to talk to a great many persons daily and (b) has, in fact, discussed this case with a great many persons, s/he may be asked such questions as (i) what proportion of the persons to whom s/he talked discussed the case; (ii) whether they expressed the view that the defendant was guilty; (iii) whether they expressed the view that the crime was atrocious or that

559

the perpetrator should be shot; and (iv) (if local practice demands this question) whether they expressed the view that the defendant could not get a fair trial in the locality. In a number of jurisdictions, a change of venue apparently depends upon the answer to this last question – obviously, a wholly unrealistic test. Counsel should urge its abandonment – and, if necessary, its unconstitutionality – on the ground that the same circumstances which are likely to make trial unfair are likely to make the local populace bad judges of whether a fair trial is possible. *Cf. Irvin v. Dowd*, 366 U.S. 717, 728 (1961); *Holbrook v. Flynn*, 475 U.S. 560, 569-70 (1986) (dictum). Usually the witness may also be asked (v) whether s/he has an opinion as to whether the defendant can receive a fair trial locally and (vi) what that opinion is. S/he will be permitted to answer only if s/he has demonstrated sufficient contact with public attitudes to qualify as an expert.

(3) *Opinion polls.* Counsel should consider commissioning an opinion poll to establish through accepted polling techniques the nature and pervasiveness of public attitudes about the defendant and the case. *See, e.g., Commonwealth v. Cohen*, 489 Pa. 167, 185-86, 413 A.2d 1066, 1076 (1980); *People v. Boss*, 261 A.D.2d 1, 6, 701 N.Y.S.2d 342, 346 (N.Y. App. Div., 1st Dep't 1999). Useful questions include: (a) Have you ever heard of . . . [name of defendant], who is accused of . . . [crime]? (b) Do you think s/he is guilty? (c) Do you know that s/he has made a confession? (d) Have you heard that s/he has a criminal record? [Other publicized inadmissible matters should be made the subject of separate questions.] (e) Have you read . . . [or seen, or heard] [specified news stories or postings on the internet or social media]? (f) Do you think that most people in . . . County believe s/he is guilty? (This question is preferable to "Do you think s/he can get a fair trial in . . . County," but local law may require that the latter question be asked. See paragraph (2) *supra.*) Commercial attitude-polling organizations or advertising firms with expertise in consumer studies may be retained to do the job. Professors of psychology, sociology, communications, or advertising at neighboring universities may be competent to design a poll and may be willing to conduct it with student assistance at a cost cheaper than that which a commercial pollster would charge.

(4) *Summoning passersby.* At the hearing on a motion for change of venue, the court may be asked to have the marshal bring in the first 20 or 25 persons who pass by on the street outside the courthouse. This procedure was developed in the era predating modern opinion-polling methods and is sometimes recognized by statute or local practice. It is obviously dangerous and should not be used if an opinion poll is possible.

(5) *Evidence of petitions, resolutions, speeches, and so forth.* If petitions relating to the case have been circulated or resolutions passed or speeches made at public meetings, these may be proved by observers. Since only the making of these sorts of declarations is to be proved and not the truth of what is declared, there is, of course, no hearsay problem.

(6) *Evidence of news conferences, press releases, and so forth by the police and the prosecutor.* It is desirable to prove, if it is so, that adverse publicity emanated from state officials. This has been an important consideration in cases holding that defendants were denied a fair trial by reason of inflammatory publicity or the publication of inadmissible evidence. *E.g., Rideau v. Louisiana*, 373 U.S. 723 (1963); *Sheppard v. Maxwell, supra*, 384 U.S. at 349; *State ex rel. Coburn v. Bennett*, 202 Mont. 20, 31-32, 655 P.2d 502, 507-08 (1982); *Commonwealth v. Cohen*,

supra, 489 Pa. at 179-83, 413 A.2d at 1073-75; *Corona v. Superior Court*, 24 Cal. App. 3d 872, 879-81, 101 Cal. Rptr. 411, 416-17 (1972); *United States ex rel. Bloeth v. Denno*, 313 F.2d 364 (2d Cir. 1963) (en banc). *See Nebraska Press Ass'n v. Stuart,* 427 U.S. 539, 554-55 (1976); Bennett Gershman, *The Prosecutor's Duty of Silence*, 79 ALBANY L. REV. 1183 (2016); *and see Attorney Grievance Commission of Maryland v. Gansler*, 377 Md. 656, 676, 835 A.2d 548, 559 (2003) ("One outside circumstance that may affect a defendant's right to a fair trial and, specifically, his right to an impartial jury, occurs when an attorney makes a publicized, out-of-court statement about the defendant's case. This is particularly true because attorneys occupy a special role as participants in the criminal justice system, and, as a result, the public may view their speech as authoritative and reliable. Attorneys involved in a particular case have greater access to information through discovery, the ability to converse privately with knowledgeable witnesses, and an enhanced understanding of the circumstances and issues. Their unique role and extensive access to information lends a degree of credibility to their speech that an ordinary citizen's speech may not usually possess. Comments by prosecuting attorneys, in particular, have the inherent authority of the government and are more likely to influence the public. When such seemingly credible information reaches the ears or eyes of the public, the jury pool may become contaminated, greatly diminishing the court's ability to assemble an impartial jury. The defendant's right to a fair trial, thus, may be compromised.").

22.2.4. *Steps to Take if the Motion is Denied*

If a pretrial motion for change of venue is denied, counsel should consider the availability of appellate review by means of a prerogative writ. See Chapter 31 *infra*. The fate of most defendants who lose pretrial motions is that they are convicted and their claims of jury bias are rejected on appeal from conviction on the ground that the trial judge did a sufficiently colorable job of jury selection at the *voir dire* stage to protect the defendant's fair-trial rights. *See, e.g., United States v. Haldeman*, 559 F.2d 31 (D.C. Cir. 1976) (en banc); *United States v. Blanton*, 719 F.2d 815 (6th Cir. 1983) (en banc). Giving a trial judge the opportunity to "cure" the dubious denial of a venue-change motion by at-trial juror screening which is often more cosmetic than corrective makes no sense if defense counsel can avoid it.

However, in many jurisdictions, pretrial appellate review is unavailable, either for want of an established prerogative-writ procedure or because of rulings that require a defendant to attempt to empanel a fair jury before s/he can complain on appeal that s/he could not get one. In these jurisdictions, counsel cannot afford to rest on the record made at the hearing on the change-of-venue motion but must also conduct intensive *voir dire* examination of prospective jurors at trial in order to establish their hostility to the defendant or their exposure to the prejudicial publicity of which counsel complains (see §§ 33.3, 33.5 subdivision (2), 33.6 *infra*). *See, e.g., Dobbert v. Florida*, 432 U.S. 282, 301-03 (1977). A challenge to the venire or the panel may also be advised. See §§ 32.4 subdivision(1), 33.2 *infra*.

Requests to the court for other protective measures – continuance, sequestration – will improve counsel's record. If prejudicial publicity has continued between the time of the pretrial hearing and the trial, counsel should submit affidavits documenting its content, extensiveness, and date of publication and should renew the motion for a change of venue on the record previously made and this augmentation of it. The same procedure should be repeated during trial and at the time of postrial motions whenever significant additional inflammatory matter is published unless the jury is sequestered. The temporal proximity of inflammatory publications to the jury's deliberations is an important factor in appellate and postconviction consideration of claims that the defendant was improperly denied a change of venue or a fair trial because of such publications (*see, e.g., Patton v. Yount,* 467 U.S. 1025 (1984)), and counsel should accordingly be careful to update the record periodically until after verdict.

22.3. *Other Grounds for a Motion for a Change of Venue*

Statutes, rules or local practice in counsel's jurisdiction will ordinarily specify other grounds for defense motions for a change of venue. These should be consulted for particulars. The available grounds may include:

(1)   *In the interest of justice, for the convenience of the parties and witnesses.* For example, if the defendant lives in a county other than the one in which the crime was alleged to have been committed, and if it would be a hardship for the defendant to travel to court, the defense can seek a change of venue to the county in which the defendant resides. Such a request may also be appropriate to accommodate the needs of "character witnesses [who are likely to reside] . . . in the district of [the defendant's] . . . residence" (*United States v. Johnson,* 323 U.S. 273, 279 (1944) (Murphy, J., concurring)). (For discussion of character witnesses, see §§ 39.21-39.24 *infra.*)

(2)   *For the purpose of the defendant's pleading guilty and disposing of the prosecution in the district of arrest.* This procedure allows a defendant to avoid the need to return to the district where the crime was alleged to have been committed if s/he is not going to contest guilt and s/he wishes to expedite a final disposition of the charges. *See, e.g.,* FED. RULE CRIM. PRO. 20.

B. *Motions for Recusal or Disqualification of the Judge*

22.4. *The Right to an Impartial Judge*

Statutes, court rules, local practice, canons of judicial ethics, and opinions rendered by a jurisdiction's professional-ethics committee or agency provide varying grounds and procedures for objecting to a particular judge's presiding at trial or on pretrial matters. The applicable statutes or court rules may or may not detail specific grounds for challenge: – personal interest in the outcome of the case, relationship to a party, bias, and so forth. *See, e.g., Liteky v. United States,* 510 U.S. 540 (1994), surveying the basic federal statutory provisions. The AMERICAN BAR ASSOCIATION MODEL CODE OF JUDICIAL CONDUCT (2007), which has been adopted *verbatim* in almost all jurisdictions, provides that "A judge shall disqualify himself or herself in any proceeding in which the judge's impartiality might reasonably be questioned, including but not limited to . . . [certain specified] circumstances" (MODEL CODE, Rule 2.11(A)). *See, e.g., United States v. Orr,* 969 F.3d 732, 738 (7th Cir. 2020). The specified circumstances address situations in which the judge or a family member has personal connections with the litigants or personal interests in a case, and also call for disqualification a/k/a recusal in three situations of particular significance in criminal matters: where –

(1) "The judge has a personal bias or prejudice concerning a party or a party's lawyer, or personal knowledge of facts that are in dispute in the proceeding" (MODEL CODE, Rule 2.11(A)(1));

(2) "The judge, while a judge or a judicial candidate, has made a public statement, other than in a court proceeding, judicial decision, or opinion, that commits or appears to commit the judge to reach a particular result or rule in a particular way in the proceeding or controversy" (MODEL CODE, Rule 2.11(A)(5)); and

(3) "The judge:

(a) served as a lawyer in the matter in controversy, or was associated with a lawyer who participated substantially as a lawyer in the matter during such association;

(b) served in governmental employment, and in such capacity participated personally and substantially as a lawyer or public official concerning the proceeding, or has publicly expressed in such capacity an opinion concerning the merits of the particular matter in controversy;

(c) was a material witness concerning the matter; or

(d) previously presided as a judge over the matter in another court." (MODEL CODE, Rule 2.11(A)(6)).

In addition to the grounds for recusal provided by the applicable ethical prescriptions, statutes and court rules, the Due Process Clause of the Fourteenth Amendment and equivalent state constitutional provisions guarantee a right to an impartial judge. *Caperton v. A.T. Massey Coal Co.*, 556 U.S. 868, 883-84 (2009); *Bracy v. Gramley*, 520 U.S. 899, 904-05 (1997); *In re Murchison*, 349 U.S. 133, 136 (1955); *Williams v. Pennsylvania*, 579 U.S. 1 (2016). *See, e.g., Hurles v. Ryan*, 752 F.3d 768 (9th Cir. 2014); *In re Ruth H.*, 26 Cal. App. 3d 77, 84-86, 102 Cal. Rptr. 534, 538-39 (1972); *State v. Sawyer*, 297 Kan. 902, 906-07, 909-12, 305 P.3d 608, 611-12, 613-15 (2013); *People v. Stevens*, 498 Mich. 162, 164, 869 N.W.2d 233, 238-39 (2015); *see also Tumey v. Ohio*, 273 U.S. 510 (1927); *Ward v. Village of Monroeville*, 409 U.S. 57 (1972); *Cain v. White*, 937 F.3d 446 (5th Cir. 2019); *Caliste v. Cantrell*, 937 F.3d 525 (5th Cir. 2019); *Harper v. Professional Probation Services, Inc.*, 976 F.3d 1236 (11th Cir. 2020) (extending the rule to a private contract probation agency) (distinguished in *Brucker v. City of Doraville*, 38 F.4th 876 (11th Cir. 2022)); *Butler v. United States*, 414 A.2d 844, 852-53 (D.C. 1980) (en banc) ("[t]he essence of the judicial role is neutrality"); *cf. Mayberry v. Pennsylvania*, 400 U.S. 455 (1971); *Johnson v. Mississippi*, 403 U.S. 212 (1971); *Taylor v. Hayes*, 418 U.S. 488 (1974); *Connally v. Georgia*, 429 U.S. 245, 247-50 (1977) (per curiam); *Withrow v. Larkin*, 421 U.S. 35, 47 (1975) (dictum); *Marshall v. Jerrico, Inc.*, 446 U.S. 238, 242-43 (1980) (dictum); *and see* Ronald Rotunda, *Judicial Disqualification in the Aftermath of* Caperton v. A.T. Massey Coal Co., 60 SYRACUSE L. REV. 247 (2010). Federal constitutional due process requires recusal in any case in which "actual," subjective bias is demonstrated and also "when, objectively speaking, 'the probability of actual bias on the part of the judge or decisionmaker is too high to be constitutionally tolerable'" (*Rippo v. Baker*, 580 U.S. 285, 287 (2017) (per curiam)). "The test does not require a showing of actual judicial bias, 'though actual bias, if disclosed, no doubt would be grounds for appropriate relief.' . . . Rather, the test requires only a showing of an undue risk of bias, based on the psychological temptations affecting an 'average judge.'" *Echavarria v. Filson*, 896 F.3d 1118, 1128-29 (9th Cir. 2018).

In *Williams v. Pennsylvania, supra,* the Supreme Court sketched the contours of the federal constitutional command of recusal of a judge for bias. "Due process guarantees 'an absence of actual bias' on the part of a judge. . . . Bias is easy to attribute to others and difficult to discern in oneself. To establish an enforceable and workable framework, the Court's precedents apply an objective standard that, in the usual case, avoids having to determine whether actual bias is present. The Court asks not whether a judge harbors an actual, subjective bias, but instead whether, as an objective matter, 'the average judge in his position is "likely" to be neutral, or whether there is an unconstitutional "potential for bias."' . . . Of particular relevance, the Court has determined that an unconstitutional potential for bias exists when the same person serves as both accuser and adjudicator in a case" (579 U.S. at 8). Refining this standard for application to the sub-set of cases in which a judge has played a role as a prosecuting attorney in the defendant's case before being appointed or elected to the bench, the Court held that "under the Due Process Clause there is an impermissible risk of actual bias when a judge earlier had significant, personal involvement as a prosecutor in a critical decision regarding the defendant's case" (*id.*). Hence, *Williams* found that Due Process obliged a state supreme court chief justice to recuse himself in a postconviction proceeding brought by a death-sentenced inmate when that justice had been the district attorney at the time of the inmate's prosecution and had personally approved the decision of his subordinates to seek the death sentence in the case. And this result was required even though the D.A.'s position was as the head of an office employing more than two hundred assistants, where the practice was that the initial decision to paper a case as capital was made by a line prosecutor and passed up the chain of command for the D.A.'s final review, and where the D.A. acted to approve dozens of capital prosecutions a year. "A prosecutor may bear responsibility for any number of critical decisions, including what charges to bring, whether to extend a plea bargain, and which witnesses to call. Even if decades intervene before the former prosecutor revisits the matter as a jurist, the case may implicate the effects and continuing force of his or her original decision. In these circumstances, there remains a serious risk that a judge would be influenced by an improper, if inadvertent, motive to validate and preserve the result obtained through the adversary process." *Id.* at 10-11. *See also Reed v. State,* 259 So.3d 718 (Fla. 2018).

22.5. *Grounds for Recusal or Disqualification of the Judge*

In some jurisdictions the mere filing of a motion for recusal or "substitution" bars the judge from presiding and requires transfer of the matter to another judge. *See, e.g.,* CAL. CODE CIVIL PRO. § 170.6, as construed in *Solberg v. Superior Court,* 19 Cal. 3d 182, 561 P.2d 1148, 137 Cal. Rptr. 460 (1977); *State v. Harrison,* 2015 WI 5, 360 Wis. 2d 246, 255-59, 858 N.W.2d 372, 377-78 (Wis. 2015). The brake against improvident use of these "judicial peremptory strike" procedures is that the lawyer who resorts to them too frequently ends up in serious disfavor with the entire local judiciary – not only the judges s/he strikes but those s/he seeks to draw.

In most jurisdictions, the defense must demonstrate specific grounds for recusal. Recusal statutes and caselaw uniformly require that a judge recuse himself or herself when s/he has a personal interest in the outcome of the case, a relationship to a party, or some actual bias or prejudice.

In any case in which there will be a bench trial – either because the criminal charge against the defendant does not entail a right to jury trial (see § 32.1 *infra*) or because the defendant has waived the right to a jury (see § 32.2 *infra*) – counsel should be alert to the possibility of obtaining recusal of the currently assigned judge if that judge is aware of unfavorable information about the defendant or the case that could impair the judge's objectivity as the finder of fact. Although there is caselaw in many jurisdictions holding that prior knowledge of the case or the defendant does not necessarily bar a judge from serving as the fact-finder in a bench trial – on the rationale that judges are presumed to be capable of ignoring inadmissible information and reaching a verdict solely on the facts elicited at trial – recusal nonetheless may be required if the information known to the judge is highly prejudicial, such as:

(1) When the information known to the judge strongly suggests that the defendant is guilty of the charges. *See, e.g., Butler v. United States,* 414 A.2d 844 (D.C. 1980) (en banc) (the defendant was deprived of due process when the judge presided over the bench trial after having been informed by defense counsel that the prosecution could prove its case beyond a reasonable doubt and that the defendant intended to commit perjury); *Brent v. State,* 63 Md. App. 197, 492 A.2d 637 (1985) (the judge should have recused himself from presiding over a bench trial after learning of the defendant's willingness to plead guilty and after having presided over the guilty plea proceedings of codefendants, at which statements were made implicating the defendant); *People v. Zappacosta,* 77 A.D.2d 928, 431 N.Y.S.2d 96 (N.Y. App. Div., 2d Dep't 1980) (the judge should have recused himself from presiding over the bench trial because the judge had presided over the guilty plea proceeding of defendant's wife, who was his co-perpetrator, and the judge thereby heard statements incriminating the defendant). *See also In re George G.,* 64 Md. App. 70, 494 A.2d 247 (1985) (the juvenile court judge should have recused himself as the trier of fact in a juvenile delinquency bench trial because the judge had previously convicted three co-perpetrators of the same crime, rejecting the same defense that the defendant intended to offer). *Cf. Watson v. State,* 934 A.2d 901, 906-08 (Del. 2007) (the Family Court judge who had convicted the juvenile in a bench trial based in part on the judge's rejection of the credibility of the juvenile's testimony, should have recused herself from a trial of the same juvenile shortly thereafter on an unrelated charge in which the juvenile's credibility would again be at issue).

(2) When the judge is aware of inadmissible evidence about the defendant's other criminal activity, prior record, or prejudicial aspects of the defendant's character or history. *See, e.g., Commonwealth v. Goodman,* 454 Pa. 358, 362 & n.4, 311

A.2d 652, 654 & n.4 (1973) (the judge who presided over the suppression hearing should have recused himself from the bench trial in a marijuana possession case because, at the suppression hearing, "an impression was left from hearsay testimony as to probable cause that the appellants were trafficking in narcotics," and this evidence was both "highly inflammatory" and "inadmissible during the trial of the cause"). *See also In re Gladys R.*, 1 Cal. 3d 855, 861-62, 464 P.2d 127, 132, 83 Cal. Rptr. 671, 676 (1970) (the judge in a juvenile delinquency bench trial committed reversible error by reviewing a social study with "negative indications about [the child's] . . . home environment"); *In the Matter of James H.*, 41 A.D.2d 667, 341 N.Y.S.2d 92 (N.Y. App. Div., 2d Dep't 1973), *appeal withheld and case remanded on an unrelated point,* 34 N.Y.2d 814, 316 N.E.2d 334, 359 N.Y.S.2d 48 (1974), *appeal dism'd,* 36 N.Y.2d 794, 330 N.E.2d 649, 369 N.Y.S.2d 701 (1975) (when the probation officer stated during a juvenile delinquency bench trial that the case was "a 'Training School' case," the judge should have granted the defense motion for disqualification to avoid an appearance of prejudice).

Even if the judge does not view himself or herself as actually biased, s/he must consent to recusal if his or her knowledge of prejudicial information would cause the proceedings to have an "appearance of partiality" (*see, e.g., Perotti v. State*, 806 P.2d 325, 328 (Alaska App. 1991) (the "appearance of partiality . . . [arising] 'in light of the objective facts'" (*id.* at 328) required that the trial judge recuse himself from serving as the sentencing judge in an adult criminal case in which he had presided over the proceeding to transfer the case from juvenile to adult court and had made a finding of non-amenability to rehabilitative treatment based on improperly-obtained psychiatric evidence); *People v. Zappacosta, supra,* 77 A.D.2d at 930, 431 N.Y.S.2d at 99 (courts must be "[s]ensitive to the imperative that we avoid any situation which allows even a suspicion of partiality"); *Commonwealth v. Goodman, supra,* 454 Pa. at 361, 311 A.2d at 654 ("[w]e have every confidence that the trial judges of this Commonwealth are sincere in their efforts to avoid consideration of incompetent inflammatory evidence in reaching these judgments but we also are acutely aware that the appearance of bias or prejudice can be as damaging to public confidence in the administration of justice as would be the actual presence of either of these elements")). *See also Caperton v. A.T. Massey Coal Co.*, 556 U.S. 868, 888 (2009) ("[T]he States have implemented . . . ["judicial reforms"] to eliminate even the appearance of partiality. Almost every State . . . has adopted the American Bar Association's objective standard: 'A judge shall avoid impropriety and the appearance of impropriety.' ABA Annotated Model Code of Judicial Conduct, Canon 2 (2004) . . . . The ABA Model Code's test for appearance of impropriety is 'whether the conduct would create in reasonable minds a perception that the judge's ability to carry out judicial responsibilities with integrity, impartiality and competence is impaired.' Canon 2A, Commentary"); *Williams v. Pennsylvania*, 579 U.S. 1, 12-14 (2016); AMERICAN BAR ASSOCIATION, STANDARDS FOR CRIMINAL JUSTICE MONITORS AND MONITORING, SPECIAL FUNCTIONS OF THE TRIAL JUDGE (4th ed. 2017), Standard 6-1.9, *Obligation to perform and circumstances requiring recusal* ("[t]he trial judge should recuse himself or herself whenever the judge has any doubt as to his or her ability to preside impartially or whenever his or her impartiality reasonably might be questioned"); *Rippo v. Baker*, 580 U.S. 285, 287 (2017) (per curiam) (summarily vacating the Nevada Supreme Court's denial of relief on a judicial bias claim and remanding the case for further proceedings because the lower court focused exclusively on the existence of actual bias rather than "ask[ing] the question our precedents require: whether, considering all the circumstances alleged, the risk of bias was too high to be constitutionally tolerable"; "Under our precedents, the Due Process Clause may sometimes demand recusal even when a judge '"ha[s] no actual bias.'" . . . Recusal is required when, objectively speaking, 'the probability of actual bias on the part of the judge or decisionmaker is too high to be constitutionally tolerable.'"); *accord, Gacho v. Wills*, 986 F.3d 1067, 1068 (7th Cir. 2021) (vacating a conviction returned in a jury trial in which the presiding judge was corrupt, without requiring a showing that the judge was actually biased against this defendant in particular: "Evidence that the presiding judge was actually biased is sufficient to establish a due-process violation but it's not necessary. Constitutional claims of judicial bias also have an objective component: the reviewing court must determine whether the judge's conflict of interest created a constitutionally unacceptable likelihood of bias for an average person sitting as judge."); *State v. Daigle*, 2018-0634 (La. 4/30/18), 241 So.3d 999, 1000 (La. 2018) (requiring recusal where "[t]he record . . . demonstrates that the trial judge had a longtime working relationship with Mrs. Vincent, the victim's widow and a court employee; has a social media relationship with Mrs. Vincent that he initially denied in a formal opinion, but later admitted under oath; and has taken steps barred by the Code of Criminal Procedure which, if not corrected by the appellate court, would have thwarted another judge from considering his recusal. Mrs. Vincent is not only the victim's widow, she is designated as a penalty phase witness in this capital case."); *People v. Towns*, 33 N.Y.3d 326, 328, 125 N.E.3d 816, 817, 102 N.Y.S.3d 151, 152 (2019) ("On this appeal, we are asked to decide whether defendant was denied the right to a fair trial when the trial court negotiated and entered into a cooperation agreement with a codefendant requiring that individual to testify against defendant in exchange for a more favorable sentence. We hold that the trial court abandoned the role of a neutral arbiter and assumed the function of an interested party, thereby creating a specter of bias that requires reversal."); *Tundidor v. State*, 2023 WL 2920534 (Fla. 2023) (requiring recusal of a judge whose comments hostile to the defense in a notorious recent capital trial had been widely reported in the media; Florida's relevant statute provides for disqualification when a "party reasonably fears that he or she will not receive a fair trial or hearing because of specifically described prejudice or bias of the judge"); *Commonwealth v. St. John*, 2023 WL 2858941 (Pa. Super. 2023) (dictum) ("Our case law has recognized several ways a litigant can establish that a judge should be disqualified due to the appearance of impropriety. First, a litigant can establish that the jurist can reasonably be considered to harbor a personal bias against the litigant. *See Commonwealth v. Darush*, 459 A.2d 727, 732 (Pa. 1983) (requiring disqualification of sentencing judge who could not refute an allegation that he had said '[w]e want to get people like him [appellant] out of Potter County'). A second method involves establishing that the jurist could reasonably be considered to have a personal interest in the outcome of the litigant's case. *See In the Interest of McFall*, 617 A.2d 707, 713 (Pa. 1992) (holding that a trial judge, who cooperated with the FBI as an undercover agent following allegations of bribery, had a real and tangible bias in the criminal cases heard by her, because she was subject to prosecution for her actions by the prosecuting authority in each of the cases before). A third way we have recognized for establishing an appearance of impropriety is a showing that a jurist has a bias against a particular class of litigants. *See Commonwealth v. Lemanski*, 529 A.2d 1085, 1089 (Pa. Super. 1987) (finding that a defendant adequately supported allegations of personal bias against a 'particular class of litigants' by reference to comments made from the bench and in a local newspaper regarding an opinion and predetermined policy that in all drug cases deserve the maximum sentence)."); *cf. Matter of Dependency of A.N.G.*, 12 Wash. App. 2d 789, 459 P.3d 1099 (2020) (in a proceeding seeking the termination of a mother's parental rights, the judge should have recused himself because he had served as the state's attorney who previously sought and obtained termination orders regarding the mother's two older children; the Court of Appeals relies, *inter alia*, on *Williams v. Pennsylvania, supra*, which sets the due process standard for recusal in cases in which a judge has formerly acted as a prosecuting attorney).

Moreover, even if recusal is not *required*, counsel can urge the judge to exercise his or her discretion in favor of recusal as a prophylactic measure to guard against any possible unconscious influences of the judge's prior knowledge on his or her fact-finding function, or any possible appearance of impropriety. Counsel can point to decisions recognizing that even when the judge intends to faithfully ignore inadmissible information, it may still have an effect upon his or her mind. *See, e.g., United States v. Walker,* 473 F.2d 136, 138 (D.C. Cir. 1972) (although a "[j]udge is presumed to have a trained and disciplined judicial intellect, . . . [this] disciplined judicial mind should not be subjected to any unnecessary strain; even the most austere intellect has a subconscious"); *People v. Zappacosta, supra,* 77 A.D.2d at 930, 431 N.Y.S.2d at 99 ("[e]ven the most learned [j]udge would have difficulty in excluding such information from his subconscious deliberations"); *In re George G., supra,* 64 Md. App. at 80, 494 A.2d at 252 (although "the sincerity [and] . . . the integrity of the trial judge" could not be doubted, "[s]ubconsciously, . . . [the impermissible information] apparently lingered on in the deep recesses of his mind"). *See also People v. Kagan,* 204 A.D.3d 695, 696, 163 N.Y.S.3d 867, 867-68 (Mem) (N.Y. App. Div., 2d Dept. 2022) (reversing a bench trial conviction because, after the trial, the judge reviewed the "transcript of the trial," "reflect[ed] on the case," and then forthrightly admitted that "his experiences as a civil rights activist 'influenced [his] analysis'" of a cross-racial homicide, causing him to "'incorrectly frame[ ] the issue as being whether the defendant was motivated in his actions by racism rather than whether or not his criminal intent was established beyond a reasonable doubt,'" and thereby preventing the judge from being "fair and impartial"; a different judge who thereafter presided over the defendant's postconviction motion to vacate the conviction was wrong to dismiss the trial judge's admissions of "'bias and prejudice . . . [as] mere afterthoughts or second guesses'"). Counsel can suggest that, at least when recusal and substitution of another judge will impose no significant burden or inconvenience upon the judiciary, these measures are warranted to guard against even the possibility of unconscious influences upon the judge. *See, e.g., United States v. Walker, supra,* 473 F.2d at 138-39 (rejecting the argument that a judge *must* recuse himself or herself after learning that one of the defendants had offered a guilty plea, but observing that "it would be better if [the judge] . . . exercised his prerogative to recuse himself [in such a situation since this rule] . . . should be easy to observe and put no burden on the administration of justice"); *People v. Smith,* 264 Cal. App. 2d 718, 722, 70 Cal. Rptr. 591, 594 (1968) (indicating that "where a motion is properly made before trial, a pretrial [suppression] hearing before another judge is . . . preferable to a determination by the trial judge"); *Banks v. United States*, 516 A.2d 524, 529 (D.C. 1986) (although the trial judge did not commit an abuse of discretion by conducting a bench trial of a defendant whose guilty plea broke down because the defendant asserted his innocence and the prosecution refused to offer an *Alford* plea, "the preferable procedure would have been for the trial judge to certify the case to another judge for trial after he rejected the plea"). The same reasoning, calling for recusal when it is not burdensome to the judicial system, would also apply to cases in which there is a potential for the appearance of impropriety. *See, e.g., State v. Lawrence,* 344 N.W.2d 227, 231 (Iowa 1984), *partially overruled on an unrelated point, State v. Liddell*, 672 N.W.2d 805 (Iowa 2003) (upholding the trial judge's exercise of discretion in favor of recusal because the judge "felt his trial rulings might be questioned in the mistaken belief that he was reacting in some way to the fact that he had been asked to step aside").

In addition to these situations in which information known to the judge may render it difficult for the judge to be an objective finder of fact at a bench trial – or would give rise to an unacceptable appearance of impropriety – the manner in which a judge conducts a bench trial may manifest such an apparent bias in favor of the prosecution that recusal is required or at least highly desirable to avoid an appearance of impropriety. *See, e.g., People v. Arnold*, 98 N.Y.2d 63, 64, 67-68, 772 N.E.2d 1140, 1142, 1144-45, 745 N.Y.S.2d 782, 784, 786-87 (2002) (the trial court abused its discretion in a bench trial by calling a police officer as a court witness to clarify an ambiguity in the prosecution's case after both sides had rested; "Although the law will allow a certain degree of judicial intervention in the presentation of evidence, the line is crossed when the judge takes on either the function or appearance of an advocate at trial"; the judge in this case "assumed the parties' traditional role of deciding what evidence to present, and introduced evidence that had the effect of corroborating the prosecution's witnesses and discrediting defendant on a key issue"); *People v. Zamorano*, 301 A.D.2d 544, 546-47, 754 N.Y.S.2d 645, 648 (N.Y. App. Div., 2d Dep't 2003) (the trial court in a bench trial abused its discretion in various ways, including taking "on the function and appearance of an advocate when, after the People's cross-examination, [the judge] asked the defendant numerous questions about the attack and tried to point out the inconsistencies and unbelievablity of his theory of defense"). *See also, e.g., In the Matter of Jacqulin M.*, 83 A.D.3d 844, 845, 922 N.Y.S.2d 111, 112-13 (N.Y. App. Div., 2d Dep't 2011) (the "Family Court Judge [in a juvenile delinquency bench trial] took on the function and appearance of an advocate by extensively participating in both the direct and cross-examination of the two . . . [prosecution] witnesses and eliciting testimony which strengthened the . . . [prosecution's] case" and by summoning the accused's probation officer to court to refute the accused's direct examination testimony that she gave "a certain document which would support her defense" to the probation officer, and by informing defense counsel that "unless he agreed to stipulate as to what . . . [the] Probation Department records would reflect, those records would be admitted into evidence through the Probation Officer's testimony"). Recusal is also required when a judge manifests bias against a class with which s/he identifies the defendant by, for example, treating the defendant's characteristics as stereotypical of the class. *See State v. Smith,* 308 Kan. 778, 423 P.3d 530 (2018) (ordering a new hearing before a different judge because the judge who made credibility findings against the defendant in a postconviction proceeding displayed unwarranted attention to the defendant's tattoos and supposed taste for rap music; "Granted, our record does not conclusively show that the district court actually relied on the irrelevant tattoo and brand information it retrieved independently – and may not have effectively shared with counsel and the parties before denying Smith's motion to file a late appeal. Nor does it conclusively show the court in fact relied on its irrelevant 'assumption' about the music Smith listened to. But a judge must avoid even 'conduct that may reasonably be perceived as prejudiced or biased.' Supreme Court Rule 601B, Canon 2, Rule 2.3, Comment [2] (2018 Kan. S. Ct. R. 436). And this information (particularly the assumption) was obviously at least considered by the court."

A judge's lack of objectivity – or even just an appearance of partisanship – can be problematic in a jury trial as well. "Although the judge in a criminal jury trial does not find facts, he or she still must make many rulings that affect the defendant's ability to obtain a fair trial. Some of these rulings rise and fall on the judge's discretion alone, and they can have dramatic impact on the evidence the jury hears as well as both parties' ability to present their arguments. . . . It nearly goes without saying that a criminal trial judge also is inevitably vested with considerable discretion at sentencing." *State v. Sawyer*, 297 Kan. 902, 911, 305 P.3d 608, 614 (2013) (rejecting the trial judge's and lower appellate court's reasoning that recusal was not necessary because "this case was tried to a jury rather than to the bench"). *See also People v. Towns, supra; Gacho v. Wills, supra*, 986 F.3d at 1076: "It is irrelevant that Gacho was convicted by a jury rather than . . . [by the biased judge] himself." Accordingly, in jury trials just as in bench trials, counsel should consider seeking recusal or disqualification if a judge has made statements evidencing a bias against the defendant or in favor of the prosecution or has manifested such a bias in the way that s/he conducted pretrial proceedings or is conducting the trial. *See Sawyer, supra*, 297 Kan. at 908, 911-12, 305 P.3d at 613, 614-15 (although defense counsel's motion for recusal did not specify bias sufficient to require recusal under the applicable state statute, the Due Process Clause required recusal because "Judge McNally had previously chosen to recuse in Sawyer's assault and battery bench trial; the judge's intemperate demeanor in Sawyer's intervening jury trial for lewd and lascivious behavior drew a stern admonition from the Court of Appeals; and Judge McNally's mere observation that this case involved a jury trial rather than a bench trial did nothing to ameliorate any earlier need for recusal"). *See also, e.g., People v. Lawhorn*, 178 A.D.3d 1466, 1467, 112 N.Y.S.3d 631, 632 (N.Y. App. Div. 4th Dep't 2019) ("the [trial] court committed reversible error when it 'negotiated and entered into a [plea] agreement with a codefendant[,] requiring that individual to testify against defendant in exchange for a more favorable sentence' . . . . Here, 'by assuming the function of an interested party and deviating from its own role as a neutral arbiter, the trial court denied defendant his due process right to "[a] fair trial in a fair tribunal"' . . . . We therefore reverse the judgment and grant a new trial before a different justice"); *State v. Malone*, 963 N.W.2d 453, 457, 466, 469 (Minn. 2021) (the judge's conduct during a pretrial proceeding on the defendant's motion to dismiss the charging paper for lack of probable cause – which included the judge's "investigat[ing] a fact not introduced into evidence, announc[ing] the findings from that investigation to the parties, rel[ying] on those findings in rejecting Malone's motion to dismiss, [and] suggest[ing] that the State might want to consider calling a second witness to testify against Malone" – "reasonably caused the judge's impartiality to be questioned" and therefore required disqualification under MINN. R. CRIM. P. 26.03 subd. 14(3) even though "Malone failed to show actual bias"; this error could not be deemed harmless on the ground that "the judge did not sit as the factfinder at Malone's [jury] trial"); *People v. Stevens*, 498 Mich. 162, 869 N.W.2d 233 (2015) ("Judicial misconduct may come in myriad forms, including belittling of counsel, inappropriate questioning of witnesses, providing improper strategic advice to a particular side, biased commentary in front of the jury, or a variety of other inappropriate actions." *Id.* at 172-73, 869 N.W.2d at 243. "A trial judge's conduct deprives a party of a fair trial if the conduct pierces the veil of judicial impartiality. A judge's conduct pierces this veil and violates the constitutional guarantee of a fair trial when, considering the totality of the circumstances, it is reasonably likely that the judge's conduct improperly influenced the jury by creating the appearance of advocacy or partiality against a party. . . . When the issue is preserved and a reviewing court determines that the trial judge's conduct pierced the veil of judicial impartiality, the court may not apply harmless-error review. Rather, the judgment must be reversed and the case remanded for a new trial." *Id.* at 164, 869 N.W.2d at 238-39.); *People v. Estevez*, 155 A.D.3d 650, 651, 64 N.Y.S.3d 236, 237 (N.Y. App. Div., 2d Dep't 2017) (reversing a conviction due to the trial judge's excessive intervention in witness examinations, even though defense counsel did not preserve the claim by "object[ing] to the court's questioning of the witnesses"; the judge "effectively took over the direct examination of one of the complaining witnesses at key moments in her testimony where she was describing how the defendant shot the victim . . . . Moreover, in its extensive questioning of the defendant, the court repeatedly highlighted apparent inconsistencies in the defendant's testimony."); *People v. Aponte*, 204 A.D.3d 1031, 1034-35, 1036, 167 N.Y.S.3d 154, 158, 159 (N.Y. App. Div., 2d Dept. 2022) (reversing a conviction because the trial judge "improperly impeded the defendant's defense of third-party culpability by limiting the defendant's cross-examination of the police witness regarding the lineup procedures, curtailing defense counsel's summation, and, sua sponte, improperly and erroneously instructing the jury and defense counsel in the presence of the jury that counsel could not argue that the lineup was unfair or suggestive, as the court had already found it fair and not suggestive"; "although the defendant's contention that he was deprived of a fair trial is unpreserved for appellate review, we reach it in the exercise of our interest of justice jurisdiction . . . and find that the cumulative effect of these errors, particularly the . . . [trial court's] intrusion into defense counsel's summation as an advocate for the People and its erroneous instructions on the law regarding the lineup, deprived the defendant of a fair trial"); *People v. Kocsis*, 137 A.D.3d 1476, 1481-82, 28 N.Y.S.3d 466, 471-72 (N.Y. App. Div. 3d Dep't 2016) (the judge in a jury trial "deprived [the defendant] of a fair trial" by providing "guidance and instructions" to the prosecutor regarding "the rules of evidence": "During the course of the trial, the ADA [Assistant District Attorney] in question demonstrated difficulty in laying the proper foundation for the admission into evidence of certain photographs and bank records and in utilizing a particular document to refresh a witness's recollection. In response, County Court conducted various sidebars, during the course of which the court, among other things, explained the nature of defense counsel's objections, outlined the questions that the ADA needed to ask of the testifying witnesses, referred the ADA to a certain evidentiary treatise and afforded him a recess in order to consult and review the appropriate section thereof."; the "County Court's assistance in this regard – although well-intentioned – arguably created the perception that the People were receiving an unfair tactical advantage"); *People v. Retamozzo*, 25 A.D.3d 73, 74, 86-87, 802 N.Y.S.2d 426, 427, 434-35 (N.Y. App. Div., 1st Dep't 2005) (the trial judge in a jury trial "deprived defendant of his constitutional right to a fair trial by excessive interference in the examination of witnesses," including asking questions and making comments during counsel's cross-examinations of prosecution witnesses that undermined the cross-examinations, and asking questions during the defendant's testimony that conveyed "considerable skepticism"; the record does not contain "a single instance of a question asked by the trial judge that plausibly could be viewed as helpful to the defense"); *People v. Chatman*, 14 A.D.3d 620, 620-21, 789 N.Y.S.2d 208, 210 (N.Y. App. Div., 2d Dep't 2005) (the trial judge in a jury trial "assumed the appearance of an advocate at the trial" by "improperly elicit[ing] from the investigating detective testimony that the defendant did not mention his alleged alibi at the time of his arrest, and refused to answer any questions" and by "extensive[ly] questioning . . . the defendant's alibi witness"); *People v. Raosto*, 50 A.D.3d 508, 509, 856 N.Y.S.2d 86, 88 (N.Y. App. Div., 1st Dept. 2008) (the trial judge in a jury trial "'unduly injected himself into the proceeding to such an extent as to deny defendant a fair and impartial trial'" by "conduct[ing] lengthy and inappropriate cross-examinations of defendant and defense witnesses, which were neither neutral nor aimed at clarification, but disrupted the flow of testimony and plainly conveyed to the jury the court's disbelief of these witnesses").

22.6. *Procedures for Seeking Recusal or Disqualification*

Local practice must be consulted with regard to the appropriate form of challenge to a judge (motion for recusal or disqualification or substitution; affidavit of bias; whatever) and the time when it must be made.

As noted in § 22.5 *supra,* in some jurisdictions the filing of a facially sufficient affidavit or motion requires that the judge recuse himself or herself, without inquiry into the truth of the matters of fact averred. Under other procedures the underlying factual questions are heard before the judge who is challenged or another judge.

The defense is entitled to put allegations of bias into the record in any manner necessary to present them to the court and save them for review. *See Holt v. Virginia,* 381 U.S. 131 (1965); *In re Little,* 404 U.S. 553 (1972). Ordinarily, a written motion with supporting affidavits is desirable to protect the record.

Procedures and preparations for dealing with a predictably hostile judge are discussed in Michael D. Cicchini, *Combating Judicial Misconduct: A Stoic Approach*, 67 BUFFALO L. REV. 1259 (2019).

In some jurisdictions there is a procedure – sometimes called a motion for change of venue, sometimes called an affidavit of bias – that is actually used (by custom) as a form of peremptory challenge to the judge. It may not require any assertion of bias, or it may require simply an allegation of bias in conclusory form that the judges do not take seriously or resent. Ordinarily, motions or affidavits for removal of a judge under these peremptory-challenge procedures are timely only if filed before the judge has taken any action in the case; sometimes they are required to be filed within a specific time after the assignment of the case to the judge.

22.7. *Tactical Considerations in Deciding Whether to Seek Recusal and in Framing the Recusal Request*

In deciding whether to seek recusal or disqualification of the judge, counsel must balance the liabilities of keeping the present judge (that is, the likely effects of the biasing factors upon the judge's rulings and, in the event of conviction, the sentence s/he imposes) against the risk of incurring judicial wrath. If the motion is denied and the judge retains the case, whatever latent biasing factors originally existed may well be exacerbated by the judge's anger over being accused of bias. A sufficiently irascible judge may also invoke sanctions against counsel. *See Dean v. Philadelphia Gas Works*, 2020 WL 7695751 (E.D. Pa. 2020). And even if the motion is granted, there may be repercussions: The judge to whom the case is transferred may resent counsel and the client for what the judge perceives as an attack upon a colleague or the judiciary in general.

In deciding whether to seek recusal, counsel also will need to compare the present judge with the other judges to whom the case might be assigned if the recusal motion is granted.

Notwithstanding whatever biases the current judge may harbor, s/he may be more prone to be fair in his or her rulings at trial and/or a more lenient sentencer than the other judges who could receive the case if it is transferred.

Counsel can both maximize the chances of gaining recusal and minimize the risks of incurring judicial wrath by the way in which the recusal request is framed. When possible, counsel should rely upon the "appearance of impropriety" as the primary basis for recusal. See § 22.5 fourth paragraph *supra*.

Depending upon the temperament of the judge and counsel's relationship with the judge, counsel may want to consider making an informal recusal request before filing a motion or invoking statutory recusal procedures. Such an initial soft-sell approach permits a graceful way out that will be accepted by some judges who would feel obliged to resist a formal motion making specific allegations of bias against them. However, some judges may resent such informal requests, viewing them as an attempt to use a back-door approach to obtain recusal for reasons that are so insubstantial that the attorney is not even willing to put them on the record.

In making the difficult decisions whether to seek recusal and how to frame recusal requests, counsel should always investigate both the general local attitudes toward these procedures and the known past reactions of the individual judge in question. In some jurisdictions, and with some judges, recusal motions are accepted as a routine forum-shopping device, which may ordinarily be safely used, without incurring judicial ire. Conversely, what is accepted as stock pleading in one locality – or to one judge – may be taken as a deadly insult in another locality or by another judge in the same locality.

Chapter 23

Motions for Severance or for Consolidation of Counts or Defendants

A. *Motions Challenging the Joinder of Counts or Seeking Consolidation of Counts*

23.1. *Introduction: The Problem of Joined Counts; Overview of the Possible Remedies*

As § 20.9 *supra* explained, prosecutors may be authorized (by state statutes, rules of court, or caselaw) to include in a single charging paper all charges arising from (1) the same event or episode (for example, housebreaking, larceny, and receiving stolen property); and possibly also (2) separate events or episodes that are (depending upon variations in local rules) (a) part of the same transaction or series of transactions, (b) part of a "common plan" or "common scheme" by the defendant, or (c) legally the same or similar (for example, housebreaking on May 5 and housebreaking on June 12).

In cases in which all the charges against the defendant arise from the same event or episode (such as the ordinary set of housebreaking-larceny-receiving charges based on a single break-in), the joinder results in little prejudice to the defendant, and thus there is little reason to seek severance. Indeed, the defendant may even derive some benefit from a joint trial: The same proof, and all the proof, would likely be admitted at separate trials; and the more trials there are, the more chance there is that the defendant will lose at least one of them. In any event, most courts will compel a joint trial in this situation, whether the defendant wants one or not.

However, in cases in which the prosecution has joined charges arising from different episodes or transactions (on the basis of the factual connection between the transactions or the legal similarity of the charges), the defendant faces a significant risk that the trier of fact, whether jury or judge, will view the aggregation of charges as increasing the likelihood that the defendant is guilty of each one. Thus, in cases that are going to trial, counsel will usually wish to challenge the joinder of the counts or seek severance. *See, e.g., People v. Hall*, 120 A.D.3d 588, 589, 991 N.Y.S.3d 114, 116 (N.Y. App. Div., 2d Dep't 2014) ("the defendant was deprived of the effective assistance of counsel, based on defense counsel's failure to make a proper pretrial motion to sever the charges of robbery from the drug charges"). In rare cases, however, there may be countervailing benefits to having the counts joined for trial, and counsel may want to leave the joinder unchallenged; or when the prosecutor has filed separate charging instruments, counsel may want to seek consolidation of the charges for a single trial. In addition, if the defendant wishes to enter pleas of guilty to separate charging instruments or wishes to enter a plea of guilty to one charging instrument upon the basis of an agreement with the prosecutor that other charges will be dismissed (see § 15.6.2 *supra*), consolidation may facilitate the implementation of a favorable plea agreement and may also enable the defendant to steer the case before the most favorable sentencing judge (see § 15.7.2 *supra*).

Section 23.2 describes the strategic variables that counsel should consider in deciding whether to challenge joinder of counts. Sections 23.3 and 23.4 then examine the motions that counsel can file to obtain dismissal or a severance on grounds of misjoinder and to obtain a severance on the grounds that the joinder, although technically valid, is prejudicial to the defendant. Section 23.5 discusses motions for consolidation.

Counsel must check local statutes, court rules, and caselaw to determine not only the terms of the joinder rules used in the jurisdiction but also the procedural requirements for raising joinder issues. In many jurisdictions objections to misjoinder and/or motions for severance must be made at arraignment or within a specified period of time after arraignment. See § 17.7 *supra.*

23.2. *Deciding Whether to Oppose a Trial on Multiple Charges*

As explained in § 23.1 *supra,* usually the only joinder of charges that the defense might want to challenge is a joinder of charges arising from different events or episodes. In deciding whether to make such a challenge, counsel should consider:

(a) *What will be the effect of the trier's knowing that the defendant is charged with several offenses, quite apart from any proof of his or her guilt of those offenses?*

Generally the more a defendant is charged with, the worse s/he looks. Jurors and even many judges in bench trials tend to operate on the principle that where there's smoke, there's fire. At the outset of the trial, when they are forming critical first impressions of the case that may affect their perceptions of much of the proof that follows, they know little about the defendant except what s/he is charged with. If the charges are several, the defendant starts with several sins.

In some cases, however, there may be countervailing considerations. If the defendant is obviously overcharged – if, for example, s/he breaks into a few vending machines and is charged, for each machine, with burglary, theft, and malicious destruction – the cumulative weight of the overcharging may make out a case of persecution that will sway a jury or judge in the defendant's favor.

(b) *What will be the effect on the trier of the cumulation of evidence?*

Again, generally the more evidence there is against a defendant, the worse. But this may depend on whether the evidence comes from several sources or from one. If two package store proprietors give the same "pretty sure" identifications of the defendant as the person who robbed them, conviction is more likely than if separate juries or judicial triers of fact heard each of the identifying witnesses. On the other hand, if a single complainant relates that the defendant committed an offense against him or her on several successive occasions, proof of an airtight alibi for one or more of those occasions may convince the jury or the judge in a bench trial that the whole story is a fabrication, particularly if the defense can point to some motive for fabricating.

(c) *Will one defense depreciate another?*

If a defendant has a weak or unconvincing defense to one charge and a more substantial defense to another, the incredibility of the former is likely to attaint the latter. Or both defenses may be believable separately but unbelievable together, as when a defendant charged with two rapes pleads alibi to the first and consent to the second.

(d) *Is it desirable to put the defendant on the stand in one case but not in the other?*

If so, separate trials are essential. Apart from problems of cross-examination, a defendant cannot practicably take the stand and leave part of the charges against him or her unanswered.

(e) *Is there a "clinching" piece of evidence in one case that would not be admissible in the other if it were tried separately?*

If so, the item may "clinch" both cases, as when a defendant charged with two holdups left a fingerprint at the scene of one.

(f) *Are there items of evidence that the prosecution would probably be forbidden to present in a separate trial of one case because they are irrelevant or unduly prejudicial but that the prosecution would probably be permitted to present in a joint trial of the two cases?*

For example, a defendant may be charged with armed robbery and also with being a felon in possession of a firearm. If the robbery count were tried separately, the evidence of the defendant's prior felony conviction would ordinarily be inadmissible. In a joint trial of the two counts, the evidence would be admissible and would be likely to sway a jury against the defendant on the more serious robbery charge as well. Under these circumstances, "[s]ome jurisdictions routinely refuse [severance] requests . . . . Instead, they seek to address the risk of prejudice with an instruction directing the jury to consider the defendant's prior convictions only when assessing the felon-in-possession charge. . . . Other jurisdictions allow parties to stipulate to the defendant's past convictions so the particulars of those crimes don't reach the jury's ears. . . . Others take a more protective approach yet and view severance requests with favor." (*Currier v. Virginia*, 138 S. Ct. 2144, 2148 (2018)). The tactical problem here is less acute (or at least less solvable) in bench trials than in jury trials because the trial judge (whether or not s/he shares the ordinary juryperson's once-a-criminal-always-a-criminal presumption) will probably be exposed to pretrial proceedings or court records revealing the prior conviction even in a separate trial. See § 40.5 *infra* and §§ 15.4.3, 22.5 subdivision (2) *supra* regarding the limited means available for dealing with the latter problem.

(g) *To what extent will a unitary wrap-up of all charges against the defendant expedite the task of gathering the requisite defense witnesses?*

Although, in an ideal world, defense witnesses would be willing to come to court again and again, the reality is that defense witnesses other than the defendant's family will soon lose patience and stop coming to court. Even when local practice makes it possible to put these witnesses "on call," they may be unwilling to be available for more than one trial date. If this is the case, then counsel might consider reducing the risk of losing witnesses by trying all charges in a joint trial.

(h) *To what extent may the process of successive prosecution cause the prosecutor to offer favorable plea bargains?*

Most prosecutors are so overburdened that they are hard pressed to find the time to try cases. Frequently, a prosecutor who is unwilling to make a good plea offer to resolve joint charges slated for a single trial will be far more amenable to offering whatever it takes to avoid the daunting prospect of a series of trials. If the various charges involve the same complainant or other witnesses, the prosecutor also may be eager to avoid repeated trials because the likelihood of prosecution witnesses losing patience and failing to appear increases with each successive court date.

(i) *To what extent will a unitary wrap-up affect sentencing?*

As explained in § 15.5 *supra,* the judge may penalize a defendant at sentencing for taking a case to trial when the evidence of guilt was obviously strong. If the defendant is facing several different charges, all of which are strong prosecution cases, and the defendant is unwilling to plead guilty to any of the charges, counsel may be well advised to try all of the cases in a single trial. If the cases are separated, and the defendant insists on going through with each trial, the court's substantial expenditure of time and resources may redound to the defendant's detriment at disposition.

In assessing the possible sentencing implications of joinder, counsel must also study the rules governing sentencing on multiple charges and the terms of recidivist sentencing laws. See §§ 48.6 subdivisions (B), (H); 48.13.1 *infra.* Increased penalties may be available for successive but not simultaneous convictions. Also, the defendant probably has a better chance of receiving concurrent sentences on two convictions after a single trial before a single judge than after two trials before different judges, or even the same judge.

As noted in § 23.1 *supra,* consolidation of charges for purposes of a plea or pleas covering all of the charges can sometimes be used to work out the details of a satisfactory plea bargain (see § 15.6.2 *supra*) and to bring the case before the judge who is known to be the most favorable sentencer (see § 15.7.2 *supra*).

(j) *Will a unitary wrap-up affect the defendant's pretrial detention status?*

If the defendant is being held in custody on bail s/he cannot afford to post, counsel should consider the potential benefits of a unitary wrap-up as a way of shortening the defendant's pretrial detention. If the defendant is likely to be acquitted of all charges or if s/he is likely to receive probation upon conviction, the resolution of all cases at once means that the defendant will be immediately released. To resolve them piecemeal probably means that the defendant will stay in custody until all of the pending charges have been resolved.

(k) *Could a unitary wrap-up affect the defendant's eligibility for parole?*

If the defendant is tried on only one of several pending charges, the prosecutor may "dead-list" the others (that is, not bring them on for trial) and may lodge them as detainers against the defendant who is committed to serve a sentence of imprisonment on the first charge. The detainers will not only hang over the defendant's head; they may make the defendant ineligible for parole. See § 15.6.1 subdivision (D) *supra*. The prosecutor may or may not be required to bring the dead-listed charges on for trial upon the defendant's demand. See § 28.5 *infra*.

23.3. *Motions Challenging the Charging Paper for Misjoinder or an Insufficient Showing of the Basis for Joinder*

As § 20.9 *supra* explained, the local statute, rule, or caselaw usually provides a basis for defense counsel to challenge the joinder of counts in an indictment or information on the ground that the applicable standards do not permit charges of this nature to be filed in a single charging paper. *See, e.g., United States v. Cousins*, 841 Fed. Appx. 885, 893-94 (6th Cir. 2021) ("In this case, the face of the indictment gives no indication that Mr. Cousins's charge forms part of the same 'act or transaction' or the 'same series of acts or transactions' as the other charges, as [Federal Criminal Rule 8(b) requires. Unlike many drug-conspiracy indictments, this [seven-count] indictment does not contain a statement of alleged facts before the list of counts; it merely states the counts that each defendant is charged with. It charges both Mr. Stewart and Mr. Moore with possession with intent to distribute certain drugs in each of counts 1 through 3, and it charges them both in count 4 with possession of two handguns in furtherance of drug-trafficking crimes. . . . ¶ . . . [T]he indictment contains nothing readily connecting the single count charging Mr. Cousins with any of the other six. . . . ¶ Although the government argues that joinder was appropriate because the offenses 'grew out of the same search,' the three defendants 'simultaneously stored guns' at the . . . [same] house, and '[t]he government's witnesses regarding the basis for the search, and the search itself, would be the same in separate trials,' there is no basis for any of those conclusions in the charging instrument. The only connection apparent from the indictment is that the offenses are all alleged to have occurred '[o]n or about November 17, 2016.' Although we construe indictments 'in favor of joinder,' . . . without knowing additional facts about the search and witnesses, we cannot infer from the coincidence in date that count 7 is related to the first six counts or that the proofs will involve common evidence. We conclude that count 7 is misjoined."); *People v. Santiago*, 190 A.D.3d 502, 502-03, 140 N.Y.S.3d 29 (N.Y. App. Div., 1st Dep't 2021) (the trial court should have granted the defendant's motion to sever charges of "leaving the scene of an incident without reporting" and "driving while ability impaired" which were based on incidents that "occurred on a different date" and "different set[s] of facts": although state law allows joinder of offenses "based on different criminal transactions if proof of one offense would be material and admissible as evidence in chief upon a trial of the other offense," the "witnesses, locations, and dates of the two crimes were completely unrelated" and "none of the proof necessary for each offense was material to the other"); *State v. Shape*, 517 N.W.2d 650 (S.D. 1994) (requiring that charges of cattle theft and of perjury committed before a grand jury roughly two years later be severed because the charged offenses were not of the same or similar character, were not based on the same act or transaction, and were not based on acts constituting a common scheme or plan.). As § 20.9 also notes, in some jurisdictions, a multi-count charging paper can be attacked for misjoinder if it fails to explicitly allege the facts ("same transaction"; "common plan"; whatever) upon which the permissibility of joinder depends.

23.4. *Motions for a Severance of Charges on the Ground of Prejudicial Joinder*

Unlike motions challenging misjoinder, see §§ 20.9, 23.3 *supra,* motions for a severance by reason of prejudicial joinder ask the court to order separate trials of properly joined counts on the ground that trying them together would unfairly disadvantage the defendant.

In seeking to persuade the court that the defendant would be prejudiced by a joint trial of two or more charges, counsel can point to the types of potential harm described in paragraphs (a) through (f) of § 23.2 *supra. See, e.g., Wiest v. State,* 542 A.2d 1193, 1195 (Del. 1988) ("The prejudice which a defendant may suffer from a joinder of offenses has been described in the following terms: 1) the jury may cumulate the evidence of the various crimes charged and find guilt when, if considered separately, it would not so find; 2) the jury may use the evidence of one of the crimes to infer a general criminal disposition of the defendant in order to find guilt of the other crime or crimes; and 3) the defendant may be subject to embarrassment or confusion in presenting different and separate defenses to different charges."). Often, there is local caselaw that can be cited in support of a severance to avoid the particular form of prejudice urged by counsel. *See, e.g., State v. Perez*, 322 Conn. 118, 139 A.3d 654 (2016) ("'[B]ecause of the unfavorable appearance of testifying on one charge while remaining silent on another, and the consequent pressure to testify as to all or none, the defendant may be confronted with a dilemma: whether, by remaining silent, to lose the benefit of vital testimony on one count, rather than risk the prejudice (as to either or both counts) that would result from testifying on the other.'" *Id.* at 134, 139 A.3d at 663. "We conclude that the trial court improperly denied the defendant's . . . motion to sever." *Id.* at 136, 139 A.3d at 664.); *United States v. Sampson*, 385 F.3d 183, 190-93 (2d Cir. 2004) (the joint trial of drug offenses occurring in 1998 with drug offenses occurring in 2000 "caused Sampson substantial prejudice with regard to the 1998 counts" because "he would have taken the stand in his defense on the 1998 counts" and he had "reasons for wanting to remain silent on the 2000 counts"); *Cross v. United States*, 335 F.2d 987, 989-91 (D.C. Cir. 1964) (the joint trial of charges of robbing a church rectory and robbing a tourist home on different dates was prejudicial because Cross "wished to testify on Count II [the tourist home robbery] and remain silent on Count I [the church rectory robbery]"); *United States v. McCarter*, 316 F.3d 536, 538-39 (5th Cir. 2002) ("We have long recognized the obvious dangers inherent in trying a felon-in-possession count together with other charges, as it acts as a conduit through which the government may introduce otherwise inadmissible evidence of the defendant's prior convictions, thereby potentially tainting the reliability of the verdict rendered by the jury on the other counts. For this reason, '"evidence of a prior conviction has long been the subject of careful scrutiny and use at trial" because of the danger that the jury might convict, not based on the evidence, but because it feels that the defendant is a 'bad person.'"' Although the potential for prejudice resulting from introduction of prior crimes evidence in connection with a felon-in-possession charge may be lessened by limiting instructions, a proper inquiry into the propriety of trying the felon count together with the other charges requires examining not only the efficacy of the limiting measures taken by the trial court, but also the strength of the evidence of the defendant's guilt. In certain cases, the translucency of the government's ill motive for adding the felon-in-possession count is also a factor in determining whether severance was warranted."); *People v. Utley*, 2019 IL App (1st) 152112, 142 N.E.3d 352, 363-64, 436 Ill. Dec. 249, 260-61 (2019) (holding defense counsel ineffective for failing to file a severance motion: "[D]efendant notes that he was charged with being an armed habitual criminal, with unlawful use of a weapon by a felon for his alleged possession of guns and ammunition, and with possession of a controlled substance with intent to deliver for his alleged possession of cocaine and heroin. Defendant further notes that, to prove the gun charges, the State was required to introduce evidence of defendant's prior convictions for aggravated battery with a firearm and delivery of a controlled substance, neither of which would have been admissible to prove the possession of a controlled substance offense. Defendant contends that, in these circumstances, defense counsel should have filed a motion to sever the gun charges and drug charges and that, had counsel done so, the court would have granted the motion. ¶ . . . [W]e find that there existed a significant risk that the jury's knowledge that defendant had previously been convicted of aggravated battery with a firearm and unlawful delivery of a controlled substance would be used in determining his guilt or innocence of the instant, unrelated, offense."); *Wallace v. Commonwealth*, 478 S.W.3d 291, 303 (Ky. 2015) ("[T]his Court . . . long ago set forth how trial courts should resolve questions of joinder and severance of multiple charges when possession of a firearm by a convicted felon is one of the charged offenses. That is, this Court made clear that a firearm charge is required to be severed from other charges to avoid the prejudice that necessarily arises from a jury learning of a defendant's otherwise inadmissible criminal history when considering guilt or innocence on other charged offenses." A trial court may sever the firearms charge entirely or may try that charge before the same jury after the conclusion of an initial trial of the other offenses.); *State v. Lozada*, 357 N.J. Super. 468, 471, 815 A.2d 1002, 1003-04 (2003) (applying and extending the holding of *State v. Chenique-Puey*, 145 N.J. 334, 343, 678 A.2d 694, 698 (1996), that "in order to avoid the prejudice to defendant resulting from the jury's knowledge of the restraining order when it tries the underlying crimes, . . . ' . . . trial courts should sever and try sequentially charges of contempt of a domestic-violence restraining order and of an underlying criminal offense when the charges arise from the same episode"); *Harris v. State*, summarized in § 36.2.3 *infra* (alternative ground) ("[b]ecause . . . almost all of the evidence needed to prove the counts . . . [charging the defendant with sex offenses based on online communications with an unrelated teenage girl] was inadmissible as to the counts . . . [charging the defendant with malice murder of his 22-month-old son and associated child cruelty in leaving the boy to die of hyperthermia in a closed car], the trial court abused its discretion by denying . . . defendant's motion to sever"). *See also People v. Martinez*, 165 A.D.3d 1288, 1290, 86 N.Y.S.3d 143, 146 (N.Y. App. Div., 2d Dep't 2018) (the trial court "improvidently exercised its discretion in granting the People's motion to consolidate" indictments for two separate crimes; although the crimes were "properly joinable," the consolidation "'compromise[d] . . . [the] defendant's fundamental right to a fair trial'" because "there was a substantial disparity in the evidence tying the defendant to the offenses contained in the separate indictments, which presented a strong possibility that the jury convicted the defendant of the offenses charged in Indictment No. 8114/13 by reason of the cumulative effect of the evidence").

When a severance motion based on a claim of anticipated prejudice has been denied but in the course of trial an unexpected evidentiary ruling or other development arising from the joinder of charges occurs and is damaging to the defense, the motion can be renewed and coupled with a motion for a mistrial. *See, e.g., City of Seattle v. Lange*, 18 Wash. App. 2d 139, 491 P.3d 156 (2021).

In many localities counsel will find that the judges are obdurate in favor of joint trials to the fullest extent allowed by law and that they are reluctant to grant a severance whenever joinder is technically permissible, because of the supposed saving of court time. In these localities particularly, the inquiry into "prejudice" is likely to turn into a balancing of the economies and other considerations favoring or disfavoring joint trial. *See, e.g., State v. Freshment*, 309 Mont. 154, 164-71, 43 P.3d 968, 976-80 (2002). Accordingly, counsel is wise to point to the lack of evidentiary overlap between the counts that s/he is asking to have severed – demonstrating (to the extent that the facts allow) that the prosecution's witnesses on one count will be completely (or substantially) different from those on the other count(s), and representing (when this is true) that the defense witnesses on the different counts will be completely (or substantially) different as well. Under these circumstances a judge might conclude that a joint trial would not save much time and, therefore, that it is not worth the judge's while to suffer the unwieldiness of numerous sets of witnesses and a lengthy proceeding, particularly in the face of the defendant's tenable (and preserved) claims of potential prejudice to his or her defense.

It is not necessarily fatal to joint trial that some charges will be tried to a jury while others are tried to the court. In a number of localities it is standard procedure to conduct simultaneous jury and bench trials, with the judge sitting as the trier of fact on the bench-tried charges and sending the others out to the jury. Other courts do not seem to do this, and in those courts the defendant can obtain a *de facto* severance by waiving jury trial on some charges but not on others. In many jurisdictions, however, the waiver is only effective if it is agreed to by the prosecutor and accepted by the court (see § 32.2.1 *infra*), and one or the other may decline to agree to a jury waiver in some, but not all, cases that would otherwise be jointly tried.

23.5. *Consolidation of Counts*

For reasons made apparent by §§ 23.1 and 23.2 *supra,* it will be the rare case in which the defense should seek consolidation for trial of charges that the prosecutor has filed in separate charging instruments.

However, as those sections also noted, a different calculus may apply to cases in which the defendant intends to enter a guilty plea covering charges in various charging instruments. If the various charging instruments are before different judges, counsel may be able to consolidate all of them, for purposes of a plea, before the judge who would be the most favorable sentencer. (If local procedure makes it impossible to predict which judge would receive the consolidated plea, it may be best to leave the cases before separate judges and then use the sequencing of sentencings to secure the best overall result. For example, if there is a reasonable chance of obtaining a sentence of probation, it may be wise to schedule the sentencing by the most favorable judge first, counting on the other judges to defer to that judge's grant of probation rather than overriding it with a sentence of incarceration in another case. If the defendant is likely to end up with a term of incarceration, then it may be best to go to the harsher sentencer first and then ask the more lenient, follow-up sentencer to make the prison term in his or her case concurrent rather than consecutive – assuming, of course, that the applicable sentencing statute does not mandate consecutive terms (see § 48.6 subdivision (H) *infra*).)

When consolidation is desired, it may be ordered on stipulation, or on joint motion of the parties, or on motion of one of them, or it may be effected informally by the prosecutor's listing the cases for trial or plea together, with the acquiescence of the defense. Consolidation can be ordered in any case in which the rules governing joinder would have permitted the joinder of counts initially. If the prosecution and defense are agreed that consolidation will serve their mutual interests, the court will probably accept a stipulation consolidating even those charges that could not technically have been joined.

B. *Motions Challenging the Misjoinder of Defendants or Seeking Severance of Defendants*

23.6. *Introduction: The Problem of Joined Defendants; Overview of the Possible Remedies*

Prosecutors almost always take advantage of local rules permitting the joinder for trial of codefendants who are charged with participating in the same offense or offenses. Joinder of defendants is ordinarily in the prosecutor's interest for several reasons: (i) it saves the prosecutor from the burden of conducting successive trials, each with the same evidence; (ii) it minimizes the risk that prosecution witnesses will lose patience and stop coming to court; and (iii) it enables the prosecutor to gain the impermissible benefit of aggregating the evidence against each defendant individually to mount a persuasive cumulative case against both.

The considerations that might lead defense counsel to favor or oppose a joint trial are listed in § 23.7 *infra*. As the discussion there indicates, it will usually be in the defendant's interest to seek a severance from joined codefendants.

Challenges to the misjoinder of defendants are described in § 23.8 *infra*. Section 23.9 takes up the constitutional, statutory, and common law grounds for severance by reason of prejudicial (although technically permissible) joinder. Section 23.10 concludes by examining defense motions for consolidation of defendants.

Many jurisdictions require that objections to joinder and motions for severance must be made at arraignment or within a specified time after arraignment. Local statutes and court rules must be consulted. See § 17.7 *supra*.

23.7. *Deciding Whether to Oppose a Joint Trial of Defendants*

The considerations favoring and disfavoring joint trial of defendants are exceedingly complex. The most significant are:

(a) *Will evidence be admitted at a joint trial that could not be admitted at the defendant's trial if s/he were tried separately?*

A principal item of concern in joint trials, and one that has generated considerable constitutional caselaw, is the admission at a joint trial of a codefendant's confession that implicates not only the codefendant but also the defendant. Section 23.9.1 *infra* examines the constitutional rules relating to this issue. For the present purpose of summarizing the considerations militating for and against a joint trial, it is sufficient to observe that the existence of a confession by the codefendant significantly impairs the defendant's chances of prevailing at a joint trial. Although the confession may not legally be considered as evidence of the defendant's guilt (see § 23.9.1), the jury or judicial trier of fact will hear it and will almost surely consider it in fact, whether consciously or unconsciously, insofar as it implicates the defendant. Even codefendants' confessions that do not explicitly implicate the defendant (or that have been redacted to remove references to the defendant, see § 23.9.1) can be extremely damaging to the defense, particularly when they factually contradict the defendant's theory of defense or when the facts are such that both defendants are probably guilty if either one is.

Certain non-confessional evidence that would be inadmissible against the defendant at a severed trial may also be admissible and hurtful at a joint trial. For example, in a robbery trial, if the defendant admits to being with the codefendant at the time the crime was committed, evidence that the codefendant was found in possession of stolen items a short while later will probably be the undoing of the defendant as well as the codefendant.

(b) *Conversely, will evidence be excluded at a joint trial that would be admitted against the defendant at a separate trial?*

Products of an illegal search and seizure of a codefendant may be admissible against the defendant because the defendant lacks standing to complain of the illegality. See § 25.15 *infra.* At a joint trial, they might have to be excluded, although this point is not clear. *See McDonald v. United States,* 335 U.S. 451 (1948).

(c) *What are the relative strengths of the defensive cases of the defendant and codefendant(s)?*

Defendants with weak defenses tend to look particularly bad in comparison to those who have stronger defenses. If the codefendant is likely to take the stand, this may cast a bad light on the defendant's failure to take the stand. (On the other hand, in a case in which the defendant should not testify because s/he could be impeached with a damaging prior record, it may be possible to present the defendant's defense through the codefendant's testimony.)

(d) *What is the apparent relative blameworthiness of the defendant and the codefendant(s)?*

Joint trial invites the trier of fact, whether jury or judge, to assess degrees of culpability. If convictions of lesser included offenses are possible, the jury may mete out a sort of rough justice among codefendants according to what appears to be their culpability. This suggests that the least culpable defendant has the most to gain from joint trial. But counsel cannot count on his or her client appearing the least culpable unless the stories of prosecution witnesses or irrefutable physical circumstances – for example, relative size and age – make the favorable comparison strongly evident. Otherwise, the codefendants and their attorneys will also be vying to look the best of the bunch. In this and other situations of antagonistic defenses, separate trial should be sought.

(e) *Is there something particularly attractive or unattractive about the codefendant(s)?*

The jury's or judge's positive or negative reactions to a codefendant may rub off on the defendant at a joint trial.

(f) *Can counsel cooperate and work well with counsel for the codefendant(s)?*

Do their defensive theories or trial strategies conflict?

(g) *Will the number of defendants tend to protract the trial and wear the jury out?* Might it leave the jury confused and unable to identify the individual defendants? In "mass trials," when there is considerable evidence of wrongdoing, the jury usually convicts everybody in sight.

(h) *What are the local rules, and what is the local practice, regarding limitation of the procedural rights of joined defendants?*

For example, will counsel's cross-examination of prosecution witnesses be cut off as "cumulative" of that of counsel for a codefendant? In a jury trial, will each joined defendant be permitted the full number of peremptory challenges to which s/he would be entitled at a separate trial, or will the defendants be required to apportion peremptories?

(i) *If trial is severed, who is likely to be tried first?*

Prior trial of the codefendants may allow defense counsel full discovery of the prosecution's case in advance of his or her own trial. On the other hand, if they are convicted, they may turn state's evidence in an attempt to win sentencing consideration.

23.8. *Motions Challenging Misjoinder of Defendants*

Statutes, court rules, and caselaw must be reviewed to determine the local rules governing joinder of defendants and also to determine whether the remedy for misjoinder is a motion to dismiss the charging paper (see § 20.9 *supra*) or a motion to sever the defendant's trial from that of the codefendant(s). In some jurisdictions, counsel will also be able to frame a motion for dismissal or severance on the technical ground that the charging paper does not expressly allege the facts required to support a joinder of defendants. See § 20.9 *supra.*

The generally prevailing rule is that defendants may be joined in a single charging paper, or their charging papers may be joined for trial, if the defendants are alleged to have participated in the same act or transaction or in the same series of acts or transactions constituting an offense or offenses. A defendant can challenge the charging paper for misjoinder if, in addition to charging offenses in which both of two defendants allegedly participated, it charges offenses that only the codefendant is accused of committing. *See, e.g., Davis v. United States,* 367 A.2d 1254, 1260-64 (D.C. 1976).

23.9. *Motions for a Severance of Defendants on the Ground of Prejudicial Joinder*

Motions for severance may request a separate trial for the defendant notwithstanding the technically proper joinder of codefendants in the charging paper. A severance may be granted if, for any reason, the defendant will suffer prejudice as a result of being tried jointly with the codefendant(s). *See, e.g., Chartier v. State,* 124 Nev. 760, 191 P.3d 1182 (2008); *Rollerson v.*

United States, 127 A.3d 1220 (D.C. 2015); *People v. Massie*, 66 Cal. 2d 899, 917, 428 P.2d 869, 882, 59 Cal. Rptr. 733, 746 (1967) ("Older cases had held almost unanimously that a court could never abuse its discretion in denying a motion for a separate trial because the jury could be admonished not to consider prejudicial testimony admissible only against a codefendant. The more recent cases, however, recognizing the impossibility of a juror's obliteration from his mind of that which he already knew, have held that the court should separate the trials of codefendants in the face of an incriminating confession, prejudicial association with codefendants, likely confusion resulting from evidence on multiple counts, conflicting defenses, or the possibility that at a separate trial a codefendant would give exonerating testimony."), quoted with approval in *People v. Gomez*, 6 Cal. 5th 243, 274, 430 P.3d 791, 818, 240 Cal. Rptr. 3d 315, 347 (2018) (dictum).

A cardinal problem here, as with the required showing of prejudice generally, is that at the time of the hearing on a pretrial motion for severance, most of what will occur at trial remains largely speculative. After trial has begun and if prejudice develops, a motion for mistrial and severance may be made; but by this time the judge has an interest in not having wasted the court hours already invested, and s/he will be particularly loth to grant the motion. Counsel can sometimes turn these several related problems to advantage, however. If, on a pretrial motion, counsel can convince the court that the case is one in which trial problems may arise depending on the nature of the prosecutor's proof, the court will frequently ask the prosecutor what the proof is going to be – for example, whether a codefendant's confession will be used and whether it will incriminate the defendant. Motions for severance, therefore, have considerable discovery potential and may result in the disclosure of advance information about the prosecution evidence that counsel could not obtain by regular discovery procedures.

The most common bases for seeking severance are the following:

23.9.1. *Severance on the Basis of a Codefendant's Confession Implicating the Defendant*

In *Bruton v. United States,* 391 U.S. 123 (1968), the Court held that the admission at a joint trial of a codefendant's confession which incriminated the defendant violated the defendant's Sixth Amendment right of confrontation despite clear instructions to the jury limiting the use of the confession to its maker. Even in the situation known as "interlocking confessions," in which the defendant and codefendant both confessed and their incriminating statements supported each other, the *Bruton* rule prohibited the introduction at a joint trial of a codefendant's statement that incriminated the defendant. *Cruz v. New York,* 481 U.S. 186 (1987) (rejecting the plurality opinion in *Parker v. Randolph,* 442 U.S. 62 (1979), and adopting the approach espoused by Justice Blackmun's concurring opinion in *Parker*). *See, e.g., Brown v. Brown,* 847 F.3d 502 (7th Cir. 2017).

During the 45 years that followed *Bruton*, the Supreme Court and the lower courts evolved a coherent set of rules for joint trials in which one or more codefendants' confessions were proffered by the prosecution. The *Bruton* rule was limited to codefendants' statements incriminating the defendant, and therefore a codefendant's confession could be introduced at a joint trial "with a proper limiting instruction when . . . the confession . . . [was] redacted to eliminate not only the defendant's name, but any reference to her existence" (*Richardson v. Marsh,* 481 U.S. 200, 211 (1987)). *See also Gray v. Maryland,* 523 U.S. 185, 192-93 (1998) (addressing "a question that *Richardson* left open" and holding that "*Bruton*'s protective rule" fully applied when the ostensible "redaction [of the codefendant's confession] . . . replaces a defendant's name with an obvious indication of deletion, such as a blank space, the word 'deleted,' or a similar symbol," with the result that "the jury will often realize that the confession refers specifically to the defendant"); *Washington v. Secretary, Pennsylvania Dep't of Corrections,* 801 F.3d 160, 162, 163, 167 (3d Cir. 2015) ("admission into evidence of a confession by a non-testifying codefendant that redacted James Washington's name and replaced it with . . . generic terms describing Washington and his role in the charged crimes" violated the Confrontation Clause because "there were two obvious alterations that notified the jury that Washington's name was deleted"); *Colon v. Rozum,* 649 Fed. Appx. 259, 263-64 (3d Cir. 2016) ("Although the reference to 'another person' in this case is less specific than the more direct reference to 'the driver' in *Washington,* this distinction is not very meaningful in this case. This is so because the jury knew that: there were only three people in the car at the time of the crime; the statement was coming from Gonzales; Gonzales referred to the second person in the car (Betancourt) by name; and, finally, the jury knew from the prosecutor that Colon was the third person in the car. By a process of elimination, it was easy for the jury to infer that Colon was the person referenced when Gonzales was asked if the 'other person' heard Betancourt say that 'he was gonna rob somebody's purse and stuff like that.'"); *United States v. Taylor,* 745 F.3d 15, 29-30 (2d Cir. 2014) (redaction of the codefendants' names from Taylor's statement failed to overcome the Confrontation Clause problem because the resulting "stilted circumlocutions" and the retention of the name of the co-perpetrator who testified for the prosecution would have made it "obvious [to the jury] that names have been pruned from the text" and "the choice of implied identity is narrow" since "[t]he unnamed persons correspond by number (two) and by role to the pair of co-defendants" on trial with Taylor); *Eley v. Erickson,* 712 F.3d 837, 854-62 (3d Cir. 2013) (the trial court violated the Confrontation Clause by denying severance and allowing the admission of a jailhouse informant's account that a non-testifying codefendant confessed to committing the charged crime with two other persons and that shooting the victim "was the other two's idea" – a circumlocution which the jury doubtless would have understood to refer to Eley and another codefendant); *Brown v. Superintendent Greene SCI,* 834 F.3d 506 (3d Cir. 2016) (the codefendant's statement was redacted to eliminate the defendant's name by using terms such as "the other guy," "one of the guys," or "the guy with the gun" to replace it, but the prosecutor in closing argument referred to the defendant by name in a way that revealed he was "the other guy"; this constituted a *Bruton* violation whether the prosecutor's action was deliberate or an inadvertent slip, and although "[t]here are some circumstances when the prosecution can commit what otherwise would be a constitutional violation but nonetheless escape a mistrial through limiting instructions[,] . . . in cases falling within the ambit of *Bruton* and its progeny, limiting instructions cannot cure the error." (*id.* at 519)); *accord, Johnson v. Superintendent Fayette SCI,* 949 F.3d 791 (3d Cir. 2020); *People v. Cedeno,* 27 N.Y.3d 110, 120-21, 50 N.E.3d 901, 907-08, 31 N.Y.S.3d 434, 440-41 (2016) (the admission of the codefendant's statement violated *Bruton* even though the "statement, as read out loud at trial, did not appear to have been obviously redacted" to remove any reference to the defendant (and "simply referred to a generic 'Latin King,' of which there were many involved in the fight"), because the "manner in which the physical, written statement itself – which was provided to the jury – was redacted [with a replacement of an "identifying description of defendant . . . with a large blank space"] made it obvious that Villanueva expressly implicated a specific Latin King" and, "[g]iven that defendant was one of three codefendants sitting at the table with . . . [the codefendant who made the statement], the statement powerfully implicated" the defendant); *Orlando v. Nassau County District Attorney's Office*, 915 F.3d 113 (2d Cir. 2019) (an investigating detective testified that while interrogating the defendant he confronted the defendant with the fact that an accomplice, during simultaneous interrogation, had made a statement incriminating the defendant and that the detective believed that the accomplice's statement was what really happened; although the contents of the accomplice's statement were not further disclosed and although the judge instructed the jury that the statement could not be used as evidence of guilt but was admitted only to show the context within which the defendant himself made certain changes in his version of relevant events, the Second Circuit finds a clear *Bruton* violation); *United States v. De Leon-De La Rosa*, 17 F.4th 175 (1st Cir. 2021) ("The government's sole contention as to why there is no *Bruton* violation . . . hinges on the fact that . . . [appellant's codefendant] did not at any point in his statements expressly assert that he had tied a controlled substance to the engine that was jettisoned. Rather, the government stresses, . . . [the codefendant] referred in those statements only to "*eso*." ¶ According to the government, that feature of . . . [the codefendant's] statements in and of itself ensures that there is no problem here under *Bruton*, because it ensures that those statements are not themselves "facially incriminating" of . . . [appellant]. According to the government, the statements became so only when linked to the other testimony at trial that explained that "*eso*" . . . [is a] common slang terms for cocaine." *Id.* at 193-94. Rejecting this argument and finding a reversible *Bruton* error, the First Circuit writes: "[W]e are confident that '[a] juror who does not know the law,' . . . would easily intuit that had the meaning of "*eso*" been ambiguous, [the interrogating] Agent . . . would have asked . . . [the codefendant] a follow up question – namely, 'What is *eso*?' Given that . . . [the agent] did not acknowledge asking such a question, a juror would immediately infer here that the meaning of '*eso*' was unambiguous to . . . [the codefendant's] interlocutor. And, in coming to that conclusion, a juror would also immediately infer that '*eso*' must obviously mean cocaine – for if it did not mean as much, then . . . [the agent] would have continued to question . . . [the codefendant] about what was on the boat to determine if he would admit to possessing, destroying, and conspiring to destroy forfeitable property." *Id.* at 195.). The *Bruton* rule was limited to cases in which the codefendant did not testify at trial in a manner that exposed him or her to cross-examination on the confession by the defendant's attorney. *Nelson v. O'Neil*, 402 U.S. 622 (1971).

In 2023, the Supreme Court revisited *Bruton*. An "originalist" majority announced that "[f]or most of our Nation's history, longstanding practice allowed a nontestifying codefendant's confession to be admitted in a joint trial so long as the jury was properly instructed not to consider it against the nonconfessing defendant." *Samia v. United States*, 2023 WL 4139001, at *6 (U.S. 2023). "This historical evidentiary practice is in accord with the law's broader assumption that jurors can be relied upon to follow the trial judge's instructions. Evidence at trial is often admitted for a limited purpose, accompanied by a limiting instruction." 2023 WL 4139001, at *6. So Bruton was *recast* as "'a narrow exception'" (2023 WL 4139001, at *7) to a general rule allowing the admission at a joint trial of any defendant's confession when (a) the jury is instructed that the confession can be considered only against its maker, not against the codefendant[s], and (b) the confession does not "directly implicate a [co]defendant" but "do[es] so [only] indirectly" (2023 WL 4139001, at *7). Under *Samia*, a defendant's confession that

587

describes incriminating activity by a codefendant is admissible with a limiting instruction if the confession is redacted by substituting words like "the other person" for the codefendant's name. "Here, the District Court's admission of . . . [a jointly tried defendant's] confession, accompanied by a limiting instruction, did not run afoul of this Court's precedents. . . . [That] confession was redacted to avoid naming Samia, satisfying *Bruton*'s rule. And, it was not obviously redacted in a manner resembling the confession in *Gray*; the neutral references to some 'other person' were not akin to an obvious blank or the word 'deleted.'" 2023 WL 4139001, at *10. The only saving grace in this revisionist interpretation of *Bruton* is the Court's observation that "it would not have been feasible to further modify . . . [the] confession to make it appear, as in *Richardson*, that . . . [the confessing defendant] had acted alone. . . . [He] was charged with conspiracy and did not confess to shooting . . . [the victim]. Consequently, the evidence of coordination between . . . [the confessing defendant] and . . . [the] killer (whether Samia or not) was necessary to prove an essential element of the Government's case." 2023 WL 4139001, at *10.

In jury trials, the pre-*Samia Bruton* rule provided a powerful argument in support of a defense motion for a severance in virtually every jury-tried case in which the prosecution intended to introduce a codefendant's statement that incriminated the defendant. *See, e.g., United States v. Truslow*, 530 F.2d 257 (4th Cir. 1975). It remains to be seen how much *Samia* will change this. When seeking a severance of jury trials based on *Bruton*, defense counsel can argue that the court should order separate trials of codefendants in order to avoid the problem of sufficiently redacting a codefendant's confession so that it passes muster under the obtuse "directly-implicate/indirectly-implicate" test and thus averts the danger of appellate reversal if the redaction proves inadequate. But many trial judges are likely to regard the cost of separate jury trials as outweighing these considerations. And, as a *coup de grace*, the concluding section of the *Samia* opinion ends by saying: "The Confrontation Clause ensures that defendants have the opportunity to confront witnesses against them, but it does not provide a freestanding guarantee against the risk of potential prejudice that may arise inferentially in a joint trial." 2023 WL 4139001, at *10.

The likelihood is even greater that motions for severance of bench trials will be denied on the ground that the trial judges are capable of instructing themselves to consider confessions only against their makers and of following their own instruction. (Before *Samia*, some jurisdictions applied the *Bruton* rule to bench trials. *See, e.g., State v. M.M.*, 133 Wash. App. 1031, 2006 WL 1731316 (2006) (per curiam). There were decisions to the contrary (*e.g., United States v. Cardenas*, 9 F.3d 1139, 1154-56 (5th Cir. 1993)), but to deny *Bruton*'s protections in bench trials is arguably at odds with the reasoning of *Lee v. Illinois*, 476 U.S. 530 (1986), a bench-trial case. The Court held in *Lee* that the trial judge's consideration of a non-testifying codefendant's confession incriminating the defendant violated the defendant's Sixth Amendment right of confrontation. *See id.* at 539-46. *See also Crawford v. Washington*, 541 U.S. 36, 58 (2004) (replacing the analytic rubric used in *Lee* and other pre-*Crawford* cases to assess Confrontation Clause claims but explaining that *Lee*'s result was "faithful to the Framers' understanding" of the requirements of the Confrontation Clause). The *Lee* case is distinguishable from the usual *Bruton* situation because the judge in *Lee* not only admitted the codefendant's confession into evidence but considered it as substantive evidence against the defendant (see § 36.5.2 *infra*), whereas typically a judge in a bench trial would profess to compartmentalize his or her mind and not consider a codefendant's statement against the defendant. The *Lee* decision is instructive, however, because the majority's opinion contains an extended discussion of the presumptive unreliability and harmfulness of codefendants' confessions even in the context of a bench trial. *See Lee, supra*, 476 U.S. at 541-46 (the "truthfinding function of the Confrontation Clause is uniquely threatened when an accomplice's confession is sought to be introduced against a criminal defendant without the benefit of cross-examination" (*id.* at 541)). *See also Crawford v. Washington, supra*, 541 U.S. at 64-65 (explaining, in the context of a jury trial, that cross-examination is essential to test the reliability of a "potential suspect['s]" statement that inculpates the accused); *Lilly v. Virginia*, 527 U.S. 116, 131 (1999) (plurality opinion) ("we have over the years 'spoken with one voice in declaring presumptively unreliable accomplices' confessions that incriminate defendants'" (quoting *Lee v. Illinois, supra*, 476 U.S. at 541)); *Williamson v. United States*, 512 U.S. 594, 601 (1994). The *Lee* Court's reasoning provides support for the conclusion that judicial self-control is not an adequate substitute for the *Bruton* rule in bench trials; and *Crawford* adds (albeit in connection with a different aspect of judicial self-control) a strong admonition that it would violate the Constitution's "intended constraint on judicial discretion" (*Crawford v. Washington, supra*, 541 U.S. at 76) to rely upon individual judges' subjective willingness and ability to protect accused persons as a substitute for "the constitutionally prescribed method of assessing reliability" (*id.* at 62) through confrontation and cross-examination. *See id.* ("The Framers . . . knew that judges, like other government officers, could not always be trusted to safeguard the rights of the people; the likes of the dread Lord Jeffreys were not yet too distant a memory. They were loath to leave too much discretion in judicial hands."). Caselaw supporting the general proposition that judges should avoid engaging in mental gymnastics in lieu of objective procedural precautions is discussed in § 22.5 *supra*.

In any event, *Samia* is a prime candidate for rejection by state courts applying state constitutional confrontation clauses. See § 17.11 *supra*. Its reasoning is so dependent upon the 2023 United States Supreme Court majority's "originalist" philosophy that it can be followed only by (a) state courts which share that philosophy and whose state constitutional confrontation clauses predate *Bruton* (because the argument is strong that any confrontation clause adopted or readopted after *Bruton* was intended to incorporate the full-fledged *Bruton* rule) or (b) state courts which hold that their state constitutional provisions are invariably coterminous with the parallel provisions of the federal constitution as most recently interpreted by the U.S. Supreme Court or (c) state courts which are predisposed to welcome any rule diminishing criminal defendants' procedural protections. Counsel should urge state judges to continue to apply the rules evolved from *Bruton* prior to *Samia*, as described in the preceding paragraphs of this section, either as a state constitutional matter or as an application of the State's subconstitutional rule excluding evidence whose prejudicial impact substantially outweighs its probative value (see § 36.2.3 *infra*).

23.9.2. *Severance on the Basis of the Defendant's Need To Call the Codefendant as a Witness*

In some jurisdictions, a statute or court rule or caselaw provides a basis for severance in those cases in which the defense can show that a codefendant's testimony would be favorable to the defendant. *See, e.g., United States v. Cobb*, 185 F.3d 1193, 1195 (11th Cir. 1999) ("the district court should have granted Stephen Cobb's motion to sever the trial so his brother and codefendant, Jerry Cobb, could provide exculpatory testimony"); *Rollerson v. United States*, 127 A.3d 1220, 1226-30 (D.C. 2015). The theory underlying this doctrine is that in a joint trial, the codefendant could elect to invoke his or her Fifth Amendment Privilege not to take the witness stand, and therefore the joint trial would prejudice the defendant by depriving him or her of a witness with exculpatory testimony. If the cases are severed and the codefendant's case is tried before the defendant's, then the codefendant is free to testify at the defendant's trial. (If the codefendant is acquitted at his or her own trial, s/he can also be subpoenaed and compelled to testify; if s/he is convicted, his or her Fifth Amendment Privilege certainly continues until s/he is sentenced and probably also continues throughout the pendency of his or her appeal, but s/he may elect to waive it in order to testify on the defendant's behalf.) Severance is similarly required when a codefendant has made an out-of-court statement which critically supports the defendant's theory of the case and which would be admissible within a hearsay exception if the defendant were tried alone but excludable upon the codefendant's objection at a joint trial. *United States v. Slatten*, 865 F.3d 767 (D.C. Cir. 2017).

Typically, the applicable standard requires that the defense show both that the codefendant has exculpatory testimony to offer on the defendant's behalf and that s/he is willing to testify for the defendant if the cases are severed. *See, e.g., State v. Sanchez*, 143 N.J. 273, 670 A.2d 535 (1996), canvassing the relevant caselaw. This showing is ordinarily made through an affidavit by counsel or the defense investigator affirming that s/he has spoken with the codefendant, recounting the substance of the codefendant's exculpatory testimony (in as little detail as possible, to avoid giving discovery to the prosecution), and relating the codefendant's willingness to testify if the cases are severed and his or her trial is held first.

Although decisions recognizing this ground for severance are usually based on a statute, rule of court, or state court's supervisory powers, counsel can argue that the right to call the codefendant as a witness – and whatever procedures such as severance are necessary to bring that about – are grounded in the Sixth Amendment rights to compulsory process and to present defensive evidence (see § 18.9.2.4 *supra*; § 39.1 *infra*; *Washington v. Texas,* 388 U.S. 14 (1967)), the Fourteenth Amendment Due Process right to a fair trial (see *Holmes v. South Carolina*, 547 U.S. 319, 324 (2006)), and cognate state constitutional guarantees. *Williams v. United States*, 884 A.2d 587 (D.C. 2005). And because, in most jurisdictions, the prosecution could secure the testimony of the codefendant *against* the defendant, if it were incriminating, by granting the codefendant immunity from prosecution, the principle of *Wardius v. Oregon,* 412 U.S. 470 (1973), discussed in § 18.9.2.7 *supra,* strongly suggests that a severance sought by the defendant in order to obtain the same codefendant's exculpatory testimony is constitutionally required in order to maintain "the balance of forces between the accused and his accuser" (412 U.S. at 474).

23.9.3. *Severance on the Basis of the Defendants' Conflicting and Irreconcilable Defenses*

State law frequently affords a basis for severance on the ground that the defense which a codefendant intends to offer irreconcilably conflicts with the defense that the defendant intends to offer. The theory underlying this ground for severance is that the benefits of judicial economy which justify a joint trial do not outweigh the concrete prejudice that the defendant suffers when a codefendant essentially proves the case for the prosecution by rebutting the defendant's witnesses with a conflicting version of the events. *See People v. Gutierrez*, 2021 COA 110, 499 P.3d 367, 368 (Colo. App. 2021) ("After a two-week trial, a jury found defendant, Andrew George Gutierrez, and his codefendant, John Orlando Sanchez, guilty of first degree murder and conspiracy to commit murder. The defendants were tried jointly, despite numerous pretrial motions to sever. At trial, the prosecution introduced evidence that the victim, Eric Schnaare, was fatally shot four times with bullets from one gun. Both defendants and the prosecution regarded this evidence, considered with the other evidence in the case, as conclusively proving that there was one shooter. Gutierrez denied shooting Schnaare and accused Sanchez of being the sole shooter, and Sanchez similarly denied being the shooter and accused Gutierrez. ¶ In this case, we conclude that Gutierrez's defense was antagonistic to Sanchez's because the two defenses specifically contradicted each other and to believe one defense meant that a jury would have to disbelieve the other. We further conclude that the joint proceedings in this case resulted in reversible prejudice because the trial saw the introduction of voluminous evidence that would likely not have been admissible in a separate trial – and also required numerous limiting instructions – and a great deal of damaging evidence introduced not by the prosecution but by the codefendant. The trial court erred by denying Gutierrez's motions for severance, so we reverse his convictions and remand for a new, separate trial."); *Santiago v. State*, 644 N.W.2d 445, 447 (Minn. 2002) ("At the hearing on Santiago's second pretrial severance motion, each party identified his respective defense theory to the court. Rodriguez told the court that his defense theory was that Santiago was the shooter. Santiago told the court that his defense theory was that Rodriguez was the shooter and that Rodriguez acted alone. . . . ¶ Because Santiago's offer of proof regarding his defense was sufficient and because the defendants had antagonistic defenses resulting in potential prejudice to Santiago, we hold that the district court erred when it denied Santiago's pretrial severance motions."); *State v. Jaramillo*, 248 Ariz. 329, 334, 460 P.3d 321, 326 (Ariz. App. 2020) (reversing a conviction because the trial court's erred in denying pretrial and repeated midtrial motions for a severance: "The core of . . . [Jaramillo's] defense was that he was merely a struggling shopkeeper who had rented space in the back room of his Boost Mobile shop to his friend, Islas, to store some tools, and he had no knowledge that Islas was actually 'warehousing drugs' there or 'dealing drugs out of his store.' Conversely, the core of Islas's defense was that Jaramillo was the drug supplier and took advantage of Islas, who had been 'nothing more than a delivery driver' for Jaramillo, with no knowledge he was delivering Jaramillo's drugs. Each defendant squarely argued that the other had singular knowledge of the heroin being stored in and sold from the Boost Mobile store. The jury could not rationally accept both theories. That is the hallmark of antagonistic, mutually exclusive defenses.").

Typically, the applicable caselaw imposes a stringent standard that a defendant must meet in order to obtain severance on this ground. The cases may require, for example, that counsel show that the defenses of the defendant and the codefendant are directly conflicting (and not merely inconsistent) or that the conflicts are such that a trier of fact could conclude, solely on the basis of the conflicts, that the defendant is guilty. *Compare United States v. Mayfield*, 189 F.3d 895, 897, 900 (9th Cir. 1999) ("Mayfield argues that the district court abused its discretion by refusing to sever the trials despite Gilbert's mutually exclusive defense and prejudicial evidence that was improperly elicited by Gilbert's counsel. Although the district court's initial denial of Mayfield's severance motion was understandable, based on pretrial representations made by the government about the evidence that would be admitted, the district court abused its discretion when at trial it gave Gilbert's counsel free rein to introduce evidence against Mayfield and act as a second prosecutor. Gilbert's counsel's trial tactics necessitated severance or some alternative means of mitigating the substantial risk of prejudice."; "Gilbert's counsel used every opportunity to introduce impermissible evidence against Mayfield, and her closing argument barely even addressed the government's evidence against her client and instead focused on convincing the jury that Mayfield was the guilty party, not her client. . . . It is beyond dispute that, if the jury accepted Gilbert's defense, which was that Mayfield was the drug ringleader who had control over the drugs, it necessarily had to convict Mayfield."), *and People v. Colon*, 177 A.D.3d 1086, 1088-89, 113 N.Y.S.3d 389, 393 (N.Y. App. Div., 3d Dep't 2019) (the trial court erred in denying the defendant's motion to sever his trial from his codefendant's based on conflicting defenses: The codefendant "denied knowledge of the cocaine's existence in his car and . . . testified that defendant had brought the . . . bag into the car, that he did not know the contents of that bag, [and] that he would not have allowed the bag in his car if he did," while the defendant "argued – through counsel and without testifying – that he lacked knowledge of the cocaine's presence in the car and that the cocaine must have belonged to [the codefendant], given that it was found in [the codefendant's] car and that he had a criminal history involving drug possession and distribution"), *and People v. McGuire*, 148 A.D.3d 1578, 1579, 51 N.Y.S.3d 726, 727-28 (N.Y. App. Div., 4th Dep't 2017) (the trial court should have severed the defendant's trial from that of his codefendants based on irreconcilable trial strategies because "both codefendants denied possessing the gun and testified it was in defendant's possession," and "the codefendants' respective attorneys 'took an aggressive adversarial stance against [defendant at trial], in effect becoming a second [and a third] prosecutor'"), *and People v. Lessane*, 142 A.D.3d 562, 564, 36 N.Y.S.3d 231, 233 (N.Y. App. Div., 2d Dep't 2016) (the trial court should have granted the defendant's motion to sever his trial from his codefendant's based on antagonistic defenses; the defendant asserted that his written and videotaped confessions were false and extracted by the interrogating officers' promises of leniency, while "[c]odefendant Steele's defense . . . was almost entirely based on accepting as true the defendant's statements, in which the defendant named three other individuals as perpetrators and omitted any mention of Steele"), *and People v. Feliciano*, 189 A.D.3d 416, 417, 419, 136 N.Y.S.3d 268, 270-71, 272 (N.Y. App. Div., 1st Dep't 2020) ("the court should have severed Feliciano's trial from that of his codefendant, Roberts, rather than conducting a joint trial before separate juries. In order to establish that both defendants participated in the crimes, the People were necessarily required to establish that both defendants were present. However, Roberts' cross examinations, mostly presented to both juries, undermined Feliciano's defense, that he was merely present with Roberts and did not share Roberts' intent to commit robbery or murder, which was antagonistic to, and irreconcilable with, Roberts' defense that he was not there at all."; "Roberts' counsel's pursuit of his client's defense, contemporaneously undermined Feliciano's. Accordingly, he effectively became a 'second prosecutor' and was able to impeach . . . witnesses to Feliciano's detriment in a manner that the People were unable to."), *with Zafiro v. United States*, 506 U.S. 534, 538-41 (1993) ("the District Court did not abuse its discretion in denying petitioners' motion to sever" under FED. RULE CRIM. PRO. 14 based on a claim of "mutually antagonistic defenses"; "Rule 14 leaves the determination of risk of prejudice and any remedy that may be necessary to the sound discretion of the district courts" and "petitioners have not shown that their joint trial subjected them to any legally cognizable prejudice"). *See also United States v. Blunt*, 930 F.3d 119 (3d Cir. 2019) (in a prosecution of a married couple for identity theft and mail fraud, it was an abuse of discretion for the trial court to deny the motions made by both defendants for a severance based on the wife's intention to testify in her defense that the husband coerced her to take part in the criminal scheme; the husband was prejudiced by the admission of emotion-rousing evidence that would not have been admitted against him in a single trial; the wife was prejudiced by being required to choose between asserting spousal privilege and taking the stand in her own defense); *People v. Davydov*, 144 A.D.3d 1170, 1172, 43 N.Y.S.3d 74, 78 (N.Y. App. Div., 2d Dep't 2016) (the defendant was denied effective assistance of counsel due to his lawyer's errors, which included "fail[ing] to request a severance of the defendant's trial from that of the codefendant . . . as soon as it became clear that their defenses were antagonistic").

23.9.4. *Severance on the Basis of the Disparity or Dissimilarity of the Evidence Against the Defendants*

State law may also provide a basis for severance when the evidence against the codefendant is much stronger than the evidence against the defendant, and the specter is thereby raised that the defendant will be found guilty by association. "It is difficult for the individual to make his own case stand on its own merits in the minds of jurors who are ready to believe that birds of a feather are flocked together." *Krulewitch v. United States,* 336 U.S. 440, 454 (1949) (concurring opinion of Justice Jackson). Usually, state law requires that the disparity of the evidence be substantial.

Although this doctrine affords a basis for severance in jury trials, it would probably be rejected as a ground for severance in a bench trial. Most judges would deny the notion that they are susceptible to being swayed by guilt-by-association. However, even in a bench trial, counsel may be able to secure severance when the evidence is not only disparate but includes items inadmissible against the defendant, admissible against the codefendant, and incriminating as to the defendant. Although the *Bruton* rule described in § 23.9.1 *supra* deals exclusively with codefendants' confessions that incriminate the defendant, the logic underlying that rule calls for severance also in this situation. *See, e.g., Zafiro v. United States*, 506 U.S. 534, 539 (1993) (dictum) (explaining that one of the types of prejudice that can justify severance under FED. RULE CRIM. PRO. 8(b) is when there is "[e]vidence that is probative of a defendant's guilt but technically admissible only against a codefendant," and citing *Bruton* as support). And § 23.9.1 makes the argument for the applicability of the *Bruton* principle to bench trials.

Prejudice sufficient to require severance of codefendants may also be found when substantial evidence of wrongdoing by one of them would be admissible only against that one and would be inadmissible in a separate trial of the other. *See, e.g., United States v. López Martinez*, 994 F.3d 1, 14-15 (1st Cir. 2021) (reversing convictions for accepting bribes and for conspiracy because the trial judge denied defendant López Martinez's motion for severance from her codefendant Rivera: "The jury before which López was tried was exposed to days of detailed evidence regarding Hernández's role in corrupting the contract bidding process at the Puerto Rico House of Representatives [by giving bribes] . . . . ¶ But, López was not herself employed by the Puerto Rico House of Representatives, let alone charged with any offense pertaining to the corruption of that bidding process. We thus cannot see how evidence of such depth and quality about the nature of the allegedly corrupt scheme at the Puerto Rico House of Representatives in which [codefendant] Rivera was charged with having a role could have been admitted at a trial against López alone on the counts that she faced. . . . ¶ . . . López's primary defense to the charges against her was that Hernández acted corruptly and intended to influence her but that she merely accepted gifts from him without any sort of quid pro quo. For that reason, the evidence about how Hernández corruptly schemed with others in connection with the Puerto Rico House of Representatives that could not have been introduced at a trial against her alone but to which her jury nonetheless was exposed did create a grave risk of spillover prejudice. Specifically, that evidence risked leading the jury in considering her charges to impute the states of mind of the employees of the Puerto Rico House of Representatives – based on the direct evidence of their intent that was introduced – to López and thereby 'prevent[ing] the jury from making a reliable judgment about [her] guilt or innocence.'"); *United States v. Islam*, 2021 WL 308272 (E.D. Pa. January 29, 2021). Judges considering a motion to sever trials of defendants on the ground that evidence admissible against some of them would be inadmissible and prejudicial at a separate trial of others are likely to balance that consideration against the economies and efficiencies of joint trial. For this reason, the advice given in the third paragraph of § 23.4 *supra* is applicable to these motions as well: Counsel should emphasize not only the probable prejudicial impact of evidence inadmissible against his or her client but also the fact – when it is the case – that there is relatively little prosecution evidence which is admissible against both his/her client and others, so that "[a] separate trial for . . . [counsel's client] will be the most efficient use of judicial resources" (*United States v. Burke*, 789 F. Supp. 2d 395, 400 (E.D. N.Y. 2011)); *Sousa v. United States*, 400 A.2d 1036, 1041-42 (D.C. 1979) ("In this case, the assault and weapon charges against Richter which were distinct in time and place, were joined with charges of first-degree murder while armed against the other defendants. The evidence of the murder was overwhelmingly the major portion of this five-week trial while there was comparatively meager evidence on the assault and weapon charges. [The murder was "bloody and grotesque' and the "defendants [were referred to] throughout the trial as the 'Richter group' thereby associating Richter in the minds of the jurors with the murder he was not charged with committing."] The evidence of the murder would not have been admissible at a separate trial of Richter on the assault and weapon charges. We conclude that the trial court erred in denying severance."); *cf. People v. Dell'Orfano*, 72 A.D.2d 749, 421 N.Y.S.2d 265 (N.Y. App. Div., 2d Dep't 1979) (co-defendant's counsel introduced evidence that would have been admissible against the defendant at a severed trial).

23.10. *Defense Motions for Consolidation of Defendants*

Although rare, there are some cases in which the defendant would benefit by being tried with codefendants. See § 23.7 *supra*. The procedures for consolidation of defendants are the same as those for consolidation of offenses, described in § 23.5 *supra*. Usually, if the prosecutor has decided for strategic reasons to try the codefendants separately, s/he will resist the defendant's motion for consolidation. In arguing the motion to the court, defense counsel should both point to whatever specific prejudice the defendant is suffering as a result of being tried separately and also advert to any economies that would be effected by a joint trial, noting previous cases in which the prosecutor has elected to conduct a single trial of multiple defendants in similar circumstances, apparently in recognition of the force of those economies. *United States v. Burdett*, 127 A.F.T.R.2d 2021-1270, 2021 WL 1063067 (E.D. La. March 19, 2021).

Chapter 24

Suppression Hearings

24.1. *The Timing of the Suppression Hearing*

Suppression motions practice varies considerably among jurisdictions. Some States require motions to suppress to be made in writing and filed by a specified pretrial deadline (see § 17.7 *supra*); other States allow the motions to be made in writing or orally at trial.

In jurisdictions that require pretrial motions, the hearing on the motion may, depending upon the jurisdiction, be conducted in advance of trial or at the trial. In some jurisdictions, evidentiary hearings on motions to suppress are routinely held days or even weeks before the trial. (Such an early scheduling of suppression hearings is particularly advantageous to the defense, since it enhances the usefulness of the hearings for discovery. See §§ 24.2, 24.4.2 *infra*.) In other jurisdictions the suppression hearing is commonly held immediately before trial – just prior to the selection and swearing of the jurors in a jury trial – and, depending upon local practice, defense counsel may or may not find it easy to obtain a continuance of the trial for the purpose of getting a transcript of the suppression hearing. In still other jurisdictions the suppression hearing (frequently called a *voir dire*) takes place in the course of trial, at the time when the first witness is asked about the challenged evidence.

The trial-objection procedure, which has fallen into disfavor in most jurisdictions as pretrial motions practice has developed, permits the defendant to object to suppressible evidence for the first time at trial. A *voir dire* hearing is then held on the objection. In jury trials, the jury is removed while the hearing proceeds, with the judge sitting as the trier of whatever issues of fact are dispositive of the defendant's suppression claims. To be sure, even in jurisdictions that require pretrial motions, the defense can request the suppression of evidence for the first time at trial in exceptional circumstances – for example, when defense counsel could not reasonably have known of the challenged evidence or the factual or legal grounds for challenging it prior to trial. See § 24.8 *infra*. Similarly, in these pretrial-motion jurisdictions the defense can renew a previously denied suppression motion at trial on the basis of newly discovered evidence. See *id.* What distinguishes the trial-objection jurisdictions is that objections to suppressible evidence are routinely entertained, with no need to show special circumstances, at the time when the evidence is presented by the prosecution in its case-in-chief at trial. But the objection must be made when the first prosecution witness begins to testify about the suppressible evidence; an objection made later in the trial will be held untimely.

24.2. *Defense Goals and Strategies at a Suppression Hearing*

Suppression hearings may be used by the defense for several different purposes. To put a hearing to the most effective use, defense counsel needs to make a preliminary determination of which purposes s/he should be pursuing in this particular case. Often, a clear-cut choice between one purpose and another will be necessary, because the purposes or important means for achieving them are inconsistent. This is ordinarily not a choice that can be put off until the time of the evidentiary hearing: Both the content of the suppression motion and the nature of counsel's pre-hearing preparation will vary considerably depending upon counsel's choice of goals and consequent strategies for the hearing.

The first and most obvious potential goal is to win the hearing and secure suppression of whatever evidence is challenged. Victory in a suppression hearing will frequently result in the prosecutor's having to dismiss the entire case against the defendant. For example, suppression of the drugs and all police testimony relating to their seizure in a drug possession case usually leaves the prosecutor without any evidence of the defendant's alleged wrongdoing. In many cases, suppression of eyewitness identification testimony or of a confession deprives the prosecution of the only available evidence of the defendant's identity as the perpetrator of the offense. Even when a defense victory at the suppression hearing does not terminate the prosecution, the suppression ruling may create major gaps in the prosecutor's proof and thereby substantially improve the chances for an acquittal at trial.

An alternative defense goal at the suppression hearing is to obtain discovery of the prosecution's theory of the case and supporting evidence on the issue of guilt. Depending upon which claims are litigated and the way in which defense counsel shapes the hearing, the prosecutor's evidence at the suppression hearing may provide a full preview of the prosecution's case-in-chief at trial. For example, if the suppression motion challenges the legality of the defendant's arrest on the ground that the arresting officers lacked probable cause, the prosecutor may be obliged to present extensive testimony regarding the facts of the crime known to the police and the facts that led the police to believe that the defendant was the perpetrator. In addition to obtaining this disclosure of the prosecution's evidence, counsel may also be able to obtain discovery of documents that would not otherwise be available until mid-trial: In some jurisdictions the prosecution's presentation of a witness in a suppression hearing activates a prosecutorial duty to turn over to the defense any prior written statements of that witness or documents prepared by that witness. *See, e.g.,* N.Y. CRIM. PRO. LAW § 240.44. Beyond this discovery of the content of the prosecution's case, defense counsel also gains a valuable opportunity to watch prosecution witnesses on the stand and acquire insights into their vulnerability to particular approaches on cross-examination. Indeed, it is often possible to use a suppression hearing to test risky lines of cross-examination in order to determine what questions can be safely used at trial. In jury trials and in bench trials in jurisdictions with liberal recusal rules permitting the defense to obtain a different judge for the trial (see § 24.8 *infra*), the ultimate trier of fact will never hear the results of defense counsel's experimentation. And even when the judge presiding at the motion hearing does sit at the defendant's bench trial, counsel can use experimentation in the motion hearing to decide what evidence should be put into the trial record. Naturally, these discovery benefits will be enhanced in jurisdictions where the suppression hearing is held in advance of trial. However, even discovery procured in a mid-trial hearing can prove immensely useful in determining what additional cross-examination would be fruitful or dangerous and in deciding other questions of trial tactics, such as whether to put the defendant on the stand or to present other defense witnesses.

A third potential goal of the suppression hearing is to extract concessions from prosecution witnesses on the record, for defense counsel's use in examining and impeaching those witnesses at trial. Often prosecutors fail to coach their witnesses prior to the suppression hearing with the same care that they employ in preparing for trial, and it will be possible to lure an unwary prosecution witness into conceding affirmatively helpful points. At the very least, counsel can circumscribe the damage that any witness will be able to do at trial, by locking him or her into a version of the facts that s/he cannot alter without being exposed to impeachment by the inconsistent testimony that s/he gave at the hearing. See §§ 24.4.3, 37.4 *infra*. Finally, the mere fact that the witness is telling his or her version of the facts twice – once at the suppression hearing and again at trial – often proves beneficial: Particularly when the suppression hearing takes place some time before trial, witnesses will change details in their stories and can then be discredited by confronting them with the discrepancies. All of these means of controlling or undercutting prosecution witnesses' trial testimony will be greatly enhanced by obtaining a transcript of the suppression hearing to use for impeachment at trial. See § 24.8 *infra*.

There are several other benefits that the defense may gain from litigating suppression motions. The most important ones are catalogued in the concluding paragraph of § 17.3 *supra*. But while these benefits should be considered as factors in counsel's initial decision whether or not to file a suppression motion and bring it on for evidentiary hearing – together with the countervailing considerations of cost and risk that such a motion may entail (see § 17.9 *supra*) – they will seldom play more than a minor role in shaping counsel's tactics and techniques for conducting the hearing. Counsel's primary determinants in preparing for and handling an evidentiary suppression hearing will almost always be strategies for pursuing one or more of the three key goals of getting prosecution evidence suppressed, obtaining discovery, and/or creating impeachment material for use at trial. When these three goals prove inconsistent, counsel will have to choose among them. See § 24.4 *infra*.

24.3. *Procedural Aspects of the Suppression Hearing*

24.3.1. *The Defense Response When a Prosecution or Defense Witness Fails To Appear*

Frequently, the prosecutor will announce that an essential prosecution witness has failed to appear and that the prosecution is therefore seeking a continuance of the suppression hearing. Police witnesses are particularly common no-shows. If the hearing is scheduled for the day of trial and the prosecutor is requesting a continuance of the trial as well, counsel should invoke any applicable speedy-trial sanctions, such as dismissal of the case or release of a defendant who is being held on bond. See § 28.4 *infra*. Even if the suppression hearing is scheduled days or weeks before trial, counsel should ask for sanctions as a result of the prosecutor's unwillingness to proceed: If the prosecutor or the judge remarks that the hearing can be re-scheduled without delaying the trial, counsel should respond that sanctions are nonetheless appropriate to deter prosecutors from cavalierly ignoring suppression hearing dates, to the detriment of the court's calendar and discouragement of defense witnesses. The apt sanction, counsel should insist, is a judicial ruling that the motion has been conceded (in essence, forfeited) by the prosecution. *See, e.g., People v. Goggans,* 123 A.D.2d 643, 506 N.Y.S.2d 908 (N.Y. App. Div., 2d Dep't 1986). If the judge seems dubious about the appropriateness of this remedy, counsel should point out that it is the closest possible analogue to the trial-date sanction of dismissal when the prosecutor declines to proceed and is the only effective deterrent of prosecutorial neglect. For discussion of *Goggans* and of remedies for prosecutorial unreadiness, see § 28.4.

Occasionally, prosecutors will attempt to get around a witness's failure to appear by going forward with hearsay testimony to cover the matters that the missing witness would have recounted. Although hearsay testimony usually is admissible in suppression hearings, counsel should point out the inherent unreliability of second-hand information that is insulated from testing by cross-examination and should argue accordingly that the hearsay testimony is not sufficient to satisfy the prosecutor's burden of persuasion at the hearing. See §§ 24.3.4, 24.3.5 *infra*.

A trickier problem for defense counsel arises when a missing prosecution witness is crucial for the *defendant's* case at the hearing and the prosecutor elects to go forward by presenting other witnesses who participated in the same events or observed them. Defense counsel is well advised to forestall this situation by subpoenaing all prosecution witnesses whom s/he may need, including police and other law enforcement personnel. See § 29.4.1 *infra*. If counsel has failed to subpoena a prosecution witness who is crucial for the defense case, counsel will need to seek a continuance, and that continuance will probably be charged to the defense for speedy-trial purposes. See §§ 28.5.2, 28.5.4 *infra*. If counsel did subpoena the prosecution witness, then counsel should explain that the witness is essential to the defense presentation and, in requesting a continuance, should ask that the continuance be charged to the prosecution – or, as a fall-back position, that the continuance be charged jointly to defense and prosecution. The prosecutor will undoubtedly argue that, because the prosecution is willing to go forward, the continuance should be charged solely to the defense; but counsel's surrebuttal is that any delay resulting from the failure of a witness to obey a court subpoena should be charged to the party with whom the witness is allied and which is best able to control the witness. If the witness is a law enforcement agent, counsel should point out that delays resulting from the dilatoriness or negligence of such personnel are ordinarily counted against the prosecution in the speedy-trial calculus, even when the prosecutors themselves have not been derelict. *See Doggett v. United States*, 505 U.S. 647, 652-53 (1992); *United States v. Velasquez*, 749 F.3d 167, 175-77, 180-81 (3d Cir. 2014).

If the missing witness is needed by the defense solely to impeach another prosecution witness in the event that the latter witness denies a prior inconsistent statement, defense counsel does not necessarily have to request a continuance. Counsel has the option of alerting the judge to the possible need for the witness and then offering to proceed without the witness, on the understanding that counsel will be given the opportunity to complete the hearing by calling the missing witness at a later date if necessary. As counsel can point out to the judge, it may never be necessary to present the missing witness, because the testifying witness may admit to making the impeaching statement. See § 37.4 *infra*. In any such colloquies with the judge, defense counsel must be careful to guard against alerting the prosecutor to the nature of the anticipated impeachment; if the court wishes a detailed proffer, counsel should insist that that proffer be made *ex parte* to avoid disclosure of defense strategies to the prosecution.

If the missing witness is solely a foundational witness (for example, a police communications division officer whose testimony will establish the standard police procedures for recording radio communications), defense counsel should consider offering to go forward if the prosecutor will stipulate to the foundational facts that counsel wishes to adduce. The stipulation should, in most cases, suffice to fill counsel's needs. It is usually advisable to make the stipulation offer in open court. Then, if the prosecutor refuses to stipulate and defense counsel is forced to ask for a continuance to obtain the missing foundational witness, the judge will know to attribute the disruption of the court's calendar to the prosecutor's obstructionism and will be more disposed to grant the continuance. Or the judge may intervene and put pressure on the prosecutor to agree to the stipulation.

Whenever defense counsel does need to seek a continuance of a suppression hearing, counsel should be ready to argue both the factual basis for the request and the defendant's legal right to obtain a continuance in order to prepare adequately for the hearing. See § 28.3 *infra*. In requesting the continuance, however, counsel should again be alert to the danger of revealing defense strategies to the prosecution. If the continuance is necessitated by a defense witness's failure to appear and if revelation of the witness's name might lead the police to interview the witness before the next hearing, counsel should simply omit the witness's name or offer to reveal it to the judge *ex parte*.

24.3.2. *Waiving the Defendant's Presence in Suppression Hearings That Involve an Identification Suppression Claim*

Counsel litigating an identification suppression claim should consider waiving the client's presence during the testimony of all witnesses whose eyewitness identifications s/he is challenging. This waiver is strongly desirable from the defense perspective for two reasons.

First, the eyewitness's observation of the defendant during the suppression hearing will aggravate the effect of prior suggestive police procedures and may ensure the witness's identification of the defendant at trial. Not only will the witness have seen the defendant for an additional, prolonged period of time, so that s/he will be more likely to feel and testify persuasively at trial that the defendant "looks familiar" but also the witness will have seen the defendant in a highly suggestive setting. (Unlike a lineup, the setting of the suppression hearing makes it quite obvious which person in the courtroom has been charged as the culprit.) Second, the presence of the defendant at the suppression hearing frustrates any hope of obtaining from the witness an unvarnished description of the perpetrator for use in arguing the suppression motion: The witness will simply describe the individual s/he is observing at counsel table, seated next to defense counsel.

In several jurisdictions the courts have recognized the accused's right to waive his or her presence at an identification suppression hearing, relying on either or both of two rationales: (i) that the constitutional protections against suggestive pretrial identification procedures entitle the defense to avoid an additional unnecessary and suggestive encounter between the accused and the eyewitness, and (ii) that the accused's right to be present during all court hearings is a personal, waivable right because it exists solely for the accused's protection and not for the protection of any governmental interests. *See, e.g., People v. Huggler,* 50 A.D.2d 471, 473-74, 378 N.Y.S.2d 493, 496-97 (N.Y. App. Div., 3d Dep't 1976); *Singletary v. United States,* 383 A.2d 1064, 1070 (D.C. 1978).

The court will usually insist that counsel demonstrate on the record that the defendant's waiver is a knowing and voluntary relinquishment of the right to be present at the hearing.

Counsel can make the requisite showing either: (i) by presenting a written waiver signed by the defendant, which sets forth the defendant's understanding of his or her right to be present, the reasons for waiving the right to be present, and the defendant's desire to waive the right; or (ii) by bringing the defendant to the hearing solely for the purpose of responding to the court's inquiry into the voluntariness of the waiver and then sending the defendant out of the courtroom before any eyewitness enters.

Whether the defendant's presence should be waived for all or only part of the hearing depends upon the roster of witnesses who will testify at the hearing. If most of the witnesses are eyewitnesses to the crime, then the defendant's presence should be waived during the entire hearing and the defendant should be kept away from any parts of the courthouse where s/he might encounter or be observed by any of the eyewitnesses. On the other hand, if there is a significant portion of the hearing that the defendant can safely attend – and naturally also if the defendant will take the stand at the hearing – then counsel should waive the defendant's presence only during the portions of the hearing when eyewitnesses will be in or around the courtroom. Counsel should make arrangements for the defendant to sit during those portions of the hearing in a location where s/he is not likely to be observed by any of the eyewitnesses and to enter and leave the courtroom by a route that will not lead to any encounters with the eyewitnesses.

24.3.3. *Enforcing the "Rule on Witnesses" in a Suppression Hearing*

Throughout a trial both parties have the right to insist that the opposing witnesses be excluded from the courtroom, in order to prevent them from hearing information that might affect their testimony. See § 34.6 *infra*. This "rule on witnesses" should similarly be invoked by the defense at a suppression hearing. At the beginning of the hearing, defense counsel should request that the courtroom be cleared of any prosecution witnesses who might testify either at the suppression hearing or at the trial. Counsel also must be alert throughout the hearing to the possibility of a prosecution witness entering and remaining in the courtroom. If, notwithstanding counsel's precautions, a prosecution witness does overhear another witness's testimony, counsel should request that the court impose the only sanction that will both remedy the violation and deter future misconduct by prosecution witnesses: exclusion of the witness's testimony at the suppression hearing and trial.

As at trial the operation of the rule on witnesses does not bar the defendant from the courtroom. S/he has a right to be present while all testimony in the case is taken. See § 34.1 *infra*. For discussion of the circumstances under which the defendant should waive his or her right to be present at a suppression hearing, see § 24.3.2 *supra*.

24.3.4. *Who Proceeds First in the Suppression Hearing: The Burdens of Production and Persuasion*

Even though the suppression motion is a defense motion, it is customary in many jurisdictions for the prosecution to proceed first and to present the testimony of all police officers and other witnesses whom the prosecution intends to call. As a result, the defense has the distinct advantage of being able to cross-examine (and thereby lead and control) the officers and other prosecution witnesses. In some jurisdictions, however, the defense is expected to proceed first, at least on some suppression issues. *See, e.g., United States v. Daniels*, 41 F.4th 412, 416 (4th Cir. 2022) ("[i]n suppression hearings, criminal defendants have the burden of putting forward evidence to support all elements of their reasonable expectation of privacy"). In these jurisdictions, defense counsel will usually want to invoke the constitutional caselaw dealing with burdens of production and persuasion, described in this section, to argue that the prosecutor should be required to proceed first. On rare occasions, the defense may reap some benefit from proceeding first and calling the police officers as defense witnesses – for example, when: (i) the officers are known to be unprepared and the prosecutor is an experienced and able examiner who can effectively shape their testimony on direct; or (ii) the rules of evidence in the particular jurisdiction permit parties to lead and impeach their own witnesses; or (iii) the judge will permit the officers and other prosecution witnesses to be called as hostile witnesses (see § 39.29 *infra*). But in most jurisdictions the greater latitude allowed for leading and impeaching witnesses on cross-examination makes it wise for defense counsel to force the prosecutor to proceed first whenever possible.

The allocation of the burden of production (also known as the burden of going forward) and of the burden of persuasion (also known as the burden of proof) varies with the constitutional issue being litigated:

(i) *Search and seizure issues.* Federal constitutional law permits the burden of going forward to be imposed on the defense (*see Rawlings v. Kentucky,* 448 U.S. 98, 104-05 (1980)), but state statutes, court rules, or state constitutional caselaw may elect to impose that burden on the prosecution instead (*see, e.g., State v. Boyd*, 275 Kan. 271, 273, 64 P.3d 419, 422 (2003); *State v. Carrawell*, 481 S.W.3d 833, 837 (Mo. 2016) (dictum); *People v. Dodt,* 61 N.Y.2d 408, 415, 474 N.Y.S.2d 441, 445, 462 N.E.2d 1159, 1163 (1984); *cf. Commonwealth v. Long*, 485 Mass. 711, 152 N.E.3d 725 (2020), summarized in § 25.28 *infra*). In jurisdictions where the defense does bear the burden of going forward on Fourth Amendment issues, that burden is easily satisfied whenever the search or seizure was made without a warrant. Once the defense has shown that a search or seizure was conducted and that the police lacked a warrant authorizing it, the Fourth Amendment shifts the burden of persuasion to the prosecution to prove that the warrantless search or seizure falls within one of the established exceptions to the warrant requirement. *Riley v. California*, 573 U.S. 373, 382 (2014) ("[i]n the absence of a warrant, a search is reasonable only if it falls within a specific exception to the warrant requirement"); *McDonald v. United States*, 335 U.S. 451, 456 (1948); *United States v. Jeffers,* 342 U.S. 48, 51 (1951); *United States v. Curry*, 965 F.3d 313, 319 (4th Cir. 2020) (en banc); *cf. Vale v. Louisiana,* 399 U.S. 30, 34 (1970); *Schneckloth v. Bustamonte,* 412 U.S. 218, 219, 222 (1973) (dictum); *Florida v. Royer,* 460 U.S. 491, 497 (1983) (plurality opinion); see § 25.2.1 *infra. And see State v. Jones*, 172 N.H. 774, 235 A.3d 119 (2020) (two police officers approached the defendant and one talked with him for about 20 minutes while the other ran a warrants check; when the latter officer learned that there was an outstanding bench warrant for the defendant, the officers arrested him; on his motion to suppress evidence seized incident to the arrest on the ground that he had been unconstitutionally seized during his conversation with officer number one, only officer number two testified, so the record contained no significant information about the interaction between officer number one and the defendant, other than officer number two's observation from beyond hearing distance that it appeared to be very laid back; the New Hampshire Supreme Court reverses the denial of suppression and the ensuing conviction on the ground that the prosecution failed to meet its burden of proving that the defendant was not seized before the officers learned of the outstanding warrant for his arrest). When the police did possess a warrant authorizing the search or seizure, federal constitutional law would appear to permit the imposition of the burden of persuasion of the invalidity of the warrant or the search upon the defense (*see, e.g., Malcolm v. United States,* 332 A.2d 917, 918-19 (D.C. 1975)), but some States impose the burden of persuasion upon the prosecution even in these cases (*see, e.g., Graddy* v. *State,* 277 Ga. 765, 596 S.E.2d 109 (2004); *State v. Heald,* 314 A.2d 820, 828-29 (Me. 1973); *State v. Martin,* 145 N.H. 362, 364, 761 A.2d 516, 518 (2000)). As for the quantum of evidence that the prosecution must present to satisfy its burden, on most issues the federal constitution requires nothing more than a preponderance of the evidence (*United States v. Matlock,* 415 U.S. 164, 177, 178 n.14 (1974); *cf. Colorado v. Connelly,* 479 U.S. 157, 167-69 (1986); *Nix v. Williams,* 467 U.S. 431, 444 n.5 (1984); *and see Bourjaily v. United States,* 483 U.S. 171, 175-76 (1987) (dictum)), although "the States are free, pursuant to their own law, to adopt a higher standard" with respect to the prosecutorial burden (*Lego v. Twomey,* 404 U.S. 477, 489 (1972)). Some States have, indeed, imposed upon the prosecution the higher standard of clear-and-convincing evidence in proving certain specific exceptions to the warrant requirement. *See, e.g., Stone v. State,* 348 Ark. 661, 669, 74 S.W.3d 591, 596 (2002) (consent searches); *Blair v. Pitchess,* 5 Cal. 3d 258, 274, 486 P.2d 1242, 1253, 96 Cal. Rptr. 42, 53 (1971) (consent searches); *People v. Zimmerman,* 101 A.D.2d 294, 475 N.Y.S.2d 127 (N.Y. App. Div., 2d Dep't 1984) (consent searches); *People v. Dorney,* 17 Ill. App. 3d 785, 788, 308 N.E.2d 646, 648 (1974) (abandonment); *State v. Ibarra,* 953 S.W.2d 242, 245 (Tex. Crim. App. 1997) (consent searches). In jurisdictions where the defense is assigned a burden of persuasion in warrant cases, the applicable standard is a preponderance of the evidence. *See, e.g., State v. Edwards,* 98 Wis. 2d 367, 297 N.W.2d 12 (Wis. 1980).

(ii) *Challenges to the admissibility of a confession.* When the issue is the voluntariness of a confession or other incriminating statement by the defendant, the prosecution bears the burden of persuasion. *Lego v. Twomey, supra,* 404 U.S. at 489 (dictum); *see also United States v. Raddatz,* 447 U.S. 667, 678 (1980); *Missouri v. Seibert,* 542 U.S. 600, 608 n.1 (2004) (plurality opinion). The quantum of proof required as a matter of federal constitutional law is "a preponderance of the evidence" (*Lego v. Twomey, supra,* 404 U.S. at 489; *accord, Missouri v. Seibert, supra,* 542 U.S. at 608 n.1 (plurality opinion)), although several States have, "pursuant to their own law, . . . adopt[ed] [the] . . . higher standard" (*Lego v. Twomey, supra,* 404 U.S. at 489) of proof beyond a reasonable doubt (*see, e.g., People v. Jiminez,* 21 Cal. 3d 595, 580 P.2d 672, 147 Cal. Rptr. 172 (1978), *partially overruled on an unrelated point, People v. Cahill,* 5 Cal. 4th 478, 853 P.2d 1037, 20 Cal. Rptr.2d 582 (1993); *State v. Carter,* 412 A.2d 56, 60 (Me. 1980); *Lowe v. State,* 800 So.2d 552, 554-55 (Miss. App. 2001)). Although the jurisdictions vary with respect to which party bears the burden of production in a confession suppression hearing, the Supreme Court's imposition of the burden of persuasion on the prosecution and the fact that it is the prosecutor who is proffering the evidence support the argument that the proper procedure is to place the burden of production on the prosecution. When the issue is a waiver of *Miranda* rights, the prosecution again bears the burden of persuasion (*Miranda v. Arizona,* 384 U.S. 436, 475-76, 479 (1966); *see also Brewer v. Williams,* 430 U.S. 387, 402-04 (1977); *Tague v. Louisiana,* 444 U.S. 469 (1980) (per curiam); *Missouri v. Seibert, supra,* 542 U.S. at 608 n.1 (plurality opinion); *J.D.B. v. North Carolina,* 564 U.S. 261, 269-70 (2011)), by a preponderance of the evidence (*Colorado v. Connelly, supra,* 479 U.S. at 167-69; *Missouri v. Seibert, supra,*

542 U.S. at 608 n.1 (plurality opinion)). Although the *Connelly* opinion states unequivocally that "[w]henever the State bears the burden of proof in a motion to suppress a statement that the defendant claims was obtained in violation of our *Miranda* doctrine, the State need prove waiver only by a preponderance of the evidence" (479 U.S. at 168), it is possible that a heavier burden of proof exists on the separate issue raised by *Edwards v. Arizona*, 451 U.S. 477 (1981), in *Miranda* cases in which "an accused has [once] invoked his right to have counsel present during custodial interrogation" (*id.* at 484). *Edwards* held that an accused person in custody who has "expressed his desire to deal with the police only through counsel, is not subject to further interrogation by the authorities until counsel has been made available to him, unless the accused himself initiates further communication, exchanges, or conversations with the police" (*id.* at 484-85). *See also Smith v. Illinois,* 469 U.S. 91, 95 (1984) (per curiam); *Minnick v. Mississippi*, 498 U.S. 146, 150-56 (1990); *Davis v. United States*, 512 U.S. 452, 458 (1994) (dictum); *Montejo v. Louisiana,* 556 U.S. 778, 794-95 (2009) (dictum); § 26.9.3 *infra.* "The [*Edwards*] rule ensures that any statement made in subsequent interrogation is not the result of coercive pressures. *Edwards* conserves judicial resources which would otherwise be expended in making difficult determinations of voluntariness, and implements the protections of *Miranda* in practical and straightforward terms." *Minnick v. Mississippi, supra*, 498 U.S. at 151. The Supreme Court has repeatedly said that "[t]he merit of the *Edwards* decision lies in the clarity of its command and the certainty of its application" – its capacity to provide ""clear and unequivocal"' guidelines to the law enforcement profession" (*id.*, quoting *Arizona v. Roberson*, 486 U.S. 675, 682 (1988)). Arguably, to preserve the clarity and firmness of "[t]his 'rigid' prophylactic rule" (*id.*), embodying an unprecedented "*per se* approach" (*Solem v. Stumes,* 465 U.S. 638, 647 (1984)), the prosecution should be required to show by clear and convincing evidence "once a suspect has invoked the right to counsel, [that] any subsequent conversation . . . was initiated by him" (*id.* at 641). *See Smith v. Illinois, supra*, 469 U.S. at 95 n.2; *and see, e.g., State v. Tidwell*, 775 S.W.2d 379, 386 (Tenn. Crim. App. 1989). The question, however, remains an open one. *Compare Commonwealth v. Gonzalez*, 487 Mass. 661, 670, 169 N.E.3d 485, 494 (2021), quoted in § 26.9.3 *infra* (applying a beyond-a-reasonable-doubt standard in holding that the prosecution failed to meet its burden on the initiation issue), *with Moore v. Berghuis*, 700 F.3d 882, 888 (6th Cir. 2012)*,* discussed in § 26.9.3 *infra*, reasoning that "[t]he government did not show by a preponderance of the evidence, and the [state] . . . trial court did not clearly find, that Moore, and not the officer, initiated further conversation" after Moore had invoked his right to counsel under *Edwards.* The Sixth Circuit opinion does not explicitly consider its choice of this quantum of proof or address possible alternatives; and because its "review [of] the district court's denial of Moore's petition for a writ of habeas corpus [was restricted by] . . . the standards of review as set forth in the Antiterrorism and Effective Death Penalty Act of 1996" (*Moore v. Berghuis, supra*, 700 F.3d at 886; see § 49.2.3.2 *infra*), its phrasing of the quantum cannot be taken as addressing the applicable burden in non-AEDPA cases.

(iii) *Identification suppression issues.* When the issue is whether the defendant's right to counsel at a post-arraignment lineup was violated, the prosecution bears the burdens of production and persuasion and must show either that counsel was actually present or that there was a valid waiver of the right to counsel. *See, e.g., United States v. Garner,* 439 F.2d 525, 526-27 (D.C. Cir. 1970). If a violation of the right to counsel is established, then the prosecution cannot elicit an in-court identification unless it shows by clear and convincing evidence that the in-court identification has an independent source. *See United States v. Wade,* 388 U.S. 218, 240 n.31 (1967); *United States ex rel. Whitmore v. Malcolm,* 476 F.2d 363, 365 n.2 (2d Cir. 1973). If the suppression motion challenges eyewitness identification procedures on due process grounds, many jurisdictions require that the defense satisfy an initial burden of showing suggestivity, with the burden then shifting to the state to show by clear and convincing evidence that the identification was nevertheless reliable. *See, e.g., People v. Monroe*, 925 P.2d 767, 774 (Colo. 1996); *People v. McTush,* 81 Ill. 2d 513, 520, 410 N.E.2d 861, 865, 43 Ill. Dec. 727 (1980); *State v. Howe*, 129 N.H. 120, 123, 523 A.2d 94, 96 (1987); *People v. Rahming,* 26 N.Y.2d 411, 417, 259 N.E.2d 727, 731, 311 N.Y.S.2d 292, 297 (1970).

In jurisdictions where the defense is ordinarily expected to proceed first at suppression hearings, defense counsel can insist that the order of procedure be reversed for any issues on which federal constitutional caselaw requires the prosecution to bear the burden of production. (Where the allocation of the burden of production has not yet been resolved by the Supreme Court but has been imposed upon the prosecution by state courts in other jurisdictions, counsel should use the logic of that caselaw to urge the local court to alter its practice.) If defense counsel once succeeds in convincing the court that the Constitution places the burden of production upon the prosecutor on at least one issue, counsel can then argue that the hearing will be too unwieldy if the defense is left to carry the burden of production on other issues. Counsel should point out that the alternation of burdens of production would result in both parties calling the same witnesses to the witness stand and alternating styles of examination depending upon the issue to which each particular question is relevant – a procedure calculated to result in numerous time-consuming objections and rulings.

If the judge is not persuaded and insists that the defense must carry the burden of production on some issues, counsel should request leave to call police officers and any other persons who are allied in interest with the prosecution as hostile witnesses, with the right to ask leading questions on direct examination. See § 39.29 *infra.* (In support of this request, counsel should point out that police personnel not only have reasons of professional pride and self-advancement for seeking to uphold the legality of arrests, searches, seizures, confessions, and identification procedures in which they have participated but are also subject to potential civil and criminal liability if their conduct in these connections is found to have violated constitutional rights. *See, e.g., Monroe v. Pape,* 365 U.S. 167 (1961) (civil liability under the federal Civil Rights Acts); *Screws v. United States,* 325 U.S. 91 (1945) (criminal liability under the federal Civil Rights Acts); § 3.3.2.4 *supra*; *and see United States v. Price,* 383 U.S. 787, 794 (1966) (criminal liability of private individuals who are "willful participant[s] in joint activity with the State or its agents").) When the defendant's burden of production can be satisfied by proving an easily-established threshold fact – for example, that the search was warrantless – counsel should seek a stipulation from the prosecutor conceding the threshold fact and, once the stipulation is made, insist that the prosecutor proceed with his or her witnesses, allowing subsequent opportunity for rebuttal testimony by the defense. As a rule, such requests should be made in open court at the beginning of the hearing so that, if the prosecutor refuses to stipulate, the judge will understand that the prosecution is the party responsible for wasting the court's time by disputing the indisputable. Counsel should then announce that s/he will present evidence only to the extent necessary to prove the threshold fact, reserving further testimony for rebuttal.

24.3.5. *The Admissibility of Hearsay Testimony in Suppression Hearings*

As a general matter, hearsay is admissible in suppression hearings. *United States v. Matlock,* 415 U.S. 164, 172-77 (1974); *United States v. Raddatz,* 447 U.S. 667, 679 (1980) (dictum). However, there are certain limitations upon the prosecution's use of hearsay. The defense has a right to confront and cross-examine the prosecution's witnesses at a suppression hearing (*see, e.g., United States v. Hodge,* 19 F.3d 51, 53 (D.C. Cir. 1994); *United States v. Salsedo,* 447 F. Supp. 1235, 1241 (E.D. Cal. 1979), *vacated on an unrelated point, United States v. Torres,* 622 F.2d 465 (9th Cir. 1980) (per curiam) (summarized in § 24.3.6 second paragraph *infra*); *People v. Edwards,* 95 N.Y.2d 486, 491, 719 N.Y.S.2d 202, 204-05, 741 N.E.2d 876, 878-79 (2000); *State v. Ehtesham,* 309 S.E.2d 82, 84 (W. Va. 1983)), and a prosecutor cannot use hearsay evidence in such a way as to deprive the defense of meaningful cross-examination of a prosecution witness (*see, e.g., State v. Terrell,* 283 N.W.2d 529, 531 (Minn. 1979) (the prosecution cannot make its case at a suppression hearing merely by submitting a transcript of grand jury testimony to show the lawfulness of a search); *People v. Kaufman,* 457 Mich. 266, 577 N.W.2d 466 (1998) (per curiam) (explaining the Michigan rule that precludes the prosecution from "relying exclusively on preliminary examination transcripts in the conduct of suppression hearings" (*id.* at 273, 577 N.W.2d at 469), and adopting a limited exception for cases in which "the lawyers . . . cho[o]se to have the motion decided on the basis of the preliminary examination transcript" (*id.* at 276, 577 N.W.2d at 471); the court observes that "[c]ertainly, there are cases in which further testimony would be harmful to the defendant's interests, and that determination is normally reserved for defense counsel" (*id.*))).

A second limitation upon the general rule of admissibility of hearsay is that the prosecutor's hearsay evidence is subject to exclusion if particularized reasons appear for doubting its reliability. Thus if defense counsel has a good-faith basis for asserting that the out-of-court declarant lacked personal knowledge of the matters s/he reportedly stated or had some bias against the defendant, the prosecutor should be required to produce the declarant for cross-examination by the defense. *See United States v. Matlock, supra,* 415 U.S. at 175-77 (in holding that hearsay evidence was admissible at a suppression hearing, the Court stresses that the witness "harbored no hostility or bias against defendant that might call her statements into question" and that the hearsay statements "were also corroborated by other evidence received at the suppression hearing" and bore "indicia of reliability"). Multiple hearsay can be challenged as particularly unreliable because of the inherent potential for errors and inaccuracies when a statement is relayed between several individuals.

Finally, even if the proffered hearsay evidence is admissible, it may be insufficiently persuasive to meet the prosecutor's burden of proof (see § 24.3.4 *supra*) on a particular suppression issue. *See, e.g., People v. Moses,* 32 A.D.3d 866, 868, 823 N.Y.S.2d 409, 411 (N.Y. App. Div., 2d Dep't 2006) (the prosecution's burden of production at a hearing on a motion to suppress identification testimony as the fruit of an unlawful *Terry* stop was not satisfied by the testimony of a police officer who transported the complainant to the location of the show-up but was not involved in the stop of the defendant, could not testify to the circumstances of the stop, and offered nothing more than a "vague and equivocal hearsay" account of a statement made by the arresting officer which "was inadequate to demonstrate" the validity of the arresting officer's actions in stopping and detaining the defendant and transporting him to the location of the show-up).

24.3.6. *The Defense Right to Disclosure of Prior Statements of Prosecution Witnesses*

In some jurisdictions, statutes or court rules give the defendant the right to obtain from the prosecutor all prior statements of witnesses who testify for the prosecution at the suppression hearing. *See, e.g.*, FED. RULE CRIM. PRO. 12(h) and 26.2(g); *United States v. Dockery*, 294 A.2d 158 (1972); N.Y. CRIM. PRO. LAW § 240.44. The prosecutor typically is obligated to disclose all written or oral statements in his or her possession or the possession of the police or other governmental agencies. The statutes and rules usually provide that this disclosure must be made after each witness has finished his or her direct examination, or "prior to the commencement of the direct examination" (N.Y. CRIM. PRO. LAW § 240.44). As a practical matter, however, counsel can often obtain the prior statements of all prosecution witnesses from the prosecutor at the beginning of the suppression hearing by requesting them at that time in the interest of efficiency. If the prosecutor refuses counsel's request and insists upon the prerogative of turning over the statements only at the technically obligatory time, counsel should inform the judge of this and explain that there may be delays during the hearing while counsel pauses to read the statements turned over by the prosecutor. Mentioning the issue before the hearing commences may lead the judge to lean on the prosecutor to turn over the statements immediately; at the least, it will improve the judge's patience when defense counsel does indeed take time to read the statements during the course of the hearing.

In jurisdictions that do not provide for disclosure by statute or court rule, counsel should nevertheless request all prior statements of each prosecution witness and should assert that the denial of access to these materials is an unconstitutional infringement upon the defendant's right to cross-examine. *Cf. United States v. Salsedo*, 477 F. Supp. 1235 (E.D. Cal. 1979), *vacated on an unrelated point, United States v. Torres*, 622 F.2d 465 (9th Cir. 1980) (per curiam) (the district court relied on a federal statute to order the government to "deliver to the defendants all documents in its possession relating to the issue of probable cause for the stop, seizure pursuant to the stop, and the fruits of the stop and seizure" (477 F. Supp. at 1244); the district court explained that "[d]epriving the defendants of the government's records as to what the agents knew at the time of the stop makes meaningful cross-examination almost impossible," and the "'deni[al] [of] the right of effective cross-examination . . . is . . . constitutional error of the first magnitude'" (*id.* at 1241, quoting *Davis v. Alaska*, 415 U.S. 308, 318 (1974)); on appeal by the government, the court of appeals vacates the district court's order because "[a]fter the filing of the district court opinion, the government delivered to the defendants the notes requested at the suppression hearing," withholding only "the surveillance logs," and then, "[a]t oral argument, the government stated: (1) it would deliver the surveillance logs to the district court for *in camera* inspection; and (2) in the event that the district court determined that the surveillance logs were relevant to the subject matter of the government agent's testimony, the logs would be released to the defendants" (622 F.2d at 465)). In the event that the judge refuses to order the production of the documents, defense counsel should request their disclosure again at trial (see § 34.7.1.1 *infra*) and then consider whether they reveal any basis for a motion to reopen the suppression hearing on the ground of newly discovered information contained in the documents.

In those jurisdictions where the defendant is expected to proceed first at the suppression hearing and is obligated to conduct direct examinations of police officers, defense counsel should nevertheless request all prior statements of the officers in the possession or control of the prosecution. To support the logic of this request, counsel can point to the disclosure provision in the Federal Rules of Criminal Procedure, which declares that, for purposes of the rules on "Producing Statements at a Suppression Hearing," "a law enforcement officer is considered a government witness." FED. RULE CRIM. PRO. 12(h). As the commentary to the federal rule explains, this provision reflects the practical consideration that a police officer's loyalty invariably belongs to the government regardless of who has called the officer as a witness; the systemic interest in testing the credibility of the officer can be effectuated only by permitting defense counsel to have access to prior statements of the witness. If the court denies access, counsel will again have to be alert to the possibility of moving to reopen the suppression hearing after obtaining the documents at trial.

24.4. *Techniques for Cross-examining Prosecution Witnesses at a Suppression Hearing*

Defense counsel must tailor his or her cross-examination style and the form of cross-examination questions to fit the goal that s/he is pursuing in litigating the suppression hearing. See § 24.2 *supra.* The nature of the cross-examination will vary considerably depending on whether counsel is trying to win the hearing, obtain discovery, or create impeachment material for use at trial.

24.4.1. *Examination Techniques When Counsel's Primary Goal Is To Win the Suppression Hearing*

If counsel has decided that winning the suppression hearing takes precedence over any other potential goals, s/he will often have to pass up tempting opportunities for discovery on cross-examination in order to avoid the risk of eliciting material that would bolster the prosecution's case on suppression issues. For example, if the defense is seeking suppression of objects seized from a defendant incident to arrest and is urging that the arrest was invalid for lack of probable cause, counsel would not cross-examine an arresting officer whose direct examination by the prosecutor established that the officer acted upon incriminating information from an informant but neglected to address the subject of the informant's veracity. See § 25.35.2 *infra.*

When the goal of winning the hearing overrides that of discovery, counsel will ordinarily proceed in the following ways:

(i) As suggested by the preceding illustration, counsel will forgo cross-examination of a prosecution witness altogether when the prosecutor's direct examination has left holes in the showing which the relevant doctrinal rules require the prosecution to make in order to sustain the legality of the law-enforcement activity which counsel is challenging. The temptation to cross-examine for discovery may be intense in this situation, precisely because counsel would like to know the omitted information and whether it could be put to defense use at trial on the issue of guilt or innocence. But that temptation has to be resisted because the witness's answers on cross or on redirect examination by the prosecutor may serve to cure the defects in the prosecution's justification for the law-enforcement agent's actions.

(ii) When counsel does choose to cross-examine a prosecution witness, s/he will tailor his or her questions to elicit only material that undermines the credibility of statements made by the witness on direct without broadening the subjects of the witness's testimony. That is, counsel will ask only questions that disparage the witness's direct testimony by eliciting some retraction or concession which limits what the witness has said explicitly on direct, and will avoid asking any questions that inject new material into the examination. The trick is to be sure to stay out of areas that could open the door to redirect questioning which adds anything to what the witness said on direct, even though those areas would be ideal for discovery. (As indicated in § 37.2.3 *infra*, redirect examination is ordinarily not permitted to go into matters that are beyond the scope of the cross.)

(iii) Counsel's cross-examination questions will be tightly framed and closed-ended – seeking yes-or-no answers or their equivalent, rather than the kind of open-ended questions suitable for discovery purposes. For example, in litigating a claim that the police did not have probable cause to arrest the defendant on the basis of the complainant's description, counsel might ask: "Officer, the description you received from Ms. [*X*] did not include any mention of a blue coat, did it?" Counsel would not ask: "What exactly did the complainant say when she was describing her assailant?" Although the latter question would provide excellent discovery, it also gives the officer the chance to bring up portions of the description that match the defendant.

(iv) During the prosecutor's direct examination of witnesses, counsel will object to all potentially inadmissible evidence that could impair the chances of winning the suppression hearing, even though counsel might like to know the inadmissible information for discovery purposes.

In addition to passing up opportunities to obtain discovery of the prosecution's case, counsel may also allow a strong prospect of winning the hearing to dictate the otherwise inadvisable course of revealing facets of the defense case (including, for example, statements taken from prosecution witnesses by defense investigators) that ordinarily would be saved until trial. And suppression hearings that have a realistic chance of winning are the only suppression hearings in which counsel should seriously consider presenting the testimony of defense witnesses and the defendant. See § 24.5 *infra*.

24.4.2. *Examination Techniques When Counsel's Primary Goal in Litigating the Suppression Motion Is To Obtain Discovery*

When counsel is contemplating using a suppression hearing for the purpose of discovery, s/he will have to engage in a cost-benefit analysis, weighing the value to the defense of each particular item of discovery in preparing for trial against the likelihood and value of winning the suppression motion and the extent to which that likelihood might be impaired by any particular discovery tactic. As implied in § 24.4.1 *supra*, defense counsel would usually be ill-advised to pursue discovery when the chances of winning the suppression of crucial prosecution evidence are very strong, since the cross-examination questions necessary for discovery often will fill gaps in the prosecutor's case at the hearing. If, however, the chances of winning the hearing are remote or if the damage that questioning for discovery could cause to those chances is minimal, then counsel can take advantage of the excellent discovery opportunities afforded by a suppression hearing.

Defense strategies and techniques in a hearing conducted primarily for discovery purposes are the converse of those just described for handling a suppression hearing aimed to produce a defense victory:

(i) Counsel should ordinarily cross-examine every prosecution witness to the maximum extent permitted by the court, covering every area that could conceivably arise at trial. But counsel should not refer to any prior statements of the witness or other documents of which the prosecutor might be unaware that could give the defense an edge at trial.

(ii) Counsel should use predominantly open-ended cross-examination questions, for example: "What was the description of the perpetrator?" "What else did the complainant say?" "What did you do next?" Follow-up questions should be used to assure that subjects are canvassed from every angle: *e.g.*, "Think back and tell us everything s/he said in describing the perpetrator." "Tell us her exact words as best you can recall them." "Anything else she said about the perpetrator's clothing?" "Anything at all about the perpetrator's facial characteristics?" Closed-ended questions should be used only to bottom out each subject of inquiry before moving to the next: "Have you now told us everything said between you and the complainant that provided you with any information which could be used to identify the perpetrator?" [Followed – unless the answer is a categorical "no" – by: "What else? We want the court to hear everything that was said."] By definition, questions calling for yes-or-no answers cannot unearth any *new* subjects of information or alert counsel to the possible existence of subjects s/he does not already know about. What's wanted are forms of questioning that invite the witness to tell everything s/he knows about the case. Counsel should use questions like, "Is there anything else you haven't mentioned about [*X topic*] [*X episode*] [*X time period*]?" and "What more can you remember about [*X topic*] [*X episode*] [*X time period*]?" to get at material that counsel may not have previously contemplated.

(iii) Counsel should not put the defendant or any defense witness on the stand at the suppression hearing. Since the hearing is not being conducted to win, there is no reason to give the prosecutor discovery of the defense case at trial or to risk producing material that the prosecutor can use for impeachment of defense witnesses at trial.

In preparing to use a suppression hearing for discovery, counsel's major task will be to construct reasonable arguments to justify every cross-examination question as relevant to some issue being litigated at the hearing. The problem here is similar to the one discussed in § 11.8.3 *supra* relating to preliminary examinations. The prosecutor will predictably object to defense cross-examination questions that appear to be aimed at obtaining discovery of the prosecution's trial evidence. (The technically correct prosecutorial objection here is irrelevancy, although many prosecutors cite the nonexistent objection that a question should be disallowed simply because it is "discovery.") When the prosecutor does object, most judges will be inclined to curb defense questioning in order to speed up the hearing, and even judges who are sympathetic to the defense effort to obtain some discovery will need to protect the record by demanding that defense counsel explain how the challenged question can produce information bearing on the suppression claim that is being adjudicated. Accordingly, for every discovery-oriented cross-examination question that counsel intends to ask, s/he will need to be prepared to demonstrate that the question is relevant to the issues at the suppression hearing. For this purpose, it is useful to keep in mind that a cross-examination question is technically relevant whenever (i) any possible answer to it would make any fact that supports the defendant's legal theory or theories on the suppression motion more probable, or would make any fact that supports the prosecution's theory or theories less probable, than it would be without the answer; *or* (ii) any possible answer would reflect adversely upon the general credibility of the witness or upon the accuracy of any fact supporting the prosecution's theory or theories which the witness's direct-examination testimony bolsters; *or* (iii) any possible answer would decrease the force of any inference that might be drawn from any piece of testimony given by the witness on direct examination in support of the prosecution's theory or theories; *or* (iv) any possible answer might begin a process of undermining the witness's confidence in any piece of testimony given on direct examination that supports the prosecution's theory or theories, so that the witness might be led eventually to retract it.

In preparing for a suppression hearing at which the primary goal is discovery, counsel will need to plan out thoroughly the sequence of cross-examination questions for each prosecution witness. Even if counsel is able to justify the questions against the prosecutor's objections of irrelevancy, the judge may increasingly lose patience with an attorney who appears to be primarily engaged in seeking discovery and may, at some point, rule out further cross-examination. Thus counsel will want to structure the cross-examination of every witness in such a way that the key questions covering the matters in which counsel is most interested are asked early in the examination, before questioning is likely to be cut off. In order to decrease judicial impatience, it is useful to intersperse questions that bear clearly and directly on the issues being litigated among counsel's more suspiciously discovery-oriented questions: Judges are far less likely to cut off cross-examination when they feel that discovery is a secondary goal rather than counsel's primary purpose. Counsel should also strive to keep the cross-examination questions flowing at a rapid-fire rate; judges with crowded calendars will not tolerate slow examination styles or delays while the attorney thinks of new questions or consults documents.

To the inexperienced practitioner it may seem that suppression hearings conducted for the purpose of discovery require little preparation. As the foregoing discussion has suggested, however, counsel will need to devote substantial time to planning before the hearing in order to take full advantage of the opportunities for discovery.

24.4.3. *Examination Techniques When Counsel's Primary Goal Is To Lay a Foundation for Impeachment at Trial*

In suppression hearings conducted primarily for the purpose of creating transcript material that can be used to impeach prosecution witnesses at trial, counsel will usually be pursuing one or more of the following objectives:

(1)   To lure the witness into making statements that are affirmatively helpful because:

(a)   They tend to negate some element of the offense (thereby preventing conviction altogether or limiting conviction to a lesser included charge);

    (b)   They tend to establish some fact that supports an affirmative defense (for example, self-defense);

    (c)   They tend to establish some fact that mitigates the gravity of the offense and will thereby help at sentencing (for example, the fact that the defendant was the look-out and was not directly involved in the beating of the complainant).

    (2)   To circumscribe unfavorable testimony so that the witness cannot make even more damaging statements at trial (for example, by pinning an eyewitness down to the statement that s/he could not have observed the face of the perpetrator for more than a minute, in order to prevent the witness from lengthening the time when s/he testifies at trial and thus enhancing the persuasiveness of his or her identification of the defendant).

Generally, in pursuing any of these objectives, counsel should make heavy use of "closed" questions – that is, forms of questioning which demand specific answers and leave the witness with the smallest possible range of choice about what to say or what words to say it in. ("At the moment when you first saw the two people standing in the doorway, how many feet were you from the closer of those two people?" "Well, when why you say 'a couple of feet,' do you mean that it was closer to two feet or closer to ten feet?" "Closer to six feet or closer to ten feet?") Questions calling for yes-or-no answers will often constitute a substantial part of this sort of cross-examination. ("You told the police officers at the scene that those two people came running at you, didn't you?" "'Running' was the word you used to describe how they came toward you, isn't that right?") An effective way to lock a witness in to unambiguous answers is to take full advantage of the cross-examiner's right to use leading questions, stating the exact factual proposition that counsel wants to extract from the witness and asking the witness only whether or not that proposition is correct. ("It is true, is it not, that as soon as you saw the two persons start running toward you, you began to run away from them?" "And when you were grabbed, you were grabbed around the neck from behind, isn't that correct?" "You had turned your face away from them by that time, right?" "As soon as you started running, you turned to look where you were running, didn't you?") Particularly when the objective of the cross-examination is to circumscribe damaging testimony, it is important to bottom out the witness's story by establishing that what s/he has described as the things s/he saw or heard or did that fall within any significant category of information constitute *all* s/he heard or saw or did within that category. This is best achieved by "nothing else" questions. ("So, the period between the first moment when you saw two people standing in the doorway and the moment when you turned to run away was the only time before the lineup when you were able to observe the features of either of those two people, was it not?" "There was no other time when you were facing them, right?" "Apart from what you told the police at the scene, you didn't observe anything else about the facial features of either of the two persons, did you?" "Except for the one word 'Hey!' that was shouted at you, you heard nothing else said by either of the two persons prior to the lineup, did you?")

Counsel should be prepared to adjust the order of subjects covered to fit the demeanor of the witness. Frequently, civilian witnesses will be fairly pliant at the beginning of a cross-examination (either because the witness is nervous and cowed or because the witness does not have any reason yet to distrust or dislike the defense attorney) and will become progressively more difficult to handle (as the nervousness wears off or as the witness comes to realize that the defense attorney is succeeding in extracting statements that are helpful to the defense). Thus it often will prove useful to lead off the cross-examination with the factual propositions that counsel is most concerned with proving or anticipates having the most difficulty extracting from the witness. On the other hand, if there are a few points that can be tied down without pushing the witness hard and without the witness perceiving that s/he is conceding anything significant or embarrassing, these points should usually be taken up before the first point on which counsel expects to have to dominate the witness perceptibly, since that will mark the end of the honeymoon period with most witnesses.

In attempting to extract concessions from hostile witnesses who are trying to out-maneuver counsel by saying the opposite of whatever counsel is seeking, it will often be productive to use false leads. This technique consists of getting the witness to believe that counsel wants the converse of what s/he really wants or of getting the witness so concerned to avoid falling into an apparent trap that s/he will back away from it and thereby fall into counsel's real trap. For example, in an identification suppression hearing at which counsel is trying to show that an eyewitness's fingering of the defendant in a lineup resulted from the witness's having selected the defendant's picture from a photo array the week before (rather than from having seen the defendant commit the crime), counsel might ask questions which appear to be aimed at disparaging the witness's perceptual abilities by showing that the photo is not a good likeness of the defendant in person. In response, the witness is likely to deny any significant dissimilarities between the defendant's picture and the defendant's appearance at the lineup, and to exaggerate the degree of confidence with which s/he recognized the defendant when s/he saw the defendant's photo in the array.

False leads can be used in four different ways in a suppression hearing:

(i)   To establish propositions that will be useful solely in attempting to win the suppression hearing (for example, that the defendant did not give consent to the search of his room that led to the recovery of contraband);

(ii)   To establish propositions that will be useful both in the suppression hearing and at trial (for example, in an identification suppression hearing: that it was dark at the time of the incident – a fact tending to establish the unreliability of the identification as a basis for suppression and also bolstering the defense of misidentification that counsel intends to present at trial);

(iii) To establish propositions that will be neither useful nor harmful at the suppression hearing but will be useful at trial (for example, at a confession suppression hearing: that the defendant was arrested less than fifteen minutes after the robbery complainant emerged from a dark alley at midnight and borrowed a cell phone to call the police – a fact irrelevant to the defendant's claim of coercion but one that bolsters the misidentification defense at trial); and

    (iv)   To establish propositions that will be harmful to the defendant at the suppression hearing but useful to his or her defense at trial.

Statements in the last of these categories can often be drawn out of an unfriendly witness, such as a police officer, precisely *because* of their evident harmfulness to the defendant's claim for suppression. Consider the following two illustrations:

    (A)   Assume that the charge is possession of drugs and that the police claim they obtained consent to search the defendant's bedroom and bureau from his brother, who shared the bedroom and the bureau. If defense counsel contests the brother's authority to consent (see § 25.18.2 *infra*) and behaves during cross-examination as if s/he is trying to get the police officer to say that the bureau was used exclusively by the defendant, the officer will probably react by strengthening his or her testimony that the brother had equal, if not greater, access to the bureau. By the end of the cross-examination, counsel will probably have gotten the officer to say that most, if not all, of the clothing in the bureau at the time of the search belonged to the brother; that most of the clothing in the drawer with the drugs belonged to the brother; that the bureau was closer to the brother's bed; and that the brother acted as if he had free and constant access to the bureau. Counsel will thereupon have lost the battle by helping the prosecution to justify the search on consent grounds. However, counsel will have won the war by acquiring material to use in impeaching the officer at trial if the officer tries to change stories when counsel springs the defendant's true defense: that the drugs belonged to the brother and were placed by the brother in his drawer of his bureau.

    (B)   Suppose that the charge is assault with a firearm and that the defendant has made a statement to the police admitting the commission of the shooting but explaining it on self-defense grounds. Counsel has a good-faith basis for challenging the voluntariness of the statement and proceeds to do so. Inevitably, when counsel begins to cross-examine police officers on the subject of voluntariness and tries to get them to agree that the defendant resisted the coercive efforts of the police, the officers will insist that the defendant willingly came forward and was absolutely cooperative. Once again, the defense will have lost the suppression hearing. But, at trial, defense counsel will be able to force the officers to admit that the defendant's actions were not those of a guilty person who has something to hide.

24.4.4. *Examination Techniques When Counsel Has a Mixture of Goals at the Suppression Hearing*

The foregoing three sections focused on cases in which counsel had a single overriding objective at the suppression hearing. In many cases, however, counsel may wish to pursue more than one goal. For example, there may be a realistic chance of winning the suppression hearing, yet counsel may be insufficiently sanguine about the probability of victory to be wholly comfortable about forgoing opportunities for discovery and creation of impeachment material.

As the previous sections have suggested, pursuing multiple goals may jeopardize them all. For example, cross-examining for discovery or to create impeachment material may unavoidably elicit facts that will destroy any chance of winning the hearing. In many cases counsel is realistically required to choose one strategy and follow it single-mindedly – unless, of course, during the hearing that strategy is proving unworkable.

There are other cases, however, in which counsel can, with careful advance planning, pursue a range of goals. For example, if counsel is litigating several different suppression claims or theories, it may be possible to seek victory on one claim or theory, while using others to obtain discovery and create impeachment material. For example, in an identification suppression hearing, counsel might seek discovery through a claim that the police lacked probable cause to arrest the defendant (see §§ 25.7 and 27.7 *infra*), might seek to pin down impeachment material by cross-examination predicated on the claim that a show-up on the scene was impermissibly suggestive (see § 27.3.1 *infra*), and might seek to win yet a third claim – that a subsequent lineup was unconstitutionally held without the presence of counsel (see § 27.6 *infra*).

In deciding whether to mix strategies, counsel will need to be completely familiar with the facts of the case and all possible legal issues that could be litigated at the suppression hearing, and s/he will need to conduct a cost-benefit analysis that considers (i) the likelihood and value of succeeding on each strategy if pursued alone, (ii) the extent to which potentially winning strategies will be impaired by mixing them with other strategies, and (iii) whether the predictable impairment is outweighed by the probable gains to be achieved from pursuing a mixture of strategies.

24.4.5. *Using Diagrams and Vidcam Recordings in Cross-Examination*

In litigating Fourth Amendment claims, counsel will often find it helpful to ask each officer to draw a diagram of the scene of the arrest, search, or seizure in issue, describing the events in detail in relation to the diagram. Diagrams drawn by each officer should be removed from view before the entry of the next police witness, and counsel should ask the court not only for leave to remove the diagram after the testimony of the first witness but also for a ruling precluding the use of that diagram by the prosecutor in examining subsequent prosecution witnesses. The policy underlying the rule on witnesses (see § 34.6 *infra*) supports such a request, and by keeping from each police witness the diagrams drawn by the others, visibly inconsistent versions of the affair can sometimes be elicited that will persuade the judge or an appellate court to discredit the officers.

In strategizing and preparing for suppression hearings, counsel should always ascertain whether any police officers or vehicles involved in relevant events were equipped with vidcams, and should request the vidcam recordings through informal and, if necessary, formal discovery proceedings. If a recording supports the defense version of the police activity at issue in the suppression hearing or appears likely to be useful in cross-examining an officer, counsel should take the necessary steps to authenticate the recording so as to assure its admissibility. See § 29.10.3 *infra*. In the latter case, counsel's cross-examination of the officer may be designed in either of two ways. (A) If the officer's direct testimony is inconsistent with events captured in the recording in ways that are directly material to the legality of the officer's conduct which produced the evidence that counsel is seeking to suppress, counsel should ordinary confine cross-examination to (1) asking the officer to reaffirm on cross his or her direct testimony; (2) introducing the recording and playing it; and (3) asking the officer whether X or Y event shown by the recording is not inconsistent with his or her current version of the episode. *Caveat:* Questioning of type (3) should be pursued only if counsel is reasonably confident that the officer cannot come up with a credible tale that reconciles his or her direct testimony with the recording. (B) If the officer's direct testimony is inconsistent with the events captured in the recording only in ways that do not bear directly on the legality of the officer's conduct, counsel can use the inconsistencies to discredit the officer's testimony generally by developing as many detailed discrepancies as possible and arguing that the officer's current version of material events is untrustworthy as a whole.

24.5. *Determining Whether to Present the Testimony of the Defendant and Other Defense Witnesses*

There are several strategic factors that must be considered in deciding whether to present the defendant or other defense witnesses in a suppression hearing. The decisions will have to be made at least tentatively at an early stage of counsel's preparation, in order to leave sufficient time to rehearse the defendant's testimony and to subpoena the other witnesses and prepare them to testify. See §§ 29.5-29.6 *infra*. (Even when a witness is loyal to the defendant, a subpoena is advisable, to make the necessary record for a continuance in the event of the witness's failure to appear. See § 29.4.1 *infra*.) On the other hand, counsel should not allow himself or herself to feel locked in to the tentatively chosen strategy; s/he must constantly re-evaluate goals and strategies and adapt them to unanticipated developments at the hearing.

24.5.1. *Testimony by the Defendant*

In deciding whether to put the defendant on the witness stand in a suppression hearing, counsel should consider that whatever testimony the defendant gives at the hearing can probably be used to impeach the defendant if s/he testifies at trial. Although a defendant's testimony in a suppression hearing cannot be used against him or her in the prosecutor's case-in-chief at trial on the issue of guilt (*Simmons v. United States,* 390 U.S. 377 (1968); *Brown v. United States,* 411 U.S. 223, 228 (1973) (dictum); *United States v. Salvucci,* 448 U.S. 83, 89-90 (1980) (dictum)), the prosecution is usually free to use it for impeachment of the defendant's trial testimony to the extent that the two are inconsistent (see §§ 39.10, subdivision (G), 39.13.1 *infra*; *cf. Harris v. New York,* 401 U.S. 222 (1971) (a confession suppressed on *Miranda* grounds can be used as a prior inconsistent statement to impeach the defendant at trial)). (Counsel can, however, argue that this kind of impeachment should be barred by *New Jersey v. Portash,* 440 U.S. 450 (1979), which holds that an accused cannot be impeached with prior testimony which s/he was compelled to give in violation of the Fifth Amendment privilege against self-incrimination. Arguably a defendant's testimony in a suppression hearing is "compelled" and involuntary in the sense that the defendant is confronted with the "Hobson's choice" (*Simmons v. United States, supra,* 390 U.S. at 391) "either to give up what he believed, with advice of counsel, to be a valid . . . [constitutional] claim [to have evidence suppressed] or, in legal effect, to waive his Fifth Amendment privilege against self-incrimination" (*id.* at 394). *Cf. Harrison v. United States,* 392 U.S. 219 (1968); *McDaniel v. North Carolina,* 392 U.S. 665 (1968) (per curiam).) Counsel may be able to limit cross-examination at the suppression hearing so as to avoid incriminating admissions (*see, e.g., People v. Lacy*, 25 A.D.2d 788, 788, 270 N.Y.S.2d 1014, 1015-16 (N.Y. App. Div., 3d Dep't 1966) (at a hearing on a motion to suppress incriminating statements, "the defendant . . . may take the stand and testify as to his request for counsel at the time of the arrest and as to all facts relevant to the proceedings . . . leading to and including the signing of the alleged confession and waiver and by so testifying, the defendant does not subject himself 'to cross-examination upon the [circumstances of the crime]'")), but often this will not be easy to do if the cross-examining prosecutor is at all capable.

If the defendant's testimony would probably be instrumental in winning the suppression hearing and if a victory at the hearing would probably necessitate the prosecutor's dismissal of the case, these prospects usually justify accepting the risks of impeachment. Even if the chances of victory at the suppression hearing are not overwhelming, testimony by the defendant at the hearing may be justified if there is little chance that the defendant will testify at trial or if the defendant's testimony at the hearing will be limited to matters that do not overlap any of the subjects about which the defendant may testify at trial. *See, e.g., People v. Lacy, supra*, 25 A.D.2d at 788, 270 N.Y.S.2d at 1015-16.

Apart from the risk of impeachment at trial, there may be tactical reasons to forgo presenting the defendant's testimony at a suppression hearing. It is often possible to establish a marginal case of unconstitutional police conduct on the basis of police testimony alone, whereas the defendant's version of the relevant events portrays the officers' behavior as considerably more egregious and blatantly unlawful. The question whether to put the defendant on the stand in this situation is particularly difficult. Many judges believe that defendants are prone to exaggerate police misconduct; these judges are slow to credit any defendant's testimony, particularly when it consists of horror stories. Therefore, calling the defendant to testify entails the risk of irritating the judge to such an extent that s/he will strain the facts and the law to uphold the police.

On the other hand, if the defendant's description of atrocious police conduct is strongly credible, and particularly if it is corroborated by independent witnesses or evidence, proof of flagrant police abuse can spell the difference between victory and defeat in a suppression hearing. The Supreme Court has held – in a decision of uncertain breadth – that the scope of taint attending an unconstitutional search and seizure may depend in part on the flagrancy of the unconstitutionality. *Brown v. Illinois,* 422 U.S. 590, 603-05 (1975); *cf. United States v. Leon,* 468 U.S. 897, 911 (1984); see § 25.41 *infra.* And, as a practical matter, trial and appellate judges who can be persuaded that the police have behaved abominably are more likely to rule in the defendant's favor on any close questions in the case.

Several collateral dangers bear upon the decision whether to put the defendant on the stand in a suppression hearing. The defendant's testimony may give the prosecutor discovery of the defenses planned for trial and thereby improve the prosecutor's presentation on the issue of guilt. In cross-examining the defendant at the suppression hearing, the prosecutor can develop a sense of the defendant's personality and susceptibility to certain cross-examination tactics and may consequently do a better job of cross-examination at trial. Finally, if the judge at the suppression hearing is the same judge who will preside at a bench trial and/or at sentencing, unpersuasive testimony by the defendant at the hearing could prove detrimental in later stages of the case: The judge's discrediting of this testimony could lead the judge also to discredit the defendant's testimony at trial. And/or the judge's belief that the defendant has perjured himself or herself could lead to a harsher sentence.

Notwithstanding all these risks, there will be many cases in which the chances of victory at the suppression hearing are sufficiently strong, and the contribution that the defendant's testimony can make is sufficiently important, that defense counsel will opt in favor of having the defendant testify. The final decision must be made by the defendant personally (see § 39.11 *infra*); counsel should explain the potential benefits and risks and advise the defendant about the best course.

When the defendant does testify at the suppression hearing, it is usually best that s/he testify last. Having heard all of the prior evidence, s/he will be in a position to rebut police testimony effectively and to explain any apparent inconsistencies in the accounts of defense witnesses. See §§ 29.6, 39.3 *infra*.

24.5.2. *Testimony by Defense Witnesses Other Than the Defendant*

Calling defense witnesses other than the defendant to testify at a suppression hearing involves significant dangers and complications. The bottom line is that defense counsel should not do so unless (1) counsel's purpose in conducting the hearing is to win suppression (see §§ 24.2, 24.4.1 *supra*); and (2) the evidence that counsel is seeking to suppress is likely to make the difference between conviction and acquittal at trial; and (3) counsel's chances of winning the suppression of this evidence are strong if counsel calls the defense witnesses and considerably weaker if s/he does not; and (4) the hearing judge insists that the defense lead off the hearing by presenting evidence sufficient to meet an applicable burden of production; and (5) defense counsel cannot get around the judge's sequence-of-proof requirement in one of the ways suggested in § 24.3.4 *supra*; and (6) counsel cannot meet the production burden with documentary evidence (like police reports and records). In this situation, counsel obviously has no choice but call at least *some* witnesses. But s/he should (a) call as few witnesses as possible, and limit the examination of each witness to material that is indispensable for satisfying the defense's production burden; (b) announce at the outset that s/he is presenting the testimony of these witnesses only under the compulsion of the judge's sequence-of-testimony ruling; (c) announce that s/he is limiting his or her examination of the witnesses to matters that bear directly on the issues of law-enforcement illegality that are the basis of the motion to suppress; and (d) scrupulously observe that limitation.

The problems – in order of complexity – are these:

(A) When counsel introduces the testimony of any witnesses, s/he risks perpetuating testimony that the prosecution can introduce in its case-in-chief at trial, within the prior-recorded-testimony exception to the hearsay rule, if the witnesses become unavailable at the time of trial. The law on this subject is vexed.

(1) Many jurisdictions have codified the prior-testimony exception in the form in

which it appears in FED. RULE EVID. 804(b)(1), allowing the admission of the former testimony of a presently unavailable witness "if the party against whom the testimony is now offered . . . had an opportunity and similar motive to develop the testimony by direct, cross, or redirect examination." Defense counsel's obvious objection to the application of this exception is that s/he did not have a "similar motive" for questioning the witness at the suppression hearing as s/he would have for cross-examining the witness at trial, inasmuch as the sole focus of the suppression hearing was the legality of the manner in which the prosecution obtained its evidence, not the reliability and probative force of the evidence in proving the defendant's guilt. But this distinction is less than clear in the case of some defense theories for suppression, like a Due Process challenge to identification testimony as unreliable (see §§ 27.2-27.4 *infra*) or a Due Process challenge to incriminating statements as involuntary when the defense claim of involuntariness relies in part on the idea that an impressionable defendant was coached to make the statements by police questioning that was "leading or suggestive" (*Fikes v. Alabama*, 352 U.S. 191, 195 (1957); *see, e.g., Jurek v. Estelle*, 623 F.2d 929, 941 (5th Cir. 1980)). And some judges might well be persuaded to find a "similar motive" in any case in which defense counsel at the suppression hearing uses some of the techniques advised in §§ 24.4.2-24.4.3 as means for developing discovery and impeachment material.

(2) Federal constitutional Confrontation-Clause analysis would proceed along much the same track to an equally uncertain conclusion. See § 36.3.3 *infra*. The principal pertinent cases are *Crawford v. Washington*, 541 U.S. 36 (2004), and *Lee v. Illinois*, 476 U.S. 530, 546 n.6 (1986). *Crawford* permits a prosecutor's use at trial of the pretrial testimony of a witness "where the . . . [witness] is unavailable [at the time of trial], and . . . where the defendant has had a prior opportunity to cross-examine" (541 U.S. at 59). *Lee* holds that the kind of "opportunity to cross-examine" contemplated by *Crawford* would not be satisfied by a defendant's cross-examination of a *prosecution* witness at a suppression hearing (*see* 476 U.S. at 546 n.6). Logically, the rationale of *Lee* – that defense counsel at a suppression hearing has no reason to go beyond matters bearing on the lawfulness of the prosecution's evidence-gathering methods and to cross-examine on subjects relating to the defendant's guilt or innocence – seems as applicable to defense suppression-hearing witnesses as to those for the prosecution. But because, as a practical matter, defense counsel takes the initiative in developing the scope of examination of a witness whom s/he calls to the stand and questions on direct, some judges might distinguish *Lee* and find *Crawford*'s "prior opportunity" test satisfied in the case of a *defense* suppression-hearing witness.

(3) As a back-up argument for precluding the prosecutor's use at trial of the testimony of such a witness who has become unavailable since the suppression hearing, counsel could invoke the rationale of *Simmons v. United States*, 390 U.S. 377 (1968). This would require extending *Simmons*'s holding – that a defendant's testimony admitting a possessory interest in property for the purpose of acquiring standing to challenge the legality of its warrantless seizure may not be used in the prosecution's case-in-chief at trial to show the defendant's possession of the instruments and proceeds of a crime because "[t]he need to choose between waiving the Fifth Amendment privilege and asserting an incriminating interest in evidence sought to be suppressed, or invoking the privilege but thereby forsaking the claim for exclusion, creates what the [*Simmons*] Court characterized as an 'intolerable' need to surrender one constitutional right in order to assert another" (*United States v. Kahan*, 415 U.S. 239, 242 (1974) (per curiam)) – to

encompass any sort of evidence that the defense is compelled to present in court (*cf. Harrison v. United States,* 392 U.S. 219 (1968)) in order to assert the defendant's rights against the governmental illegality that necessitated the motion to suppress. *Cf. Fisher v. United States,* 425 U.S. 391, 399-400 n.5 (1976) (dictum); *Andresen v. Maryland,* 427 U.S. 463, 472 & n.6 (1976) (dictum). Such an extension is not predictable (*see United States v. Kahan, supra,* 415 U.S. at 243; *cf. United States v. Nobles,* 422 U.S. 225, 233-34 (1975)), and counsel cannot afford to rely on it in the present state of the law.

(4) The upshot, then, is that the risk of perpetuating potential prosecution trial evidence by calling defense witnesses at a suppression hearing is considerable in some circumstances and difficult to calculate in others.

(B) Even if the prosecution were forbidden to use a defense witness's suppression-hearing testimony in its case-in-chief at trial, it could almost certainly use that testimony to impeach the witness if his or her trial testimony deviates at all from what s/he said at the hearing. *See* § 17.9 *supra*; § 34.7.2 *infra*. The defense might argue that the logic of *New Jersey v. Portash,* 440 U.S. 450 (1979), § 24.5.1 *supra,* prohibits this use of the prior testimony because the defendant was "compelled" to present it in order to vindicate the constitutional rights at issue in the suppression hearing; but the argument requires extensions of both *Portash* and *Simmons* in the teeth of *United States v. Nobles, supra,* 422 U.S. at 233-34 (see §§ 18.12-18.13 *supra*), and *Kansas v. Cheever,* 571 U.S. 87, 93-95 (2014) (see § 16.6.1 *supra*); and the chances of winning all of these uphill battles under current constitutional doctrine are slim.

(C) Finally, apart from the dangers of prosecutorial use of the testimony at trial, counsel who calls defense witnesses at a suppression hearing may give the prosecutor discovery of the version of the facts that the defense intends to present at trial, together with "batting practice" in cross-examining potential defense trial witnesses.

So defense counsel's wisest practice is to present defense testimony only under the circumstances described in the first paragraph of this section and, even when those circumstances exist, to take the precautions advised there. Any witness whom counsel is obliged to call should be painstakingly prepared to testify, by rehearsals that teach the witness to give the shortest practicable responsive answers to all questions asked on either direct or cross-examination. See §§ 29.5-29.6 *infra*. Direct examination questions should be tightly framed to avoid opening the door to wide-ranging cross-examination by the prosecutor. And when defense counsel later prepares the same witness to testify at trial, counsel will need to take the witness through a detailed review of the transcript of his or her suppression-hearing testimony, to minimize the likelihood that the witness will inadvertently diverge from it and expose himself or herself to avoidable impeachment.

24.6. *Arguing the Motion*

24.6.1. *Timing of the Argument; Reasons for Seeking a Continuance*

After the conclusion of the evidence-taking at a suppression hearing, counsel for both parties will ordinarily be expected to proceed immediately to make their legal arguments for and against the motion. Defense counsel needs to be ready to present his or her position succinctly, integrating the applicable legal principles with the facts adduced at the hearing. For this purpose, counsel will find it useful to have taken notes, during the testimony of the principal witnesses, of key points made by each of them. Motions judges are often impatient with extended argument, and counsel will want to zero in promptly on crucial details.

In rare cases counsel may have to request a continuance of oral argument because the evidence has generated new legal issues that counsel had not anticipated and now needs to research or because counsel's notes and memory of the evidence are not sufficient and counsel wants to review a transcript of the hearing in preparation for argument. Since judges will usually be resistant to continuing the arguments (particularly when trial is scheduled to begin shortly after the suppression hearing), counsel may be required to explain precisely why the additional research or transcript is essential to his or her ability to represent the defendant competently in arguing the motion. If the court nevertheless denies the request for a continuance, counsel will have to proceed with the oral argument. In this situation counsel should consider requesting leave to submit a supplementary written memorandum based upon counsel's additional research and review of the transcript. If the court denies even that request and immediately rules on the motion, counsel should thereafter conduct the contemplated legal research, acquire the transcript, or both, and should incorporate any favorable new legal authorities or transcript references in a motion for reconsideration of the ruling. When trial begins immediately on the heels of the suppression hearing, counsel should inform the judge of his or her intention to submit a memorandum in support of reconsideration and should ask the judge to instruct the prosecutor not to mention during jury-selection *voir dire* or in an opening statement the evidence which counsel is continuing to contend should be suppressed. See § 18.14 *supra*; § 33.4.1 *infra*. Counsel will have to promise the court to produce the memorandum promptly, so that the judge can consider it before the trial progresses to a point at which the prosecution's presentation of the challenged evidence cannot practicably be further delayed.

24.6.2. *Order of the Parties' Arguments*

In oral arguments on suppression motions, it is customary in most jurisdictions for the defense to proceed first because the defendant is the moving party. On issues on which the prosecution bears the burden of persuasion (see § 24.3.4 *supra*), defense counsel could perhaps insist that the prosecutor argue first. However, it is usually in defense counsel's interest to argue first, so as to gain the advantage of framing the issues and also – in jurisdictions where rebuttal argument is conventional – to get the last word.

24.6.3. *Using Burdens of Production and Persuasion*

When arguing the motion, defense counsel should make aggressive use of the applicable burdens of production and persuasion. (See § 24.3.4 *supra*.) If the evidentiary record is bare or insufficient on an issue on which the prosecution bears the burden of production or persuasion, it will usually reward counsel's effort to remind the judge that the prosecutor had an obligation to establish the missing facts and that, therefore, any deficiency of evidence on the issue is fatal to the prosecution.

24.6.4. *Factors to Consider in Constructing Legal and Factual Arguments*

The essence of a good suppression argument is to highlight the facts adduced at the evidentiary hearing that bring the case within the legal principles on which counsel is relying. Those principles – established by precedent, by constitutional or statutory text, or by logical extrapolation from the extant caselaw – are background. Facts are foreground. Having just heard the evidence, the judge wants to know what to make of it. Ordinarily, having just heard at least as much unimportant evidence as important evidence, the judge wants to be told exactly what counsel is asserting is important. Zeroing in on key details is the way to persuade the judge to rule in counsel's favor. It is also the way to obtain specific findings of fact that will insulate a favorable ruling from appellate reversal in jurisdictions where the prosecutor can appeal from a suppression order or get the order reviewed by prerogative writ proceedings.

Because form optimally mirrors function, it will usually be most effective for counsel to shape his or her argument by presenting the applicable legal principles not in the manner of a doctrinal primer but rather as a framework for identifying and emphasizing critical, favorable facts. Thus, for example, in a case in which a police officer stopped the defendant on the street and then frisked him or her (as a result of which the officer found a gun), counsel might structure the argument in the following manner:

(i)   Begin the argument by explaining that the defendant is moving for suppression on two separate and independent grounds: on the ground that the officer's stop of the defendant amounted to an unconstitutional seizure, and the gun therefore must be suppressed as a fruit of the seizure; and on the alternative ground that even if the officer had a lawful basis to stop the defendant, s/he did not have a lawful basis to frisk the defendant, and the gun therefore must be suppressed as a fruit of this unlawful search of the defendant's person.

(ii)   In arguing the first claim (that the stop was unconstitutional), begin by stating that there is no dispute about the fact that the officer did indeed stop the defendant; then tersely state the applicable legal standard for gauging whether a stop constitutes a "seizure" within the meaning of the Fourth Amendment (and/or the state constitution) and move on quickly to a detailed recitation of facts adduced at the hearing which demonstrate that the officer's actions did indeed constitute such a "seizure" – beginning with the most dramatic or legally crucial such facts; then tersely state the applicable standard for assessing whether the officer had an adequate basis for stopping the defendant, and similarly promptly move on to the facts demonstrating that s/he did not – mustering the evidence in the same way, strongest first; and conclude by stating the legal principle that the unconstitutionality of the stop requires suppression of the gun as a fruit of an unlawful seizure.

(iii) In arguing the second claim (that the frisk was unconstitutional), begin by stating that there is no dispute about the fact that a frisk amounting to a "search of the person" took place; then tersely state the applicable legal standard for determining the constitutionality of a frisk and get rapidly into the evidence showing that the officer did not have the requisite information to meet that standard; and conclude by stating the legal principle that the gun must be suppressed as a fruit of the unlawful frisk even if it is not suppressed as a fruit of the unlawful stop.

When the relevant legal principles are well settled (like the federal constitutional standards for determining the validity of a stop or frisk), counsel should ordinarily keep the discussion of the law quite brief. As a general rule, counsel should state the legal principles simply and concisely, and then devote most of the argument to fitting facts into the legal framework. Even when the law is not so well settled and the issues in the case make it necessary for counsel to argue law, counsel is well advised to refrain from reciting strings of citations of court decisions or engaging in complex legal analysis in oral argument. See § 19.6 *supra*. If counsel's legal position does require intricate reasoning or reference to authorities that are not the staple stuff of suppression motions in counsel's jurisdiction, s/he does best by handing up a concise written memorandum of law or highlighted photocopies of purportedly controlling judicial opinions. See §§ 19.6-19.7 *supra*.

In arguing facts, counsel should consider the availability and strategic advisability of various grounds for urging the court to find that the testimony of the other side's witness(es) is incredible. Since judges are often loth to disbelieve witnesses – particularly police officers and others who make a respectable appearance – counsel should ordinarily (a) include in his or her argument any legally sustainable theories that do *not* require the judge to reject the testimony of an opposing witness; (b) argue that opposing witnesses are mistaken rather than lying, to the extent that s/he is obliged to contest their testimony and can plausibly assert that it is innocently erroneous; and (c) contest the testimony of as few opposing witnesses – and as little of the testimony of each – as s/he needs to contest in order to win. However, when counsel's position does demand that s/he ask the judge to discredit an opposing witness, s/he should be prepared to argue, for example, that a police officer's testimony should be found to be incredible and rejected because:

(1) The officer's account of actions or events defies "common sense" or "common knowledge" (*see, e.g., People v. Lastorino*, 185 A.D.2d 284, 285, 586 N.Y.S.2d 26, 27 (N.Y. App. Div., 2d Dep't 1992) (rejecting, as incredible, a police officer's testimony "that the defendant, who was aware he was under surveillance for at least several minutes, exited his vehicle and left the driver's door open and a loaded gun visible on the seat, virtually inviting the police to discover the gun"); *People v. Void*, 170 A.D.2d 239, 241, 567 N.Y.S.2d 216, 217 (N.Y. App. Div., 1st Dep't 1991) (rejecting, as incredible, a police officer's testimony "that the defendant consented to a police search of the apartment, where a substantial amount of cocaine was stored in plain view in the kitchen sink – a location where the drugs could be readily discovered"); *People v. Addison*, 116 A.D.2d 472, 474, 496 N.Y.S.2d 742, 744 (N.Y. App. Div., 1st Dep't 1986) (in rejecting a police officer's testimony that he had reasonable grounds to believe that the defendant was armed and dangerous because the defendant "reach[ed] for his waistband as the . . . officer approached," the court observes that there were five police cars and several officers on the scene, and "we find it incredible that defendant, in the face of such a show of force, would . . . reach for his waistband"); *United States v. Loines*, 56 F.4th 1099 (6th Cir. 2023), summarized in § 25.22.2 *infra*).

(2) At the hearing, counsel impeached the officer with a prior inconsistent statement or statements. *See, e.g., People v. Miret-Gonzalez*, 159 A.D.2d 647, 552 N.Y.S.2d 958 (N.Y. App. Div., 2d Dep't 1990), *app. denied*, 76 N.Y.2d 739, 558 N.Y.S.2d 901 (1990) (the court finds a police officer's testimony incredible, in part because the officer's account of the car stop and search was contradicted by his incident report); *People v. Lebron*, 184 A.D.2d 784, 785-87, 585 N.Y.S.2d 498, 550-02 (N.Y. App. Div., 2d Dep't 1992) (the police officer's testimony was contradicted by statements and omissions in prior police reports).

(3) The officer has a motive to present perjurious testimony. *See, e.g., People v. Berrios*, 28 N.Y.2d 361, 368, 270 N.E.2d 709, 713, 321 N.Y.S.2d 884, 889 (1971) (acknowledging that "[s]ome police officers . . . may be tempted to tamper with the truth" at a suppression hearing in order to justify their actions in conducting a search or seizure).

(4) The officer's "demeanor" on the witness stand or the witness's "mode of telling his [or her] story" indicates that s/he is not telling the truth (*People v. Perry*, 128 Misc. 2d 430, 432, 488 N.Y.S.2d 977, 979 (N.Y. Sup. Ct., N.Y. Cty. 1985)). *See also People v. Carmona*, 233 A.D.2d 142, 144-45, 649 N.Y.S.2d 432, 434 (N.Y. App. Div., 1st Dep't 1996) (in an opinion rejecting the officer's testimony as incredible, the appellate court refers disparagingly to the officer's testimony "that he approached the defendant merely to exercise a common law right of inquiry" as a "well-rehearsed claim").

(5) The officer's account was refuted, in whole or in part, by a defense witness's testimony. *See, e.g., People v. Torres*, 54 Misc. 3d 1220(A), 54 N.Y.S.3d 612 (Table), 2017 WL 740983, at *3 (N.Y. County Court, Monroe Cty, January 15, 2017) (rejecting the police officer's testimony that he observed that the defendant's "vehicle's taillights were not working" and stopped the car for that reason, and instead crediting the "directly contradict[ory] . . . testimony of the defendant's girlfriend," who "testified with no obvious contradiction, nervousness or hesitation").

Finally, counsel should anticipate the judge's reactions to the legal and factual issues in the case and should frame arguments so as to meet the judge's likely concerns. For example, as suggested in § 19.7 *supra*, counsel can foresee the reluctance of a trial judge to announce any broad legal rules which go beyond the boundaries of settled precedent, and counsel can forestall that concern by taking pains to explicitly, narrowly delineate the limits of the ruling s/he is advocating.

24.7. *The Prospect of Appellate Review; Obtaining or Avoiding Findings by the Motions Judge in Order to Improve the Defendant's Chances on Appeal*

If the motion to suppress is denied, the defense typically cannot take an interlocutory appeal but can obtain appellate review after conviction and sentencing. See § 31.1 *infra*. If the motion to suppress is granted, the prosecution in some jurisdictions has a statutory or common-law right to take an interlocutory appeal or to challenge the suppression ruling by a petition for a prerogative writ. See §§ 17.5.2, 20.8.2.1 *supra*. If the motion was granted in part and denied in part, an interlocutory appeal by the prosecutor may activate a defense right to cross-appeal on rulings adverse to the defendant. *See, e.g., People v. Fenelon,* 88 Ill. App. 3d 191, 410 N.E.2d

451, 43 Ill. Dec. 451 (1980); *Commonwealth v. Mottola,* 10 Mass. App. Ct. 775, 412 N.E.2d 1280 (1980), *review denied,* 383 Mass. 890, 441 N.E.2d 1042 (1981). When the prosecutor forgoes interlocutory review (or is not entitled to pursue it) and goes to trial without the suppressed evidence, a defendant's acquittal insulates the suppression ruling from appellate reversal. See § 20.8.2.1 *supra.*

In some jurisdictions the judge is required to record specific findings of fact and conclusions of law in ruling on suppression motions. In other jurisdictions the judge is permitted to announce a yea-or-nay ruling on the motion without explaining it. Depending on the nature of the judge's decision and the lay of the evidence, defense counsel may wish to ask the judge to make or clarify particular findings of fact or legal rulings, in order to improve the defendant's posture in appellate review proceedings.

If the judge has ruled in the defendant's favor and counsel anticipates that the prosecutor will appeal, counsel obviously has an incentive to aid the judge in insulating the ruling from reversal. Counsel should consider requesting that the judge amend or revise any troublesome or ambiguous findings of fact or legal conclusions. It is particularly in the defendant's interest for counsel to urge the judge to rest his or her decision explicitly on record-specific factual grounds, both because appellate review of *nisi prius* fact-finding is more limited than appellate review of *nisi prius* legal reasoning and because appellate judges will be more inclined to upset a motions judge's pro-defense rulings in proportion to the breadth of their potential precedential impact.

If the judge has ruled against the defendant on a ground which counsel suspects is legally erroneous but which the judge did not spell out clearly on the record, counsel may wish to request elaboration of the judge's reasoning. Absent an overt articulation of incorrect legal reasoning, many appellate courts will uphold a trial court's ruling if the appellate judges can conjecture any possible permissible rationale for it. However, if a request for clarification will likely lead a judge to seek out more unassailable bases for the denial of a suppression motion or to bolster the denial by making additional findings of fact contrary to the defense, counsel will be wiser to leave ambiguities in the record and decide later what possible use to make of them in appellate arguments. As in most other matters, it is important for counsel to know as much about the judge's predilections, temperament, opinion-writing habits and intelligence as counsel can learn from discussing these subjects with experienced local defense attorneys.

24.8.   *After the Suppression Hearing: Protecting the Defendant's Rights at Trial and Preserving Appellate Remedies*

When the prosecution seeks interlocutory review of a suppression order, counsel with a client in custody should request the trial court to release the client on his or her own recognizance (see § 4.02 *supra*) pending appeal. Counsel can argue that the trial court's suppression ruling provides the best basis for predicting the outcome of the appeal and that it is highly unfair to subject the defendant to protracted incarceration for a crime for which s/he will probably never be convicted. If the trial court does not release the defendant pending appeal, counsel should ask the appellate court to do so, by a motion filed in the appeal, by a separate appeal of the trial court's refusal to grant release, or by a petition for a writ of habeas corpus (see §§ 3.8.3-3.8.4 *supra*), as local practice makes appropriate. Counsel may request in the alternative that the appellate court hear the appeal of the suppression ruling on an expedited basis.

If the defense loses the suppression motion or if the defense wins and the prosecutor elects to forgo interlocutory appellate review, many judges will insist upon proceeding immediately to trial. Often, the defense will want a continuance in order to obtain the transcript of the suppression hearing for use in impeaching prosecution trial witnesses. If, without revealing defense strategy imprudently, counsel can articulate specific ways in which the transcript would assist the defense at trial, counsel should advert to them as supporting a motion for a continuance for the purpose of effectuating the defendant's constitutional rights to effective assistance of counsel, confrontation, and a fair trial. See § 28.3 *infra*. When the defendant is indigent, counsel should move that a transcript be made and furnished to him or her at state expense, under the Sixth and Fourteenth Amendment doctrines noted in §§ 5.2-5.3, 11.5.3 and 18.9.2.1 *supra*.

If the trial will be a bench trial – either because the charges are not eligible for jury trial or because the defendant has concluded that a bench trial is preferable to a jury trial – and if the usual procedure in the jurisdiction is for the judge who presided at the suppression hearing to also serve as the finder at fact in a bench trial, counsel will need to consider whether to seek recusal of the judge. In presiding over a suppression hearing, a judge often hears testimony, such as hearsay evidence, that would be inadmissible under the more stringent rules of evidence applicable at trial. Moreover, if the judge suppressed evidence (such as a confession or an identification), the judge will surely find it difficult to put it completely out of mind in deciding the defendant's guilt or innocence at trial. For the standards governing recusal, tactical considerations in deciding whether to seek recusal, and suggestions for the framing of recusal requests, see §§ 22.4-22.7 *supra*.

Counsel litigating suppression motions must familiarize themselves with the idiosyncratic local requirements for obtaining appellate review of suppression rulings. In some jurisdictions the pretrial denial of a motion to suppress evidence can be reviewed on appeal only if defense counsel renews the motion or objects to the admission of the evidence at trial. In some jurisdictions a suppression ruling unfavorable to the defense can be appealed even after a guilty plea (or a conditional guilty plea) (see § 14.8 *supra*); in other jurisdictions the right to appeal can be preserved only by going through the motions of a "stipulated trial" (see § 36.7.2 *infra*); in still others the defendant must plead not guilty and go through a full-fledged trial in order to obtain appellate review of the suppression ruling.

Occasionally, in cases in which the defense has lost a suppression motion, new facts emerge at trial that would have significantly strengthened the original motion or provided an independent basis for suppression. Under these circumstances counsel should move to reopen the suppression hearing. *See Gouled v. United States,* 255 U.S. 298, 305, 312-13 (1921) ("where, in the progress of a trial, it becomes probable that there has been an unconstitutional seizure of papers, it is the duty of the trial court to entertain an objection to their admission, or a motion for their exclusion, and to consider and decide the question as then presented, even where a motion to return the papers may have been denied before trial"); *United States v. Raddatz,* 447 U.S. 667, 678 n.6 (1980) (dictum) (recognizing that a federal "district court's authority to consider anew a suppression motion previously denied is within its sound judicial discretion"); *cf. Murray v.*

Carrier, 477 U.S. 478, 488 (1986) (holding, in the context of collateral challenges to a criminal conviction, that defense counsel's reasonable lack of knowledge of the facts giving rise to a legal claim constitutes sufficient cause to excuse counsel's failure to pursue the claim in timely fashion). *See also, e.g., Commonwealth v. Haskell,* 438 Mass. 790, 792, 784 N.E.2d 625, 627-28 (2003) ("renewal [of a suppression motion] 'is appropriate where new or additional grounds are alleged which could not reasonably have been known when the motion was originally filed,' . . . but the remedy is not restricted to those circumstances" since "[a] judge's power to reconsider his own decisions during the pendency of a case is firmly rooted in the common law"). And in cases in which the defense learns for the first time at trial that prosecution evidence may have been obtained by unlawful means warranting suppression, a motion for a mistrial and for a suppression hearing in support of that motion are in order. *See, e.g., United States v. Shelton,* 997 F.3d 749 (7th Cir. 2021).

Chapter 25

Motions To Suppress Tangible Evidence

A. *Introduction: Tools and Techniques for Litigating Search and Seizure Claims*

25.1. *Overview of the Chapter and Bibliographical Note*

The Fourth Amendment to the Constitution of the United States, forbidding "unreasonable searches and seizures," is the subject of an extensive jurisprudence. Issues raised by the numerous Fourth Amendment doctrines are multiple and complex; the law is often uncertain and in flux. The best general treatment of the subject is WAYNE R. LAFAVE, SEARCH AND SEIZURE (5th ed. & Supp.). *See also* JOSEPH G. COOK, CONSTITUTIONAL RIGHTS OF THE ACCUSED – PRETRIAL RIGHTS 175-461 (1972); JOHN WESLEY HALL, JR., SEARCH AND SEIZURE (3d ed. 2000); ARNOLD MARKLE, THE LAW OF ARREST AND SEARCH AND SEIZURE (1974); WILLIAM E. RINGEL, SEARCHES & SEIZURES, ARRESTS & CONFESSIONS (2d ed. 2003 & Supp.); JOSEPH A. VARON, SEARCHES, SEIZURES AND IMMUNITIES (2d ed. 1974). There are voluminous law review articles of good quality on specific subtopics.

Rather than attempt still another doctrinal discourse, this chapter approaches the law of search and seizure from a different angle. After a brief description of the major constitutional guarantees that defense counsel may invoke to challenge the legality of police searches and seizures and thereby the admissibility of prosecution evidence produced by those activities (§ 25.2 *infra*), the text sets out a checklist of questions that counsel can ask and answer (with minimal investigation) about the facts of any particular case s/he is handling (§ 25.3 *infra*). The references following each question will direct counsel to subsequent sections containing functional analyses of the law applicable to the basic factual situation targeted by the question. These analyses should assist counsel in identifying particular aspects of law enforcement activity that may be assailable in each situation, together with the theoretical grounds and supporting authorities for assailing them.

Counsel should particularly heed the advice in § 17.11 *supra* to invoke state statutory and constitutional provisions as well as the federal Fourth Amendment when challenging searches or seizures. This is an area in which state constitutional law has increasingly become more defense-friendly than federal constitutional law. *See* LaKeith Faulkner & Christopher R. Green, *State-Constitutional Departures from the Supreme Court: The Fourth Amendment*, 89 MISS. L. J. 197 (2020); *State v. Short*, 851 N.W.2d 474, 486 (Iowa 2014) ("As a result of the United States Supreme Court's retreat in the search and seizure area, there has been a sizeable growth in independent state constitutional law. A survey of jurisdictions in 2007 found that a majority of the state supreme courts have departed from United States Supreme Court precedents in the search and seizure area to some degree.").

25.2. *Constitutional and Statutory Restraints on Searches and Seizures*

25.2.1. *General Principles of Fourth Amendment Law*

The Fourth Amendment's proscription of unreasonable searches and seizures governs federal prosecutions by its express terms and state prosecutions by incorporation into the Due Process Clause of the Fourteenth Amendment. *Mapp v. Ohio,* 367 U.S. 643 (1961). It regulates the actions of the police, other law enforcement agents, other government officials (see §§ 25.15.2 subdivision (v), 25.36, 25.38 *infra*) and private citizens acting in league with government agents (*see, e.g., United States v. Shelton*, 997 F.3d 749 (7th Cir. 2021); *State v. Scrotsky*, 39 N.J. 410, 189 A.2d 23 (1963); *Milan v. Bolin*, 795 F.3d 726, 729 (7th Cir. 2015) (dictum); *cf. Wilson v. Layne*, 526 U.S. 603, 614 (1999) (dictum) ("We hold that it is a violation of the Fourth Amendment for police to bring members of the media or other third parties into a home during the execution of a warrant when the presence of the third parties in the home was not in aid of the execution of the warrant")).

Perhaps the simplest way of viewing the vast array of Fourth Amendment caselaw is by breaking it down into five categories of cases:

(i) Caselaw defining the powers of police officers to conduct a search of a person, place, or thing, and to seize items discovered in that search, without the benefit of a search warrant. The Supreme Court has repeatedly declared that "searches conducted outside the judicial process, without prior approval by judge or magistrate, are *per se* unreasonable under the Fourth Amendment – subject only to a few specifically established and well-delineated exceptions" (*Katz v. United States,* 389 U.S. 347, 357 (1967)). *See, e.g., Carpenter v. United States*, 138 S. Ct. 2206, 2221 (2018); *Riley v. California*, 573 U.S. 373, 382 (2014); *Georgia v. Randolph*, 547 U.S. 103, 109 (2006); *Kyllo v. United States*, 533 U.S. 27, 31 (2001); *Minnesota v. Dickerson*, 508 U.S. 366, 372-73 (1993); *Thompson v. Louisiana,* 469 U.S. 17, 19-20 (1984); *United States v. Karo,* 468 U.S. 705, 714-15, 717 (1984). The "jealously and carefully drawn" exceptions to the warrant requirement (*Jones v. United States,* 357 U.S. 493, 499 (1958)) include searches and seizures made with the valid consent of an authorized person (see § 25.18 *infra*), incident to a valid arrest (see § 25.8 *infra*), under "exigent circumstances" (see § 25.20 *infra*), in an operable motor vehicle that there is probable cause to believe contains criminal objects (see § 25.24 *infra*), and after an officer's observation of contraband or crime-related objects in "plain view" (see § 25.22.2 *infra*). In addition to these specific exceptions to the warrant requirement, the courts also will excuse the absence of a warrant and will test a search or seizure under the standard of "general reasonableness" in situations in which the "intrusion on the individual's Fourth Amendment interests" is minimal (*United States v. Place,* 462 U.S. 696, 703 (1983); *see, e.g., Samson v. California*, 547 U.S. 843 (2005); *United States v. Sczubelek*, 402 F.3d 175, 184-87 (3d Cir. 2005)), or the police activity at issue is of a type that "historically has not been, and as a practical matter could not be, subjected to the warrant procedure" (*Terry v. Ohio,* 392 U.S. 1, 20 (1968); *see, e.g., Illinois v. McArthur*, 531 U.S. 326, 330-37 (2001); *Delaware v. Prouse,* 440 U.S. 648, 653-55 (1979); *Michigan v. Summers,* 452 U.S. 692, 699-701 (1981)), or "'in those exceptional circumstances in which special needs, beyond the normal need for law enforcement, make the warrant . . . requirement impracticable'" (*O'Connor v. Ortega,* 480 U.S. 709, 720 (1987) (plurality opinion)) "and where the 'primary purpose' of the searches is '[d]istinguishable from the general interest in crime control'" (*City of Los Angeles v. Patel*, 576 U.S. 409, 420 (2015); *see, e.g., Board of Education of Independent School District No. 92 of Pottawatomie County v. Earls*, 536 U.S. 822 (2002); *Griffin v. Wisconsin,* 483 U.S. 868 (1987); *New Jersey v. T.L.O.,* 469 U.S. 325 (1985); §§ 25.36-25.38 *infra*).

(ii) Caselaw concerning warrantless seizures of the person, either in the form of an "arrest" or in the form of the less extensive restraint first differentiated in *Terry v. Ohio*, 392 U.S. 1 (1968), and commonly called a *"Terry* stop." See §§ 25.4-25.14 *infra.*

(iii) Caselaw dealing with searches and seizures made pursuant to a search warrant. See § 25.17 *infra.*

(iv) Caselaw pertinent to the procedural issue of when a defendant has a sufficient interest in the area searched or the item seized to mount a challenge to the search or seizure. See §§ 25.15, 25.23, 25.32 penultimate paragraph, 25.33 *infra.*

(v) Caselaw addressing the procedural question of whether, if a search or seizure was unconstitutional, the prosecution may nevertheless use particular items of evidence at trial because they are not viewed as "tainted" by the unlawful search or seizure. See §§ 25.39-25.42 *infra.*

25.2.2. *State Constitutional Protections Against Searches and Seizures*

As explained in § 17.11 *supra,* many state courts in recent years have begun to construe state constitutional provisions as providing greater protections than the parallel provisions of the Constitution of the United States as interpreted by the Supreme Court of the United States. This has occurred particularly in the area of searches and seizures. *See, e.g., State v. Short*, 851 N.W.2d 474, 486 (Iowa 2014) ("A survey of jurisdictions in 2007 found that a majority of the state supreme courts have departed from United States Supreme Court precedents in the search and seizure area to some degree."). Quite a few state courts have developed an extensive body of state constitutional law on searches and seizures, rejecting major doctrines that limit Fourth Amendment rights. Although the state constitutional decisions are too numerous to survey systematically, some of the most significant ones will be noted in the relevant subsections of this chapter. As § 17.11 advises, defense counsel should always invoke state constitutional provisions in addition to the federal Fourth Amendment, even when there are no state constitutional precedents on the issue. This is a cost-free practice, and the advantages of winning a search-and-seizure claim on state-law grounds always make that possibility worth pursuing. See the concluding paragraph of § 17.11.

25.2.3. *Statutory Provisions Relating to Searches and Seizures*

There is a federal statute (18 U.S.C. §§ 2510-2520) – and, in several jurisdictions, there are state statutes – governing police use of electronic surveillance. See §§ 25.31-25.32 *infra.*

In many jurisdictions there are statutes (i) delineating the circumstances under which a police officer or a private citizen may make an arrest for a felony or misdemeanor (see § 25.7

infra), (ii) limiting the degree of force that may be employed in the course of an arrest (*cf.* § 25.7 concluding paragraph); and (iii) enacting "knock-and-announce" requirements under which a police officer must give adequate warning of the officer's identity and intention to enter a dwelling before entering forcibly (see § 25.21 *infra*). Other statutory regulations of searches and seizures are found in some States and may provide grounds for suppression motions. *See, e.g., State v. Gilman*, 173 Vt. 110, 787 A.2d 1238 (2001); *Casillas v. People*, 2018 CO 78M, 427 P.3d 804 (Colo. 2018) (alternative ground).

25.3. *Analyzing Search and Seizure Issues: The Questions to Ask*

In examining a case for possible search and seizure issues, counsel should begin by breaking down the series of governmental actions into their component parts, since each specific act by a government agent may give rise to a separate claim for relief. For example, in a case in which the police stop a person, pat the person down, arrest the person, and seize objects from the person's possession, counsel should consider all of the following issues: Did the police have a sufficient basis for making the initial *Terry* stop? Even if the police had the requisite basis for a *Terry* stop, did they have the additional "specific and articulable facts" necessary for a *Terry* frisk? If there was an adequate basis for the *Terry* frisk, did the manner in which the frisk was conducted exceed constitutional limits for a pat-down? Did the police thereafter have an adequate basis for an arrest? Did the subsequent search incident to arrest exceed constitutional limits? If not, was the seizure of each particular object that the search uncovered constitutionally justified? Any of the distinct police actions identified in these questions could generate a basis for suppressing evidence.

The following questions should be asked in analyzing search and seizure claims:

(1)   Was the defendant stopped, accosted, arrested, or taken into custody by government agents at any time?

(a)   If so, is it in the interest of the defense to characterize the agents' action as an arrest or as a *Terry* stop? See § 25.5 *infra.* Do the facts support the preferred characterization? See § 25.6 *infra.*

(b)   If the agents' action is characterized as an arrest:

(i)   Did the agents have the requisite probable cause to make the arrest? See §§ 25.7, 25.11 *infra.*

(ii)   Did the agents search the defendant incident to the arrest? If so, did the search comply with the requirements for searches incident to arrest? See § 25.8 *infra.*

(iii)   Did the post-arrest custodial treatment of the defendant comport with constitutional and statutory requirements? See §§ 25.8.3, 25.14 *infra.*

(c) If the agents' action is characterized as a *Terry* stop:

    (i) Did the agents have the requisite factual basis for a *Terry* stop? See §§ 25.9, 25.11 *infra.*

    (ii) Did the agents conduct a *Terry* frisk? If so, did they have the requisite facts to support a *Terry* frisk? See §§ 25.10-25.11 *infra.*

    (iii) Was the period of the stop unduly extended or the post-stop investigation conducted in a manner that exceeded the justifications for search activities incidental to the stop? See §§ 25.6.1, 25.27, 25.28 *infra.*

(d) Did the agents search any closed containers that the defendant had in his or her possession? See §§ 25.8.2, 25.12 *infra.*

(e) Was the defendant's body or clothing inspected? Was any physical examination of the defendant made? Were any tests conducted on the defendant's body or on any object or fluid, hair, or like substance taken from the defendant's body? See § 25.14 *infra.*

(f) Did the incident occur in a school setting? See § 25.38 *infra.*

(2) Did government agents enter or search the defendant's home, any premises with which s/he had more than transitory connections, or any premises in which the defendant was legitimately present at the time of the agents' entry or search?

(a) If so, does the defendant have a constitutionally protected interest that permits him or her to challenge the agents' entry into the premises, the agents' search of areas within the premises, or both? See § 25.15 *infra.*

(b) If the defendant does have the requisite interest:

    (i) Was the agents' entry and was the search authorized by a search warrant? If so, was the warrant validly issued, and was it validly executed? See § 25.17 *infra.*

    (ii) Was the agents' entry and was the search authorized by an arrest warrant? If so, did the agents limit their activities to arresting the subject of the warrant or use the arrest entry to conduct an impermissible search? See §§ 25.19, 25.22 *infra.*

    (iii) Was the agents' entry and was the search authorized by exigent circumstances? If so, did the agents confine their activities to a range within the scope of this justification? See §§ 25.20, 25.22 *infra.*

(iv)   Was the agents' entry and was the search authorized by the consent of the defendant? If so, was the defendant's consent voluntary? See § 25.18.1 *infra.*

(v)   Was the agents' entry and was the search authorized by the consent of some individual other than the defendant? If so, did that individual have the authority to consent to the search of the area? Was the consent voluntary? See § 25.18.2 *infra.*

(vi)   Was the agents' entry purportedly made for "regulatory" or "administrative" purposes? See § 25.36 *infra.* Was it purportedly made to enforce parole or probation regulations? See § 25.37 *infra.* Did it occur on school premises? See § 25.38 *infra.*

(c)   Did the agents at any time after they entered the premises detain or search the person of the defendant? If so:

(i)   Did the agents have the requisite basis for detaining the defendant? See § 25.22.3 *infra.*

(ii)   Did the agents have the requisite basis for searching the person of the defendant? See § 25.22.3 *infra.*

(d)   Did the agents seize any item that was allegedly in plain view? If so, did the seizure comport with the rules governing the plain view exception to the warrant requirement? See § 25.22.2 *infra.*

(e)   Did the agents comply with the rules requiring them to announce their identity and intention to enter before effecting a forcible entry of a dwelling? See § 25.21 *infra.*

(3)   Did the agents stop, search, or seize any motor vehicle?

(a)   If so, does the defendant have a constitutionally protected interest that permits him or her to challenge the agents' conduct in stopping, searching or seizing the vehicle? See § 25.23 *infra.*

(b)   If the defendant does have the requisite interest:

(i)   Did the agents stop the vehicle while it was moving? If so, did the agents have the requisite factual basis for a *Terry* stop? See § 25.27 *infra.*

(ii)   Did the agents order the defendant out of the vehicle? If so, did they have the requisite basis to issue that order? See § 25.28 *infra.*

(iii) Did the agents conduct a search of the vehicle incident to an arrest of the defendant? If so, was the arrest valid? Was the search properly limited in scope? See § 25.26 *infra.*

(iv) Did the agents conduct an evidentiary search of the vehicle? If so, did they have the requisite probable cause for that search? See § 25.24 *infra.*

(v) During the stop or search of the vehicle, did the agents seize any item that was allegedly in plain view? If so, did the seizure comport with the rules governing the plain view exception to the warrant requirement? See § 25.22.2 *infra.*

(vi) Was the asserted basis for the stop of the vehicle a traffic infraction? See § 25.28 *infra.*

(vii) Was the vehicle impounded and thereafter searched in an "inventory search"? If so, was the search conducted pursuant to standardized procedures? Was the alleged inventory a mere pretext for an otherwise impermissible evidentiary search? See § 25.25 *infra.*

(viii) Did the agents open any closed containers that were in the vehicle? See § 25.24 *infra.*

(4) Did government agents use electronic surveillance and/or other forms of surveillance to gather information about the defendant? If so:

(a) Was surveillance of any sort maintained by agents into or around the defendant's home, any premises with which s/he had more than transitory connections, or any premises in which the defendant was legitimately present at the time of the surveillance? See §§ 25.31, 25.33 *infra.*

(b) Was any telephone owned or used by the defendant tapped? See § 25.32 *infra.*

(5) Did government agents search or seize any physical object belonging to the defendant, whether or not on premises in which s/he has an interest? See § 25.15.4 *infra.*

(6) Did government agents act on the basis of information obtained from informants, whether those informants were "special agents," police spies, or private citizens? See § 25.35 *infra.*

In the preceding paragraphs, the phrase "government agents" is used advisedly. The personnel to whom the Fourth Amendment's strictures are most commonly applied in criminal litigation are police and other law enforcement officers, but the Amendment is held to govern the conduct of many other government employees as well. *See, e.g., Ferguson v. City of Charleston,* 532 U.S. 67, 76 (2001) ("[b]ecause . . . [the hospital operated by the Medical University of South Carolina] is a state hospital, the members of its staff are government actors, subject to the strictures of the Fourth Amendment"); *New Jersey v. T.L.O.,* 469 U.S. 325, 333 (1985) ("the Fourth "Amendment's prohibition on unreasonable searches and seizures applies to searches conducted by public school officials"); *State v. Bee,* 2021 ND 61, 956 N.W.2d 380 (N.D. 2021) (Police officers accompanied a social worker who went to the defendant's home to remove her child; the defendant fled out of the house with the child and was restrained by the police outside the house; the "social worker [then] entered the residence to obtain personal belongings for the child, and an officer followed. Once the officer was inside, the social worker pointed out a glass smoking pipe. Bee was subsequently charged with Child Neglect; Possession of Methamphetamine; Possession of Drug Paraphernalia; and Refusal to Halt." *Id.* at 382. Here, regardless of their intent, the officers violated the Fourth Amendment by crossing the threshold of the residence without a warrant. The State's argument that the officers were merely acting in the regular course of duty to assist social services is unavailing because the social workers are also bound by the Fourth Amendment. . . . The State has not provided persuasive reasoning or authority to avoid application of the exclusionary rule in these circumstances." *Id.* at 383.); *Dyas v. Superior Court,* 11 Cal. 3d 628, 522 P.2d 674, 114 Cal. Rptr. 114 (1974) (uniformed, armed Housing Authority patrol officer). At the least, any government employee who is acting in collaboration with law enforcement, at the instance of law enforcement authorities (as a general matter or in the particular case at bar), or with the aim of furthering criminal law enforcement is subject to Fourth Amendment regulation. *See, e.g., Piazzola v. Watkins,* 316 F. Supp. 624, 626-27 (M.D. Ala. 1970), *aff'd,* 442 F.2d 284 (5th Cir. 1971); *Picha v. Wielgos,* 410 F. Supp. 1214, 1219-21 (N.D. Ill. 1976); *M.J. v. State,* 399 So.2d 996, 998 (Fla. App. 1981); and see § 25.18.3 *infra.* A rare case finding that a government employee's conduct was not constrained by the Amendment is *United States v. Johnlouis,* 44 F.4th 331 (5th Cir. 2022). In that case, a U.S. Postal Service letter carrier accidentally stuck her thumb through a preexisting hole in a package she was delivering, felt something she believed to be marijuana, lifted a torn flap of the package to examine the contents further, and saw what she took to be methamphetamine. Loth to deliver meth to a location where there were lots of children, she took the package to a private individual who was the property manager for the house to which the package was addressed as well as for a number of adjacent houses, and she suggested that this person call the police. The property manager did so, and law-enforcement follow-up resulted in the confiscation of the meth and then in Johnlouis's prosecution. The Fifth Circuit's opinion rejecting Johnlouis' contention that the letter carrier was a government agent for Fourth Amendment purposes notably contains the following observations: "Of course, we have 'never limited the [Fourth] Amendment's prohibition on unreasonable searches and seizures to operations conducted by the police. *New Jersey v. T.L.O.,* 469 U.S. 325, 335 (1985). '[W]e have held the Fourth Amendment applicable to the activities of civil as well as criminal authorities,' including building inspectors, firefighters, teachers, healthcare workers, and, yes, even USPS employees. *Id.* After all, '[t]he basic purpose of this Amendment . . . is to safeguard the privacy and security of individuals against arbitrary invasions by governmental officials." *Camara v. Mun. Ct. of City & Cnty. of S.F.,* 387 U.S. 523, 528 (1967). 'Because the individual's interest in privacy and personal security suffers whether the government's motivation is to investigate violations of criminal laws or breaches of other statutory or regulatory standards, it would be anomalous to say that the individual and his private property are fully protected by the Fourth Amendment only when [he] is suspected of criminal behavior. *New Jersey*, 469 U.S. at 335. . . . ¶ But the building inspectors, firefighters, teachers, healthcare workers, and USPS employees that courts have identified as government actors to whom the Fourth Amendment applies were all carrying out law enforcement functions. The same cannot be said of . . . [the letter carrier here]. 44 F.4th at 336-37. In addition, the *Johnlouis* opinion is at pains to point out that: "Ordinarily, this resolution would not dispose of Johnlouis's Fourth Amendment claim because he could argue that . . . [the letter carrier] was a private person acting in the capacity of a government agent by searching the package with the knowledge of, or in order to assist, law enforcement. . . . Where a search is conducted by someone other than 'an agent of the government,' this court has held that it still violates the Fourth Amendment if (1) 'the government knew of and acquiesced in the intrusive conduct' and (2) 'the party performing the search intended to assist law enforcement efforts or to further his own ends.' . . . But Johnlouis explicitly disclaims any such alternative argument . . . [and] has thus abandoned any argument that the Fourth Amendment applies to . . . [the letter carrier] outside of his contention that her employment by USPS per se renders her subject to the Fourth Amendment" [see §§ 25.18.3-25.18.4 *infra*]." 44 F.4th at 337. *See also State v. Ellingsworth*, 966 P.2d 1220, 1224 (Utah App. 1998), and cases cited (holding that the actions of a Workers Compensation Fund investigator were not subject to Fourth Amendment constraint and quoting *Commonwealth v. Cote*, 15 Mass. App. Ct. 229, 234, 444 N.E.2d 1282, 1286 (1983): "'Perhaps the single general principle which may be distilled from cases is the precept that mere employment by an arm of government is not enough to make an actor a government agent for purposes of the Fourth Amendment. Rather, the nature of the actor's employment, his specific duties and authority to act for the State and the circumstances of the search are all taken into account in deciding whether a search was 'private' or governmental in nature.'").

When law enforcement activity that may give rise to search and seizure issues has occurred, it is important to think comprehensively about all the items that could be suppressed as a result of a ruling that the search or seizure was unconstitutional. For example, if an arrest is found to be unlawful, the suppressible fruits of that arrest may include any physical object or substance seized at or after the time of the arrest, any show-up or lineup observations made at or after the time of the arrest, identifications of the defendant's photograph in a photographic array that was made possible because the defendant was photographed upon arrest, confessions or statements of the defendant made in custody after the arrest or otherwise induced by pressures flowing from the arrest, any physical object or substance or observation obtained by a search or seizure whose validity depends upon consent given while the defendant was in custody after the arrest or upon consent otherwise induced by pressures flowing from the arrest, testimony of witnesses whose identity was learned by interrogation of the defendant following the arrest, and fingerprint identification evidence based upon exemplars taken at the time of the arrest. See § 25.39 *infra*. While some of these potential fruits of the arrest may be found eventually to be too far removed from the illegality to require suppression, see *id.*, counsel cannot afford to overlook any conceivably viable suppression arguments.

In analyzing the validity of a search or seizure, it is crucial to isolate the facts and circumstances known to the police at the time of the search or seizure from those facts later learned by the police. The constitutionality of police officers' conduct "must [be] judge[d] . . . in light of the information available to them at the time they acted" (*Maryland v. Garrison,* 480 U.S. 79, 85 (1987)). *See also Florida v. J.L.,* 529 U.S. 266, 271 (2000) ("The reasonableness of official suspicion must be measured by what the officers knew before they conducted their search."); *United States v. Jacobsen,* 466 U.S. 109, 115 (1984) ("[t]he reasonableness of an official invasion of the citizen's privacy must be appraised on the basis of the facts as they existed at the time that invasion occurred"); *Terry v. Ohio,* 392 U.S. 1, 21-22 (1968) (the constitutionality of a search or seizure is determined by asking "would the facts available to the officer at the moment of the seizure or the search 'warrant a man of reasonable caution in the belief' that the action taken was appropriate?"); *State v. Amstutz,* 169 Idaho 144, 150, 492 P.3d 1103, 1109 (2021) (same); *United States v. Thomas,* 65 F.4th 922, 925 (7th Cir. 2023) ("[t]he validity of a search depends on what law enforcement knew when they conducted the search"); *United States v. Frazier,* 30 F.4th 1165, 1174 (10th Cir. 2022), summarized in § 25.6.1 *infra* ("we consider only those facts known to the trooper at the point he diverted from his traffic-based mission to arrange the dog sniff"); *United States v. Hurtt,* 31 F.4th 152, 159 (3d Cir. 2022) ("[a]fter the *Rodriguez* moment, 'nothing later in the stop can inform our reasonable suspicion analysis'"); *State v. Deuble,* 2020-Ohio-3970, 2020 WL 4532961, at *6 (Ohio App. 2020) (a prosecutor's investigator posing as a 15-year-old girl on a social-media site posted a provocative message that triggered a series of interchanges with one "EY" in which EY proposed to have sex with "her" and arranged to meet "her" in a designated park at a specified time; police surveilled the park, knowing nothing more about EY than that he was a thin white male, 21 to 25 years old, who drove a green Honda; they saw no green Honda but did observe Deuble, a thin, young white male, playing basketball; the investigator initiated a series of messages to EY and the police observed that whenever a message was posted, Deuble stopped playing basketball and used his cell phone; the police moved in – four or more officers surrounding Deuble – and handcuffed him; the investigator then picked Deuble's cell phone up off the ground and sent a test message which confirmed that Deuble was EY; the court of appeals "find[s] that . . . probable cause did not occur until after the police arrested Deuble. Prior to Deuble's arrest, the police knew that he was present at the meeting place, and he was using a cell phone at the same time the suspect was using a cell phone. He matched the suspect's description, but that description was vague, indicating race, gender, a 'thin' build, and approximate age. Furthermore, there was no sign of the green Honda the suspect was purportedly driving"; Deuble's arrest therefore violated the Fourth Amendment, and all evidence resulting from it, including information on his cell phone and a confession, should have been suppressed); *White v. Commonwealth,* 2005 WL 2807242 (Ky. App. 2005), summarized in § 25.37 *infra.* It is not always easy to determine what facts were known by the police at the time of a search or seizure. For example, police officers often amend the complaint report, supposedly containing the facts learned from the victim on the scene (see §§ 9.18, 9.20 first subdivision *supra*), to add a detailed description of the defendant based upon the officers' observations of the defendant after arrest. Counsel should not accept these reports at face value but must cross-examine the police officer to ascertain what precise facts were known to him or her when s/he undertook the search or seizure.

In a few categories of cases, the Supreme Court has held that an unlawful police search or seizure may not require suppression if the actions of the police were so obviously in "good faith" and objectively reasonable that suppression would not further the exclusionary rule's rationale of deterring police misconduct. The context in which this principle is most often invoked – a police officer's good faith reliance on a search warrant issued by a magistrate which turns out to have been defective because the magistrate was mistaken in finding probable cause – is discussed in § 25.17 *infra*. The other situations in which the Court has recognized a "good faith" exception to the exclusionary rule are (1) when the police, in making an arrest, reasonably relied on a computer record of a warrant which a court clerk erroneously failed to update to reflect the later quashing of the warrant (*Arizona v. Evans*, 514 U.S. 1, 14-16 (1995)); (2) when an arresting officer's reasonable but erroneous belief in the existence of "an outstanding arrest warrant" stemmed from "a negligent bookkeeping error by another police employee" who failed to update the police computers when the warrant was recalled (*Herring v. United States*, 555 U.S. 135, 137 (2009)), although this version of the "good faith" rule would be inapplicable and "exclusion [of the fruits of the arrest] would certainly be justified" "[i]f the police have been shown to be reckless in maintaining a warrant system, or to have knowingly made false entries to lay the groundwork for future false arrests" or if "systemic errors" in a warrant system were so "routine or widespread" as to make it "reckless for officers to rely on . . . [the] unreliable warrant system" (*id.* at 146-47); (3) "when the police conduct a search in compliance with binding precedent that is later overruled" (*Davis v. United States*, 564 U.S. 229, 232 (2011)); and (4) "when officers act in objectively reasonable reliance upon a *statute* authorizing . . . [certain] searches, but where the statute is ultimately found to violate the Fourth Amendment" (*Illinois v. Krull*, 480 U.S. 340, 342 (1987)). The Supreme Court also has held that a police officer's "mistake of law can . . . give rise to the reasonable suspicion necessary to uphold . . . [a] seizure under the Fourth Amendment" as long as the mistake was "*objectively* reasonable" (*Heien v. North Carolina*, 574 U.S. 54, 57, 68 (2014) (upholding the validity of a police officer's stop of a car "because one of its two brake lights was out" and "[i]t was . . . objectively reasonable for an officer . . . to think that [the] . . . faulty right brake light was a violation of North Carolina law" even though "a [North Carolina appellate] court later determined that a single working brake light was all the law required" (*id.* at 57, 68)); *compare People v. Owen*, 2019 WL 3312531 (Mich. App. 2019) (finding a Fourth Amendment violation requiring suppression of evidence obtained through a traffic stop where the officer knew all of the facts necessary to establish that the speed limit on the road where the stop was made was 55 m.p.h. but believed that the limit was 25 m.p.h. because he was ignorant of the statutory law which precluded a village from reducing the state speed limit without meeting certain posting requirements: "The deputy in this case did not make a reasonable mistake of law because the Motor Vehicle Code since 2006 established the rule of law regarding speed limits throughout Michigan. Under the Motor Vehicle Code, unposted roads were 55 miles per hour. . . . The deputy's testimony does not reflect a reasonable interpretation of the Motor Vehicle Code or even a plausible understanding of the applicable law. The record indicates that he never considered the Motor Vehicle Code at all. We conclude that the deputy did not have an objectively reasonable belief that probable cause existed to stop defendant because the totality of the circumstances established that he made an unreasonable mistake of law merely based on an unsupported hunch that the speed limit was 25 miles per hour because other roads were posted elsewhere in the village with that speed limit. However, since 2006, nearly 10 years before the traffic stop, the Motor Vehicle Code repealed blanket village-wide speed limits. The circuit court erred because it essentially held that a law enforcement officer's unreasonable ignorance of the law was equivalent to a reasonable mistake of the law.")). See also § 25.28 *infra*. Finally, as discussed, in § 25.21 *infra*, the Supreme Court has withdrawn the exclusionary rule as a remedy for violations of the Fourth Amendment's "knock and announce" requirement. *See Hudson v. Michigan*, 547 U.S. 586, 588, 594 (2006). In some States, one or more of the foregoing limitations on the availability of suppression have been rejected by the state courts as a matter of state constitutional law. See, *e.g.*, § 25.17 *infra* (citing state caselaw that relies on the state constitution to reject the Supreme Court's good faith rule for search warrants issued without probable cause); *and see State v. Scott*, 619 N.W.2d 371 (Iowa 2000). See generally § 17.11 *supra*.

B. *On-the-Street Encounters with the Police: Arrests, Searches Incident to Arrest,* **Terry** *Stops,* **Terry** *Frisks, and Other Encounters*

25.4. *The Spectrum of On-the-Street Encounters Between Citizens and the Police: – Contacts;* **Terry** *Stops; Arrests*

As the Supreme Court has observed, "[s]treet encounters between citizens and police officers are incredibly rich in diversity. They range from wholly friendly exchanges of pleasantries or mutually useful information to hostile confrontations of armed men involving arrests, or injuries, or loss of life." (*Terry v. Ohio,* 392 U.S. 1, 13 (1968)). The Court thus far has identified three categories of encounters, which have differing ramifications for police prerogatives and citizens' rights: contacts, *Terry* stops, and arrests.

25.4.1. *Contacts*

The Fourth Amendment is not called into play by "law enforcement officers . . . merely approaching an individual on the street or in another public place, by asking him if he is willing to answer some questions, by putting questions to him if the person is willing to listen . . . [even if] the officer identifies himself as a police officer. . . . The person approached, however, need not answer any question put to him; indeed, he may decline to listen to the questions at all and may go on his way. . . . He may not be detained even momentarily without [triggering Fourth Amendment protections that require] reasonable, objective grounds for doing so; and his refusal to listen or answer does not, without more, furnish those grounds" (*Florida v. Royer,* 460 U.S. 491, 497-98 (1983) (plurality opinion)). *Compare Kolender v. Lawson,* 461 U.S. 352 (1983), *with Hiibel v. Sixth Judicial District Court of Nevada*, 542 U.S. 177 (2004), discussed in § 25.11.2 *infra*.

25.4.2. *The Dividing Line Between Contacts and "Seizures" Within the Meaning of the Fourth Amendment*

If a police officer, going beyond this kind of detention-free contact, "accosts [the] individual and restrains his freedom to walk away, he has 'seized' that person" within the meaning of the Fourth Amendment's restrictions upon "seizures" (*Terry v. Ohio,* 392 U.S. 1, 16 (1968); *Brown v. Texas,* 443 U.S. 47, 50 (1979); *Brendlin v. California*, 551 U.S. 249, 254-55 (2007)). The restraint may be physical (*Sibron v. New York,* 392 U.S. 40, 67 (1968)), or it may take the form of a command to "stand still" or to "come along" or any other gesture or expression indicating that the person is not free to go as s/he pleases (*Dunaway v. New York,* 442 U.S. 200, 203, 207 n.6 (1979); *see Florida v. Royer,* 460 U.S. 491, 501-03 & n.9 (1983) (plurality opinion); *id.* at 511-12 (concurring opinion of Justice Brennan); *Brendlin v. California, supra*, 551 U.S. at 254-55). "What has evolved from our cases is a determination that an initially consensual encounter between a police officer and a citizen can be transformed into a seizure or detention within the meaning of the Fourth Amendment, 'if, in view of all the circumstances surrounding the incident, a reasonable person would have believed that he was not free to leave.'" *Immigration and Naturalization Service v. Delgado,* 466 U.S. 210, 215 (1984). The touchstone of a Fourth Amendment seizure of a person is whether the police behavior "would . . . have communicated to a reasonable person that he was not at liberty to ignore the police presence and go about his business" (*Michigan v. Chesternut,* 486 U.S. 567, 569 (1988)). *Accord, Kaupp v. Texas,* 538 U.S. 626, 629 (2003) (per curiam); *and see Baude v. Leyshock,* 23 F.4th 1065, 1071 (8th Cir. 2022) ("[w]hen a person is surrounded by officers on all sides, he would reasonably believe that he is no longer free to leave and that he has been seized"); *United States v. Washington,* 490 F.3d 765, 771-72 (9th Cir. 2007) ("We have identified several non-exhaustive situations where an officer's actions escalate a consensual encounter into a seizure: 'when a law enforcement officer, through coercion, physical force, or a show of authority, in some way restricts the liberty of a person,' . . . or 'if there is a threatening presence of several officers, a display of a weapon by an officer, some physical touching of the person of the citizen, or the use of language or tone of voice indicating that compliance with the officer's request might be compelled.' . . . [We have] identified several factors to consider in determining if a person was seized, any one of which, if present, could constitute a seizure: (1) the number of officers; (2) whether weapons were displayed; (3) whether the encounter occurred in a public or non-public setting; (4) whether the officer's tone or manner was authoritative, so as to imply that compliance would be compelled; and (5) whether the officers informed the person of his right to terminate the encounter."); *United States v. Lopez,* 907 F.3d 472, 486-87 (7th Cir. 2018) ("The government argues that the stop here was not excessively long because, when the officer asked Lopez for permission to search his house, he was no longer being detained by police and was free to leave. The officer had told Lopez 'that he was not under arrest, that he didn't have to speak' to officers, and that 'he was free to go.' In assessing whether a person has been seized, we look to the totality of the circumstances and ask whether 'a reasonable person would feel free to terminate the encounter.' . . . ¶ . . . [W]hile one officer was assuring Lopez that he was free to go, the other officers still had Lopez's keys, van, and cellphone. At least eight officers remained on the scene at his garage and house. In this case, no reasonable person in Lopez's shoes would conclude that one officer's words meant more than all eight officers' actions. Lopez remained in police detention for as long as officers functionally blocked his exit by the overwhelming physical presence of eight officers and by retaining his van, car keys, and cellphone."); *see also Brendlin v. California, supra,* 551 U.S. at 254-55, 262 ("A police officer may make a seizure by a show of authority and without the use of physical force, but there is no seizure without actual submission; otherwise, there is at most an attempted seizure, so far as the Fourth Amendment is concerned. . . . When the actions of the police do not show an unambiguous intent to restrain or when an individual's submission to a show of governmental authority takes the form of passive acquiescence, there needs to be some test for telling when a seizure occurs in response to authority, and when it does not. The test was devised by Justice Stewart in *United States v. Mendenhall,* 446 U.S. 544 (1980), who wrote that a seizure occurs if 'in view of all of the circumstances surrounding the incident, a reasonable person would have believed that he was not free to leave,' *id.,* at 554 (principal opinion). Later on, the Court adopted Justice Stewart's touchstone . . . but added that when a person 'has no desire to leave' for reasons unrelated to the police presence, the 'coercive effect of the encounter' can be measured better by asking whether 'a reasonable person would feel free to decline the officers' requests or otherwise terminate the encounter' . . . . [W]hat may amount to submission depends on what a person was doing before the show of authority: a fleeing man is not seized until he is physically overpowered, but one sitting in a chair may submit to authority by not getting up to run away."). *See, e.g., United States v. Smith*, 794 F.3d 681, 682, 684-88 (7th Cir. 2015); *United States v. Black*, 707 F.3d 531, 537-39 (4th Cir. 2013); *Clark v. State*, 994 N.E.2d 252, 263 (Ind. 2013); *State v. White*, 887 N.W.2d 172, 176-77 (Iowa 2016). *Cf. United States v. Drayton*, 536 U.S. 194, 203-04 (2002) (police questioning of passengers on a bus did not amount to a "seizure" for Fourth Amendment purposes when "[t]he officers gave the passengers no reason to believe that they were required to answer the officers' questions," "left the aisle free so that [passengers] could exit," and did "[n]othing . . . that would suggest to a reasonable person that he or she was barred from leaving the bus or otherwise terminating the encounter"); *California v. Hodari D.*, 499 U.S. 621 (1991) (there was no "seizure" for purposes of the Fourth Amendment when police officers chased a suspect who failed to comply with their directive to halt; therefore, the officers' lack of a basis for the directive and the pursuit provided no Fourth Amendment ground for suppression of contraband the suspect discarded during the chase; the Court says that "the so-called *Mendenhall* test, formulated by Justice Stewart's opinion in *United States v. Mendenhall,* 446 U.S. 544, 554 (1980), and adopted by the Court in later cases . . . [citing *Chesternut* and *Delgado*] states a *necessary,* but not a *sufficient,* condition for seizure – or, more precisely, for seizure effected through a 'show of authority.' *Mendenhall* establishes that the test for existence of a 'show of authority' is an objective one: not whether the citizen perceived that he was being ordered to restrict his movement, but whether the officer's words and actions would have conveyed that to a reasonable person" (*id.* at 627-28); if, after such a show of authority, the citizen does not attempt to flee or resist but rather "yield[s]," s/he is deemed to have been seized (*id.* at 626; *see also id.* at 629); but if, instead of complying with the show of authority, the citizen flees, no "seizure" is effected until s/he is thereafter physically restrained or submits to restraint (*id.* at 628-29)). *Compare Torres v. Madrid*, 141 S. Ct. 989, 993-94 (2021) ("The question in this case is whether a seizure occurs when an officer shoots someone who temporarily eludes capture after the shooting. The answer is yes: The application of physical force to the body of a person with intent to restrain is a seizure, even if the force does not succeed in subduing the person."); *Campbell v. Cheatham County Sheriff's Department*, 47 F.4th 468, 479 (6th Cir. 2022) ("'When an officer fires a gun at a person,' but 'the bullet does not hit the person, the "show of authority . . . ha[s] the intended effect of contributing to [the person]'s immediate restraint"' and under our caselaw is a seizure.['] . . . By firing at the Campbells' home, Fox made a show of authority. This show of authority restricted the Campbells' movement such that a reasonable person, under these circumstances, would not feel free to leave. Therefore, Fox seized the Campbells under the Fourth Amendment."); *Johnson v. VanderKooi*, 509 Mich. 524, 983 N.W.2d 779 (2022) ("Fingerprinting an individual without probable cause, a warrant, or an applicable warrant exception violates an individual's Fourth Amendment rights." *Id.* at 529-30, 983 N.W.2d N.W.2d at 782. "As directed by [*United States v.*] *Jones*[, 565 U.S. 400 (2012)] and *Grady* [*v. North Carolina*, 575 U.S. 306 (2015)] [see § 25.33 *infra*], we consider whether there was a physical trespass on a constitutionally protected area and whether there was an attempt to obtain information. Again, the Fourth Amendment protects both the right of people to be secure in their own persons as well as in their houses and effects. The fingerprinting of each of the plaintiffs in these cases constituted a physical trespass onto a person's body, a constitutionally protected area. That the act of fingerprinting is done for the very *purpose* of obtaining information is clear; defendants' entire argument justifying the P&P policy [a police department policy of photographing and fingerprinting individuals stopped without probable cause whenever an officer deemed photographing and fingerprinting necessary given the facts and circumstances] was that fingerprinting was necessary under these circumstances to confirm an individual's identity. Accordingly, we hold that fingerprinting pursuant to the P&P policy constitutes a search under the Fourth Amendment." *Id.* at 537-38, 983 N.W.2d at 786-87.); *United States v. Gaines*, 918 F.3d 793 (10th Cir. 2019) (while the defendant was seated in his car in a parking lot, two marked police cars came up behind him and stopped with their roof lights flashing; one uniformed officer signaled the defendant to get out of his car and told him that the police had a report he was there selling PCP; during this conversation, the other officer circled the defendant's car and looked inside; when he saw an open container of alcohol and smelled PCP, he advised the defendant that the defendant would be detained; the defendant then grabbed a pouch from the car and fled but was caught and arrested; distinguishing *Hodari D.*, the court holds that the defendant was seized for Fourth Amendment purposes and yielded to a show of authority before his flight; thus, evidence found on his person had to be suppressed); *Commonwealth v. Adams*, 651 Pa. 440, 450, 205 A.3d 1195, 1200-01 (2019) (an officer approached a car parked at night in a lot behind commercial properties, saw that the driver's seat was occupied, and knocked on the window; the occupant started to open the door; the officer, fearing for his safety, pushed it shut and told the occupant to open his window: "We agree with Adams that he was 'seized' for Fourth Amendment purposes when [the] Officer . . . would not allow Adams to exit his vehicle, closing the door as Adams opened it. This action, constituting both an act of physical force and a show of authority, is precisely the type of escalatory factor that compels a finding that a seizure occurred."); *United States v. Bowman*, 884 F.3d 200 (4th Cir. 2018) (following a traffic stop, a highway patrol officer instructed the driver to sit in the patrol car while the officer verified his license and registration information; the officer then issued the driver a warning citation, returned his license and registration documents, and shook his hand but told him to stay in the patrol car while the officer questioned a passenger who had remained in the stopped vehicle; the directive to stay in the patrol car – to which the driver responded "okay" – was a seizure of the driver and violated the Fourth Amendment in the absence of reasonable suspicion); *United States v. Peters*, 60 F.4th 855, 863 (4th Cir. 2023) ("[W]e find that Peters was seized approximately one minute into the encounter when Officer Butler threatened to exercise his authority to take Peters to jail for trespass and suggested that Peters should consent to a pat down. Both the officers were in uniform, with their service weapons holstered, and exited their patrol car upon seeing Peters and Garrison. They spoke in 'stern' and 'authoritative' tones of voice while asking Peters and Garrison if they were armed and to lift their shirts. . . . Although the Government maintains that the officers' interaction with Peters constituted a consensual encounter, we find otherwise.. . . ¶ A reasonable person would not feel free to leave if an officer says he can take the person to jail for a specific crime, or threatens that he will do so. This is especially true after being accused of the specific crime several times."); *United States v. McKinney*, 980 F.3d 485, 491 (5th Cir. 2020) ("When [an] Officer . . . jumped out of the police SUV and approached the group [of three men and a woman standing on a sidewalk], he shined his flashlight on the woman who appeared to be walking away and ordered that she return. No reasonable person would have felt free to walk away. As a result, each person in the group was seized at that moment."); *Commonwealth v. Cost*, 224 A.3d 641, 650-51 (Pa. 2020) (observing the defendant and two other men in an alley in a high-crime neighborhood, police officers parked at the mouth of the alley, announced that they were police, and asked the men for identification; all three handed ID cards to the officers, who retained the ID's while phoning in for a warrants check; meanwhile, the defendant removed his backpack and an officer asked him whether there was anything in it that the police should know about; the defendant admitted that the backpack contained a gun, which the police then seized; applying "the 'free-to-leave' standard," the Pennsylvania Supreme Court finds that a Fourth Amendment seizure occurred and, unsupported by reasonable suspicion, requires suppression of the gun; the court stops short of adopting the *per se* rule established by some courts that recognize "'the impractical and unrealistic option of a reasonable person in modern society to abandon one's identification'" and walk away leaving it in the hands of a police officer, but concludes that "the retention by police of an identification card to conduct a warrant check will generally be a material and substantial escalating factor within the totality assessment.").

As a doctrinal matter, these rules involve a strictly objective inquiry; they do not turn either on the suspect's subjective belief that s/he is or is not free to leave (*Brendlin v. California, supra*, 551 U.S. at 258 n.4) or on the officer's unmanifested intentions to restrain the suspect if the suspect attempts to leave (*id*. at 259-62) (the passenger in a stopped automobile was "seized" within the meaning of the Fourth Amendment even though the record did not establish that the officer "'was even aware [the passenger] was in the car prior to the vehicle stop'" and thus the officer may not have intended to stop the passenger: "the objective *Mendenhall* test of what a reasonable passenger would understand . . . leads to the intuitive conclusion that all the occupants were subject to like control by the successful display of authority"); *accord, Villanueva v. California*, 986 F.3d 1158, 1166 (9th Cir. 2021) (a passenger in a truck was "seized" for Fourth Amendment purposes when police fired at the vehicle and killed the driver, bringing the truck to a stop: "[a] person is seized under the Fourth Amendment 'when there is a governmental termination of freedom of [his] movement through means intentionally applied.'"). *See also Kaupp v. Texas, supra*, 538 U.S. at 632 (handcuffing of a suspect was a significant factor in the classification of police conduct as a seizure tantamount to an arrest notwithstanding evidence that the sheriff's department "'routinely'" used handcuffs for safety reasons when transporting individuals: "the officers' motivation of self-protection does not speak to how their actions would reasonably be understood" by the suspect); *United States v. Mendenhall, supra*, 446 U.S. at 554 n.6 (opinion of Justice Stewart, announcing the judgment of the Court); *Berkemer v. McCarty*, 468 U.S. 420, 442 (1984); *United States v. Hensley*, 469 U.S. 221, 234-35 (1985); *Nieves v. Bartlett*, 139 S. Ct. 1715, 1724-25 (2019). *Cf. United States v. Guerrero*, 19 F.4th 547, 549 (1st Cir. 2021) (recognizing that "the Supreme Court has issued opinion after opinion interpreting (in various contexts) the Constitution's reasonableness command as not depending on the officer's 'actual motivations' – and that is because the Fourth Amendment generally prefers 'objective' inquiries over 'subjective' ones."). However, as a practical matter, judges conducting a suppression hearing in the first instance often tend to be moved in the direction of finding a "seizure" when the officers can be gotten to concede that they would not have permitted the suspect to leave if the suspect had attempted to do so. Therefore, counsel may be well advised to ask the officer or officers a question like: "If [the client] had simply ignored you, turned [his] [her] back on you and walked away, are we to understand that you would have done nothing to prevent [him] [her] from taking off?" Officers with an ego will commonly be unwilling to say that they would have done nothing in this insulting situation; and, if they do say so, the question and answer will have done the defense no harm under the ultimate "objective *Mendenhall* test" (*Brendlin v. California, supra*, 551 U.S. at 260). Prosecutorial objections to the question can be met by the observation that U.S. Supreme Court opinions attach significance to the information that the question seeks to elicit (*see, e.g., Florida v. Royer, supra*, 460 U.S. at

503 (plurality opinion) ("the State conceded in the Florida courts that Royer would not have been free to leave the interrogation room had he asked to do so. Furthermore, the state's brief in this Court interprets the testimony of the officers at the suppression hearing as indicating that had Royer refused to consent to a search of his luggage, the officers would have held the luggage and sought a warrant to authorize the search."); *Dunaway v. New York*, *supra*, 442 U.S. at 203, 212 ("although . . . [Dunaway] was not told he was under arrest, he would have been physically restrained if he had attempted to leave"); *id.* at 212 (Dunaway "was never informed that he was 'free to go'; indeed, he would have been physically restrained if he had refused to accompany the officers or had tried to escape their custody")) – perhaps because an officer's subjective intentions will frequently manifest themselves in subtle, visible appearances or "actions . . . [that] show an unambiguous intent to restrain" (*Brendlin v. California*, *supra*, 551 U.S. at 255). Janus-like observations quoting officers' statements which reveal that the reasons which drove their actions were impermissible and appearing to rely on those statements to condemn their actions while simultaneously disavowing any such reliance are found in numerous judicial opinions. *E.g.*, *United States v. McKinney*, 980 F.3d 485, 493 (5th Cir. 2020), summarized in § 25.11.1 *infra* ("The record strongly supports a finding that the comments we have already quoted from the officers were the actual and insufficient reasons for the stop. Officer Carmona said his 'reasonable suspicion' was that there had been multiple shootings. Officer Holland believed it was enough to stop people who 'are hanging out over here,' especially if the people are members of a gang – presumably meaning anyone wearing red. Even though the articulated reasons fail, the test to be applied is objective, meaning it does not depend on what the officers claimed as reasons. . . . We look at the remainder of the relevant evidence to determine whether other facts known to these officers objectively justified the stop.").

Also, notwithstanding the dogma that the subjective perceptions of the parties are not to be considered in determining whether police-civilian interactions amount to a constitutionally prohibited seizure of the person, "race is an appropriate circumstance to consider in conducting the totality of the circumstances seizure analysis. *See State v. Hight*, 146 N.H. 746, 750-51, 781 A.2d 11 (2001) (considering the races of a Caucasian police officer and an African-American suspect in deciding whether the state purged the taint of an unlawful detention followed by a consent to search). "As the Seventh Circuit has concluded, 'race is "not irrelevant" to the question of whether a seizure occurred,' but 'it is not dispositive either.' [*United States v.*] *Smith*, 794 F.3d [681] at 688 [(2015)]; *see United States v. Mendenhall*, 446 U.S. 544, 558 . . . (1980) (noting that the defendant's race was 'not irrelevant' to determining whether she consented to accompany police officers)." *State v. Jones*, 172 N.H. 774, 780, 235 A.3d 119, 126 (2020). *See also Dozier v. United States*, 220 A.3d 933, 937, 942-45 (D.C. 2019) (concluding that the African-American defendant's race was "relevant in evaluating the coercive character of the overall setting of the encounter" with the police and in holding that the trial court was incorrect to find that the defendant "voluntarily agreed to a pat-down": "Even the innocent person we posit in our Fourth Amendment analysis might well fear that he is perceived with particular suspicion by hyper-vigilant police officers expecting to find criminal activity in a particular area. ¶ This fear is particularly justified for persons of color, who are more likely to be subjected to this type of police surveillance. As is known from well-publicized and documented examples, an African-American man facing armed policemen would reasonably be especially apprehensive. The fear of harm and resulting protective conditioning to submit to avoid harm at the hands of police is relevant to whether there was a seizure because feeling 'free' to leave or terminate an encounter with police officers is rooted in an assessment of the consequences of doing so. . . . We cannot turn a blind eye to the reality that not all encounters with the police proceed from the same footing, but are based on experiences and expectations, including stereotypical impressions, on both sides. . . . In the isolated setting where the encounter took place, appellant, who is African-American, reasonably could have feared that unless he complied with the police requests, he would be vulnerable to police violence, without hope that anyone would come to his aid or witness what happened."); *Commonwealth v. Warren*, 475 Mass. 530, 58 N.E.3d 333 (2016), and *Miles v. United States*, 181 A.3d 633 (D.C. 2016), quoted in § 25.11.2 *infra*; *Millan-Hernandez v. Barr*, 965 F.3d 140 (2d Cir. 2020) (per curiam), quoted in § 25.28 *infra*; *United States v. Washington, supra*, 490 F.3d at 775-76; *D.Y. v. State*, 28 N.E.2d 249, 256 (Ind. App. 2015); *State v. Sum*, 199 Wash. 2d 627, 630-31, 511 P.3d 92, 97 (2022) (holding that the "circumstances" a court must consider in "determin[ing] whether a person has been seized" "include[ ] the race and ethnicity of the allegedly seized person": "we now clarify that a person is seized for purposes of article I, section 7 [of the Washington Constitution] if, based on the totality of the circumstances, an objective observer could conclude that the person was not free to leave, to refuse a request, or to otherwise terminate the encounter due to law enforcement's display of authority or use of physical force. For purposes of this analysis, an objective observer is aware that implicit, institutional, and unconscious biases, in addition to purposeful discrimination, have resulted in disproportionate police contacts, investigative seizures, and uses of force against Black, Indigenous, and other People of Color (BIPOC) in Washington.").

Some state courts extend their state constitutional guarantees against unreasonable searches and seizures to police conduct that would not be characterized as a "seizure" under the federal Fourth Amendment caselaw. *See, e.g., People v. McIntosh*, 96 N.Y.2d 521, 755 N.E.2d 329, 730 N.Y.S.2d 265 (2001) (striking down a seizure as violating state law under factual circumstances which the U.S. Supreme Court in *United States v. Drayton*, 536 U.S. at 203-04, viewed as not constituting a seizure); *People v. Holmes*, 81 N.Y.2d 1056, 1057-58, 619 N.E.2d 396, 397-98, 601 N.Y.S.2d 459, 460-61 (1993) (finding a police officer's pursuit of an individual to be an unlawful seizure even though the U.S. Supreme Court in *Hodari D.*, 499 U.S. at 629, declined to classify police pursuits as "seizures"). See generally § 17.11 *supra* (strategies and techniques for using state court caselaw that construes state constitutional provisions as providing greater protections than the U.S. Constitution).

25.4.3. Terry *Stops*

There is a "general rule that seizures of the person require probable cause to arrest" (*Florida v. Royer*, 460 U.S. 491, 499 (1983) (plurality opinion)), but the Court in *Terry v. Ohio* "created a limited exception to this general rule: certain seizures are justifiable under the Fourth Amendment if there is articulable suspicion that a person has committed or is about to commit a crime" (*Florida v. Royer, supra*, 460 U.S. at 498 (plurality opinion)). "The predicate permitting seizures on suspicion short of probable cause is that law enforcement interests warrant a limited intrusion on the personal security of the suspect. The scope of the intrusion permitted will vary to some extent with the particular facts and circumstances of each case. This much, however, is clear: an investigative detention must be temporary and last no longer than is necessary to effectuate the purpose of the stop. Similarly, the investigative methods employed should be the least intrusive means reasonably available to verify or dispel the officer's suspicion in a short period of time." *Id.* at 500. For further discussion of the circumstances justifying a *Terry* stop, see §§ 25.9, 25.11 *infra*; for discussion of the rules governing *Terry* frisks, see § 25.10 *infra*.

25.4.4. *Arrests*

The divider that separates *Terry* stops from arrests is described as the "point [at which] . . . police procedures [are] . . . qualitatively and quantitatively . . . so intrusive with respect to a suspect's freedom of movement and privacy interests as to trigger the full protection of the Fourth and Fourteenth Amendments" (*Hayes v. Florida,* 470 U.S. 811, 815-16 (1985)). Plainly, that line is not always easy to pinpoint. As the Court itself has observed, its decisions in "*Terry* [*v. Ohio,* 392 U.S. 1 (1968)], *Dunaway* [*v. New York,* 442 U.S. 200 (1979)], [*Florida v.*] *Royer*[*,* 460 U.S. 491 (1983)] and [*United States v.*] *Place,* [462 U.S. 696 (1983)] considered together, may in some instances create difficult line-drawing problems in distinguishing an investigative stop from a *de facto* arrest" (*United States v. Sharpe,* 470 U.S. 675, 685 (1985)). Certainly, any time the police "forcibly remove a person from his home or other place in which he is entitled to be and transport him to the police station, where he is detained, although briefly, for investigative purposes," the police have "crossed" the line between *Terry* stops and arrests and have effected a "seizure[ ] . . . sufficiently like [an] arrest[ ] to invoke the traditional rule that arrests may constitutionally be made only on probable cause" (*Hayes v. Florida, supra*, 470 U.S. at 816.) *Accord, Kaupp v. Texas,* 538 U.S. 626, 631-32 (2003) (per curiam) (a seizure requiring probable cause occurred when "a group of police officers rous[ed] . . . [the 17-year-old defendant] out of bed in the middle of the night," handcuffed him and took him to the police station in his underwear, and then questioned him in an interrogation room, even though the officers said "'we need to go and talk,'" the defendant verbally acquiesced, and the sheriff's department routinely used handcuffs for transporting individuals); *Dunaway v. New York, supra,* 442 U.S. at 212 (when the police removed the defendant from his home, transported him to the police station against his will and interrogated him, the defendant's "detention . . . was in important respects indistinguishable from a traditional arrest"). With respect to lesser intrusions upon an individual's freedom, the point of arrest is flexible, determined on a case-by-case basis by whether the circumstances of the detention were "more intrusive than necessary to effectuate an investigative detention otherwise authorized by the *Terry* line of cases" (*Florida v. Royer, supra,* 460 U.S. at 504 (plurality opinion). *See United States v. Bailey,* 743 F.3d 322, 340-41 (2d Cir. 2014) (the police "exceeded the reasonable bounds of a *Terry* stop when they handcuffed Bailey": although "not every use of handcuffs automatically renders a stop an arrest requiring probable cause," the "government failed to make . . . [the requisite] showing" that the police had "a reasonable basis to think that the person detained pose[d] a present physical threat and that handcuffing [was] the least intrusive means to protect against that threat"); *Mareska v. Bernalillo County,* 804 F.3d 1301, 1310 (10th Cir. 2015) ("the deputies, by ordering the Marescas out of the car one-by-one at gunpoint, making them lie on the ground, handcuffing four of them and placing them in separate patrol cars, effected an arrest"); *Reid v. State,* 428 Md. 289, 293, 51 A.3d 597, 599 (2012) (police officer's "use of a Taser to fire two metal darts into Reid's back converted what otherwise may have been a *Terry* stop into a *de facto* arrest for Fourth Amendment purposes"). *Accord, Michigan v. Summers,* 452 U.S. 692, 696-97 (1981) (to escape "the general rule that an official seizure of the person must be supported by probable cause, even if no formal arrest is made," the detention must be "significantly less intrusive than an arrest"). The criteria normally considered in making that assessment are described in § 25.6 *infra*. For further discussion of the standards for making an arrest, see § 25.7 *infra*.

There are some situations that do not fit neatly into the ordinary set of categories – contacts, *Terry* stops, arrests – used to adjudicate Fourth Amendment claims arising from the restraint or detention of a person. For example, in *United States v. Conley*, 69 F.4th 519 (8th Cir. 2023), the defendant was admitted to a hospital with a gunshot wound and placed on a gurney in a stabilization room. When medical personnel urged him to allow them to remove his clothing so that they could examine him completely, he refused to cooperate; a hospital security officer placed a hand on the defendant to get him to lie down flat on the gurney; the defendant struggled and attempted to get off the gurney; and two additional security officers came to the aid of the first and held him down. One of the officers felt a handgun in the defendant's pocket and alerted a sheriff's deputy who seized the gun. Charged with being a felon in possession of a weapon, the defendant moved to suppress the gun, arguing that the security officers' restraint of his body was an unconstitutional seizure of the person. The Eighth Circuit agreed that the defendant had been seized for Fourth Amendment purposes and characterized the issue as the constitutionality of a noninvestigatory seizure. "A noninvestigatory seizure can be justified by an officer's reasonable belief 'that an emergency exists requiring the officer's attention.'" *Id.* at 523. "We recently explained that 'all seizures – whether brief detentions or arrests – done for noninvestigatory purposes are governed by the Fourth Amendment's reasonableness balancing test.' *Graham v. Barnette*, 5 F.4th 872, 885 (8th Cir. 2021). Under the balancing test, 'the greater the intrusion on a citizen, the greater the justification required for that intrusion to be reasonable.' . . . Noninvestigatory seizures are reasonable if they are 'based on specific articulable facts' and the 'governmental interest' in effectuating the seizure in question 'outweighs the individual's interest in being free from arbitrary government interference.'" *Id.* Except in cases of violent or prolonged restraint, counsel wants to avoid this kind of unconventional analysis if possible, because defendants fare better under the more rule-bound tripartite category structure that calls into play the specific precedents governing contacts, *Terry* stops and arrests respectively. A fluid "balancing" test is characteristically invoked when judges want to work outside the framework of clear-cut Fourth Amendment protective doctrines in order to justify governmental seizures (or searches) that strike them as not particularly offensive. *Cf.* §§ 25.2.1 subdivision (i), 25.36, 25.37 *infra*.

25.4.5. *"Custody" for Purposes of the* Miranda *Doctrine*

It should be noted that there is one other constitutionally significant point on the spectrum of intrusiveness of police contacts with citizens. The protections established in *Miranda v. Arizona,* 384 U.S. 436 (1966), and its progeny, are triggered by the police placing a criminal defendant in "custody." See § 26.6.1 *infra*. In *Berkemer v. McCarty,* 468 U.S. 420 (1984), the Court made clear that the *Miranda* concept of custody envisions a greater degree of intrusiveness than a *Terry* stop. *See id.* at 439-40. It is uncertain, however, whether the *Miranda* concept of "custody" is synonymous with the Fourth Amendment concept of "arrests" that require probable cause. For detailed discussion of what constitutes "custody" under *Miranda*, see § 26.6.1.

25.5. *Tactical Reasons for Seeking a Categorization of Police Conduct as an Arrest or as a Terry Stop*

Because there is no "litmus-paper test for distinguishing a consensual encounter from a seizure or for determining when a seizure exceeds the bounds of an investigative stop" (*Florida v. Royer,* 460 U.S. 491, 506 (1983) (plurality opinion)), the classification of the police action in each case will depend substantially upon the facts that defense counsel elicits from the witnesses and on the quality of counsel's arguments.

Obviously, it is always in the interest of the defense to characterize a police action as a seizure of the person rather than a "consensual encounter," because only seizures trigger the protections of the Fourth Amendment. The determination whether the defense stands to gain by characterizing the seizure as a *Terry* stop or as an arrest is not quite so clear-cut. Before the criteria for classifying seizures are discussed, it is useful to examine the strategic considerations that may make one or the other of the two classifications more beneficial to the defendant.

Ordinarily, defense counsel will wish to establish that a particular restraint was an arrest rather than a *Terry* stop (or, in cases in which the degree of police restraint escalated over a period of time, that the arrest occurred earlier, rather than later, in the sequence of events). The arrest categorization usually favors the defense because the preconditions for a valid arrest are more demanding than those for a *Terry* stop (see §§ 25.7, 25.9 *infra*), making it more difficult for the prosecution to justify the seizure. Moreover, in certain cases, the classification of the seizure as an "arrest" will provide additional grounds for suppression apart from the central claim that the invalidity of the seizure tainted all evidence derived from it. (For discussion of the concept of "derivative evidence," see § 25.39 *infra*.) For example, in cases involving confessions or other statements of the defendant, the greater level of custody involved in an arrest will ordinarily guarantee *Miranda* protection. See § 26.6.1 *infra; Orozco v. Texas,* 394 U.S. 324, 327 (1969); *compare Berkemer v. McCarty,* 468 U.S. 420, 434 (1984) ("there can be no question that respondent was 'in custody' at least as of the moment he was formally placed under arrest and instructed to get into the police car"), *with id.* at 439-42; *cf.* § 25.4.5 *supra*. And the greater degree of coerciveness inherent in an arrest will be a factor for consideration in determining the voluntariness both of incriminating statements (see § 26.3 *infra; cf. Payne v. Arkansas,* 356 U.S. 560, 567 (1958)) and of consents to search or seizure (see § 25.18.1 *infra; cf. Schneckloth v. Bustamonte,* 412 U.S. 218, 240 n.29 (1973) (dictum) ("courts have been particularly sensitive to the heightened possibilities for coercion when the 'consent' to a search was given by a person in custody").

In certain cases, however, it may be in the interest of the defense to characterize a restraint as a *Terry* stop rather than an arrest. One of the most important examples of this is when the classification of the restraint as a *Terry* stop can be used to invalidate a subsequent search of the defendant. If the restraint were characterized as an arrest and the arrest was lawful because the police had probable cause to arrest, then any post-arrest search of the person would be valid as a search incident to arrest. See § 25.8 *infra*. On the other hand, if the restraint were classified as a *Terry* stop and if the police lacked the requisite basis for a *Terry* frisk – specific and articulable facts warranting a reasonable conclusion that the defendant was armed and dangerous, see § 25.10 *infra* – then the frisk would be invalid (*see Thomas v. Dillard,* 818 F.3d

864, 874-86 (9th Cir. 2016) (dictum) and cases collected) and the fruits of the frisk would have to be suppressed. (When considering the latter strategy, counsel should also consider whether s/he can bring the case within the general rule that "a search incident to a lawful arrest may not precede the arrest" (*Sibron v. New York,* 392 U.S. 40, 67 (1968)), and can avoid the narrow exception to that rule permitting a search incident to arrest to be made immediately preceding the arrest as a part of a single course of action (see § 25.8.4 *infra*).)

25.6. ***Criteria for Categorizing a Restraint (That Is, Any Seizure of the Person) as a* Terry *Stop on the One Hand or an Arrest on the Other***

As already explained, the defense will always want to classify a police action as a "seizure of the person" in order to bring the Fourth Amendment's protections into play. This initial step of showing that a "seizure" occurred is ordinarily achieved by establishing that the police made some "show of official authority" (*Florida v. Royer,* 460 U.S. 491, 502 (1983) (plurality opinion)), that would cause a "'reasonable person'" to believe "'that he was not free to leave'" (*id.*). See § 25.4.2 *supra.* Thus, in *Royer,* the plurality concluded that a Fourth Amendment "seizure" had occurred when officers approached a suspect in an airport concourse, identified themselves as narcotics agents, told the defendant that he was suspected of transporting drugs, asked him to accompany them to the police room while retaining his airplane ticket and driver's license, and in no way indicated that he was free to leave. *Id.* at 502-03. *See also Reid v. Georgia,* 448 U.S. 438 (1980) (per curiam).

The next step is to categorize the seizure as either a *Terry* stop or, conversely, an arrest. *See, e.g., Mareska v. Bernalillo County,* 804 F.3d 1301, 1308-10 (10th Cir. 2015). "There is no simple test for determining at which point a prolonged investigative stop turns into a de facto arrest, but important factors include unnecessary delays, handcuffing the suspect, confining the suspect in a police car, transporting the suspect, isolating the suspect, and the degree of fear and humiliation engendered by the police conduct." *State v. Shaw,* 237 N.J. 588, 612-13, 207 A.3d 229, 243 (2019) ("Once it was determined that Shaw was unarmed and had no outstanding warrants . . . there was no particularized suspicion that Shaw was engaged in criminal activity that would justify Shaw's further detention. We do not accept the State's argument that a person's mere presence in the car of a suspected drug dealer warrants indefinite detention without any individualized suspicion. Rather than conducting a true investigatory stop, the officers appear to have been operating from the assumption that the passengers were . . . [the dealer's] confederates. While such a hunch may be reasonable, it is insufficient to justify the extent of the investigatory detention here. . . . ¶ . . . [T]he State failed to demonstrate any reason for continuing the investigatory detention of Shaw after his warrant check returned negative. . . . [I]solating Shaw in the back of a patrol car despite a negative warrant check was a de facto and an unlawful arrest." *Id.* at 613-13, 207 A.3d at 243.). Counsel should consider developing the facts on each of the following subjects that bear upon the stop-*versus*-arrest classification.

25.6.1. *The Length of the Restraint*

On numerous occasions the Court has said that one of the factors that distinguish *Terry* stops from arrests is the relative brevity of a *Terry* stop. *See, e.g., United States v. Place,* 462 U.S. 696, 709 (1983) (explaining that "[a]lthough we have recognized the reasonableness of seizures longer than the momentary ones involved in *Terry*, . . . the brevity of the invasion of the individual's Fourth Amendment interests is an important factor in determining whether the seizure is so minimally intrusive as to be justifiable on reasonable suspicion," and then invalidating a 90-minute detention of an air traveler's luggage on reasonable suspicion: "[A]lthough we decline to adopt any outside time limitation for a permissible *Terry* stop, we have never approved a seizure of the person for the prolonged 90-minute period involved here and cannot do so on the facts presented by this case"); *Florida v. Royer*, 460 U.S. 491, 500 (1983) (plurality opinion) ("This much, however, is clear: an investigative detention must be temporary and last no longer than is necessary to effectuate the purpose of the stop"); *Dunaway v. New York*, 442 U.S. 200, 212 (1979) (stops are limited to "brief and narrowly circumscribed intrusions"); *United States v. Brignoni-Ponce*, 422 U.S. 873, 878, 880-82 (1975); *Terry v. Ohio, supra*, 392 U.S. at 10. *See also, e.g., United States v. Arvizu*, 534 U.S. 266, 273 (2002) (dictum) ("brief investigatory stops"). *Cf. United States v. Sokolow*, 490 U.S. 1, 10-11 (1989) (dictum).

In *United States v. Sharpe*, 470 U.S. 675 (1985), the Court retreated somewhat from an iron-clad rule that a *Terry* stop must be no longer than momentary. While continuing to recognize that "'brevity . . . is an important factor'" (*id.* at 685, quoting *United States v. Place, supra*), the Court in *Sharpe* stressed that "our cases impose no rigid time limitations on *Terry* stops" (*Sharpe, supra*, 470 U.S. at 685) and stated:

> "[W]e have emphasized the need to consider the law enforcement purposes to be served by the stop as well as the time reasonably needed to effectuate those purposes. . . . In assessing whether a detention is too long in duration to be justified as an investigative stop, we consider it appropriate to examine whether the police diligently pursued a means of investigation that was likely to confirm or dispel their suspicions quickly, during which time it was necessary to detain the defendant. . . . A court making this assessment should take care to consider whether the police are acting in a swiftly developing situation . . . ." (*Id.* at 685-86.)

Applying this standard in *Sharpe*, the Court concluded that the 20-minute investigative detention there was a *Terry* stop, not an arrest, because: (i) the police officer "pursued his investigation in a diligent and reasonable manner" and "proceeded expeditiously": there was no indication "that the officers were dilatory in their investigation"; (ii) to perform the investigation it was necessary to detain the suspect during the 20-minute period; (iii) the police were acting in a swiftly developing situation; and (iv) "[t]he delay in this case was attributable almost entirely to the evasive actions" of one of the suspects and, in the absence of that suspect's "maneuvers, only a short and certainly permissible pre-arrest detention would likely have taken place" (*id.* at 687-88).

In the wake of the *Sharpe* decision, the primary question is whether the detention exceeded the "time reasonably needed to effectuate" the "law enforcement purposes to be served by the stop" (*id.* at 685). *Accord, Rodriguez v. United States*, 575 U.S. 348, 350 (2015) ("We hold that a police stop exceeding the time needed to handle the matter for which the stop was made violates the Constitution's shield against unreasonable seizures."); *Illinois v. Caballes*, 543 U.S. 405, 407 (2005) (dictum) ("A seizure . . . can become unlawful if it is prolonged beyond the time reasonably required to complete th[e] mission" justifying the seizure); *Illinois v. McArthur*,

531 U.S. 326, 332 (2001) (dictum) ("this time period was no longer than reasonably necessary for the police, acting with diligence, to [complete the activity that justified the suspect's restraint]"); *and see, e.g., Johnson v. Thibodeaux City*, 887 F.3d 726, 733-35 (5th Cir. 2018); *United States v. Jenson*, 462 F.3d 399, 404 (5th Cir. 2006); *State v. Coles*, 218 N.J. 322, 344-47, 95 A.3d 136, 148-50 (2014). (The predicate for this question – and thus another necessary element for characterizing a police action as a stop rather than as an arrest – is that the purposes served by the officer's actions are consistent with the function of a *Terry* stop: to confirm or dispel an officer's suspicions by nonintrusive methods of investigation. *See, e.g., People v. Ryan*, 12 N.Y.3d 28, 30-31, 904 N.E.2d 808, 809-10, 876 N.Y.S.2d 672, 673-74 (2009) (even assuming that the police had reasonable suspicion to stop the defendant, the detention exceeded the permissible bounds of a *Terry* stop and became a seizure requiring probable cause when the police held the defendant at the location for 13 minutes while they conducted a photo identification procedure, apparently "to make it convenient for the police to arrest defendant if a positive identification subsequently occurred")). When, as in *United States v. Place, supra*, the police seized a suspect's luggage for 90 minutes in order to arrange for a narcotics-sniffing dog and when the police had forewarning of the suspect's arrival which would have permitted them to make advance preparations and thereby shorten the detention period, a reviewing court could properly conclude that the police failed to act diligently. *See United States v. Sharpe, supra*, 470 U.S. at 684-85 (explaining the holding in *Place*); *United States v. Frazier*, 30 F.4th 1165 (10th Cir. 2022) ("Under *Rodriguez*, . . . an unlawful seizure occurs when an officer (1) diverts from the traffic-based mission of the stop to investigate ordinary criminal conduct, (2) in a way that "prolongs" (i.e., adds time to) the stop, and (3) the investigative detour is unsupported by any independent reasonable suspicion. . . . Even de minimis delays caused by unrelated inquiries violate the Fourth Amendment in the absence of reasonable suspicion. ¶ . . . [W]e think it clear that the trooper's efforts to arrange for a dog sniff diverted from the traffic-based mission of the stop and thereby extended its duration." *Id*. at 1173. "Consequently, because the trooper lacked reasonable suspicion to extend the stop by several minutes to arrange for the dog sniff, Mr. Frazier's seizure violated the Fourth Amendment." *Id*. at 1178); *accord, United States v. Hurtt*, 31 F.4th 152, 160 (3d Cir. 2022) (the Court of Appeals adds that "police may not vary from the original mission and thereby create an exigency to support the resulting delay and any subsequent arrest. This police-created exigency doctrine prevents the government from deliberately creating its own exigent circumstances to justify otherwise unconstitutional intrusions."); *compare United States v. Rederick*, 65 F.4th 961 (8th Cir. 2023). But diligence is not the only issue. The most diligent of police officers is not permitted to extend a *Terry* stop indefinitely simply because the purpose of the stop cannot be achieved in a finite period of time. As the Court acknowledged in elaborating its new standard in *Sharpe*, "[o]bviously, if an investigative stop continues indefinitely, at some point it can no longer be justified as an investigative stop." 470 U.S. at 685. And the Court in *Sharpe*, when describing the need for allowing the police to pursue their investigations, specified that it was contemplating investigations that were to be conducted "quickly" (*id*. at 686). *Compare United States v. Lopez*, 907 F.3d 472, 486 (7th Cir. 2018) ("Even if the initial stop had been justified, it lasted too long. A *Terry* stop may 'last no longer than is necessary to effectuate' its purpose. . . . ¶ In this case, the officers clearly extended the stop beyond the time necessary to complete any investigation based on the claimed reasonable suspicion. There was not a sufficient justification for the *Terry* stop in the first place, but even that inadequate justification evaporated when the officers looked inside the paper bags in the garage. . . . ¶ This case presents a wrinkle not present

in *Rodriguez v. United States*, where the police search occurred after the defendant had refused the officers' request to conduct the search. Here, by contrast, Lopez consented to the search. So one might think that a person's consent to a search might absolve the officers' illegal extension of the search. To the contrary, '[q]uestioning that prolongs the detention, yet cannot be justified by the purpose of such an investigatory stop, is unreasonable under the fourth amendment.' . . . . ¶ The question does not depend on exactly how many minutes the stop lasts. It depends on whether law enforcement has detained the person longer than needed to carry out the investigation that was justified by the reasonable suspicion."), *and Mahaffy v. State*, 486 P.3d 170 (Wyo. 2021) (two deputy sheriffs stopped a car when a passenger tossed a lit cigarette out of the window; while writing up a citation for this violation, they summoned a drug-sniffing dog; "About twelve minutes into the stop, . . . [the passenger was asked] to get out of the car and . . . [walk] to the front of . . . [the deputies'] patrol car. Eleven seconds later, . . . [the deputy] completed the citation and asked . . . [the passenger], 'Is there a reason you guys are so nervous while I'm talking to you?' That discussion lasted approximately thirty seconds. . . . [The deputy] then proceeded to explain the citation." *Id*. at 172. The dog alerted to the presence of drugs and the deputy who was issuing the citation was informed of this while he was still explaining the citation to the passenger. "Twenty-three seconds later, . . . [the deputy] completed his explanation and began to inquire about drugs in the car. The entire extension of the stop, from the time . . . [the deputy] finished writing the citation to the time he began questioning about drugs, took approximately one and a half minutes." *Id*. Finding a Fourth Amendment violation that required the suppression of drugs found in the car, the Wyoming Supreme Court writes that "the United States Supreme Court soundly rejected the argument that a *de minimis* extension of a stop is acceptable in *Rodriguez*, 575 U.S. at 350-53 . . . . [The deputy] unlawfully extended the duration of the traffic stop after he had completed the citation by asking unrelated questions about nervousness." 486 P.3d at 176.), *and Baxter v. Roberts*, 54 F.4th 1241 (11th Cir. 2022) (similar), *with United States v. Cole*, 21 F.4th 421, 425 (7th Cir. 2021) (en banc) (holding that a vehicle stop for a traffic violation was not unduly prolonged when the trooper questioned the driver about his travel plans: ("[W]e hold that travel-plan questions ordinarily fall within the mission of a traffic stop. Travel-plan questions, however, like other police inquiries during a traffic stop, must be reasonable under the circumstances. And here they were. The trooper inquired about the basic details of Cole's travel, and his follow-up questions were justified given Cole's less-than-forthright answers. The stop itself was lawfully initiated, and the trooper developed reasonable suspicion of other criminal activity before moving the initial stop to the gas station for . . . [a] dog sniff. We therefore affirm the district court's denial of Cole's motion to suppress [drugs found in a search of the vehicle after the dog alerted to their presence]."), *and United States v. Nault*, 41 F.4th 1073, 1078 (9th Cir. 2022) ("An officer's 'mission' includes certain 'ordinary inquiries incident to the traffic stop,' even if they are not required to investigate a particular traffic violation [quoting *Rodriguez*, 575 U.S. at 355]. . . . Those inquiries '[t]ypically . . . involve checking the driver's license, determining whether there are outstanding warrants against the driver, and inspecting the automobile's registration and proof of insurance.' *Id*. Such routine checks 'ensur[e] that vehicles on the road are operated safely and responsibly.' *Id*. By contrast, unrelated inquiries such as dog sniffs or other nonroutine checks, which are 'aimed at "detect[ing] evidence of ordinary criminal wrongdoing,"' lack the same 'close connection to roadway safety,' and must be justified by independent reasonable suspicion. *Rodriguez*, 575 U.S. at 355-56 . . . ; *see* [*United States v.*] *Landeros*, 913 F.3d . . . [862,] 868 [9th Cir. 2019] (requesting passenger's identification was not part of an officer's traffic stop mission because '[t]he identity of a passenger . . . will ordinarily have no relation to a driver's safe operation of a vehicle'. . . ."); *cf. Johnson v. VanderKooi*, 509 Mich. 524, 540, 983 N.W.2d 779, 788 (2022), summarized in § 25.4.2 *supra* ("Fingerprinting pursuant to the . . . [photographing and fingerprinting] policy exceeded the permissible scope of a *Terry* stop because it was not reasonably related in scope to the circumstances that justified the stop"); *and see United States v. Foreste*, 780 F.3d 518, 525 & n.4 (2d Cir. 2015) (if police officers conduct successive stops of the same individual based on the "same reasonable suspicion," and if "the officer conducting the subsequent investigation is aware of the prior investigation and the suspicion that supported it, the investigations' duration and scope must be both individually and collectively reasonable under the Fourth Amendment"; "The same would be true were the suspicion justifying the second investigation generated from the first investigation rather than if it were identical to it. In either case, the second stop can be viewed as an extension of the first stop, justifying the stops' joint evaluation for reasonableness under the Fourth Amendment.").

25.6.2. *Whether the Police Transported the Defendant from the Location of the Stop*

The police frequently transport a suspect from the place of initial accosting to another location, either to conduct questioning in a more private setting, or to display the suspect to an eyewitness in a show-up identification procedure, or for some other investigative purpose. In *Hayes v. Florida*, 470 U.S. 811 (1985); *Dunaway v. New York*, 442 U.S. 200 (1979); *Florida v. Royer*, 460 U.S. 491 (1983); and *Kaupp v. Texas*, 538 U.S. 626 (2003) (per curiam), the ambulatory nature of the detention was a significant factor in the Court's classification of the detention as an arrest rather than a *Terry* stop.

In *Hayes v. Florida*, the Court concluded that the forcible removal of a suspect from his home and the non-consensual transportation of the suspect to the police station constituted such an "intrusi[on] with respect to a suspect's freedom of movement and privacy interests as to trigger the full protection of the Fourth and Fourteenth Amendments." 470 U.S. at 816. Similarly, in *Dunaway v. New York,* two of "[t]he pertinent facts relied on by the Court" in finding that the detention was an arrest "were that (1) the defendant was taken from a private dwelling; [and] (2) he was transported unwillingly to the police station" (*United States v. Sharpe, supra*, 470 U.S. at 684 n.4 (explaining the holding in *Dunaway*)).

In *Royer,* one of the factors that transformed "[w]hat had begun as a consensual inquiry in a public place" (460 U.S. at 503) into a full arrest was the transportation of the defendant some 40 feet to a small airport room for questioning. In condemning this movement of the suspect, the plurality in *Royer* stressed that "[t]he record does not reflect any facts which would support a finding that the legitimate law enforcement purposes which justified the detention in the first instance were furthered by removing Royer to the police room prior to the officer's attempt to gain his consent to a search of his luggage" (460 U.S. at 505). *See also United States v. Sharpe, supra*, 470 U.S. at 684 (discounting the portion of the *Royer* opinion that seemed to rely on the length of the detention, and defining the opinion as being concerned primarily with "the fact that the police confined the defendant in a small airport room for questioning").

In the *per curiam* opinion in *Kaupp v. Texas*, the Court relied on the reasoning in *Hayes v. Florida* and *Dunaway v. New York* to hold that the police conducted a seizure that was "'in important respects indistinguishable from a traditional arrest' and therefore required probable cause or judicial authorization" when they removed the 17-year-old defendant from his home in the middle of the night in handcuffs, "placed [him] in a patrol car, dr[o]ve[ ] [him] to the scene of a crime and then to the sheriff's offices, where he was taken into an interrogation room and questioned" (*Kaupp v. Texas, supra,* 538 U.S. at 631). "[W]e have never 'sustained against Fourth Amendment challenge the involuntary removal of a suspect from his home to a police station and his detention there for investigative purposes . . . absent probable cause or judicial authorization.'" *Id.* at 630 (quoting *Hayes v. Florida, supra,* 470 U.S. at 815). The Court in *Kaupp* reiterated that "[s]uch involuntary transport to a police station for questioning is 'sufficiently like arres[t] to invoke the traditional rule that arrests may constitutionally be made only on probable cause'" (*Kaupp v. Texas, supra,* 538 U.S. at 630 (quoting *Hayes v. Florida, supra,* 470 U.S. at 816)).

25.6.3. *The Nature of the Setting in Which the Detention Takes Place*

In *Berkemer v. McCarty,* 468 U.S. 420 (1984), in the course of holding *Miranda* inapplicable to roadside questioning of motorists detained pursuant to traffic stops, the Court made some general observations concerning the distinction between *Terry* stops and arrests. Explaining that typical traffic stops differ from the usual *Miranda* custodial setting in that the "exposure to public view . . . diminishes the motorist's fear that, if he does not cooperate, he will be subjected to abuse," the Court then commented that in this respect, "the usual traffic stop is more analogous to a so-called 'Terry* stop' . . . than to a formal arrest" (*id.* at 438-39). The Court noted that *Terry* stops are normally characterized by "[t]he comparatively non-threatening character of [the] detentions" (*id.* at 440).

Non-public setting played an important part in the decision in *Florida v. Royer, supra.* In condemning the transportation of the suspect, the plurality stressed that the effect of the move was to shift the suspect from a "public place" to "a small room – a large closet . . . [where] [h]e was alone with two police officers" (460 U.S. at 502). Although the *Royer* plurality did not expressly characterize the change in location as designed to increase the pressure on the suspect, that conclusion is implicit in the plurality's strong criticism of the lack of any "legitimate law enforcement purposes" in "removing Royer to the police room prior to the officers' attempt to gain his consent to a search of his luggage" (*id.* at 505).

Significantly, the progenitors of the "stop" doctrine, *Terry v. Ohio* and *Sibron v. New York,* originally recognized the "stop" power in the context of stops made on the street or in a public place. In extending that power to cases in which police officers board a bus and question passengers, the Court in *United States v. Drayton,* 536 U.S. 194 (2002), and *Florida v. Bostick,* 501 U.S. 429 (1991), said that "[t]he fact that an encounter takes place on a bus does not on its own transform standard police questioning of citizens into an illegal seizure" (*Drayton, supra,* 536 U.S. at 204; *Bostick, supra,* 501 U.S. at 439-40). Acknowledging that "[w]here the encounter takes place is one factor" in assessing whether a "seizure" has taken place (*Bostick, supra,* 501 U.S. at 437), the Court explained that "an encounter [that] takes place on a bus" may be no more intrusive than one that "occurred on the street" "because many fellow passengers are present to witness [the] officers' conduct, [and thus] a reasonable person may feel even more secure in his or her decision not to cooperate with police on a bus than in other circumstances"

(*Drayton, supra*, 536 U.S. at 195).

Except for a pair of scenarios – one of which the Supreme Court has addressed in several decisions – all of the Court's rulings upholding stops have involved "on-the-street" situations (*Dunaway v. New York, supra*, 442 U.S. at 210-11), or encounters in similarly public places, such as buses or airport concourses (*United States v. Mendenhall*, 446 U.S. 544, 560-66 (1980) (plurality opinion on this point)). The first exception is a situation in which officers who are executing a valid search warrant for contraband in a home detain an occupant of the premises during the search – a scenario the Court addressed in *Michigan v. Summers*, 452 U.S. 692 (1981), and again in *Muehler v. Mena*, 544 U.S. 93 (2005). See § 25.22.3 *infra*. In *Summers*, the Court held that in this situation, officers executing a valid search warrant have "the limited authority to detain the occupants of the premises while a proper search is conducted" (452 U.S. at 705). *Accord, Los Angeles County v. Rettele*, 550 U.S. 609, 613-14 (2007) (per curiam). *Cf. Bailey v. United States*, 568 U.S. 186, 193 (2013) (*Summers* doctrine is strictly limited to "cases [in which] the occupants detained were found within or immediately outside a residence at the moment the police officers executed the search warrant"); *United States v. Watson*, 703 F.3d 684, 691-92 (4th Cir. 2013). In *Muehler*, the Court added that the police also may engage in the additional intrusion of handcuffing an occupant during the search if this measure is necessitated by "inherently dangerous" circumstances such as those that existed in the *Muehler* case, where the "warrant authoriz[ed] a search for weapons and a wanted gang member reside[d] on the premises" and there was a "need to detain multiple occupants" (544 U.S. at 100). But, as the Court emphasized in establishing the general rule in *Summers*, the police officers' possession of a search warrant in these cases precludes any possibility that the police have arranged for detention in a non-public place for the sake of exploiting the coercive atmosphere to gain information or consent to a search or seizure. The *Summers* Court made a point of explaining that "the type of detention imposed here is not likely to be exploited by the officer" to extract information from the suspect since "the information the officers seek normally will be obtained through the search and not through the detention" (*Summers, supra*, 452 U.S. at 701). *See also Muehler, supra*, 544 U.S. at 101-02 (explaining that, although the police questioned the handcuffed suspect about her immigration status, the case did not require that the Court consider the constitutionality of "questioning that extended the time [the detainee] . . . was detained" or that otherwise "constitute[d] an independent Fourth Amendment violation"). Moreover, in this scenario, extraction of a consent to search or seize would be superfluous since the officers already have a warrant.

The second exceptional scenario is *Illinois v. McArthur*, 531 U.S. 326 (2001), where the Court upheld the conduct of police who, after discussions with a homeowner on his front porch, refused to permit him to enter his home unaccompanied by a police escort during a two-hour period while they were seeking a search warrant for the home, based on probable cause to believe there was marijuana inside. The Court justified the restraint of the homeowner's freedom because "the police had good reason to fear that, unless restrained, . . . [he] would destroy the drugs before they could return with a warrant (*id.* at 332), and it noted that, on the two or three occasions when a police officer accompanied the homeowner into the house during the two-hour wait, the homeowner had "reentered simply for his own convenience, to make phone calls and to obtain cigarettes" and had given his consent to the officer's escorting him inside for these purposes (*id.* at 335). *See United States v. Curry*, 965 F.3d 313, 326-29 (4th Cir. 2020) (en banc) (reading *MacArthur* narrowly).

Accordingly, in situations other than the *Summers-Muehler* and *McArthur* scenarios, counsel can argue that any detention of a suspect in a "'police dominated'" setting (*Berkemer v. McCarty, supra*, 468 U.S. at 439), where no or few other members of the public are "present to witness officers' conduct" (*United States v. Drayton, supra*, 536 U.S. at 204) and to reinforce "[t]he comparatively nonthreatening character of [the] detention[ ]" (*Berkemer v. McCarty, supra*, 468 U.S. at 440), transforms what might otherwise be merely a *Terry* stop into an arrest requiring probable cause. The argument has particular force when the police have moved the suspect from a public location to a setting of that sort – a particularly intimidating action. See the discussion of *Florida v. Royer, supra*, in the second paragraph of this section.

25.6.4. *Whether the Detention Was for the Purpose of Interrogation*

If the purpose of police detention of a suspect is interrogation, the courts are particularly likely to view the interrogation as an arrest requiring probable cause rather than a *Terry* stop. In *Dunaway v. New York, supra*, the Court concluded that when the police transported the suspect to the police station for the purpose of interrogation, the "detention . . . was in important respects indistinguishable from a traditional arrest" (442 U.S. at 212). *See also United States v. Sharpe, supra*, 470 U.S. at 684 n.4 (explaining the holding in *Dunaway*). In *Kaupp v. Texas, supra*, the Court applied the reasoning of *Dunaway* to hold that the police had conducted a seizure that was "'in important respects indistinguishable from a traditional arrest' and therefore required probable cause or judicial authorization" when they removed the 17-year-old defendant from his home in the middle of the night in handcuffs and drove him "to the sheriff's offices, where he was taken into an interrogation room and questioned" (538 U.S. at 631 (quoting *Dunaway v. New York, supra*, 442 U.S. at 212)). Such "involuntary transport to a police station *for questioning*," the Court explained, is "'sufficiently like arres[t] to invoke the traditional rule that arrests may constitutionally be made only on probable cause'" (*Kaupp v. Texas, supra*, 538 U.S. at 630 (emphasis added)). Similarly, in *Florida v. Royer, supra*, it was deemed significant that the police transported the defendant to the police room for the purpose of interrogation rather than legitimate "reasons of safety and security" (460 U.S. at 504-05 (plurality opinion)). By contrast, in *Michigan v. Summers, supra*, 452 U.S. at 701-02 & n.15, the Court emphasized that the detention of the suspect, which the Court classified as a *Terry* stop, was not designed to extract information from the suspect.

Because the general rule for evaluating police conduct under the Fourth Amendment turns on the officer's behavior – in theory, an objective test that eschews any inquiry into the officer's motivation (*see Whren v. United States*, 517 U.S. 806 (1996), and cases cited together with *Whren* in § 25.4.1 *infra*; *but see State v. Arreola*, 176 Wash. 2d 284, 294, 290 P.3d 983, 989 (2012) ("[p]retextual traffic stops are unconstitutional under article I, section 7" of the Washington Constitution); *Schuster v. State Department of Taxation and Revenue, Motor Vehicle Division*, 2012-NMSC-025, 283 P.3d 288, 297 (2012) (citing *State v. Gonzales*, 2011-NMSC-012, 150 N.M. 74, 257 P.3d 894, 896, 897-98 (2011), and *State v. Ochoa*, 2009-NMCA-002, 146 N.M. 32, 206 P.3d 143 (N.M. App. 2008): "New Mexico has departed from United States Supreme Court precedent in *Whren v. United States* . . . by holding that pretextual traffic stops are constitutionally unreasonable. . . . '[A] pretextual stop [is] a detention supportable by reasonable suspicion or probable cause to believe that a traffic offense has occurred, but is executed as a pretense to pursue a "hunch," a different[,] more serious investigative agenda for which there is no reasonable suspicion or probable cause.'")) – the *purpose of interrogation* criterion depends for the most part on whether the police do indeed interrogate a detained individual. But doctrine does not always hobble judges who can be persuaded by the glaring facts of a case that the police were acting from an illicit motive and using a *Terry* stop as a pretext to justify some impermissible investigative technique. The several criteria for a valid *Terry* stop have sufficient flexibility to provide a tenable counterstrategy for holding such a stop or its protraction unconstitutional. *See, e.g., United States v. Frazier*, 30 F.4th 1165 (10th Cir. 2022), summarized in § 25.6.1 *supra*; *United States v. Hurtt*, 31 F.4th 152 (3d Cir. 2022); *United States v. Walker*, 965 F.3d 180 (2d Cir. 2020); *United States v. Blair*, 524 F.3d 740 (6th Cir. 2008); *cf. United States v. Williams*, 731 F.3d 678, 686-87 (7th Cir. 2013), summarized in § 25.10 *infra* (invalidating a manifestly pretextual *Terry* frisk).

25.6.5. *The Intrusiveness of the Restraint; Police Behavior Conventionally Associated with Arrest*

Handcuffing or otherwise physically restraining an individual is a factor that counts in favor of characterizing police action as an arrest. *See, e.g., Mwangangi v. Nielsen*, 48 F.4th 816, 826-27 (7th Cir. 2022) ("'[T]he use of handcuffs substantially aggravates the intrusiveness of a *Terry* stop' and, as a meaningful 'restraint[] on freedom of movement,' is '*normally* associated with arrest.' . . . While there is no categorical rule that an officer's decision to place a suspect in handcuffs *always* transforms the interaction from a *Terry* stop into an arrest, it is the 'rare case' in which 'common sense and ordinary human experience convince us that an officer believed reasonably that an investigative stop could be effectuated safely only in this manner.' . . . [S]ee also *United States v. Howard*, 729 F.3d 655, 661 (7th Cir. 2013) ('Handcuffs in a *Terry* stop and frisk are not and should not be the norm.')."); *White v. United States*, 68 A.3d 271, 279 (D.C. 2013) ("Handcuffing does not necessarily transform an investigative detention into an arrest, but it is recognized as "'a hallmark of a formal arrest."'"); *Reagan v. Idaho Transportation Department*, 169 Idaho 689, 697, 502 P.3d 1027, 1035 (2021) ("Handcuffing a suspect alone does not automatically convert an investigative detention into an arrest where 'the use of handcuffs was a reasonable precaution for the officer's safety.'. . . However, the threshold for showing that handcuffs were a reasonable precaution for officer safety is high. . . . ¶ Here, the act of handcuffing Reagan exceeded the bounds of what was reasonably intrusive in conducting an investigative detention and so requires this Court to conclude that the use of handcuffs converted the investigative detention into an arrest. Nothing indicates that Reagan posed any threat to officer safety. Indeed, the officer made no attempt to articulate that such a threat even existed. The alleged crime did not involve violence."); *State v. Snyder*, 240 Ariz. 551, 555, 382 P.3d 109, 113 (Ariz. App. 2016) ("A significant factor in determining whether an arrest has occurred 'is the extent that freedom of movement is curtailed and the degree and manner of force used.' . . . 'Another significant factor is the display of official authority, such that "a reasonable person would . . . not [feel] free to leave."' . . . 'Handcuffing a suspect is an indicia [sic] of arrest.'"); *compare Longshore v. State*, 399 Md. 486, 924 A.2d 1129 (2007) ("generally, a display of force by a police officer, such as putting a person in handcuffs, is considered an arrest" (399 Md. at 502, 924 A.2d 1129, 1138); "Maryland has recognized very limited instances in which a show of force, such as placing a suspect in handcuffs, is not an arrest. This Court has upheld the use of such force when done to protect the officer . . . and the intermediate appellate court has upheld use of such force when done to prevent a suspect's flight . . . ." 399 Md. at 509, 924 A.2d at 1142; "Because Longshore was neither a flight nor safety risk, there was no justification for placing Longshore in handcuffs. This was, therefore, no mere detention; it was, in fact, an arrest." 399 Md. at 515, 924 A.2d 1129, 1145.), *with Chase v. State*, 449 Md. 283, 309, 144 A.3d 630, 645 (2016) ("Chase's reliance on *Longshore* . . . is misplaced. In that case, the officers presented no particularized observations nor did they indicate a belief that Longshore was armed, dangerous or that they were concerned with their safety. Under those circumstances, we held that the officers had no justification for placing Longshore in handcuffs. The instant case differs significantly from *Longshore* in that Detective Melnyk testified that the 'reason for the handcuffs were solely based on the safety of everybody involved, based on the furtive movements that we observed inside the vehicle as we were approaching the vehicle.'"); *and see United States v. Coulter*, 41 F.4th 451 (5th Cir. 2022) (a 2-1 panel decision holding that the defendant was not in custody for *Miranda* purposes although he was handcuffed during a traffic stop by a lone officer who had reason to suspect that he had a gun). More generally, "[a] *Terry* stop becomes an arrest if officers use more force than reasonably necessary to facilitate the detention." *United States v. Stevenson*, 66 F.4th 1143, 1145 (8th Cir. 2023) (dictum). "Giving a defendant *Miranda* warnings is also 'considered a factor weighing in favor of concluding that there was an arrest because most people associate the warnings with arrest.'" *State v. Snyder, supra*, 240 Ariz. at 555, 382 P.3d at 113. And an explicit statement that the individual is under arrest is likely to be decisive. *See United States v. Mota*, 982 F.2d 1384, 1387 (9th Cir. 2004); *Reagan v. Idaho Transportation Department, supra*, 169 Idaho at 698, 502 P.3d at 1036.

25.7. *Circumstances Justifying an Arrest*

25.7.1. *Authorization by Statute or Common Law*

"Whether an officer is authorized to make an arrest ordinarily depends, in the first instance, on state law." *Michigan v. DeFillipo*, 443 U.S. 31, 36 (1979). *See, e.g., Sweetin v. City of Texas City*, 48 F.4th 387 (5th Cir. 2022). In virtually all jurisdictions the conditions for a valid arrest are specified by either statute or caselaw. *See, e.g., N.S. v. Hughes*, 335 F.R.D. 337 (D. D.C. 2020); *State of New York v. U.S. Immigration and Customs Enforcement*, 466 F. Supp. 3d 439 (S.D. N.Y. 2020); *accord, Doe v. U.S. Immigration and Customs Enforcement*, 490 F. Supp. 3d 672 (S.D. N.Y. 2020). State law may require the suppression of evidence obtained as a consequence of a legally unauthorized arrest (*see, e.g., Commonwealth v. Le Blanc*, 407 Mass. 70, 75, 551 N.E.2d 906, 909 (1990) ("The police officer in this case acted without statutory or common law authority both when he stopped the defendant and when he arrested him. Our case law supports exclusion of evidence when such conduct prejudices the defendant. . . . The requirement that a police officer have lawful authority when he deprives individuals of their liberty is closely associated with the constitutional right to be free from unreasonable searches and seizures."); *Commonwealth v. Clark*, 558 Pa. 157, 165-66, 735 A.2d 1248, 1253 (1999); *People v. Alesi*, 89 Cal. App. 3d 537, 152 Cal. Rptr. 623 (1979); *cf. City of Billings v. Whalen*, 242 Mont. 293, 790 P.2d 471 (1990)), but such an arrest does not *eo ipso* violate the Fourth Amendment or require suppression as a matter of federal constitutional law (*Virginia v. Moore*, 553 U.S. 164, 176-77 (2008); *Cornel v. Hawai'i*, 37 F.4th 527, 533-34 (9th Cir. 2022)). The state-law validity of an arrest may also have other consequences unaffected by federal law: In many States, for example, a defendant can be convicted of the crime of resisting arrest only if the arrest is lawful. *E.g., State v. Robinson,* 6 Ariz. App. 424, 433 P.2d 75 (1967); *People v. Peacock,* 68 N.Y.2d 675, 496 N.E.2d 683, 505 N.Y.S.2d 594 (1986); *State v. Mobley,* 240 N.C. 476, 83 S.E.2d 100 (1954).

25.7.2. *Arrest Warrants*

In cases in which a defendant is arrested on an arrest warrant, the defense can challenge the validity of the warrant, and thereby the validity of the arrest, by arguing that the warrant was issued without a showing of probable cause to believe that the defendant committed an offense. *See Giordenello v. United States,* 357 U.S. 480 (1958), as explained in *Aguilar v. Texas,* 378 U.S. 108, 112 n.3 (1964); *Steagald v. United States,* 451 U.S. 204, 213 (1981) (dictum). In determining whether such an argument is viable, counsel will need to obtain the affidavit or sworn complaint submitted by the police or prosecutor in support of the request for the arrest warrant and examine the sufficiency of the facts presented to the magistrate or judge who issued the warrant. In cases in which an arrest warrant does not correctly name the defendant and instead is issued on the basis of an alias, a nickname, or a description of the person sought, counsel also may be able to challenge the validity of the warrant on the grounds that it does not identify the defendant with the requisite particularity. *See, e.g., United States v. Doe,* 703 F.2d 745 (3d Cir. 1983). "'[A] seizure conducted pursuant to an arrest warrant must conform to the terms of that warrant.'" *Simon v. City of New York,* 893 F.3d 83, 94 (2d Cir. 2018). The arresting officer's deviation from those terms will render the arrestee's detention unconstitutional under the general Fourth Amendment principle that "because a warrant generally authorizes no more than what it expressly provides, to act unreasonably beyond the terms of a warrant is akin to acting without a warrant at all" (*id.*). *Cf.* § 25.17.7 penultimate paragraph *infra. And see Arizmendi v. Gabbert,* 919 F.3d 891, 901 (5th Cir. 2019) (dictum) ("*Vance* [*v. Nunnery,* 137 F.3d 270 (5th Cir. 1988)] rejected the possibility that an officer could arrest someone based on a warrant and then, on its challenge, retroactively justify his conduct by arguing that he had probable cause to arrest the person without a warrant for a different offense").

The practical value of challenging arrest warrants has been drastically curtailed by the holdings in *United States v. Leon,* 468 U.S. 897 (1984), and *Massachusetts v. Sheppard,* 468 U.S. 981 (1984), that the exclusionary rule does not apply to evidence obtained through police actions taken in "good faith" reliance upon an apparently valid warrant issued as a consequence of a magistrate's erroneous finding of probable cause. For discussion of this complicated subject, see §§ 25.17 – 25.17.1, 25.17.3 – 25.17.5 *infra*.

25.7.3. *Arrests Without a Warrant: The Basic Authorizations for Warrantless Arrest*

In most jurisdictions the requirements for a warrantless arrest depend upon whether the underlying crime is a felony or a misdemeanor.

(A) If the underlying crime is a felony, a warrantless arrest can be made whenever the arresting officer (or the officer who ordered or requested the arrest) was in possession of facts providing probable cause to believe that the crime was committed and that the person to be arrested had committed it. *Maryland v. Pringle,* 540 U.S. 366, 370 (2003); *United States v.*

Watson, 423 U.S. 411 (1976); *United States v. Santana,* 427 U.S. 38 (1976); *Michigan v. DeFillippo,* 443 U.S. 31, 36 (1979). This is the ubiquitous state-law rule and is also the rule of the Fourth Amendment.

(B) If the underlying crime is a misdemeanor, the rule in most jurisdictions is that a warrantless arrest can be made only when the offense was committed in the presence of the arresting officer. *See, e.g., State v. Amstutz,* 169 Idaho 144, 146-47, 492 P.3d 1103, 1105-06 (2021); *Juliano v. State,* 260 A.3d 619, 628, 632 (Del. 2021); *Roseborough v. Commonwealth,* 281 Va. 233, 704 S.E.2d 414 (2011); *cf. People v. Hammerlund,* 504 Mich. 442, 939 N.W.2d 129 (2019) (anticipating *Lange v. California,* 141 S. Ct. 2011 (2021), summarized in § 25.20 *infra,* in holding that when an officer has personal knowledge of all of the elements of a minor misdemeanor, it is unreasonable, and a violation of the Fourth Amendment, to arrest an individual in his or her home for such an offense); *and see Atwater v. City of Lago Vista,* 532 U.S. 318, 355-60 (2001) ("Appendix to Opinion of the Court," listing and quoting state statutes). The Supreme Court has explicitly reserved the question "whether the Fourth Amendment [also] entails an 'in the presence' requirement for purposes of misdemeanor arrests" (*see id.* at 341 n. 11, citing, with a "*cf.*" signal, Justice White's statement in a dissent in *Welsh v. Wisconsin,* 466 U.S. 740, 756 (1984), that the "'requirement that a misdemeanor must have occurred in the officer's presence to justify a warrantless arrest is not grounded in the Fourth Amendment'"). The answer to that question is important because "violations of state arrest law" are not necessarily "also violations of the Fourth Amendment" (*Virginia v. Moore,* 553 U.S. 164, 173 (2008)). See § 25.7.1 *supra.*

(1) Counsel contending that the Fourth Amendment does embody the majority state-law rule limiting misdemeanor arrests to offenses committed in the presence of the arresting officer can point to passages in a number of Supreme Court opinions which treat that proposition as axiomatic. *See Virginia v. Moore, supra,* 553 U.S. at 171 ("In a long line of cases, we have said that when an officer has probable cause to believe a person committed even a minor crime in his presence, . . . [t]he arrest is constitutionally reasonable."); *id.* at 178 ("When officers have probable cause to believe that a person has committed a crime in their presence, the Fourth Amendment permits them to make an arrest"); *Maryland v. Pringle,* 540 U.S. 366, 370 (2003) ("A warrantless arrest of an individual in a public place for a felony, or a misdemeanor committed in the officer's presence, is consistent with the Fourth Amendment if the arrest is supported by probable cause."); *Atwater v. City of Lago Vista, supra,* 532 U.S. at 354 ("[i]f an officer has probable cause to believe that an individual has committed even a very minor criminal offense in his presence, he may, without violating the Fourth Amendment, arrest the offender.").

(2) The argument for a "presence" requirement also has strong historical support. Most of the common-law authorities extensively canvassed in the *Atwater* opinion, 532 U.S. at 326-43, condition an officer's arrest power in misdemeanor cases upon the circumstance that the misdemeanor was "committed in the presence of the arresting officer" (JACOB W. LANDYNSKI, SEARCH AND SEIZURE AND THE SUPREME COURT – A STUDY IN CONSTITUTIONAL INTERPRETATION 45 (Johns Hopkins University Studies in Historical and Political Science, Ser. 84, No. 1, 1966), quoted in *Atwater, supra,* 532 U.S. at 336; *and see* the earlier American commentaries cited in *id.* at 343) or "committed in his view" (see the English treatises quoted in

Atwater, supra, 532 U.S. at 330-31), or that the offender was found or "taken in the very act" (*Money v. Leach*, 3 Burr. 1742, 1766, 97 Eng. Rep. 1075, 1088 (K.B.1765), quoted in *Atwater, supra*, 532 U.S. at 332 n.6).

(3) Pre-*Atwater* decisions of the federal courts of appeals in several Circuits had rejected the "presence" requirement as a Fourth Amendment precondition for valid arrest upon probable cause, and it is unclear to what extent *Atwater* will spark a reconsideration of those precedents. *See, e.g., United States v. Laville*, 480 F.3d 187, 191-94 (3d Cir. 2007); *United States v. Dawson*, 305 Fed. Appx. 149, 160 n.9 (4th Cir. 2008); *United States v. McNeill*, 484 F.3d 301, 311 (4th Cir. 2007); *Rockwell v. Brown*, 664 F.3d 985, 996 (5th Cir. 2011); *Hall v. Hughes*, 232 Fed. Appx. 683, 684-85 (9th Cir. 2007); *Graves v. Mahoning County*, 821 F.3d 772 (6th Cir. 2016) ("[I]t's an open question at the Supreme Court . . . 'whether the Fourth Amendment' requires officers to get a warrant 'for purposes of misdemeanor arrests' committed '[outside] the[ir] presence.' *Atwater* . . . . ¶ But it's not an open question at our court. The 'requirement that a misdemeanor must have occurred in the officer's presence to justify a warrantless arrest,' we have explained, 'is not mandated by the Fourth Amendment.' . . . This may be why the plaintiffs don't mention the issue in their appellate brief or for that matter distinguish the rules for misdemeanor and felony arrests. ¶ Other circuits agree with our approach." 821 F.3d at 778. "All the while, though, no court has devoted much more than a line or two to this issue. ¶ There are, to be sure, some sound reasons for our court's position . . . ." *Id.* at 779. "But there are valid competing arguments that deserve to be addressed at some point. The common law, most sources say, prohibited an officer from 'mak[ing] a [warrantless] arrest for a misdemeanor [unless] the crime was committed in his presence.' . . . What was reasonable at common law often tells us what is reasonable under the Fourth Amendment. It 'sheds light on the obviously relevant, if not entirely dispositive,' meaning of 'reasonable.'" *Id.* at 779-80. "Some state courts, following this logic, have constitutionalized the common law rule. They have held that statutes that 'authorize[ ] an arrest, without a warrant, for a misdemeanor not committed in the presence of the officer making the arrest' are unconstitutional . . . . ¶ With sound arguments on each side, it's no wonder that the Court has left the question open, even while deciding related questions about warrantless arrests. . . . And it's no wonder that some judges have flagged the issue. . . . Today, however, is not the day to address it." *Id.* at 780.); *United States v. Barajas*, 517 F. Supp. 3d 1008, 1021 (N.D. Cal. 2021) ("[t]he Sixth Circuit's recent opinion in *Graves* . . . appears to be the most in depth analysis on this issue to date"); *Veatch v. Bartels Lutheran Home*, 627 F.3d 1254, 1258 (8th Cir. 2010) ("[T]he Supreme Court has not decided whether the Fourth Amendment permits a warrantless arrest for a misdemeanor when the alleged offense did not occur in the presence of the arresting officer. *See Atwater* . . . . Although the weight of authority holds that the Fourth Amendment does not impose an 'in the presence' requirement of this type, . . . this circuit has not decided the point, . . . and we need not address the issue in this case."). Pending Supreme Court resolution of the issue, counsel should press the claim, when relevant, that the Fourth Amendment does prohibit misdemeanor arrests for offenses of which the arresting officer has no personal, observational knowledge, so that s/he is relying solely on third parties for the information necessary to establish probable cause.

(C) If the arrest is for a mental health evaluation, probable cause is required. *Graham v. Barnette*, 5 F.4th 872, 886 (8th Cir. 2021) ("[W]e now make explicit that which has long been implicit in our case law and align our circuit with the unanimous consensus in all other circuits.

We conclude that only probable cause that a person poses an emergent danger – that is, one calling for prompt action – to herself or others can tip the scales of the Fourth Amendment's reasonableness balancing test in favor of the government when it arrests an individual for a mental-health evaluation because only probable cause constitutes a sufficient 'governmental interest' to outweigh a person's 'interest in freedom.'").

25.7.4. *The Probable Cause Requirement for Arrest*

As indicated in the preceding two sections, a showing of "probable cause" is the minimum precondition for a valid arrest, with or without a warrant.

Much of the law of the Fourth Amendment is concerned with the concept of "probable cause." Not only arrest warrants but also search warrants are issued upon a magistrate's or a judge's finding of probable cause; not only warrantless arrests but also many types of warrantless searches depend upon the officer's possession of probable cause. Whether the issue is the validity of an arrest or a search, the constitutional phrase *probable cause* means "'a reasonable ground for belief'" (*Brinegar v. United States,* 338 U.S. 160, 175 (1949)). "Probable cause exists where 'the facts and circumstances within . . . [the officers'] knowledge and of which they had reasonably trustworthy information [are] sufficient in themselves to warrant a man of reasonable caution in the [requisite] belief . . . .'" *Id.* at 175-76. *Accord, Florida v. Harris*, 568 U.S. 237, 243-44 (2013) ("A police officer has probable cause to conduct a search when 'the facts available to [him] would "warrant a [person] of reasonable caution in the belief"' that contraband or evidence of a crime is present. . . . The test for probable cause is not reducible to 'precise definition or quantification.' . . . All we have required is the kind of 'fair probability' on which 'reasonable and prudent [people,] not legal technicians, act.'"); *Safford Unified School District # 1 v. Redding*, 557 U.S. 364, 371 (2009) ("a 'fair probability' . . . or a 'substantial chance'"); *District of Columbia v. Wesby*, 138 S. Ct. 577, 586 (2018); *Maryland v. Pringle, supra*, 540 U.S. at 370-71; *Wong Sun v. United States,* 371 U.S. 471, 479 (1963); *Braun v. Village of Palatine*, 56 F.4th 542, 545, 549 (7th Cir. 2022) (finding probable cause to arrest a driver for DWI after his car crashed into a telephone pole: although he passed a breathalyzer test, he failed other standard field sobriety tests; he had slurred speech, bloodshot and glassy eyes, and difficulty balancing; he told the arresting officer that "he lived in 'Chicago-Miami'"; he acknowledged drinking a beer earlier in the evening; he did not inform the officer that he was subject to seizures – which, in retrospect, likely explained both the accident and the symptoms of intoxication; "probable cause [was not] eliminated because an innocent explanation for the crash and Braun's behavior emerged later"). *Cf. Carpenter v. United States*, 138 S. Ct. 2206, 2221 (2018) (holding that a showing of "'reasonable grounds' for believing that . . . records were 'relevant and material to an ongoing investigation . . .' . . . [fell] well short of the probable cause required for a warrant" because "[t]he Court usually requires 'some quantum of individualized suspicion' before a search or seizure may take place"). *See, e.g., Bickford v. Hensley*, 832 Fed. Appx. 549, 554-55 (10th Cir. 2020) (a Facebook message asserting that one "Chaz" was in possession of marijuana did not establish probable cause for Bickford's arrest: "First, the Facebook message between third-parties constitutes hearsay. Although the fact that hearsay evidence would be inadmissible at trial 'does not make it unusable as a source of probable cause for a warrantless arrest,' . . . longstanding legal principles generally consider hearsay statements to be inherently unreliable. . . . Second, the Facebook message did not mention . . . [Bickford] by name, but merely referred to someone named 'Chaz,' who Deputy Hensley *thinks* is . . . [Bickford]. The lack of specific identification of . . . [Bickford] in an uncorroborated conversation that did not even involve . . . [Bickford] further undermines the ability of the message to establish probable cause of any offense."). "The 'totality of the circumstances'" known to the officer must be considered (*District of Columbia v. Wesby*, 138 S. Ct. at 588); *Johnson v. City of Minneapolis*, 901 F.3d 963 (8th Cir. 2018); *Gilliam v. Sealey*, 932 F.3d 216, 234 (4th Cir. 2019) ("In making . . .[the probable-cause] inquiry, we consider only the information the officers had at the time of the arrest. . . . ¶ . . . A coerced or fabricated confession that police know to be coerced – . . . based on the use of coercive interrogation tactics, the age and intellectual disabilities of . . . [suspects] and the inconsistencies between the confessions and the crime scene – does not give police probable cause to arrest the suspect as a matter of law."); *Ouza v. City of Dearborn Heights, Michigan*, 969 F.3d 265, 282 (6th Cir. 2020) (a police officer investigated a domestic dispute and concluded that an ex-husband had assaulted his wife; responding to a second call shortly after the first, the officer was met by the husband outside the residence and told by the husband that the wife had assaulted him; the wife and a daughter disputed this, but the officer arrested the wife; these facts permitted a finding of lack of probable cause: "a person has a right to be free from arrest based solely on an eyewitness account that is in some way untruthful or unreliable."); *Nichols v. Macias*, 695 Fed. Appx. 291 (9th Cir. 2017) ("if 'specific intent is a required element of the offense, the arresting officer must have probable cause for that element in order to reasonably believe that a crime has occurred'"); *Rieves v. Town of Smyrna, Tennessee*, 959 F.3d 678, 696 (6th Cir. 2020) (the actions of two prosecutors in pressing the police to make arrests of the proprietors of stores selling legal cannabidiol products "were objectively unreasonable because their probable cause determinations rested on the inconclusive results in . . . [laboratory] reports. It is unreasonable to submit an innocuous product to a lab test that is incapable of determining its legality, then rely on that inconclusive evidence to say that the substance was probably illegal."); *Nichols v. City of Riverside*, 775 Fed. Appx. 845, at 845 (9th Cir. 2019) ("the existence of a dispute over the amount of a bill or the right to possess are civil in nature and ordinarily do not give rise to probable cause to arrest"); *Reynaga Hernandez v. Skinner*, 969 F.3d 930, 938 (9th Cir. 2020) (a deputy sheriff "conducted a Terry stop when he confronted . . . [a Mexican national] outside the courtroom [in which a witness had testified that the suspect was an illegal alien], asked him questions regarding his immigration status, and requested identification"; "The parties agree that at the time . . . [the deputy] conducted the stop, the only relevant information available to . . . [him] was . . . [a] statement [by the presiding judge] that he had heard sworn testimony that . . . [the suspect] was 'not a legal citizen.'"; this information was inadequate to provide "reasonable suspicion or probable cause to conduct the stop and [a subsequent] arrest, respectively": "Unlike illegal *entry* into the United States – which is a crime under 8 U.S.C. § 1325 – illegal *presence* is not a crime.")); *Friend v. Gasparino*, 61 F.4th 77 (2d Cir. 2023), summarized in § 25.11.2 *infra* (there is no probable cause for arrest when the arrestee's conduct is, as a matter of law, beyond the reach of the statute that purportedly underlies the arrest); *Gorsky v. Guajardo*, 2023 WL 3690429 (5th Cir. 2023) (an arrest for interfering with a police officer's investigation would lack probable cause if it was based on the arrestee's refusal of the officer's demand to bring the arrestee's wife out of their home to talk with the officer; interfering with a police officer in the performance of his or her duties requires active obstruction, not mere failure to obey the officer's commands); *Duncan v. City of Sandy Springs*, 2023 WL 3862579 (11th Cir. 2023). Specifically, probable cause to *arrest* is established when there are reasonable grounds to believe that the particular person sought to be arrested has committed a crime; probable cause for a *search* is established when there are reasonable grounds to believe that objects connected to criminal activity or otherwise subject to seizure are presently located in the particular place to be searched. *Zurcher v. Stanford Daily,* 436 U.S. 547, 556-57 n.6 (1978); *Steagald v. United States,* 451 U.S. 204, 213 (1981); *Safford Unified School District # 1 v. Redding, supra,* 554 U.S. at 370; *State v. Thompson,* 419 S.C. 250, 797 S.E.2d 716 (2017). There are elaborate definitions of the concept of probable cause (*e.g., Gerstein v. Pugh,* 420 U.S. 103, 111-12 (1975); *Dunaway v. New York,* 442 U.S. 200, 208 n.9 (1979)), and innumerable constructions of it in individual factual situations.

The topic of probable cause for the issuance of warrants will be taken up in discussing search warrants. See § 25.17 *infra.* With respect to warrantless arrests, the probable cause requirement must be "strictly enforced" (*Henry v. United States,* 361 U.S. 98, 102 (1959)) because "the informed and deliberate determinations of magistrates empowered to issue warrants as to what searches and seizures are permissible under the Constitution are to be preferred over the hurried action of officers and others . . . while acting under the excitement that attends the capture of persons accused of crime" (*United States v. Lefkowitz,* 285 U.S. 452, 464 (1932)).

> "The point of the Fourth Amendment, which often is not grasped by zealous officers, is not that it denies law enforcement the support of the usual inferences which reasonable men draw from evidence. Its protection consists in requiring that those inferences be drawn by a neutral and detached magistrate instead of being judged by the officer engaged in the often competitive enterprise of ferreting out crime. Any assumption that evidence sufficient to support a magistrate's disinterested determination to issue a search warrant will justify the officers in making a search without a warrant would reduce the Amendment to a nullity and leave the people's homes secure only in the discretion of police officers. . . . When the right of privacy must reasonably yield to the right of search is, as a rule, to be decided by a judicial officer, not by a policeman or Government enforcement agent." (*Johnson v. United States,* 333 U.S. 10, 13-14 (1948).)

Accord, United States v. Watson, 423 U.S. 411, 432 n.6 (1976) (Powell, J., concurring) (emphasizing the Court's "longstanding position that . . . [such a warrantless arrest] should receive careful judicial scrutiny").

In determining whether the police had probable cause to arrest, the central question is what facts the police knew before the arrest. *See, e.g., Michael v. Trevena,* 899 F.3d 528 (8th Cir. 2018). "[A]n arrest is not justified by what the subsequent search discloses." *Henry v. United States, supra,* 361 U.S. at 104. *See also Maryland v. Pringle, supra,* 540 U.S. at 371 ("To determine whether an officer had probable cause to arrest an individual, we examine the events leading up to the arrest, and then decide 'whether these historical facts, viewed from the standpoint of an objectively reasonable police officer, amount to' probable cause"); *Florida v. Harris,* 568 U.S. 237, 249 (2013) ("we do not evaluate probable cause in hindsight, based on what a search does or does not turn up"); *cf. Wright v. City of Euclid,* 962 F.3d 852, 873-74 (6th Cir. 2020) (an officer "conceded that he did not have probable cause to arrest Wright until he started 'resisting.' This puts the cart before the horse. When an underlying arrest is for resisting arrest and nothing more, 'the officers could not, as a matter of law, have probable cause to arrest [Wright] where the underlying arrest was not lawful.'"); and see § 25.3 penultimate paragraph *supra*. "If probable cause is established at any early stage of the investigation, it may be dissipated if the investigating officer later learns additional information that decreases the likelihood that the defendant has engaged, or is engaging, in criminal activity. A person may not be arrested, or must be released from arrest, if previously established probable cause has dissipated. 'As a corollary . . . of the rule that the police may rely on the totality of facts available to them in establishing probable cause, they also may not disregard facts tending to dissipate probable cause.'" *United States v. Ortiz-Hernandez*, 427 F.3d 567, 574 (9th Cir. 2005); *accord, Hicks v. Ferreyra*, 64 F.4th 156, 170 (4th Cir. 2023) ("The jury's findings in the special interrogatories, which the officers do not challenge, make plain the officers' violation of Hicks's Fourth Amendment rights. The . . . [vehicle] stop began when Officer Ferreyra conducted a 'welfare check' on the well-being of the driver, Hicks, in a car parked on the side of a highway. Even if we assume that Officer Ferreyra's observation of the gun on the front passenger seat gave rise to an objectively reasonable suspicion of criminal activity, that justification ceased when Ferreyra confirmed that Hicks, as a Secret Service agent, was authorized to carry a firearm. . . . Moreover, as the jury found, the . . . [U.S. Park Police] did not have a customary practice that a supervisor come to the scene before an officer could release an individual who had displayed a weapon. Thus, the prolonged first detention of nearly an hour after any justification ceased plainly violated Hicks's Fourth Amendment right to be free from unreasonable seizures."); *Nicholson v. Guttierrez*, 935 F.3d 685 (9th Cir. 2019); *Barnett v. MacArthur*, 956 F.3d 1291 (11th Cir. 2020); *United States v. Brinkley*, 980 F.3d 377, 387 (4th Cir. 2020). *See also Haynes v. Minnehan*, 14 F.4th 830, 836 (8th Cir. 2021), summarized in the last paragraph of this section (saying, in a *Terry*-stop context, that "as new information flows in, a reasonable belief can dissolve into an unreasonable one"); *Sanders v. Jones*, 728 Fed. Appx. 563, 566 (6th Cir. 2018) (holding, in the context of a Fourth Amendment malicious prosecution action, that the probable cause provided by a confidential informant's identification of Sanders as the individual who sold him drugs would be dissipated if the police officer who received the informant's report subsequently viewed a videotape of the controlled drug buy and "knew or strongly suspected from viewing the video that the person who sold the confidential informant the drugs was not Sanders"); *cf. Neal v. Ficcadenti*, 895 F.3d 576, 581 (8th Cir. 2018) (saying, in the context of an excessive-force claim, that "a reasonable officer is not permitted to ignore changing circumstances and information that emerges once arriving on scene"); *Harris v. Klare*, 902 F.3d 630 (6th Cir. 2018), summarized in § 25.39 subdivision (d) *infra*. "[I]n determining whether there is probable cause, officers are charged with knowledge of any 'readily available exculpatory evidence' that they unreasonably fail to ascertain. . . . '[T]he probable cause standard of the Fourth Amendment requires officers to reasonably interview witnesses readily available at the scene, investigate basic evidence, or otherwise inquire if a crime has been committed at all before invoking the power of warrantless arrest and detention.'" *Mareska v. Bernalillo County*, 804 F.3d 1301, 1310 (10th Cir. 2015); *accord, Harris v. City of Saginaw*, 62 F.4th 1028 (6th Cir. 2023) (sustaining a claim that Harris was arrested without probable cause: "The Officers were required to 'consider the totality of the circumstances, recognizing both the inculpatory *and exculpatory* evidence, before determining if [they have] probable cause to make an arrest.'" *Id*. at 1034. "[O]fficers cannot ignore these facts and circumstances to insulate themselves: It is clearly established that probable cause is lacking when officers effect 'hasty, unsubstantiated arrests' without investigation." *Id*. at 1033. "The Officers generally assert that they had probable cause for Harris's arrest based on the . . . statements [of an individual whom Harris had accused of pointing a gun at him], Harris's inconsistent stories, and the security footage. But their assertions are belied by evidence that the Officers had seemingly made up their minds prior to speaking to the clerks, viewing the security footage, or hearing Harris's later clarifications. A reasonable jury could conclude as much, finding that the Officers merely sought out whatever would support their decision after Harris's initial description. In other words, a reasonable jury could conclude that . . . the . . . officers were 'simply turn[ing] a blind eye toward potentially exculpatory evidence' in order to arrest Harris." *Id.* at 1034). *See, e.g., Ross v. City of Jackson, Missouri,* 897 F.3d 916, 922 (8th Cir. 2018) (holding that a claim of arrest without probable cause was sustainable when a suspect was arrested based on an ambiguous facebook comment regarding weapons: "In this case, even a 'minimal further investigation' would have revealed that Ross's post was not a true threat. . . . The officers conducted no investigation into the context of the statement, Ross's history of violence, or Ross's political beliefs about gun ownership or gun control measures. . . . Ross tried to explain what was meant by his comment and provide the officers with more context about the post, but the officers did not give him that opportunity until after he was booked at the police station."); *Sital v. City of New York,* 60 A.D.3d 465, 466, 875 N.Y.S.2d 22, 23 (N.Y. App. Div., 1st Dep't 2009) ("Regarding the false arrest cause of action, the evidence demonstrates that a rational jury could have found that there was no probable cause for plaintiff's arrest because the accusation from an identified citizen, which was the sole basis for the arrest, was not sufficiently reliable, given that the investigating officer had doubts about the witness's credibility . . . . The identification of plaintiff was also arguably contradicted by physical evidence from the crime scene that was consistent with a conflicting statement of an independent eyewitness, and the jury heard testimony showing that the investigating officer recognized plaintiff based on a prior arrest, at which time he had referred to plaintiff as 'an animal.' Under these circumstances, a rational jury could have determined that the officer's failure to make further inquiry of potential eyewitnesses was unreasonable under the circumstances, and evidenced a lack of probable cause . . . ."); *Abercrombie v. Bean,* 728 Fed. Appx. 918, 926 (11th Cir. 2018) ("Abercrombie has offered evidence that Beam 'elect[ed] not to obtain easily discoverable facts, such as . . . whether witnesses were available to attest to' what occurred during the incident. . . . ¶ Not only that, but . . . Beam's actions could be construed as preventing Abercrombie, Bryant, and Diamond from offering information relevant to the investigation. . . . Beam . . . refused to tell Abercrombie why he was being arrested and instead 'just told [him] to shut up.' As for Bryant, Beam likewise told her to 'shut up' if she did not want to be arrested . . . In light of evidence that Beam not only failed to interview available witnesses but also actively dissuaded some of them from talking to him, we must conclude that a triable issue exists as to whether Beam conducted an objectively reasonable and unbiased investigation into the alleged assault."); *Greve v. Bass,* 805 Fed. Appx. 336, 346 (6th Cir. 2020) ("[E]ven if we assume that Bass had reasonable suspicion to detain Greve initially, he never investigated at all the potentially exculpatory evidence or explanation that Greve had explicitly called to his attention, so that suspicion could not mature into probable cause for arrest."); *Humbert v. Mayor and City Council of Baltimore City,* 866 F.3d 546 (4th Cir. 2017) ("Trial testimony indicates that Humbert closely matched a generic physical description [which a rape victim gave of her assailant] – a 5'7", African-American male in his late 30s to early 40s who was fairly well-spoken – and a generic looking composite sketch of an African-American male. Humbert was also stopped *eight days* after the assault in the Charles Village neighborhood, [a location that was within blocks of the victim's home where the rape occurred but was also] near . . . [Humbert's] homeless shelter and a couple of miles away from where his family members resided. These facts cannot reasonably support the probable cause needed for his arrest." *Id.* at 559. "[T]he

Officers can find no solace in the victim's so-called tentative identification, as the evidence demonstrates that the Officers improperly influenced the investigation from its inception. Jones asked the victim multiple times whether her assailant was homeless, and it is undisputed that Humbert was homeless at the time he was stopped. Jones also showed the victim Humbert's picture and identified him as her attacker a day after the assault occurred, either during or after she completed the composite sketch and only a few days before she saw his photo in the photobook. Again, drawing all reasonable inferences in Humbert's favor, the evidence indicates that Jones inappropriately affected the victim's ability to complete the composite sketch and identify her attacker. Such suggestive acts unquestionably nullified the Officers' ability to rely on the victim's initial reaction to Humbert's photo." *Id.* at 560.). *And see Hurt v. Wise*, 880 F.3d 831 (7th Cir. 2018), *partially overruled on an unrelated point in Lewis v. City of Chicago*, 914 F.3d 472, 475 & n.1, 478-79 (7th Cir. 2019) (arrestees stated a Fourth Amendment false-arrest claim when their arrests rested upon confessions "replete with easily verified and contemporaneous evidence of inaccuracy and unreliability" (*id.* at 837); the arresting officers "insist that there was at least arguable probable cause to arrest . . . based on . . . [the] 'confessions' because neither of those confessions was coerced. . . . [T]his argument is misplaced with respect to a Fourth Amendment false-arrest claim. Reliability, not coercion, is the gravamen of probable cause." (*Id.* at 841.)); *Dean v. Searcy*, 893 F.3d 504 (8th Cir. 2018) (affirming liability for claims of arrest and imprisonment resulting from a reckless investigation, manufactured false evidence, and coerced confessions). For discussion of some of the factors commonly considered by the courts in assessing whether there was probable cause, see § 25.11 *infra*.

When an arrest is made (with or without a warrant) upon probable cause to believe that a particular individual has committed an offense but the police arrest the wrong individual, their arrest is nonetheless legal if (i) they honestly believe that the person arrested is the individual sought and (ii) they have probable cause for this belief. *Hill v. California,* 401 U.S. 797 (1971). *Cf. Garcia v. City of Riverside*, 817 F.3d 635, 641 (9th Cir. 2016) ("Whether . . . [the police] had to investigate in the face of . . . [an arrested individual's] protests and complaints that he wasn't the person described in the outstanding warrant is an important question. No person deserves to be incarcerated without good reason, and incarceration on a warrant without a reasonable investigation of identity, when the circumstances demand it, is subject to review under the Due Process Clause. The issue is whether LASD's treatment of Plaintiff's contention that he was not the warrant subject was so superficial, under the circumstances, that it ignored a duty to investigate and offended due process. ¶ . . . [T]he warrant . . . matched only his first and last name and date of birth. Garcia is nine inches taller and forty pounds heavier than the warrant subject. Even a cursory comparison of Garcia to the warrant subject should have led officers to question whether the person described in the warrant was Garcia. Information that raised questions about Garcia's identity should have prompted the LASD to investigate more deliberately."); *Cozzi v. City of Birmingham*, 892 F.3d 1288, 1297 (11th Cir. 2018) ("We need not decide whether the evidence Thomas possessed – the statements of two tipsters that Cozzi resembled the perpetrator shown in the *Crime Stoppers* video, confirmation that the informant had accurately provided Cozzi's address and a description of his vehicle, and a plastic bag with 32 pills found inside Cozzi's home – was sufficient to establish arguable probable cause because we must also consider the information tending to exculpate Cozzi that was available to Thomas when he made the arrest. Thomas had been told the readily verifiable exculpatory fact that the perpetrator's multiple tattoos did not match Cozzi's single tattoo. And setting aside the 32 pills we have already discussed, the search of his residence had failed to turn up even arguable evidence of the robberies. . . . ¶ Despite having been given plainly exculpatory and easily verifiable information, Thomas did not look at Cozzi's tattoo before arresting him. Under our precedent, this failure was unreasonable.").

Fourth Amendment restrictions on the amount of physical force that can be used to effect an arrest or other seizure are the subject of a body of case law emanating from *Tennessee v. Garner*, 471 U.S. 1 (1985), and *Graham v. Connor*, 490 U.S. 386 (1989). *See, e.g., Kisela v. Hughes*, 138 S. Ct. 1148, 1152 (2018); *County of Los Angeles v. Mendez*, 581 U.S. 420, 427-28 (2017); *White v. Pauly*, 580 U.S. 73, 79-80 (2017) (per curiam), *explicated on remand in Pauly v. White*, 874 F.3d 1197 (10th Cir. 2017); *Plumhoff v. Rickard*, 572 U.S. 765 (2014); *Tolan v. Cotton*, 572 U.S. 650 (2014); *Mullenix v. Luna*, 577 U.S. 7, 12-15 (2015) (per curiam); *Franklin v. City of Charlotte*, 64 F.4th 519, 530 (4th Cir. 2023) ("'[a]ll claims that law enforcement officers have used excessive force – deadly or not – in the course of an arrest, investigatory stop, or other "seizure" of a free citizen should be analyzed under the Fourth Amendment and its "reasonableness" standard'"); *Franco v. Gunsalus*, 2023 WL 3590102, at *3 (2d Cir. 2023) ("We have held that a police officer violates a clearly established Fourth Amendment right when he 'use[s] significant force against an arrestee who is no longer resisting and poses no threat to the safety of officers or others.'"); *Shumate v. City of Adrian, Michigan*, 44 F.4th 427 (6th Cir. 2022) (exhaustively analyzing "the three *Graham* factors" (*id.* at 440) used to determine whether police use of force is reasonable – "(1) the severity of the crime at issue; (2) whether the suspect posed an immediate threat to the officer or others; and (3) whether the suspect was actively resisting arrest or attempting to evade arrest by flight" (*id.*), the Sixth Circuit finds that a police officer employed excessive force by tasing, beating and kneeing an individual who insulted him, cursed at him, and then backed away when the officer tried to handcuff him); *Cobbins v. Sollie*, 2023 WL 4015303, at *6 (5th Cir. 2023) ("precedent makes it clear to all reasonable officers that tasing a subject who is suspected of no more than a misdemeanor, is pinned to the ground, is surrounded by law enforcement officers and unable to escape, is unarmed, and is offering no more than passive resistance, amounts to excessive force in violation of the Fourth Amendment"); *Tenorio v. Pitzer*, 802 F.3d 1160, 1164 (10th Cir. 2015) ("The Fourth Amendment permits an officer to use deadly force only if there is 'probable cause to believe that there [is] a *threat of serious physical harm to [the officer]* or to others'"); *Callahan v. Wilson*, 863 F.3d 144, 149 (2d Cir. 2017) ("'the use of force highly likely to have deadly effects is unreasonable unless the officer had probable cause to believe that the suspect posed a significant threat of death or serious physical injury to the officer or to others'"); *Harris v. Pittman*, 927 F.3d 266, 268-69 (4th Cir. 2019) ("even where an initial use of deadly force is reasonable, the repeated use of force may be constitutionally excessive if circumstances change in a material way"); *Longoria v. Pinal County*, 873 F.3d 699, 705 (9th Cir. 2017) ("[t]he 'most important' factor is whether . . . [the suspect] posed an *immediate* threat"); *Lewis v. Charter Township of Flint*, 660 Fed. Appx. 339, 343 (6th Cir. 2016) ("It has long been established that '[t]he use of deadly force to prevent the escape of all felony suspects, whatever the circumstances, is constitutionally unreasonable.' . . . Where a person attempts to flee in a vehicle, 'police officers are "justified in using deadly force against a driver who objectively appears ready to drive into an officer or bystander with his car,' but 'may not use deadly force once the car moves away, leaving the officer and bystanders in a position of safety.'"'"); *accord, Williams v. Strickland*, 917

F.3d 763 (4th Cir. 2019); *Edwards v. Oliver*, 31 F.4th 925 (5th Cir. 2022); *Newmaker v. City of Fortuna*, 842 F.3d 1108, 1116 (9th Cir. 2016) ("Excessive force claims are analyzed under a Fourth Amendment reasonableness inquiry. . . . In conducting this analysis, a court must balance the severity of the intrusion on the individual's Fourth Amendment rights against the government's need to use force."); *Burwell v. Peyton*, 131 F. Supp. 3d 268, 292 (D. Vt. 2015), *aff'd*, 670 Fed. Appx. 734 (2d Cir. 2016) ("'In order to establish that the use of force to effect an arrest was unreasonable and therefore a violation of the Fourth Amendment, . . . [claimants] must establish that the government interests at stake were outweighed by "the nature and quality of the intrusion on [plaintiffs'] Fourth Amendment interests"'"); *accord, E.W. v. Dolgos*, 884 F.3d 172, 176, 179-85 (4th Cir. 2018) (dictum) ("a school resource officer's decision to handcuff a calm, compliant elementary school student for fighting with another student three days prior" constituted excessive force in violation of the Fourth Amendment); *Strickland v. City of Detroit, Michigan*, 995 F.3d 495, 508 (6th Cir. 2021) (confirming that a "right to be free of excessive handcuffing" was clearly established as early as 2014); *Neal v. Ficcadenti*, 895 F.3d 576, 581 (8th Cir. 2018) (a police officer's use of an arm-bar takedown on an unresisting suspect constituted excessive force in violation of the Fourth Amendment); *Richmond v. Badia*, 47 F.4th 1172 (11th Cir. 2022) (a school resource officer used excessive force in violation of the Fourth Amendment when he used an arm-bar takedown to slam a seventh grader to the floor after the boy, arriving at school with his mother, had pushed her away because she had tried to pull off his hoodie); *Michael v. Trevena*, 899 F.3d 528, 533 (8th Cir. 2018) (Michael "was a nonviolent misdemeanant who neither fled nor actively resisted arrest, and posed no threat to the officers or other members of the public. . . . Under these circumstances, it is objectively unreasonable to make an arrest by grabbing the suspect by the throat . . . or using a baton with sufficient force to break the suspect's arm . . . ."); *Rokusek v. Jansen*, 899 F.3d 544 (8th Cir. 2018) (face-first takedown of an unresisting offender constitutes excessive force in violation of the Fourth Amendment); *Rice v. Morehouse*, 989 F.3d 1112 (9th Cir. 2021) (allegations that after a motorist was stopped for a traffic violation several officers pulled him out of his car, tripped him so that he fell to the ground face first, pinned him down, and handcuffed him, causing long-term physical injuries and emotional distress, state a claim of excessive force in violation of the Fourth Amendment); *Andrews v. City of Henderson*, 35 F.4th 710 (9th Cir. 2022) ("A physical tackle that results in severe injury may constitute a significant use of force. . . . ¶ In this case, the detectives forcibly tackled Andrews to the ground with enough force to fracture his hip. The injury resulted in 'excruciating pain' and required two surgeries. Under these circumstances, we conclude that this use of force by the detectives was 'substantial' and, therefore, 'must be justified by the need for the specific level of force employed.'" *Id.* at 716. "Armed robbery is a serious crime that poses an obvious risk of violence, and this factor suggests that the government may have an interest in using force to effect an arrest. . . . But we must consider this fact in the full context that the officers faced, including that Andrews was not engaged in any violent or nonviolent criminal conduct when he was tackled without warning by the detectives. Moreover, taking the evidence in the light most favorable to Andrews, the detectives knew that he was not armed when they tackled him . . . . Thus, the risk of violence attributable to Andrews's suspected crimes was mitigated by the specific circumstances in which the officers chose to act." *Id.* at 716-17. . . . Given this broader context, the nature of Andrews's suspected crime does not establish a strong governmental interest in using significant physical force against him." *Id.* at 717.); *El v. City of Pittsburgh*, 975 F.3d 327 (3d Cir. 2020) (grabbing a suspect by the wrist and neck, slamming him into the wall of building, and taking him to the ground constituted excessive force in violation of the Fourth Amendment although apparently the only damage suffered by the suspect was a contusion to his hip); *Deasey v. Slater*, 789 Fed. Appx. 17 (9th Cir. 2019) (applying asphyxiating pressure to a prone individual by kneeling on his back while hogtying him constituted excessive force in violation of the Fourth Amendment); *Timpa v. Dillard*, 20 F.4th 1020 (5th Cir. 2021) (allegations that officers knelt on the back of a struggling individual for an extended period of time, resulting in his death, stated a claim for violation of the Fourth Amendment: "[t]he risks of asphyxiation in this circumstance should have been familiar to . . . [the officer who applied his body weight for more than fourteen minutes] because he had received training on the use of a prone restraint to control subjects in a state of excited delirium"); *Wright v. City of Euclid, supra* (tasing and pepper spraying the driver of an automobile who initially backs away when approached by visibly armed plainclothes officers but stops the car as soon as one of them displayed a badge constituted excessive force in violation of the Fourth Amendment); *Briceno v. Williams*, 2022 WL 1599254, at *1 (9th Cir. May 20, 2022) ("[p]unching a face-down suspect constitutes significant force"); *State v. White*, 2015-Ohio-492, 142 Ohio St. 3d 277, 280-85, 29 N.E.3d 939, 944-47 (2015); *Wilkins v. City of Tulsa, Oklahoma*, 33 F.4th 1265, 1273 (10th Cir. 2022) (allegations that three police officers pepper-sprayed a man found sleeping in his parked car and whom they arrested for drunk driving stated a viable claim of excessive force in violation of the Fourth Amendment: "In *Graham v. Connor*, the Supreme Court identified three non-exclusive factors to evaluate whether a use of force was excessive: (1) 'the severity of the crime at issue,' (2) 'whether the suspect poses an immediate threat to the safety of the officers or others,' and (3) 'whether he is actively resisting arrest or attempting to evade arrest by flight.' . . . ¶ Under the first factor, a minor offense supports only the use of minimal force."); *and see Haynes v. Minnehan, supra*, 14 F.4th at 835 (upholding a claim of Fourth Amendment violation in connection with a *Terry* stop (see § 25.4.3): "*Terry* analysis examines whether: (1) the stop began lawfully; and (2) the way officers conducted the stop 'was reasonably related in scope to the circumstances which justified the interference in the first place.' . . . ¶ . . . [B]ecause handcuffs constitute 'greater than a de minimus intrusion,' their use 'requires the [officer] to demonstrate that the facts available to the officer would warrant a man of reasonable caution in [believing] that the action taken was appropriate.' . . . In particular, *Terry* 'requires some reasonable belief that the suspect is armed and dangerous or that the restraints are necessary for some other legitimate purpose, evaluated on the facts of each case.' . . . We have already held that handcuffing 'absent any concern for safety' violates the second *Terry* prong."). In some circumstances, violations of these restrictions may require the exclusion of evidence produced by the excessive force. *See Rochin v. California,* 342 U.S. 165 (1952); *cf.* § 25.14 *infra*, discussing *Winston v. Lee*, 470 U.S. 753 (1985), and cognate cases. And counsel will want to investigate and document a client's claims of police use of excessive force in connection with his or her arrest even when that abuse produced no evidentiary consequences: well-founded claims of this sort can be a valuable bargaining chip in plea negotiation (see § 15.12 *supra*); they may sometimes persuade a prosecutor to drop charges against a badly abused client (see § 8.2.3 *supra*); and the client may also want to seek damages in a civil-rights action under 28 U.S.C. § 1343(3) and 42 U.S.C. § 1983 or under state tort law for any injuries s/he suffered.

25.8. Searches Incident to Arrest

25.8.1. The "Search Incident to Arrest" Doctrine

Warrantless searches of an arrested person's clothing and body surfaces are routinely permitted incident to a valid arrest. *United States v. Robinson,* 414 U.S. 218 (1973); *Gustafson v. Florida,* 414 U.S. 260 (1973); *Birchfield v. North Dakota,* 579 U.S. 438, 457-61, 471-73 (2016); *United States v. Chadwick,* 433 U.S. 1, 14 (1977) (dictum). "[A] lawful custodial arrest creates a situation which justifies the contemporaneous search without a warrant of the person arrested and of the immediately surrounding area." *New York v. Belton,* 453 U.S. 454, 457 (1981). The rationale for this exception to the warrant requirement is that "[w]hen a custodial arrest is made, there is always some danger that the person arrested may seek to use a weapon, or that evidence may be concealed or destroyed. To safeguard himself and others, and to prevent the loss of evidence, it has been held reasonable for the arresting officer to conduct a prompt, warrantless 'search of the arrestee's person and the area "within his immediate control" construing that phrase to mean the area from within which he might gain possession of a weapon or destructible evidence.'" (*United States v. Chadwick, supra,* 433 U.S. at 14.) This rationale has crucial implications for the *scope* of the search permitted incident to arrest (see the following paragraphs) but does not require any case-by-case factual showing of a likelihood that any particular arrestee possesses a weapon or destructible evidence. Rather, what has evolved – in the interest of a bright-line rule – is the treatment of a valid arrest as *generically* posing the requisite likelihoods and *categorically* authorizing a search calculated to address them. "The constitutionality of a search incident to an arrest does not depend on whether there is any indication that the person arrested [actually] possesses weapons or evidence. The fact of a lawful arrest, standing alone, authorizes a search." *Michigan v. DeFillippo,* 443 U.S. 31, 35 (1979). *See also Birchfield v. North Dakota, supra,* 579 U.S. at 473 (under "the search-incident-to-arrest exception, . . . [the arresting officer's] authority [to search the arrestee's person] is categorical. It does not depend on an evaluation of the threat to officer safety or the threat of evidence loss in a particular case."); *Illinois v. LaFayette,* 462 U.S. 640, 644-45 (1983) (dictum); *Michigan v. Long,* 463 U.S. 1032, 1048, 1049 & n.14 (1983) (dictum). *But see State v. Conn,* 278 Kan. 387, 391-94, 99 P.3d 1108, 1112-13 (2003) ("In Kansas, the permissible circumstances, purposes, and scope of a search incident to arrest are controlled by statute." Because the statute authorizing search incident to arrest states the permissible "purpose" of such a search as being "'(a) Protecting the officer from attack'"; "'(b) Preventing the person from escaping'"; or "'(c) Discovering the fruits, instrumentalities, or evidence of the crime'" . . . this court rejected the view that case law applying the Fourth Amendment . . . meant that a search of an automobile could automatically be conducted when an occupant was arrested." Because "the trooper in this case did not indicate any concern for safety," "the search cannot be justified as a search incident to arrest."). A search incident to arrest may be made either at the site of the arrest (*United States v. Robinson, supra,* 414 U.S. at 224-26, 236), or at the stationhouse to which the arrested person is taken (*United States v. Edwards,* 415 U.S. 800 (1974)).

The rule's rationales do circumscribe it in two principal ways. First, they preclude the extension of the authority for warrantless search to generic situations that are *not* conceived to be akin to arrests from the standpoint of inciting probable armed resistance or evidence destruction. *See, e.g., Knowles v. Iowa,* 525 U.S. 113, 116-19 (1998) (the rationales of the "search incident to

670

arrest" doctrine do not justify a full search of a vehicle when the police stop a motorist for speeding and issue a citation rather than arresting him); *Virginia v. Moore*, 553 U.S. 164, 176-77 (2008) (reaffirming *Knowles*) (dictum); *Sibron v. New York,* 392 U.S. 40, 67 (1968) ("a search incident to a lawful arrest may not precede the arrest"). Second, searches that are innately too intrusive or too expansive to be justified by concerns about armed resistance or evidence destruction cannot be sustained under the search-incident-to-arrest exception to the warrant requirement. *See, e.g., Riley v. California*, 573 U.S. 373, 401 (2014), discussed further in § 25.8.2 *infra* ("when a cell phone is seized incident to arrest," a search "warrant is generally required before . . . a search" may be made of digital information on the phone); *Commonwealth v. Morales*, 462 Mass. 334, 335, 344, 968 N.E.2d 403, 405, 411-12 (2012) (a search incident to arrest that resulted in exposure of the defendant's buttocks to public view on a public street constituted a "strip search" that violated both the federal and state constitutions). *Cf. Birchfield v. North Dakota, supra*, 579 U.S. at 462-63, 474-76 (holding that a motorist who has been arrested for drunk driving can be compelled to submit to a warrantless breath test to determine his or her intoxication level but cannot be compelled to submit to a blood draw because "[b]lood tests are significantly more intrusive, and their reasonableness must be judged in light of the availability of the less invasive alternative of a breath test" (*id.* at 474)).

"[T]he search-incident-to-arrest rule actually comprises 'two distinct propositions': 'The first is that a search may be made of the *person* of the arrestee by virtue of the lawful arrest. The second is that a search may be made of the area within the control of the arrestee.'" *Id.* at 460. The limits of the latter proposition have been established by a series of Supreme Court decisions whose upshot is that searches incident to arrest are restricted to "the arrestee's person and the area 'within his immediate control' – construing that phrase to mean the area from within which he might gain possession of a weapon [to attack the arresting officer] or destructible evidence" (*Chimel v. California, 395* U.S. 752, 763 (1969)). *See also United States v. Chadwick,* 433 U.S. 1, 14 (1977); *Lo-Ji Sales, Inc. v. New York,* 442 U.S. 319, 326 (1979). "That limitation, which . . . define[s] the boundaries of the exception, ensures that the scope of a search incident to arrest is commensurate with its purposes of protecting arresting officers and safeguarding any evidence of the offense of arrest that an arrestee might conceal or destroy. . . . If there is no possibility that an arrestee could reach into the area that law enforcement officers seek to search, both justifications for the search-incident-to-arrest exception are absent and the rule does not apply." *Arizona v. Gant,* 556 U.S. 332, 339 (2009). Police officers could not, for example, predicate their entry and search of a house on the arrest of a defendant outside the house. *See, e.g., Vale v. Louisiana,* 399 U.S. 30 (1970); *Shipley v. California,* 395 U.S. 818 (1969). *See also Arizona v. Gant, supra*, 556 U.S. at 343-44 (narrowing previous rulings in *New York v. Belton supra*, and *Thornton v. United States*, 541 U.S. 615, 617 (2004), to "hold that the *Chimel* rationale authorizes police to search a vehicle incident to a recent occupant's arrest only when the arrestee is unsecured and within reaching distance of the passenger compartment at the time of the search," but announcing an additional rule, which "does not follow from *Chimel*," to permit a search incident to arrest in certain "circumstances unique to the vehicle context" (see § 25.26 *infra*)).

Within the "wingspan" area defined by *Chimel*, a warrantless search incident to arrest is valid if – but only if – the arrest itself is valid under the doctrines summarized in § 25.7 *supra. See, e.g., Beck v. Ohio,* 379 U.S. 89 (1964).

25.8.2. *Searches of Containers in the Possession of Arrested Persons*

An issue that frequently arises in cases of searches incident to arrest or *Terry* frisks is whether these warrantless search powers extend to a closed container that the defendant is carrying, such as a knapsack or gym bag.

In *United States v. Chadwick,* 433 U.S. 1 (1977), the Court implied that large locked receptacles, such as luggage, may be taken from an arrested person as a matter of routine incident to arrest. But the Court also stated explicitly (although in *dictum*) that containers seized in this manner may not thereafter be *opened* without a warrant based upon probable cause. *Id.* at 14-16 & n.10. *See also Horton v. California,* 496 U.S. 128, 142 n.11 (1990) (dictum); *United States v. Place,* 462 U.S. 696, 701 n.3 (1983) (dictum).

In *New York v. Belton,* 453 U.S. 454 (1981), which the Court later circumscribed in *Arizona v. Gant,* 556 U.S. 332 (2009), the Court appeared to take a contrary position. *Belton* upheld an arresting officer's opening of a zippered pocket in a leather jacket found on the seat of a car following arrest of the car's occupants. In *dictum* the Court in *Belton* stated a very broad rule that the scope of search incident to arrest of a motorist extends to "the contents of any containers found within the passenger compartment" (*Belton, supra,* 453 U.S. at 460), including "luggage, boxes, [and] bags" (*id.* at 460-61 n.4), "whether [the container] . . . is open or closed" (*id.* at 461).

The subsequent opinion in *United States v. Ross,* 456 U.S. 798 (1982), further compounds the confusion. First, the Court in *Ross* gratuitously comments that "[a] container carried at the time of arrest *often* may be searched without a warrant and even without any specific suspicion concerning its contents" (*id.* at 823 (emphasis added)). Second, the Court asserts (in the different context of a *Carroll* vehicle search (see § 25.24 *infra*)), that "a traveler who carries a toothbrush and a few articles of clothing in a paper bag or knotted scarf [may] claim an equal right to conceal his possessions from official inspection as the sophisticated executive with the locked attaché case" (*id.* at 822). The latter observation appears to rule out any distinction between "paper bags, locked trunks, lunch buckets, and orange crates" (*id.*), so far as the Fourth Amendment privacy interests of the respective possessors of these containers is concerned. Within the framework of the search-incident-to-arrest doctrine, the containers might still be distinguished, allowing search of the paper bag and not the trunk, on the ground that the arrestee's ability to seize weapons or destructible evidence from the former is greater. That distinction is, however, difficult to reconcile with the holding of *United States v. Robinson, supra,* 414 U.S. at 235, that "[t]he authority to search the person incident to a lawful custodial arrest, while based upon the need to disarm and to discover evidence, does not depend on what a court may later decide was the probability in a particular arrest situation that weapons or evidence would in fact be found upon the person of the suspect." *Belton* not merely quotes this *Robinson* language but draws from it the conclusion that the power of search incident to arrest encompasses "containers [which are] . . . such that they could hold neither a weapon nor evidence of the criminal conduct for which the suspect was arrested" (453 U.S. at 461). Differences in the accessibility of various containers to the arrestee can hardly be thought decisive of the application of a doctrine that permits search of containers that could not hold a weapon or evidence in the first place. *See Thornton v. United States*, 541 U.S. 615, 623 (2004) (the *Belton* rule does not "depend[ ] on differing estimates of what items were or were not within reach of an arrestee at any particular moment"). So *Belton* rests the search-incident-to-arrest power not upon the risk that the arrestee may grab the contents of the container but upon the concept that a "lawful custodial arrest justifies the infringement of any privacy interest the arrestee may have" in containers within his or her reach (*id.*). But if this is so, the question arises why the search-incident-to-arrest power is restricted to the area within the arrestee's reach, as *Belton* concedes that it is (*id.* at 457-58, 460), and as *Gant* declares unequivocally that it is (*see Arizona v. Gant, supra*, 556 U.S. at 335 ("a vehicle search incident to a recent occupant's arrest" is not constitutionally "authorize[d]" "after the arrestee has been secured and cannot access the interior of the vehicle")). *Chadwick* squarely holds that the privacy interests inhering in "property in the possession of a person arrested in public" (433 U.S. at 14) but outside of his or her reach are *not* dissipated by the fact of a lawful custodial arrest (433 U.S. at 13-16). And it adds that "[u]nlike searches of the person, *United States v. Robinson,* 414 U.S. 218 (1973) . . . , searches of possessions within an arrestee's immediate control cannot be justified by any reduced expectations of privacy caused by the arrest" (433 U.S. at 16 n.10).

This area of Fourth Amendment law was muddied still further when the Court in *California v. Acevedo*, 500 U.S. 565 (1991), revised the rules governing a *Carroll* vehicle search (see § 25.24 *infra*) to eliminate the distinction that *Ross*, in explaining the import of *Chadwick* and *Arkansas v. Sanders*, 442 U.S. 753 (1979), drew between what the police may do when they have probable cause to believe that a seizable object is concealed in a vehicle and what they may do when they have probable cause merely to believe that a seizable object may be contained within some particular receptacle carried in the vehicle. The *Acevedo* decision concerned solely a *Carroll* vehicle search and accordingly did not address the nature and scope of the "search incident to arrest" doctrine.

In *Arizona v. Gant supra*, in 2009, the Court disavowed the lower courts' "broad reading of *Belton*" as authorizing "a vehicle search . . . incident to every arrest of a recent occupant notwithstanding that in most cases the vehicle's passenger compartment will not be within the arrestee's reach at the time of the search" (*Gant, supra*, 556 U.S. at 343). Explaining this curtailment of the lower courts' expansive applications of *Belton*, the *Gant* Court stated:

> "To read *Belton* as authorizing a vehicle search incident to every recent occupant's arrest would . . . untether the rule from the justifications underlying the *Chimel* exception – a result clearly incompatible with our statement in *Belton* that it 'in no way alters the fundamental principles established in the *Chimel* case regarding the basic scope of searches incident to lawful custodial arrests.' 453 U.S., at 460, n. 3. Accordingly, we reject this reading of *Belton* and hold that the *Chimel* rationale authorizes police to search a vehicle incident to a recent occupant's arrest only when the arrestee is unsecured and within reaching distance of the passenger compartment at the time of the search." (*Id.*)

Although the five-Justice majority in *Gant* characterized its decision as merely a "narrow reading of *Belton*" (*Gant, supra,* 556 U.S. at 348 n.9), the four dissenting Justices viewed the *Gant* majority opinion as "effectively overrul[ing]" both *Belton* and *Thornton v. United States* (*Gant, supra,* 556 U.S. at 355 (Justice Alito, dissenting, joined in pertinent part by Chief Justice Roberts and Justices Kennedy and Breyer)). *And see People v. Lopez*, 8 Cal. 5th 353, 358, 453 P.3d 150, 153, 255 Cal. Rptr. 3d 526, 530 (2019) (finding a Fourth Amendment violation when police officers who had arrested a motorist for driving without a license and handcuffed her outside the car conducted a search of the car's cabin for the purpose of obtaining identification documents: "*Gant* held that a vehicle search incident to arrest is justified only if it is reasonable to believe the suspect can gain access to weapons inside the vehicle or that evidence of the offense of arrest might be found inside the vehicle."). Even by the shoddy standards for clarity and durability that characterize the U.S. Supreme Court's Fourth Amendment jurisprudence generally (see Justice Frankfurter's classic statement that "[t]he course of true law pertaining to searches and seizures . . . has not – to put it mildly – run smooth" (*Chapman v. United States*, 365 U.S. 610, 618 (1961) (concurring opinion)), the *Belton-Gant* caselaw is a disaster area. Its unprincipled and unstable quality gives counsel an especially strong argument for urging state high courts to reject it and adopt more protective state constitutional rules to govern this sector, as suggested in § 17.11 *supra*. *See, e.g., State v. Gaskins*, 866 N.W.2d 1, 12-13 (Iowa 2015) ("declining to adopt *Gant*'s broad evidence-gathering purpose as a rationale for warrantless searches of automobiles and their contents incident to arrest under article I, section 8 of the Iowa Constitution" and invalidating a warrantless search of a small portable locked safe found in an automobile following the driver's arrest for marijuana possession and removal to a squad car; "We now agree with the approach taken by the courts that have rejected the *Belton* rule that authorized warrantless searches of containers without regard to the *Chimel* considerations of officer safety and protecting evidence. 'When lines need to be drawn in creating rules, they should be drawn thoughtfully along the logical contours of the rationales giving rise to the rules, and not as artificial lines drawn elsewhere that are unrelated to those rationales' . . . . ¶ . . . [W]e decline to adopt *Gant*'s alternative evidence-gathering rationale for warrantless searches incident to arrest under the Iowa Constitution because it would permit the SITA exception to swallow completely the fundamental textual rule in article I, section 8 that searches and seizures should be supported by a warrant. In other words, 'use of a [SITA] rationale to sanction a warrantless search that has nothing to do with its underlying justification – preventing the arrestee from gaining access to weapons or evidence – is an anomaly.'").

Even though *Gant* did not address (and had no reason to address) the preexisting rules governing searches of containers incident to the arrest of an individual outside the automobile context, *Gant* throws into question some of the lower court caselaw on this subject because that caselaw was expressly predicated on *Belton. See, e.g., State v. Roach*, 234 Neb. 620, 627-30, 452 N.W.2d 262, 267-69 (1990) (concluding that *Belton* applies outside the automobile context and relying on the court's own and other courts' broad readings of *Belton* to uphold a search of a closed container in the possession of an individual arrested inside a house). Given *Gant*'s repudiation of a broad reading of *Belton*, counsel can argue that the best source of Supreme Court guidance on the proper handling of container searches incident to arrest is *Chadwick*. In States in which the courts relied on *Belton* to authorize container searches even when the container was not physically accessible to the arrestee at and after the time s/he was seized by the arresting officers, counsel can challenge that rule by invoking *Gant*'s explanation that, in the absence of "circumstances unique to the automobile context" (*Arizona v. Gant, supra*, 556 U.S. at 335), the "search-incident-to-arrest . . . rule does not apply" when "there is no possibility that an arrestee could reach into the area that law enforcement officers seek to search" (*id.* at 339). *See United States v. Davis*, 997 F.3d 191, 193 (4th Cir. 2021) (the warrantless search of an arrestee's nearby backpack "while . . . [he] was handcuffed with his hands behind his back and lying on his stomach" violated the Fourth Amendment: "The issue we confront in this appeal is whether the Supreme Court's holding in *Gant* applies beyond the automobile context to the search of a backpack. We join several sister circuits in answering, yes."); *United States v. Knapp*, 917 F.3d 1161, 1168 (10th Cir. 2019) (police officer's warrantless search of a handcuffed defendant's purse after it had been taken from her and remained out of her reach for a period of time was not justified under the search-incident-to-arrest doctrine or "by either the need to preserve evidence or the need to disarm [her]"); *State v. Burroughs*, 2022-Ohio-2146, 169 Ohio St. 3d 79, at 79, 202 N.E.3d 611, 612-13 (2022) ("While executing an arrest warrant, police discovered a closed bookbag with a plastic baggie stuck in its zipper. Without obtaining a search warrant, they opened the bookbag [after the arrestee had been removed from the arrest scene and taken to a squad car] and discovered illegal drugs. The question for us is whether the warrantless search comports with the Fourth Amendment under the 'single-purpose-container exception' to the warrant requirement [– an "exception [that] can be traced to a footnote in *Arkansas v. Sanders*, [442 U.S. 753, 764 n. 13 (1979)], a . . . case involving the warrantless search of luggage in a car based on an anonymous tip [and] . . . observ[ing] that 'some containers (for example a kit of burglar tools or a gun case) by their very nature cannot support any reasonable expectation of privacy because their contents can be inferred from their outward appearance'"]. We hold that it does not. The exception applies only when the illegal nature of the contents of a package are readily apparent because of the distinctive characteristics of the package. A bookbag could hold a variety of items – some illegal, some not. ¶ Because there was no valid basis to search the bookbag without a warrant, the trial court erred in failing to grant a motion to suppress the evidence."); *United States v. Johnson*, 43 F.4th 1100, 1112 (10th Cir. 2022) (an officer's palping of a large black, opaque, oblong-shaped bundle inside the backpack belonging to validly arrested individual who had placed it under the seat next to him on a bus constituted an unconstitutional Fourth Amendment search: ("[A]n officer may conduct a warrantless search of a container in plain view if its contents are a foregone conclusion. . . . But the foregone-conclusion standard is high: It requires 'virtual certainty' that a container holds contraband. . . . This is 'a degree of certainty as to the contents . . . equivalent to the plain view of the [contraband] itself'; and the officer's observations here did not warrant that degree of certainty); *State v. Carrawell*, 481 S.W.3d 833, 837, 845 (Mo. 2016) (dictum) ("It matters not whether this bag was more akin to luggage or more akin to a purse. Neither is part of the person. It matters only whether the bag was within Carrawell's immediate control. Because it was not, there was not a valid search incident to arrest."); *see also, e.g., State v. Lamay*, 140 Idaho 835, 839-40, 103 P.3d 448, 452-53 (2004) (pre-*Gant* decision that rejected *Belton* as inapplicable outside the automobile context and held that the customary rules on searches incident to arrest inside a dwelling do not permit the search of an arrestee's knapsack if the arrestee is handcuffed and the knapsack is "nearly fifteen feet away . . . and located in a different room"); *People v. Gokey*, 60 N.Y.2d 309, 311, 313-14, 457 N.E.2d 723, 724, 725, 469 N.Y.S.2d 618, 619, 620 (1983) (state high court, which had previously rejected *Belton* in favor of a state constitutional rule that resembles the rule the Supreme Court eventually adopted in *Gant*, applies its state constitutional rule to hold that a warrantless search of an arrestee's duffel bag was unlawful, even though the bag was "within the immediate control or 'grabbable area'" of the arrestee "at the time of his arrest" because the "defendant's hands were handcuffed behind his back and he was surrounded by five police officers and their dog" and thus the circumstances did not "support a reasonable belief that the suspect may gain possession of a weapon or be able to destroy evidence located in the bag").

In *Riley v. California*, 573 U.S. 373 (2014), the Court addressed the question "whether the police may, without a warrant, search digital information on a cell phone seized from an individual who has been arrested" (*id.* at 378). Distinguishing between "physical objects" and "digital content on cell phones," the Court concluded that the two governmental interests underlying "*Robinson*'s categorical rule" for searches of "physical objects" – the risks of "harm to officers and destruction of evidence" – do not have "much force with respect to digital content on cell phones" (*id.* at 386). Moreover, while "*Robinson* regarded any privacy interests retained by an individual after arrest as significantly diminished by the fact of the arrest itself," "[c]ell phones . . . place vast quantities of personal information literally in the hands of individuals," and "[a] search of the information on a cell phone bears little resemblance to the type of brief physical search considered in *Robinson*" (*ibid.*). *See also id.* at 393 ("Modern cell phones, as a category, implicate privacy concerns far beyond those implicated by the search of a cigarette pack, a wallet, or a purse."); *ibid.* ("Cell phones differ in both a quantitative and a qualitative sense from other objects that might be kept on an arrestee's person. The term 'cell phone' is itself misleading shorthand; many of these devices are in fact minicomputers that also happen to have the capacity to be used as a telephone."); *id.* at 403 ("Modern cell phones[,] . . . [w]ith all they contain and all they may reveal, . . . hold for many Americans 'the privacies of life'" (quoting *Boyd v. United States*, 116 U.S. 616, 630 (1886))). Accordingly, the Court "decline[d] to extend *Robinson* to searches of data on cell phones, and h[e]ld instead that officers must generally secure a warrant before conducting such a search" (*Riley v. California, supra*, 573 U.S. at 403). *See also id.* at 386 ("even though the search incident to arrest exception does not apply to cell phones, other case-specific exceptions may still justify a warrantless search of a particular phone"); *United States v. Camou*, 773 F.3d 932, 939, 940-41, 943 (9th Cir. 2014) (a Border Patrol agent's search of an arrestee's cell phone, which was retrieved from the arrestee's vehicle, "was not roughly contemporaneous with Camou's arrest and, therefore, was not incident to arrest," because "one hour and twenty minutes passed between Camou's arrest and Agent Walla's search of the cell phone" and "a string of intervening acts occurred between Camou's arrest and the search of his cell phone" that "signaled the arrest was over" by the time of the cell phone search; the search also was not justifiable under the exigent circumstances exception because the search "occurred one hour and twenty minutes after [Camou's] arrest," and, furthermore, "even if we were to assume that the exigencies of the situation permitted a search of Camou's cell phone to prevent the loss of cell data, the search's scope was impermissibly overbroad" in that it "went beyond contacts and call logs to include a search of hundreds of photographs and videos stored on the phone's internal memory"; the search also was not justifiable under the automobile exception because *Riley*'s reasoning requires that cell phones be classified as "*non*-containers for purposes of the vehicle exception to the warrant requirement"); *United States v. Lopez-Cruz*, 730 F.3d 803, 805-06, 808 (9th Cir. 2013) (discussed in § 25.15.4 concluding paragraph *infra*); *State v. K.C.*, 207 So.3d 951 (Fla. App. 2016) (discussed in § 25.13 subdivision (d) *infra*); *United States v. Pratt*, 915 F.3d 266, 272-73 (4th Cir. 2019) (condemning the inspection of data on a seized cell phone because the authorities delayed 31 days after seizing the phone before obtaining a warrant to search its files: "Pratt had an undiminished possessory interest in the cellphone – he didn't consent to the seizure and he wasn't allowed to retain any of the phone's files. . . . Given Pratt's undiminished interest, a 31-day delay violates the Fourth Amendment where the government neither proceeds diligently nor presents an overriding reason for the delay.); *Commonwealth v. Fulton*, 645 Pa. 296, 318-19, 179 A.3d 475, 486, 488-89

(2018) (rejecting the prosecution's argument that "no search of the phone occurred because police navigated the menus of the [defendant's] phone only to obtain the phone's assigned number"; "The act of powering on Fulton's flip phone constituted a search, i.e., an intrusion upon a constitutionally protected area (Fulton's cell phone) without Fulton's explicit or implicit permission. . . . Turning on the phone exposed to view portions of the phone that were previously concealed and not otherwise authorized by a warrant or an exception to the warrant requirement. . . . Powering on the phone is akin to opening the door to a home. It permitted police to obtain and review a host of information on the cell phone, including viewing its wallpaper, reviewing incoming text messages and calls, and accessing all of the data contained in the phone. . . . ¶ Detective Harkins engaged in a second warrantless search when he obtained the phone's assigned number. After powering on the phone, Detective Harkins navigated through the menus of the flip phone to obtain its number. . . . The act of navigating the menus of a cell phone to obtain the phone's number is unquestionably a search that required a warrant. . . . ¶ Detective Harkins conducted a third warrantless search of the phone when he monitored incoming calls and text messages. . . . ¶ Contrary to the finding of the trial court and the argument advanced by the Commonwealth before this Court, there is little difference between monitoring the internal and external viewing screens on a cell phone and searching the phone's call logs. Both result in accessing 'more than just phone numbers,' but also 'any identifying information that an individual might add' to his or her contacts, including the caller's photograph, the name assigned to the caller or sender of the text message. . . . Further, and unlike a call log, monitoring a phone's incoming text messages allows the viewer to see the content of a text message, which indisputably constitutes private data. This is all information that, pursuant to *Riley/Wurie*, cannot be accessed by police without a warrant. ¶ The rule created by *Riley/Wurie* is exceedingly simple: if a member of law enforcement wishes to obtain information from a cell phone, get a warrant."); *Jones v. United States*, 168 A.3d 703, 713 (D.C. 2017) (police "use of a cell-site simulator to locate . . . [the defendant's] phone invaded a reasonable expectation of privacy and was thus a search" that violated the Fourth Amendment in the absence of a search warrant); *State v. Terrell*, 372 N.C. 657, 658, 669, 831 S.E.2d 17, 18, 25 (2019) (rejecting the prosecution's argument that the "private search" doctrine (see § 25.18.3 *infra*) authorized "a law enforcement officer's warrantless search of defendant's USB drive, following a prior search of the USB drive by a private individual": "We cannot agree that the mere opening of a thumb drive and the viewing of as little as one file automatically renders the entirety of the device's contents 'now nonprivate information' no longer afforded any protection by the Fourth Amendment. . . . An individual's privacy interest in his or her effects is not a liquid that, taking the shape of its container, wholly evaporates merely upon the container's opening, with no regard for the nature of the effects concealed therein. This is particularly true in the context of digital storage devices, which can retain massive amounts of various types of information and which organize this information essentially by means of containers within containers. . . . Unlike rifling through the contents of a cardboard box, a foray into one folder of a digital storage device will often expose nothing about the nature or the amount of digital information that is, or may be, stored elsewhere in the device."); *Commonwealth v. Mauricio*, 477 Mass. 588, 593, 594, 80 N.E.3d 318, 323, 324 (2017) (construing the state constitution to "hold, for the same reasons articulated by the Supreme Court in *Riley* [*v. California, supra*] . . . , that digital cameras may be seized incident to arrest, but that the search of data contained in digital cameras falls outside the scope of the search incident to arrest exception to the warrant requirement"; "Although digital cameras do not allow storage of information as diverse and far ranging as a cell phone, they nevertheless possess the capacity to store enormous quantities of photograph and often video recordings, dating over periods of months and even years, which can reveal intimate details of an individual's life."). *And cf. United States v. Saulsberry,* 878 F.3d 946 (10th Cir. 2017) (police who detained a driver on reasonable suspicion that he was smoking marijuana in his parked car could search a bag on the floor of the driver's seat for marijuana, but the officer's seizure and examination of a stack of credit cards found in the bag exceeded the justification for the search and violated the Fourth Amendment).

If the police lawfully seize a cellphone and thereafter obtain a search warrant to search the contents of the phone, an issue that may arise is whether the state can obtain a court order compelling the defendant to provide the password for accessing the device. A number of court decisions recognize that the defendant can challenge such an order as violating federal and/or state constitutional protections against self-incrimination, although these courts have employed differing approaches to analyze the issue, with the result that differing challenges are available in different jurisdictions. *Compare Commonwealth v. Davis,* 656 Pa. 213, 217, 239-40, 220 A.3d 534, 537, 551 (2019) ("we hold that the compelled recollection of Appellant's password ["to allow the Commonwealth access to the defendant's lawfully-seized, but encrypted, computer"] is testimonial in nature, and, consequently, privileged under the Fifth Amendment to the United States Constitution. Furthermore, until the United States Supreme Court holds otherwise, we construe the foregone conclusion rationale to be one of limited application, and, consistent with its teachings in other decisions, believe the exception to be inapplicable to compel the disclosure of a defendant's password to assist the Commonwealth in gaining access to a computer."), *and G.A.Q.L. v. State,* 257 So.3d 1058 (Fla. App. 2018) (same rulings regarding a cellphone), *and Seo v. State,* 148 N.E.3d 952, 953 (Ind. 2020) ("Forcing Seo to unlock her iPhone [which the state sought to do by obtaining a "warrant that ordered Seo to unlock her iPhone," and then, when "[s]he refused, . . . the trial court held her in contempt"] would violate her Fifth Amendment right against self-incrimination. By unlocking her smartphone, Seo would provide law enforcement with information it does not already know, which the State could then use in its prosecution against her. The Fifth Amendment's protection from compelled self-incrimination prohibits this result."), *with Commonwealth v. Jones,* 481 Mass. 540, 117 N.E.3d 702 (2019) ("when the Commonwealth seeks an order . . . compelling a defendant to decrypt an electronic device by entering a password, art. 12 [of the state constitution] requires the Commonwealth to prove that the defendant knows the password beyond a reasonable doubt" in order to show that "the act of entering the password would not amount to self-incrimination because the defendant's knowledge of the password was already known to the Commonwealth, and was therefore a 'foregone conclusion' under the Fifth Amendment and art. 12" (*id.* at 541-43, 117 N.E.3d at 706-07); [however, the court concludes that "the Commonwealth met its burden in this case" (*id.* at 543, 117 N.E.3d at 707)]), *and State v. Pittman,* 367 Or. 498, 479 P.3d 1028 (2021) ("Here, defendant was ordered to unlock the phone using a passcode. . . . [D]efendant's performance of that act would communicate that she knew the passcode. If the court had ordered defendant to do something different, what would be communicated by compliance with the order may have been different as well. For example, had the phone been one that could be unlocked by placing a finger on the phone, and had the court ordered defendant to place her finger on the phone, then, by performing that act, defendant would communicate only that she knew how to move her finger, not that she knew how to unlock the phone. If, however, the court had ordered defendant to unlock the phone, without specifying the means she should use to do so, then any act that she performed that served to unlock the phone would communicate her knowledge – that she knew how to comply with the court's order and how to access the phone's contents. Here, as the state acknowledges, the court's order was of that ilk. It required defendant to unlock the phone using a passcode, and compliance with that order would communicate that defendant knew that passcode. We conclude that the act of unlocking the phone was an act that would provide incriminating testimonial evidence." *Id.* at 517-18, 479 P.3d at 1043. "[W]e construe Article I, section 12 [of the state constitution], to permit an order compelling a defendant to unlock a cell phone [only] so long as the state (1) has a valid warrant authorizing it to seize and search the phone; (2) already knows the information that the act of unlocking the phone, by itself, would communicate; and (3) is prohibited from using defendant's act against defendant, except to obtain access to the contents of the phone." *Id.* at 525, 479 P.3d at 1047.). A minority view is that the act of producing a cellphone's passcode is "non-testimonial" (see § 36.3.3 *infra*) and can therefore be compelled without implicating the privilege against self-incrimination. *See, e.g., People v. Sneed*, 2023 IL 127968, 2023 WL 4003913 (Ill. 2023). For discussion of Fifth Amendment doctrines bearing on judicial orders that require putative defendants to disclose various sorts of potentially incriminating material, see § 18.12 *supra*. For discussion of the rules governing the issuance and execution of search warrants, see § 25.17 *infra*.

25.8.3. *"Inventory" Searches Incident to Incarceration*

If an arrested person is to be incarcerated, the police may remove, examine, and inventory everything in his or her possession at the lockup. *Illinois v. LaFayette,* 462 U.S. 640, 646-48 (1983). This "inventory search" power permits the opening, without a warrant, of any container carried by the person, whether or not the police have any reason to suspect its contents and whether or not they could practically secure the container during the period of the person's incarceration without opening it up. *Id.* Presumably the rule of *Riley v. California,* 573 U.S. 373 (2014) – which bars the application of the "search incident to arrest" doctrine to the digital content of a cell phone because "[c]ell phones differ in both a quantitative and a qualitative sense from other objects that might be kept on an arrestee's person" (*id.* at 393; see § 25.8.2 *supra*, discussing *Riley*) – applies as well in the context of "inventory" searches incident to incarceration and requires that such a search be authorized either by a search warrant or by some "case-specific exception[ ]" that "justif[ies] a warrantless search of a particular phone" (*id.* at 401-02). *See Commonwealth v. Mauricio,* 477 Mass. 588, 595, 80 N.E.3d 318, 325 (2017) (police conducting a stationhouse inventory search of an arrestee's backpack found a digital camera; "suspecting that the camera was stolen, [they] took steps to investigate its ownership by activating the camera and viewing the stored images"; this search "exceeded the bounds of the inventory search exception to the warrant requirement because it was investigatory in nature" and it was therefore impermissible without a warrant under the Massachusetts constitution); *see also State v. Granville,* 423 S.W.3d 399, 402 (Tex. Crim. App. 2014) (pre-*Riley* decision holding that a search warrant was needed for the police to examine the contents of a cell phone that was taken from the defendant "during the booking procedure and placed in the jail property room": the arrestee, a "high-school student[,] did not lose his legitimate expectation of privacy in his cell phone simply because it was being stored in the jail property room"; the officer "could have seized appellant's phone and held it while he sought a search warrant, but, even with probable cause, he could not 'activate and search the contents of an inventoried cellular phone' without one"). *And cf. United States v. Saulsberry,* 878 F.3d 946 (10th Cir. 2017) (police who detained a driver on reasonable suspicion that he was smoking marijuana in his parked car could search a bag on the floor of the driver's seat for marijuana, but the officer's seizure and examination of a stack of credit cards found in the bag exceeded the justification for the search and violated the Fourth Amendment). The inventory-search exception to the warrant requirement is limited to effects that are in the physical possession of an arrestee at the time of the arrest; it does not authorize the arresting officers to seize the arrestee's belongings from even a nearby location which they have no other constitutional justification to access. *State v. Banks-Harvey,* 2018-Ohio-201, 152 Ohio St. 3d 368, 374, 96 N.E.3d 262, 269-70 (2018) (police stopped a car for speeding and asked the driver to step out of the vehicle; they placed her in the back seat of their patrol cruiser while conducting a warrants check, then arrested her when they learned that she had outstanding arrest warrants for drug offenses; she had left her purse in the vehicle, which was owned by a friend who was present as a passenger; police returned to the vehicle, seized the purse, and searched it pursuant to a policy of conducting "inventory searches" of all arrestees; "Certainly we take no issue with the reasonableness of an administrative policy requiring the search and inventory of personal items that necessarily come into police custody as a result of an arrest. Indeed, . . . [an Ohio statute] requires law-enforcement agencies to keep safe any lawfully seized property that comes into their custody. However, this is not a case in which personal items came into the custody of the police as an incident of lawful police conduct. In this case, the trooper retrieved a personal item belonging to an arrestee from a place that is protected under the Fourth Amendment (the car). At the time the trooper retrieved the appellant's purse, her identity had already been confirmed and she was handcuffed and under arrest in the trooper's vehicle. Neither her purse, nor the vehicle that contained her purse, came into police custody as a result of her arrest. On these facts, the state has failed to show that this search fits under the inventory-search exception to the Fourth Amendment's warrant requirement.").

Inventory searches must be conducted "in accordance with established inventory procedures" (*Illinois v. LaFayette, supra,* 462 U.S. at 648). *See id.* at 644 (explaining that the validity of inventory searches is to be determined by the principles of *Delaware v. Prouse,* 440 U.S. 648, 654 (1979), a decision that calls for standardized procedures to control "'the discretion of the official in the field'" (440 U.S. at 655)); *see also Colorado v. Bertine,* 479 U.S. 367, 372-76 (1987) (analogizing inventory searches of automobiles to inventory searches of arrested individuals and reaffirming that inventory searches of automobiles must be conducted in accordance with "standard criteria"); *Florida v. Wells,* 495 U.S. 1, 4 (1990); *City of Indianapolis v. Edmond,* 531 U.S. 32, 45 (2000).

Jail personnel may also conduct an intrusive visual search of the body – including body cavities – of an individual who is being admitted into the general population of a holding facility, for the purpose of detecting and confiscating any materials that would compromise the facility's security. *Florence v. Board of Chosen Freeholders of County of Burlington,* 566 U.S. 318 (2012). *But see Hinkle v. Beckham County Board of County Commissioners,* 962 F.3d 1204 (10th Cir. 2020) ("Under *Florence,* the jail could (1) decide that Hinkle 'will be' housed in the jail's general population, and (2) then strip search him before placing him in the general population. . . . Here, the County did not decide that Hinkle 'will be' placed in the jail's general population, in fact just the opposite. By acting as it did, the County set the cart before the horse – it strip searched Hinkle before committing itself to admit him into its jail's general population."

Id. at 1237. "*Florence* does not sanction such a policy – strip searching detainees not destined for the jail's general population, or even as here, for the jail itself." *Id.* at 1238. "Before subjecting a detainee to the abject abasement of a body-cavity strip search, jail officials should first conclusively decide whether that detainee will be housed in their jail's general population." *Id.* at 1242. "[F]or detainees like Hinkle who will not be housed in the jail's general population, the County needs far more to justify a body-cavity strip search – probable cause that detainee is secreting evidence of a crime." *Id.* at 1239.).

25.8.4. *Search Prior to the Point of Arrest*

The general rule is that "a search incident to a lawful arrest may not precede the arrest" (*Sibron v. New York,* 392 U.S. 40, 67 (1968)). However, the Court has recognized two narrow exceptions to this rule.

If the search and the arrest are parts of a single course of events and "the formal arrest followed quickly on the heels of the challenged search" (*Rawlings v. Kentucky,* 448 U.S. 98, 111 (1980)), then it is not "particularly important that the search preceded the arrest rather than vice versa" (*id.*). However, the police officer must, of course, have "probable cause to place [the defendant] under arrest" at the time of the search (*id.*), and "[t]he fruits of the search of [the defendant's] person . . . [cannot be] necessary to support probable cause to arrest" (*id.* at 111 n.6). *Accord, Sibron v. New York, supra,* 392 U.S. at 63 ("[i]t is axiomatic that an incident search may not precede an arrest and serve as part of its justification"). *See also People v. Reid,* 24 N.Y.3d 615, 617, 619, 620, 26 N.E.3d 237, 238, 239, 240, 2 N.Y.S.3d 409, 410, 411, 412 (2014) (Although a search can precede an arrest as long as "the two events were substantially contemporaneous," the officer "testified [that], but for the search there would have been no arrest at all," notwithstanding that "probable cause to arrest the driver existed before the search," and "[w]here that is true, to say that the search was incident to the arrest does not make sense."; "[T]he 'search incident to arrest' doctrine, by its nature, requires proof that, at the time of the search, an arrest has already occurred or is about to occur. Where no arrest has yet taken place, the officer must have intended to make one if the 'search incident' exception is to be applied.").

In cases in which the search and the arrest are not a single course of events, a search prior to arrest nevertheless may be valid if it is restricted to the "very limited search necessary to preserve" some evidence of "ready destructibility" that the suspect would otherwise likely destroy (*Cupp v. Murphy,* 412 U.S. 291, 296 (1973)). Thus, in *Cupp,* the Court approved the officers' taking scrapings of what appeared to be dried blood from the fingernails of a suspect, at a point in time when the police already had probable cause to arrest the suspect, even though the formal arrest did not occur until a month later. The Court emphasized that the scope of the search must be strictly limited to the measures needed to "preserve . . . highly evanescent evidence" (*id.* at 296), and that "a full *Chimel* search [the type of extensive search permitted incident to arrest upon probable cause] would [not be] . . . justified . . . without a formal arrest and without a warrant" (*id.*) See the discussion in *Illinois v. McArthur,* 531 U.S. 326, 331-34 (2001), of police authority to prevent alerted suspects from destroying evidence; and see the cases dealing with a similar issue in the context of building searches, discussed in § 25.22.3 *infra.* Note that this authority depends upon the possession by the police of probable cause to believe that seizable evidence exists and is within the capacity of the suspect to destroy. *See Illinois v. McArthur, supra*, 531 U.S. at 334 ("We have found no case in which this Court has held unlawful a temporary seizure *that was supported by probable cause* and was designed to prevent the loss of evidence . . . . (emphasis added)); *Knowles v. Iowa*, 525 U.S. 113, 116 (1998) (in cases in which *there is probable cause to arrest a suspect*, "the need to preserve evidence for later use at trial" is one of the justifications for allowing a warrantless search incident to arrest). If the police lack probable cause either (i) to search for seizable evidence or (ii) to arrest a suspect, they have no power to seize evidence in the first place (*see, e.g., Minnesota v. Dickerson*, 508 U.S. 366, 373 (1993)), so they cannot justify a "preventive" search on the theory that it is necessary to preserve destructible evidence.

25.9. *Circumstances Justifying a* Terry *Stop*

In *Terry v. Ohio,* 392 U.S. 1 (1968), the Supreme Court held that a state could constitutionally authorize its law enforcement officers to conduct a "stop" – a brief on-the-street detention for the purpose of inquiry and observation – under circumstances giving rise to a rational suspicion of criminal activity but not amounting to the probable cause necessary for arrest. *Terry* "created an exception to the requirement of probable cause, an exception whose 'narrow scope' . . . [the Supreme] Court 'has been careful to maintain'" (*Ybarra v. Illinois,* 444 U.S. 85, 93 (1979)). *See also Dunaway v. New York,* 442 U.S. 200, 207-10 (1979); *Florida v. Royer,* 460 U.S. 491, 499 (1983) (plurality opinion); *id.* at 509-11 (concurring opinion of Justice Brennan); *Kaupp v. Texas,* 538 U.S. 626, 630 (2003).

A *Terry* stop must rest upon specific, identifiable facts that, "judged against an objective standard" (*Terry v. Ohio, supra,* 392 U.S. at 21; *see Delaware v. Prouse,* 440 U.S. 648, 654 (1979)), give rise to "a reasonable and articulable suspicion that the person seized is engaged in criminal activity" (*Reid v. Georgia,* 448 U.S. 438, 440 (1980) (per curiam); *see Brown v. Texas,* 443 U.S. 47, 51-53 (1979)); *United States v. Curry*, 965 F.3d 313, 324, 325-26 (4th Cir. 2020) (en banc) (rejecting the argument that the "exigent circumstances" doctrine (see § 25.20 *infra*) justifies a *Terry* stop without reasonable suspicion: "There are relatively few cases that purport to extend the exigent circumstances exception to suspicionless, investigatory seizures of a person. But in each of these cases, officers typically have searched for a suspect implicated in a known crime in the immediate aftermath of that crime, and – per that objective – have isolated a geographic area with clear boundaries or a discrete group of people to engage in minimally intrusive searches. ¶ In sum, the exigent circumstances exception may permit suspicionless seizures when officers can narrowly target the seizures based on specific information of a known crime and a controlled geographic area. This reading of the exception does not transform it into individualized suspicion by another name. . . . Nor does it require that officers be virtually certain that one of the individuals they stop is the suspect. But officers must support their 'objectively reasonable belief' that there is an emergency with 'specific articulable facts and reasonable inferences.' . . . Allowing officers to bypass the individualized suspicion requirement based on the information they had here – the sound of gunfire and the general location where it may have originated – would completely cripple a fundamental Fourth Amendment protection and create a dangerous precedent."). Considering "the totality of the circumstances," the "detaining officers must have a particularized and objective basis for suspecting the particular person stopped of criminal activity" (*United States v. Cortez,* 449 U.S. 411, 417-18 (1981)). *See also Arizona v. Johnson*, 555 U.S. 323, 327 (2009); *United States v. Arvizu,* 534 U.S. 266, 273-

74 (2002); *Illinois v. Wardlow*, 528 U.S. 119, 123-24 (2000); *Ornelas v. United States*, 517 U.S. 690, 696 (1996); *United States v. Sokolow*, 490 U.S. 1, 7-8 (1989) (dictum); *Kolender v. Lawson*, 461 U.S. 352, 356 n.5 (1983) (dictum); *Thomas v. Dillard*, 818 F.3d 864, 877 (9th Cir. 2016) (dictum) ("Just as a suspicion must be reasonable and individualized, it must be based on the totality of the circumstances known to the officer."). Conduct or circumstances that "describe a very large category of presumably innocent [persons]" will not suffice (*Reid v. Georgia, supra,* 448 U.S. at 441; *Brown v. Texas, supra*, 443 U.S. at 52; *cf. Ybarra v. Illinois, supra*, 444 U.S. at 91; *compare United States v. Sokolow, supra*, 490 U.S. at 8-11). *See United States v. Walker*, 965 F.3d 180, 187 (2d Cir. 2020) (finding a *Terry* stop unlawful because the "attributes derived from the photograph" of a suspect which were the basis for the stop of the defendant – "black male, medium-to-dark skin tone, glasses, facial hair, and long hair" – "fit too many people to constitute sufficient articulable facts"); *Commonwealth v. Hicks*, 652 Pa. 353, 401, 208 A.3d 916, 945 (2019) (visual observation of an individual carrying a firearm and concealing it on his person is insufficient to establish reasonable suspicion for a stop; the person may have had a license for the weapon, as in this case he did: "When many people are licensed to do something, and violate no law by doing that thing, common sense dictates that the police officer cannot assume that any given person doing it is breaking the law. Absent some other circumstances giving rise to a suspicion of criminality, a seizure upon that basis alone is unreasonable."); *United States v. Peters*, 60 F.4th 855, 868 (4th Cir. 2023) (finding no reasonable suspicion for a *Terry* stop, the Fourth Circuit disparages the government's reliance upon, *inter alia*, evidence that "confidential sources informed . . . [an officer that] 'men specifically were wearing skinny jeans drawn tightly with a belt and would wedge a firearm in their waistband[.]'" ¶ . . . A general tip 'that men specifically were wearing skinny jeans' to 'wedge a firearm in their waistband' does not justify the seizure here, because it is not at all particular to Peters."); *Reynaga Hernandez v. Skinner*, 969 F.3d 930 (9th Cir. 2020), summarized in § 25.7.4 second paragraph *supra*; *cf. United States v. Feliciana*, 974 F.3d 519, 523 (4th Cir. 2020) (a Park Police Officer stopped a delivery truck driver on the George Washington Memorial Parkway, where commercial vehicles require permits; the officer asked to see the driver's permit; the driver had none but did have marijuana; the Fourth Circuit orders the marijuana suppressed because the officer lacked reasonable suspicion for the stop: the officer "did not articulate any reason to suspect that Feliciana did not possess the requisite permit to drive a commercial vehicle on the Parkway. The entire factual basis he offered for conducting the traffic stop was that he saw a vehicle requiring a permit on the Parkway. But that fact by itself is wholly innocent."); *People v. McCloud*, 2021 WL 1596498, at *4 (Mich. App. 2021) (in connection with a police team's entry into a social club suspected of selling liquor without a license, two officers were assigned to remove any security personnel from the club so that the rest of the team would not be searched for weapons when they entered undercover to determine whether liquor was being sold on the premises; these officers detained and frisked two men who identified themselves as security and found that both were carrying handguns; the Court of Appeals orders the handguns suppressed because the officers lacked the requisite reasonable belief that the security men "possessed a weapon or intended to commit an assault"; " the mere act of working security at an afterhours club being investigated for the possibility that it was selling liquor without a license did not provide reasonable suspicion for a *Terry* stop."). Rather, the "particularized suspicion" must be focused upon "the particular individual being stopped" (*United States v. Cortez, supra*, 449 U.S. at 418). *See also, e.g., United States v. Black*, 707 F.3d 531, 540-41 (4th Cir. 2013); *State v. Teamer*, 151 So.3d 421, 427-28 (Fla. 2014) ("The discrepancy between the vehicle registration and the color

the deputy observed does present an ambiguous situation, and the Supreme Court has recognized that an officer can detain an individual to resolve an ambiguity regarding suspicious yet lawful or innocent conduct. . . . However, the suspicion still must be a reasonable one. . . . In this case, there simply are not enough facts to demonstrate reasonableness. . . . [T]he color discrepancy here is not 'inherently suspicious' or 'unusual' enough or so 'out of the ordinary' as to provide an officer with a reasonable suspicion of criminal activity, especially given the fact that it is not against the law in Florida to change the color of your vehicle without notifying the DHSMV. ¶ The law allows officers to draw rational inferences, but to find reasonable suspicion based on this single noncriminal factor would be to license investigatory stops on nothing more than an officer's hunch. Doing so would be akin to finding reasonable suspicion for an officer to stop an individual for walking in a sparsely occupied area after midnight simply because that officer testified that, in his experience, people who walk in such areas after midnight tend to commit robberies. Without more, this one fact may provide a 'mere suspicion,' but it does not rise to the level of a reasonable suspicion."); *Bey v. Falk*, 946 F.3d 304 (6th Cir. 2019) ("McKinley violated Bey's Fourth Amendment rights by directing a stop without reasonable suspicion. When McKinley directed . . . [another officer] to initiate the stop, he knew only that three young men had driven an old minivan to three different stores [the first and third of which were open for business] in the early morning [at about 2:30 a.m.], at one time reversing direction on the highway. . . . [A member of McKinley's surveillance unit] had followed them around the third store and had not observed any criminal, or even suspicious, behavior; in fact, she had watched them stand in line at the cash register, 'flip[] through some [credit] cards to . . . pick a card,' and pay for the items in their shopping cart with the card. . . . ¶ McKinley testified that '[c]riminals frequently use stolen old vehicles that cannot be traced to them if they flee the scene,' and points to his testimony that the paper registration on . . . [Bey's] van's window did not appear in a records search. He likewise contends that Bey's reversal on the interstate was 'consistent with a cleaning maneuver.' But even taken together, these meager observations are not enough to constitute reasonable suspicion." *Id.* at 313. In addition, Bey, who is African-American, stated a cognizable claim of racial discrimination; "the district court determined that 'McKinley's explanation for why he started following the minivan in the first place,' his failure to 'stop the minivan once they learned of the "no record" plates,' and McKinley's suggestion that he 'did not know the race of . . . [Bey] and his friends prior to . . . [their arrival at the third store] created a genuine issue of material fact with respect to McKinley's intent." *Id.* at 320.); *United States v. Martinez*, 910 F.3d 1309 (10th Cir. 2018) (a state trooper's testimony that white Cadillacs are a rare sight on the section of I-40 where he stopped a white Cadillac was insufficient to warrant a reasonable suspicion that the Cadillac he stopped was the one wanted in connection with a bank robbery and which had last been reported sighted 130 miles away from where he made the stop). Information "completely lacking in indicia of reliability would either warrant no police response or require further investigation before a forcible stop of a suspect would be authorized" (*Adams v. Williams,* 407 U.S. 143, 147 (1972) (dictum)). *See, e.g., Florida v. J.L.*, 529 U.S. 266, 271 (2000) (an anonymous tip which lacks "moderate indicia of reliability" will not justify a stop, and this is the rule even where the tip contains an "accurate description of a subject's . . . location and appearance"; "[t]he reasonable suspicion here at issue requires that a tip be reliable in its assertion of illegality, not just in its tendency to identify a determinate person"; and the *Terry* requirement of "standard pre-search reliability testing" in terms of reasonable suspicion is not relaxed in cases where the tip asserts that the subject is in possession of an illegal firearm); *United States v. Lopez*, 907 F.3d 472, 480-81 (7th Cir. 2018) ("Tips that come from more trustworthy sources will require less independent corroboration than those obtained from more questionable sources. . . . ¶ In this case, officers knew the informant's identity but nothing else. Without corroborating any incriminating or predicted information, and without knowing anything about the informant's reliability, they seized Lopez and deprived him of his liberty. When officers know the bare identity but little else about an informant, they still must conduct and rely upon independent investigation to corroborate a tip before seizing a person. In this case, police corroborated only the name-and-address match for Fausto Lopez – 'easily obtained facts' that '[a]nyone could have "predicted."' " . . . They verified no facts that would indicate the tip was 'reliable in its allegation of illegality,' as required by *Florida v. J.L.*"); *United States v. Drakeford*, 992 F.3d 255, 263-64 (4th Cir. 2021) ("This court has previously noted, '[T]ips fall somewhere on a spectrum of reliability, and under the Fourth Amendment a reviewing court may – indeed must – take into account all the facts surrounding a tip in assessing the totality of the circumstances supporting a stop.' . . . Here, officers' testimony on the reliability of the confidential informant is scant. When asked how many cases the informant had assisted with, Detective Moore testified, 'Approximately 50.' . . . However, Detective Moore never opined on the number of convictions the informant aided in, if any, or any other facts that credit the reliability of the informant. ¶ . . . Of note, despite the informant's ability to communicate with . . . [the suspect], detectives never attempted to confirm the informant's allegation by setting up a controlled buy between the informant and . . . [the suspect] nor did they seek any predictive information that would lend to her credibility. Thus, the information provided by the informant as to . . . [the suspect's] alleged illegal activities deserves little weight in the totality of the circumstances."); *United States v. Brown*, 925 F.3d 1150 (9th Cir. 2019); *United States v. Freeman*, 735 F.3d 92, 97-103 (2d Cir. 2013); *United States v. Brown*, 448 F.3d 239 (3d Cir. 2006); *United States v. Patterson*, 340 F.3d 368 (6th Cir. 2003); *United States v. Mallides,* 473 F.2d 859 (9th Cir. 1973); *Irwin v. Superior Court,* 1 Cal. 3d 423, 462 P.2d 12, 82 Cal. Rptr. 484 (1969), *modified in In re Tony C.,* 21 Cal. 3d 888, 894, 582 P.2d 957, 960, 148 Cal. Rptr. 366, 369 (1978); *cf. Navarette v. California*, 572 U.S. 393, 395, 398-401, 404 (2014); *United States v. Ramsey,* 431 U.S. 606, 612-15 (1977); *Jernigan v. Louisiana*, 446 U.S. 958, 959-60 (1980) (opinion of Justice White, dissenting from the denial of *certiorari*). *And see* Shawn E. Fields, *Stop and Frisk in a Concealed Carry World,* 93 WASH. L. REV. 1675 (2018); *United States v. Willy*, 40 F.4th 1074 (9th Cir. 2022); *United States v. Brown, supra*; *Commonwealth v. Hicks, supra*. As is the case regarding probable cause to arrest (see § 25.7.4 fourth paragraph *supra*), officers making a judgment whether there is reasonable suspicion for a *Terry* stop may not cherry-pick incriminating information and disregard exculpatory information. *See United States v. Drakeford, supra*, 992 F.3d at 258 ("In order to sustain reasonable suspicion, officers must consider the totality of the circumstances and, in doing so, must not overlook facts that tend to dispel reasonable suspicion. . . . [Here the officers overlooked] the facts that the interaction took place in a public space, in broad daylight, outside of the vehicles, and in front of a security camera; and after the interaction, . . . [the suspect] went into a store, rather than immediately leaving the scene. On these facts, we . . . [find] that the officers did not have more than a mere hunch that criminal activity was afoot when they stopped . . . [the suspect]" for a supposed hand-off sale of narcotics).

The power of the police to conduct a *Terry* stop is more limited when the stop is for the purpose of "investigat[ing] past criminal activity . . . rather than . . . to investigate ongoing criminal conduct" (*United States v. Hensley,* 469 U.S. 221, 228 (1985)). The *Terry* decision itself and almost all of the caselaw establishing standards for *Terry* stops involved situations in which the "police stopped or seized a person because they suspected he was about to commit a crime . . . or was committing a crime at the moment of the stop" (469 U.S. at 227). In such situations the stop is justified by the exigencies of crime prevention and the need to avert an imminent threat to public safety. *Id.* at 228. "A stop to investigate an already completed crime does not necessarily promote the interest of crime prevention as directly . . . [and] officers making a stop to investigate past crimes may have a wider range of opportunity to choose the time and circumstances of the stop." *Id.* at 228-29. To conduct a stop for the purpose of investigating a completed crime, a police officer must "have a reasonable suspicion, grounded in specific and articulable facts, that [the] . . . person . . . was involved in or is wanted in connection with a completed felony" (*id.* at 229). Moreover, in authorizing such investigatory stops in *United States v. Hensley*, the Court strongly indicated that these stops may be conducted only in cases in which the police previously "have been unable to locate [the] . . . person" (469 U.S. at 229) and therefore need to exercise the "stop" power in order to prevent "a person they encounter" (*id.*) from "flee[ing] in the interim and . . . remain[ing] at large" (*id.*) *See id.* at 234-35 (emphasizing that the defendant was "at large" and that the officers who conducted the stop could reasonably conclude, on the basis of a "wanted flyer," that "a warrant might have been obtained in the period after the flyer was issued"). It is only the inability to find the defendant in a fixed location – to fully "choose the time and circumstances of the stop" (*id.* at 228-29) – that creates the exigency necessary to conduct a stop for the purpose of investigating a completed crime. *See id.* at 228-29; *see also Brown v. Texas, supra*, 443 U.S. at 51. Thus, at least arguably, when the police have known the defendant's address and failed to avail themselves of the opportunity of conducting a purely voluntary "contact" at the defendant's home (see § 25.4.1 *supra*), they may not use their suspicions about the defendant's involvement in a completed crime to conduct a *Terry* stop.

For discussion of some of the factors commonly considered by the courts in gauging whether there was an adequate basis for a *Terry* stop, see § 25.11 *infra.*

25.10. *Circumstances Justifying a* **Terry** *Frisk; The Plain Touch Doctrine*

In *Terry v. Ohio,* 392 U.S. 1 (1968), the Court ruled that a state could constitutionally authorize not only a "stop" but also, under appropriate circumstances, a "frisk": – that is, a pat-down for weapons or a similar "self-protective" search. The frisk must be made incidental to a valid accosting or stop. *See, e.g., State v. Serna*, 235 Ariz. 270, 275, 331 P.3d 405, 410 (2014) (a *Terry* frisk could not be conducted during a consensual encounter between a civilian and a police officer even though the civilian admitted to having a gun because "the initial stop was based on consent, not on any asserted suspicion of criminal activity," and "*Terry* allows a frisk only if two conditions are met: officers must reasonably suspect both that criminal activity is afoot and that the suspect is armed and dangerous").

A *Terry* frisk cannot be conducted for the purpose of seeking evidence; it can only be conducted for the purpose of discovering weapons that might be used against the officer. *See Sibron v. New York,* 392 U.S. 40, 64-65 (1968); *Ybarra v. Illinois,* 444 U.S. 85, 93-94 (1979); *Michigan v. Long,* 463 U.S. 1032, 1049-52 & n.16 (1983); *Minnesota v. Dickerson,* 508 U.S. 366, 373 (1993); *Florida v. J.L.,* 529 U.S. 266, 269-70 (2000). To justify a frisk, the officer needs more than the reasonable suspicion of criminal activity that will justify a stop and needs more than merely a hunch that the suspect might be armed. *See, e.g., United States v. McKinney*, 980 F.3d 485, 496 (5th Cir. 2020) ("[e]ven if the officers had reasonable suspicion to initiate the stop, the pat-down needs its own justification"). The officer must be able to "point to specific and articulable facts which, taken together with rational inferences from those facts, reasonably warrant" the conclusion that the officer "is dealing with an armed and dangerous individual" (*Terry v. Ohio, supra*, 392 U.S. at 21, 27). *See Sibron v. New York, supra*, 392 U.S. at 63-64; *Ybarra v. Illinois, supra*, 444 U.S. at 92-93; *Michigan v. Long, supra*, 463 U.S. at 1049-52 & nn.14, 16; *Minnesota v. Dickerson, supra*, 508 U.S. at 373; *Florida v. J.L., supra*, 529 U.S. at 269-72; *Arizona v. Johnson*, 555 U.S. 323, 327 (2009); *Dunaway v. New York*, 442 U.S. 200, 209 n.11 (1979) (dictum); *United States v. Howell*, 958 F.3d 589, 600 (7th Cir. 2020) (holding a frisk that followed a valid stop unconstitutional: "Here what matters perhaps most is that the 911 call in no way suggested that the suspect was armed or dangerous. The caller did not so much as hint at violence, injuries, or weapons."); *United States v. Williams*, 731 F.3d 678, 686-87 (7th Cir. 2013) ("The government asserts that the following facts supported Officer Jesberger's decision to frisk Mr. Williams: the fact that the group [of eight to ten persons standing in a parking lot], in general, avoided eye contact with the officers and started to move away from the area upon the officers' arrival; the fact that Mr. Williams, in particular, had his hands in his pocket or near his waistband, avoided eye contact, and began to move away from the area; the fact that this all occurred in a high crime area; and the fact that the police were responding to a 911 call reporting weapons. ¶ None of those facts, alone or together, could have supported a reasonable suspicion that Mr. Williams was armed and dangerous."); *Thomas v. Dillard*, 818 F.3d 864, 877 (9th Cir. 2016) (dictum) ("Even where certain facts might support reasonable suspicion a suspect is armed and dangerous when viewed initially or in isolation, a frisk is not justified when additional or subsequent facts dispel or negate the suspicion. Just as a suspicion must be reasonable and individualized, it must be based on the totality of the circumstances known to the officer. Officers may not cherry pick facts to justify the serious Fourth Amendment intrusion a frisk imposes."); *State v. Serna, supra*, 235 Ariz. at 275, 331 P.3d at 410 ("mere knowledge or suspicion that a person is carrying a firearm" will not suffice because *Terry* requires "that a suspect be 'armed *and* presently dangerous'"); *Norman v. State*, 452 Md. 373, 424, 156 A.3d 940, 970 (2017) ("that a law enforcement officer must have specific reasons for believing a suspect is armed and dangerous supports the conclusion that the mere odor of marijuana emanating from [a] vehicle with multiple occupants would not give rise to reasonable articulable suspicion that an occupant is armed and dangerous"). *But cf. Samson v. California*, 547 U.S. 843, 846, 851-52 (2006) (a police officer, "who was aware that [Samson] was on parole" and stopped him based on a belief that there was "an outstanding parole warrant" for him but then confirmed that no such warrant had been issued, could nonetheless frisk Samson because Samson's expectation of privacy was diminished by having signed a statutorily-required agreement to a parole condition of being subject to a "'search or seizure by a parole officer or other peace officer . . . with or without cause'"); *compare State v. Ochoa*, 792 N.W.2d 260, 291 (Iowa 2010) ("reject[ing] the holding of *Samson* under the Iowa Constitution" and "conclud[ing] that a parolee may not be subjected to broad, warrantless searches by a general law enforcement officer without any particularized suspicion or limitations to the scope of the search").

In addition to limiting the situations in which an officer can make a frisk, the Fourth Amendment also regulates the manner in which frisks may be conducted. A frisk must be "limited to that which is necessary for the discovery of weapons" (*Terry v. Ohio, supra*, 392 U.S. at 26). *See Sibron v. New York, supra*, 392 U.S. at 65-66; *United States v. Brignoni-Ponce,* 422 U.S. 873, 880-82 (1975); *Pennsylvania v. Mimms,* 434 U.S. 106, 111-12 (1977) (per curiam); *Florida v. Royer,* 460 U.S. 491, 500 (1983) (plurality opinion); *id.* at 509-11 (concurring opinion of Justice Brennan). "If the protective search goes beyond what is necessary to determine if the suspect is armed, it is no longer valid under *Terry* and its fruits will be suppressed." *Minnesota v. Dickerson, supra*, 508 U.S. at 373. Emphasizing that the frisk approved in *Terry* consisted of "a limited patting of the outer clothing of the suspect for concealed objects which might be used as instruments of assault" and that it was only after the discovery of such objects that "the officer in *Terry* place[d] his hands in the pockets of the men he searched," the Court in *Sibron v. New York, supra*, condemned a frisk in which the officer, "with no attempt at an initial limited exploration for arms, . . . thrust his hand into [the defendant's] pocket" (392 U.S. at 65). *Accord, United States v. Brown*, 996 F.3d 998 (9th Cir. 2021); *and see also State v. Privott*, 203 N.J. 16, 31-32, 999 A.2d 415, 424-25 (2010) (a police officer exceeded the permissible scope of a *Terry* frisk by "lift[ing] defendant's tee-shirt to expose defendant's stomach, and in doing so, observ[ing] a plastic bag with suspected drugs in the waistband of defendant's pants"). In *Minnesota v. Dickerson, supra*, 508 U.S. at 378-79, the Court held that a "police officer . . . overstepped the bounds of the 'strictly circumscribed' search for weapons allowed under *Terry*" by "continu[ing] exploration of defendant's pocket after having concluded that it contained no weapon." The frisk must be "limited to those areas in which a weapon may be placed or hidden" (*Michigan v. Long, supra*, 463 U.S. at 1049 (during a *Terry* search of the passenger compartment of an automobile, the *Terry* frisk doctrine permits officers to search only those areas that could contain a weapon and were accessible to the suspect)). *See also United States v. Baker*, 58 F.4th 1109 (9th Cir. 2023), summarized in § 25.13 *infra; United States v. Zavala*, 541 F.3d 562 (5th Cir. 2008); *Harris v. Commonwealth*, 241 Va. 146, 400 S.E.2d 191 (1991); *United States v. Askew*, 529 F.3d 1119, 1123, 1127-44 (D.C. Cir. 2008) (en banc) (police officers' partial unzipping of the defendant's outer jacket during a show-up to allow the victim to see whether the defendant's sweatshirt matched that of the perpetrator exceeded the lawful bounds of a *Terry* frisk).

If, in the course of a *Terry* frisk, "a police officer lawfully pats down a suspect's outer clothing and feels an object whose contour or mass makes its identity [as contraband] immediately apparent," the officer may be able to seize the object pursuant to the "plain touch" (sometimes called the "plain feel") doctrine (*Minnesota v. Dickerson, supra*, 508 U.S. at 373, 375-76). For the "plain touch" doctrine to justify a seizure, "the officer who conducted the search . . . [had to have been] acting within the lawful bounds marked by *Terry*" at the time s/he discovered the contraband (*id.* at 377); the "incriminating character of the object . . . [had to have been] immediately apparent" to the officer without, for example, engaging in "'squeezing, sliding and otherwise manipulating the contents of the defendant's pocket'" after it was already apparent that the "pocket . . . contained no weapon" (*id.* at 378-79); the officer's recognition of the contraband nature of the object must reach the level of "probable cause" (*id.* at 377); and it must be evident from the circumstances that the officer was not exploiting an authorized *Terry* frisk for weapons to engage in "the sort of evidentiary search that *Terry* expressly refused to authorize . . . and that [the Court has] . . . condemned in subsequent cases" (*id.* at 378); *and see United States v. Crutchfield*, 2023 WL 3317992, at *1 (D. Minn. 2023) (ordering suppression of a cell phone seized during a traffic stop because the officer who seized it in order to "preserve evidence" lacked "a 'reasonable, articulable suspicion, premised on objective facts, that [Crutchfield's phone] . . . contain[ed] contraband or evidence of a crime'"). *But cf. People v. Diaz*, 81 N.Y.2d 106, 110-12 & n.2, 612 N.E.2d 298, 301-02 & n.2, 595 N.Y.S.2d 940, 943-44 & n.2 (1993) (rejecting the "plain touch" doctrine altogether on state constitutional grounds).

25.11. *Factors Commonly Relied on by the Police to Justify an Arrest or a* Terry *Stop or Frisk*

Invariably, the police invoke the same general factors in case after case to justify their decisions to arrest or to conduct a *Terry* stop and frisk. In part, this may be due to police experience that these factors are reliable indicators of criminal conduct. In part, it may be because police officers have learned the proper formulaic responses necessary in order to obtain judicial ratification of their actions. The following subsections discuss some of the more controversial factors in the standard litany. In addressing these factors, counsel should be alert to the reality that they are heavily skewed by racial stereotypes and often constitute vestiges of *de jure* race discrimination, and to the possibility that some judges can be convinced to discredit or discount them for that reason. *See* Daniel S. Harawa, Lemonade: *A Racial Justice Reframing of The Roberts Court's Criminal Jurisprudence*, 110 CAL. L. REV. 681 (2022); *and see, e.g., United States v. Black*, 707 F.3d 531, 542 (4th Cir. 2013), quoted in § 25.11.1 *infra*; *Commonwealth v. Warren*, 475 Mass. 530, 58 N.E.3d 333 (2016), quoted in § 25.11.2 *infra*; *United States v. Brinkley*, 980 F.3d 377, 391 (4th Cir. 2020), quoted in § 25.11.3 *infra*; *State v. Sum*, 199 Wash. 2d 627, 511 P.3d 92 (2022), quoted in § 25.4.2 *supra*.

25.11.1. *"High Crime Neighborhood"*

Police routinely cite the high crime rate in a neighborhood to justify a stop or an arrest. Although the prevalence of crime in a certain area may be of some relevance in determining probable cause or articulable suspicion (*see Carroll v. United States,* 267 U.S. 132, 159-60 (1925); *Illinois v. Wardlow*, 528 U.S. 119, 124 (2000); *United States v. Darrell*, 945 F.3d 929 (5th Cir. 2019)), the Supreme Court has indicated that this factor should be given little weight as a predicate for either an arrest or a *Terry* stop. In *Brown v. Texas,* 443 U.S. 47 (1979), the Court invalidated a *Terry* stop that was based in part on the crime-prone character of the neighborhood, saying: "The fact that appellant was in a neighborhood frequented by drug users, standing alone, is not a basis for concluding that appellant himself was engaged in criminal conduct" (*id.* at 52). *Accord, Illinois v. Wardlow, supra*, 528 U.S. at 124 ("An individual's presence in an area of expected criminal activity, standing alone, is not enough to support a reasonable, particularized suspicion that the person is committing a crime" (citing *Brown v. Texas, supra*)); *United States v. Hurtt*, 31 F.4th 152, 160 (3d Cir. 2022) ("mere presence in a high-crime area obviously does not, without more, justify an otherwise unconstitutional intrusion"); *United States v. Blair*, 524 F.3d 740, 750 (6th Cir. 2008) ("[t]hat a given locale is well known for criminal activity will not by itself justify a Terry stop, although it may be taken into account with other factors"); *United States v. McKinney*, 980 F.3d 485, 488, 492 (5th Cir. 2020) (patrol officers accosted, stopped and frisked a group of four persons who were standing at 9:00 p.m. "on a sidewalk near a gas station . . . [that] had in recent days been the location of ["multiple gang-related"] drive-by shootings, one as recent as 4:00 a.m. that day"; the court holds the stop unsupportable under *Terry*: "a person's 'presence in an area of expected criminal activity, standing alone, is not enough to support a reasonable, particularized suspicion that the person is committing a crime.'"); *United States v. Massenburg*, 654 F.3d 480, 488 (4th Cir. 2011) ("The fact that this was a 'high-drug, high-crime area' adds little to the anonymous tip [even though "the city police 'usually get complaints . . . [for] random gunfire' in this area" and had, on the present occasion, received an anonymous report of eight gunshots in the general vicinity] . . . . This counts among the totality of the circumstances we consider, but it does little to support the claimed particularized suspicion as to Massenburg."); *accord, Wingate v. Fulford*, 987 F.3d 299, 306 (4th Cir. 2021) ("simply being in an area where crime is prevalent is minimally probative in the reasonable suspicion analysis"); *United States v. Black*, 707 F.3d 531, 542 (4th Cir. 2013) ("In our present society, the demographics of those who reside in high crime neighborhoods often consist of racial minorities and individuals disadvantaged by their social and economic circumstances. To conclude that mere presence in a high crime area at night is sufficient justification for detention by law enforcement is to accept *carte blanche* the implicit assertion that Fourth Amendment protections are reserved only for a certain race or class of people. We denounce such an assertion."); *People v. Shabaz*, 424 Mich. 42, 60-61, 378 N.W.2d 451, 459 (1985); *People v. Holmes*, 81 N.Y.2d 1056, 1058, 619 N.E.2d 396, 398, 601 N.Y.S.2d 459, 461 (1993) (suspect's presence in a "known narcotics location," even when combined with his flight from the police and a "bulge in the pocket of his jacket," did not provide the requisite basis for a *Terry* stop: "Given the unfortunate reality of crime in today's society, many areas of New York City, at one time or another, have probably been described by the police as 'high crime neighborhoods' or 'narcotics-prone locations.'"); *Commonwealth v. Cost*, 224 A.3d 641 (Pa. 2020), summarized in § 25.4.2 *supra*. Mere presence in a crime-ridden locale also cannot supply the predicate for a *Terry* frisk. *See Ybarra v. Illinois*, 444 U.S. 85, 93-96 (1979) (holding that the defendant's presence in a sparsely occupied one-room bar "at a time when the police had reason to believe that the bartender would have heroin for sale" (444 U.S. at 91) did not justify a reasonable belief that the defendant was armed and dangerous); *Perez Cruz v. Barr*, 926 F.3d 1128, 1138 (9th Cir. 2019) (the detention of a worker on factory premises which Immigration and Customs Enforcement agents suspected of employing undocumented aliens violated the Fourth Amendment in the absence of probable cause to believe that the worker himself was undocumented: "That ICE suspected . . . [the factory] was employing undocumented workers did not provide reasonable suspicion that Perez Cruz himself was undocumented."); *cf. United States v. Segoviano*, 30 F.4th 613, 623 (7th Cir. 2022) ("[U]nder well-established Fourth Amendment jurisprudence, it was not enough for Segoviano to merely be present in a building in which the agents believed that . . . [a person for whom they had an arrest warrant charging the shooting of a federal agent] could be located; the mere propinquity to . . . [the assailant's girlfriend] or to a place in which . . . [the assailant] might be located was insufficient to provide reasonable suspicion to detain Segoviano, whose only connection to the facts known to the agents was his residence in the building. The Fourth Amendment at its core protects the sanctity of the home – whether that is an apartment connected to other homes by common hallways or houses connected to other homes by yards and sidewalks. Apartments within a building are individual homes entitled to the same protection as homes on a street, and a suspicion that a person may be in the area is not a justification to seize residents of all of the apartments in a building – just as it would be insufficient to seize the residents of all the homes on a street if . . . [the assailant's girlfriend] was seen in the area of those homes and . . . [the assailant's] cell phone had been detected there."); *and see United States v. Rickmon*, 952 F.3d 876 (7th Cir. 2020) (discussing the weight that should be accorded to proximity to a location identified by ShotSpotter technology as the site of gunfire).

25.11.2. *Failure to Respond to Police Inquiry; Flight; Hassling the Police*

Frequently the police detain or arrest an individual because the individual refused to answer questions or because s/he walked or ran away when the police attempted to question him or her.

When suspects choose to answer the questions of the police, "the responses they give to [the] officers' questions" can be considered in the calculus of probable cause or articulable suspicion (*United States v. Ortiz*, 422 U.S. 891, 897 (1975)). *See United States v. Bowman*, 884 F.3d 200 (4th Cir. 2018) (reasonable suspicion was not warranted by driver's claim that he did not recall the address at which he had picked up a passenger 30 minutes earlier but that the address would be found in the car's on-board GPS). It is not clear, however, whether (and, if so, to what extent) a refusal to answer inquiries may be given weight in justifying a stop or arrest. In a number of cases, a majority or plurality of the Supreme Court or an individual Justice has stated that a suspect's refusal to answer police questions cannot provide a predicate for satisfaction of the Fourth Amendment criteria for a *Terry* stop or an arrest. *See Illinois v. Wardlow*, 528 U.S. 119, 125 (2000) ("when an officer, without reasonable suspicion or probable cause, approaches an individual, the individual has a right to ignore the police and go about his business"; an individual has the "right to . . . remain silent in the face of police questioning"); *Florida v. Bostick*, 501 U.S. 429, 437 (1991) (a suspect's "refusal to cooperate, without more, does not furnish the minimal level of objective justification needed for a detention or seizure"); *Berkemer v. McCarty*, 468 U.S. 420, 439 (1984) (a "detainee is not obliged to respond" to a police officer's questions); *Kolender v. Lawson*, 461 U.S. 352, 365 (1983) (Justice Brennan, concurring) (a *Terry* suspect "must be free . . . to decline to answer the questions put to him"); *Florida v. Royer*, 460 U.S. 491, 498 (1983) (plurality opinion) (a suspect's "refusal to listen [to police questions] or answer does not, without more, furnish . . . grounds" for a *Terry* stop); *Terry v. Ohio, supra*, 392 U.S. at 34 (Justice White, concurring) (a suspect's "refusal to answer furnishes no basis for an arrest"). Similar statements can be found in lower court opinions. *See, e.g., Moya v. United States*, 761 F.2d 322, 325 (7th Cir. 1985); *People v. Howard*, 50 N.Y.2d 583, 591-92, 408 N.E.2d 908, 914, 430 N.Y.S.2d 578, 584 (1980). In *Hiibel v. Sixth Judicial District Court of Nevada*, 542 U.S. 177 (2004), however, the Court rejected a Fourth Amendment challenge to a "stop and identify" statute that allowed an officer to detain a person to "'ascertain his identity'" if the "'circumstances . . . reasonably indicate that the person has committed, is committing or is about to commit a crime'" and that permitted the suspect's failure to give the officer his or her name under these circumstances to be punished criminally as "'obstruct[ing] and delay[ing] . . . a public officer in attempting to discharge his duty'" (*id.* at 181-82). In upholding the statute, the Court stated that "[t]he principles of *Terry* permit a State to require a suspect to disclose his name in the course of a *Terry* stop," as long as the "statute does not alter the nature of the stop itself . . . [–] does not change its duration . . . or its location" (*id.* at 187-88, 189). The *Hiibel* ruling is expressly limited to situations (and, thus, jurisdictions) in which a statute authorizes an arrest of an individual for refusing to divulge his or her name during a *Terry* stop. *See id.* at 187-88 (explaining that prior Court statements, such as those quoted above, regarding a suspect's right to refuse to answer questions concern the nature and import of Fourth Amendment protections while the *Hiibel* "case concerns a different issue, . . . [in that] the source of the legal obligation arises from Nevada state law, not the Fourth

Amendment"). *See also, e.g.*, *City of Topeka v. Grabauskas*, 33 Kan. App. 2d 210, 222, 99 P.3d 1125, 1134 (2004) (rejecting the prosecution's *Hiibel* argument because "[u]nlike the State of Nevada, we have no statute requiring persons to identify themselves . . . [and thus] *Hiibel* is clearly distinguishable from this case"). Moreover, even in jurisdictions possessing a statute such as the one upheld in *Hiibel*, "the statutory obligation does not go beyond answering an officer's request to disclose a name" (*Hiibel, supra*, 542 U.S. at 187), and thus a suspect's failure to answer police questions about other matters presumably cannot be factored into the calculus of probable cause or articulable suspicion. *See id.* at 185 (explaining that "the Nevada Supreme Court . . . [had] interpreted . . . [the applicable statute] to require only that a suspect disclose his name. . . . 'The suspect is not required to provide private details about his background, but merely to state his name to an officer when reasonable suspicion exists' . . . . As we understand it, the statute does not require a suspect to give the officer a driver's license or any other document. Provided that the suspect either states his name or communicates it to the officer by other means – a choice, we assume, that the suspect may make – the statute is satisfied and no violation occurs."); *and see id.* at 187-88 (explaining that a state statutory requirement that "a suspect . . . disclose his name in the course of a valid *Terry* stop is consistent with" "the purpose, rationale, and practical demands of a *Terry* stop" and "does not alter the nature of the stop itself"). Finally, even under a statute such as the one upheld in *Hiibel*, the initial stop that prompts the question about identity must be "based on reasonable suspicion, satisfying the Fourth Amendment requirements" for *Terry* stops (*id.* at 184; *see id.* at 188; *see also, e.g.*, *Commonwealth v. Ickes*, 582 Pa. 561, 873 A.2d 698 (2005) (striking down a "stop and identify" statute that, unlike the one in *Hiibel*, failed to require a valid *Terry* stop as a predicate for the request for identification)); "an officer may not arrest a suspect for failure to identify himself if the request for identification is not reasonably related to the circumstances justifying the stop" (*Hiibel, supra*, 542 U.S. at 188); and it must be apparent from the circumstances that "[t]he officer's request [for identification] was . . . not an effort to obtain an arrest for failure to identify after a *Terry* stop yielded insufficient evidence" (*id.* at 189); *Johnson v. Thibodeaux City*, 887 F.3d 726, 733 (5th Cir. 2018) ("According to the officers, they had probable cause to arrest Johnson for failing to provide identification, an alleged violation of Louisiana Revised Statute 14:108. That statute requires an 'arrested or detained party' to provide identification only when the officer is making 'a *lawful* arrest' or a '*lawful* detention.' ¶ The statute could not extend more broadly. Under the Fourth Amendment, police officers may not require identification absent an otherwise lawful detention or arrest based on reasonable suspicion or probable cause. . . . ¶ . . . Thus, under both Louisiana law and the Constitution, Johnson was required to provide identification only if she was otherwise lawfully stopped. The officers would have no probable cause to arrest if the request for identification came during an illegal seizure."); *Wingate v. Fulford*, 987 F.3d 299, 310 (4th Cir. 2021) ("Read together, *Brown* [*v. Texas*, 443 U.S. 47 (1979)], and *Hiibel* illustrate that a valid investigatory stop, supported by *Terry*-level suspicion, is a constitutional prerequisite to enforcing stop and identify statutes. Necessarily so. The prevailing seizure jurisprudence flows from the idea that, short of an investigatory stop, a person is 'free to disregard the police and go about his business.' *Cf. California v. Hodari D.*, 499 U.S. 621, 628 (1991); *Brendlin v. California*, 551 U.S. 249, 254–55 (2007) . . . .").

Flight may be relevant to the determination of probable cause or articulable suspicion (*see Illinois v. Wardlow, supra*, 528 U.S. at 124-25; *Sibron v. New York*, 392 U.S. 40, 66-67 (1968); *United States v. Darrell, supra*), but it is not dispositive and cannot, in and of itself, supply the basis for an arrest or a stop. *See, e.g., Illinois v. Wardlow, supra,* 528 U.S. at 124 ("flight," although "suggestive" of "wrongdoing," "is not necessarily indicative of wrongdoing"); *United States v. Brown,* 925 F.3d 1150 (9th Cir. 2019); *United States v. Green,* 670 F.2d 1148, 1152 (D.C. Cir. 1981); *People v. Holmes,* 81 N.Y.2d 1056, 1058, 619 N.E.2d 396, 398, 601 N.Y.S.2d 459, 461 (1993) (suspect's flight from the police, even when combined with his presence in a "known narcotics location" and a "bulge in the pocket of his jacket," did not provide the requisite basis for a *Terry* stop). Moreover, unless the flight occurs under circumstances in which it is reasonable to infer guilty knowledge, the flight cannot be considered at all. *See, e.g., Wong Sun v. United States,* 371 U.S. 471, 482-83 (1963) ("when an officer insufficiently or unclearly identifies his office or his mission, the occupant's flight . . . must be regarded as ambiguous conduct [and] . . . afford[s] no sure . . . inference of guilty knowledge"); *People v. Shabaz, supra,* 424 Mich. at 64, 378 N.W.2d at 461; *Commonwealth v. Warren,* 475 Mass. 530, 58 N.E.3d 333 (2016) ("Although flight is relevant to the reasonable suspicion analysis in appropriate circumstances, we add two cautionary notes regarding the weight to be given this factor. ¶ First, we perceive a factual irony in the consideration of flight as a factor in the reasonable suspicion calculus. Unless reasonable suspicion for a threshold inquiry already exists, our law guards a person's freedom to speak or not to speak to a police officer. A person also may choose to walk away, avoiding altogether any contact with police. . . . Where a suspect is under no obligation to respond to a police officer's inquiry, we are of the view that flight to avoid that contact should be given little, if any, weight as a factor probative of reasonable suspicion. Otherwise, our long-standing jurisprudence establishing the boundary between consensual and obligatory police encounters will be seriously undermined. . . . ¶ Second, . . . where the suspect is a black male stopped by the police on the streets of Boston, the analysis of flight as a factor in the reasonable suspicion calculus cannot be divorced from the findings in a recent Boston Police Department (department) report documenting a pattern of racial profiling of black males in the city of Boston. . . . According to the study, based on FIO [Field Interrogation and Observation] data collected by the department, . . . black men in the city of Boston were more likely to be targeted for police-civilian encounters such as stops, frisks, searches, observations, and interrogations. . . . Black men were also disproportionally targeted for repeat police encounters. . . . We do not eliminate flight as a factor in the reasonable suspicion analysis whenever a black male is the subject of an investigatory stop. However, in such circumstances, flight is not necessarily probative of a suspect's state of mind or consciousness of guilt. Rather, the finding that black males in Boston are disproportionately and repeatedly targeted for FIO encounters suggests a reason for flight totally unrelated to consciousness of guilt. Such an individual, when approached by the police, might just as easily be motivated by the desire to avoid the recurring indignity of being racially profiled as by the desire to hide criminal activity. Given this reality for black males in the city of Boston, a judge should, in appropriate cases, consider the report's findings in weighing flight as a factor in the reasonable suspicion calculus." (*Id.* at 539-40, 58 N.E.3d at 341-42.) "[I]n the circumstances of this case, the [defendant's] flight from [officer] Anjos during the initial encounter added nothing to the reasonable suspicion calculus" (*id.* at 539, 58 N.E.3d at 342) because the police, who "were handicapped from the start with only a vague description of the perpetrators," had "far too little information to support an individualized suspicion that the defendant had committed the breaking and entering," and therefore, "[u]ntil the point when [officer] Carr seized the defendant, the investigation failed to transform the defendant from a random black male in dark clothing traveling the streets of Roxbury on a cold December night into a suspect in the crime of breaking and entering." (*Id.* at

540, 58 N.E.3d at 342-43.)); *Miles v. United States*, 181 A.3d 633, 641-42, 645 (D.C. 2016) ("Mr. Miles's flight was too equivocal to reasonably corroborate the anonymous tip that the man had a gun" and thus "the police lacked reasonable suspicion to subject Mr. Miles to a *Terry* stop": "There are myriad reasons an innocent person might run away from the police. In *In re D.J.* [532 A.2d 138, 142 n.4 (D.C. 1987)], we explained that '[a]n individual may be motivated to avoid the police by a natural fear or dislike of authority, a distaste for police officers based upon past experience, an exaggerated fear of police brutality or harassment, a fear of being apprehended as the guilty party, or other legitimate personal reasons.' . . . As to this 'fear of police brutality,' Mr. Miles states in his brief that 'the proliferation of visually documented police shootings of African-Americans that has generated the Black Lives Matter protests' suggests that the court was misinformed in *In re D.J.* when it characterized such fear as 'exaggerated.' . . . In any event, an investigatory stop and frisk is not a 'petty indignity'– '[i]t is a serious intrusion upon the sanctity of the person,' *Terry*, 392 U.S. at 16–17 – and though we lack adequate empirical grounds for fathoming the extent to which innocent people might flee to avoid being subjected to one, it seems safe to say that the number is not insignificant."). *See also Illinois v. Wardlow, supra*, 528 U.S. at 128-29, 131-35 (Justice Stevens, concurring in part and dissenting in part, joined by Justices Souter, Ginsburg, and Breyer) (identifying a variety of "instances in which a person runs for entirely innocent reasons" and scenarios in which "[f]light to escape police detection . . . may have an entirely innocent motivation"). *Compare id.* at 124 (majority opinion) (*Terry* stop was justified by the totality of circumstances, including the suspect's "unprovoked," "[h]eadlong flight" "upon noticing the police"), *with Miles v. United States, supra*, 181 A.3d at 643-44 ("The *Wardlow* defendant's flight was probative of guilt because it was 'unprovoked.' . . . Mr. Miles fled after Officer Sanchez pulled his police cruiser in front of Mr. Miles as he was walking, blocking off his path. . . . Officer Sanchez then got out of the vehicle and told Mr. Miles to 'stop'; before that, Officer James was walking behind Mr. Miles. . . . [T]he experience of being followed by a police officer on foot, blocked by a police cruiser, and then told to 'stop' would be startling and possibly frightening to many reasonable people. There was thus a reason other than consciousness of guilt for Mr. Miles to have fled. . . . ¶ Moreover, . . . there was nothing about the character of Mr. Miles's flight that seemed particularly incriminating."), *and Banks v. Commonwealth*, 2015 WL 3533197 (Ky. App. 2016), summarized in § 25.11.3 *infra*.

Police will often invoke charges of disorderly conduct and similar public-order misdemeanors or petty offenses to justify arresting persons who berate or verbally hassle them. These arrests will seldom pass constitutional muster. *See, e.g., Villarreal v. City of Laredo, Texas*, 44 F.4th 363, 367 (5th Cir. 2022) ("If the First Amendment means anything, it surely means that a citizen journalist has the right to ask a public official a question, without fear of being imprisoned. Yet that is exactly what happened here: Priscilla Villarreal was put in jail for asking a police officer a question. ¶ If that is not an obvious violation of the Constitution, it's hard to imagine what would be."); *Croland v. City of Atlanta*, 782 Fed. Appx. 753, 757 (11th Cir. 2019) ("On this record, no objective officer under the same circumstances and possessing Officer Camille's knowledge could have believed reasonably that probable cause existed to arrest Plaintiff. Plaintiff's conduct consisted of yelling at Officer Camille in front of a group of people. Plaintiff made no physical gestures with her hands and took no steps toward Officer Camille, who was then about 11 steps away."); *Friend v. Gasparino*, 61 F.4th 77 (2d Cir. 2023) (the plaintiff in this civil-rights action stood on a public sidewalk and displayed a sign reading "Cops

Ahead" two blocks before a checkpoint at which the police were ticketing drivers for using cellphones while driving; an officer confiscated plaintiff's sign and arrested him for interfering with the officers; the Second Circuit holds that on these facts the plaintiff's First Amendment right to free speech was violated and that the arrest also violated his Fourth Amendment right against arrest without probable cause because the interfering-with-an-officer statute, as a matter of law, prohibited only physical interference and "fighting words" tending to produce a breach of the peace); *Garcia v. City of New Hope*, 984 F.3d 655 (8th Cir. 2021) (allegations that a police officer arrested a motorist for disorderly conduct and a license-plate violation in retaliation for his flipping the bird at her state a claim of violation of the First Amendment); *Cruise-Gulyas v. Minard*, 918 F.3d 494 (6th Cir. 2019) (an officer ticketed a driver for a minor traffic violation; as she left the scene, the driver flipped the bird at the officer; he stopped her vehicle a second time and amended the ticket to charge a more severe offense; allegation of these facts stated a claim that the second stop constituted a violation of the Fourth and First Amendments); *Wood v. Eubanks*, 25 F.4th 414, 418 (6th Cir. 2022) ("Michael Wood wore a shirt bearing the words 'Fuck the Police' to the county fair. According to Wood, the defendant police officers ordered him to leave and escorted him from the fairgrounds because of his shirt. While leaving, Wood made his displeasure known through numerous coarse insults levied at the police and the fairground's administrator. The defendants then arrested Wood for disorderly conduct. After the charges were dismissed, Wood filed this § 1983 action against the officers, alleging false arrest and retaliation. The district court granted summary judgment to the defendants. We reverse because Wood's speech was protected by the First Amendment."); *Ballentine v. Tucker*, 28 F.4th 54 (9th Cir. 2022) (allegations that a police officer arrested the activists in retaliation for their chalking anti-police slogans on a sidewalk state a First Amendment violation); *Alston v. Swarbrick*, 954 F.3d 1312, 1319 (11th Cir. 2020) (allegations that a police officer arrested a homeowner for disorderly conduct when, in the course of a police investigation of a reported domestic dispute, the homeowner refused to answer the officer's questions and said "Fuck you" stated a claim for violation of the Fourth Amendment: ""by 2011, it was clearly established that words alone cannot support probable cause for disorderly conduct – including profanity regarding police officers."); *see also Chestnut v. Wallace*, 947 F.3d 1085, 1090 (8th Cir. 2020) (police approached a jogger who had stopped to watch an officer make two traffic stops; when asked for identification, he provided his name and the last four digits of his social security number but refuse to provide the whole number; he was then detained and handcuffed; allegation of these facts stated a claim that the detention was unsupported by reasonable suspicion and violated the Fourth Amendment: "Every circuit court to have considered the question has held that a person has the right to record police activity in public."); *Quraishi v. St. Charles County, Missouri*, 986 F.3d 831, 839 (8th Cir. 2021) ("it is clearly established that using an arrest (that lacks arguable probable cause) to interfere with First Amendment activity is a constitutional violation"); *Watkins v. Bigwood*, 797 Fed. Appx. 438 (11th Cir. 2019); Anthony G. Amsterdam, *Federal Constitutional Restrictions on the Punishment of Crimes of Status, Crimes of General Obnoxiousness, Crimes of Displeasing Police Officers, and the Like*, 3 (No. 4) CRIM. L. BULLETIN 205 (1967); Anthony G. Amsterdam, *A Selective Survey of Supreme Court Decisions in Criminal Law and Procedure*, 9 (No. 5) CRIM. L. BULLETIN 389, 390-96 (1973).

25.11.3. *Furtive Gestures; Nervousness*

Frequently, a "furtive gesture" of the defendant's will be the impetus for a stop or an arrest. Although "deliberately furtive actions" may be considered (*Sibron v. New York, supra*, 392 U.S. at 66), the purported furtiveness of the gestures must be carefully scrutinized to determine whether they could be equally consistent with innocent behavior. *See, e.g., Reid v. Georgia,* 448 U.S. 438, 441 (1980) (per curiam) (invalidating a *Terry* stop because the allegedly furtive "manner in which the petitioner and his companion walked through the airport" was "too slender a reed to support the seizure"); *Brown v. Texas, supra*, 443 U.S. at 52 (striking down a *Terry* stop that was based upon the defendant's "'look[ing] suspicious'" and appearing to be walking away from a companion upon the arrival of the police, while in a "'high drug problem area'" (*id.* at 49)); *compare Florida v. Rodriguez,* 469 U.S. 1 (1984) (per curiam). If the officer's assertions about "furtive gestures" are vague, defense counsel should consider pinning the officer down on precisely which gestures s/he viewed as suspicious, in order to be able to argue that these actions are consistent with innocent conduct. *See, e.g., Thomas v. Dillard*, 818 F.3d 864, 884 (9th Cir. 2016) ("As one additional reason to believe [that defendant] Thomas was armed, [police officer] Dillard points to Thomas' demeanor, suggesting Thomas appeared 'startled and fidgety.' We do not see how either of these observations support even minimally the inference that Thomas was armed, however. Although Dillard testified Thomas and [his companion] Husky may have appeared 'a little startled' when he first confronted them, he also explained that this was 'a common reaction . . . when a police officer arrives on the scene.' By fidgety, Dillard meant only that Thomas and Husky exhibited normal hand movements, noting that it is not natural for people to stand in a perfectly still, statuesque form. Thomas and Husky, in other words, behaved normally."); *Banks v. Commonwealth*, 2015 WL 3533197, at *3 (Ky. App. 2016) (although the arresting officer "viewed Banks's act of walking away [from a crowd that "peacefully dispersed" upon the officers' emergence from their vehicle] as suspicious behavior," and the officer "explained that people with something to conceal often might step away from a group," the court of appeals rejects this reasoning and states: "in this case, the group *dispersed*; there was no longer a group from which to separate. We are not persuaded that peacefully walking away from a gathering is unusual conduct – or at least conduct so noteworthy as to justify a stop and search."). However, if counsel knows from interviews with the defendant or witnesses that the defendant's actions really were suspicious, counsel should refrain from giving the officer an opportunity to clarify a vague account.

"'[A] driver's nervousness is not a particularly good indicator of criminal activity, because most everyone is nervous when interacting with the police.' . . . '[M]ere nervousness 'is of limited value to reasonable suspicion analyses'. . . ." *United States v. Bowman*, 884 F.3d 200, 214 (4th Cir. 2018) (dismissing an officer's contentions that the driver and passenger of a stopped car "appeared to be nervous. . . . [The driver,] Bowman's hands were shaking as he handed over his vehicle registration and driver's license after the initial stop; . . . when . . . [the officer] initially approached the car, [the passenger,] Alvarez stared straight ahead instead of looking him in the eye; . . . in both men 'the carotid artery was beating very hard and rapidly,' . . . signaling an increased heart rate and nervousness; . . . Bowman 'couldn't sit still' in the patrol vehicle while . . . [the officer] was processing his license and registration"); *United States v. Massenburg*, 654 F.3d 480, 489 (4th Cir. 2011) (here "'nervous behavior" was . . . [the officer's] characterization of Massenburg's repeated refusal to consent to a voluntary pat-down": "The evidence . . . [the officer] cites for Massenburg's nervousness is slight: Massenburg was standing a foot or two from the other three, who were lined up shoulder-to-shoulder, and '[l]ooked down' or failed to make eye contact as . . . [the officer] repeatedly asked him if he would consent to a search."). *See also United States v. Howell*, 958 F.3d 589, 600 (7th Cir. 2020) ("Nervousness alone, at least not as a categorical matter, does not create reasonable suspicion that a suspect is armed and dangerous. See [*United States v.*] *Williams*, 731 F.3d [678] at 687 [(7th Cir. 2013)] (recognizing that '[m]ost people, when confronted by a police officer, are likely to act nervous, avoid eye contact, and even potentially shift their bodies as if to move away from the area')."); *Clinton v. Garrett*, 49 F.4th 1132, 1143 (8th Cir. 2022) (affirming summary judgment on a Fourth Amendment claim in favor of a driver whose car was stopped by police officers who asserted that they were unable to make out any writing on the temporary vehicle tag on the car's rear window: "The officers argue that there is no clearly established right to drive with a nervous passenger through a high crime neighborhood with a temporary tag that is unable to be read by officers following the vehicle. . . . Clinton's nervous passenger and the area where he was driving . . . , in isolation, do not support a conclusion that Clinton's vehicle was connected to unlawful activity in general, much less to the specific kind of unlawful activity for which the officers pulled him over – a possible temporary tag violation. Nor can a driver rightly be held responsible for ambient conditions that render a tag illegible."); *Klaver v. Hamilton County, Tennessee*, 2022 WL 16647970 (6th Cir. 2022) ("[D]eputy sheriffs from Hamilton County, Tennessee, stopped William Klaver for a tinted-window violation. They eventually requested a drug-sniffing dog because Klaver was shaking and refusing to say why. After the dog 'alerted,' the deputies searched Klaver's vehicle but found nothing illegal." *Id.* at *1. The Sixth Circuit holds that on these facts, "the deputies violated clearly established Fourth Amendment law" (*id.*): "We have a mountain of caselaw indicating that heightened nerves represent weak evidence of wrongdoing and cannot be the primary justification for a stop." *Id.* at *7.); *United States v. Brinkley*, 980 F.3d 377, 391 (4th Cir. 2020) (discounting police observations of nervousness on the part of a homeowner who had answered a knock at her door: she "could have been nervous at the prospect of exposing any number of people – for example, an elderly parent or a young child [as distinguished from the person sought by the police] – to five armed policemen. . . . [She] might also have feared for herself. Recent events have underscored how quickly police encounters with Black Americans may escalate, at times fatally.").

25.11.4. *Arrests and* Terry *Stops Based on Tips from Informants*

Frequently, a police officer's decision to make an arrest or a *Terry* stop is based on information obtained from a third party – either an ordinary citizen or a covert police informer. The standards regulating police reliance on such information are the same in these cases as in other contexts, such as automobile searches (see § 25.24 *infra*) and "hot pursuit" or "exigent circumstances" entries into premises (see §§ 25.19-25.20 *infra*) and are discussed in § 25.35 *infra. See also United States v. Peters*, 60 F.4th 855, 865 (4th Cir. 2023) ("Peters's criminal history as outlined in the police records does not justify Officer Butler's suspicion that he was trespassing. . . ¶ In [*United States v.*] *Powell*, [666 F.3d 180, 186 (4th Cir. 2011)], we evaluated the usefulness of similar police database information, labeled 'caution data,' and ultimately found that it could not provide the police officer with grounds for reasonable suspicion without additional facts. . . . (noting that 'caution data' – information indicating the defendant had 'priors' and a suspended license – lacked specificity, because there was no information as to when the data was collected or if it resulted in a conviction). Likewise, the record here is silent as to what led the officers to create the alerts, whether doing so led to further action, and whether the information had been updated since collected. Therefore, without more specific facts, these alerts do not heighten any suspicion that Peters was engaged in crime.); *United States v. Sprinkle,* 106 F.3d 613, 617 (4th Cir. 1997) (finding that an individual 'recently finish[ing] a sentence' and having a criminal record alone cannot show reasonable suspicion).

25.12. *Police Seizures of Objects from the Defendant's Person; Police Demands That a Defendant Hand Over an Object in His or Her Possession*

Any activity by a police officer or other state agent that is "designed to obtain information . . . by physically intruding on a subject's body . . . [is] a Fourth Amendment search" (*Grady v. North Carolina,* 575 U.S. 306, 310 (2015) (per curiam)). Frequently, in the course of an on-the-street encounter between a defendant and the police, a police officer will seize an object from the defendant. Such "a seizure of personal property [is] . . . *per se* unreasonable within the meaning of the Fourth Amendment unless it is accomplished pursuant to a judicial warrant . . . [or is justified by] some . . . recognized exception to the warrant requirement" (*United States v. Place,* 462 U.S. 696, 701 (1983)). *See, e.g., Beck v. Ohio,* 379 U.S. 89 (1964); *Torres v. Puerto Rico,* 442 U.S. 465 (1979). Objects may be seized from the defendant's person and may be searched without a warrant pursuant to the doctrine of "search incident to arrest" if all of the requirements of that doctrine, including probable cause to arrest, are satisfied. See § 25.8 *supra.* And if the defendant is carrying an object that is visibly contraband, in plain view of the officer, then the seizure and search of that object may be justifiable under the "plain view" doctrine. See § 25.22.2 *infra.* But if the object is a closed container, the power to seize it does not include the power to search inside it – or to manipulate it physically in order to detect its contents – without a search warrant. *Bond v. United States*, 529 U.S. 334 (2000); *United States v. Johnson,* 43 F.4th 1100 (10th Cir. 2022), quoted in § 25.8.2 *supra.*

Under certain narrowly defined exigent circumstances – for example, when "the seizure is minimally intrusive and operational necessities render it the only practicable means of detecting certain types of crime" (*Arizona v. Hicks,* 480 U.S. 321, 327 (1987)) – the police may be able to conduct a *"Terry*-type investigative [detention]" of an object (*United States v. Place, supra,* 462 U.S. at 709). However, this limited extension of the *Terry* doctrine has thus far been applied only in cases of "investigative detention of [a] vehicle suspected to be transporting illegal aliens" (*see Arizona v. Hicks, supra,* 480 U.S. at 327, citing *United States v. Cortez,* 449 U.S. 411 (1981), and *United States v. Brignoni-Ponce,* 422 U.S. 873 (1975)) and in a case involving a "seizure of [a] suspected drug dealer's luggage at [an] airport to permit exposure to [a] specially trained dog" (*see Arizona v. Hicks, supra,* 480 U.S. at 327, citing *United States v. Place, supra*). In each of the cited cases, the Court demanded "reasonable suspicion" of the criminal nature of the object seized, in the ordinary sense of the *Terry* doctrine (see § 25.9 *supra*), as a necessary precondition of the seizure.

The police cannot avoid these constitutional restrictions upon seizures by simply ordering the defendant to turn over the object rather than physically taking it from the defendant's possession. *See, e.g., Kelley v. United States,* 298 F.2d 310, 312 (D.C. Cir. 1961) (police officers' demand that "appellant systematically disclose the contents of his clothing, first one pocket, then another, and then another, was no less a search . . . than if the police had themselves reached into the appellant's pockets"); *United States v. Hallman,* 365 F.2d 289, 291-92 (3d Cir. 1966); *In the Matter of Bernard G.,* 247 A.D.2d 91, 94, 679 N.Y.S.2d 104, 105 (N.Y. App. Div.,

1st Dep't 1998) (police officers' "ask[ing] . . . [a juvenile] to empty his pockets . . . was the equivalent of searching his pockets themselves"); *M.J. v. State*, 399 So.2d 996, 997 (Fla. App. 1981) ("a demand to disclose or produce a concealed object is treated as a search"). In cases in which the police officers frame their demand in the form of a request and purportedly obtain the defendant's consent to the officers' taking control of the object or searching it, the constitutionality of their actions will ordinarily turn on whether there was a valid, voluntary "consent" under the principles set forth in § 25.18.1 *infra*. *See, e.g., Florida v. Royer,* 460 U.S. 491 (1983); *People v. Gonzalez,* 115 A.D.2d 73, 499 N.Y.S.2d 400 (N.Y. App. Div., 1st Dep't 1986), *aff'd,* 68 N.Y.2d 950, 502 N.E.2d 1001, 510 N.Y.S.2d 86 (1986); *United States v. Butler,* 2023 WL 3719025 (11th Cir. 2023), summarized in § 25.18 *infra*. But when the sole justification for the encounter is a *Terry*-type investigative detention, a request for consent to conduct a search of the defendant's person or possessions which is unrelated to that justification has been held impermissible, tainting the ensuing consent and a search pursuant to it. *State v. Smith*, 286 Kan. 402, 184 P.3d 890 (2008).

25.13. *The Defendant's Alleged Abandonment of Contraband Upon the Arrival of the Police: The "Dropsie" Problem*

Police officers frequently testify that, when approached or accosted, the defendant threw away an incriminating object, which was then picked up by the officer, or that the defendant disclosed the object to their sight in an attempt to hide it somewhere away from his or her person. This testimony is calculated to invoke the doctrines that the observation of objects "placed . . . in plain view" is not a search (*Rawlings v. Kentucky,* 448 U.S. 98, 106 (1980) (dictum); *see, e.g., Rios v. United States,* 364 U.S. 253, 262 (1960)), and that it is neither a search nor a seizure to pick up "abandoned" objects (*see, e.g., United States v. Thomas*, 864 F.2d 843 (D.C. Cir. 1989); *United States v. Ferebee*, 957 F.3d 406 (4th Cir. 2020)) thrown on a public road (*California v. Greenwood,* 486 U.S. 35 (1988); *California v. Hodari D.*, 499 U.S. 621, 624 (1991)). *See, e.g., Lee v. United States,* 221 F.2d 29 (D.C. Cir. 1954)).

In these "dropsie" or "throw-away" cases, the defense can prevail by showing that:

(a) The alleged abandonment of the property was itself the product of unlawful police action. Thus abandonment will not be found if (i) the defendant was illegally arrested or illegally detained prior to the time of the alleged "drop" (*see Reid v. Georgia,* 448 U.S. 438 (1980) (per curiam); *United States v. Beck,* 602 F.2d 726 (5th Cir. 1979); *Commonwealth v. Harris,* 491 Pa. 402, 421 A.2d 199 (1980); *State v. Bennett,* 430 A.2d 424 (R.I. 1981)); (ii) the police were engaged in an unlawful search prior to the time of the alleged "drop" (*see United States v. Newman,* 490 F.2d 993 (10th Cir. 1974); *State v. Dineen,* 296 N.W.2d 421 (Minn. 1980)); or (iii) the police were in the course of unlawfully pursuing the defendant at the time of the alleged "drop." (Prior to the decision in *California v. Hodari D.*, *supra*, there were a number of state high court decisions holding that if police officers initiated visible pursuit of an individual without the requisite justification for an arrest or a *Terry* stop (see §§ 25.7, 25.9 *supra*) and if the individual responded by fleeing and tossing away an incriminating object, an unconstitutional "seizure" of the individual had occurred at the time when the pursuit became manifest (because, for example, the police activated a flasher or a siren or called to the individual to stand still), and the discarded object was tainted by this illegality and therefore subject to suppression. *See, e.g.,*

People v. Shabaz, 424 Mich. 42, 378 N.W.2d 451 (1985); *People v. Torres,* 115 A.D.2d 93, 499 N.Y.S.2d 730 (N.Y. App. Div., 1st Dep't 1986); *Commonwealth v. Barnett,* 484 Pa. 211, 398 A.2d 1019 (1979). As a matter of federal constitutional law, those decisions have been cast in doubt by the holding in *Hodari D.* that an individual who flees when accosted by police is not "seized" for Fourth Amendment purposes until s/he is caught and physically restrained (see § 25.4.2 first paragraph *supra*). However, the pre-*Hodari* caselaw should continue to obtain in jurisdictions where (A) state law requires a justification for the initial accosting, and that justification is lacking (*see, e.g., People v. Holmes*, 81 N.Y.2d 1056, 619 N.E.2d 396, 601 N.Y.S.2d 459 (1993)) or (B) the state courts have rejected *Hodari* as a matter of state law and continue to hold that a "seizure of the person" occurs at the point of initiation of a manifest police pursuit (*see, e.g., State v. Oquendo*, 223 Conn. 635, 613 A.2d 1300 (1992); *Commonwealth v. Stoute*, 422 Mass. 782, 665 N.E.2d 93 (1996); *Commonwealth v. Barros*, 435 Mass. 171, 755 N.E.2d 740 (2001)). *See State v. Quino*, 74 Hawai'i 161, 840 P.2d 358 (1992).

(b) The "dropped" object fell into a constitutionally protected area. *See, e.g., Rios v. United States, supra*, 364 U.S. at 262 n.6 (a taxicab "passenger who lets a package drop to the floor of the taxicab in which he is riding can hardly be said to have 'abandoned' it"); *United States v. Ramirez*, 67 F.4th 693 (5th Cir. 2023) (finding no abandonment where the defendant tossed his jacket – later found to contain a handgun – over a fence so that it landed on top of a trash bin in the yard of his mother's home); *Work v. United States,* 243 F.2d 660, 662-63 (D.C. Cir. 1957) (the trash receptacle into which the defendant placed a phial of narcotics upon police officers' entry into a house was within the constitutionally protected "curtilage" of the home); *Commonwealth v. Straw*, 422 Mass. 756, 665 N.E.2d 80 (1996), summarized in subdivision (e) *infra*; *Commonwealth v. Ousley*, 393 S.W.3d 15, 18, 26-29, 33 (Ky. 2013) (police officers' search of "closed trash containers," which were near the defendant's home, was unlawful because "[t]he containers had not been put out on the street for trash collection" and were within the "curtilage" of the home). (Section 25.15.3 *infra* discusses the concept of "curtilage" in detail.)

(c) The police "dropsie" story is a fabrication, as it often is. *See, e.g., People v. Quinones*, 61 A.D.2d 765, 766, 402 N.Y.S.2d 196, 198 (N.Y. App. Div. 1st Dep't 1978). In seeking to show that the police officers are fabricating, defense counsel should cross-examine the officers on what they did prior to the "drop" that caused the defendant to disclose to them incriminating matters that were otherwise well-concealed. If plainclothes police are involved, this fact, together with the fact that the defendant had not previously encountered the officers, should be brought out. Even the habitual credulity of judges with regard to police testimony is sometimes shaken by accounts of a defendant's tossing away incriminating (and often highly valuable) objects at the approach of unannounced, unknown, and unidentifiable police.

(d) The object seized was a repository of information enjoying special Fourth Amendment protection because of its peculiarly private nature and its owner's efforts to preserve that privacy interest. *See State v. K.C.*, 207 So.3d 951 (Fla. App. 2016) (police chased a speeding car; it pulled into a shopping plaza and stopped; its two occupants fled; the pursuing officers seized several cell phones left in the vehicle; a detective later retrieved the contents of one of the phones, which was password-protected; "[h]e did not obtain a search warrant because he believed that the phone was abandoned." *Id.* at 952. "The State . . . claims that it could search the cell phone without a warrant under the abandonment exception." *Id.* at 955. "While we acknowledge that the physical cell phone in this case was left in the stolen vehicle by the individual, and it was not claimed by anyone at the police station, its contents were still protected by a password, clearly indicating an intention to protect the privacy of all of the digital material on the cell phone or able to be accessed by it. Indeed, the password protection that most cell phone users place on their devices is designed specifically to prevent unauthorized access to the vast store of personal information which a cell phone can hold when the phone is out of the owner's possession." *Id.* "As the Supreme Court held [in *Riley v. California*, 573 U.S. 373 (2014), discussed in § 25.8.2 *supra*] that a categorical rule permitting a warrantless search incident to arrest of a cell phone contravenes the Fourth Amendment protection against unreasonable searches and seizures, we hold that a categorical rule permitting warrantless searches of abandoned cell phones, the contents of which are password protected, is likewise unconstitutional." *Id.* at 956.). *See also State v. Worsham*, 227 So.3d 602 (Fla. App. 2017), summarized in § 25.25 *infra*.

(e) The police activity producing the material that the defendant contends should be suppressed involved the handling of some object belonging to the defendant which the defendant did not intentionally discard, or the invasion of some interest of the defendant that s/he did not intentionally relinquish. *See United States v. Baker*, 58 F.4th 1109 (9th Cir. 2023) (After a *Terry* frisk turned up no evidence of any weapon, an officer seized an auto key fob from the defendant's belt; the officer asked whether the defendant had a car, and the defendant said that he did not; the officer activated the key fob, causing a car in a nearby parking to flash its lights; the officer then searched the car and seized a handgun from it. The Ninth Circuit holds that the seizure of the key fob exceeded the scope of a permissible frisk because it occurred after the officer had determined that the defendant was carrying no weapon, then rejects the government's argument that the defendant "abandoned" the car by disclaiming that he had one: "The Government's . . . argument fails to persuade because Baker's statements concerning the car did not constitute abandonment of a possessory interest in the key hanging from his belt. Because abandonment is 'a question of intent,' we must consider the totality of the circumstances to determine whether an individual, by their words, actions, or other objective circumstances, so relinquished their interest in the property that they no longer retain a reasonable expectation of privacy in it at the time of its search or seizure. . . . '[N]one of our "abandonment" cases has held that mere disavowal of ownership, without more, constitutes abandonment of a person's reasonable expectation of privacy in that property.' . . . ¶ Based on the totality of the circumstances, we conclude that Baker did not objectively demonstrate his intent to abandon the car key. Baker never disclaimed any ownership or possessory interest in the key itself, nor did he voluntarily relinquish possession or control over the key." *Id.* at 1118.); *and see Smith v. Ohio*, 494 U.S. 541, 543-44 (1990) (per curiam) ("a citizen who attempts to protect his private property from inspection, after throwing it on a car to respond to a police officer's inquiry, clearly has not abandoned that property"); *United States v. Perea*, 986 F.2d 633 (2d Cir. 1993), *and* 848 F. Supp. 1101 (E.D. N.Y. 1994); *Commonwealth v. Straw*, 422 Mass. 756, 759, 665 N.E.2d 80, 83 (1996) (after the police had knocked on the door of the defendant's home and announced that they had an arrest warrant for him, he threw a briefcase out of a second floor window into the back yard; the Massachusetts Supreme Judicial Court holds that there was no abandonment for Fourth Amendment purposes: "[T]he briefcase and its contents would be abandoned for Fourth Amendment purposes only if the defendant had voluntarily surrendered all control over the briefcase in a way which demonstrated that he had relinquished any continued expectation of privacy. . . . ¶ We conclude that the defendant intended to protect his property from any public scrutiny because he placed the property in a closed and locked briefcase and disposed of the briefcase by throwing it into the fenced-in curtilage of his family's home, an area enjoying full Fourth Amendment protection from search by the authorities.").

25.14. *Post-arrest Custodial Treatment of the Defendant*

The post-arrest treatment of persons in custody is regulated by statute or caselaw in virtually all jurisdictions. The typical post-arrest procedures are described in § 3.2 *supra*. Counsel should be alert to the possibility that an arresting officer's failure to follow a constitutionally or statutorily required procedure rendered the post-arrest confinement unlawful and supplies a basis for suppressing evidence obtained during the post-arrest period. For example, if the police keep the defendant at the stationhouse for an undue length of time instead of bringing him or her to court expeditiously for arraignment, this will almost certainly violate local statutory requirements and may also fall afoul of the constitutional protections in this area (see § 11.2 *supra*), thereby tainting evidence such as confessions or lineup identifications obtained during the period of undue delay. See § 26.11 *infra; cf.* § 27.7 *infra*. Police brutality during the post-arrest period (*see, e.g., Kingsley v. Hendrickson*, 576 U.S. 389 (2015); *Shuford v. Conway*, 666 Fed. Appx. 811 (11th Cir. 2016)) may render any subsequent confessions or consents to searches unlawful. See § 26.3.1 *infra*.

The post-arrest period is often the stage at which the police or prosecution investigators conduct physical examinations, extractions of body fluids, hair, and so forth from arrested persons. An individual's body is protected by the Fourth and Fourteenth Amendments' prohibition of unreasonable searches of the person, including any procedure that is "designed to obtain information" and that involves "physically intruding on a subject's body" (*Grady v. North Carolina*, 575 U.S. 306, 310 (2015) (per curiam)). *See Birchfield v. North Dakota*, 579 U.S. 438, 455 (2016) ("our cases establish that the taking of a blood sample or the administration of a breath test is a search" for Fourth Amendment purposes). Searches that intrude into the body or breach the body wall – and perhaps other intimate personal examinations – are governed by a set of constitutional principles originating in *Schmerber v. California,* 384 U.S. 757 (1966), and *Winston v. Lee,* 470 U.S. 753 (1985), and elaborated in *Birchfield*. The "individual's interests in privacy and security are weighed against society's interests in conducting the [search] procedure . . . [in order to determine] whether the community's need for evidence outweighs the substantial privacy interests at stake" (*Winston v. Lee, supra*, 470 U.S. at 760). *Compare, e.g., Florence v. Board of Chosen Freeholders of County of Burlington,* 566 U.S. 318, 322, 330, 339 (2012) (jail's policy of requiring that "every detainee who will be admitted to the general population . . . undergo a close visual inspection while undressed," notwithstanding the absence of "reasonable suspicion of a concealed weapon or other contraband," did not violate the Fourth Amendment, given the "undoubted security imperatives involved in jail supervision" and the "reasonable balance [that had been struck] between inmate privacy and the needs of the institution[ ]"), *with United States v. Fowlkes,* 804 F.3d 954, 958, 966 (9th Cir. 2015) ("the forcible removal of an unidentified item of unknown size from Fowlkes' rectum [during processing at jail after a strip search] by officers without medical training or a warrant violated his Fourth Amendment rights"; "the record is devoid of any evidence from which the officers reasonably might have inferred that evidence would be destroyed if they took the time to secure a warrant and summon medical personnel. . . . ¶ Similarly, the record contains no evidence that a medical emergency existed. . . . Thus, there was time to take steps – potentially including, *inter alia*, securing medical personnel, a warrant, or both – to mitigate the risk that the seizure would cause physical and emotional trauma."), *and People v. Hall*, 10 N.Y.3d 303, 312-13, 886 N.E.2d 162, 169, 856 N.Y.S.2d 540, 547 (2008) ("manual body cavity search" of a suspect at the police station to remove contraband observed during a lawfully conducted strip search violated the Fourth Amendment because there were no exigent circumstances preventing the police from obtaining a warrant). In the application of this balancing test, the following factors are central to an assessment of the "reasonableness," and thereby of the constitutionality, of the search:

(a) Whether the police officers obtained a search warrant; or, if they failed to obtain a warrant, whether their failure to obtain a warrant was justified because the imminent disappearance of the evidence made it impracticable to obtain a warrant. *Schmerber, supra*, 384 U.S. at 770; *Winston v. Lee, supra*, 470 U.S. at 761. *See, e.g., Missouri v. McNeely*, 569 U.S. 141, 156, 165 (2013) ("in drunk-driving investigations, the natural dissipation of alcohol in the bloodstream does not constitute an exigency in every case sufficient to justify conducting a blood test without a warrant"; "while the natural dissipation of alcohol in the blood may support a finding of exigency in a specific case, as it did in *Schmerber*, it does not do so categorically"). *Compare Birchfield v. North Dakota, supra*, 579 U.S. at 456, discussed in subdivision (d) of this section, *with Mitchell v. Wisconsin*, 139 S. Ct. 2525 (2019) (plurality opinion) ("in . . . [the] narrow but important category of cases . . . in which the driver is unconscious and therefore cannot be given a breath test. . ., the exigent-circumstances rule almost always permits a blood test without a warrant" (*id.* at 2531) but "[w]e do not rule out the possibility that in an unusual case a defendant would be able to show that his blood would not have been drawn if police had not been seeking BAC information, and that police could not have reasonably judged that a warrant application would interfere with other pressing needs or duties" (*id.* at 2539)); *and see People v. Schaufele*, 2014 CO 43, 325 P.3d 1060, 1068 (Colo. 2014) ("the trial court properly adhered to *McNeely* in suppressing evidence of Schaufele's blood draw" because *McNeely* holds "that the Fourth Amendment requires officers in drunk-driving investigations to obtain a warrant before drawing a blood sample when they can do so without significantly undermining the efficacy of the search . . . ."); *McGuire v. State*, 493 S.W.3d 177, 197-98 (Tex. App. 2016) ("Fort Bend County had a process in place to assist officers in obtaining warrants. It had assistant district attorneys on call at all hours. Officers, or the assistant district attorneys, could fax transmissions to any of "about 20" Fort Bend County judges at their homes to process a warrant or the officers could take a warrant request to the judges personally. Nonetheless, no effort was made to obtain a warrant by any of the seven officers at the scene. . . . ¶ . . . The State argues that it may have proven difficult to locate a judge to sign a warrant, but, without any effort to do so, the testimony is only speculation. ¶ Having examined the totality of the circumstances, we conclude that the State failed to demonstrate an exigency to excuse the requirement of a warrant."); *Commonwealth v. Jones-Williams*, 279 A.3d 508, 518 (Pa. 2022) (holding that the Fourth Amendment was violated when police obtained a sample of an unconscious defendant's blood from the hospital where he had been taken after a traffic accident: the blood had been drawn and preserved by hospital personnel before the arrival of the police; there was no danger of dissipation of any alcohol it may have contained, so "it is [that] clear exigent circumstances did not exist to justify the warrantless seizure of . . . [the defendant's] blood"; the Pennsylvania

Supreme Court relies in part upon its decision in *Commonwealth v. Trahey*, 658 Pa. 340, 228 A.3d 520 (Pa. 2020), which it summarizes as "applying *Mitchell* and *Birchfield* to hold that there were no exigent circumstances for a warrantless seizure of blood where a breath test could have been taken to test for the presence of alcohol and there was time to secure a warrant to test blood for controlled substances" (*id.* at 518).).

(b) Whether the search was justified by a "clear indication" that incriminating evidence would be found. *Schmerber, supra*, 384 U.S. at 770; *see Winston v. Lee, supra*, 470 U.S. at 762 (quoting the *Schmerber* "clear indication" standard). The Court in *United States v. Montoya de Hernandez*, 473 U.S. 531, 540 (1985), subsequently glossed the "clear indication" standard as requiring nothing more than probable cause, but there remains room to argue that a particularly exacting judicial review of the probable-cause determination is appropriate in cases of physical intrusion on the body because the degree of justification required for a search always depends upon the extent of "the invasion which the search entails" (*Camara v. Municipal Court*, 387 U.S. 523, 536-37 (1967); *see, e.g., Terry v. Ohio*, 392 U.S. 1, 21 (1968); *Tennessee v. Garner*, 471 U.S. 1, 7-9 (1985)), and "'intrusions into the human body' . . . perhaps implicate[ ] . . . [the] most personal and deep-rooted expectations of privacy" (*Winston v. Lee, supra*, 470 U.S. at 760). *Compare Sloley v. VanBramer*, 945 F.3d 30, 33 (2d Cir. 2019) (holding that "*visual* body cavity searches must be justified by specific, articulable facts supporting reasonable suspicion that an arrestee is secreting contraband inside the body cavity to be searched" (emphasis added)).

(c) "[T]he extent to which the procedure may threaten the safety or health of the individual." *Winston v. Lee, supra*, 470 U.S. at 761. With respect to this factor it is particularly relevant to consider whether: "all reasonable medical precautions were taken"; any "unusual or untested procedures were employed"; and "the procedure was performed 'by a physician in a hospital environment according to accepted medical practices'" (*id.; Schmerber v. California, supra*, 384 U.S. at 771-72).

(d) "[T]he extent of intrusion upon the individual's dignitary interests in personal privacy and bodily integrity." *Winston v. Lee, supra*, 470 U.S. at 761. With regard to this consideration, it is relevant to examine whether the procedure involved any "'trauma, or pain'" or violated "the individual's interest in 'human dignity'" (*id.* at 762 n.5). *See, e.g., Maryland v. King*, 569 U.S. 435, 446, 465 (2013) ("DNA identification of arrestees is a reasonable search that can be considered part of a routine booking procedure . . . [w]hen officers make an arrest supported by probable cause to hold for a serious offense and they bring the suspect to the station to be detained in custody"; the Court observes that "[a] buccal swab [to obtain a DNA sample] is a far more gentle process than a venipuncture to draw blood . . .[; it] involves but a light touch on the inside of the cheek . . . [and] no 'surgical intrusions beneath the skin'"; and there are "significant state interests in identifying . . . [the arrestee] not only so that the proper name can be attached to his charges but also so that the criminal justice system can make informed decisions concerning pretrial custody"); *compare Birchfield v. North Dakota, supra* (upholding state implied-consent laws requiring that drunk-driving arrestees submit to breath tests without a warrant because "breath tests do not 'implicat[e] significant privacy concerns . . .'"; "the physical intrusion is almost negligible," in that "[b]reath tests 'do not require piercing the skin' and entail 'a minimum of inconvenience. . .'"; the "effort is no more demanding than blowing up a party balloon"; "there is nothing painful or strange about . . . [the procedure of taking a tube into one's mouth, which is akin to] use of a straw to drink beverages"; "the process [does not] put into the possession of law enforcement authorities a sample from which a wealth of additional, highly personal information could potentially be obtained"; it "results in a BAC [blood alcohol concentration] reading on a machine, nothing more"; and "participation in a breath test is not an experience that is likely to cause any great enhancement in the embarrassment that is inherent in any arrest" (579 U.S. at 461-63), *with id.* ("[b]lood tests are a different matter" (*id.* at 463) and cannot be compelled without a warrant under "the search incident to arrest doctrine" (*id.* at 476) because "[t]hey 'require piercing the skin' and extract a part of the subject's body"; "for many [people], the process [of having blood drawn, even for medical diagnostic purposes] is not one they relish"; and "a blood test, unlike a breath test, places in the hands of law enforcement authorities a sample that can be preserved and from which it is possible to extract information beyond a simple BAC reading. Even if the law enforcement agency is precluded from testing the blood for any purpose other than to measure BAC, the potential remains and may result in anxiety for the person tested.") (*id.* at 463-64)). *See also State v. Thompson,* 886 N.W.2d 224 (Minn. 2016) (applying the *Birchfield* analysis to invalidate a statute providing that driving a vehicle constitutes implied consent to urine testing); *Mann v. City of San Diego,* 907 F.3d 1154, 1165-66 (9th Cir. 2018) (invalidating a county practice of subjecting children who are the suspected victims of abuse to physical examinations at a children's center without a warrant or parental consent: These "medical examinations are significantly intrusive, as children are subjected to visual and tactile inspections of their external genitalia, hymen, and rectum, as well as potentially painful tuberculosis and blood tests. . . . Children are forced to undress and are inspected, by strangers, in their most intimate, private areas. . . . The County's argument that the examinations are 'minimally intrusive' because they are 'adjusted to the children's comfort level,' ignores that the County routinely subjects children to these objectively intimate and potentially upsetting procedures. And while the County argues that the test results 'were used only for health-related rather than law enforcement purposes,' the dual purposes of the search necessarily mean that the examinations could result in the disclosure of information to law enforcement, which would further intrude on the children's privacy."). A prime example of a deprivation of dignity sufficient to violate the Due Process Clause occurred in *Rochin v. California,* 342 U.S. 165 (1952), when "police officers broke into a suspect's room, attempted to extract narcotics capsules he had put into his mouth, took him to a hospital, and directed that an emetic be administered to induce vomiting" (*Winston v. Lee, supra,* 470 U.S. at 762 n.5). *See also Sims v. Labowitz,* 885 F.3d 254, 261 (4th Cir. 2018) (having obtained a search warrant authorizing the photographing of a sexting suspect's penis, a detective instructed the suspect to masturbate in order to raise an erection; "Although the intrusion suffered by Sims was neither physically invasive nor put him at risk of direct physical harm, the search nonetheless was exceptionally intrusive" and therefore violated the Fourth Amendment.); *United States v. Booker,* 728 F.3d 535, 537 (6th Cir. 2013) (applying the Fourth Amendment to suppress contraband that was removed from the defendant's rectum by an emergency-room doctor to whom the police brought the defendant, "reasonably suspecting that Booker had contraband hidden in his rectum" and who "intubated Booker for about an hour, rendered him unconscious for twenty to thirty minutes, and paralyzed him for seven to eight minutes"; "Even though the doctor may have acted for entirely medical reasons, the unconsented procedure while Booker was under the control of the police officers must, in the circumstances of this case, be attributed to the state for Fourth Amendment purposes. The unconsented procedure, moreover, shocks the conscience at least as much as the stomach pumping that the Supreme Court long ago held to violate due process.");

State v. Brown, 932 N.W.2d 283, 296 (Minn. 2019) (holding that although officers have obtained a search warrant based upon probable cause and authorizing a physician to remove a baggie from a defendant's rectum, "forcing . . . [him] to undergo an anoscopy against his will and under sedation in the presence of nonmedical personnel is a serious invasion of . . . [his] dignitary interests in personal privacy and bodily integrity that outweighs the State's need to retrieve relevant evidence of drug possession"); *Ioane v. Hodges*, 939 F.3d 945, 949, 957 (9th Cir. 2019) (federal agents obtained a search warrant to investigate tax-fraud charges against a homeowner; during the lawful execution of the warrant, a female IRS agent insisted on escorting the homeowner's wife to the bathroom and monitored her while she relieved herself; this conduct violated the wife's "Fourth Amendment right to bodily privacy," and "a reasonable officer in . . . [the agent's] position would have known that such a significant intrusion into bodily privacy, in the absence of legitimate government justification, is unlawful."); *Robinson v. Hawkins*, 937 F.3d 1128 (8th Cir. 2019) (finding that a clear Fourth Amendment violation is stated by allegations that a female police officer conducted strip and body-cavity searches of a female marijuana-possession suspect in a public parking lot within the view of male officers). "[D]ue process concerns could be involved if the police initiate[ ] physical violence while administering the [blood alcohol] test, refuse[ ] to respect a reasonable request to undergo a different form of testing, or respond[ ] to resistance with inappropriate force." *South Dakota v. Neville,* 459 U.S. 553, 559 n.9 (1983) (dictum); *see also id.* at 563. *Cf. Kingsley v. Hendrickson*, 576 U.S. 389 (2015) (recognizing that the use of "excessive force" against a pretrial detainee violates Due Process).

(e) Whether there is a "compelling need" (*Winston v. Lee, supra,* 470 U.S. at 766) for the intrusion or examination because it represents the most accurate and effective method for detecting facts critical to the issue of guilt or innocence. Thus a blood test was approved in *Schmerber* because the test is "'a highly effective means of determining the degree to which a person is under the influence of alcohol'" and "the difficulty of proving drunkenness by other means . . . [rendered the] results of the blood test . . . of vital importance if the State were to enforce its drunken driving laws" (*Winston v. Lee, supra,* 470 U.S. at 762-63 (explaining the holding in *Schmerber*)). Conversely, the Court concluded in *Winston v. Lee* that the state had not shown a "compelling need" for the surgical removal of a bullet from the defendant's body, since the state possessed "substantial" alternative evidence of guilt (*see id.* at 765-66).

Certain types of physical examinations conducted by law enforcement investigators or consultants may run afoul of other constitutional prohibitions. Tests and examinations that involve the eliciting of "communications" from the accused (such as polygraph tests or the use of "truth serums") – and perhaps others that require his or her willed cooperation – are impermissible in the absence of a valid waiver of the privilege against self-incrimination. *See Estelle v. Smith,* 451 U.S. 454 (1981) (psychiatric examination); *Schmerber v. California, supra,* 384 U.S. at 764 (dictum) ("lie detector tests"); *South Dakota v. Neville, supra,* 459 U.S. at 561 n.12 (dictum) (same); § 16.6.1 *supra.* A physical examination that is extremely abusive, degrading, or unfair may violate the Due Process Clause of the Fourteenth Amendment. *See Rochin v. California*, 342 U.S. 165 (1952); *Taglavore v. United States*, 291 F.2d 262 (9th Cir. 1961) (alternative ground); *United States v. Townsend,* 151 F. Supp. 378 (D. D.C. 1957). *See also Kingsley v. Hendrickson*, 576 U.S. 389, 391-92 (2015) (clarifying that when "an individual detained in a jail prior to trial" brings a claim under 42 U.S.C. § 1983 against "jail officers, alleging that they used excessive force against him, in violation of the Fourteenth Amendment's Due Process Clause," the detainee needs not show that "the officers were *subjectively* aware that their use of force was unreasonable," and instead needs show "only that the officers' use of that force was *objectively* unreasonable"). Finally, to an extent that is not yet clear, tests and examinations whose reliability depends upon careful administration are impermissible if conducted in the absence of counsel and without a valid waiver of the right to counsel, following the initiation of adversary judicial proceedings. *See Winston v. Lee, supra*, 470 U.S. at 763 n.6 (reserving the question). *Compare United States v. Wade,* 388 U.S. 218 (1967), *and Moore v. Illinois,* 434 U.S. 220 (1977), *with Gilbert v. California,* 388 U.S. 263, 267 (1967); and see §§ 26.10, 27.6 *infra.*

C. *Police Entry and Search of Dwellings or Other Premises*

25.15. *The Threshold Issue: Defendant's Expectation of Privacy*

25.15.1. *Introduction to the Concepts of Constitutionally Protected Interests and "Standing" To Raise Fourth Amendment Claims*

In the preceding discussion of arrests and *Terry* stops, it was unnecessary to deal with the question whether the police conduct adversely affected any constitutionally protected interest of the defendant. A defendant always has a sufficient interest in the privacy and security of his or her own body to provide a basis for challenging a seizure of the person in the form of an arrest or a *Terry* stop or to challenge a search of the person incident to an arrest or stop. *See, e.g., People v. Burton*, 6 N.Y.3d 584, 588, 848 N.E.2d 454, 457, 815 N.Y.S.2d 7, 10 (2006). When addressing issues raised by searches of dwellings or other premises, however, it becomes necessary to inquire whether the defendant has the kind of relationship to the premises that permits him or her to complain if the Constitution is violated in searching them.

Prior to *Rakas v. Illinois,* 439 U.S. 128 (1978), this inquiry was framed in terms of whether a criminal defendant had "standing" to challenge the violation. *Rakas* changed the terminology to "whether the disputed search and seizure has infringed an interest of the defendant which the Fourth Amendment was designed to protect" (*id.* at 140). *See also United States v. Payner,* 447 U.S. 727, 731-32 (1980); *United States v. Salvucci,* 448 U.S. 83, 95 (1980); *Rawlings v. Kentucky,* 448 U.S. 98, 104-06 (1980); *United States v. Ross,* 963 F.3d 1056, 1062 (11th Cir. 2020) (en banc); *United States v. Waddell*, 840 Fed. Appx. 421, 430 (11th Cir. 2020) (reviewing the federal caselaw regarding the standing of a corporate executive to challenge a government agent's electronic search of the publicly inaccessible areas of a website owned by the corporation: "[a]sking whether a defendant has standing to challenge a search is another way of asking whether the defendant had a 'legitimate expectation of privacy' in the searched website"); *Commonwealth v. DeJesus*, 489 Mass. 292, 295-96, 182 N.E.3d 280, 284 (2022) (dictum)] (under traditional standing rules that require a defendant to have a possessory interest in the place or thing searched or seized or to be present at the time of a search or seizure, a defendant whose encrypted text message was acquired from the receiving device by law enforcement officers would likely be unable to challenge the search of that device, but under *Rakas* this defendant's reasonable expectation of privacy will enable him or her to contest the search and seizure). But *Rakas* also recognized that this terminological change would seldom affect either the nature of the traditional inquiry or its result (439 U.S. at 138-39); and the term "standing" continues to be used in some jurisdictions as a convenient label for the *Rakas* determination that a particular defendant "is entitled to contest the legality of [the law enforcement conduct which s/he challenges as the basis for invoking the exclusionary rule]" (*Rakas, supra*, 439 U.S. at 140). *See, e.g., United States v. Payner, supra*, 447 U.S. at 731; *Byrd v. United States*, 138 S. Ct. 1518, 1530 (2018) ("The concept of standing in Fourth Amendment cases can be a useful shorthand for capturing the idea that a person must have a cognizable Fourth Amendment interest in the place searched before seeking relief for an unconstitutional search"); *Warick v. Commonwealth*, 592 S.W.3d 276 (Ky. 2019).

The historical starting point for contemporary understanding of what kinds of "interest" can claim Fourth Amendment protection is *Katz v. United States*, 389 U.S. 347 (1967), summarized in § 25.31 *infra*. Dealing with electronic surveillance conducted by attaching a monitoring device to the outside of a public telephone booth, *Katz* famously said that "electronically listening to and recording . . . words [spoken in an area of] . . . privacy upon which [a person] . . . justifiably relied . . . constituted a 'search and seizure' within the meaning of the Fourth Amendment" (389 U.S. at 353). That formulation established the mantra that dominates post-*Katz* Fourth Amendment analysis: "A 'search' occurs when an expectation of privacy that society is prepared to consider reasonable is infringed." (*United States v. Jacobsen,* 466 U.S. 109, 113 (1984)). *See, e.g., United States v. Karo,* 468 U.S. 705, 714 (1984); *Kyllo v. United States*, 533 U.S. 27, 32-33 (2001).

"'. . . Expectations of privacy protected by the Fourth Amendment . . . need not be based on a common-law interest in real or personal property, or on the invasion of such an interest.' . . . Still, 'property concepts' are instructive in 'determining the presence or absence of the privacy interests protected by that Amendment.' . . . ¶ Indeed, more recent Fourth Amendment cases have clarified that the test most often associated with legitimate expectations of privacy, which was derived from the second Justice Harlan's concurrence in *Katz* v. *United States*, 389 U. S. 347 (1967), supplements, rather than displaces, 'the traditional property-based understanding of the Fourth Amendment.'" (*Byrd v. United States, supra*, 138 S. Ct. at 1526.)

"Although the Court has not set forth a single metric or exhaustive list of considerations to resolve the circumstances in which a person can be said to have a reasonable expectation of privacy, it has explained that '[l]egitimation of expectations of privacy by law must have a source outside of the Fourth Amendment, either by reference to concepts of real or personal property law or to understandings that are recognized and permitted by society.' . . . The two concepts . . . are often linked. 'One of the main rights attaching to property is the right to exclude others,' and, in the main, 'one who owns or lawfully possesses or controls property will in all likelihood have a legitimate expectation of privacy by virtue of the right to exclude.'" (*Id.* at 1527.)

Compare United States v. Dixon, 984 F.3d 814, 816, 820 (9th Cir. 2020) (holding that "the insertion of a car key into a lock on the vehicle's door for the sole purpose of aiding the police in ascertaining its ownership or control is a 'search' within the meaning of the Fourth

Amendment"), *with United States v. Beaudion*, 979 F.3d 1092 (5th Cir. 2020), summarized in § 25.33 *infra*.

But "privacy" interests not linked to the possession of any "property" are also protected. "[W]hile property rights are often informative, our cases by no means suggest that such an interest is 'fundamental' or 'dispositive' in determining which expectations of privacy are legitimate." *Carpenter v. United States*, 138 S. Ct. 2206, 2214 n.1 (2018). After repeating that "no single rubric definitively resolves which expectations of privacy are entitled to protection" (*id.* at 2213-14), the Court in *Carpenter* observed that:

"the analysis is informed by historical understandings 'of what was deemed an unreasonable search and seizure when [the Fourth Amendment] was adopted.' . . . On this score, our cases have recognized some basic guideposts. First, that the Amendment seeks to secure 'the privacies of life' against 'arbitrary power.' . . . Second, and relatedly, that a central aim of the Framers was 'to place obstacles in the way of a too permeating police surveillance.'" (*Id.* at 2214.)

Applying these concepts, *Carpenter* held that "the Government conducts a search under the Fourth Amendment when it accesses historical cell phone records that provide a comprehensive chronicle of the user's past movements" (*id.* at 2211). See § 25.31 *infra*.

25.15.2. *Expectation of Privacy; Areas in Which a Defendant Will Ordinarily Be Deemed To Have the Requisite Expectation*

The test of a defendant's right to base a suppression claim upon an unconstitutional search of premises is whether the defendant "had an interest in connection with the searched premises that gave rise to 'a reasonable expectation [on his or her part] of freedom from governmental intrusion' upon those premises" (*Combs v. United States,* 408 U.S. 224, 227 (1972); *Sgaggio v. Suthers,* 2023 WL 3055572, at *2-*3 (10th Cir. 2023)). An individual may have "a legitimate expectation of privacy in the premises he was using and therefore . . . claim the protection of the Fourth Amendment with respect to a governmental invasion of those premises, even though his 'interest' in those premises might not have been a recognized property interest at common law" (*Rakas v. Illinois, supra,* 439 U.S. at 143 (dictum)). When the defendant's relationship to searched premises is such that s/he "could legitimately expect privacy in the areas which were the subject of the search and seizure [that s/he seeks] . . . to contest," s/he is entitled to challenge the legality of the search and seizure (*id.* at 149 (dictum)).

All of the following are examples of premises for which a defendant can claim the requisite expectation of privacy:

(i) The defendant's home. *See, e.g., Kyllo v. United States*, 533 U.S. 27, 31 (2001) ("'At the very core' of the Fourth Amendment 'stands the right of a man to retreat into his home and there be free from unreasonable governmental intrusion'"); *Wilson v. Layne*, 526 U.S. 603, 610 (1999) ("The Fourth Amendment embodies th[e] centuries-old principle of respect for the privacy of the home"); *United States v. Karo,* 468 U.S. 705, 714 (1984) ("[a]t the risk of belaboring the obvious, private residences are places in which the individual normally expects privacy free of governmental intrusion not authorized by a warrant, and that expectation is plainly one that society is prepared to recognize as justifiable"); *United States v. Johnson,* 457 U.S. 537, 552 n.13 (1982) ("the Fourth Amendment accords special protection to the home"); *Collins v. Virginia,* 138 S. Ct. 1663, 1670 (2018); *Payton v. New York,* 445 U.S. 573, 589-90 (1980); *Minnesota v. Carter,* 525 U.S. 83, 99 (1998) (Justice Kennedy, concurring) ("it is beyond dispute that the home is entitled to special protection as the center of the private lives of our people"); *cf. United States v. Segoviano,* 30 F.4th 613, 623 (7th Cir. 2022), quoted more fully in § 25.11.1 *supra* ("[a]partments within a building are individual homes entitled to the same protection as homes on a street"). *See also State v. Brown,* 216 N.J. 508, 517, 529, 535-36, 83 A.3d 45, 50, 57, 61 (2014) ("in determining whether a defendant has a possessory or proprietary interest in a building or residence and therefore standing to object to a warrantless search" under the New Jersey Constitution when the state asserts that "the building was abandoned or, alternatively, . . . [that the defendant was a] trespasser[ ]," "the focus must be whether, in light of the totality of the circumstances, a police officer had an objectively reasonable basis to conclude that a building was abandoned or a defendant was a trespasser before the officer entered or searched the home"; "the record supports the trial court's finding that the State did not meet its burden of . . . establish[ing] that the property ["a dilapidated row house in the City of Camden"], although in decrepit condition ["with one or more windows broken, the interior in disarray, the front door padlocked, and the back door off its hinges but propped closed"], was abandoned or that defendants were trespassers"; "The constitutional protections afforded to the home make no distinction between a manor estate in an affluent town and a ramshackle hovel in an impoverished city.").

(ii) An unleased room that is occupied from time to time by the defendant, in rental property owned by the defendant's parents. *Murray v. United States,* 380 U.S. 527 (1965) (per curiam), *vacating* 333 F.2d 409 (10th Cir. 1964); *People v. Hill,* 153 A.D.3d 413, 416, 60 N.Y.S.3d 23, 27 (N.Y. App. Div., 1st Dep't 2017) (the defendant had standing to challenge a police search of his uncle's "apartment and surrounding curtilage" because the defendant "had stayed with his [uncle's] family 'on and off' since he was five years old," and, "although [the] defendant did not have his own room in the apartment and slept on the couch, he stored all of his clothes in the living room, and received mail at the apartment"). *See also United States v. Murphy,* 516 F.3d 1117, 1124 (9th Cir. 2008), *superseded on another issue by Fernandez v. California,* 571 U.S. 292 (2014) (the rent-paying lessee of various storage units "testified that he allowed Murphy to stay in the storage units [rent-free] . . . and gave him a key that opened all of the units"; "Murphy's living situation was unconventional, but the record shows that the storage units were the closest thing that he had to a residence. He was sleeping in unit 14 and storing his belongings in unit 17. For the purposes of the Fourth Amendment, this is sufficient to create an expectation of privacy and thus the authority to refuse a search.").

(iii) A home that the defendant is visiting as a social guest at the invitation of the homeowner or another resident. *See Minnesota v. Carter, supra,* 525 U.S. at 109 n.2 (Justice Ginsburg, dissenting) (explaining that although the Court majority ruled that there was no reasonable expectation of privacy under the facts of the case, it is "noteworthy that five Members of the Court [one of whom joined the majority opinion and also issued a concurring opinion, one of whom concurred in the judgment, and three of whom dissented] would place under the Fourth Amendment's shield, at least, 'almost all social guests'" (quoting *id.* at 99 (Justice Kennedy, concurring))); *State v. Talkington*, 301 Kan. 453, 483, 345 P.3d 258, 278-79 (2015) (defendant had "a reasonable expectation of privacy as a social guest in his host's residence," which extended to "standing to assert a reasonable, subjective expectation of privacy in the backyard, *i.e.*, curtilage, of his host's residence"). *See also Minnesota v. Olson*, 495 U.S. 91, 98 (1990) (accused had a reasonable expectation of privacy in a friend's duplex in which he was "[s]taying overnight" as a "houseguest"); *Jones v. United States*, 362 U.S. 257 (1960), as explained in *Rakas v. Illinois, supra*, 439 U.S. at 141, and *Minnesota v. Carter, supra*, 525 U.S. at 89-90 (majority opinion). *Cf. id.* at 102 (Justice Kennedy, concurring) (although, "as a general rule, social guests will have an expectation of privacy in their host's home," "[t]hat is not the case before us" in that "defendants have established nothing more than a fleeting and insubstantial connection with . . . [the] home"; they were using the "house simply as a convenient processing station" for packaging cocaine; they had never "engaged in confidential communications with [the homeowner] . . . about their transaction"; they "had not been to . . . [the] apartment before, and [they]. . . left it even before their arrest").

(iv) A hotel room in which the defendant is staying, however temporarily or sporadically. *Stoner v. California,* 376 U.S. 483 (1964); *United States v. Jeffers,* 342 U.S. 48 (1951) (a hotel room rented by defendant's aunts, who had given defendant a key and permission to use the room at will; he "often entered the room for various purposes" (*id.* at 50)). *See also United States v. Ramos*, 12 F.3d 1019 (11th Cir. 1994) (the lessee of a condominium had an expectation of privacy in his condo unit even after the check-out time for moving to another unit had passed; a briefcase which he left in the old unit and which was collected together with his other belongings by cleaners in anticipation of occupancy by a new lessee was not "abandoned" but remained protected by the Fourth Amendment against warrantless search by state police); *State v. M.B.W.*, 276 So.3d 501 (Fla. App. 2019) (a male juvenile who accompanied a female juvenile while she rented a hotel room under an alias and who accompanied her into it had an expectation of privacy in the room); *State v. Leonard*, 943 N.W.2d 149, 152, 157-58 (Minn. 2020) ("We hold that the law enforcement officers conducted a search under Article I, Section 10 of the Minnesota Constitution when they examined the [hotel's] guest registry. We hold further that law enforcement officers must have at least a reasonable, articulable suspicion to search a guest registry."; "In *State v. Jorden,* [160 Wash.2d 121, 156 P.3d 893 (2007)], the Supreme Court of Washington held that the Washington Constitution afforded individuals a reasonable expectation of privacy in their guest registry information because 'an individual's very presence in a motel or hotel may in itself be a sensitive piece of information.' . . . The court noted that the anonymity of hotels may provide necessary space for people engaged in consensual – but deeply private – relationships or confidential business negotiations, for celebrities, and for people experiencing domestic violence who hope to 'remain[ ] hidden from an abuser.' . . . ¶ We find the reasoning in *Jorden* persuasive. . . . The particular role that hotels play in society makes a guest's presence at that location sensitive information that warrants privacy protections. To conclude otherwise would deprive Minnesotans of rights that we have the duty to safeguard.").

(v) A defendant's office or work area, even if it is shared with other employees. *O'Connor v. Ortega,* 480 U.S. 709, 714-19 (1987) (a public employee's office); *United States v. Lefkowitz,* 285 U.S. 452 (1932) (a business office); *Marshall v. Barlow's, Inc.,* 436 U.S. 307, 311-15 (1978) (employees' work areas in a factory building); *Tidwell v. State*, 285 Ga. 103, 674 S.E.2d 272 (2009) (a wooden locker maintained by a livestock auction employee just outside his workplace sleeping quarters); *Serpas v. Schmidt*, 1983 WL 2192 (N.D. Ill. 1983) (grooms' living quarters at a public racetrack); *Mancusi v. DeForte,* 392 U.S. 364 (1968) (a union office shared by defendant and other union officials); *Villano v. United States,* 310 F.2d 680 (10th Cir. 1962), *limited on an unrelated point, United States v. Price,* 925 F.2d 1268 (10th Cir. 1991) (an employee's desk in a retail store); *United States v. Blok,* 188 F.2d 1019 (D.C. Cir. 1951) (an employee's desk in a government office); *United States v. Shelton,* 997 F.3d 749, 764 (7th Cir. 2021) (the desk and office of the administrative assistant to a township trustee; this office was the antechamber "to the inner sanctum of the Trustee herself, on the top floor of a secure building that largely contained administrative offices. Only four employees worked on that floor. Although she could not exclude [the] Trustee . . . from her office, . . . the assistant had a door that she could and did close to other employees . . . . She kept personal items in her office, and turned down papers on her desk when she wished to keep them private from visitors entering the space.").

(vi) "Public" places in which it is customary to allow temporary exclusive occupancy with a measure of privacy, such as taxicabs (*Rios v. United States,* 364 U.S. 253, 262 n.6 (1960); *but cf. Rakas v. Illinois, supra,* 439 U.S. at 149 n.16 (dictum)), pay telephone booths (*Katz v. United States,* 389 U.S. 347 (1967)), public lavatory cabinets (*Bielicki v. Superior Court,* 57 Cal. 2d 602, 371 P.2d 288, 21 Cal. Rptr. 552 (1962); *People v. Mercado,* 68 N.Y.2d 874, 501 N.E.2d 27, 508 N.Y.S.2d 419 (1986); *People v. Vinson,* 161 A.D.3d 493, 77 N.Y.S.3d 26 (N.Y. App. Div., 1st Dep't 2018)), and rented lockers in commercial storage facilities (*United States v. Karo, supra,* 468 U.S. at 720 n.6 (dictum)). *Compare Hudson v. Palmer,* 468 U.S. 517 (1984); *Bell v. Wolfish,* 441 U.S. 520, 556-58 (1979).

For discussion of privacy rights in the interior of automobiles, see § 25.23 *infra.*

25.15.3. *"Curtilage" and "Open Fields"; Multifamily Apartment Complexes*

The "curtilage" of a home – that is, "the area immediately surrounding a dwelling house" (*United States v. Dunn,* 480 U.S. 294, 300 (1987)) – is treated as "part of the home itself for Fourth Amendment purposes" (*Oliver v. United States,* 466 U.S. 170, 180 (1984)) and thus receives the same "Fourth Amendment protections" (*id.* (dictum)). *Accord, Florida v. Jardines,* 569 U.S. 1, 6 (2013) ("the curtilage of the house . . . enjoys protection as part of the home itself"); *United States v. Banks,* 60 F.4th 386, 387 (7th Cir. 2023) ("[A] front porch – part of a home's so-called curtilage – receives the same protection as the home itself. And no exception to the warrant requirement saves the officers' actions here [in making a warrantless entry onto the porch to arrest the homeowner with probable cause to believe that he was a felon in possession of a gun]. We therefore reverse the district court's denial of Banks's motion to suppress."); *State v. Kruse,* 306 S.W.3d 603 (Mo. App. 2010).

In determining whether any particular area is or is not within the curtilage, "the extent of the curtilage is determined by factors that bear upon whether an individual reasonably may expect that the area in question should be treated as the home itself. . . . [C]urtilage questions should be resolved with particular reference to four factors: the proximity of the area claimed to be curtilage to the home, whether the area is included within an enclosure surrounding the home, the nature of the uses to which the area is put, and the steps taken by the resident to protect the area from observation by people passing by. . . . [T]hese factors are useful analytic tools . . . to the degree that, in any given case, they bear upon the centrally relevant consideration – whether the area in question is so intimately tied to the home itself that it should be placed under the home's 'umbrella' of Fourth Amendment protection" (*United States v. Dunn, supra*, 480 U.S. at 300-01). Applying this four-part analysis in *Dunn,* the Court concluded that "the area near a barn, located approximately 50 yards from a fence surrounding a ranch house" (*id.* at 296) and "60 yards from the house itself" (*id.* at 302) "lay outside the curtilage of the ranch house" (*id.* at 301) and was not entitled to Fourth Amendment protection because (i) "the substantial distance" from not only the house but also the fence surrounding the house "supports no inference that the barn should be treated as an adjunct of the house" (*id.* at 302); (ii) "[v]iewing the physical layout of defendant's ranch in its entirety, . . . it is plain that the fence surrounding the residence serves to demark a specific area of land immediately adjacent to the house that is readily identifiable as part and parcel of the house," and the area in question "stands out as a distinct portion of defendant's ranch, quite separate from the residence" (*id.*); (iii) "the law enforcement officials possessed objective data indicating . . . that the use to which the barn was being put could not fairly be characterized as so associated with the activities and privacies of domestic life that the officers should have deemed the barn as part of defendant's home" (*id.* at 302-03); and (iv) "[r]espondent did little to protect the barn area from observation by those standing in the open fields . . . [since] the fences were designed and constructed to corral livestock, not to prevent persons from observing what lay inside the enclosed areas" (*id.* at 303). *Compare Collins v. Virginia*, 138 S. Ct. 1663 (2018) (holding that a police officer made a warrantless and hence unconstitutional entry into the curtilage of a home when he walked down the driveway adjacent to a residence and inspected a tarp-covered motorcycle which he had reason to believe was stolen and had outrun police in two traffic-violation incidents; the location is described by the Court as follows: "[T]he driveway runs alongside the front lawn and up a few yards past the front perimeter of the house. The top portion of the driveway that sits behind the front perimeter of the house is enclosed on two sides by a brick wall about the height of a car and on a third side by the house. A side door provides direct access between this partially enclosed section of the driveway and the house. . . . [T]he motorcycle . . . was parked inside this partially enclosed top portion of the driveway that abuts the house." *Id.* at 1670-71. "[T]he Fourth Amendment's protection of curtilage has long been black letter law.' . . . [T]he Court considers curtilage – 'the area "immediately surrounding and associated with the home"' – to be '"part of the home itself for Fourth Amendment purposes."' . . . ¶ When a law enforcement officer physically intrudes on the curtilage to gather evidence, a search within the meaning of the Fourth Amendment has occurred. . . . Such conduct thus is presumptively unreasonable absent a warrant." *Id.* at 1670.). *Cf. United States v. Jones,* 893 F.3d 66 (2d Cir. 2018), distinguishing *Collins* and upholding a warrantless search of a truck parked in a multi-family parking lot: "The lot was a common area accessible to other tenants of 232 Westland Street and to tenants of a multi-family building next door, and therefore Jones could not reasonably expect that it should be treated as part of his private home." *Id.* at 72.

In the urban context, application of the four-part test of *United States v. Dunn* will ordinarily produce the result that "curtilage" is coextensive with a fenced yard. *See Oliver v. United States, supra*, 466 U.S. at 182 n.12 ("for most homes, the boundaries of the curtilage will be clearly marked"); *California v. Ciraolo*, 476 U.S. 207, 212-13 (1986) (treating the area within a fenced yard as curtilage under an analysis that anticipates *Dunn*'s); *Estate of Smith v. Marasco*,

430 F.3d 140, 156-58 (3d Cir. 2005); *Lucibella v. Town of Oak Ridge*, 2023 WL 2822126 (11th Cir. 2023); *People v. Morris*, 126 A.D.3d 813, 814, 4 N.Y.S.3d 305, 307 (N.Y. App. Div., 2d Dep't 2015); *People v. Theodore*, 114 A.D.3d 814, 816-17, 980 N.Y.S.2d 148, 151 (N.Y. App. Div., 2d Dep't 2014). This is consistent with pre-*Dunn* caselaw. *See, e.g., Weaver v. United States,* 295 F.2d 360 (5th Cir 1961); *Hobson v. United States,* 226 F.2d 890 (8th Cir. 1955); *State v. Parker,* 399 So.2d 24 (Fla. App. 1981), *review denied,* 408 So.2d 1095 (Fla. 1981); *People v. Pakula,* 89 Ill. App. 3d 789, 411 N.E.2d 1385, 44 Ill. Dec. 919 (1980). Separate closed structures on residential property – garages, for example – are generally held protected by the Fourth Amendment without reference to the ordinary indicia of "curtilage," such as fencing in. *Taylor v. United States,* 286 U.S. 1 (1932); *see, e.g., Mendez v. County of Los Angeles*, 815 F.3d 1178, 1187 (9th Cir. 2016), *aff'd after remand,* 897 F.3d 1067 (9th Cir. 2019); *State v. Daugherty,* 94 Wash. 2d 263, 616 P.2d 649 (1980). When properties are unfenced or only partially fenced, the rule of thumb is that police may enter walkways leading to a front door but not into side- and backyard areas. *See, e.g., Morgan v. Fairfield County,* 903 F.3d 553, 563 (6th Cir. 2018) ("[T]he officers' right to enter the property like any other visitor comes with the same limits of that 'traditional invitation': 'typically . . . approach the home by the front path, knock promptly, wait briefly to be received, and then (absent invitation to linger longer) leave.' . . . Certainly, '[a] visitor cannot traipse through the garden, meander into the backyard, or take other circuitous detours that veer from the pathway that a visitor would customarily use.' . . . Neither can the police."); *Florida v. Jardines,* 569 U.S. 1 (2013) (the activity of the police in bringing a narcotics-sniffing dog onto the front porch of a residence constitutes a search within the curtilage and, in the absence of a warrant, violates the Fourth Amendment); *Bovat v. Vermont,* 141 S. Ct. 22, 22 (2020) (statement of Justice Gorsuch respecting the denial of certiorari) ("*Jardines* acknowledged that a doorbell or knocker on the front door often signals a homeowner's consent allowing visitors to 'approach the home by the front path, knock promptly, wait briefly to be received, and then (absent invitation to linger longer) leave.' . . . The Court recognized, too, that law enforcement agents, like everyone else, may take up this 'implied license' to approach. But, the Court stressed, officers may not abuse the limited scope of this license by snooping around the premises on their way to the front door. Whether done by a private person or a law enforcement agent, that kind of conduct is an unlawful trespass – and, when conducted by the government, it amounts to an unreasonable search in violation of the Fourth Amendment."); *State v. Chute,* 908 N.W.2d 578, 586-87 (Minn. 2018) ("In this case, the district court found that Chute had given members of the public an implied license to access his land to seek 'a back door entrance to the house and garage' by using the driveway and turnaround area on which the camper was parked. The court supported this factual finding by noting that the driveway was a 'well-worn dirt area' that exhibited a 'definable pathway,' and that two other vehicles were parked near the camper. . . . ¶ Because Chute had impliedly granted the public access to his backyard to seek 'a back door entrance to the house and garage,' we must next consider whether the officer acted within the scope of this implied license while on the property. The scope of the implied license 'is limited not only to a particular area but also to a specific purpose.' . . . The license, therefore, has a spatial limitation and a purpose limitation. . . . ¶ Viewed objectively, the evidence demonstrates that the officer's purpose for entering the curtilage was to conduct a search. . . . [T]he camper was parked at the end of Chute's driveway, past the house, in the back corner of Chute's backyard. To inspect the camper, the officer had to deviate substantially from the route that would take him to the back door of the house or to the garage. The officer walked directly to the camper, inspected it thoroughly, both inside and out, and only turned back toward

the house when he was satisfied that the camper was stolen. Anyone observing the officer's actions objectively would conclude that his purpose was not to question the resident of the house, but to inspect the camper, 'which is not what anyone would think he had license to do.' . . . ¶ . . . ¶ In sum, under *Jardines*, the officer's implied license to enter Chute's property was limited to what 'any private citizen might do' when visiting another's property. . . . Just as a private citizen would not be impliedly invited to explore Chute's backyard and snoop in a parked camper, the officer had no right to inspect the camper without attempting to contact Chute first."); *French v. Merrill*, 15 F.4th 116 (1st Cir. 2021) (Officers having probable cause to arrest French went to the front door of his rooming house at 5:00 a.m. and knocked; no one answered; an officer walked down the next-door neighbor's driveway and shined a flashlight into a basement window of the rooming house, whereupon someone inside covered the window and turned off the basement lights; the officer returned to the front door and knocked again, then observed that "more lights were quickly being turned off in the residence. Window coverings which looked like blankets were drawn over the open windows as well." *Id.* at 129. "Instead of honoring the clear signals that the occupants of the home did not wish to receive visitors, . . . [one officer] walked back onto the property and, peering through a drawn window covering, saw that a light remained on in the kitchen." *Id.* He and another officer next "walked through the curtilage along the narrow strip of grass and located what they had reason to believe was French's bedroom window. They knocked forcefully on the window frame and yelled for French to come out and talk. . . . [One officer] also shined his light into the bedroom. At the same time, . . . [a third officer] returned to the front porch, knocked on the front door, and told French to come outside." *Id.* A divided Court of Appeals holds that these repeated entries of the curtilage of the rooming house violated the clearly established "principle at the heart of *Jardines*: the scope of the knock and talk exception to the warrant requirement is controlled by the implied license to enter the curtilage." *Id.* at 133.); *Brennan v. Dawson*, 752 Fed. Appx. 276, 283 (6th Cir. 2018) (dictum) ("[a] police officer simply cannot linger and continue to search the curtilage of the home if his knocking at the front door goes unanswered"); *People v. Frederick*, 500 Mich. 228, 895 N.W.2d 541 (2017) (Narcotics enforcement officers knocked at the front doors of two homes at 4:00 a.m and 5:00 a.m. respectively and asked the homeowners about marijuana butter that the officers suspected the homeowners possessed. After *Miranda* warnings, each homeowner consented to a search of the residence, which turned up marijuana. These activities amounted to a Fourth Amendment search and invalidated the resulting seizures, unless the consents were found to be attenuated from the warrantless searches. "We believe, as the Supreme Court suggested in *Jardines*, that the scope of the implied license to approach a house and knock is time-sensitive. . . . Just as there is no implied license to bring a drug-sniffing dog to someone's front porch, there is generally no implied license to knock at someone's door in the middle of the night. . . . [A] knock and talk is not considered a governmental intrusion precisely because its contours are defined by what anyone may do. . . . When the officers stray beyond what any private citizen might do, they have strayed beyond the bounds of a permissible knock and talk; in other words, the officers are trespassing. That is what happened here." *Id.* at 238-39, 895 N.W.2d at 546. "[W]e next turn to whether the police were seeking 'to find something or to obtain information,' such that the Fourth Amendment is implicated. . . . A police officer walking through a neighborhood who takes a shortcut across the corner of a homeowner's lawn has trespassed. Yet that officer has not violated the Fourth Amendment because, without some information-gathering, no search has occurred. . . . In these cases, however, the police were seeking information; therefore, their conduct implicated the Fourth Amendment. . . . The officers approached each house to obtain information about the marijuana butter they suspected each defendant possessed. . . . *Id.* at 240-41, 895 N.W.2d at 547. "That the officers intended to get permission to search for the marijuana butter does not alter our analysis. . . . ¶ What matters is that they sought to gather information by way of a trespass on Fourth-Amendment-protected property." *Id.* at 241-42, 895 N.W.2d at 547-48.); *Commonwealth v. Ousley*, 393 S.W.3d 15, 27-29 (Ky. 2013) (trash cans, which were "sitting on the driveway very near the home," were within the "curtilage" even though "the area in question" was not "enclosed by a fence": "The home was in an urban area that does not lend itself to enclosures" and a resident's decision to forgo fencing "(for example, because the lot on which his home sits is small) cannot deprive him of having curtilage surrounding his home"); *United States v. Alexander*, 888 F.3d 628 (2d Cir. 2018) (backyard area in front of a shed a few steps from the back door of defendant's residence, accessible from the street by traversing defendant's driveway, which he used for parking, barbecues and relaxation is Fourth-Amendment protected curtilage); *State v. Chute, supra*, 908 N.W.2d at 585 (applying the four-part test of *United States v. Dunn, supra*, to conclude that "the area of Chute's backyard on which the [stolen] camper [trailer] was parked" was within the curtilage of Chute's home because "[t]he part of Chute's dirt driveway on which the trailer was parked is in close proximity to his suburban home"; "[a]erial photographs admitted at trial show that the backyard and dirt driveway are bordered on three sides by a tall, opaque fence on the east side, quite close to where the trailer was parked, a wooded area with a pond to the south, and trees to the west side"; "the driveway and turnaround were 'regularly used by cars carrying persons seeking a back door entrance to the house and garage,'" and "Chute stored scrap materials near the turnaround," and "in the center of th[e] turnaround was a fire pit with a horizontal log upon which persons could sit to enjoy a fire," and "[t]hese activities are closely related to the home and associated with the privacies of life"; and, although "the dirt driveway where the camper was parked is visible from County Road D if an observer stands at its northern end and looks directly down it[,] . . . [t]he curtilage of a home . . . need not be completely shielded from public view"); *State v. Kruse*, 306 S.W.3d 603, 611-12 (Mo. App. 2010) ("The State argues that Kruse did not have an expectation of privacy in his backyard. The State notes that there were no gates or objects to hinder entrance into the backyard. Nothing obstructed a person's view into the back yard except the buildings. There appears to be a well-travelled route from the driveway to the rear of the property, marked by large pieces of wood resembling railroad ties. The two 'no trespassing' signs were posted on doors, which the State says implies that access was denied to the interior of the residence or shed without permission. ¶ We cannot agree that there was no expectation of privacy in the backyard. The officers arrived at the Kruse residence after midnight. No exterior lights were on to welcome the public to come on the premises. The entrance to the residence is in the front yard. The 'no trespassing' signs would ordinarily be understood to assert a privacy interest on the entire property. The back yard could not be seen from the road and was not in plain view. The back yard and backdoor were enclosed by trees on three sides and the home on the fourth side. ¶ By entering into the back yard, the police were entering onto property as to which there was a privacy interest protected by the Fourth Amendment"). *Cf. State v. Kuuttila*, 965 N.W.2d 484, 486-87 (Iowa 2021) (applying *State v. Wright*, 961 N.W.2d 396 (Iowa 2021), in which "we held law enforcement officers conducted an unreasonable and thus unconstitutional seizure and search in violation of article I, section 8 of the Iowa Constitution when they seized and searched garbage bags left out for collection without first obtaining a warrant"; municipal ordinances applicable in both cases "prohibited any person, other than an authorized trash collector, from taking or collecting trash left out for collection," and these ordinances, "like similar municipal ordinances, . . . [are] positive evidence of a societal expectation that trash left out shall remain private and not disturbed by anyone other than an authorized collector"; a police officer is "not a licensed [waste] collector," and therefore the officer in each case "violated this expectation of privacy in seizing and searching . . . [the defendant's] trash without a warrant").

With respect to tenants living in multifamily apartment complexes, some courts have viewed their curtilage as very limited. *See, e.g., Commonwealth v. Thomas,* 358 Mass. 771, 774-75, 267 N.E.2d 489, 491 (1971). However, if the building is secured against entry by the general public, then any of the tenants may be able to rely upon the collective expectation of privacy in the corridors and hallways (*e.g., United States v. Heath,* 259 F.3d 522 (6th Cir. 2001); *United States v. Carriger,* 541 F.2d 545, 549-52 (6th Cir. 1976); *United States v. Booth,* 455 A.2d 1351 (D.C. 1983); *see also Hicks v. Scott,* 958 F.3d 421, 432 (6th Cir. 2020) (officers' warrantless entry into the separate foyer, stairwell and upstairs hallway of a duplex residence consisting of two units, upstairs and downstairs, provides the basis for a Fourth Amendment claim of illegal entry: " [T]there is no documentary or testimonial evidence to support the view that these areas were anything other than interior portions of the rear apartment unit. ¶ The layout of the duplex further evidences that the . . . [officers] entered a constitutionally protected area. The only kitchen and bathroom associated with the rear unit are located on the second floor and are connected to the third-floor bedroom via the landing. It would be anomalous to find – let alone at summary judgment – that the conduit between these core living spaces is a public corridor, especially when there is evidence that the foyer, stairwell, and landing were controlled and used by only one person: . . . [the upstairs resident]. Moreover, even if the foyer and stairwell could be described as distinct from the core living spaces, they are still 'intimately tied' to the apartment's interior."); *United States v. Whitaker,* 820 F.3d 849, 853-54 (7th Cir. 2016) (although the defendant, who lived in a multi-apartment building with "closed hallways," did not have "a reasonable expectation of complete privacy in the hallway," this "does not also mean that he had no reasonable expectation of privacy against persons in the hallway snooping into his apartment using sensitive devices not available to the general public"; accordingly, the "police engaged in a warrantless search within the meaning of the Fourth Amendment when they had a drug-sniffing dog come to the door of the apartment and search for the scent of illegal drugs"); *accord, People v. Bonilla,* 2018 IL 122484, 120 N.E.3d 930 (2018)) and the basement (*e.g., Garrison v. State,* 28 Md. App. 257, 345 A.2d 86 (1975)). *Compare McDonald v. United States,* 335 U.S. 451 (1948), *with United States v. Dunn,* 480 U.S. 294 (1987). Similarly, if the back yard to the building is not accessible to the general public, and particularly if it is surrounded by a fence, the back yard area may be "sufficiently removed and private in character that [a tenant] . . . could reasonably expect privacy" (*Fixel v. Wainwright,* 492 F.2d 480, 484 (5th Cir. 1974)). *See also United States v. Burston,* 806 F.3d 1123, 1125, 1127-28 (8th Cir. 2015) (even though the defendant lived in an "eight-unit apartment building," and even though the lawn in front of his apartment window "was not in an enclosed area" and "the public [was not] physically prevented from entering or looking at that area other than by the physical obstruction of . . . [a] bush," the court nonetheless classifies the area as curtilage under the four-part analysis of *United States v. Dunn, supra,* because the area "was in close proximity to Burston's apartment – six to ten inches"; "Burston made personal use of the area by setting up a cooking grill between the door and his window"; and "[o]ne function of the bush," which was "planted in the area in front of the window, [and] which partially covered the window," "was likely to prevent close inspection of Burston's window by passersby"). Counsel urging these results can argue that, in light of the established principle that "the Fourth Amendment accords special protection to the home" (*United States v. Johnson,* 457 U.S. 537, 552 n.13 (1982); *see, e.g., Groh v. Ramirez*, 540 U.S. 551, 559 (2004); *Kyllo v. United States*, 533 U.S. 27, 31 (2001); *Wilson v. Layne*, 526 U.S. 603, 610 (1999); *Welsh v. Wisconsin,* 466 U.S. 740, 748 (1984); *Florida v. Jardines, supra*, 569 U.S. at 6; *Minnesota v. Carter*, 525 U.S. 83, 99 (1998) (Justice Kennedy, concurring)), it would be anomalous to deny at least as much protection to shared residential facilities as is given to shared workplace facilities (see § 25.15.2 subdivision (v) *supra*).

The Fourth Amendment's protection of the home and its curtilage does not extend to "'the open fields'" (*United States v. Dunn, supra*, 480 U.S. at 300; *see Oliver v. United States, supra*, 466 U.S. at 180; *Hester v. United States,* 265 U.S. 57 (1924)). "[O]pen fields do not provide the setting for those intimate activities that the [Fourth] Amendment is intended to shelter from government interference or surveillance. There is no societal interest in protecting the privacy of those activities, such as the cultivation of crops, that occur in open fields. Moreover, as a practical matter these lands usually are accessible to the public and the police in ways that a home, an office, or commercial structure would not be. It is not generally true that fences or 'No Trespassing' signs effectively bar the public from viewing open fields in rural areas." *Oliver v. United States, supra*, 466 U.S. at 179.

Moreover, if a police officer, while situated in an "open field" – or in any area accessible to the general public – engages in "naked-eye observation of the curtilage" (*California v. Ciraolo,* 476 U.S. 207, 213 (1986)), that observation is not treated as a "search" subject to Fourth Amendment restrictions. See §§ 25.22.2, 25.33 *infra*.

25.15.4. *Police Search or Seizure of an Object Belonging to the Defendant from Premises in Which the Defendant Has No Privacy Interest*

Even if the defendant does not have a privacy interest in any premises searched by the police, s/he may nevertheless challenge a police examination or seizure of an object during a police search of the premises if the defendant is the owner of that object. As the Court observed in *United States v. Jacobsen,* 466 U.S. 109, 113 (1984), "an individual's possessory interests in [a certain piece of] . . . property" confer upon that individual a Fourth Amendment right to challenge a police officer's "meaningful interference with [his or her] . . . possessory interests in that property" (*id.*) *See, e.g., United States v. Johnson*, 43 F.4th 1100 (10th Cir. 2022). Thus, in *Jacobsen,* the Court concluded that the defendant had the requisite privacy interest to challenge government agents' assertion of control over, and search of, a package which the defendant had consigned to a private freight carrier, even though the defendant obviously had no privacy interest in the Federal Express office where the search took place. *Id.* at 114-15. *See also, e.g., Safford Unified School District # 1 v. Redding*, 557 U.S. 364, 374 n.3 (2009); *Bond v. United States*, 529 U.S. 334, 336-37, 338-39 (2000); *Walter v. United States,* 447 U.S. 649 (1980); *Recchia v. City of Los Angeles Department of Animal Services*, 889 F.3d 553 (9th Cir. 2018) (a homeless person stated a valid claim of Fourth Amendment violation when animal control officers without a warrant seized twenty pet birds which he kept in covered cardboard boxes and cages on the public sidewalk); *Garcia v. City of Los Angeles*, 11 F.4th 1113 (9th Cir. 2021) (homeless persons stated a valid claim of Fourth Amendment violation when their bulky property such as crates, sleeping pallets, and storage bins was seized and destroyed by city sanitation workers); *United States v. Barber*, 777 F.3d 1303, 1305 (11th Cir. 2015) (a passenger in a car stopped by the police had standing to challenge the search of the bag at his feet, "even if he lacked standing to contest the search of the car," because it was "his bag" and he "had a reasonable expectation of privacy in his bag"); *State v. Crane*, 2014-NMSC-026, 329 P.3d 689, 694-95 (N.M. 2014) (construing the state constitution to hold that a motel occupant had a reasonable expectation of privacy in garbage that was placed in "opaque garbage bags," which were "sealed from plain view . . . [and] placed directly in the dumpster, rather than being left in the motel room for disposal by the housekeeping staff"); *State v. Lien*, 364 Or. 750, 763-64, 441 P.3d 185, 193 (2019) ("Based on social and legal norms, . . . we conclude that, for purposes of Article I, section 9 [of the Oregon Constitution], defendants in this case had privacy interests in their garbage that had been placed within a closed, opaque container and put out at curbside for collection by the sanitation company. . . . [W]e recognize, given the realities of living in modern society, which is experiencing . . . significant social and technological changes, that privacy norms exist notwithstanding some limited public exposure of information, in this case, putting out garbage in a closed bin for pickup by the sanitation company at curbside, an area accessible to members of the public other than the sanitation company."). *But see United States v. Rose*, 3 F.4th 722 (4th Cir. 2021) (acknowledging that "[b]oth senders and recipients of letters and other sealed packages ordinarily have a legitimate expectation of privacy in those items even after they have been placed in the mail" (*id.* at 728), but holding that a cocaine-distribution defendant who arranged for FedEx shipments of packages addressed to a friend's deceased brother at the friend's residence where the defendant picked them up, paying the friend for his participation in this scheme, had no standing to contest the search of the packages at a FedEx processing facility).

The individual's privacy interest in objects that s/he owns extends to "[l]etters and other sealed packages [since these objects] are in the general class of effects in which the public at large has a legitimate expectation of privacy" (*United States v. Jacobsen, supra*, 466 U.S. at 114). *See also Love v. State*, 543 S.W.3d 835, 844-45 (Tex. Crim. App. 2016) ("appellant had a reasonable expectation of privacy in the contents of the text messages he sent," and "[c]onsequently, the State was prohibited from compelling Metro PCS to turn over appellant's content-based communications without first obtaining a warrant supported by probable cause"; "Text messages are analogous to regular mail and email communications. Like regular mail and email, a text message has an 'outside address "visible" to the third-party carriers that transmit it to its intended location, and also a package of content that the sender presumes will be read only by the intended recipient.'"). This is the case as well for the contents of a cell phone. *See Riley v. California*, 573 U.S. 373, 403 (2014) (discussed in § 25.8.2 *supra*) ("Modern cell phones[,] . . . [w]ith all they contain and all they may reveal, . . . hold for many Americans 'the privacies of life'" (quoting *Boyd v. United States*, 116 U.S. 616, 630 (1886))); *United States v. Pratt*, 915 F.3d 266 (4th Cir. 2019), summarized in § 25.8.2 *supra*; *United States v. Lopez-Cruz*, 730 F.3d 803, 805-06, 808 (9th Cir. 2013) (pre-*Riley* decision holding that the defendant, whose car was stopped by border patrol agents and who agreed to the agents' request to inspect and search two cell phones that the defendant identified as belonging to a friend of his, "had a reasonable expectation of privacy in the phones" and could challenge an agent's actions in accepting an incoming call and "passing himself as Lopez" and thereby obtaining information that incriminated Lopez: "Lopez had possession of the phones and was using them. He certainly had the right to exclude others from using the phones. He also had a reasonable expectation of privacy in incoming calls and a reasonable expectation that the contents of those calls 'would remain free from governmental intrusion.'"); *State v. Peoples*, 240 Ariz. 244, 246, 248-49, 378 P.3d 421, 423, 425-26 (2016) ("an overnight guest who left his cell phone in his host's apartment . . . did not lose his expectation of privacy in his phone" by leaving "his cell phone behind when he ran from the apartment to direct paramedics" even though "'numerous other individuals were present [in the apartment], including police officers,'" and this privacy expectation also was not diluted on the ground that "no passcode was required to activate" the phone since "personal belongings need not be locked for a legitimate expectation of privacy to exist" and "[c]ell phones are intrinsically private, and the failure to password protect access to them is not an invitation for others to snoop"); *State v. K.C.*, 207 So.3d 951 (Fla. App. 2016) (discussed in § 25.13 subdivision (d) *supra*). See also § 25.33 *infra* (caselaw recognizing a defendant's privacy right in cellphone site location information that can be used to ascertain his or her location at the present time and/or to trace his or her whereabouts in the past).

25.15.5. *"Automatic Standing"*

In some States, criminal defendants have "automatic standing" to challenge seizures of contraband whenever they are charged with possession of that contraband: They need not show any proprietary interest or expectation of privacy in the place from which the contraband was seized. This "automatic standing" rule was the law of the Fourth Amendment before *United States v. Salvucci,* 448 U.S. 83 (1980). When the Supreme Court abolished it in *Salvucci,* some state courts responded by reinstating the rule as a matter of state constitutional law. *E.g., State v. Shaw*, 237 N.J. 588, 611, 207 A.3d 229, 242 (2019) ("The New Jersey Constitution provides greater protections from warrantless searches and seizures than the Fourth Amendment of the Constitution of the United States. . . . ¶ Our standard both incorporates the legitimate expectation of privacy standard and offers broader protections that advance three important State interests. . . . The first is the State's interest in protecting defendants from having to admit possession to vindicate their constitutional right against unreasonable searches and seizures. . . . The second is to prevent the State from arguing a defendant should be subject to criminal liability for possessing contraband, while asserting the same defendant had no privacy interest in the area from which police obtained the contraband without a warrant. . . . Our third aim is to increase privacy protections for our citizens and to promote respect for our Constitution by discouraging law enforcement from carrying out warrantless searches and seizures where unnecessary."); *State v. Settle,* 122 N.H. 214, 447 A.2d 1284 (1982); *Commonwealth v. Porter P.*, 456 Mass. 254, 261 n.5, 923 N.E.2d 36, 45 n.5 (2010); *Commonwealth v. Sell,* 504 Pa. 46, 470 A.2d 457 (1983); *State v. Simpson,* 95 Wash. 2d 170, 622 P.2d 1199 (1980); *see also People v. Millan,* 69 N.Y.2d 514, 508 N.E.2d 903, 516 N.Y.S.2d 168 (1987) (adopting a version of automatic standing that grants standing whenever a charge of criminal possession is based upon a statutory presumption of constructive possession); *Commonwealth v. DeJesus*, 489 Mass. 292, 296-97, 182 N.E.3d 280, 285 (2022) (dictum) ("In one limited situation, . . . a defendant may rely on another's reasonable expectation of privacy: where the defendant has been charged with possessing contraband at the time of the search and, also at the time of the search, the property was in the actual possession of a codefendant or in a place where the codefendant had a reasonable expectation of privacy, the defendant may assert the same reasonable expectation of privacy as the codefendant. . . . '[O]therwise the person who carried the contraband might go free (because of suppression of the evidence) and the defendant confederate would not.'"). In States that have not reconsidered the "automatic standing" issue since *Salvucci,* counsel should draw upon the reasoning of these decisions to urge the state courts to restore "automatic standing." See § 17.11 *supra.*

25.16. *Police Entry of Premises: General Principles*

An entry into a building is a "search" within the Fourth Amendment. *Lo-Ji Sales, Inc. v. New York,* 442 U.S. 319, 325 (1979). *See Sause v. Bauer*, 138 S. Ct. 2561, 2563 (2018) (per curiam); *Mendez v. County of Los Angeles*, 815 F.3d 1178, 1187 (9th Cir. 2016), *aff'd after remand*, 897 F.3d 1067 (9th Cir. 2019); *Commonwealth v. Martin*, 2021 PA Super 128, 253 A.3d 1225 (Pa. Super. 2021) (police officers responded to a call from Holiday Inn staff who reported that they smelled marijuana smoke emanating from a particular room; the officers approached the room and confirmed the odor; one officer knocked on the door without announcing that he was a policeman; a woman opened the door and the officer leaned in; with his body half-way through the door, he saw the defendant reach over a chair; fearing that the defendant was reaching for a weapon, the officer entered, gun drawn, and ordered the defendant to put his hands on his head; the officer then observed a bulge in the defendant's pants pocket which, in a pat-down search, proved to be a gun; the Superior Court holds that the officer's entry half-way into the room was a search for Fourth Amendment purposes and was unconstitutional in the absence of a warrant or consent; the subsequent discovery and seizure of the gun were tainted by the unconstitutional entry and were required to be suppressed). To be constitutional, any police entry of a building must either: (i) be authorized by a search warrant (see § 25.17 *infra*), or (ii) "fall[ ] within one of the narrow and well-delineated exceptions to the warrant requirement" (*Flippo v. West Virginia*, 528 U.S. 11, 13 (1999) (quoting *Katz v. United States,* 389 U.S. 347, 357 (1967)); see §§ 25.18-25.20 *infra*). *E.g., Groh v. Ramirez*, 540 U.S. 551, 559 (2004) ("Because '"the right of a man to retreat into his own home and there be free from unreasonable governmental intrusion"' stands '"[a]t the very core" of the Fourth Amendment,' . . . , our cases have firmly established the '"basic principle of Fourth Amendment law" that searches and seizures inside a home without a warrant are presumptively unreasonable'" (quoting *Payton v. New York,* 445 U.S. 573, 586 (1980)); *id.* at 590 ("the Fourth Amendment has drawn a firm line at the entrance to the house"); *Kyllo v. United States*, 533 U.S. 27, 31 (2001) ("With few exceptions, the question whether a warrantless search of a home is reasonable and hence constitutional must be answered no."); *United States v. Karo,* 468 U.S. 705, 714-15 (1984) ("[s]earches and seizures inside a home without a warrant are presumptively unreasonable absent exigent circumstances"); *Welsh v. Wisconsin,* 466 U.S. 740, 750 (1984) (a "presumption of unreasonableness . . . attaches to all warrantless home entries"); *Florida v. Jardines*, 569 U.S. 1, 6 (2013) ("when it comes to the Fourth Amendment, the home is first among equals"); *accord, Lange v. California*, 141 S. Ct. 2011, 2018 (2021); *Caniglia v. Strom*, 141 S. Ct. 1596 (2021) (holding that the doctrine permitting certain vehicle searches to be made without a warrant when the police are exercising "community caretaking functions" (such as dealing with disabled automobiles on a public road or investigating accidents) does not apply to home entries); *accord, State v. Gill*, 2008 ND 152, 755 N.W.2d 454, 459-60 (N.D. 2008) (citing and agreeing with similar holdings by four federal circuits). *See also State v. Jackson*, 742 N.W.2d 163, 177 (Minn. 2007) ("in order to be constitutionally reasonable, nighttime searches [of the home] require additional justification beyond the probable cause required for a daytime search"); *United States v. Bute*, 43 F.3d 531,

535 (10th Cir. 1994) (finding a Fourth Amendment violation when a police officer, seeing the garage door of an old cinderblock building – formerly a honey manufacturing plant – standing open, entered without a warrant for the stated purpose of determining whether the building had been burglarized or vandalized: the court refuses to extend the so-called "community caretaking exception" of *Cady v. Dombrowksi*, 413 U.S. 433 (1973) (see § 25.25 subdivision (iii) *infra*), from automobile-search cases to a building search; it "decline[s] to recognize the security check exception to the warrant requirement of the Fourth Amendment and conclude[s] that the protection of property exception is inapplicable under the facts of this case.").

If a police entry of a building violates the applicable Fourth Amendment rules, all observations made by the police within the building and all objects seized by the entering officers are excludable. *Johnson v. United States,* 333 U.S. 10 (1948); *Chapman v. United States,* 365 U.S. 610 (1961); *Work v. United States,* 243 F.2d 660 (D.C. Cir. 1957); *United States v. Merritt,* 293 F.2d 742 (3d Cir. 1961). *Cf. United States v. Shrum*, 908 F.3d 1219 (10th Cir. 2018) (a homeowner phoned 911 to report his wife's sudden illness; EMS responded and took the couple to a hospital, where she died; police, with no reason to believe the death suspicious, secured the perimeter of the house and refused the homeowner reentry; he was interrogated and gave consent to search the house for his wife's prescription drugs, to determine her cause of death; during the search, an officer saw ammunition which he reported to federal ATF agents who used this information to obtain a search warrant; the search disclosed firearms; on these facts, the home was "seized" for Fourth Amendment purpose; this warrantless seizure was unconstitutional; the search warrant was tainted, and the firearms were required to be suppressed.). Evidence derived from these observations or things is also excludable. See § 25.39 *infra*.

For discussion of whether a police officer's use of a flashlight or other implement or technological device to see into or obtain information about a private area constitutes a "search" for Fourth Amendment purposes, see § 25.33 *infra*.

25.17. *Entry of Premises Pursuant to a Search Warrant*

Search warrants are issued by a magistrate (or, in some jurisdictions, by a judge) in an *ex parte* proceeding. Defense attorneys are almost never in a position to contest the sufficiency of the application for a warrant before the warrant is executed. Their first opportunity to challenge a search made pursuant to a search warrant ordinarily comes after the search has been completed, the defendant arrested, and charges filed.

The reason for "the Fourth Amendment rule ordinarily prohibiting the warrantless entry of a person's house [or other protected location] as unreasonable *per se" (Georgia v. Randolph, 547 U.S. 103, 109 (2006))* "is not that it denies law enforcement the support of the usual inferences which reasonable men draw from evidence. Its protection consists in requiring that those inferences be drawn by a neutral and detached magistrate instead of being judged by the officer engaged in the often competitive enterprise of ferreting out crime" (*Johnson v. United States*, 333 U.S. 10, 13-14 (1948)). To assure that that protective function is served, the affidavit or other materials presented to the magistrate as the basis for a warrant must be fact-specific and sufficiently detailed to enable the magistrate to make an independent judgment whether the information known to the authorities adds up to probable cause. See § 25.17.1 *infra*. The magistrate, not the affiant, must draw the inferences that mediate between concrete factual observations and the ultimate finding of probable cause. *See, e.g., United States v. Gifford*, 727 F.3d 92, 99-100 (1st Cir. 2013); *United States v. Button*, 653 F.2d 319, 323-24 (8th Cir. 1981); *United States v. Flanagan*, 423 F.2d 745, 746-47 (5th Cir. 1970); *Gillespie v. United States*, 368 F.2d 1, 4-6 (8th Cir. 1966). Therefore, when the affidavit supporting a search warrant asserts as empirical fact an undisclosed inference on the part of the affiant, a reviewing court must "'[d]etermine whether the hidden inference was so significant as to cross the line between permissible interpretation and usurpation. * * * A hidden inference should be deemed significant if it can be fairly concluded that it had a substantial bearing on the magistrate's determination of probable cause in each of two respects: ¶ (1) Relevance : The more directly relevant the inference is to the magistrate's inquiry, the more substantial its bearing and the more significant it will be. * * * ¶ (2) Complexity : The more complex and attenuated the logical process by which a relevant conclusion is reached, the more important it is that the magistrate receive an opportunity to test the inference for validity as part of his neutral and detached function. Conversely, an inference so straightforward, and so patently within the affiant's area of expertise, as to be a matter of "routine interpretation" for the affiant is probably not so significant as to require the magistrate's review even though the conclusion thus reached is highly relevant.'" *State v. Castagnola*, 2015-Ohio-1565, 145 Ohio St. 3d 1, 12-13, 46 N.E.3d 638, 652 (2015), summarized in § 25.17.2 *infra*.

In *United States v. Leon,* 468 U.S. 897 (1984), and *Massachusetts v. Sheppard,* 468 U.S. 981 (1984), the Supreme Court limited the grounds for such challenges. *Leon* and *Sheppard* held that evidence obtained by a search conducted under a search warrant should not be suppressed if the police officers executing the warrant reasonably relied on the magistrate's determination of probable cause in issuing the warrant, even though the magistrate's finding of probable cause was erroneous. *See, e.g., United States v. Morton*, 46 F.4th 331 (5th Cir. 2022) (en banc). *Leon* and *Sheppard* are not substantive constitutional decisions; they do not modify the explicit Fourth Amendment rule that a search warrant issued without probable cause is unconstitutional (*see, e.g., State v. Thompson*, 419 S.C. 250, 797 S.E.2d 716 (2017)); they simply withdraw the ordinary Fourth Amendment exclusionary rule as a means of enforcing this particular constitutional command. *Cf. United States v. Werdene*, 883 F.3d 204 (3d Cir. 2018) (extending the good-faith doctrine to preclude the exclusion of evidence obtained under a search warrant that violated the Fourth Amendment because it exceeded the territorial jurisdiction of the issuing magistrate "and was not authorized by any positive law" (*id.* at 214)). In a decision that ignores the basic rationale of *Leon* – that the exclusionary rule exists to guarantee police compliance with the Fourth Amendment and should not be applied when a violation is the fault of a magistrate alone – and flouts the explicit statement in *Leon* that the Court's analysis of "the deterrent effect of excluding evidence obtained in reasonable reliance on a subsequently invalidated warrant assumes, of course, that the officers properly executed the warrant and searched only those places and for those objects that it was reasonable to believe were covered by the warrant" (468 U.S. at 918 n. 19), the Court of Appeals for the First Circuit has applied *Leon*'s "good faith" doctrine to uphold the search of the third floor of a residence by officers serving a search warrant for the second floor. *United States v. Pimentel*, 26 F.4th 86 (1st Cir. 2022). *Pimentel*'s exact holding is questionable because its murky opinion also relies to some extent on the alternative ground that the warrant was ambiguous and on the idiosyncratic circumstance that "the notation '2nd floor' was not included in the original warrant application; rather, it was added in handwriting at the request of the issuing judge's clerk, who had sought clarification regarding where in the building Pimentel lived" (*id.* at 88). In any event, the First Circuit's expansive view of the "good faith" justification for admitting evidence obtained through Fourth Amendment violations (see also *United States v. Moore-Bush*, 36 F.4th 320 (1st Cir. 2022) (en banc) (concurring opinion of three judges)) may signal a trend in that direction among the lower federal courts. *See United States v. Aigbekaen*, 943 F.3d 713 (4th Cir. 2019); *United States v. Skaggs*, 25 F.4th 494 (7th Cir. 2022); *United States v. Taylor*, 54 F.4th 795 (4th Cir. 2022). Compare the concluding paragraph of § 25.3 *supra*, describing the relatively narrow roster of circumstances in which the Supreme Court has recognized a "good faith" exception to the exclusionary rule *a là Leon* and *Sheppard*.

In the wake of *Leon* and *Sheppard*, there are essentially eight situations in which defense counsel can seek suppression of the proceeds of a search conducted pursuant to a search warrant: (i) when the affidavit submitted in support of the issuance of the warrant states merely "'bare bones'" conclusions (*United States v. Leon, supra*, 468 U.S. at 923 n.24, 926) or is "'so lacking in indicia of probable cause as to render official belief in its existence entirely unreasonable'" (*id.* at 923); (ii) when the police knowingly or negligently fail to limit their application for a warrant to the pertinent unit of a multi-unit building; (iii) when "the magistrate or judge in issuing a warrant was misled by information in an affidavit that the affiant knew was false or would have known was false except for his reckless disregard of the truth" (*id.* at 923); (iv) when the affidavit includes information obtained by an earlier unconstitutional search or seizure and this information is necessary to sustain a finding of probable cause; (v) when the magistrate who issues the warrant is not neutral and detached, thereby rendering reliance on the warrant unreasonable (*id.*); (vi) when the warrant is "so facially deficient – *i.e.,* in failing to particularize the place to be searched or the things to be seized – that the executing officers cannot reasonably presume it to be valid" (*id.*); (vii) when the police, in executing the warrant, exceeded the authority granted by it; and (viii) when an officer who executed the warrant was also the person who submitted to the issuing magistrate the information purporting to establish probable cause, and the deficiency of the warrant is the result of the deficiency of that information. These eight situations are discussed in greater detail in the following subsections.

The retraction of the Fourth Amendment exclusionary rule in *Leon* and *Sheppard* does not, of course, control the evidentiary consequences of state constitutional violations in the issuance of warrants. Defense counsel can and should ask state courts to reject *Leon* and *Sheppard* as a matter of state constitutional law and to continue to suppress evidence obtained by any search made pursuant to a warrant issued without probable cause. *See, e.g., State v. Novembrino,* 105 N.J. 95, 157-58, 519 A.2d 820, 856-57 (1987); *People v. Bigelow,* 66 N.Y.2d 417, 426-27, 488 N.E.2d 451, 457-58, 497 N.Y.S.2d 630, 636-37 (1985). The argument for state constitutional repudiation of regressive criminal-procedure decisions handed down by the post-Warren Supreme Court of the United States (see § 17.11 *supra*) is particularly forceful in this context. Over the past half-century the "basic conclusion" of the Kerner Commission that "[o]ur nation is moving toward two societies, one black, one white – separate and unequal" (NATIONAL ADVISORY COMMISSION ON CIVIL DISORDERS, REPORT 1 (1968)), has proved increasingly prophetic. More and more, police activity has become the paradigmatic, iconic locus for the fact and for the public awareness that government treats white people differently than people of color. More and more, minority communities have focused their disillusionment, their outrage, their anger, and their fear upon the police as the prime agency of governmental oppression. Ferguson Missouri, Staten Island New York, Minneapolis Minnesota, and their prominent precursors and progeny are only the most obvious demonstrations of this. In a world where minority communities fundamentally distrust the police, any legal ruling that visibly countenances illegal activity carried out by police officers will enhance that distrust. And this is a matter that should concern state judges of every ideological bent, because minority-community bitterness against the police specifically and against law-enforcement processes more generally is all too likely to increase the level of violence which it is the purpose of policing and of the criminal law to prevent. Particularly for ghetto-dwellers who are "without means of escape from an oppressive urban environment" (FINAL REPORT OF THE NATIONAL COMMISSION ON THE CAUSES AND PREVENTION OF VIOLENCE: TO ESTABLISH JUSTICE, TO ENSURE DOMESTIC TRANQUILITY ["EISENHOWER COMMISSION"] xxi (1969)) and for whom the police stand as the primary agents and symbols of that oppression (*see, e.g.*, ALICE GOFFMAN, ON THE RUN: FUGITIVE LIFE IN AN AMERICAN CITY (2014)), any retrenchment of visible judicial control over the police can only add to the legitimate feelings of frustration which are "poisoning the spirit of trust and cooperation that is essential to [the] . . . proper functioning" of legal institutions (EISENHOWER COMMISSION xv-xvi). Rulings like *Leon* and *Sheppard*, which forswear judicial redress for *conceded* constitutional violations committed by police officers as a result of systemic failings that the police themselves cannot prevent, can only subvert law enforcement as well as the rule of law.

Search warrant cases involving the seizure or search of a computer, cellphone, or tablet may give rise to a variety of issues. For example, the affidavit submitted in support of the issuance of the warrant may have been impermissibly "bare bones" (see § 25.17.1 *infra*); the search warrant may lacked the requisite degree of particularity (see §§ 25.17.2, 25.17.6 *infra*); or the police may have exceeded the scope of the warrant by seizing or searching the electronic device (see § 25.17.7 *infra*). If a lawfully seized computer or other electronic device is password-protected and the police or prosecution seek a court order compelling the defendant to supply the password, the defendant can object on self-incrimination grounds. See § 25.8.2 *supra*, discussing the self-incrimination issue in the context of cellphone searches.

25.17.1. *"Bare Bones" Affidavits*

The "'test for whether the good faith exception applies is "whether a reasonably well trained officer would have known that the search was illegal despite the magistrate's authorization"'" (*United States v. Caesar*, 2 F.4th 160, 170 (3d Cir. 2021); *United States v. Hodson*, 543 F.3d 286 (6th Cir, 2008); *State v. Henderson*, 2019-Ohio-1974, 136 N.E.3d 848 (Ohio App. 2019)). In *United States v. Leon, supra*, the Court recognized that a search warrant and a search conducted pursuant to that warrant are patently invalid if the affidavit submitted in support of the issuance of the warrant states merely "'bare bones'" conclusions (*Leon, supra*, 468 U.S. at 923 n.24, 926), or is "'so lacking in indicia of probable cause as to render official belief in its existence entirely unreasonable'" (*id.* at 925). *Accord, Malley v. Briggs*, 475 U.S. 335, 344-45 (1986). The inadequacy of such an affidavit is so well settled in Fourth Amendment jurisprudence that an officer would be grossly derelict not to know it. *See, e.g., Nathanson v. United States,* 290 U.S. 41 (1933); *Aguilar v. Texas,* 378 U.S. 108 (1964); *Riggan v. Virginia,*

384 U.S. 152 (1966) (per curiam); *Illinois v. Gates,* 462 U.S. 213, 239 (1983) (dictum) ("[a]n officer's statement that '[a]ffiants have received reliable information from a credible person and do believe' that heroin is stored in a home, is likewise inadequate"). "To elude the 'bare bones' label, the affidavit must state more than 'suspicions, or conclusions, without providing some underlying factual circumstances regarding veracity, reliability, and basis of knowledge' and make '*some* connection' between the illegal activity and the place to be searched." *United States v. Ward*, 967 F.3d 550, 554 (6th Cir. 2020) (affirming the suppression of evidence seized under a bare-bones affidavit); *accord, State v. Schubert*, 2022-Ohio-4604, 2022 WL 17836574, at *3 (Ohio 2022); *State v. Baldwin*, 664 S.W.3d 122 (Tex. Crim. App. 2022) ("We granted review to answer this question: under what circumstances may boilerplate language about cell phones be considered in a probable cause analysis? We hold that boilerplate language may be used in an affidavit for the search of a cell phone, but to support probable cause, the language must be coupled with other facts and reasonable inferences that establish a nexus between the device and the offense." *Id.* at 123. Here "the affidavit contained insufficient particularized facts to allow the magistrate to determine probable cause for a warrant to search the phone. Insofar as the court of appeals affirmed the trial court's order granting the motion to suppress evidence obtained from the cell phone found in Baldwin's vehicle, we affirm." *Id.* at 135-36. The following excerpts from the affidavit are illustrative of the boilerplate held insufficient: "based on your Affiant's training and experience, Affiant knows from other cases he [sic] has investigated and from training and experiences that it is common for suspects to communicate about their plans via text messaging, phone calls, or through other communication applications. Further, Affiant knows from training and experiences that someone who commits the offense of aggravated assault or murder often makes phone calls and/or text messages immediately prior and after the crime. ¶ Affiant further knows based on training and experience, often times, in a moment of panic and in an attempt to cover up an assault or murder that suspects utilize the internet via their cellular telephone to search for information." *Id.* at 126.). When a warrant is based upon bare-bones conclusory allegations or upon grossly inadequate showings of probable cause, the logic of *Leon* – to preserve the exclusionary rule in warrant cases when any adequately trained police officer would know that a search warrant is unconstitutional – implies that suppression is required. *See United States v. Lopez-Zuniga,* 909 F.3d 906, 909-10 (8th Cir. 2018) (approving suppression of evidence obtained through GPS tracking based on a warrant entirely lacking in probable cause: "On appeal, the government has abandoned its argument that probable cause supported the first warrant; it argues only that the good-faith exception saves evidence obtained from the issuance of the first warrant from suppression. We disagree. Lopez-Zuniga makes only a brief appearance in the affidavit in support of the first warrant application, and the only information about him is that he dropped off someone appearing to be Garcia-Jimenez at his apartment and then days later picked him up to go to a restaurant and mall. The first affidavit does not connect Lopez-Zuniga to any of Garcia-Jimenez's suspected illicit activities. As the magistrate judge in this case said, if this amounts to probable cause, 'then *anyone* who drops a drug trafficker off at the trafficker's residence and travels with the trafficker for innocent activity, such as the trafficker's grandmother or mere acquaintance, would be subject to search.' We agree, and we think the warrant was so lacking in indicia of probable cause that belief in its existence would have been entirely unreasonable."); *United States v. Waide*, 60 F.4th 327, 336, 342 (6th Cir. 2023) ("The only information contained in the [search warrant] affidavit that is proffered to support a finding of probable cause is the statement of an unidentified person made to the unidentified property owner, and then communicated second-hand to . . . [the fire department investigator

726

who executed the affidavit], regarding an unknown person entering the property and removing items from the shed around the unspecified time of the fire. When presented with such hearsay information from an undisclosed source, 'a court must consider the veracity, reliability, and the basis of knowledge for that information as part of the totality of the circumstances for evaluating the impact of that information.'. . . '[I]n the absence of any indicia of the informants' reliability, courts insist that the affidavit contain substantial independent police corroboration.' . . . ¶ . . . Here . . . the uncorroborated information is not sufficiently reliable to support a finding of probable cause. ¶ . . . In sum, the . . . warrant was 'based on an affidavit "so lacking in indicia of probable cause as to render official belief in its existence entirely unreasonable."' . . . The *Leon* good-faith exception is therefore inapplicable."); *State v. Johndro*, 2013 ME 106, 82 A.3d 820, 824-26 (Me. 2013) ("[T]he affidavit indicates that both witnesses saw a 'suspicious car' in the area of the burglarized homes around noon on the day the burglaries were discovered. It provides no indication as to what time the burglaries occurred, or what time they were reported. A vehicle being driven down the road in the middle of the day, and even pulling in and out of several driveways, without more, is not a sufficient nexus to criminal activity, notwithstanding the subjective feelings of the witnesses who observed this behavior. . . . ¶ [T]he justice of the peace . . . [could] consider . . . [Johndro's] prior burglary convictions as part of the probable cause analysis. . . . Standing alone, however, this history would not give a prudent person reason to believe that evidence of the burglaries would exist in Johndro's home. . . . ¶ This is especially true because there is no indication that Johndro was the person driving the car near the crime scenes. According to the affidavit, one witness observed that the operator was male; no further description was provided. The affidavit's failure to identify Johndro as the operator renders the weak connection between the vehicle and Johndro's home even more tenuous. . . . ¶ . . . Because nothing in the affidavit establishes a connection between the burglaries and Johndro's residence, officers' reliance on the warrant was not objectively reasonable" and *Leon*'s good faith exception to the exclusionary rule is inapplicable); *People v. Rojas*, 2013 IL App (1st) 113780, 998 N.E.2d 567, 575-76, 376 Ill. Dec. 25, 33-34 (Ill. App. 2013) ("While the 20–page complaint is not bare-bones in and of itself, *it is* bare-bones *with regard to defendant's . . . [home] address.* . . . [T]he nearly two pages of "probable cause" evidence attempting to create a nexus between defendant's criminal drug trafficking activity and his family's Cromwell home was entirely lacking. . . . Probable cause regarding the other [five] locations [covered by the same warrant] cannot be bootstrapped to supply probable cause, and by implication, good faith, for the Cromwell location. If we allow . . . [the affiant officer's] conjecture that people involved in drug trafficking keep records of their drug activity in their homes to provide the 'indicia' of probable cause necessary for application of the good-faith exception here, we fear we would be opening up any criminal to the official search of his home – as most people keep records in their homes."); *People v. Gutierrez*, 222 P.3d 925 (Colo. 2009) ("[T]his case involves contrasting interpretations of the probable cause required to support the government's search of the files found on the premises of Amalia's Tax Service. The district attorney contends that the State only needed probable cause to search the premises of Amalia's Tax Service generally, and that this would permit a search of each file found on those premises. . . . ¶ Although precedent is sparse, our review of Fourth Amendment law leads us to conclude that probable cause is required to intrude upon (through search and seizure) each constitutionally protected privacy interest an individual may have, irrespective of whether that interest is in his person or his tax returns." *Id.* at 937. ¶ . . . To summarize, probable cause may not be analyzed merely in relation to the property or premises searched. Rather, unless the custodian or business itself is pervaded by fraud, probable cause must be analyzed in relation to each individual's constitutionally protected interests. *Id.* at 940. ¶ . . . The affidavit did not provide probable cause to search Gutierrez's individual file. Nowhere in the affidavit is Gutierrez's name mentioned, and the affidavit offers no facts which could 'provide the magistrate with a substantial basis,' . . . for finding probable cause to believe that evidence of criminal impersonation or identity theft would be found in his particular tax return or client file. . . . *Id.* ¶ . . . The supporting affidavit in the present case does not merely fail to establish a 'sufficient nexus' between Gutierrez's tax return and the suspected criminal activity, it fails to establish any connection at all between Gutierrez and criminal activity. . . . *Id.* at 943. ¶ . . . Accordingly, we hold that *Leon's* good faith exception is inapplicable and suppression of Gutierrez's tax records is appropriate." *Id.* at 944.)). *But see United States v. Barnes*, 895 F.3d 1194 (9th Cir. 2018) (holding that an arrest warrant issued pursuant to a municipal court practice under which judges routinely rubber-stamped the prosecutors' complaints with no independent examination of their basis "was inexcusably infirm . . . [because of this] judicial abandonment" (*id.* at 1201): "We . . . join our sister circuits in concluding that a defendant may show judicial abandonment through any one of the following ways: (1) the magistrate was biased against the defendant or otherwise personally interested in issuing the warrant; (2) the magistrate functionally occupied a different, non-neutral role while making the probable cause determination; or (3) the magistrate failed to review the requisite affidavits or materials prior to making a probable cause determination." *Id.* at 1202. However, "[we also] conclude, consistent with the Fifth, Sixth, and Tenth Circuits, that the exclusionary rule [as limited by *Leon* and *Sheppard*] only applies if the issuing judge abandoned his or her judicial role *and* law enforcement officers knew or should have known of the abandonment" (*id.* at 1203).). Searches based on wholly conclusionary affidavits – those that merely recite the ultimate fact in issue or the affiant's belief of it (for example, that *X* has a sawed-off shotgun in a certain house) – thus remain challengeable under *Leon* and *Sheppard*. *Cf. Luke v. Gulley*, 50 F.4th 90, 96 (11th Cir. 2022) (finding that an arrest and prosecution pursuant to an arrest warrant violated the Fourth Amendment: "Detective Gulley does not dispute that his affidavit lacked sufficient information to provide the magistrate judge probable cause to issue the warrant to arrest Luke for Lewis's murder. The detective's affidavit is skeletal, consisting of a conclusory allegation that Luke killed Lewis by 'sho[oting] at the truck Lewis was driving' 'based on the [detective]'s Investigation, and eye witness verbal statements.' The affidavit is devoid of relevant and reliable facts from which one could infer that Luke murdered Lewis. . . . That Detective Gulley told the magistrate judge there was a 'gang shooting' added no information to implicate Luke in Lewis's death. And we do not consider in the calculus of probable cause that the detective relied on the investigative file and his intuition to identify Luke as a suspect because no record exists that he submitted the file to or explained his thought processes to the magistrate judge. *See Whitely* [*v. Warden*, 401 U.S. 560,] . . . 565 n.8 [(1971)] ('[A]n otherwise insufficient affidavit cannot be rehabilitated by testimony concerning information possessed by the affiant when he sought the warrant but not disclosed to the issuing magistrate'). Because Detective Gulley's affidavit 'consists of nothing more than [his] conclusion that . . . [Luke] perpetrated the offense described,' it 'could not support the independent judgment of [the] disinterested magistrate' judge."). Conclusory assertions that the person to be arrested or whose house is to be searched is a "known criminal" or is "known" to deal in narcotics should be accorded "no weight" (*see Spinelli v. United States,* 393 U.S. 410, 414, 418-19 (1969)). Allegations that the person named in the warrant *consorts* with "known" criminals, narcotics dealers, and the like, are doubly worthless (*see United States v. Hatcher,* 473 F.2d 321 (6th Cir. 1973); *United States v. Herron,* 215 F.3d 812 (8th Cir. 2000)). *Cf. Dollard v. Whisenand,* 946 F.3d 342, 359 (7th Cir. 2019) (probable cause to believe that the professional staff of an addiction treatment clinic were operating an illegal pill mill was insufficient to justify a warrant for arrest of the clinic's parking valet: "'The concept of guilt by association is repugnant to our notion of elemental justice and fair play.'"). *And see United States v. Mora,* 989 F.3d 794, 801 (10th Cir. 2021) ("Although the totality of the circumstances established probable cause that Defendant engaged in alien smuggling, the government failed to articulate how evidence of alien smuggling justified the search of his home. . . . ¶ [T]he government identifies a few general statements in the affidavit about commonly owned items. The affiant stated, based on his training and experience, that alien smugglers often use electronic communication devices, GPS devices, and electronic banking systems to conduct operations and store records. None of those boilerplate statements, however, are specific to Defendant's crime or circumstances. *See United States v. Zimmerman,* 277 F.3d 426, 433 (3d Cir. 2002) (observing that '[r]ambling boilerplate recitations designed to meet all law enforcement needs do not produce probable cause'. . . .").); *United States v. Sanders,* 59 F.4th 232 (6th Cir. 2023) (finding that a search violated the Fourth Amendment because the authorizing warrant "failed to establish a nexus between the drug activity and the . . . apartment" searched (*id.* at 242): "[T]he [police] affiant included few facts that support a nexus between the drug evidence officers sought and the Yellowstone Parkway apartment that the officers searched. Initially, the affiant stated that he received a tip from a confidential informant that "[Defendant] was selling Heroin/Fentanyl from [the Yellowstone Parkway apartment]." *Id.* at 238. "Acting on this information, . . . [the affiant] set up two controlled purchases." *Id.* at 235. "Next, pertaining to the first controlled purchase, officers observed Defendant drive directly from the controlled purchase location to the Yellowstone Parkway apartment. Finally, pertaining to the second controlled purchase, officers observed Defendant exit the Yellowstone Parkway apartment and drive directly to the controlled purchase location, and then drive directly back from that location to the Yellowstone Parkway apartment, which Defendant then entered. *Id.* at 238. "Nothing in the affidavit establishes that evidence of drug dealing existed in the Yellowstone Parkway apartment rather than in the vehicle in which the two controlled purchases occurred." *Id.* at 241.).

25.17.2. *Improper Multi-unit Warrant Applications; Overly Broad Warrants*

If officers seeking a warrant know "or even if they should have known" that the premises described in their application includes separate units with different occupants, they are constitutionally obliged to limit the application to the unit that they are presenting probable cause to search (*Maryland v. Garrison,* 480 U.S. 79, 85-87 (1987) (dictum); *see also United States v. Voustianiouk,* 685 F.3d 206, 215 (2d Cir. 2012)). A violation of this obligation should entail exclusion of any evidence seized from the other units, because the rationale of *Leon* and *Sheppard* is to withdraw the exclusionary rule as a remedy for *magistrates'* errors in the search warrant process but preserve it as a remedy for *police errors.*

Similarly, warrants authorizing searches which extend to materials having no connection with the crimes that the warrant affidavits justify investigating are challengeable for overbreadth. *See, e.g., State v. Missak,* 2023 WL 3635471 (N.J. App. 2023) (holding that a warrant to search the entire contents of a cell phone violates the Fourth Amendment and Article I, ¶ 7 of the New Jersey Constitution because it purports to authorize "searches of information and data within the phone for which . . . [the supporting affidavit] does not adequately establish probable cause" (*id.* at *9): the affiant, claiming expertise in searches of electronic devices, asserted two justifications for searching materials that were not tied to the offenses for which her affidavit presented probable cause: (a) "proving who used, controlled, or accessed an electronic device, and who entered, controlled, or saw data on it, is generally important to an investigation and 'requires examination of data that, on its face, might be innocent, such as registry information and files accessed around that time.' Based on that assertion, and the other facts set forth in the . . . [affidavit, the affiant] stated [that] a 'forensic examiner must be allowed to access and examine ALL of the data on a computer, electronic device, or storage media'" (*id.* at *2), and (b) "'a suspect may try to conceal criminal evidence' and 'might store it in random order with deceptive file names . . . [so that] the search may require an examination of 'all the stored data to determine which particular files are evidence or instruments of crimes'" (*id.*); but the court holds that these purported justifications "fall[ ] short of the constitutional mark, . . . because establishing probable cause for a search requires more than a showing of what 'may' have occurred' (*id.* at *8), and "[t]he progress of two-hundred-thirty-two years since the ratification of the Bill of Rights has not tempered . . . [the federal and state constitutions'] denunciation of general searches" (*id.* at *6).); *Burns v. United States*, 235 A.2d 758, 772-73 (D.C. 2020) ("The privacy interests underlying . . . fundamental Fourth Amendment principles may be at their most compelling when police wish to search the contents of a modern smart phone. . . . ¶ A search warrant for data on a modern smart phone . . . must fully comply with the requirements of the Warrant Clause. It is not enough for police to show there is probable cause to arrest the owner or user of the cell phone, or even to establish probable cause to believe the phone contains some evidence of a crime. To be compliant with the Fourth Amendment, the warrant must specify the particular items of evidence to be searched for and seized from the phone and be strictly limited to the time period and information or other data for which probable cause has been properly established through the facts and circumstances set forth under oath in the warrant's supporting affidavit. Vigilance in enforcing the probable cause and particularity requirements is thus essential to the protection of the vital privacy interests inherent in virtually every modern cell phone and to the achievement of the 'meaningful constraints' contemplated in *Riley* [*v. California* (summarized in § 25.8.2 *supra*)]"); *State v. Castagnola*, 2015-Ohio-1565, 145 Ohio St. 3d 1, 46 N.E.3d 638 (2015) (a warrant which authorized a search of "Records and documents either stored on computers, ledgers, or any other electronic recording device to include hard drives and external portable hard drives, cell phones, printers, storage devices of any kind" (*id.* at 18, 46 N.E.3d at 657) "lacked particularity and was therefore invalid" (*id.* at 21, 46 N.E.3d at 659): "[D]etails regarding the records or documents stored on the computer should have been included in the search warrant to guide and control the searcher and to sufficiently narrow the category of records or documents subject to seizure. . . . [T]his degree of specificity was required, since the circumstances and the nature of the activity under investigation permitted the affiant to be this specific." *Id.* at 20-21, 46 N.E.3d at 658.); *United States v. Galpin*, 720 F.3d 436 (2d Cir. 2013) ("The chief evil that prompted the framing and adoption of the Fourth Amendment was the 'indiscriminate searches and seizures' conducted by the British 'under the authority of "general warrants."' . . . ('[T]he central concern underlying the Fourth Amendment [is] the concern about giving police officers unbridled discretion to rummage at will among a person's private effects.'). To prevent such 'general, exploratory rummaging in a person's belongings' and the attendant privacy violations, . . . the Fourth Amendment provides that 'a warrant may not be issued unless probable cause is properly established and the scope of the authorized search is set

730

out with particularity.'" *Id.* at 445. "Where, as here, the property to be searched is a computer hard drive, the particularity requirement assumes even greater importance." *Id.* at 446. "The district court determined, and the government does not dispute, that insofar as the warrant generally authorized officers to search Galpin's physical property and electronic equipment for evidence of violations of 'NYS Penal Law and or Federal Statutes,' the warrant violated the Fourth Amendment's particularity requirement." *Id.* at 446. "[W]e agree that the warrant was facially overbroad and thus violated the Fourth Amendment . . . ." *Id.* at 446.); *United States v. Abrams*, 615 F.2d 541 (1st Cir. 1980) ("The warrant, after describing the location of the doctors' offices, states: ¶ ['](T)here is now being concealed certain property, namely evidence of a crime, to wit, certain business and billing and medical records of patients of Doctors Abrams, London, Braun, and Abrams, London and Associates, Inc. which show actual medical services performed and fraudulent services claimed to have been performed in a scheme to defraud the United States and to submit false medicare and medicaid claims for payments to the United States or its agents; in violation of Title 18 . . . [§ 1001.'] ¶ In executing the warrant, all of the Medicare and Medicaid records in the doctors' offices were seized. In addition, approximately twenty medical records of non-Medicare-Medicaid patients were seized. The search and seizure started at 2:40 P.M. and was terminated at 5:57 P.M. on the same day. *Id.* at 542. "The general warrant and the unrestricted search that follows have been condemned by Americans since Colonial days." *Id. at* 543. "The warrant at issue fails to meet the requirement of particularity. The officers' discretion was unfettered, there is no limitation as to time and there is no description as to what specific records are to be seized. As a result of this general description, the executing officers seized all of the Medicare and Medicaid records of the three doctors and, in addition, records of non-Medicare-Medicaid patients. It seems clear that the executing officers could not or made no attempt to distinguish bona fide records from fraudulent ones so they seized all of them in order that a detailed examination could be made later. This is exactly the kind of investigatory dragnet that the fourth amendment was designed to prevent." *Id.*); *People v. Coke*, 461 P.3d 508, 516 (Colo. 2020) ("A search conducted pursuant to a warrant is typically reasonable. . . . However, so-called 'general warrants,' which permit 'a general, exploratory rummaging in a person's belongings,' are prohibited. . . . ¶ Here, the warrant allowed officers to search Coke's phone for the following: ¶ • Data which tends to show possession, dominion and control over said equipment; including but not limited to system ownership information, phone number, pictures, or documents bearing the owners name or information; ¶ • Any electronic data that would be illegal to possess (contraband), or fruits or proceeds of a crime, or data intended to be used in the commission of a crime; ¶ • All telephone contact lists, phone books and telephone logs; ¶ • Any text messages and Multimedia Messaging Service (MMS) stored, sent, received or deleted; ¶ • Any photographs or images stored, sent, received or deleted; ¶ • Any videos stored, sent, received or deleted[;] ¶ • Any electronic data packets stored, sent, received or deleted. ¶ The trial court found that the warrant was overbroad because phones 'are a repository of almost everything that is private and personal and deserving of [heightened] protection' and the warrant gave the officers virtually unfettered access to it. We agree.").

United States v. Christine, 687 F.2d 749 (3d Cir. 1982) is a leading case regarding "the question whether a partially invalid search warrant may be redacted so that evidence obtained pursuant to valid, severable portions of the warrant need not be suppressed" (*id.* at 750). "After examining the purposes of the warrant requirement and the means by which those purposes are served, we conclude that the practice of redaction is fully consistent with the Fourth Amendment and should be utilized to salvage partially invalid warrants." *Id.* at 750-51. *See, e.g., United States v. Sells*, 463 F.3d 1148 (10th Cir. 2006) ("Under the severability doctrine, '[t]he infirmity of part of a warrant requires the suppression of evidence seized pursuant to that part of the warrant, but does not require the suppression of anything described in the valid portions of the warrant (or lawfully seized – on plain view grounds, for example – during . . . execution [of the valid portions]).' . . . We [have] adopted the doctrine . . . [but in *United States v. Naugle*, 997 F.2 819, 822-23 (10th Cir. 1993),] we limited the applicability of the doctrine by holding that it applies only if 'the valid portions of the warrant [are] sufficiently particularized, distinguishable from the invalid portions, and make up the greater part of the warrant.'"); *Cassady v. Goering*, 567 F.3d 628, 638-41 (10th Cir. 2009) (applying *Sells* analysis to invalidate the whole of a warrant: "The warrant here can be divided into three general parts: (1) the section authorizing seizure of narcotics and related illegal contraband; (2) the section authorizing seizure of all other evidence of criminal activity; and (3) the section authorizing seizure of Mr. Cassady's personal property if its seizure is authorized on a number of enumerated grounds totally unrelated to a narcotics operation. Only the first of these sections – directing officers to seize '[a]ny & all narcotics, to wit; marijuana plants, and/or marijuana' and illegal contraband related to marijuana distribution – is arguably valid. And this is true only if we assume that everything in the sentence beginning, 'Any and all illegal contraband including but not limited to,' is meant to be narrowed by a requirement that the illegal contraband be related 'to the transportation, ordering, purchasing, and distribution of controlled substances, in particular a Schedule I controlled substance, to wit: marijuana,' which appears at the end of this convoluted sentence. . . . Even assuming we view the reference to 'contraband' narrowly as contraband related to a marijuana operation, which is supported by the crime for which there was probable cause, severance would still be improper in this case for the following reasons. . . . ¶ The second and third sections are clearly invalid. The second section expressly permits seizure of "all other evidence of criminal activity," without any limitation or reference to a specific crime. . . . The third section authorizes seizure of ¶ [']articles of personal property tending to establish the identity of the person or persons in control or possession of the place or vehicle . . . *[upon the grounds] that this property is stolen or embezzled; or is designed or intended for use as a means of committing a criminal offense;* or is or has been used as a means of committing a criminal offense; or the possession of which is illegal; or would be material evidence in a subsequent criminal prosecution in this state or another state; or the *seizure of which is expressly required, authorized or permitted by any statute of this state.[']* ¶ . . . Neither section is linked in any way to marijuana cultivation; instead, both sections appear intended to give officers as few limits as possible. . . . ¶ In sum, then, the warrant contains one mostly valid and two invalid sections. While the severance analysis does not end with a 'mere counting of provisions, . . . the 'number of valid versus invalid provisions is one element in the analysis of which portion makes up the greater part of the warrant' . . . ¶ Here, the invalid portions of the warrant are sufficiently 'broad and invasive' so as to 'contaminate the whole warrant.' . . . [T]he warrant's invalid provisions 'allow for the seizure of evidence, whether or not related to [marijuana possession and distribution], and largely subsume those provisions that would have been adequate standing alone.' . . . The warrant epitomizes a general warrant, and the officers treated it as such.").

25.17.3. *Affidavits Containing "Deliberate Falsehoods" or Statements Manifesting a "Reckless Disregard for the Truth"*

In *Franks v. Delaware,* 438 U.S. 154 (1978), the Court held

"that, where the defendant makes a substantial preliminary showing that a false statement knowingly and intentionally, or with reckless disregard for the truth, was included by the affiant in the warrant affidavit, and if the allegedly false statement is necessary to the finding of probable cause, the Fourth Amendment requires that a hearing be held at the defendant's request. In the event that at that hearing the allegation of perjury or reckless disregard is established by the defendant by a preponderance of the evidence, and, with the affidavit's false material set to one side, the affidavit's remaining content is insufficient to establish probable cause, the search warrant must be voided and the fruits of the search excluded to the same extent as if probable cause was lacking on the face of the affidavit." (*Id.* at 155-56.)

See, e.g., Harte v. Board of Commissioners of County of Johnson, Kansas, 864 F.3d 1154 (10th Cir. 2017); *Humbert v. Mayor and City Council of Baltimore City*, 866 F.3d 546 (4th Cir. 2017); *Frimmel Management, LLC v. United States*, 897 F.3d 1045 (9th Cir. 2018). *And see Bickford v. Hensley*, 832 Fed. Appx. 549 (10th Cir. 2020) (applying *Franks* to sustain a challenge to an arrest warrant); *accord, Terwilliger v. Reyna*, 4 F.4th 270 (5th Cir. 2021); *Goldring v. Henry*, 2021 WL 5274721, at *4 (11th Cir. November 12, 2021) (same: "[t]he law is clearly established . . . that the Constitution prohibits a police officer from knowingly making false statements in an arrest affidavit about the probable cause for an arrest in order to detain a citizen if such false statements were necessary to the probable cause'"); *Tlapanco v. Elges*, 969 F.3d 638 (6th Cir. 2020) (applying *Franks* to sustain challenges to both search and arrest warrants). A *Franks* hearing is also required if a defendant makes a substantial showing that an officer applying for a search warrant deliberately or recklessly omitted significant exculpatory information from the affidavit (*see, e.g., Washington v. Napolitano*, 29 F.4th 93, 98-99 (2d Cir. 2022) ("[W]e hold that, if a police officer finds an individual's statements regarding his lack of intent to commit a crime to be credible in light of the totality of the circumstances, or if (at the very least) such exculpatory statements could materially impact the probable cause determination by a neutral magistrate judge, that officer cannot then use the incriminating portions of those statements as the foundation for probable cause in an arrest warrant affidavit for that individual, while either knowingly or recklessly concealing from the judge that credibility assessment (if it has been reached) and/or the exculpatory details of those statements.); *Gregory v. City of Louisville*, 444 F.3d 725 (6th Cir. 2006); *Burke v. Town of Walpole*, 405 F.3d 66 (1st Cir. 2005); *DeLoach v. Bevers*, 922 F.2d 618 (10th Cir. 1990); *Phillips v. Whittington*, 2022 WL 797418, at *5, *7 (5th Cir. March 15, 2022); *Dahlin v. Frieborn*, 859 Fed. Appx. 69 (Mem) (9th Cir. 2021); *State v. Missouri*, 337 S.C. 548, 524 S.E.2d 394 (1999); *State v. Jardine*, 118 Idaho 288, 796 P.2d 165 (Idaho App. 1990), and cases cited) or that casts significant doubt upon the credibility of the officer's sources, such as the fact that the officer's confidential informant was a paid informer or was facing criminal charges and hoped to receive a reduced sentence by informing (*e.g., United States v. Clark*, 935 F.3d 558 (7th Cir. 2019); *cf. United States v. Taylor*, 63 F.4th 637 (7th Cir. 2023) (failure to include in a search warrant affidavit the facts that the affiant police officer and another retired police officer involved in the investigation had sexual relations with the individual who was the source of most of the affidavit's incriminating information – together with the misleading characterization of that individual as a "female friend" who "approached" the officers with this information – would call for a *Franks* analysis)) or the known lack of qualifications of professional personnel whose purported expert opinions form the basis for factual conclusions recited in the warrant application (*Camm v. Faith*, 937 F.3d 1096 (7th Cir. 2019)) or that suggests that the information adduced and necessary to support the issuance of the warrant was tainted by earlier unconstitutional activity on the part of law enforcement agents (*United States v. Tate*, 524 F.3d 449 (4th Cir. 2008)). The rule of *Franks* "has a limited scope, both in regard to when exclusion of the seized evidence is mandated, and when a hearing on allegations of misstatements must be accorded" (*Franks v. Delaware*, 438 U.S. at 167).

> "To mandate an evidentiary hearing, the challenger's attack must be more than conclusory and must be supported by more than a mere desire to cross-examine. There must be allegations of deliberate falsehood or of reckless disregard for the truth, and those allegations must be accompanied by an offer of proof. They should point out specifically the portion of the warrant affidavit that is claimed to be false; and they should be accompanied by a statement of supporting reasons. Affidavits or sworn or otherwise reliable statements of witnesses should be furnished, or their absence satisfactorily explained. Allegations of negligence or innocent mistake are insufficient. The deliberate falsity or reckless disregard whose impeachment is permitted . . . is only that of the affiant, not of any nongovernmental informant. Finally, if these requirements are met, and if, when material that is the subject of the alleged falsity or reckless disregard is set to one side, there remains sufficient content in the warrant affidavit to support a finding of probable cause, no hearing is required. On the other hand, if the remaining content is insufficient, the defendant is entitled, under the Fourth and Fourteenth Amendments, to his hearing." (*Id.* at 171-72.)

Accord, United States v. Leon, supra, 468 U.S. at 914, 925; *compare United States v. Sandalo*, 70 F.4th 77 (2d Cir. 2023), *with United States v. Lauria*, 70 F.4th 106 (2d Cir. 2023). "That said, individuals have a clearly established Fourth Amendment right to be free from malicious prosecution by a . . . [government agent] who has 'made, influenced, or participated in the decision to prosecute the plaintiff' by, for example, 'knowingly or recklessly' making false statements that are material to the prosecution either in reports or in affidavits filed to secure warrants." *King v. Harwood*, 852 F.3d 568, 582-83 (6th Cir. 2017). *See, e.g., Rainsberger v. Benner*, 913 F.3d 640, 647 (7th Cir. 2019) ("An officer violates the Fourth Amendment if he intentionally or recklessly includes false statements in a warrant application and those false statements were material to a finding of probable cause. . . . An officer similarly violates the Fourth Amendment if he intentionally or recklessly withholds material information from a probable cause affidavit. . . . We use a straightforward method to determine whether the alleged lies or omissions are material: 'We eliminate the alleged false statements, incorporate any allegedly omitted facts, and then evaluate whether the resulting "hypothetical" affidavit would establish probable cause.'"); *Winfrey v. Rogers*, 901 F.3d 483 (5th Cir. 2018) (same); *United States v. Glover*, 755 F.3d 811, 819-21 (7th Cir. 2014) ("The government's response to Glover's motion to suppress revealed Doe's history as an informant, his multiple convictions, his prior gang affiliation, his use of aliases, and his interest in being paid for useful information. Glover renewed his request for a hearing under *Franks v. Delaware*, . . . to determine whether the officer acted with reckless disregard for the truth by omitting the credibility information from the probable cause affidavit. To obtain a *Franks* hearing, the defendant must make a 'substantial preliminary showing' of (1) a material falsity or omission that would alter the probable cause determination, and (2) a deliberate or reckless disregard for the truth. . . . This is a burden of production. Proof by a preponderance of the evidence is not required until the *Franks* hearing itself. . . . ¶ In this case, the omitted credibility information was clearly material . . . .¶ The district court did not show that it considered whether the credibility omissions themselves, even in the absence of more direct evidence of the officer's state of mind, provide sufficient circumstantial evidence to support a reasonable and thus permissible inference of reckless disregard for the truth. We hold that they do. . . . ¶ On remand the government may provide a satisfactory explanation for the omission of the damaging information about the informant's credibility, but Glover is entitled to test its explanation. We therefore REVERSE the denial of defendant's motion to suppress and REMAND for a *Franks* hearing."); *United States v. Carneiro,* 861 F.2d 1171 (9th Cir. 1988) (material omissions and misstatements in an application for an electronic-surveillance warrant rendered the warrant invalid); *State v. Douglass,* 544 S.W.3d 182, 188 (Mo. 2018) (an officer submitting an application and supporting affidavit for a search warrant also attached a standard form listing items to be seized; he check-marked many categories including "any deceased human fetus or corpse" although the only offenses for which the affidavit stated probable cause were theft crimes; he "testified he checked the corpse clause because, if a corpse was found during the search, he would be required to obtain a 'piggyback warrant' – by checking the box, he was just saving the police from having to stop the search to obtain an additional search warrant if a corpse was found"; the court treats the check mark as a deliberate falsehood for *Franks* purposes); *State v. Tichenor,* 2016 WL 4151375, at *3 (Ariz. App. 2016) ("A defendant may challenge an affiant's statements at an evidentiary hearing after establishing by a preponderance of the evidence, that the affiant 'knowingly and intentionally, or with reckless disregard for the truth' made a false, material statement or omitted a material fact in the affidavit. . . . If the trial court finds the affiant intentionally or recklessly made a false material statement or omitted a material fact, the court then must redraft the affidavit by removing the false statement or adding the omitted fact before determining whether sufficient probable cause remains to support the warrant."). *Cf. United States v. Cordero-Rosario,* 786 F.3d 64, 72 (1st Cir. 2015) (the *Leon-Sheppard* doctrine does not save a warrant-based search where the agent who made it was relying on warrants that were constitutionally inadequate because of his own failure to provide the facts in the affidavits that could have supported their issuance").

25.17.4. *Warrants Based on Tainted Evidence*

If an affidavit for a search warrant includes information that is the product of an earlier unconstitutional search or seizure by the police and does not contain sufficient independent evidence to make out probable cause without reference to the tainted information, the resulting warrant and any search made under its authority are invalid. *Florida v. Jardines,* 569 U.S. 1 (2013); *United States v. Karo,* 468 U.S. 705, 719-21 (1984) (dictum); *United States v. Waide,* 60 F.4th 327 (6th Cir. 2023), summarized in § 25.39 *infra*; *United States v. Mora,* 989 F.3d 794 (10th Cir. 2021); *United States v. Wilson,* 13 F.4th 961 (9th Cir. 2021), summarized in § 25.18.3 *infra*; *United States v. Lopez-Zuniga,* 909 F.3d 906, 910 (8th Cir. 2018); *State v. Harris,* 369 Or. 628, 650, 509 P.3d 83, 96-97 (2022); *People v. Bonilla,* 2018 IL 122484, 120 N.E.3d 930 (2018); see § 25.42 *infra.* To the extent that the earlier unconstitutionality was the consequence of improper police conduct rather than improper magisterial conduct, it continues to invoke the exclusionary sanction that *Leon* and *Sheppard* retain as a curb on the police and withdraw only as a curb on magistrates. *United States v. Bagley*, 877 F.3d 1151 (10th Cir. 2017); *United States v. Nora*, 765 F.3d 1049, 1058-60 (9th Cir. 2014). *Cf. Frimmel Management, LLC v. United States*, 897 F.3d 1045 (9th Cir. 2018) (evidence obtained through an Immigration and Customs Enforcement notice of inspection and subpoena had to be suppressed when ICE's investigation was triggered by information received from a local sheriff's department that had seized a restaurant's employment records during the course of a raid based on search warrants containing reckless omissions and distortions).

25.17.5. *A Neutral and Detached Magistrate*

Exclusion of evidence seized under a warrant is obligatory, even when the police acted in "good faith," if the magistrate who issued the warrant was not neutral and detached. *Leon, supra*, 468 U.S. at 925. This principle would include situations "where the issuing magistrate wholly abandoned his judicial role in the manner condemned in *Lo-Ji Sales, Inc. v. New York*, 442 U.S. 319 (1979)" (*Leon, supra*, 468 U.S. at 923), "allow[ing] himself to become a member, if not the leader, of the search party which was essentially a police operation . . . [and] acting . . . as an adjunct law enforcement officer" (*Lo-Ji, supra*, 442 U.S. at 327). It would also include situations in which the magistrate "'serve[s] merely as a rubber stamp for the police'" (*Leon, supra*, 468 U.S. at 914).

25.17.6. *The Particularity Requirement*

The *Leon/Sheppard* doctrine does not alter the longstanding Fourth Amendment requirement that a warrant must identify the premises to be searched and the things to be seized with reasonable particularity. *See Leon, supra*, 468 U.S. at 923; *Sheppard, supra*, 468 U.S. at 988 n.5; *and see, e.g., Groh v. Ramirez*, 540 U.S. 551, 557-63 (2004); *Maryland v. Garrison*, 480 U.S. 79, 84 (1987) (dictum). The Supreme Court has "clearly stated that the presumptive rule against warrantless searches applies with equal force to searches whose only defect is a lack of particularity in the warrant" (*Groh v. Ramirez, supra*, 540 U.S. at 559). "The manifest purpose of this particularity requirement [is] . . . to prevent general searches. By limiting the authorization to search to the specific areas and things for which there is probable cause to search, the requirement ensures that the search will be carefully tailored to its justifications, and will not take on the character of the wide-ranging exploratory searches the Framers [of the Fourth Amendment] intended to prohibit." *Maryland v. Garrison, supra*, 480 U.S. at 84 (dictum). *See also Groh v. Ramirez, supra*, 540 U.S. at 557-58 ("The fact that the *application* [for the warrant] adequately described the 'things to be seized' does not save the warrant from its facial invalidity. The Fourth Amendment by its terms requires particularity in the warrant, not in the supporting documents."; the Court declines to reach the question of whether "the Fourth Amendment prohibits a warrant from cross-referencing other documents," noting that "most Courts of Appeals have held that a court may construe a warrant with reference to a supporting application or affidavit if the warrant uses appropriate words of incorporation, and if the supporting document accompanies the warrant"); *Lo-Ji Sales, Inc. v. New York, supra*, 442 U.S. at 325-26; *Stanford v. Texas,* 379 U.S. 476 (1965); *Dalia v. United States,* 441 U.S. 238, 255-56 (1979) (dictum); *United States v. Suggs*, 998 F.3d 1125, 1132-33, 1139 (10th Cir. 2021) (holding the particularity requirement violated by a residential search warrant that "targeted some particular items but also included a catch-all phrase authorizing the search and seizure of '[a]ny item identified as being involved in crime'"; "The . . . question as to severability is whether the valid portions 'make up the greater part of the warrant.'. . . They do not. Because the warrant has two valid and two invalid sections, we might have had a draw if the 'greater part' inquiry was limited to merely counting parts. But given the scope and invasiveness of the invalid parts – particularly the 'miscellaneous' catch-all section authorizing officers to search for and seize '[a]ny item identified as being involved in crime'—the valid parts do not constitute the greater part of the warrant."); *United States v. Dunn*, 719 Fed. Appx. 746, 748-49 (10th Cir. 2017) (per curiam) ("the particularity requirement was violated" and therefore "the good-faith exception to the exclusionary rule does not apply"; "The warrant here listed particular items to be searched, but prefaced the list with a catch-all phrase, stating that the items to be searched 'include but are not limited to' the listed items. . . . ¶ The qualifying phrase, 'not limited to,' is frequently included with particular categories in a warrant. In those situations, we have held that the 'not limited to' language does not taint a warrant when the language serves only to modify one or more categories in the list. . . . ¶ But here, the phrase 'not limited to' is used in connection with the entire warrant, not just particular categories. Thus, the addition of this phrase allowed officers to search for any item for any reason."); *State v. Douglass*, 544 S.W.3d 182 (Mo. 2018) (a search warrant listed numerous categories of items to be seized; some categories specifically described objects that there was ample probable cause to find and seize; others included overbroad or catch-all clauses or authorizations unsupported by probable cause; the court holds that the warrant is a constitutionally prohibited 'general warrant' and requires suppression of even the items seized within the pinpoint categories; it rejects the argument that "the invalid portion of the warrant . . . could be redacted pursuant to the 'severance doctrine' . . . [so that] all items . . . seized under the valid portions of the warrant" would escape suppression: "Severance is appropriate under the doctrine *only* 'if the valid portions of the warrant [are] sufficiently particularized, distinguishable from the invalid portions, and make up the greater part of the warrant.'" *Id.* at 189-90 (emphasis in original).); *People v. Gordon*, 36 N.Y.3d 420, 422-23, 429, 436, 166 N.E.3d 514, 515, 519, 525, 142 N.Y.S.3d 440, 441, 445, 451 (2021) ("a search warrant authorizing a search of Mr. Gordon's 'person' and the 'entire premises' . . . did not encompass the search of two vehicles located outside the residence, and the police lacked probable cause to search those vehicles": "The requirement that warrants must describe with particularity the places, vehicles, and persons to be searched is vital to judicial supervision of the warrant process"; "Although some federal courts of appeals have interpreted the Fourth Amendment in a manner that might permit the search here, we decline to follow suit. Instead, we exercise our independent authority to follow our existing state constitutional jurisprudence, even if federal constitutional jurisprudence has changed, because 'we are persuaded that the proper safeguarding of fundamental constitutional rights requires that we do so'"); *United States v. Galpin*, 720 F.3d 436, 446 (2d Cir. 2013) ("Where, as here, the property to be searched is a computer hard drive, the particularity requirement assumes even greater importance. As numerous courts and commentators have observed, advances in technology and the centrality of computers in the lives of average people have rendered the computer hard drive akin to a residence in terms of the scope and quantity of private information it may contain."); *State v. Harris*, 369 Or. 628, 650, 509 P.3d 83, 96-97 (2022) (affirming the suppression of evidence resulting from the acquisition of cell-phone data pursuant to an overbroad search warrant "Overbreadth is an aspect of the requirement in Article I, section 9 [of the Oregon Constitution], that warrants issue only 'upon probable cause, *** and particularly describing the place to be searched, and the person or thing to be seized.' . . . The constitutional requirement means that, 'even if the warrant is sufficiently specific, it must not authorize a search that is broader than the supporting affidavit supplies probable cause to justify.'"); *State v. Castagnola, supra,* 2015-Ohio-1565, 145 Ohio St. 3d at 19-21, 46 N.E.3d at 657-59 ("the search warrant lacked particularity and was therefore invalid" because the authorization to search "'[r]ecords and documents stored on computers'" in the defendant's home "did not contain any description or qualifiers of the 'records and documents stored on the computer' that the searcher was permitted to look for"); *Wheeler v. State,* 135 A.3d 282, 304-05 (Del. 2016) ("warrants, in order to satisfy the particularity requirement, must describe what investigating officers believe will be found on electronic devices with as much specificity as possible under the circumstances. . . . ¶ . . .Where, as here, the investigators had available to them a more precise description of the alleged criminal activity that is the subject of the warrant, such information should be included in the instrument and the search and seizure should be appropriately narrowed to the relevant time period so as to mitigate the potential for unconstitutional exploratory rummaging"); *State v. Henderson,* 289 Neb. 271, 289, 854 N.W.2d 616, 633 (2014) ("a warrant for the search of the contents of a cell phone must be sufficiently limited in scope to allow a search of only that content that is related to the probable cause that justifies the search"); *and see United States v. Lyles,* 910 F.3d 787, 795-96 (4th Cir. 2018) ("This case, ultimately, touches on the Fourth Amendment's independent requirement that 'all searches and seizures must be reasonable.' . . . Reasonableness has many dimensions. One must be proportionality between the gravity of the offense and the intrusiveness of the search. That was absent here. In this case, the 'underlying offense . . . [was] relatively minor' . . . . First-time possession of less than ten grams of marijuana in Maryland, while unlawful, is a civil infraction 'punishable by a fine not exceeding $100.'. . .The warrant here, on the other hand, permitted an intrusion that was anything but minor. It foretold a major incursion into a person's belongings and effects. The magnitude of the intrusion relative to the seriousness of any offense 'is of central relevance to determining reasonableness,'. . . and this is especially the case when 'any and all' is the warrant's insistent refrain with respect to almost every category of personality that might conceivably be in a house."); *and see United States v. Taylor,* 63 F.4th 637 (7th Cir. 2023) (where a typed search warrant signed by the issuing judge described the subject of the search as evidence of child pornography but the warrant had been amended by the handwritten addition of authorization to search for evidence of bestiality, a hearing was required to determine whether the addition had been approved by the judge; if not, the amendment of the warrant by the executing officers would violate the particularity requirement of the Fourth Amendment). *Cf. In re Appeal of Application for Search Warrant,* 2012 VT 102, 71 A.3d 1158, 1162, 1172, 1174, 1181, 1183 (Vt. 2012) (a judicial officer who "granted a warrant to search the residence and to seize electronic devices to be searched at an off-site facility" had the authority to attach *ex ante* conditions "requiring that the search [of the electronic devices] be performed by third parties or trained computer personnel separate from the investigators and operating behind a firewall," "requiring that the information be segregated and redacted prior to disclosure," "requiring police to use focused search techniques," and "prohibiting the use of specialized search tools without prior court authorization"; "Because modern computers contain a plethora of private information, exposing them to wholesale searches presents a special threat of exposing irrelevant but damaging secrets."; "especially in a nonphysical context, particularity may be achieved through specification of how a search will be conducted"). *But cf. United States v. Grubbs,* 547 U.S. 90, 98-99 (2006) ("The Fourth Amendment does not require that the warrant set forth the magistrate's basis for finding probable cause," and, in the case of an anticipatory search warrant, "does not require that the triggering condition . . . be set forth in the warrant itself").

For a discussion of the additional protections grounded in the Sixth Amendment right to counsel, in the attorney-client privilege, and in the work-product doctrine when a warrant authorizes search of a lawyer's files or of material that includes attorney-client communications, *see In re Search Warrant Issued June 13, 2019*, 942 F.3d 159 (4th Cir. 2019); *Harbor Healthcare System, L.P., v. United States*, 5 F.4th 593 (5th Cir. 2021); *In re Sealed Search Warrant and Application for a Warrant by Telephone or Other Reliable Electronic Means*, 11 F.4th 1235 (11th Cir. 2021).

25.17.7. *Scope of the Search Permitted in Executing a Warrant*

The "good faith" doctrine of *Leon* and *Sheppard* does not affect the courts' obligation to review "the reasonableness of the manner in which [a search warrant] . . . was executed" (*Maryland v. Garrison,* 480 U.S. 79, 84 (1987)).

The permissible scope of a search pursuant to a warrant is strictly limited to the premises specified in the warrant. *Id.* at 86-87. *See, e.g., United States v. Bershchansky*, 788 F.3d 102, 105, 111-12 (2d Cir. 2015) (Department of Homeland Agents, who were authorized by a warrant to search "Apartment 2 at the location where Bershchansky lived," exceeded the scope of the warrant "by searching Apartment 1 instead"); *People v. Moore*, 195 A.D.3d 1585, 1586-87, 148 N.Y.S.3d 599, 600-01 (N.Y. App. Div., 4th Dep't 2021) (evidence seized by the police during the execution of a search warrant is suppressed because the area from which the evidence was seized was not one of the locations itemized in the warrant: the warrant authorized a search of the upper apartment and "common areas" of a 2½ story house but the evidence was "found by the police behind a doorway on stairs leading to the attic," which "cannot be considered a part of the upper apartment itself," and the defendant "testified that the door to the attic was closed and locked, and that during the execution of the warrant, the door was broken down by the police" and so "it cannot be said that the attic was accessible to all tenants and their invitees" and thus a "common area"); *Manriquez v. Ensley*, 46 F.4th 1124, 1126-27 (9th Cir. 2022) ("The Fourth Amendment specifically requires a warrant to include a description of the 'place to be searched.' The police officers here – at first – complied with that requirement, obtaining a warrant that listed a motel room suspected of being a hub for drug trafficking. The officers then decided to search the suspect's home as well, and asked the judge over the phone to expand the scope of the warrant to include the home. The judge agreed, but the officers did not physically amend the warrant. ¶ We agree with the district court that the officers violated the Fourth Amendment because the warrant was facially defective. While a judge had orally approved the search of the home, the text of the Fourth Amendment still requires the warrant to specify the place to be searched. ¶ But we hold that the district court erred in denying the officers qualified immunity because it was not clearly established at the time that the search would violate the Fourth Amendment."). When the officers who are applying for a warrant know or should know that a particular building contains multiple units, their application and the warrant are required to specify the individual unit to be searched. See § 25.17.2 *supra*. If, however, they reasonably believe that the entire building is a single unit and in good faith obtain a warrant for the building as a whole, their "failure to realize the overbreadth of the warrant" will be deemed "objectively understandable and reasonable" (*Maryland v. Garrison, supra*, 480 U.S. at 88), and their search of any portion of the building will be sustained until such time as it discloses that separate units do exist within the building (*id.* at 86-89). At that time a continuation of the search beyond the unit for which probable cause was shown to the magistrate – and perhaps any further search at all until the warrant is reissued with a more limited specification of the place to be searched – is unconstitutional (*id.* at 86-87), and the products of the search are suppressible.

Within the premises specified by the warrant, "the scope of a lawful search is 'defined by the object of the search and the places in which there is probable cause to believe that it may be found'" (*id.* at 84; see § 25.22.1 *infra*). This is a corollary of the pervasive Fourth Amendment principle that "'[t]he scope of [a] search must be "strictly tied to and justified by" the circumstances which rendered its initiation permissible'" (*New York v. Belton,* 453 U.S. 454, 457 (1981) (dictum). *See also Birchfield v. North Dakota*, 579 U.S. 438, 469 (2016) (dictum) ("Search warrants protect privacy in two main ways. First, they ensure that a search is not carried out unless a neutral magistrate makes an independent determination that there is probable cause to believe that evidence will be found. . . . Second, if the magistrate finds probable cause, the warrant limits the intrusion on privacy by specifying the scope of the search – that is, the area that can be searched and the items that can be sought."). The officers may search "the entire area in which the object of the search may be found," performing whatever additional "acts of entry or opening may be required to complete the search. Thus a warrant that authorizes an officer to search a home for illegal weapons also provides authority to open closets, chests, drawers, and containers in which the weapon might be found." (*United States v. Ross,* 456 U.S. 798, 820-21 (1982) (dictum)). *Cf. Dalia v. United States,* 441 U.S. 238, 257-58 (1979) (dictum). However, the search may not extend into areas that could not contain the objects specified in the warrant. *See United States v. Ross, supra*, 456 U.S. at 824 (dictum). "[A] warrant to search for a stolen refrigerator would not authorize the opening of desk drawers." *Walter v. United States,* 447 U.S. 649, 657 (1980) (plurality opinion) (dictum).

A search warrant valid when issued may cease to support a constitutional search if changes in circumstances between the time of its issuance and the time of its execution deprive the magistrate's probable-cause finding of continuing force. "[P]robable cause may cease to exist after a warrant is issued. The police may learn, for instance, that contraband is no longer located at the place to be searched. . . . Or the probable-cause showing may have grown 'stale' in view of the time that has passed since the warrant was issued." *United States v. Grubbs*, 547 U.S. 90, 95 n.2 (2006); *United States v. Dalton*, 918 F.3d 1117, 1127-28 (10th Cir. 2019) (dictum) ("There is a plethora of cases in nearly every circuit explaining the circumstances in which a time delay will nullify probable cause as found in the warrant. . . .¶ . . . [T]here are far fewer examples of cases where new information, rather than the passage of time, nullifies the probable cause articulated in a warrant. . . .¶ . . . [But] we are persuaded that probable cause becomes stale when new information received by the police nullifies information critical to the earlier probable cause determination before the warrant is executed."). Or information obtained by the officers executing the warrant may provide an innocent explanation for the apparently incriminating facts upon which the magistrate's finding was based. *See Harte v. Board of Commissioners of County of Johnson, Kansas*, 864 F.3d 1154, 1182-83 (10th Cir. 2017) (opinion of Judge Phillips). In the case of anticipatory warrants (search warrants issued on a showing of probable cause that requires the occurrence of a future "triggering" event), the warrant may not be executed unless the triggering event is observed to happen in the manner that the warrant describes. *United States v. Perkins*, 887 F.3d 272 (6th Cir. 2018).

Nor may the officers seize anything not specified in the warrant. *Marron v. United States,* 275 U.S. 192, 196-98 (1927); *Bivens v. Six Unknown Named Agents of Federal Bureau of Narcotics,* 403 U.S. 388, 394 n.7 (1971) (dictum); *Marshall v. Barlow's, Inc.,* 436 U.S. 307, 323 (1978) (dictum); *see also Dahlin v. Frieborn,* 859 Fed. Appx. 69, 71 (Mem) (9th Cir. 2021) ("'the law is clearly established that a search may not exceed the scope of the search warrant'"); *United States v. Ganias,* 755 F.3d 125, 137-38 (2d Cir. 2014) (government exceeded the scope of a "warrant for the seizure of particular [business record] data on a computer" by retaining a forensic mirror image of the computer's hard drive for two-and-a-half years "until [the government] finally developed probable cause to search and seize" computer files containing "personal financial records . . . not covered by the . . . [original search] warrant"); *United States v. Sedaghaty,* 728 F.3d 885, 910-15 (9th Cir. 2013) ("The question we consider de novo is whether the search was unreasonable because agents relied on the affidavit in support of the warrant to expand the authorized scope of items detailed in the warrant itself." "The plain text of the warrant . . . clearly delineates what is to be seized." "May a broad ranging probable cause affidavit serve to expand the express limitations imposed by a magistrate in issuing the warrant itself? We believe the answer is no. The affidavit as a whole cannot trump a limited warrant."); *cf. Lo-Ji Sales, Inc. v. New York, supra,* 442 U.S. at 325.

The sole exception to the four-corners-of-the-warrant limitation upon objects that can be seized is grounded in the "plain view" doctrine discussed in § 25.22.2 *infra*: Objects not encompassed by the warrant's terms but which the officer encounters while conducting a search of the limited scope described in the preceding paragraph may be seized if, but only if, their appearance and situation give the officer probable cause to believe that they are contraband or otherwise subject to seizure. *Arizona v. Hicks,* 480 U.S. 321 (1987); *Texas v. Brown,* 460 U.S. 730 (1983) (plurality opinion).

When a warrant contains specific restrictions regarding the time or manner of service, violation of those restrictions renders its execution unconstitutional. *Jones v. Kirchner,* 835 F.3d 74, 85 (D.C. Cir. 2016) ("In this case the magistrate, as clearly indicated on the face of the warrant, affirmatively denied the Defendants permission to search Jones's house before 6:00 AM. The plaintiff alleges the Defendants nonetheless executed the warrant at 4:45 AM. Just as a warrant is 'dead,' and a search undertaken pursuant to that warrant invalid, after the expiration date on the warrant, *Sgro v. United States,* 287 U.S. 206, 212 . . . (1932), a warrant is not yet alive, and a search is likewise invalid, if executed before the time authorized in the warrant. If the Defendants executed the warrant when the magistrate said they could not, then they exceeded the authorization of the warrant and, accordingly, violated the Fourth Amendment."). "[B]ecause a warrant generally authorizes no more than what it expressly provides, to act unreasonably beyond the terms of a warrant is akin to acting without a warrant at all." *Simon v. City of New York,* 893 F.3d 83, 94 (2d Cir. 2018); *accord, Zuniga-Perez v. Sessions,* 897 F.3d 114, 123, 126 (2d Cir. 2018).

Regarding searches of *persons* found on the premises, see § 25.22.3 *infra*.

25.17.8. *Deficiency of the Warrant Due to Deficiency of Information Supplied by the Same Officer Who Later Executes the Warrant*

See United States v. Sheehan, 70 F.4th 36 (1st Cir. 2023) ("Sheehan argues that the . . . affidavit's description of 'pictures consist[ing] of images of prepubescent penises that lacked pubic hair' is . . . insufficient to ground a showing of probable cause." *Id.* at 45. "[C]hild nudity alone does not make an image pornographic" (*id.*); the "affidavit's description of the images on Sheehan's phone could only have established probable cause by providing enough detail for the magistrate to determine . . . that the images seen by the state trooper were sufficiently 'lewd,' such that they were indicative of child pornography." *Id.* at 46. "We hold that the affidavit failed to cross this threshold. Its cursory description . . . did little more than signify that the images contained child nudity. That description offered no detail as to the focus of the images, how the children were positioned in the images, or whether the images were sexually provocative in any other respect." *Id.* Such a description, "coupled with the unconnected fact that the defendant was charged with indecent assault and battery of a child, does not, without further elaboration and factual support, suffice to show probable cause of possession of child pornography." *Id.* at 48. "[A]n officer's reliance on a magistrate's approval of a facially deficient warrant is especially unreasonable when those 'deficiencies arise from the failure of the [officer] conducting the search to provide the required supporting information in the affidavit.' . . . ; *cf. Groh v. Ramirez*, 540 U.S. 551, 563-65 (2004) ('[B]ecause petitioner himself prepared the invalid warrant, he may not argue that he reasonably relied on the Magistrate's assurance that the warrant contained an adequate description of the things to be seized and was therefore valid.'). In such circumstances, suppression 'remains an appropriate remedy.'" *Id.* at 51.).

25.18. *Warrantless Entries of Buildings and Searches on Consent*

The police may enter a building without a warrant whenever they obtain the valid consent of a party who has the authority to admit persons to the building. *Washington v. Chrisman*, 455 U.S. 1, 9-10 (1982). "The standard for measuring the scope of a suspect's consent under the Fourth Amendment is that of 'objective' reasonableness – what would the typical reasonable person have understood by the exchange between the officer and the suspect?" *Florida v. Jimeno*, 500 U.S. 248, 251 (1991). *Compare United States v. Jones*, 22 F.4th 667, 678 (7th Cir. 2022) (officers told the occupant of a motel room that they had an arrest warrant for a third party and wanted to enter the room to search places where a person might be hidden; the occupant's response, "that's fine," is held to be effective consent to the officers' looking under a bed with a 6" to 10" clearance from the floor; "[A] reasonable person would likely believe looking underneath the beds in . . . [the] motel room was well within the scope of his consent. Again, the officers explained they would look only "where a person could be." . . . [I]t seems perfectly reasonable that someone could be hiding under a bed to evade arrest even if it was a tight squeeze."), *with, e.g., People v. Hickey*, 172 A.D.3d 745, 747, 98 N.Y.S.3d 287, 289 (N.Y. App. Div., 2d Dep't 2019) ("Contrary to the People's contention, the consent of the defendant's mother to the police to enter the home to speak with the defendant did not constitute a consent to Officer Temple's search of the living room" after the defendant reacted to the police entry by "dart[ing] to the back of the house to the living room," tossing an object "underneath a chair in the living room as he ducked behind a wall," and then "compl[ying] with the officers' requests to come out with his hands up"), *and Commonwealth v. Ortiz*, 478 Mass. 820, 820, 90 N.E.3d 735,

736-37 (2018) ("In this case we must decide whether a driver's consent to allow the police to search for narcotics or firearms 'in the vehicle' authorizes a police officer to search under the hood of the vehicle and, as part of that search, to remove the vehicle's air filter. We hold that it does not. A typical reasonable person would understand the scope of such consent to be limited to a search of the interior of the vehicle, including the trunk."). *Compare United States v. Lopez-Cruz*, 730 F.3d 803, 805-06, 808 (9th Cir. 2013) (although the defendant consented to a border patrol agent's request to inspect and search two cell phones that the defendant identified as belonging to a friend of his, "the agent's answering of the phone [which led to the acquisition of information that incriminated the defendant] exceeded the scope of the consent that [the agent] obtained and, thus, violated Lopez's Fourth Amendment right"), *and State v. Mefford*, 2022 MT 185, 410 Mont. 146, 155, 517 P.3d 210, 218 (2022) (alerted by a GPS monitor that a parolee was out of his home in potential violation of his curfew condition, a parole officer interviewed the parolee to investigate; the parolee explained that he had lost cell-phone access in his home and had gone out to sit in his automobile in the parking lot to message his daughter through Facebook Messenger; the parole officer requested the cell phone to confirm this story; the parolee handed it over; the phone showed an outgoing message at the relevant time but the parole officer, suspecting that that communication was not made to the parolee's daughter, opened the digital photo application on the phone and discovered child porn photos; the Montana Supreme Court, finding that the search exceeded the parolee's consent, holds that it violated the state and federal constitutions: "'[w]hen an official search is properly authorized – whether by consent or by the issuance of a valid warrant – the scope of the search is limited by the terms of the authorization'"), *with United States v. Butler*, 2023 WL 3719025 (11th Cir. 2023) (the defendant, knowing that agents were investigating electronic child pornography, handed his cell phone to an agent at the agent's request; the agent asked for permission to search the phone and the defendant granted it and unlocked the phone, again at the agent's request; the Eleventh Circuit holds that an intensive forensic search and of all of the contents of the phone a month later was within the scope of the defendant's consent).

25.18.1. *Voluntariness of the Consent*

In order to be valid, the consent must be voluntary. *Amos v. United States,* 255 U.S. 313 (1921). *See, e.g., Harris v. Klare*, 902 F.3d 630 (6th Cir. 2018). It must "not be coerced, by explicit or implicit means, by implied threat or covert force . . . no matter how subtly . . . applied" (*Schneckloth v. Bustamonte,* 412 U.S. 218, 228 (1973) (dictum)). "'[W]hen a prosecutor seeks to rely upon consent to justify the lawfulness of a search, he has the burden of proving [by a preponderance of the evidence (*see United States v. Matlock,* 415 U.S. 164, 177, 177-78 n.14 (1974))] that the consent was, in fact, freely and voluntarily given.'" *Schneckloth v. Bustamonte, supra*, 412 U.S. at 222, and cases cited; *see also Florida v. Royer,* 460 U.S. 491, 497 (1983) (plurality opinion); *United States v. Mendenhall,* 446 U.S. 544, 557 (1980) (dictum).

As with confessions, see § 26.2 *infra*, the test of voluntariness is said to turn upon "the totality of all surrounding circumstances" (*Schneckloth v. Bustamonte, supra*, 412 U.S. at 226): "[A]ccount must be taken of subtly coercive police questions, as well as the possibly vulnerable subjective state of the person who consents" (*id.* at 229; *cf. United States v. Watson,* 423 U.S. 411, 424-25 (1976)). Factors that may render a person "vulnerable" and particularly susceptible to coercion include youth, emotional disturbance, lack of education, and mental deficiency. *See, e.g., State v. Butler*, 232 Ariz. 84, 88-89, 302 P.3d 609, 613-14 (2013); *In re J.M.*, 619 A.2d 497, 502-04 (D.C. 1992); and see § 26.4 *infra.*

Courts are loth to find voluntary consent when police entry is sought under an apparent show of authority to enter and is merely acquiesced in by the occupant. *Johnson v. United States,* 333 U.S. 10 (1948); *Bumper v. North Carolina,* 391 U.S. 543 (1968); *Lo-Ji Sales, Inc. v. New York,* 442 U.S. 319, 329 (1979). *See also United States v. Shaw,* 707 F.3d 666, 669 (6th Cir. 2013) ("An officer may not falsely tell a homeowner that he has an arrest warrant for a house, then use that falsity as the basis for obtaining entry into the house."); *cf. State v. Valenzuela,* 239 Ariz. 299, 306-07, 371 P.3d 627, 634-35 (2016) ("[W]e conclude that the State failed to prove by a preponderance of the evidence that Valenzuela's consent was voluntary. *Bumper* and *Johnson* direct this outcome. By telling Valenzuela multiple times that Arizona law required him to submit to and complete testing to determine AC or drug content, the officer invoked lawful authority and effectively proclaimed that Valenzuela had no right to resist the search. ¶ . . . [T]he . . . officer here . . . informed Valenzuela that Arizona law required him to submit to testing or his license would be suspended. The implied consent law, however, nowhere 'requires' a DUI arrestee to submit to testing, and the DPS officer's admonition therefore did not mirror the statute. . . . But even assuming that the officer accurately paraphrased the law, this distinction is immaterial. The *Bumper* Court's ruling turned on the grandmother's acquiescence to the officer's assertion of lawful authority to search regardless of the truthfulness of the officer's claim to possess a warrant. . . . The officer's claim of authority to search was 'instinct with coercion' whether or not he actually possessed a valid warrant."). Valid consent may be obtained from an individual who is in police custody (*United States v. Watson, supra,* 423 U.S. at 424), but "courts have been particularly sensitive to the heightened possibilities for coercion when the 'consent' to a search was given by a person in custody" (*Schneckloth v. Bustamonte, supra,* 412 U.S. at 240 n.29). *See, e.g., United States v. Hall,* 565 F.2d 917, 920 (5th Cir. 1978); *Guzman v. State,* 283 Ark. 112, 120, 672 S.W.2d 656, 659-60 (1984); *Commonwealth v. Smith,* 470 Pa. 220, 228, 368 A.2d 272, 277 (1977). *Cf. Kaupp v. Texas,* 538 U.S. 626, 631 (2003) (per curiam) (police officers' removal of a 17-year-old suspect from his home in the middle of the night and transporting of him to the stationhouse could not be deemed "consensual" even though the suspect said "'Okay'" in response to an officer's statement "'we need to go and talk'" because there was "no reason to think [the suspect's] answer was anything more than 'a mere submission to a claim of lawful authority'"). Consent during a period of *illegal* custody is *eo ipso* ineffective. *See Florida v. Royer, supra,* 460 U.S. at 507-08 (plurality opinion); *id.* at 508-09 (concurring opinions of Justices Powell and Brennan); *United States v. Lopez,* 907 F.3d 472, 487 (7th Cir. 2018), quoted in § 25.39 *infra; Harris v. Klare, supra,* 902 F.3d at 637, quoted in § 25.39 *infra; United States v. Murphy,* 703 F.3d 182, 190 (2d Cir. 2012); *State v. Betts,* 2013 VT 53, 194 Vt. 212, 219-21, 75 A.3d 629, 635-36 (2013) (the rule that "consent obtained during an illegal detention is invalid" necessarily calls for holding as well that "consent for a search is not voluntary when obtained in response to the threat of an unlawful detention"). *See also People v. Frederick,* 500 Mich. 228, 231, 238, 895 N.W.2d 541, 542-43, 546 (2017) (police officers' "predawn" knocking on the front doors of the defendants' homes (at 4 a.m. in one case and 5:30 a.m. in the other) exceeded "the scope of the implied license to approach a house and knock" – which is "time-sensitive" and does not include "knock[ing] at someone's door in the middle of the night" – and therefore "the defendants' consent to search – even if voluntary – is invalid unless it is sufficiently attenuated from the illegality"). And see § 25.39 *infra.*

At least with regard to persons who have not been taken to the stationhouse or other place of closed confinement, the police may obtain valid consent for a warrantless search without first warning the consenting party of his or her Fourth Amendment rights. *Coolidge v. New Hampshire,* 403 U.S. 443, 484-90 (1971); *Schneckloth v. Bustamonte, supra,* 412 U.S. at 234; *United States v. Matlock, supra,* 415 U.S. at 167 n.2; *United States v. Watson, supra,* 423 U.S. at 424-25; *Edwards v. Arizona,* 451 U.S. 477, 483-84 (1981) (dictum)). "[K]nowledge of a right to refuse is not a prerequisite of a voluntary consent." *Schneckloth v. Bustamonte, supra,* 412 U.S. at 234. *See also United States v. Drayton,* 536 U.S. 194, 206 (2002); *Ohio v. Robinette,* 519 U.S. 33, 39-40 (1996). Even with respect to persons at large in the world, however, "knowledge of the right to refuse consent is one factor to be taken into account" in determining the voluntariness of consent for federal Fourth Amendment purposes (*Schneckloth v. Bustamonte, supra,* 412 U.S. at 227; *see also United States v. Drayton, supra,* 536 U.S. at 206; *United States v. Mendenhall, supra,* 446 U.S. at 558-59), and the Court has not rejected the argument that explicit warnings should be required in the case of persons who are in police custody "in the confines of the police station" (*United States v. Watson, supra,* 423 U.S. at 424), or in similar settings where "the techniques of police questioning and the nature of custodial surroundings produce an inherently coercive situation" (*Schneckloth v. Bustamonte, supra,* 412 U.S. at 247), in which the reasoning of *Miranda v. Arizona,* 384 U.S. 436 (1966) (see §§ 26.5-26.9 *infra*) appears to be fully applicable (*see Berkemer v. McCarty,* 468 U.S. 420, 437-40 (1984); *Arizona v. Roberson,* 486 U.S. 675, 685-86 (1988); *United States v. Washington,* 431 U.S. 181, 187 n.5 (1977) (dictum); *Roberts v. United States,* 445 U.S. 552, 560-61 (1980) (dictum). *And see Schneckloth v. Bustamonte, supra,* 412 U.S. at 240 n.29, 247 n.36. *Cf. Ohio v. Robinette, supra,* 519 U.S. at 35 (a motorist who was stopped for speeding on the open road, and who was thereafter given a verbal warning and received his driver's license back from the police officer, did not have to be "advised that he is 'free to go'" in order for his consent to the officer's request to search the car to be "recognized as voluntary"). Several state high courts have declined to follow *Schneckloth* in construing their state constitutions and have held that consent to a search is ineffective unless preceded by an explicit warning and waiver of the right not to undergo the search. *E.g., State v. Brown,* 356 Ark. 460, 466, 156 S.W.3d 722, 726 (2004) (reviewing such decisions in other jurisdictions and concluding "that the circuit judge correctly construed the Arkansas Constitution to require law enforcement officers to advise home dwellers of their right to refuse to consent to a search"); *State v. Budd,* 185 Wash. 2d 566, 573, 374 P.3d 137, 141 (2016) (reaffirming a state constitutional rule that when the police engage in a so-called "knock and talk," in which they "go to a home without a warrant and ask for the resident's consent to search the premises," the "police 'must, prior to entering the home, inform the person from whom consent is sought that he or she may lawfully refuse to consent to the search and that they can revoke, at any time, the consent that they give, and can limit the scope of the consent to certain areas of the home'"; "Officers must give these warnings before entering the home because the resident's knowledge of the privilege is a 'threshold requirement for an intelligent decision as to its exercise.'"). See generally § 17.11 *supra*.

When law enforcement agents employ subterfuge to obtain consent, the courts "distinguish between 'undercover' entries, where a person invites a government agent who is concealing that he is a government agent into her home, and 'ruse' entries, where a known government agent misrepresents his purpose in seeking entry. . . . The former does not violate the

Fourth Amendment, as long as the undercover agent does not exceed the scope of his invitation while inside the home. . . . But '[a] ruse entry when the suspect is informed that the person seeking entry is a government agent but is misinformed as to the purpose for which the agent seeks entry cannot be justified by consent.'" *Whalen v. McMullen*, 907 F.3d 1139, 1147 (9th Cir. 2018) (dictum) (concluding that a detective investigating welfare fraud violated the Fourth Amendment when he obtained consent to enter a suspect's home by falsely purporting to be investigating an identity theft ring and assuring her that she was neither under suspicion nor in danger of having her identity compromised: "McMullen appealed to Whalen's trust in law enforcement and her sense of civic duty to assist him in his 'identity theft' investigation. . . . But there was no identify theft investigation underway. McMullen lied to Whalen about his real purpose – to investigate her for possible social security fraud. Whalen's consent to McMullen's entry into her home is vitiated by his deception." *Id.* at 1147-48.) *Accord, United States v. Harrison*, 639 F.3d 1273 (10th Cir. 2011) (ATF agents investigating possible narcotics and firearms offenses gained consent to enter an apartment by representing that they had received an anonymous phone call indicating that there were drugs and bombs in the apartment and that "'any time we get a phone call like this, you know, our boss makes us come out and investigate it further and see if there's any threat or danger to the community.'" *Id.* at 1276. "[T]he ATF had no reason to believe there were bombs in the apartment, but . . . planned to say this to . . . 'in an effort to gain . . . consent to search.'" *Id.* "Notwithstanding the legality of searches conducted by undercover agents, the 'Fourth Amendment can certainly be violated by guileful as well as by forcible intrusions into a constitutionally protected area.' . . . We have repeatedly held that deception and trickery are among the factors that can render consent involuntary. . . . When government agents seek an individual's cooperation with a government investigation by misrepresenting the nature of that investigation, this deception is appropriately considered as part of the totality of circumstances in determining whether consent was gained by coercion or duress. We should be especially cautious when this deception creates the impression that the defendant will be in physical danger if he or she refuses to consent to the search." *Id.* at 1278-79.); *Pagán-González v. Moreno*, 919 F.3d 582 (1st Cir. 2019) (requiring the suppression of evidence obtained from a computer when ten FBI agents came to the home of its 21-year-old owner and his parents and obtained their consent to take and search it by misrepresenting that it was "'sending a signal and/or viruses to computers in Washington'" (*id.* at 587), and that the agents would try to fix the faulty modem or would replace it at FBI expense if it were not reparable: Although consents obtained by government agents who pose as private citizens may be found voluntary, "[t]he dynamic is meaningfully different . . . when police officers identify themselves as such but misrepresent their purpose. Because citizens will respond to law enforcement with a sense of obligation and presumption of trustworthiness, multiple courts have held facially consensual searches to be invalid where the 'consent' was elicited through officers' lies about the nature or scope of their investigations." (*Id.* at 592.) "[D]espite the broadly framed objections of courts to deception by known government agents, the general consensus in the case law is that such deception, including lying about the purpose of an investigation, is not categorically off-limits in obtaining consent to search. The question instead is whether the deception in context rendered the consent involuntary." *Id.* at 593-94. "[C]ourts have regularly held that coercion is implicit when officers falsely present a need for urgent action." *Id.* at 595. "Roughly ten FBI agents appeared at appellant's door with the alarming news that computers in Washington, D.C. – the heart of the country's political and military operations – were receiving signals or viruses from a computer at appellant's location. If the report of a virus infecting technology in the nation's capital was not itself enough to convey an urgent need to address a pressing threat, the show of force by the federal agents elevated the seriousness of the situation and communicated that the problematic computer posed a substantial threat – perhaps even to the nation's security." *Id.* at 597. "[T]he virus ruse falls squarely within the 'body of relevant case law' in which consent premised on a fabricated emergency was found invalid." *Id.* at 600.); *cf. United States v. Boyd*, 910 F. Supp. 2d 995, 1003 (W.D. Mich. 2011) (suppressing evidence obtained in an apartment search which the Government sought to justify as consensual: "The interaction between the officers and the occupants of the apartment began with a lie. After Investigator Millard knocked twice, Ms. Martin asked who was at the door. Instead of telling the truth about his identity, Investigator Millard lied, telling whoever was on the other side of the door that he was 'Tim from maintenance.' . . . The officers used this lie about their identity purposefully. By Investigator Millard's own admission, the false identification was designed to induce contact with the apartment's occupants. The officers' deceit had the exact manipulative effect Investigator Millard wanted, as Ms. Martin eventually opened the door.").

The extent to which state law can require *ex ante* blanket consent to certain searches and seizures as a condition of receiving various licenses, privileges, or benefits is largely an open question. The convoluted reasoning in *United States v. Knights*, 534 U.S. 112 (2001), summarized in § 25.37 third paragraph *infra*, plainly implies that a state cannot condition a convict's release on probation upon his or her agreement to be subject to searches and seizures that would violate the Fourth Amendment in the case of non-probationers. Since Knights "signed . . . [a] probation order, which stated immediately above his signature that "I HAVE RECEIVED A COPY, READ AND UNDERSTAND THE ABOVE TERMS AND CONDITIONS OF PROBATION AND AGREE TO ABIDE BY SAME," and since one of those terms was "that Knights would '[s]ubmit his . . . person, property, place of residence, vehicle, personal effects, to search at anytime, with or without a search warrant, warrant of arrest or reasonable cause by any probation officer or law enforcement officer" (*id.* at 114), the case would have been a no-brainer if consents of this sort were legally effective. Conspicuously avoiding this straightforward approach (which the Government forcefully advocated), the Court wrote that it "need not decide whether Knights' [sic] acceptance of the search condition constituted consent in the *Schneckloth* sense of a complete waiver of his Fourth Amendment rights, . . . because we conclude that the search of Knights was reasonable under our general Fourth Amendment approach of 'examining the totality of the circumstances,' . . . with the probation search condition being a salient circumstance (*id.* at 118) because "[t]he probation condition . . . significantly diminished Knights' [sic] reasonable expectation of privacy" (*id.* at 119-20). *See also Samson v. California*, 547 U.S. 843, 846, 851-52 (2006), summarized in § 25.37 *infra*; *United States v. Beechler*, 68 F.4th 358, 365 (7th Cir. 2023) ("When assessing the privacy expectations of a person subject to a correctional system, salient factors include the level of punishment or supervision to which the individual has been subjected, whether the individual has agreed to waive some or all Fourth Amendment rights in exchange for more freedom within the correctional system, and expectations of privacy formed pursuant to state law. . . . On the other side of the scale, a court must consider the government's interest in protecting the public, reducing recidivism, and promoting reintegration into society."). *Compare United States v. Fletcher*, 978 F.3d 1009, 1015, 1018-19 (6th Cir. 2020) ("while [*Knights* holds that] the privacy interest of a probationer has been 'significantly diminished,' it is still substantial" and was violated when a probation officer searched the contents of a probationer's cell phone in purported reliance on a state statute authorizing warrantless searches of a probationer's "'person[,] tangible or intangible personal property, or . . . real property upon reasonable suspicion'"; this statute, unlike the applicable provision in *Knights*, did not "clearly or unambiguously include[ ] a cell phone" [see the discussion of *Knights* in § 25.37 *infra*]; and "[t]he Supreme Court in *Riley* [*v. California*, 573 U.S. 373 (2014), discussed in § 25.8.2 *supra*] recognized that the search of a cell phone is unique and – as compared to the search of a home – infringes far more on individual privacy"). A generation later, in *Birchfield v. North Dakota*, 579 U.S. 438 (2016), summarized in § 25.14 subdivision (d) *supra*, the Supreme Court, "[h]aving concluded that the search incident to arrest doctrine does not justify the warrantless taking of a blood sample" from a motorist arrested for drunk driving (*id.* at 476), was required to address the question whether "such tests are justified based on the driver's legally implied consent to submit to them" (*id.*) under state "implied-consent laws" that "go beyond" the "typical penalty for . . . [refusal to submit to blood testing for sobriety – namely,] suspension or revocation of the motorist's license" – and "make it a crime for a motorist to refuse to be tested after being lawfully arrested for driving while impaired" (*id.* at 444). The Court answered that question in the negative, but on extremely narrow grounds. "Our prior opinions have referred approvingly to the general concept of implied-consent laws that impose civil penalties and evidentiary consequences on motorists who refuse to comply. . . . Petitioners do not question the constitutionality of those laws, and nothing we say here should be read to cast doubt on them. ¶ It is another matter, however, for a State not only to insist upon an intrusive blood test, but also to impose criminal penalties on the refusal to submit to such a test. There must be a limit to the consequences to which motorists may be deemed to have consented by virtue of a decision to drive on public roads. ¶ . . . [R]easonableness is always the touchstone of Fourth Amendment analysis, . . . [a]nd applying this standard, we conclude that motorists cannot be deemed to have consented to submit to a blood test on pain of committing a criminal offense." *Id.* at 476-77. In the wake of *Birchfield*, lower courts have continued to uphold the suspension of driver's licenses under implied-consent laws as a sanction for refusal to submit to blood-draw testing (*e.g.*, *Renfroe v. Commonwealth, Pennsylvania Department of Transportation*, 179 A.3d 644 (Pa. Commonwealth Ct. 2017)); they have found that blood draws performed upon drivers who consented to them after being warned that a refusal would result in the suspension of their operating privileges are not *per se* unconstitutional (*see State v. Fleckenstein*, 907 N.W.2d 365, 369 (N.D. 2018)); they have found that refusals to consent may be used in criminal prosecutions as evidence of consciousness of guilt (*Fitzgerald v. People*, 2017 CO 26, 394 P.3d 671 (Colo. 2017); *Commonwealth v. Bell*, 653 Pa. 515, 211 A.3d 761 (2019)) or as the basis for a mandatory minimum sentence on a DWI conviction (*State v. LeMeunier-Fitzgerald*, 2018 ME 85, 188 A.3d 183 (Me. 2018)); *but see Commonwealth v. McCarthy*, 628 S.W.3d 18, 23 (Ky. 2021) ("We conclude the trial court properly held that under *Birchfield* McCarthy's refusal to submit to a blood test could not be used to enhance his criminal penalty for DUI and, under controlling Kentucky precedent, could not be used as evidence that he was guilty of DUI. The trial court erred, however, in allowing the Commonwealth to introduce the refusal evidence to explain to the jury the lack of scientific evidence as to McCarthy's blood alcohol content . . . ."). And a dictum in a plurality opinion in *Mitchell v. Wisconsin*, 139 S. Ct. 2525, 2532-33 (2019), gives its blessing to "'the general concept of implied-consent laws that impose civil penalties and evidentiary consequences on motorists who refuse to comply'" with a request for a blood draw. (After noting that "our decisions [dealing with "implied consent" laws] have not rested on the idea that these laws do what their popular name might seem to suggest" – that is, create actual consent to all the searches they authorize" and that "[i]nstead, we have based our decisions on the precedent regarding the specific constitutional claims in each case," the plurality says specifically that "punishing . . . [drivers'] refusal [to submit to a blood draw requested by an arresting officer] with automatic license revocation does not violate drivers' due process rights if they have been arrested upon probable cause . . . ; on the contrary, this kind of summary penalty is 'unquestionably legitimate.'") The *Mitchell* plurality opinion and the post-*Birchfield* lower-court cases that uphold such sanctions observe correctly that *Birchfield* explicitly declined to address their constitutionality, but neither *Birchfield* nor its progeny to date have explained how the enforcement of implied consent through administrative sanctions and adverse evidentiary consequences is consistent with the settled general principle that consents extracted *ex ante* as the price for receiving government "privileges" are ineffective. *See Garrity v. New Jersey*, 385 U.S. 493 (1967); *Gardner v. Broderick*, 392 U.S. 273 (1968); *Lefkowitz v. Turley*, 414 U.S. 70 (1973); *Lefkowitz v. Cunningham*, 431 U.S. 801, 805 (1977) ("when a State compels testimony by threatening to inflict potent sanctions unless the constitutional privilege is surrendered, that testimony is obtained in violation of the Fifth Amendment and cannot be used against the declarant in a subsequent criminal prosecution"). In each of these Fifth Amendment cases, the "potent sanctions" threatened were nothing more or less than the termination of public employment or of "the opportunity to secure public contracts" (*id.* at 806) – advantages which the states have no greater obligation to bestow than driver's licenses. Pending authoritative resolution of the question left undecided by *Birchfield* whether the Fourth Amendment permits searches that involve significant intrusions upon person, privacy or property on the basis of anterior general consents extracted as the condition of state-conferred licenses or benefits, counsel are warranted in taking the position that the answer is no. Counsel should rely primarily on their state constitutional guarantees and rules against coerced waivers of those guarantees (*see Commonwealth v. Norman*, 484 Mass. 330, 335, 142 N.E.3d 1, 6-7 (2020) (holding that the requirement of submission to GPS tracking as a condition of pretrial release violates the state constitution: "Although consent can justify a warrantless search, 'the Commonwealth bears the burden of proof that consent was freely and voluntarily given, meaning it was unfettered by coercion, express or implied' . . . . ¶ Here, the only evidence of consent is the fact that the defendant signed the form [of consent required as a condition for release]. If he had not, the consequence presumably would have been pretrial detention . . . . . The Commonwealth has not met its burden of showing free and voluntary consent."); *Commonwealth v. Feliz*, 486 Mass. 510, 515, 159 N.E.3d 661, 667 (2020) ("In examining the reasonableness of a condition of probation that authorizes suspicionless searches without probable cause or reasonable suspicion, courts weigh the government's need for the search and the degree of invasion of the reasonable expectations of privacy that the search entails. . . . ¶ Some conditions, such as those that authorize blanket suspicionless searches of a probationer's home, are so invasive that they are not permissible under art. 14 [of the Massachusetts Constitution]."); *State v. Ochoa*, 792 N.W.2d 260 (Iowa 2010), summarized in § 25.10 *supra*; and see § 17.11 *supra*) but also argue as a backstop that, as a matter of federal Fourth Amendment law, the *Garrity-Gardner-Lefkowitz* principle trumps the plurality's dictum in *Mitchell*. *See Serpas v. Schmidt*, 1983 WL 2192 (N.D. Ill. 1983) (invalidating a requirement that grooms employed by a public racetrack consent to searches of their living quarters at the track and of their persons as a condition for occupational licensure: "[i]t has long been held by the Supreme Court that the government may deny an individual a benefit for legitimate reasons; it may not, however, deny a benefit for a reason which infringes an individual's constitutional rights" (*id.* at *10)). Alternatively, counsel can argue that at the least the compulsion exerted by such sanctions is a factor to be considered under *Schneckloth*'s "totality-of-the-circumstances" analysis in determining the voluntariness of a defendant's consent. *See Commonwealth v. Myers*, 640 Pa. 653, 164 A.3d 1162 (2017) (an encyclopedic, cautious plurality opinion invoking constitutional restraints as a basis for construing the State's implied-consent law to forbid the taking of a blood draw from an unconscious driver: "In recent years, a multitude of courts in our sister states have interpreted their respective – and similar – implied consent provisions and have concluded that the legislative proclamation that motorists are deemed to have consented to chemical tests is insufficient to establish the voluntariness of consent that is necessary to serve as an exception to the warrant requirement." *Id.* at 673, 164 A.3d at 1173. "Even where implied consent statutes establish a clear right of refusal . . . numerous state courts have concluded that implied consent laws which provide that motorists are deemed to consent to chemical tests do not, in themselves, serve as exceptions to the warrant requirement." *Id.* at 674, 164 A.3d at 1174. "Although it does not squarely resolve the question of whether implied consent may serve as an independent warrant exception, the *Birchfield* decision does not suggest any contrary conclusion. To be sure, *Birchfield* (like our own precedents) provides a general if uncontroversial endorsement of the concept of implied consent. . . . But *Birchfield* in no way suggests that the existence of a statutory implied consent provision obviates the constitutional necessity that consent to a search must be voluntarily given . . . ." *Id.* at 681, 164 A.3d at 1178. "We . . . agree with Professor LaFave that *Birchfield* does not cast doubt upon the principle that the consent exception to the warrant requirement requires analysis under the totality of the circumstances, and may not be satisfied merely by legislative proclamation. . . . We find it particularly doubtful that the Court, while relying upon the seminal *Schneckloth* decision in discussing the necessity of voluntariness, would sweep away decades of jurisprudence by implication only, and would alter dramatically the mechanics of the consent exception without explicitly so declaring." *Id.* at 684, 164 A.3d at 1180.); *State v. Prado*, 2021 WI 64, 397 Wis. 2d 719, 960 N.W.2d 869 (Wis. 2021) (an implied-consent statute which "provides: 'A person who is unconscious or otherwise not capable of withdrawing consent is presumed not to have withdrawn [the] consent' . . . [statutorily implied in the case of any person operating a vehicle on a public highway, and which thereby authorizes] a law enforcement officer [who] has probable cause to believe that an incapacitated person has violated the . . . [drunk driving] statutes . . . [to] take blood from the person for testing without a search warrant" (397 Wis. 2d at 731, 960 N.W.2d at 875) is facially unconstitutional under the Fourth Amendment; "In the context of warrantless blood draws, consent 'deemed' by statute is not the same as actual consent, and in the case of an incapacitated driver the former is incompatible with the Fourth Amendment. Generally, in determining whether constitutionally sufficient consent is present, a court will review whether consent was given in fact by words, gestures, or conduct. . . . This inquiry is fundamentally at odds with the concept of 'deemed' consent in the case of an incapacitated driver because an unconscious person can exhibit no words, gestures, or conduct to manifest consent." 397 Wis. 2d at 739, 960 N.W.2d at 879. "The State's essential argument in this case boils down to an assertion that the incapacitated driver provision is constitutional because exigent circumstances may have been present. This argument conflates the consent and exigent circumstances exceptions to the warrant requirement. The incapacitated driver provision of the implied consent statute is not focused on exigent circumstances. As the moniker 'implied consent' connotes, the statute addresses consent, which is an exception to the warrant requirement separate and apart from exigent circumstances. 397 Wis. 2d at 738-39, 960 N.W.2d at 875).)

25.18.2. *Authority To Consent: Consent by a Party Other Than the Defendant*

The test of a third party's authority to consent is whether the third party possessed – or reasonably appeared to the police to possess – "common authority over or other sufficient relationship to the premises or effects sought to be inspected" (*United States v. Matlock*, 415 U.S. 164, 171 (1974)). *See also Georgia v. Randolph*, 547 U.S. 103, 109 (2006) ("the exception for consent extends even to entries and searches with the permission of a co-occupant whom the police reasonably, but erroneously, believe to possess shared authority as an occupant"); *Illinois v. Rodriguez*, 497 U.S. 177, 186 (1990). "Common authority is, of course, not to be implied from the mere property interest a third party has in the property. The authority which justifies the third-party consent does not rest upon the law of property, . . . but rests rather on mutual use of the property by persons generally having joint access or control for most purposes, so that it is reasonable to recognize that any of the co-inhabitants has the right to permit the inspection in his own right and that the others have assumed the risk that one of their number might permit the common area to be searched." *United States v. Matlock, supra*, 415 U.S. at 171 n.7. *See also Frazier v. Cupp*, 394 U.S. 731, 740 (1969); *Georgia v. Randolph, supra*, 547 U.S. at 111-12 ("The constant element in assessing Fourth Amendment reasonableness in the consent cases . . . is the great significance given widely shared social expectations, which are naturally enough influenced by the law of property, but not controlled by its rules."; "[W]hen it comes to searching through bureau drawers, there will be instances in which even a person clearly belonging on premises as an occupant may lack any perceived authority to consent; 'a child of eight might well be considered to have the power to consent to the police crossing the threshold into that part of the house where any caller, such as a pollster or salesman, might well be admitted,' . . . , but no one would reasonably expect such a child to be in a position to authorize anyone to rummage through his parents' bedroom"); *Payton v. New York*, 445 U.S. 573, 583 (1980) (a three-year old child's opening of the door to the house could not constitute valid consent to a police entry to arrest the child's father); *Stoner v. California*, 376 U.S. 483 (1964) (a hotel manager's consent to the entry of a guest's room is ineffective); *Chapman v. United States*, 365 U.S. 610 (1961) (a landlord's consent to the entry of a tenant's house is ineffective); *United States v. Thomas*, 65 F.4th 922, 923-24 (7th Cir. 2023) (requiring suppression of evidence seized in the search of a condominium although the landlord consented to the search and the defendant had leased the condo under "a bogus name in order to avoid arrest on multiple warrants": the Government "conceded that the lease gave Thomas a subjective expectation of privacy in the condo. But it argued that this is not an expectation that society is prepared to accept as reasonable, because Thomas had obtained the lease by deceiving the landlord about his identity, which is a crime in Georgia." The Seventh Circuit rejects this argument because "Georgia has codified . . . [a condo lessee's] expectation that his tenancy could not be revoked without notice and an opportunity for judicial process . . . [; no judicial revocation proceedings were held before the search of Thomas's condo; therefore,] his expectation of privacy . . . is one that society recognizes as reasonable."); *United States v. Terry*, 915 F.3d 1141, 1143 (7th Cir. 2019) ("Is it reasonable for officers to assume that a woman who answers the door in a bathrobe has authority to consent to a search of a male suspect's residence? We hold that the answer is no. The officers could reasonably assume that the woman had spent the night at the apartment, but that's about as far as a bathrobe could take them. Without more, it was unreasonable for them to conclude that she and the suspect shared access to or control over the property."); *United States v. Peyton*, 745

F.3d 546, 552-56 (D.C. Cir. 2014) (defendant's great-great-grandmother, with whom he shared a one-bedroom apartment, lacked both actual and apparent authority to consent to a search of a closed shoebox of his that was next to his bed: "The fact that a person has common authority over a house, an apartment, or a particular room, does not mean that she can authorize a search of anything and everything within that area."); *United States v. Moran*, 944 F.3d 1 (1st Cir. 2019) (arrestee's sister had neither actual nor apparent authority to consent to a warrantless search of closed, opaque black trash bags containing his personal effects which he had asked her to hold for him in her storage unit); *State v. Jackson*, 878 N.W.2d 422 (Iowa 2016) (finding a Fourth Amendment violation where an "officer relied on a third party's consent in conducting the search. The third party possessed actual authority to consent to a search of the bedroom the backpack was in but lacked actual authority to consent to a search of the backpack itself." *Id.* at 424. "[A] warrantless search is not authorized when the circumstances would cause a reasonable officer to doubt whether the party consenting had authority to consent with respect to the location to be searched. The mere fact that an officer subjectively relied on third-party consent does not render that reliance reasonable. . . . Reliance on apparent authority to authorize a search is only reasonable when the authority of the person consenting is actually apparent with respect to the location to be searched. Thus, when the totality of the circumstances indicates a reasonable officer would have conducted further inquiry to determine whether the person who consented to a premises search had authority to consent to a search of a closed container, the government must demonstrate the officer did just that in order to establish the search of the container was reasonable." *Id.* at 438.); *Reeves v. Warden*, 346 F.2d 915 (4th Cir. 1965) (a co-tenant cannot consent to entry of an area reserved for defendant's private occupancy and use); *State v. Colvard*, 296 Ga. 381, 381-82, 383, 768 S.E.2d 473, 474, 475 (2015) (defendant's uncle, in whose apartment the defendant lived, did not have authority to consent to a search of the defendant's bedroom, which was "used exclusively" by the defendant, and had a lock on the door for which the uncle did not have a key; the uncle "could not go into the bedroom when the door was locked," and the bedroom door was locked at the time of the police entry, although "it did not appear that the bedroom door was securely fastened" since the police were able to "pop [it] open" easily).

Although "voluntary consent of an individual possessing [or reasonably appearing to possess the requisite] authority" may suffice "*when the suspect is absent*" (*Georgia v. Randolph, supra*, 547 U.S. at 109 (emphasis added)), a different standard applies when a co-occupant "who later seeks to suppress the evidence . . . is present at the scene and expressly refuses to consent" (*id.* at 106). In *Randolph*, the Court addressed the latter scenario and held that "a physically present inhabitant's express refusal of consent to a police search is dispositive as to him, regardless of the consent of a fellow occupant" (*id.* at 122-25). *Accord, Fernandez v. California*, 571 U.S. 292, 300-01 (2014) (dictum). *See also Clemons v. Couch*, 3 F.4th 897, 902 n.3 (6th Cir. 2021) (after a domestic squabble, a homeowner ordered his daughter-in-law out of the house where she and her husband had been staying; she returned with a state trooper to retrieve her personal belongings, and they entered the house; the homeowner ordered the trooper to leave; the Sixth Circuit concludes that the homeowner's "demand that . . . [the trooper] leave negated any consent that . . . [the trooper] may have had to enter the home.); *United States v. Johnson*, 656 F.3d 375, 377-79 (6th Cir. 2011) (the defendant's objection to the search at the scene was sufficient to override the consent given by his wife and her grandmother, even though the defendant "was not a full-time resident of the home and his possessory interest was therefore inferior to that of" the consenting individuals, "who lived there full-time": the Supreme Court in *Randolph* "expressly avoided making . . . distinctions" between "relative degrees of possessory interest among residential co-occupants"). *Compare Fernandez v. California, supra*, 571 U.S. at 294, 303 (a domestic violence victim's consent to police entry of the home she shared with the defendant was valid, notwithstanding the defendant's objection at the time the police arrived, because the "consent was provided by [the] . . . abused woman well after her male partner had been [lawfully] removed" by the police: when "an occupant . . . is absent due to a lawful detention or arrest," the absent occupant "stands in the same shoes as an occupant who is absent for any other reason"; the Court emphasizes, however, that the defendant did not "contest the fact that the police had reasonable grounds for removing him from the apartment so that they could speak with . . . an apparent victim of domestic violence, outside of [the defendant's] . . . potentially intimidating presence," and did "not even contest the existence of probable cause to place him under arrest"), *with State v. Coles*, 218 N.J. 322, 328, 347-48, 95 A.3d 136, 139, 150-51 (2014) ("As the United States Supreme Court's *Fernandez* opinion makes clear, valid third-party consent is subject to the exception that the third party's consent cannot be manufactured through the unlawful detention of the defendant"; the New Jersey Supreme Court holds on state constitutional grounds, "bolstered by Fourth Amendment principles," that the officers' initially valid detention of the defendant became unlawful once his identity and residence were confirmed and thus he "was being unlawfully detained by police, a few houses away from his home" at the time the police obtained consent from his aunt to search his bedroom in her house; the "asserted consent-based search" was unlawful because "[t]he officer's action detaining defendant in a patrol car when probable cause to arrest was lacking effectively prevented any objection from defendant" and "[it] also prevented him from disputing his aunt's statements in response to police inquiries about control over the room").

25.18.3. *"Private Searches"*

A situation analytically distinct from third-party consent searches but sometimes entangled with it is presented when a private citizen unconnected with law enforcement makes a search or seizure of property or premises in which that person has no protected interest but the defendant does. If the private citizen is not acting in collaboration or coordination with any government agent at the time of the search or seizure, neither that initial action nor the subsequent delivery of its fruits to law enforcement officers implicates the Fourth Amendment. *Burdeau v. McDowell*, 256 U.S. 465 (1921); *United States v. Phillips*, 32 F.4th 865 (9th Cir. 2022); *United States v. Miller,* 982 F.3d 412 (6th Cir. 2020); *Commonwealth v. Shaffer*, 653 Pa. 258, 209 A.3d 957 (2019). *Compare United States v. Meals*, 21 F.4th 903, 905 (5th Cir. 2021) (as required by statute (18 U.S.C. §2258A(a)), Google sent an electronic CyberTipline report to the National Center for Missing and Exploited Children (NCMEC) that Meals and a 15-year-old were exchanging messages about their past and future sexual encounters via Facebook; NCMEC reported this to law enforcement authorities who used the tip to obtain a warrant for Meals's electronic devices; Meals's motion to suppress evidence obtained in executing the warrant was denied, and the Court of Appeals affirms "because Facebook did not act as a government agent and NCMEC's search, assuming that it is a government agent, did not exceed the scope of Facebook's cyber tip"), *and United States v. Rosenow*, 50 F.4th 715 (9th Cir. 2022) (same), *and United States v. Sykes*, 65 F.4th 867 (6th Cir. 2023) (essentially the same), *with United States v. Ackerman*, 831 F.3d 1292 (10th Cir. 2016) (alternative ground) (holding that NCMEC's Cyber

Tipline activities are subject to Fourth Amendment constraint: "[W]hen an actor *is* endowed with law enforcement powers beyond those enjoyed by private citizens, courts have traditionally found the exercise of the public police power engaged. . . . ¶ NCMEC's law enforcement powers extend well beyond those enjoyed by private citizens – and in this way it seems to mark it as a fair candidate for a governmental entity. NCMEC's two primary authorizing statutes . . . mandate its collaboration with federal (as well as state and local) law enforcement in over a dozen different ways, many of which involve duties and powers conferred on and enjoyed by NCMEC but no other private person. For example, NCMEC is statutorily obliged to operate the official national clearinghouse for information about missing and exploited children, to help law enforcement locate and recover missing and exploited children, to 'provide forensic technical assistance . . . to law enforcement' to help identify victims of child exploitation, to track and identify patterns of attempted child abductions for law enforcement purposes, to 'provide training . . . to law enforcement agencies in identifying and locating non-compliant sex offenders,' and of course to operate the CyberTipline as a means of combating Internet child sexual exploitation. . . . This special relationship runs both ways, too, for NCMEC is also empowered to call on various federal agencies for unique forms of assistance in aid of its statutory functions."), *and United States v. Wilson*, 13 F.4th 961 (9th Cir. 2021) (Google sent a CyberTipline report to the NCMEC that Wilson had uploaded four images of apparent child pornography to his email account as email attachments. "No one at Google had opened or viewed Wilson's email attachments; its report was based on an automated assessment that the images Wilson uploaded were the same as images other Google employees had earlier viewed and classified as child pornography. Someone at NCMEC then, also without opening or viewing them, sent Wilson's email attachments to the San Diego Internet Crimes Against Children Task Force (ICAC), where an officer ultimately viewed the email attachments without a warrant. The officer then applied for warrants to search both Wilson's email account and Wilson's home, describing the attachments in detail in the application." *Id.* at 964. The Ninth Circuit holds that the ICAC officer's warrantless viewing of the images was a violation of the Fourth Amendment: "Viewing Wilson's email attachments . . . substantively expanded the information available to law enforcement far beyond what the label [affixed to Wilson's attachments: "A1," indicating an image of a sex act involving a prepubescent minor] alone conveyed, and was used to provide probable cause to search further and to prosecute. The government learned at least two things above and beyond the information conveyed by the CyberTip by viewing Wilson's images: First, Agent Thompson learned exactly what the image showed. Second, Agent Thompson learned the image was in fact child pornography. Until he viewed the images, they were at most 'suspected' child pornography. . . . ¶ . . . Because the government saw more from its search than the private party had seen, it exceeded the scope of the private search." *Id.* at 973-74.), *and State v. Terrell*, 372 N.C. 657, 658, 671, 831 S.E.2d 17, 18, 26 (2019) (rejecting the prosecution's argument that the "private search" doctrine authorized "a law enforcement officer's warrantless search of defendant's USB drive, following a prior search of the USB drive by a private individual" who gave the thumb drive to the police after viewing images stored on it: "It is clear that . . . [the private individual's] limited search did not frustrate defendant's legitimate expectation of privacy in the *entire* contents of his thumb drive and that Detective Bailey's follow-up search . . . was not permissible under [*United States v.*] *Jacobsen*[, 466 U.S. 109 (1984)] because he did not possess 'a virtual certainty that nothing else of significance was in the [thumb drive] and that a manual inspection of the [thumb drive] and its contents would not tell him anything more than he already had been told'" by the private individual); *United States v. Donnes*, 947 F.2d 1430,

1434-35 (10th Cir. 1991) (ordering suppression of methamphetamine found by officers when they opened a camera lens case inside a glove that had been picked up by a private citizen and handed to an officer because it looked suspicious: "In *United States v. Jacobsen*, 466 U.S. 109 (1984), the Supreme Court recognized a standard for evaluating the actions of law enforcement officials when presented with evidence uncovered during a private search. The Court stated that '[t]he additional invasions of [defendant's] privacy by the Government agent must be tested by the degree to which they exceeded the scope of the private search. *Id.* at 115. The district court found that . . . [the private individual here] gave the glove and its contents to the officer immediately after seeing the syringe inside the glove. . . . [The private individual] did not himself open the camera lens case which was also inside the glove."); *United States v. Runyan*, 275 F.3d 449, 461 (5th Cir. 2001) (similar holding: "Language from the Supreme Court's *Jacobsen* opinion suggests that the critical inquiry under the Fourth Amendment is whether the authorities obtained information with respect to which the defendant's expectation of privacy has not already been frustrated. Thus, *Jacobsen* directs courts to inquire whether the government learned something from the police search that it could not have learned from the private searcher's testimony and, if so, whether the defendant had a legitimate expectation of privacy in that information.").

The Fourth Amendment does regulate the search or seizure "if the private party acted as an instrument or agent of the Government." *Skinner v. Railway Labor Executives' Association*, 489 U.S. 602, 614 (1989). *See, e.g., United States v. Shelton*, 997 F.3d 749 (7th Cir. 2021); *United States v. Ackerman, supra*, 831 F.3d at 1300-04 (alternative ground); *United States v. Hardin*, 539 F.3d 404 (6th Cir. 2008) (acting under an arrest warrant for parole violation by an armed-robbery convict, government investigators went to the apartment of a woman whom they had been informed was his girlfriend; they "told the apartment manager that 'we need to see if he is there' and . . . '*asked* him to go ahead and under a ruse check to see if a water leak was in the apartment to see if he was there'" (*id.* at 407) (emphasis in original); although they testified without contradiction "that the apartment manager was shocked and worried about . . . [the parolee's] potential presence in the apartment complex" (*id.*), the court holds that "because the officers urged the apartment manager to investigate and enter the apartment, and the manager, independent of his interaction with the officers, had no reason or duty to enter the apartment, . . . the manager was acting as an agent of the government" (*id.* at 420)); *United States v. Walther*, 652 F.2d 788 (9th Cir. 1981) ("[T]wo of the critical factors in the "instrument or agent" analysis are: (1) the government's knowledge and acquiescence, and (2) the intent of the party performing the search." *Id.* at 792. An airline employee who opened a freight package in an airport baggage terminal is held to be a government agent under this test: "Though . . . [the employee] testified that he believed that a federal regulation gave the airlines the right to open any piece of luggage consigned to them for shipping, he also testified that the only reason why he opened the case was his suspicion that it contained illegal drugs. Thus, legitimate business considerations such as prevention of fraudulent loss claims were not a factor. The record contained sufficient evidence for the [district] court to conclude also that . . . [the employee] opened the case with the expectation of probable reward from the DEA. . . . [The employee] acknowledged that there was no reason that he should not expect a reward, and the testimony of a DEA agent established that it would be reasonable for him to have such an expectation. . . . We are thus satisfied that . . . [the employee] opened the package with the requisite mental state of an "instrument or agent." *Id.* ¶ "We are also satisfied that . . . [the employee's] prior experience with the DEA provides proof of the government's acquiescence in the search. While the DEA had no prior knowledge that this particular search would be conducted and had not directly encouraged . . . [the employee] to search this overnight case, it had certainly encouraged . . . [him] to engage in this type of search. . . . [The employee] had been rewarded for providing drug-related information in the past. He had opened Speed Paks before, and did so with no discouragement from the DEA. The DEA thus had knowledge of a particular pattern of search activity dealing with a specific category of cargo, and had acquiesced in such activity." *Id.* at 793.); *United States v. Reed*, 15 F.3d 928, 930-33 (9th Cir. 1994) (dictum); *State v. Moninger*, 957 So.2d 2 (Fla. App. 2007), *review dismissed as improvidently granted*, 982 So.2d 682 (Fla. 2008); *State v. Lien*, 364 Or. 750, 776-81, 441 P.3d 185, 200-02 (2019); *Fogg v. United States*, 247 A.3d 306 (D.C. 2021); *but see United States v. Bebris*, 4 F.4th 551 (7th Cir. 2021). "The decisive factor in determining the applicability of the . . . [Amendment] is the actuality of a share by a . . . [government] official in the total enterprise of securing and selecting evidence by other than sanctioned means. It is immaterial whether a . . . [government] agent originated the idea or joined in it while the search was in progress. So long as he was in it before the object of the search was completely accomplished, he must be deemed to have participated in it." *Lustig v. United States*, 338 U.S. 74, 79 (1949) (plurality opinion). "'Whether a private party should be deemed an agent or instrument of the government for Fourth Amendment purposes necessarily turns on the degree of the government's participation in the private party's activities, a question that can only be resolved in light of all the circumstances.' . . . In evaluating agency in the Fourth Amendment context, our court has focused on three relevant factors: '[1] whether the government had knowledge of and acquiesced in the intrusive conduct; [2] whether the citizen intended to assist law enforcement or instead acted to further his own purposes; and [3] whether the citizen acted at the government's request.' . . . A defendant bears the burden of proving by a preponderance of the evidence that a private party acted as a government agent." *United States v. Highbull*, 894 F.3d 988, 992 (8th Cir. 2018); *United States v. Fortney*, 772 Fed. Appx. 269, 273, 275 (6th Cir. 2019) (discussing two theories of official involvement in private searches – the state-compulsion test and the symbiotic relationship or nexus test – and applying the latter test to find a Fourth Amendment violation: "'Under the symbiotic relationship or nexus test, the action of a private party constitutes state action when there is a sufficiently close nexus between the state and the challenged action of the regulated entity so that the action of the latter may be fairly treated as that of the state itself.' . . . The test requires demonstrating that the state was 'intimately involved in the challenged private conduct' such that the conduct can 'be attributed to the state[.]' . . . The district court found that Fortney did not satisfy this test because the 'three officers on site did not play an active role in the search.' Here we part ways with the district court. . . . ¶ . . . Fortney unambiguously objected to the search. By everyone's account, Fortney attempted to promptly and independently retrieve his property after he was fired but stopped this effort because three police officers triangulated around him. Then, as the three officers looked on – and in contrast to his earlier refusal – he allowed . . . [his employment supervisor, who had just fired him] to search every pocket of his bag, remove his wallet, and hand the wallet to the police so that they could go through its contents."); *Meier v. City of St. Louis*, 934 F.3d 824, 829 (8th Cir. 2019) (a private towing company acting at the direction of a police dispatcher picked up, towed, and held a truck that was listed by police as "wanted" because of possible involvement in a hit-and-run incident; the Eighth Circuit concludes that the towing company is a state actor because "an act violating the Constitution is considered to have occurred under color of law if it is 'fairly attributable' to a governmental entity."); *State v. Collins*, 367 Md. 700, 717-18, 790 A.2d 660, 670 (2002) (holding that two bail bond agents were state actors for Fourth Amendment purposes because they were accompanied to the door of the defendant's apartment by a police officer who initially knocked on the door and asked the defendant "if *we* could check the residence for a wanted subject" (not the defendant himself) but who remained outside while the bondsmen insisted on entering; the bondsmen had taken the initiative in the episode, telling the officer that they wished to apprehend a wanted subject and requesting his aid pursuant to an established practice whereby officers "stood by" bondsmen to intervene if, but only if, the officer witnessed a crime being committed: however, "[i]n the case *sub judice,* the actions of . . . [the officer] in relation to the bail bond agents and . . . [defendant] was more akin to non-incidental and impliedly supportive conduct, as opposed to mere standby protection services. In conjunction with the inherent nature of the bail bond process, the extra actions of the officer under the specific circumstances here present, transformed the actions of the bail bond persons into 'State action' subjecting the search to Fourth Amendment analysis."). And see § 25.38 *infra.*

25.18.4. *Application of the "Private Search" Doctrine to Home Entries by Law Enforcement Officers*

This subject is canvassed thoroughly, with discussion of the relevant authorities, in *State v. Wright*, 221 N.J. 456, 459-78, 114 A.3d 340, 342-53 (2015):

> "In this case, we consider whether the 'third-party intervention' or 'private search' doctrine applies to a warrantless search of a home.
>
> "The doctrine originally addressed situations like the following: Private actors search an item, discover contraband, and notify law enforcement officers or present the item to them. The police, in turn, replicate the search without first getting a warrant. *See, e.g., United States v. Jacobsen*, 466 U.S. 109 (1984) [§ 25.22.2 subdivision (ii) *infra*]. Because the original search is carried out by private actors, it does not implicate the Fourth Amendment. And if the officers' search of the item does not exceed the scope of the private search, the police have not invaded a defendant's protected privacy interest and do not need a warrant.
>
> "The State now seeks to expand the doctrine to a very different setting: the search of a private home. In this case, a resident reported a leak in her apartment to her landlord, who showed up the following day with a plumber. The landlord and plumber entered the apartment while no one was home, spotted the leak in the kitchen, and checked elsewhere for additional leaks. In the rear bedroom, the plumber saw drugs on top of a nightstand and inside an open drawer. He and the landlord notified the police.
>
> "Instead of using that information to apply for a search warrant, an officer walked into the apartment and looked around the kitchen and bedroom area. He, too, noticed the drugs and found a scale as well. The police conducted a full search moments later, with the resident's consent, and found other contraband.
>
> " . . . .

"Relying on the protections in the State Constitution, we conclude that the private search doctrine cannot apply to private dwellings. Absent exigency or some other exception to the warrant requirement, the police must get a warrant to enter a private home and conduct a search, even if a private actor has already searched the area and notified law enforcement.

"To be sure, whenever residents invite someone into their home, they run the risk that the third party will reveal what they have seen to others. . . . A landlord, like any other guest, may tell the police about contraband he or she has observed. And the police, in turn, can use that information to apply for a search warrant. . . . But that course of events does not create an exception to the warrant requirement.

" . . . .

"We recognize that residents have a reduced expectation of privacy in their home whenever a landlord or guest enters the premises. But residents do not thereby forfeit an expectation of privacy as to the police. In other words, an invitation to a plumber, a dinner guest, or a landlord does not open the door to one's home to a warrantless search by a police officer.

" . . . .

"The proper course under the State and Federal Constitutions is the simplest and most direct one. If private parties tell the police about unlawful activities inside a person's home, the police can use that information to establish probable cause and seek a search warrant. In the time it takes to get the warrant, police officers can secure the apartment or home from the outside, for a reasonable period of time, if reasonably necessary to avoid any tampering with or destruction of evidence. *Illinois v. McArthur*, 531 U.S. 326, 334 . . . (2001) [§ 25.6.3, fifth paragraph *supra*]. But law enforcement cannot accept a landlord's invitation to enter a home without a warrant unless an exception to the warrant requirement applies."

Accord, *State v. Shaw*, 237 N.J. 588, 611, 207 A.3d 229, 242 (2019) (extending *Wright* to motel rooms; "[w]e note, as a general matter, that the third-party intervention doctrine is a poor fit to living spaces"); *State v. Rodriguez*, 521 S.W.3d 1 (Tex. Crim. App. 2017).

25.19. *Warrantless Entry for the Purpose of Making a Valid Arrest*

Before the decisions in *Payton v. New York*, 445 U.S. 573 (1980), and *Steagald v. United States,* 451 U.S. 204 (1981), there was a substantial body of caselaw holding that police officers who had probable cause to arrest an individual could constitutionally enter premises (including residential premises) to make the arrest without a search or arrest warrant. In *Payton*, the Supreme Court held that "the Fourth Amendment . . . prohibits the police from making a warrantless and nonconsensual entry into a suspect's home in order to make a routine felony arrest" (445 U.S. at 576). *See, e.g., Collins v. Virginia*, 138 S. Ct. 1663, 1672 (2018) ("it is a 'settled rule that warrantless arrests in public places are valid,' but, absent another exception such as exigent circumstances, officers may not enter a home to make an arrest without a warrant, even when they have probable cause"); *United States v. McCraw*, 920 F.2d 224, 228 (4th Cir. 1990) ("Mathis's suppression motion presents the question of whether officers without an arrest warrant but with probable cause may, absent exigent circumstances, force their way into a hotel room and arrest the occupant who, from inside his room, partially opens the door to determine the identity of officers knocking on the door. We hold that a person does not surrender his expectation of privacy nor consent to the officers' entry by so doing, and that his arrest inside his room under such circumstances is contrary to the fourth amendment and the United States Supreme Court's decision in *Payton* . . . .). This holding has generally been understood to require an arrest warrant – not a search warrant – as the precondition for police entry into a building to effect the arrest of someone believed to be inside; dictum at the end of the opinion said that "an arrest warrant founded on probable cause implicitly carries with it the limited authority to enter a dwelling in which the suspect lives when there is reason to believe the suspect is within" (*id.* at 603). The reference to a "routine" arrest is conventionally read as distinguishing cases in which there is a demonstrated need to apprehend the suspect immediately, without the delay that applying for a warrant would entail. *See, e.g., Bailey v. Swindell*, 940 F.3d 1295, 1303 (11th Cir. 2019) (a police officer went to the front door of Bailey's parents' home and asked to speak with him about an incident involving his estranged wife; Bailey came out onto the porch but refused to talk with the officer; they argued briefly; Bailey retreated into the house; the officer followed him through the doorway, tackled him and arrested him: "Because . . . [the officer] can point to no exigency, he violated the Fourth Amendment when he crossed the threshold to effectuate a warrantless, in-home arrest.").

In *Steagald*, the Court held that "a law enforcement officer may [not] legally search for the subject of an arrest warrant in the home of a third party without first obtaining a search warrant[,] absent exigent circumstances or consent" (451 U.S. at 205-06). The gap between *Steagald*'s "third-party"-home holding and *Payton*'s "suspect's"-home dictum left unclear such questions as (1) whether a search warrant is required for "arrest entries" into nonresidential premises; (2) whether a particular residence should be treated as that of the "suspect" in joint-occupancy situations, situations in which the suspect is living as a guest (more or less transiently or permanently) in someone else's home, and other complicated multi-person living arrangements (and also what degree of well-founded belief police officers must have that a particular dwelling satisfies the criteria for the suspect's residence rather than a third party's); and (3) whether "reason to believe the suspect is within" a particular residence means *probable cause* (see § 25.7.4 *supra*) or some other degree of founded belief. Concerning the second and third questions, *see United States v. Brinkley*, 980 F.3d 377 (4th Cir. 2020): (a) "Pursuant to *Payton* and *Steagald*, the officers needed to establish reason to believe not just that Brinkley was *staying* in the Stoney Trace apartment but that he *resided* there. If Brinkley was merely staying as a guest in someone else's home, *Steagald* would require the officers to obtain a search warrant before they could enter it. Detective Stark's discovery that Brinkley was involved with Chisholm, and that Chisholm was associated with the Stoney Trace apartment, certainly provided additional evidence that Brinkley might well have stayed at Chisholm's home, but it did not speak to whether he did so as a resident or as Chisholm's overnight guest. . . . Further investigation was necessary to establish probable cause that Brinkley *resided* there." *Id.* at 387-88. (b) "The courts of appeals have unanimously interpreted *Payton*'s standard – 'reason to believe the suspect is within,' . . . – to require a two-prong test: the officers must have reason to believe both (1) 'that the location is the defendant's residence' and (2) 'that he [will] be home' when they enter. . . . But the quantum of proof necessary to satisfy *Payton* has divided the circuits, with some construing 'reason to believe' to demand less than probable cause and others equating the two standards. *See United States v. Vasquez-Algarin*, 821 F.3d 467, 474–77 (3d Cir. 2016) (collecting cases). ¶ It seems to us that interpreting reasonable belief to require probable cause hews most closely to Supreme Court precedent and most faithfully implements the special protections that the Fourth Amendment affords the home. For these reasons, we join those courts 'that have held that reasonable belief in the *Payton* context "embodies the same standard of reasonableness inherent in probable cause."'" *Id.* at 384, 386; *see also, e.g., United States v. Gorman*, 314 F.3d 1105 (9th Cir. 2002); *and see United States v. Vasquez-Algarin*, 821 F.3d 467, 469 (3d Cir. 2016) ("Law enforcement officers need both an arrest warrant and a search warrant to apprehend a suspect at what they know to be a third party's home. If the suspect resides at the address in question, however, officers need only an arrest warrant and a 'reason to believe' that the individual is present at the time of their entry. This case sits between these two rules and calls on us to decide their critical point of inflection: how certain must officers be that a suspect resides at and is present at a particular address before forcing entry into a private dwelling? ¶ A careful examination of the Supreme Court's Fourth Amendment jurisprudence reveals that the standard cannot be anything less than probable cause. Because here, law enforcement acted on information that fell short of the standard, we will vacate the conviction and remand to the District Court."). *But see Cunningham v. Baltimore County*, 246 Md. App. 630, 677, 232 A.3d 278, 306-07 (2020) ("Based on our review of the case law, we are persuaded, consistent with the majority of state courts addressing the reasonable belief standard in the context of an entry into the home pursuant to an arrest warrant, that the 'reason to believe' standard does not rise to the level of probable cause. Rather, we hold, consistent with the decision in *Taylor*, that the term 'reason to believe' in the context of the execution of an arrest warrant is akin to reasonable suspicion.").

More basically, *Steagald*'s rationale casts doubt on the logical foundation of the *Payton* dictum itself:

> "[W]hile an arrest warrant and a search warrant both serve to subject the probable-cause determination of the police to judicial review, the interests protected by the two warrants differ. An arrest warrant is issued by a magistrate upon a showing that probable cause exists to believe that the subject of the warrant has committed an offense and thus the warrant primarily serves to protect an individual from an unreasonable seizure. A search warrant, in contrast is issued upon a showing of probable cause to believe that the legitimate object of a search is located in a particular place, and therefore safeguards an individual's interest in the privacy of his home and possessions against the unjustified intrusion of the police." (451 U.S. at 212-13.)

An individual whose arrest is sought and justified on the ground of probable cause that s/he has committed a crime has no less interest in "the privacy of his home" than any other person. This proposition is the necessary predicate and implication of the well-settled rule of *Chimel v. California*, 395 U.S. 752 (1969), discussed in § 25.8.1 *supra*. Chimel was arrested in his home on a valid arrest warrant but a search of areas of his house beyond his "wingspan" was held to violate the Fourth Amendment in the absence of a search warrant for the premises. *See also Vale v. Louisiana,* 399 U.S. 30, 33-35 (1970); *Wilson v. Layne,* 526 U.S. 603, 609-11 (1999); *Maryland v. Buie,* 494 U.S. 325, 335 (1990) (dictum). So, in the "routine" arrest situation contemplated by *Payton,* where "officers were able to procure . . . warrants for . . . [homeowners'] arrest[s and] . . . [t]here is . . . no reason . . . to suppose that it was impracticable for them to obtain a search warrant as well" (*Vale v. Louisiana, supra,* 399 U.S. at 35), they should be required to do so.

The lower courts have reached discordant results when wrestling with issues clouded by *Payton-Steagald* fallout. *See* 3 Wayne R. LaFave, Search and Seizure: A Treatise on the Fourth Amendment § 6.1(b) (5th ed. & Supp.). In the current murky state of the law, counsel should not hesitate to take the position that both a search warrant and an arrest warrant are required in order to justify the police entering any premises in which an individual has a Fourth-Amendment-protected interest (see § 25.15 *supra*) for the purpose of arresting him or her, except when they are "in 'hot pursuit' of a fugitive" (*Steagald v. United States, supra,* 451 U.S. at 221) or under other "exigent circumstances" (see § 25.20 *infra*) that make it impracticable to obtain a warrant (*Steagald v. United States, supra,* 451 U.S. at 213-16, 218, 221-22; *Minnesota v. Olson,* 495 U.S. 91, 100-01 (1990) (elaborated in § 25.20). This position is supported by the lead opinion in *Commonwealth v. Romero,* 646 Pa. 47, 183 A.3d 364 (2018), which meticulously analyzes the pertinent authorities and concludes that

> "the Fourth Amendment requires that, even when seeking to execute an arrest warrant, a law enforcement entry into a home must be authorized by a warrant reflecting a magisterial determination of probable cause to search that home, whether by a separate search warrant or contained within the arrest warrant itself. Absent such a warrant, an entry into a residence is excused only by a recognized exception to the search warrant requirement." (646 Pa. at 114, 183 A.3d at 405-06.)

On its facts, the *Romero* case did not involve a police entry into the home of the person they were seeking to arrest; the home they thought was his turned out to be his half-brother's; and it was the half-brother's family whose Fourth Amendment rights the Pennsylvania Supreme Court's lead opinion held *ex post* to have been violated. But the logic of the opinion would require the same result if the house had been his, because the police action and its justification are identical *ex ante* in the two situations. It is hornbook Fourth Amendment law that the lawfulness of a search or seizure depends on the circumstances as they appeared to officers at the time they acted (see § 25.7.4 fourth paragraph *supra*): its "reasonableness . . . must be measured by what the officers knew before they conducted their search" (*Florida v. J.L.,* 529 U.S. 266, 271 (2000)).

At the least, *Payton*'s requirement that arresting officers have "reason to believe" that the person named in their arrest warrant "lives [in]" and is currently "within" the premises they enter should be construed as demanding probable cause for belief that these two preconditions exist. *See Maryland v. Buie,* 494 U.S. 325, 332 (1990) (dictum) (an arrest entry can be sustained only when the officers "[p]ossessing an arrest warrant . . . [have] probable cause to believe [that the person named in the warrant] was in his home"); *Lankford v. Gelston,* 364 F.2d 197 (4th Cir. 1966); *United States v. Vasquez-Algarin,* 821 F.3d 467 (3d Cir. 2016) (surveying conflicting federal circuit court decisions and concluding that the better rule is that a valid arrest entry requires probable cause (*id.* at 477-80) to believe "that the arrestee resided at and was present within the targeted home" (*id.* at 472)). Similarly, if the police act without an arrest warrant in reliance on a claim of exigent circumstances, "there must be at least probable cause to believe" that facts exist which give rise to "'the need to prevent a suspect's escape, or the risk of danger to the police or to other persons inside or outside the dwelling'" or which presage the "'imminent destruction of evidence.'" *Minnesota v. Olson,* 495 U.S. 91, 100 (1990). The mere "'inherent mobility' of persons" sought to be arrested does not suffice to establish the requisite exigency because the police can cope with that problem "simply by waiting for a suspect to leave the [premises]" (*cf. Steagald v. United States, supra,* 451 U.S. at 221 n.14).

Police making any of the permissible types of arrest entry without a search warrant – entries pursuant to an arrest warrant and "hot pursuit" entries or entries under exigent circumstances (both discussed in § 25.20 *infra*) – are governed by the following rules:

(i)   The intended arrest itself must be valid within the principles of § 25.7 *supra.* If the arrest is not valid, the arrest entry falls with it. *E.g., Massachusetts v. Painten,* 368 F.2d 142 (1st Cir. 1966), *cert. dismissed,* 389 U.S. 560 (1968).

(ii)   Upon entry, the police may "search anywhere in the house that . . . [the person sought] might . . . [be] found" (*id.* at 330). However, the entry and search may not exceed the bounds appropriate in hunting for a person (*id.* at 335-36), and they may not intrude into closed areas too small to contain a human being (*see United States v. Ross,* 456 U.S. 798, 824 (1982) (dictum)), unless the officers have probable cause to believe that the person sought to be arrested is armed and that they therefore "need to check the entire premises [for weapons] for safety reasons" (*Payton v. New York, supra,* 445 U.S. at 589 (dictum); *see Warden v. Hayden,* 387 U.S. 294, 298-300 (1967)). *Cf. Arizona v. Hicks,* 480 U.S. 321 (1987), elaborated in § 25.22.2 *infra.*

(iii)   "Once . . . [the person sought has been] found, . . . the search for him . . . [is] over, and there . . . [is] no longer that particular justification for entering any rooms that had not yet been searched." *Maryland v. Buie, supra,* 494 U.S. at 333. "[A]s an incident to the arrest the officers could, as a precautionary matter and without probable cause or reasonable suspicion, look in closets and other spaces immediately adjoining the place of arrest from which an attack could be immediately launched." *Id.* at 334. See also § 25.8 *supra.* "Beyond that, however, . . . [the only basis for continuing the search or entering additional rooms after the arrest is the "protective sweep" doctrine described in § 25.22.4 *infra,* which requires] articulable facts which, taken together with the rational inferences from those facts, would warrant a reasonably prudent officer in believing that the area to be swept harbors an individual posing a danger to those on the arrest scene." *Maryland v. Buie, supra,* 494 U.S. at 334.

Another limited exception to the search warrant requirement is a kind of hybrid of "arrest entry" reasoning and "consent" reasoning. In *Washington v. Chrisman,* 455 U.S. 1 (1982), the United States Supreme Court held that when a person who has been validly arrested in a location other than his or her home requests and receives permission from the arresting officer to return home before being taken to the lockup, the officer may accompany that person into the home, as an exercise of "the arresting officer's authority to maintain custody over the arrested person" (*id.* at 6). *Contra, State v. Chrisman,* 100 Wash. 2d 814, 676 P.2d 419 (1984) (on remand, the Washington Supreme Court rejects the *Washington v. Chrisman* holding on state constitutional grounds).

To bring the *Payton* and *Steagald* warrant requirements into play, it is not always necessary that the police have entered closed quarters before effecting an arrest. Arrests on the threshold of a residence or just outside it are sufficient. *See, e.g., United States v. Allen,* 813 F.3d 76, 79, 85-86 (2d Cir. 2016) (defendant, who opened his apartment door at police officers' request and spoke to the officers from "'inside the threshold' while the officers stood on the sidewalk," "was under arrest" when "[t]he officers told Allen that he would need to come down to the police station to be processed for the assault," and the police thereby violated *Payton* even though the police had not yet physically entered the apartment: "While it is true that physical intrusion is the 'chief evil' the Fourth Amendment is designed to protect against, . . . we reject the government's contention that this fact requires that *Payton*'s warrant requirement be limited to cases in which the arresting officers themselves cross the threshold of the home before effecting an arrest. The protections of the home extend beyond instances of actual trespass. . . . By advising Allen that he was under arrest, and taking control of his further movements, the officers asserted their power over him *inside his home*."); *United States v. Nora,* 765 F.3d 1049, 1054, 1060 (9th Cir. 2014) ("The government properly concedes that the police arrested Nora 'inside' his home for purposes of the *Payton* rule. Although officers physically took Nora into custody outside his home in the front yard, they accomplished that feat only by surrounding his house and ordering him to come out at gunpoint. We've held that forcing a suspect to exit his home in those circumstances constitutes an in-home arrest under *Payton*." "Although Nora's arrest was supported by probable cause, the manner in which officers made the arrest violated *Payton*. Evidence obtained as a result of Nora's unlawful arrest must be suppressed."); *People v. Gonzales,* 111 A.D.3d 147, 148-50, 972 N.Y.S.2d 642, 643-44 (N.Y. App. Div., 2d Dep't 2013) (police who were told by a complainant that her cousin's boyfriend had assaulted her in a basement apartment went to the door of that apartment accompanied by the complainant; they knocked; "[w]hen the defendant opened the door, the police asked the complainant if he was the person who had assaulted her, and she said yes. The defendant, who had never left the apartment, even partially, tried to close the door, but the police pushed their way inside and handcuffed him. Minutes later, still inside the apartment, the defendant made an inculpatory statement. . . . ¶ In *Payton v. New York,* 445 U.S. 573 . . . the United States Supreme Court announced a clear and easily applied rule with respect to warrantless arrests in the home: 'the Fourth Amendment has drawn a firm line at the entrance to the house. Absent exigent circumstances, that threshold may not reasonably be crossed without a warrant' . . . . The rule under the New York Constitution is the same (see N.Y. Const., art. 1, § 12; *People v. Levan,* 62 N.Y.2d 139, 144, 476 N.Y.S.2d 101, 464 N.E.2d 469). *Payton* and *Levan* require suppression of the defendant's statement under the clear, undisputed facts of this case.").

25.20. *Warrantless Entry Under "Exigent Circumstances"*

As mentioned in § 25.19 *supra,* police may make a warrantless entry for the purpose of effecting an arrest under "exigent circumstances" that preclude the acquisition of an arrest warrant. Thus, in *Warden v. Hayden,* 387 U.S. 294 (1967), the Court approved a building entry by officers without a warrant for the purpose of arresting a fugitive armed robbery suspect under circumstances of "hot pursuit": The police observed the defendant flee from the crime scene, saw him enter the building, and reached the building less than five minutes after the defendant. *Cf. United States v. Santana,* 427 U.S. 38, 42-43 & n.3 (1976); *Steagald v. United States,* 451 U.S. 204, 218, 221-22 (1981) (dictum). In *Lange v. California,* 141 S. Ct. 2011 (2021), the Supreme Court left open the question whether *Hayden* and *Santana* establish a categorical rule allowing "hot pursuit" entries in all felony cases or whether the authority to follow a fleeing felon into a residence must be justified by exigency on a case-by-case basis. But the Court clarified that "the pursuit of a fleeing misdemeanor suspect" does not "always – or more legally put, categorically – qualif[y] as an exigent circumstance. . . . A great many misdemeanor pursuits involve exigencies allowing warrantless entry. But whether a given one does so turns on the particular facts of the case." (141 S. Ct. at 2016.). "Under the . . . case-specific view, an officer can follow . . . [a fleeing] misdemeanant when, but only when, an exigency . . . allows insufficient time to get a warrant." *Id.* at 2018. "When the totality of circumstances shows an emergency – such as imminent harm to others, a threat to the officer himself, destruction of evidence, or escape from the home – the police may act without waiting. And those circumstances . . . include the flight itself. But the need to pursue a misdemeanant does not trigger a categorical rule allowing home entry, even absent a law enforcement emergency. When the nature of the crime, the nature of the flight, and surrounding facts present no such exigency, officers must respect the sanctity of the home – which means that they must get a warrant." *Id.* at 2021-22.

The more general "exception . . . for exigent circumstances . . . applies when 'the exigencies of the situation make the needs of law enforcement so compelling that [a] warrantless search is objectively reasonable.' . . . The exception enables law enforcement officers to handle 'emergenc[ies]' – situations presenting a 'compelling need for official action and no time to secure a warrant.' . . . Over the years, this Court has identified several such exigencies. An officer, for example, may 'enter a home without a warrant to render emergency assistance to an injured occupant[,] to protect an occupant from imminent injury,' or to ensure his own safety. . . . So too, the police may make a warrantless entry to 'prevent the imminent destruction of evidence' or to 'prevent a suspect's escape.' . . . In those circumstances, the delay required to obtain a warrant would bring about 'some real immediate and serious consequences' – and so the absence of a warrant is excused." *Lange, supra,* 141 S. Ct. at 2017. But "the police bear a heavy burden when attempting to demonstrate an urgent need that might justify warrantless searches or arrests" (*Welsh v. Wisconsin,* 466 U.S. 740, 749-50 (1984)). "Before agents of the government may invade the sanctity of the home, the burden is on the government to demonstrate exigent circumstances that overcome the presumption of unreasonableness that attaches to all warrantless home entries." *Id.* at 750. *Accord, Vale v. Louisiana,* 399 U.S. 30, 34-35 (1970); *G.M. Leasing Corp. v. United States,* 429 U.S. 338, 358-59 (1977); *Mincey v. Arizona,* 437 U.S. 385, 393-94 (1978); *Brigham City v. Stuart,* 547 U.S. 398, 403 (2006). "[I]n the absence of hot pursuit there must be at least probable cause to believe that [facts constituting exigent circumstances – such as the "'imminent destruction of evidence, . . . or the need to prevent a suspect's escape, or the risk of danger to the police or to other persons inside or outside the dwelling'" – are] . . . present." *Minnesota v. Olson,* 495 U.S. 91, 100 (1990). *See, e.g., United States v. Collins,* 510 F.3d 697, 701 (7th Cir. 2007) (the government's claim of "exigent circumstances" for a warrantless entry of a dwelling, based on an asserted risk of destruction of evidence, is rejected because "[t]he government has failed to show that in this case the police had probable cause to believe that evidence was being, or was about to be, destroyed when they entered"); *United States v. Ramirez*, 676 F.3d 755, 762 (8th Cir. 2012) (a hotel room occupant's "attempt to shut the door once he became aware of the police presence outside [the] room" (by partially opening the door in response to an officer's knocking and claiming to be housekeeping staff) did not provide a reasonable basis for believing that "the destruction of evidence was imminent"; the occupant "was under no obligation to allow the officers to enter the premises at that point and was likewise within his bounds in his attempt to close the door"); *accord, Williams v. Maurer*, 9 F.4th 416, 434-35 (6th Cir. 2021); *Lucibella v. Town of Oak Ridge*, 2023 WL 2822126 (11th Cir. 2023) (a report of gunshots in an area that included the defendant's residence did not give rise to probable cause of an emergency situation justifying police entry into the back yard where the police could see, through a wrought-iron gate, the defendant and a companion (who was an off-duty police lieutenant) sitting with beverages on a patio); *United States v. Rodríguez-Pacheco*, 948 F.3d 1 (1st Cir. 2020) (police officers were dispatched to make a warrantless arrest of the defendant – a fellow officer – upon a complaint of domestic violence; local standard procedure called for retrieving an arrested officer's service weapon before explaining the complaint to him and placing him under arrest; when the arresting officers arrived at the defendant's residence, he came out the front door; they told him that they needed to retrieve his weapon; he offered to go in and get it; they insisted on accompanying him into the residence, where they found incriminating material that he moved before trial to suppress; the court rejects a claim that the exigent circumstances exception justified this entry: the domestic violence complaint did not involve the use of a weapon and the arresting officers had no reason to believe that the defendant would use his service weapon to resist arrest or for any other improper purpose.); *Turrubiate v. State*, 399 S.W.3d 147, 149, 154 (Tex. Crim. App. 2013) (an exigent circumstances exception is not supported by "probable cause to believe that illegal drugs are in a home coupled with an odor of marijuana from the home and a police officer making his presence known to the occupants"; there must be "additional evidence of . . . attempted or actual destruction based on an occupant's movement in response to the police knock"); *People v. Hickey*, 172 A.D.3d 745, 746-47, 98 N.Y.S.3d 287, 288-89 (N.Y. App. Div., 2d Dep't 2019) (the police could not rely on the exigent circumstances exception to enter and search the living room of the defendant's home after the defendant "complied with the officers' requests to come out [of the living room] with his hands up": even though an officer had seen the defendant "reach[ ] into his waistband, remove[ ] an object, and toss[ ] it underneath a chair in the living room as he ducked behind a wall," and even though the defendant's psychiatrist had told a 911 operator that "the defendant was armed as a result of purchasing a shotgun and had a history of possessing firearms, making threats to police, and paranoia," and the police knew from an "'officer safety alert'" that "the defendant previously had made threats to shoot a police officer and had a shotgun confiscated," nonetheless the exigent circumstances exception did not apply because "any exigency abated once the defendant [exited the living room and] was detained"). *Compare Kentucky v. King*, 563 U.S. 452, 455, 462, 471 (2011) (if the police had a reasonable basis to believe that evidence in a dwelling was at risk of imminent destruction, which the Court "assume[s] for purposes of argument," the exigent circumstances exception could justify a warrantless entry of the dwelling even though "the police, by knocking on the door of a residence and announcing their presence, cause[d] the occupants to attempt to destroy evidence." As long as "[t]he conduct of the police prior to their entry into the apartment was entirely lawful," and "the police did not create the exigency by engaging or threatening to engage in conduct that violates the Fourth Amendment," "the exigent circumstances rule applies"), *with King v. Commonwealth*, 386 S.W.3d 119, 122 (Ky. 2012), *cert. denied*, 569 U.S. 954 (2013) (on remand of *Kentucky v. King* from the U.S. Supreme Court, the Kentucky Supreme Court holds that "the Commonwealth failed to meet its burden of demonstrating exigent circumstances justifying a warrantless entry" because "the sounds . . . [from inside the dwelling that the police] described at the suppression hearing [as evidencing efforts to destroy evidence] were indistinguishable from ordinary household sounds, and were consistent with the natural and reasonable result of a knock on the door"), *and State v. Campbell*, 300 P.3d 72, 74, 78-79 (Kan. 2013) ("the exigent circumstances exception does not apply in light of the officer's unreasonable actions in creating the exigency" by not "simply knock[ing] on the door and wait[ing] for an answer . . . [or "announc[ing] his presence" but instead] covering the peephole and positioning himself to block the occupant's ability to determine who was standing at the door," thereby causing an occupant to "open[ ] the door about a third of the way" while visibly armed with a gun).

In *Welsh v. Wisconsin, supra*, the Court held that in cases of arrest entries under a claim of exigent circumstances, "an important factor to be considered in determining whether any exigency exists is the gravity of the underlying offense for which the arrest is being made" (466 U.S. at 753). Explaining that "application of the exigent-circumstances exception in the context of a home entry should rarely be sanctioned when there is probable cause to believe that only a minor offense . . . has been committed" (*id.*), the Court in *Welsh* struck down a warrantless home entry to make an arrest for the offense of driving while intoxicated. The Court found that "the best indication of the State's interest in precipitating an arrest" was the State's classification of the offense as "a noncriminal, civil forfeiture offense" and refused to allow an arrest entry for such an offense, notwithstanding the risk that "evidence of the petitioner's blood-alcohol level might have dissipated while the police obtained a warrant" (*id.* at 754). The *Welsh* opinion did not go quite as far as holding that "warrantless entry to arrest a misdemeanant is never justified, but only that such entry should be rare" (*Stanton v. Sims*, 571 U.S. 3, 9 (2013) (per curiam)). There is, however, language in the *Welsh* opinion that supports a categorical rule limiting warrantless arrest entries under exigent circumstances to felony arrests. *See Welsh v. Wisconsin, supra*, 466 U.S. at 750 n.12, 752-53. At the very least, *Welsh* "counsel[s] that suspicion of minor offenses should give rise to exigencies only in the rarest of circumstances" (*White v. Stanley*, 745 F.3d 237, 240-41 (7th Cir. 2014) ("smell of burning marijuana" inside a house did not provide a basis for exigent-circumstances entry of the house); *Lange v. California, supra*, 141 S. Ct. at 2020 (quoting *Welsh* to the effect that "'[A]pplication of the exigent-circumstances exception in the context of a home entry should rarely be sanctioned when there is probable cause to believe that only a minor offense' is involved."); *O'Kelley v. Craig*, 781 Fed. Appx. 888 (11th Cir. 2019) (property owner's misdemeanor "terroristic threat" against hunters who had trespassed on his property did not provide a basis for exigent-circumstances entry of the house)). *See also Minnesota v. Olson, supra*, 495 U.S. at 100-01 (holding that the lower court "applied essentially the correct standard in determining . . . that in assessing the risk of danger, the gravity of the crime and likelihood that the suspect is armed should be considered," and approving the lower court's "fact-specific application of th[is] . . . proper legal standard . . . [to reject a claim of exigent circumstances even though the] grave crime [of murder] was involved . . . [because] defendant 'was known not to be the murderer but thought to be the driver of the getaway car,' . . . and . . . the police had already recovered the murder weapon"); *Harris v. O'Hare*, 770 F.3d

224, 235 (2d Cir. 2014). *Cf. Brigham City v. Stuart, supra,* 547 U.S. at 405 (distinguishing *Welsh v. Wisconsin* on the ground that "*Welsh* involved a warrantless entry by officers to arrest a suspect for driving while intoxicated" and "the 'only potential emergency' confronting the officers was the need to preserve evidence (i.e., the suspect's blood-alcohol level)" whereas "[h]ere, the officers were confronted with ongoing violence occurring within the home"); *compare Stanton v. Sims, supra,* 571 U.S. at 8-9 (noting that in *Welsh* "'there was no immediate or continuous pursuit of [Welsh] from the scene of a crime'" and cautioning that "despite our emphasis in *Welsh* on the fact that the crime at issue was minor – indeed, a mere nonjailable civil offense – nothing in the opinion establishes that the seriousness of the crime is equally important *in cases of hot pursuit*"; the "federal and state courts nationwide are sharply divided on the question whether an officer with probable cause to arrest a suspect for a misdemeanor may enter a home without a warrant while in hot pursuit of that suspect" (*id.* at 6 (citing cases))), *with Coffey v. Carroll,* 933 F.3d 577, 586 (6th Cir. 2019) (sustaining a claim of violation of the Fourth Amendment when officers sought to justify a home entry under the "hot pursuit" rationale but the circumstances were "neither 'hot' nor in 'pursuit,' in any fair sense of those words. The sequence of events lacked an emergency. At most, Coffey had attempted (and failed) to commit a non-violent property crime earlier in the day, meaning that when the officers arrived at his house sometime later, their pursuit was lukewarm at best. Nor were the officers truly in pursuit of Coffey, as that term is understood in the case law. Pursuit is defined as an effort to catch and detain an individual following an attempted arrest and subsequent escape. . . . But here, the officers encountered Coffey for the first time *after* they entered the home; it was only then that they began to arrest him. In other words, this was not pursuit following a failed arrest. The district court thus correctly concluded that the search was not justified by an exigent emergency.").

When the police make a valid arrest entry in "hot pursuit," they may lawfully observe anything in the building that comes into "plain view" while they are seeking out the suspect and effecting his or her arrest, and they may seize objects in "plain view" if, but only if, there is probable cause to believe that the objects are contraband or crime-related. See § 25.22.2 *infra.* They may not search the premises more intensively or intrusively than is necessary to find the person sought to be arrested (*see Arizona v. Hicks,* 480 U.S. 321 (1987)), except when that person is known to be armed. In *Warden v. Hayden, supra,* the Court did allow police who entered a building in "hot pursuit" of an armed fugitive to make a warrantless search within the building to the extent necessary to find weapons. 387 U.S. at 298-300. *But see, e.g., People v. Jenkins,* 24 N.Y.3d 62, 65, 20 N.E.3d 639, 641, 995 N.Y.S.2d 694, 696 (2014) (although the police lawfully broke down the door of an apartment as they pursued an armed suspect into the apartment and also acted lawfully in searching the apartment and arresting the defendant and another man who were hiding under a bed, the officers' subsequent search of a closed box – which was found to contain a gun – was unlawful and therefore the gun should have been suppressed: "by the time [the] Officer . . . opened the box, any urgency justifying the warrantless search had abated" because "[t]he officers had handcuffed the men and removed them to the living room where they (and the two women) remained under police supervision," and thus "the police 'were in complete control of the house'" and "there was no danger that defendant would dispose of or destroy the weapon . . . , nor was there any danger to the public or the police"; accordingly, "the police were required to obtain a warrant prior to searching the box").

In addition to "hot pursuit" arrest entries, law enforcement officers may make warrantless building entries in the "exigent circumstances" presented by a manifest need to render assistance to an occupant who is in physical danger or to prevent serious bodily injury. *See City and County of San Francisco v. Sheehan*, 575 U.S. 600, 611-12 (2015) (police officers, who were dispatched to a group home for mentally ill residents to help take a resident to a secure ward at a hospital, did not violate the Fourth Amendment by using a social worker's key to enter the resident's room when she did not respond to the officers' knocking on her door, announcing their identity, and saying that they wanted to help her; the officers' subsequent reentry of the apartment, after they initially retreated in the face of the resident's approaching them with a knife and threatening to kill them, also was justified as "'part of a single, continuous'" entry in a "'continuing emergency'" in which the police "knew that delay could make the situation more dangerous"); *Michigan v. Fisher,* 558 U.S. 45, 47-49 (2009) (per curiam) (the "emergency aid exception" to the warrant requirement – which permits "law enforcement officials . . . [to] 'enter a home without a warrant to render emergency assistance to an injured occupant or to protect an occupant from imminent injury'" – justified a warrantless entry of a home by police officers who "respond[ed] . . . . to a report of a disturbance" and, upon "arriv[ing] at the scene," "encountered a tumultuous situation in the house," "found signs of a recent injury, perhaps from a car accident, outside," and "could see violent behavior inside" the house; the circumstances were sufficient to justify a reasonable belief on the officers' part that an occupant "had hurt himself (albeit non-fatally) and needed treatment that in his rage he was unable to provide, or that [the occupant] was about to hurt, or had already hurt someone else."); *Brigham City v. Stuart, supra*, 547 U.S. at 403 ("law enforcement officers may enter a home without a warrant to render emergency assistance to an injured occupant or to protect an occupant from imminent injury"); *Michigan v. Tyler,* 436 U.S. 499, 509-10 (1978) (firefighting officials require neither "a warrant [n]or consent before entering a burning structure to put out the blaze" (*id.* at 509); and, because "[f]ire officials are charged not only with extinguishing fires, but with finding their causes" (*id.* at 510), they "need no warrant [or consent] to remain in a building for a reasonable time to investigate the cause of a blaze after it has been extinguished" (*id.*)). *See also, e.g., Ryburn v. Huff,* 565 U.S. 469, 474-77 (2012) (per curiam); *United States v. Barone,* 330 F.2d 543 (2d Cir. 1964); *United States v. Sanders*, 4 F.4th 672, 677-78 (8th Cir. 2021) ("Although the presence of a domestic violence suspect in a home with children cannot alone justify a warrantless entry, here the officers were confronted with 'facts indicating that the suspect was a threat to the child[ren] or others.'"); *Mincey v. Arizona, supra,* 437 U.S. at 392-93 (dictum), and authorities cited; *but see Carlson v. Fewins,* 801 F.3d 668 (6th Cir. 2015) (exigency dissipated). Officers alerted to an emergency situation in a particular residence must make a reasonable effort to assure that the residence they enter is the one in which the emergency is believed to be occurring; they may not enter premises without "'a reasonable effort to ascertain and identify the [correct] place intended to be searched.'" *Gerhart v. Barnes*, 724 Fed. Appx. 316, 322 (5th Cir. 2018), quoting *Maryland v. Garrison,* 480 U.S. 79 (1987), referenced in § 25.17.2 *supra*.

In *dicta,* the Supreme Court has frequently suggested the existence of a more general "exigent circumstances" exception to the warrant requirement. *See, e.g., Johnson v. United States,* 333 U.S. 10, 14-15 (1948); *United States v. Jeffers,* 342 U.S. 48, 51 (1951); *Chapman v. United States,* 365 U.S. 610, 615 (1961); *Mincey v. Arizona, supra,* 437 U.S. at 392-94; *Michigan v. Summers,* 452 U.S. 692, 702 n.17 (1981); *Birchfield v. North Dakota,* 579 U.S. 438, 456-57 (2016); *cf. Torres v. Puerto Rico,* 442 U.S. 465, 471 (1979); *New York v. Belton,* 453

U.S. 454, 457 (1981). However, the Court has never sustained a warrantless building entry on the "exigent circumstances" theory when the purpose of the entry was to make a *search* unassociated with an arrest or with the peacekeeping responsibilities of the police to provide emergency aid and to avert serious bodily injury. Probably the "exigent circumstances" exception extends no further than "hot pursuit" and "emergency assistance" cases (*see Vale v. Louisiana, supra*, 399 U.S. at 34-35; *Mincey v. Arizona, supra*, 437 U.S. at 392-93), although the tenor of some of the Supreme Court *dicta* does. *See State v. Vargas*, 213 N.J. 301, 305, 313-17, 321-26, 63 A.3d 175, 177, 182-84, 187-89 (2013) (reviewing relevant decisions of the U.S. Supreme Court and concluding that these decisions do not support treating the "community-caretaking" function of the police – as manifested here by the police officers' seeking to "check on the welfare of a resident" in response to concerns expressed by the landlord – as "a justification for the warrantless entry and search of a home in the absence of some form of an objectively reasonable emergency"); *United States v. Curry*, 965 F.3d 313, 321, 322 (4th Cir. 2020) (en banc) ("[L]ike all exceptions to the warrant requirement, the exigent circumstances exception is a 'narrow' one that must be 'well-delineated in order to retain [its] constitutional character.' ¶ Though the 'emergency-as-exigency approach . . .' . . . may sound broad in name, it is subject to important limitations and thus is quite narrow in application. For example, the requirement that the circumstances present a true 'emergency' is strictly construed – that is, an emergency must be 'enveloped by a sufficient level of urgency.' . . . Indeed, standing alone, even a 'possible homicide' does not present an 'emergency situation' demanding 'immediate [warrantless] action.'").

25.21. *"Knock and Announce" Requirements: Restrictions upon the Manner of Police Entry*

The preceding sections deal with restrictions upon the *circumstances* under which building entries can be made. There are also legal restrictions upon the *manner* of police entry.

In most jurisdictions, "knock and announce" statutes require that the police announce their presence and identity as officers, explain the purpose of their intended entry, and request to be admitted peaceably, before they may break and enter. *See, e.g., Miller v. United States*, 357 U.S. 301 (1958) (construing 18 U.S.C. § 3109 and the local law of the District of Columbia). Although these statutes are commonly framed in terms of police "breaking" open a door, their requirements are usually held to apply whenever the police open any door, whether locked or unlocked, forcibly or nonforcibly (*see Sabbath v. United States*, 391 U.S. 585 (1968)), and in some jurisdictions the statutes are also applied to police entries through an already open door (*People v. Buckner,* 35 Cal. App. 3d 307, 313-14, 111 Cal. Rptr. 32, 36-37 (1973)).

The statutes or cases construing the statutes usually provide for emergency exceptions to the "knock and announce" requirement. The exceptions commonly include situations in which there is reasonable ground to believe that an announcement would (i) jeopardize the safety of the entering officer, (ii) cause the destruction of evidence, or (iii) be a useless gesture because it is apparent from the surrounding circumstances that the occupants of the premises already know of the authority and purpose of the police. *See, e.g., Miller v. United States, supra*, 357 U.S. at 308-10; *Sabbath v. United States, supra*, 391 U.S. at 591; *cf. Dalia v. United States,* 441 U.S. 238, 247-48 (1979); *Washington v. Chrisman,* 455 U.S. 1, 10 n.7 (1982).

The Supreme Court has recognized that "knock and announce" requirements are embodied in the Fourth Amendment. *See Wilson v. Arkansas*, 514 U.S. 927 (1995) (the "common-law 'knock and announce' principle forms a part of the reasonableness inquiry under the Fourth Amendment"). *Accord, United States v. Banks*, 540 U.S. 31, 36-37 (2003); *United States v. Ramirez*, 523 U.S. 65, 70 (1998); *Richards v. Wisconsin*, 520 U.S. 385, 387 (1997); *and see Jones v. Kirchner*, 835 F.3d 74, 79-80 (D.C. Cir. 2016); *Terebesi v. Torresso*, 764 F.3d 217, 241-43 (2d Cir. 2014). *Cf. Carroll v. Carman*, 574 U.S. 13 (2014) (per curiam). The Court has held, however, that the exclusionary rule is not available to suppress evidence obtained in the course of a building entry that is unconstitutional solely because the entering officers violated the Fourth Amendment "knock and announce" rule. *Hudson v. Michigan*, 547 U.S. 586, 599-600, 602 (2006). *See id.* at 602-03 (Justice Kennedy, concurring in part and concurring in the judgment, thus supplying the vote necessary to produce a 5-Justice majority, but writing separately to "underscore[ ]" the following "[t]wo points": "First, the knock-and-announce requirement protects rights and expectations linked to ancient principles in our constitutional order . . . [and] [t]he Court's decision should not be interpreted as suggesting that violations of the requirement are trivial or beyond the law's concern. Second, the continued operation of the exclusionary rule, as settled and defined by our precedents, is not in doubt. Today's decision determines only that in the specific context of the knock-and-announce requirement, a violation is not sufficiently related to the later discovery of evidence to justify suppression."). Because *Hudson v. Michigan* concerned only the consequences of a federal Fourth Amendment violation, it does not preclude state courts from enforcing their respective state-law "knock and announce" requirements by exclusion and suppression. *See, e.g., State v. Jean-Paul*, 2013-NMCA-032, 295 P.3d 1072, 1076 (N.M. App. 2013) (adhering to New Mexico's pre-*Hudson* exclusionary rule: "[W]hile both the federal and state constitutions include the knock-and-announce requirement, the remedies for a violation under the two constitutions are not the same."); *State v. Rockford*, 213 N.J. 424, 453, 64 A.3d 514, 530 (2013) (reserving the question "whether the exclusionary rule is the appropriate remedy for an unconstitutional execution of a knock-and-announce warrant under our State Constitution" in the wake of *Hudson*); § 17.11 *supra*. For the reason stated in § 25.17 concluding paragraph *supra*, the case for state-law rejection of *Hudson* is a strong one. *See, e.g., State v. Cable*, 51 So.3d 434 (Fla. 2010) ("[I]n *Benefield v. State*, 160 So.2d 706 (Fla.1964), . . . this Court held that a violation of Florida's knock-and-announce statute vitiated the ensuing arrest and required the suppression of the evidence obtained in connection with the arrest." *Id.* at 435. "[T]he [*Benefield*] Court noted that '[s]ection 901.19, Florida Statutes, . . . appears to represent a codification of the English common law . . . . ¶ 'Entering one's home without legal authority and neglect to give the occupants notice have been condemned by the law and the common custom of this country and England from time immemorial. It was condemned by the yearbooks of Edward IV, before the discovery of this country by Columbus. . . . ¶ This sentiment has moulded our concept of the home as one's castle as well as the law to protect it. The law forbids the law enforcement officers of the state or the United States to enter before knocking at the door, giving his name and the purpose of his call. There is nothing more terrifying to the occupants than to be suddenly confronted in the privacy of their home by a police officer decorated with guns and the insignia of his office. This is why the law protects its entrance so rigidly.'" *Id.* at 439. "[B]ecause *Hudson* does not address the remedy for state-created statutory violations, *Hudson* does not require us to recede from *Benefield*." *Id.* at 442.); *Berumen v. State*, 182 P.3d 635 (Alaska App. 2008) ("[T]he issue before us is one of state law, so the United States Supreme Court's decision in *Hudson* does not bind us." *Id.* at 637. "The police officers in this case violated a longstanding requirement of Alaska law that is designed to protect the privacy and dignity of this state's citizens. On the issue of whether the police must announce their claimed authority and purpose, and on the related issue of whether the police are allowed to break into a building if they have neither sought nor been refused admittance, the statute is written in clear and unambiguous terms. . . . ¶ . . . [T]he evidence found in the hotel room was 'secured through such a flagrant disregard' of the procedure specified by the Alaska legislature that it 'cannot be allowed to stand without making the courts themselves accomplices in [willful] disobedience of [the] law.'" *Id.* at 642.).

Police entries that involve SWAT-squad tactics or other exercises of massive force can be challenged both as unreasonable searches under the Fourth Amendment and as violations of Due Process under the Fourteenth (*see, e.g., Estate of Smith v. Marasco*, 430 F.3d 140, 151-53 (3d Cir. 2005); *Milan v. Bolin*, 795 F.3d 726 (7th Cir. 2015); *Carlson v. Fewins*, 801 F.3d 668 (6th Cir. 2015); *Greer v. City of Highland Park, Michigan*, 884 F.3d 310 (6th Cir. 2018); *Campbell v. Cheatham County Sheriff's Department*, 47 F.4th 468 (6th Cir. 2022); *Torres v. City of St. Louis*, 39 F.4th 494 (8th Cir. 2022)), and state law if they are excessively violent. *Hudson* should not withdraw the Fourth Amendment exclusionary remedy in such cases, because they would evoke the independent principle of *Rochin v. California*, 342 U.S. 165 (1952), which is, at its root, a prohibition against *"convictions* . . . brought about by methods that offend 'a sense of justice'" (*id.* at 173 (emphasis added)) or governmental "conduct that shocks the conscience" (*id.* at 172). And see §§ 8.23, 15.12 *supra* regarding the utility of police misconduct claims in urging prosecutors to drop or reduce charges or to make concessions in plea negotiation.

25.22. *Scope of Permissible Police Activity after Entering the Premises*

25.22.1. *The Requisite Relationship Between Police Activity Inside the Dwelling and the Purpose of the Entry*

The scope of an officer's investigatory powers, once inside a building, is defined by the circumstances that permitted his or her entry under the principles of §§ 25.16-25.20 *supra*. *United States v. King*, 227 F.3d 732, 750-54, 755 (6th Cir. 2000); *United States v. Sedaghaty*, 728 F.3d 885, 910-15 (9th Cir. 2013); *United States v. Angelos*, 433 F.3d 738, 746 (10th Cir. 2006). This is a corollary of the general rule that "the purposes justifying a police search strictly limit the permissible extent of the search" (*Maryland v. Garrison*, 480 U.S. 79, 87 (1987) (dictum)). *Accord, id.* at 84 ("the scope of a lawful search is 'defined by the object of the search and the places in which there is probable cause to believe that it may be found'"). *See also, e.g., Wilson v. Layne*, 526 U.S. 603, 611 (1999) (dictum) ("the Fourth Amendment . . . require[s] that police actions in execution of a warrant be related to the objectives of the authorized intrusion"); *New York v. Belton*, 453 U.S. 454, 457 (1981) (dictum) ("'[t]he scope of [a] search must be "strictly tied to and justified by" the circumstances which rendered its initiation permissible'"); *Horton v. California*, 496 U.S. 128, 140 (1990) (dictum) ("[i]f the scope of the search exceeds that permitted by the terms of a validly issued warrant or the character of the relevant exception from the warrant requirement, the subsequent seizure is unconstitutional without more"). A search must be "carefully tailored to its justifications," so as to avoid "tak[ing] on the character of the wide-ranging exploratory searches the Framers [of the Fourth Amendment] intended to prohibit" (*Maryland v. Garrison, supra*, 480 U.S. at 84). *See also Maryland v. Buie*, 494 U.S.

325, 335-36 (1990); *cf. United States v. Foster*, 100 F.3d 846, 849 (10th Cir. 2006) ("Under the law of this circuit, 'even evidence which is properly seized pursuant to a warrant must be suppressed if the officers executing the warrant exhibit "flagrant disregard" for its terms.' . . . The basis for blanket suppression when a search warrant is executed with flagrant disregard for its terms 'is found in our traditional repugnance to "general searches" which were conducted in the colonies pursuant to writs of assistance.' . . . To protect against invasive and arbitrary general searches, the Fourth Amendment mandates that search warrants 'particularly describ[e] the place to be searched and the persons or things to be seized.'").

Thus, as explained in § 25.17.7 *supra,* when the police enter a dwelling or other premises pursuant to a search warrant, the search ordinarily may not extend into areas that are not covered by the warrant or into areas that could not contain the objects specified in the warrant. If the entry was predicated upon the consent of a member of the household, the officers' movement within the home is limited by the scope of the consent that was given and the extent of the individual's authority to consent. See § 25.18 *supra.* If the entry was made for the purpose of effecting an arrest, whether with or without a warrant, the officers possess only the freedom of movement necessary to locate and to apprehend the person sought to be arrested (see § 25.19 *supra*), unless they can justify a further search of the premises as a "protective sweep" (see § 25.22.4 *infra*). If the entry was made in the exercise of the officers' peacekeeping functions, they may not undertake even the most minimal search beyond the needs of those functions. *Arizona v. Hicks,* 480 U.S. 321 (1987). *See, e.g., In the Matter of the Welfare of J.W.L.,* 732 N.W.2d 332, 339 (Minn. App. 2007) (a police officer, who lawfully entered a dwelling without a warrant under the exigent circumstances exception due to a 911 call from inside the dwelling, thereafter violated the Fourth Amendment by taking photographs of graffiti in a bedroom that were subsequently used to connect the defendant to graffiti incidents).

25.22.2. *Police Officers' Search and Seizure of Objects While Searching the Premises; The "Plain View" Exception to the Warrant Requirement*

Often, while inside a building, dwelling unit, or other premises, police officers catch sight of an object that they believe to be contraband or evidence of a crime. The officer will then inspect the object further or will seize it.

As explained in § 25.15.4 *supra,* a defendant has a constitutionally protected interest against the search or seizure of an object that belongs to him or her, regardless of whether s/he is on the premises at the time the search or seizure takes place, and regardless of whether s/he has any privacy interest in the premises. Like other searches and seizures made without a warrant, "warrantless searches of such effects are presumptively unreasonable" (*United States v. Jacobsen,* 466 U.S. 109, 114-15 (1984)), and must be brought within one of the exceptions to the warrant requirement in order to be valid. *See United States v. Loines*, 56 F.4th 1099 (6th Cir. 2023) (police officers testified they peered through the closed windows of a parked car and observed a bag of dope in plain view in the car's center console; to support this testimony, the prosecution presented photographs that showed the view inside the vehicle from the purported position of the officers outside, but the Court of Appeals finds the photos too obscure to demonstrate anything relevant; police towed the car, made an inventory search of it without a warrant, and found various items of contraband; the Court of Appeals holds the search unconstitutional in an opinion that manifestly rests solely on the ground that the officers were lying about seeing a bag through the car window (although the district court judge who heard and denied the defendant's suppression motion must have believed the officers): the government's argument "that the bag with the narcotics was in plain view . . . has not been substantiated" (*id.* at 1106).

However, an officer's mere observation of an object from a location where the officer is entitled to be is not considered a "search" within the meaning of the Fourth Amendment. See § 25.33 *infra.* "[O]bjects falling in the plain view of an officer who has a right to be in the position to have that view" may be scrutinized without any further justification and without Fourth Amendment limitation (*Harris v. United States,* 390 U.S. 234, 236 (1968); *see Arizona v. Hicks,* 480 U.S. 321, 325 (1987) (dictum)). As long as the officer's entry and movement to the location were justified by either a warrant or an exception to the warrant requirement, the "viewing of the object in the course of a lawful search is as legitimate as it would have been in a public place" (*id.* at 327).

Although simple observation of the object is not a constitutionally regulated "search," any action by the police that "'meaningfully interfere[s]' with [a] defendant's possessory interest in [an object] . . . amount[s] to a seizure" within the Fourth Amendment (*Arizona v. Hicks, supra,* 480 U.S. at 324; *Horton v. California, supra,* 496 U.S. at 136-37). And any physical manipulation of the object that reveals its hidden features or contents is a "search" of the object. *Bond v. United States,* 529 U.S. 334 (2000); *United States v. Johnson,* 43 F.4th 1100 (10th Cir. 2022). Thus, in *Hicks,* when officers who had entered a residence in an emergency peace-keeping situation observed what they suspected to be stolen stereo equipment, the Court acknowledged in *dictum* that their "mere recording" of a stereo component's serial number would not constitute a search or seizure if the serial number was in plain view (480 U.S. at 324), but the Court held that when the officers went beyond merely observing the stereo equipment and moved it slightly for the purpose of disclosing serial numbers that were *not* in plain view, their action constituted a "*search* of objects in plain view" (*id.* at 327). This was an "independent search," "unrelated to the objectives of the authorized intrusion" into the residence, which "produce[d] a new invasion of defendant's privacy," and it consequently violated the Fourth Amendment in the absence of adequate justification (*id.* at 325).

To justify a "seizure" or a "search" of an object which is in "plain view," the prosecution must demonstrate that the following three conditions are satisfied:

(i) The officer must be lawfully in the location from which s/he observed the object. *See, e.g., Arizona v. Hicks, supra,* 480 U.S. at 326 ("'the initial intrusion that brings the police within plain view of such [evidence] [must be] . . . supported . . . by one of the recognized exceptions to the warrant requirement,' . . . such as the exigent-circumstances [exception]"); *Collins v. Virginia,* 138 S. Ct. 1663, 1672 (2018) ("'any valid warrantless seizure of incriminating evidence' requires that the officer 'have a lawful right of access to the object itself'"); *Horton v. California, supra,* 496 U.S. at 137 (dictum) ("[i]t is, of course, an essential predicate to any valid warrantless seizure of incriminating evidence that the officer did not violate the Fourth Amendment in arriving at the place from which the evidence could be plainly viewed"); *State v. Kruse,* 306 S.W.3d 603 (Mo. App. 2010); *cf. Florida v. Jardines,* 569 U.S. 1 (2013); *Minnesota v. Dickerson*, 508 U.S. 366, 375 (1993), discussed in § 25.10 *supra* (police must be "lawfully in a position from which they view an object").

(ii) The seizure or search of the object must be justified by "probable cause to believe the [object] . . . was stolen" (*Arizona v. Hicks, supra*, 480 U.S. at 328) or is "contraband" (*id.* at 327), or was an instrument or is evidence of a crime. *Cf. Minnesota v. Dickerson, supra*, 508 U.S. at 375 (police must have "probable cause to believe that an object in plain view is contraband"). As the Court explained in *Arizona v. Hicks,* a seizure or search of an object discovered "during an unrelated search and seizure" must be justified under the same "standard of *cause*" that "would have been needed to obtain a warrant for that same object if it had been known to be on the premises" (*id.* at 327). The "incriminating character [of the object] must . . . be 'immediately apparent'" (*Horton v. California, supra*, 496 U.S. at 136). *Cf. Minnesota v. Dickerson, supra*, 508 U.S. at 375 ("If . . . the police lack probable cause to believe that an object in plain view is contraband without conducting some further search of the object – *i.e.,* if 'its incriminating character [is not] "immediately apparent,"' . . . – the plain-view doctrine cannot justify its seizure."). Thus, in *Coolidge v. New Hampshire,* 403 U.S. 443 (1971), the plain view exception did not justify a police seizure of "two automobiles parked in plain view on the defendant's driveway . . . [because even though] the cars were obviously in plain view, . . . their probative value remained uncertain until after the interiors were swept and examined microscopically" (*Horton v. California, supra*, 496 U.S. at 134-37 (explaining the holding in *Coolidge*)). *Compare id.* at 142 (upholding a police seizure of firearms and stun guns in plain view under circumstances in which "it was immediately apparent to the officer that they constituted incriminating evidence"). *See also, e.g., People v. Sanders*, 26 N.Y.3d 773, 775, 777-78, 47 N.E.3d 770, 771-72, 27 N.Y.S.3d 491, 492-93 (2016) (a police officer's warrantless seizure of the hospitalized defendant's clothes, which "were in a clear plastic bag that rested on the floor of a trauma room a short distance away from the stretcher on which defendant was situated in a hospital hallway," was not justified by the plain view exception because, although the officer "knew defendant to have been shot," the officer did not have "probable cause to believe that defendant's clothes were the instrumentality of a crime" since the officer did not know at that time "that entry and exit wounds were located on an area of defendant's body that would have been covered by the clothes defendant wore at the time of the shooting."). If a police officer has probable cause to believe that a substance seized in plain view is a narcotic, then the additional seizure involved in destroying a minute amount of the substance in the course of a narcotics "field test" does not necessitate a search warrant. *United States v. Jacobsen, supra*, 466 U.S. at 124-26.

(The probable-cause requirement just described is subject to a narrow exception under exigent circumstances when "the seizure is minimally intrusive and operational necessities render it the only practicable means of detecting certain types of crime" (*Arizona v. Hicks, supra*, 480 U.S. at 327). The limits of this principle are discussed in the second paragraph of § 25.12 *supra*.)

(iii) In cases in which a police seizure of an object involves an invasion of the defendant's interests above and beyond the initial observation of the object, the additional intrusion also must be constitutionally justified. "[N]ot only must the officer be lawfully located in a place from which the object can be plainly seen, but he or she must also have a lawful right of access to the object itself" (*Horton v. California,* 496 U.S. 128, 137 (1990)). *Cf. Minnesota v. Dickerson, supra,* 508 U.S. at 375 ("the officers [must] have a lawful right of access to the object"). *Cf. United States v. Saulsberry,* 878 F.3d 946 (10th Cir. 2017), summarized in § 25.8.3 *supra.* Thus, for example, "'[i]ncontrovertible testimony of the senses that an incriminating object is on premises belonging to a criminal suspect may establish the fullest possible measure of probable cause. But even where the object is contraband, this Court has repeatedly stated and enforced the basic rule that the police may not enter and make a warrantless seizure'" (*Horton v. California, supra,* 496 U.S. at 137 n.7). *See, e.g., People v. Vega,* 276 A.D.2d 414, 414, 714 N.Y.S.2d 291, 291-92 (N.Y. App. Div., 1st Dep't 2000) (police officers who observed contraband in the defendant's room from the officers' "lawful vantage point" in "the hallway in th[e] residential hotel" could not rely on the "plain view" doctrine to enter the room and seize the contraband: "it was still necessary to establish that the police had lawful access to the [interior of the defendant's room] . . . either by way of a search warrant or some exception to the warrant requirement, such as exigent circumstances.").

In *Coolidge v. New Hampshire, supra,* a plurality of the Court concluded that the plain view doctrine should also be subject to a requirement that "the discovery of [the] evidence in plain view . . . be inadvertent" (403 U.S. at 469). Subsequently, in *Horton v. California,* a majority of the Court rejected this rule, holding that "even though inadvertence is a characteristic of most legitimate 'plain view' seizures, it is not a necessary condition" (496 U.S. at 130). However, in the two decades between the *Coolidge* and *Horton* decisions, state court decisions in 46 States had followed the *Coolidge* plurality's approach of recognizing an "inadvertent discovery" requirement for "plain view" searches and seizures. *Horton, supra,* 496 U.S. at 145 (dissenting opinion of Justice Brennan); *see id.* at 149-52, Appendix A (listing the state court decisions). In many of these States, it may be possible to persuade the state courts to retain the "inadvertent discovery" rule as a matter of state constitutional law. *See, e.g., State v. Meyer,* 78 Hawai'i 308, 314 & n.6, 893 P.2d 159, 165 & n.6 (1995); *Commonwealth v. Balicki,* 436 Mass. 1, 9-10, 762 N.E.2d 290, 298 (2002). See generally § 17.11 *supra.*

25.22.3. *Detention and Searches of Persons Found on the Premises*

Sometimes, in executing a search warrant for a building, the police detain and search one or more individuals who were on the premises at the time the police entered.

If the search warrant specifically names a certain person and authorizes the search of that person, then the police may conduct the search as long as the warrant and the search comply with the requirements described in § 25.17 *supra.* If the warrant does not authorize the search of individuals but merely authorizes a search of the premises to find certain objects, then the officers cannot extend their search of the premises to the individuals present on the premises. "[A] warrant to search a place cannot normally be construed to authorize a search of each individual in that place." *Ybarra v. Illinois,* 444 U.S. 85, 92 n.4 (1979). *See also United States v. Watson,* 703 F.3d 684, 689-94 (4th Cir. 2013). If the police have specific and articulable facts giving rise to a reasonable belief that a particular individual on the premises is armed and dangerous, then the officers may conduct a *Terry* frisk of that individual. See § 25.10 *supra.* But "[t]he 'narrow scope' of the *Terry* exception does not permit a frisk for weapons on less than reasonable belief or suspicion directed at the person to be frisked, even though that person happens to be on premises where an authorized . . . search is taking place" (*Ybarra v. Illinois, supra*, 444 U.S. at 94).

In *Ybarra,* the Court struck down a police pat-down of a patron of a bar, who was on the premises during the execution of a search warrant for the bar and the bartender. The Court explained that "a person's mere propinquity to others independently suspected of criminal activity does not, without more, give rise to probable cause to search that person" (444 U.S. at 91). As several lower courts have recognized, the principles established in *Ybarra* necessarily apply not only to searches of patrons of a commercial establishment but also to searches of individuals who are visiting a private home at the time that the police effect an entry and search of the home. *E.g., United States v. Clay,* 640 F.2d 157, 161-62 (8th Cir. 1981); *People v. Tate,* 367 Ill. App. 3d 109, 853 N.E.2d 1249, 304 Ill. Dec. 883 (2006); *State v. Vandiver*, 257 Kan. 53, 891 P.2d 350 (1995); *Beeler v. State,* 677 P.2d 653 (Okla. Crim. App. 1984); *Lippert v. State,* 664 S.W.2d 712 (Tex. Crim. App. 1984). *Cf. Leveto v. Lapina,* 258 F.3d 156, 163-65 (3d Cir. 2001) (Alito, J.) (IRS agents executing a search warrant could not validly frisk a homeowner in the absence of justification for a *Terry* frisk). *See also Guy v. Wisconsin,* 509 U.S. 914, 914-15 (1993) (Justice White, dissenting from denial of *certiorari*) (describing a division of authority among lower courts with regard to "whether this Court's holding in *Ybarra v. Illinois* . . . applies where a search warrant for drugs is executed in a private home").

In *Michigan v. Summers*, 452 U.S. 692, 705 (1981), and *Muehler v. Mena*, 544 U.S. 93 (2005), the Court did hold that an owner or resident of premises may be detained and prevented from leaving the premises while the police execute a search warrant of the premises. *See also Bailey v. United States*, 568 U.S. 186 (2013); *Los Angeles County v. Rettele*, 550 U.S. 609 (2007) (per curiam); *Illinois v. McArthur*, 531 U.S. 326 (2001), discussed in § 25.6.3 *supra*. Using broad language, the Court stated in *Summers*, and reiterated in *Muehler*, that "a warrant to search for contraband . . . implicitly carries with it the limited authority to detain the occupants of the premises while a proper search [of the premises themselves] is conducted" (*Summers, supra*, 452 U.S. at 705; *Muehler, supra*, 544 U.S. at 98 (quoting *Summers*); *Los Angeles County v. Rettele, supra*, 550 U.S. at 613 (quoting *Summers*); *Bailey, supra*, 568 U.S. at 208 (quoting *Summers*)). However, the facts of these cases and the reasoning of the opinions demonstrate that the phrase "occupant[ ] of the premises" is meant to refer solely to "residents" (terms that are used interchangeably by the *Summers* Court (*see id.* at 701-03; *see also Rettele, supra*, 550 U.S. at 609, 615; *Muehler, supra*, 544 U.S. at 106, 110 (Justice Stevens, concurring) [the concurring opinion, representing the views of 4 Justices, describes occupants as "resident[s]," each of whom "had his or her or own bedroom"]) and not to persons who happen to be visiting the premises at the time when the police effect their entry. In *Summers*, in which the Court announced the rule that an occupant may be detained while the police search a home pursuant to a warrant, the defendant owned the house that was searched and several of the Court's rationales for upholding the detention were predicated upon the defendant's status as the owner of the premises. The Court explained that the defendant, as owner of the house, could facilitate the search by "open[ing] locked doors or locked containers to avoid the use of force that is . . . damaging to property" (452 U.S. at 703); the Court pointed out that "residents" like the defendant would ordinarily wish to "remain in order to observe the search of their possessions" (*id.* at 701); and it observed that since the place of detention was the detainee's own residence, the seizure would "add only minimally to the public stigma associated with the search itself" (*id.* at 702). In

Muehler, the Court did not revisit the reasoning for the rule, treating its earlier holding in *Summers* as "categorical[ly]" authorizing the detention of a resident who "was asleep in her bed" when the police executed the warrant and "entered her bedroom" (544 U.S. at 96, 98), and the Court focused on a new question presented by the facts of *Muehler*: whether the police improperly engaged in the additional intrusion of handcuffing this resident for the duration of the search. The Court concluded that handcuffing is permissible if this measure is necessitated by "inherently dangerous" circumstances such as those that existed in the *Muehler* case, where the "warrant authoriz[ed] a search for weapons and a wanted gang member reside[d] on the premises" and there was a "need to detain multiple occupants" (*id.* at 100). *But cf. id.* at 102 (Justice Kennedy, concurring and thus supplying the vote necessary to produce a 5-Justice majority: "[t]he restraint should . . . be removed if, at any point during the search, it would be readily apparent to any objectively reasonable officer that removing the handcuffs would not compromise the officers' safety or risk interference or substantial delay in the execution of the search."). In *Bailey*, the Court made clear that the *Summers* rule is strictly limited to "cases [in which] the occupants detained were found within or immediately outside a residence at the moment the police officers executed the search warrant" (568 U.S. at 193). "A spatial constraint defined by the immediate vicinity of the premises to be searched is . . . required for detentions incident to the execution of a search warrant. The police action permitted here – the search of a residence – has a spatial dimension, and so a spatial or geographical boundary can be used to determine the area within which both the search and detention incident to that search may occur. Limiting the rule in *Summers* to the area in which an occupant poses a real threat to the safe and efficient execution of a search warrant ensures that the scope of the detention incident to a search is confined to its underlying justification. Once an occupant is beyond the immediate vicinity of the premises to be searched, the search-related law enforcement interests are diminished and the intrusiveness of the detention is more severe." *Id.* at 201. *Dicta* in the *Bailey* opinion use the term "occupant" without specifying the precise connection that it implies between the premises being searched and the individual whose detention is in question under *Summers* (*see id.* at 193-99), but the Court does describe the *Summers* rule as involving a "detention [that] occurs in the individual's own home" (*id.* at 200), and the Court emphasizes that the "exception [that *Summers* created] to the Fourth Amendment rule prohibiting detention absent probable cause must not diverge from its purpose and rationale" (*id.* at 194).

As some lower courts have concluded, the *Summers* rule cannot be construed as authorizing detentions of individuals who happen to be visiting the premises at the time of a police entry. *See, e.g., Lippert v. State*, 664 S.W.2d 712 (Tex. Crim. App. 1984); *State v. Broadnax*, 98 Wash. 2d 289, 654 P.2d 96 (1982). *See also Commonwealth v. Catanzaro*, 441 Mass. 46, 51-52 & n.10, 803 N.E.2d 287, 291 & n.10 (2004). In order to detain visitors, the police must have the specific and articulable facts necessary to conduct a *Terry* stop. *See* § 25.9 *supra*. Nor does the *Summers* rule authorize a *frisk* of anyone – visitor, resident or owner – in the course of executing a search warrant for premises. *See, e.g., Leveto v. Lapina*, 258 F.3d 156, 163-66 (3d Cir. 2001) (Alito, J.); *Denver Justice and Peace Committee, Inc. v. City of Golden*, 405 F.3d 923, 928-32 (10th Cir. 2005). As § 25.10 *supra* indicates, the power to detain an individual briefly for investigation, whether under *Terry* or under *Summers*, carries with it no automatic power to frisk that individual; any frisk must be justified by a particularized and objectively reasonable suspicion that the detainee is armed and dangerous. *See, e.g., id.* at 932.

25.22.4. *"Protective Sweep" of the Premises*

"A 'protective sweep' is a quick and limited search of a premises, incident to an arrest and conducted to protect the safety of police officers or others. It is narrowly confined to a cursory visual inspection of those places in which a person might be hiding." *Maryland v. Buie,* 494 U.S. 325, 327 (1990). When the police "effect[ ] the arrest of a suspect in his home pursuant to an arrest warrant, [the police] may conduct a warrantless protective sweep of all or part of the premises . . . if the searching officer 'possesse[s] . . . a reasonable belief based on "specific and articulable facts which, taken together with the rational inferences from those facts, reasonably warrant[ ] . . ." the officer in believing' . . . that the area swept harbor[s] . . . an individual posing a danger to the officer or others" (*id.* at 327-28). *See also id.* at 334, 335-37; *United States v. Serrano-Acevedo,* 892 F.3d 454 (1st Cir. 2018) (holding a putative "protective sweep" unconstitutional for lack of reasonable grounds for such a belief). The Court in *Buie* "emphasize[d] that such a protective sweep, aimed at protecting the arresting officers, if justified by the circumstances, is . . . not a full search of the premises, but may extend only to a cursory inspection of those spaces where a person may be found. . . . The sweep lasts no longer than is necessary to dispel the reasonable suspicion of danger and in any event no longer than it takes to complete the arrest and depart the premises" (*id.* at 335-36). *See, e.g., United States v. Hernandez-Mieses,* 931 F.3d 134, 141-45 (1st Cir. 2019); *United States v. Green,* 231 A.3d 398, 407-08 (D.C. 2020); *United States v. Bagley,* 877 F.3d 1151 (10th Cir. 2017) ("Deputy U.S. Marshals obtained a search warrant allowing entry into a house solely to locate and arrest Mr. Bagley ["a convicted felon who was named in an arrest warrant for violating the terms of his supervised release"]. . . . When they arrived, Mr. Bagley was allegedly in the southeast bedroom. He eventually surrendered and was handcuffed near the front door. ¶ The deputy marshals then conducted a protective sweep of the entire house. In the southeast bedroom, deputy marshals found two rounds of ammunition and a substance appearing to be marijuana. . . . ¶ . . . Mr. Bagley may have been in the living room when the protective sweep began. . . . ¶ The government argues that it doesn't matter where Mr. Bagley was at the time of the protective sweep because he had earlier been 'arrested' in the southeast bedroom. With this focus on the place of the purported earlier arrest, the government argues that the deputy marshals could enter the southeast bedroom because Mr. Bagley had announced his surrender when he was in the southeast bedroom, rendering him under 'arrest' at that time. . . . We disagree. . . . . ¶ . . . The deputy marshals could conduct a protective sweep only if the protective sweep was justified at the time of the arrest; the deputy marshals could not conduct the arrest and later conduct a protective sweep based on an earlier arrest somewhere in the house." *Id.* at 1153-55. Nor could the sweep be justified on the theory that some dangerous person other than Bagley may have been in the house. "When the deputy marshals entered the southeast bedroom, Mr. Bagley, his girlfriend, and her children had already left the house. The deputy marshals had no way of knowing, one way or another, whether anyone besides Mr. Bagley was still in the house. . . . ¶ . . . [L]ack of knowledge cannot constitute the specific, articulable facts required . . . ." *Id.* at 1156.); *State v. Sanders,* 2008 WI 85, 311 Wis. 2d 257, 270-71, 752 N.W.2d 713, 720 (Wis. 2008) (officers accosted the defendant in his back yard, where he was observed holding a small cannister; he fled into his house and took refuge in a bedroom; after a minute, he came out of the bedroom and was arrested; the officers made a "protective sweep" of the bedroom; either then or thereafter, they retrieved and searched the cannister, which was hidden under the bed; on the assumption that the cannister was found during the "protective sweep," the court orders its suppression as unjustified under *Buie*: "Accepting for the moment the State's position that articulable facts exist to demonstrate that the officer had reasonable suspicion that other persons may be lurking in the defendant's bedroom who would pose a danger to the officers and that a protective search of the bedroom was therefore justified, we nevertheless must conclude that . . . [the] search of the canister and seizure of its contents clearly were not within the purpose of the protective sweep. The search of the canister and seizure of its contents were not part of a search for persons who might pose a danger to law enforcement officers or to others. No person could be hiding in the canister. Furthermore, the officers had no articulable suspicion that weapons were involved in the instant case. The search of the canister and seizure of its contents therefore do not fall within the 'protective sweep' exception to the search warrant requirement.").

D. *Automobile Stops, Searches, Inspections, and Impoundments*

25.23. *The Threshold Issue: Defendant's Interest in the Automobile or Expectation of Privacy Inside it*

Just as a defendant who seeks to challenge a police entry and search of premises must have a constitutionally protected interest or legitimate expectation of privacy in the premises, see § 25.15 *supra,* so, too, a defendant who seeks to challenge a police stop or search of an automobile must have a sufficient possessory or privacy interest in the vehicle – or, alternatively, a sufficient personal interest in its unhindered movement – to complain about the particular police action in question.

A defendant has the requisite interest to complain of an unconstitutional automobile search in each of the following situations:

(i)   The automobile belongs to the defendant, even though it is out of his or her possession at the time of the search (*see, e.g., Cash v. Williams,* 455 F.2d 1227, 1229-30 (6th Cir. 1972); *United States v. Powell,* 929 F.2d 1190, 1196 (7th Cir. 1991) (an absentee owner has standing to challenge the search of a vehicle although s/he does not have standing to challenge the mere stopping of the vehicle for a purported traffic violation); *State v. Foldesi,* 131 Idaho 778, 963 P.2d 1215 (Idaho App. 1998)), as long as the defendant has not given up possession of the vehicle in a manner that deprives him or her of any remaining legitimate expectation of privacy in it (*United States v. Jenkins,* 92 F.3d 430, 434-35 (6th Cir. 1996); *see generally Rakas v. Illinois,* 439 U.S. 128 (1978)).

(ii)   The automobile is in the defendant's lawful possession under circumstances that comport the possessor's ordinary right to exclude undesired intrusions by others. *See Rakas v. Illinois, supra,* 439 U.S. at 144 n.12 (dictum). This includes situations in which the defendant is driving a family member's or friend's automobile with the permission of the owner. *See, e.g., United States v. Valdez Hocker,* 333 F.3d 1206 (10th Cir. 2003); *People v. Lewis,* 217 A.D.2d 591, 593, 629 N.Y.S.2d 455, 457 (N.Y. App. Div., 2d Dep't 1995). *Cf. Minnesota v. Olson,* 495 U.S. 91, 96-100 (1990); *Jones v. United States,* 362 U.S. 257 (1960), as explained in *Rakas v. Illinois, supra,* 439 U.S. at 141. It includes situations in which the defendant has rented the vehicle from a car rental agency (*United States v. Walton*, 763 F.3d 655 (7th Cir. 2014) (granting standing even though the renter's driving license was suspended); *United States v. Cooper*, 133 F.3d 1394 (11th Cir. 1998) (granting standing even though the rental agreement had expired before the search); *United States v. Henderson*, 241 F.3d 638, 646-47 (9th Cir. 2000) (dictum) (same)) or is "listed on a rental agreement as an authorized driver" (*United States v. Walker*, 237 F.3d 845, 849 (7th Cir. 2001), and cases cited). It also includes persons to whom the renter has entrusted the vehicle, even if s/he does so in violation of terms in the rental agreement that restrict authorized drivers to designated individuals. *Byrd v. United States*, 138 S. Ct. 1518 (2018) ("[A]s a general rule, someone in otherwise lawful possession and control of a rental car has a reasonable expectation of privacy in it even if the rental agreement does not list him or her as an authorized driver." *Id.* at 1524. "The Court sees no reason why the expectation of privacy that comes from lawful possession and control and the attendant right to exclude would differ depending on whether the car in question is rented or privately owned by someone other than the person in current possession of it." *Id.* at 1528. "[T]he mere fact that a driver in lawful possession or control of a rental car is not listed on the rental agreement will not defeat his or her otherwise reasonable expectation of privacy." *Id.* at 1531. A "car thief would not have a reasonable expectation of privacy in a stolen car" but anyone in "lawful possession" does (*id.* at 1529.).

(iii)   The vehicle is a taxicab in which the defendant is a lawful passenger. *See Rios v. United States,* 364 U.S. 253, 262 n.6 (1960).

(iv)   The defendant is a lawful occupant of the vehicle at the time of the search (*United States v. Mosley*, 454 F.3d 249 (3d Cir. 2006) ("when a vehicle is illegally stopped by the police, no evidence found during the stop may be used by the government against any occupant of the vehicle unless the government can show that the taint of the illegal stop was purged" (*id.* at 251)), and cases cited; *see also United States v. Kimball*, 25 F.3d 1, 5-6 (1st Cir. 1994)) and the search invades an area of the vehicle in which, as a lawful occupant, the defendant has "any legitimate expectation of privacy" (*Rakas v. Illinois, supra*, 439 U.S. at 150 n.17 (dictum)). *See also Bond v. United States*, 529 U.S. 334, 338-39 (2000) ("a bus passenger [who] places a bag in an overhead bin" has a reasonable expectation that "other passengers," "bus employees," and police officers will not "feel the bag in an exploratory manner"); *accord, United States v. Johnson*, 43 F.4th 1100 (10th Cir. 2022).

A defendant can complain of an unconstitutional *stop* of an automobile if s/he was in the vehicle at the time of the stop. *Brendlin v. California*, 551 U.S. 249, 251, 257 (2007) ("When a police officer makes a traffic stop, the driver of the car is seized within the meaning of the Fourth Amendment. . . . We hold that a passenger is seized as well and so may challenge the constitutionality of the stop."; "A traffic stop necessarily curtails the travel a passenger has chosen just as much as it halts the driver"); *United States v. Grant*, 349 F.3d 192, 196 (5th Cir. 2003). If the defendant was not in the automobile at the time of the stop, s/he can nevertheless challenge the stop if s/he is the owner of the automobile (*see Cash v. Williams, supra*, 455 F.2d at 1229-30) or if s/he has established a sufficient privacy interest in the automobile through repeated use to invoke the same rights as an owner (*cf. Jones v. United States*, 362 U.S. 257 (1960), as explained in *Rakas v. Illinois, supra*, 439 U.S. at 141; *Minnesota v. Olson, supra*, 495 U.S. at 96-100).

Even when an individual has the requisite possessory interest or expectation of privacy in an automobile, s/he cannot claim any privacy rights with respect to the car's Vehicle Identification Number (VIN) located on the dashboard "because of the important role played by the VIN in the pervasive governmental regulation of the automobile and the efforts by the Federal Government to ensure that the VIN is placed in plain view" (*New York v. Class*, 475 U.S. 106, 114 (1986)). In *Class*, the Court held that the public nature of the VIN empowers the police to move papers obstructing the VIN, in order to view the number in the course of a valid stop for a traffic violation, at least under circumstances in which the driver on his or her own initiative leaves the vehicle and therefore is not in a position to accede to a lawful request to move the papers so that the number can be inspected. *See id.* at 114-16. *Contra, People v. Class*, 67 N.Y.2d 431, 494 N.E.2d 444, 503 N.Y.S.2d 313 (1986) (reaffirming, on state constitutional grounds, the opinion reversed in *New York v. Class, supra*). In cases in which an entry into a car was not justified by a traffic violation, some lower courts have ruled that the public nature of the VIN does not justify the opening of the vehicle for the purpose of inspecting the VIN. *See People v. Piper*, 101 Ill. App. 3d 296, 427 N.E.2d 1361, 56 Ill. Dec. 815 (1981); *State v. Simpson*, 95 Wash. 2d 170, 622 P.2d 1199 (1980); *but see United States v. Forrest*, 620 F.2d 446 (5th Cir. 1980).

For discussion of the "automatic standing" principle and of the evolution of the general concepts governing "standing" to challenge searches and seizures, see § 25.15 *supra*.

25.24. *Evidentiary Searches of Automobiles: The "Automobile Exception" to the Warrant Requirement*

Automobiles are the subject of a specialized Fourth Amendment jurisprudence stemming from *Carroll v. United States*, 267 U.S. 132 (1925). As presently interpreted, *Carroll* permits warrantless stopping and search of moving vehicles if, but only if, the searching officers have probable cause to believe that seizable objects are concealed in the vehicle. *Almeida-Sanchez v. United States*, 413 U.S. 266 (1973); *Marshall v. Barlow's, Inc.*, 436 U.S. 307, 315 n.10 (1978) (dictum); *Wyoming v. Houghton*, 526 U.S. 295, 300-01 (1999); *compare Chambers v. Maroney*, 399 U.S. 42 (1970), *and Colorado v. Bannister*, 449 U.S. 1 (1980) (per curiam), *and Maryland v. Dyson*, 527 U.S. 465 (1999) (per curiam), *with Preston v. United States*, 376 U.S. 364 (1964), *and Dyke v. Taylor Implement Mfg. Co.*, 391 U.S. 216 (1968), *and United States v. Davis*, 997 F.3d 191 (4th Cir. 2021). *See also California v. Carney*, 471 U.S. 386 (1985) (extending the *Carroll* rule to a motor home parked in a downtown parking lot); *Florida v. White*, 526 U.S. 559, 565, 566 (1999) (the *Carroll* rule permitting search of a vehicle based on probable cause to believe that it contains contraband justified the seizure of a car based on "probable cause to believe that the vehicle *itself* was contraband" where "the warrantless seizure . . . did not involve any invasion of defendant's privacy" because the vehicle was in "a public area"); *Bell v. City of Chicago*, 835 F.3d 736, 739 (7th Cir. 2016) (rejecting a Fourth Amendment challenge to a municipal ordinance that authorizes seizure and impounding of vehicles upon probable cause to believe they have been "used in an illegal manner or in connection with an illegal act, such as possession of illegal drugs in a vehicle, drag racing, or solicitation of a prostitute"). *Compare Commonwealth v. Alexander*, 243 A.3d 177, 180-81 (Pa. 2020) (holding that the state constitution "affords greater protection to our citizens" than the "federal automobile exception": "the Pennsylvania Constitution requires both a showing of probable cause and exigent circumstances to justify a warrantless search of an automobile").

If there is probable cause to believe that seizable objects may be concealed in any part of the vehicle, then the police may search every part of the vehicle and every container within it which is capable of holding the seizable object. *Wyoming v. Houghton, supra*, 526 U.S. at 307; *California v. Acevedo*, 500 U.S. 565, 580 (1991); *United States v. Ross,* 456 U.S. 798 (1982); *United States v. Johns,* 469 U.S. 478, 482-83 (1985). The only limitation on the scope of the search is that it may not extend into areas incapable of holding the object, including containers that are not "capable of concealing the object of the search" (*Wyoming v. Houghton, supra*, 526 U.S. at 307 (dictum); *United States v. Ross, supra*, 456 U.S. at 820-21, 823-24 (dictum)).

The *Carroll* decision and its progeny establishing special rules for automobile searches and seizures are based in substantial part upon the inherent mobility of automobiles, which renders the securing of a warrant impracticable. *See Wyoming v. Houghton, supra*, 526 U.S. at 304; *Pennsylvania v. Labron*, 518 U.S. 938, 940 (1996) (per curiam); *California v. Carney, supra*, 471 U.S. at 390-91. (The caselaw also mentions two other factors that distinguish automobiles from buildings: – the lesser degree of privacy that an automobile offers (*e.g.*, *Pennsylvania v. Labron, supra*, 518 U.S. at 940; *South Dakota v. Opperman,* 428 U.S. 364, 367 (1976)), and the fact that automobiles are subject to extensive noncriminal regulation by the state (*e.g.*, *Pennsylvania v. Labron, supra*, 518 U.S. at 940; *Cady v. Dombrowski,* 413 U.S. 433, 441 (1973)). But the latter factors have never been invoked independently to uphold a warrantless police search that invades what privacy an automobile *does* afford, in a case where no noncriminal regulatory concern drew police attention to a particular vehicle.) Accordingly, in *Coolidge v. New Hampshire,* 403 U.S. 443 (1971), the Court held that an almost totally immobilized automobile could not be searched without a warrant. *Coolidge* arguably forbids the application of *Carroll*'s automobile exception to the warrant requirement in situations in which there are no reasonable grounds to apprehend that a vehicle may be moved before a warrant can be obtained. *See id.* at 462 (plurality opinion) (except "where 'it is not practicable to secure a warrant,' . . . the 'automobile exception,' despite its label, is simply irrelevant"); *Preston v. United States,* 376 U.S. 364 (1964); *United States v. Bradshaw*, 490 F.2d 1097 (4th Cir. 1974); *State v. LeJeune*, 276 Ga. 179, 182-83, 576 S.E.2d 888, 892-93 (2003) (alternative ground); *United States v. Bazinet*, 462 F.2d 982, 986 n.3 (8th Cir. 1972) (dictum); *United States v. McCormick*, 502 F.2d 281 (9th Cir. 1974); *cf. State v. Gonzales*, 236 Or. App. 391, 236 P.3d 834 (2010), *subsequent history in* 265 Or. App. 655, 337 P.3d 129 (2014). The *Carroll* rule applies, in other words, only "[w]hen a vehicle is being used on the highways, or if it is readily capable of such use and is found stationary in a place not regularly used for residential purposes – temporary or otherwise" (*California v. Carney, supra*, 471 U.S. at 392). *Compare State v. Witt*, 223 N.J. 409, 447-48, 126 A.3d 850, 872-73 (2015) ("In . . . [*State v. Alston*, 88 N.J. 211, 233, 440 A.2d 1311 (1981)] we held that the automobile exception authorized the warrantless search of an automobile only when the police have probable cause to believe that the vehicle contains contraband or evidence of an offense and the circumstances giving rise to probable cause are unforeseeable and spontaneous. . . . ¶ Here, we part from the United States Supreme Court's interpretation of the automobile exception under the Fourth Amendment and return to the *Alston* standard, this time supported by Article I, Paragraph 7 of our State Constitution. *Alston* properly balances the individual's privacy and liberty interests and law enforcement's investigatory demands. *Alston*'s requirement of 'unforeseeability and spontaneity,' . . . does not place an undue burden on law enforcement. For example, if a police officer has probable cause to search a car and is looking for that car, then it is reasonable to expect the officer to secure a warrant if it is practicable to do so. In this way, we eliminate the . . . fear that 'a car parked in the home driveway of vacationing owners would be a fair target of a warrantless search if the police had probable cause to believe the vehicle contained drugs.' . . . In the case of the parked car, if the circumstances giving rise to probable cause were foreseeable and not spontaneous, the warrant requirement applies."); *State v. Smart*, 253 N.J. 156, 159-60, 172, 289 A.3d 469, 471, 478 (2023) (applying the state constitutional rule of *State v. Witt, supra*, to hold that a warrantless search of a vehicle after an investigative stop was unlawful, notwithstanding the parties' "agree[ment that] the investigative stop was legal" and the officers' reliance on a canine sniff of the exterior of the vehicle to establish probable cause that drugs were in the vehicle, because the "circumstances giving rise to probable cause were not 'unforeseeable and spontaneous'" in that the police had received information "a month earlier from a confidential informant (CI) that helped link" the defendant and the vehicle to "narcotics trafficking in the area," and, after the police observed the defendant enter the vehicle, they "surveilled it for almost an hour" before stopping the car: "the investigative stop was deliberate, orchestrated, and wholly connected with the reason for the subsequent seizure of the evidence").

In *Collins v. Virginia*, 138 S. Ct. 1663 (2018) (summarized in § 25.15.3 *supra*), the Supreme Court held that a police officer violated the Fourth Amendment when, without a warrant, he entered the curtilage of a home to inspect a tarp-covered motorcycle parked in the driveway adjacent to the house. The Court rejected Virginia's argument "that this Court's precedent indicates that the automobile exception is a categorical one that permits the warrantless search of a vehicle anytime, anywhere, including in a home or curtilage" (*id*. at 1673). Because the Court's *ratio decidendi* was that an illegal search occurred at the point at which the officer trespassed on the curtilage, it was unnecessary for the Court to reach the question whether the bike's lack of mobility would have insulated it from warrantless search and seizure if it had been similarly parked and draped somewhere other than on private residential premises. There are, however, hints in the opinion which suggest that the answer to this question should be yes. The Court parsed the *Carroll* doctrine by saying: "The 'ready mobility' of vehicles served as the core justification for the automobile exception for many years. . . . Later cases then introduced an additional rationale based on 'the pervasive regulation of vehicles capable of traveling on the public highways.'" *Id*. at 1669-70. But the latter-day "additional rationale" would seem to be applicable to Collins' motorcycle no matter where it was parked, and the Court does not discuss it further. (As noted above, no Supreme Court decision has ever sustained a warrantless vehicle search solely on the basis of the regulatory rationale.) By contrast, the *Collins* Court does recur to the "ready mobility" rationale in distinguishing *Scher* v. *United States*, 305 U.S. 251 (1938): "Whereas Collins' motorcycle was parked and unattended when Officer Rhodes intruded on the curtilage to search it, the officers in *Scher* first encountered the vehicle when it was being driven on public streets, [and] approached the curtilage of the home only when the driver turned into the garage, and searched the vehicle." *Id.* at 1674. Thus, the immobility of Collins' bike played a significant albeit inexplicit role in the outcome. *And see Commonwealth v. Loughnane*, 173 A.3d 733 (2017), a pre-*Collins* decision also involving a warrantless police search of a vehicle parked in a residential driveway. The Pennsylvania Supreme Court invalidated the search not only out of concern for the vehicle's proximity to the defendant's residence, but because of the perceived inapplicability of *Carroll*'s mobility rationale. "Absent exigent circumstances, the concern about the inherent mobility of the vehicle does not apply, as the chance to search and/or seize the vehicle is not fleeting. . . . The vehicle is parked where the defendant lives and it will typically either remain there or inevitably return to that location." *Id.* at 745. There is language in *id.* at 744, suggesting that a vehicle parked in a public parking lot differs from one parked in a residential driveway because a public parking facility "'is typically an interim destination, but a home's driveway is often the end of that day's travels.'" Nevertheless, *Collins* and *Loughnane* justify counsel's advocating the position that a warrantless search of an immobile, unattended vehicle in any location falls outside the *Carroll* "automobile exception" (*Collins*, 138 S. Ct. at 1669). *See also People v. Rorabaugh*, 74 Cal. App. 5th 296, 289 Cal. Rptr. 3d 393 (2022) (holding that the warrantless seizure, impoundment and search of a car which was located just inside the property line of a farm with permission of the farm owner (for whom the defendant did mechanical work in return for the farmer's permission to leave the car on his property) violated the Fourth Amendment; in rejecting the state's argument that the car was "readily mobile," the court notes that the farmer did not have the keys to it and that the defendant, who did, had been arrested at another location and was already in custody at the time the police seized the vehicle).

When the police have probable cause to make a warrantless search of a vehicle under *Carroll* but, instead of searching it on the street, they lawfully impound it, they may exercise the *Carroll* prerogative to search it without a warrant later at the police station (*e.g., Chambers v. Maroney, supra*, 399 U.S. at 52; *Michigan v. Thomas,* 458 U.S. 259, 261-62 (1982) (per curiam); *Florida v. Meyers,* 466 U.S. 380 (1984) (per curiam); *and see United States v. Ross, supra*, 456 U.S. at 807 n.9 ("if an immediate search on the street is permissible without a warrant, a search soon thereafter at the police station is permissible if the vehicle is impounded")), at least when no additional invasion of privacy interests results from their delay in making the search and when the delay is not inordinate (*see United States v. Johns, supra*, 469 U.S. at 487 (dictum), citing Justice White's dissenting opinion in *Coolidge v. New Hampshire, supra*, 403 U.S. at 525). The same rule permitting delayed searches applies to closed containers found in the vehicle. *United States v. Johns, supra*, 469 U.S. at 482-83. *But see State v. Witt, supra,* 223 N.J. at 448-49, 126 A.3d at 873 ("We also part from federal jurisprudence that allows a police officer to conduct a warrantless search at headquarters merely because he could have done so on the side of the road. . . . 'Whatever inherent exigency justifies a warrantless search at the scene under the automobile exception certainly cannot justify the failure to secure a warrant after towing and impounding the car' at headquarters when it is practicable to do so. . . . Warrantless searches should not be based on fake exigencies. Therefore, under Article I, Paragraph 7 of the New Jersey Constitution, we limit the automobile exception to on-scene warrantless searches.").

25.25. *Inventory Searches of Impounded Vehicles; Consent Searches of Vehicles*

(A) The immediately preceding section dealt with the circumstances under which the police can conduct warrantless searches of automobiles "for the purpose of investigating criminal conduct, with the validity of the searches . . . dependent on the application of the probable cause and warrant requirements of the Fourth Amendment" (*Colorado v. Bertine,* 479 U.S. 367, 371 (1987)). "By contrast, an inventory search may be 'reasonable' under the Fourth Amendment even though it is not conducted pursuant to a warrant based upon probable cause." *Id.*

The police may conduct an "inventory search" of the contents of an impounded automobile, including an examination of the contents of containers found in the automobile (*id.* at 374-75), if the inventory search complies with the following four requirements:

(i) The search must be conducted in accordance with "standardized procedures" (*id.* at 372), based upon "reasonable police regulations relating to inventory procedures" (*id.*). *Accord, Florida v. Wells,* 495 U.S. 1, 4 (1990) ("standardized criteria . . . or established routine"); *South Dakota v. Opperman,* 428 U.S. 364, 366, 376 (1976). *See, e.g., Wells, supra,* 495 U.S. at 4-5 (suppressing contraband found in the course of an alleged inventory search because "the Florida Highway Patrol had no policy whatever with respect to the opening of closed containers encountered during an inventory search . . . [and] absent such a policy, the instant search was not sufficiently regulated to satisfy the Fourth Amendment").

(ii) The police must not be acting "in bad faith or for the sole purpose of investigation" (*Colorado v. Bertine, supra,* 479 U.S. at 372). *See also id.* at 374 (speaking of "reasonable police regulations relating to inventory procedures administered in good faith"); *id.* at 376 (noting that "[t]here was no showing that the police chose to impound Bertine's van in order to investigate suspected criminal activity"); *Florida v. Wells, supra,* 495 U.S. at 4 ("an inventory search must not be a ruse for a general rummaging in order to discover incriminating evidence"); *South Dakota v. Opperman, supra,* 428 U.S. at 376 (police had no "investigatory . . . motive"); *Cady v. Dombrowski,* 413 U.S. 433, 447 (1973) (officer conducting the search had no purpose to look for criminal evidence); *United States v. Woodard,* 5 F.4th 1148, 1150 (10th Cir. 2021) ("[w]hen the police use pretext to impound . . . [a] car, the Fourth Amendment typically prohibits introduction of the evidence obtained from the search"); *United States v. Del Rosario-Acosta,* 968 F.3d 123, 128 (1st Cir. 2020) ("All in all, it seems inescapable that the officers seized Del Rosario's car so that they could search it for evidence of a crime, and that they later sought to justify the search by invoking the community-caretaking exception. And while that exception might well apply even if there were also other motives for seizing the car, here the exception fits so poorly that it does not suffice to lift our eyes from the obvious conclusion that the seizure served no purpose other than facilitating a warrantless investigatory search under the guise of an impoundment inventory."); *United States v. Johnson,* 889 F.3d 1120, 1125-26 (9th Cir. 2018) ("The government argues that, regardless what the officers' personal motivations were for searching Johnson's car, such motivations are simply not relevant to our Fourth Amendment inquiry. In most contexts, that is true. . . . ¶ However, in an opinion published after the district court's decision in this case, our court held that administrative searches conducted without individualized suspicion – such as drunk-driving checkpoints or vehicular inventory searches – are an exception to this general rule. . . . Thus, an administrative search may be invalid where the officer's 'subjective purpose was to find evidence of crime.' . . . However, the mere 'presence of a criminal investigatory motive' or a 'dual motive – one valid, and one impermissible –' does not render an administrative stop or search invalid; instead, we ask whether the challenged search or seizure 'would . . . have occurred in the absence of an impermissible reason.'"). *Cf.* § 25.36, concluding paragraph *infra*; *and see generally City of Indianapolis v. Edmond*, 531 U.S. 32, 45-46 (2000) (dictum) (discussing the "inventory search" caselaw).

(iii) The automobile must be lawfully "in the custody of the police" (*Colorado v. Bertine, supra*, 479 U.S. at 372), in the sense that an adequate justification exists for the police to impound it (*see South Dakota v. Opperman, supra*, 428 U.S. at 365-66, 375; *Cady v. Dombrowski, supra*, 413 U.S. at 443). "[T]he threshold question in inventory cases is whether the impoundment itself was proper. . . . '[W]here the circumstances show that the police had no authority to impound the vehicle, or that police custodial care of the vehicle was not necessary, the inventory search was unlawful.'" *Fair v. State*, 627 N.E.2d 427, 431 (Ind. 1993). *Accord, United States v. Rosario-Acosta, supra*, 968 F.3d at 127, 128 (following the defendant's arrest while running away from his car, which "was parked legally on a quiet residential street one street over from where . . . [he] lived with his family," police impounded and searched the vehicle; the impounding and search are held unsustainable under the community caretaking function: "The only . . . factor favoring the government is that ostensibly there was no one else to move the car. But the relevance of that factor only arises when there is a need to move the car."). "[W]hen the impoundment is not specifically directed by state law, the risk increases that a decision to tow will be motivated solely by the desire to conduct an investigatory search. . . . ¶ . . . [Thus] we hold that to prevail on the question of whether an impoundment was warranted in terms of the community caretaking function, the prosecution must demonstrate: (1) that the belief that the vehicle posed some threat or harm to the community or was itself imperiled was consistent with objective standards of sound policing, . . . *and* (2) that the decision to combat that threat by impoundment was in keeping with established departmental routine or regulation." *Fair v. State, supra*, 627 N.E.2d at 433. Depending upon state law, the police may be empowered to impound an automobile for traffic or parking violations (*South Dakota v. Opperman, supra*, 428 U.S. at 365-66, 375); incident to the arrest of the driver (*Colorado v. Bertine, supra*, 479 U.S. at 368 & n.1); and in connection with routine highway management duties, such as the removal of a disabled vehicle that was "a nuisance along the highway" (*Cady v. Dombrowski, supra*, 413 U.S. at 443). But the Fourth Amendment regulates the permissible duration of the impound. *Brewster v. Beck*, 859 F.3d 1194 (9th Cir. 2017) (although police could lawfully impound a vehicle on the ground that its owner's driving license had been suspended, the protraction of the impound period under a state statute providing that a "vehicle so impounded shall be impounded for 30 days" (*id.* at 1195) violated the Fourth Amendment: "The exigency that justified the seizure vanished once the vehicle arrived in impound and Brewster showed up with proof of ownership and a valid driver's license." ¶ "A seizure is justified under the Fourth Amendment only to the extent that the government's justification holds force. Thereafter, the government must cease the seizure or secure a new justification. Appellees have provided no justification here." *Id.* at 1196-97.). *Compare Sandoval v. County of Sonoma*, 912 F.3d 509 (9th Cir. 2018) (holding that a California statute authorizing warrantless impounding of a vehicle operated by a driver without a valid state operator's license cannot, consistently with the Fourth Amendment, be applied so as to justify the seizure or retention of a vehicle if the driver provides another person, who has such a license, to take over the driving), *and Commonwealth v. Goncalves-Mendez*, 484 Mass. 80, 138 N.E.3d 1038 (2020) (police violated the Fourth Amendment when they impounded and later searched a vehicle driven by the defendant who was validly stopped for a traffic violation and arrested on an outstanding warrant: a passenger in the car was a licensed driver; therefore the police were required to offer the defendant the alternative of having the passenger take the vehicle to a safe location of the defendant's choice), *with United States v. Trujillo*, 993 F.3d 859, 864 (10th Cir. 2021) ("The search of Defendant's vehicle was justified on two separate community caretaking grounds. First, impoundment of the vehicle was proper . . . . When an unoccupied vehicle would impede traffic and the registered owner cannot readily arrange for someone to drive it away, law-enforcement officers may impound the vehicle. Second, officers may take reasonable steps to protect the public by removing firearms (and searching for additional firearms) from unattended vehicles under their control in areas accessible to the public."), *and United States v. Anderson*, 56 F.4th 748 (9th Cir. 2022) (applying the caretaking-function rationale to sustain the impounding and inventorying of a truck illegally parked in the driveway of a private residence whose owner told sheriff's deputies that he wanted the truck removed; the driver had no valid driver's license, had no passengers, was not from the area, and had a record as a career criminal), *and United States v. Treisman*, 71 F.4th 225 (4th Cir. 2023) (applying the community-caretaking-function rationale to sustain the impounding and inventorying of a van that was parked overnight in a bank parking lot: the bank manager had phoned the police and the responding officers observed through the passenger-side window an assault rifle, a handgun box, an ammunition box, a container of pills and a suitcase; possession of these items was not illegal but the officers testified – credibly, the district court found – that (1) it would be unsafe to leave a van containing weapons unattended, and (2) the officers feared that someone might be living in the van and might be in heat distress in the rear area).

(iv) The search may not intrude into repositories of electronic information akin to those protected by the rule of *Riley v. California*, 573 U.S. 373 (2014) (discussed in § 25.8.2 *supra*). *See State v. Worsham*, 227 So.3d 602, 603 (Fla. App. 2017) ("Without a warrant, the police downloaded data from the 'event data recorder' or 'black box' located in Worsham's impounded vehicle. We affirm [the granting of Worsham's suppression motion], concluding there is a reasonable expectation of privacy in the information retained by an event data recorder and downloading that information without a warrant from an impounded car in the absence of exigent circumstances violated the Fourth Amendment.").

In approving an inventory search in *South Dakota v. Opperman, supra*, the Court emphasized that the car's owner was "not present to make other arrangements for the safekeeping of his belongings" (428 U.S. at 375). In its subsequent decision in *Colorado v. Bertine,* the Court held that the Fourth Amendment does not require the police to forgo an inventory search in favor of the "'less intrusive'" procedure of offering a driver "the opportunity to make other arrangements for the safekeeping of his property" (479 U.S. at 373). Arguably, *Bertine* means only that the police need not opt for "'less intrusive'" procedures in deciding whether to conduct an inventory search incident to impoundment, whereas *Opperman* implies that the police do have to consider less intrusive alternatives in determining whether it is necessary to impound the car in the first place. The *Bertine* opinion recognizes that impoundments must be based on "standardized criteria, related to the feasibility and appropriateness of parking and locking [the] . . . vehicle rather than impounding it" (479 U.S. at 376), but because the only challenge made to the impoundment in *Bertine* was a claim that the applicable police regulation gave too much discretion to individual officers (*see id.* at 375-76), the Court there did not elaborate this parking-and-locking passage or consider what other constitutional requirements, if any, govern impoundments as a distinct species of Fourth

Amendment "seizures" of automobiles. Some state courts have found impoundments to be unreasonable and violative of the Fourth Amendment when the sole purpose of the impoundment was safekeeping of the automobile while the driver was in custody and that goal could have been achieved by the less intrusive measures of turning the car over to an unarrested passenger (*Virgil v. Superior Court,* 268 Cal. App. 2d 127, 73 Cal. Rptr. 793 (1968)), or leaving the car parked in a legal parking space if this would not be unduly time-consuming for the police and would not expose the car to undue risk of theft or vandalism (*State v. Slockbower,* 79 N.J. 1, 397 A.2d 1050 (1979); *State v. Simpson,* 95 Wash. 2d 170, 662 P.2d 1199 (1980)).

If the police have the authority to impound an automobile and to conduct an inventory search of it, they can make the search at the scene, at the police station, or at other locations. *Colorado v. Bertine, supra,* 479 U.S. at 373 (inventory search was not rendered unreasonable simply because the vehicle "was towed to a secure, lighted facility"). "[T]he security of the storage facility does not completely eliminate the need for inventorying; the police may still wish to protect themselves or the owners of the lot against false claims." *Id.*

The state courts have been active in developing independent state constitutional restrictions upon inventory searches. *See, e.g., State v. Daniel,* 589 P.2d 408, 417 (Alaska 1979) (police cannot open "closed, locked or sealed luggage, containers, or packages contained within a vehicle" during an inventory search); *State v. Opperman,* 247 N.W.2d 673, 675 (S.D. 1976) ("noninvestigative police inventory searches of automobiles without a warrant must be restricted to safeguarding those articles which are within plain view of the officer's vision"). This is an area in which defense counsel is particularly advised to follow the suggestion of § 17.11 *supra* and invoke state-law principles as alternative grounds for challenging searches and seizures.

(B) Vehicles may also be searched without a warrant or cause if an authorized party consents to the search (*e.g., Florida v. Jimeno,* 500 U.S. 248 (1991); *State v. Akuba,* 2004 S.D. 94, 686 N.W.2d 406 (S.D. 2004)) – including a party other than the defendant who is contesting the search (*e.g., United States v. Dewilfond,* 54 F.4th 578 (8th Cir. 2022) (upholding the monitoring of a GPS device placed on a car belonging to a government informer who consented to its installation before lending it to the defendant for a drug buy); *People v. Mendoza,* 234 Ill. App. 3d 826, 599 N.E.2d 1375, 175 Ill. Dec. 361 (1992)) – provided that the search does not exceed the scope of the consent (*see, e.g., United States v. Neely,* 564 F.3d 346 (4th Cir. 2009) (a driver's consent to search of his car's trunk did not authorize searching the back passenger area); *United States v. Cotton,* 722 F.3d 271 (5th Cir. 2013) (a driver's consent to search his luggage did not authorize searching areas of the car that could not contain luggage)).

25.26. *Searches of Automobiles Incident to the Arrest of the Driver or Occupants*

Automobiles may be subjected to a warrantless search of limited scope incidental to the valid arrest of their drivers or occupants, under the doctrine of "search incident to arrest" (see § 25.8 *supra*), as modified by the Supreme Court in *Arizona v. Gant,* 556 U.S. 332 (2009), to account for certain "circumstances unique to the vehicle context" (*id.* at 343). Such searches may be made without a warrant only at the immediate time and place of the arrest. *See Preston v. United States,* 376 U.S. 364 (1964); *Dyke v. Taylor Implement Mfg. Co.,* 391 U.S. 216 (1968); *Chambers v. Maroney* 399 U.S. 42, 47 (1970); *Cardwell v. Lewis,* 417 U.S. 583, 591-92 n.7

(1974); *id.* at 599 n.4 (Stewart, J., dissenting); *United States v. Chadwick,* 433 U.S. 1, 14-15 (1977). This "search incident to arrest" rule applies not only in "situations where the officer makes contact with the occupant [of a vehicle] while the occupant is inside the vehicle" but also "when the officer first makes contact with the arrestee after the latter has stepped out of his vehicle" (*Thornton v. United States*, 541 U.S. 615, 617 (2004)). In accordance with the search-incident-to-arrest rule that applies to all situations including the automobile context, the search may "include 'the arrestee's person and the area "within his immediate control" – construing that phrase to mean the area from within which he might gain possession of a weapon or destructible evidence'" (*Arizona v. Gant, supra,* 556 U.S. at 339; *see also id.* at 343 (narrowing *New York v. Belton,* 453 U.S. 454 (1981), to clarify that the customary search-incident-to-arrest rule "authorizes police to search a vehicle incident to a recent occupant's arrest only when the arrestee is unsecured and within reaching distance of the passenger compartment at the time of the search")). *See People v. Lopez*, 8 Cal. 5th 353, 453 P.3d 150, 255 Cal. Rptr. 3d 526 (2019), summarized in § 25.8.2 *supra.* In *Gant*, the Court responded to "circumstances unique to the vehicle context" by holding that police officers also may search a vehicle incident to the arrest of a "recent occupant" "when it is 'reasonable to believe evidence relevant to the crime of arrest might be found in the vehicle'" (*id.*). *See also id.* at 343-44 (explaining that "[i]n many cases, as when a recent occupant is arrested for a traffic violation, there will be no reasonable basis to believe the vehicle contains relevant evidence," "[b]ut in others, including *Belton* and *Thornton*, the offense of arrest will supply a basis for searching the passenger compartment of an arrestee's vehicle and any containers therein"; the Court applies its new rule to hold a vehicle search unlawful because "Gant clearly was not within reaching distance of his car at the time of the search" and thus the search could not be justified under the customary search-incident-to-arrest rule, and "Gant was arrested for driving with a suspended license – an offense for which police could not expect to find evidence in the passenger compartment of Gant's car"). *See also State v. Noel*, 236 W. Va. 335, 779 S.E.2d 877 (2015). *Compare State v. Snapp*, 174 Wash. 2d 177, 181-82, 275 P.3d 289, 291 (2012) (construing the state constitution to reject that portion of the *Gant* rule that allows a search of a vehicle incident to the arrest of a recent occupant when "it is reasonable to believe evidence relevant to the crime of arrest might be found in the vehicle").

When an automobile is stopped to ticket the driver for a traffic violation, a warrantless "search of the passenger compartment of [the] . . . automobile, limited to those areas in which a weapon may be placed or hidden, is permissible if the police officer possesses a reasonable belief . . . that the suspect [driver or occupant] is dangerous and the suspect may gain immediate control of weapons [from the vehicle]" (*Michigan v. Long,* 463 U.S. 1032, 1049 (1983)). Unlike a search incident to arrest, which is authorized by the mere fact of a valid arrest, this latter sort of weapons search requires *both* a valid stop *and* reasonable grounds to believe that the driver or occupant is dangerous and may grab a weapon from the car to use against the officers. *Id.* at 1046-53 & nn.14, 16. *See, e.g., United States v. Hussain*, 835 F.3d 307, 314-17 (2d Cir. 2016).

So far as the Fourth Amendment is concerned, an officer who sees a driver violate the traffic laws may choose either to make an arrest and thereby acquire the full power of search incident to arrest or to issue a ticket or other form of summons and acquire only the relatively limited search power described in *Long. See Virginia v. Moore*, 553 U.S. 164, 176-77 (2008); *Knowles v. Iowa*, 525 U.S. 113, 114, 118-19 (1998); *United States v. Robinson,* 414 U.S. 218 (1973); *Gustafson v. Florida,* 414 U.S. 260 (1973). Even if state law categorizes the traffic infraction as one that must be handled by a ticket or other form of summons rather than a full-scale arrest, an arrest which thus violates state law does not give rise to a Fourth Amendment basis for suppressing evidence unless either the arrest or the search incident to that arrest violated the Fourth Amendment rules summarized in §§ 25.7.2-25.8.4 *supra. See Virginia v. Moore*, *supra*, 553 U.S. at 167, 171, 177-78 (even though police officers' arrest of Moore for driving on a suspended license violated Virginia state law, which restricted the officers to "issu[ing] Moore a summons instead of arresting him," the arrest satisfied the applicable Fourth Amendment standard of "probable cause to believe a person committed . . . [a] crime in [the officer's] presence," and accordingly the contraband obtained by the police in a valid search incident to arrest was not suppressible under the Fourth Amendment). Suppression in such cases may be available, however, on state constitutional grounds. *See, e.g., Commonwealth v. Hernandez*, 456 Mass. 528, 531-32, 924 N.E.2d 709, 711-12 (2010); and see § 17.11 *supra*.

25.27. "Terry *Stops" of Automobiles and Attendant Searches*

"The law is settled that in Fourth Amendment terms a . . . stop [of a moving vehicle] entails a seizure of the driver [and any passengers in the vehicle] 'even though the purpose of the stop is limited and the resulting detention quite brief.'" *Brendlin v. California*, 551 U.S. 249, 255 (2007). *See also Arizona v. Johnson*, 555 U.S. 323, 327 (2009). *Cf. United States v. Delaney*, 955 F.3d 1077, 1080, 1083, 1085 (D.C. Cir. 2020) ("a seizure occurred when the officers pulled into the parking lot, [and] partially blocked Delaney's vehicle" – "stopp[ing] their [police] cruiser near the parking lot's entrance, 'more than 3 feet away from the nose of the [defendant's] Jeep,'" and, "[a]lthough 'the marked police car did not completely block the Jeep from exiting the parking lot, . . . it would have taken some maneuvering, a number of turns for the Jeep to get out of the parking lot'" – "and [the police also] activated their take-down light": "'officers need not totally restrict a citizen's freedom of movement in order to convey the message that walking away is not an option'"); *People v. Suttles*, 171 A.D.3d 1454, 1455, 98 N.Y.S.3d 682, 683 (N.Y. App. Div., 4th Dep't 2019) ("police officers effectively seized the [parked] vehicle" in which the defendant was seated in the passenger seat "when their two patrol cars entered the parking lot in such a manner as to prevent the vehicle from being driven away"). By analogy to the *Terry* stop doctrine (§ 25.9 *supra*), "law enforcement agents may briefly stop a moving automobile to investigate a reasonable suspicion that its occupants are involved in criminal activity" (*United States v. Hensley*, 469 U.S. 221, 226 (1985)). *See, e.g., Kansas v. Glover*, 140 S. Ct. 1183 (2020); *United States v. Sharpe*, 470 U.S. 675 (1985); *Delaware v. Prouse*, 440 U.S. 648 (1979) (dictum). In limited circumstances, the police can also conduct a *Terry* stop of an automobile "to investigate past criminal activity" (*United States v. Hensley, supra*, 469 U.S. at 228). See § 25.9 *supra*. Neither sort of investigative stop may be made in the absence of "reasonable suspicion" (*Brendlin v. California, supra*, 551 U.S. at 254 n.2, 255-56). *See also United States v. Feliciana*, 974 F.3d 519 (4th Cir. 2020), summarized in § 25.9 *supra*; *United States v. Mosley*, 454 F.3d 249 (3d Cir. 2006). The standard of "reasonable suspicion" for an automobile stop is the same as that for a pedestrian stop, discussed in § 25.9 *supra. See, e.g., United States v. Uribe*, 709 F.3d 646, 649-50 (7th Cir. 2013); *United States v. Cohen*, 481 F.3d 896 (6th Cir. 2007); *State v. Teamer*, 151 So.3d 421, 427-30 (Fla. 2014). *And see Kansas v. Glover, supra*, holding that standard satisfied when a police officer ran a license plate check on a moving vehicle and learned that the vehicle was registered to an individual whose driver's license had been revoked. "The fact that the registered owner of a vehicle is not always the driver of the vehicle does not negate the reasonableness of . . . [the officer's] inference. Such is the case with all reasonable inferences. The reasonable suspicion inquiry "falls considerably short" of 51% accuracy, . . . for, as we have explained, '[t]o be reasonable is not to be perfect . . .'." 140 S. Ct. at 1188. However, "the presence of additional facts might dispel reasonable suspicion . . . . For example, if an officer knows that the registered owner of the vehicle is in his mid-sixties but observes that the driver is in her mid-twenties, then the totality of the circumstances would not 'raise a suspicion that the particular individual being stopped is engaged in wrongdoing.'" (*id.* at 1191). *Compare United States v. Forjan*, 66 F.4th 739, 746-47 (8th Cir. 2023) (considered dictum) ("[T]he district court found . . . that Deputy Hook was mistaken in his belief that Forjan's license plate sticker revealed he had an expired registration. However, after finding the relevant Missouri statutes ambiguous and Deputy Hook's testimony regarding his mistaken belief credible, the district court determined that Deputy Hook's mistake was objectively reasonable. We disagree. . . . Taken together, Missouri statutes and regulations contain no ambiguity: a registration is valid through the month and year displayed on the tag of the vehicle's license plate. Thus, a license plate bearing a December 2016 tag means that the vehicle's registration is not expired until the first day of January 2017. ¶ The district court noted that its decision that Deputy Hook's mistake was reasonable was based on Deputy Hook's credibility. . . . But '[t]he Fourth Amendment tolerates only reasonable mistakes, and those mistakes – whether of fact or of law – must be objectively reasonable. We do not examine the subjective understanding of the particular officer involved.' Heien v. North Carolina, 574 U.S. 54, 66 (2014). Regardless of Deputy Hook's understanding, it was not objectively reasonable for an officer in his position to believe that a tag bearing the date December 2016 was expired on December 20, 2016. See id. at 67. ('[A]n officer can gain no Fourth Amendment advantage through a sloppy study of the laws he is duty bound to enforce.'). The license plate tag bearing that registration date thus did not provide reasonable suspicion to initiate the traffic stop.").

Whether an unmoving vehicle has been "stopped" for purposes of *Terry*'s reasonable-suspicion requirement is a vexed issue. As cases like *Delaney* and *Sutttles*, cited in the preceding paragraph, illustrate, a "stop" is ordinarily found where the vehicle was motionless at the time when the police arrived on the scene if they position themselves or a police car so as to restrict the vehicle's movement. *Accord, United States v. Jones*, 562 F.3d 768 (6th Cir. 2009); *United States v. Gross*, 662 F.3d 393 (6th Cir. 2011); *United States v. Cloud*, 994 F.3d 233 (4th Cir. 2021) (considered dictum). The Pennsylvania and California Supreme Courts have found a "stop" when a police car pulls up beside or behind a parked vehicle and activates its emergency lights. *Commonwealth v. Livingstone*, 644 Pa. 27, 174 A.3d 609 (2017); *People v. Brown*, 61 Cal. 4th 968, 353 P.3d 305, 190 Cal. Rptr. 3d 583 (2015) (considered dictum); *accord, In re Edgerrin J.*, 57 Cal. App. 5th 752, 271 Cal. Rptr. 3d 610 (2020) (alternative ground). The Fourth Circuit has analyzed as a vehicle "stop" the actions of an officer who initially approached a parked car for a "welfare check" (to determine whether the driver needed assistance) and then, observing a holstered handgun on the front seat, detained the driver for about an hour. *Hicks v. Ferreyra*, 64 F.4th 156, 170 (4th Cir. 2023), summarized in § 25.7.4 *supra. See also United States v. Campbell*, 549 F.3d 364 (6th Cir. 2008) (apparently assuming that a "stop" occurred when an officer in a patrol car, seeing a vehicle parked on a dark, secluded, privately owned railway access road, activated the patrol car's flasher, spot lights and siren). The Eighth Circuit has found no "stop" in a case factually indistinguishable from the California and Pennsylvania Supreme Court cases, *United States v. Cook*, 842 F.3d 597 (8th Cir. 2016); the Tenth Circuit has found no "stop" when a police car pulls up in front of a parked vehicle – but without blocking the vehicle's path – and activates its takedown lights (as distinguished from its emergency flasher), *United States v. Tafuna*, 5 F.4th 1197 (10th Cir. 2021); and the First Circuit has found no "stop" when a police car pulls up at the scene of a vehicle which has crashed into a snow bank. *United States v. Howard*, 66 F.4th 33 (1st Cir. 2023). *See also the fractured panel decision in United States v. Robertson*, 864 F.3d 1118 (10th Cir. 2017).

"[A]s in the case of a pedestrian reasonably suspected of criminal activity," the *Terry* frisk doctrine permits "a patdown of the driver or a passenger [of a lawfully stopped vehicle] during a . . . [vehicle] stop" if the police have "reasonable suspicion that the person subjected to the frisk is armed and dangerous" (*Arizona v. Johnson, supra*, 555 U.S. at 327). Also by analogy to *Terry*, police who validly stop a vehicle may search some areas of it for weapons if the officers possess a reasonable belief, based on specific and articulable facts, that a detained suspect is dangerous and that s/he can gain immediate control of weapons from the vehicle. *Michigan v. Long*, 463 U.S. 1032, 1049 (1983). The search must, however, be "limited to those areas [of the vehicle] in which a weapon may be placed or hidden" (*id.*). In the absence of reasonable grounds to believe that the vehicle or its occupants conceal a weapon, any police intrusion into the vehicle constitutes an unconstitutional search. *United States v. Ngumezi*, 980 F.3d 1285, 1288, 1289 (9th Cir. 2020) ("We . . . consider whether police officers who have reasonable suspicion sufficient to justify a traffic stop – but who lack probable cause or any other particularized justification, such as a reasonable belief that the driver poses a danger – may open the door to a vehicle and lean inside. We conclude they may not."; "Although the intrusion here may have been modest, the Supreme Court has never suggested that the magnitude of a physical intrusion is relevant to the Fourth Amendment analysis. . . . [W]e apply a bright-line rule that opening a door and entering the interior space of a vehicle constitutes a Fourth Amendment search.").

25.28. *Traffic Stops and Attendant Searches*

Automobiles may, of course, be stopped for traffic violations (*see United States v. Robinson*, 414 U.S. 218 (1973); *Whren v. United States*, 517 U.S. 806 (1996)) if – but only if – the police have "reasonable suspicion" to justify the traffic stop. *See Arizona v. Johnson*, 555 U.S. 323, 327 (2009); *Brendlin v. California*, 551 U.S. 249, 254 n.2, 255-56 (2007); *Heien v. North Carolina*, 574 U.S. 54, 60 (2014). (*Heien* also holds that a police officer's "*objectively* reasonable" mistake of law – a plausible interpretation of an ambiguous traffic-code provision which is subsequently construed by a state appellate court in a manner contrary to the officer's "reasonably, even if mistakenly" advised reading of it (*id.* at 59) – does not invalidate the "reasonable suspicion" required for a traffic-violation stop if the officer's visual observations of the vehicle bring it, factually, within his mistaken reading. See § 25.3 concluding paragraph *supra.*). *See also Melendres v. Arpaio*, 695 F.3d 990 (9th Cir. 2012), *permanent injunctions affirmed in relevant part in Melendres v. Arpaio*, 784 F.3d 1254 (9th Cir. 2015) *and in Melendres v. Maricopa County*, 897 F.3d 1217 (9th Cir. 2018) (racial profiling of Hispanics for automobile stops by county police officers in a border State violated the Fourth Amendment: "[B]ecause mere unauthorized presence [of an alien in the United States] is not a criminal matter, suspicion of unauthorized presence alone does not give rise to an inference that criminal activity is 'afoot.'" 695 F.3d at 1001. "[U]nlike illegal entry, mere unauthorized presence . . . is not a crime." 695 F.3d at 1000. "Absent suspicion that a 'suspect is engaged in, or is about to engage in, criminal activity,' law enforcement may not stop or detain an individual." *Id.*); *United States v. Paniagua-Garcia*, 813 F.3d 1013, 1014 (7th Cir. 2016) ("The government failed to establish that the officer [who stopped the defendant's car] had probable cause or a reasonable suspicion that Paniagua was violating the no-texting [while driving] law. The officer hadn't seen any texting; what he had seen was consistent with any one of a number of lawful uses of cellphones."); *Campbell v. Mack*, 777 Fed. Appx. 122, 131 (6th Cir. 2019) (allegations that an officer stopped a motorist for a license plate violation although a temporary plate was taped to the back window of his vehicle in a manner that was clearly visible stated a claim for violation of the Fourth Amendment: "We apply different standards for ascertaining whether a traffic stop comports with the Constitution depending on the nature of the alleged infraction. . . . Generally, an officer needs probable cause to stop a vehicle for a civil infraction and only reasonable suspicion to stop a vehicle for a criminal violation."); *United States v. Murphy*, 703 F.3d 182, 188 (2d Cir. 2012) (the trial court did not err in rejecting, as incredible, a police officer's testimony at a suppression hearing that he observed the defendant's car exit the interstate without signaling and thus in violation of traffic laws); *State v. Kooima*, 833 N.W.2d 202, 210 (Iowa 2013) ("Cases decided by us and other courts require a personal observation of erratic driving, other facts to substantiate the allegation the driver is intoxicated, or details not available to the general public as to the defendant's future actions in order to spawn a reasonable inference . . . [that an anonymous] tipster had the necessary personal knowledge that a person was driving while intoxicated and the stop comports with the requirements of the Fourth Amendment. To hold otherwise would cause legitimate concern because such tips would let the police stop persons on anonymous tips that might have been called in for vindictive or harassment purposes or based solely on a hunch or rumor."); *People v. Mott*, 389 Ill. App. 3d 539, 906 N.E.2d 159, 329 Ill. Dec. 314 (2009) (finding that an officer lacked the reasonable suspicion necessary to stop a driver for material obstruction of her front windshield); *Commonwealth v. Long*, 485 Mass. 711, 713, 152 N.E.3d 725, 731 (2020) (construing the state constitution's Equal Protection Clause to establish a standard for suppressing the fruits of a "racially motivated traffic stop[ ]": if the defendant's suppression motion "point[s] to specific facts" supporting "a reasonable inference that the officer's decision to initiate the stop was motivated by race or another protected class," then "the defendant is entitled to a hearing at which the Commonwealth would have the burden of rebutting the inference," and "[a]bsent a successful rebuttal, any evidence derived from the stop would be suppressed"); *People v. Hinshaw*, 35 N.Y.3d 427, 432-34, 156 N.E.3d 812, 815-17, 132 N.Y.S.3d 90, 93-95 (2020) (holding that New York law requires that "an officer . . . have probable cause to stop a vehicle for a traffic infraction," and explaining that "New York . . . provides greater protections than does federal law for traffic infraction vehicle stops" to ensure that "'[d]iscriminatory law enforcement has no place in our law,'" and that "when a traffic violation, not a crime, is the predicate of an officer's forcible stop of a motorist, greater scrutiny is required to prevent 'a policemen's badge . . . [from] be[ing] considered a license to oppress'").

An officer making a traffic-violation stop may order the driver out of the car, whether the officer proposes to arrest the driver or merely to give the driver a summons. *Pennsylvania v. Mimms,* 434 U.S. 106 (1977) (per curiam). In the former case, the officer may conduct a complete search of the driver's person and may also search the passenger compartment of the car incident to the driver's arrest, to the extent indicated in § 25.26 *supra*; in the latter, the officer may frisk the driver and search the passenger compartment of the car for weapons if, but only if, the requisite conditions for a *Terry* frisk (see §§ 25.10, 25.26 *supra*) are met. If the officer invokes the *Mimms* doctrine to order the driver out of the car, the officer can detain the driver outside the car for the period necessary to conduct an inquiry and inspect the Vehicle Identification Number. *New York v. Class,* 475 U.S. 106, 115-16 (1986); *Arizona v. Johnson, supra,* 555 U.S. at 333; see § 25.23 *supra. See also Rodriguez v. United States,* 575 U.S. 348, 355 (2015) (traffic stops often "include[ ] 'ordinary inquiries incident to [the traffic] stop,'" which "[t]ypically . . . involve checking the driver's license, determining whether there are outstanding warrants against the driver, and inspecting the automobile's registration and proof of insurance"; an officer may conduct these checks but "may not do so in a way that prolongs the stop, absent the reasonable suspicion ordinarily demanded to justify detaining an individual."). *Compare Sharp v. United States,* 132 A.3d 161, 169-70 (D.C. 2016) (when "the encounter does not begin with a stop for a traffic violation" – as in this case of a defendant who was seated behind the wheel of a lawfully parked car – an officer cannot ask the driver to exit the vehicle in a manner that would appear to a reasonable person to foreclose "a genuine choice to decline the request and stay in the car," absent "reasonable articulable suspicion to justify the seizure"); *State v. Keaton,* 222 N.J. 438, 442, 448, 450, 119 A.3d 906, 908, 912, 913 (2015) (a police officer does not have "a legal right to enter an overturned car in order to obtain registration and insurance information for the vehicle, without first requesting permission, or allowing defendant an opportunity to retrieve the documents himself"; although a police officer who conducts a lawful traffic stop "may search the car for evidence of ownership" "[i]f the vehicle's operator is unable to produce proof of registration," such a "warrantless search of a vehicle is only permissible after the driver has been provided the opportunity to produce his credentials and is either unable or unwilling to do so."). Regarding DWI sobriety testing, see § 25.14 subdivision (d) *supra.*

The *Mimms* doctrine also allows "an officer making a traffic stop . . . [to] order passengers to get out of the car pending completion of the stop" (*Maryland v. Wilson,* 519 U.S. 408, 415 (1997)). *See Arizona v. Johnson, supra,* 555 U.S. at 333 ("The temporary seizure of driver and passengers ordinarily continues, and remains reasonable, for the duration of the stop."); *but see Maryland v. Wilson, supra,* 519 U.S. at 415 n.3 (expressly reserving the question whether "an officer may forcibly detain a passenger for the entire duration of the stop"); *and cf. United States v. Hensley,* 469 U.S. 221, 235-36 (1985); *People v. Porter,* 136 A.D.3d 1344, 1345, 24 N.Y.S.3d 470, 472 (N.Y. App. Div., 4th Dep't 2016) (the police unlawfully detained the passenger of a lawfully stopped car, who had "asked whether he could leave the scene," by telling him that "he must remain present with them until the inventory search [of the arrested driver's car] was complete"; "the justification for th[e] stop [of the car and for detaining the passenger pursuant to that stop] ended once the driver had been arrested for th[e] [traffic] offense."). The officer also can conduct a protective "patdown of . . . a passenger during a [lawful] traffic stop" under the customary *Terry* frisk standard if the officer has a "reasonable suspicion that the person subjected to the frisk is armed and dangerous" (*Arizona v. Johnson, supra,* 555 U.S. at 327, 333; see § 25.10 *supra*). Search activity exceeding the scope of a *Terry* frisk is not permitted; and when an officer, during a traffic stop, requests and receives permission from a passenger to conduct a search of his or her possessions for evidence unrelated to the traffic violation that justified the stop, the request has been held impermissible, the consent tainted, and the ensuing search and seizure unconstitutional. *State v. Smith,* 286 Kan. 402, 184

P.3d 890 (2008). *See also Harris v. Klare*, 902 F.3d 630 (6th Cir. 2018), summarized in § 25.39 subdivision (d) *infra*.

Because "[t]emporary detention of individuals during the stop of an automobile by the police, even if only for a brief period and for a limited purpose, constitutes a [Fourth Amendment] 'seizure' of 'persons'" (*Whren v. United States, supra*, 517 U.S. at 809), and because "a police stop exceeding the time needed to handle the matter for which the stop was made violates the Constitution's shield against unreasonable seizures," a "seizure justified only by a police-observed traffic violation . . . 'become[s] unlawful if it is prolonged beyond the time reasonably required to complete th[e] mission' of issuing a ticket for the violation" (*Rodriguez v. United States, supra*, 575 U.S. at 350-51). "Authority for the seizure . . . ends when tasks tied to the traffic infraction are – or reasonably should have been – completed." *Id.* at 349. "On-scene investigation into other crimes . . . detours [*that's a verb*] from that mission," as do "safety precautions taken in order to facilitate such detours" (*id.* at 356). Accordingly, the Court held in *Rodriguez* that a dog sniff of a car stopped for a traffic infraction, which resulted in the dog's alerting to the presence of drugs and an ensuing search of the car and seizure of drugs violated the Fourth Amendment because it was "conducted after completion of . . . [the] traffic stop" and thus "'prolonged [the traffic stop] beyond the time reasonably required to complete th[e] mission' of issuing a ticket for the violation" (*id.* at 350-51). *See also United States v. Bowman*, 884 F.3d 200 (4th Cir. 2018); *Millan-Hernandez v. Barr*, 965 F.3d 140, 149 (2d Cir. 2020) (per curiam) (the immigration judge improperly denied Millan-Hernandez an evidentiary hearing to establish a *prima facie* case for suppression of the fruits of a traffic stop on the ground that "her prolonged detention [during a traffic stop of a vehicle in which she was a passenger] was unlawful and that the reason for the prolongation was her race or ethnicity": "the officer's words ('You're not legal, right?') and his request for the passenger's 'papers,' . . . coupled with the absence of probable cause to suspect that Millan-Hernandez (or, for that matter, the driver) had committed any crime, . . . strongly suggest that a racial or ethnic impetus could have been the reason for the detention").

If the police request and receive valid consent from a driver before the expiration of the allowable period for a stop, they may search the driver's person and the vehicle to the extent – but only to the extent – authorized by that consent. *See Commonwealth v. Ortiz*, 478 Mass. 820, 820, 90 N.E.3d 735, 736-37 (2018), summarized in § 25.18 *supra*. For additional restrictions upon the power of the police to obtain consent in this setting, *see State v. Smith, supra; Harris v. Klare*, summarized in § 25.39 subdivision (d) *infra; State v. Shaw*, 237 N.J. 588, 619, 207 A.3d 229, 246 (2019) ("New Jersey's Constitution also provides greater protections than the federal constitution when it comes to consent searches. . . . Law enforcement must have a 'reasonable and articulable suspicion to believe that an errant motorist or passenger has engaged in, or is about to engage in, criminal activity,' before officers may ask for consent to search a vehicle. . . . This prophylactic rule protects the public from the unjustified extension of motor vehicle stops and from fishing expeditions unrelated to the reason for the initial stop."). *See also Demarest v. City of Vallejo, California*, 44 F.4th 1209 (9th Cir. 2022) (holding that the City's systematic addition of driver's license examinations at a sobriety checkpoint is permissible).

Concerning breath and blood tests of drivers of vehicles stopped and suspected of DWI, see §§ 25.14, 25.18.1 *supra*.

25.29. *License Checks; Stops of Automobiles at Roadblocks and Checkpoints*

In *Delaware v. Prouse,* 440 U.S. 648 (1979), the Court condemned the previously widespread practice of "spot checks" of vehicles selected by roving patrols. The Court in *Prouse* held that the Fourth Amendment does not permit the flagging down of selected automobiles for the purpose of "check[ing] [the] . . . driver's license and the registration of the automobile" unless "there is at least articulable and reasonable suspicion that a motorist is unlicensed or that an automobile is not registered" (440 U.S. at 663).

The Court in *Prouse* suggested, however, that it might sustain other "methods for spot checks that involve less intrusion or that do not involve the unconstrained exercise of discretion" by police officers (*id.*). It included "[q]uestioning of all oncoming traffic at roadblock-type stops [as] . . . one possible [constitutional] alternative" (*id.*). In the subsequent case of *Michigan Department of State Police v. Sitz,* 496 U.S. 444 (1990), the Court upheld the constitutionality of "a State's use of highway sobriety checkpoints" (*id.* at 447), where motorists passing through selected sites were "briefly stopped" (*id.* at 455), "briefly examined for signs of intoxication" (*id.* at 447), and asked some questions (*id.*), in accordance with established "guidelines setting forth procedures governing checkpoint operations [and] . . . site selection" (*id.*). "The average delay for each vehicle was approximately 25 seconds." *Id.* at 448. The Court acknowledged that "a Fourth Amendment 'seizure' occurs when a vehicle is stopped at a checkpoint" (*id.* at 450). *Accord, City of Indianapolis v. Edmond,* 531 U.S. 32, 40 (2000) ("It is well established that a vehicle stop at a highway checkpoint effectuates a seizure within the meaning of the Fourth Amendment."). The *Sitz* Court concluded, however, that "the balance of the State's interest in preventing drunken driving, the extent to which this system can reasonably be said to advance that interest, and the degree of intrusion upon individual motorists who are briefly stopped" (496 U.S. at 455) provided the requisite constitutional justification for the use of the sobriety checkpoint procedure. The Court emphasized that the "'objective' intrusion [upon seized motorists], measured by the duration of the seizure and the intensity of the investigation, [w]as minimal" (*id.* at 452) and that the procedure did not suffer from the same "degree of 'subjective intrusion' and . . . potential for generating fear and surprise [on the part of seized motorists]" (*id.*) as did the roving-patrol stops condemned in *Prouse* (*see Sitz, supra,* 496 U.S. at 452-53). The Court in *Sitz* further distinguished the sobriety checkpoint procedure from the roving-patrol stops on the grounds that the "checkpoints are selected pursuant to . . . guidelines, and uniformed police officers stop every approaching vehicle" (*id.* at 453), thereby avoiding the "'kind of standardless and unconstrained discretion [which] is the evil the Court has discerned . . . in previous cases'" (*id.* at 454 (quoting *Prouse, supra,* 440 U.S. at 661)), and the state in *Sitz* presented "empirical data" (*id.*) demonstrating that the checkpoint procedure made at least some measurable contribution to controlling "the drunken driving problem" (*id.* at 451; *see id.* at 454-55). Finally, the Court in *Sitz* took pains to make clear "what our inquiry is *not* about" (*id.* at 450). Explaining that the issue "address[ed] [was] only the initial stop of each motorist passing through a checkpoint and the associated preliminary questioning and observation by checkpoint officers[,]" the Court noted that "[d]etention of particular motorists for more extensive field sobriety testing may require satisfaction of an individualized suspicion standard" (*id.* at 450-51). The Court further cautioned that "[n]o allegations are before us of unreasonable treatment of any person after an actual detention at a particular checkpoint" (*id.* at 450).

Thereafter, in *City of Indianapolis v. Edmond, supra*, the Court struck down a "highway checkpoint program whose primary purpose . . .[was] the discovery and interdiction of illegal narcotics" (531 U.S. at 34), and in which the police stopped a predetermined number of vehicles, conducted a license and registration check, and walked around each stopped car with a narcotics-detection dog (*see id.* at 34-35). In holding this practice unconstitutional, the Court distinguished *Sitz* and also an earlier decision that had upheld the routine stopping of vehicles and the brief questioning of their occupants by immigration authorities at designated checkpoints near an international border (*United States v. Martinez-Fuerte*, 428 U.S. 543 (1976), discussed in § 25.30 *infra*). "In none of these cases," the Court explained, "did we indicate approval of a checkpoint program whose primary purpose was to detect evidence of ordinary criminal wrongdoing" (*Edmond, supra*, 531 U.S. at 38). Emphasizing that "our checkpoint cases have recognized only limited exceptions to the general rule that a seizure must be accompanied by some measure of individualized suspicion" (*id.* at 41), the Court declared that "[w]e decline to suspend the usual requirement of individualized suspicion where the police seek to employ a checkpoint primarily for the ordinary enterprise of investigating crimes" (*id.* at 44). *See also id.* at 34, 41-42, 48; *Singleton v. Commonwealth*, 364 S.W.3d 97, 104-06 (Ky. 2012) (applying *Edmond* to strike down a traffic checkpoint that was designed to catch violators of a city ordinance requiring that motor vehicles display a "city sticker" that shows residence or employment within city limits).

The Court returned to these issues in *Illinois v. Lidster*, 540 U.S. 419 (2003), rejecting a Fourth Amendment challenge to "a highway checkpoint where police stopped motorists to ask them for information about a recent hit-and-run accident" (*id.* at 421). The Court distinguished *Edmond* on the ground that that case "involved a checkpoint at which police stopped vehicles to look for evidence of drug crimes committed by occupants of those vehicles" (*id.* at 423) whereas the "primary law enforcement purpose [of the checkpoint in *Lidster*] was *not* to determine whether a vehicle's occupants were committing a crime, but to ask vehicle occupants, as members of the public, for their help in providing information about a crime in all likelihood committed by others [and] . . . [t]he police expected the information elicited to help them apprehend, not the vehicle's occupants, but other individuals" (*id.* at 425). Applying the criteria the Court had previously employed in *Sitz*, the Court upheld the checkpoint in *Lidster* because "[t]he relevant public concern was grave" in that "[p]olice were investigating a crime that had resulted in a human death . . . [a]nd the stop's objective was to help find the perpetrator of a specific and known crime, not of unknown crimes of a general sort"; "[t]he stop advanced this grave public concern to a significant degree" in that "[t]he police appropriately tailored their checkpoint stops to fit important criminal investigatory needs"; and, "[m]ost importantly, the stops interfered only minimally with liberty of the sort the Fourth Amendment seeks to protect," in that "each stop required only a brief wait in line – a very few minutes at most," "[c]ontact with the police lasted only a few seconds," "[p]olice contact consisted simply of a request for information and the distribution of a flyer," and, "[v]iewed subjectively, the contact provided little reason for anxiety or alarm" since "[t]he police stopped all vehicles systematically" and "there is no allegation here that the police acted in a discriminatory or otherwise unlawful manner while questioning motorists during stops" (*id.* at 427-28).

In addition to approving the checkpoints in *Sitz* and *Lidster* and border stops by immigration authorities in *Martinez-Fuerte*, the Court has indicated that it is likely to accept standardized checkpoint procedures in other settings if the stops are not protracted, do not involve any physical searches of the car or occupants, and are not made solely at the discretion of officers in the field. In *Texas v. Brown,* 460 U.S. 730 (1983), the Court and all parties appear to have assumed the constitutionality of a "routine driver's license checkpoint" (*see id.* at 733 (plurality opinion)). And in *Prouse,* the Court noted that its holding did not "cast doubt on the permissibility of roadside truck weigh-stations and inspection checkpoints, at which some vehicles may be subject to further detention for safety and regulatory inspection than are others" (440 U.S. at 663 n.26).

In light of the Court's opinions in these cases, the validity of various spot-check practices (for example, pollution emission tests, agricultural produce inspections, and game wardens' inspections, as well as driver's license and registration inspections) involving the brief stopping of vehicles without a reasonable suspicion that the particular vehicle stopped is being operated in violation of an applicable regulatory law appears to turn upon four considerations:

First is whether the "primary purpose [of the checkpoint program] was to detect evidence of ordinary criminal wrongdoing" (*City of Indianapolis v. Edmond, supra,* 531 U.S. at 41) by one or more of the "vehicle's occupants" (*Illinois v. Lidster, supra,* 540 U.S. at 423). Such situations are governed by "an *Edmond*-type rule of automatic unconstitutionality" (*id.* at 424). The Court stated in *dicta* in *Edmond* that an exception to this rule may apply to "emergency" situations, such as where the police set up "an appropriately tailored roadblock . . . to thwart an imminent terrorist attack or to catch a dangerous criminal who is likely to flee by way of a particular route" (*Edmond, supra,* 531 U.S. at 44). But, in the absence of such "exigencies" (*id.*), *Edmond* prohibits a checkpoint "program whose primary purpose is ultimately indistinguishable from the general interest in crime control," except when, as in *Lidster,* "[t]he stop's primary law enforcement purpose was *not* to determine whether a vehicle's occupants were committing a crime, but to ask vehicle occupants, as members of the public, for their help in providing information about a crime in all likelihood committed by others" and "[t]he police expected the information elicited to help them apprehend, not the vehicle's occupants, but other individuals" (*Lidster, supra,* 540 U.S. at 423).

Second is the extent to which some sort of spot check is necessary and will likely be effective to enforce the regulatory scheme in question. *See Illinois v. Lidster, supra,* 540 U.S. at 427; *Michigan Department of State Police v. Sitz, supra,* 496 U.S. at 451; *Delaware v. Prouse, supra,* 440 U.S. at 658-61. Counsel challenging a checkpoint stop should contend that the standard of necessity is high. In approving the use of sobriety checkpoints in *Sitz,* the Court cited statistical and anecdotal evidence of the extent of "alcohol-related death and mutilation on the Nation's roads" (496 U.S. at 451 & n.*) and observed that "[n]o one can seriously dispute the magnitude of the drunken driving problem or the States' interest in eradicating it" (*id.* at 451; *accord, id.* at 455-56 (Justice Blackmun, concurring)). Similarly, in sustaining immigration checkpoint stops in border regions (see § 25.30 *infra*), the Supreme Court has repeatedly emphasized "the enormous difficulties of patrolling a 2,000-mile open border" (*United States v. Cortez,* 449 U.S. 411, 418 (1981)), and the vital national importance of patrolling it effectively (*see, e.g., Almeida-Sanchez v. United States,* 413 U.S. 266, 273 (1973); *United States v. Brignoni-Ponce,* 422 U.S. 873, 878-79, 881 (1975); *United States v. Martinez-Fuerte, supra,* 428 U.S. at 551-57). And, in upholding a "highway checkpoint where police stopped motorists to ask them for information about a recent hit-and-run accident," the Court in *Illinois v. Lidster* explained that "[t]he relevant public concern was grave . . . [in that] [p]olice were investigating a crime that had resulted in a human death . . . [and] [t]he stop advanced this grave public concern to a significant degree" (540 U.S. at 421, 427). *See also id.* at 425 ("voluntary requests [of "members of the public in the investigation of a crime"] play a vital role in police investigatory work"). With regard to the assessment of "'the degree to which . . . [a checkpoint procedure] advances the public interest'" (*Sitz, supra*, 496 U.S. at 453), the Court has made clear that reviewing courts may not strike down a law enforcement technique that is a reasonable means of dealing with the problem simply because some "[e]xperts in police science" might view a different technique as "preferrable" [sic] (*id.*). However, a procedure may be found to violate the Fourth Amendment if the state fails to present empirical data justifying the procedure (*see Sitz, supra*, 496 U.S. at 454-55) or if the procedure falls below an as-yet unspecified threshold of effectiveness (*see Sitz, supra*, 496 U.S. at 454-55 (finding that the sobriety checkpoint procedure under review sufficiently advanced the state's interest in controlling drunk driving because it resulted in arrests of "approximately 1.6 percent of the drivers passing through the checkpoint," which compared favorably with the "0.5 percent" "ratio of illegal aliens detected to vehicles stopped" by the immigration checkpoint procedure approved in *Martinez-Fuerte*)).

Third is the extent to which the visibility and regularity of the spot-check practice are likely to reduce motorists' apprehensions of danger and the feeling that they are being singled out for official scrutiny. *See Illinois v. Lidster, supra*, 540 U.S. at 425, 427-28; *Michigan Department of State Police v. Sitz, supra*, 496 U.S. at 452-53; *Delaware v. Prouse, supra*, 440 U.S. at 657.

Fourth is the extent to which the spot-check procedures limit and control the exercise of discretion by individual officers in determining which vehicles to stop and which ones to detain for longer or shorter periods. *See Michigan Department of State Police v. Sitz, supra*, 496 U.S. at 452-53; *Delaware v. Prouse, supra*, 440 U.S. at 653-55, 661-63. This latter factor is probably the most significant, for the Supreme Court's Fourth Amendment decisions have increasingly recognized that restricting police discretion in the execution of the search-and-seizure power is the Amendment's central purpose. *See, e.g., Johnson v. United States*, 333 U.S. 10, 13-17 (1948); *McDonald v. United States*, 335 U.S. 451, 455-56 (1948); *Beck v. Ohio*, 379 U.S. 89, 97 (1964); *See v. City of Seattle*, 387 U.S. 541, 545 (1967); *United States v. United States District Court for the Eastern District of Michigan*, 407 U.S. 297, 316-17 (1972); *United States v. Martinez-Fuerte, supra*, 428 U.S. at 558-59, 566; *G.M. Leasing Corp. v. United States*, 429 U.S. 338, 357 (1977); *Marshall v. Barlow's, Inc.*, 436 U.S. 307, 323-24 (1978); *Mincey v. Arizona*, 437 U.S. 385, 394-95 (1978); *Brown v. Texas*, 443 U.S. 47, 51 (1979); *Steagald v. United States*, 451 U.S. 204, 220 (1981); *Donovan v. Dewey*, 452 U.S. 594, 599, 601, 605 (1981); *New York v. Burger*, 482 U.S. 691, 703 (1987) (dictum). As in other fields of constitutional law in which excessive discretion embodied in a statutorily or administratively prescribed procedure may void it, factual evidence of divergent and particularly of discriminatory police practices in the administration of the procedure should be admissible and persuasive on this last issue. *See, e.g., Yick Wo v. Hopkins*, 118 U.S. 356 (1886); *Niemotko v. Maryland*, 340 U.S. 268 (1951); *Shuttlesworth v. City of Birmingham*, 394 U.S. 147 (1969).

25.30. *Border Searches*

The "border search" doctrine allows customs and immigration officials to stop and search all vehicles (or persons or articles) entering the United States from abroad. "Routine searches of the persons and effects of entrants are not subject to any requirement of reasonable suspicion, probable cause, or warrant, and first-class mail may be opened without a warrant on less than probable cause . . . . Automotive travelers may be stopped at fixed checkpoints near the border without individualized suspicion even if the stop is based largely on ethnicity . . . and boats on inland waters with ready access to the sea may be hailed and boarded with no suspicion whatever." *United States v. Montoya de Hernandez*, 473 U.S. 531, 538 (1985). "This court has held that the border-search exception applies not only to entrants into the country but also to those departing." *United States v. Tenorio*, 55 F.4th 465, 468 (5th Cir. 2022); *accord, United States v. Xiang*, 67 F.4th 895, 899 (8th Cir. 2023) ("it blinks at reality to assert that CBP's seizure and search of the electronic devices Xiang was about to carry abroad was not a 'border search'"). This unfettered search power is, however, limited to the "border itself [or] . . . its functional equivalents" (*Almeida-Sanchez v. United States*, 413 U.S. 266, 272 (1973)). *See also United States v. Flores-Montano*, 541 U.S. 149, 154 (2004) ("the expectation of privacy is less at the border than it is in the interior"). And even at border points of entry, the power may be limited in the case of particularly intrusive search techniques. The federal circuits are divided as to whether the principle of *Riley v. California*, 573 U.S. 373 (2014) [discussed in § 25.8.2 *supra*], has any application at the border and therefore whether technological searches of cell phones and other digital devices by border officials must be justified by individualized reasonable suspicion of illegality or need no justification. *Compare United States v. Aigbekaen*, 943 F.3d 713 (4th Cir. 2019), *and United States v. Cano*, 934 F.3d 1002 (9th Cir. 2019), *with United States v. Touset*, 890 F.3d 1227, 1231 (11th Cir. 2018) (alternative ground); *and Alasaad v. Mayorkas*, 988 F.3d 8 (1st Cir. 2021); *cf. United States v. Williams,* 942 F.3d 1187 (10th Cir. 2019). Although "[t]he circuits are divided over whether reasonable suspicion is required for a forensic search of a cell phone at the border . . . every circuit to have addressed the issue has agreed that no individualized suspicion is required for the government to undertake a manual border search of a cell phone." *United States v. Castillo*, 70 F.4th 894, 895 (5th Cir. 2023).

Other than at the border and its functional equivalents, customs and immigrations *searches* of automobiles may not be made without a warrant or probable cause. *Almeida-Sanchez v. United States, supra*, 413 U.S. at 274-75 (condemning a warrantless "roving patrol" search without probable cause); *United States v. Ortiz,* 422 U.S. 891 (1975) (condemning a warrantless "fixed check point" search without probable cause). Roving patrols of customs or immigration agents are permitted to make brief warrantless *stops* of vehicles in regions near the border on the basis of "reasonable suspicion" that a particular vehicle contains smuggled goods or illegal aliens. *United States v. Brignoni-Ponce,* 422 U.S. 873, 880-84 (1975); *United States v. Villamonte-Marquez,* 462 U.S. 579, 587-88 (1983) (dictum) (discussing the border-search doctrines applicable to automobiles while developing a somewhat different rule for ships "located in waters offering ready access to the open sea"). These roving-patrol stops are akin to domestic *Terry* stops and are governed by similar rules. See §§ 25.4-25.6, 25.9, 25.27 *supra*. "The officer may question the driver and passengers about their citizenship and immigration status, and he may ask them to explain suspicious circumstances, but any further detention or search must be based on consent or probable cause." *United States v. Brignoni-Ponce, supra*, 422

U.S. at 881-82.

Equally limited stops of all or selected vehicles may be made routinely at fixed checkpoints in the border area, without a warrant, probable cause, or reasonable suspicion. *United States v. Martinez-Fuerte,* 428 U.S. 543 (1976). But the "claim that a particular exercise of [administrative] discretion in locating or operating a checkpoint is unreasonable is subject to post-stop judicial review" (*id.* at 559). Routine checkpoint stops, like roving-patrol stops made upon "reasonable suspicion," must be restricted to "brief questioning" and may not include either prolonged detention or search in the absence of "consent or probable cause" (*id.* at 566-67). *See also United States v. Flores-Montano, supra,* 541 U.S. at 155 n.2 (reserving "the question 'whether, and under what circumstances, a border search might be deemed "unreasonable" because of the particularly offensive manner in which it is carried out'").

The opinions in *Ortiz* and *Brignoni-Ponce* purport to reserve the question whether searches and more extensive detentions in connection with immigration stops (either by roving patrols or at fixed checkpoints) may be made without reasonable suspicion or probable cause concerning the individual vehicle stopped, under the authorization of a search warrant "issued to stop cars in a designated area on the basis of conditions in the area as a whole" (*Brignoni-Ponce, supra,* 422 U.S. at 882 n.7; *see also Ortiz, supra,* 422 U.S. at 897 n.3). This question was generated by Justice Powell's concurring opinion in *Almeida-Sanchez,* which adopts the concept of an "area" search warrant from the Supreme Court's building-code cases (*see Camara v. Municipal Court,* 387 U.S. 523 (1967); § 25.36 *infra*) and suggests that such a warrant might validate immigration searches in border areas. Because Justice Powell's concurrence was necessary to make up a 5-4 majority in *Almeida-Sanchez* and the Court has not become more sympathetic to Fourth Amendment rights since his departure, the likelihood is strong that "area" search warrants will be sustained in border-region immigration cases. *See also United States v. Martinez-Fuerte, supra,* 428 U.S. at 555, 564 n.18.

The "border search" principles described in this section are limited to *international* borders and do not apply to interstate boundary lines. *Torres v. Puerto Rico,* 442 U.S. 465, 472-73 (1979); *One 1958 Plymouth Sedan v. Pennsylvania,* 380 U.S. 693, 702 (1965) (by implication); *see also United States v. Flores-Montano, supra,* 541 U.S. at 152 ("The Government's interest in preventing the entry of unwanted persons and effects is at its zenith at the international border."); *United States v. Montoya De Hernandez,* 473 U.S. 531, 538 (1985) ("the Fourth Amendment's balance of reasonableness is qualitatively different at the international border than in the interior"); *id.* at 544 ("at the international border, . . . the Fourth Amendment balance of interests leans heavily to the Government").

E. *Surveillance by Law Enforcement Agents*

25.31. *Electronic Eavesdropping and Wiretapping*

Traditionally, governmental surveillance into premises without a physical trespass upon the premises was thought not to be a Fourth Amendment "search." Tom-peeping and eavesdropping were insulated from Fourth Amendment restriction by the doctrine that "the eye cannot commit a search," nor can the ear. *See, e.g., Polk v. United States,* 291 F.2d 230 (9th Cir.

1961), 314 F.2d 837 (9th Cir. 1963); *Anspach v. United States*, 305 F.2d 48, 960 (10th Cir. 1962). The Supreme Court applied these concepts in *Olmstead v. United States*, 277 U.S. 438 (1928), to hold that telephone wiretapping was not a "search" and in *Goldman v. United States*, 316 U.S. 129 (1942), to hold that no "search" had been conducted by officers who monitored conversations in a suspect's room by means of an electronic sound-amplifying device placed against the party wall in an adjoining room. During almost 40 years, the Court – although indicating increasing disaffection with *Olmstead* – subjected electronic surveillance to Fourth Amendment restriction only when the surveillance involved some form of physical trespass. *See Silverman v. United States*, 365 U.S. 505 (1961) (involving an electronic device inserted within the perimeter of a suspect's premises); *Clinton v. Virginia*, 377 U.S. 158 (1964) (per curiam), *rev'g* 204 Va. 275, 130 S.E.2d 437 (1963) (same); *Hoffa v. United States*, 387 U.S. 231 (1967) (involving an electronic device planted on a suspect's premises by trespassing officers); *Berger v. New York*, 388 U.S. 41 (1967) (same). Eventually, *Olmstead* and *Goldman* were expressly overruled in *Katz v. United States*, 389 U.S. 347 (1967). *Katz* held specifically that the monitoring of conversations through an electronic listening and recording device attached to the outside of a public telephone booth was a Fourth Amendment search; and it said more generally that "electronically listening to and recording . . . words [spoken in an area of] . . . privacy upon which [a person] . . . justifiably relied" would constitute a search without regard to "the presence or absence of a physical intrusion into any given enclosure" (389 U.S. at 353). "In *Katz* . . . we established that 'the Fourth Amendment protects people, not places,' and expanded our conception of the Amendment to protect certain expectations of privacy as well." *Carpenter v. United States*, 138 S. Ct. 2206, 2213 (2018). See also § 25.33 *infra*.

Congress responded to *Katz* by legislation comprehensively regulating the subject of electronic surveillance (together with telephone wiretapping, § 25.32 *infra*). The Omnibus Crime Control and Safe Streets Act of 1968, Pub. L. No. 90-351, § 802, 82 Stat. 212, codified as 18 U.S.C. §§ 2510-2520, broadly prohibits electronic eavesdropping and wiretapping, creates criminal and civil liability for violators, declares the fruits of forbidden electronic eavesdropping or wiretapping inadmissible in any state or federal judicial, administrative, or legislative proceedings, but also excepts from these bans eavesdropping and tapping conducted for law enforcement purposes under the authorization of 18 U.S.C. §§ 2516-19. The latter sections authorize:

(a) the issuance of electronic surveillance or wiretap orders by federal judges, upon application of the Attorney General, Deputy Attorney General, Associate Attorney General, or any federal prosecutor of a specified grade "specially designated by the Attorney General" (*see United States v. Giordano*, 416 U.S. 505 (1974)), for the purpose of investigating specified federal offenses; and

(b) the issuance of similar orders by state judges, in States that so provide by statute, upon application of the "principal prosecuting attorney" of the State or of one of its political subdivisions (*see, e.g., Villa v. Maricopa County, Arizona*, 865 F.3d 1224, 1230-34 (9th Cir. 2017)), for the purpose of investigating specified state-law offenses punishable by imprisonment for more than one year and "designated in [the] applicable State statute" (18 U.S.C. § 2516).

In either instance, judges may issue orders only upon written and sworn applications containing detailed averments of the matters described in 18 U.S.C. § 2518(1) and upon finding:

(1)   that there is probable cause to believe that a person is committing, has committed, or is about to commit one of the specified offenses;

(2)   that there is probable cause to believe that particular communications concerning the offense will be obtained through the authorized surveillance or tap;

(3)   that there is probable cause to believe that the facilities or places to be tapped or put under surveillance are used in connection with the commission of the offense, or are leased to, listed in the name of, or commonly used by, the person committing the offense; and

(4)   that "normal investigative procedures have been tried and have failed or reasonably appear to be unlikely to succeed if tried or to be too dangerous." (18 U.S.C. § 2518(3).)

See, e.g., United States v. Gonzalez, 412 F.3d 1102, 1113-15 (9th Cir. 2005) (wiretap evidence is suppressed because the government did not satisfy 18 U.S.C. § 2518(1)(c)'s "necessity" requirement: the government "did not establish that adequate traditional tools were tried before the wiretap was sought or that these untried alternatives were reasonably unlikely to be productive," and the government "makes no claim that normal investigative procedures were reasonably determined to be too dangerous to try"); *United States v. Blackmon*, 273 F.3d 1204, 1206 (9th Cir. 2001) (wiretap evidence is suppressed because "the wiretap application contained material misstatements and omissions, and because the application does not otherwise make a particularized showing of necessity").

The application and order must set forth the name of every person who is reasonably believed to be committing the offense and whose communications are expected to be intercepted (*United States v. Donovan*, 429 U.S. 413, 423-28 (1977)), but it needs not name persons likely to be overheard unless there is probable cause (see § 25.7.4 *supra*) to believe that they are implicated in the offense (*United States v. Kahn*, 415 U.S. 143 (1974)). (The *Kahn* opinion contains *dictum* to the effect that "when there is probable cause to believe that a particular telephone is being used to commit an offense but no particular person is identifiable, a wire interception order may, nevertheless, properly issue under the statute" (*id.* at 157).)

A surveillance order impliedly authorizes covert entry into private premises for the purpose of installing listening devices. No "explicit authorization of the entry is . . . required" (*Dalia v. United States*, 441 U.S. 238, 259 n.22 (1979)), although "the 'preferable approach' would be for Government agents . . . to make explicit to the authorizing court their expectation that some form of surreptitious entry will be required to carry out the surveillance" (*id.*), and their failure to do so may perhaps be deemed relevant when "the manner in which a warrant is executed is subject[ed] to later judicial review as to its reasonableness" (*id.* at 258).

The authorizing order must contain specified recitations restricting its scope (18 U.S.C.

§ 2518(4)), and it may not authorize surveillance or taps "for any period longer than is necessary to achieve the objective of the authorization, nor in any event longer than thirty days" (18 U.S.C. § 2518(5)), although extensions may be granted upon new showings sufficient to authorize initial issuance of an order (*id.*). "The plain effect of the detailed restrictions of § 2518 is to guarantee that wiretapping or bugging occurs only when there is a genuine need for it and only to the extent that it is needed." *Dalia v. United States, supra,* 441 U.S. at 250 (dictum). Warrantless eavesdropping and tapping are authorized only in "an emergency situation" involving conspiracies that threaten the national security or characterize "organized crime," and, in these cases, subsequent judicial approval must be obtained within 48 hours (18 U.S.C. § 2518(7)).

Detailed provisions are made concerning the execution of surveillance orders (*see, e.g., Scott v. United States,* 436 U.S. 128 (1978) (construing the provision of Section 2518(5) requiring that surveillance be conducted "in such a way as to minimize the interception of [noncriminal] communications")); the *post facto* service of inventories upon persons affected (*see United States v. Donovan, supra; United States v. Chun,* 503 F.2d 533 (9th Cir. 1974)); recording and sealing of surveillance logs and documents (*see, e.g., Villa v. Maricopa County, Arizona, supra,* 865 F.3d at 1235-36), pretrial service of the surveillance applications and orders upon parties to any proceeding when the fruits of a surveillance or tap are to be offered in evidence, and motions to suppress the evidentiary use of these fruits (18 U.S.C. § 2518(8)-(10)).

Violations of some, but not all, of the procedural provisions of the statute require the suppression of evidence obtained through electronic surveillance (*Dahda v. United States,* 138 S. Ct. 1491 (2018); *United States v. Chavez,* 416 U.S. 562 (1974); *United States v. Giordano, supra; United States v. Donovan, supra,* 429 U.S. at 432-40; *United States v. Lomeli,* 676 F.3d 734, 739, 741-42 (8th Cir. 2012); *United States v. Lambus,* 897 F.3d 368 (2d Cir. 2018) (applying *Donovan* to hold that the statutory exclusionary rule did not require suppression of evidence obtained by a wiretap order issued on the basis of an affidavit that "erroneously stated that a check of law enforcement agency databases indicated that there had been no previous wiretap application or authorization for any of the target subjects" (*id.* at 395), but recognizing that this conclusion "does not end the suppression inquiry . . . [because in] addressing a motion to suppress the proceeds of a wiretap on the ground that the application contained misrepresentations or omissions, we, like every other Circuit Court of Appeals, have concluded that the appropriate analytical framework is that set forth in *Franks* [*v. Delaware,* 438 U.S. 154 (1978), discussed in § 25.17.3 *supra*]" (*id.* at 396), and therefore reversing a suppression order only after finding that the erroneous statements in the affidavit were not material and were neither intentional nor made in reckless disregard for the truth); *State v. Harris,* 369 Or. 628, 509 P.3d 83 (2022) (requiring the suppression of evidence obtained through a wiretap authorized by a prosecutor who was not the "principal prosecuting attorney" of the county; state law allowing district attorneys to delegate their power to authorize wiretaps cannot expand the scope of wiretapping permissible under 18 U.S.C. § 2516(2); and "[a]lthough *Giordano* [*v. United States, supra*] predates the [United States Supreme] Court's adoption of a 'good faith' exception to the Fourth Amendment exclusionary rule, *Giordano* remains controlling precedent on the question of whether evidence intercepted through an unlawful wiretap must be suppressed" (*id.* at 645, 509 P.3d at 94))), whereas violations of the Fourth Amendment uniformly entail suppression (*Berger v. New York, supra; Katz v. United States, supra*), subject only to the qualifications of § 25.3 concluding paragraph, and §§ 25.17 and 25.21 *supra*. (Concerning electronic surveillance of communications between an individual and his or her attorney, see § 26.13 *infra*.)

Counsel handling an electronic surveillance case should consult the statutory provisions against the background of the constitutional restrictions upon electronic surveillance announced in *Berger, supra*, 388 U.S. at 53-64; *Katz, supra*, 389 U.S. at 354-59; and *Osborn v. United States*, 385 U.S. 323, 327-30 (1966) – restrictions that are similar, but may not be identical, to those of the statute. *Dicta* throughout the opinion in *United States v. United States District Court for the Eastern District of Michigan*, 407 U.S. 297 (1972), appear to give the Supreme Court's constitutional blessing to the statute in general (*see also Nixon v. Administrator of General Services*, 433 U.S. 425, 463-65 (1977) (dictum)), but they would not preclude attack upon particular aspects or instances of statutorily authorized surveillance under the constitutional standards of *Berger, Katz*, and *Osborn*. *See United States v. Chun, supra*, 503 F.2d at 537-38. The *Eastern District* decision rejected the Government's contention that warrantless electronic surveillance approved by the President was constitutional in certain "national security" cases involving suspected domestic subversion. It did not determine what constitutional restrictions might apply to electronic surveillance in "foreign intelligence" cases. The latter subject is now regulated in detail by Title I of the Foreign Intelligence Surveillance Act of 1978, Pub. L. No. 95- 511, 92 Stat. 1783, codified as 50 U.S.C. §§ 1801-13.

Electronic interception of any communication is permissible without a warrant or other prerequisite – that is, with no requirement of probable cause, reasonable suspicion, necessity, or other justification – by a law enforcement officer (or by any person, under most relevant circumstances) if the officer (or person) "is a party to the communication or [if] one of the parties to the communication has given prior consent to such interception" (18 U.S.C. § 2511(2)(c), (d)). This statutory provision appears to broaden somewhat the exception that *Rathbun v. United States*, 355 U.S. 107 (1957), carved out of former Section 605 of the Federal Communications Act, which had prohibited most wiretapping prior to *Katz* (see § 25.32 *infra*). Its validity – now that electronic surveillance generally has been brought within the purview of the Fourth Amendment by *Katz* – raises questions akin to those raised by "bugged" informers (§ 26.10.2 *infra*). Although the law on the latter subject is a conceptual shambles (see *id.*), the present practical bottom line is plain enough: "Neither the Constitution nor any Act of Congress [imposes any restraints upon electronic monitoring or recording of conversations] . . . by Government agents with the consent of one of the conversants" (*United States v. Caceres*, 440 U.S. 741, 744 (1979); see *id.* at 749-52). The exception to this generalization is surreptitious government surveillance of communications between a consenting conversant and defense counsel. *See State v. Martinez*, 461 N.J. Super. 249, 255, 220 A.3d 498, 501-02 (2019) ("[W]e hold that mere compliance with the Wiretap Act does not mean that . . . secret taping [through a body wire of an interview of a government informer and prospective trial witness by defense counsel] is permissible . . . . Specifically, without appropriate limitations, such recording can have the capacity to infringe upon a criminal defendant's constitutional right to fair and unimpeded access by his counsel to interview government witnesses, and the capacity to reveal attorney work product. The surveillance of attorney interviews also can implicate ethical norms, particularly those governing prosecutors.").

Fourth Amendment protection against particularly intrusive forms of electronic surveillance got a significant boost in *Carpenter v. United States*, 138 S. Ct. 2206 (2018). On its facts, *Carpenter* holds that the Government's acquisition from a wireless carrier of an individual's cell phone records which "provide a comprehensive chronicle of the user's past movements" (*id.* at 2211) constitutes a Fourth Amendment "search," and that "the Government must generally obtain a warrant supported by probable cause before acquiring such records" (*id.* at 2221), except in "case-specific" situations where exigent circumstances such as "the need to pursue a fleeing suspect, protect individuals who are threatened with imminent harm, or prevent the imminent destruction of evidence" (*id.* at 2222-23) """"make the needs of law enforcement so compelling that [a] warrantless search is objectively reasonable under the Fourth Amendment"""" (*id.* at 2222). The Court reasons that the Fourth Amendment protects "a person's expectation of privacy in his physical location and movements" (*id.* at 2215). It observes that because "a phone goes wherever its owner goes, conveying to the wireless carrier not just dialed digits, but a detailed and comprehensive record of the person's movements" (*id.* at 2217), "cell phone location information is detailed, encyclopedic, and effortlessly compiled" (*id.* at 2216) and "provides an intimate window into a person's life, revealing not only his particular movements, but through them his 'familial, political, professional, religious, and sexual associations'" (*id.* at 2217), so that "[t]hese location records 'hold for many Americans the "privacies of life"'" (*id.*). These realities bring into play the principle that "[a]s technology has enhanced the Government's capacity to encroach upon areas normally guarded from inquisitive eyes, this Court has sought to 'assure[ ] preservation of that degree of privacy against government that existed when the Fourth Amendment was adopted'" (*id.* at 2214). The latter declaration has potential beyond the specific, narrow holding in *Carpenter*. It suggests, *inter alia*, that some electronic surveillance practices now regarded as regulated only by 18 U.S.C. §§ 2510-2520 may also be subject to Fourth Amendment restrictions. If they are, then violations of those restrictions would require Fourth Amendment exclusion of any evidence that the violations produce (subject, again, only to the qualifications of § 25.3 concluding paragraph, and §§ 25.17 and 25.21 *supra*) – a substantially more robust version of the exclusionary rule than the courts have been applying under 18 U.S.C. §§ 2510-2520. *See also Commonwealth v. Almonor*, 482 Mass. 35, 120 N.E.3d 1183 (2019) (holding that police pinging of a cellphone to determine the location of its owner constitutes a search under the state constitution's unreasonable-search-and-seizure clause and may be conducted only with a warrant or under exigent circumstances, but finding sufficient exigency on the facts of the case – involving a suspect fleeing from a shotgun-murder scene – to justify a warrantless ping).

In a number of States, there are statutes regulating electronic eavesdropping that may be construed as more protective than the federal statutes or Constitution. *See, e.g., State v. Catania*, 85 N.J. 418, 436-39, 427 A.2d 537, 546-48 (1981); *State v. Thompson*, 191 Conn. 360, 371, 464 A.2d 799, 807 (1983), and cases cited; *cf. People v. Davis*, 2021 IL 126435, 185 N.E.3d 1223, 1226, 452 Ill. Dec. 487, 490 (2021) (the state concedes that an audio recording made by a wired informant pursuant to an eavesdropping exemption application that named another person, not the defendant, as the target of the eavesdropping was illegally obtained and had to be suppressed).

25.32. *Telephone Wiretapping*

Telephone wiretapping was banned by § 605 of the Federal Communications Act of 1934, 48 Stat. 1103, 47 U.S.C. § 605 (1964). The Supreme Court construed the statute as rendering wiretap evidence inadmissible in federal prosecutions, even when the tap was made by state officers acting without federal participation and in compliance with a state law allowing tapping. *Benanti v. United States*, 355 U.S. 96 (1957). In *Schwartz v. Texas*, 344 U.S. 199 (1952), the Court held that Section 605 did not require the exclusion of wiretap evidence in state criminal prosecutions; but *Schwartz* was overruled in *Lee v. Florida*, 392 U.S. 378 (1968). *See Fuller v. Alaska*, 393 U.S. 80 (1968) (per curiam). Section 605 was then amended to conform to the detailed congressional regulation of wiretapping and electronic eavesdropping contemporaneously enacted as 18 U.S.C. §§ 2510-20. That regulation is described in § 25.31 *supra*. The only substantive points requiring additional mention here are:

(A) A party has standing to complain of an unlawful wiretap if either (1) s/he is a party to the tapped conversation or (2) his or her telephone is tapped, whether or not s/he is a party to the conversation. *Alderman v. United States*, 394 U.S. 165, 176-80 (1969); *Rakas v. Illinois*, 439 U.S. 128, 144 n.12 (1978) (dictum); *United States v. Karo*, 468 U.S. 705, 716-17 n.4 (1984) (dictum).

(B) The use of a "pen register" to record the numbers dialed from a telephone (or other such "dialing, routing, addressing, or signaling information" from other "instrument[s] or facilit[ies] from which a wire or electronic communication is transmitted" (18 U.S.C. § 3127(3))) – but without monitoring the "contents of any communication" (*id.*) – is not subject to the restrictions of 18 U.S.C. §§ 2510-20 (*United States v. New York Telephone Co.*, 434 U.S. 159 (1977)), and does not constitute a "search" subject to Fourth Amendment constraints (*Smith v. Maryland*, 442 U.S. 735 (1979)). Pen registers and their technological counterparts are regulated by 18 U.S.C. § 3121-27, but violations of those sections do not entail exclusionary consequences. *See, e.g.*, *United States v. Thompson*, 936 F.2d 1249 (11th Cir. 1991) (the Communications Assistance for Law Enforcement Act of 1994, which was enacted "after the Supreme Court's holding in *Smith v. Maryland* . . . made no provision for exclusion" (936 F.2d at 1252); hence, "information obtained from a pen register placed on a telephone can be used as evidence in a criminal trial even if the court order authorizing its installation does not comply with the statutory requirements." (*id.* at 1249-50)); *cf. United States v. Forrester*, 495 F.3d 1041, as amended, 512 F.3d 500, 504, 510 n.6 (9th Cir. 2008) ("computer surveillance that enabled the government to learn the to/from addresses of . . . [the defendant's] e mail messages, the Internet protocol ("IP") addresses of the websites that he visited and the total volume of information transmitted to or from his account . . . was analogous to the use of a pen register that the Supreme Court held in *Smith v. Maryland* . . . did not constitute a search for Fourth Amendment purposes. Moreover, whether or not the surveillance came within the scope of the then-applicable federal pen register statute, . . . [the defendant] is not entitled to the suppression of the evidence obtained through the surveillance because there is no statutory or other authority for such a remedy" (495 F.3d at 1043); "Surveillance techniques that enable the government to determine not only the IP addresses that a person accesses but also the uniform resource locators ("URL") of the pages visited might be more constitutionally problematic. A URL, unlike an IP address, identifies the particular document within a website that a person views and thus reveals much more information about the person's Internet activity." (512 F.3d at 503 n.6)).

25.33. *Other Forms of Electronic and Nonelectronic Surveillance*

If the police use a device or technology merely as a means to view what was already exposed to observation by the public at large, then there is no "search" for Fourth Amendment purposes. *See, e.g., Texas v. Brown,* 460 U.S. 730, 740 (1983) (plurality opinion) (an officer's use of a flashlight to examine the interior of an automobile was not a "search" since "the interior of an automobile . . . may be viewed from outside the vehicle by either inquisitive passersby or diligent police officers"); *United States v. Dunn,* 480 U.S. 294, 305 (1987) ("the officers' use of the beam of a flashlight, directed through the essentially open front of defendant's barn, did not transform their observations into an unreasonable search within the meaning of the Fourth Amendment"). *See also, e.g., California v. Ciraolo,* 476 U.S. 207, 215 (1986) (warrantless observation of marijuana plants in the fenced yard of a home, made possible because police officers flew over the yard in a private plane and observed it from an altitude of 1,000 feet, did not violate the homeowner's reasonable expectation of privacy because the marijuana plants were "visible to the naked eye," albeit only with the assistance of the aircraft); *Florida v. Riley,* 488 U.S. 445, 451 (1989) (police flew a helicopter at an altitude of 400 feet above a backyard greenhouse and thus observed marijuana invisible from the ground because of enclosing walls, fences, and foliage; "[a]ny member of the public could legally have been flying over Riley's property in a helicopter at the altitude of 400 feet and could have observed Riley's greenhouse"). *Cf. Dow Chemical Co. v. United States,* 476 U.S. 227, 237-39 (1986) (in the context of inspections of commercial property, where "the Government has 'greater latitude,'" the Court approves the use of an aerial camera that enhanced human vision "somewhat" but was not "so revealing of intimate details as to raise constitutional concerns"; the Court notes that use of "[a]n electronic device to penetrate walls or windows so as to hear and record confidential discussions of chemical formulae or other trade secrets would raise very different and far more serious questions.").

But if the police use an electronic device or other artificial contrivance to extend their surveillance into an area or into a field of information that is normally inaccessible to public observation, then a "search" has occurred for purposes of the Fourth Amendment. *See, e.g., Silverman v. United States,* 365 U.S. 505, 506-07, 509, 511 (1961) (police violated the Fourth Amendment by eavesdropping on conversations in defendants' house by means of a microphone that was inserted into a heating duct in what amounted to an "unauthorized physical penetration into the premises"); *Regalado v. California,* 374 U.S. 497 (1963) (per curiam) (police surveillance through peepholes routinely drilled in hotel room doors – apparently by collaboration of the police and hotel management in "high crime" areas – was a Fourth Amendment search); *Kyllo v. United States,* 533 U.S. 27, 29, 31 (2001) ("the use of a thermal-imaging device aimed at a private home from a public street to detect relative amounts of heat within the home constitutes a 'search' within the meaning of the Fourth Amendment": "obtaining by sense-enhancing technology any information regarding the interior of the home that could not otherwise have been obtained without physical 'intrusion into a constitutionally protected area,' . . . constitutes a search – at least where (as here) the technology in question is not in general public use."). *See also Florida v. Jardines,* 569 U.S. 1, 11-12 (2013) ("The government's use of trained [drug-sniffing] police dogs to investigate the home and its immediate surroundings is a 'search' within the meaning of the Fourth Amendment."); *State v. Howard,* 169 Idaho 379, 381, 496 P.3d 865, 867 (2021) ("Howard appeals from the denial of a motion to suppress evidence obtained after a police drug-sniffing dog put its nose through the open window of a car Howard had been driving. Howard argues the intrusion of the dog into the physical space of the car was a trespass, and therefore, an unlawful search under the common law trespassory test articulated in *United States v. Jones*, 565 U.S. 400 (2012). We agree . . . [and] reverse the denial of Howard's motion to suppress." [Jones is summarized in the following paragraph of this manual.]); *United States v. Burston*, 806 F.3d 1123, 1125, 1127-28 (8th Cir. 2015) (a police officer conducted an unlawful search by releasing a drug-sniffing dog "off-leash to sniff the air" in an area within the curtilage of the defendant's apartment while the officer "remained six feet from the apartment"); *People v. McKnight*, 2019 CO 36, 446 P.3d 397, 400 (2019) (following the legalization of marijuana in Colorado, the state constitution requires probable cause of the presence of illegal drugs before police can arrange a sniff by a dog trained to alert to marijuana as well as the latter drugs: "a sniff from a drug-detection dog that is trained to alert to marijuana constitutes a search under article II, section 7 of the Colorado Constitution because that sniff can detect lawful activity".); *United States v. Correa*, 908 F.3d 208, 214 (7th Cir. 2018) (DEA agents seized an electronic garage-door opener from the defendant during a consent search after a traffic stop; an agent "first took the openers at least three blocks away from the scene of Correa's arrest to test them on the garage of the building from which the unidentified men had emerged with the cash eight days earlier. When the openers did not work there, he tried them on 'a bunch of townhouses with garages attached to them right in that area.' And when that did not work, he 'did a grid system.' We believe that seeing this kind of approach – driving a car up and down streets and alleys testing multiple garage door openers, but backing up after one garage door opened, waiting for it to close, and then opening it again – would strike the layperson as an obvious search" (*id.* at 218), and the Seventh Circuit therefore finds that these activities constitute a search for Fourth Amendment purposes, although it holds the search reasonable even without a warrant "at least where the search disclose[d] no further information . . . because these searches produced only an address, not any meaningful private information about the interior or contents of the garage. Correa had no reasonable expectation of privacy in that information. Officers routinely obtain that kind of information without a warrant as booking information and in searches incident to arrest." (*id.* at 219)); *State v. Kraft*, 301 So.3d 981 (Fla. App. 2020) (suppressing evidence obtained by video surveillance from cameras surreptitiously placed in massage parlors under a warrant authorizing surveillance to detect suspected prostitution: the warrant contained no minimization provisions and so allowed indiscriminate observation and recording); *compare Killgore v. City of South El Monte*, 3 F.4th 1186 (9th Cir. 2021), summarized in § 25.36 *infra*.

The basic principle in this area was established by *Katz v. United States*, 389 U.S. 347, 353 (1967), holding that "electronically listening to and recording . . . words [spoken in a zone of] . . . privacy upon which [a person] . . . justifiably relied" is a "search" for Fourth Amendment purposes, without regard to "the presence or absence of a physical intrusion into any given enclosure." The principle is illustrated by comparing the decisions in *United States v. Knotts*, 460 U.S. 276 (1983), and *United States v. Karo*, 468 U.S. 705 (1984). In *Knotts*, the Court held that police officers' tracing of the movements of an automobile by means of an electronic beeper planted in a can of chloroform purchased by a drug manufacturing suspect was not a "search" since it revealed nothing more than what could be observed through "[v]isual surveillance from public places" (460 U.S. at 282). In *Karo*, the police employed the same tactic of installing an electronic beeper in a can of ether, but the can thereafter ended up inside a private home.

Distinguishing the *Knotts* case as limited to surveillance of a public area, the Court in *Karo* held that "the monitoring of a beeper in a private residence, a location not open to visual surveillance, violates the Fourth Amendment rights of those who have a justifiable interest in the privacy of the residence" (468 U.S. at 714). *See Carpenter v. United States*, 138 S. Ct. 2206 (2018), discussed in § 25.31 *supra; and compare United States v. Jones*, 565 U.S. 400, 404-05, 409 (2012) ("hold[ing] that the Government's installation of a GPS [Global-Positioning-System] device on a target's vehicle, . . . and its use of that device to monitor the vehicle's movements, constitutes a 'search'" – although basing this ruling on a "common-law trespassory test" rather than "the *Katz* reasonable-expectation-of-privacy test" – and concluding that the government's attachment of the GPS tracking device to the underside of Jones' vehicle constituted a "physical intrusion" into "private property for the purpose of obtaining information" and thus a "'search' within the meaning of the Fourth Amendment when it was adopted"), *with id.* at 418-19, 430 (Alito, J., concurring in the judgment, joined by Ginsburg, Breyer & Kagan, JJ.) (rejecting the majority's reliance on "18th-century tort law" and reaching the same result as the majority by "asking whether defendant's reasonable expectations of privacy were violated by the long-term monitoring of the movements of the vehicle he drove," and concluding that although "relatively short-term monitoring of a person's movements on public streets accords with expectations of privacy that our society has recognized as reasonable," "the use of longer term GPS monitoring" – such as occurred in this case, where "law enforcement agents tracked every movement that defendant made in the vehicle he was driving" for "four weeks" – "impinges on expectations of privacy" and thus constitutes a "search" for purposes of the Fourth Amendment). *And see Grady v. North Carolina*, 575 U.S. 306, 310 (2015) (per curiam) (applying *United States v. Jones, supra,* to hold that a satellite-based monitoring program for recidivist sex offenders, which tracked program participants by means of a tracking device that participants were required to "wear . . . at all times," "effect[ed] a Fourth Amendment search": "a State . . . conducts a search when it attaches a device to a person's body, without consent, for the purpose of tracking that individual's movements"; "The State's program is plainly designed to obtain information. And since it does so by physically intruding on a subject's body, it effects a Fourth Amendment search.").

Courts are increasingly finding a privacy interest in various other forms of electronic data and requiring that the police obtain a warrant in order to obtain that data. *See, e.g., Leaders of a Beautiful Struggle v. Baltimore Police Department*, 2 F.4th 330 (4th Cir. 2021) (en banc) (holding that plaintiffs seeking a preliminary injunction against the maintenance of data from Baltimore's experimental aerial surveillance [AIR] program have shown a likelihood of succeeding on their claim that the program violates the Fourth Amendment: "*Carpenter* [*v. United States, supra*] solidified [the teaching of Supreme Court precedents since 2001 drawing] the line between short-term tracking of public movements – akin to what law enforcement could do '[p]rior to the digital age' – and prolonged tracking that can reveal intimate details through habits and patterns. . . . The latter form of surveillance invades the reasonable expectation of privacy that individuals have in the whole of their movements and therefore requires a warrant." *Id.* at 341. ". . . [Th]e AIR program's surveillance is not 'short-term' and transcends mere augmentation of ordinary police capabilities. People understand that they may be filmed by security cameras on city streets, or a police officer could stake out their house and tail them for a time. . . . But capturing everyone's movements outside during the daytime for 45 days goes beyond that ordinary capacity." *Id.* at 345.). Intensive police surveillance of residences by cameras mounted on utility poles which record the comings and goings of homeowners and visitors for extended periods of time have divided the courts, with some state high courts and the federal Fifth Circuit finding that this kind of activity constitutes a search for Fourth Amendment purposes, two other federal circuits finding that it does not, and the First Circuit splitting 3-to-3 on the issue. *Compare People v. Tafoya*, 2021 CO 62, 494 P.3d 613 (2021), *and State v. Jones*, 2017 S.D. 59, 903 N.W.2d 101 (S.D. 2017) (dictum), *and United States v. Cuevas-Sanchez*, 821 F.2d 248 (5th Cir. 1987) (dictum), *with United States v. Tuggle*, 4 F.4th 505 (7th Cir. 2021), *and United States v. Houston*, 813 F.3d 282 (6th Cir. 2016); *see United States v. Moore-Bush*, 36 F.4th 320 (1st Cir. 2022) (en banc); *cf. Commonwealth v. Mora*, 485 Mass. 360, 361, 150 N.E.3d 297, 301-02 (2020) ("Over a period of seven months, the Attorney General investigated an alleged drug distribution network based in Essex County. At different times during the course of the investigation, officers installed a total of five hidden video cameras on public telephone and electrical poles. Three of these cameras were aimed towards homes of alleged members of the drug conspiracy. Using the video footage collected by these 'pole cameras,' in addition to other evidence, the Commonwealth secured indictments against twelve defendants, including the defendants . . . . ¶ We conclude that the continuous, long-term pole camera surveillance targeted at the residences of Mora and Suarez well may have been a search within the meaning of the Fourth Amendment, a question we do not reach, but certainly was a search under [Massachusetts Declaration of Rights] art. 14."). *See also Tracey v. State*, 152 So.3d 504, 522, 525-26 (Fla. 2014) (an individual has a reasonable "expectation of privacy of location as signaled by one's cell phone – even on public roads"; "Simply because the cell phone user knows or should know that his cell phone gives off signals that enable the service provider to detect its location for call routing purposes, and which enable cell phone applications to operate for navigation, weather reporting, and other purposes, does not mean that the user is consenting to use of that location information by third parties for any other unrelated purposes."; "no warrant based on probable cause authorized the use of Tracey's real time cell site location information to track him," so police officers' use of "cell site location information emanating from his cell phone in order to track him in real time" was an unlawful search and "the evidence obtained as a result of that search was subject to suppression."); *Jones v. United States*, 168 A.3d 703, 713 (D.C. 2017) (police "use of a cell-site simulator to locate . . . [the defendant's] phone invaded a reasonable expectation of privacy and was thus a search" that violated the Fourth Amendment in the absence of a search warrant); *Commonwealth v. Augustine*, 467 Mass. 230, 231, 232, 4 N.E.3d 846, 849, 850 (2014) (construing the state constitution to hold that the state must obtain a search warrant in order to acquire "historical cell site location information for a particular cellular telephone" from "a cellular telephone service provider"; the court observes that although the information "at issue here is a business record of the defendant's cellular service provider, he had a reasonable expectation of privacy in it"); *Commonwealth v. Fredericq*, 482 Mass. 70, 71, 77-78, 121 N.E.3d 166, 171, 175 (2019) ("the defendant has standing to challenge the Commonwealth's warrantless CSLI [cell site location information] search because, by monitoring the . . . CSLI [of a telephone which, although registered to the defendant, was used solely by another individual], the police effectively monitored the movement of a vehicle in which . . . [the defendant] was a passenger"; "For all practical purposes, the CSLI monitoring of the cellular telephone tracked the defendant's location when he was in the vehicle in much the same way as would GPS tracking of that vehicle."); *State v. Earls*, 214 N.J. 564, 569, 70 A.3d 630, 633 (2013) (construing the state constitution to hold that "cell-phone users have a reasonable expectation of privacy in their cell-phone location information, and that police must obtain a search warrant before accessing that information"); *State v. Reid*, 194 N.J. 386, 399, 945 A.2d 26, 33-34 (2008) (the state constitution "protects an individual's privacy interest in the subscriber information he or she provides to an Internet service provider"). Concerning geofence searches, *see, e.g., Matter of Search of Information Stored at Premises Controlled by Google*, 481 F. Supp. 3d 730 (N.D. Ill. 2020); *Matter of Search of Information that is Stored at Premises Controlled by Google*, 542 F. Supp. 3d 1153 (D. Kan. 2021). *But see City of Ontario v. Quon*, 560 U.S. 746, 761-62 (2010) (upholding a police department's review of text messages sent and received on a government-owned pager that was issued to a police officer and that was reviewed by the department for the purpose of "determin[ing] whether [the officer's] overages were the result of work-related messaging or personal use," where the officer had been given advance notice "that his [text] messages were subject to auditing"); *United States v. Beaudion*, 979 F.3d 1092, 1098 (5th Cir. 2020) (a defendant lacked standing to complain that law enforcement officers violated the Fourth Amendment by obtaining a GPS tracking warrant for his girlfriend's cell phone: the court rejects Beaudion's contention that "the Government's search extended beyond . . . [the girlfriend] and her phone to include Beaudion and the car in which he and . . . [the girlfriend] were traveling . . . [and that] '[t]he purpose of the search warrant was to track the movements of [t]he car by using the GPS location of the cell phone inside of the car.'").

In cases involving advanced surveillance technology with which the courts are not familiar, a defendant challenging its use is entitled to make a record that contains sufficient information to enable appellate review of the way in which the specific instrument works and the extent to which it intrudes upon privacy. *See, e.g., Andrews v. Baltimore City Police Department*, 8 F.4th 234, 238 (4th Cir. 2020) ("Absent a more detailed understanding of the Hailstorm simulator's configuration and surveillance capabilities, we cannot address the issues necessary for resolution of this case. Despite the government's use of a sophisticated, wide-reaching, and hard-to-detect new surveillance tool – one with potentially significant implications for constitutional privacy – we know very little about how many searches it conducted, of whom, and what data it collected and stored. We thus cannot strike the appropriate 'balance between the public interest and the individual's right to personal security free from arbitrary interference by law officers' that is central to the Fourth Amendment analysis. . . . We therefore remand this matter so that the district court may resolve certain factual issues and, if necessary, provide updated conclusions of law as to whether the Hailstorm simulator's use was a constitutional violation."); *cf.* SMITH-HURD ILL. COMP. STAT. ANN. ch. 725, § 137/15; WEST'S REV. CODE WASH. ANN. § 9.73.260(4)(c)(ii). Defense counsel should move for discovery of this information (see § 18.9.1 fifth paragraph *supra*) and, if necessary, for funding to retain an expert consultant to evaluate it (see §§ 5.2-5.4 *supra*).

Search warrants or surveillance orders that authorize Fourth Amendment "searches" may be issued on probable cause. *See, e.g., United States v. Gibson*, 996 F.3d 451 (7th Cir. 2021). Absent probable cause, they are invalid. *Carpenter v. United States*, 138 S. Ct. 2206 (2018). Suppression issues arising from searches conducted under these warrants are apparently governed by the *Leon/Sheppard* rules discussed in §§ 25.17 – 25.17.6 *supra. See, e.g., United States v. Friend,* 992 F.3d 728 (8th Cir. 2021); *United States v. Goldstein*, 989 F.3d 1178 (11th Cir. 2021) (alternative ground); *United States v. Goldstein*, 914 F.3d 200 (3d Cir. 2019) (alternative ground).

F. *Probable Cause or Articulable Suspicion Based on Information Obtained from Other Police Officers or Civilian Informants*

25.34. *Police Action Based on Information Learned from Other Police Officers*

Frequently, Officer *A* concludes that a person is guilty of an offense and conveys that conclusion to Officer B – directly or through some form of police bulletin or dispatch or "wanted flyer" – in connection with a request or directive that the person be arrested or held for questioning. Some courts were inclined to sustain *B*'s arrest or stop of the person in this situation, even though *A* lacked probable cause or articulable suspicion for *A*'s conclusion, on the theory that *B* had probable cause or articulable suspicion generated by a communication from an apparently reliable informant – namely, fellow officer *A*. This bootstrap has, however, been firmly rejected by the Supreme Court on the obvious ground that "an otherwise illegal arrest cannot be insulated from challenge by the decision of the instigating officer to rely on fellow officers to make the arrest" (*Whiteley v. Warden,* 401 U.S. 560, 568 (1971)). *Accord, United States v. Hensley,* 469 U.S. 221, 230 (1985). Police dispatches gain no credibility from the mere fact of their internal transmission. *Cf. Franks v. Delaware, supra*, 438 U.S. at 163-64 n.6.

Thus, when police officers rely on a flyer or dispatch to make an arrest, the admissibility of evidence uncovered during a search incident to that arrest "turns on whether the officers who *issued* the flyer [or dispatch] possessed probable cause to make the arrest" (*United States v. Hensley, supra*, 469 U.S. at 231 (dictum); *United States v. Balser,* 70 F.4th 613 (1st Cir. 2023)). *See, e.g., People v. Powell,* 101 A.D.3d 756, 758, 955 N.Y.S.2d 608, 610 (N.Y. App. Div., 2d Dep't 2012). Similarly, in cases of *Terry* stops based on a flyer or dispatch, "[i]f the flyer [or dispatch] has been issued in the absence of a reasonable suspicion, then a stop in the objective reliance upon it violates the Fourth Amendment" (*United States v. Hensley, supra*, 469 U.S. at 232). Of course, this adequacy of the underlying information is only the necessary condition – not a sufficient condition – for the validity of a detention based upon internal police communications. In addition, the officer who effects the detention must be aware of the communication and must be able to identify the person detained as the individual sought. *See State v. Gardner,* 2012-Ohio-5683, 135 Ohio St. 3d 99, 104-05, 984 N.E.2d 1025, 1029-30 (2012) (even if there is a valid arrest warrant for an individual, a police seizure of that individual cannot be predicated on the existence of the warrant unless the arresting officer "knew that there was a warrant for the individual's arrest"). If the circumstances give rise to questions about the reliability of the communication or the identity of a suspect as the individual sought, police officers are obliged to take reasonable measures to verify the information and their conclusions before taking action. *See, e.g., Mareska v. Bernalillo County,* 804 F.3d 1301, 1310-12 (10th Cir. 2015) (a police officer who arrested a truck's occupants based upon an erroneously-received stolen vehicle report for a different vehicle was obliged to "confirm the accuracy of her information in light of the disparity between the vehicle described on the stolen vehicle report and that driven by the Marescas"; "[I]n determining whether there is probable cause, officers are charged with knowledge of any 'readily available exculpatory evidence' that they unreasonably fail to ascertain. . . . '[T]he probable cause standard of the Fourth Amendment requires officers to reasonably interview witnesses readily available at the scene, investigate basic evidence, or otherwise inquire if a crime has been committed at all before invoking the power of warrantless arrest and detention.'").

When arrests are made or ordered by two or more officers, prosecutors sometimes invoke a so-called "collective knowledge" or "fellow officer" doctrine to argue that facts known to some of the officers but not to others can be aggregated to add up to the probable cause required for an arrest or to the reasonable suspicion required for a *Terry* stop. This should be impermissible because the only way in which the probable-cause and reasonable-suspicion standards for any warrantless police action can be enforced is to insist that some single officer be responsible for making the determination that the factual information at hand satisfies the applicable standard. For an excellent discussion of this subject, *see United States v. Massenburg*, 654 F.3d 480, 491-96 (4th Cir. 2011); *and see, e.g., United States v. Hussain*, 835 F.3d 307, 316 n.8 (2d Cir. 2016) ("we decline to extend the collective [police] knowledge doctrine to cases where, as here, there is no evidence that an officer has communicated his suspicions with the officer conducting the search, even when the officers are working closely together at a scene"); Derik T. Fettig, *Who Knew What When: A Critical Analysis of the Expanding Collective Knowledge Doctrine*, 82 U. Mo. Kan. City L. Rev. 663 (2014). *Cf. Furlow v. Belmar*, 52 F.4th 393, 402 (8th Cir. 2022) (dictum) ("[b]ecause the Wanteds System routinely imputes a single officer's finding of probable cause to officers potentially anywhere in the country – without any showing of a joint investigation – this Wanteds System cannot be saved under the collective knowledge doctrine").

Information obtained from law-enforcement databases may be so unreliable that it fails to provide an adequate factual basis for a determination of probable cause. In these cases, arresting officers' uncritical reliance on the information, without independently verifying it, will render an arrest or an application for an arrest warrant susceptible to Fourth Amendment challenge. *See Hart v. Hillsdale County, Michigan,* 973 F.3d 627 (6th Cir. 2020).

25.35. *Police Action Based on Information Learned from a Civilian Informant*

25.35.1. *The General Standard*

Unless a police officer witnessed the crime or some objective manifestation of criminal conduct, police action – whether it be an arrest, a search, a *Terry* stop or a *Terry* frisk – will usually depend upon information learned from civilians. The source of the information may be either an ordinary citizen (a complainant or an eyewitness) or a "police informer" who is trading the information for cash or leniency on criminal charges to which s/he is subject. The identity of the source of the information may not even be known to the police, as in the case of an anonymous phone tip or an informant relaying information that s/he heard "on the street" without revealing the precise source of the information.

Defense attorneys usually confront the issue of informants' tips in either of two contexts: (i) when the officer presented the information to a magistrate in support of a request for a search warrant or arrest warrant and defense counsel is challenging a search or arrest made pursuant to the resulting warrant, or (ii) when the officer relied on the informant's tip in making a warrantless arrest, search, stop, or frisk. If the officer acted pursuant to a warrant, the scope of review of the magistrate's reliance upon information derived from nonpolice informants will be quite limited under Fourth Amendment doctrine, although it may be more expansive under state constitutional law. See § 25.17 *supra.* Essentially, the issue in warrant cases is whether the informant's information, as presented in the police affidavit in support of the warrant, was "'so lacking in indicia of probable cause as to render'" the issuance of a warrant manifestly unreasonable (*United States v. Leon,* 468 U.S. 897, 923 (1984)). See § 25.17.1 *supra.*

In cases in which the officer acted without a warrant, the reviewing court must engage in a far more piercing examination of the reliability and sufficiency of the informant's communications to the police. Judicial review of police reliance on information from informants was formerly governed by a two-pronged test of "veracity" and "basis of knowledge" established in *Aguilar v. Texas,* 378 U.S. 108 (1964), and *Spinelli v. United States,* 393 U.S. 410 (1969). The *Aguilar-Spinelli* standard has been preserved in several States as a matter of state constitutional law (*see, e.g., Commonwealth v. Upton,* 394 Mass. 363, 476 N.E.2d 548 (1985); *People v. Johnson,* 66 N.Y.2d 398, 405-07, 488 N.E.2d 439, 444-45, 497 N.Y.S.2d 618, 623-24 (1985); *State v. Jackson,* 102 Wash. 2d 432, 443, 688 P.2d 136, 143 (1984)), but federal Fourth Amendment doctrine is now controlled by the opinion in *Illinois v. Gates,* 462 U.S. 213 (1983). Although the *Gates* case itself involved a warrant, its rules have generally been accepted as governing warrantless police action based on hearsay information.

Under the *Gates* opinion, the question whether information received from an informant supplies the requisite predicate for a search or seizure (whether that predicate be probable cause or articulable suspicion) is to be determined by the "totality of the circumstances," including, *inter alia,* the "informant's 'veracity,' 'reliability,' and 'basis of knowledge'" (462 U.S. at 230-39). Whereas the *Aguilar-Spinelli* standard treated "veracity" and "basis of knowledge" as separate criteria, both of which had to be satisfied, the *Gates* standard treats them as intertwined aspects of a "totality-of-the-circumstances analysis" in which "a deficiency in one [aspect] may be compensated for, in determining the overall reliability of a tip, by a strong showing as to the other, or by some other indicia of reliability" (426 U.S. at 233). In *Gates,* the Court concluded that it was possible to overlook the lack of direct evidences of "veracity" and "basis of knowledge" of an anonymous letter because the information in the letter was so detailed as to imply that the informant must be highly knowledgeable and accurate, and "independent investigative work" by the police had corroborated substantial portions of the details relating to conduct by the suspects which "at least suggested" criminal activity (*id.* at 243-46). *See also Navarette v. California,* 572 U.S. 393, 395, 398-401, 404 (2014) (an anonymous 911 call reporting that "a vehicle had run [the caller] . . . off the road" "bore adequate indicia of reliability for the officer to credit the caller's account" and to rely on this information in conducting a traffic stop because (1) the caller's report that "she had been run off the road by a specific vehicle – a silver Ford F-150 pickup, license plate 8D94925 – . . . necessarily claimed eyewitness knowledge of the alleged dangerous driving" and "[t]hat basis of knowledge lends significant support to the tip's reliability"; (2) police confirmation of "the truck's location near mile marker 69 (roughly 19 highway miles south of the location reported in the 911 call) at 4:00 p.m. (roughly 18 minutes after the 911 call) . . . suggests that the caller reported the incident soon after she was run off the road," and "[t]hat sort of contemporaneous report has long been treated as especially reliable"; and (3) "the caller's use of the 911 emergency system," which has "features that allow for identifying and tracing callers," is an additional "indicator of veracity," although this is not "to suggest that tips in 911 calls are *per se* reliable"; the Court majority in this 5-4 decision acknowledges that "this is a 'close case.'"). *Compare Florida v. J.L.,* 529 U.S. 266, 270, 271-72 (2000) (an anonymous tip that a certain individual at a particular location was in possession of a gun did not provide the police with an adequate basis for a stop and frisk, even though the police found a person matching the description at that precise location, because "'an anonymous tip alone seldom demonstrates the informant's basis of knowledge or veracity'" and, although "there are situations in which an anonymous tip, suitably corroborated, exhibits 'sufficient indicia of reliability to provide reasonable suspicion to make the investigatory stop,'" the "unknown, unaccountable informant . . . neither explained how he knew about the gun nor supplied any basis for believing he had inside information about [the subject]" and the police confirmation of the accuracy of the tipster's "description of [the] subject's readily observable location and appearance . . . does not show that the tipster has knowledge of concealed criminal activity": "The reasonable suspicion here at issue requires that a tip be reliable in its assertion of illegality, not just in its tendency to identify a determinate person."); *United States v. Freeman*, 735 F.3d 92, 94, 97-103 (2d Cir. 2013) (an anonymous caller's two calls to 911 reporting that an individual "'is possibly armed with a firearm' and was 'arguing with a female'" and describing this individual's appearance in detail and giving his precise location "did not provide the police with the reasonable suspicion needed to stop Freeman": "[t]he fact that the call was recorded and that the caller's apparent cell phone number is known does not alter the fact that the identity of the caller is still unknown, leaving no way for the police (or for the reviewing court) to determine her credibility and reputation for honesty"; the detailed information about the individual's appearance and location "does nothing to 'show that the tipster has knowledge of concealed criminal activity'"; and "the facts that the stop occurred at night in a 'high crime' area" do not "enhance the reliability of the phone call by confirming in it some individualized detail."); *United States v. Martinez*, 486 F.3d 855, 863 (5th Cir. 2007) (finding no reasonable suspicion where the "police had verified information that the person in the car they stopped was the 'Angel' whom the informant desired to accuse" but "had no verified information . . . that linked Martinez to any criminal behavior" and "[t]he informant also provided no verifiable predictive information about Martinez's future behavior that would have indicated any 'inside knowledge' about Martinez"); *United States v. Brown*, 448 F.3d 239, 252 (3d Cir. 2006) (concluding that "an excessively general description, combined with an honest but unreliable location tip [*i.e.*, a tip by a citizen whose identity is known but whose reliability is not known to the police,] in the absence of corroborating observations by the police, does not constitute reasonable suspicion under the 'narrowly drawn authority' of *Terry v. Ohio*"); *State v. Kooima*, 833 N.W.2d 202, 210-11 (Iowa 2013) ("we hold a bare assertion [of drunk driving] by an anonymous tipster, without relaying to the police a personal observation of erratic driving, other facts to establish the driver is intoxicated, or details not available to the general public as to the defendant's future actions does not have the requisite indicia of reliability to justify an investigatory stop. Such a tip does not meet the requirements of the Fourth Amendment.").

The pre-*Gates* caselaw applying the *Aguilar-Spinelli* test contains extensive discussion of the concepts of "veracity" and "basis of knowledge" with respect to informants' tips. Although *Gates* overrules the *Aguilar-Spinelli* approach of treating these factors as separate and independent criteria, it acknowledges the relevance of both and does not undermine the earlier judicial analyses of "veracity" and "basis of knowledge."

25.35.2. *"Veracity" of the Informant*

The "veracity" inquiry examines whether there are facts showing either that the informant is generally credible or that the information that s/he gave on this particular occasion is reliable. *Aguilar v. Texas, supra*, 378 U.S. at 114-15. Information from an informant of unknown or doubtful reliability is worth little. *E.g., Wong Sun v. United States,* 371 U.S. 471, 480-81 (1963); *Taylor v. Alabama,* 457 U.S. 687, 688-89 (1982); *Florida v. J.L., supra,* 529 U.S. at 270-71. *See, e.g., United States v. Glover,* 755 F.3d 811, 815-16 (7th Cir. 2014) ("Officer Brown's affidavit did not include any available information on Doe's credibility. . . . ¶ . . . The complete omission of information regarding Doe's credibility is insurmountable, and it undermines the deference we would otherwise give the decision of the magistrate to issue the search warrant."). "Even a known informant's information may require corroboration if an affidavit supplies little information concerning that informant's reliability." *United States v. Clay,* 630 Fed. Appx. 377, 385 (6th Cir. 2015).

"[T]he ordinary citizen who has never before reported a crime to the police" is generally viewed as "more reliable than one who supplies information on a regular basis" (*United States v. Harris,* 403 U.S. 573, 599 (1971) (Harlan, J., dissenting)). If the source of information is an informant who supplies information on a regular basis, then a critical question is whether the information supplied in prior cases proved to be accurate. *See, e.g., McCray v. Illinois,* 386 U.S. 300, 303-04 (1967); *United States v. Ross,* 456 U.S. 798, 817 n.22 (1982). Mere conclusory allegations about the accuracy of the informant in prior cases are insufficient (*see Gates, supra,* 462 U.S. at 239; *Aguilar v. Texas, supra,* 378 U.S. at 114-15); details must be supplied concerning the number of times the informant has provided information in the past and the extent to which that information led to arrests and convictions. *See, e.g., State v. Robinson,* 2009 VT 1, 185 Vt. 232, 239, 969 A.2d 127, 132 (2009) ("The mere statement that the informant had in the past provided unspecified, albeit purportedly 'creditable,' 'accurate,' or "reliable' information that 'concerned' drug deals or dealers does not establish the informant's inherent credibility"); *United States v. Neal,* 577 Fed. Appx. 434, 441 (6th Cir. 2014) ("This Court has repeatedly held that an affidavit that furnishes details of an informant's track record of providing reliable tips to the affiant can substantiate the informant's credibility, such that other indicia of reliability may not be required when relying on the informant's statements. ¶ However, where the affidavit does not aver facts showing the relationship between the affiant and the informant, or detail the affiant's knowledge regarding the informant providing prior reliable tips that relate to the same type of crimes as the current tip concerns, this Court has generally found that other indicia of reliability must be present to substantiate the informant's statements."). *Compare McCray v. Illinois, supra,* 386 U.S. at 303-04 (credibility of an informant was sufficiently established by the informant's having supplied information on fifteen to twenty prior occasions that proved accurate and resulted in numerous arrests and convictions), *with State v. Betts,* 194 Vt. 212, 224-25, 75 A.3d 629, 638-39 (2013) (trooper's affidavit, which "indicated that the confidential informant [who was the source of the information upon which the police relied] had 'provided . . . information in the past that has led to the arrest of at least three separate individuals for various narcotics offenses'" – but which "contain[ed] no indication as to the actual nature of the informant's cooperation or information in the past, how the information 'led' to the alleged arrests, or the final outcome of any of the cases in which he or she was involved" – failed to provide the reviewing court with a sufficient "basis upon which to discharge its constitutional duty to independently analyze the informant's credibility"). In cross-examining a police officer on the issue of prior performance of an informant, defense counsel should try to pin down precisely how many *bad* tips the informant has given in the past. Although the courts have not squarely confronted the question of how high a "batting average" is necessary to establish the credibility of an informant and although it certainly is not "required that informants used by the police be infallible" (*Illinois v. Gates, supra*, 462 U.S. at 245 n.14), there will be a point at which the number of prior instances of inaccuracy tips the scales in favor of a finding of unreliability. *See id.* at 234 (courts must engage in "a balanced assessment of the relative weights of all the various indicia of reliability (and unreliability) attending an informant's tip"); *Massachusetts v. Upton,* 466 U.S. 727, 732 (1984) (per curiam) (dictum) (same).

Apart from the general credibility of the informant, information given on a particular occasion gains reliability if it is an admission against penal interest. *See, e.g., United States v. Harris, supra*, 403 U.S. at 583-85 (plurality opinion); *Spinelli v. United States, supra*, 393 U.S. at 425 (Justice White, concurring); *United States v. Ruiz*, 623 Fed. Appx. 378 (9th Cir. 2015). Conversely, when the informant is known to have an incentive to give incriminating information – when, for example, the informant was paid for the information – there is reason to distrust the information. *See, e.g., Rutledge v. United States,* 392 A.2d 1062, 1066 (D.C. 1978) ("the expectation of reward for services is an ambiguous variable which very well could furnish reason to be honest and accurate in the hope of being utilized again or, conversely, reason to distort or fabricate, in order to earn at least one payment"). For an excellent enumeration and analysis of the factors to be considered in evaluating the veracity of a citizen informant, *see United States v. Brown*, 448 F.3d 239, 249-51 (3d Cir. 2006).

The necessary showing of veracity "requires that a tip be reliable in its assertion of illegality, not just in its tendency to identify a determinate person" (*Florida v. J.L.*, 529 U.S. 266, 272 (2000) ("Florida contends that the tip was reliable because its description of the suspect's visible attributes proved accurate: There really was a young black male wearing a plaid shirt at the bus stop. . . . These contentions misapprehend the reliability needed for a tip to justify a *Terry* stop. ¶ An accurate description of a subject's readily observable location and appearance is of course reliable in this limited sense: It will help the police correctly identify the person whom the tipster means to accuse. Such a tip, however, does not show that the tipster has knowledge of concealed criminal activity. . . . *Cf.* 4 W. LaFave, Search and Seizure § 9.4(h), p. 213 (3d ed.1996) (distinguishing reliability as to identification, which is often important in other criminal law contexts, from reliability as to the likelihood of criminal activity, which is central in anonymous-tip cases).").

25.35.3. *The Informant's "Basis of Knowledge"*

"It is axiomatic that a proper finding of probable cause requires the affidavit to show not only the affiant's knowledge but also that the affiant has sufficient basis for the knowledge." *State v. Schubert*, 2022-Ohio-4604, 2022 WL 17836574, at *3 (Ohio 2022). Whereas the "veracity" inquiry focuses on whether the informant is likely to be telling the truth, the inquiry into the informant's "basis of knowledge" is concerned with whether the informant has a sufficient basis for knowing the information s/he relates, even assuming that s/he is telling the truth. In *Aguilar v. Texas, supra*, the Court held that one of the principal defects in a police officer's affidavit was its failure to reveal "some of the underlying circumstances from which the informant concluded that the narcotics were where he claimed they were" (378 U.S. at 114).

The "basis of knowledge" concern is satisfied whenever the informant asserts a direct perceptual basis for knowing the facts: when, for example, the informant personally saw criminal behavior or contraband (*see, e.g., United States v. Bruner*, 657 F.2d 1278, 1297 (D.C. Cir. 1981)), or was a participant in the crime (*see, e.g., United States v. Estrada*, 733 F.2d 683, 686 (9th Cir. 1984)). Mere conclusory recitations, such as that "the informant had personal knowledge," will not suffice (*United States v. Long*, 439 F.2d 628, 630-31 (D.C. Cir. 1971); *People v. Leftwich*, 869 P.2d 1260, 1266-67 (Colo. 1994); *State v. Baca*, 1982-NMSC-016, 97 N.M. 379, 381, 640 P.2d 485, 487 (1982)); there must be some concrete, factual indication of the basis for the informant's "personal knowledge" (*see, e.g., United States v. Wall*, 277 Fed. Appx. 704 (9th Cir. 2008)).

The Court explained in *Spinelli v. United States, supra*, that "[i]n the absence of a statement detailing the manner in which the information was gathered, it is especially important that the tip describe the accused's criminal activity in sufficient detail that the magistrate may know that he is relying on something more substantial than a casual rumor circulating in the underworld or an accusation based merely on an individual's general reputation" (393 U.S. at 416). When testing this sort of "self-verifying detail" (*United States v. Gifford*, 727 F.3d 92, 99 (1st Cir. 2013)), the courts must critically consider whether the details are such that they must have been derived from direct observation or insider information, as distinguished from scuttlebutt. *See id.* at 100 ("While the Government offers the informant's statements regarding the contemporaneous state of the marijuana grow as well as the autumn grow as self-authenticating, without any statements as to the informant's basis of knowledge, there is no means of determining whether that information was obtained first-hand or through rumor. The information is not so specific and specialized that it could only be known to a person with inside information. Further, information about Gifford's former and current occupation are not so self-verifying to establish the reliability of the informant."). *See also, e.g., United States v. Martinez*, 486 F.3d 855, 861-64 (5th Cir. 2007) (finding no reasonable suspicion where an informant "provided no verifiable predictive information . . . that would have indicated any 'inside knowledge'"); *United States v. Bush*, 647 F.2d 357, 364 & n.6 (3d Cir. 1981) (the informant's statement that two men had flown to New York to obtain heroin and would return that evening was not an adequate "self-verifying detail," since it was not the type of fact that "arguably would only be known to someone with reliable information" and it was "surely equally probable that the informant was merely repeating a rumor overheard on the street"); *Shivers v. State*, 258 Ga. App. 253, 573 S.E.2d 494 (2002); *West v. State*, 137 Md. App. 314, 768 A.2d 150 (2000).

25.35.4. *Partial Corroboration of the Informant's Statement Through Police Investigation*

In upholding reliance on the informant's tip in *Illinois v. Gates, supra*, the Court stressed that the information "had been corroborated in major part" as a result of police investigation (462 U.S. at 243). The Court explained that "[t]he corroboration of the letter's predictions that the Gateses' car would be in Florida, that Lance Gates would fly to Florida in the next day or so, and that he would drive the car north toward Bloomingdale all indicated, albeit not with certainty, that the informant's other assertions also were true" (*id.* at 244). These events, though not necessarily dispositive of criminal activity, were viewed by the Court as "suggestive of a prearranged drug run" (*id.* at 243). In contrast, in *Florida v. J.L., supra*, the Court held that an anonymous tip that a certain individual at a particular location was in possession of a gun did not provide the police with an adequate basis for stopping and frisking that individual, even though the police observations corroborated that there was a person matching the description at that precise location, because the corroborating observations must support the reliability of the tip's "assertion of illegality," not just the reliability of its "identif[ication] [of] a determinate person" (529 U.S. at 272; see § 25.35.2 concluding paragraph, *supra*). Thus, in gauging whether an informant's tip has been adequately corroborated through police investigation, the courts have been careful to require that the activity witnessed by the police be at least "suspicious" (*Rutledge v. United States,* 392 A.2d 1062, 1066-67 (D.C. 1978)), or "suggestive of . . . criminal activity" (*People v. Elwell,* 50 N.Y.2d 231, 241, 406 N.E.2d 471, 477, 428 N.Y.S.2d 655, 662 (1980)). *See also, e.g., United States v. Reaves*, 512 F.3d 123, 127-28 (4th Cir. 2008).

In some circumstances, the corroboration can come from prior reports of criminal activity. Thus, in *Massachusetts v. Upton,* 466 U.S. 727 (1984), the Court found that an informant's tip describing stolen goods concealed in her former boyfriend's motor home was partially corroborated by police reports of recent burglaries in which the descriptions of certain of the items stolen "tallied with" the informant's descriptions of the stolen goods (*see id.* at 733-34). The police observations offered by the prosecution as corroborating an informant must be sufficiently specific and factually detailed to support the conclusion that the behavior observed is criminal, not innocent. *See, e.g., State v. Novembrino,*105 N.J. 95, 127-28, 519 A.2d 820, 839 (1987) (applying the state constitution to find corroboration inadequate: ("[T]he affidavit is utterly devoid of specific facts witnessed by the officers from which the judge could have independently concluded that their suspicions were reasonable. The affidavit does not state with particularity what the officers observed or why the officers believed that drugs were being sold. It does not inform the judge in what respect the transactions observed by the officers differed from routine service station transactions. The only specific allegation offered is that an identification check was made with respect to one vehicle that entered the service station that day – after its occupant completed 'a transaction' with defendant – and the check revealed that the vehicle's owner had been arrested on charges related to drugs. That factual insertion is insufficient to overcome the deficiencies in detail and substance to which we have averted. ¶ . . . [T]his affidavit, read tolerantly and nontechnically, simply does not pass constitutional muster. . . . The conclusory allegations of the officers are even less certain and less persuasive than the conclusory and vague allegations of the informant. Our common-sense review of these circumstances leads to the conclusion that the officers, after an abbreviated investigation, were uncertain whether they had seen drug sales and their informant was vague about what he had seen and silent as to when he had seen it. Read together, the allegations of the informant and of the officers did not provide the issuing judge with sufficient facts on which to base an independent determination as to the existence of probable cause.").

25.35.5. *Disclosure of the Informant's Name at the Suppression Hearing*

In cases in which a search or seizure was based either wholly or partly on an informant's tip, defense counsel almost invariably will want to obtain the informant's name from the police or the prosecutor, so as to be able to make an independent investigation of the informant's prior "track record," the informant's "basis of knowledge," and any bias that the informant may have against the defendant. Disclosure of the informant's identity is not available as a matter of right, but can be ordered in the discretion of the judge presiding at a suppression hearing. *See, e.g., Schmid v. State*, 615 P.2d 565, 570-71 (Alaska 1980). The so-called "informer's privilege" and its effect upon the defendant's right to disclosure of the names of confidential informers at a suppression hearing is discussed in § 18.10.1 *supra*.

G. Settings Governed by Specialized Fourth Amendment Standards

25.36. *"Administrative" Searches of Commercial Premises*

Entries and inspections of commercial premises are the subject of specialized canons of Fourth Amendment doctrine usually identified by the rubrics "searches of licensed dealers in regulated industries" and "administrative searches." Warrantless entries and inspections are permissible in the case of a few "'pervasively regulated business[es],' . . . and . . . 'closely regulated' industries 'long subject to close supervision and inspection'" (*Marshall v. Barlow's Inc.*, 436 U.S. 307, 313 (1978)), but this category is a narrow one. *See City of Los Angeles v. Patel*, 576 U.S. 409, 424 (2015) ("Over the past 45 years, the Court has identified only four industries that 'have such a history of government oversight that no reasonable expectation of privacy . . . could exist for a proprietor over the stock of such an enterprise,' *Barlow's, Inc.*, 436 U.S., at 313 . . . . Simply listing these industries refutes petitioner's argument that hotels should be counted among them. Unlike liquor sales, *Colonnade Catering Corp. v. United States*, 397 U.S. 72 . . . (1970), firearms dealing, *United States v. Biswell*, 406 U.S. 311. . . (1972), mining, *Donovan v. Dewey*, 452 U.S. 594 . . . (1981), or running an automobile junkyard, *New York v. Burger*, 482 U.S. 691 . . . (1987), nothing inherent in the operation of hotels poses a clear and significant risk to the public welfare. ¶ Moreover, '[t]he clear import of our cases is that the closely regulated industry . . . is the exception.'"). For a detailed discussion of the regulated-industries doctrine and its limits, s*ee Liberty Coins, LLC v. Goodman*, 880 F.3d 274 (6th Cir. 2018); *EZ Pawn Corp. v. City of New York*, 90 F. Supp. 3d 403 (E.D. N.Y. 2019). *Compare Calzone v. Olson*, 931 F.3d 722 (8th Cir. 2019), *and Owner-Operator Independent Drivers Association, Inc. v. United States Department of Transportation*, 840 F.3d 679 (7th Cir. 2016), *and In the Matter of Owner Operator Independent Drivers Association, Inc., v. New York State Department of Transportation*, 2023 WL 3956619 (N.Y. Ct. App. 2023) (commercial trucking is a closely regulated industry), *and Killgore v. City of South El Monte*, 3 F.4th 1186 (9th Cir. 2021) (massage parlors are a closely regulated industry), *with Zadeh v. Robinson*, 928 F.3d 457, 466 (5th Cir. 2019) (dictum) ("the medical industry as a whole is not a closely regulated industry"), *and Cotropia v. Chapman*, 978 F.3d 282, 287 (5th Cir. 2020) (dictum) (same). *And see Verdun v. City of San Diego*, 51 F.4th 1033 (9th Cir. 2022) (chalking tires comes within the administrative search exception to the warrant requirement).

For "administrative" searches and inspections of other sorts of business premises and commercial enterprises, a search warrant or subpoena is required but may be issued without an individualized showing of cause. *Camara v. Municipal Court*, 387 U.S. 523 (1967); *See v. City of Seattle*, 387 U.S. 541 (1967). What is required in these latter cases, "in order for an administrative search to be constitutional, [is that] the subject of the search must be afforded an opportunity to obtain precompliance review before a neutral decisionmaker" (*City of Los Angeles v. Patel, supra*, 576 U.S. at 420). *See, e.g., Michigan v. Tyler*, 436 U.S. 499, 507-08 (1978) ("To secure a warrant to investigate the cause of a fire, an official must show more than the bare fact that a fire has occurred. The magistrate's duty is to assure that the proposed search will be reasonable, a determination that requires inquiry into the need for the intrusion on the one hand, and the threat of disruption to the occupant on the other. For routine building inspections, a reasonable balance between these competing concerns is usually achieved by broad legislative or administrative guidelines specifying the purpose, frequency, scope, and manner of conducting the inspections. In the context of investigatory fire searches, which are not programmatic but are responsive to individual events, a more particularized inquiry may be necessary. The number of prior entries, the scope of the search, the time of day when it is proposed to be made, the lapse of time since the fire, the continued use of the building, and the owner's efforts to secure it against intruders might all be relevant factors. Even though a fire victim's privacy must normally yield to the vital social objective of ascertaining the cause of the fire, the magistrate can perform the important function of preventing harassment by keeping that invasion to a minimum."). A line of Ninth Circuit cases holds that searches made under the regulatory-search doctrine and other exceptions to the requirement of particularized probable cause or reasonable suspicion violate the Fourth Amendment if it is shown that they were conducted for the illicit purpose of apprehending suspected perpetrators or seizing evidence of criminal activity. *Perez Cruz v. Barr*, 926 F.3d 1128, 1139-40 (9th Cir. 2019) ("Under these no-probable-cause circumstances, 'the exemption from the need for probable cause (and warrant), which is accorded to searches made for the purpose of inventory or administrative regulation, is not accorded to searches that are not made for those purposes.' *Whren [v. United States]*, 517 U.S. [806] at 811–12 [(1996)]. Without an inquiry into purpose, these exceptions would provide officers with 'a purposeful and general means of discovering evidence of crime,' which the Fourth Amendment forbids."); *United States v. Orozco*, 858 F.3d 1204 (9th Cir. 2017); *and see United States v. Johnson*, 889 F.3d 1120, 1125-26 (9th Cir. 2018), quoted in § 25.25 *supra*; *cf. United States v. Grey*, 959 F.3d 1166, 1183 (9th Cir. 2020) ("Where, as here, law enforcement officers are called upon to assist in the execution of an administrative warrant providing for the inspection of a private residence, the execution of the warrant is consistent with the Fourth Amendment only so long as the officers' primary purpose in executing the warrant is to assist in the inspection. If the person challenging the execution of the warrant shows that the officers' primary purpose was to gather evidence in support of an ongoing criminal investigation, the conduct does not satisfy the Fourth Amendment."); *United States v. Feliciana*, 974 F.3d 519, 526 (4th Cir. 2020), summarized in § 25.9 *supra* (rejecting a regulatory-search justification for stopping a commercial vehicle when the officer who conducted the stop did so for a purpose other than that underlying the regulatory scheme and was not within the class of officers authorized to enforce the regulatory scheme: "the Government cannot justify the constitutionality of this traffic stop by relying on a regulatory scheme that was not the basis for the stop").

25.37. *Searches of a Probationer's or Parolee's Residence*

In *Griffin v. Wisconsin*, 483 U.S. 868 (1987), the Supreme Court upheld a warrantless search of a probationer's home by probation officers, pursuant to a state regulation that authorized "any probation officer to search a probationer's home without a warrant as long as his supervisor approves and as long as there are 'reasonable grounds' to believe the presence of contraband – including any item that the probationer cannot possess under the probation conditions" (*id*. at 871). Acknowledging that "[a] probationer's home, like anyone else's, is protected by the Fourth Amendment's requirement that searches be 'reasonable,'" and that "we usually require that a search be undertaken only pursuant to a warrant (and thus supported by probable cause, as the Constitution says warrants must be)" (*id.* at 873), the Court nevertheless concluded that "[a] State's operation of a probation system, like its operation of a school [see § 25.38 *infra*], government office or prison, or its supervision of a regulated industry [see § 25.36 *supra*], . . . presents 'special needs' beyond normal law enforcement that may justify departures from the usual warrant and probable-cause requirements" (*id.* at 873-74). The Court held that "the special needs of Wisconsin's probation system make the warrant requirement impracticable and justify replacement of the standard of probable cause by 'reasonable grounds'" (*id.* at 876) and that "[t]he search of Griffin's residence was 'reasonable' within the meaning of the Fourth Amendment because it was conducted pursuant to a valid regulation governing probationers" (*id.* at 880). *See also United States v. Payne*, 181 F.3d 781, 784, 786-87, 791 (6th Cir. 1999) (upholding the constitutionality of a Kentucky parole department policy similar to the probation regulation upheld in *Griffin*, *supra*, because "the Kentucky policy is sufficiently specific and adopts a standard that is at least as demanding as the standard upheld in *Griffin*," but suppressing the items seized by the parole officers because their "searches of the trailer [which "the government and Payne's attorney have treated . . . as Payne's residence"] and Payne's truck were not justified by a reasonable suspicion that he possessed contraband"). *Compare State v. Mefford*, 2022 MT 185, 410 Mont. 146, 167, 517 P.3d 210, 225 (2022), summarized in § 25.18 *supra*] (holding a parole officer's search of the digital photo application of a parolee's cell phone unconstitutional because the officer knew no "specific facts upon which the officer reasonably suspected violations of probation or the criminal law. . . . [N]othing that . . . [the officer] expected to discover in Mefford's photo gallery had any connection to the initial crime that landed him on parole or to the admitted curfew violation that . . . [the officer was] investigating. Mefford was paroled on drug and assault convictions, not for sex crimes or crimes involving minors. The contents of his photo gallery bore no relation to the reasons for his parole.").

The *Griffin* rule is, by its terms and its underlying rationale, limited to "a 'special needs' search conducted by a probation officer monitoring whether the probationer is complying with probation restrictions" (*United States v. Knights*, 534 U.S. 112, 117 (2001)). *Compare Keating v. Pittston City*, 643 Fed. Appx. 219 (3d Cir. 2016), *with United States v. Carnes*, 309 F.3d 950, 960-61 (6th Cir. 2002) ("The government's argument . . . that the special needs of law enforcement allowed the government to seize and listen to the six tapes seized at 1731 Harmon, is unavailing. . . . At the suppression hearing, the government argued that the tapes were seized to help establish a violation of the residency requirement of Carnes's parole agreement. . . . The fact that the tapes were not listened to until well after the parole hearing shows that they were not originally seized, nor subsequently listened to, pursuant to the special authority granted the government for supervising parolees. . . . Where the government claims that 'special needs' of law enforcement justify an otherwise illegal search and seizure, a court must look to the 'actual motivations of individual officers'. . . . Here, there is no evidence that the officers who seized the six tapes on January 14, 1997, were motivated by a desire to establish a violation of the residency requirement of Carnes's parole agreement. Rather, the government's failure to listen to the tapes until well after the parole hearing suggests some other motivation."); *White v. Commonwealth*, 2005 WL 2807242, at *4 (Ky. App. 2005) ("the record is void of any evidence suggesting the police officer was aware of the consent form [executed by White as a condition of his participation in a drug court program and allowing any law enforcement agency to search his person, automobile, or residence pursuant to drug-court procedures] prior to the search. . . . ¶ . . .

[W]e now hold that a search condition cannot justify an otherwise unlawful search if a law enforcement officer was unaware of the condition at the time the search was conducted. Accordingly, we are of the opinion the search of appellant's trunk was unlawful and the circuit court erred by denying appellant's motion to suppress the evidence seized therefrom."). And where, as in *Griffin*, the applicable probation- or parole-release provision authorizes warrantless searches only if a probation or parole officer has reasonable grounds to believe that the releasee is violating the law or some condition of his or her release, a search unsupported by reasonable suspicion violates the Fourth Amendment. *See, e.g., United States v. Fletcher*, 978 F.3d 1009 (6th Cir. 2020); *United States v. Payne, supra*.

In *United States v. Knights, supra*, the Court addressed the distinct scenario of a defendant who had been placed on probation pursuant to a California statute that established a probation condition that the probationer will "'[s]ubmit his . . . person, property, place of residence, vehicle, personal effects, to search at anytime [sic], with or without a search warrant, warrant of arrest or reasonable cause by any probation officer or law enforcement officer'" (534 U.S. at 114) and who signed a probation order agreeing to abide by this condition and thus "was unambiguously informed of it" (*id.* at 114, 119). The question before the Court was "whether a [warrantless] search [of the probationer's residence] pursuant to this probation condition, and supported by reasonable suspicion, satisfied the Fourth Amendment" (*id.*). Distinguishing the *Griffin* rule and its limitations, the Court observed that "nothing in the condition of probation suggests that it was confined to searches bearing upon probationary status and nothing more" (*id.* at 116). Nor did the Fourth Amendment "limit[ ] searches pursuant to this probation condition to those with a 'probationary' purpose" (*id.*). Analyzing the totality of the circumstances, and factoring in "the probation search condition . . . [as] a salient circumstance" (*id.* at 118) because it "significantly diminished Knights' [sic] reasonable expectation of privacy" (*id.* at 120), the Court concluded that "the balance of the[ ] considerations requires no more than reasonable suspicion to conduct a search of this probationer's house" (*id.* at 121). Because "Knights concede[d] . . . that the search in this case was supported by reasonable suspicion" (*id.* at 122), the Court upheld the warrantless search. *Compare People v. Johns*, 342 Ill. App. 3d 297, 301-03, 795 N.E.2d 433, 438-39, 277 Ill. Dec. 66, 71-72 (2003) ("It is implicit in the Court's statements in *Knights* and *Griffin* that probation searches are limited by some reasonable and legally protectible privacy interest. . . . ¶ By mandating that we balance the government's interests against the privacy interests of a probationer, and by declaring the individual's privacy interests to be diminished, but not extinguished, the Supreme Court has made it clear that in the case of searches pursuant to probation conditions, the ordinary search requirements are to be relaxed but not eliminated. ¶ Unlike in every suspicionless search [case in which the search was] approved . . . , law enforcement authorities [here] entered an individual's home. We have considered the totality of the circumstances, balancing the degree to which the search intruded upon defendant's privacy and the degree to which the intrusion is needed for the promotion of legitimate governmental interests. Based upon the unique facts and circumstances of this case, and given the holdings in *Knights* and *Griffin,* we find that some reasonable suspicion was required to justify the search of the dresser drawer in defendant's bedroom."); *United States v. Dixon*, 984 F.3d 814, 818, 822 (9th Cir. 2020) (when a parolee is "'subject to a warrantless, suspicionless search condition'" this "authority is not limitless"; "to conduct a search of property pursuant to this condition, the individual subject to it must 'exhibit[ ] a sufficiently strong connection to [the property in question] to demonstrate "control" over it.' . . . ¶ We hold that before conducting a warrantless search of a vehicle pursuant to a supervised release condition, law enforcement must have probable cause to believe that the supervisee owns or controls the vehicle to be searched."). In *Samson v. California*, 547 U.S. 843 (2006), summarized in § 25.10 second paragraph *supra*, the Supreme Court revisited *Knights* "in the context of a parolee search" (*id.* at 850) and held that "parolees have fewer expectations of privacy than probationers, because parole is more akin to imprisonment than probation is to imprisonment." On this ground, the Court upheld a California statute providing "that every prisoner eligible for release on state parole 'shall agree in writing to be subject to search or seizure by a parole officer or other peace officer at any time of the day or night, with or without a search warrant and with or without cause'" (*id.* at 846). The application of the statute to justify a police officer's search of the person of a parolee in a street encounter was consistent with the Fourth Amendment, the *Samson* Court held, even though the officer had no warrant, probable cause, or even reasonable suspicion. *See also United States v. Estrella*, 69 F.4th 958, 961 (9th Cir. 2023) (in a case involving the same parole condition as *Samson*, the Ninth Circuit writes: "It is firmly established that '[a] search of a parolee that complies with the terms of a valid search condition will usually be deemed reasonable under the Fourth Amendment.' . . . As a threshold requirement, we have held that 'an officer must know of a detainee's parole status before that person can be detained and searched pursuant to a parole condition.' However, this Court has yet to specifically address how precise that knowledge must be. ¶ . . . [W]e now hold that a law enforcement officer must have probable cause to believe that a person is on active parole before he may be detained and searched pursuant to a parole condition. Although a law enforcement officer must have 'advance knowledge' that the detainee remains on active parole, . . . the officer need not 'know to an absolute certainty,' with precise day-by-day or minute-by-minute information of the detainee's parole status . . . . It is sufficient for the officer to determine, using the well-established rules governing probable cause, that the individual to be detained and searched is on active parole, and that an applicable parole condition authorizes the challenged search or seizure."). *But see State v. Ochoa*, 792 N.W.2d 260 (Iowa 2010), summarized in § 25.10 *supra*; *and compare State v. Ballard*, 874 N.W.2d 61, 70, 72 (N.D. 2016) ("Here, Ballard was an unsupervised probationer, not a parolee like *Knights*. . . . ¶ By contrast to *Samson,* Ballard pleaded guilty to two misdemeanor drug crimes. For one he was fined $200 and was sentenced to 180 days in jail with 150 days suspended. . . . ¶ Ballard's minimal unsupervised probation conditions stand in stark contrast to Samson's extensive parole restraints, limitations and loss of liberty after prison time. Ballard pleaded guilty to two misdemeanors, as opposed to Samson's felony conviction. Ballard was not incarcerated after his guilty pleas; Samson was paroled after time in prison. Ballard was not subject to supervision for either conviction. Samson was heavily supervised and his liberty was severely curtailed in virtually every respect important to a law-abiding person. Samson's associational rights were severely curtailed. Samson's travel rights were similarly limited. Samson was required to report his movements and changes in employment while Ballard had no similar constraints. Samson was subject to onerous and intrusive changes to his parole conditions, including psychiatric treatment or other special conditions. Ballard faced no such uncertainty and suffered no comparable loss of liberty. ¶ The United States Supreme Court described a criminal defendant's Fourth Amendment privacy interests as a 'continuum.' *Samson*, 547 U.S. at 850 . . . Based on that continuum, we do not equate Samson's extensive parole constraints with Ballard's modest conditions of unsupervised probation. We therefore cannot conclude the governmental interest outweighs Ballard's expectation of privacy so that Ballard's suspicionless search of his person and his home is reasonable under the Fourth Amendment."); *Commonwealth v. Feliz*, 486 Mass.

510, 515, 159 N.E.3d 661, 667 (2020), quoted in § 25.18.1 *supra.*

The rules of *Samson* and *Knights* respectively are self-evidently limited to cases in which a probation or parole condition clearly authorizes the search and in which the defendant was "unambiguously informed" of this condition (*Knights, supra,* 534 U.S. at 119); *State v. Howell,* 2008 WL 732128 (Tenn. App. 2008). *Compare United States v. Williams,* 880 F.3d 713 (5th Cir. 2018), *and United States v. Lambus,* 897 F.3d 368 (2d Cir. 2018), *with Jones v. State,* 282 Ga. 784, 787-88, 653 S.E.2d 456, 459 (2007) (the *Knights* rule does not apply because the state has not identified any "valid law, legally authorized regulation, or sentencing order" that limited the defendant's "right not to have his home searched without a warrant" as a result of his probationary status and that provided him with adequate "notice of that deprivation of rights"), *and State v. Vanderkolk,* 32 N.E.3d 775 (Ind. 2015) ("A probationer or community corrections participant may, by a valid advance consent or search term in the conditions of release, authorize a warrantless search of his or her premises without reasonable suspicion. Because the search term in this case informed the participant that he was consenting only to searches made upon probable cause, we reverse the partial denial of the defendant's motion to suppress." (*Id.* at 775.) "In determining that the warrantless search of a probationer's residence based on reasonable suspicion was reasonable in *United States v. Knights,* the United States Supreme Court considered that the probation order 'clearly expressed the search condition' and 'unambiguously informed [the defendant] of it.' . . . In the present case, the search condition was not clearly expressed and the defendant was not unambiguously informed. The defendant consented only to searches upon probable cause, not to the type of search conducted in the present case. The ensuing search and seizures were thus unlawful under the Fourth Amendment, and the resulting evidence must be suppressed." *Id.* at 778.), *and Brennan v. Dawson,* 752 Fed. Appx. 276, 284 (6th Cir. 2018) (dictum) ("Brennan was subject to at least some warrantless intrusions because his probation required him to take randomly administered breath tests on demand. But that condition did not expose his home to warrantless searches . . . . [A] court may subject a probationer to warrantless searches of his home if it so chooses, yet Brennan's probation contains no such condition. We infer from the lack of such condition that Brennan was not subject to warrantless searches of his home. Indeed, Brennan was as secure in his home as a non-probationer."), *and United States v. Lara,* 815 F.3d 605, 607, 611-12 (9th Cir. 2016) (the probation agreement that the defendant signed, authorizing the state to search his "'person and property, including any residence, premises, [or] container,'" did not authorize the probation officers' "warrantless, suspicionless searches of his cell phone" during a search of his home; the defendant's "privacy interest in his cell phone and the data it contained . . . was substantial in light of the broad amount of data contained in, or accessible through, his cell phone," and the probation agreement did not "clear[ly] and unequivocal[ly] . . . authoriz[e] . . . cell phone searches"). *Cf. State v. Bennett,* 288 Kan. 86, 98, 200 P.3d 455, 462-63 (2009) ("The Kansas Legislature has not authorized suspicionless searches of probationers or parolees. Kansas' procedures for parole supervision specifically inform parolees that they have an expectation that searches will not be conducted unless an officer has a (reasonable) suspicion that such a search is necessary to enforce the conditions of parole. Put another way, parolees in Kansas have an expectation that they will not be subjected to suspicionless searches. ¶ It logically follows from this conclusion that because probationers have a greater expectation of privacy than parolees, searches of probationers in Kansas must also be based on a reasonable suspicion. Thus, the condition of Bennett's probation subjecting him to random, nonconsensual, suspicionless searches violates his rights under the Fourth Amendment and Kansas Constitution Bill of Rights.").

State courts that can be persuaded to find the Fourth Amendment rules of *Griffin*, *Knights* and *Samson* too confusing or oppressive are free to adopt a more protective set of rules under their state constitutions. *See, e.g., State v. Short*, 851 N.W.2d 474, 504-06 (Iowa 2014) ("[*State v.*] *Cullison* [, 173 N.W.2d 533 (1970)] rejected reasoning designed to strip or dilute constitutional protections for probationers home searches. . . . So should we. ¶ That leaves the additional constitutional requirements of obtaining a warrant from a neutral magistrate describing the place to be searched and the things to be sought with particularity. Whatever else may have been true in the past, obtaining a warrant from a judicial officer is not particularly onerous. ¶ The factual assertion in *Griffin* that it was impracticable for a probation officer to obtain a warrant was wrong then and it is even more wrong today. . . . ¶ . . . [U]nder the search and seizure provision of article I, section 8 of the Iowa Constitution, a valid warrant is required for law enforcement's search of a parolee's home."); *Commonwealth v. LaFrance*, 402 Mass. 789, 790, 792-95, 525 N.E.2d 379, 380, 381-83 (1988) ("[B]oth art. 14 of the Massachusetts Declaration of Rights and the Fourth Amendment to the Constitution of the United States forbid the search of a probationer or her premises unless the probation officer has at least a reasonable suspicion that a search might produce evidence of wrongdoing. The requirement that the probation officer have reasonable suspicion should be set forth expressly in any order imposing such a special condition. . . . ¶ . . .We accept for art. 14 purposes the principle that a reduced level of suspicion, such as 'reasonable suspicion,' will justify a search of a probationer and her premises. . . . ¶ . . .We need not define here the limits of reasonable suspicion. . . . It may be that *Terry v. Ohio* . . . [see § 25.9 *supra*] will provide guidance in defining reasonable suspicion. . . . ¶ The Supreme Court divided in the *Griffin* case over the question whether under the Fourth Amendment a warrant was required in support of the search of the probationer's home. . . . ¶ We are persuaded that a warrantless search of a probationer's home, barring the appropriate application of a traditional exception to the warrant requirement, cannot be justified under art. 14. Mr. Justice Blackmun's dissent in the *Griffin* case (joined on this point by Justices Brennan and Marshall) has the better of the argument concerning the propriety of a warrantless search of a probationer's home. . . . We agree with Justice Abrahamson of the Supreme Court of Wisconsin, dissenting in *State v. Griffin*, that the issuance of a search warrant on a proper showing of reasonable cause 'is not an undue burden on the probation officer and provides the protection for the probationer guaranteed by the constitution[ ]. . . .'"); see generally § 17.11 *supra*.

25.38. *Searches and Seizures of Students in School*

The Fourth Amendment clearly applies to searches and seizures made by police officers inside a school building. *See, e.g., Piazzola v. Watkins,* 316 F. Supp. 624, 626-27 (M.D. Ala. 1970), *aff'd,* 442 F.2d 284 (5th Cir. 1971). It is equally clear that if a school official conducts a search or seizure of a student at the behest of the police, the school official is acting as an agent of the police and is subject to the same restrictions that would govern police conduct under the circumstances. *See, e.g., Picha v. Wielgos,* 410 F. Supp. 1214, 1219-21 (N.D. Ill. 1976); *Piazzola v. Watkins, supra,* 316 F. Supp. at 626-27; *M.J. v. State,* 399 So.2d 996 (Fla. App. 1981); *State v. Heirtzler,* 147 N.H. 344, 349-52, 789 A.2d 634, 638-41 (2001). *See generally* § 25.18.3 *supra*; Michael Pinard, *From the Classroom to the Courtroom: Reassessing Fourth Amendment*

Standards in Public School Searches Involving Law Enforcement Authorities, 45 ARIZ. L. REV. 1067 (2003).

Absent police involvement, searches of students in public schools by teachers, principals, or other school officials are governed by Fourth Amendment rules originating in *New Jersey v. T.L.O.*, 469 U.S. 325 (1985). The *T.L.O.* case established the premise that "the school setting requires some easing of the restrictions to which searches by public authorities are ordinarily subject" (*id.* at 340), including the warrant requirement and the probable cause requirement (*id.* at 340-41). Thus, "the legality of a search of a student . . . depend[s] simply on the reasonableness, under all the circumstances, of the search" (*id.* at 341). The determination of "the reasonableness of any search involves a two-fold inquiry: first, one must consider 'whether the . . . action was justified in its inception,' . . .; second, one must determine whether the search as actually conducted 'was reasonably related in scope to the circumstances which justified the interference in the first place'" (*id.*). *Compare id.* at 345-47 (applying the standard to the facts of the *T.L.O.* case and concluding that (i) the school vice-principal's "decision to open T.L.O.'s purse was reasonable" because a teacher had observed T.L.O. smoking cigarettes in the girls' bathroom in violation of school rules and it was therefore reasonable to suspect that T.L.O. had cigarettes in her purse; (ii) when the vice-principal, in opening and removing a pack of cigarettes, observed a package of rolling papers, the "reasonable suspicion that T.L.O. was carrying marihuana as well as cigarettes in her purse . . . justified further exploration of T.L.O.'s purse, which turned up more evidence of drug-related activities: a pipe, a number of plastic bags of the type commonly used to store marihuana, a small quantity of marihuana, and a fairly substantial amount of money"; and (iii) "[u]nder these circumstances, it was not unreasonable to extend the search to a separate zippered compartment of the purse; and when a search of that compartment revealed an index card containing a list of 'people who owe me money' as well as two letters, the inference that T.L.O. was involved in marihuana trafficking was substantial enough to justify [the vice-principal] . . . in examining the letters to determine whether they contained any further evidence."), *with Safford Unified School District # 1 v. Redding*, 557 U.S. 364, 368-69, 373-77 (2009) (applying the *T.L.O.* standard and concluding that (i) an assistant principal had adequate "suspicion . . . to justify a search of [a student's] . . . backpack and outer clothing" in the student's "presence and in the relative privacy of [the assistant principal's] . . . office," based upon information from other students giving rise to a reasonable suspicion that the student was "giving out contraband pills" in violation of a school rule and that the student was "carrying [such pills] . . . on her person and in the [backpack]"; but that (ii) when the school nurse and an administrative assistant thereafter conducted a more intrusive search of the student's person in the nurse's office, directing the student to "remove her clothes down to her underwear, and then 'pull out' her bra and the elastic band on her underpants," "thus exposing her breasts and pelvic area to some degree," this "quantum leap from outer clothes and backpacks to exposure of intimate parts" violated the Fourth Amendment because the facts known to the school officials did not indicate that there was "danger to the [other] students from the power of the drugs [that the student was "reasonably suspected of carrying" – which were "common pain relievers"] or their quantity, . . . [or] any reason to suppose that . . . [the student] was carrying pills in her underwear."), *and T.R. by and through Brock v. Lamar County Board of Education*, 25 F.4th 877, 885 (11th Cir. 2022) (allegations that strip searches of a student by school officials stated a clearly established claim of violation of the Fourth Amendment; "Here, the district court reasoned that because school officials could not find marijuana in T.R.'s backpack, then they had reason to suspect that they would find marijuana in T.R.'s underwear or bra. Thus, according to the district court, the school officials had sufficient reason to suspect T.R. contained drugs under her clothing, which made this case factually distinguishable from *Safford*. However, this type of reasoning is of the sort that the Supreme Court expressly forbade in *Safford*. There, the court rejected the school's argument that 'as a truth universally acknowledged . . . students . . . hide contraband in or under their clothing[.]' . . . The Court classified this reasoning as a 'general background possibilit[y]' that a student could be hiding contraband under their clothing. . . . This type of general possibility is insufficient when considering 'the categorically extreme intrusiveness of a search down to the body of an adolescent.'"), *and Littell v. Houston Independent School District*, 894 F.3d 616, 623 (5th Cir. 2018) ("the Supreme Court has 'ma[d]e it clear' that a search of a student's underwear is impermissibly intrusive unless the school officials reasonably suspect either that the object of the search is dangerous, or that it is actually likely to be hidden in the student's underwear"), *and G.C. v. Owensboro Public Schools*, 711 F.3d 623, 633-34 (6th Cir. 2013) (in a decision issued even before the Supreme Court's announcement of strict privacy protections for cell phones' digital content in *Riley v. California*, 573 U.S. 373 (2014), the court of appeals holds that school officials' search of a cell phone confiscated from a student violated *T.L.O.*, notwithstanding the school officials' "background knowledge of [G.C.'s] drug abuse . . . [and] depressive tendencies," because "there is no evidence in the record to support the conclusion . . . that the school officials had any specific reason at the inception of the . . . search to believe that G.C. then was engaging in any unlawful activity or that he was contemplating injuring himself or another student"), *and In the Interest of Dumas*, 357 Pa. Super. 294, 298, 515 A.2d 984, 986 (1986) (striking down a school search under the *T.L.O.* standard because the assistant principal "was unable to articulate any reasons for [ ]his suspicion" that the student who had been caught smoking cigarettes was "involved with marijuana"), *and Coronado v. State*, 835 S.W.2d 636, 637, 641 (Tex. Crim. App. 1992) (although "the first prong of *T.L.O.* is met" in that the assistant principal had "reasonable grounds to suspect that [the student] was violating school rules by 'skipping'" class and leaving school early, the assistant principal's "searches of . . . [the student's] clothing and person, locker, and vehicle were excessively intrusive in light of the infraction of skipping school," notwithstanding the assistant principal's reasons for suspecting that the student was selling drugs to other students).

The Court in *T.L.O.* expressly reserved "the question, not presented by th[at] case, whether a schoolchild has a legitimate expectation of privacy in lockers, desks, or other school property provided for the storage of school supplies," and what "standards (if any) govern[ ] searches of such areas by school officials or by other public authorities acting at the request of school officials" (469 U.S. at 337 n.5). A number of lower court decisions have concluded that students have a reasonable expectation of privacy in their lockers, at least in the absence of an express school policy or state regulation that could render such an expectation unreasonable. *See, e.g., State v. Jones*, 666 N.W.2d 142, 147-48 (Iowa 2003) (citing caselaw from other jurisdictions); *Commonwealth v. Snyder*, 413 Mass. 521, 526, 597 N.E.2d 1363, 1366 (1992) (citing caselaw from other jurisdictions). In situations involving a school policy or state regulation establishing a school's right of access to the contents of students' lockers, some courts have found that students lacked a reasonable expectation of privacy in their lockers (*see, e.g., In Interest of Isiah B.*, 176 Wis. 2d 639, 649-50, 500 N.W.2d 637, 641 (Wis. 1993)), or had a reduced expectation of privacy in their lockers (*see, e.g., Commonwealth v. Cass*, 551 Pa. 25, 38-

39, 709 A.2d 350, 356-57 (1998)), while other courts have held that students possess an undiminished expectation of privacy in their lockers despite such policies or regulations (*see, e.g., State v. Jones*, 666 N.W.2d 142, 147-48 (Iowa 2003)).

Another question reserved in *T.L.O.* was "whether individualized suspicion is an essential element of the reasonableness standard . . . for searches by school authorities" (469 U.S. at 342 n.8.). Thereafter, the Court has twice upheld a program of random drug testing, without individualized suspicion, of students who voluntarily participated in extracurricular activities. *See Board of Education of Independent School District No. 92 of Pottawatomie County v. Earls*, 536 U.S. 822, 830-38 (2002) (in upholding a school district's policy of random drug testing of students voluntarily participating in competitive extracurricular activities, the Court applies a three-pronged standard – which considers the nature of the privacy interest affected; the character of the intrusion; and the nature and immediacy of the government's concerns and the efficacy of the policy in meeting them – and concludes that (1) the privacy interests of the children were diminished because they voluntarily chose to participate in extracurricular activities which were highly regulated; (2) urinalysis was a "negligible" intrusion, especially given that the test results were not turned over to law enforcement officials, the only consequence of refusing to participate in drug testing was nonparticipation in the extracurricular activity, and students did not face expulsion or suspension or any other school-related sanctions even if they tested positive; and (3) there was sufficient evidence of student use of drugs to justify the need for the drug testing program.); *Vernonia School District 47J v. Acton*, 515 U.S. 646, 648, 654-65 (1995) (in upholding a school district's policy of "random urinalysis drug testing of students who participate in the District's school athletics programs," the Court applies the same three-pronged analytic apparatus employed in *Earls*, and concludes that (1) the very nature of school sports results in a lesser degree of privacy, and student athletes "voluntarily subject themselves to a degree of regulation even higher than that imposed on students generally"; (2) the urinalysis testing process, as administered under the district's guidelines, involved a "negligible" degree of intrusion; and (3) there was concrete evidence of a significant increase in the use of drugs by the student body, "'particularly those involved in interscholastic athletics,'" and there was a basis for concluding that in the case of "drug use by school athletes, . . . the risk of immediate physical harm to the drug user or those with whom he is playing his sport is particularly high."). As the Court's analyses in *Acton* and *Earls* make clear, the constitutionality of a search of students without individualized suspicion turns upon a balancing of context-specific facts and circumstances. *See, e.g., Doe ex rel. Doe v. Little Rock School District*, 380 F.3d 349, 351, 354-56 (8th Cir. 2004) (rejecting a school district's attempt to apply *Acton* and *Earls* to justify a district practice of "subject[ing] secondary public school students to random, suspicionless searches of their persons and belongings," and explaining that, "[u]nlike the suspicionless searches of participants in school sports and other competitive extracurricular activities that the Supreme Court approved in *Vernonia* and *Earls*, in which 'the privacy interests compromised by the process' of the searches were deemed 'negligible,' . . . the type of search at issue here invades students' privacy interests in a major way"; "[i]n sharp contrast to these cases, the fruits of the searches at issue here are apparently regularly turned over to law enforcement and are used in criminal proceedings against students whose contraband is discovered"; and the district had failed to present the kinds of "particularized evidence" offered by the school districts "[i]n both *Vernonia* and *Earls* . . . to 'shore up' their assertions of a special need to institute administrative search programs for extracurricular-activity participants."); *B.C. v. Plumas*

Unified School District, 192 F.3d 1260, 1268 & nn.10-11 (9th Cir. 1999) (rejecting a school district's attempt to apply *Acton* to justify the use of a drug-sniffing dog to sniff all of the students in a classroom for drugs, and explaining that, "[i]n contrast [to *Acton*], the search in this case took place in a classroom where students were engaged in compulsory, educational activities," and that, "[i]n sharp contrast" to *Acton*, "the record here does not disclose that there was any drug crisis or even a drug problem" at the school at the time of the search); *Kittle-Aikeley v. Strong*, 844 F.3d 727, 741 (8th Cir. 2016) ("We conclude that the district court properly applied [*National Treasury Employees Union v.*] *Von Raab*, [489 U.S. 656 (1989)] when it conducted a program-by-program analysis. The category of students who may be drug tested as a condition of attending Linn State is composed only of those students who enroll in safety-sensitive educational programs. By requiring all incoming students to be drug tested, Linn State defined the category of students to be tested more broadly than was necessary to meet the valid special need of deterring drug use among students enrolled in safety-sensitive programs."). *See also York v. Wahkiakum School District No. 200*, 163 Wash. 2d 297, 299, 178 P.3d 995, 997 (2008) (rejecting *Vernonia School District 47J v. Acton* on state constitutional grounds and holding that "warrantless random and suspicionless drug testing of student athletes violates the Washington State Constitution").

 T.L.O.'s special rules for searches and seizures inside a school building may apply as well to external areas that are clearly part of the school grounds, but *T.L.O.*'s applicability presumably ends at the boundary line between school property and public-use areas adjacent to a school. *Compare Gonzalez v. Huerta*, 826 F.3d 854, 855, 858-59 (5th Cir. 2016) (a school district police officer, who was sued for detaining a school employee's husband in the school parking lot for refusing to show identification, was entitled to qualified immunity notwithstanding two "prior Supreme Court cases [that] have held that police may not detain an individual solely for refusing to provide identification," because "neither of those cases dealt with incidents occurring on school property," and "[t]his is no small distinction, as the Supreme Court has routinely reconsidered the scope of individual constitutional rights in a school setting."), *with J.P. ex rel. A.P. v. Millard Public Schools*, 285 Neb. 890, 830 N.W.2d 453 (2013) ("*T.LO.*['s] school-needs exception . . . for the search of students on school grounds" (*id.* at 905, 830 N.W.2d at 465) did not apply to a school official's "search of a student's pickup truck that was parked on a public street across from the school" (*id.* at 892, 830 N.W.2d at 457) and thus "was not in the school environment or under the dominion and control of the school" (*id.* at 909, 830 N.W.2d at 467). Although some courts "have expanded *T.L.O.*'s reasonable suspicion standard to a school's search of a student's vehicle parked on school grounds" and some courts have "extend[ed] the *T.L.O.* standard to school searches conducted while a student was attending a school-sponsored class or activity that was held off campus," the court explains that "none of these cases, nor any that we have found, recognize a right of school officials to conduct off-campus searches of a student's person or property which are unrelated to school-sponsored activities. To the contrary, courts have held that school officials lack authority to conduct such searches." (*Id.* at 900-01, 830 N.W.2d at 462.)).

H. *Derivative Evidence: Fruits of Unlawful Searches and Seizures*

25.39. *The Concept of "Derivative Evidence": Evidence That Must Be Suppressed as the Fruits of an Unlawful Search or Seizure*

When government agents have violated the restrictions of the Fourth Amendment or state constitutional or statutory protections against unlawful searches or seizures, the court must suppress not only evidence directly obtained by the violation but also "derivative evidence" – that is, evidence to which the police are led "'by the exploitation of that illegality'" (*Wong Sun v. United States*, 371 U.S. 471, 488 (1963)). *See also Brown v. Illinois*, 422 U.S. 590, 597-603 (1975); *Silverthorne Lumber Co. v. United States*, 251 U.S. 385 (1920); *Oregon v. Elstad*, 470 U.S. 298, 305-06 (1985) (dictum); *Vega v. Tekoh*, 142 S. Ct. 2095, 2103 (2022) (dictum). "Under the Court's precedents, the exclusionary rule encompasses both the 'primary evidence obtained as a direct result of an illegal search or seizure' and . . . 'evidence later discovered and found to be derivative of an illegality,' the so-called "'fruit of the poisonous tree.'"" *Utah v. Strieff*, 579 U.S. 232, 237 (2016) (dictum).

"*Wong Sun* . . . articulated the guiding principle for determining whether evidence derivatively obtained from a violation of the Fourth Amendment is admissible against the accused at trial: 'The exclusionary prohibition extends as well to the indirect as the direct products of such invasions.' 371 U.S., at 484. . . . As subsequent cases have confirmed, the exclusionary sanction applies to any 'fruits' of a constitutional violation – whether such evidence be tangible, physical material actually seized in an illegal search, items observed or words overheard in the course of the unlawful activity, or confessions or statements of the accused obtained during an illegal arrest and detention." *United States v. Crews*, 445 U.S. 463, 470 (1980) (dictum). *See, e.g., United States v. Garcia*, 974 F.3d 1071 (9th Cir. 2020). It also applies to the testimony of witnesses that has a sufficiently close "causal connection" to the constitutional violation (*United States v. Ceccolini*, 435 U.S. 268, 274 (1978); *see id.* at 274-75 (dictum); *Jones v. United States*, 168 A.3d 703, 723-26 (D.C. 2017)), although in order to exclude "live-witness testimony . . . , a closer, more direct link between the illegality and that kind of testimony is required" (*id.* at 278; *see also id.* at 280), except perhaps "where the search was conducted by the police for the specific purpose of discovering potential witnesses" (*id.* at 276 n.4; *see also id.* at 279-80).

The possible chains of causal connection may be elaborate (*e.g., Smith v. United States*, 344 F.2d 545 (D.C. Cir. 1965); *United States v. Tane*, 329 F.2d 848 (2d Cir. 1964)), and counsel should be alert to follow them out. "[T]he question" determining the excludability of any particular piece of evidence is said to be "whether the chain of causation proceeding from the unlawful conduct has become so attenuated or has been interrupted by some intervening circumstance so as to remove the 'taint' imposed upon that evidence by the original illegality" (*United States v. Crews, supra*, 445 U.S. at 471). *Accord, Utah v. Strieff, supra*, 579 U.S. at 237-38; *compare Dunaway v. New York*, 442 U.S. 200, 216-19 (1979), *and Taylor v. Alabama*, 457 U.S. 687 (1982), *with Rawlings v. Kentucky*, 448 U.S. 98, 106-10 (1980); *and see United States v. Ceccolini, supra*, 435 U.S. at 276 ("we have declined to adopt a *'per se* or "but for" rule' that would make inadmissible any evidence, whether tangible or live-witness testimony, which somehow came to light through a chain of causation that began with an illegal arrest"); *id.* at

273-74.

Categories of derivative evidence that have been held tainted by a defendant's unconstitutional arrest or detention, so as to require their suppression include:

(a) *Any physical object or substance seized without a warrant at or after the time of arrest, the validity of whose seizure depends on the arrest. Beck v. Ohio*, 379 U.S. 89 (1964); *Sibron v. New York,* 392 U.S. 40, 62-66 (1968); *Whiteley v. Warden,* 401 U.S. 560 (1971). Searches incident to arrest (§ 25.8 *supra*) and "frisks" incident to a *Terry* stop (§ 25.10 *supra*) are unconstitutional if the arrest or stop is unconstitutional. *E.g., United States v. Di Re*, 332 U.S. 581 (1948); *Henry v. United States,* 361 U.S. 98 (1959). Similarly, if an unconstitutionally arrested or detained person attempts to drop or throw away objects or exposes them to the police when attempting to discard them, their observation and seizure are tainted by the arrest or detention. *Reid v. Georgia,* 448 U.S. 438 (1980) (per curiam); see § 25.13 *supra*. A defendant needs not have independent standing to complain about the search or seizure of an object if its obtention by the government was the consequence of an earlier search or seizure that s/he does have standing to contest. *Jones v. United States*, 168 A.3d 703, 722 (D.C. 2017) ("'[w]hile the fruit of the poisonous tree doctrine applies only when the defendant has standing regarding the Fourth Amendment *violation* which constitutes the poisonous tree, the law imposes no separate standing requirement regarding the *evidence* which constitutes the fruit of that poisonous tree'"); *Commonwealth v. Fredericq*, 482 Mass. 70, 78, 121 N.E.3d 166, 176 (2019) ("Evidence may be suppressed as fruit of the poisonous tree even if it is found in a place where the defendant has no reasonable expectation of privacy. This principle is as old as the fruit of the poisonous tree doctrine itself.").

(b) *Any observations made in the course of effecting the arrest – before, during, or after the arrest – whose validity depends on the arrest. Johnson v. United States*, 333 U.S. 10 (1948). Thus, when police enter a building pursuant to the "arrest entry" doctrine (§ 25.19 *supra*), unconstitutionality of the arrest or intended arrest will invalidate their observations of objects in "plain view" (§ 25.22.2 *supra*) within the building and their subsequent searches or seizures of those objects. *See Johnson v. United States, supra*, 333 U.S. at 12-13, 17; *Massachusetts v. Painten*, 368 F.2d 142 (1st Cir. 1966), *cert. dismissed,* 389 U.S. 560 (1968).

(c) *Confessions or statements made in custody after the arrest or otherwise induced by pressures flowing from the arrest* "unless intervening events break the causal connection between the illegal arrest and the confession so that the confession is '"sufficiently an act of free will to purge the primary taint"'" (*Taylor v. Alabama, supra,* 457 U.S. at 690). *See Wong Sun v. United States, supra,* 371 U.S. at 484-88; *Brown v. Illinois, supra,* 422 U.S. at 597-603; *Dunaway v. New York, supra,* 442 U.S. at 216-19; *Lanier v. South Carolina*, 474 U.S. 25 (1985) (per curiam); *Kaupp v. Texas*, 538 U.S. 626, 632-33 (2003) (per curiam); *United States v. Bocharnikov*, 966 F.3d 1000, 1003, 1004 (9th Cir. 2020) ("Bocharnikov argues that his statements in March 2018 should be suppressed because they were tainted by the illegality of his detention and the seizure of the laser in July 2017. . . . ¶ . . . [E]ight months is a considerable time for the memory of the violation to dissipate in Bocharnikov's mind. But one of the first things that Agent Hoover said to Bocharnikov was that he was there to 'ask some follow-up questions.' That phrase was innocent enough, identifying in conversational fashion why Agent

Hoover wished to speak with Bocharnikov, but it also served to refer Bocharnikov back to his prior detention and confession. In our view, referring back to the initial illegality by using the 'follow-up' phrasing made the second encounter a de facto extension of the first incident, the passage of time notwithstanding."); *State v. Shaw*, 237 N.J. 588, 611, 614-15, 207 A.3d 229, 244 (2019) ("The length of time between the unlawful arrest and the confession is the least determinative due to its ambiguity; a long detention could suggest increasing pressure or dissipation of the initial shock of arrest, and a short detention could indicate the confession was a product of the initial shock or that the confession was unrelated to the arrest. . . . The conditions of the unlawful detention should be considered because they 'can be as important as the temporal proximity.' . . . ¶ The presence of intervening circumstances that break the causal connection between the arrest and confession can be the most important consideration. . . . ¶ And, finally, the purposefulness and flagrancy of the police misconduct is particularly relevant in determining whether a confession was the fruit of an unlawful arrest and has justified suppression where the illegal conduct was 'calculated to cause surprise, fright, and confusion.'"); *Commonwealth v. Goncalves-Mendez,* 484 Mass. 80, 138 N.E.3d 1038 (2020) (requiring the suppression of a driver's admission that a gun found in an unreasonable inventory search of his vehicle was his); *Jones v. United States*, 168 A.3d 703, 722 (D.C. 2017) (requiring the suppression of an incriminating statement made by a defendant when accosted and arrested by police who had located him through the use of a cell-site simulator held to constitute a Fourth Amendment search unconstitutional for lack of a search warrant). *Compare Rawlings v. Kentucky,* 448 U.S. 98, 106-10 (1980); *and cf. United States v. Ceccolini, supra*, 435 U.S. at 273-79 (dictum). *But cf. New York v. Harris*, 495 U.S. 14, 21 (1990) ("where the police have probable cause to arrest a suspect, the exclusionary rule does not bar the State's use of a statement made by the defendant outside of his home, even though the statement is taken after an arrest made in the home in violation of *Payton* [*v. New York*, 445 U.S. 573 (1980)]"). *Compare State v. Luuertsema*, 262 Conn. 179, 192-97, 811 A.2d 223, 231-34 (2002), *partially overruled on an unrelated point, State v. Salamon*, 287 Conn. 509, 949 A.2d 1092 (2008) (rejecting the *New York v. Harris* rule as a matter of state constitutional law); *People v. Harris*, 77 N.Y.2d 434, 568 N.Y.S.2d 702, 570 N.E.2d 1051 (1991) (same).

(d) *Any physical object or substance or observation obtained by a search or seizure whose validity depends upon consent, when the consent is given in custody after the arrest or otherwise induced by pressures flowing from the arrest.* Consent to a police search or seizure (§ 25.18 *supra*) is ineffective if given during an unlawful confinement (*Florida v. Bostick*, 501 U.S. 429, 433-34 (1991) (if Bostick's consent to search had been obtained during a period of unlawful detention, the results of that search "must be suppressed as tainted fruit"); *Florida v. Royer,* 460 U.S. 491, 507-08 (1983) (plurality opinion); *id.* at 509 (concurring opinion of Justice Powell); *id.* (concurring opinion of Justice Brennan); *United States v. Lopez*, 907 F.3d 472, 487 (7th Cir. 2018) ("Since Lopez was being detained in violation of the Fourth Amendment, his consent to search the house cannot be deemed voluntary. No time had elapsed, there were no intervening circumstances, and the detention was not even arguably justified after the search of the garage turned up nothing incriminating. . . . The evidence obtained pursuant to the search of the house may not be admitted as evidence against Lopez."); *Harris v. Klare*, 902 F.3d 630, 637 (6th Cir. 2018) (a 17-year-old girl's consent to an intrusive pat-down search was ineffective because it was given during a period of detention that violated the Fourth Amendment; any reasonable suspicion that she was involved in drug activity was dispelled when a drug-sniffing dog failed to alert to controlled substances in the minivan in which the girl was riding: "Because a reasonable jury could credit . . . [the girl's] deposition testimony that she was not escorted to the restroom until after the drug dog had investigated the minivan, a reasonable jury could conclude that the officers did not reasonably suspect drug activity at the time of her search and that therefore she was unlawfully detained, rendering her consent to the search invalid."); *United States v. Murphy,* 703 F.3d 182, 190 (2d Cir. 2012); *Watson v. United States,* 249 F.2d 106 (D.C. Cir. 1957); *United States v. Klapholz,* 230 F.2d 494 (2d Cir. 1956)), just as a confession or incriminating statement would be (see § 26.15 *infra*). *And see United States v. Serrano-Acevedo,* 892 F.3d. 454, 461 (1st Cir. 2018) ("Agent Rivera sought and received consent immediately after the SWAT team told him that they saw money in the house during . . . [a] "protective" sweep [that the court holds was a search unjustifiable under the Fourth Amendment] and once Diaz was already in handcuffs. The record provides no indication that Diaz would have consented to the search if not for the unconstitutional sweep and what it uncovered. In response to this strong factual connection, the government 'makes no argument as to why [Diaz's] consent was not the tainted fruit of the unlawful sweep.'"); *United States v. Shrum,* 908 F.3d 1219, 1233 (10th Cir. 2018), summarized in § 25.16 *supra* ("Where an unlawful seizure of a home precedes a 'consensual' search of the home and the discovery of incriminating evidence then used to procure a search warrant, the Government's burden to prove the primary taint of the illegality has been purged, *i.e.*, that the search warrant and its 'fruits' are valid, is two-fold. . . . The Government must prove the voluntariness of a defendant's consent . . . . But in addition, the Government must demonstrate a break in the causal chain somewhere between the illegality and discovery of the incriminating evidence used to support the defendant's prosecution."). Consent given by persons not themselves arrested but who share possession of property with an unconstitutionally arrested or detained individual and who have been informed of that person's arrest is also tainted. *United States v. Maez*, 872 F.2d 1444 (10th Cir. 1989); *United States v. Oaxaca*, 233 F.3d 1154 (9th Cir. 2000); *and see United States v. Cordero-Rosario*, 786 F.3d 64 (1st Cir. 2015).

(e) *Fingerprint exemplars taken after the arrest* (*Davis v. Mississippi,* 394 U.S. 721 (1969); *Hayes v. Florida,* 470 U.S. 811 (1985); *Bynum v. United States,* 262 F.2d 465 (D.C. Cir. 1958); *see Taylor v. Alabama, supra*, 457 U.S. at 692-93 (dictum)), and, by the same logic, any other evidence obtained through physical custody of the defendant – lineup identifications, body-test results, and so forth (see § 25.14 *supra*). *E.g., United States v. Crews*, 445 U.S. 463, 472 (1980) (the Court assumes the Government is correct in conceding that pretrial photo and lineup identifications following an arrest made without probable cause must be suppressed); *Young v. Conway*, 698 F.3d 69, 84-85 (2d Cir. 2012) (a state-court order suppressing the complainant's lineup identification as the fruit of an unconstitutional arrest without probable cause also should have precluded an in-court identification by the complainant because "the State failed to meet its burden to prove an independent basis [for an in-court identification] by clear and convincing evidence"); *People v. Teresinki*, 30 Cal. 3d 822, 832, 180 Cal. Rptr. 617, 622-23, 640 P.3d 753, 758-59 (1982) (a pretrial identification by an eyewitness to a robbery based upon booking photos resulting from a vehicle stop and investigative detention made without reasonable suspicion must be suppressed); *Ferguson v. State*, 301 Md. 542, 547-53, 483 A.2d 1255, 1257-60 (1984) (an identification by a robbery victim in a holding cell show-up following an arrest without probable case must be suppressed); *State v. Le*, 103 Wash. App. 354, 360-67, 12 P.3d 653, 656-60 (2000) (an identification by a police officer who had witnessed a fleeing burglar and was called to view the defendant in a show-up at the scene of the defendant's warrantless arrest in his home – a dwelling entry that violated the rule of *Payton v. New York* – should have been suppressed, although the trial court's failure to suppress it was harmless error because of other overwhelming evidence of guilt); 6 WAYNE R. LAFAVE, SEARCH AND SEIZURE § 11.4(g) (5th ed. & Supp.); *but see United States v. Olivares-Rangel*, 458 F.3d 1104, 1112-16 (10th Cir. 2006) (holding that the exclusion of physical evidence obtained by routine processing of an arrestee following an unconstitutional arrest – in this case, an arrest tainted by an investigative stop without reasonable suspicion – is required only if the arrest was made for the purpose of obtaining that evidence). Different kinds of police lawlessness may entail different evidentiary consequences. *Compare People v. Gethers*, 86 N.Y.2d 159, 654 N.E.2d 102, 630 N.Y.S.2d 281 (1995) (a police-arranged identification following an arrest without probable cause must be excluded), *with People v. Jones*, 2 N.Y.3d 235, 810 N.E.2d 415, 778 N.Y.S.2d 133 (2004) (a police-arranged identification following a warrantless home arrest in violation of *Payton v. New York* ordinarily needs not be excluded).

(f) *Evidence obtained through observations made by means of an earlier unconstitutional search or seizure. See, e.g., Johnson v. United States,* 333 U.S. 10, 16 (1948); *Arizona v. Hicks,* 480 U.S. 321 (1987), summarized in § 25.22.2 *supra; Collins v. Virginia,* 138 S. Ct. 1663 (2018); *United States v. Alexander,* 888 F.3d 628 (2d Cir. 2018); *United States v. Ngumezi,* 980 F.3d 1285 (9th Cir. 2020); *State v. Christian,* 310 Kan. 229, 445 P.3d 183 (2019); *State v. Bennett,* 430 A.2d 424 (R.I. 1981); *Commonwealth v. Martin,* 2021 PA Super 128, 253 A.3d 1225 (Pa. Super. 2021), summarized in § 25.16 *supra; cf. United States v. Williams,* 615 F.3d 657 (6th Cir. 2010) (following a *Terry* stop which is held illegal for lack of reasonable suspicion, the defendant acknowledged that that there was an outstanding warrant for his arrest and that he was carrying a gun; the Court of Appeals affirms the district court's suppression of the statement and gun); *United States v. Camacho,* 661 F.3d 718 (1st Cir. 2011) (following a *Terry* stop which is held unconstitutional for lack of reasonable suspicion, an officer patted down the defendant, felt a gun, and seized it; the Court of Appeals orders the gun suppressed as the tainted fruit of the invalid stop).

(g) *Evidence obtained through warrants, subpoenas and other legal process issued on the basis of information uncovered in an earlier unconstitutional search or seizure, and evidence obtained through investigations triggered by such information. See* § 25.17.4 *supra.*

(h) *Evidence derived from any of the foregoing sources. See, e.g., United States v. Bagley,* 877 F.3d 1151 (10th Cir. 2017); *United States v. Nora,* 765 F.3d 1049 (9th Cir. 2014); *Perez Cruz v. Barr,* 926 F.3d 1128, 1135-37, 1145-46 (9th Cir. 2019) (suppressing a birth certificate obtained from Mexican authorities by the Immigration and Customs Enforcement agency, which was led to make the request because an individual detained by ICE agents in violation of the Fourth Amendment had admitted to them that he was a Mexican national); *Commonwealth v. Norman,* 484 Mass. 330, 142 N.E.3d 1 (2020) (the defendant was required to submit to GPS tracking as a condition of pretrial release; after holding that this requirement violated the state constitutional guarantee against unreasonable searches and seizures, the Supreme Judicial Court excludes evidence that the GPS data placed the defendant at the scene of a later home invasion; evidence obtained under a search warrant issued for a building address on the basis of GPS data indicating that the defendant had been at that address before and after the home invasion; and evidence that one of the home-invasion victims identified the defendant in a photo array).

However, evidence obtained by the police following an unconstitutional search or seizure is not suppressible if the prosecution shows that (i) the police officers' knowledge of the evidence and access to it derived from an "independent source" unconnected with the search or seizure (*Segura v. United States,* 468 U.S. 796 (1984); *Murray v. United States,* 487 U.S. 533 (1988); *United States v. Miller,* 68 F.4th 1065, 1070 (7th Cir. 2023) ("An exception to the exclusionary rule, the independent-source doctrine permits the admission of the fruit of an unlawful search if the government obtained the evidence 'via an independent legal source, like a warrant.' . . . Here the officers recovered the gun in the execution of a valid warrant to search the car. Under the independent-source doctrine, we ask two questions: (1) did the evidence obtained from the officer's use of the key fob [which the court assumes *arguendo* constituted an unlawful search] affect the judge's decision to issue a warrant; and (2) did that evidence affect the officers' decision to apply for a warrant?"); *State v. Wilson,* 2023 WL 3065140 (N.J. Super. 2023); *and see United States v. Saelee,* 51 F.4th 327, 335 (9th Cir. 2022) ("To establish that 'evidence initially acquired unlawfully' has later been independently obtained through an untainted source, the Government must show 'that no information gained' from the Fourth Amendment violations 'affected either [1] the law enforcement officers' decision to seek a warrant or [2] the magistrate's decision to grant it.'" (quoting *Murray,* 487 U.S. at 539-40))), or (ii) the evidence "ultimately or inevitably would have been discovered by lawful means" in the course of events even if the search or seizure had not produced it (*Nix v. Williams,* 467 U.S. 431, 444 (1984) (a Sixth Amendment decision placed on grounds equally applicable to the Fourth Amendment exclusionary rule); *but compare Commonwealth v. Davis,* 656 Pa. 213, 217, 239-40, 220 A.3d 534, 537, 551 (2019), summarized in § 25.8.2 *supra.*); or (iii) "the connection between unconstitutional police conduct and the evidence is remote or has been interrupted by some intervening circumstance, so that 'the interest protected by the constitutional guarantee that has been violated would not be served by suppression of the evidence obtained'" (*Utah v. Strieff,* 579 U.S. 232, 238 (2016)). This third exception to the exclusionary rule goes by the name of "the attenuation doctrine" (*id.*). Applying it in the *Strieff* case, the Court held that the "doctrine applies when an officer makes an unconstitutional investigatory stop; learns during that stop that the suspect is subject to a valid arrest warrant; and proceeds to arrest the suspect and seize incriminating evidence during a search incident to that arrest" (*id.* at 235). "The three factors articulated in *Brown v. Illinois,* 422 U.S. 590 (1975), guide our analysis. First, we look to the 'temporal proximity' between the unconstitutional conduct and the discovery of evidence to determine how closely the discovery of evidence followed the unconstitutional search. . . . Second, we consider 'the presence of intervening circumstances.' . . . Third, and 'particularly' significant, we examine 'the purpose and flagrancy of the official misconduct.'" *Utah v. Strieff,* 579 U.S. at 239. The latter two considerations were determinative, the Court wrote, because (a) "the second factor, the presence of intervening circumstances, strongly favors the State"; "the warrant was valid, it predated . . . [the] investigation [which generated the *Terry* stop of Strieff], and it was entirely unconnected with the stop. And once . . . [the investigating officer] discovered the warrant, he had an obligation to arrest Strieff." (*Utah v. Strieff,* 579 U.S. at 240); and (b) the investigating officer "was at most negligent . . . [i]n stopping Strieff": he made "errors in judgment" but "there is no indication that this unlawful stop was part of any systemic or recurrent police misconduct. To the contrary, all the evidence suggests that the stop was an isolated instance of negligence that occurred in connection with a bona fide investigation of a suspected drug house": "[I]t is especially significant that there is no evidence that . . . [this] illegal stop reflected flagrantly unlawful police misconduct." (*Id.* at 241-42.) *See also United States v. Forjan*, 66 F.4th 739 (8th Cir. 2023); *but compare United States v. Baker*, 58 F.4th 1109 (9th Cir. 2023) (the suppositious "intervening event" must precede the search that produced the evidence sought to be suppressed); *United States v. Waide*, 60 F.4th 327 (6th Cir. 2023) ("[T]he Supreme Court has made no distinction between actual and threatened violations of the Fourth Amendment with regard to the suppression of unlawfully obtained evidence. . . . [T]he fruit-of-the-poisonous-tree doctrine may be used to suppress evidence derived from the threatened use of an unlawful warrant [here, a warrant lacking probable cause because based on triple hearsay]. *Id.* at 338. There were no "intervening circumstances between the threatened execution of the unlawful . . . warrant and the discovery of the challenged evidence. The affidavits that sought the narcotics warrants authorizing searches of the two . . . apartments satisfied the probable-cause requirement only because of information that had been obtained by that threat. . . . [T]he primary basis for the narcotics warrants was Waide's confession about the presence of marijuana in his apartment. ¶ But Waide confessed only because of the officials' threat to execute the unlawful . . . warrant. When . . . [a fire department investigator] informed Waide that the officials intended to execute the . . . warrant, [a narcotics officer accompanying the investigator] affirmatively 'interjected at one point and asked him – advised him, you know, if he had any drugs in the apartment, if that's what he was worried about and so forth.' And a confession 'made in response to a question posed by [an officer] [ ] is not the kind of 'intervening spontaneous action' that typically supports attenuation." *Id.* at 340.); *People v. McWilliams*, 14 Cal. 5th 429, 434-35, 524 P.3d 768, 770-71, 304 Cal. Rptr. 3d 779, 782 (2023) ("As a general rule, evidence seized as a result of an unlawful search or seizure is inadmissible against the defendant in a subsequent prosecution. But the law permits use of the evidence when the causal connection 'between the lawless conduct of the police and the discovery of the challenged evidence has "become so attenuated as to dissipate the taint."' . . . Here, the Court of Appeal held that the officer's discovery of McWilliams's parole search condition sufficiently attenuated the connection between the unlawful detention and the contraband found in McWilliams's vehicle. The Court of Appeal relied on cases allowing the admission of evidence seized incident to arrest on a valid warrant, where the warrant was discovered during an unlawful investigatory stop. (*Utah v. Strieff* . . . .) ¶ We now reverse. Unlike an arrest on an outstanding warrant, a parole search is not a ministerial act dictated by judicial mandate . *Strieff, supra*, . . .), but a matter of discretion. We conclude the officer's discretionary decision to conduct the parole search did not sufficiently attenuate the connection between the officer's initial unlawful decision to detain McWilliams and the discovery of contraband. The evidence therefore was not admissible against him."); *United States v. Garcia,* 974 F.3d 1071 (9th Cir. 2020); *United States v. Walker*, 965 F.3d 180, 188-90 (2d Cir. 2020); *United States v. Gaines*, 918 F.3d 793 (10th Cir. 2019); *United States v. Shrum*, 908 F.3d 1219 (10th Cir. 2018).

25.40. *Prosecutorial Burden of Disproving "Taint" of Unlawful Search and Seizure*

When unconstitutional activity by the police or other government agents has been shown that may have led to evidence proffered by the prosecution, the "'[t]he government has the burden to show that the evidence is not "the fruit of the poisonous tree"'" (*United States v. Ngumezi*, 980 F.3d 1285, 1291 (9th Cir. 2020)). *Harrison v. United States,* 392 U.S. 219, 224-26

(1968); *Brown v. Illinois,* 422 U.S. 590, 604 (1975); *Dunaway v. New York,* 442 U.S. 200, 218 (1979); *Rawlings v. Kentucky,* 448 U.S. 98, 107, 110 (1980); *Taylor v. Alabama,* 457 U.S. 687, 690 (1982); *Kaupp v. Texas,* 538 U.S. 626, 633 (2003) (per curiam); *United States v. Suggs,* 998 F.3d 1125, 1142 (10th Cir. 2021); *United States v. Paroutian,* 299 F.2d 486 (2d Cir. 1962), *aff'd after remand,* 319 F.2d 661 (2d Cir. 1963); *United States v. Serrano-Acevedo,* 892 F.3d 454, 459-60 (1st Cir. 2018); *cf. Alderman v. United States,* 394 U.S. 165, 183 (1969) (dictum); *and compare Mt. Healthy City School District Board of Education v. Doyle,* 429 U.S. 274, 286-87 (1977). This requirement is the point of entry of the "inevitable discovery" doctrine. "'[T]he inevitable discovery doctrine allows for the admission of evidence that would have been discovered even without the unconstitutional source.'" *United States v. Cooper*, 24 F.4th 1086 (6th Cir. 2022). "Our cases recognize two scenarios in which inevitable discovery operates. First, the doctrine applies when there is 'an independent, untainted investigation' that was bound to uncover the same evidence. . . . Inevitable discovery also applies when 'other compelling facts' demonstrate that discovery was inevitable. . . . A few paradigmatic examples of 'other compelling facts' demonstrate what we mean. The doctrine applies when the evidence would have been discovered pursuant to a 'routine procedure,' such as an airline's standard policy of opening lost luggage. . . . And it has repeatedly been employed when, after seizing evidence during an illegal search, police obtain and execute a search warrant based on probable cause developed before the illegal search." *Id.* at 1091. "That test necessarily involves some hypothesizing. We must ask: '[V]iewing affairs as they existed at the instant before the unlawful search, what would have happened had the unlawful search never occurred[?]'" *Id.* at 1092. "Because inevitable discovery asks what would have happened had the illegality not occurred, courts may rely on post-illegality events only if they would have occurred in that counterfactual scenario." *Id.* at 1095. The *Cooper* court accordingly holds that the district judge erred by applying the inevitable discovery rule to justify the admission into evidence of a gun found in an unlawful search of the home of an arrested suspect's girlfriend based upon her consent to search the house *after* the gun was found and seized, although that consent itself was found by the district judge to have been unaffected by the illegality of the search under the "attenuation" principle discussed in § 25.39 *supra.* "On remand the court should focus on the following questions: If the . . . [unlawful search] had never happened, would officers have sought . . . [the girlfriend's] consent to search? Would . . . [the girlfriend] have given her consent in such a hypothetical world? And would the ensuing consent search have led to the gun? The inevitable discovery exception applies only if the answer to all three questions is 'yes.'" 24 F.4th at 1096). *See also, e.g., United States v. Stokes,* 733 F.3d 438, 446 (2d Cir. 2013) (the trial court erred in finding that the government had satisfied its burden of proving "by a preponderance of the evidence that the guns and ammunition would inevitably have been discovered": the trial court "failed to account for all of the demonstrated historical facts in the record, and in doing so, failed adequately to consider . . . plausible contingencies that might not have resulted in the guns' discovery"); *State v. Banks-Harvey,* 2018-Ohio-201, 152 Ohio St. 3d 368, 375-76, 96 N.E.3d 262, 271-72 (2018) ("The state argues that the local police officer's observation of an empty capsule on the vehicle's floorboard provided probable cause to believe the vehicle contained contraband and, thus, to conduct a warrantless search of the vehicle under the automobile exception to the warrant requirement . . . . ¶ It was only *after* the trooper removed the appellant's purse from the vehicle [in violation of the Fourth Amendment], began to search it, and stated that he had found narcotics in it that the local officer approached the trooper and told him that he was 'pretty sure' he had observed a capsule on the vehicle's floorboard. . . . ¶ Even assuming that the local officer's observation of the capsule afforded him probable cause to search the vehicle, the inevitable-discovery exception would not apply if the local officer based his decision to search the vehicle on knowledge of the contraband found in the unlawful search of the appellant's purse. . . . ¶ [Thus,] the . . . [record] fail[s] to demonstrate by a preponderance of the evidence a reasonable probability that the local officer would inevitably have discovered the contraband in the appellant's purse apart from the trooper's removal and search of the purse in violation of the appellant's Fourth Amendment rights."); *Rodriguez v. State*, 187 So.3d 841, 849 (Fla. 2015) ("The question before this Court is whether the inevitable discovery rule requires the prosecution to demonstrate that the police were in the process of obtaining a warrant prior to the misconduct or whether the prosecution need only establish that a warrant could have been obtained with the information available prior to the misconduct."; "Because the exclusionary rule works to deter police misconduct by ensuring that the prosecution is not in a better position as a result of the misconduct, the rule cannot be expanded to allow application where there is only probable cause and no pursuit of a warrant. If the prosecution were allowed to benefit in this way, police misconduct would be encouraged instead of deterred, and the rationale behind the exclusionary rule would be eviscerated."); *Brown v. McClennen*, 239 Ariz. 521, 524-525, 373 P.3d 538, 542-543 (2016) ("The [inevitable discovery] exception does not turn on whether the evidence would have been discovered had the deputy acted lawfully in the first place. . . . Rather, the exception applies if the evidence would have been lawfully discovered despite the unlawful behavior and independent of it."); *Gore v. United States*, 145 A.3d 540, 548-49 (D.C. 2016) ("The inevitable discovery doctrine shields illegally obtained evidence from the exclusionary rule if the government can show, by a preponderance of the evidence, that the evidence 'ultimately or inevitably *would* have been discovered by lawful means.' . . . 'Would' – not 'could' or 'might' – is the word the Supreme Court used in *Nix v. Williams*[, *infra*] and is, therefore, the 'constitutional standard.' . . . ¶ The requirements of the inevitable discovery doctrine were not met in this case. At the time the police officers illegally entered appellant's room, and even when they seized Mr. Ward's property from her bathroom, the 'lawful process' that supposedly would have ended in the inevitable discovery of that property there – the putative application for a search warrant for the room – had not begun. Indeed, it was never begun; we have only Officer Tobe's statement that he 'could' have applied for a warrant in the event a hypothetical search of nearby dumpsters (which itself had not been commenced and was hardly certain to have been performed) was unproductive. Of course, whenever police officers disregard the warrant requirement, they 'could' have applied for a warrant instead. But in this case, there is no solid evidence that the officers *would* have done so."); *United States v. Lauria*, 70 F.4th 106, 123 (2d Cir. 2023) ("[T]he inevitable discovery doctrine requires that the means by which the evidence would inevitably be discovered is independent from the means by which the evidence was actually – and unlawfully – discovered. Consistent with this principle, the investigation supporting a claim of inevitable discovery cannot itself have occurred only because the misconduct resulting in actual discovery was exposed. . . . ¶ This comports with the requirement for 'a high level of confidence that each of the contingencies required' for lawful inevitable discovery of the disputed evidence 'would in fact have occurred.' . . . ('We have previously characterized the Government's obligation as one of "certitude" that the evidence would have been discovered.'). In other words, the inevitable discovery doctrine does not apply simply because 'a reasonable police officer *could have*' lawfully discovered the evidence at issue; rather, it applies where the record establishes 'with a sufficiently high degree of certainty that a reasonable police officer *would have*' lawfully discovered the evidence regardless of the disclosure of any legal defect in the actual discovery of the evidence."); *Jones v. United States*, 168 A.3d 703, 722 (D.C. 2017) ("[T]he government is asking us to find inevitable discovery where the police had mutually exclusive options and, for whatever reason, chose the option that turned out to be unlawful. The inevitable-discovery doctrine does not apply in this type of situation. . . . '("[T]he argument that 'if we hadn't done it wrong, we would have done it right' is far from compelling.")'"). *Compare United States v. Alexander*, 54 F.4th 162, 164-65 (3d Cir. 2022) ("The police entered the homes of both Alexander and his girlfriend, without search warrants. In law enforcement parlance, the officers at each location conducted a 'hit-and-hold;' that is, they entered and secured the premises before getting a warrant, a tactic sometimes used to respond to emergency circumstances. Once inside, and having secured the premises, the officers at Alexander's home waited to conduct a search until a warrant for that house was issued. Those who entered Alexander's girlfriend's home likewise secured the premises and were in the process of applying for a warrant, which was all but certain to issue, when they received what they understood as consent to a search. Because the government has shown that the evidence from both locations would have been discovered in any event, we need not consider the lawfulness of the hit-and-holds or subsequent searches . . . .").

In *Nix v. Williams*, 467 U.S. 431, 444 n.5 (1984), the Supreme Court implied that "the usual burden of proof" on this issue is "a preponderance of evidence." It may, however, be greater in situations in which the illegality is peculiarly likely to have tainted the sort of evidence that the prosecution is offering or when there is peculiar "difficulty in determining" questions of cause and effect because these involve "speculative elements" (*id.*). Both considerations were mentioned in *Nix* as distinguishing *United States v. Wade*, 388 U.S. 218, 240 (1967), which held that the prosecutor's burden of proof in showing that in-court identification testimony is not tainted by the witness's exposure to the accused in an earlier, unconstitutional identification confrontation is "clear and convincing evidence." *See also Moore v. Illinois*, 434 U.S. 220, 225-26 (1977) (dictum). *And see Kastigar v. United States*, 406 U.S. 441, 461-62 (1972), holding that when an individual has given compelled testimony under an immunity grant, the prosecution bears "the heavy burden of proving that all of the evidence it proposes to use was derived from legitimate independent sources." *See also Braswell v. United States*, 487 U.S. 99, 117 (1988); *United States v. Hubbell*, 530 U.S. 27, 40 & n.22 (2000). Both *Nix* and *Wade* were Sixth Amendment right-to-counsel cases; *Kastigar* and *Braswell* and *Hubbell* were Fifth Amendment self-incrimination cases; the Supreme Court has not squarely addressed the prosecutor's burden of proving its evidence untainted following a Fourth Amendment search-and-seizure violation. But there appears to be no reason to distinguish among kinds of constitutional violations when it comes to the standards for determining whether derivative evidence is "'purged of the primary taint'" (*Johnson v. Louisiana*, 406 U.S. 356, 365 (1972)). The *Nix* opinion derived its statement of the "usual burden of proof at suppression hearings" from Fourth and Fifth Amendment caselaw (*see also Colorado v. Connelly*, 479 U.S. 157, 167-69 (1986)); *Wade*'s companion case, *Gilbert v. California*, 388 U.S. 263, 272-73 (1967), expressly adopted principles of taint that were first announced in the Fourth Amendment context (*see also Moore v. Illinois, supra*, 434 U.S. at 226, 231); the Court in *Harris v. New York*, 401 U.S. 222, 224-25 (1971), relied upon a Fourth Amendment case (*Walder v. United States*, 347 U.S. 62 (1954)) when deciding the exclusionary consequences of a *Miranda* violation; and it later treated *Harris* as authoritative in another Fourth Amendment case (*United States v. Havens*, 446 U.S. 620, 624-27 (1980)). The exclusionary rules that enforce the Fourth, Fifth, and Sixth Amendments are said to have the same essential purpose: "to deter – to compel respect for the constitutional guaranty in the only effectively available way – by removing the incentive to disregard it" (*Elkins v. United States,* 364 U.S. 206, 217 (1960)). *See Colorado v. Connelly, supra,* 479 U.S. at 166; *Linkletter v. Walker,* 381 U.S. 618, 633, 636-37 (1965) (Fourth Amendment); *Stone v. Powell,* 428 U.S. 465, 484-88 (1976) (same); *Illinois v. Krull,* 480 U.S. 340, 347 (1987) (same); *Johnson v. New Jersey,* 384 U.S. 719, 729-31 (1966) (Fifth Amendment); *Stovall v. Denno,* 388 U.S. 293, 297 (1967) (Sixth Amendment); *cf. United States v. Payner,* 447 U.S. 727, 735-36 n.8 (1980); *United States v. Johnson,* 457 U.S. 537, 561 (1982). Rules for litigating issues of taint under all three Amendments are therefore presumptively similar. *But see Oregon v. Elstad,* 470 U.S. 298, 304-09 (1985).

State constitutional decisions may heighten the prosecution's burden of dissipating taint. *See, e.g., State v. Rodrigues,* 128 Hawai'i 200, 211-15, 286 P.3d 809, 820-24 (2012) (discussing and applying a state constitutional rule that follows Justice Brennan's dissent in *Nix v. Williams* by requiring that the prosecution "'satisfy a heightened burden of proof'" of "clear and convincing evidence" in order to rely on the inevitable discovery exception); and see generally § 17.11 *supra.*

25.41. *Relevance of the "Flagrancy" of the Police Conduct in Ascertaining "Taint"*

A passage in *Brown v. Illinois,* 422 U.S. 590, 604 (1975), indicates that "the purpose and flagrancy of . . . official misconduct are . . . relevant" in determining the scope of taint that flows from Fourth Amendment violations. *See also Dunaway v. New York,* 442 U.S. 200, 218 (1979); *Rawlings v. Kentucky,* 448 U.S. 98, 109-10 (1980); *Taylor v. Alabama,* 457 U.S. 687, 693 (1982); *Kaupp v. Texas,* 538 U.S. 626, 633 (2003) (per curiam).

The *Brown* case itself involved the question of the admissibility of a confession following an illegal arrest (as did *Dunaway, Rawlings, Taylor*, and *Kaupp*). The *Brown* majority opinion leaves unclear whether the "flagrancy" principle is limited to that issue or is applicable to determinations of taint in other contexts. Arguably, "flagrancy" is particularly relevant in connection with the inquiry whether confessions – "(verbal acts, as contrasted with physical evidence)" (422 U.S. at 600) – are tainted by unconstitutional police treatment of a suspect because the *degree* of official disregard of a suspect's rights is particularly likely to affect the suspect's choice to confess. *See Oregon v. Elstad,* 470 U.S. 298, 312 (1985). The *Brown* majority notes specifically that "[t]he manner in which Brown's arrest was effected gives the appearance of having been calculated to cause surprise, fright, and confusion" (422 U.S. at 605). If this is the rationale for considering "flagrancy" as a factor in the exclusionary calculus in confession cases, then "flagrancy" should also be considered in cases involving motions to suppress the tangible fruits of searches and seizures based on consent given after an unconstitutional arrest or stop, or in unconstitutional detention, or as a result of other unconstitutional police conduct that is potentially intimidating. And the courts do consistently consider the "flagrancy of . . . official misconduct" in consent-search cases. *E.g., United States v. Martinez,* 486 F.3d 855, 865 (5th Cir. 2007) (applying the flagrancy principle in determining to exclude firearms seized in a dwelling search based upon consent given following a stop made without reasonable suspicion); *United States v. Robeles-Ortega,* 348 F.3d 679, 684-85 (7th Cir. 2003) (applying the flagrancy principle in determining to exclude drugs seized in a dwelling search based upon consent given following a forcible, warrantless entry by five DEA agents with drawn guns); *United States v. Jones*, 234 F.3d 234, 243 (5th Cir. 2000) (applying the flagrancy principle in determining to exclude drugs seized in a vehicle search based on consent given after a vehicle stop was unconstitutionally prolonged); *State v. Munroe*, 2001 WI App 104, 244 Wis. 2d 1, 13-14, 630 N.W.2d 223, 228-29 (Wis. App. 2001) (applying the flagrancy principle in determining to exclude drugs seized in a motel-room search based on consent given after an entry to request identification was unconstitutionally prolonged).

But the "flagrancy" principle appears to apply more broadly than in cases involving intimidating police conduct that may influence a suspect's will to confess or consent. The *Brown* majority supports its "flagrancy" statement with a footnote citing lower court decisions that involved both confessional and nonconfessional evidence (*Brown v. Illinois, supra*, 422 U.S. at 604 n.9); and it purports, at the outset of its opinion, to be explicating the principles announced in *Wong Sun v. United States,* 371 U.S. 471 (1963), "to be applied where the issue is whether statements *and other evidence* obtained after an illegal arrest or search should be excluded" (422 U.S. at 597 (emphasis added)). A concurring opinion by Justice Powell explains the relevance of "flagrancy" by reference to a notion which has appeared in a few other Supreme Court decisions (*see, e.g., United States v. Peltier,* 422 U.S. 531, 542 (1975); *United States v. Janis,* 428 U.S. 433, 454 n.28, 458-59 n.35 (1976)), that the exclusionary rule "is most likely to be effective" in cases of willful or gross police violations of the Constitution (422 U.S. at 611); *see also United States v. Rush,* 808 F.3d 1007, 1010 (4th Cir. 2015), quoting *Davis v. United States,* 564 U.S. 229, 238 (2011). If *this* is the rationale for the "flagrancy" principle – or any part of its rationale – then the principle should apply to all exclusionary-rule issues. "In view of the deterrent purposes of the exclusionary rule[,] consideration of official motives may play some part in determining whether application of the exclusionary rule is appropriate. . . ." *Scott v. United States,* 436 U.S. 128, 135-36 (1978) (dictum). *See also id.* at 139 n.13; *United States v. Leon,* 468 U.S. 897, 911 (1984). Strong support for the proposition that "flagrancy" is relevant in this broader manner to the adjudication of issues bearing on the excludability of derivative evidence is provided by the Supreme Court's opinion in *Utah v. Strieff,* 579 U.S. 232 (2016), summarized in § 25.39 subdivision (g) *supra*. As noted there, *Strieff* repeatedly refers to the "'flagrancy of the official misconduct" as "'particularly' significant" (*id.* at 239) and "especially significant" (*id.* at 242) and explains that its consideration "reflects . . . [the exclusionary rule's core deterrent] rationale by favoring exclusion only when the police misconduct is most in need of deterrence – that is, when it is purposeful or flagrant" (*id.* at 241). For additional cases that take account of the flagrancy of unconstitutional police conduct in applying the exclusionary rule to evidence other than confessions and the products of consent searches, *see, e.g., United States v. Torres,* 2022 WL 13983627 (6th Cir. 2022) (in a case involving the seizure of firearms, the court discusses the "blanket suppression" principle – *i.e.,* the suppression of evidence obtained through the portion of a search which is constitutionally permissible when other aspects of the same search are flagrantly unconstitutional); *United States v. Garcia,* 974 F.3d 1071 (9th Cir. 2020) (requiring the exclusion of methamphetamine and other physical evidence obtained during the second police entry into a residence following their first illegal entry); *United States v. Fletcher*, 978 F.3d 1009 (6th Cir. 2020) (requiring the exclusion of pornographic photographs found in the search of a cell phone under a warrant issued on the basis of information obtained through an anterior unconstitutional warrantless search); *United States v. Walker*, 965 F.3d 180, 188-90 (2d Cir. 2020) (requiring the suppression of narcotics seized from the person of a defendant following a *Terry* stop held flagrantly unconstitutional for lack of reasonable suspicion); *People v. Sampson*, 86 Ill. App. 3d 687, 694, 408 N.E.2d 3, 9, 41 Ill. Dec. 657, 663 (1980) (requiring a hearing on a motion to suppress a lineup identification following an arrest without probable cause); *Ferguson v. State*, 301 Md. 542, 549-53, 483 A.2d 1255, 1258-60 (1984) (excluding a show-up identification following an arrest without probable cause); *Hill v. State*, 692 S.W.2d 716, 723 (Tex. Crim. App. 1985) (excluding a lineup identification following an arrest without probable cause or any legal authorization, made for the purpose of exhibiting the defendant in the lineup); *State v. Le*, 103 Wash. App. 354, 360-62, 12 P.3d 653, 657-58 (2000) (holding that a pretrial identification by a police officer who had witnessed a fleeing burglar and was called to view the defendant in a show-up at the scene of the defendant's warrantless home arrest in violation of the rule of *Payton v. New York*, 445 U.S. 573 (1980), should have been suppressed, although its admission was harmless because of other overwhelming evidence of guilt); *Yoc-Us v. Attorney General*, 932 F.3d 98 (3d Cir. 2019) (applying the principle in alien removal proceedings in which the government relies on evidence obtained through an unconstitutional seizure made by a state officer); *and cf. United States v. Olivares-Rangel*, 458 F.3d 1104, 1112-16 (10th Cir. 2006) (holding that the exclusion of physical evidence obtained by routine processing of an arrestee following an unconstitutional arrest is required only if the arrest was made for the purpose of obtaining that evidence). *Compare Brendlin v. California*, 551 U.S. 249, 259-61, 263 (2007) (rejecting a lower court approach that would have permitted a police claim of lawful intent to *uphold* a seizure – by treating an officer's assertion that s/he had no intent to seize an individual as a basis for finding that no such seizure took place – and instead announcing a rule that is designed to avert the "powerful incentive" that police have to engage in certain "kind[s] of" conduct the Court has previously found to be unlawful). *But cf. Whren v. United States*, 517 U.S. 806 (1996) (rejecting the argument that an objectively valid traffic stop is unconstitutional when it is used as a pretext for an impermissible investigative search, and stating more generally that, in making the initial determination whether police action is constitutional, the Supreme Court has "never held . . . that an officer's motive invalidates objectively justifiable behavior under the Fourth Amendment" (*id.* at 812); thus, that "[s]ubjective intentions play no role in ordinary, probable-cause Fourth Amendment analysis" (*id.* at 813)); *Arkansas v. Sullivan*, 532 U.S. 769 (2001) (per curiam) (same); *Devenpeck v. Alford*, 543 U.S. 146, 153 (2004) ("Our cases make clear that an arresting officer's state of mind (except for the facts that he knows) is irrelevant to the existence of probable cause."); *United States v. Brooks*, 987 F.3d 593, 599 (6th Cir. 2021) ("Brooks says that the officers' seatbelt 'excuse' did not permit the stop because it was 'pretextual' and the officers were really engaged in a fishing expedition to uncover crime in a high-crime area. He misunderstands black-letter law. Under the Fourth Amendment, officers may stop a car as long as they objectively have probable cause that an occupant of the car has committed a traffic offense, even if they subjectively do so for a different reason. *Whren*, 517 U.S. at 811–16. '*Whren* puts an end to inquiries' like Brooks's 'about an officer's state of mind in conducting a traffic stop.' . . . And while the Equal Protection Clause does bar officers from pretextually stopping a car based on such unlawful motivations as the occupants' race, Brooks asserts no equal-protection claim here.").

See § 24.5.1, third paragraph *supra* for a tactical *caveat* regarding defense recourse to "flagrancy" analysis.

25.42. *Unavailability of "Tainted" Evidence as Justification for Any Subsequent Police Action*

Illegally obtained evidence or information that may not be used in court also may not be used to justify any subsequent police action. The fruits of an illegal search, for example, may not be used to supply the probable cause required for a later arrest (*Johnson v. United States,* 333 U.S. 10 (1948)), or search (*see United States v. Paroutian,* 299 F.2d 486 (2d Cir. 1962), *aff'd after remand,* 319 F.2d 661 (2d Cir. 1963); *State v. Harris,* 369 Or. 628, 650, 509 P.3d 83, 96-97 (2022); *cf. New Jersey v. T.L.O.,* 469 U.S. 325, 344 (1985) (dictum)), or for the issuance of a warrant (*United States v. Giordano,* 416 U.S. 505, 529-34 (1974); *Florida v. Jardines,* 569 U.S. 1 (2013); *Steagald v. United States,* 451 U.S. 204 (1981) (by implication); *Hair v. United States,* 289 F.2d 894 (D.C. Cir. 1961); *United States v. Lopez-Zuniga,* 909 F.3d 906, 910 (8th Cir. 2018); *United States v. Drakeford,* 992 F.3d 255 (4th Cir. 2021); *United States v. Shelton,* 997 F.3d 749 (7th Cir. 2021); *People v. Bonilla,* 2018 IL 122484, 120 N.E.3d 930 (2018); see also § 25.17.4 *supra*). When they are so used, the products of the second police action are tainted by the illegality of the first (*see Alderman v. United States,* 394 U.S. 165, 177 (1969) (dictum); *United States v. Karo,* 468 U.S. 705, 719 (1984) (dictum)), unless the prosecution shows "sufficient untainted evidence" (that is, information not derived in any way from the first action) to justify the later one (*id.*). This evidence must be "genuinely independent of [the] . . . earlier, tainted [police action]," a condition that cannot be met if either (1) the police "decision to seek [a] . . . warrant [or conduct the second search] was prompted by what they had seen during the initial entry," or (2) "information obtained during that entry was presented to the Magistrate and affected his decision to issue the warrant [or is necessary to justify the second search without a warrant, if it was so made]" (*Murray v. United States,* 487 U.S. 533, 542 (1988)). *Cf. United States v. Hubbell,* 530 U.S. 27 (2000), discussed in § 12.6.4.1 *supra*.

Chapter 26

Motions To Suppress Confessions, Admissions, and Other Statements of the Defendant

A. *Introduction*

26.1. *Strategic Reasons for Seeking Suppression of the Defendant's Statements, Whether Inculpatory or Exculpatory*

The doctrines described in this chapter supply grounds for suppressing not only confessions but any statement by the defendant – "whether inculpatory or exculpatory – that the *prosecution* may seek to introduce at trial" (*Rhode Island v. Innis,* 446 U.S. 291, 301 n.5 (1980) (emphasis in original); *see also Miranda v. Arizona,* 384 U.S. 436, 476-77 (1966)).

Ordinarily, counsel will want to suppress all statements made by the defendant. In the case of a confession or a damaging admission, this is self-evident; the confession or admission is frequently the most damning thing the prosecutor has. In cases involving ostensibly exculpatory statements, a suppression motion is also the prudent course, since the facts that emerge at trial may render the statement more damaging than counsel can predict. For example, a statement asserting self-defense may prove to be detrimental in a case in which the state has no other persuasive proof that the defendant was the person who committed the assault. Also, counsel's pursuit of a suppression motion may serve the ancillary goals of discovery and creation of transcript material for use in impeaching prosecution witnesses at trial. See §§ 24.2, 24.4.2-24.4.3 *supra.*

B. *Involuntary Statements*

26.2. *General Standard for Assessing Voluntariness*

As noted in § 24.3.4 subdivision (ii) *supra,* whenever the defense claims that a defendant's statement was "involuntary" and is therefore inadmissible in evidence as a matter of Due Process, the prosecution bears the burden of proving by a preponderance of the evidence (and, in some jurisdictions, by proof beyond a reasonable doubt) that the statement was voluntarily made.

"The [Due Process] question in each case is whether a defendant's will was overborne at the time he confessed" (*Reck v. Pate,* 367 U.S. 433, 440 (1961); *cf. United States v. Washington,* 431 U.S. 181, 188 (1977)): – "whether the behavior of the State's law enforcement officials was such as to overbear . . . [the defendant's] will to resist and bring about confessions not freely self-determined" (*Rogers v. Richmond,* 365 U.S. 534, 544 (1961)), or whether the confession was "the product of an essentially free and unconstrained choice by its maker" (*Culombe v. Connecticut,* 367 U.S. 568, 602 (1961) (plurality opinion), approved in *Schneckloth v. Bustamonte,* 412 U.S. 218, 225-26 (1973)). This question is said to be determined "on the 'totality of the circumstances' in any particular case" (*Boulden v. Holman,* 394 U.S. 478, 480 (1969)). *See, e.g., Koh v. Ustich*, 933 F.3d 836, 844 (7th Cir. 2019) ("'The voluntariness of a confession depends on the totality of the circumstances, including both the characteristics of the accused and the nature of the interrogation. If those circumstances reveal that the interrogated person's will was overborne, admitting the resulting confession violates the Fifth Amendment.'").

Despite the psychological flavor of the "voluntariness" label, the Supreme Court's involuntary-statement caselaw has gradually evolved to focus as much upon police mistreatment of suspects for its own sake as upon the effects of the mistreatment in wearing the suspect down. *See, e.g., Spano v. New York,* 360 U.S. 315, 320-21 (1959); *Blackburn v. Alabama,* 361 U.S. 199, 206-07 (1960); *Jackson v. Denno,* 378 U.S. 368, 385-86 (1964); *Beecher v. Alabama,* 389 U.S. 35 (1967) (per curiam); *Sims v. Georgia,* 389 U.S. 404 (1967) (per curiam); *Brooks v. Florida,* 389 U.S. 413 (1967) (per curiam); *Crane v. Kentucky,* 476 U.S. 683, 687-88 (1986); *but see Moran v. Burbine,* 475 U.S. 412, 432-34 (1986).

> "This Court has long held that certain interrogation techniques either in isolation or as applied to the unique characteristics of a particular suspect, are so offensive to a civilized system of justice that they must be condemned under the Due Process Clause of the Fourteenth Amendment. . . . Although these decisions framed the legal inquiry in a variety of different ways, usually through the 'convenient shorthand' of asking whether the confession was 'involuntary,' . . . the Court's analysis has consistently been animated by the view that 'ours is an accusatorial and not an inquisitorial system,' . . . and that, accordingly, tactics for eliciting inculpatory statements must fall within the broad constitutional boundaries imposed by the Fourteenth Amendment's guarantee of fundamental fairness." (*Miller v. Fenton,* 474 U.S. 104, 109-10 (1985).)

Indeed, *some* coercive behavior on the part of government agents is an indispensable ingredient of an involuntary-statement claim: In *Colorado v. Connelly,* 479 U.S. 157 (1986), the Court rejected a defendant's contention that his confession was involuntary solely because his mental illness drove him to confess. But this does not mean that a defendant's mental, emotional, or physical vulnerability is immaterial. To the contrary, *Connelly* reaffirms the clear holding of *Blackburn v. Alabama,* 361 U.S. 199 (1960), that mental illness is "relevant to an individual's susceptibility to police coercion" (479 U.S. at 165); and in *Yarborough v. Alvarado,* 541 U.S. 652 (2004), the Court definitively declared that "whether 'the defendant's will was overborne,' . . . [is] a question that logically can depend on 'the characteristics of the accused'" (*id.* at 667-68), so "we do consider a suspect's age and experience" – together with other "characteristics of the accused . . . [including] the suspect's . . . education, and intelligence, . . . as well as a suspect's prior experience with law enforcement" as bearing on "the voluntariness of a statement" (*id.*). *See also Haley v. Ohio,* 332 U.S. 596, 599 (1948), discussed in § 26.4.1 *infra.* Personal qualities and conditions relevant to the assessment of a suspect's susceptibility to coercion include intellectual disability (*Reck v. Pate, supra,* 367 U.S. at 441-44; *Culombe v. Connecticut, supra,* 367 U.S. at 620-21, 624-25, 635), educational privation (*Payne v. Arkansas,* 356 U.S. 560 (1958); *Fikes v. Alabama,* 352 U.S. 191 (1957)), physical pain and drug ingestion (*Townsend v. Sain,* 372 U.S. 293 (1963); *Beecher v. Alabama,* 408 U.S. 234 (1972)), and any "unique characteristics of a particular suspect" (*Miller v. Fenton, supra,* 474 U.S. at 109) that impair the suspect's "powers of resistance to overbearing police tactics" (*Reck v. Pate, supra,* 367 U.S. at 442). In addition, the propriety or impropriety of police conduct is itself measured, to a large extent, by its tendency to weaken the suspect's will. *See, e.g., Spano v. New York,* 360 U.S. 315 (1959); *Lynumn v. Illinois,* 372 U.S. 528 (1963); *cf. Moran v. Burbine, supra,* 475 U.S. at 423 ("[a]lthough highly inappropriate, even deliberate deception of an attorney [that keeps the attorney from coming to the police station to advise a suspect who is undergoing interrogation] could not possibly affect a suspect's decision to waive his *Miranda* rights unless he were at least aware of the incident"). State constitutional protections may exclude statements found to be involuntary for reasons wholly apart from any inappropriate police behavior. *See State v. Rees,* 2000 ME 55, 748 A.2d 976, 977, 978-79 (Me. 2000) (construing the state constitution to reject *Colorado v. Connelly's* holding that "'coercive police activity is a necessary predicate to the finding that a confession is not "voluntary" within the meaning of the Due Process Clause'"; the state supreme court affirms a trial court's finding of involuntariness which was based entirely on the defendant's "'dementia,'" and which "'stressed that this ruling makes no finding of improper or incorrect conduct upon the part of the investigating officers'"). And see § 17.11 *supra.*

Thus the caselaw provides a basis for presenting involuntary-statement claims from any one or more of three perspectives:

(a)   with an emphasis upon the *behavior* of the police as constituting "coercive government misconduct" (*Colorado v. Connelly, supra,* 479 U.S. at 163) that is "'revolting to the sense of justice'" (*id.,* quoting *Brown v. Mississippi,* 297 U.S. 278, 286 (1936); *see, e.g., Brooks v. Florida, supra,* 389 U.S. at 414-15; *cf. Crowe v. County of San Diego,* 608 F.3d 406, 432 (9th Cir. 2010) ("One need only read the transcripts of the boys' interrogations, or watch the videotapes, to understand how thoroughly the defendants' conduct in this case 'shocks the conscience.' Michael and Aaron – 14 and 15 years old, respectively – were isolated and subjected to hours and hours of interrogation during which they were cajoled, threatened, lied to, and relentlessly pressured by teams of police officers. 'Psychological torture' is not an inapt description. In *Cooper* [*v. Dupnik,* 963 F.2d 1220, 1223 (9th Cir. 1992)], we held that police violated an adult suspect's substantive due process rights when they 'ignored Cooper's repeated requests to speak with an attorney, deliberately infringed on his Constitutional right to remain silent, and relentlessly interrogated him in an attempt to extract a confession.' . . . The interrogations of Michael and Aaron are no less shocking. Indeed, they are more so given that the boys' interrogations were significantly longer than Coopers's, the boys were minors, and Michael was in shock over his sister's brutal murder. The interrogations violated Michael's and Aaron's Fourteenth Amendment rights to substantive due process."));

(b)   with an emphasis upon the *effects* of the police behavior on the accused's psychological state, considering the accused's individual weaknesses and vulnerabilities (*see, e.g., Culombe v. Connecticut, supra,* 367 U.S. at 620-21, 624-25, 635; *Davis v. North Carolina,* 384 U.S. 737 (1966); *Colorado v. Spring,* 479 U.S. 564, 573-74 (1987) (dictum)), as bearing on the question whether the confession was "'"the product of a rational intellect and a free will"'" (*Mincey v. Arizona,* 437 U.S. 385, 398 (1978); *see also Townsend v. Sain, supra,* 372 U.S. at 308 ("[a]ny questioning by police officers which *in fact* produces a confession which is not the product of a free intellect renders that confession inadmissible" (emphasis in the original); *and see* Dean A. Strang, *Inaccuracy and the Involuntary Confession: Understanding Rogers v. Richmond Rightly*, 110 J. CRIM. L. & CRIMINOLOGY 69 (2020) (arguing that accuracy of factual details in a confession cannot properly be considered as evidence of voluntariness but that inaccuracy should be considered as evidence of involuntariness)); or

(c)   with an emphasis upon the *tendency* of the police behavior to overbear the will of someone in the accused's position and condition (*see, e.g., Sims v. Georgia*, 389 U.S. 404 (1967); *Miller v. Fenton, supra*, 474 U.S. at 116 ("the admissibility of a confession turns as much on whether the techniques for extracting the statements, as applied to *this* suspect, are compatible with a system that presumes innocence and assures that a conviction will not be secured by inquisitorial means as on whether the defendant's will was in fact overborne" (emphasis in the original)).

Defense counsel should select the perspective or perspectives that will make the most of the facts of the particular case.

It should be noted that although the lower courts occasionally confuse or interweave analyses of involuntariness and *Miranda* claims, the two claims are separate and distinct. *See, e.g., Dickerson v. United States*, 530 U.S. 428, 432-35 (2000); *Miller v. Fenton, supra*, 474 U.S. at 109-10; *Oregon v. Elstad,* 470 U.S. 298, 303-04 (1985); *Colorado v. Connelly, supra*, 479 U.S. at 163-71; *cf. United States v. Patane*, 542 U.S. 630, 636-41 (2004) (plurality opinion). The doctrines may overlap in their application to the facts of a particular case: for example, the facts showing the involuntariness of the statement will usually also show the involuntariness of the defendant's waiver of *Miranda* rights. *Cf. Colorado v. Connelly, supra*, 479 U.S. at 169-70. But counsel should be precise in identifying the constitutional basis of the claim, both because it may significantly affect the appropriate analysis (see, *e.g., Yarborough v. Alvarado, supra*, 541 U.S. at 667 ("the objective *Miranda* custody inquiry could reasonably be viewed as different from doctrinal tests that depend on the actual mindset of a particular suspect")) and because it may affect the scope of relief for any constitutional violation that is found. For example, a statement suppressed on *Miranda* grounds cannot be used in the prosecution's case in chief but can be used to impeach the defendant if s/he testifies at trial, whereas a statement suppressed because of a finding of involuntariness under the Due Process Clause cannot be used by the prosecution for any purpose. See § 26.19 *infra*. And the scope of exclusion of derivative evidence is broader in the case of involuntary statements than in the case of statements obtained in violation of *Miranda*. See § 26.16 *infra*.

26.3. *Police Coercion Rendering a Statement Involuntary*

As explained in § 26.2 *supra*, "coercive police activity is a necessary predicate to the finding that a confession is not 'voluntary' within the meaning of the Due Process Clause of the Fourteenth Amendment" (*Colorado v. Connelly*, 479 U.S. 157, 167 (1986)). "While each confession case has turned on its own set of factors justifying the conclusion that police conduct was oppressive, all have contained a substantial element of coercive police conduct." *Id.* at 163-64. The concept of "coercive police activity" includes physical force or the threat of force (see

§ 26.3.1 *infra*), excessively long detention or intimidating circumstances of detention (see § 26.3.2 *infra*), promises of leniency or threats of adverse governmental action (see § 26.3.3 *infra*), and certain tricks and artifices (see § 26.3.4 *infra*).

26.3.1. *Physical Force or Threat of Force*

As the Supreme Court observed in *Sims v. Georgia,* 389 U.S. 404, 407 (1967) (per curiam): "It needs no extended citation of cases to show that a confession produced by violence or threats of violence is involuntary and cannot constitutionally be used against the person giving it." *See, e.g., Arizona v. Fulminante*, 499 U.S. 279, 287-88 (1991) ("Fulminante's will was overborne in such a way as to render his confession the product of coercion" as a result of a fellow inmate, who was a government agent, offering to protect him from other inmates if he confessed: "Our cases have made clear that a finding of coercion need not depend upon actual violence by a government agent; a credible threat is sufficient."); *Payne v. Arkansas,* 356 U.S. 560 (1958) (a confession was rendered involuntary by the totality of police conduct "and particularly the culminating threat" (*id.* at 567) that the Chief of Police was preparing to admit a lynch mob into the jail); *State v. Hilliard,* 318 S.E.2d 35, 36 (W. Va. 1983) (a confession was rendered involuntary when a police officer told the accused he would "knock [his] . . . head off" if he didn't confess).

Serious physical abuse or the threat of it will ordinarily be held to render subsequent statements involuntary even when it is not closely related in time or circumstances to police interrogation or the making of the statements. *See, e.g., Sims v. Georgia, supra*, 389 U.S. at 405-07 (on the facts of the case, set forth at greater length in *Sims v. Georgia,* 385 U.S. 538 (1967), a confession was rendered involuntary because the defendant was physically abused, even though the abuse took place several hours prior to, and in a different location from, the confession); *Beecher v. Alabama,* 389 U.S. 35 (1967) (per curiam), as construed in *Colorado v. Connelly, supra,* 479 U.S. at 163 n.1 (the "crucial element of police overreaching" was holding a gun to the head of the wounded defendant at the time of his arrest, five days prior to the interrogation and confession).

26.3.2. *Intimidating or Overbearing Circumstances of Interrogation or Detention*

The coerciveness of interrogation increases with the length of the interrogation (*see, e.g., Haley v. Ohio,* 332 U.S. 596 (1948) (15-year-old questioned from midnight to 5 a.m.); *Spano v. New York,* 360 U.S. 315 (1959) (adult interrogated for eight hours); *Doody v. Ryan,* 649 F.3d 986, 990, 1023 (9th Cir. 2011) (en banc) ("sleep-deprived" 17-year-old interrogated by a "tag team of detectives" in a "relentless, nearly thirteen-hour interrogation"); *In the Interest of Jerrell C.J.,* 2005 WI 105, 283 Wis. 2d 145, 162-63, 699 N.W.2d 110, 118-19 (Wis. 2005) (14-year-old questioned for five-and-a-half hours)) and with the length of time that the suspect is held incommunicado by the police (*see, e.g., Haley v. Ohio, supra,* 332 U.S. at 600 (15-year-old held incommunicado and denied access to his mother for five days); *Gallegos v. Colorado,* 370 U.S. 49 (1962) (14-year-old held incommunicado for five days); *In the Interest of Jerrell C.J., supra,* 2005 WI 105, 283 Wis. 2d at 162-63, 699 N.W.2d at 118-19 ("In this case, [14-year-old] Jerrell was handcuffed to a wall and left alone for approximately two hours. He was then interrogated for five-and-a-half more hours before finally signing a written confession . . . . The duration of

Jerrell's custody and interrogation was longer than the five hours at issue in *Haley*. Indeed, it was significantly longer than most interrogations. Under these circumstances, it is easy to see how Jerrell would be left wondering 'if and when the inquisition would ever cease.'" (footnote omitted.))). *See also Crowe v. County of San Diego*, 608 F.3d 406, 432 (9th Cir. 2010) (holding, in a civil rights action, that the police interrogations of two juvenile suspects violated their "Fourteenth Amendment rights to substantive due process" because the 14-year-old and 15-year-old youths "were isolated and subjected to hours and hours of interrogation during which they were cajoled, threatened, lied to, and relentlessly pressured by teams of police officers"). Prolonged detention under oppressive or debilitating conditions can render a confession involuntary even in the absence of extensive interrogation. *See Brooks v. Florida*, 389 U.S. 413, 414-15 (1967) (per curiam) ("Putting to one side quibbles over the dimensions of the windowless sweatbox into which Brooks was thrown naked with two other men, we cannot accept his statement as the voluntary expression of an uncoerced will. For two weeks this man's home was a barren cage fitted only with a hole in one corner into which he and his cell mates could defecate. For two weeks he subsisted on a daily fare of 12 ounces of thin soup and eight ounces of water. For two full weeks he saw not one friendly face from outside the prison, but was completely under the control and domination of his jailers. These stark facts belie any contention that the confession extracted from him within minutes after he was brought from the cell was not tainted by the 14 days he spent in such an oppressive hole.").

Even if the period of detention is not excessively long, unusually harsh conditions of confinement preceding the confession, such as deprivations of food, sleep, or medication, can render the confession involuntary. *See, e.g., Greenwald v. Wisconsin,* 390 U.S. 519 (1968) (denial of food, sleep, and medication for high blood pressure); *Reck v. Pate,* 367 U.S. 433 (1961) (inadequate food and medical attention); *Payne v. Arkansas,* 356 U.S. 560 (1958) (three days with little food); *State v. Garcia*, 301 P.3d 658, 666-67, 668 (Kan. 2013) (a confession was rendered involuntary by "coercive tactics" of "withholding requested relief for an obviously painful untreated gunshot wound over the course of a several-hours-long interrogation" ("[e]ven if Garcia did not confess solely to obtain medical treatment") and by the officer's assurance to the suspect that "a murder charge and accompanying life sentence could be avoided by admitting to the robbery and testifying against" another (even though "[i]t appears that Garcia refused to take the bait because he thought it was a trick").).

26.3.3. *Promises of Leniency or Threats of Adverse Governmental Action*

A confession is involuntary if "'obtained by any direct or implied promises, however slight, [or] by the exertion of any improper influence'" (*Hutto v. Ross,* 429 U.S. 28, 30 (1976) (per curiam), quoting *Bram v. United States*, 168 U.S. 532, 542-43 (1897)). *See, e.g., Lynumn v. Illinois,* 372 U.S. 528, 534 (1963) (a confession was rendered involuntary largely because police told the defendant "that state financial aid for her infant children would be cut off, and her children taken from her, if she did not 'cooperate'"); *Haynes v. Washington,* 373 U.S. 503, 514 (1963) (a confession was rendered involuntary in part because of "the express threat of continued incommunicado detention and . . . the promise of communication with and access to family"); *Koh v. Ustich*, 933 F.3d 836, 847 (7th Cir. 2019) (an interrogating officer's statement "that they could be there for 'days and days and days,'" if found to be a threat, would be probative of coercion, rendering a confession involuntary); *Sharp v. Rohling*, 793 F.3d 1216, 1219 (10th Cir.

2015) (a confession was rendered involuntary by the interrogating officer's promise of "leniency – no jail"); *United States v. Young*, 964 F.3d 938 (10th Cir. 2020) (holding a confession involuntary: "The district court found that Agent Brown made false representations to Young when he stated that he was 'on your side' and that he had discussions with the judge about Young's charges and sentence. It also found Agent Brown's statement that Young could 'buy down' his time by answering questions truthfully was a promise of leniency." (*Id*. at 942-43.) "Although we do not require a law enforcement officer to inform a suspect of the penalties for all the charges he may face, if he misrepresents these penalties, then that deception affects our evaluation of the voluntariness of any resulting statements. In this interrogation, Agent Brown misrepresented the law to Young, a factor that weighs in favor of concluding his actions were coercive. (*Id*. at 944.)); *United States v. Lopez*, 437 F.3d 1059, 1066 (10th Cir. 2006) ("the federal agents' promising Lopez that he would spend 6 rather than 60 years in prison if he admitted to killing Box by mistake and the Agents' misrepresenting the strength of the evidence they had against Lopez, resulted in Lopez's first confession being coerced and, thus, involuntary"; "although Lopez's second confession came after a night's sleep and a meal, and almost twelve hours elapsed between confessions, the coercion producing the first confession had not been dissipated."); *United States ex rel. Everett v. Murphy,* 329 F.2d 68 (2d Cir. 1964) (a confession was rendered involuntary when police falsely promised assistance in arranging less serious charges than they knew would be brought); *Rincher v. State*, 632 So.2d 37, 40 (Ala. Crim. App. 1993) (a 17-year-old's stationhouse statement was "coerced" because a police captain "promised . . . [him] that he could go home if he made a statement"); *People v. Perez*, 243 Cal. App. 4th 863, 866-67, 196 Cal. Rptr. 3d 871, 875 (2016) ("Perez's statements were clearly motivated by a promise of leniency, rendering the statements involuntary": "a police sergeant told Perez that if he '[told] the truth' and was 'honest,' then, 'we are not gonna charge you with anything'"); *People v. Ramadon*, 2013 CO 68, 314 P.3d 836, 838, 844-45 (Colo. 2013) (the defendant's statements were rendered involuntary by the interrogating officer's telling him "that, if he did not tell the truth, he would likely be deported to Iraq" and "insinuat[ing] that Ramadon would not be deported if he admitted to committing the sexual assault"); *State v. Howard*, 825 N.W.2d 32, 34, 41 (Iowa 2012) (an interrogating detective "crossed the line into an improper promise of leniency" and thereby rendered the confession inadmissible by repeatedly referring to "getting help" for the suspect (who had been arrested for sexually abusing a minor) and overtly suggesting that "if Howard admitted to sexually abusing A.E. he merely would be sent to a treatment facility similar to that used to treat drug and alcohol addiction in lieu of further punishment"); *State v. Polk*, 812 N.W.2d 670, 676 (Iowa 2012) (an interrogating officer "crossed the line" and rendered the resulting confession involuntary by "combining statements that county attorneys 'are much more likely to work with an individual that is cooperating' with suggestions . . . [that the defendant] would not see his kids 'for a long time' unless he confessed"); *In the Interest of J.D.F.*, 553 N.W.2d 585, 589 (Iowa 1996) ("J.D.F.'s inculpatory admission was induced by the police promising that they would take him home rather than to the juvenile intake center"); *State v. Brown*, 286 Kan. 170, 182 P.3d 1205 (2008) (a child welfare agency worker unconstitutionally coerced a statement by pressuring the defendant to admit culpability for his child's injury or else risk losing custody of his children); *Dye v. Commonwealth*, 411 S.W.3d 227, 232-34 (Ky. 2013) (police coerced a confession by falsely telling the 17-year-old defendant that the only way to avoid the death penalty was to confess, even though the police "knew, or should have known, that . . . [he] was not death-eligible," and by telling the defendant that "a confession is the only way he will avoid daily prison assault");

State v. Wiley, 2013 ME 30, 61 A.3d 750, 760 (Me. 2013) (an interrogating officer's "concrete representation of a short jail sentence followed by probation in exchange for Wiley's cooperation" was a "primary motivating force for the ensuing confession" and rendered it involuntary); *State v. Smith,* 203 Neb. 64, 66, 277 N.W.2d 441, 443 (1979) (a confession was rendered involuntary when police promised to "attempt to have the matter transferred to juvenile court" if defendant cooperated). *Cf.* the cases holding that the Fifth Amendment is violated when a witness is compelled to testify in formal proceedings under threat of the withdrawal of government benefits if s/he does not: *Stevens v. Marks*, 383 U.S. 234 (1966); *Garrity v. New Jersey*, 385 U.S. 493 (1967); *Gardner v. Broderick*, 392 U.S. 273 (1968); *Lefkowitz v. Turley*, 414 U.S. 70 (1973); *Lefkowitz v. Cunningham*, 431 U.S. 801 (1977).

Statements made to government agents such as parole and probation officers in settings in which a defendant has reason to believe that s/he is obliged to answer incriminating questions or suffer revocation of conditional release represent the "'classic penalty situation' [that] arises when a person must choose between incriminating himself, on the one hand, or suffering government-threatened punishment for invoking his Fifth Amendment privilege to remain silent, on the other" (*McKathan v. United States*, 969 F.3d 1213, 1217 (11th Cir. 2020)). "[T]he Supreme Court has . . . identified a solution to this problem: when a 'classic penalty situation' occurs, the Fifth Amendment privilege is self-executing, and the government is deemed to have compelled the speaker's statements in violation of the Fifth Amendment . . . [citing *Minnesota v. Murphy*, 465 U.S. 420, 435 (1984)]. As a result, the statements are rendered inadmissible in a criminal prosecution." *McKathan, supra*, 969 F.3d at 1217. However, *Murphy* and *United States v. Linville*, 60 F.4th 890 (4th Cir. 2023), erect a strict test that the releasee must meet to obtain exclusion of incriminating statements made without an explicit claim of privilege in this situation. The release conditions must either (1) "actually require a choice between asserting the Fifth Amendment and revocation of supervised release" (*id.* at 897) or (2) give rise to "a reasonable basis for . . . [the releasee] to believe they do" in the factual setting in which the releasee is called upon to answer (*id.*). Ordinarily, when the conditions "'merely require[ ] . . . [the releasee] to appear and give testimony about matters relevant to his [or her] probationary status'" (*id.*), this test is not met. But "[i]f the government 'expressly or by implication [ ] asserts that invocation of the privilege would lead to revocation of . . . [release], it would have created the classic penalty situation, the failure to assert the privilege would be excused, and the . . . [releasee's] answers would be deemed compelled and inadmissible in a criminal prosecution.'" *Id.*

Outside the context of police interrogation as well, incriminating disclosures which an individual is legally required to make in order to avoid forfeitures or similar adverse consequences are regarded as involuntary (*see Lacy v. Butts*, 922 F.3d 371 (7th Cir. 2019), summarized in § 16.6.1 *supra*) and cannot be used as evidence of guilt in the prosecution's case in chief. *See State v. Melendez*, 240 N.J. 268, 222 A.3d 639 (2020), summarized in § 16.6.1 *supra*.

26.3.4. *Tricks or Artifices*

Although the Supreme Court has never ruled a confession involuntary solely because it was induced by tricks or artifices, the Court has cited trickery as one of the factors considered when holding a confession involuntary in the light of "the totality of the situation" (*Spano v. New York,* 360 U.S. 315, 323 (1959) (a police officer who was a close childhood friend of the defendant's misleadingly told the defendant that he, the officer, would get in trouble with the police force if the defendant failed to confess). *See also Colorado v. Spring,* 479 U.S. 564, 576 n.8 (1987) (dictum) (citing *Spano, supra,* and *Lynumn v. Illinois, supra*).

Lower courts have similarly treated police artifice as a factor in the "totality of the circumstances" leading to a finding of involuntariness. *See, e.g., Dye v. Commonwealth*, 411 S.W.3d 227, 232-34 (Ky. 2013), summarized in § 26.3.3 *supra; United States v. Lall,* 607 F.3d 1277, 1287 (11th Cir. 2010) ("Gaudio explicitly assured Lall that anything he said would not be used to prosecute him. . . . Gaudio's promise was deceptive. . . . Gaudio told him he would not be charged for any statements or evidence collected on the night of the robbery. . . . It is inconceivable that Lall, an uncounseled twenty-year-old, understood at the time that a promise by Gaudio that he was not going to pursue any charges did not preclude the use of the confession in a federal prosecution. Indeed, it is utterly unreasonable to expect any uncounseled layperson, especially someone in Lall's position, to so parse Gaudio's words. On the contrary, the only plausible interpretation of Gaudio's representations, semantic technicalities aside, was that the information Lall provided would not be used against him by Gaudio or anyone else. Under these circumstances, Gaudio's statements were sufficient to render Lall's confession involuntary and to undermine completely the prophylactic effect of the *Miranda* warnings Gaudio previously administered."); *United States v. Lopez,* 437 F.3d 1059, 1065 (10th Cir. 2006) ("in this case, the agents' misrepresentation of the evidence against Lopez, together with Agent Hopper's promise of leniency to Lopez if he confessed to killing Box by mistake, are sufficient circumstances that would overbear Lopez's will and make his confession involuntary"); *United States v. Morales,* 233 F. Supp. 160 (D. Mont. 1964) (a juvenile's statement was rendered involuntary partly because he was falsely told that his accomplices had signed statements implicating him); *Gray v. Commonwealth,* 480 S.W.3d 253, 260-61 (Ky. 2016) (the police "overbore Gray's free will" by showing him "falsified documents purporting to represent the official results of a state-police lab's DNA examination" and making false statements about other evidence inculpating him); *In re Elias V.,* 237 Cal. App. 4th 568, 571, 579, 583, 588, 188 Cal. Rptr. 3d 202, 204, 211, 214, 218 (2015) (a 13-year-old's confession was rendered involuntary because his will was "'overborne'" by the police officers' use of "the type of coercive interrogation techniques condemned in *Miranda*," including the so-called "'Reid Technique,'" which uses "a 'cluster of tactics' [termed "'maximization/ minimization'"] designed to convey . . . 'the interrogator's rock-solid belief that the suspect is guilty and that all denials will fail' [and] 'to provide the suspect with moral justification and face saving excuses for having committed the crime in question,'" and also including police claims of fictitious evidence implicating the suspect, notwithstanding that even "the most recent edition of the Reid manual on interrogations notes that . . . 'this technique should be avoided when interrogating a youthful suspect with low social maturity' because such suspects 'may not have the fortitude or confidence to challenge such evidence and depending on the nature of the crime, may become confused as to their own possible involvement if the police tell them evidence clearly indicates they committed the crime.'"); *State v. Swindler*, 296 Kan. 670, 680-81, 294 P.3d 308, 315-16 (2013) (a statement was rendered involuntary because the police obtained it by using a "bait and switch" tactic of assuring the defendant that "he was free to terminate the interrogation and leave at any time" but then breaking these "rules of engagement . . . as soon as they thought Swindler might slip away without telling them what they wanted to hear"); *People v. Thomas*, 22 N.Y.3d 629, 642-43, 8 N.E.3d 308, 314-15, 985 N.Y.S.2d 193, 199-200 (2014) (police officers' "highly coercive deceptions" – threatening the defendant that if he "continued to deny responsibility for his child's injury, his wife would be arrested and removed from his ailing child's bedside," and falsely asserting that "his disclosure of the circumstances under which he injured his child was essential to assist the doctors attempting to save the child's life" – "were of a kind sufficiently potent to nullify individual judgment in any ordinarily resolute person and were manifestly lethal to self-determination when deployed against defendant, an unsophisticated individual without experience in the criminal justice system"); *Young v. State,* 670 P.2d 591, 594-95 (Okla. Crim. App. 1983) (a statement was rendered involuntary partly because of a polygraph examiner's "gross misstatement of the law" that the defendant would have to convince the judge and jury that he was "'perfectly innocent'"); *State v. Caffrey,* 332 N.W.2d 269, 272-73 (S.D. 1983) (a juvenile's statement was rendered involuntary partly because of the "interrogating officers['] deliberately mislead[ing] [him] . . . into thinking that he would be compelled to submit to a lie detector test"); *United States v. Anderson*, 929 F.2d 96 (2d Cir. 1991) (a DEA agent gave defendant Anderson *Miranda* warnings and "then proceeded to tell Anderson that if he asked for an attorney, no federal agents would be able to speak to him further; the agent added 'this [is] the time to talk to us, because once you tell us you want an attorney we're not able to talk to you and as far as I [am] concerned, we probably would not go to the U.S. Attorney or anyone else to tell them how much [you] cooperated with us.' The 'if you want a lawyer you can't cooperate' language was repeated three times." (*id.* at 97); "[T]hese statements were false and/or misleading. It is commonplace for defendants who have acquired counsel to meet with federal law enforcement officials and agree to cooperate with the government." (*id.* at 100). "Under the totality of the circumstances, Agent Valentine's statements contributed to the already coercive atmosphere inherent in custodial interrogation and rendered Anderson's . . . confession involuntary as a matter of law." *Id.* at 102.); *In the Interest of Jerrell C.J.*, 2005 WI 105, 283 Wis. 2d 145, 163-64, 699 N.W.2d 110, 119 (Wis. 2005) ("pressures brought to bear on the [14-year-old] defendant" included police officers' use of "psychological techniques" during interrogation: "Not only did the detectives refuse to believe Jerrell's repeated denials of guilt, but they also joined in urging him to tell a different 'truth,' sometimes using a 'strong voice' that 'frightened' him. Admittedly, it does not appear from the record that Jerrell was suffering from any significant emotional or psychological condition during the interrogation. Nevertheless, we remain concerned that such a technique applied to a juvenile like Jerrell over a prolonged period of time could result in an involuntary confession."). *Cf. State v. Matsumoto*, 145 Hawai'i 313, 324, 327, 452 P.3d 310, 321, 324 (2019) ("A police officer's use of subterfuge to induce a suspect to make an incriminating statement may rise to the level of coercion, rendering the statement involuntary, untrustworthy, and inadmissible. . . . When measuring 'the legitimacy of the use of "deception" by the police in eliciting confessions or inculpatory statements from suspects and arrestees,' Hawai'i courts evaluate the use of falsehoods regarding information intrinsic to the case differently from deception that is extrinsic to the facts of the alleged offense. . . . When the police use 'deliberate falsehoods extrinsic to the facts of the alleged offense, which are of a type reasonably likely to procure an untrue statement or to influence an accused to make a confession regardless of guilt, [they] will be regarded as coercive per se.' . . . ¶ Examples of extrinsic falsehoods include assurances of divine salvation upon confession; promises of mental health treatment in exchange for a confession; assurances of treatment in a 'nice hospital' in lieu of incarceration, in exchange for a confession; promises of more favorable treatment in the event of a confession; and misrepresentations of legal principles, such as misrepresenting the consequences of a 'habitual offender' conviction and holding out that the defendant's confession cannot be used against the defendant at trial. . . . ¶ . . . Thus, inculpatory statements elicited during a custodial interrogation from a suspect whom has previously been given falsified polygraph results in the interrogation process are coercive per se and are inadmissible at trial."). *See generally* Christopher Slobogin, *Manipulation of Suspects and Unrecorded Questioning: After 50 Years of Miranda Jurisprudence, Still Two (or Maybe Three) Burning Issues*, 97 B.U. L. REV. 1157 (2017); Michael J. Zydney Mannheimer, *Fraudulently Induced Confessions*, 96 NOTRE DAME L. REV. 79 (2020).

Beyond their bearing on the issue of voluntariness, deceptive interrogation practices may affect the admissibility and weight of incriminating statements under other evidentiary principles. When interrogating officers ply a suspect with misleading information or use psychological ploys that create a significant risk of eliciting false admissions, counsel should urge the exclusion of any inculpatory responses as unreliable, under the court's authority to refuse to admit evidence which is substantially more prejudicial than probative. See § 36.2.3 *infra*. In *Aleman v. Village of Hanover Park*, 662 F.3d 897, 906-07 (7th Cir. 2011), Circuit Judge Posner wrote for the court that "[t]he question of coercion is separate from that of reliability" and that "a trick that is as likely to induce a false as a true confession renders a confession inadmissible because of its unreliability even if its voluntariness is conceded. . . . If a question has only two answers – A and B – and you tell the defendant [untruthfully] that the answer is not A, and he has no basis for doubting you, then he is compelled by logic to 'confess' that the answer is B. . . . A confession so induced is worthless as evidence, and as a premise for an arrest." (Judge Posner's concluding phrase implies that if the defendant's inculpatory statements are indispensable to the probable cause required for a subsequent arrest or search, the arrest or search is unconstitutional and any evidence which they produce is excludable on that account. See, *e.g.*, §§ 25.7, 25.16, 25.24, 25.26, 25.39, 25.42 *supra*; § 26.15 *infra*.) And even if the court refuses to entirely exclude a deception-induced inculpatory statement, defendant's counsel is free to argue to the trier of fact at trial (see § 26.18 *infra*) that the deceptive interrogation procedure renders the statement incredible (*see* Brian L. Cutler & Richard A. Leo, *Analyzing Videotaped Interrogations and Confessions*, 40-DEC THE CHAMPION 40 (December 2016); Brian L. Cutler & Richard A. Leo, *False Confessions in the 21st Century*, 40-MAY THE CHAMPION 46 (May 2016); Bryan L. Cutler, Jeffrey S. Neuschatz & Charles R. Honts, *An Overview of Expert Psychological Testimony in False Confession Cases*, 44-JUN THE CHAMPION 30 (2020); JAMES L. TRAINUM, HOW THE POLICE GENERATE FALSE CONFESSIONS: AN INSIDE LOOK AT THE INTERROGATION ROOM (2016)) and also casts doubt upon "the reliability of the investigation" as a whole by "'discrediting . . . the police methods employed in assembling the case'" (*cf. Kyles v. Whitley*, 514 U.S. 419, 446 (1995)).

Under some circumstances there may be a constitutionally significant distinction between "affirmative misrepresentations" by the police and their misleading of a suspect through "mere silence" (*Colorado v. Spring, supra*, 479 U.S. at 576 & n.8). In *Spring,* the Supreme Court reversed the finding of two state appellate courts that a suspect's waiver of the privilege against self-incrimination was invalid and that his incriminating statements were improperly obtained when the interrogating officers who gave him his *Miranda* warnings (see § 26.5 *infra*) failed to inform him of the specific crimes about which he would be questioned (and when the context of the interrogation did not make these apparent). The Court rejected this finding on the broad ground that a suspect's knowledge of the topic of an interrogation is not a necessary precondition for a valid waiver of the Fifth Amendment privilege and that interrogating officers are therefore not obliged to inform suspects on this subject. However, in dealing with Spring's argument that his interrogators had practiced a form of trickery by failing to tell him what crimes they were investigating, the Court emphasized both that "the Colorado courts made no finding of official trickery" (479 U.S. at 575), and that "mere silence by law enforcement officials as to the subject matter of an interrogation" (*id.* at 576) is distinguishable from the "affirmative misrepresentations by the police [that were found] sufficient to invalidate a suspect's waiver of the Fifth Amendment privilege" in *Spano v. New York* [360 U.S. 315 (1959)] . . . and *Lynumn v. Illinois* [372 U.S. 528, 534 (1963)] . . ." (479 U.S. at 576 n.8). "In this case, we are not confronted with an affirmative misrepresentation by law enforcement officials as to the scope of the interrogation and do not reach the question whether a waiver of *Miranda* rights would be valid in such a circumstance." *Id. Cf. Moran v. Burbine,* 475 U.S. 412, 422-24 (1986), noted in § 26.8.1 *infra. See generally* WELSH S. WHITE, *MIRANDA'S* WANING PROTECTIONS: POLICE INTERROGATION PRACTICES AFTER *DICKERSON* 209-15 (2001); Welsh S. White, *Police Trickery in Inducing Confessions,* 127 U. PA. L. REV. 581 (1979); Rinat Kitai-Sangero, *Extending Miranda: Prohibition on Police Lies Regarding the Incriminating Evidence,* 54 SAN DIEGO L. REV. 611 (2017).

26.4. *Characteristics of the Defendant That Are Relevant to the Assessment of Voluntariness*

The Supreme Court has long recognized that personal characteristics of a suspect that render him or her particularly vulnerable to coercion – such as youth, mental illness, intellectual disability, limited intellect, limited education, intoxication, and the effects of drugs – are significant factors in the "totality of the circumstances" that determine the voluntariness of a statement. *See, e.g., Haley v. Ohio,* 332 U.S. 596 (1948) (age of 15); *Culombe v. Connecticut,* 367 U.S. 568 (1961) (I.Q. of 64, illiteracy); *Fikes v. Alabama,* 352 U.S. 191 (1957) (less than third-grade education). See § 26.2, fourth paragraph, *supra.*

In *Colorado v. Connelly,* 479 U.S. 157 (1986), the Court made clear that a claim of involuntariness for Fourteenth Amendment Due Process purposes cannot be based *solely* on the personal frailties of a suspect. Reversing a lower court finding of involuntariness predicated exclusively on the accused's mental illness, the Court emphasized that federal constitutional protections are triggered only by "'state action'" (*id.* at 165), and it accordingly held that some form of "coercive police activity is a necessary predicate to the finding that a confession is not 'voluntary' within the meaning of the Due Process Clause" (*id.* at 167). *Connelly* does, however, reaffirm in dictum that a suspect's "mental condition is surely relevant to an individual's susceptibility to police coercion" (*id.* at 165): "as interrogators have turned to more subtle forms of psychological persuasion, courts have found the mental condition of the defendant a more significant factor in the 'voluntariness' calculus" (*id.* at 164). And in *Yarborough v. Alvarado,* 541 U.S. 652 (2004), the Court repeated (again in dictum) that "we do consider a suspect's age and [extent of prior] experience [with the criminal justice system]" when gauging, for purposes of assessing the "voluntariness of a statement," whether "'the defendant's will was overborne,'" . . . a question that logically can depend on 'the characteristics of the accused'" (*id.* at 667-68; *and see id.* at 668 (the "characteristics of the accused" relevant to this assessment "can include the suspect's age, education, and intelligence, . . . as well as a suspect's prior experience with law enforcement")). *See also Procunier v. Atchley,* 400 U.S. 446, 453-54 (1971) (dictum) (a suspect's "[l]ow intelligence, denial of the right to counsel and failure to advise of the right to remain silent were not in themselves coercive [but] . . . were relevant . . . in establishing a setting in which actual coercion might have been exerted to overcome the will of the suspect"); *State v. Carrillo,* 156 Ariz. 125, 136, 750 P.2d 883, 894 (1988) (dictum) ("[W]e do not believe *Connelly* forbids consideration of the accused's subjective mental state. Certainly the police are not permitted to take advantage of the impoverished, the mentally deficient, the young, or the inexperienced by employing artifices or techniques that destroy the will of the weakest but leave the strong, the tough, and the experienced untouched."). Thus a suspect's vulnerable state of mind can lend coercive force to police words and actions that would not be deemed coercive in the case of a suspect with normal powers of resistance. *See, e.g., Reck v. Pate,* 367 U.S. 433, 442 (1961) (the defendant's "youth, his subnormal intelligence, and his lack of previous experience with the police" impaired "his powers of resistance to overbearing police tactics"); *Haley v. Ohio, supra,* 332 U.S. at 599 (five hours of incommunicado interrogation rendered a confession involuntary because the defendant was only 15 years old, and "[t]hat which would leave a man cold and unimpressed can overawe and overwhelm a lad in his early teens"); *United States v. Preston,* 751 F.3d 1008, 1028 (9th Cir. 2014) (en banc) ("Even if we would reach a different conclusion regarding someone of normal intelligence, we hold that the officers' use of the [interrogation] methods employed here to confuse and compel a confession from the intellectually disabled eighteen-year-old before us produced an involuntary confession"); *United States v. Blocker,* 354 F. Supp. 1195, 1201-02 (D. D.C. 1973) ("[i]n this case, defendant's age [21] and limited mental ability suggest that the defendant would be particularly susceptible to psychological coercion in the form of threats and promises of leniency"). Moreover, personal characteristics such as youth and intellectual disability may be sufficient in and of themselves to render a statement inadmissible under state-law doctrines of involuntariness. See § 26.12 *infra.*

The following are common factors that may be considered as bearing on voluntariness under a federal constitutional analysis:

26.4.1. *Youth*

The Supreme Court "has emphasized that admissions and confessions of juveniles require special caution" (*In re Gault,* 387 U.S. 1, 45 (1967)), and that the courts must take "the greatest care . . . to assure that the [juvenile's] admission was voluntary, in the sense not only that it was not coerced or suggested, but also that it was not the product of ignorance of rights or of adolescent fantasy, fright, or despair" (*id.* at 55 (footnote omitted)). In reversing the conviction of a 15-year-old in *Haley v. Ohio,* 332 U.S. 596, 599 (1948), the Court wrote:

> "What transpired would make us pause for careful inquiry if a mature man were involved. And when, as here, a mere child – an easy victim of the law – is before us, special care in scrutinizing the record must be used. Age 15 is a tender and difficult age for a boy of any race. He cannot be judged by the more exacting standards of maturity. That which would leave a man cold and unimpressed can overawe and overwhelm a lad in his early teens."

The Court similarly stressed the inherent vulnerability of young people in finding in *Gallegos v.*

Colorado, 370 U.S. 49, 54 (1962), that a 14-year-old's confession was involuntary:

> "[A] 14-year-old boy, no matter how sophisticated, is unlikely to have any conception of what will confront him when he is made accessible only to the police. . . . He cannot be compared with an adult in full possession of his senses and knowledgeable of the consequences of his admissions."

In *Yarborough v. Alvarado,* the Court reiterated that the "characteristics of the accused [relevant to the assessment of the "voluntariness of a statement"] can include the suspect's age, education, and intelligence, . . . as well as a suspect's prior experience with law enforcement" (541 U.S. at 668) (dictum). *See also id.* at 667-68 ("we do consider a suspect's age and experience" when gauging, for purposes of assessing the "voluntariness of a statement," whether "'the defendant's will was overborne'"). *Cf. Miller v. Alabama,* 567 U.S. 460, 471 (2012) (explaining, in the context of criminal sentencing, that the Court has recognized, based on "science and social science" as well as "common sense" and "what 'any parent knows,'" that "children 'are more vulnerable . . . to . . . outside pressures'").

The lower courts have similarly treated the youth of the suspect as a highly significant factor in assessing the voluntariness of a confession. *See, e.g., Woods v. Clusen,* 794 F.2d 293 (7th Cir. 1986); *Williams v. Peyton,* 404 F.2d 528 (4th Cir. 1968); *Shelton v. State,* 287 Ark. 322, 699 S.W.2d 728 (1985); *State in the Interest of A.A.,* 240 N.J. 341, 354, 222 A.3d 681, 689 (2020) ("Juveniles receive heightened protections when it comes to custodial interrogations for obvious reasons. Common sense tells us that juveniles – teenagers and children alike – are typically less mature, often lack judgment, and are generally more vulnerable to pressure than adults."); *State in the Interest of S.H.,* 61 N.J. 108, 293 A.2d 181 (1972); *People v. Ward,* 95 A.D.2d 351, 466 N.Y.S.2d 686 (N.Y. App. Div., 2d Dep't 1983); *State v. Caffrey,* 332 N.W.2d 269 (S.D. 1983); *In the Interest of Jerrell C.J.,* 2005 WI 105, 283 Wis. 2d 145, 159, 699 N.W.2d 110, 117 (Wis. 2005) ("Simply put, children are different than adults, and the condition of being a child renders one 'uncommonly susceptible to police pressures.' . . . We therefore view Jerrell's young age of 14 to be a strong factor weighing against the voluntariness of his confession."). In urging courts to recognize the need for particular solicitude to assure that juveniles' inculpatory statements are not admitted into evidence unless they are truly voluntary, counsel can point to empirical findings that a disproportionately high percentage of documented instances of false confessions (about 33%) involve juvenile suspects. Steven A. Drizin & Richard A. Leo, *The Problem of False Confessions in the Post-DNA World,* 82 N.C. L. REV. 891, 941-43 (2004). *See also* Steven A. Drizin & Greg Luloff, *Are Juvenile Courts a Breeding Ground for Wrongful Convictions?,* 34 N. KY. L. REV. 257 (2007); Saul M. Kassin, Steven A. Drizin, Thomas Grisso, Gisli H. Gudjonsson, Richard A. Leo & Allison D. Redlich, *Police-Induced Confessions: Risk Factors and Recommendations,* 34 LAW & HUM. BEHAV. 3, 8-9, 19, 30-31 (2010); Allison D. Redlich, *The Susceptibility of Juveniles to False Confessions and False Guilty Pleas,* 62 RUTGERS L. REV. 943 (2010); Joshua A. Tepfer, Laura H. Nirider & Lynda Tricarico, *Arresting Development: Convictions of Innocent Youth,* 62 RUTGERS L. REV. 887, 904-08 (2010); *J.D.B. v. North Carolina,* 564 U.S. 261, 269 (2011) ("[T]he pressure of custodial interrogation is so immense that it 'can induce a frighteningly high percentage of people to confess to crimes they never committed.' *Corley v. United States,* 556 U.S. 303, 329 (2009) (citing Drizin & Leo, . . . [*supra*]); see also *Miranda,* 384 U.S., at 455, n. 23. . . . That risk is all the more troubling – and recent studies suggest, all the more acute – when the subject of custodial interrogation is a juvenile. See Brief for Center on Wrongful Convictions of Youth et al. as *Amici Curiae* 21–22 (collecting empirical studies that 'illustrate the heightened risk of false confessions from youth').")"; *In the Matter of Jimmy D.*, 15 N.Y.3d 417, 431, 938 N.E.2d 970, 979, 912 N.Y.S.2d 537, 546 (2010) (Lippman, C.J., dissenting) ("So long as juveniles cannot be altogether preserved from rigors of police interrogation, it would behoove us not to minimize the now well-documented potential for false confessions when suggestible and often impulsive and impaired children are ushered into the police interview room."; "Children do resort to falsehood to alleviate discomfort and satisfy the expectations of those in authority, and, in so doing, often neglect to consider the serious and lasting consequences of their election. There are developmental reasons for this behavior which we ignore at the peril of the truth-seeking process."). A reference to these findings in briefing and argument is often useful for a couple of reasons. First, although the voluntariness and the reliability of confessions are analytically distinct issues (see § 26.18 *infra*), a judge who is persuaded that a confession poses significant risks of unreliability will, as a practical matter, be more prone to suppress it as involuntary. Second, in courts where the judge who presides at the suppression hearing is likely to be the same judge who will also sit as the trier of fact in a subsequent bench trial of the issue of the defendant's guilt or innocence (see § 24.8 *supra*), the defendant's interests are obviously best served by persuading the judge during the suppression hearing that any inculpatory statement s/he hears is not only technically suppressible but probably inaccurate.

26.4.2. *Mental Illness*

A factor such as mental illness, which impairs the suspect's "mental condition[,] is surely relevant to an individual's susceptibility to police coercion" (*Colorado v. Connelly, supra*, 479 U.S. at 165 (discussing *Blackburn v. Alabama*, 361 U.S. 199 (1960))). *See also, e.g., Spano v. New York,* 360 U.S. 315, 322 & n.3 (1959) (emotional instability); *Fikes v. Alabama,* 352 U.S. 191, 193, 196 (1957) (schizophrenia); *Eisen v. Picard,* 452 F.2d 860, 863-66 (1st Cir. 1971) (psychotic-depressive reaction); *Jackson v. United States,* 404 A.2d 911, 924 (D.C. 1979) ("Here, there was compelling evidence to show that appellant was mentally ill at the time of his statements: his history of mental illness, the incoherent nature of his statement, the testimony of Detective Wood and Dr. Papish, and the trial court's acknowledgement of the irrationality of appellant's statement."); William C. Follette, Richard A. Leo, & Deborah Davis, *Mental Health and False Confessions*, in ELIZABETH KELLEY (ed.), REPRESENTING PEOPLE WITH MENTAL DISABILITIES 95 (2018).

26.4.3. *Intellectual Disability*

A suspect may be rendered particularly vulnerable to police coercion by intellectual disability. *See, e.g., Sims v. Georgia,* 389 U.S. 404 (1967) (limited mental capacity); *Davis v. North Carolina,* 384 U.S. 737 (1966) (low level of intelligence); *Reck v. Pate,* 367 U.S. 433 (1961) (intellectual disability); *Culombe v. Connecticut,* 367 U.S. 568 (1961) (I.Q. of 64); *United States v. Preston*, 751 F.3d 1008, 1027-28 (9th Cir. 2014) (en banc) (18-year-old with an I.Q. of 65); *Shelton v. State,* 287 Ark. 322, 699 S.W.2d 728 (1985) (juvenile who was nearly 18 but had marginal intelligence and maturity); *In the Interest of Thompson,* 241 N.W.2d 2 (Iowa 1976) (I.Q. of 71); *State in the Interest of Holifield,* 319 So.2d 471 (La. App. 1975) (intellectual disability; I.Q. of 67); *People v. Knapp*, 124 A.D.3d 36, 46, 995 N.Y.S.2d 869, 877 (N.Y. App. Div., 4th Dep't 2014) (I.Q. of 68; a defense expert testified that the "defendant is 'a suggestible and overly compliant individual, which is not unusual in [intellectually disabled] . . . individuals who are frequently "yea-saying," in turn causing him to be easily intimidated by the interrogation process'"); *In the Interest of Jerrell C.J., supra*, 2005 WI 105, 283 Wis. 2d at 160, 699 N.W.2d at 117 ("low average intelligence"). *See also Atkins v. Virginia*, 536 U.S. 304, 320 & n.25 (2002) (observing that there is a "possibility of false confessions" in cases of intellectually disabled defendants, and noting that the "disturbing number of inmates on death row [who] have been exonerated . . . included at least one [intellectually disabled] . . . person who unwittingly confessed to a crime that he did not commit."); Drizin & Leo, *supra* at 970-73.

26.4.4. *Limited Education*

Educational privation and illiteracy also are factors that can cause a suspect to be less capable of resisting domination by the police. *See, e.g., Sims v. Georgia*, 389 U.S. 404 (1967) (third-grade education and illiteracy); *Clewis v. Texas*, 386 U.S. 707 (1967) (fifth-grade education); *Culombe v. Connecticut*, 367 U.S. 568, 620-21, 624-25, 635 (1961) (illiteracy); *Fikes v. Alabama, supra*, 352 U.S. at 196 (defendant was "uneducated"); *State v. Graham*, 277 Ark. 465, 642 S.W.2d 880 (1982) (limited education and illiteracy); *In the Interest of Jerrell C.J., supra*, 2005 WI 105, 283 Wis. 2d at 160, 699 N.W.2d at 117 ("limited education" coupled with "low average intelligence"). *Cf. Koh v. Ustich*, 933 F.3d 836, 845 (7th Cir. 2019) ("It was clear that Mr. Koh did not speak fluent English . . . . [Findings could be made that] Mr. Koh did not just suffer from a language barrier, but rather that Mr. Koh suffered a lack of understanding and confusion and that the officers were aware of this. . . . ¶ . . . The extent of Mr. Koh's understanding and the degree of his confusion are key to determining whether his confession was involuntary and coerced.").

26.4.5. *Effects of Drugs or Alcohol*

As the Supreme Court has recognized, a suspect's will and ability to resist interrogation can be impaired by the effects of drugs. *See, e.g., Beecher v. Alabama*, 389 U.S. 35 (1967) (morphine); *Townsend v. Sain*, 372 U.S. 293 (1963) (scopolamine, a drug with "truth serum" properties). *See also Colorado v. Connelly, supra*, 479 U.S. at 165-66 (discussing *Townsend v. Sain*). *Accord, United States v. Taylor*, 745 F.3d 15, 19-20, 23-26 (2d Cir. 2014) (xanax); *In re Cameron*, 68 Cal. 2d 487, 439 P.2d 633, 67 Cal. Rptr. 529 (1968) (thorazine); *People v. Fordyce*, 200 Colo. 153, 612 P.2d 1131 (1980) (morphine).

Several lower court decisions have recognized that intoxication by alcohol can have the same resistance-impairing effects as drugs and should be considered in assessing the voluntariness of a statement. *See, e.g., State v. Mikulewicz*, 462 A.2d 497 (Me. 1983); *State v. Discoe*, 334 N.W.2d 466 (N.D. 1983).

26.4.6. *Lack of Prior Experience With the Police*

The Supreme Court has repeatedly recognized that "lack of previous experience with the police" can impair a suspect's "powers of resistance to overbearing police tactics" (*Reck v. Pate*,

367 U.S. 433, 442 (1961)). *See, e.g., Clewis v. Texas,* 386 U.S. 707, 712 (1967); *Spano v. New York,* 360 U.S. 315, 321-22 (1959); *Yarborough v. Alvarado,* 541 U.S. 652, 667-68 (2004) (dictum). *Accord, Woods v. Clusen,* 794 F.2d 293, 297 (7th Cir. 1986); *In the Interest of Jerrell C.J., supra,* 2005 WI 105, 283 Wis. 2d at 161, 699 N.W.2d at 117 (limited "experience with law enforcement" – two prior arrests for misdemeanor offenses that never resulted in a delinquency finding – "may have contributed to . . . [a 14-year-old's] willingness to confess"). *See also Fare v. Michael C.,* 442 U.S. 707, 726-29 (1979) (dictum) (prior "experience with the police" is relevant to assessment of the voluntariness of *Miranda* waivers). *Cf. United States v. Young,* 964 F.3d 938, 946 (10th Cir. 2020) (although "Young had prior experience with the criminal justice system," which "is relevant to our analysis of voluntariness," his "prior experience was solely in the state system" and "did not necessarily make him less susceptible to believing promises of leniency and misrepresentations by a *federal* law enforcement officer explaining his access to a federal judge and how Young could 'buy down' his sentence").

26.4.7. *Combination of Factors*

Frequently, counsel's case will feature more than one of the foregoing factors and others – physical exhaustion, pain resulting from physical injuries, emotional depression, and so forth. Counsel should argue that the several factors combined to render the defendant particularly susceptible to coercion. *See, e.g., A.M. v. Butler,* 360 F.3d 787, 800-01 (7th Cir. 2004) (11-year-old with no prior court experience); *Woods v. Clusen,* 794 F.2d 293 (7th Cir. 1986) (16-year-old with no prior court experience); *Thomas v. North Carolina,* 447 F.2d 1320 (4th Cir. 1971) (15-year-old with an I.Q. of 72 and limited education); *In the Interest of Thompson,* 241 N.W.2d 2 (Iowa 1976) (17-year-old with an I.Q. of 71 and a fourth-grade reading level); *State in the Interest of Holifield,* 319 So.2d 471 (La. App. 1975) (intellectually disabled 14-year-old with an I.Q. of 67); *In the Interest of Jerrell C.J., supra,* 2005 WI 105, 283 Wis. 2d at 159, 699 N.W.2d at 117 (14-year-old with an I.Q. of 84 and limited prior involvement with the juvenile justice system); *Koh v. Ustich,* 933 F.3d 836, 846 (7th Cir. 2019) ("[b]oth [lack of] sleep and medication are relevant to the inquiry of whether an individual is susceptible to coercion"). *Cf. Edmonds v. Oktibbeha County,* 675 F.3d 911, 914, 915, 916 (5th Cir. 2012) (recognizing, in the context of a section 1983 suit against police deputies, that the "thirteen-year-old[accused]'s separation from his mother, his desire to please adults, and his inexperience with the criminal justice system all weigh against [a finding of] voluntariness [of his confession]," but ultimately concluding that voluntariness was established by the totality of the circumstances, including the accused's disclosure "in his videotaped retraction (and also later on national television)" that he falsely confessed in order "to help his sister" and that "the deputies did not coerce him into confessing."). *And see* Nicole Weis, Note, *The "Fool's Gold" Standard of Confession Evidence: How Intersecting, Disadvantaged Identities Heighten the Risk of False Confession,* 22 NEV. L.J. 1179 (2022).

Despite the robust doctrinal recognition that suspects' weaknesses are important in the analysis of the voluntariness *vel non* of an incriminating statement, the courts are often blinded by unrealistic preconceptions of the "hardened" character of the class of persons likely to be interrogated – particularly the "usual" non-white-collar criminal suspect – when applying the doctrine to the facts of specific cases. *See, e.g.,* Scott E. Sundby, *The Court and the Suspect: Human Frailty, The Calculating Criminal, and the Penitent in the Interrogation Room,* 98

WASHINGTON U. L. REV. 123 (2020). Breaking this image is an important function that can be served by a defense expert witness both in confession-suppression hearings and in challenging the reliability of inculpatory admissions at trial. See § 30.1 subdivision 14 *infra*.

C. Miranda *Violations*

26.5. *The* Miranda *Doctrine Generally*

The rule of *Miranda v. Arizona*, 384 U.S. 436 (1966), excludes any incriminating response made to custodial interrogation unless the response was preceded by specified warnings of the defendant's rights and an effective waiver by the defendant of those rights. "In order to be able to use statements obtained during custodial interrogation of the accused, the State must warn the accused prior to such questioning of his right to remain silent and of his right to have counsel, retained or appointed, present during interrogation." *Fare v. Michael C.*, 442 U.S. 707, 717 (1979) (dictum). *See, e.g., Dickerson v. United States*, 530 U.S. 428 (2000) (reaffirming the *Miranda* doctrine and clarifying that, notwithstanding the Court's previous references to the "*Miranda* warnings as 'prophylactic'" (*id.* at 437), "*Miranda* announced a constitutional rule" (*id.* at 444)); *Doyle v. Ohio*, 426 U.S. 610, 617 (1976); *Michigan v. Mosley*, 423 U.S. 96, 99-100 & n.6 (1975) (dictum).

"Custodial interrogation" is a term of art. The *Miranda* doctrine applies only when a defendant is in "custody" – or its "functional equivalent" – (see § 26.6.1 *infra*) and makes statements in response to "interrogation" (see § 26.6.2 *infra*).

If these two conditions are satisfied, *Miranda* requires the suppression of the defendant's statements whenever (a) the required warnings were not given or were defective (see § 26.7 *infra*); (b) the defendant's waiver of *Miranda* rights was involuntary (see § 26.8.1 *infra*) or was not "knowing and intelligent" (see § 26.8.2 *infra*); or (c) the police failed to honor the defendant's assertion of the right to remain silent or the right to counsel (see § 26.9 *infra*).

The *Miranda* rule governs statements made by a person in custody for any criminal offense, "regardless of the nature or severity of the offense of which he is suspected or for which he was arrested" (*Berkemer v. McCarty*, 468 U.S. 420, 434 (1984) (finding constitutional error in the admission of unwarned incriminating statements made after an arrest for a "misdemeanor traffic offense" (*id.* at 429))). The Supreme Court has created only two exceptions to the *Miranda* rule. First, in *New York v. Quarles*, 467 U.S. 649 (1984), the Supreme Court recognized "a narrow exception to the *Miranda* rule" (467 U.S. at 658), when police officers, "in the very act of apprehending a suspect [who had been reported to be armed and who was found to be wearing an empty shoulder holster when arrested], were confronted with the immediate necessity of ascertaining the whereabouts of a gun which they had every reason to believe the suspect had just removed from his empty holster and discarded in [a public] . . . supermarket" (*id.* at 657). "[O]n these facts" (*id.* at 655), and when the only question asked by the arresting officer was "about the whereabouts of the gun" (*id.* at 657), the Court held that "there is a 'public safety' exception to the requirement that *Miranda* warnings be given before a suspect's answer may be admitted into evidence" (467 U.S. at 655). *Quarles* has since been described as holding that "when the police arrest a suspect under circumstances presenting an imminent danger to the public safety, they may without informing him [or her] of [the *Miranda*] . . . rights ask questions essential to elicit information necessary to neutralize the threat to the public" (*Berkemer v. McCarty, supra*, 468 U.S. at 429 n.10). *Compare Cronk v. State*, 443 N.E.2d 882, 887 (Ind. App. 1983) (the public safety exception applied to the police officers' questions to the defendant about the location of a bomb that he said he had planted but "the emergency . . . expired" after state police troopers found and dismantled the bomb, and therefore the subsequent questioning of the defendant at the jail about the bomb required *Miranda* warnings). Second, in *Pennsylvania v. Muniz*, 496 U.S. 582 (1990), the Court recognized "a 'routine booking question' exception which exempts from *Miranda*'s coverage questions to secure the '"biographical data necessary to complete booking or pretrial services,"'" such as "name, address, height, weight, eye color, date of birth, and current age," as long as the questions asked are "reasonably related to the police's administrative concerns" and are not "'designed to elicit incriminatory admissions'" (*id*. at 601-02 & n.14). *Compare United States v. Pacheco-Lopez*, 531 F.3d 420, 423-24 (6th Cir. 2008) (the "booking exception" of *Pennsylvania v. Muniz* did not apply to an officer's questions to the defendant about "where he was from, how he had arrived at the house, and when he had arrived" because the house was "ostensibly linked to a drug sale" and therefore questions about the defendant's "origin" and his connections to the house were "'reasonably likely to elicit an incriminating response,' thus mandating a *Miranda* warning"); *United States v. Williams*, 842 F.3d 1143, 1145, 1147-49 (9th Cir. 2016) (the "booking exception" did not apply to a deputy sheriff's question to the defendant "whether he was a gang member" and the defendant's resulting admission of gang membership, because the officer had "'reason to know that . . . [the] answer may incriminate'" the defendant; even though "no gang-related charges were then pending," a defendant "charged with a violent crime in California who is a gang member is subject to far greater jeopardy than those who are not gang members . . . [a]nd, the same is true under federal law"); *People v. Hiraeta*, 117 A.D.3d 964, 964, 986 N.Y.S.2d 217, 218-19 (N.Y. App. Div., 2d Dep't 2014) (the booking exception did not apply to "the defendant's statement to a detective regarding his gang affiliation, which was probative of his identity as one of the victim's attackers"); *United States v. Phillips*, 146 F. Supp. 3d 837, 848 (E.D. Mich. 2015), *ruling on another issue aff'd*, 677 Fed. Appx. 294 (6th Cir. 2017) ("the Defendant's responses to the officer's questions regarding his criminal history and the location of his vest resulted from a 'custodial interrogation,' not biographical questioning subject to the booking exception"). With these sole exceptions, "[i]n the years since the decision in *Miranda*, we have frequently reaffirmed the central principle established by that case: if the police take a suspect into custody and then ask him [or her] questions without informing him [or her] of the [*Miranda*] rights . . . , [the] responses cannot be introduced into evidence to establish . . . guilt" (*Berkemer v. McCarty, supra*, 468 U.S. at 429).

26.6. *The Precondition for Applicability of* Miranda *Protections: "Custodial Interrogation"*

26.6.1. *"Custody"*

Miranda comes into play only "after a person has been taken into custody or otherwise deprived of his freedom of action in any significant way" (*Miranda v. Arizona*, 384 U.S. 436, 444 (1966)). *See also id*. at 477, 478; *Estelle v. Smith*, 451 U.S. 454, 466-67 (1981).

Thus, the *Miranda* warnings and waivers are not required when investigating officers interview an unarrested suspect in his or her residence, even though "the 'focus' of [a criminal] . . . investigation may . . . have been on [him or her]" (*Beckwith v. United States,* 425 U.S. 341, 347 (1976)); they are not required when a suspect comes voluntarily to the police station in response to an officer's telephonic request for an interview, at least when the suspect is "immediately informed that [s/he is] . . . not under arrest" and when "there is no indication that [his or her] . . . freedom to depart [is] . . . restricted in any way" (*Oregon v. Mathiason,* 429 U.S. 492, 495 (1977) (per curiam); *see also California v. Beheler,* 463 U.S. 1121 (1983) (per curiam)); and they are not required when a probationer is questioned by his or her probation officer during a probation-supervision conference in the latter's office, even when attendance at such conferences is a condition of probation enforceable by its possible revocation (*Minnesota v. Murphy,* 465 U.S. 420 (1984) ("Murphy was not 'in custody' for purposes of receiving *Miranda* protection since there was no '"formal arrest or restraint on freedom of movement" of the degree associated with a formal arrest'" (*id.* at 430)). *Cf. United States v. Mandujano,* 425 U.S. 564, 578-82 (1976) (plurality opinion) (alternative ground) (subpoenaed grand jury witness has no right to *Miranda* warnings or to have counsel present in the grand jury room). "[T]he roadside questioning of a motorist detained pursuant to a traffic stop [does not] . . . constitute custodial interrogation" (*Berkemer v. McCarty,* 468 U.S. 420, 423 (1984)), nor does questioning during a "'*Terry* stop'" (468 U.S. at 439-40; see §§ 25.4-25.6.4 *supra*)), unless the person stopped "is subjected to treatment that renders him [or her] 'in custody' for practical purposes" (468 U.S. at 440), under the "settled [principle] that the safeguards prescribed by *Miranda* become applicable as soon as a suspect's freedom of action is curtailed to a 'degree associated with formal arrest'" (468 U.S. at 440). *See, e.g., United States v. Perdue,* 8 F.3d 1455, 1464-65 (10th Cir. 1993) ("The traditional view . . . is that *Miranda* warnings are simply not implicated in the context of a valid *Terry* stop. . . . This view has prevailed because the typical police-citizen encounter envisioned by the Court in *Terry* usually involves no more than a very brief detention without the aid of weapons or handcuffs, a few questions relating to identity and the suspicious circumstances, and an atmosphere that is 'substantially less "police dominated" than that surrounding the kinds of interrogation at issue in *Miranda.*' . . . ¶ The last decade, however, has witnessed a multifaceted expansion of *Terry*. Important for our purposes is the trend granting officers greater latitude in using force in order to 'neutralize' potentially dangerous suspects during an investigatory detention. . . . Thus, today, consonant with this trend, we held [earlier in the opinion] that police officers acted reasonably under the Fourth Amendment when they, without probable cause and with guns drawn, stopped Mr. Perdue's car, forced him to get out of his car, and demanded that he lie face down on the ground. . . . ¶ One cannot ignore the conclusion, however, that by employing an amount of force that reached the boundary line between a permissible *Terry* stop and an unconstitutional arrest, the officers created the 'custodial' situation envisioned by *Miranda* and its progeny. Mr. Perdue was forced out of his car and onto the ground at gunpoint. He was then questioned by two police officers while police helicopters hovered above. During the questioning, Mr. Perdue remained face down on the ground while the officers kept their guns drawn on him and his pregnant fiancee. . . . ¶ . . . A reasonable man in Mr. Perdue's position could not have misunderstood the fact that if he did not immediately cooperate, his life would be in danger. Any reasonable person in Mr. Perdue's position would have felt 'completely at the mercy of the police.' . . . We therefore find as a matter of law that Mr. Perdue was in police custody during the initial questioning by Officer Carreno."). And see §§ 25.4.4-25.4.5, 25.6-25.6.4 *supra.*

However, *Miranda* applies to the questioning of a person who is handcuffed and surrounded by police officers, even in a public place. *New York v. Quarles,* 467 U.S. 649, 654 n.4, 655 (1984) (dictum); *and see Berkemer v. McCarty, supra,* 468 U.S. at 441 n.34, 442 n.36, giving other examples of street-arrest questioning that constitute "custodial interrogation." *Compare United States v. Coulter,* 41 F.4th 451 (5th Cir. 2022), summarized in § 25.6.5 *supra.* And it applies to any questioning of a person involuntarily detained in closed quarters, even though those quarters may be the person's own home and even though the questioning may be wholly unrelated to the reason for the detention. *Mathis v. United States,* 391 U.S. 1 (1968) (a state prison inmate questioned in prison by a federal revenue agent shortly before federal authorities decide to pursue a criminal tax investigation); *Orozco v. Texas,* 394 U.S. 324 (1969) (a suspect arrested and questioned by police officers in his boardinghouse bedroom); *United States v. Hashime,* 734 F.3d 278, 280-81, 283-84, 285 (4th Cir. 2013) (the interrogation of a 19-year-old was "custodial" even though it took place in his home, the officers said that "they were not there to arrest anyone but rather to execute a search warrant," "the door to the room in which he was interrogated was open," the officers told him that he "was free to leave," and the officers offered him "multiple breaks" during the interrogation: although these factors "do cut against custody, they are decidedly outweighed" by the "sheer length" of the three-hour interrogation, the number of federal and state law enforcement officers who "streamed into the house with their guns drawn," and the fact that Hashime "'was rousted from bed at gunpoint, . . . not allowed to move unless guarded, and ultimately separated from his family'" during the interrogation.); *United States v. Craighead,* 539 F.3d 1073, 1084-89 (9th Cir. 2008) (the court finds an in-home interrogation "custodial" for *Miranda* purposes under a standard that considers: "(1) the number of law enforcement personnel and whether they were armed; (2) whether the suspect was at any point restrained, either by physical force or by threats; (3) whether the suspect was isolated from others; and (4) whether the suspect was informed that he was free to leave or terminate the interview, and the context in which any such statements were made."); *In re I.J.,* 906 A.2d 249, 262-63 (D.C. 2006) (a 16-year-old juvenile, who was residing in a youth center pursuant to a court order of probation, was in "custody" for *Miranda* purposes when he was questioned by a police officer, in an office of the center, about a crime the youth allegedly committed on the premises). *See also State v. McKenna,* 166 N.H. 671, 675, 686, 103 A.3d 756, 760, 769 (2014) (the court holds on state constitutional grounds that a defendant was in "custody" for *Miranda* purposes when police officers questioned him as he was walking around the grounds of his restaurant and campground for an hour and a half, at least at the point at which they stopped him from walking into a wooded area and told him to remain in the open areas; "Although the defendant was informed that he was not under arrest, there is no evidence that the officers ever informed the defendant that he was free to terminate the interrogation. In addition, we accord substantial weight to the fact that the officers' questions were accusatory and focused on the defendant's alleged criminal activity."). *Cf. Howes v. Fields,* 565 U.S. 499, 512, 515 (2012) (questioning of a prison inmate does not automatically trigger *Miranda*'s requirements because "service of a term of imprisonment, without more, is not enough to constitute *Miranda* custody"; *Miranda* "custody" was not established on a record showing that the inmate was taken aside and questioned in private about "events that took place outside the prison" because "'[a]ll of the[ ] objective facts are consistent with an interrogation environment in which a reasonable person would have felt free to terminate the interview and leave'": the inmate "was told at the outset of the interrogation, and was reminded again thereafter, that he could leave and go back to his cell whenever he wanted"; the inmate "was not physically restrained or threatened and was interviewed in a well-lit, average-sized conference room, where he was 'not uncomfortable'"; and the inmate "was offered food and water, and the door to the conference room was sometimes left open.").

The determination "whether a suspect is 'in custody' is an objective inquiry" that involves the following "'[t]wo discrete inquiries'":

> "'first, what were the circumstances surrounding the interrogation; and second, given those circumstances, would a reasonable person have felt he or she was at liberty to terminate the interrogation and leave. Once the scene is set and the players' lines and actions are reconstructed, the court must apply an objective test to resolve the ultimate inquiry: was there a formal arrest or restraint on freedom of movement of the degree associated with formal arrest.'" (*J.D.B. v. North Carolina*, 564 U.S. 261, 270 (2011) (quoting *Thompson v. Keohane*, 516 U.S. 99, 112 (1995))).

Accord, Berkemer v. McCarty, supra, 468 U.S. at 442; *Stansbury v. California*, 511 U.S. 318, 322-25 (1994) (per curiam). In the case of a minor, the Supreme Court has recognized that this "reasonable person" test must take into account the age of the child "so long as the child's age was known to the officer at the time of police questioning, or would have been objectively apparent to a reasonable officer" (*J.D.B. v. North Carolina, supra*, 564 U.S. at 277). *See id.* at 264-65 ("It is beyond dispute that children will often feel bound to submit to police questioning when an adult in the same circumstances would feel free to leave. Seeing no reason for police officers or courts to blind themselves to that commonsense reality, we hold that a child's age properly informs the *Miranda* custody analysis."); *id.* at 269 ("By its very nature, custodial police interrogation entails 'inherently compelling pressures.' . . . Even for an adult, the physical and psychological isolation of custodial interrogation can 'undermine the individual's will to resist and . . . compel him to speak where he would not otherwise do so freely.' . . . Indeed, the pressure of custodial interrogation is so immense that it 'can induce a frighteningly high percentage of people to confess to crimes they never committed.' . . . That risk is all the more troubling – and recent studies suggest, all the more acute – when the subject of custodial interrogation is a juvenile."). *See also Matter of D.A.H.*, 2021-NCCOA-135, 277 N.C. App. 16, 17, 27-29, 857 S.E.2d 771, 775, 781-82 (2021) (addressing the question "whether a juvenile is entitled to *Miranda* warnings prior to being interrogated by his school principal, when the school resource officer ('SRO') is present but does not ask questions": "Today we harmonize our prior opinions on this issue in light of the United States Supreme Court's holding in *J.D.B.* and the holdings of our sister courts in other states. There can be no doubt that educators and law enforcement are increasing their collaboration in the school setting and that school officials are increasingly becoming active participants in the criminal justice system. While potentially warranted for both the educational and safety needs of our children, this cooperation must be consistent with the Fifth Amendment's guarantee against self-incrimination. As the United States Supreme Court recognized in *J.D.B.*, the Fifth Amendment requires that minors under criminal investigation be protected against making coerced, inculpatory statements, even when – and perhaps, in some cases, particularly because – they are on school property. *J.D.B.* . . . . Increased cooperation between educators and law enforcement cannot allow the creation of situations where no *Miranda* warnings are required just because a student is on school property. ¶ . . . [W]hen a student is interrogated in the presence of an SRO – even when the SRO remains silent

– the presence of the officer can create a coercive environment that goes above and beyond the restrictions normally imposed during school, such that a reasonable student would readily believe they are not free to go. This holding recognizes the 'reality that courts cannot simply ignore' – that juveniles are uniquely susceptible to police pressure and may feel compelled to confess when a reasonable adult would not. *J.D.B.*"); *State v. Ahmad*, 246 N.J. 592, 252 A.3d 968 (2021) (the 17-year-old defendant had been shot several times and was taken to a hospital where he was heavily medicated and underwent surgery to remove a bullet from his leg; at the hospital, he was asked by a detective where he had been shot and how he was brought to the hospital; his reply portrayed himself as the innocent victim of a shooting; when he was released from the hospital on crutches, he was told that he had to report to the police, and officers drove him to a stationhouse in a squad car; after several hours, he and his father were told to go to a prosecutor's office for questioning and were escorted there by police; the defendant was then questioned by two detectives, one of whom testified at a suppression hearing that they did not, at that time, suspect the defendant of having committed a crime; the trial court found that his unwarned questioning was not custodial for *Miranda* purposes because he "was interrogated as a shooting victim, not a suspect" (*id.* at 604, 252 A.3d at 975), but the New Jersey Supreme Court finds a *Miranda* violation and reverses his conviction, concluding that he was in custody because: "Defendant was a minor, still in high school. He suffered the significant trauma of being shot multiple times. Immediately upon release from the hospital, he was placed in the back of a patrol car – where arrestees are normally held – and taken to the police station. We doubt there are many, if any, reasonable 17-year-olds who would think they were free to leave after such events. Accordingly, our decision today simply honors the long-held standard of whether a reasonable person in the defendant's position would have believed they were free to leave." *Id.* at 613-14, 252 A.3d at 980.).

If the defendant was formally arrested or was placed under physical restraint "of the 'degree associated with a formal arrest,'" this plainly suffices to establish "custody" for *Miranda* purposes (*New York v. Quarles, supra*, 467 U.S. at 655 (dictum)). If s/he was not, the custody inquiry requires "'examin[ation] [of] all of the circumstances surrounding the interrogation,' . . . including any circumstance that 'would have affected how a reasonable person' in the suspect's position 'would perceive his or her freedom to leave'" (*J.D.B. v. North Carolina, supra*, 564 U.S. at 271). *See also id.* (the custody test "ask[s] how a reasonable person in the suspect's position would understand his freedom to terminate questioning and leave"; "On the other hand, the 'subjective views harbored by either the interrogating officers or the person being questioned' are irrelevant."). Relevant factors include (i) whether the detention was merely "temporary and brief" or was "prolonged" (*Berkemer v. McCarty, supra*, 468 U.S. at 437-38; *see also id.* at 441); (ii) whether the defendant was subjected to only a "modest number of questions" or was subjected to "'persistent questioning'" (*id.* at 442 & n.36; *see also id.* at 438); and (iii) whether the questioning took place in a public location, where "exposure to public view both reduces the ability of an unscrupulous policeman to use illegitimate means to elicit self-incriminating statements and diminishes the [suspect's] . . . fear that, if he does not cooperate, he will be subjected to abuse" (*id.* at 438). "Some of the factors relevant to whether a reasonable person would believe he was free to leave include 'the purpose, place, and length of interrogation,' along with 'the extent to which the defendant is confronted with evidence of guilt, the physical surroundings of the interrogation, the duration of the detention, and the degree of pressure applied to the defendant.'" *State v. Snell*, 2007-NMCA-113, 142 N.M. 452, 456, 166

P.3d 1106, 1110 (N.M. App. 2007), quoting *State v. Munoz*, 1998-NMSC-048, 126 N.M. 535, 544, 972 P.2d 847, 856 (N.M. 1998); *United States v. Mora-Alcaraz*, 986 F.3d 1151 (9th Cir. 2021), finding the questioning of a suspect in a public shopping mall "custodial" under a multi-factor test: "These factors are: '(1) the language used to summon the individual; (2) the extent to which the defendant is confronted with evidence of guilt; (3) the physical surroundings of the interrogation; (4) the duration of the detention; and (5) the degree of pressure applied to detain the individual.'" *Id.* at 1156. "Here, the police took physical custody of Mora-Alcaraz's seven-year-old son and eventually led him inside a large store and out of Mora-Alcaraz's sight. Despite the lack of physical restraints, Mora-Alcaraz was subjected to severe pressure as a result of the police separating him from his son. Although the government argues the situation was relatively benign, because there was no threat of harm to the child, the police were well aware that a father would not walk away from a public place and leave his young son with strangers. No physical restraint of Mora Alcaraz was necessary so long as the police kept him separated from his son. He could not leave." *Id.* at 1156-57. *And see State v. E.R.*, 123 N.E.3d 675, 677-78 (Ind. 2019) (affirming a trial-court order finding that police questioning was custodial and excluding the defendant's incriminating statements under *Miranda*: "In granting the motion, the court recognized – rightly – that whether E.R. was in custody turns on objective circumstances. It then determined that the environment was 'a police setting' in which multiple officers questioned E.R. in an accusatory and focused way in a room behind several closed doors. The court observed that although E.R. went to the police station on his own, he 'had to be buzzed into the area or taken into the area of a secure room.' And although the first officer told E.R. he could walk out of the interrogation-room door, the court found that statement, in this specific context, would not make a reasonable person feel free to leave. The court emphasized that after the second officer later entered the room, shut the door, and took on the role of interrogator, E.R. was not told that he could leave or that the first officer's initial statement remained valid."). When officers are able to testify credibly that a suspect was told s/he was not under arrest but expressed a willingness to answer police questioning and cooperated with their investigation, the chances that the court will find the interrogation "custodial" are drastically reduced, despite the presence of factors that would otherwise plainly establish custody. *See United States v. Leal*, 1 F.4th 545 (7th Cir. 2021) (FBI agents lured the defendant to a residence that they used as the center of a sting operation; he became suspicious and fled in his car; three federal officers pursued him and stopped the car; they asked him for his car keys (which he gave them and which they retained throughout the episode); they asked him to return to the sting site and he agreed to do so; there he was confronted by several additional federal law enforcement officers and subjected to an audiotaped interrogation by two of them in a closed room; he began making incriminating statements two minutes into an eighteen-minute interview; the Seventh Circuit credits the officers' testimony that he willingly agreed to participate in this entire scenario, and it therefore finds that he was never in custody until formally arrested after he confessed.); *United States v. Woodson*, 30 F.4th 1295 (11th Cir. 2022).

26.6.2. *"Interrogation"*

The *Miranda* concept of "interrogation" encompasses:

"express questioning or its functional equivalent. That is to say, the term 'interrogation' under *Miranda* refers not only to express questioning, but also to any words or actions on the part of the police (other than those normally attendant to arrest and custody) that the police should know are reasonably likely to elicit an incriminating response from the suspect" (*Rhode Island v. Innis,* 446 U.S. 291, 300-01 (1980)).

Accord, Arizona v. Mauro, 481 U.S. 520, 525-27 (1987); *Grueninger v. Director, Virginia Department of Corrections*, 813 F.3d 517, 524-28 (4th Cir. 2016); *State v. Wright*, 444 N.J. Super. 347, 363-67, 133 A.3d 656, 666-68 (2016).

As the Supreme Court has explained, the *police-should-know* test "focuses primarily upon the perceptions of the suspect, rather than the intent of the police. This focus reflects the fact that the *Miranda* safeguards were designed to vest a suspect in custody with an added measure of protection against coercive police practices, without regard to objective proof of the underlying intent of the police" (*Rhode Island v. Innis, supra*, 446 U.S. at 301). The assessment of the suspect's perceptions is predicated upon a "reasonable person" standard rather than a subjective standard, because "the police surely cannot be held accountable for the unforeseeable results of their words or actions" (*id.* at 301-02). Accordingly, "the definition of interrogation can extend only to words or actions on the part of police officers that they *should have known* were reasonably likely to elicit an incriminating response" (*id.* at 302 (emphasis in original)).

"In deciding whether particular police conduct is interrogation," the courts have been admonished to "remember the purpose behind [the] . . . decisions in *Miranda* and *Edwards* [*v. Arizona,* 451 U.S. 477 (1981)]: preventing government officials from using the coercive nature of confinement to extract confessions that would not be given in an unrestrained environment" (*Arizona v. Mauro, supra*, 481 U.S. at 529-30). Thus if the police set in motion "compelling influences [or] . . . psychological ploys" (*id.* at 529) that "implicate this purpose" (*id.* at 530) and create an "atmosphere of oppressive police conduct" (*id.* at 528 n.5), their behavior "properly could be treated as the functional equivalent of interrogation" (*id.* at 527).

In urging that police conduct short of explicit questioning amounted to "interrogation," counsel can point to the following sorts of factors:

(i)   "the police carried on a lengthy harangue in the presence of the suspect" rather than simply "a few offhand remarks" (*Rhode Island v. Innis, supra*, 446 U.S. at 303).

(ii)   "under the circumstances, the officers' comments were particularly 'evocative'" (*id.*). *See, e.g., State v. Bond*, 2000 WI App 118, 237 Wis. 2d 633, 642-43, 647, 614 N.W.2d 552, 556-57, 558 (Wis. App. 2000) (a police officer's statement to the defendant in a witness-intimidation case that "'you're the man behind the man,'" implying that the defendant was "'the man who does the dirty work, . . . the muscle,'" was "'particularly "evocative"' or provocative," and "the functional equivalent of interrogation"); *People v. Stephans*, 168 A.D.3d 990, 995, 93 N.Y.S.3d 317, 324 (N.Y. App. Div., 2d Dep't 2019) ("Officer Persaud should have known that in telling the defendant that she needed to come to the precinct station house in connection with his investigation into the allegations her husband had made against her [that she had assaulted him], allegations about which she had already been told she would be arrested, placing her in an interview room, and then confronting her with the allegations and the evidence against her, including the existence of the order of protection, he was reasonably likely to elicit from the defendant an incriminating response").

(iii)   the police used "psychological ploys, such as to 'posi[t]' 'the guilt of the subject,' to 'minimize the moral seriousness of the offense,' and 'to cast blame on the victim or on society'" (*Rhode Island v. Innis, supra*, 446 U.S. at 299 (quoting *Miranda, supra*, 384 U.S. at 450)). *See also Arizona v. Mauro, supra*, 481 U.S. at 526, 529. The *Miranda* opinion cites a number of police manuals describing sophisticated interrogation techniques; counsel will often find it helpful to peruse these and other "police science" hornbooks because any similarity between the techniques they advise to elicit incriminating statements and the behavior of the officers in counsel's own case will be highly persuasive that the latter behavior was "interrogation." *See, e.g., Hill v. United States*, 858 A.2d 435, 443 (D.C. 2004) (finding that the officer's statement to the defendant that "'he was being charged with second-degree murder and that . . . [his friend] "told [the police] what happened"'" was the "functional equivalent of interrogation" because the officer employed "classic interrogation techniques" recommended in the Reid manual on criminal interrogations, which was cited in the *Miranda* opinion); *United States v. Rambo*, 365 F.3d 906, 909-10 (10th Cir. 2004) ("While the district court concluded that the lack of questions indicated there was no interrogation by Moran, the use of questions is not required to show that interrogation occurred. . . . ¶ The portion of the interview available on videotape opens with Moran informing Rambo that much of the blame will fall on Rambo's shoulders. As the Supreme Court has recognized, one of the techniques used by police during interrogation is to 'posit the guilt of the subject.' . . . Thus, Moran's first comments are an example of interrogation explicitly recognized by the Supreme Court. Moreover, other questions and comments recorded on the videotape support the conclusion that Rambo was under interrogation. ¶ Given the context, Moran's comment 'if you want to talk to me about this stuff, that's fine,' is fairly understood as an attempt to refocus the discussion on the robberies. Moran reiterates this invitation four times during the course of the interview. . . . ¶ While the government claims that Moran's only goal was to obtain a waiver of the right to remain silent, that assertion ignores the appropriate test for determining if an interrogation occurred. It is true that an investigating officer's intention may be relevant, but it is the objectively measured tendency of an action to elicit an incriminating response which is ultimately determinative. . . . Moran's interaction with Rambo was reasonably likely to produce incriminating information and, therefore, Rambo was under interrogation."); *In re Elias V.*, 237 Cal. App. 4th 568, 571, 579, 583, 588, 188 Cal. Rptr. 3d 202, 204, 211, 214, 218 (2015), quoted in § 26.3.4 second paragraph *supra*. *See also* the Cutler & Leo articles cited in the penultimate paragraph of § 26.3.4.

(iv)   the police were aware that the suspect was:

(A)   "unusually disoriented or upset at the time of his arrest" (*Rhode Island v. Innis, supra*, 446 U.S. at 302-03). *See, e.g., Xu v. State*, 191 S.W.3d 210, 217 (Tex. App. 2005) ("the officers should have known their interrogation would result in Xu's oral statement. . . . The detectives described Xu as emotional and upset throughout the day. He was described as 'hysterical.' He repeatedly wept and clutched a picture of his wife and daughter. The detectives knew Xu's English was broken and that he came from China, where the culture is far different than that of the United States.").

(B)   "unusual[ly] susceptib[le] . . . to a particular form of persuasion" (*Rhode Island v. Innis, supra*, 446 U.S. at 302 n.8) because of young age, intellectual disability, mental illness, or the effects of alcohol or other substances. *See, e.g., Benjamin v. State*, 116 So.3d 115, 123 (Miss. 2013) (a police officer's "tactics" of "foster[ing] the suspect's mistaken belief that talking would allow him to avoid a night in jail" and encouraging the suspect's mother to "pressure" him to talk to the police "constituted the functional equivalent of interrogation" because the police should have known that these "psychological ploys . . . were reasonably likely to elicit an incriminating response from fourteen-year-old Benjamin"); *In the Matter of Ronald C.*, 107 A.D.2d 1053, 486 N.Y.S.2d 575 (N.Y App. Div., 4th Dep't 1985) (because the defendant was only 13 years old and was unaccompanied by a parent or counsel, the police should have known that placing the alleged burglar's tools in front of him was likely to elicit an incriminating response). *See also State in the Interest of A.A.*, 240 N.J. 341, 345, 222 A.3d 681, 684 (2020) (the police engaged in "the functional equivalent of interrogation" by summoning the 15-year-old arrestee's mother to the police station (as state law required), bringing "her to see him at her request," and then "listen[ing] to the conversation between mother and son – which took place on opposite sides of the gate of a holding cell").

(C)   "unusual[ly] susceptib[le]" (*Rhode Island v. Innis, supra*, 446 U.S. at 302 n.8) to priming for any other reason. *See, e.g., State v. Juranek*, 287 Neb. 846, 856, 844 N.W.2d 791, 801 (2014) ("the detective knew about Juranek's propensity to talk without being interrogated and should have expected that if asked about the incident, Juranek would confess again").

(v)   the police *intended* to elicit an admission. Even though the officers' intentions are not controlling, the "intent of the police . . . may well have a bearing on whether the police should have known that their words or actions were reasonably likely to evoke an incriminating response" (*Rhode Island v. Innis, supra*, 446 U.S. at 301 n.7, 303 n.9). *See, e.g., Drury v. State*, 368 Md. 331, 332, 341, 793 A.2d 567, 568, 573 (2002) (a police officer's action in showing the defendant "physical evidence" and telling him "that the evidence would be processed for fingerprints" was the "functional equivalent of interrogation": the officer's "actions were aimed at invoking an incriminating remark"; "indeed, there is no explanation for his conduct but that he expected to elicit such statements."); *State v. Brooks*, 2013 VT 27, 193 Vt. 461, 464, 468, 70 A.3d 1014, 1016-17, 1019 (2013) ("the interaction [between the detective and the defendant] at the holding cell" – in which the "[d]efendant asked 'what was going on' in the case, and Detective Plusch informed him of the current police investigation," whereupon the defendant made an incriminating statement – "was an interrogation, regardless of how casual a conversation it might appear. Detective Plusch admitted that he hoped informing defendant about the investigation would produce some admission of guilt."). *Cf.* § 25.4.2, second paragraph *supra*.

26.7. *Validity of the* Miranda *Warnings*

Miranda requires that the police preface any custodial interrogation with the following warnings to the suspect:

(a)   that s/he has a right to remain silent (*Miranda v. Arizona, supra*, 384 U.S. at 467-68);

(b)   that any statement s/he makes can and will be used in court as evidence against him or her (*id.* at 469; *Estelle v. Smith*, 451 U.S. 454, 466-67 (1981));

(c)   that s/he has a right "to consult with a lawyer and to have the lawyer with him [or her] during interrogation" (*Miranda v. Arizona, supra*, 384 U.S. at 471); and

(d)   that if s/he cannot afford a lawyer, s/he has a right to have a lawyer appointed "prior to interrogation," to represent him or her without cost (*id.* at 474).

See generally id. at 444, 467-73.

Each of the *Miranda* warnings must be given expressly, and an incriminating statement made during custodial interrogation is inadmissible unless a foundation is laid for it by an affirmative showing in the trial record that all of the warnings were given. *See Clark v. Smith*, 403 U.S. 946 (1971) (per curiam) (reversing a conviction for admission of a confession made after three of the four *Miranda* warnings were given; only the right of an indigent to have state-paid counsel was omitted); *accord, Michigan v. Tucker*, 417 U.S. 433, 445 (1974) (dictum). Proof by the prosecution that the defendant knew his or her *Miranda* rights will not excuse a failure to warn. *Miranda v. Arizona, supra*, 384 U.S. at 468-69, 471-73.

The police need not precisely parrot the language of *Miranda* when they give *Miranda* warnings. *Duckworth v. Eagan*, 492 U.S. 195, 201 (1989) (upholding a warning which included the statement "'We have no way of giving you a lawyer, but one will be appointed for you, if you wish, if and when you go to court'" (*id.* at 198), on the ground that the warning *also* said explicitly, "'You have a right to talk to a lawyer for advice before we ask you any questions, and to have him with you during questioning'" (*id.*); the Court viewed this combination of advice as conveying the accurate information that, although the police were not obliged to furnish the arrested person with a lawyer, they were obliged to stop questioning him if he requested a lawyer (*id.* at 202-03).); *Florida v. Powell*, 559 U.S. 50, 53, 62 (2010) (the *Miranda* requirement that an individual must be "'clearly informed,' prior to custodial questioning, that he has, among other rights, 'the right to consult with a lawyer and to have the lawyer with him during interrogation'" was satisfied by a police officer's advising the defendant that he "has 'the right to talk to a lawyer before answering any of . . . [the law enforcement officers'] questions'"; that "'[i]f you cannot afford to hire a lawyer, one will be appointed for you without cost and before any questioning'"; and that "'[y]ou have the right to use any of these rights at any time you want during this interview'" (*id.* at 53), because "[i]n combination, the two warnings reasonably conveyed . . . [the suspect's] right to have an attorney present, not only at the outset of interrogation, but at all times."); *see also California v. Prysock,* 453 U.S. 355 (1981) (per curiam). What is required is that the warnings be "'*a fully effective equivalent*'" of the *Miranda* cautions (*Duckworth v. Eagan, supra,* 492 U.S. at 202, quoting *Miranda, supra,* 384 U.S. at 476 (emphasis in the original *Duckworth* opinion)) and "reasonably 'conve[y] to [a suspect] his rights as required by *Miranda*'" (*Duckworth, supra,* 492 U.S. at 203, quoting *California v. Prysock, supra,* 453 U.S. at 361). *Cf. United States v. Botello-Rosales*, 728 F.3d 865, 867-68 (9th Cir. 2013) (per curiam) ("the Spanish-language [*Miranda*] warning administered to Botello before he was interrogated failed to 'reasonably convey'" the "government's obligation to appoint an attorney for an indigent suspect who wishes to consult one" because "the Spanish word 'libre' [used by the detective] to mean 'free,' or without cost" actually "translates to 'free' as being available or at liberty to do something"; this "constitutional infirmity" was not "cure[d]" by the officers' prior administration of "correct *Miranda* warnings in English to Botello" because "[e]ven if Botello understood the English-language warnings, there is no indication in the record that the government clarified which set of warnings was correct."); *Commonwealth v. Rosario*, 99 Mass. App. Ct. 1118, 167 N.E.3d 892 (Table), 2021 WL 1263892 (2021) (among other defects in the administration of *Miranda* warnings, a Spanish translation telling the defendant "If you don't have a lawyer to pay, the state gets you one" did not unequivocally convey the information that the lawyer would be provided without cost); *Soares v. State*, 248 Md. App. 395, 241 A.3d 981 (Ct. Special App. 2020) (finding numerous problems in the implementation of *Miranda* when an interpreter overstepped his proper role both in the police interrogation itself and in the suppression hearing); *United States v. Murphy*, 703 F.3d 182, 193 (2d Cir. 2012) (a police officer's "instruct[ion] [to] the defendants that they could 'decide at anytime to give up these rights, *and* not talk to us' . . . ¶ . . . failed to 'ensure that the person in custody ha[d] sufficient knowledge of his . . . constitutional rights relating to the interrogation'": the officer's "incorrect formulation strongly suggested that the defendants *should* talk if they wished to exercise their rights – or, put another way, that they would waive their rights if they remained silent."); *United States v. Wysinger*, 683 F.3d 784 (7th Cir. 2012) (an admonition to a suspect that he had the "'right to talk to a lawyer for advice before we ask any questions or have one – have an attorney with you during questioning'" (*id.* at 798) was inadequate because it told the suspect "that he could talk to an attorney before questioning *or* during questioning" when "[i]n fact, Wysinger had a right to consult an attorney both before *and* during questioning" (*id.*): "A person given a choice between having a lawyer with him before questioning or during questioning might wait until it is clear that questioning has begun before invoking his right to counsel" (*id.* at 800); here, the interrogating agent "implied that Wysinger could decide whether to exercise his rights after [the] Agent . . . 'la[id] it out for' him and told him 'what the story is,' and that, in the meantime, he should 'listen for a minute.' The time to invoke his rights, in other words, had not yet arrived." (*id.* at 801); an incorrectly worded *Miranda* warning, one that suggests that *Miranda* rights apply only to direct questioning or to the time before direct questioning, followed by diversionary tactics that redirect the suspect away from asserting those rights, frustrates the purpose of the *Miranda* protections" (*id.* at 800)); *State v. Dorff*, 468 N.J. Super. 633, 260 A.3d 904 (2021) (after being given *Miranda* warnings, the defendant said she did not know how to trust the officers and that "That's why I feel I might need a lawyer"; a detective told her "But if you didn't do anything, you certainly don't need to have, I mean that's — " and the defendant responded: "I didn't. I feel like I didn't do anything wrong"; thereafter, the defendant and detectives engaged in an extensive dialogue in which she repeatedly asked whether she should get a lawyer; they repeatedly replied that that was a decision she alone could make; their replies increasingly expressed impatience and an insistence that she make the decision one way or the other; finally, they told her "That's up to you. Do you want to talk to us?"; she said "As much as I, as much as I feel comfortable with yeah, if that's okay?" and went on to make damaging admissions (468 N.J. Super. at 641-43, 260 A.3d at 909-10); the court finds that this scenario violated *Miranda* and *Edwards v. Arizona*, 451 U.S. 477 (1981) (discussed in § 26.9.3 *infra*) because "the State bears the burden to show scrupulous compliance with *Miranda* and *Edwards*": "Nor does it matter whether the detective's offhand remark was 'an attempt to coerce a confession.' In determining whether *Miranda* rights were scrupulously honored, we do not examine whether an interrogating officer intended to undermine the *Miranda* warnings and coerce a confession, but rather whether the officer's words and actions complied with *Miranda*'s strict requirements. There is no 'good faith' exception to *Miranda*." 468 N.J. Super. at 651-52, 260 A.3d at 915-16); *People v. Mathews*, 324 Mich. App. 416, 438, 922 N.W.2d 371, 383 (2018) (reviewing the conflicting *Miranda* caselaw and concluding that "a warning preceding a custodial interrogation is deficient when the warning contains only a broad reference to the 'right to an attorney' that does not, when the warning is read in its entirety, reasonably convey the suspect's right to consult with an attorney and to have an attorney present during the interrogation"); *Lujan v. Garcia*, 734 F.3d 917, 931-32 (9th Cir. 2013) ("The problem here is that the words used by law enforcement did not reasonably convey to Petitioner that he had the right to speak with an attorney present at all times – before and during his custodial interrogations. In the end, we find that the 'choice' communicated to Petitioner was that he could speak without an attorney or he could remain silent throughout his interrogations. Speaking with an attorney present was not an option presented to Petitioner. Thus, *Miranda* was never satisfied. ¶ Before his first interrogation, Petitioner was told the following regarding his *Miranda* rights: ¶ Your rights are you have the right to remain silent, whatever we talk about or you say can be used in a court of law against you, and if you don't have money to hire an attorney one's appointed to represent you free of charge. So, those are your rights. If you have questions about the case, if you want to tell us about what happened tonight, we'll take your statement, take your statement from beginning to end. We'll give you an opportunity to explain your side of the story. That's what we're looking for and we're looking for the truth. So you understand all that? ¶ . . . [The state] argues that, during Petitioner's third interrogation, Detective Rodriguez provided an 'enhanced *Miranda* warning' that advised Petitioner above what the *Miranda* warning itself provides by telling Petitioner that his legal counsel would likely advise against making any statements to the police. The detective advised Petitioner, 'I doubt that if you hire an attorney they'll let you make a statement, usually they don't. That's the way it goes. So, that's your prerogative, that's your choice.' This advice did not inform Mr. Lujan of his constitutional right to counsel. It was improper, unauthorized legal advice."); *United States v. San Juan-Cruz*, 314 F.3d 384, 388-89 (9th Cir. 2002) (a Border Patrol agent's administration of the *Miranda* warning about the right to a lawyer free of cost was rendered ineffective by the agent's having previously informed the defendant, who was a Mexican national questioned "about his immigration status and intent," that he had the right under immigration laws "to have an attorney present during questioning but 'not at the [G]overnment's expense'"; "When a warning, not consistent with *Miranda*, is given prior to, after, or simultaneously with a *Miranda* warning, the risk of confusion is substantial, such that the onus is on the Government to clarify to the arrested party the nature of his or her rights under the Fifth Amendment."); *People v. Dunbar*, 24 N.Y.3d 304, 308, 316, 23 N.E.3d 946, 947-48, 953, 998 N.Y.S.2d 679, 680, 681, 686 (2014) (a local booking practice, in which a detective investigator from the D.A.'s office advised suspects that "'this is your opportunity to tell us your story,' and 'your only opportunity' to do so before going before a judge," fatally "undermined the subsequently-communicated *Miranda* warnings" by conveying to suspects that "remaining silent or invoking the right to counsel would come at a price – they would be giving up a valuable opportunity to speak with an assistant district attorney, to have their cases investigated or to assert alibi defenses. . . . By advising them that speaking would facilitate an investigation, the interrogators implied that these defendants' words would be used to help them, thus undoing the heart of the warning that anything they said could and would be used against them."); *People v. Alfonso*, 142 A.D.3d 1180, 1180-81, 38 N.Y.S.3d 566, 568-69 (N.Y. App. Div., 2d Dep't 2016) (the interrogating detective "undermined the *Miranda* warnings and rendered them ineffective" by saying to the defendant that he had "'an opportunity now to tell [his] side of the story, if [he] want[ed] to,'" and that "'obviously, anything that you say can also help you and benefit you in certain ways, you know what I mean' . . . 'potentially'"; "indicat[ing] that in his 'younger days,' he [the detective] would have bounced the defendant off 'about . . . five walls'"; "reiterat[ing] that he was going to give the defendant an opportunity to give his side of the story, and promis[ing] him that he 'potentially [could] help [himself]'"; and, as "the defendant ultimately began to give a statement, . . . interrupt[ing] him and, referring to the *Miranda* warnings form, [and] indicat[ing] that it was a 'bullshit form that [he] had to get past'"). A state court is, of course, free to construe its state constitution as requiring strict conformity with the language of *Miranda*. See § 17.11 *supra*.

26.8. *Validity of the Defendant's Waiver of* **Miranda** *Rights*

In addition to showing that the defendant received valid *Miranda* warnings (see § 26.7 *supra*), the prosecution must show that the defendant made a voluntary, knowing, and intelligent waiver of the *Miranda* rights. *Edwards v. Arizona,* 451 U.S. 477, 482-84 (1981); *see, e.g., Garner v. United States,* 424 U.S. 648, 657 (1976) (dictum); *Fare v. Michael C.,* 442 U.S. 707, 724-27 (1979) (dictum); *United States v. Garibay,* 143 F.3d 534 (9th Cir. 1998); *United States v. Lall,* 607 F.3d 1277, 1282-84 (11th Cir. 2010). The element of "voluntariness" is discussed in § 26.8.1 *infra,* and the "knowing and intelligent" element in § 26.8.2.

A waiver needs not be express: "[I]n at least some cases waiver can be clearly inferred from the actions and words of the person interrogated" (*North Carolina v. Butler,* 441 U.S. 369, 373 (1979)). In certain circumstances, "a waiver of *Miranda* rights may be implied through 'the defendant's silence, coupled with an understanding of his rights and a course of conduct indicating waiver'" (*Berghuis v. Thompkins,* 560 U.S. 370, 385 (2010) (quoting *Butler, supra,* 441 U.S. at 376)). *See Berghuis, supra,* 560 U.S. at 385-86 ("The record in this case shows that Thompkins waived his right to remain silent," notwithstanding the absence of an explicit waiver, because "[t]here was more than enough evidence in the record to conclude that Thompkins understood his *Miranda* rights" and thus that "he chose not to invoke or rely on those rights when he did speak; Thompkins's answer to the interrogating officer's question was "a 'course of conduct indicating waiver' of the right to remain silent," and "there is no evidence that Thompkins's statement was coerced.").

For discussion of the state's burden of persuasion in showing a waiver *of Miranda* rights, see § 24.3.4 *supra*.

26.8.1. *The Requirement That* Miranda *Waivers Be Voluntary*

A waiver of *Miranda* rights, "[o]f course, . . . must at a minimum be 'voluntary' to be effective against an accused" (*Colorado v. Connelly,* 479 U.S. 157, 169 (1986) (dictum); *Miranda, supra,* 384 U.S. at 444, 476.) "'[T]he relinquishment of the right must have been voluntary in the sense that it was the product of a free and deliberate choice rather than intimidation, coercion, or deception.'" *Colorado v. Spring,* 479 U.S. 564, 573 (1987) (dictum); *Moran v. Burbine,* 475 U.S. 412, 420 (1986) (dictum); *Fare v. Michael C., supra,* 442 U.S. at 725 (dictum).

The Court has indicated that the "indicia of coercion" recognized in the context of the due process issue of the voluntariness of statements (see §§ 26.2-26.4.7 *supra*) are also relevant to the voluntariness of a waiver of *Miranda* rights (*see Colorado v. Spring, supra,* 479 U.S. at 573-74; *Colorado v. Connelly, supra,* 479 U.S. at 169-70). The decisive question is whether the defendant's "'will [was] overborne and his capacity for self-determination critically impaired' because of coercive police conduct" (*Colorado v. Spring, supra,* 479 U.S. at 574). In making that inquiry, the courts may consider: "'the duration and conditions of detention . . . , the manifest attitude of the police toward . . . [the accused], his physical and mental state, [and] the diverse pressures which sap or sustain his powers of resistance and self-control'" (*id.* (quoting *Culombe v. Connecticut,* 367 U.S. 568, 602 (1961) (opinion of Justice Frankfurter))).

Excessively long detention or detention under oppressive conditions can suffice to render a *Miranda* waiver involuntary. See § 26.3.2 *supra*. *Miranda* says expressly that the fact that an accused's statement was made after "lengthy interrogation *or* incommunicado incarceration . . . is inconsistent with any notion of a voluntary relinquishment of the privilege [against self-incrimination]" (*Miranda v. Arizona, supra,* 384 U.S. at 476 (emphasis added)).

The voluntariness of a *Miranda* waiver can also be undermined by a police officer's use of force or the threat of force (see § 26.3.1 *supra*) or by police promises of leniency or threats of adverse governmental action (see § 26.3.3 *supra*). "[E]vidence that the accused was . . . tricked . . . into a waiver will, of course, show that the defendant did not voluntarily waive his [Fifth Amendment] privilege." *Miranda, supra,* 384 U.S. at 476. *Accord, United States v. Lall,* 607 F.3d 1277, 1282-84 (11th Cir. 2010), summarized in § 26.3.3 second paragraph *supra*. *See also Miranda, supra,* 384 U.S. at 449-55 (describing the methods by which "interrogators . . . induce a confession out of trickery" (*id.* at 453)). *Cf. Moran v. Burbine,* 475 U.S. 412 (1986) (accepting the basic proposition that police "'trick[ery]' . . . can vitiate the validity of a waiver" (*id.* at 423), but concluding that police misrepresentations to the suspect's attorney did not undermine the voluntariness of waivers by a suspect who was unaware of the misrepresentations). And see the discussion of *Colorado v. Spring*, 479 U.S. 564 (1987), in the concluding paragraph of § 26.3.4 *supra*; *see generally* Christopher Slobogin, *Manipulation of Suspects and Unrecorded Questioning: After 50 Years of Miranda Jurisprudence, Still Two (or Maybe Three) Burning Issues*, 97 B.U. L. REV. 1157 (2017).

As in the due process voluntariness context (see § 26.4 *supra*), the defendant's "mental condition is surely relevant to an individual's susceptibility to police coercion" (*Colorado v. Connelly, supra*, 479 U.S. at 165 (dictum); *see J.D.B. v. North Carolina*, 564 U.S. 261, 272 (2011) (discussed in § 26.6.1 *supra*)), and thereby to the assessment of the voluntariness of a waiver of *Miranda* rights (*Colorado v. Spring, supra*, 479 U.S. at 573-74 (dictum); *see also Fare v. Michael C., supra*, 442 U.S. at 725 (dictum)). Counsel should develop any factor bearing on a defendant's psychological or emotional vulnerability. *See, e.g., Rodriguez v. McDonald*, 872 F.3d 908, 922-23 (9th Cir. 2017) (14-year-old with "Attention Deficit Hyperactivity Disorder and a 'borderline' I.Q. of seventy-seven"); *Woods v. Clusen*, 794 F.2d 293 (7th Cir. 1986) (16-year-old with no prior court experience); *United States v. Blocker*, 354 F. Supp. 1195 (D. D.C. 1973) (21-year-old with "low intelligence" and only one prior arrest); *In re Estrada*, 1 Ariz. App. 348, 403 P.2d 1 (1965) (14-year-old with a low level of education and literacy); *In re Roderick P.*, 7 Cal. 3d 801, 500 P.2d 1, 103 Cal. Rptr. 425 (1972) (intellectually disabled 14-year-old with no prior arrests); *In re S.W.*, 124 A.3d 89, 104 (D.C. 2015) ("emphasiz[ing] the role of [the 15-year-old] appellant's juvenile status" in the court's conclusion that the interrogating detective's "veiled threat to throw appellant to the 'lions'" rendered the youth's *Miranda* waiver involuntary; "in the juvenile context, . . . [the] courts must exercise 'special caution' in conducting a voluntariness analysis."); *In the Interest of Thompson*, 241 N.W.2d 2 (Iowa 1976) (17-year-old with an I.Q. of 71); *State in the Interest of Holifield*, 319 So.2d 471 (La. App. 1975) (14-year-old with an I.Q. of 67); *Commonwealth v. Cain*, 361 Mass. 224, 279 N.E.2d 706 (1972) (15-year-old with no prior experience with police, who was denied access to his father).

26.8.2. *The Requirement That* Miranda *Waivers Be "Knowing and Intelligent"*

A *Miranda* waiver "must have been made with a full awareness both of the nature of the right being abandoned and the consequences of the decision to abandon it. Only if the 'totality of the circumstances surrounding the interrogation' reveal both an uncoerced choice and the requisite level of comprehension may a court properly conclude that the *Miranda* rights have been waived" (*Moran v. Burbine*, 475 U.S. 412, 421 (1986) (dictum); *see Colorado v. Spring*, 479 U.S. 564, 573-74 (1987) (dictum)). *And see People v. Bernasco*, 138 Ill. 2d 349, 357, 562 N.E.2d 958, 961, 150 Ill. Dec. 155, 158 (1990) ("where a defendant confesses after being given *Miranda* warnings . . . , both intelligent knowledge and voluntariness remain requirements for assuring that a defendant's *Miranda* waiver reflects *Miranda*'s 'carefully drawn approach': its 'subtle balance' between the need for police questioning and the coercive pressures inherent in such questioning."); *In re T.B.*, 2010 PA Super 197, 11 A.3d 500, 505 (Pa. Super. 2010) ("[r]egardless of whether a waiver of *Miranda* is voluntary, the Commonwealth must prove by a preponderance of the evidence that the waiver is also *knowing and intelligent*."); *Ramirez v. State*, 739 So.2d 568, 575-76 (Fla. 1999) (holding that a confession should have been suppressed because the defendant's waiver of *Miranda* rights was not knowing, voluntary or intelligent: "The 'totality of the circumstances' to be considered in determining whether a waiver of

Miranda warnings [sic] is valid based on the two-pronged approach of *Moran* may include factors that are also considered in determining whether the confession itself is voluntary. . . . The factors that we consider relevant here include: (1) the manner in which the *Miranda* rights were administered, including any cajoling or trickery . . . ; (2) the suspect's age, experience, background and intelligence . . . ; (3) the fact that the suspect's parents were not contacted and the juvenile was not given an opportunity to consult with his parents before questioning . . . ; (4) the fact that the questioning took place in the station house . . . ; and (5) the fact that the interrogators did not secure a written waiver of the *Miranda* rights at the outset."); *State v. Lujan*, 634 S.W.3d 862, 865-66 (Tex. Crim. App. 2021) (after the defendant was given *Miranda* warnings at a police station in what she was told was "a formal interview," she waived her rights and confessed to involvement in a homicide; she then agreed to accompany detectives in a squad car to show them the site where she had last seen the victim's body; as they left the interrogation room, one detective told the defendant "when we come back, we can continue, if you like, okay?"; during the squad-car ride, a detective electronically recorded the conversation without the defendant's knowledge as she gave an extensive, free-wheeling recounting of her role in the crime; the Texas Court of Criminal Appeals, applying *Miranda* and a Texas statute implementing *Miranda*, affirms a trial-court ruling suppressing this recounting because it was not made with the requisite understanding: "The waiver's validity depends on, among other things, a showing that the defendant 'was aware of the State's intention to use his statements to secure a conviction[.]' *Burbine* . . . Deception is relevant to the waiver inquiry if the deception 'deprives a defendant of knowledge essential to his ability to understand the nature of his rights and the consequences of abandoning them.'").

Personal characteristics of a defendant that were identified in previous sections as bearing on the voluntariness of a statement (see § 26.4 *supra*) and the voluntariness of a *Miranda* waiver (see § 26.8.1 *supra*) also are relevant to a determination of whether a defendant's waiver of *Miranda* rights was "knowing and intelligent." Thus, a defendant may have been unable to comprehend the language employed in *Miranda* warnings and/or the concepts embodied in the warnings because of:

(1)   *Youth. See, e.g., A.M. v. Butler*, 360 F.3d 787, 801 n.11 (7th Cir. 2004) (in the course of finding that a juvenile's *Miranda* waiver was involuntary, the court states that "[t]here is no reason to believe that this 11-year-old could understand the inherently abstract concepts of the *Miranda* rights and what it means to waive them," and cites an empirical study "finding that 96 percent of 14-year-olds lack an adequate understanding of the consequences of waiving their rights"); *State v. Benoit,* 126 N.H. 6, 13-14, 18-19, 490 A.2d 295, 300-01, 304 (1985) (establishing a heightened state constitutional standard for determining the constitutionality of a juvenile's waiver of *Miranda* rights, and citing empirical studies that "have concluded that, due to their immaturity, many children are incapable of exercising informed judgment concerning the substance and significance of waiving their constitutional rights and that, hence, certain procedural safeguards should be employed to insure that waivers by children are genuinely knowing, intelligent and voluntary"); *In the Matter of B.M.B.*, 264 Kan. 417, 429-33, 955 P.2d 1302, 1310-13 (1998) (discussing the empirical data on juveniles' comprehension of *Miranda* rights and adopting a categorical rule that when a juvenile suspect is

under 14, the police must advise not only the juvenile but also his or her parent or guardian of the juvenile's "right to an attorney and to remain silent," and must afford the juvenile an "opportunity to consult with his or her parent, guardian, or attorney as to whether he or she will waive his or her rights to an attorney and against self-incrimination"); *Commonwealth v. A Juvenile (No. 1), 389 Mass. 128, 131-35, 449 N.E.2d 654, 656-58 (1983) (discussing the empirical studies "suggest[ing] that most juveniles do not understand the significance and protective function of these rights even when they are read the standard *Miranda* warnings," and holding that a finding of "a knowing and intelligent waiver by a juvenile" requires that "the State must first prove that the juvenile and his parent, or if a parent is not available, someone in loco parentis, were fully advised of the juvenile's right against self-incrimination through administration of the standard *Miranda* warnings"; "in most cases it should show that a parent or an interested adult was present, understood the warnings, and had the opportunity to explain his rights to the juvenile so that the juvenile understands the significance of waiver of these rights"; this showing is indispensable for juveniles under the age of 14 and important, albeit not decisive, for older children.); *State in the Interest of S.H.,* 61 N.J. 108, 115, 293 A.2d 181, 184-85 (1972) (treating it as axiomatic that "[r]ecitation of the *Miranda* warnings to a boy of 10 even when they are explained is undoubtedly meaningless"); *In the Interest of Jerrell C.J.,* 2005 WI 105, 283 Wis. 2d 145, 151, 159 n.6, 699 N.W.2d 110, 113, 117 n.6 (Wis. 2005) (in the course of holding that a 14-year-old's confession was involuntary and establishing a general rule requiring that "all custodial interrogations of juveniles in future cases be electronically recorded where feasible, and without exception when questioning occurs at a place of detention," the court observes that "scholarly research" supports the proposition that, "[b]ecause their intellectual capacity is not fully developed, children are less likely to understand their *Miranda* rights"). *Cf. Miller v. Alabama,* 567 U.S. 460, 471 (2012) (explaining that the Court has recognized, based on "science and social science" as well as "common sense" and "what 'any parent knows,'" that "children are constitutionally different from adults for purposes of sentencing" because, *inter alia,* "children have a "'lack of maturity and an underdeveloped sense of responsibility,'" leading to recklessness, impulsivity, and heedless risk-taking," and "children 'are more vulnerable . . . to . . . outside pressures'"). *See generally* Barry C. Feld, *Behind Closed Doors: What Really Happens When Cops Question Kids,* 23 CORNELL J.L. & PUB. POL'Y 395 (2013).

(2)   *Intellectual disability. See, e.g., Cooper v. Griffin,* 455 F.2d 1142, 1145-46 (5th Cir. 1972) (two juveniles, who were 15 and 16 years old, and whose I.Q. "was said to range between 61 and 67" (*id. at* 1145) "could not have made a 'knowing and intelligent' waiver of their rights" (*id. at* 1146): they "surely had no appreciation of the options before them or of the consequences of their choice. Indeed it is doubtful that they even comprehended all of the words that were read to them" (*id.*)); *People v. Jiminez,* 863 P.2d 981, 982, 985 (Colo. 1993) (the defendant, who was found by a psychologist to be "'function[ing] at about the 6 year old level,'" and who had never been to school and had "'a very limited

vocabulary,'" did not make a "knowing and intelligent" waiver of his *Miranda* rights); *Smith v. State*, 918 A.2d 1144 (Del. 2007) (an intellectually disabled 14-year-old, who "was functioning at a second grade level" (*id. at* 1151), "could not sign his name because he did not know how" (*id.*) and who "could not read the *Miranda* warnings himself, [and] so was given a quick and confusing explanation of what they supposedly meant" (*id.*) did not make a "knowing" waiver of his *Miranda* rights (*id.*)); *State v. Thorpe*, 274 N.C. 457, 461, 164 S.E.2d 171, 174 (1968) (an intellectually disabled 20-year-old, "who had left school before he completed the third grade," did not make a valid waiver of his right to counsel during questioning); *People v. Kadow*, 2021 IL App (4th) 190103, 182 N.E.3d 814, 450 Ill. Dec. 1002 (2021). For a discussion of the relevant forensic testing materials, *see* Sydnee L. Erickson, Karen L. Salekin, Lauren N. Johnson & Stephanie C. Doran, *The Predictive Power of Intelligence: Miranda Abilities of Individuals with Intellectual Disability*, 44 (No. 1) LAW AND HUMAN BEHAVIOR 60 (2020).

(3)   *Mental illness. See, e.g., Commonwealth v. Hilton*, 443 Mass. 597, 603, 607, 823 N.E.2d 383, 390, 393 (2005) (defendant who "suffer[ed] from schizophenia and ha[d] a schizotypal personality disorder," did not understand "the *Miranda* warnings" and thus could not have made a "knowing and intelligent" waiver).

(4)   *Intoxication or the effects of drugs. See, e.g., Commonwealth v. Anderl*, 329 Pa. Super. 69, 81, 477 A.2d 1356, 1362 (1984) ("we conclude that the appellee's waiver of his *Miranda* rights was vitiated by his intoxication and that the statements made by the appellee while in custody should be suppressed"); *State v. Young*, 1994-NMCA-061, 117 N.M. 688, 692, 875 P.2d 1119, 1123 (1994) ("[V]oluntary intoxication is relevant to determining whether a waiver was knowing and intelligent. See . . . 1 Wayne R. LaFave & Jerold H. Israel, Criminal Procedure § 6.9, at 527 (1984). On remand, the trial court shall consider the evidence of Defendant's intoxication in determining whether Defendant knowingly and intelligently waived his rights."); *State v. Kinn*, 288 Minn. 31, 36, 178 N.W.2d 888, 891 (1970), *partially overruled on an unrelated point* in *State v. Herem*, 384 N.W.2d 880 (Minn. 1986) ("The lower court's attention is called to the fact that the evidence indicates that defendant was obviously intoxicated during all of the time that the investigation and arrest took place. In view of this circumstance, the court should consider the evidence as it bears upon the question of whether defendant was mentally competent to waive his constitutional rights at any point."); *People v. Knedler*, 2014 CO 28, 329 P.3d 242, 245-46 (Colo. 2014) (recognizing that "a defendant's level of intoxication at the time of the *Miranda* advisement is relevant to a waiver's validity" and that a defendant may be so "intoxicated that he or she could not have made a knowing and intelligent waiver," and explaining the "set of subfactors to [be used in] assess[ing] a defendant's competence in cases involving intoxication," but ultimately concluding that the totality of the circumstances adequately established that "Knedler's decision to waive his rights was informed and deliberate"); *and see United States v. Harris*, 64 F.4th 999, 1002 (8th Cir. 2023) ("[I]ntoxication alone

does not preclude a valid waiver. . . . ¶ Harris's intoxication did not cause his will to be overborne. The district court found Harris was 'alert, aware of his criminal liability, and appropriately responding to questions' while talking with the officers. It credited the officers' testimony that he 'appeared coherent and did not tell them that he was intoxicated or under the influence of drugs.' His behavior was 'consistent with someone who understood the nature of his crimes,' and he 'did not appear to be intoxicated.' The court also noted that Harris's extensive criminal history –including five arrests and convictions – supported this conclusion.").

In cases in which counsel will argue that a defendant was disabled from making a "knowing and intelligent" waiver due to one of the foregoing circumstances, the key to prevailing on the claim will often be to present a mental health expert to testify to the defendant's capacity to comprehend the language and/or the concepts in the *Miranda* warnings. *See, e.g., People v. Jiminez, supra,* 863 P.2d at 982-83 (the trial court's finding that the defendant did not make a "knowing and intelligent waiver" relied on "the testimony of . . . a psychologist, who had examined the defendant initially to determine his competency," and who was called by the defense to testify to the defendant's cognitive impairments, lack of education, and "'very limited vocabulary'"); *Commonwealth v. Hilton, supra,* 443 Mass. at 603, 823 N.E.2d at 390 (the judge at the suppression hearing "credited expert testimony proffered by the defense concerning the defendant's significant mental impairments" and "[s]pecifically . . . found that the defendant is [intellectually disabled] . . . , functionally illiterate, and given to 'delusional and bizarre thinking[,]' . . . [that] [s]he has 'a tenuous connection to reality, poor judgment, and a tendency to misinterpret events and their meaning,' with 'little ability to understand abstract concepts' . . . [and that she] suffers from schizophrenia and has a schizotypal personality disorder"). *See also In re Ariel R.,* 98 A.D.3d 414, 417, 419, 950 N.Y.S.2d 17, 20-21 (N.Y. App. Div., 1st Dep't 2012) (the defendant's treating psychiatrist, who was called as a witness for the defense at a confession suppression hearing, should have been allowed to "render an opinion as to whether [the juvenile] appellant could have understood the juvenile *Miranda* warnings read to him"; although the psychiatrist "did not perform any tests on appellant that were specifically designed to determine appellant's competency to waive *Miranda,*" his "evaluations of appellant's receptive communication skills and IQ . . . [were] sufficient to enable him to form an opinion as to the ultimate question of whether appellant had adequate language and cognitive skills to understand the *Miranda* warnings."); *Smith v. State,* 918 A.2d 1144 (Del. 2007) (the denial of a suppression motion presented without the benefit of expert testimony was required to be reversed in the light of expert testimony presented at a subsequent competency hearing). For general discussion of the use of expert witnesses and the right to court funds for retention of experts when representing indigent defendants, see §§ 5.1.2-5.4, 16.2-16.3 *supra.* If the defendant is still in school, and especially if the defendant is in special education, counsel should obtain the defendant's school records and should consult any special education teachers who might be able to testify about the defendant's reading and comprehension abilities. *See, e.g., Cooper v. Griffin, supra,* 455 F.2d at 1143-46 (on the basis of special education teachers' testimony concerning the low I.Q. scores and comprehension levels of the defendants, the court concludes that their *Miranda* waivers were not "knowing and intelligent"). Counsel might also consider putting the defendant on the witness stand at the suppression hearing to testify about his or her understanding of the meaning of the various *Miranda* warnings. *See, e.g., State in the Interest of*

Holifield, 319 So.2d 471, 472-73 (La. App. 1975) ("The defendant juvenile also was called to the witness stand. His testimony leaves considerable doubt regarding his capacity to understand the meaning of words used in the normal criminal process.").

Even if a defendant had the intellectual capacity to comprehend *Miranda* warnings, there will be substantial questions about whether a waiver was "knowing and intelligent" in any case in which s/he was not a native English speaker and in which the *Miranda* warnings were read to him or her in English rather than in his or her native language. *See, e.g., United States v. Barry,* 979 F. Supp. 2d 715, 719 (M.D. La. 2013) (a *Miranda* waiver was not voluntary, knowing and intelligent because "the warnings were not in Barry's native tongue, there was no use of a translator, the rights were not explained to him at length, and his understanding was assumed but not confirmed"); *see also United States v. Botello-Rosales,* 728 F.3d 865, 867-68 (9th Cir. 2013) (per curiam), summarized in § 26.7 third paragraph *supra*; Aneta Pavlenko, Elizabeth Hepford & Scott Jarvis, *An illusion of understanding: How native and non-native speakers of English understand (and misunderstand) their* Miranda *rights,* 26 (No. 6) INTERNATIONAL JOURNAL OF SPEECH, LANGUAGE AND THE LAW 181 (2019).

26.9. Statements Taken after the Defendant Has Asserted His or Her Miranda Rights to Silence or Counsel

The discussion in § 26.8 *supra* described the normal standard for assessing waivers of *Miranda* rights. If, instead of making an immediate and final waiver of *Miranda* rights, the defendant asserts at any time the right to silence or the right to counsel, there are more stringent standards for determining the validity of any subsequent *Miranda* waivers.

Provided that the defendant has used language adequate to assert the right (see § 26.9.1 *infra*), the standard to be applied following an assertion of the right to silence is the one discussed in § 26.9.2 *infra,* and the standard to be applied after an assertion of the right to counsel is the one discussed in § 26.9.3 *infra.*

26.9.1. Sufficiency of the Language Used in Asserting the Right

An assertion of *Miranda* rights needs not expressly refer to the rights. As long as the defendant's statements manifest a "clear indication[ ]" of his or her desire to exercise a particular right, they are sufficient to invoke the right (*Brewer v. Williams,* 430 U.S. 387, 404-05, 412 n.1 (1977) (discussing invocation of the right to counsel). *See Miranda v. Arizona, supra,* 384 U.S. at 444-45 (the right to counsel is asserted whenever the suspect "indicates in any manner" that s/he wants a lawyer); *Davis v. United States,* 512 U.S. 452, 459 (1994) (dictum) (the right to counsel is invoked if a suspect makes a "'statement that can reasonably be construed to be an expression of a desire for the assistance of an attorney'"). *See, e.g., Michigan v. Mosley,* 423 U.S. 96 (1975) (by implication) (the right to silence was invoked when a suspect told the police that he did not want to say "[a]nything about the robberies" (*id.* at 105 n.11)); *Smith v. Illinois,* 469 U.S. 91 (1984) (per curiam) (the right to counsel was invoked when, in response to administration of *Miranda* warnings, defendant said: "'Uh, yeah, I'd like to do that'" (*id.* at 93)). *See also Arizona v. Roberson,* 486 U.S. 675, 681-84 (1988); *Connecticut v. Barrett,* 479 U.S. 523, 529 (1987) (dictum); *Johnson v. Zerbst,* 304 U.S. 458, 464 (1938); *Jones v. Harrington,* 829

F.3d 1128 (9th Cir. 2016) (the defendant "simply and unambiguously" invoked the right to silence (*id.* at 1142) by saying, after "hours of questioning," "'I don't want to talk no more'" (*id.* at 1132), which "means the government cannot use against Jones anything he said after his invocation. And that includes using Jones's subsequent statements to 'cast retrospective doubt on the clarity of [Jones's] initial request itself.'" (*id.*)); *Garcia v. Long*, 808 F.3d 771 (9th Cir. 2015) (the defendant asserted his right to silence by responding to the officer's question "'do you wish to talk to me?'" with "a simple 'no'" (*id.* at 773); notwithstanding "other statements Garcia made during the interview" (*id.*), "'no' meant 'no.'"(*id.*)); *Tobias v. Arteaga*, 996 F.3d 571, 580-81 (9th Cir. 2021) ("Tobias's statement – 'Could I have an attorney? Because that's not me' – was an unequivocal invocation of his right to counsel under clearly established law. . . . In modern usage, 'Can I' and 'Could I' are both well understood ways of asking a direct question – the only distinction is that 'could' is considered a more polite form of request than 'can.' . . . . The second half of Tobias's statement, 'Because that's not me,' does nothing to undermine his initial question . . . . ¶ The LAPD detectives suggest that Tobias's question was not clearly established as unambiguous because we have found statements such as 'I think I would like to talk to a lawyer,' 'Maybe he ought to see an attorney,' and '[I] might want to talk to a lawyer,' ambiguous. . . . Tobias, by contrast, 'did not equivocate in his invocation by using words such as "maybe" or "might" or "I think."' . . . . He asked directly for an attorney, a request the officers ignored."); *Hurd v. Terhune*, 619 F.3d 1080, 1088-89 (9th Cir. 2010) ("Hurd unambiguously invoked his right to silence when the officers requested that he reenact the shooting . . . [and] Hurd responded to the officers' requests by saying, among other things, 'I don't want to do that,' 'No,' 'I can't,' and 'I don't want to act it out because that – it's not that clear.'"); *compare United States v. Abdallah*, 911 F.3d 201 (4th Cir. 2018) (Halfway through an initial reading of the *Miranda* warnings, the defendant interrupted to tell the interrogating officers that he "wasn't going to say anything at all." An interrogator responded by stating, "Well, just let me finish your Warning first." After the warning, the interrogator asked, "Do you even know why you're under arrest?" Defendant responded, "No, tell me." The interrogator then repeated the *Miranda* warnings; the defendant did not interrupt; he indicated that he understood his rights; he made incriminating statements. The court finds a *Miranda* violation because the defendant's invocation of the right to silence was unambiguous.), *with Smith v. Boughton*, 43 F.4th 702 (7th Cir. 2022) (in a case involving a factual scenario essentially indistinguishable from that in *Abdallah*, but in which federal adjudication is constrained by AEDPA's limitation on federal *habeas corpus* review of state-court decisions (see § 49.2.3.2 *infra*), a Seventh Circuit panel holds 2-to-1 that the Wisconsin Supreme Court was not unreasonable in finding some ambiguity in the defendant's invocation of his right to remain silent); *and see United States v. Rodriguez*, 518 F.3d 1072, 1077-78, 1081 (9th Cir. 2008) (the defendant, who responded to a question whether he wanted to talk to a law enforcement official by stating "'I'm good for tonight,'" had "at best, [made] an ambiguous invocation of the right to silence," but his subsequent statement had to be suppressed "because his interrogator failed to clarify [defendant's] . . . wishes with regard to his *Miranda* warnings" before commencing interrogation); *Anderson v. Terhune*, 516 F.3d 781, 787 (9th Cir. 2008) (en banc) ("Following the issuance of *Miranda* in 1966 and the literally thousands of cases that repeat its rationale, we rarely have occasion to address a situation in which the defendant not only uses the facially unambiguous words 'I plead the Fifth,' but surrounds that invocation with a clear desire not to talk any more. The state court accurately recognized that under *Miranda*, 'if [an] individual indicates in any manner, at any time prior to or during questioning, that he wishes to remain silent, the interrogation must cease,' . . . but then went on to eviscerate that conclusion by stating that the comments were 'ambiguous in context ¶ . . . because they could have been interpreted as not wanting officers to pursue the particulars of his drug use as opposed to not wanting to continue the questioning at all. By asking defendant what he meant by pleading the fifth, the officer asked a legitimate clarifying question.' ¶ Using 'context' to transform an unambiguous invocation into open-ended ambiguity defies both common sense and established Supreme Court law. It is not that context is unimportant, but it simply cannot be manufactured by straining to raise a question regarding the intended scope of a facially unambiguous invocation of the right to silence."); *Deviney v. State*, 112 So.3d 57 (Fla. 2013) (a suspect's repeated declarations during interrogation that he was "done" and "ready to go home" (*id.* at 77) "represented an unequivocal invocation of his right to remain silent" (*id.*) particularly when "Deviney further indicated his desire to end questioning by standing and attempting to leave the interrogation room" (*id.* at 78)); *State v. Maltese*, 222 N.J. 525, 546, 120 A.3d 197, 209 (2015) (the "defendant affirmatively asserted his right to remain silent" by "repeatedly stat[ing] that he wanted to speak with his uncle, whom he considered 'better than a freaking attorney,' before answering any further questions," and "specifically stat[ing] that he wanted to consult with his uncle about 'what to do'"); *State v. King*, 2013-NMSC-014, 300 P.3d 732, 733 (N.M. 2013) ("King clearly invoked his right to remain silent" (*id.* at 735) when he responded to the officer's inquiry "'Do you wish to answer any questions?'" by stating "'Not at the moment. Kind of intoxicated.'" (*id.* at 733): "There is nothing ambiguous about his statement, which made it clear that he did not want to speak with the police. The adverb 'not' is unequivocally a negative expression" (*id.* at 735); "Although King's statement suggested that he might want to talk at a later time, there was absolutely no respite from the interrogation in this case (*id.* at 736)"); § 26.9.3 *infra* (further discussing the standards governing the invocation of the right to counsel).

If the defendant's initial assertion is adequately clear, then it is not rendered ambiguous by subsequent statements indicating a willingness to speak with the police. *Smith v. Illinois*, 469 U.S. 91 (1984) (per curiam). *Accord, Jones v. Harrington, supra*, 829 F.3d at 1132, 1136, 1140. Such "subsequent statements are relevant only to the question whether the accused [later] waived the right he had invoked. Invocation and waiver are entirely distinct inquiries, and the two must not be blurred" (*Smith v. Illinois, supra*, 469 U.S. at 98).

The courts will honor a partial assertion of *Miranda* rights and give effect to the limitations established by the suspect if those limitations are clearly and unequivocally stated. Thus, in *Connecticut v. Barrett*, 479 U.S. 523 (1987), the Court recognized that the defendant's statement "'he was willing to talk about [the incident] verbally but he did not want to put anything in writing until his attorney came'" (*id.* at 526) constituted an invocation of the right to counsel with respect to written, but not oral, statements. *See also United States v. Jumper*, 497 F.3d 699, 706 (7th Cir. 2007) (the defendant asserted his right to silence with respect to specific questions by saying, in answer to these questions, "'I don't want to answer that'.").

The defendant can invoke his or her right to silence or to counsel even after initially waiving such rights. "The mere fact that he may have answered some questions or volunteered some statements on his own does not deprive him of the right to refrain from answering any further inquiries until he has consulted with an attorney and thereafter consents to be questioned." *Miranda v. Arizona, supra*, 384 U.S. at 444-45.

26.9.2. *Assertion of the Right to Silence*

"If the individual indicates in any manner, at any time prior to or during questioning, that he wishes to remain silent, the interrogation must cease." *Miranda v. Arizona, supra*, 384 U.S. at 473-74; *see Michigan v. Mosley*, 423 U.S. 96, 100-01 (1975) (dictum). However, this does not mean that an arrested individual who has once declined to answer questions "can never again be subjected to custodial interrogation by any police officer at any time or place on any subject" (*Mosley, supra*, 423 U.S. at 102).

In *Mosley*, the Court sustained the admission of a murder confession by a defendant, notwithstanding his earlier assertion of his right to silence, because the unusual facts of the case showed that his assertion had been "'scrupulously honored'" (*id.* at 104) by the police. The defendant had been arrested for several robberies and, upon administration of full *Miranda* warnings, told the arresting officer that he did not want to say "'[a]nything about the robberies'" (*id.* at 105 n.11). The arresting officer respected that assertion of the right to silence by "promptly ceas[ing] the interrogation" (*id.* at 97), and the defendant was never again questioned about the robberies for which he had been arrested (*see id.* at 105-06). "After an interval of more than two hours" (*id.* at 104), the defendant was taken from his cell to "another location" in the building (*id.*) "by another police officer" (*id.*), who was not shown to have had any connection with the earlier questioning (*see id.* at 105). This second police officer gave the defendant another complete set of *Miranda* warnings and then questioned the defendant "about an unrelated holdup murder" (*id.* at 104). In response to the second administration of *Miranda* warnings, the defendant signed a *Miranda* "notification form" and proceeded to answer questions, initially denying the murder and then, within 15 minutes, admitting guilt (*see id.* at 98). During all of these proceedings the defendant never asked to see a lawyer. *Id.* at 101 n.7. The Supreme Court held that "the admissibility of statements obtained after [a] . . . person in custody has decided to remain silent depends under *Miranda* on whether his 'right to cut off questioning' was 'scrupulously honored'" (*id.* at 104), and that, on this record, Mosley's "'right to cut off questioning' was fully respected" (*id.*). "This is not a case . . . where the police failed to honor a decision of a person in custody to cut off questioning, either by refusing to discontinue the interrogation upon request or by persisting in repeated efforts to wear down his resistance and make him change his mind." *Id.* at 105-06.

Under *Mosley*, the courts will find that the police failed to "scrupulously honor" a suspect's invocation of the right to remain silent and will suppress any ensuing statement if the police (a) do not cease questioning as soon as the suspect invokes his or her right to silence (*see, e.g., Anderson v. Smith,* 751 F.2d 96, 102-03 (2d Cir. 1984); *State v. Aguirre*, 301 Kan. 950, 349 P.3d 1245 (2015)), or (b) engage in "repeated rounds of questioning to undermine the will of the person being questioned" (*Michigan v. Mosley, supra*, 423 U.S. at 102; *see, e.g., United States v. Hernandez,* 574 F.2d 1362, 1368-69 (5th Cir. 1978); *United States v. Rambo*, 365 F.3d 906, 910-911 (10th Cir. 2004) ("If Rambo invoked his right to remain silent and Moran failed to 'scrupulously honor[ ]' that right, Rambo's confession must be suppressed. . . . The government contends that it was Rambo who reinitiated communication after invoking his right to remain silent and, therefore, Moran was not required to terminate the interview. That argument ignores Moran's active role in continuing the interview after Rambo invoked his rights. When Rambo stated that he did not want to discuss the robberies, Moran made no move to end the encounter. Instead he acknowledged Rambo's request, but told Rambo that he would be charged with two aggravated robberies and that other agencies would want to speak with Rambo. Those comments reflect both further pressure on Rambo to discuss the crimes and a suggestion that despite Rambo's present request to terminate discussion of the topic, he would be questioned further."); *People v. Jackson*, 103 A.D.3d 814, 816-17, 959 N.Y.S.2d 540, 543 (N.Y. App. Div., 2d Dep't 2013) (an "arresting officer failed to 'scrupulously honor' the defendant's [assertion of the right to silence] . . . when he deliberately engaged the defendant in conversation . . . [and] told the defendant that, unless someone confessed to ownership of the gun, all three occupants of the car would be charged with its possession, . . . [thereby] engaging in the functional equivalent of interrogation in that he knew or should have known that his comments were reasonably likely to elicit an incriminating response").

When litigating cases in which interrogation was resumed after a defendant's assertion of the right to silence, counsel may be advised to seek a state constitutional ruling forbidding such a resumption even under circumstances in which *Mosley* would allow it. *See, e.g., State v. O'Neill*, 193 N.J. 148, 176-78, 936 A.2d 438, 454-55 (2007); and see generally § 17.11 *supra*.

26.9.3. *Assertion of the Right to Counsel*

"If the individual states that he wants an attorney, the interrogation must cease until an attorney is present." *Miranda v. Arizona, supra*, 384 U.S. at 474; *Lujan v. Garcia*, 734 F.3d 917, 932 (9th Cir. 2013). A request for an attorney triggers "additional safeguards" beyond those recognized in *Mosley* as attending an invocation of the right to remain silent (*Edwards v. Arizona*, 451 U.S. 477, 484 (1981); *Radovsky v. State*, 296 Md. 386, 464 A.2d 239 (1983)).

> "[W]e . . . hold that when an accused has invoked his right to have counsel present during custodial interrogation, a valid waiver of that right cannot be established by showing only that he responded to further police-initiated custodial interrogation even if he has been advised of his rights. We further hold that an accused, . . . having expressed his desire to deal with the police only through counsel, is not subject to further interrogation by the authorities until counsel has been made available to him, unless the accused himself initiates further communication, exchanges, or conversations with the police." (*Id.* at 484-85.)

See also Minnick v. Mississippi, 498 U.S. 146, 150 (1990); *Shea v. Louisiana*, 470 U.S. 51, 54-55 (1985); *Commonwealth v. Gonzalez*, 487 Mass. 661, 670, 169 N.E.3d 485, 494 (2021) ("We conclude that there was no error in the judge's findings . . . that the Commonwealth failed to meet its burden to show, beyond a reasonable doubt, that the defendant had reinitiated conversation with police. Accordingly, the order allowing suppression of the defendant's statements after he invoked his right to counsel must be affirmed."); *Moore v. Berghuis*, 700 F.3d 882 (6th Cir. 2012) (a murder suspect turned himself in and asked the police to call the number on his attorney's business card; an officer called and got the attorney's answering service; the officer told the suspect that he had reached only the attorney's answering device, not the attorney (*id.* at 884). The officer then "'asked [Moore] did he want to talk to [the officer] and [Moore] said yes he did.' The officer . . . then had Moore sign a form waiving his constitutional rights, and 'asked [Moore] could he tell [the officer] about . . . the fatal shooting . . . '" (*id.* at 888). "[T]o demonstrate that Moore waived his asserted right to counsel and was therefore 'not subject to further interrogation by the authorities until counsel [was] made available to him,' the government must have shown that Moore 'himself initiate[d] further communication, exchanges, or conversations with the police.' *Edwards*, . . . Though the Supreme Court in [*Berghuis v.*] *Thompkins*, [560 U.S. 370 (2010), summarized in § 26.8] recently addressed the issue of waiver of *Miranda* rights, we do not read *Thompkins*'s waiver analysis to alter the *Edwards* rule regarding waiver of the right to counsel. In *Thompkins*, the Court did not alter, or even speak to, the *Edwards* analysis regarding the waiver of the right to counsel; instead, *Thompkins* clarifies the waiver analysis for the right to remain silent." 700 F.3d at 888.); *Davis v. United States*, 512 U.S. 452, 458 (1994) (dictum); *McNeil v. Wisconsin*, 501 U.S. 171, 176-77 (1991) (dictum); *Montejo v. Louisiana*, 556 U.S. 778, 794-95 (2009) (dictum). *But see Maryland v. Shatzer*, 559 U.S. 98, 109, 110 (2010) (the *Edwards* rule does not bar "reinterrogat[ion] after a break in custody that is of sufficient duration to dissipate . . . [the] coercive effects" of the initial period of "*Miranda* custody"; this will ordinarily be the case when the "break in custody" has been at least "14 days," a period of time that "provides plenty of time for the suspect to get reacclimated to his normal life, to consult with friends and counsel, and to shake off any residual coercive effects of his prior custody."); *United States v. Rought*, 11 F.4th 178, 182-83 (3d Cir. 2021) ("In *Connecticut v. Barrett*, 479 U.S. 523 (1987) [summarized in § 26.9.1 third paragraph *supra*], the Supreme Court held that invocations of the right to counsel during custodial interrogations can be 'limited.' . . . After a limited invocation, interrogation can continue on topics not covered by the invocation. If the suspect, without prompting from law enforcement, then voluntarily reinitiates discussion of a covered topic and waives her previously invoked rights, it 'is quite consistent with the Fifth Amendment' for the suspect's statements about a covered topic to be admissible at trial.").

"*Edwards* set forth a 'bright-line rule' that all questioning must cease after an accused requests counsel." *Smith v. Illinois*, 469 U.S. 91, 98 (1984) (per curiam). "*Edwards* is 'designed to prevent police from badgering a defendant into waiving his previously asserted *Miranda* rights.' . . . The rule ensures that any statement made in subsequent interrogation is not the result of coercive pressures." *Minnick v. Mississippi, supra*, 498 U.S. at 150-51. *See also Smith v. Illinois, supra*, 469 U.S. at 97-99 (rejecting arguments that a request for counsel made partway through the administration of *Miranda* warnings was insufficient to trigger the *Edwards* rule and that equivocations in the suspect's responses to the remaining warnings could be considered as rendering his initial request for counsel ambiguous). "The *Edwards* rule . . . is *not* offense specific: Once a suspect invokes the *Miranda* right to counsel for interrogation regarding one offense, he may not be reapproached regarding *any* offense unless counsel is present." *McNeil v. Wisconsin, supra*, 501 U.S. at 177 (dictum). *Accord, Arizona v. Roberson*, 486 U.S. 675, 682 (1988); *Vega v. Tekoh*, 142 S. Ct. 2095, 2104 (2022) (dictum). "Furthermore, it is well settled that, where a defendant directs a request for counsel to one police officer, the knowledge of that request is imputed to all other officers. . . . 'To hold otherwise could make it possible to nullify an accused's request for the assistance of counsel by the expedient of transferring his custody for questioning to an officer who would be unaware of the request for an attorney.'" *People v. Williams*, 2021 IL App (3d) 180282, 185 N.E.3d 848, 852, 452 Ill. Dec. 443, 447 (2021).

"Invocation of the *Miranda* right to counsel 'requires, at a minimum, some statement that

can reasonably be construed to be an expression of a desire for the assistance of an attorney.'
. . . [I]f a suspect makes a reference to an attorney that is ambiguous or equivocal in that a
reasonable officer in light of the circumstances would have understood only that the suspect
might be invoking the right to counsel, . . . [the Supreme Court's] precedents do not require the
cessation of questioning. . . . Although a suspect need not 'speak with the discrimination of an
Oxford don,' . . . he must articulate his desire to have counsel present sufficiently clearly that a
reasonable police officer in the circumstances would understand the statement to be a request for
an attorney." *Davis v. United States, supra,* 512 U.S. at 459. S*ee also id.* at 462 (upholding the
determination of the "courts below . . . that . . . [Davis'] remark to the . . . agents – 'Maybe I
should talk to a lawyer' – was not a request for counsel" and that the agents could continue
questioning "to clarify whether [Davis] . . . in fact wanted a lawyer"); *Connecticut v. Barrett,*
479 U.S. 523, 529 (1987) (the *Edwards* rule was not triggered by a defendant's announcement
that he would not give the police a written statement unless his lawyer was present but had no
problem in talking about the incident: "Barrett's limited requests for counsel . . . were
accompanied by affirmative announcements of his willingness to speak with the authorities.").
Compare Sessoms v. Grounds, 776 F.3d 615, 617-18, 630-31 (9th Cir. 2015) (en banc) (the
defendant's question to the interrogating officers "'There wouldn't be any possible way that I
could have a – a lawyer present while we do this?'" combined with his follow-up statement
"'that's what my dad asked me to ask you guys . . . uh, give me a lawyer,'" constituted "an
unambiguous request for counsel, which should have cut off any further questioning"); *United
States v. Hunter,* 708 F.3d 938, 948 (7th Cir. 2013) ("Given the decisive language and the prior
context of Hunter's request to Detective Karzin, we find that Hunter's request, 'Can you call my
attorney?' was an unambiguous and unequivocal request for counsel"); *United States v.
Wysinger,* 683 F.3d 784, 795-96 (7th Cir. 2012) (the defendant unequivocally invoked his right
to counsel in an exchange with the interrogating officer that began with the defendant's asking
"'I mean, do you think I should have a lawyer? At this point?,'" to which the officer responded
"'If you want an attorney, by all means, get one,'" and the defendant replied "'I mean, but can I
call one now? That's what I'm saying.'"); *Wood v. Ercole,* 644 F.3d 83, 92 (2d Cir. 2011) (the
defendant "unambiguously asserted his right to counsel" by saying "'I think I should get a
lawyer'"); *Yenawine v. Motley,* 402 Fed. Appx. 997, 998 (6th Cir. 2010) (the defendant's request
for counsel was sufficient to trigger *Edwards*'s protection and to require the exclusion of his
inculpatory statement where "(1) the . . . [defendant] was under police interrogation when he
stated, '[M]aybe I should talk to an attorney'; (2) the . . . [defendant] named his attorney and
gave the police officer his attorney's business card; and (3) shortly thereafter, the police
continued questioning the . . . [defendant] and he gave a statement"); *People v. Henderson,* 9
Cal. 5th 1013, 1020, 1023-24, 470 P.3d 71, 77, 79, 266 Cal. Rptr. 3d 365, 372, 374 (2020) (the
defendant's statement, "I . . . uh, want to, speak to an attorney first, because I, I take
responsibility for me, but there's other people that . . . ." was unequivocal and triggered
Edwards' protection: the prosecution's argument that "a reasonable officer could understand
defendant's reference to taking responsibility as an indication that he was willing to continue
speaking to the officers about his own liability notwithstanding his request for counsel" is
untenable: "Defendant clearly said he wanted to talk to a lawyer. Although not required, he went
on to explain why he wanted counsel. Further, his explanation did not create an ambiguity. There
is nothing inconsistent or ambiguous about wanting to speak to an attorney before taking
responsibility, and defendant made clear that he wanted to speak to an attorney 'first.' One can
take responsibility in ways other than giving an uncounseled confession to the police."); *State v.*

Negrete, 630 S.W.3d 460 (Tex. App. 2021) (finding that the defendant made "an unambiguous and unequivocal invocation of his right to counsel" (*id.* at 468) and rejecting the State's arguments that the defendant's "statement, 'I don't want to snitch without a lawyer,' was not an unambiguous invocation of his Fifth Amendment right to counsel because the word 'snitch' is informal or slang and 'it is not exactly clear when a criminal defendant snitches,' thus, making the term 'snitch' itself ambiguous . . . [and f]urther, . . . [that the defendant's] statement only indicated that his 'desire for an attorney [was] condition[ed] on when he snitche[d],' and it was not a blanket request for an attorney" (*id.* at 466)); *People v. Firestine*, 2019 IL App (5th) 180264, 132 N.E.3d 886, 889, 892-93, 433 Ill. Dec. 636, 639, 642-43 (2019) (asked whether he shot his brother in the foot, the defendant responded, 'I don't want to answer that question without my lawyer'; interrogation continued and the defendant made incriminating statements which trial judge suppressed under *Miranda*; on appeal from the suppression order, the State invokes *Connecticut v. Barrett*, *supra*, to argue that, "by using the phrase 'that question,' the defendant unambiguously made only a limited invocation of his right to counsel", but the Appellate Court distinguishes *Barrett* and affirms the suppression order: "Here, unlike in *Barrett*, the defendant's invocation of his right to counsel was not accompanied by an affirmative statement that there were any topics he was willing to discuss. . . . ¶ The defendant refused to answer the first question he was asked about the incident in which his brothers were shot. Under these circumstances, we believe it should have been clear to a reasonable police officer that he did not wish to discuss that incident further without an attorney."); *N.J.O. v. State*, 292 So.3d 491, 495-96 (Fla. App. 2020) (a juvenile respondent's statement, made after he was read the *Miranda* warnings and was given a *Miranda* waiver form to sign, "I don't know what all these legal questions mean, so I want to, like have somebody with me. I'm not trying to be difficult or anything. Like, I just don't know, because you guys word stuff funny sometimes" was sufficient to invoke his right to counsel and require interrogation to stop); *Ballard v. State*, 420 Md. 480, 491, 24 A.3d 96, 102 (2011) (the defendant "unambiguous[ly] and unequivocal[ly] assert[ed] . . . the right to counsel" by stating: "'You mind if I not say no more and just talk to an attorney about this?'"); *People v. Slocum*, 133 A.D.3d 972, 975-76, 20 N.Y.S.3d 440, 444 (N.Y. App. Div., 3d Dep't 2015) (the defendant unequivocally invoked his right to counsel by responding to the officer's question "'if he felt that he should have an attorney or if he wanted to be represented by the Public Defender's office'" by saying "'Yeah, probably.'"); *State v. Rose*, 604 A.2d 24 (Me. 1992) (the defendant was indicted in Maine while incarcerated in an Arizona prison; he transmitted to Maine authorities a written request for trial under the Interstate Agreement on Detainers (see § 28.5.3 *infra*), circling the statement "I request the court to appoint counsel" on the I.A.D. form; a Maine police officer sent to bring the defendant to Maine for trial told the defendant that, once aboard the plane, the officer would advise the defendant of his *Miranda* rights and then, if the defendant wished to talk with the officer, he could; the defendant replied that he might want to talk with a lawyer but would think about it; after being *Mirandized* on the plane, he waived his rights and made inculpatory statements which were admitted against him at trial; the Maine Supreme Court holds that his submission of the written I.A.D. form requesting the appointment of counsel constituted an effective invocation of this Sixth Amendment right and required the suppression of the statements made on the plane; note that although the court's decision was grounded on the Sixth Amendment rule of *Michigan v. Jackson*, which has since been overruled (see § 26.10.3 *infra*), its finding that the defendant effectively invoked his right to counsel should be equally persuasive under *Edwards v. Arizona*). *Cf. State v. Culbreath*, 340 Conn. 167, 263 A.3d 350 (2021) (in *State v. Purcell*, 331 Conn. 318, 321, 203 A.3d 542, 544-45

(2019) "we held . . . that article first, § 8, of the Connecticut constitution provides greater protection for a criminal defendant's *Miranda* rights than the federal constitution. . . . 'In *Davis v. United States*, 512 U.S. 452, 459-60 (1994) . . . , the United States Supreme Court determined that, after a defendant has been informed of his *Miranda* rights, the police officers conducting a custodial interrogation have no obligation to stop and clarify an ambiguous invocation by the defendant of his right to have counsel present. Instead, they must cease interrogation only upon an objectively unambiguous, unequivocal invocation of that right. . . .' . . . In *Purcell*, we held that *Davis'* clear and unequivocal standard fails to satisfy the state constitution and that, 'to adequately safeguard the right against compelled self-incrimination under article first, § 8, of the Connecticut constitution, police officers are required to clarify an ambiguous request for counsel before they can continue the interrogation.' . . . Thus, 'our state constitution requires that, if a suspect makes an equivocal statement that arguably can be construed as a request for counsel, interrogation must cease except for narrow questions designed to clarify the earlier statement and the suspect's desire for counsel.' 340 Conn. at 183, 263 A.3d at 361. Here "defendant . . . invoked his right to counsel approximately three hours . . . [into] the interview, when he asked, '[i]s there anybody I can talk to . . . [l]ike an attorney or something?' The defendant's question about the availability of 'an attorney' or someone else to 'talk to' is precisely the type of conditional and equivocal inquiry that reasonably can be construed as a request for counsel. . . . Accordingly, . . . [Detective Rykowski] had an obligation . . . to stop the interview and to clarify whether the defendant desired the presence of counsel or, alternatively, to terminate the interview altogether. ¶ The state contends that Rykowski complied with *Purcell*'s 'stop and clarify' rule by asking clarifying questions, such as '[i]s that what you want,' and stopping the interview for approximately twenty minutes. We disagree for two reasons. First, although some of Rykowski's responses sought clarification of the defendant's intent to invoke his right to counsel, other responses plainly 'attempted to convince the defendant that it was against his interests not to continue the interview.' . . . Rykowski informed the defendant that, if he had an attorney present, the attorney 'probably won't let me talk to you,' and 'the cards [will] fall the way they will' without the defendant telling the 'story' of 'the why or the who or the what reason.' . . . Furthermore, Rykowski's suggestion that an attorney's financial interest would induce the attorney to advise the defendant, contrary to the defendant's interests, to stop answering questions was entirely inappropriate. We conclude that these statements exceeded the 'limited inquiry permissible after an equivocal request for legal counsel. . . .'") 340 Conn. at 188-90, 263 A.3d at 364-65.); *State v. Gonzalez*, 249 N.J. 612, 619-20, 268 A.3d 329, 333 (2022) ("In the middle of the [police] interview, defendant asked, 'But now what do I do about an attorney and everything?' Rather than seek clarification, the interviewing detective merely advised defendant, 'That is your decision. I can't give you an opinion about anything.' . . . ¶ . . . We conclude that defendant's question about the attorney was an ambiguous invocation of her right to counsel and that, under settled New Jersey law, *see, e.g.*, . . . [*State v. Reed*, 133 N.J. 237, 253, 627 A.2d 630 (1993)], the detective was required to cease questioning and clarify whether defendant was requesting counsel during the interview.").

"[I]f a suspect requests counsel [with the degree of clarity described in the preceding paragraph] at any time during the interview, he is not subject to further questioning until a lawyer has been made available or the suspect himself reinitiates conversation." *Davis v. United States, supra*, 512 U.S. at 458 (dictum). With the sole exception of the situation in which the suspect has "reinitiate[d] conversation," the invocation of the *Miranda* right to counsel "bar[s] police-initiated interrogation unless the accused has counsel with him at the time of questioning" (*Minnick v. Mississippi*, *supra*, 498 U.S. at 153). *See also id.* ("when counsel is requested, interrogation must cease, and officials may not reinitiate interrogation without counsel present, whether or not the accused has consulted with his attorney"); *Martinez v. Cate*, 903 F.3d 982 (9th Cir. 2018) (after Martinez invoked his right to counsel and "[a]fter Detective Navarro told Martinez that he was not sure if his lawyer was available, Detective Navarro stated, '[a]ll I wanted was your side of the story. That's it. OK. So, I'm pretty much done with you then. Um, I guess I don't know another option but to go ahead and book you. OK. Because . . . .' Martinez cut in, '[w]hat am I being booked under?' to which Navarro replied '[y]our [sic] going to be booked for murder because I only got one side of the story. OK.'" (*Id.* at 994.) These statements "constituted the functional equivalent of express questioning" (*id.*) and required the suppression of Martinez's ensuing admissions as a violation of *Edwards*.).

In order to sustain the admissibility of an incriminating statement under the *Edwards* exception for a suspect's reinitiation of discussions with the police, the prosecution must show not only that the defendant took the initiative in resuming the interchange by broaching or specifically requesting further conversation with police officers or prosecuting authorities but also that, in the ensuing interchange, any responses made by the defendant to police interrogation (as defined in § 26.6.2 *supra*) manifested a valid waiver of the rights to remain silent and to have counsel (under the standards described in § 26.8 *supra*). *See Minnick v. Mississippi*, *supra*, 498 U.S. at 156 ("*Edwards* does not foreclose" further police questioning if "the accused . . . initiated the conversation or discussions with the authorities" and if there was "a waiver of Fifth Amendment protections"); *Smith v. Illinois*, *supra*, 469 U.S. at 94-95 ("if the accused invoked his right to counsel, courts may admit his responses to further questioning only on finding that he (a) initiated further discussions with the police, and (b) knowingly and intelligently waived the right he had invoked"); *Oregon v. Bradshaw*, 462 U.S. 1039, 1044 (1983) (plurality opinion) (dictum) ("even if a conversation . . . is initiated by the accused, where reinterrogation follows, the burden remains upon the prosecution to show that subsequent events indicated a waiver of the Fifth Amendment right to have counsel present during the interrogation"); *Rodriguez v. McDonald*, 872 F.3d 908, 924-25 (9th Cir. 2017) ("[B]y suggesting to Mr. Rodriguez that he would be imminently charged with murder but that cooperation would result in more lenient treatment from the court, the probation office, and from the police themselves, the officers 'effectively told [Mr. Rodriguez] he would be penalized if he exercised rights guaranteed to him under the Constitution of the United States.' . . . Because this pressure followed Mr. Rodriguez's invocation of his right to counsel, it constituted 'badgering' in direct violation of *Miranda* and *Edwards*. . . . Particularly in light of Mr. Rodriguez's special vulnerabilities to coercion [due to his young age of 14, Attention Deficit Hyperactivity Disorder, and "borderline" I.Q. of 77], . . . we hold that these coercive police tactics overbore Mr. Rodriguez's will, and that his waiver of his previously invoked right to counsel was not voluntary."); *Benjamin v. State*, 116 So.3d 115, 123 (Miss. 2013) (even if the police officer's post-assertion interactions with the 14-year-old suspect had been initiated by the suspect himself rather than improperly engineered by the officer, the resulting statement nonetheless would have to be suppressed because "we cannot say that the record demonstrates that Benjamin's waiver was made with full awareness of the nature of the right and the consequences of abandoning it": "Benjamin's youth rendered him particularly susceptible to parental pressure" and "[i]t is manifestly apparent that Benjamin conceded to pressure from his mother and to his desire to avoid a night in jail in deciding to waive his rights.").

The Supreme Court has not yet established definitive criteria for the kind of communication from a detained individual to his or her custodians that will satisfy the "initiation" prong of the *Edwards* rule. In *Oregon v. Bradshaw,* the Court split 4-to-4 on whether a defendant's question to officers "'Well, what is going to happen to me now?'" manifested a "willingness and a desire for a generalized discussion about the investigation" or was "merely a necessary inquiry arising out of the incidents of the custodial relationship" that could not "be fairly said to represent a desire on the part of an accused to open up a more generalized discussion relating directly or indirectly to the investigation" (462 U.S. at 1045-46 (plurality opinion)). The confession in *Bradshaw* was held admissible, but only through the concurring vote of Justice Powell, who adopted an analysis that was rejected by all eight other members of the Court. *Compare Martinez v. Cate, supra,* 903 F.3d at 996-97 ("The government argues that Martinez initiated further conversation by asking, '[w]hat am I being booked under?'" . . . ¶ No fairminded jurist could interpret Martinez's statement as a re-initiation of the conversation. For one, the conversation between [Detective] Navarro and Martinez never stopped. Initiate means 'to begin' and no reasonable jurist could review the transcript of the interaction between Detective Navarro and conclude that Martinez *began* the exchange about being booked for murder. . . . ¶ Similarly, Martinez's question 'what did you want to talk to me about?' also came in the same conversation. In every other case where the Supreme Court has held that a defendant initiated the communication with the police, there was some break in questioning."); *Ferguson v. Commonwealth,* 52 Va. App. 324, 663 S.E.2d 505 (2008) (en banc) (a police investigator began a police-station interview of the defendant by requesting permission to search the defendant's car for the proceeds of a burglary; the defendant replied "Nah, I want a lawyer, you know what I'm saying?"; the investigator said, "Okay. But anyway . . . ," read the defendant his *Miranda* rights, and continued: "I'll just tell you what the offense was that we were talking about uh, do you want to go ahead and talk with me?"; the defendant responded: "Uh, my moma [sic] said that if I get in any more trouble I need a lawyer"; the investigator said: "Okay, well, you don't have to talk to me. Let me talk to you now" and told the defendant that the police had a positive identification of the defendant's car leaving the burglary site, so "[i]f you want to go ahead and talk to me about this fine, if you don't, you know you're in trouble right now"; after a few additional questions, the investigator told defendant that he was going to let him "sit here for a few minutes" and that "this concludes the interview," turned off the tape recorder, and went out of the room, leaving the defendant and the police chief – who had some previous acquaintance with the defendant – sitting together in silence; after about 20 minutes, the defendant said either "I messed up" or "This is messed up"; the chief "testified that they then began to discuss . . . [defendant's] family and his job status, and . . . [the chief] told . . . [the defendant] that 'he needed to help his [sic] self'" (*id.* at 332, 663 S.E.2d at 509) ; the chief called the investigator back into the room and read the defendant his *Miranda* rights again before asking whether the defendant would feel more comfortable speaking with the chief than with the investigator; the defendant said he would and proceeded to make incriminating statements; the court holds that the defendant unequivocally invoked his right to counsel ("nothing in . . . [his] first statement indicated that he wanted a lawyer only if the police were going to search his vehicle" (*id.* at 337, 663 S.E.2d at 511), and that the defendant did not thereafter re-initiate conversation with the police: "Any consideration of whether a defendant 're-initiated' the dialogue with police necessarily presumes that police officers have stopped the interrogation upon a defendant's request for counsel. . . . Here . . ., despite . . .[defendant's] invocation of his right to counsel, the interview never ceased." *Id.* at 340, 663 S.E.2d at 512.); *Commonwealth v. Frein*, 651 Pa. 635, 670, 206 A.3d 1049, 1069-70 (2019) (dictum) (holding that the defendant's statements during a post-arrest videotaped interrogation should have been suppressed but finding that their admission into evidence was harmless error: "We reject the Commonwealth's suggestion that Appellant's question to Corporal Clark and Trooper Mulvey as to whether the officers were fathers, and Appellant's subsequent observation that "[t]here was a father that didn't come home [apparently referring to the murder victim]," amounted to an initiation of further conversation with police as contemplated by *Edwards*. First, we note that, unlike *Bradshaw* . . . in the instant case, there was *no break* in questioning once Appellant stated that he did not want to talk about the crimes, or, indeed, at any time during the interview. Rather, Corporal Clark and Trooper Mulvey continued their questioning of Appellant for more than three hours, simply redirecting the subject of the conversation whenever Appellant indicated that he did not want to talk about his crimes or stated that he did not want to provide the police with additional information without first speaking with a lawyer. Without a stop or a break in conversation, we fail to see how there could be a subsequent *reinitiation* of conversation. Further, unlike the officer in *Bradshaw*, Corporal Clark and Trooper Mulvey did not remind Appellant that he had a right not to speak." (emphasis in original)). *But see United States v. Jackson*, 70 F.4th 1005 (7th Cir. 2023) ("Jackson barely took a breath between saying he would rather have a lawyer and then asking: 'What is there more I can do to help myself?' . . . [T]hat question had the legal effect under *Miranda* and *Edwards* of opening the interrogation back up, so . . . ¶ . . . Jackson initiated 'further communication, exchanges, or conversations with the police,'" and "[t]he detective was then free to seek clarity on whether this was a knowing and voluntary waiver." *Id.* at 1011. "Even after the detective several times informed Jackson that he did not have to talk to him, Jackson still said, 'I understand that' and 'of course I'm willing to talk to you." . . . Jackson initiated further conversation and knowingly, intelligently, and voluntarily waived his right to counsel." *Id.* at 1012.).

In applying the "initiation" requirement, the lower courts have found waivers to be invalid when the police prompted or stimulated the suspect's initiation of communications by, for example, reciting incriminating evidence in detail (*see, e.g., Wainwright v. State*, 504 A.2d 1096 (Del. 1986); *Koza v. State,* 718 P.2d 671 (Nev. 1986)), or informing the suspect that his or her accomplices have given confessions incriminating him or her (*see, e.g., State v. Quinn*, 64 Md. App. 668, 498 A.2d 676 (1985)), or telling the suspect about further investigation that police officers are conducting to gather incriminating evidence (*State v. McKnight*, 131 Hawai'i 379, 393-34, 319 P.3d 298, 312-13 (2013) (officer told the defendant "that they planned to execute a search warrant on his residence")). *Cf. United States v. Rambo*, 365 F.3d 906, 910-11 (10th Cir. 2004), summarized in § 26.9.2, third paragraph, *supra.*

D. *Other Constitutional, Common-Law, and Statutory Bases for Suppressing Statements*

26.10. *Suppression under the Sixth Amendment Right to Counsel: The* Massiah *Principle*

In *Massiah v. United States*, 377 U.S. 201 (1964), the Court held that the Sixth Amendment right to counsel required the exclusion of an incriminating statement made by a defendant to an electronically bugged police undercover informer in the absence of the defendant's lawyer after indictment. As construed in subsequent cases, the *Massiah* rule reaches all statements "'deliberately elicited'" by any overt or covert government agent from an accused who neither has a lawyer present nor has waived the right to have a lawyer present at any time after the "initiation of adversary . . . proceedings" (*United States v. Henry*, 447 U.S. 264, 273-74 n.11 (1980)). *See Maine v. Moulton,* 474 U.S. 159, 171-76 (1986); *Kuhlmann v. Wilson,* 477 U.S. 436, 456-59 (1986) (dictum); *Kansas v. Ventris,* 556 U.S. 586, 590 (2009) (dictum); *see also State v. Marshall*, 882 N.W.2d 68, 81-106 (Iowa 2016) (a thoroughgoing analysis of all elements of the *Massiah* doctrine, based on an extensive collection of caselaw); *Blakeney v. State*, 236 So.3d 11, 24-26 (Miss. 2017).

Unlike the *Miranda* doctrine (see § 26.6.1 *supra*), the *Massiah* principle is not limited to situations in which the accused is in custody. *Rhode Island v. Innis,* 446 U.S. 291, 300 n.4 (1980) (dictum); *United States v. Henry, supra*, 447 U.S. at 273-74 & n.11 (dictum); *Massiah, supra*, 377 U.S. at 206. Massiah himself was at large on bond when he made his incriminating statement, and the circumstances of its making were in no way coercive. *See id.* at 202-03.

The central issues in applying *Massiah* are whether the defendant's statement was made at a "critical stage" of the proceedings (§ 26.10.1 *infra*), whether it was "deliberately elicited" (§ 26.10.2 *infra*), and by a government actor (*id.*; *compare United States v. Chandler*, 56 F.4th 27 (2d Cir. 2022)), and in cases in which the prosecution claims that the defendant waived the right to counsel, whether that waiver was valid (§ 26.10.3 *infra*).

26.10.1. *"Critical Stages" of the Proceedings*

The *Massiah* doctrine applies to "any interrogation occurring after the first formal charging proceeding, the point at which the Sixth Amendment right to counsel initially attaches" (*Moran v. Burbine,* 475 U.S. 412, 428 (1986) (dictum); *see also id.* at 429-32). "[O]nce the adversary judicial process has been initiated, the Sixth Amendment guarantees a defendant the right to have counsel present at all 'critical' stages of the criminal proceedings," and "[i]nterrogation by the State is such a stage" (*Montejo v. Louisiana*, 556 U.S. 778, 786 (2009) (dictum)). *See also Brewer v. Williams,* 430 U.S. 387, 398 (1977) ("a person is entitled to the help of a lawyer at or after the time that judicial proceedings have been initiated against him – 'whether by way of formal charge, preliminary hearing, indictment, information or arraignment'"); *Rothgery v. Gillespie County, Texas*, 554 U.S. 191, 194 (2008) ("the right to counsel guaranteed by the Sixth Amendment applies at the first appearance before a judicial officer at which a defendant is told of the formal accusation against him and restrictions are imposed on his liberty"); *id.* at 198, 213; § 11.5.1 *supra*. *Compare Gerstein v. Pugh,* 420 U.S. 103, 122-25 (1975) (when the "state system[ ] of criminal procedure" (*id.* at 123) assigns only a "limited function and . . . nonadversary character" (*id.* at 122) to probable cause determinations, such determinations are not "critical stages" for purposes of the right to counsel).

The Supreme Court has rejected the proposition that *Massiah* applies prior to the commencement of adversary proceedings on a particular charge if the suspect is already represented by an attorney in connection with other charges on which adversary proceedings have commenced. *See Texas v. Cobb,* 532 U.S. 162, 168 (2001) ("a defendant's statements regarding offenses for which he ha[s] not been charged . . . [are] admissible notwithstanding the [prior] attachment of his Sixth Amendment right to counsel on other charged offenses," even if those other charges are "'factually related'"; the attachment of the right to counsel on one charge will carry over to other offenses only when those offenses, whether or not formally charged, "would be considered the same offense [as the charged offense] under the . . . test [of *Blockburger v. United States*, 284 U.S. 299 (1932), discussed in § 20.8.2.2 *supra*]"); *McNeil v. Wisconsin*, 501 U.S. 171, 175-76 (1991); *Moran v. Burbine, supra*, 475 U.S. at 428-32; *see also Maine v. Moulton, supra*, 474 U.S. at 180 n.16 (dictum); *Honeycutt v. Donat*, 535 Fed. Appx. 624, 629 (9th Cir. 2013). This is the rule in most jurisdictions. *See, e.g., State v. Sparklin*, 296 Or. 85, 672 P.2d 1182 (1983); *State v. Clawson*, 270 S.E.2d 659 (W. Va. 1980). *Cf. Rubalcado v. State*, 424 S.W.3d 560, 571-73 (Tex. Crim. App. 2014) (applying the rule of *Texas v. Cobb* but nonetheless concluding that the attachment of the right to counsel in a case in one county required the suppression of statements a police agent elicited from the defendant about uncharged conduct in another county because those statements "incriminate[d] [the] defendant with regard to [the] two separate offenses simultaneously" and the state ultimately used the statements against the defendant at trial in the case in which the right to counsel had already attached). Nevertheless, in States in which the courts have not yet ruled on the protections afforded by the state constitutional right to counsel in this context, counsel should urge them to adopt a state constitutional rule that an accused has the right to have counsel present during interrogation once the accused is represented by an attorney, regardless of whether that representation is on the charges about which the suspect is being interrogated or on other charges. *See, e.g., People v. Cohen*, 90 N.Y.2d 632, 638-39 & n.*, 687 N.E.2d 1313, 1316-17 & n.*, 665 N.Y.S.2d 30, 33-34 & n.* (1997) (the attachment of the state constitutional right to counsel on one charge will bar questioning on another, not-yet-charged offense if "the two criminal matters are so closely related transactionally, or in space or time, that questioning on the unrepresented matter would all but inevitably elicit incriminating responses regarding the matter in which there had been an entry of counsel" or if the "defendant is in custody on the charge upon which the right to counsel has indelibly attached," regardless of whether the new matter is "related or unrelated" to the charge for which the defendant is in custody); and see generally § 17.11 *supra*.

In *Escobedo v. Illinois*, 378 U.S. 478 (1964), the Court indicated that a suspect's retention of counsel before interrogation can activate the Sixth Amendment right to counsel during pre-arraignment interrogation, at least when the suspect explicitly requests the presence of counsel during interrogation. Later cases have, however, reinterpreted *Escobedo* as based on the Fifth Amendment privilege against self-incrimination rather than the Sixth Amendment (*see Moran v. Burbine, supra*, 475 U.S. at 428-31; *United States v. Gouveia*, 467 U.S. 180, 188 n.5 (1984)), and have rejected the argument that pre-arraignment retention of an attorney alters the general rule that Sixth Amendment protections commence at the first formal charging proceeding (*Moran v. Burbine, supra*, 475 U.S. at 429-32). Counsel can urge the state courts to adopt a more protective rule on state constitutional grounds. *See, e.g., People v. Grice*, 100 N.Y.2d 318, 321, 794 N.E.2d 9, 10-11, 763 N.Y.S.2d 227, 229 (2003) ("A suspect's [state constitutional] right to counsel can . . . attach before an action is commenced when a person in custody requests to speak to an attorney or when an attorney who is retained to represent the suspect enters the matter under investigation"); *People v. Houston*, 42 Cal. 3d 595, 724 P.2d 1166, 230 Cal. Rptr. 141 (1986) (abrogated by a subsequent initiative constitutional amendment) (rejecting *Moran v. Burbine* on state constitutional grounds and holding that the right to counsel protects a suspect's relationship with retained counsel even earlier than the first formal charging proceeding); *State v. Stoddard,* 206 Conn. 157, 537 A.2d 446 (1988) (rejecting *Moran v. Burbine* on state constitutional grounds and construing the due process clause of the state constitution to require that "a suspect . . . be informed promptly of timely efforts by counsel to render pertinent legal assistance [and that] . . . [a]rmed with that information, the suspect . . . be permitted to choose whether he wishes to speak with counsel, in which event interrogation must cease" (206 Conn. at 166-67, 537 A.2d at 452)); and see generally § 17.11 *supra.*

26.10.2. *Statements "Deliberately Elicited" by the Government*

The *Massiah* protections apply to ordinary police interrogation (*see Brewer v. Williams,* 430 U.S. 387 (1977); *Montejo v. Louisiana,* 556 U.S. 778, 786-87 (2009) (dictum)), to court-ordered psychiatric examinations of the defendant whose products are used to incriminate him or her (*Estelle v. Smith,* 451 U.S. 454, 469-71 & n.14 (1981); *Powell v. Texas,* 492 U.S. 680 (1989) (per curiam); *People v. Guevara,* 37 N.Y.3d 1014, 174 N.E.3d 1240, 152 N.Y.S.3d 866 (2021)), to conversations between the defendant and police spies or state-activated jailhouse snitches (*United States v. Henry,* 447 U.S. 264 (1980)), and to similar "investigatory techniques that are the equivalent of police interrogation" (*Kuhlmann v. Wilson,* 477 U.S. 436, 459 (1986) (dictum)). *See also, e.g., Randolph v. People,* 380 F.3d 1133, 1138 (9th Cir. 2004) ("if the State places a cooperating informant in a jail cell with a defendant whose right to counsel has attached, and if the informant then makes a successful effort to stimulate a conversation with the defendant about the crime charged, the State thereby violates the defendant's Sixth Amendment rights under *Massiah*"); *State v. Ashby,* 336 Conn. 452, 483-84, 247 A.3d 521, 541-42 (2020) (finding a Sixth Amendment violation after an exhaustive canvass of the *Massiah* caselaw: ("[Detective] Weaver met with Pladsen[,] . . . [who was jailed with the defendant, after Pladsen had initiated contact by writing to Weaver that Pladsen had information about the defendant that would be useful to Weaver. Weaver] expressed an interest in obtaining verifiable evidence of incriminating statements from this particular defendant regarding this particular case. Although there was no 'agreement,' 'contract,' 'mutual understanding,' or 'meeting of the minds,' the two expressly discussed Pladsen's desire for a benefit in exchange for his cooperation in the present case, and, in fact, the state actually provided such a benefit to Pladsen after the desired evidence was produced. Although the record does not evince any particular 'plan' or 'instruction,' Weaver knew from the initial letter that Pladsen had strong incentives to cooperate as the result of his incarceration and consecutive sentences, had already gained the defendant's trust, and was in a uniquely strong position to question the defendant at length. After Weaver told Pladsen that he was interested in hearing new evidence relating to the victim's death – by, for example, suggesting the use of a wire – additional control would have been superfluous. We conclude that the state either knew or should have known that such a conversation was likely to end in further deliberate elicitation"); *United States v. Anderson,* 523 F.2d 1192 (5th Cir. 1975) (the defendant was a medical doctor indicted for possession of amphetamines with intent to distribute; a week before trial, Drug Enforcement Administration agents sent a paid informer to induce him to give her illegal drug prescriptions; he did, and her testimony was admitted at the trial of the amphetamines charges for the purpose of showing the defendant's specific intent; the Court of Appeals holds that this testimony violated *Massiah*); *Commonwealth v. Hilton,* 443 Mass. 597, 603-04, 614-15, 823 N.E.2d 383, 391, 398-99 (2005) ("for purposes of a Sixth Amendment analysis, court officer Marrin ["whose job responsibilities included the transportation of detainees between the holding cells and the court room, maintaining order in the court room, and providing security for the judges and the public" and who conversed with the defendant as "Marrin was escorting the defendant back to the holding area"] must be viewed as an agent of law enforcement"; "[o]nce the Sixth Amendment right to counsel has attached, the *Massiah* line of cases . . . prohibits '*government efforts* to elicit information from the accused' . . . , including interrogation by '*the government* or someone acting on its behalf'"; references in the caselaw to "the Sixth Amendment as prohibiting questioning by 'the police' and their agents . . . do not mean that the Sixth Amendment's protections are implicated only by actions involving the 'police,' but merely operate to describe the most common fact pattern raised by such cases."); *State v. Oliveira*, 961 A.2d 299, 310-11 (R.I. 2008) (a child protective services investigator was an "agent of the state" for Sixth Amendment purposes, even though she "did not interview defendant at the direct behest of the police or prosecution," because the agency's "protocol required that she work cooperatively with law enforcement personnel," she had already "exchanged information" with the police about the case, and she acknowledged that "one of her purposes in interviewing defendant was to 'add to the evidence'"); *People v. Desjardins*, 196 A.D.3d 1177, 1178, 150 N.Y.S.3d 488, 490 (N.Y. App. Div., 4th Dep't 2021) ("[a]lthough social workers are not automatically considered agents of the police, they may be so considered under certain circumstances," and "we conclude that the CPS [Child Protective Services] caseworker here had a 'cooperative working arrangement' with police such that she was acting as an agent of the police when she interviewed defendant and relayed his incriminatory statements": "the CPS caseworker . . . was aware that defendant was being held on criminal charges and that he was represented by counsel. . . . [S]he worked on a multidisciplinary task force composed of social services and law enforcement agencies, through which she received training on interviewing individuals accused of committing sexual offenses. Additionally, in keeping with task force protocol directing her to report to law enforcement any inculpatory statements made during CPS interviews, the CPS caseworker called the investigating officer immediately following the interview with defendant and promptly went to his office to report defendant's statements."); *Rubalcado v. State*, 424 S.W.3d 560, 574-76 (Tex. Crim. App. 2014) (the complaining witness was a "government agent" for Sixth Amendment purposes because the "police encouraged [her] to call appellant for the purpose of eliciting a confession" and "supplied [her] with the recording equipment, and an officer was present during those calls").

When a police officer, informer, or agent "stimulate[s]" conversations with the defendant for the purpose of "elicit[ing] [incriminating] information," this "'indirect and surreptitious interrogatio[n]'" comes within *Massiah*'s strictures against deliberately eliciting incriminating statements (*United States v. Henry, supra*, 447 U.S. at 273). Similarly, if the agent engages the defendant "in active conversation about [his or her] . . . upcoming trial [in a manner that is] . . . certain to elicit" incriminating statements, the agent's "mere[ ] participat[ion] in this conversation [will be deemed] . . . 'the functional equivalent of interrogation'" in violation of *Massiah* (*Maine v. Moulton, supra*, 474 U.S. at 177 n.13; *Kuhlmann v. Wilson, supra*, 477 U.S. at 459 (dictum)). *See also, e.g., Fellers v. United States*, 540 U.S. 519, 524-25 (2004) (the lower court "erred in holding that the absence of an 'interrogation' foreclosed petitioner's [Sixth Amendment] claim": "the officers in this case 'deliberately elicited' information from petitioner" by informing him, upon "arriving at petitioner's house, . . . that their purpose in coming was to discuss his involvement in the distribution of methamphetamine and his association with certain co-conspirators" as well as to arrest him in connection with his indictment on a methamphetamine conspiracy charge; the Sixth Amendment right to counsel applies in this situation even though the interchange between the petitioner and the arresting officers was no longer than 15 minutes and the petitioner apparently made his inculpatory admissions immediately upon being advised of the arresting officers' purpose.); *Ayers v. Hudson*, 623 F.3d 301, 311-12 (6th Cir. 2010) ("agency in the *Massiah* context [is not limited] to cases where the State gave the informant instructions to obtain evidence from a defendant"; "[t]o hold otherwise would allow the State to accomplish 'with a wink and a nod' what it cannot do overtly").

On the other hand, there is no *Massiah* violation if the police plant a stool pigeon in an accused's jail cell as a cellmate but the "police and their informant" take no additional "action, beyond merely listening, that [is] . . . designed deliberately to elicit incriminating remarks" (*Kuhlmann v. Wilson, supra*, 477 U.S. at 459). "[A] defendant does not make out a violation of [*Massiah*] . . . simply by showing that an informant, either through prior arrangement or voluntarily, reported his incriminating statements to the police." *Kuhlmann v. Wilson, supra*, 477 U.S. at 459.

If a civilian informer deliberately elicits statements from an accused within the foregoing principles, the courts will find a *Massiah* violation even though the government agents who employed the informer instructed him or her to refrain from questioning the accused (*United States v. Henry, supra*, 447 U.S. at 268, 271) or to refrain from inducing the suspect to make incriminating statements (*Maine v. Moulton, supra*, 474 U.S. at 177 n.14). *Compare Kulhmann v. Wilson, supra*, 477 U.S. at 460-61 (finding no *Massiah* violation when the informant not only was instructed to refrain from questioning or eliciting incriminating statements but "followed those instructions").

26.10.3. *Waiver*

"[T]he Sixth Amendment right to counsel may be waived by a defendant, so long as relinquishment of the right is voluntary, knowing, and intelligent." *Montejo v. Louisiana*, 556 U.S. 778, 786 (2009) (citing, *inter alia, Johnson v. Zerbst*, 304 U.S. 458, 464 (1938)). *See also, e.g., Carnley v. Cochran*, 369 U.S. 506, 513-16 (1962); *Montejo, supra*, 556 U.S. at 797-98 (remanding so that Montejo can "press any claim he might have that his Sixth Amendment waiver was not knowing and voluntary, *e.g.*, his argument that the waiver was invalid because it was based on misrepresentations by police as to whether he had been appointed a lawyer"). It is "incumbent upon the State to prove 'an intentional relinquishment or abandonment of a known right or privilege' . . . [and] courts [assessing "an alleged waiver of the right to counsel" must] indulge in every reasonable presumption against waiver" (*Brewer v. Williams*, 430 U.S. 387, 404 (1977)). *See also Satterwhite v. Texas*, 486 U.S. 249, 256 (1988).

When the defendant's incriminating statement was made to any sort of a police spy, there can obviously be no waiver: The fact that the accused is unaware s/he is making a statement for government consumption suffices to exclude the possibility of a waiver as defined by *Johnson v. Zerbst, supra*, 304 U.S. at 464: – that is, an "intentional relinquishment or abandonment of a known right or privilege." When the statement was made to a person whom the defendant knew to be a government agent, the test of a valid waiver of the right to counsel is basically similar in the Sixth Amendment context of *Massiah* and in the Fifth Amendment context of *Miranda*. *See*

Patterson v. Illinois, 487 U.S. 285 (1988); *Montejo v. Louisiana, supra,* 556 U.S. at 786, 794-95. The principles and precedents discussed in § 26.8 *supra* are generally controlling. *See, e.g., Brewer v. Williams, supra,* 430 U.S. at 401-06. For example, a waiver made after administration of the ordinary *Miranda* warnings will "typically" be effective (*Montejo v. Louisiana, supra,* 556 U.S. at 786, 794-95; *Patterson v. Illinois, supra,* 487 U.S. at 300). However, because the Sixth Amendment imposes on "the prosecutor and the police . . . an affirmative obligation not to act in a manner that circumvents and thereby dilutes the protection afforded by the right to counsel" (*Maine v. Moulton, supra,* 474 U.S. at 171), some waivers that would be valid in the *Miranda* setting are not valid in the *Massiah* setting (*see Patterson v. Illinois, supra,* 487 U.S. at 297 n.9 (dictum) ("we have permitted a *Miranda* waiver to stand where a suspect was not told that his lawyer was trying to reach him during questioning [citing *Moran v. Burbine,* 475 U.S. 412 (1986)]; in the Sixth Amendment context, this waiver would not be valid"); *cf. Powell v. Texas,* 492 U.S. 680 (1989) (per curiam) (holding, in the context of a court-ordered pretrial psychiatric examination, that a determination that "the defendant waived his Fifth Amendment privilege by raising a mental-status defense [at trial] . . . [does] not suffice to resolve the defendant's separate Sixth Amendment claim" (*id.* at 685), and that the lower court erred by "conflat[ing] . . . the Fifth and Sixth Amendment analyses" (*id.* at 683) and by treating the defendant's waiver of his Fifth Amendment right to remain silent as also waiving the Sixth Amendment right to counsel)).

In *Michigan v. Jackson,* 475 U.S. 625 (1986), the Supreme Court established a now-defunct "prophylactic rule that once a criminal defendant invokes his Sixth Amendment right to counsel, a subsequent waiver of that right – even if voluntary, knowing, and intelligent under traditional standards – is presumed invalid if secured pursuant to police-initiated conversation" (*Michigan v. Harvey,* 494 U.S. 344, 345-46 (1990)). In *Montejo v. Louisiana, supra,* the Court overruled *Jackson* and eliminated this "prophylactic rule," explaining that even "after arraignment, when Sixth Amendment rights have attached," a defendant is adequately protected by the "three layers of prophylaxis" that apply both before and after arraignment: "Under *Miranda*'s prophylactic protection of the right against compelled self-incrimination, any suspect subject to custodial interrogation has the right to have a lawyer present if he so requests, and to be advised of that right. 384 U.S., at 474. Under *Edwards* [*v. Arizona*]'[s] prophylactic protection of the *Miranda* right, once such a defendant 'has invoked his right to have counsel present,' interrogation must stop. 451 U.S. [477], at 484 [(1981)]. And under *Minnick* [*v. Mississippi*]'s prophylactic protection of the *Edwards* right, no subsequent interrogation may take place until counsel is present, 'whether or not the accused has consulted with his attorney.' 498 U.S. [146], at 153 [(1990)]." (*Montejo, supra,* 556 U.S. at 794-95.) State courts are free to retain the *Jackson* rule as a matter of state constitutional law. *See, e.g., State v. Bevel,* 231 W. Va. 346, 348, 745 S.E.2d 237, 239 (2013) ("we decline to adopt *Montejo* and find that the right to counsel that has been recognized in this state for more than a quarter century continues to be guaranteed by article III, section 14 of the West Virginia Constitution"); and see generally § 17.11 *supra.*

26.11. *Statements Obtained During a Period of Unnecessary Delay Following Arrest*

In *McNabb v. United States,* 318 U.S. 332 (1943), and *Mallory v. United States,* 354 U.S. 449 (1957), the Supreme Court exercised its supervisory powers over the federal courts to enforce prompt-arraignment requirements (currently contained in Federal Rule of Criminal Procedure 5(a)) by excluding confessions obtained from arrested persons during a period of unlawful delay in bringing them before a judicial officer for a determination of probable cause. As a result of subsequent legislative enactments described in detail in *Corley v. United States*, 556 U.S. 303 (2009), the "*McNabb-Mallory* rule" has been modified to provide a basis for excluding confessions obtained during "unreasonable or unnecessary" delays of more than six hours before preliminary arraignment in federal prosecutions (*Corley*, 556 U.S at 322). *See, e.g., United States v. Thompson*, 772 F.3d 752, 762-63 (3d Cir. 2014) ("Thompson's confession[,] [which] came considerably after the six-hour period had run," is suppressed under the *McNabb-Mallory* rule because "the government delayed Thompson's arraignment so that they could continue to persuade him to cooperate," and the court "hold[s] that pursuit of cooperation is not a reasonable excuse for delay in presentment"); *United States v. Pimental*, 755 F.3d 1095, 1101, 1104 (9th Cir. 2014) (suppressing "incriminating statements that Torres Pimental made to Agent Aradanas on Sunday morning, about forty-eight hours after his Friday morning arrest, and before he was presented to a magistrate judge on Tuesday," because "[i]t is undisputed that Torres Pimental's incriminating statements . . . were made more than six hours after his . . . arrest and before his . . . initial appearance," and this "delay was not a result of the distance to be traveled to the nearest available magistrate holding a presentment calendar that Friday," and the "delay in presenting Torres Pimental [also] does not fall within" other "'reasonable delays apart from transportation, distance, and the availability of a magistrate'").

In most States the criminal code contains a provision requiring prompt delivery of a newly arrested defendant to court for arraignment. Such provisions supply a predicate for a state-law exclusionary rule analogous to the *McNabb-Mallory* rule. *See generally* Romualdo P. Eclavea, Annot., *Admissibility of Confession or Other Statement Made by Defendant as Affected by Delay in Arraignment – Modern State Cases*, 28 A.L.R.4th 1121 (1984 & Supp.).

Arguably, the decision in *Gerstein v. Pugh*, 420 U.S. 103 (1975), lays a federal constitutional foundation for something akin to the *McNabb-Mallory* exclusionary rule in state prosecutions. As explained in § 11.2 *supra*, *Gerstein* establishes a Fourth Amendment right to a prompt judicial determination of probable cause following a warrantless arrest. *See, e.g., Manuel v. City of Joliet, Ill.*, 580 U.S. 357 (2017); *Fisher v. Washington Metropolitan Area Transit Authority*, 690 F.2d 1133, 1140 (4th Cir. 1982); *Lively v. Cullinane,* 451 F. Supp. 1000, 1004-05 (D. D.C. 1978). Accordingly, when the police hold a defendant beyond the period prescribed by *County of Riverside v. McLaughlin*, 500 U.S. 44 (1991), as the limit of permissible detention without a probable-cause determination (see § 11.2 *supra*), counsel can argue that the Fourth Amendment requires the suppression of any statements made by the defendant during the unlawfully protracted custody. *See, e.g., State v. Huddleston*, 924 S.W.2d 666, 675-76 (Tenn. 1996) (suppressing a statement obtained by the police during a 72-hour period in which the defendant was held without a judicial determination of probable cause in violation of *Gerstein* and *County of Riverside v. McLaughlin*); *Norris v. Lester*, 545 Fed. Appx. 320, 321, 327 (6th Cir. 2013) ("appellate counsel was ineffective for failing to argue [under *County of Riverside v. McLaughlin*] that [Norris'] confession was obtained after the violation of his constitutional right to a prompt probable-cause determination"). The general Fourth Amendment rule excluding statements made in confinement following an unconstitutional arrest (§ 26.15 *infra*) supports this result. However, as the Supreme Court observed in *Powell v. Nevada*, 511 U.S. 79, 85 n.* (1994), the Court has not yet ruled on the specific question whether "a suppression remedy applies" to a *Gerstein* violation of "failure to obtain authorization from a magistrate for a significant period of pretrial detention."

26.12. *State Common-law Doctrines Requiring the Suppression of Statements as Involuntary*

In addition to the federal constitutional doctrine excluding coerced confessions, see §§ 26.2-26.4.7 *supra,* there are state common-law doctrines that may exclude a confession on the ground that it is "involuntary." *See Colorado v. Connelly,* 479 U.S. 157, 167 (1986); *Rogers v. Richmond,* 365 U.S. 534, 540-44 (1961); *State v. Kelly,* 61 N.J. 283, 290-93, 294 A.2d 41, 45-46 (1972). Although the issue under the federal Constitution (and many state constitutional self-incrimination and due process clauses) is whether the defendant's will was overborne, the issue under the state's common law is likely to be whether the confession was made in circumstances that render it untrustworthy or unreliable.

In addition, the common-law doctrine affords a basis for suppressing statements coerced by private citizens. Whereas coercive behavior by private citizens cannot supply the "state action" necessary for a due process violation (*see Colorado v. Connelly, supra*, 479 U.S. at 165-67), it may render a defendant's statement unreliable and thus inadmissible under state common law (*see, e.g., State v. Kelly, supra*, 61 N.J. at 292-94, 294 A.2d at 46-47 (holding a statement coerced by a private security guard inadmissible under state law because it was unreliable although not unconstitutionally involuntary)).

The substantive details and procedural aspects of the common-law doctrine of involuntariness vary considerably among jurisdictions, and counsel must consult local statutes and caselaw. In a number of jurisdictions, for example, the prosecutor must lay a foundation for the introduction of any statement of the defendant by showing that it was made "without the slightest hope of benefit" and "without the remotest fear of injury." *See, e.g., State v. Ritter*, 268 Ga. 108, 109-10, 485 S.E.2d 492, 494 (1997) ("Under Georgia law, only voluntary incriminating statements are admissible against the accused at trial. OCGA § 24–3–50. When not made freely and voluntarily, a confession is presumed to be legally false and can not be the underlying basis of a conviction. . . . To make a confession admissible, it must have been made voluntarily, i.e., 'without being induced by another by the slightest hope of benefit or remotest fear of injury.' OCGA § 24–3–50. . . . A reward of lighter punishment is generally the 'hope of benefit' to which OCGA § 24–3–50 refers. . . . The State bears the burden of demonstrating the voluntariness of a confession by a preponderance of the evidence."); *State v. Crank*, 105 Utah 332, 142 P.2d 178, 184-85 (1943) ("When the state seeks to put the confession before the jury it must establish its competency to the court. To do this it must show that the confession was given by the accused as his voluntary act; as an expression of his independent and free will, uninfluenced by fear of punishment or by hope of reward; that it was not induced or influenced by any advantages or benefits that might accrue to him or those near or dear to him, nor was it given to lighten any penalties or punishments the law might impose on him if tried and convicted without confessing; and that it was not giver [*sic* in 142 P.2d at 184; spelled correctly as "given" in 105 Utah at 347] as a result of a desire to escape or avoid any misery, threats, acts, or conduct of any other person, having it in their power, or whom he believed had it in their power, to inflict upon him, or upon those whom it was his duty or privilege to protect.").

In cases in which the facts provide defense counsel with a viable state common-law challenge to a defendant's statement, counsel should ordinarily attempt to litigate that claim in a pretrial hearing even if the normal practice is to raise the issue by an evidentiary objection at trial. A mid-trial ruling excluding the statement as unreliable will come too late to prevent the trier of fact from hearing the contents of the statement in a bench trial; and even in a jury trial there is a risk of the jurors' getting wind that the question being litigated while they are sent out to wait involves a confession by the defendant. Accordingly, in jurisdictions that permit motions *in limine,* counsel will usually want to raise the common-law contention as an *in limine* matter and, if the statement is excluded, counsel should consider moving to recuse the motions judge from sitting as fact-finder at a bench trial. See §§ 17.5, 22.5 *supra.* If the jurisdiction is one in which the court may entertain or decline to entertain motions *in limine* at its discretion, counsel will increase the likelihood of obtaining a pretrial adjudication of the common-law ground by joining it with a constitutional ground (see §§ 26.2-26.11 *supra* and §§ 26.15-26.16 *infra*) on which pretrial suppression motions are authorized by statute or court rule or which are customarily litigated on pretrial motions *in limine* under local practice. Since the facts bearing on the common-law and constitutional grounds will invariably overlap, counsel can present strong arguments of judicial convenience for hearing the two (or more) claims at the same time. (An exception to this strategy is the situation in which the suppression hearing will be conducted by a pro-prosecution judge and there is a realistic prospect that the trial judge will be more defense-friendly.)

26.13. *Statements Obtained by Eavesdropping on a Conversation Between the Defendant and Defense Counsel*

The Supreme Court has forbidden prosecutorial use of statements obtained by government agents through electronic eavesdropping on conversations between an accused and his or her lawyer. *Black v. United States,* 385 U.S. 26 (1966) (per curiam); *O'Brien v. United States,* 386 U.S. 345 (1967) (per curiam); *Roberts v. United States,* 389 U.S. 18 (1967) (per curiam); *see also Hoffa v. United States,* 385 U.S. 293, 306-09 (1966) (dictum). The lower courts also have steadfastly excluded evidence produced by eavesdropping that intrudes upon attorney-client communications. *See, e.g., State v. Beaupre,* 123 N.H. 155, 459 A.2d 233 (1983) (an officer was in the room with the suspect while he telephoned his attorney); *State v. Sugar,* 84 N.J. 1, 417 A.2d 474 (1980) (the police used an electronic device to listen in on a conversation between the suspect and counsel in an interrogation room). *See also State v. Lenarz,* 301 Conn. 417, 425, 22 A.3d 536, 542 (2011) (holding that a prosecution had to be dismissed because the contents of the defendant's computer, seized by police executing a valid search warrant in the course of their investigations and later transmitted to the forensics lab and the prosecutor, contained extensive information about defense strategy that was protected by attorney-client privilege: "[W]e conclude generally that prejudice may be presumed when the prosecutor has invaded the attorney-client privilege by reading privileged materials containing trial strategy, regardless of whether the invasion of the attorney-client privilege was intentional."); *Matter of Neary,* 84 N.E.3d 1194, 1197 (Ind. 2017) (imposing disciplinary sanctions for professional misconduct upon a prosecutor who monitored audio and video feeds of a stationhouse interview between one arrestee and his attorney and also viewed the DVD recording of another arrestee's discussions with defense counsel during a "break" in a negotiated statement-taking session; "the constitutional imperative of honoring and protecting the confidentiality of a defendant's communications with counsel is a principle '[w]e would have hoped . . . too obvious to mention.'"); *United States v. Spaeth*, 69 F.4th 1190, 1192 (10th Cir. 2023) (condemning the conduct of a United States Attorney's office that, in investigating the smuggling of drugs into a federal pretrial detention facility, arranged to have phone calls between detainees and their attorneys routinely recorded – although the court holds that this misconduct provides no basis for setting aside a defendant's voluntary and adequately counseled guilty plea).

Although the rule is clear, its doctrinal underpinnings are murky. In *Weatherford v. Bursey,* 429 U.S. 545 (1977), the Court characterized its *Black* and *O'Brien* decisions as grounded upon the Fourth Amendment, but in *United States v. Morrison,* 449 U.S. 361, 364-65 (1981) (dictum), it treated them as based upon the Sixth Amendment right to counsel. Later decisions treat *Weatherford* itself as a Sixth Amendment case. *See, e.g., State v. Robinson*, 209 A.3d 25 (Del. 2019) (finding a Sixth Amendment violation where a prosecution investigator, instructed by prosecutors to search the defendant's jail cell for evidence that defense counsel had violated a protective order by informing the defendant of the identity of prosecution witnesses, seized documents contained in numerous envelopes bearing defense counsel's letterhead, which were then reviewed before trial by a paralegal on the prosecution team); *State v. Bain*, 292 Neb. 398, 872 N.W.2d 777 (2016) (finding a Sixth Amendment violation where prosecutors, in reviewing discovery materials, were unintentionally exposed to documents containing attorney client-communications that revealed defense trial strategy; the opinion canvasses a wide range of post-*Weatherford* caselaw); *Schillinger v. Haworth*, 70 F.3d 1132 (10th Cir. 1995) (finding a Sixth Amendment violation where, at the insistence of the sheriff, a deputy was present in a courtroom during several sessions in which defense counsel prepared the defendant to testify). The Sixth Amendment analysis is complicated further by the subsequent holding in *Moran v. Burbine,* 475 U.S. 412 (1986), that the Sixth Amendment does not protect the attorney-client relationship prior to the attachment of the right to counsel at the first formal charging proceeding.

In this unsettled state of the law, counsel is advised to advance alternative grounds for any motion to suppress statements obtained by police eavesdropping on attorney-client conversations. Counsel should urge that the statements be suppressed under the Fourth Amendment (*see Weatherford v. Bursey, supra; Gennusa v. Canova,* 748 F.3d 1103, 1112-13 (11th Cir. 2014)); the Sixth Amendment (*see United States v. Morrison, supra*); state constitutional protections of the right to counsel (*see, e.g., People v. Grice*, 100 N.Y.2d 318, 321, 794 N.E.2d 9, 10-11, 763 N.Y.S.2d 227, 229 (2003), summarized in § 26.10.1 concluding paragraph *supra*); state constitutional protections against unreasonable searches and seizures (§ 25.2.2 *supra*); the statutory or common-law privilege for attorney-client communications (*see, e.g., State v. Beaupre, supra*, 123 N.H. at 159, 459 A.2d at 236); and, in cases of electronic eavesdropping, the federal and state statutory restrictions upon electronic surveillance (*see* §§ 25.31-25.32 *supra*). For a discussion of the interrelated protections provided the Sixth Amendment, attorney-client privilege, and work-product doctrine (discussed in § 18.13 *supra*) in the context of a search warrant for lawyer's files, *see In re Search Warrant Issued June 13, 2019,* 942 F.3d 159 (4th Cir. 2019).

26.14. *Electronic Recording of Interrogations*

In a number of jurisdictions, the police are required to electronically record interrogations, usually with video-recording equipment. In some jurisdictions, this requirement was established by a court decision (*see, e.g., Stephan v. State*, 711 P.2d 1156, 1157 (Alaska 1986) ("we hold that an unexcused failure to electronically record a custodial interrogation conducted in a place of detention violates a suspect's right to due process, under the Alaska Constitution, . . . and that any statement thus obtained is generally inadmissible"); *State v. Scales*, 518 N.W.2d 587, 592 (Minn. 1994) (adopting the requirement by means of the court's "supervisory power to insure the fair administration of justice")); in others, it was established by a statute (*see, e.g.*, SMITH-HURD ILL. COMP. STAT. ANN. ch. 725, § 5/103-2.1; WIS. STAT. ANN. § 968.073) or court rule (*see, e.g.*, IND. RULE EVID. 617). Typically, the police are required to record "all custodial interrogation including any information about rights, any waiver of those rights, and all questioning" (*State v. Scales, supra*, 518 N.W.2d at 592). *See also Commonwealth v. Adonsoto*, 475 Mass. 497, 507-08 & n.9, 58 N.E.3d 305, 315-16 & n.9 (2016) (establishing "a new protocol" that, "where practicable, . . . all [police] interviews and interrogations using interpreter services will be recorded," and "[t]he defendant must be advised that the conversation is being recorded"; "The implementation of this protocol will provide significantly enhanced protections and assurances of reliability for defendants who speak through an interpreter. Reliability is an essential factor of due process to the defendant. . . . A recording allows defendants and judges to independently evaluate accuracy, and thus, the reliability of interpreter services."). There may be exceptions for situations in which recording is not feasible (*see, e.g.*, IND. RULE EVID. 617(a); WIS. STAT. ANN. § 972.115(2)(a)). Some statutes confer upon the prosecution a procedural benefit at the suppression hearing if a statement was electronically recorded; counsel should be alert to the possibility of challenging such provisions on constitutional grounds. *See, e.g., State v. Barker*, 2016-Ohio-2708, 149 Ohio St. 3d 1, 73 N.E.3d 365 (2016) (holding that a statute on electronic recording of juveniles' custodial statements, which provided that statements "'are presumed to be voluntary if . . . electronically recorded'" (*id.* at 1, 73 N.E.3d at 368), "may not supersede the constitutional rule announced in *Miranda*" and therefore "cannot lessen the protections announced in *Miranda* by removing the state's burden of proving a suspect's knowing, intelligent, and voluntary waiver of rights prior to making a statement during a custodial interrogation" (*id.* at 8, 73 N.E.3d at 373); and holding further that such a statutory presumption, at least as applied to juveniles, violates due process, because the "[a]pplication of the statutory presumption would remove all consideration of the juvenile's unique characteristics from the due-process analysis unless the juvenile introduced evidence to disprove voluntariness when the interrogation was electronically recorded" and "there is no rational relationship between the existence of an electronic recording and the voluntariness of a suspect's statement[,] . . . especially . . . where, as with R.C. 2933.81(B), the statute requires only that the *statement* sought to be admitted, not the entire interrogation, be recorded" (*id.* at 12, 73 N.E.3d at 377)).

Although video-recording provides a degree of protection against abusive police practices, it is not nearly as protective as proponents of this reform may believe. A crafty detective or officer can do an end-run around the recording requirement by making promises or threats (or engaging in other types of psychological manipulations of the defendant) before the video-camera is turned on. Moreover, if the interrogation is protracted, the police presumably will turn off the camera periodically to allow the defendant to use the bathroom or to take a break from interrogation. During these breaks, the police have additional opportunities to engage in off-camera manipulations of the defendant. As a result, the video the judge eventually sees at a suppression hearing (and that the jury may see at trial) is often a carefully stage-managed performance, with the police as both on-stage actors and behind-the-scenes directors. In such cases, the use of a recording actually may make things worse for the defendant because the video images provide the judge and jury with a compelling – but dangerously false – appearance of careful, responsible police work.

Accordingly, defense attorneys in jurisdictions with electronic recording of interrogations need to be alert to the possibility that police improprieties took place off-camera. Counsel should interview the client carefully about what the police said and did before the video camera was turned on and during all breaks in the recording. Although litigation about such off-camera statements and actions of the police will usually come down to the defendant's word against the officers', counsel can at least use the police reports and the time counters in the video to document all of the opportunities the police had to apply pressure on the defendant off-camera (*e.g.*, at the scene of the arrest, in the police car on the way to the station, during booking, in the interrogation room before the camera was turned on, and during breaks in the interrogation). Naturally, counsel should also watch for any indications of alterations in the video. Some state statutes prescribe safeguards against alterations (*see, e.g.*, SMITH-HURD ILL. COMP. STAT. ANN. ch. 725, § 5/103-2.1(b)(2)).

26.15. *Statements Obtained Through Violation of the Defendant's Fourth Amendment Rights or Illegal Eavesdropping*

The derivative-evidence principle described in §§ 25.39-25.42 *supra* requires the suppression of statements that are the "fruits" of a Fourth Amendment violation. *See Wong Sun v. United States,* 371 U.S. 471 (1963). Potential fruits include:

(a)   statements obtained from a defendant following his or her unconstitutional arrest or detention (*e.g., Brown v. Illinois,* 422 U.S. 590 (1975); *Dunaway v. New York,* 442 U.S. 200 (1979); *Lanier v. South Carolina,* 474 U.S. 25 (1985) (per curiam); *Kaupp v. Texas,* 538 U.S. 626, 632-33 (2003) (per curiam); *Perez Cruz v. Barr,* 926 F.3d 1128, 1135-37, 1145-46 (9th Cir. 2019); *United States v. Segoviano,* 30 F.4th 613 (7th Cir. 2022); *but cf. New York v. Harris,* 495 U.S. 14, 21 (1990) (summarized in § 25.39 subdivision (c) *supra*));

(b)   statements obtained by means of eavesdropping following an unlawful entry into protected premises (*e.g., Berger v. New York,* 388 U.S. 41 (1967); see § 25.31 *supra*);

(c)   statements obtained by means of electronic eavesdropping in violation of the constitutional doctrines governing electronic surveillance (*e.g., Katz v. United States,* 389 U.S. 347 (1967); see §§ 25.31, 25.33 *supra*); and

(d)   statements made in response to being told of illegally seized evidence or in response to being confronted with the evidence itself (*e.g., Commonwealth v. Goncalves-Mendez,* 484 Mass. 80, 138 N.E.3d 1038 (2020); *Ruiz v. Craven,* 425 F.2d 235 (9th Cir. 1970); *State v. Blair,* 691 S.W.2d 259 (Mo. 1985); *cf. Fahy v. Connecticut,* 375 U.S. 85 (1963)).

As indicated in § 25.40 *supra*, the rules requiring suppression of derivative evidence are limited by a dissipation-of-taint principle. Thus, for example, statements made in police custody following an unconstitutional arrest or *Terry* stop are inadmissible unless "intervening events break the causal connection between the illegal arrest [or stop] and the confession so that the confession is "'sufficiently an act of free will to purge the primary taint'"" (*Taylor v. Alabama,* 457 U.S. 687, 690 (1982)). *Accord, Kaupp v. Texas, supra,* 538 U.S. at 632-33; *compare Rawlings v. Kentucky,* 448 U.S. 98, 106-10 (1980). In determining whether the prosecution has met its burden of showing a break in the connection (see § 25.40), "[t]he temporal proximity of the arrest and the confession, the presence of intervening circumstances, . . . and, particularly, the purpose and flagrancy of the official misconduct are all relevant" (*Brown v. Illinois,* 422 U.S. 590, 603-04 (1975)). *Accord, Kaupp v. Texas, supra,* 538 U.S. at 632-33. More particularly, the Supreme Court has recognized that illegal detentions "designed to provide an opportunity for interrogation [are] . . . likely to have coercive aspects likely to induce self-incrimination" (*Michigan v. Summers,* 452 U.S. 692, 702 n.15 (1981) (dictum)). The relevant Fourth Amendment restrictions on arrest and investigative detention are discussed in §§ 25.4-25.14 *supra*.

Statements obtained by electronic eavesdropping in violation of some, but not all, of the statutory regulations codified in 18 U.S.C. §§ 2510-2520 must also be suppressed. *Compare United States v. Chavez,* 416 U.S. 562 (1974), *and United States v. Giordano,* 416 U.S. 505 (1974), *with United States v. Donovan,* 429 U.S. 413 (1977). *See, e.g., United States v. North,* 735 F.3d 212 (5th Cir. 2013). See §§ 25.31-25.32 *supra*.

26.16. *Statements Tainted by Prior Ones That Were Unlawfully Obtained: The "Cat Out of the Bag" Doctrine*

Prior to *Oregon v. Elstad,* 470 U.S. 298 (1985), the finding that an incriminating statement had been taken from an accused in violation of either the due process requirement of voluntariness or the *Miranda* rules commonly led to the suppression of any subsequent statement of the accused on the same subject before consulting a lawyer. This result was not commanded by any majority opinion of the Supreme Court of the United States but appeared to be required by the Court's *per curiam* decision in *Robinson v. Tennessee,* 392 U.S. 666 (1968), approving Justice Harlan's concurring opinion in *Darwin v. Connecticut,* 391 U.S. 346, 349-51 (1968). Justice Harlan there reasoned that once an accused has given the police a confession, his or her subsequent statements to them about the crime are more likely to be the products of a belief that the "cat is out of the bag" than of an independent choice to commit a fresh act of self-incrimination. Thus, if the first confession was constitutionally inadmissible, it tainted all later statements made by the accused without the legal advice necessary to place the first confession in perspective.

In *Elstad,* the Court rejected similar reasoning as the basis for an argument that "an initial failure of law enforcement officers to administer the warnings required by *Miranda . . .* , without more, 'taints' subsequent admissions made after a suspect has been fully advised of and has waived his *Miranda* rights" (470 U.S. at 300). *Elstad* holds that if the only illegality in obtaining a first incriminating statement is a *Miranda* violation, "a careful and thorough administration of

Miranda warnings serves to cure the condition that rendered the unwarned statement inadmissible" (*id.* at 310-11). Thus, the "admissibility of any subsequent statement . . . turn[s] . . . solely on whether it is knowingly and voluntarily made" (*id.* at 309).

As a result of the analysis in *Elstad* and later Supreme Court decisions elaborating *Elstad*, the federal scope-of-taint rule to be applied in successive-statement situations now turns upon the reason the first statement is found to be unconstitutional.

26.16.1. *Statements Tainted by a Prior Statement Taken in Violation of the Due Process Clause and the Self-Incrimination Clause of the Fifth Amendment*

In *Elstad*, the Supreme Court recognized that "[t]here is a vast difference between the direct consequences flowing from coercion of a confession by physical violence or other deliberate means calculated to break the suspect's will and the uncertain consequences of disclosure of a 'guilty secret' freely given in response to an unwarned but noncoercive question . . . ." (470 U.S. at 312). Accordingly, *Elstad*'s repudiation of the concept of presumptive taint is limited to *Miranda* violations (§§ 26.5-26.9.3 *supra*) and does not extend to involuntary confessions (§§ 26.2-26.4 *supra*). E.g., *United States v. Lopez*, 437 F.3d 1059, 1066-67 & n.4 (10th Cir. 2006); *Shelton v. State,* 287 Ark. 322, 699 S.W.2d 728 (1985). The *Elstad* opinion says that "[w]hen a prior statement is actually coerced" (470 U.S. at 310), or perhaps even when it is simply "obtained through overtly or inherently coercive methods which raise serious Fifth Amendment and Due Process concerns" (*id.* at 312 n.3),"the time that passes between confessions, the change in place of interrogations, and the change in identity of the interrogators all bear on whether that coercion has carried over into the second confession" (*id.* at 310); and the admissibility of the second confession is subject to a "requirement of a break in the stream of events" (*id.,* citing *Westover v. United States,* decided with *Miranda v. Arizona,* 384 U.S. 436 (1966)). *See also Brown v. Illinois,* 422 U.S. 590, 605 n.12 (1975); *cf. Clewis v. Texas,* 386 U.S. 707, 710 (1967) (requiring the exclusion of a third incriminating statement made after two earlier ones where there was "no break in the stream of events . . . sufficient to insulate the [later] statement from the effect of all that went before"). In these due process cases, a second confession must be shown to be "an act independent of the [previous] confession" (*Reck v. Pate,* 367 U.S. 433, 444 (1961)), and the prosecution plainly bears the burden of proof on that issue (*Nix v. Williams,* 467 U.S. 431 (1984) (dealing with the exclusionary consequences of a confession obtained in violation of the Sixth Amendment and suggesting that the prosecution's burden of proving the dissipation of taint – "by a preponderance of the evidence" (467 U.S. at 444) – is the same in Fifth Amendment cases (*see id.* at 442 & n.3)), discussed in § 25.40 *supra*). *See, e.g., People v. Guilford*, 21 N.Y.3d 205, 209, 213, 991 N.E.2d 204, 206, 209, 969 N.Y.S.2d 430, 432, 435 (2013) (suppressing a statement as the fruit of an earlier involuntary statement because the prosecution failed to prove that the defendant had been "restored to the status of one no longer under the influence" of the coercion that tainted the earlier statement "so as to render plausible the characterization of [the] subsequent admission as voluntary": Although the 49½-hour interrogation that produced the involuntary first statement was followed by an "eight-hour 'break,'" during which the defendant was arraigned and had an opportunity to confer with counsel, these circumstances could not "attenuate[ ] the taint of the wrongful interrogation" and "transform . . . [the defendant's] coerced capitulation into a voluntary disclosure."); *United States v. Anderson*, 929 F.2d 96, 102 (2d Cir. 1991) ("[A]gent Valentine coerced Anderson's first confession with improper tactics. Moreover, nothing in the record suggests that the taint clinging to the first confession was dissipated. No significant time elapsed between the first questioning by agent Valentine and when Anderson made his statement to agent Moorin. The suspect was at all times in custody and under close police supervision with the same agents present on both occasions. Agent Moorin made no effort to dispel the original threat. In fact, his statement that Anderson 'could only help himself by cooperating' only reaffirmed agent Valentine's earlier coercive statements [that if Anderson exercised his *Miranda* rights, he could not thereafter cooperate with the Government and gain the benefits of cooperation]. The district court correctly found a continuing presumption of compulsion applied to the second statement. Hence, Anderson's waiver, tainted by the earlier, coerced confession, was also involuntary and should be suppressed. Moreover, suppression of the second statement here also serves the objectives of deterrence and trustworthiness. It operates as a disincentive for police to coerce a confession by threatening a defendant with false and/or misleading statements. The fact-finding process is also enhanced since a confession obtained in the manner this one was may be untrustworthy.").

26.16.2. *Statements Tainted by a Prior Statement Taken in Violation of* Miranda

Although *Elstad* rejected a general rule of presumptive taint in the *Miranda* context, a violation of *Miranda* in the taking of one statement may nonetheless provide a basis for suppressing a subsequent statement as a fruit of the earlier violation in certain circumstances. *See State v. Alexander*, 2019-01664 (La. 12/20/19), 285 So.3d 1091, 1091-92 (La. 2019) ("This Court previously ordered the suppression of a statement defendant made after a detective assured him anything he said would stay in the interrogation room, finding this guarantee to have subverted the *Miranda* warning that anything defendant might say would be used against him in a court of law. . . . ¶ The State now seeks to introduce a subsequent statement defendant made to his mother outside of the detective's presence but after the detective's direction that defendant 'apologize to his mother for what he did' and representation to defendant's mother that 'nobody needs to know the specifics of what we talk about in here.' This second statement is closely related in time, circumstance, and content to the one previously ordered suppressed, and there were no intervening factors to break the chain between the two. . . . Importantly, the second statement occurred in the very interrogation room in which the detective promised defendant his statements would remain confidential. Thus, it, too, is inadmissible. Further, while defendant's mother was not a state actor, the statement defendant made to her was the direct result of state action sufficient to render it involuntary and inadmissible."); *State v. Carrion*, 249 N.J. 253, 260, 265 A.3d 115, 119 (2021) (applying a state-law ruling implementing *Miranda* in cases in which "a confession, given after *Miranda* warnings, . . . [is proffered by the prosecution] when the suspect has previously been subjected to unwarned questioning in which he confessed" (*id.* at 275, 265 A.3d at 128.) and holding such a confession inadmissible in the case at bar; "In [*State v.*] *O'Neill*, [193 N.J. 148, 936 A.2d 438 (2007),] we expressed our view that the key concern is whether the warnings provided in the second interrogation 'function[ ] effectively,' so as to limit the potential psychological burdens that the previous confession may have placed on the defendant and that could otherwise affect the voluntariness of the defendant's waiver. . . . We stated that, to assess how effectively the warnings in the second interrogation functioned, ¶ [']courts should consider all relevant factors, including: (1) the extent of questioning and the nature of any admissions made by defendant before being informed of his Miranda rights; (2) the proximity in time and place between the pre- and post-warning questioning; (3) whether the same law enforcement officers conducted both the unwarned and warned interrogations; (4) whether the officers informed defendant that his pre-warning statements could not be used against him; and (5) the degree to which the post-warning questioning is a continuation of the pre-warning questioning.'" *Id.* at 276, 265 A.3d at 129.).

The Court in *Elstad* distinguished the case before it from cases "concerning suspects whose invocation of their rights to remain silent and to have counsel present were flatly ignored while police subjected them to continued interrogation" (470 U.S. at 313 n.3). Thus, as Justice Brennan observed in his dissenting opinion in *Elstad,* "the Court concedes that its new analysis does *not* apply where the authorities have ignored the accused's actual invocation of his *Miranda* rights to remain silent or to consult with counsel. . . . In such circumstances, courts should continue to apply the traditional presumption of tainted connection" (470 U.S. at 346 n.28 (emphasis in original)). *See, e.g., State v. Hartley,* 103 N.J. 252, 511 A.2d 80 (1986) (concluding that the "cat out of the bag" doctrine has continuing vitality in cases in which the initial statement is suppressed on grounds of police failure to scrupulously honor a suspect's invocation of the rights to counsel or to remain silent).

In *Missouri v. Seibert,* 542 U.S. 600 (2004), the Court addressed the applicability of *Elstad* to a situation in which police officers question a suspect without *Miranda* warnings and then administer the warnings and re-question the suspect for the purpose of obtaining an admissible, *Mirandized* statement. A majority of the Court ruled that, in at least some circumstances, such a sequence of interrogations renders *Elstad* inapplicable and requires the suppression of the second statement as a fruit of the *Miranda* violation in obtaining the first statement. A four-Justice plurality concluded that the admissibility of the subsequent *Mirandized* statement turns on "whether it would be reasonable to find that in these circumstances the warnings could function 'effectively' as *Miranda* requires" (542 U.S. at 611-12). The inquiry into effectiveness involves the questions whether "the warnings [could] effectively advise the suspect that he had a real choice about giving an admissible statement at that juncture" and whether the warnings could "reasonably convey that [the suspect] could choose to stop talking even if he had talked earlier" (*id.* at 612). Relevant factors include "the completeness and detail of the questions and answers in the first round of interrogation, the overlapping content of the two statements, the timing and setting of the first and the second, the continuity of police personnel, and the degree to which the interrogator's questions treated the second round as continuous with the first" (*id.* at 615). It is also a plausible reading of the *Seibert* plurality opinion that *Miranda* warnings and other corrective procedures administered after a suspect has made initial admissions in violation of *Miranda* cannot "function 'effectively' as *Miranda* requires" (*id.* at 611-12) if they do not inform the suspect that those earlier admissions cannot be used in evidence against him or her, so that the suspect is no longer laboring under the impression that "what he has just said will be used, with subsequent silence being of no avail" (*id.* at 613). On the facts of the *Seibert* case itself, the plurality concluded that the midstream *Miranda* warnings were ineffective because "[t]he warned phase of questioning proceeded after a pause of only 15 to 20 minutes, in the same place as the unwarned segment," with "the same officer" doing the questioning; "he said nothing to counter the probable misimpression that the advice that anything Seibert said could be used against her also applied to the details of the inculpatory statement previously elicited"; and "[i]n particular, the police did not advise

. . . [Seibert] that her prior statement could not be used" (*id.* at 616). (A footnote to the sentence making the latter point says: "We do not hold that a formal addendum warning that a previous statement could not be used would be sufficient to change the character of the question-first procedure to the point of rendering an ensuing statement admissible, but its absence is clearly a factor that blunts the efficacy of the warnings and points to a continuing, not a new, interrogation" (*id.* at 616 n.7).) Justice Kennedy concurred in the judgment in *Seibert*, providing the fifth vote for suppression of Seibert's statement, on the narrower ground that "in the infrequent case, such as we have here, in which the two-step interrogation technique was used in a calculated way to undermine the *Miranda* warning" (*id.* at 622), "postwarning statements that are related to the substance of prewarning statements must be excluded unless curative measures are taken before the postwarning statement is made . . . to ensure that a reasonable person in the suspect's situation would understand the import and effect of the *Miranda* warning and of the *Miranda* waiver" (*id.*), and "[n]o curative steps were taken in this case" (*id.*). Under Justice Kennedy's approach, "a substantial break in time and circumstances between the prewarning statement and the *Miranda* warning may suffice in most circumstances, as it allows the accused to distinguish the two contexts and appreciate that the interrogation has taken a new turn"; and "[a]lternatively, an additional warning that explains the likely inadmissibility of the prewarning custodial statement may be sufficient" (*id.*). *See also Bobby v. Dixon*, 565 U.S. 23, 32 (2011) (per curiam) ("the effectiveness of th[e] [*Miranda*] warnings was not impaired by the sort of 'two-step interrogation technique' condemned in *Seibert*" because "there was simply 'no nexus' between Dixon's unwarned admission to forgery and his later, warned confession to murder" and there was a "significant break in time and dramatic change in circumstances" between the two interrogations, "creat[ing] 'a new and distinct experience'" and "ensuring that Dixon's prior unwarned interrogation did not undermine the effectiveness of the *Miranda* warnings he received before confessing to Hammer's murder"). *Compare Reyes v. Lewis*, 833 F.3d 1001 (9th Cir. 2016) ("Reyes's postwarning confession should have been suppressed" because the "police officers deliberately employed a two-step interrogation technique, and . . . they did not take appropriate 'curative measures,' in violation of [*Missouri v.*] *Seibert*" (*id.* at 1033); during the administration of the *Miranda* warnings, Detective Brandt "played down their importance," saying he "wanted 'just to clarify stuff,' [and] suggesting by his use of the word 'clarify' that the 'stuff' had already been conveyed in the earlier interview, and that the only purpose of the later interview was clarification. Brandt then said he wanted to 'read you your rights' because 'you've been sitting in that room and the door was locked and you're not free to leave.' An experienced officer in Brandt's position would have known that to a reasonable person not trained in the law, let alone a fifteen-year-old high school freshman, these stated reasons were hardly an effective means of conveying the fact that the warning he was about to give could mean the difference between serving life in prison and going home that night." (*id.* at 1032); "After Brandt read the *Miranda* warnings, he said, 'Do you understand each of these rights that I've explained to you? Yeah? OK. Can we talk about the stuff we talked about earlier today? Is that a yes?' While giving the *Miranda* warnings, Brandt did not pause to ask 'Is that a yes?' after asking if Reyes understood 'each of the rights' listed. Only after the *Miranda* warnings had been completed and after Brandt asked whether 'we [can] talk about the stuff we talked about earlier today' did Brandt finally ask 'Is that a yes?' and wait for a response. In contrast to the interrogation in *Seibert*, Brandt did not ask Reyes for a signed waiver of rights or a signed acknowledgment of having read and understood the *Miranda* warnings. ¶ The psychological, spatial, and temporal break between the unwarned and warned interrogations was not enough to cure the violation.

Perhaps most important, Brandt had been a continuous presence throughout." *Id.*); *United States v. Barnes*, 713 F.3d 1200, 1203, 1205-07 (9th Cir. 2013) (per curiam) ("the interrogation was a 'deliberate two-step' approach in contravention of *Missouri v. Seibert*": the "evidence reflects that the agents deliberately employed the two-step interrogation tactic"; "[t]here was no break or dividing point in the interrogation"; "[t]he agents treated the second round of interrogation as continuous with the first"; and "the agents took no curative measures to mitigate their error" such as "tak[ing] a substantial time break in the interrogation or warn[ing] Barnes that what he had said before the warnings could not be used against him."); *United States v. Capers*, 627 F.3d 470, 477, 483, 485 (2d Cir. 2010) (resolving an issue that "Justice Kennedy had no reason to explore" – "how a court should determine when a two-step interrogation had been executed deliberately" – by "hold[ing] that the burden rests on the prosecution to disprove deliberateness," and applying this rule to require suppression of the defendant's second (post-warning) confession because "the Government has failed to meet its burden of demonstrating that Capers was not subjected to a [deliberate] two-step interrogation" and because "there were no curative measures to ensure that the defendant was not misled with regard to his rights prior to his second confession"); *Kelly v. State*, 997 N.E.2d 1045, 1053-55 (Ind. 2013) (post-warning statements were the "product of the 'question-first' interrogation practice disapproved of in *Seibert* and therefore inadmissible" because the pre-warning and post-warning statements "concern the same subject . . . [and] were made in the same location, mere minutes apart, in response to the same officer. Most significantly, however, Chief Kiphart and another officer referred to Kelly's pre-warning admission three times during the post-warning interrogation. . . . Such references, we believe, inevitably diluted the potency of the *Miranda* warning such that it was powerless to cure the initial failure to warn, even if that failure was a product of good-faith mistake."); *State v. Navy*, 386 S.C. 294, 303-04, 688 S.E.2d 838, 842 (2010) (*Seibert* requires suppression of two postwarning statements, given the absence of "the curative measures suggested by Justice Kennedy," even though the record does not show that this was a case of a "deliberate" police use of a "'question first' strategy"); *Martinez v. State*, 272 S.W.3d 615, 626-27 (Tex. Crim. App. 2008) (applying Justice Kennedy's analysis in *Seibert* to suppress a videotaped statement obtained with a "deliberate two-step strategy" because "the officers did not apprise appellant of his *Miranda* rights when they began custodial interrogation and failed to apply any curative measures in order to ameliorate the harm caused by the *Miranda* violation").

Elstad does not govern cases in which a defendant testifies at trial in order to rebut or explain an incriminating pretrial statement that was erroneously admitted in violation of *Miranda*. That situation continues to be governed by the exclusionary rule of *Harrison v. United States*, 392 U.S. 219 (1968). *See Lujan v. Garcia*, 734 F.3d 917, 924-30 (9th Cir. 2013) (in *Harrison* the "Court held that if Harrison had testified 'in order to overcome the impact of confessions illegally obtained and hence improperly introduced, then his testimony was tainted by the same illegality that rendered the confessions themselves inadmissible'" (*id.* at 925); "*Harrison* outlines a clear exclusionary rule that applies to the States" (*id.* at 927); "The opinions of *Elstad* and *Harrison* should not be conflated to create ambiguity where there is none. *Harrison* sets forth a clearly established rule that has not been undermined by *Elstad*. ¶ Under the *Harrison* exclusionary rule, when a criminal defendant's trial testimony is induced by the erroneous admission of his out-of-court confession into evidence as part of the government's case-in-chief, that trial testimony cannot be introduced in a subsequent prosecution, nor can it be used to support the initial conviction on harmless error review, because to do so would perpetuate the underlying constitutional error." *Id*. at 930.).

Even in cases in which a defendant's second statement is not subject to federal constitutional suppression as the fruit of an earlier *Miranda* violation because of the rule of *Elstad* and the limitations of *Seibert*, counsel can urge the state courts to reject *Elstad* as a matter of state constitutional law and to preserve the "cat out of the bag" doctrine in its entirety. *See, e.g., State v. O'Neill*, 193 N.J. 148, 180-81, 936 A.2d 438, 457 (2007); *People v. Bethea*, 67 N.Y.2d 364, 493 N.E.2d 937, 502 N.Y.S.2d 713 (1986); *State v. Aguirre*, 301 Kan. 950, 961-62, 349 P.3d 1245, 1252 (2015) ("In *State v. Matson*, 260 Kan. 366, 374, 921 P.2d 790 (1996), this court said that the validity of a *Miranda* waiver, after a suspect has previously invoked those rights, depends on whether 'the accused (a) initiated further discussions with the police and (b) knowingly and intelligently waived the previously asserted right.' . . . The State failed the *Matson* test by reinitiating the second interrogation. ¶ Consequently, the taint of the *Miranda* rights violation in the first interview was not sufficiently attenuated to validate the rights waiver for the second interview, and the statements obtained in the second interview should have been suppressed, as well."); and see generally § 17.11 *supra*.

26.16.3. *Statements Tainted by a Prior Statement Taken in Violation of the Sixth Amendment*

The Supreme Court has expressly reserved the question "whether the rationale of *Elstad* applies when a suspect makes incriminating statements after a knowing and voluntary waiver of his right to counsel notwithstanding earlier police questioning in violation of [the] Sixth Amendment standards" discussed in § 26.10 (*Fellers v. United States*, 540 U.S. 519, 525 (2004)). The analytic approach the Court used in *Elstad* to reject the concept of presumptive taint for fruits of a *Miranda* violation and to distinguish the situation of a coerced confession (see §§ 26.16-26.16.1 *supra*) would seem to render *Elstad* inapplicable when the interests at stake are those protected by the Sixth Amendment right to counsel. As in the due process context, the prosecution bears the burden of proving that a Sixth Amendment violation in taking the previous statement did not taint the subsequent statement. *See Nix v. Williams*, 467 U.S. 431, 441-48 (1984).

26.16.4. *Statements Tainted by a Prior Statement Taken in Violation of the Fourth Amendment*

The reasoning of *Elstad* and the distinction that it drew between *Miranda* violations and coercion in violation of the Due Process Clause (see §§ 26.16-26.16.1 *supra*) also suggest that *Elstad* does not limit the pre-*Elstad* caselaw governing suppression of a second statement following a previous statement obtained in violation of the Fourth Amendment (*see Dunaway v. New York*, 442 U.S. 200, 218 n.20 (1979) (dealing with "subsequent statements . . . which . . . were 'clearly the result and the fruit of the first'" where an initial statement was the product of an arrest without probable cause). As in the other contexts discussed in §§ 26.16.1 and 26.16.3 *supra*, the prosecution bears the burden of proving dissipation of taint. *See Nix v. Williams*, *supra*, 467 U.S. at 441-48 (addressing the prosecutorial burden of disproving taint in the Sixth Amendment context and suggesting that the same rule applies in Fourth Amendment cases (*id*. at 442)).

26.16.5. *Potential Implications of* Elstad *for Physical Fruits of an Unconstitutionally Obtained Statement*

The principles discussed in the preceding subparts have to do with suppression of *statements* as the fruits of a constitutional violation in obtaining a previous statement. In *United States v. Patane*, 542 U.S. 630 (2004), a plurality of three Justices, joined by two other Justices on narrower reasoning, employed the rationale of *Elstad* to conclude that a *Miranda* violation in obtaining a statement does not provide a basis for suppressing "the physical fruits of the suspect's unwarned but voluntary statements" (*id.* at 634, 636 (plurality opinion)). *Accord, id.* at 644-45 (Justice Kennedy, concurring in the judgment, joined by Justice O'Connor). Here again, the Court limited its analysis to *Miranda* violations, distinguishing them from the situation of a coerced statement. *See id.* at 634 (plurality opinion); *id.* at 645 (Justice Kennedy, concurring in the judgment). *See, e.g., Dye v. Commonwealth*, 411 S.W.3d 227, 236-38 (Ky. 2013) (suppression of the defendant's statement as involuntary in violation of Due Process also required the suppression of the physical "evidence seized pursuant to the . . . search warrant . . . which was issued upon information contained in his involuntary confession"). Even with respect to *Miranda* violations, counsel can seek a more protective rule on state constitutional grounds. *See, e.g., State v. Farris*, 2006-Ohio-3255, 109 Ohio St. 3d 519, 529, 849 N.E.2d 985, 996 (2006) ("We . . . join the other states that have already determined after *Patane* that their state constitutions' protections against self-incrimination extend to physical evidence seized as a result of pre-*Miranda* statements"); *State v. Knapp*, 2005 WI 127, 285 Wis. 2d 86, 89, 130, 700 N.W.2d 899, 901, 921 (Wis. 2005) (after the Supreme Court's *vacatur* and remand of the state supreme court's previous decision in light of *United States v. Patane*, the Wisconsin Supreme Court relies on the state constitution to reinstate its previous result that physical evidence had to be suppressed as a fruit of a *Miranda* violation); *State v. Peterson*, 2007 VT 24, 181 Vt. 436, 446-47, 923 A.2d 585, 592-93 (2007) ("agree[ing] with" decisions of the Massachusetts Supreme Judicial Court, Ohio Supreme Court, and Wisconsin Supreme Court that rejected *United States v. Patane* on state constitutional grounds, and construing "the Vermont Constitution and our exclusionary rule" to hold that "[p]hysical evidence gained from statements obtained under circumstances that violate *Miranda* is inadmissible in criminal proceedings as fruit of the poisonous tree"); and see generally § 17.11 *supra*.

E. *Trial Issues in Cases Involving Incriminating Statements by the Defendant*

26.17. *Prosecutorial Proof of* Corpus Delicti

In some jurisdictions, a trial judge can refuse to admit a confession into evidence before the prosecution has presented a *prima facie* case of the commission of the offense charged. This preliminary showing is commonly called the *corpus delicti. See, e.g., State v. Curlew*, 459 A.2d 160, 163-64 (Me. 1983) ("Maine case law . . . leaves the order of proof within the sound judicial discretion of the trial judge. . . . [T]he exercise of discretion . . . should be guided by a strong preference for proof of the corpus delicti prior to admitting in evidence a confession or admission of the defendant."). The *corpus delicti* needs not include proof of the identity of the defendant (although, of course, it is possible that some of the evidence comprising the *corpus delicti* will *also* tend to identify the defendant). *See, e.g., Stano v. State*, 473 So.2d 1282, 1287

(Fla. 1985) ("There are three elements to the corpus delicti of a homicide: 1) The fact of death; 2) the criminal agency of another; and 3) the identity of the victim."). In other jurisdictions the term "*corpus delicti*" simply expresses the near-universal rule that a defendant's confession must be corroborated in order to make a submissible case for the prosecution; *corpus delicti* analysis relates to the standard of proof for a directed verdict and does not control the order of proof. *See, e.g., Allen v. Commonwealth*, 287 Va. 68, 752 S.E.2d 856 (2014); § 41.2.2 subdivision (1) *infra*.

Jurisdictions that do enforce the *corpus delicti* principle as regulating the order of proof ordinarily give the trial judge discretion to permit the prosecutor to vary the order and to prove the confession prior to the *corpus*, subject to "connecting up." *See, e.g., State v. Hendrickson*, 140 Wash. App. 913, 921-24, 168 P.3d 42, 424-26 (2007). Defense counsel should object to the confession and resist any variance in the order of proof. Frequently the prosecution's case on *corpus delicti* is borderline, and a judge who has heard the details of a confession will tend to lean somewhat against the accused in determining whether the *corpus* has been proved.

26.18. *The Right of the Defense to Show the Circumstances Under Which the Statement Was Made*

When a defense motion to suppress an incriminating statement of the defendant has been denied and the prosecution introduces the statement at trial, the defense will frequently want to show the coercive circumstances that prompted the statement, so as to persuade the trier of fact that the statement should be accorded little weight in the assessment of guilt or innocence. In *Crane v. Kentucky,* 476 U.S. 683 (1986), the Court made clear that a defendant cannot be precluded from presenting evidence of this sort at trial despite the denial of a pretrial motion challenging the confession as involuntary on the basis of the same evidence. The Court explained that the guarantees of "procedural fairness" embodied in the Sixth and Fourteenth Amendments (*id.* at 689-90) require that the defense be permitted to present evidence at trial concerning "the physical and psychological environment that yielded the confession . . . regardless of whether the defendant marshaled the same evidence earlier in support of an unsuccessful motion to suppress, and entirely independent of any question of voluntariness" (*id.* at 689). *See also People v. Bedessie*, 19 N.Y.3d 147, 149, 161, 970 N.E.2d 380, 381, 388-89, 947 N.Y.S.2d 357, 358, 365-66 (2012) (recognizing that, "in a proper case," the accused is entitled to present "expert testimony [at trial] on the phenomenon of false confessions" because "there is no doubt that experts in such disciplines as psychiatry and psychology or the social sciences may offer valuable testimony to educate a jury about those factors of personality and situation that the relevant scientific community considers to be associated with false confessions"); *State v. Perea*, 2013 UT 68, 322 P.3d 624, 640-41 (Utah 2013) ("expert testimony regarding the phenomenon of false confessions should be admitted so long as it meets the standards set out in rule 702 of the Utah Rules of Evidence and it is relevant to the facts of the specific case": "[f]alse confessions are an unsettling and unfortunate reality of our criminal justice system"; "expert testimony about factors leading to a false confession assists a 'trier of fact to understand the evidence or to determine a fact in issue'"; "[r]ecent laboratory-based studies have identified several factors that increase the likelihood of false confessions"; and "[t]o require a defendant to testify regarding the factors that contributed to his alleged false confession, rather than allow the use of an expert witness, opens the defendant up to cross-examination and impinges on his constitutionally guaranteed right against self-incrimination."); *and see* the Cutler, Neuschatz & Honts article cited in § 30.1 subdivision 14 *infra*. The Cutler & Leo articles cited in the penultimate paragraph of § 26.3.4 *supra* provide information and insights that will be helpful to defense counsel in arguing that the trier of fact should discredit incriminating statements produced by commonplace police interrogation tactics as unreliable. *See also* SAUL KASSIN, DUPED: WHY INNOCENT PEOPLE CONFESS – AND WHY WE BELIEVE THEIR CONFESSIONS (2022); Richard A. Leo, *Interrogation and Confessions*, in ERIK LUNA, ed., REFORMING CRIMINAL JUSTICE, Vol. 2: POLICING, pp. 233-58 (Academy for Justice 2017), *available at* https://law.asu.edu/sites/default/files/pdf/academy_for_justice/Reforming-Criminal-Justice_Vol_2.pdf; Richard A. Leo, Report on Sedley Alley, *available at* https://papers.ssrn.com/sol3/papers.cfm?abstract_id=3791645&dgcid=ejournal_htmlemail_evidence:evidentiary:procedure:ejournal_abstractlink; JAMES L. TRAINUM, HOW THE POLICE GENERATE FALSE CONFESSIONS: AN INSIDE LOOK AT THE INTERROGATION ROOM (2016); KYLE C. SCHERR & ALLISON D. REDLICH, CUMULATIVE DISADVANTAGE: A PSYCHOLOGICAL FRAMEWORK FOR UNDERSTANDING HOW INNOCENCE CAN LEAD TO CONFESSION, WRONGFUL CONVICTION, AND BEYOND (2020).

26.19. *The Prosecutor's Power to Use a Suppressed or Suppressible Statement for Impeachment*

The rules governing prosecutorial use of suppressed or suppressible statements to impeach a defendant's trial testimony vary, depending upon the constitutional doctrine under which the statement was suppressed.

If a statement is suppressed or suppressible on grounds of involuntariness (§§ 26.2-26.4 *supra*), then the statement is inadmissible for impeachment or any other purpose at trial. *Mincey v. Arizona,* 437 U.S. 385, 397-98, 402 (1978); *see New Jersey v. Portash,* 440 U.S. 450, 458-60 (1979); *Kansas v. Ventris,* 556 U.S. 586, 590 (2009) (dictum); *Vega v. Tekoh,* 142 S. Ct. 2095, 2103 (2022) (dictum).

If a statement is suppressed or suppressible on *Miranda* grounds (§§ 26.5-26.9.3 *supra*) but was not found involuntary, federal constitutional law does not forbid the prosecutor to use that statement for impeachment of the defendant's inconsistent testimony at trial. *Harris v. New York,* 401 U.S. 222 (1971); *Oregon v. Hass,* 420 U.S. 714 (1975); *Vega v. Tekoh, supra,* 142 S. Ct. at 2103 (dictum).

Statements suppressed or suppressible on Sixth Amendment grounds (§§ 26.10-26.10.3 *supra*) may be used by the prosecution to impeach a defendant's inconsistent testimony at trial. In *Kansas v. Ventris, supra,* the Court held that a statement which had been deliberately elicited by a jailhouse informant acting as an agent for law enforcement officers and which had not been preceded by a valid waiver of the right to counsel was "concededly elicited in violation of the Sixth Amendment" but "was admissible to challenge [the defendant's] . . . inconsistent testimony at trial." 556 U.S. at 594.

Statements suppressed on Fourth Amendment grounds (§ 25.39 subdivision (c) *supra*) also may be used to impeach a defendant's inconsistent testimony at trial (*United States v.*

Havens, 446 U.S. 620 (1980), subject to the meager restrictions spelled out in § 39.10 subdivision (H) *infra*.

So far as federal constitutional law is concerned, the only suppressed or suppressible matters that are inadmissible even for impeachment of a defendant's testimony are his or her involuntary admissions (*Mincey v. Arizona*, 437 U.S. 385 (1978)) and statements compelled under a grant of immunity (*New Jersey v. Portash*, 440 U.S. 450 (1979)), uncounseled prior convictions (*Loper v. Beto*, 405 U.S. 473 (1972)) and possibly other unconstitutionally obtained priors (see § 14.8 subdivisions (a), (d), (g) *supra*; *cf.* § 48.9 third paragraph *infra*), and any out-of-court testimonial statements by other persons which are rendered inadmissible by the Sixth Amendment right to confrontation (*Hemphill v. New York*, 142 S. Ct. 681 (2022)).

State courts may take a dim view of the prosecutor's use of illegally obtained statements for impeachment, and counsel should argue that the state constitution prohibits prosecutors from using statements suppressed on *Miranda* or Sixth Amendment grounds for any purpose at trial. *See, e.g., People v. Disbrow*, 16 Cal. 3d 101, 113, 545 P.2d 272, 280, 127 Cal. Rptr. 360, 368 (1976) (abrogated by a subsequent initiative constitutional amendment); *State v. Santiago*, 53 Hawai'i 254, 265-66, 492 P.2d 657, 664 (1971); *see also State v. Brunelle*, 148 Vt. 347, 351-55, 534 A.2d 198, 202-04 (1987) (construing the state constitution's explicit guarantee of "the right to testify on one's own behalf" and the state constitution's due process clause to "hold that previously suppressed evidence is unavailable to the State for impeachment purposes except when it is clear that the defendant has testified during direct examination" to "facts contradicted by previously suppressed evidence bearing directly on the crime charged"; "We believe this rule will achieve a fair balance between defendant's right to testify on his or her own behalf and the State's interest in preventing perjury. To permit the use of suppressed evidence to impeach testimony first brought out on cross-examination would upset this balance and impose an untenable chilling effect on defendant's right to testify."); and see generally § 17.11 *supra*.

Even under the federal constitutional rule permitting statements obtained in violation of *Miranda* and the Sixth Amendment to be used for impeachment of the defendant, they cannot be used to impeach defense witnesses other than the defendant. *See, e.g., James v. Illinois*, 493 U.S. 307 (1990) (the state court erred in "expanding the scope of the impeachment exception to permit prosecutors to use illegally obtained evidence to impeach the credibility of defense witnesses" (*id.* at 313); the "impeachment exception [is] limited to the testimony of [the] defendant[ ]" (*id.* at 320)); *Smiley v. Thurmer*, 542 F.3d 574, 579 n.2 (7th Cir. 2008); ("[t]he Supreme Court has limited the impeachment exception to *Miranda*, first articulated in *Harris v. New York*, . . . to situations in which the defendant elects to testify at trial"); *and see Kuntz v. McCaughtry*, 806 F. Supp. 1373 (E.D. Wis. 1992) (holding it constitutional error – albeit harmless error on the record of the case at bar – to permit the prosecution to impeach one of its own witnesses with the defendant's statement taken in violation of *Miranda* and *Edwards v. Arizona* (*see* § 26.9.3 *supra*): "If impeachment of other *defense* witnesses by use of an illegally obtained statement is prohibited, as it is under *James*, use of the statement to impeach *prosecution* witnesses is foreclosed a *fortiori*. The Court's concern in *James* was the chilling effect on presentation of other defense witnesses. That concern about a fair trial is magnified in regard to prosecution witnesses. Allowing the prosecution to use the illegal statement during the presentation of its case – even if used to impeach its own witness – would virtually negate the exclusionary rule altogether. The prosecution would have free reign to present witnesses just for their impeachment value in order to get the illegal statement before the jury. Although defendants should not be able to "'pervert" the exclusion of illegally obtained evidence into a shield for perjury, . . . it seems no more appropriate for the State to brandish such evidence as a sword . . . .'" *Id.* at 1380.).

26.20. *Admissibility of Evidence of the Defendant's Pre- or Post-arrest Silence*

Prosecutors commonly offer evidence of a defendant's pretrial failure to avow innocence or to deny guilt in either of two contexts. First, proof that the defendant failed to deny accusations made in his or her presence by police or private citizens may be offered (usually in the prosecution's case-in-chief) as "adoptive admissions," or "tacit admissions." Evidence of silence for this purpose is admissible only if some accusatory assertion has been directed to the defendant, and the only use that can be made of the evidence is as the basis for an inference that the defendant admitted the accusation. *See Trigg v. Commonwealth*, 460 S.W.3d 322, 330-32 (Ky. 2015); *State v. Ervin B.*, 202 Conn. App. 1, 12-13, 243 A.3d 799, 806-07 (2020). Second, proof that the defendant did not tell the police – or did not tell anyone before trial – the exculpatory story that s/he relates in his or her trial testimony may be offered (usually on cross-examination of the defendant, but sometimes through prosecution witnesses called in rebuttal) to impeach the defendant's testimony as a "recent fabrication."

Common-law rules of evidence regarding these two kinds of proof vary considerably from State to State. Some States have precluded prosecutorial use of an accused's pretrial silence because the evidence has low probative value (given that the accused's taciturnity may have been motivated by an awareness of the right to silence or of the risks of responding to police questioning, by distrust of the police, or by any of a host of other factors) and there is a high risk that the introduction of the evidence will prejudice the accused. *See, e.g., People v. Williams*, 25 N.Y.3d 185, 190-93, 31 N.E.3d 103, 105-08, 8 N.Y.S.3d 641, 643-46 (2015); *and see State v. Easter*, 130 Wash. 2d 228, 235 n.5, 922 P.2d 1285, 1289 n.5 (1996) (citing caselaw from other States in which the courts "ruled on evidentiary grounds [that] pre-arrest silence is not admissible because of its low probative value and high potential for undue prejudice"); *Weitzel v. State*, 384 Md. 451, 456, 461, 863 A.2d 999, 1002, 1005 (2004) ("We think the better view is that . . . evidence is too ambiguous to be probative when the 'pre-arrest silence' is in the presence of a police officer, and join the increasing number of jurisdictions that have so held. . . . ¶ . . . We hold that pre-arrest silence in police presence is not admissible as substantive evidence of guilt under Maryland evidence law."). *Cf. State v. Rutherford*, 2019 ME 128, 214 A.3d 27, 29, 33 (Me. 2019) (the trial court violated state rules of evidence by "admitt[ing] the [out-of-court] statement of the [defendant's] friend" – in which the friend said to a police officer at the scene of a car accident, in Rutherford's presence, that Rutherford "had missed the turn, thus indicating that Rutherford had been driving" – "as an admission adopted by Rutherford" because "Rutherford had been standing two feet away from his friend when they were both questioned . . . [and] had not disputed her representation that he was the driver": "At the time of his friend's statement, Rutherford had not waived his right to remain silent. . . . Accordingly, Rutherford's silence, which he had the right to maintain when his friend spoke, cannot be construed as an adoption of the friend's statement. Conduct or words manifesting adoption of the statement were required, and the State did not offer evidence of such conduct or words of adoption by

Rutherford. The friend's statement should not have been admitted as an adoptive admission, *see* M.R. Evid. 801(d)(2)(B); it remained inadmissible hearsay, *see* M.R. Evid. 801(c), 802.").

Apart from such common-law evidentiary doctrines, proof of the defendant's silence to show an "adoptive admission" or "recent fabrication" raises federal and state constitutional issues. The constitutional analysis is affected by whether the silence that the prosecutor seeks to prove occurred (1) before or after arrest and (2) before or after administration of the *Miranda* warnings described in § 26.7 *supra*.

In *Doyle v. Ohio,* 426 U.S. 610, 619 (1976), the Supreme Court held that an accused's "silence, at the time of arrest and after receiving *Miranda* warnings" is constitutionally inadmissible against him or her, even for the purpose of impeaching the accused's trial testimony as a recent fabrication. The reasoning of *Doyle* is that the *Miranda* warnings implicitly assure the person to whom they are given that s/he may remain silent with impunity, and it is fundamentally unfair and a violation of due process to use the person's subsequent silence as incriminating evidence (426 U.S. at 617-19), particularly inasmuch as the silence is "insolubly ambiguous because of what the State is required to advise the person arrested" (*id.* at 617). *See also Vega v. Tekoh*, 142 S. Ct. 2095, 2104 (2022) (dictum); *Portuondo v. Agard*, 529 U.S. 61, 74-75 (2000) (dictum); *Brecht v. Abrahamson*, 507 U.S. 619, 628 (1993) (dictum); *Hurd v. Terhune*, 619 F.3d 1080, 1088-89 (9th Cir. 2010); *People v. Shafier*, 483 Mich. 205, 218-19, 768 N.W.2d 305, 313 (2009); *People v. Clary*, 494 Mich. 260, 833 N.W.2d 308 (2013); *State v. Brooks*, 304 S.W.3d 130, 133-34 (Mo. 2010). The *Doyle* doctrine prohibits the state from "mak[ing] use of the defendant's exercise of [his] . . . rights [to remain silent] in obtaining his conviction" (*Wainwright v. Greenfield,* 474 U.S. 284, 292 (1986)), and thus bars not only the use of silence to impeach the accused but also any use of the accused's assertion of his *Miranda* rights as proof of sanity in a case in which an insanity defense is asserted (*id.* at 295). *See also Engle v. Lumpkin*, 33 F.4th 783, 791, 792-93 (5th Cir. 2022) (in a trial in which the defendant presented a defense of temporary insanity due to involuntary intoxication, the prosecutor violated the Due Process Clause by "elicit[ing] testimony that Engle had invoked his [state statutory] right to terminate police interrogation after being advised of this right" and by "argu[ing] to the jury during his summation that Engle's termination of the interview was evidence that Engle was sane at the time of the offense"; the court rejects the state's attempt to distinguish *Doyle v. Ohio* on the ground that it involved "the warnings required by *Miranda*, whereas Engle invoked his right to terminate police questioning in reliance on a warning required by Article 38.22 of the Texas Code of Criminal Procedure": "It makes no difference whether the assurance given to the defendant was required by the federal Constitution or instead by statute, as in this case; it is the defendant's *frustrated reliance* on an official assurance that violates the Constitution.").

In *Greer v. Miller,* 483 U.S. 756 (1987), the Court held that *Doyle* did not require the invalidation of a conviction when the prosecutor asked a single impermissible question touching on the defendant's silence after *Miranda* warnings and the trial court immediately sustained a defense objection and gave a curative instruction. *Greer* illustrates the desirability of filing a pretrial motion for an order *in limine* forbidding the prosecutor's use or attempted use of evidence that is inadmissible under *Doyle*. See § 17.5 *supra* regarding the utility of such motions, at least in jurisdictions where the defendant is entitled to a jury trial and those in which it is possible to litigate motions *in limine* before a judge other than the one who will sit at a bench trial of the issue of guilt or innocence (§ 22.5 *supra*).

Doyle concerned the implications of the administration of *Miranda* warnings and thus does not govern prosecutorial evidence of either a defendant's pre-arrest silence (*Jenkins v. Anderson*, 447 U.S. 231, 239-40 (1980)), or post-arrest silence when no *Miranda* warnings were given (*Fletcher v. Weir*, 455 U.S. 603, 606-07 (1982) (per curiam)). In *Jenkins* and *Fletcher*, the Court rejected Fifth and Fourteenth Amendment challenges to the prosecution's use of un-*Mirandized* defendants' silence to cross-examine them at trial. Significantly, the defendants in *Jenkins* and *Fletcher* had not combined their silence with an explicit invocation of the Fifth Amendment privilege against self-incrimination. Moreover, because the prosecutorial use of silence in both cases occurred during the cross-examination of a testifying defendant at trial, the cases fit within the principle that once an accused has chosen to abandon his or her position of silence by testifying, the prosecution has an overriding interest in being permitted to test the accused's story for veracity through "'the traditional truth-testing devices of the adversary process'"(*Jenkins v. Anderson, supra*, 447 U.S. at 238). "The majority of federal courts considering the issue have ruled pre-arrest silence cannot be used in the state's case in chief. . . . ¶ Courts in Utah, Nebraska, Wyoming, and Wisconsin have also found the use of pre-arrest silence violates the Fifth Amendment. . . . ¶ The Fifth Amendment right to silence extends to situations prior to the arrest of the accused. An accused's right to remain silent and to decline to assist the State in the preparation of its criminal case may not be eroded by permitting the State in its case in chief to call to the attention of the trier of fact the accused's pre-arrest silence to imply guilt." *State v. Easter, supra*, 130 Wash. 2d at 239-40, 243, 922 P.2d at 1291, 1293. *See also, e.g., State v. Tsujimura*, 140 Hawai'i 299, 312, 400 P.3d 500, 513 (2017) ("[w]e agree with the federal circuit courts of appeals and the several States that have held as unconstitutional the use of prearrest silence as substantive evidence of guilt"); *State v. Moore*, 131 Idaho 814, 820, 965 P.2d 174, 180 (Idaho 1998) (dictum) ("[w]e believe the better rule is that which holds that the defendants' Fifth Amendment right not to have their silence used against them in a court proceeding is applicable pre-arrest and pre-*Miranda* warnings").

In *Salinas v. Texas*, 570 U.S. 178 (2013), the Court granted *certiorari* on the question "[w]hether or under what circumstances the Fifth Amendment's Self-Incrimination Clause protects a defendant's refusal to answer law enforcement questioning before he has been arrested or read his *Miranda* rights" (Petition for a Writ of *Certiorari* at i, *Salinas v. Texas* (No. 12-246), 2012 WL 3645103, at *i). *Salinas* once again involved a defendant who did not expressly invoke his Fifth Amendment privilege against self-incrimination, but the case differed from *Jenkins* and *Fletcher* in that the prosecutor used the defendant's prearrest, non-*Mirandized* silence in the prosecution's case-in-chief. In a 5-4 decision, the Court rejected the defendant's Fifth Amendment claim, but the majority was unable to agree on a rationale. A plurality opinion, authored by Justice Alito and joined by Chief Justice Roberts and Justice Kennedy, concluded that Salinas's "Fifth Amendment claim fails because he did not expressly invoke the privilege against self-incrimination in response to the officer's question" (*Salinas, supra*, 570 U.S. at 181 (plurality opinion)). Justices Thomas and Scalia concurred in the judgment on the broader rationale that "Salinas' claim would fail even if he had invoked the privilege because the prosecutor's comments regarding his precustodial silence did not compel him to give self-incriminating testimony" (*id.* at 192 (Thomas J., concurring in the judgment, joined by Scalia, J., arguing for the overruling of the entire jurisprudence of *Griffin v. California* and its progeny (see

§ 39.9 *infra*))). The four dissenting Justices concluded that even when there has been no express invocation of the Fifth Amendment Privilege, use of an accused's silence in the prosecution's case-in-chief is nonetheless barred if "an exercise of the Fifth Amendment's privilege" can be "fairly infer[red] from an individual's silence and surrounding circumstances" (*id.* at 203 (Breyer J., dissenting, joined by Ginsburg, Sotomayor, and Kagan, JJ.)).

In the wake of *Salinas*, it seems readily apparent that a suspect's explicit invocation of the Fifth Amendment privilege against self-incrimination *will* bar the prosecution from using the suspect's silence as evidence in its case in chief at trial. *See, e.g., United States v. Okatan*, 728 F.3d 111 (2d Cir. 2013) (Okatan, seated in his automobile, was approached by a border patrol agent who questioned Okatan about his reasons for being in the area, then "warned Okatan that lying to a federal officer is a criminal act and asked whether he was there to pick someone up. Okatan said that he wanted a lawyer" and the agent then arrested him (*id.* at 114). "[E]ven when an individual is not in custody, because of 'the unique role the lawyer plays in the adversary system of criminal justice in this country,' . . . a request for a lawyer in response to law enforcement questioning suffices to put an officer on notice that the individual means to invoke the privilege [against self-incrimination]" (*id.* at 119). "[W]e conclude that where, as here, an individual is interrogated by an officer, even prior to arrest, his invocation of the privilege against self-incrimination and his subsequent silence cannot be used by the government in its case in chief as substantive evidence of guilt." *Id.* at 120.). Although Justice Alito's plurality opinion in *Salinas* only addresses the question of what happens when a suspect fails to invoke the Privilege explicitly, the opinion's wording and reasoning convey that the plurality surely would have reached the opposite result if the Privilege *had* been invoked explicitly. Moreover, even if only a single member of the plurality were to support a bar to the use of silence in such a situation, that single vote would combine with the four *Salinas* dissenters' votes to create a majority in favor of a prohibitory rule.

The prosecution should also be barred from using a suspect's silence in its case in chief if the suspect explicitly invoked the right to counsel. *State v. Lovejoy*, 2014 ME 48, 89 A.3d 1066, 1074 (Me. 2014) ("We distinguish the factual context before us from that which arises when, as in *Salinas*, . . . a defendant is voluntarily speaking with law enforcement officers and then simply ceases speaking without any clear indication of an intention to exercise the right not to be a witness against himself. . . . In contrast to those facts, Lovejoy specifically terminated communication by first telling the investigating detective during a telephone conversation that he wanted to speak with a lawyer and then remaining silent by not returning the detective's telephone calls."). When an individual understands that s/he has a right to a lawyer's help and explicitly claims that right, his or her refusal to speak to authorities in the absence of counsel should command the protections of the *Doyle* exclusionary rule because the prosecution's use of silence under these circumstances would work the same type of unfairness that was condemned in *Doyle*. And even when an accused has not claimed any privilege, *Salinas* does not justify the admission of evidence of his or her silence after s/he has been taken into "custody" within the meaning of § 26.6.1 *supra. See State v. Pinson*, 183 Wash. App. 411, 418-19, 333 P.3d 528, 532 (2014) ("*Salinas* does not apply here. Although Deputy Nault testified that Pinson allowed the officers to talk with him, Pinson testified that at the time of the interview he had been handcuffed and taken to the front porch. As a result, Pinson's interrogation was custodial rather than voluntary. . . . The Court stated in *Salinas* that 'a suspect who is subjected to the "inherently compelling pressures" of an unwarned custodial interrogation need not invoke the privilege.' *Salinas*, . . . [citing Justice Alito's plurality opinion].").

In any event, this is another area in which state constitutional guarantees may offer more protection than their federal parallels. See § 17.11 *supra*. Some state courts have concluded that their respective constitutions bar prosecutorial use of a suspect's pretrial silence, either categorically (*see Commonwealth v. Molina*, 628 Pa. 465, 502, 104 A.3d 430, 452 (2014) (the state constitution "is violated when the prosecution uses a defendant's silence whether pre or post-arrest as substantive evidence of guilt"); *People v. Pavone*, 26 N.Y.3d 629, 47 N.E.3d 56, 26 N.Y.S.3d 728 (2015) (dictum) (holding that the prosecution's use of the defendant's pretrial silence violates the state constitution's due process guarantee, "whether the People use defendant's silence as part of the case-in-chief or for impeachment purposes" (*id.* at 641, 47 N.E.3d at 66, 26 N.Y.S.3d at 738) and "reject[ing] the People's artificial distinction between defendants who are arrested and remain silent before *Miranda* warnings have been provided, and those who remain silent afterwards" (*id.* at 642, 47 N.E.3d at 67, 26 N.Y.S.3d at 739): "Indeed this Court has even held that *pre-arrest* silence cannot be used against a defendant in the People's case-in-chief." *Id.*); *State v. Horwitz*, 191 So.3d 429, 441-42 (Fla. 2016) ("We decline to apply the reasoning of the plurality in *Salinas* to whether a non-testifying defendant's privilege against self-incrimination under the Florida Constitution is violated by the State's use of his or her pre-arrest, pre-*Miranda* silence as substantive evidence of the defendant's guilt. . . . ¶ . . . [T]o allow the State to introduce evidence of and comment on a defendant's pre-arrest, pre-*Miranda* silence burdens the defendant's privilege against self-incrimination *at trial*. Particularly, when a defendant exercises the privilege against self-incrimination at trial by not taking the stand, the defendant may be doing so, in part, to prevent the State from having the opportunity for impeachment. Allowing the defendant's previous silence to be used as substantive evidence of consciousness of guilt would penalize the defendant for exercising that right at trial. The defendant should not be compelled to make the choice between testifying – with the possibility that his or her earlier silence might be used to impeach him or her – and not testifying – thereby, under the State's view, allowing the State to use the defendant's earlier silence as substantive evidence of the defendant's guilt. . . . ¶ . . . [W]e conclude that a defendant's privilege against self-incrimination guaranteed under article I, section 9 of the Florida Constitution is violated when his or her pre-arrest, pre-*Miranda* silence is used against the defendant at trial as substantive evidence of the defendant's consciousness of guilt.")), or at least if it took place after arrest (*State v. Hoggins*, 718 So.2d 761 (Fla. 1998) (the state constitutional privilege against self-incrimination forbids the use of a defendant's silence at the time of arrest but before receipt of *Miranda* warnings to impeach his or her trial testimony); *State v. Davis,* 38 Wash. App. 600, 686 P.2d 1143 (1984) (the state Due Process Clause forbids use of a defendant's post-arrest silence as substantive evidence of guilt)) or "'at or near' the time of arrest, during official interrogation, or while in police custody" (*State v. Muhammad*, 182 N.J. 551, 569, 868 A.2d 302, 312 (2005) (the state constitutional privilege against self-incrimination forbids use of silence under these circumstances, either as substantive evidence of guilt or for impeachment)); *accord, State v. Irizarry*, 2017 WL 2535950 (N.J. App. 2017)).

Concerning evidence that prior to the defendant's arrest s/he retained counsel and refused to cooperate with the police investigation, see *State v. Angel T.*, 292 Conn. 262, 973 A.2d 1207 (2009), summarized in § 43.2.1 *infra*.

26.21. *Statements Taken Through an Interpreter*

Interrogating officers who do not speak a suspect's or an arrestee's language often take a statement through an interpreter. If the prosecution offers the statement at trial only through the interrogator and does not tender the interpreter, hearsay and confrontation issues arise that are the subject of conflicting decisions among the state and lower federal courts. These are summarized in Zachary C. Bolitho, *The Hearsay and Confrontation Clause Problems Caused by Admitting What a Non-Testifying Interpreter Said the Criminal Defendant Said*, 49 NEW MEXICO L. REV. 193 (2019).

Chapter 27

Motions To Suppress Identification Testimony

27.1. *Introduction and Overview*

In a substantial proportion of criminal cases, the prosecution proves the defendant's identity as the perpetrator through an in-court identification of the defendant: The complainant or an eyewitness testifies that the individual seated next to defense counsel is the person who committed the crime. (The exceptions are cases in which the perpetrator's identity is proved through scientific evidence (such as DNA, fingerprint, or serology evidence), documentary evidence, circumstantial evidence (such as the defendant's possession of the fruits of a recent crime), the defendant's confession, and/or the testimony of a turncoat accomplice.)

Although some cases may involve a defendant who is a longstanding acquaintance of the complainant or eyewitness, most identifications in criminal cases are based upon the complainant's or eyewitness's momentary observation of a stranger. Frequently, that identification has been shaped (or at least affected) by the witness's participation in one or more of the following police identification procedures:

(a)   A "lineup" in which the witness observes the defendant standing among a group (usually ranging from seven to ten persons) and is asked to select the perpetrator.

(b)   A "show-up" in which the witness is shown only the defendant and asked whether the defendant was the perpetrator.

(c)   A "photographic identification procedure" in which the witness is shown:

      (i)   a group of photographs (a "photo array" usually consisting of five to ten "mug shots"; an entire book of mug shots, known as a "mug-book"; or a set of mug shot photos displayed on a computer screen) and asked to select the perpetrator; or

      (ii)   a single photograph and asked whether the person depicted was the perpetrator.

As the Supreme Court has recognized, a "witness' recollection of the stranger can be distorted easily by the circumstances or by later actions of the police" (*Manson v. Brathwaite,* 432 U.S. 98, 112 (1977)), and "'[t]he influence of improper suggestion upon identifying witnesses probably accounts for more miscarriages of justice than any other single factor – perhaps it is responsible for more such errors than all other factors combined'" (*United States v. Wade,* 388 U.S. 218, 229 (1967)). *See also Perry v. New Hampshire*, 565 U.S. 228, 245 (2012) ("'the annals of criminal law are rife with instances of mistaken identification'" (quoting *Wade, supra,* 388 U.S. at 228)).

The Court has established three separate constitutional doctrines regulating the use of identification testimony, each of which provides a basis for suppressing identification testimony by the complainant and any eyewitnesses:

(a) *The Due Process doctrine:* Testimony concerning pretrial identifications at police-staged confrontations that are "so impermissibly suggestive as to give rise to a very substantial likelihood of irreparable misidentification" are constitutionally inadmissible (*Simmons v. United States,* 390 U.S. 377, 384 (1968) (dictum)). *Accord, Perry v. New Hampshire, supra,* 565 U.S. at 238-40 (dictum); *State v. Dickson,* 322 Conn. 410, 141 A.3d 810 (2016). See §§ 27.2-27.5 *infra.*

(b) *The Sixth Amendment doctrine:* Police-staged lineups and show-ups held after the right to counsel has attached may be unconstitutional if they were conducted in the absence of counsel for the defendant. See § 27.6 *infra.*

(c) *The Fourth Amendment doctrine:* Testimony regarding a lineup or other custodial identification made as a result of an illegal arrest or detention is inadmissible. See § 27.7 *infra.*

State-law doctrines may provide additional bases for objecting to identification testimony. See § 27.8 *infra.*

In a number of jurisdictions, statutes or court rules provide for a pretrial hearing on a defense motion to suppress identification testimony. At such a hearing the prosecutor ordinarily presents the police officer who conducted the identification procedure and the complainant or eyewitness who made the identification. (In some jurisdictions the prosecutor presents only the police officer, taking advantage of the admissibility of hearsay evidence in a suppression hearing (see § 24.3.5 *supra*) to have the officer testify to the witness's identification as well as the witness's account of his or her ability to observe the perpetrator.) In any pretrial identification suppression hearing at which an identifying witness will testify, it is advisable for the defense to waive the defendant's presence during the witness's testimony. See § 24.3.2 *supra.*

In other jurisdictions defense objections to identification testimony or motions to suppress it are litigated in a mid-trial hearing or a series of *voir dire* examinations of the prosecution's identification witnesses. In jury trials it "may often be advisable [and,] . . . [i]n some circumstances . . . may be constitutionally necessary" to conduct such hearings outside the presence of the jury (*Watkins v. Sowders,* 449 U.S. 341, 349 (1981)), although there is no "*per se* [constitutional] rule compelling such a procedure in every case" (*id.*). Here, too, counsel should arrange that the defendant be removed from the courtroom during the *voir dire* proceedings litigating the admissibility of identification testimony.

This chapter examines the various doctrines governing suppression or exclusion of identification testimony. Procedural requirements governing suppression motions and strategic considerations in drafting the motions are discussed in §§ 17.3-17.11. Techniques for conducting a suppression hearing are discussed in Chapter 24.

A. *Due Process Grounds for Suppressing an Identification as Unreliable*

27.2. *The Due Process Standard*

Police-staged identification procedures that are unduly suggestive may impair the reliability of the resulting identification and render it inadmissible. *Foster v. California*, 394 U.S. 440 (1969); *Finch v. McCoy*, 914 F.3d 292 (4th Cir. 2019). The focus of the Due Process standard for admissibility of identification testimony is the interplay between (1) actions by law enforcement agents that may undermine the reliability of an identification, and (2) the susceptibility of each identifying witness's testimony to distortion by those actions. As in the case of confessions (see § 26.2 *supra*), unreliability alone – unaffected by any governmental behavior that could contribute to it – will not support suppression or exclusion of identification testimony. Some state activity conducing to inaccuracy is necessary. *See Perry v. New Hampshire*, 565 U.S. 228, 248 (2012), discussed in § 27.5 *infra*. Once that activity is shown, "[i]t is the reliability of identification evidence that primarily determines its admissibility" (*Watkins v. Sowders*, 449 U.S. 341, 347 (1981); *Manson v. Brathwaite*, 432 U.S. 98, 113-14 (1977)). *See Sexton v. Beaudreaux*, 138 S. Ct. 2555, 2559-60 (2018) (per curiam) (dictum).

Under current Due Process doctrine, the admissibility of an identification is determined by weighing "the corrupting effect of the suggestive identification" against factors showing the identification to be reliable notwithstanding the suggestiveness of the police-staged confrontation (*Manson v. Brathwaite, supra*, 432 U.S. at 114). *See also Neil v. Biggers,* 409 U.S. 188, 199 (1972) (the "central question" is whether "the identification procedure was reliable even though the confrontation procedure was suggestive"). In gauging the reliability of the identification, "[t]he factors to be considered . . . include the opportunity of the witness to view the criminal at the time of the crime, the witness' degree of attention, the accuracy of his prior description of the criminal, the level of certainty demonstrated at the confrontation, and the time between the crime and the confrontation" (*Manson v. Brathwaite, supra*, 432 U.S. at 114). *See also Neil v. Biggers, supra*, 409 U.S. at 199-200; *Simmons v. United States,* 390 U.S. 377, 385 (1968). If a suggestive police identification procedure created a "very substantial likelihood of irreparable misidentification," then the court must suppress both the pretrial identification (*Neil v. Biggers, supra*, 409 U.S. at 197 (dictum)) and any in-court identifications tainted by the constitutionally defective pretrial identification (*see Coleman v. Alabama,* 399 U.S. 1, 4-6 (1970) (dictum)).

Thus, the prevailing federal Due Process inquiry has two distinct components. The court determines, first, whether any police identification procedure was suggestive. If it was suggestive, then the distorting influence of the procedure is weighed against considerations indicating that the identification is nevertheless reliable. *See, e.g., State v. Thamer*, 777 P.2d 432, 435 (Utah 1989) ("We apply a two-step test to determine whether a pre-indictment or pre-information photo array is so suggestive that the subsequent admission of an in-court identification violates the due process clause. First, we must determine whether there was a pretrial photographic identification procedure used which was so impermissibly suggestive as to give rise to a very substantial likelihood of irreparable misidentification. . . . Second, if the photo array is impermissibly suggestive, then the in-court identification must be based on an untainted, independent foundation to be reliable."); *State v. Novotny*, 297 Kan. 1174, 1180-83, 307 P.3d 1278, 1284-86 (2013) (essentially the same). Section 27.3 *infra* examines the factors involved in assessing the suggestiveness of a police identification procedure, and § 27.4 examines the reliability factors. Section 27.5 explores the possible arguments that a defendant is entitled to suppression of an unreliable identification even when there was no police suggestiveness.

Of course, the state courts are free to construe their state constitutions as establishing a more protective due process standard than the federal test for admission of identification testimony. *See, e.g.*, *State v. Martinez*, 2021-NMSC-002, 478 P.3d 880 (N.M. 2020) ("In light of the significant, recurrent, and deeply troubling problems caused by unnecessarily suggestive, police-arranged identification procedures, we take this opportunity to consider our state constitutional jurisprudence as it relates to the admission of this type of powerful yet problematic evidence in New Mexico courts. We ultimately hold that the *Manson* test does not satisfy due process under . . . [the due process clause] of the New Mexico Constitution . . . ." *Id.* at 886. "Under the per se exclusionary rule we adopt herein, if a witness makes an identification of a defendant as a result of a police identification procedure that is unnecessarily suggestive and conducive to irreparable misidentification, the identification and any subsequent identification by the same witness must be suppressed." *Id.* at 905.); *Young v. State*, 374 P.3d 395 (Alaska 2016) (construing the state constitution to "depart from *Manson v. Brathwaite* and the Alaska cases that relied on it as the touchstone" because "[d]evelopments in the science related to the reliability of eyewitness identifications, and courts' responses to those developments, have significantly weakened our confidence in the *Brathwaite* test as a tool for preventing the admission of unreliable evidence at trial, and therefore its capacity for protecting the due process rights afforded by the Alaska Constitution" (*id.* at 413); "we are convinced that the *Brathwaite* test does not adequately assess the reliability of eyewitness identifications and thus allows the admission of very persuasive evidence of doubtful reliability" (*id.* at 416); the court replaces "the [*Neil v.*] *Biggers* factors" with a list that reflects the "scientific literature" on "the factors that can affect the reliability of eyewitness identifications" (*id.* at 417); the court also holds that a defendant's presentation of "'some evidence of suggestiveness'" is sufficient to require "an evidentiary hearing on the issue," that "a defendant need not show that a procedure was 'unnecessarily suggestive' in order to get a hearing," and that "[a]t the hearing the State must present evidence that the identification is nonetheless reliable" (*id.* at 427); the court further holds that "[i]f eyewitness identification is a significant issue in a case, the trial court should issue an appropriate jury instruction that sets out the relevant factors affecting reliability." (*id.* at 428)); *State v. Henderson*, 208 N.J. 208, 287 n.10, 288-93, 27 A.3d 872, 919 n.10, 919-922 (2011) (construing the state constitution's due process clause to remedy the "shortcomings" of the Supreme Court's *Manson v. Braithwaite* standard by adopting a "new framework" that "allows judges to consider all relevant factors that affect reliability in deciding whether an identification is admissible; that is not heavily weighted by factors that can be corrupted by suggestiveness; that promotes deterrence in a meaningful way; and that focuses on helping jurors both understand and evaluate the effects that various factors have on memory."); *People v. Adams*, 53 N.Y.2d 241, 423 N.E.2d 379, 440 N.Y.S.2d 902 (1981) (rejecting the "totality of the circumstances" analysis of *Neil v. Biggers*, *supra*, and *Manson v. Brathwaite*, *supra*, in favor of the Supreme Court's earlier analytical approach, which looked first at the suggestiveness of the identification and, upon finding it unduly suggestive, excluded the identification unless the prosecution could show that the identification had an "independent source"); *Commonwealth v. Johnson*, 420 Mass. 458, 463, 472, 650 N.E.2d 1257, 1260, 1265 (1995) (same as *People v. Adams*, *supra*: "reject[ing] *Brathwaite*" on state constitutional grounds and "adher[ing] to the stricter rule of per se exclusion previously followed by the Supreme Court and first set forth in the *Wade-Gilbert-Stovall* trilogy"); *State v. Lawson*, 352 Or. 724, 740, 761-62, 291 P.3d 673, 685, 696-97 (2012) ("Based on [an] . . . extensive review of the current scientific research and literature," the state supreme court takes "judicial notice of the data contained in those various sources as legislative facts" to revise the state-law "test governing the admission of eyewitness testimony." *Inter alia*, the burden rests on "the state as the proponent of the eyewitness identification" to "establish all preliminary facts necessary to establish admissibility of the eyewitness evidence"; then, "[i]f the state satisfies its burden," the burden shifts to the defendant to establish that, "although the eyewitness evidence is otherwise admissible, the probative value of the evidence is substantially outweighed by the danger of unfair prejudice, confusion of the issues, misleading the jury, or by considerations of undue delay or needless presentation of cumulative evidence."); *see also Dennis v. Secretary, Pennsylvania Department of Corrections*, 834 F.3d 263, 336-40 (3d Cir. 2016) (en banc) (McKee, C.J., concurring) (discussing the above-cited opinions of the New Jersey and Oregon Supreme Courts as examples of state courts' "creat[ion] [of] new procedures and evidentiary frameworks that minimize the risks associated with erroneous eyewitness identifications"); and see generally § 17.11 *supra*.

27.3. *Suggestiveness of Police Identification Procedures*

There are a number of useful reference works that will assist counsel to identify the suggestive features in any particular police-staged identification confrontation. *See* NATIONAL RESEARCH COUNCIL OF THE NATIONAL ACADEMIES, IDENTIFYING THE CULPRIT: ASSESSING EYEWITNESS IDENTIFICATION (National Academies Press 2014); BRANDON L. GARRETT, CONVICTING THE INNOCENT: WHERE CRIMINAL PROSECUTIONS GO WRONG (2011); ELIZABETH F. LOFTUS, EYEWITNESS TESTIMONY (1996); ELIZABETH LOFTUS, JAMES M. DOYLE & JENNIFER E. DYSART, EYEWITNESS TESTIMONY: CIVIL AND CRIMINAL (4th ed. 2007); NATHAN R. SOBEL, EYEWITNESS IDENTIFICATION – LEGAL AND PRACTICAL PROBLEMS (2d ed. 2002); PATRICK M. WALL, EYEWITNESS IDENTIFICATION IN CRIMINAL CASES (1965); A. DANIEL YARMEY, THE PSYCHOLOGY OF EYEWITNESS TESTIMONY (1979); Brandon L. Garrett, *Eyewitnesses and Exclusion*, 65 VAND. L. REV. 451 (2012); John B. Gould & Richard A. Leo, *One Hundred Years Later: Wrongful Convictions After a Century of Research*, 100 J. CRIM. L. & CRIM. 825, 841-43 (2010); Radha Natarajan, Note, *Racialized Memory and Reliability: Due Process Applied to Cross-Racial Eyewitness Identifications*, 78 N.Y.U. L. REV. 1821 (2003); Gary L. Wells & Elizabeth A. Olson, *The Other Race Effect in Eyewitness Identification*, 7 (No. 1) PSYCHOLOGY, PUBLIC POLICY, AND LAW 230 (2001); Fredric D. Woocher, Note, *Did Your Eyes Deceive You? Expert Psychological Testimony on the Unreliability of Eyewitness Identification,* 29 STAN. L. REV. 969 (1977); *cf.* Samuel R. Gross & Michael Shaffer, *Exonerations in the United States 1989-2012: Report by the National Registry of Exonerations, available at* https://www.law.umich.edu/special/exoneration/Documents/exonerations_us_1989_2012_full_report.pdf (June 2012), pp. 40-56; Cory S. Clements, *Perception and Persuasion in Legal Argumentation: Using Informal Fallacies and Cognitive Biases to Win The War of Words*, 2013 B.Y.U. L. REV. 319. *See also Dennis v. Secretary, Pennsylvania Department of Corrections*, 834 F.3d 263, 314-45 (3d Cir. 2016) (en banc) (McKee, C.J., concurring) (documenting and analyzing factors that undermine the reliability of eyewitness identifications); *United States v. Nolan*, 956 F.3d 71, 75 (2d Cir. 2020) (same: "[e]yewitness identification testimony is notoriously prone to error"); *Bey v. Superintendent Greene SCI*, 856 F.3d 230, 240 & nn.50-51

(3d Cir. 2017) ("The scientific community has understood for decades that eyewitness identifications that are certain and confident are not necessarily accurate. . . . Rather, a witness may honestly hold beliefs about what he or she saw that are distorted, inaccurate, or even completely wrong."); *Commonwealth v. Gomes*, 470 Mass. 352, 369-76, 22 N.E.3d 897, 910-16 (2015) (discussing five principles of eyewitness identification that "we determine to have achieved a near consensus in the relevant scientific community and therefore are 'so generally accepted' that it is appropriate that they now be included in a revised model jury instruction regarding eyewitness identification," and "also summariz[ing] the research that informed our conclusions as to each generally accepted principle"); *Commonwealth v. Bastaldo*, 472 Mass. 16, 18, 32 N.E.3d 873, 877 (2015) (supplementing the court's decision in *Gomes, supra*, by further discussing cross-racial and cross-ethnic identifications, and holding that "[i]n criminal trials that commence after the issuance of this opinion, a cross-racial instruction should always be included when giving the model eyewitness identification instruction, unless the parties agree that there was no cross-racial identification," and that trial judges have the "discretion to include a cross-ethnic eyewitness identification instruction in appropriate circumstances"); *People v. Boone*, 30 N.Y.3d 521, 529-30, 535-36, 91 N.E.3d 1194, 1198-99, 1202-03, 69 N.Y.S.3d 215, 219-20, 223-24 (2017) ("In light of our discussion of the cross-race effect, which has been accepted by a near consensus in the relevant scientific community of cognitive and social psychologists, and recognizing the very significant part that inaccurate identifications play in wrongful convictions, we reach the following holding: in a case in which a witness's identification of the defendant is at issue, and the identifying witness and defendant appear to be of different races, a trial court is required to give, upon request, during final instructions, a jury charge on the cross-race effect, instructing (1) that the jury should consider whether there is a difference in race between the defendant and the witness who identified the defendant, and (2) that, if so, the jury should consider (a) that some people have greater difficulty in accurately identifying members of a different race than in accurately identifying members of their own race and (b) whether the difference in race affected the accuracy of the witness's identification." ¶ Such an instruction is needed because "[t]here is . . . a significant disparity between what the psychological research shows and what uninstructed jurors believe." ¶ "Expert testimony on the cross-race effect is not a precondition of a jury charge on the subject."); *State v. Henderson*, 208 N.J. 208, 27 A.3d 872 (2011) (a comprehensive discussion of the dangers of unreliability of eyewitness identification, summarizing the scientific literature on the subject, and specifically requiring a cautionary instruction on cross-racial identifications whenever such identifications are at issue); *People v. Lemcke*, 11 Cal. 5th 644, 486 P.3d 1077, 278 Cal. Rptr. 3d 849 (2021) (suspending the portion of California's pattern jury instruction on identification testimony which advises jurors that in evaluating eyewitness identification testimony they should consider, as a factor, how certain the witness was of his or her identification; this opinion also provides a wide-ranging discussion of eyewitness-identification problems, including a comprehensive canvass of the empirical studies and judicial decisions on the subject of the lack of correlation between certainty and reliability.); *State v. Martinez*, 2021-NMSC-002, 478 P.3d 880 (N.M. 2020), summarized in § 27.2 *supra* (an exhaustive opinion collecting the empirical literature and legal materials that document the fallibility of eyewitness identification testimony). The following subsections discuss recurring features of identification procedures that judicial opinions have recognized as suggestive. Counsel should emphasize these when they are present but should also consult the social-science literature cited above to document other factors that tend to make identifications unreliable.

A model for best practices in staged identification proceedings is set out in Louisiana Code of Criminal Procedure, Title V-a (articles 251-253), signed into law on May 23, 2018, and constitutes a valuable resource for defense counsel as illustrating state-of-the-art understanding of how these proceedings should be conducted. It requires agencies administering identification procedures to adopt policies designed to reduce erroneous eyewitness identifications and to enhance the reliability and objectivity of such identifications. All agencies must either adopt the model policy recommended by the Louisiana Sheriff's Executive Management Institute or draft their own policies based on "[c]redible field, academic, or laboratory research on eyewitness memory." LA. CODE CRIM. PRO. art. 253(B)(1)(a). The policies must include, *inter alia*, the following information regarding evidence-based practices:

> "(a) Procedures for selecting photograph and live lineup filler photographs or participants to ensure that the photographs or participant:
> > "(i) Are consistent in appearance with the description of the alleged perpetrator.
> > "(ii) Do not make the suspect noticeably stand out.
> "(b) Instructions given to a witness before conducting a photograph or live lineup identification procedure shall include a statement that the person who committed the offense may or may not be present in the procedure.
> "(c) Procedures for documenting and preserving the results of a photograph or live lineup identification procedure, including the documentation of witness statements, regardless of the outcome of the procedure.
> "(d) Procedures for administering a photograph or live lineup identification procedure to an illiterate person or a person with limited English language proficiency.
> "(e) For a live lineup identification procedure, if practicable, procedures for assigning an administrator who is unaware of which member of the live lineup is the suspect in the case or alternative procedures designed to prevent opportunities to influence the witness.
> "(f) For a photograph identification procedure, procedures for assigning an administrator who is capable of administering a photograph array in a blind manner or in a blinded manner consistent with other proven or supported best practices designed to prevent opportunities to influence the witness."

Id., art. 253(B)(2). The policies must "[p]rovide [(i)] that a witness who makes an identification based on a photograph or live lineup identification procedure be asked immediately after the procedure to state, in the witness's own words, how confident the witness is in making the identification" and (ii) that these witness statements be documented and preserved. *Id.*, art. 253(B)(3). "A video record of identification procedures shall be made or, if a video record is not practicable, an audio record shall be made. If neither a video nor audio record are practicable, the reasons shall be documented in writing, and the lineup administrator shall make [and preserve] a full and complete written record of the lineup . . . ." *Id.*, art. 253(F). Noncompliance with the procedures is not alone grounds for exclusion of identification testimony but "[e]vidence of failure to comply . . . (1) [m]ay be considered by the . . . court in adjudicating motions to suppress an eyewitness identification" and (2) [m]ay be admissible in support of any claim of eyewitness misidentification . . . ." *Id.*, art. 253(H).

In 2020 the Minnesota Legislature amended the State's statutes to provide a similar, although less detailed, set of requirements fully effective on February 1, 2021. MINN. STAT. ANN.

§ 626.8433. California had enacted similar legislation in 2018, effective January 1, 2020. CAL. PENAL CODE § 859.7. Counsel challenging eyewitness identifications can point to the increasing legislative and administrative recognition of the need for meticulous procedures to assure reliability. *See also* Thomas D. Albright & Brandon L. Garrett, *The Law and Science of Eyewitness Evidence, available at:* https://ssrn.com/abstract=3675055; *2019 Report of the United States Court of Appeals for the Third Circuit Task Force on Eyewitness Identifications,* 92 TEMPLE L. REV. 1 (2019); Andrew Hemming, *Reform of the Evidential Rules for Eyewitness Identification in the United States – Advice from the Antipodes*, 43 HOUSTON J. INT'L. L. 1 (2020).

27.3.1. *Show-ups*

The Supreme Court has recognized that show-up identification procedures, in which the accused is exhibited to the witness in a one-on-one confrontation, are inherently suggestive. *See, e.g., United States v. Wade,* 388 U.S. 218, 234 (1967) ("[i]t is hard to imagine a situation more clearly conveying the suggestion to the witness that the one presented is believed guilty by the police"); *Stovall v. Denno*, 388 U.S. 293, 302 (1967) (dictum) ("[t]he practice of showing suspects singly to persons for the purpose of identification, and not as part of a lineup, has been widely condemned"). The empirical evidence strongly supports these points. *See, e.g.*, Stephen P. Bertelsman, Note, *Defending Due Process: The Case for Abolition of the Show-Up Line-Up*, 68 WASH. U. J. LAW & POLICY 245 (2022).

Notwithstanding the inherent suggestiveness of show-ups, the Court has sustained a show-up in the victim's hospital room against due process challenge when the use of this procedure was "imperative" because the witness was so gravely wounded that it was impossible to "kn[o]w how long . . . [the witness] might live" (*Stovall v. Denno, supra*, 388 U.S. at 302). Under these circumstances the Court found that the show-up was not *"unnecessarily* suggestive" (*id.*; emphasis added): "the police followed the only feasible procedure" (*id.*). Several lower courts have similarly sustained immediate, on-the-scene show-ups as justified by the need to find the perpetrator rapidly. However, show-ups will not be approved when the lapse of time between the crime and the show-up rendered it unnecessary to employ the inherently suggestive show-up procedure. *See, e.g., People v. Cruz*, 129 A.D.3d 119, 122, 125, 10 N.Y.S.3d 214, 218, 220 (N.Y. App. Div., 1st Dep't 2015) (a show-up which took place "approximately one hour after the 911 telephone call had been placed" was unnecessarily suggestive because there were no "exigent circumstances warranting a showup identification": "The 55 year old complainant, though bruised and visibly shaken, was not suffering from any life threatening wounds that would have made her otherwise unable or unavailable to make an identification at a later time or at the precinct where she was already located."); *People v. Brown*, 121 A.D.2d 733, 504 N.Y.S.2d 457 (N.Y. App. Div., 2d Dep't 1986) (a show-up which was "conducted an hour after the crime was committed" was not justified by "'exigent circumstances'" or a showing that "it would have been unduly burdensome . . . 'to form some kind of lineup'"); *People v. Knox*, 170 A.D.3d 1648, 1649-50, 96 N.Y.S.3d 811, 812-13 (N.Y. App. Div., 4th Dep't 2019) (suppressing a show-up identification as insufficiently ""'justified by exigency or temporal and spatial proximity [to the crime]'"" because the police had already obtained an identification of the suspect by the complainant prior to the challenged show-up (with an eyewitness), and "[t]he People have proffered no reason that a lineup identification procedure would have been unduly burdensome" given that the show-up occurred "approximately 90 minutes after the crime, about five miles from the scene of the crime").

The inherent suggestiveness of a show-up is exacerbated by the police officers' use of procedures that:

(a)   provide the witness with additional reasons for believing that the person being shown is the perpetrator (*see, e.g., Velez v. Schmer,* 724 F.2d 249 (1st Cir. 1984) (the police used suggestive language: "'This is him, isn't it?'"); *Styers v. Smith,* 659 F.2d 293 (2d Cir. 1981) (a show-up at the police station after a police officer told the victim that he was leaving to pick up the robbery suspects); *People v. Adams,* 53 N.Y.2d 241, 248-49, 423 N.E.2d 379, 382, 440 N.Y.S.2d 902, 905 (1981) ("[s]howing the suspects together also enhanced the possibility that if one of them were recognized the others would be identified as well . . . [and] permitting the victims as a group to view the suspects . . . increased the likelihood that if one of them made an identification the others would concur"); *People v. Buckery,* 130 A.D.3d 640, 641, 12 N.Y.S.3d 291, 292 (N.Y. App. Div., 2d Dep't 2015) (before the show-up of the defendant and three others for a robbery committed by four people, a police officer "walked up to the complainant, holding the wallet [which had been "recovered from one of the suspects other than the defendant"], and . . . the complainant identified it immediately before being asked by the police whether he recognized any of the suspects"); *State v. Moore,* 343 S.C. 282, 287, 540 S.E.2d 445, 448 (2000) ("the witness was brought to a location where two individuals, wearing clothing similar to that described by the witness, were surrounded by uniformed police officers"); *State v. Williams,* 162 W. Va. 348, 249 S.E.2d 752 (1978) (the police told the victim that his money was found in the possession of the three suspects whom he was about to view)), or

(b)   magnify the custodial features of the situation, so as to enhance the impression that the police are certain of the defendant's guilt (*see, e.g., Clark v. Caspari,* 274 F.3d 507, 511 (8th Cir. 2001) (during the show-up, the two suspects were handcuffed and "surrounded" by police officers, "one of whom was holding a shotgun"); *United States ex rel. Hudson v. Brierton,* 699 F.2d 917 (7th Cir. 1983) (the defendant was locked in a jail cell at the time of viewing); *People v. Williams,* 127 A.D.3d 1114, 1116, 7 N.Y.S.3d 434, 437 (N.Y. App. Div., 2d Dep't 2015) ("the defendant was the only person standing in the street, in handcuffs, surrounded by the police with high-beam headlights shining on his face, during the showup proceeding"); *People v. Brown,* 121 A.D.2d 733, 504 N.Y.S.2d 457 (NY. App. Div., 2d Dep't 1986) (during the show-up the suspects were surrounded by several police officers and had handcuffs dangling from their wrists).

27.3.2. *Lineups*

A lineup is impermissibly suggestive if some aspect of the defendant's appearance (age, race, skin complexion, height, weight, attire) renders him or her distinctive from the others in the line, especially if the unique characteristic makes the defendant the only person in the line who fits the known description of the perpetrator. *See, e.g., Raheem v. Kelly*, 257 F.3d 122, 135–37 (2d Cir. 2001) (a lineup was suggestive in the case of two witnesses because they had given a description of the perpetrator as wearing a black leather coat and the defendant was the only person in the line wearing a black leather coat); *United States v. Downs*, 230 F.3d 272, 273, 275 (7th Cir. 2000) (a lineup was suggestive because the witnesses had described the perpetrator as "lightly unshaven" and the defendant "was the only man in a line-up of five who lacked a moustache"); *Martin v. Indiana*, 438 F. Supp. 234 (N.D. Ind. 1977), *aff'd*, 577 F.2d 749 (7th Cir. 1978) (a lineup was suggestive because the perpetrator had been described as a tall black man in his mid-thirties, and the only black man in the line other than the defendant was short and eighteen years old); *State v. Henderson*, 116 Ariz. 310, 569 P.2d 252 (1977) (a lineup was suggestive because the perpetrator had been described as being in his early to middle thirties, and the defendant was 36 years old but the other five persons in the lineup were in their early to middle twenties); *People v. Colsen*, 181 A.D.3d 618, 618, 117 N.Y.S.3d 580, 580 (N.Y. App. Div., 2d Dep't 2020) (a lineup was suggestive because "[t]he defendant was the only person in the lineup with dreadlocks, and dreadlocks featured prominently in the description of one of the assailants that the complainant gave to the police," and "the dreadlocks were distinctive and visible despite the fact that the defendant and the fillers all wore hats"); *People v. Perry*, 133 A.D.3d 410, 410, 18 N.Y.S.3d 539, 539 (N.Y. App. Div., 1st Dep't 2015) (a lineup was suggestive because the defendant was the only participant who matched the complainant's description of the perpetrator as having a "'deformed right eye'"; notwithstanding "the practical difficulties in finding fillers with similarly defective eyes," a "'simple eye patch provided to each of the lineup participants or a hand over an eye would have sufficed to remove any undue suggestiveness of the procedure.'"); *People v. Robinson*, 123 A.D.3d 1062, 1062, 999 N.Y.S.2d 499, 500 (N.Y. App. Div., 2d Dep't 2014) (a lineup was suggestive where "three [of the four] fillers appear[ed] visibly older than the defendant" and "[t]he age disparity was sufficiently apparent as to orient the viewer toward the defendant as a perpetrator of the crimes charged"); *People v. Pena*, 131 A.D.3d 708, 709, 16 N.Y.S.3d 184, 184 (N.Y. App. Div., 2d Dep't 2015) (a lineup was suggestive where the defendant "was the only lineup participant dressed in a red shirt, the item of clothing which figured prominently in the description of the assailant's clothing that the complainant gave to the police"); *People v. Sapp*, 98 A.D.2d 784, 469 N.Y.S.2d 803 (N.Y. App. Div., 2d Dep't 1983) (a lineup was suggestive where the defendant was the only person in the line wearing the type of jacket that the witness had described the perpetrator as wearing); *State v. Boykins*, 173 W. Va. 761, 765-66, 320 S.E.2d 134, 138 (1984) (a lineup was suggestive where the defendant "was the only person in the lineup who wore a dark blue or black toboggan: the type of clothing the culprit allegedly wore," and "all but one of the people in the lineup was [sic] taller than" the defendant). *See also People v. Perkins*, 28 N.Y.3d 432, 437, 68 N.E.3d 679, 682, 45 N.Y.S.3d 860, 863 (2016) (a "distinctive feature" that causes a defendant to stand out in a lineup can render the lineup "unduly suggestive" even if that feature did not "figure[ ] prominently in the witness's description" of the perpetrator).

The manner in which the police conduct the lineup can also make it impermissibly suggestive. *See, e.g., United States v. Wade*, 388 U.S. 218, 234 (1967) (dictum) (practice of permitting witnesses to be present during each other's viewing of a lineup is "a procedure said to be fraught with dangers of suggestion"); *People v. Boyce*, 89 A.D.2d 623, 452 N.Y.S.2d 676 (N.Y. App. Div., 2d Dep't 1982) (suggestive post-lineup remarks by the police).

27.3.3. *Photographic Identifications*

Courts have consistently recognized that:

"improper employment of photographs by police may sometimes cause witnesses to err in identifying criminals. A witness may have obtained only a brief glimpse of a criminal, or may have seen him under poor conditions. Even if the police subsequently follow the most correct photographic identification procedures and show him the pictures of a number of individuals without indicating whom they suspect, there is some danger that the witness may make an incorrect identification. This danger will be increased if the police display to the witness only the picture of a single individual who generally resembles the person he saw, or if they show him the pictures of several persons among which the photograph of a single such individual recurs or is in some way emphasized. The chance of misidentification is also heightened if the police indicate to the witness that they have other evidence that one of the persons pictured committed the crime. Regardless of how the initial misidentification comes about, the witness thereafter is apt to retain in his memory the image of the photograph rather than of the person actually seen, reducing the trustworthiness of subsequent lineup or courtroom identification." (*Simmons v. United States,* 390 U.S. 377, 383-84 (1968).)

Showing a potential identification witness a single photograph is both highly suggestive and unnecessarily so because – in the absence of extraordinary circumstances – the police can easily put together a photo array. *See Manson v. Brathwaite,* 432 U.S. 98, 99, 109, 117 (1977) (dictum) (accepting the state's concession); *United States v. Dailey,* 524 F.2d 911, 914 (8th Cir. 1975); *State v. Al-Bayyinah,* 356 N.C. 150, 157, 567 S.E.2d 120, 124 (2002). In *Simmons* and *Manson,* the Supreme Court declined to adopt a "per se rule" (*Manson,* 432 U.S. at 112) excluding identifications that follow a single-photo display, but both cases allow the admission of such identifications only after conducting the two-step analysis described in § 27.2 *supra* and finding a strong showing that, "'under the "totality of the circumstances[,]" the identification was reliable even though the confrontation procedure was suggestive'" (*Manson,* 432 U.S. at 106). *See also, e.g., State v. Ostrem,* 535 N.W.2d 916, 921 (Minn. 1995) ("In determining whether pretrial eyewitness identification evidence must be suppressed, a two-part test is applied. . . . The first inquiry focuses on whether the procedure was unnecessarily suggestive. . . . Whether a pretrial identification procedure is unnecessarily suggestive turns on whether the defendant was unfairly singled out for identification. . . . Single photo line-up identification procedures have been widely condemned as unnecessarily suggestive. . . . However, under the second prong of the test, the identification evidence, even if suggestive, may be admissible if the totality of the circumstances establishes that the evidence was reliable. . . . If the totality of the circumstances shows the witness' identification has adequate independent origin, it is considered to be reliable despite the suggestive procedure. . . . The test is whether the suggestive procedures created a very substantial likelihood of irreparable misidentification."). *Compare State v. Jackson,* 454 So.2d 398, 400-01 (La. App. 1984) ("In the present case, the witness was shown a two-view mug shot of the defendant from the D.A.'s file. There can be little doubt that this procedure was impermissibly suggestive. The display of a single photograph of the defendant rather than an array of photographs depicting different individuals has repeatedly been held to be improper. . . .

¶ . . . [T]he photographic identification took place some eight months after the crime. This substantial lapse of time, coupled with the relatively brief period of observation and the absence of a physical description, casts grave doubt upon the reliability of the in-court identification. . . . ¶ Weighing these indicia of reliability against the corrupting effect of the one photograph show-up, we conclude there was a substantial likelihood of misidentification. Accordingly, the trial judge committed reversible error in admitting the identification testimony."); *Wise v. Commonwealth*, 6 Va. App. 178, 367 S.E.2d 197 (1988) (a police investigator showed bank-robbery eyewitnesses "a bank surveillance photograph depicting a man who had robbed a Maryland bank" and then showed them "a photo array consisting of six photographs" (*id.* at 180, 367 S.E.2d at 198); "We believe that significant problems are inherent in the use of a single-photograph identification procedure. . . '[A] single photograph display is one of the most suggestive methods of identification and is always to be viewed with suspicion.' . . . [S]ince the police showed Phelps and Wampler a single photograph of Wise as part of their out-of-court identification procedure, we find the out-of-court identification process was unduly suggestive. ¶ . . . In the present case, both Phelps and Wampler first identified Wise five months after the robbery when shown a single photograph of him. The record shows that both witnesses were unable to describe the robber's facial features at any time prior to seeing the single photograph. Further, Phelps could not pick him out of the photo array in January 1986, one month prior to seeing the single photograph. Wampler was not shown the photo array at that time. We believe that these facts demonstrate an absence of other indicia of reliability and require us to find that the trial court erred in admitting evidence of their out-of-court identifications. ¶ . . . [S]ince we find that neither Wampler's nor Phelps' in-court identifications originated independently of their out-of-court identifications, we conclude that the trial court erred in admitting this evidence at trial." (*Id.* at 184-87, 367 S.E.2d at 200-02.)); *People v. Marshall*, 26 N.Y.3d 495, 506-08, 45 N.E.3d 954, 962-64, 25 N.Y.S.3d 58, 66-68 (2015) (even if the defendant's photograph was shown to the witness by the prosecutor as part of "trial preparation" and "not for purposes of an identification," the witness's exposure "to defendant's likeness" creates a risk that "the display was unduly suggestive, and therefore, tainted an in-court identification"); *Morales v. United States*, 248 A.3d 161 (D.C. 2021) (reversing a conviction for error in admitting a police officer's in-court identification of the defendant where "[t]he salient facts are: (1) a police officer caught a two-to-three second glimpse of a fleeing suspect's face more than four months before trial, (2) the officer did not identify the defendant before trial – no show-up, lineup, photographic array, or any other type of pretrial identification procedure was conducted – but (3) on the cusp of trial, the prosecuting attorney handed the officer a single mugshot of the defendant to study 'in preparation for this case.'" (*id.* at 166). "We disagree with the [trial] court's assessment both as to the suggestivity of the mugshot display and as to the reliability of the officer's in-court identification. . . . ¶ It was constitutional error to permit the officer to make an in-court identification of Mr. Morales." *Id.* at 167.).

A "photo array" – a group of photographs (usually mug shots) including the defendant's photograph – will be found suggestive if the defendant's photograph is the only one that matches the description of the perpetrator (*see, e.g., United States v. Sanders,* 479 F.2d 1193 (D.C. Cir. 1973) (only the defendant's photograph depicted facial hair that was in any way comparable to the witness's description of the perpetrator); *Commonwealth v. Thornley*, 406 Mass. 96, 99-101, 546 N.E.2d 350, 352-53 (1989) (a thirteen-photograph array was suggestive because both witnesses had described the perpetrator as wearing glasses, and "the defendant's picture was the only one in the array with glasses"); *Butler v. State*, 102 So.3d 260, 263, 265-66 (Miss. 2012) (a photo of a lineup stage was impermissibly suggestive because the witness described the perpetrator as "around five-feet-five-inches tall," the accused is "actually five-feet-six-inches tall," the "other suspects in the photo lineup were between five-feet-eleven-inches and six-feet-four-inches tall," and their relative heights would have been apparent because the suspects "were pictured standing beside a height marker")) or if the defendant's photograph differs from the others in some way that would give it special salience (*see, e.g., Sloan v. State*, 584 S.W.2d 461, 467 (Tenn. Crim. App.1978) ("the photographic identification procedure was suggestive in that the photograph of defendant was emphasized by the fact that it was a portrait of him in a Navy uniform, and the other photographs were mugshots"); *People v. Smith*, 122 A.D.3d 1162, 1163, 997 N.Y.S.2d 534, 535-36 (N.Y. App. Div., 3d Dep't 2014) (a photo array was unduly suggestive, even though "[t]he array depicts six individuals of equivalent age and ethnicity who are reasonably similar in appearance," because of a formatting difference between the defendant's photo and the other photos: "[W]hile the other five photos depict individuals from the shoulders up with the upper portion of their photos consisting of nothing more than a blank, gray background, defendant is shown from the chest up with the top of his head reaching to the very top of the photo," and "[t]hus, defendant's face occupies the space that, in all of the other photos, is bare.")).

As with lineups, see § 27.3.2 *supra,* a police officer's comments or the way in which the police conduct the photographic identification can render even a properly constituted photo array suggestive. *See, e.g., Simmons v. United States, supra*, 390 U.S. at 383 ("[t]he chance of misidentification is also heightened if the police indicate to the witness that they have other evidence that one of the persons pictured committed the crime"); *United States v. Trivette,* 284 F. Supp. 720 (D. D.C. 1968) (a detective drew the witness's attention to the defendant's photograph by asking "'Is that the man?'"); *Young v. State*, 374 P.3d 395, 399-400, 407 (Alaska 2016) (a "detective's comment made . . . [the photo array] identification procedure 'so suggestive as to create "a very substantial likelihood of irreparable misidentification"'": after the eyewitness – who was "a criminal defense lawyer and former prosecutor" – "put his finger tentatively on Young's photograph, . . . the detective told him to 'trust your instincts'"; although the witness "testified that he 'was kind of going there' in selecting Young as the shooter and may well have picked Young anyway, he also testified that he took the detective's comment to mean 'that's the guy we want you to pick' and that it ended his deliberations."); *People v. Jones*, 173 A.D.3d 1062, 1065, 102 N.Y.S.3d 265, 269 (N.Y. App. Div., 2d Dep't 2019) ("[b]y showing [the complainant] . . . [a video on] the cell phone and telling him that the phone was recovered from the scene of the robbery, the detective suggested that the phone may belong to one of the perpetrators of the robbery"; during the robbery, the perpetrator had threatened the complainant with a taser; the video displayed the defendant tasing a sleeping individual; "the procedure employed by the detective in showing . . . [the complainant] the cell phone videos was a police-arranged identification procedure, even though the police did not arrange the content of the videos on the phone"; "[t]he People failed to meet their initial burden of establishing the reasonableness of the police conduct and the lack of any undue suggestiveness created by the video identification procedure."); *People v. Fernandez*, 82 A.D.2d 922, 440 N.Y.S.2d 677 (N.Y. App. Div., 2d Dep't 1981) (four eyewitnesses were permitted to view photographs together). A roster of safeguards aimed at assuring the reliability of photo displays is found in United States Department of Justice, Memorandum for Heads of Department Law Enforcement Components,

All Department Prosecutors, *Eyewitness Identification: Procedures for Conducting Photo Arrays* (January 6, 2017), *available at* https://apps.npr.org/documents/document.html?id=3254083-DAG-Memo-Procedures-for-Photo-Arrays (policies, *e.g.*, governing the number and nature of photos displayed, directing federal investigators to document or record an eyewitness's confidence in an identification at the time the i.d. is made, and encouraging "blind" or "blinded" photo arrays [*i.e.*, arrangements that keep the agent conducting the session ignorant of information that could tip the witness off as to which photo represents the prime suspect]). Counsel arguing that the photographic identification procedure used in his or her case was unduly suggestive can usefully contrast them with these DOJ guidelines. See also the Louisiana statutory model summarized in § 27.3 *supra. And see* Andrew Hemming, *Reform of the Evidential Rules for Eyewitness Identification in the United States – Advice from the Antipodes*, 43 HOUSTON J. INT'L. L. 1, 11 (2020) ("Telling the witness that the suspect's photograph may not be among the photographs that the witness views is of special significance. This is so because otherwise a witness will likely select the photograph that most resembles the recalled image of the person he or she saw at the time the crime was committed . . . .").

If the police or the prosecution failed to preserve the photo array used in the identification procedure, counsel should ask the court to apply a presumption that the array was impermissibly suggestive. *See, e.g., United States v. Honer*, 225 F.3d 549, 553 (5th Cir. 2000) ("when the government fails to preserve the photographic array used in a pretrial line-up 'there shall exist *a presumption* that the array is impermissibly suggestive'"); *People v. Holley*, 26 N.Y.3d 514, 517, 45 N.E.3d 936, 937, 25 N.Y.S.3d 40, 41 (2015) (dictum) ("When using a photo array as an identification procedure, the People should preserve a record of what was viewed. Failure to do so gives rise to a rebuttable presumption that the array was unduly suggestive. The obligation to preserve is not diminished by the type of system used. Computer screen or mug shots book, the People's obligation is the same.").

27.3.4. *Aggregation of Identification Procedures*

Frequently, a witness is exposed to a combination of identification procedures. For example, a witness who identifies the defendant in a show-up or a photographic identification display is thereafter shown the defendant in a lineup. The employment of successive identification procedures all involving the defendant is itself suggestive because the witness learns to recognize the defendant from the previous police-arranged viewing(s). *See Foster v. California,* 394 U.S. 440, 442-43 (1969).

27.4. *Reliability of the Identification*

As explained in § 27.2 *supra,* under the federal Due Process rule, even unduly suggestive police procedures will not render an identification inadmissible if the factors indicating its reliability outweigh the suggestiveness of the police conduct.

The factors to be considered in assessing the reliability of an identification "include the opportunity of the witness to view the criminal at the time of the crime, the witness' degree of attention, the accuracy of his prior description of the criminal, the level of certainty demonstrated at the confrontation, and the time between the crime and the confrontation" (*Manson v.*

Brathwaite, 432 U.S. 98, 114 (1977)). Thus, in *Manson,* the Court held that the identification was reliable because:

(a) The witness had a good "opportunity to view" the perpetrator: the scene was well-lit and the witness was "within two feet" of the perpetrator and "looked directly at" him for "two to three minutes" (*id.* at 114).

(b) The witness's "degree of attention" was excellent, in that the witness was "a specially trained, assigned, and experienced officer [who] . . . could be expected to pay scrupulous attention to detail, for he knew that subsequently he would have to find and arrest [the perpetrator] . . . [and] that his claimed observations would be subject later to close scrutiny and examination at any trial" (*id.* at 115). In addition, since the witness was of the same race as the defendant, there were no problems of cross-racial identification. *Id.*

(c) The description given by the witness was extremely detailed and accurate, including the perpetrator's "race, his height, his build, the color and style of his hair, and the high cheekbone facial feature" as well as the "clothing the [perpetrator] . . . wore" (*id.*).

(d) The witness was absolutely certain of the identification, stating, "'There is no question whatsoever'" (*id.*).

(e) The witness gave his description to the investigating officer "within minutes of the crime" and "[t]he photographic identification took place only two days later" (*id.* at 116).

In cases not exhibiting the indicia of reliability that marked the identification in *Manson,* lower courts have held that the suggestiveness of police procedures outweighed the identification's reliability. *See, e.g., Raheem v. Kelly,* 257 F.3d 122, 138-40 (2d Cir. 2001) (the witnesses to a robbery and shooting in a bar were "drinking scotch" and were not paying attention to the robbers until the witnesses "heard the shot and saw the shooter holding a gun, [and] the hold-up was announced," and "[p]lainly their attention was immediately focused more on th[e] man" who "brandished his gun at them" than at the other robber, and "[f]urther, it is human nature for a person toward whom a gun is being pointed to focus his attention more on the gun than on the face of the person pointing it"); *Velez v. Schmer,* 724 F.2d 249, 251-52 (1st Cir. 1984) (the witnesses had only about a minute to observe the perpetrator and gave virtually no description); *Dickerson v. Fogg,* 692 F.2d 238, 245 (2d Cir. 1982) (the victim was "frightened and agitated . . . having just had his life threatened and a gun at his neck"); *Jackson v. Fogg,* 589 F.2d 108 (2d Cir. 1978) (the eyewitnesses had only a few seconds to observe the gunman before running for cover); *United States v. Dailey,* 524 F.2d 911 (8th Cir. 1975) (the witness had limited opportunity to observe the perpetrator, seeing him for no more than 30 seconds in heavy rain, and there was a discrepancy between the description and the defendant's appearance); *People v. Fuller,* 71 A.D.2d 589, 418 N.Y.S.2d 427 (N.Y. App. Div., 1st Dep't 1979) (there was a gross discrepancy between the appearance of the 17-year-old defendant and the witness's description of the perpetrator's age and build); *State v. Moore,* 343 S.C. 282, 289, 540 S.E.2d 445, 449

(2000) (the eyewitness "saw the two defendants for only a very brief period of time, at some distance"; her "attention was likely not as acute as it might have been had she been the victim of a crime"; and "the degree of accuracy of [her] description is tenuous, at best . . . [inasmuch as] [h]er descriptions were based primarily on the suspects' clothing and race, and that one was taller than the other"); *United States v. Emanuele*, 51 F.3d 1123 (3d Cir. 1995); *State v. Williams*, 162 W. Va. 348, 249 S.E.2d 752 (1978); *State v. Gomez*, 937 So.2d 828 (Fla. App. 2006); *State v. Almaraz*, 154 Idaho 584, 301 P.3d 242 (Idaho 2013); *State v. Jones*, 224 N.J. 70, 128 A.3d 1096 (2016); *State v. Cooper*, 2018 WL 4167696 (N.J. Super. 2018).

Counsel should be aware that *Manson*'s factor (d) – the witness's certainty in the correctness of his or her identification – has been empirically discredited in the more than four decades since *Manson* was decided. A consistent body of persuasive research has accumulated demonstrating that there is no significant correlation between confidence and accuracy (*see* the sources collected in *People v. Lemcke*, 11 Cal. 5th 644, 661-68, 486 P.3d 1077, 1090-95, 278 Cal. Rptr. 3d 849, 865-70 (2021)); and the courts have begun to take the research seriously (see the *Lemcke*, *Bey*, *Gomes*, and *Henderson* opinions summarized in § 27.3 *supra*). Because jurors do tend to find an eyewitness identification more persuasive in proportion to the witness's degree of confidence in it (*see* Brandon L. Garrett, Alice Liu, Karen Kafadar, Joanne Yaffe & Chad S. Dodson, *Factoring the Role of Eyewitness Evidence in the Courtroom*, 17 J. EMPIRICAL LEGAL STUDIES 556 (2020)), counsel in jurisdictions where the courts have not yet recognized the fallacy of the certainty-accuracy equation may be well advised to prepare expert testimony for use in challenging the reliability of testimony by eyewitnesses who claim to be sure of their identification of the defendant. *See, e.g., United States v. Stevens*, 935 F.2d 1380, 1384 (3d Cir. 1991) (the trial court abused its discretion in excluding proffered testimony by a defense expert "concerning the lack of a correlation between confidence and accuracy in eyewitness identifications. Both of the victims expressed a great deal of confidence in their identifications of Stevens. To counteract this highly damaging testimony, Stevens offered expert testimony that, contrary to popular belief, scientific studies have shown 'a fairly weak relationship' between confidence and accuracy. We conclude that the district court erred in holding that there was no 'fit' between this testimony and the facts at bar. We also are satisfied that such testimony would have proven helpful to the jury in assessing the victims' identifications."); *Jones v. United States*, 262 A.3d 1114, 1125-28 (D.C. 2021) (vacating a conviction on the ground of ineffective assistance of counsel where the defendant's lawyer failed to present expert testimony regarding the factors that render eyewitness identifications inaccurate: "Courts across the country now accept that certain factors can greatly affect the accuracy of eyewitness identification testimony. A non-exhaustive list of factors includes: (1) transference, which occurs when a person seen in one context is confused with a person seen in another; (2) the weak correlation between confidence and accuracy regarding an identification; (3) the diminishing reliability of an identification caused by the witness's focus on a weapon; and (4) the negative impact of high stress at the time of the observation on the ability to retain an accurate perception of events. We reiterate that numerous other factors are generally accepted as well. . . . ¶ . . . Although these findings are widely accepted by scientists and, to a lesser extent, recognized by judges and attorneys, they remain largely unfamiliar to the average person and often run counter to the beliefs of jurors. . . . ¶ . . . We are convinced that a satisfactory understanding of the eyewitness testimony reliability factors 'require[s] information beyond that ordinarily attributable to the average juror.'"); *cf. State v. Lawson*, 352 Or. 724, 761, 291 P.3d 673, 696 (2012) ("Because many of the system and estimator variables that we described earlier are either unknown to the average juror or contrary to common assumptions, expert testimony is one method by which the parties can educate the trier of fact concerning variables that can affect the reliability of eyewitness identification. Expert testimony may also provide an avenue to introduce and explain scientific research or other indicia of reliability not specifically addressed by our opinion in these cases. In that regard, the use of experts may prove vital to ensuring that the law keeps pace with advances in scientific knowledge, thus enabling judges and jurors to evaluate eyewitness identification testimony according to relevant and meaningful criteria.").

27.5. *Suppression of an Identification as Unconstitutionally Unreliable Even Though Police Action Is Minimal or Non-existent*

Under the federal due process standard for suppressing an identification as unconstitutionally unreliable, "a preliminary judicial inquiry into the reliability of an eyewitness identification" is required only if the identification was "procured under unnecessarily suggestive circumstances arranged by law enforcement" (*Perry v. New Hampshire*, 565 U.S. 228, 248 (2012)). *See id.* at 232-33 ("We have not extended pretrial screening for reliability to cases in which the suggestive circumstances were not arranged by law enforcement officers. . . . Our decisions . . . turn on the presence of state action and aim to deter police from rigging identification procedures, for example, at a lineup, showup, or photograph array. When no improper law enforcement activity is involved, . . . it suffices to test reliability through the rights and opportunities generally designed for that purpose, notably, the presence of counsel at postindictment lineups, vigorous cross-examination, protective rules of evidence, and jury instructions on both the fallibility of eyewitness identification and the requirement that guilt be proved beyond a reasonable doubt.").

In States that have not already chosen to follow the federal constitutional standard on this issue, counsel can argue that the state constitution or state statutes or rules should be construed to afford a suppression remedy for unreliable identifications even in the absence of suggestive police conduct. *See, e.g., State v. Chen*, 208 N.J. 307, 310-11, 27 A.3d 930, 932 (2011) ("Recent social science research reveals that suggestive conduct by private actors, as well as government officials, can undermine the reliability of eyewitness identifications and inflate witness confidence. We consider that evidence in light of the court's traditional gatekeeping role to ensure that unreliable, misleading evidence is not presented to jurors. We therefore hold [under N.J. RULE EVID. 104] that, even without any police action, when a defendant presents evidence that an identification was made under highly suggestive circumstances that could lead to a mistaken identification, trial judges should conduct a preliminary hearing, upon request, to determine the admissibility of the identification evidence."). *See also State v. Hibl*, 2006 WI 52, 290 Wis. 2d 595, 610-13, 618, 714 N.W.2d 194, 202-03, 206 (Wis. 2006) (even when an identification does not stem from a "police procedure," as in cases of "'spontaneous' identifications resulting from 'accidental' confrontations" between an eyewitness and the suspect, the "circuit court still has a limited gatekeeping function to exclude such evidence under [WIS. STAT.] § 904.03"). See generally § 17.11 *supra. Compare State v. Johnson*, 312 Conn. 687, 688-90, 700, 703-05, 94 A.3d 1173, 1174-75, 1180-81, 1183-84 (2014) (rejecting the argument that "the due process clauses of the Connecticut constitution provide protection against allegedly unduly suggestive eyewitness identification procedures undertaken by a private actor," but recognizing that due process principles are implicated if "the [identification] evidence is so extremely unreliable that its admission would deprive the defendant of his right to a fair trial" and furthermore recognizing that state evidentiary law "goes above and beyond minimal constitutional requirements" and provides a basis for excluding, at trial, "unreliable identification evidence that is tainted by unduly suggestive private conduct").

In seeking to persuade a state court to construe the state constitution to provide a suppression remedy for unconstitutionally unreliable identifications even though police action is minimal or non-existent, counsel will often find it useful to direct the court's attention to the extensive empirical evidence on the unreliability of eyewitness identifications even when the police were not involved. *See, e.g.*, the sources cited in § 27.3 *supra* and in *State v. Chen, supra*, 208 N.J. at 938-40, 27 A.3d at 320-23; *Perry v. New Hampshire, supra*, 565 U.S. at 262-65 & nn.5-11 (Sotomayor, J., dissenting).

27.5.1. *Identifications Made for the First Time in Court*

In *State v. Dickson*, 322 Conn. 410, 141 A.3d 810 (2016), the Connecticut Supreme Court observed that "[t]he United States Supreme Court has not yet addressed the question of whether first time in-court identifications are in the category of unnecessarily suggestive procedures that trigger due process protections" (*id.* at 422, 141 A.3d at 821), but it agreed with Dickson's contention that "first time in-court identifications are inherently suggestive and implicate a defendant's due process rights no less than unnecessarily suggestive out-of-court identifications" (*id.* at 423, 141 A.3d at 822). "[W]e are hard-pressed to imagine how there could be a *more* suggestive identification procedure than placing a witness on the stand in open court, confronting the witness with the person who the state has accused of committing the crime, and then asking the witness if he can identify the person who committed the crime." *Id.* (original emphasis). "Accordingly, we conclude that first time in-court identifications, like in-court identifications that are tainted by an unduly suggestive out-of-court identification, implicate due process protections and must be prescreened by the trial court." *Id.* at 426, 141 A.3d at 825. "[W]e now set forth the specific procedures that the parties and the trial court must follow. Preliminarily, we take this opportunity to emphasize that, in cases in which the identity of the perpetrator is at issue and there are eyewitnesses to the crime, the best practice is to conduct a nonsuggestive identification procedure as soon after the crime as is possible." *Id.* at 444-45, 141 A.3d at 835. "In cases in which there has been no pretrial identification, however, and the state intends to present a first time in-court identification, the state must first request permission to do so from the trial court." *Id.* at 445, 141 A.3d at 835. "The trial court may grant such permission only if it determines that there is no factual dispute as to the identity of the perpetrator, or the ability of the particular eyewitness to identify the defendant is not at issue." *Id.* at 446, 141 A.3d at 835-36.

> "If the trial court determines that the state will not be allowed to conduct a first time identification in court, the state may request permission to conduct a nonsuggestive identification procedure, namely, at the state's option, an out-of-court lineup or photographic array, and the trial court ordinarily should grant the state's request. If the witness previously has been unable to identify the defendant in a nonsuggestive identification procedure, however, the court should not allow a second nonsuggestive identification procedure unless the state can provide a good reason why a second bite at

the apple is warranted. If the eyewitness is able to identify the defendant in a nonsuggestive out-of-court procedure, the state may then ask the eyewitness to identify the defendant in court.

"If the trial court denies a request for a nonsuggestive procedure, the state declines to conduct one, or the eyewitness is unable to identify the defendant in such a procedure, a one-on-one in-court identification should not be allowed. The prosecutor may still examine the witness, however, about his or her observations of the perpetrator at the time of the crime, but the prosecutor should avoid asking the witness if the defendant resembles the perpetrator." (*Id.* at 446-47, 141 A.3d at 836-37.)

Accord, State v. Torres, 175 Conn. App. 138, 167 A.3d 365 (2017). *Dickson* is a seminal decision supported by a well-reasoned opinion; counsel in other jurisdictions would do well to urge its adoption on both federal and state due process grounds (see §§ 17.11, 27.2 last paragraph *supra*) and alternatively as an appropriate application of judicial authority to prescribe common-law evidentiary rules that avert the danger of unreliable criminal verdicts (*Commonwealth v. Crayton*, 470 Mass. 228, 21 N.E.3d 157 (2014)). *Cf. State v. Lawson*, 352 Or. 724, 291 P.3d 673 (2012), quoted in § 27.4 *supra* (establishing rigorous conditions for the admission of eyewitness identification evidence).

B. *Other Grounds for Suppressing Identification Testimony*

27.6. *Violations of the Sixth Amendment Right to Counsel*

Sections 26.10 and 26.10.1 *supra* describe the doctrine establishing that the Sixth Amendment right to counsel attaches at the time of commencement of adversary judicial proceedings. As noted in that section, some state courts have relied upon state constitutional guarantees to afford the protections of the right to counsel even earlier in the criminal process.

Once the right to counsel has attached, the defendant is entitled to the assistance of counsel at a lineup or show-up. *United States v. Wade,* 388 U.S. 218 (1967); *Garcia v. Hepp*, 65 F.4th 945 (7th Cir. 2023). The violation of that right requires the suppression of testimony relating to any identification made at the lineup or show-up. *Moore v. Illinois,* 434 U.S. 220, 231-32 (1977); *Gilbert v. California,* 388 U.S. 263, 272-74 (1967). In cases in which the right to counsel was violated, witnesses who participated in the unconstitutional lineup or show-up are also precluded from making an in-court identification of the defendant unless the prosecution proves "by clear and convincing evidence that the in-court identifications [are] . . . based upon observations of the suspect other than the lineup [or show-up] identification" (*see United States v. Wade, supra*, 388 U.S. at 240).

Unlike lineups and show-ups, photographic identification procedures do not require the presence of counsel under the Sixth Amendment caselaw. *United States v. Ash,* 413 U.S. 300 (1973).

27.7. *Violations of the Fourth Amendment: Identifications Resulting from an Illegal Arrest or* Terry *Stop*

If a lineup, show-up, or other identification exhibition is held while the defendant is in custody following an illegal arrest or *Terry* stop, any resulting identification must be suppressed as the fruit of the Fourth Amendment violation. See § 25.39 subdivision (e) *supra.* In-court identifications tainted by the illegality of the earlier ones would also be inadmissible. *See United States v. Crews,* 445 U.S. 463, 472-73 (1980) (dictum); *Young v. Conway,* 698 F.3d 69, 84-85 (2d Cir. 2012).

A fact pattern that arises with considerable frequency and provides fertile grounds for suppression of identifications is that an eyewitness gives a very vague description of the perpetrator, the police arrest or detain the defendant because s/he matches the description, and an identification procedure is then held. If the defense succeeds in invalidating the arrest or *Terry* stop on the ground that the vague description failed to provide the requisite probable cause or articulable suspicion, see §§ 25.7.4, 25.9 *supra,* the identification must be suppressed.

27.8. *State Law Grounds of Objection to Identifications*

In addition to the constitutional rules that may require suppression of an identification, some jurisdictions have evidentiary doctrines that afford a basis for objecting to identification testimony. In some jurisdictions, police officers and other observers of an out-of-court identification are barred from recounting the identification, either by rules prohibiting third-party bolstering of identifications (*see, e.g., People v. Walston,* 99 A.D.2d 847, 472 N.Y.S.2d 453 (N.Y. App. Div., 2d Dep't 1984); *Brownfield v. State,* 668 P.2d 1165 (Okla. Crim. App. 1983); *Lyons v. State,* 388 S.W.2d 950 (Tex. Crim. App. 1965)), or by a hearsay-based rule barring such testimony generally or in specific circumstances such as when the eyewitness does not testify at trial (*see, e.g., People v. Johnson,* 68 Ill. App. 3d 836, 842, 386 N.E.2d 642, 647, 25 Ill. Dec. 371, 376 (1979)) or when the eyewitness takes the stand but is unable to make an in-court identification (*see generally* Francis M. Dougherty, Annot., *Admissibility and weight of extrajudicial or pretrial identification where witness was unable or failed to make in-court identification,* 29 A.L.R.4th 104 (1984 & Supp.)). Some jurisdictions recognize an objection to identification evidence when the identification is so unreliable that its probative value is outweighed by its prejudicial nature. *See, e.g., State v. Lawson,* 352 Or. 724, 740, 761-62, 291 P.3d 673, 685, 696-97 (2012), summarized in § 27.2 concluding paragraph, *supra; State v. Johnson,* 312 Conn. 687, 700, 94 A.3d 1173, 1180-81 (2014), summarized in § 27.5 second paragraph *supra;* and see § 36.2.3 *infra.*

Made in United States
Troutdale, OR
10/01/2024

23313165R00306